America's #1 Selling Price Guide

2011 PRICE GUIDE • 27th Edition

Published by

Krause Publications, a division of F+W Media, Inc.
700 East State Street • Iola, WI 54990-0001
715-445-2214 • 888-457-2873
www.krausebooks.com

To order books or other products call toll-free 1-800-258-0929
or visit us online at www.krausebooks.com or www.Shop.Collect.com

ISSN 1536-2884

ISBN-13: 978-1-4402-1233-8
ISBN-10: 1-4402-1233-3

Cover Design by Wendy Wendt & Heidi Zastrow
Designed by Wendy Wendt
Edited by Dan Brownell

Printed in United States of America

Front cover, clockwise from top:
Teapot, cov., William IV era, mark of Paul Storr, 1832, 7 3/4" h., **$2,820**
Stoneware jug, F. Stetzenmeyer & G. Goetzman, ca. 1857, 2 gal., 11" h., **$1,430**
Dress clip, flower design, w/red, blue, green, amber rhinestone petals, 1 3/4" d., **$30-$45**
Webb cameo vase, 8" h., signed "Thomas Webb & Sons," **$10,063**
Queen Anne highboy, cherry, 18th c., 20 1/2 x 39", 83 1/2" h., **$5,750**

Back cover:
Soda water bottle, Harris (J.W.) New Haven, Conn., ca. 1845-60, 1/2 pt., **$364**
Pocket watch, Vacheron, 18k gold, jeweled lever escapement, early 20th c., **$646**

America's #1 Selling Price Guide

Antique Trader® ANTIQUES & COLLECTIBLES

2011 PRICE GUIDE • 27th Edition

More Great Books in the Antique Trader® Series

Antique Trader® Book Collector's Price Guide

Antique Trader® Bottles Identification and Price Guide

Antique Trader® Collectible Cookbooks Price Guide

Antique Trader® Collectible Paperback Price Guide

Antique Trader® Furniture Price Guide

Antique Trader® Guide to Fakes & Reproductions

Antique Trader® Jewelry Price Guide

Antique Trader® Kitchen Collectibles Price Guide

Antique Trader® Perfume Bottles Price Guide

Antique Trader® Pottery & Porcelain Ceramics Price Guide

Antique Trader® Salt and Pepper Shaker Price Guide

Antique Trader® Tools Price Guide

Contents

Market Reports

Introduction

Listings

Welcome to Antique Trader 2011

Welcome to the 2011 edition of *Antique Trader Antiques & Collectibles Price Guide.* It's a pleasure to compile identification and pricing information for our readers year after year. We strive to bring you the latest and most reliable information to help you make informed buying and selling decisions. We thank you, our readers, for your support. We also want to thank contributors, auction houses, and dealers who have supplied photos and sales results. Also, thank you again to Wendy Wendt, who spent countless hours designing this edition.

A Brief Overview of the Past Year

The past year has seen a partial recovery in the economy, but there's no question the antiques and collectibles market, like the rest of the economy, is still feeling the painful effects of the recession. Whether one sees the glass as half empty or half full, however, depends on perspective.

Some dealers are clinging to outdated business models. Others recognize that the economy is changing and consider it an opportunity rather than a threat. They are willing to study the change carefully and adjust as necessary while stagnant competition drops away, leaving more of the remaining market available for them.

Customers are still decorating, collecting, and investing, so merchandise will continue to sell; the question is which dealers will do the selling. Those who are the most responsive will have the most success.

The Market is Alive and Well

Just as Mark Twain once said, "Reports of my death have been greatly exaggerated," the same is true with the antiques and collectibles market. The market hasn't died; it is evolving. Proof that antiques and collectibles are still in demand is evident in the intense interest in television shows such as the *Antiques Roadshow,* which is in its 14th season and still going strong. *Pawn Stars* and *American Pickers* are also wildly successful even during the recession. In fact, perhaps their success is not in spite of the recession but because of it. Some people want to clean out their attics, cellars, garages, and barns to raise needed cash, while others are motivated to look for bargains. The recession, while slowing the economy, hasn't stopped cash flow; it has just redirected it.

Six Keys to Success

Dealers need to follow at least six principles to succeed in today's market. 1) Follow the trends. Customers will buy what they want, not necessarily what you want to sell. 2) Sell online to open your store to the world rather than just your neighborhood. 3) Focus on quality rather than quantity. Quality always sells. 4) Provide excellent customer service. Buyers will appreciate and remember it. 5) Aggressively market your business and develop innovative promotions. You can't expect people to patronize your shop if you haven't effectively communicated what you have to offer. 6) Observe successful shops and adopt their practices.

The future is brighter for those who are willing to flow with the economy rather than fight against it. Use the changes to your advantage. Best wishes for the coming year!

Dan Brownell

American Pickers: Saving Antiques One at a Time

American Pickers, a reality television show featuring antique and collectible treasure hunters Mike Wolfe and Frank Fritz, debuted on the History Channel on January 18, 2010, with 3.2 million viewers and was the highest rated new cable series for viewers aged 25 to 54. The two "pickers" (buyers who typically resell to dealers) operate their business Antique Archaeology (antiquearchaeology.com) from their van as they travel around the country hunting for overlooked treasures in old barns and other out-of-the way places. Meanwhile, their office manager, Danielle Colby Cushman, working from their headquarters in LeClaire, Iowa, relies on her networking skills to follow leads looking for potential buyers and sellers. Wolfe and Fritz essentially work as antiques and collectible "flippers," buying and reselling items as quickly as possible on their field trips.

Some of their buys come from leads that Cushman has provided, while others are a result of what Wolf and Fritz call "freestyling," driving around at random and stopping at homes and farms that look promising. Sometimes they find a "honeyhole," sometimes not. They frequently encounter hoarders who have a stash of interesting items but, because of an emotional attachment, are unable to part with any. Wolfe and Fritz have a strategy for such occasions. They try to prime the pump by getting the owner to quickly sell one or more items, sometimes at higher prices than they would like to pay, in order to generate excitement with the cash that they peel off.

No doubt that with the sluggish economy and the lure of making a quick buck, some naïve viewers have gotten the idea that it would be easy to make a living copying Wolfe and Fritz's strategies. Not true. What these viewers may not realize is that success depends on an encyclopedic knowledge of antiques and collectibles, an uncanny ability to spot a deal and negotiate successfully, a keen insight into human nature, and an extensive network of dealers to sell to.

Their profit margin is actually fairly slim, with their average anticipated resale valued at double their purchase price. The 100 percent markup is considered standard in the retail business. The markup not only has to produce their profit, but cover all their overhead as well. And it has to cover their mistakes, which happens from time to time. No one is an expert in every area, and inevitably all pickers lose money now and then. Losses can be caused by paying too much, by accidentally buying a fake or reproduction, or by not being able to resell an item because there are no interested buyers.

Fritz overpaid in one episode when he impulsively negotiated the sale of a 1939 Plymouth while on a trip to the Northeast. He paid $5,500, plus the cost of having it hauled back to Iowa. Upon returning home, he discovered the car was only worth $3,000 to $4,000 and the cost of restoration would be more than that. The episode closed with Fritz making some discouraging phone calls looking for a buyer to cut his losses.

The show sparked considerable controversy, especially in early episodes, as some viewers accused the pair of taking advantage of unsuspecting elderly people by making unethically large profits off them. Actually, there have been relatively few times when either has gotten an especially good deal. One incident in particular incensed critics. Wolfe bought a saddle from a World War II veteran for $75 that was later valued for as much as $5,000 if restored and sold out West. As viewers have seen in subsequent episodes, this was an unusual opportunity rather than a typical event. And the expected bonanza never actually took place.

Even if Wolfe and Fritz had made a big profit, there is another side to the story. First, Wolfe explained that he didn't know anything about saddles and didn't know its value. Second, he offered $75 and the owner was satisfied and accepted that. Third, the $5,000 estimate was a best-case scenario, and in order for the saddle to receive its full value, it would have to be restored. In addition, Wolfe would need to sell it in a Western market. That would mean finding a buyer in that area of the country. Finally, to get maximum price, Wolfe would have to sell it to an end user rather than a middleman. If he sold to a dealer, he would likely get only half the value to allow for dealer markup, and if he sold it without restoring it first, he would likely make even less money.

The saddle was valued at $5,000 *if* restored and *if* sold to the right person in the right market. Unfortunately, items don't always sell for their appraised value. According to a WCFCourier.com article posted online June 27, 2010, they were unable to get a $199 bid for the saddle on eBay, so they sold it to a couple for $150. After restoration costs, their total profit was $45. So it wasn't a windfall after all.

Another aspect that some viewers have overlooked is that many antiques are rusting or rotting in barns and junkyards. If it weren't for pickers taking the initiative to track them down and purchase them, they would undoubtedly end up in a landfill and a piece of American history would be lost. It seems fitting then, that Wolfe and Fritz named their business Antique Archaeology, as archaeology is in fact what they do. They are explorers who find antiques and collectibles and return them to useful service.

We have to wonder how many wonderful antiques have disintegrated in dumps over the last 100 years because their owners didn't realize their value. Unfortunately for those pieces, there were no pickers like Wolfe and Fritz to rescue them. Those involved in the antiques trade—sellers, buyers, collectors, and dealers—can be thankful for the service that pickers provide for the trade and for posterity preserving a record of our cultural history.

How Much is This Worth?: An Overview of Valuation

"How much is this worth?" is a common question. An appraiser will likely respond with the comment, "It all depends." As frustrating as this might be to the owner, the appraiser would be correct. It all depends on what kind of appraisal the owner needs. The owner is most likely seeking the retail value (fair market value), which is also the value used in the listings in this book. But there are some circumstances in which appraising for retail value would not serve the owner's purpose.

Because of the dominance of fixed prices in chain stores, we're conditioned to think of items having a single value. A single item can be considered to have multiple values, however, because they can be used for multiple purposes, each appropriate for its own use, and each having its own objective criteria.

These values are acknowledged and defined both by law and by the Uniform Standards of Professional Appraisal Practice (USPAP). A number of factors affect the value of an item, including the intended use of the value, the type of value, the valuation approach used, the highest and best use of the item, and the inherent characteristics of the item. In addition, values should be distinguished from prices, as they are not the same.

Intended Use

Values can be calculated for a number of purposes, such as fair market value, insurance, charitable donation, bankruptcy, estate tax, and equitable distribution for divorce or inheritance. The value for each will be estimated based on appropriate criteria for that purpose. For example, a fair market value for buying or selling an item can be researched by checking completed sales for comparable items at auctions or online.

Values can also be assigned for **insurance coverage**. In that case, coverage can be for "replacement value" or "actual cash value." Replacement value is the amount of money needed to replace an item with a new one of similar design, material, and quality of workmanship. Actual cash value, on the other hand, is replacement value minus depreciation.

In addition, values can be assigned to assets named in **bankruptcy proceedings**. Accurate values help the courts liquidate property and provide appropriate compensation to those who are owed debts.

Values can also be used for **tax calculations**, such as deductions for donation to charity and for determining taxes due upon inheritance. And values can be used for **distributing property** between divorcing spouses or among those inheriting property. It can be challenging to devise an equitable distribution of objects, as it's not practical to physically divide tangible property. Often, appraisers are asked to value the items so they can be distributed and inequities settled monetarily.

Types of Values

Fair Market Value: This is the retail value, which is the most common use of the word "value." According to U.S. Treasury regulations, subchapter B, sec. 20.2031-1, "the fair market value is the price at which the property would change hands between a willing buyer and a willing seller, neither being under any compulsion to buy or to sell and both having reasonable knowledge of relevant facts." This would describe a buyer purchasing an antique at a typical antiques shop, show, auction, etc., where the dealer has knowledge of his field and the buyer has enough access to the item to be able to make an informed decision. In this case, neither the seller or buyer are forced to buy or sell. If an object is bought or sold without adequate knowledge, the sale may be perfectly legal and ethical, but the sale price may not necessarily reflect its fair market value, as it may have traded for too little or too much. The fair market value also reflects the age, wear, and condition of the item. If an item is well worn or damaged, the fair market value will be correspondingly less than the value of the same item in new condition because of depreciation.

Replacement Value: This value describes the amount that would have to be paid to replace an item with a similar one of equivalent quality and workmanship at current prices and does not count depreciation. Thus, since a replacement cost insurance policy provides higher coverage than actual cash value, a replacement cost policy is usually more expensive.

Actual Cash Value: Actual cash value is replacement value minus depreciation.

Forced Liquidation Value: Liquidation value applies to a sale in which a person is required to sell quickly, such as a court-ordered sale to settle debts because of a bankruptcy. In such a case, the seller does not have the option to wait for what he would normally consider an acceptable price. Liquidation value would normally be significantly lower than fair market value.

Valuation Approach

There are various ways to calculate value. The most common is the **"comparable cost approach,"** which takes into consideration recent prices paid for comparable items, with adjustments made for differences such as condition and regional and seasonal demand, and for inflation or strength or weakness of the market. The comparable cost approach is only practical for items that are commonly traded and therefore have available sale prices to research. An excellent way to research comparable costs is to consult auction prices from regional, national, or international auction houses. These prices can be found in "realized price" lists compiled by the auction houses after auctions have been completed. Published price lists are generally only produced for auctions that sell relatively valuable antiques and collectibles rather than lower end items. For lower value items, collectors may have to look for completed prices on eBay or track prices manually at local auctions.

Next is the **"cost approach,"** which is used when comparable sales are not available. This approach calculates the cost of reproducing or replacing the item with an item of similar design, material, and quality of workmanship.

The final method, the **"income approach,"** is used much less often than the first two. It is used when an object generates revenue. For example, if an antique counter were used in an ice cream shop, it could be assigned a value based on its use in creating income. If the counter burned in a fire or was otherwise ruined, the loss can be measured not only in the loss of decorative value, but in the loss of future income.

Highest and Best Use

The term **"highest and best use"** refers to the principle that an object should be appraised according to the market that offers the highest value for it. For example, an antique gold watch could be valued either by its precious metal content or by its value as an antique. If it is a rare watch by a well-known and highly prized maker, the watch's value as antique could easily surpass its precious metal value. This is important because it would be tragic for the watch to be melted down for a mere fraction of the value that it could obtain at a specialized watch auction with eager, deep-pocketed buyers waiting to purchase it for its higher value as an antique. The highest value should always be carefully considered and sought.

Inherent Characteristics

Age: A common misconception is that age is the primary characteristic determining value. Nothing could be further from the truth. An antique can be very old yet not particularly valuable. For example, many coins from Roman times are less valuable than rarer coins minted in the last century. Rarity is a much more significant factor. The misconception is probably connected to the fact that age often contributes to rarity. It is true that the older an item is, the more likely that it is scarcer, either because other items like it have been lost because of neglect, damage, or disposal or because few of the items—especially handmade items—were made to begin with.

Quality: Quality involves a number of factors such as the quality of materials used. For instance, mahogany is a more valuable material than pine, not just because mahogany is scarcer but because of its inherent properties such as its finer grain and its greater density, which makes it less vulnerable to warping and better for carving, as it can hold intricate details.

Also, a well designed antique will show superior artistic qualities such as pleasing proportion, symmetry, use of colors, etc. And a quality piece will show excellent workmanship.

Period and Style: As demographics change, decorating trends change as well. For instance, Gen X (post Baby Boomers) and Gen Y (Millennials) prefer simplified modern design rather than fussy Victorian styles.

Original vs. Reproduction: Reproductions normally have less value than original pieces because they are generally of lower quality and greater quantity than the originals.

Condition: An antique that is in excellent condition with its original finish and an attractive patina will be more desirable and, therefore, have more value than one that has not been as well preserved.

Alterations/Restorations/Repairs/ Additions/Missing Parts: The more repairs and missing or replaced parts an item has the lower its value will be in the marketplace.

Maker: Certain company lines, like Rookwood, have achieved fame for their workmanship. Objects made by these companies enjoy premium values.

Artist: Individual artists have also reached legendary status for their skill. Pieces signed by famous artists such as Kataro Shirayamadami also have greater value.

Size: Items such as furniture and advertising signs that are very large can have lower values if they are impractical to use or display.

Value vs. Price

Value and price aren't the same. Value is the amount of money an item is estimated to be worth. Price, on the other hand, is the amount of money being asked for an item. Using real estate as an example, a homeowner could put a house on the market at a price of $250,000. But its actual value could be much less. The value would be affected by relatively objective and measurable criteria such as square footage, quality of building materials, and quality of construction, and by more subjective ones like location, architectural style, and market demand. Part of a real estate agent's job is to help estimate property value by evaluating these criteria and by compiling comparables—recent sales of homes with similar characteristics—and encouraging their clients to set prices in accordance with those values. The same principle applies to antiques and collectibles. The value of an item is determined by inherent qualities and sales of comparable items, and prices should be set accordingly.

Conclusion

The *Antique Trader Antiques and Collectibles Price Guide* lists retail values (fair market values) and relies primarily on comparable costs derived from two sources. For mid-range to high-end items, values are normally derived from results at cataloged auctions. For low-value items usually not sold at cataloged auctions, experts in the category are consulted for values based on their knowledge of sales results in other venues.

It's wise to study all the factors that can affect value and price. Consult this book and specialized price guides, experts in the field, and, if necessary, for very expensive items or complex situations like a divorce or estate liquidation, hire a reputable experienced appraiser who can apply years of study and practical experience to establish credible values and recommend likely sales results in various venues. Your investment will be well worth it and will save money in the long run.

SPECIAL CONTRIBUTORS AND ADVISORS
Index by Subject

ABC Plates: Joan M. George
Black Americana: Leonard Davis and Caroline Torem-Craig
Character Collectibles: Dana Cain
Chase Brass & Copper Company: Donald-Brian Johnson
Cloisonné: Arlene Rabin
Compacts & Vanity Cases: Roselyn Gerson
Decals: Jim Trautman
Eyewear: Donald-Brian Johnson
Jewelry (Costume): Marion Cohen
Kitchenwares:
- **Cow Creamers:** LuAnn Riggs
- **Egg Cups:** Joan M. George
- **Egg Timers:** Ellen Bercovici
- **Pie Birds:** Ellen Bercovici
- **Reamers:** Bobbie Zucker Bryson
- **String Holders:** Ellen Bercovici

Lighting: Carl Heck
Lighting Devices:
- **1930s Lighting:** Donald-Brian Johnson
- **Moss Lamps:** Donald-Brian Johnson

Nativity Sets: Donald-Brian Johnson
Plant Waterers: Bobbie Zucker Bryson
Pop Culture Collectibles: Dana Cain and Emmett Butler
Ribbon Dolls: Bobbie Zucker Bryson
Steins: Andre Ammelounx
Vintage Clothing: Nancy Wolfe and Madeleine Kirsh

CERAMICS

Abingdon: Elaine Westover
American Painted Porcelain: Dorothy Kamm
Amphora-Teplitz: Les and Irene Cohen
Bauer Pottery: James Elliott-Bishop
Belleek (American): Peggy Sebek
Belleek (Irish): Del Domke
Blue & White Pottery: Steve Stone
Blue Ridge Dinnerwares: Marie Compton and Susan N. Cox
Brayton Laguna Pottery: Susan N. Cox
Buffalo Pottery: Phillip Sullivan
Caliente Pottery: Susan N. Cox
Catalina Island Pottery: James Elliott-Bishop
Ceramic Arts Studio of Madison: Donald-Brian Johnson
Clarice Cliff Designs: Laurie Williams
Cleminson Clay: Susan N. Cox
deLee Art: Susan N. Cox
Doulton/Royal Doulton: Reg Morris, Louise Irvine and Ed Pascoe
East Liverpool Potteries: William and Donna J. Gray
Flow Blue: K. Robert and Bonne L. Hohl
Franciscan Ware: James Elliott-Bishop
Frankoma Pottery: Susan N. Cox
Gonder Pottery: James R. and Carol S. Boshears
Hall China: Marty Kennedy
Harker: William A. and Donna J. Gray
Hull: Joan Hull
Ironstone: General - Bev Dieringer; Tea Leaf - The Tea Leaf Club International
Limoges: Debby DuBay
Majolica: Michael Strawser
McCoy: Craig Nissen
Mettlach: Andre Ammelounx
Noritake: Tim Trapani
Old Ivory: Alma Hillman
Pacific Clay Products: Susan N. Cox
Phoenix Bird & Flying Turkey: Joan Collett Oates
Pierce (Howard) Porcelains: Susan N. Cox
Quimper: Sandra Bondhus
Red Wing: Gail Peck
Royal Bayreuth: Mary McCaslin
Rozart Pottery: Susan N. Cox
R.S. Prussia: Mary McCaslin

Russel Wright Designs: Kathryn Wiese
Schoop (Hedi) Art Creations: Susan N. Cox
Shawnee: Linda Guffey
Shelley China: Mannie Banner; David Chartier; Bryand Goodlad; Edwin E. Kellogg; Gene Loveland and Curt Leiser
Stoneware and Spongeware: Bruce and Vicki Waasdorp
Vernon Kilns: Pam Green
Warwick China: John Rader, Sr.
Zeisel (Eva) Designs: Kathryn Wiese
Zsolnay: Federico Santi/ John Gacher

GLASS:

Animals: Helen and Bob Jones
Cambridge: Helen and Bob Jones
Carnival Glass: Jim and Jan Seeck
Central Glass Works: Helen and Bob Jones
Consolidated Glass: Helen and Bob Jones
Depression Glass: Linda D. Carannante
Duncan & Miller: Helen and Bob Jones
Fenton: Helen and Bob Jones
Fostoria: Helen and Bob Jones
Fry: Helen and Bob Jones
Heisey: Helen and Bob Jones
Higgins Glass: Donald-Brian Johnson
Imperial: Helen and Bob Jones
McKee: Helen and Bob Jones
Morgantown: Helen and Bob Jones
New Martinsville: Helen and Bob Jones
Opalescent Glass: James Measell
Paden City: Helen and Bob Jones
Pattern Glass: Green Valley Auctions
Phoenix Glass: Helen and Bob Jones
Wall Pocket Vases: Bobbie Zucker Bryson
Westmoreland: Helen and Bob Jones

Contributors and Advisors Contact Directory

Andre Ammelounx
P.O. Box 136
Palatine, IL 60078
(847) 991-5927

Mannie Banner
126 S.W. 15th St.
Pembroke Pines, FL 33027

Belleek Collectors International Society
Belleek Pottery Ltd.
3 Main Street
Belleek
Co. Fermanagh
N. Ireland
BT93 3FY
44(0)28 6865 8501
e-mail: collector@belleek.ie

Ellen Bercovici
360 -11th Ave. So.
Naples, FL 34102

Sandra Bondhus
P.O. Box 100
Unionville, CT 06085
e-mail: nbondhus@pol.net

James R. and Carol S. Boshears
375 W. Pecos Rd., #1033
Chandler, AZ 85225
(480) 899-9757

Bobbie Zucker Bryson
Bluffton, SC
Napkindoll@aol.com

Emmett Butler
Denver, CO
(303) 840-1649

Dana Cain
5061 S.Stuart Ct.
Littleton CO 80123
e-mail: dana.cain@att.net

CAS Collectors
206 Grove St.
Rockton, IL 61072
Web: www.cascollectors.com
www.ceramicartstudio.com

Linda D. Carannante
TLC Antiques
Pottstown, PA
(610) 246-5241

David Chartier
1171 Waterside
Brighton, MI 48114

Les and Irene Cohen
Pittsburgh, PA
or
Amphora Collectors International
21 Brooke Dr.
Elizabethtown, PA 17022
e-mail: tombeaz@comcast.net

Marion Cohen
14 Croyden Ct.
Albertson, NY 11507
(516) 294-0055

Neva Colbert
69565 Crescent Rd.
St. Clairsvville, OH 43950
(740) 695-2355
e-mail: georgestreet@1st.net

Marie Compton
M&M Collectibles
1770 So. Randall Rd., #236
Geneva, IL 60134-4646
eBay: brdoll

Susan N. Cox
El Cajon, CA
e-mail: antiquefever@aol.com

Caroline Torem-Craig
New York, New York

Leonard Davis
New York, New York

Bev Dieringer
P.O. Box 536
Redding Ridge, CT 06876
e-mail: dieringer1@aol.com

Janice Dodson
P.O. Box 957
Bloomfield Hills, MI 48303

Del E. Domke
16142 N.E. 15th St.
Bellevue, WA 98008-2711
(425) 746-6363
e-mail: delyicious@comcast.net

Debby DuBay
Limoges Antiques Shop
62 Merchants Row
Rutland, VT 05701
(802) 773-6444

Joan M. George
67 Stevens Ave.
Oldbridge, NJ 08856
e-mail: drjgeorge@nac.net

Roselyn Gerson
12 Alnwick Rd.
Malverne, NY 11565
(516) 593-8746
e-mail: compactlady@aol.com

William A. and Donna J. Gray
2 Highland Colony
East Liverpool, OH 43920
e-mail: harkermate@comcast.net

Pam Green
You Must Remember This
P.O. Box 822
Hollis, NH 03049
e-mail: ymrt@aol.com
Web: www.ymrt.com

Green Valley Auctions
2259 Green Valley Lane
Mt. Crawford, VA 22841
(540) 434-4260
Web: www.greenvalleyauctions.com

Linda Guffey
2004 Fiat Court
El Cajon, CA 92019-4234
e-mail: Gufantique@aol.com

Carl Heck
Box 8516
Aspen, CO 81612
(970) 925-8011
Web: www.carlheck.com

Alma Hillman
197 Coles Corner Rd.
Winterport, ME 04496
e-mail: oldivory@adelphia.net

K. Robert and Bonne L. Hohl
47 Fawn Dr.
Reading, PA 19607

Joan Hull
1376 Nevada S.W.
Huron, SD 57350

Hull Pottery Association
11023 Tunnel Hill N.E.
New Lexington, OH 43764

Louise Irvine
England: (020) 8876-7739
e-mail: louiseirvine@blueyonder.co.uk

Helen and Bob Jones
Berkeley Springs, WV
e-mail: Bglances@ aol.com

Donald-Brian Johnson
3329 South 56th St., #611
Omaha, NE 68106
e-mail: donaldbrian@msn.com

Dorothy Kamm
10786 Grey Heron Ct.
Port St. Lucie, FL 34986
e-mail: dorothykamm@adelphia.net

Edwin E. Kellogg
4951 N.W. 65th Ave.
Lauderhill, FL 33319

Madeleine Kirsh
C. Madeleine's
13702 Biscayne Blvd.
North Miami Beach, FL 33181
(305) 945-7770

Curt Leiser
National Shelley China Club
12010 - 38th Ave. NE
Seattle, WA 98125
(206) 362-7135
e-mail: curtispleiser@cs.com

Gene Loveland
11303 S. Alley Jackson Rd.
Grain Valley, MO 64029

Mary McCaslin
6887 Black Oak Ct. E.
Avon, IN 46123
(317) 272-7776
e-mail: Maryjack@indy.rr.com

Metz Superlatives Auction
P.O. Box 18185
Roanoke, VA 24014
(540) 985-3185
Web: www.metzauction.com

Reg G. Morris
2050 Welcome Way
The Villages, FL 32162
e-mail: modexmin@comcast.net

Craig Nissen
P.O. Box 223
Grafton, WI 53024-0223

Joan C. Oates
1107 Deerfield Lane
Marshall, MI 49068
e-mail: JOATES120@broadstripe.net

Gail Peck
Country Crock Antiques
2121 Pearl St.
Fremont, NE 68025
(420) 721-5721

Arlene Rabin
P.O. Box 243
Fogelsville, PA 18051
e-mail: arjw9299@verizon.net

John Rader, Sr.
Vice President, National Assn. of Warwick China & Pottery Collectors
780 S. Village Dr., Apt. 203
St. Petersburg, FL 33716
(727) 570-9906
Author of "Warwick China" (Schiffer Publishing, 2000)
or

Betty June Wymer
28 Bachmann Dr.
Wheeling, WV 26003, (304) 232-3031) Editor, "The IOGA" Club Quarterly, newsletter

LuAnn Riggs
1781 Lindberg Dr.
Columbia, MO 65201
e-mail: artichokeannies@bessi.net

Tim and Jamie Saloff
P.O. Box 339
Edinboro, PA 16412
e-mail: tim.salofff@verizon.net

Federico Santi
The Drawing Room Antiques
152 Spring St.
Newport, RI 02840
(401) 841-5060
Web: www.drawrm.com

Peggy Sebek
3255 Glencairn Rd.
Shaker Heights, OH 44122
e-mail: pegsebek@earthlink.net

Jim and Jan Seeck
Seeck Auctions
P.O. Box 377
Mason City, IA 50402
(641) 424-1116
e-mail: jimjan@seeckauction.com

Steve Stone
12795 W. Alameda Pkwy.
Lakewood, CO 80225
e-mail: Sylvanlvr@aol.com

Michael G. Strawser Auctions
P.O. Box 332
Wolcottville, IN 46795
(260) 854-2859
Web: www.majolicaauctions.com

Phillip Sullivan
P.O. Box 69
South Orleans, MA 02662
(508) 255-8495

Mark and Ellen Supnick
7725 NW 78th Ct.
Tamarac, FL 33321
e-mail: saturdaycook@aol.com

Tea Leaf Club International
P.O. Box 377
Belton, MO 64012
Webb: www.tealeafclub.com

Tim Trapani
7543 Northport Dr.
Boynton Beach, FL 33437

Jim Trautman
R.R. 1
Orton, Ontario CANADA L0N 7N0
e-mail: trautman@sentex.net

Bruce and Vicki Waasdorp
P.O. Box 434
Clarence, NY 14031
(716) 759-2361
Web: www.antiques-stoneware.com

Elaine Westover
210 Knox Hwy. 5
Abingdon, IL 61410-9332

Kathryn Wiese
Retrospective Modern Design
P.O. Box 305
Manning, IA 51455
e-mail: retrodesign@earthlink.net

Laurie Williams
Rabbitt Antiques and Collectibles
(408) 248-1260
e-mail: rabbitt3339@yahoo.com

Nancy Wolfe
Galena, IL 61036

Auction Houses Providing Color Digital Images:

American Pottery Auction
Vicki and Bruce Waasdorp
P.O. Box 434
Clarence, NY 14031
(716) 759-2361
Web: www.antiques-stoneware.com
(Stoneware Pottery)

Garth's Arts & Antiques
P.O. Box 369
Delaware, OH 43015
(740) 362-4771
Web: www.garths.com
(Americana)

Green Valley Auctions
2259 Green Valley Lane
Mt. Crawford, VA 22841
(540) 434-4260
Web: www.greenvalleyauctions.com
(American Glass & Lighting)

Glass Works Auctions
Box 180
East Greenville, PA 18041
(2150 679-5849
Web: www.glswrk-auction.com

Heritage Auction Galleries
3500 Maple Avenue
Dallas, TX 75219-3941
(800) 835-3243
Web: www.HertiageAuctions.com
(Victoriana)

Morphy Auctions
2000 N. Reading Road
Denver, PA 17517
(717) 335-3435
Web: morphyauctions.com
(Advertising, Toys, Games, Disney)

Neal Auction Company
4038 Magazine St.
New Orleans, LA 70115
(504) 899-5329
Web: www.nealauctions.com
(Americana)

Seeck Auction Company
Jim and Jan Seeck
P.O. Box 377
Mason City, IA 50402
Web: www.seeckauction.com

Skinner, Inc.
357 Main St.
Bolton, MA 01740
(978) 779-6241
Web: www.skinnerinc.com
(Americana & Jewelry)

Other Auction Houses Providing Photographs:

Charlton Hall Auctioneers
912 Gervais St.
Columbia, SC 29201

Christie's New York
20 Rockefeller Plaza
New York, NY 10020

Cincinnati Art Galleries
225 East Sixth St.
Cincinnati, OH 45202

Fontaines Auction Gallery
1485 W. Housatonic St.
Pittsfield, MA 01210

Guyette & Schmidt, Inc.
P.O. Box 522
West Farmington, ME 04922

Norman Heckler & Company
79 Bradford Corner Road
Woodstock Valley, CT 06282

Jackson's International Auctioneers & Appraisers
2229 Lincoln St.
Cedar Falls, IA 50613

James D. Julia, Inc.
P.O. Box 830
Fairfield, ME 04937

McMasters-Harris Auction Company
P.O. Box 755
Cambridge, OH 43725

New Orleans Auction Gallery
1330 St. Charles Ave.
New Orleans, LA 70130

Past Tyme Pleasures
39 California Ave., Suite 105
Pleasanton, CA 94566

Rago Art & Auction Center
333 No. Main St.
Lambertville, NJ 08530

Slater's Americana, Inc.
5335 No. Tacoma Ave., Suite 24
Indianapolis, IN 46220

Michael G. Strawser Majolica Auctions
P.O. Box 332
Wolcottville, IN 46795

John Toomey Gallery
818 North Blvd.
Oak Park, IL 60301

Treadway Gallery, Inc.
2029 Madison Road
Cincinnati, OH 45208

Other Photographs Provided By:

Susan Eberman, Bedford, IN; Ellen R. Hill, Bennington, NH; Mary Ann Johnston, New Cumberland, WV; Vivian Kromer, Bakersfield, CA; Pat Moore, San Francisco, CA; Margaret Payne, Columbus, IN, John Petzold, and Dr. Leslie Piña.

ADVERTISING ITEMS

Thousands of objects made in various materials, some intended as gifts with purchases, others used for display or given away for publicity, are now being collected. Also see various other categories and *Antique Trader Advertising Price Guide*.

Balloon inflator, "Buster Brown Shoes," figural winking Buster Brown in-store display that fits over standard helium tank, one-piece molded fiberglass head w/inflation valve that sits atop gas cylinder & two-piece vinyl cape & sheath that slides over cylinder, sheet metal base, 24 x 24" head **$230**

Calendar illustration, 1924, "Edison Mazda," Maxfield Parrish illustration titled "The Venetian Lamplighter," for large size 1924 Edison Mazda calendar, 15 3/4 x 25" (ILLUS. framed) **$1,208**

Calendar, 1901, "The Capewell Horse Nail," illustration of winter scene w/two horse-drawn sleighs racing, the name dripping w/images of icicles, full pad for 1901, Gray Litho, New York, 10 x 13 1/2" **$546**

American illustrator Maxfield Parrish (1870-1966) was especially well known for his vivid colors and dynamic energy, which made him an ideal artist for advertisements.

Bigger is not always better, nor does it necessarily make an advertising item more valuable. Very large advertising items are harder to sell because few collectors have the room to display them. However, there is a limited market for them among restaurants and other businesses who use them for decorating large spaces.

Clock, "Clapperton's Thread," figure-8 style, wood w/papier-mâché bezels, Roman numerals, the upper bezel reading "Clapperton's Six Cord Spool Cotton," the lower bezel reading "Is the Best," w/pendulum & key, 18 1/2" w., 31" h. **$1,035**

Clock, "OshKosh B'gosh Work Clothes," electric wall neon-type, octagonal case w/a green reverse-painted outer border over the neon, orange wording on dial, sweep seconds hand, ca. 1938, apparently not working, 19" w. **$316**

Clock, "Fireman's Insurance Co. - Newark, NJ," cast gilt-metal, an upright ornate scroll-cast case w/advertising below the round inset dial w/Arabic numerals, the top cast w/the figure of a standing fireman holding a fire horn & leaning on a fire hydrant, 1905, clock not working, 9 1/4" h. **$651**

Clock, "L.O. Grothe & Co. - Montreal - the Boston Cigar - The Peg-Top Cigar," cast gilt-metal, long oblong base w/a cast three-quarters figure of an elegant gentleman w/advertising on his chest at one end & another figure of a man holding an open cigar box w/advertising at the other end, an inset round clock dial w/Roman numerals & framed by leaves in the center, bronzed finish, ca. 1890s, keys present, clock not running, 16" l., 11 1/4" h. **$1,854**

Counter display box, "Fairbanks Fairy Soap," square wood w/each side printed in black & gold w/advertising, original color-printed label inside the lid decorated w/red roses, early 20th c., 17" w., 8" h. **$489**

Coin purse, "Jake's Place," leather w/metal frame, one side of frame embossed w/clover leaves, horseshoe & head of a woman w/flowing hair, the other w/celluloid advertising panel reading "Compliments of Jake's Place - Wines, Liquors and Cigars - Volga, S.D.," 3 x 3" **$121**

Counter display box, "Alma Polish," square wood w/hinged lift top w/color printed label inside in black, white & red, further advertising on the sides & front, all-original, early 20th c., 15 1/2" w., 7" h. **$115**

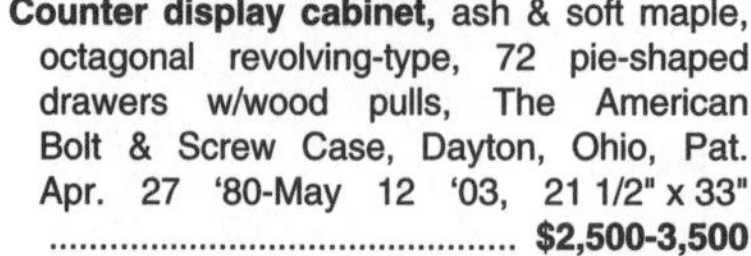

Counter display cabinet, ash & soft maple, octagonal revolving-type, 72 pie-shaped drawers w/wood pulls, The American Bolt & Screw Case, Dayton, Ohio, Pat. Apr. 27 '80-May 12 '03, 21 1/2" x 33" **$2,500-3,500**

Counter display cabinet, "Belding Silk," walnut, wording on ornate crestrail centered by a clock dial, thirty drawers w/curved glass fronts on upper drawers, mirrors center door at top, ca. 1890, 17 x 34", 45" h. **$3,500-4,500**

Counter display, "Carborundum Sharpening Stone," rectangular holder supporting the double-sided well-used stone, holder in red w/black & white lettering reading "Step up and Sharpen Your Pocket Knife on the Genuine Carborundum Sharpening Stone," early 20th c. (ILLUS. top left with Lufkin Rules cabinet)............. **$85**

Counter display cabinet, "Lufkin Spring Joint Rules," a long rectangular oak cabinet w/glass front over interior slots for eight rules, back acts as storage for sale stock, full decals, early 20th c. (ILLUS. bottom left with Carborundum Sharpening Stone display)................................ **$240**

Point of sale sign, "The Simonds Saw," color-printed tin, rectangular, a large silver circular saw blade surrounding the head of a workman carrying an ax, brown wood grain background w/red & white wording, early 20th c., minor wear, 13 x 17" (ILLUS. right with Lufkin Rules display cabinet) **$140**

Counter display, "Wrigley's Chewing Gum," tin w/gilt paint, half-cylinder base reading "Be sure its [sic] Wrigley's" around side, the die-cut marquee featuring Wrigley arrow figure w/smiling face pointing to panel reading "WRIGLEY'S," 6 x 13", 13" h. **$2,875**

Counter display, "Red Goose Shoes," chalkware figural goose painted red w/"Red Goose Shoes" in yellow on breast, yellow bill & feet, on green base, 11 1/2" h. **$144**

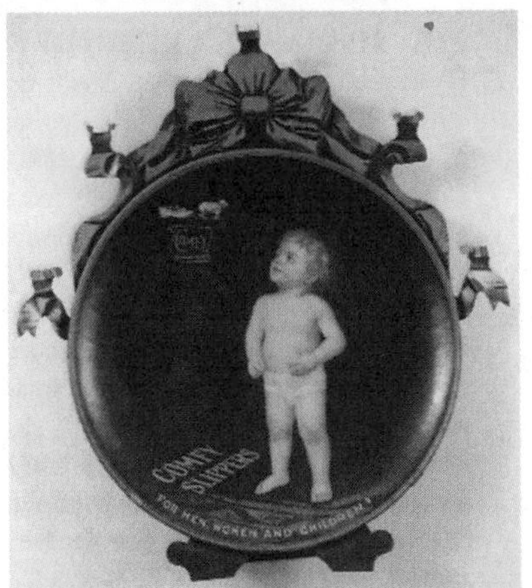

Counter display, "Comfy Slippers," 24" d. charger set within elaborate die-cut tin easel probably meant to hold five samples of Comfy slippers, the charger w/illustration of toddler gazing up at the Comfy logo of a sheep-drawn blue shoe, "Comfy Slippers - For Men, Women and Children" printed at bottom, 30" w., 32" h. **$1,639**

Counter display, "Purity Butter Pretzels," cardboard, die-cut easel-back type w/color illustration of fair-haired boy in white shirt w/ sleeves rolled up & red tie holding giant pretzel, red rectangular panel at bottom reads "Purity Butter Pretzels - Purity Pretzel Co." in white lettering along w/location & proprietor, 12 1/2 x 22" **$121**

Counter display, "Sego Milk," die-cut color-printed cardboard, tri-fold, arched w/the center panel in black w/white lettering above a can of the product, the smaller side panels printed in muted colors w/a scene of a lady or gentleman eating, ca. 1930s, only light wear, 47" l., 27" h........ **$193**

Display box, "Mason's Challenge Shoe Blacking," wood, rectangular, inside of lid w/color illustration of black boy & white boy w/oversized black & red boots, the front panel of box reading "3 doz. - No. 2 - Mason's - Challenge - Blacking," 9 x 12", 3" h. **$110**

Hatbox, "Dobbs Fifth Avenue Hats," cardboard, miniature size, given to customers for gift-giving as one would give a gift certificate, the recipient returning it to the store to redeem for the right size hat, sides illustrated w/color scene of fancy horse-drawn carriage being driven through a snowy city street, the lid w/name of company around rim & stencil on top reading "Dobbs Fifth Avenue Hats New York" & "For" followed by space for names of recipient & gift giver, 1935 .... **$75**

Hand mirror, "See yourself in Buster Brown Shoes," flat round handled printed composition back w/an image of Buster Brown & Tige & wording in black, pink rose border, light surface soil, mirror surface very worn, early 20th c., 4 1/4" l. **$55**

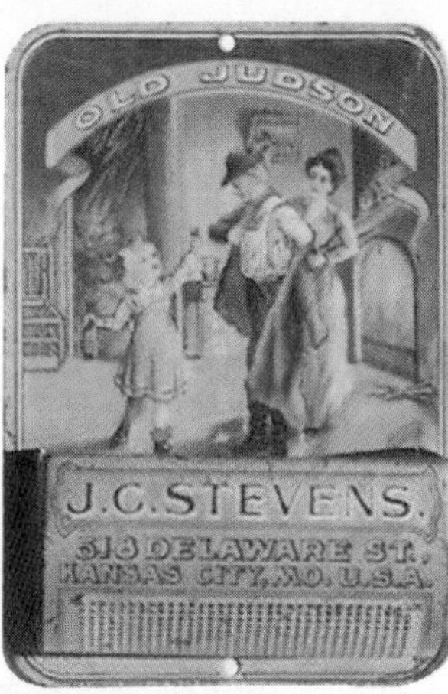

Match holder/striker, "Old Judson Whiskey," tin litho w/color illustration of cozy setting w/ woman helping man off w/his coat as little girl reaches up toward him, under banner reading "Old Judson" & over pocket for holding matches that reads "J.C. Stevens - 518 Delaware St. - Kansas City, Mo. U.S.A.," w/area for striking immediately below, by Foster & Reed of Kansas City, 3 1/2 x 5" **$176**

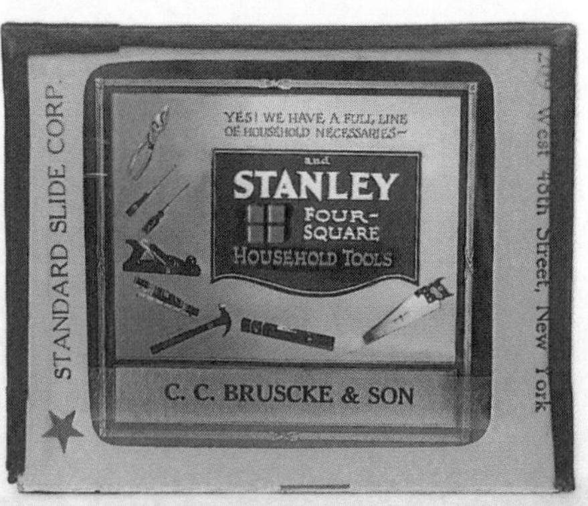

Movie house slide, color-printed glass, a rectangular matted slide w/color logo & various tools & reading "Yes! We have a full line of household necessaries - and Stanley Four-Square Household Tools - C.C. Bruscke & Son," early 20th c. **$700**

Pinback button, "Sportsman's League," celluloid, round, gold-colored edge reading "Sportsman's League" in black, the center w/illustration of fishing lure in orange & grey & reading "Johnson - Wet Fly for Trout," 1 1/2" d. **$88**

Paperweight, "Victor Spring Beds," glass, rectangular w/rounded corners, milk glass bottom, reading "Victor Spring Beds - Noiseless, Will never sag. - Guaranteed for Five Years - McElroy-Shannon Spring Bed Mfg. Co. - Louisville - Philadelphia," made by Kyle Advertising Co. of Louisville, 2 1/2 x 4", 1" h. **$77**

Pinback button, "Ducks Unlimited," celluloid, round, w/color illustration of duck flying over marsh, above "Ducks Unlimited - 1949," by Western Badge & Novelty Co. of St. Paul, Minnesota, 1 1/4" d. **$77**

Pocket mirror, "Studebaker," oval, celluloid, lithograph scene of automobile production plant by Bastian Bros., marked "Studebaker Vehicle Works - Largest in the World - South Bend, Ind. U.S.A.," ca. 1900, 1 3/4 x 2 3/4" **$200-250**

Pocket mirror, "Travelers Insurance Company," oval, celluloid, depicts approaching train engine w/skyline in background, "The Travelers Insurance Company - Hartford, Conn." in red letters above & "The Railroad Men's Reliance" in red lettering below, ca. 1900, 1 5/8 x 2 3/8" **$125-175**

Store display, "Jell-O," cardboard, three-panel die-cut display, Maxfield Parrish illustration of royal court valet presenting molded gelatin dessert to king & queen, above illustration a banner reading "Jell-O" & below illustration a box reading "The King and Queen Might Eat Thereof and Noblemen Besides," ca. 1921, 9 1/2 x 41 1/2" **$10,638**

Store display, "Wilson Rugs," miniature wooden loom w/6 x 8" rug still on the loom & connected to its balls of yarn in grey, white, red, black, cream & pink, "WILSON" spelled out in black letters on cream panel at top of rug, 1930s-40s, 11 x 14 1/2" **$125**

String holder, "Red Goose Shoes," two-piece cast-iron figural goose painted red w/"Red Goose Shoes" embossed on wing, grey ovoid base, 15" l. **$1,725**

String holder, "La Touraine Coffee," tin painted black, two identical sides, pouch decorated w/image of Arab, yellow text reading "La Touraine - The Perfect Coffee, Fresh Roasted, Ground to Order," mounts for spools, made by W.S. Quinby Co., Boston and Chicago, 20" w. x 17" h. ... **$719**

Well-known brand names are generally more desirable and therefore more valuable than lesser known brands. Look for names such as Coca-Cola, Hires Root Beer, Pepsi-Cola, Jell-O, Heinz, Cracker Jack, and Planter's Peanuts. However, because these brands command a premium, they are far more likely to be the targets of fakes and reproductions. Be cautious and examine every piece carefully.

String holder, "Red Goose Shoes," die-cut tin goose reading "Red Goose Shoes" on both sides, wire string holder hanging below display, 18" w., 26" h. **$2,530**

Thermometer, "5/A Horse Blankets," round, yellow metal w/paper face, black numbers & black diamond shape in center marked "We've Got 'Em - You Want 'Em - 5/A Horse Blankets," & marked along bottom near frame "Standard Thermometer and Electric Company, Peabody, Massachusetts, Pat. May 8, 1888," 9 1/4" d. **$200-250**

Thermometer, "Red Crown Gasoline - for Power Mileage," porcelain, hanging-type, long narrow rectangular type printed in white, black & orange, produced for Polarine, early 20th c., couple of large chips on lower left & top center, redwood frame appears original, 20" w., 73" h. **$1,140**

Thermometer, "Gillette," barometer & thermometer, blue porcelain, reads "Blue Gillette Blades" beneath picture of razor blade at top, thermometer in center & barometer at bottom, reads "Blue Gillette Blades" 6 1/4" w., 27 1/2" h. **$1,925**

Thermometer, "Atlas Perma-Guard," metal tapering oblong, marked "Atlas Perma-Guard Anti-Freeze Coolant" above in white lettering on red, "Year-round Protection" in blue lettering below, red, white & blue sun w/ray design, 8" w., 24" h. (scratches, soiling, paint chips) **$83**

"Motley's Big Roller Flour," wood w/rounded top, painted "Motley's Big Roller Flour, Rochester, N.Y., Moseley & Motley Milling Co." in circle above, "High Quality Bread Flour, Buy It Here" on side below, 9" w., 20 1/2" h. **$58**

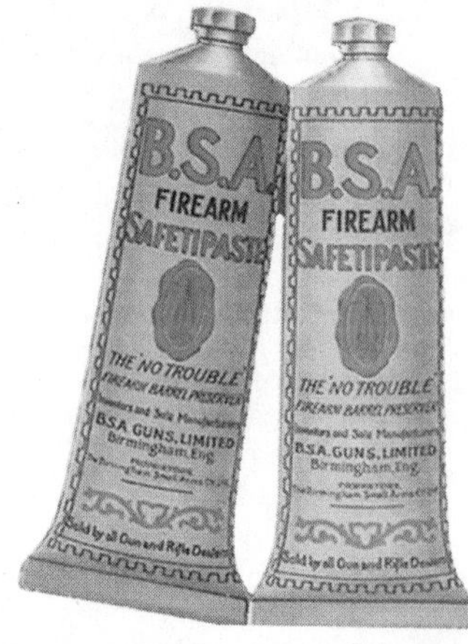

Trade card, "B.S.A. Firearm Safetipaste," die-cut fold-out card shaped like two labeled tubes of the product, each reading "B.S.A. Firearm Safetipaste" above logo, "The No Trouble Firearm Barrel Preserver" & company information below, 2 x 5 1/4" **$44**

Mercury is toxic and can be absorbed through the skin. If a mercury thermometer breaks, wear gloves to clean the spill.

ARCHITECTURAL ITEMS

In recent years the growing interest in and support for historic preservation has spawned a greater appreciation of the fine architectural elements that were an integral part of early building, both public and private. Where, in decades past, structures might be razed and doors, fireplace mantels, windows, etc., hauled to the dump, today all interior and exterior details from unrestorable buildings are salvaged to be offered to home restorers, museums and even builders who want to include a bit of history in a new construction project.

Building ornament, cast iron, large spread-winged model of an eagle perched on a half-round hemisphere, painted silver, American, late 19th c., 46 1/2" w., 18" h. **$1,293**

Door, bronze, decorated w/three tall narrow pierced Gothic-style upper panels above three smaller square panels & three vertical molded panels, the frame mounted w/ large diamond-shaped bolt heads, the inside fitted w/a hinged glazed panel & lock, some denting to lock are, loose back panel top left, glass missing from one panel, 19th c., 33 5/8" w., 76 1/8" h. **$1,610**

Frontispiece, bronze & brass, Art Deco style, probably from the interior of a bank, a tall single door w/an openwork vertical design of diamonds & small scrolls, along w/two high fence panels & four uprights w/cast fish scale designs, apparently complete except for glass insert & possibly some missing pieces from the door, 1930s, fence sections 60" w., 74" h., door 30 1/2" w., 85" h., the group **$460**

Window cornice, giltwood & burl walnut & walnut, Victorian Renaissance Revival style, the long molded top centered by a carved upright acanthus leaf on a raised medallion & w/carved palmette finials at each end above the dentil-carved frieze band. shaped & blocked end bracket supports w/turned finial drops, American-made, ca. 1870s, 63" l., 30" h. **$748**

ART DECO

Interest in Art Deco, a name given an art movement stemming from the Paris International Exhibition of 1925, continues to grow today. This style flowered in the 1930s and actually continued into the 1940s. A mood of flippancy is found in its varied characteristics - zigzag lines resembling the lightning bolt, sometimes steps, often the use of sharply contrasting colors such as black and white and others. Look for prices for the best examples of Art Deco design to continue to rise.

Bar, portable-type, brown Bakelite, the narrow long oval base w/chrome side rail handles & cream Bakelite tab end handles, each end w/an opening to hold a square liquor bottle w/a taller center compartment to hold six gilt-edged glasses, ca. 1950, 24" l. **$259**

Dresser box, cov., wood & copper, figural, Egyptian Revival style, model of an ancient Egyptian sarcophagus, bentwood form overlaid in embossed copper w/Egyptian designs & blue opaque glass scarabs, the sides trimmed in tooled leather, dark rich patina w/verdigris oxidation, silk-lined, ca. 1925, 12" l. **$460**

Book ends, wrought iron, modeled as a large stylized coiled cobra ready to strike, designed & signed by Edgar Brandt, ca. 1930, 7 1/2" h., pr. **$23,900**

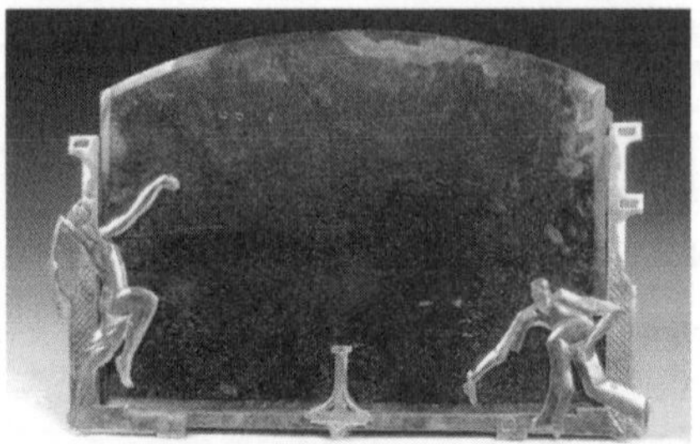

Mirror, table model, a long rectangular arched beveled mirror plate framed along the sides & base w/a silvered bronze frame depicting a pair of stylized tennis players, probably France, ca. 1920s, some minor loss to mirror silvering, 16 x 24" **$345**

Mirror, inlaid straw marqueterie, wide flat rectangular frame w/diamond-shaped corner panels & an inlaid compass star at the center top, in the style of Jean-Michel Frank, France, ca. 1940, 16 3/4 x 20 5/8" **$2,629**

Tea set, cov. teapot, cov. coffeepot, creamer & open sugar bowl; silver plate, each piece of stepped cylindrical form w/stepped & canted feet, the coffeepot w/a taupe-colored finial, teapot w/ black composition finials & handle, Wm. Hutton & Sons & J. Dixon & Sons, Sheffield, England, ca. 1930, coffeepot 6 1/4" h., the set (wear, replaced teapot handle) **$288**

Wall scones, bronze, each w/a shaped rectangular back plate supporting a single curved socket arm, polished, in the manner of Emile-Jacques Ruhlmann, unsigned, France, ca. 1925, 18" h, pr. **$3,335**

Vase, 11 3/8" h., cylindrical form w/rounded base & shoulder, w/ continuous frieze of relief-molded men & women going about their chores in a city, glazed bluish grey & cream, ca. 1920, inscribed "MOUGIN - NANCY - 257.J - Legrand dc," impressed "L" & enameled France **$1,495**

Panels, cast & wrought iron, each tall rectangular piece composed of vertical bars accented w/angular bars & an applied wrought foliate pendant at the top & scrolling bars near the base, Europe, ca. 1920s, three panels 43 1/2 x 70 1/4", two panels 37 1/2 x 70 1/4", set of five (ILLUS. of part)................ **$2,760**

←

Jean-Michel Frank (1895-1941)—a cousin of the famous Jewish World War II diarist Anne Frank—was a French interior designer who initially intended to be a lawyer, but changed plans because of the traumatic effect of the loss of two brothers during World War I, and the loss of his mother and father soon after. In the late 1920s, he was inspired by the artistic ideals of Eugenia Errazuriz and adopted her minimalist style. Beginning in 1932, he worked with Adolph Chanaux, a Parisian decorator, for nearly 10 years and helped design for wealthy patrons like the Rockefellers. He traveled to the United States just before World War II and died in New York in 1941.

ART NOUVEAU

Art Nouveau's primary thrust was between 1890 and 1905, but commercial Art Nouveau productions continued until about World War I. This style was a rebellion against historic tradition in art. Using natural forms as inspiration, it is primarily characterized by undulating or wavelike lines and whiplashes. Many objects were made in materials ranging from glass to metals. Figural pieces with seductive maidens with long, flowing hair are especially popular in this style. Interest in Art Nouveau remains high, with the best pieces by well known designers bringing strong prices.

Bust of a young woman, cast bronzed metal, the maiden wearing a fancy ruffled & flared bonnet & a wrapped gown w/wide ruffled sleeves, embossed mark "H. Jacobs - copyright 1904 by Napoleon Alliot," 18" h. **$100-200**

Card tray, silver plate, figural, a large oblong flattened shape forming a pond w/water lilies & pads & an Art Nouveau maiden rising from the water at one end, leaf & vine-formed feet, by WMF, Germany, late 19th - early 20th c., 7 3/4 x 10 1/2" **$210**

Pieces marked "silver plate," "triple plate," "EPNS," or "A1" are not sterling silver. They are made of a base metal covered with a thin silver layer.

Charger, porcelain, large round form h. p. w/a large colorful bust portrait of a partially veiled maiden w/red poppies in her black hair, against a stippled gilt ground w/stylized scattered light green flowers, the wide border decorated w/alternating swimming white swans & yellow iris w/green leaves within a dark blue outer band, artist-signed in the lower left w/a date of 1900, unmarked by maker, iron armature for hanging, 20" d. **$1,006**

Ewer, silver-mounted ivory, tall cylindrical ivory body mounted around the base w/an undulating sterling silver flaring band chased w/design of morning glories & wavy vines, the rim w/a matching wide band w/a high arched spout, rim & base joined by a long serpentine chased handle, Martelé silver by Gorham Mfg. Co., Providence, Rhode Island, 1897, 14 1/4" h. **$31,070**

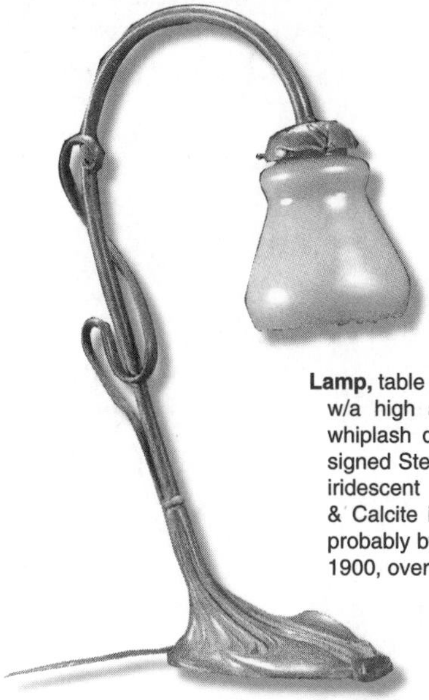

Lamp, table model, the bronze base w/a high arched stem cast w/a whiplash design & suspending a signed Steuben glass shade w/an iridescent golden brown exterior & Calcite interior, unsigned base probably by Majorelle, France, ca. 1900, overall 18 1/2" h......... **$633**

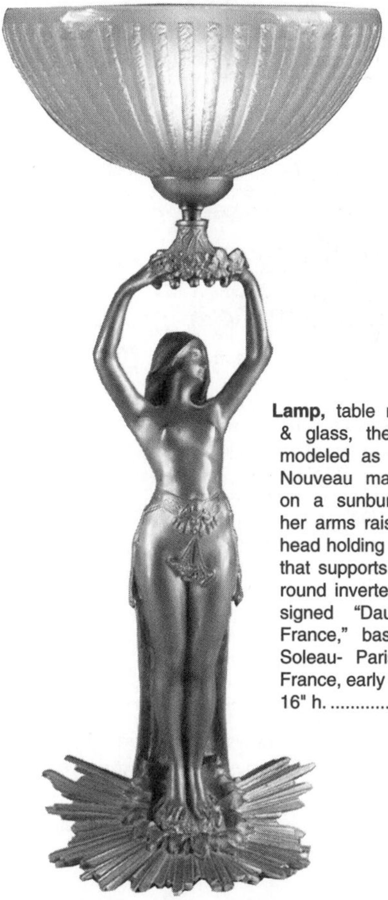

Pitcher, cov., silver-mounted cut glass, the swelled slightly tapering cylindrical glass body rock crystal-cut w/large rounded stylized blossoms among swirling bands, thick applied handle w/leaves, the low domed sterling silver hinged cover w/thumbrest & a small chased shell & floral design, cover marked inside by Tiffany & Co., New York, 1886, 9" h...................... **$4,541**

Lamp, table model, bronze & glass, the figural base modeled as an exotic Art Nouveau maiden standing on a sunburst-style base, her arms raised above her head holding a floral wreath that supports a ribbed half-round inverted glass shade signed "Daum Nancy - France," base signed "E. Soleau- Paris - A. Fery," France, early 20th c., overall 16" h. **$2,990**

Punch bowl & ladle, sterling silver, the rounded lobed & ruffled foot supporting the wide rounded bowl w/a deeply ruffled flaring rim, the sides chased w/pears, fuschia & leaves, two loop side handles, matching ladle, Martelé silver by Gorham Mfg. Co., Providence, Rhode island, 1918, bowl 21" l., 2 pcs. **$50,190**

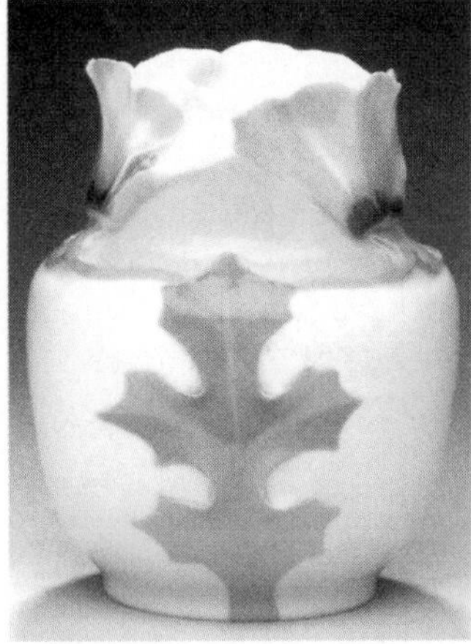

Vase, porcelain, footed bulbous body in white molded w/large light green oak leaves up the sides below the wide rounded pale green shoulder & a wide neck composed of light purple molded poppy blossoms, crowned mark of the Rorstrand Porcelain Factory w/painted numbers & monograms, ca. 1910, 5 3/4" h. **$359**

Vase, chalkware, creamy white, a bulbous squatty gently swirled base tapering to a tall cylindrial neck molded up the side w/an Art Nouveau maiden wearing a long flowing gown clinging to the flowering vines drooping around the two-lobed mouth, late 19th - early 20th c., 22 1/4" h. ... **$144**

Beware of ads in local newspapers headlined: "Antiques Wanted; Free Appraisals." It is an unethical ploy to buy antiques. Find out what your items are worth on your own before contacting potential buyers.

ASIAN MARKET REPORT

Isadore Chait , who runs I.M. Chait Gallery/Auctioneers (www.chait.com), in Beverly Hills, California, is considered the top Asian antiques specialist in the United States, and has been selling Asian antiques since 1967.

According to Chait, China is the dominant player in the Asian antiques market. "China has a gigantic middle class with an increasing amount of disposable income," he said. "Japan's market has been soft, and while South Korea's is starting to build, it's still a much smaller market. Hong Kong, Taiwan, Singapore, Malaysia, Indonesia, and a number of other countries around the world have strong Chinese markets because of their large Chinese population." He added that many mainland customers purchase their goods through Chinese buying agents bidding on their behalf at major European and American auctions.

While China is a Communist country, its relatively open and free economy has nurtured a healthy economy fueled by an immense American appetite for Chinese consumer goods. Having considerable discretionary income is not the only factor motivating the Chinese to acquire antiques. They want to buy back their heritage from Americans and Europeans who bought Chinese antiques in the 19th and 20th centuries. Since the Chinese opened Beijing's Forbidden City in the 1990s, ordinary Chinese citizens have been able to view the Royal Palace, which had previously been closed to the public. The visitors are awed by the treasures and aspire to connect with their ancestors by owning comparable items.

The Chinese government is favorable to its citizens returning its artifacts to their homeland, so bureaucratic red tape is kept to a minimum. This is helped by the fact that some of the biggest movers and shakers in the market are retired Chinese government or military leaders who still hold considerable influence.

Besides buying antiques for personal enjoyment, the Chinese also purchase them for long-term investment and for giving gifts. Gift giving is a deeply ingrained cultural tradition that helps forge not only personal but business relationships. It plays a much more important role in business in China than in Western culture. In China, it's considered a social obligation and courtesy. For example, in order to arrange an appointment with an official, a businessman would give a gift to his secretary. And in return for an official's approval of a business deal, the businessman may be expected to donate an expensive gift, such as an antique, to a local museum.

According to Chait, a number of areas in the Chinese antiques market are especially strong, such as Qing Dynasty imperial quality porcelains, lacquerware, 19th century or earlier cloisonné, jade (especially white jade), and large ivory objects. Chait emphasized that only top quality antiques are in great demand. Second-rate quality pieces are not. For example, much of the furniture that was exported from China to the United States in the early 20th century was produced in large quantity and is of mediocre quality, making it hard to sell at any price.

Chait said he sells 80 percent of his Asian antiques to out-of-town buyers, and at least 50 percent of that is purchased by overseas buyers. Chait also sells online through Artifact. He typically has 300 online bidders per auction and estimates that 20 to 30 percent of his sales are online purchases.

As with all areas of antiques and collectibles, Asian antiques are plagued with fakes and reproductions. Some can be quite difficult to detect. Chait said he visits China several times a year now, not to buy antiques as much as to visit the large retail areas to keep up with trends in reproductions. The bulk of the fakes are coming from the Chinese themselves, who are masters at the craft.

Chait pointed out that three primary factors influence value: material, workmanship, and age. Chinese artisans have access to some high quality materials, sometimes indistinguishable from that of genuine antiques. They can also produce workmanship that is comparable to the originals. The sole difference between an original and a copy may only be the age, which isn't always easy to determine. This is true for jade, for example. Old and new jade artifacts are made of the same material and can exhibit similar superb craftsmanship. The reproduction can legitimately be highly valued for these two attributes, but should not be valued the same as a comparable piece that is hundreds of years older.

"The biggest problem is with porcelain," Chait said. "Skilled Chinese artists can duplicate the workmanship of the originals, but the pieces don't have comparable materials or the age that makes the originals so valuable." Scroll paintings have also been widely faked, he said.

Chait warned that "the vast majority of Asian items on eBay are modern copies." Unfortunately, people sometimes let their eagerness cloud their judgment and hurriedly purchase an item only to discover later, when it's too late, that they've been fooled. He recommends buying and selling through a reputable dealer or auction house that will guarantee its goods are genuine.

Chait doesn't see any slowdown in the growth of the Chinese economy or its buying trends. In fact, he predicts "a geometric expansion in the market generated by Chinese citizens who want a connection to dynastic China." The state of the American economy will not halt the demand. "The U.S. recession slowed only the lower end of the Asian antiques market. The high end was totally unaffected, as there will always be buyers with money, who can afford to buy the most expensive pieces," he said.

The future is bright for the Asian market, especially Chinese antiques. Chait said Americans have become much more knowledgeable about Asian antiques in recent years due to movies and other media exposure. Those who study the category the most, however, will be in the best position to capitalize on this growing market.

JADE

Boulder, natural oblong stone w/a finely carved interior w/a Guanyin figure in light green tones, jade, polished amber-colored exterior, Oriental, 20th c., 13" h. **$805**

Figure of diety, the elderly man w/a large bald head & long beard wearing long flowing robes & standing beside a fruiting tree w/ small children climbing up beside him near an inscribed plaque, jade, white, lavender & green w/a polished finish, Oriental, 20th c., 18" h. **$1,495**

Model of a horse, Tang-style animal standing w/a caparison, jade, mottled green & lavender w/polished finish, on a carved & fitted wood base, repaired stone fissures, Oriental, 20th c., 19" h. **$431**

The stone known as "jade," is actually found in two forms: nephrite and jadeite. The English word jade comes from a term that means loin stone, for its reputed healing properties of the loins and kidneys.

Model of phoenixes, the two birds standing facing different directions but w/their heads turned looking back at each other, standing on a rockwork & vine base, pale green nephrite, Oriental, 20th c., 12" h. **$690**

Bowl, cov., squatty bulbous base w/ a carved scale design w/two flower bud handles w/rings, raised on four small feet, the low domed cover w/a hollow ball finial mounted by three mythological animals, jade, spinach green, one figure on cover chipped, small interior chips, one foot possibly restored, China, mid-20th c., 6" w., 4" h. (ILLUS. at left with carved jade jar & vase) **$633**

BANKS

Original early mechanical and cast-iron still banks are in great demand with collectors. Their scarcity has caused numerous reproductions of both types and the novice collector is urged to exercise caution. The early mechanical banks are especially scarce and some versions are seldom offered for sale but, rather, are traded with fellow collectors attempting to upgrade an existing collection. Numbers after the bank name in mechanical banks refer to those in John Meyer's *Handbook of Old Mechanical Banks*. However, another book *Penny Lane—A History of Antique Mechanical Toy Banks*, by Al Davidson, provides updated information and the number from this new volume is indicated in parenthesis at the end of each mechanical bank listing.

In past years, our standard reference for cast-iron still banks was Hubert B. Whiting's book *Old Iron Still Banks*, but because this work is out of print and a well illustrated book, The Penny Lane Bank Book—Collecting Still Banks by Andy and Susan Moore pictures and describes numerous additional banks, we will use the Moore numbers as a reference after the name of each listing. Other newer books on still banks include Iron Safe Banks by Bob and Shirley Peirce (SBCCA publication), The Bank Book by Bill Norman (N), Coin Banks by Banthrico by James Redwine (R), and Monumental Miniatures by Madua & Weingarten (MM). We will indicate the Whiting or other book reference number, with the abbreviation noted above, in parenthesis at the end.

The still banks listed are old and in good original condition with good paint and no repair unless otherwise noted. An asterisk (*) indicates this bank has been reproduced at some time.

Mechanical

Boy Scout Camp - 21 - tent w/boy, tree w/owl & two other figures, multicolored, repair to base, PL 52 .... **$5,175**

Artillery Bank (Rectangular Trap) - 6 - soldier shoots cannon into block house, original painted finish, Shepard Hardware, 1892, PL 11 .... **$1,528**

Butting Goat - 116 - cast iron, when coin is placed in tray & mechanism activated, billy goat slides forward to ram coin into gold-painted tree stump, 4 3/4", PL 91 .... **$360**

Eagle & Eaglets - 75 - bending mother eagle & rising young, w/bellows that simulate birds chirping, grey, white & yellow, green grass version known, J. & E. Stevens, ca. 1883, PL 165.... **$2,300**

Elephant Howdah - "Pull Tail" - 80 - white body w/red & blue howdah, Hubley Mfg. Coo., 1930s, PL 174 .... **$201**

Elephant Howdah - "Pull Tail" - 80 - brown body w/red & blue howdah, Hubley Mfg. Coo., 1930s, 5 1/2" h., PL 174 .... **$999**

Jonah & the Whale - 138 - Jonah in boat w/whale in water, multicolored, Shepard Hardware, pat. July 15, 1890, pedestal base version much rarer, fair paint, PL 282 .... **$2,013**

Professor Pug Frog's Great Bicycle Feat - 201-Mother Goose reading w/frog riding bicycle & clown holding large basket, multicolored, J. & E. Stevens, ca. 1886 (PL 400)............ **$7,475**

Uncle Sam w/Satchel & Umbrella - 231 - coin is dropped into open satchel, w/moving hand & mouth, red, white, blue & gold, Shepard Hardware, fair paint, trap replaced, some paint touch-up, PL 493 .... **$1,035**

William Tell - 237 - figure firing rifle at boy w/apple on head, into the tower & strikes the bell, multicolored, good paint, J. & E. Stevens, ca. 1896, PL 565 .... **$3,450**

Pottery

Chest of drawers, upright rectangular form molded w/two small drawers over two long drawers, overall dark brown Rockingham glaze, probably early 20th c., 2 3/4" h. **$99**

Still

"Andy Gump Savings Bank" - 219 - lead, standing figures of Andy flank a bank building, plain finish, General Thrift Products, ca. 1920s, missing bottom insert, 5 3/4 x 5 3/4" **$115**

Duck - Round Duck - 619 - cast iron, original paint, large Kenton-type trap, blue & red paint, Kenton Mfg. Co., 1936-40, 4 7/8" d., 4" h., W. 325 .... **$633**

Elephant on Wheels - 446 - cast iron w/gold wash, circus elephant w/howdah standing on base w/ red-spoked wheels, original paint, 4" h. **$201**

Examine every object carefully before buying. Check for chips, cracks, hidden repairs and other defects that will lower value.

Windmill - conical brick structure w/a domed roof & moveable blade, cast iron w/nickeled finish, w/original tray, 5" h. **$115**

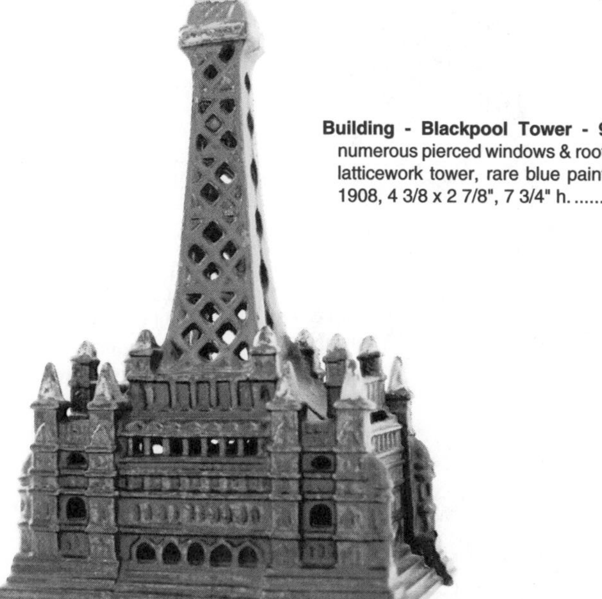

Building - Blackpool Tower - 984 - cast iron, large building w/ numerous pierced windows & roof turrets all centered by a tall pointed latticework tower, rare blue paint, Chamberlain & Hill, England, ca. 1908, 4 3/8 x 2 7/8", 7 3/4" h. **$978**

BARBERIANA

A wide variety of antiques related to the tonsorial arts have been highly collectible for many years, especially 19th- and early-20th-century shaving mugs and barber bottles. Occupational shaving mugs representing unusual jobs are highly sought after and can bring high prices.

Barber Bottles

Cobalt blue, ovoid optic-ribbed body tapering to a lady's leg neck w/rolled lip, the sides h.p. in an Art Nouveau style decorated w/gold bands & stripes highlighted by stylized white & green blossoms, pontiled base, ca. 1900, 8 3/8" h. **$392**

Cranberry cased in clear, Hobnail patt., bulbous body tapering to a three-ringed cylindrical neck w/a tooled mouth, one hob w/small tip chip, ca. 1900, 7" h. **$123**

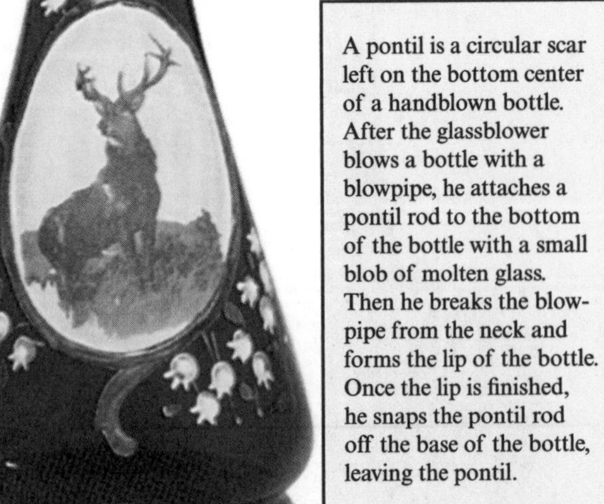

Cobalt blue, footed optic-ribbed tapering conical shape, large oval reserve on the front w/a color transfer print of a large stag based on the Monarch of the Glen painting, gold scroll border & white enameled lily-of-the-valley trim, tooled lip, pontiled base, ca. 1900, 8" h.... **$392**

A pontil is a circular scar left on the bottom center of a handblown bottle. After the glassblower blows a bottle with a blowpipe, he attaches a pontil rod to the bottom of the bottle with a small blob of molten glass. Then he breaks the blowpipe from the neck and forms the lip of the bottle. Once the lip is finished, he snaps the pontil rod off the base of the bottle, leaving the pontil.

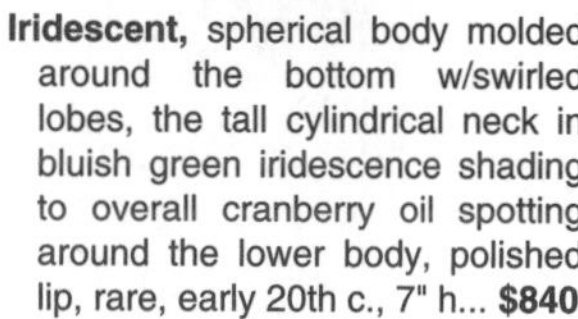

Iridescent, spherical body molded around the bottom w/swirled lobes, the tall cylindrical neck in bluish green iridescence shading to overall cranberry oil spotting around the lower body, polished lip, rare, early 20th c., 7" h... **$840**

Mary Gregory, cobalt blue Coinspot patt. w/bulbous base tapering to a lady's leg neck w/rolled lip & pontiled base, one decorated in white enamel w/ a Victorian girl playing tennis & the other w/a boy playing tennis, one w/minor content stain, the other w/a small sliver chip on edge of base, late 19th c., 8 1/4" h., facing pr. **$364**

Milk glass, ringed slightly tapering cylindrical body w/a tall ringed neck, peach-colored ground h. p. w/a large orange & blue bird above a personalized white ribbon reading "A.J. Davis - Bay Rum," original metal screw cap, smooth base, ground lip, ca. 1900, 9 1/2" h. **$532**

Milk glass, conical body w/a tall cylindrical neck, the side decorated w/a transfer-printed color scene of three frolicking cherubs surrounded by a h.p. green wreath & pink blossoms, tiny orange sprigs & blue blossoms on a yellow ground at the base, ca. 1900, base pontil, tooled mouth, 7 5/8" h. .. **$146**

Mugs

Occupational

Electric trolley driver, a large h.p. colorful scene of a red open-sided trolley full of passengers, name in worn gold at top, gold bands below, "J. & C. - Bavaria" mark on base, ca. 1900, 3 7/8" h....... **$476**

Oil driller, large color scene of an oil derrick w/steam pump house & holding tank, name above, gold banding, probably from Pennsylvania, ca. 1900, 3 1/2" h. **$728**

Railroad engineer, decorated w/a large picture of a steam locomotive marked "N.Y.C. & H. R.R.R." & tender marked "Empire State Express," name above in gold, gold band trim, 3 5/8" h. **$476**

Grocer, h.p. color scene of a grocery store front below the large gold name at the top framed w/delicate gold vining scrolls, gold band trim, ca. 1900, 3 1/2" h. **$336**

Plumber, h.p. large color scene of a plumber working on a boiler w/a pedestal sink in the background, name in gold above & gold trim bands, "Germany" impressed in the base, ca. 1900, 3 3/4" h. **$532**

Telegraph operator, decorated w/a detailed color scene of a telegraph operator standing behind a counter w/a window, flanked by pink floral clusters w/green leaves, name at the top, gold banding, ca. 1900, 3 7/8" h. **$840**

Mailman, decorated w/a scene of a horsedrawn mail wagon & driver, side of wagon marked "R.F.D. Mail Wagon," name at top & gold bands, 4" h. **$960**

Printer, decorated w/a large black & white photo of The Duplex Press, name in gold above & gold banding, Limoges blank, ca. 1900, 3 5/8" h. **$672**

Yachtsman, scene of two men sailing a small schooner, full blue wrap, name at top, Haviland blank, ca. 1900, 3 7/8" h. **$1,232**

General Items

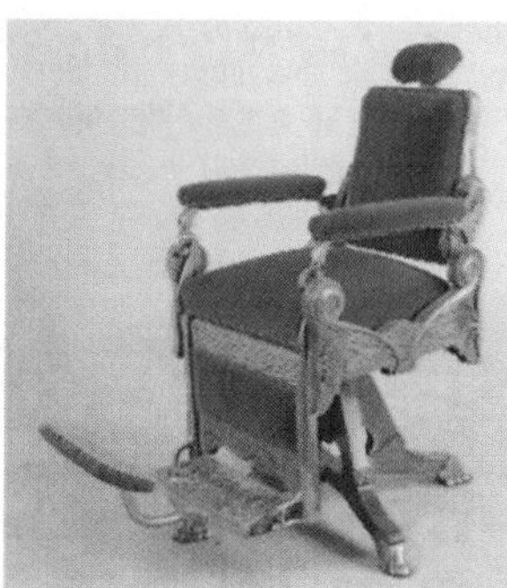

Barber chair, carved oak frame reupholstered in burgundy fabric, adjustable foot & neck rest w/ nickel-plate trim, brass lion paw feet, patent-dated 1891, one repair to the frame, 48" h. **$1,035**

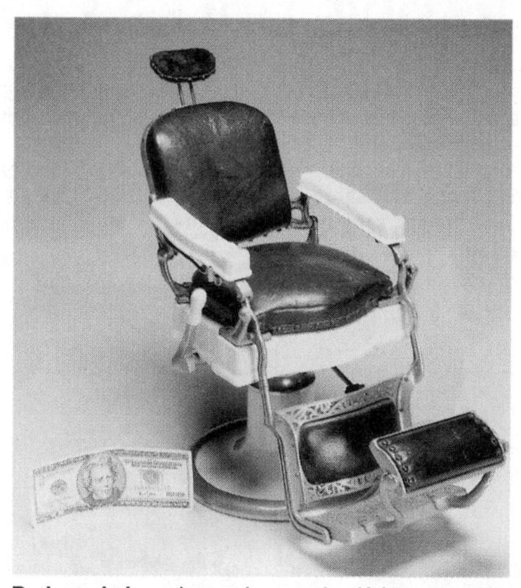

Barber chair, salesman's sample, Koken porcelain & leather miniature chair complete w/nickeled footrest w/pierced scrolling & leather pads, hydraulic mechanism, early 20th c., 14 1/2" h. **$24,000**

Barber pole, electric floor model, porcelainized metal & leaded glass, a tall hexagonal lime green porcelain on cast iron base supporting the cylindrical red & white swirled leaded glass pole framed by six nickel-plated rods, the porcelain top cap mounted w/a milk glass globe, by Koken, early 20th c., a few paint chips, overall 86" h. **$3,105**

Barber pole, wooden floor model, a multi-faceted cylindrical base section w/red, white & blue painted stripes supporting the tall multi-faceted & slightly tapering post painted w/red, white & blue swirled stripes below a small striped top section w/a red cap topped by a painted silver ball finial, probably an older repaint, late 19th c., overall 83" h..................... **$1,668**

Barber pole, leaded glass & porcelain electric model, tall tapering hexagonal design w/a white porcelain top & base, the paneled sides composed of angled bands of red & white leaded glass separated by cast-aluminum framing, missing back panel, by Koken, early 20th c., 33" h. **$720**

BARBIE DOLLS & COLLECTIBLES

At the time of her introduction in 1959, no one could have guessed that this statuesque doll would become a national phenomenon and eventually the most famous girl's plaything produced.

Over the years, Barbie and her growing range of family and friends have evolved with the times, serving as an excellent mirror of the fashion and social changes taking place in American society. Today, after more than 40 years of continuous production, Barbie's popularity remains unabated among both young girls and older collectors. Early and rare Barbies can sell for remarkable prices, and it is every Barbie collector's hope to find a mint condition "#1 Barbie."

Dolls

Barbie, "#4 Ponytail Barbie," straight-leg, brunette hair, red lips, earring holes, nostril, finger & toe paint, wearing "Candy Striper" outfit, doll in fair condition w/stiff & fuzzy ponytail, some fading, discoloration & repainting, outfit w/ blouse, pinafore & cap only age discolored, frayed & yellowed $225

Barbie, "American Girl Barbie," bent-leg, ash blonde hair, light beige lips, red finger paint, wearing American Airlines stewardess outfit, eyebrows slightly faded, back of torso slightly scuffed, left leg loose, the outfit near mint $155

Barbie, "American Girl Barbie," bent-leg, platinum blonde hair, pale peach lips, finger paint, wearing "Midnight Blue" outfit, doll in good condition, several tiny indentations & tiny holes, outfit good w/age discoloration, no purse $275

Barbie, "Bubblecut Barbie," brunette hair, coral lips, earring holes, finger & toe paint, one pearl earring, detached wrist tag, black wire stand & booklet, wearing American Airlines Stewardess outfit, minor wear & fading, discolored & worn box w/ Registered Nurse label.................... $275

More than a billion Barbie dolls have been sold since their introduction in 1959. According to Mattel, there are more than 100,000 Barbie collectors, and the average collector is 40 years old.

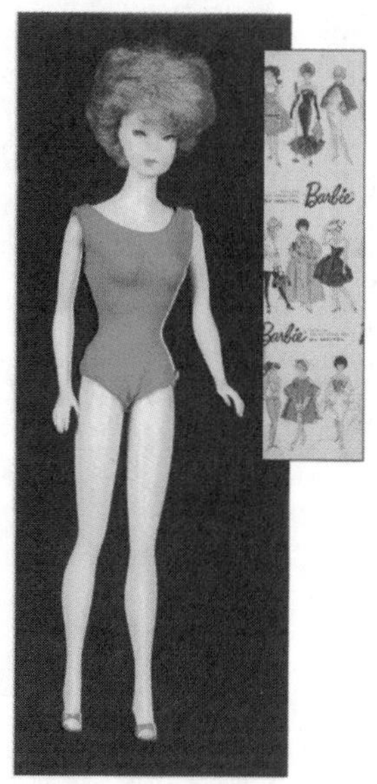

Barbie, "Bubblecut Barbie," straight-leg, titian hair, finger & toe paint, earring holes, wearing red nylon swimsuit, red open-toed shoes, pearl earrings, gold wire stand, very good condition w/some fading & discoloration, box in good condition, no box insert **$130**

Barbie, "Swirl Ponytail Barbie" in case, straight-leg, brunette hair in original set w/ yellow hair ribbon & metal hairpin, beige lips w/tint of orange, nostril, finger & toe paint, wearing original gold & white-striped swimsuit, in case w/ white open-toed shows & Fashion Booklet & in cellophane bag, new mint.................... **$675**

Barbie, "Twist 'n Turn Barbie," bent-leg, brunette hair w/plastic cover, pink lips, cheek blush, original colorful swimsuit, wrist tag, clear plastic stand & booklet, apparently never removed from box...................... **$345**

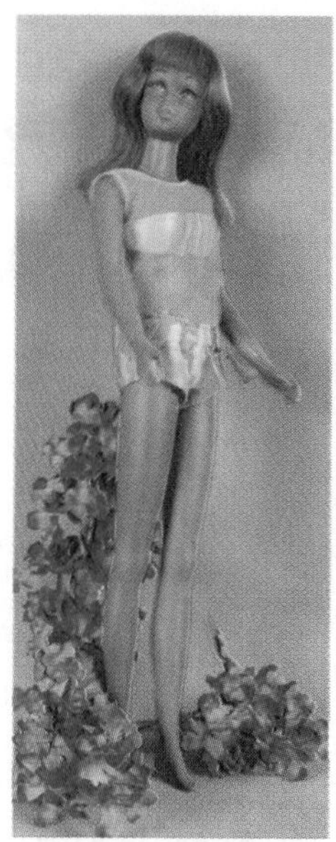

Francie, "Twist 'n Turn Francie,"blackcomplexion w/dark titian hair, bright pink lips, wearing original swimsuit, wrist tag, good condition w/some darkening & green toning, swimsuit age discolored, lightly soiled & w/hole in mesh at front **$600**

Ken, "Mod Hair Ken," No. 4224, never removed from box, 1972 ..... **$65**

Ken, straight-leg model, painted blonde hair, beige lips, wearing "Time For Tennis" outfit, apparently never removed from box, 1960s **$325**

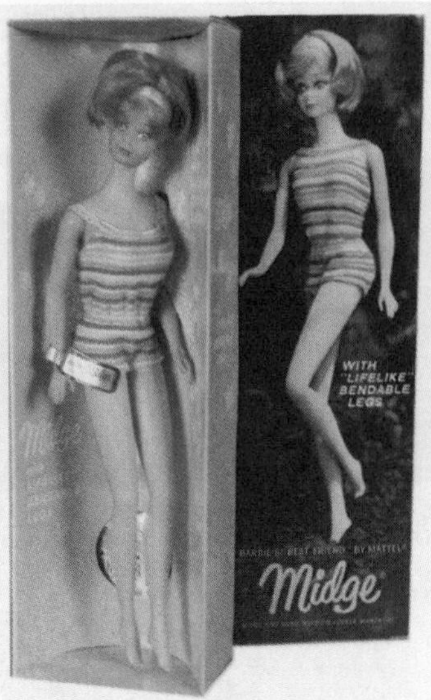

Midge, bent-leg model, ash blonde hair, dark pink lips, finger & toe paint, apparently never removed from box, hair stiff................ **$295**

P.J., "New 'n Groovy," blonde hair, pink lips, bright pink swimsuit, never removed from box................... **$1,195**

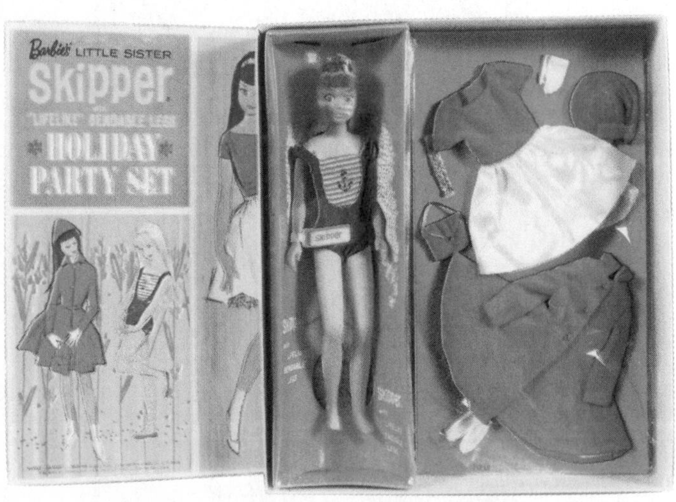

Skipper Holiday Party Gift Set, bent-leg, titian hair w/metal hairband & plastic cover, wearing one-piece swimsuit, wrist tag in box w/stand, booklet, accessories, cellophane cover, includes "Silk 'n Fancy" outfit, never removed from box **$875**

Skipper, straight-leg, brunette hair w/metal hair band, pink lips, wearing original red & white one-piece swimsuit, w/wrist tag, booklet & accessories in cellophane bag, gold wire stand, mint in box **$145**

Barbie's boyfriend Ken (ex-boyfriend, as of 2004) was introduced in 1961; her friend Midge, in 1963; friend Skipper, in 1964; and cousin P.J., in 1969.

BASEBALL MARKET REPORT

Baseball collectibles are still by far the most popular of all sports memorabilia, mainly because of their much longer history, which goes back to the late 1800s, compared to other sports that didn't really catch on until 25 to 50 years later. According to T.S. O'Connell, editor of Krause Publication's *Sports Collectors Digest* magazine, "There has been some decline in the number of bidders in the baseball collectibles market, but the highest end items are still holding their value." The middle and lower range items and eBay have seen the most impact from the current economy, he added. In addition, the steroid controversy in baseball has caused cards of tainted players to drop in value.

Prices of vintage cards (pre-1970s) aren't as volatile as more recent collectibles, as their supply is relatively small. Early baseball cards were produced as inexpensive toys for kids and only later became collectibles. The cards were frequently lost, thrown away, or mangled, so their rarity, especially in mint condition, sustains their high prices. Newer cards (post-1970s), on the other hand, are made in much larger quantities and are created as collectibles from the start, so a far higher percentage survive in pristine condition. Thus, post-70s cards are generally have much lower values. Notable exceptions are cards featuring Stephen Strasburg, the phenom Washington Nationals pitcher. For example, one of his cards, a one-of-a-kind 2010 Bowman Chrome Superfractor, exceeded $17,000 in a May 2010 eBay auction. This is considered a fluke associated with Strasburg's spectacular skill, rather than a growing trend in contemporary cards. Even Strasburg's prices pale in comparison to the value of the oldest and rarest baseball cards. For instance, in the same month that the Strasburg card sold, a vintage Honus Wagner card, in the lowest grade possible, sold for $282,000. The same card in a high grade sold for $2.8 million in late 2007. High value vintage cards make up only a small fraction of the total market, however, and are at the very top of the card collecting food chain.

By the late 1980s to early 1990s, sports card prices had matured to the point that there was less room for dramatic price increases each year. Because of this, other sports memorabilia, especially game-used equipment, like uniforms, bats, and balls, filled the void for investment potential items. Seventy-five percent of the increase in the value of these items has occurred in the last 15 years. Another development during this time has been the move to third-party authentication, slabbing, and grading services, which has helped to create and standardize the premium for the highest condition cards, which had previously been undervalued relative to those of lower condition.

Because altered cards can be a significant problem, collectors won't risk money on unauthenticated items of substantial value ($1,000 and up), so to be successfully traded, these items need to have third-party authentication. This leaves fakes and forgeries predominantly at the lower ends of the market. Third-party authentication assures that items are already carefully inspected, so a personal, hands-on evaluation is not as essential before purchasing. Consequently, most trading is done via auction by Internet and telephone.

"The worst time to sell is when you need the money the most. If you sell because of financial pressure, you're almost certain to leave money on the table," O'Connell said. Dealers, for instance, commonly acquire their best deals from someone who's going through a divorce, he explained. To get the most money for your collection, plan your budget so it doesn't force you to rely on raising extra cash by selling prematurely.

BASEBALL MEMORABILIA

Baseball was reputedly invented by Abner Doubleday as he laid out a diamond-shaped field with four bases at Cooperstown, New York. A popular game from its inception, by 1869 it was able to support its first all-professional team, the Cincinnati Red Stockings. The National League was organized in 1876, and though the American League was first formed in 1900, it was not officially recognized until 1903. Today, the "national pastime" has millions of fans, and collecting baseball memorabilia has become a major hobby with enthusiastic collectors seeking out items associated with players such as Babe Ruth, Lou Gehrig, and others who became legends in their own lifetimes. Although baseball cards, issued as advertising premiums for bubble gum and other products, seem to dominate the field, there are numerous other items available.

Advertising display, " 'Reach' Sporting Goods," color-printed cardboard, large red lettering outlined in gold printed over the large standing image of an early pitcher atop a baseball w/ the company logo, good color, fragile, early 20th c., 10 1/2 x 19" **$1,180**

Album-scorecard, printed on stiff paper, from the 1910 World Series, white cover printed in black & white w/images of a walking bear cub approaching a rearing elephant, reads "Players in the World's Series - Baseball Championship- 1910 - Issued by The Chicago Daily News," 48 pp., 3 3/4 x 6 1/4" **$513**

Baseball bat, autographed by Hank Aaron, H&B Louisville Slugger Pro Model 125, ca. 1964-1972.... **$926**

Baseball bat, autographed by Mickey Mantle, signed "My Best Wishes Mickey Mantle 9/18/65," this was "Mickey Mantle Day" at Yankee Stadium, H&B Louisville Slugger.............................. **$5,421**

Baseball bat, Jackie Robinson, game-used, H&B Louisville Slugger, Pro Model 125 "rookie-era," ca. 1947-48, uncracked, shows some game wear.... **$6,722**

Baseball bat, Joe Jackson, game-used, H&B Louisville Slugger, Pro-Model 125, used after Jackson's banishment from baseball, ca. 1922-26, w/letter of authenticity (uncracked, heavy use, some dry rot on reverse of barrel) **$6,722**

To get top dollar for valuable sports cards, consider having them authenticated and condition graded by a professional grading company, Each card is graded by impartial experts and then sealed in a tamper-proof clear plastic case, giving potential buyers the confidence that they can invest safely.

Bank, plastic, modeled as a conical red bat rack holding ten creamy yellow snap-on bats, sold via mail-order by Hillerich & Bradsby w/a red & blue cardboard tag & original cardboard shipping box w/company logo, 1960s, rack 6" h. (ILLUS. of bank & box)........ **$327**

Baseball card set, 1955 Topps set, includes Clemente, Banks, Robinson, Hodges, Spahn, Killebrew, Mays, Williams, Aaron, Koufax, Berra & more, overall graded VG-EX-EX, the set (ILLUS. of part).............. **$3,580**

Baseball card set, 1956 Topps set, includes Koufax, Hodges, Robinson, Snider, Williams, Campanella, Mantle, Reese, Aaron, Clemente & more, various grades from excellent to good, complete set of 340 (ILLUS. of part)................................ **$2,241**

Baseball card set, 1960 Topps set, includes Mays, Clemente, Mantle, Musial, Maris, Aaron, Koufax, Spahn, Berra & more, graded EX to EX-MT, the set (ILLUS. of part).. **$2,195**

Baseball cards wax box, "1953 Topp's Baseball Picture Cards," cardboard printed in red, white & blue, two-piece, meant to hold sets of the baseball cards, very good condition........ **$307**

Baseball card, Ty Cobb, Detroit, Piedmont Cigarette series, advertising on the reverse, bright colors, early 20th c., rare, mounted in plastic block, card 1 1/2 x 2 1/2" **$720**

Baseball cards wax box, "1958 Topp's Baseball Bubble Gum," cardboard printed in orange, green & white, meant to hold sets of the baseball cards, excellent condition **$193**

Baseball glove, leather, first baseman's style, autographed by Luke Appling, made by Spalding, very good condition **$863**

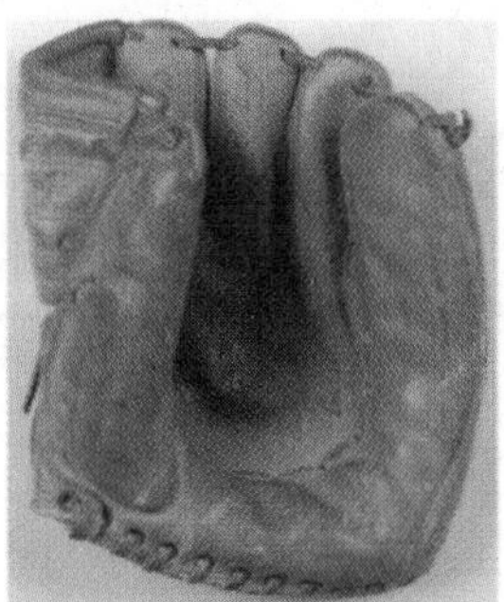

Baseball glove, leather, team-signed by the 29 members of the 1955 Milwaukee Braves, a Bob Dillinger model by Rawlings signed in ballpoint pen by Mathews, Conley, Crandall, Pendleton, Spahn & more, missing wrist button but overall excellent condition (ILLUS. of two views)... **$449**

Baseball, 1927 St. Louis Browns team-signed ball, features 20 signatures including Wingard, Stewart, Bennett, Nevers & many more, shellacked **$493**

Baseball, 1989 Oakland Athletics team-signed ball, includes 24 team members from the World Champion team **$598**

Baseball, New York Yankees team member-signed ball, includes 1927 team members Babe Ruth, Hoyt, Meusel, Reuther, Pat Collins, Myles Thomas, Fletcher, Gazella, Dugan & Bob O'Farrell, heavily worn, darkly toned Official American League ball....... **$1,091**

When autographing baseballs to fans, Hall of Fame player Ty Cobb often advised applying a coating of clear shellac to autographed baseballs to keep the ink from fading. This old practice is now considered detrimental to autographed baseballs.

Baseball, New York Yankees team member-signed ball, signed by Maris, Mantle, Skowron, Richardson, Ford & Berra, ca. 1960-62, white Official American League model (ILLUS. of two views)................................ **$900**

Baseball, signed by Bill McGowan, lightly off-white unofficial ball, rare **$1,730**

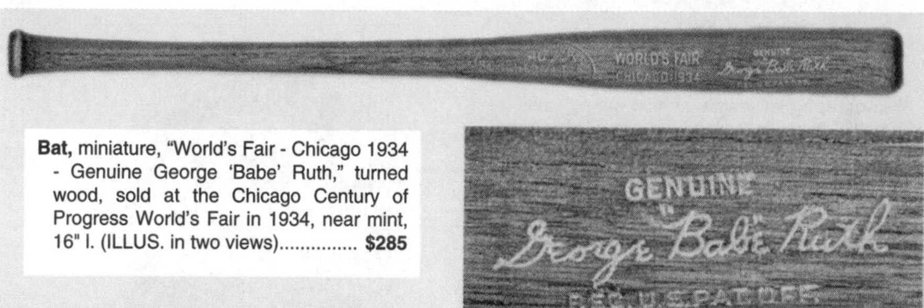

Bat, miniature, "World's Fair - Chicago 1934 - Genuine George 'Babe' Ruth," turned wood, sold at the Chicago Century of Progress World's Fair in 1934, near mint, 16" l. (ILLUS. in two views)............... **$285**

Pennant, printed felt, Chicago Cubs, dark green w/white animal mascots & wording, reads "World Series - Chicago Cubs - 1945," small hole through reinforcing felt, overall excellent condition, 25" l.. **$543**

Pennant, printed felt, New York Yankees, blue w/white wording & pink & red top hat logo, reads "American League Champions - New York Yankees - 1960," roster list of players at wide end, fine condition **$150**

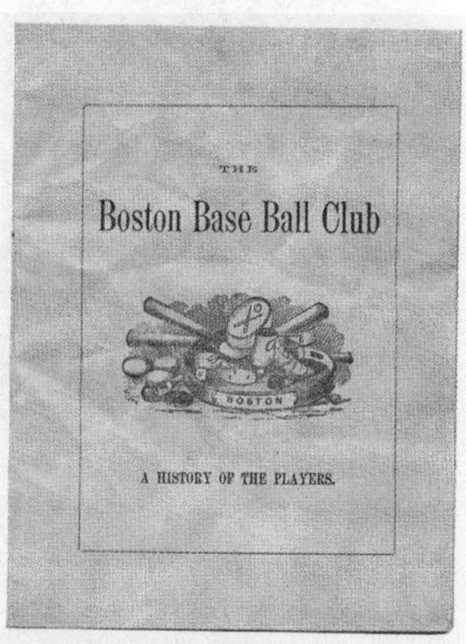

Pamphlet, "The Boston Base Ball Club - A History of the Players," published in 1873 to promote the credibility of baseball in general, biographical sketches of players, yellow paper covers, 16 pp., overall excellent condition, 4 1/4 x 5 1/2" **$1,558**

Photograph, full-length printed photo pose of Jackie Robinson swinging a bat, boldly signed by him, the reverse of this page w/a photo of Pee Wee Reese & also signed by him, from Big-Time Baseball, near mint, 8 x 10 1/2"................. **$991**

Photograph, team-issued color portrait of Roberto (Bob) Clemente, printed signature & actual blue ink autograph on the photo, ca. late 1960s, near mint.. **$1,072**

Photograph, sepia-toned photo of Babe Ruth in a batting pose, inscribed to a teammate, Jimmie Reese, and dated 1931, overall excellent condition, 3 x 4".. **$1,454**

Pinback button, advertising-type, "Morton's Buster Brown Bread," yellow ground printed w/a picture of Buster Brown in red, blue & white along w/the small figure of a tiger leaning on a baseball bat, a large circle w/ a black & white photo image of a smiling Ty Cobb, produced around 1908-1910 to appeal to fans of the Detroit Tigers baseball team, overall excellent condition, 1 1/4" d. **$1,475**

Press pin, enameled metal, pennant-shaped, white ground w/wording in black & blue reading "World Series - Dodgers - 1955 - 1959 - 1963 - 1965," 1966 World Series issue, near mint **$95**

Press pin, enameled metal, round w/red outer ring w/metal wording around a central white baseball w/blue numbers reading "All Star Baseball Game - 1947," excellent condition **$668**

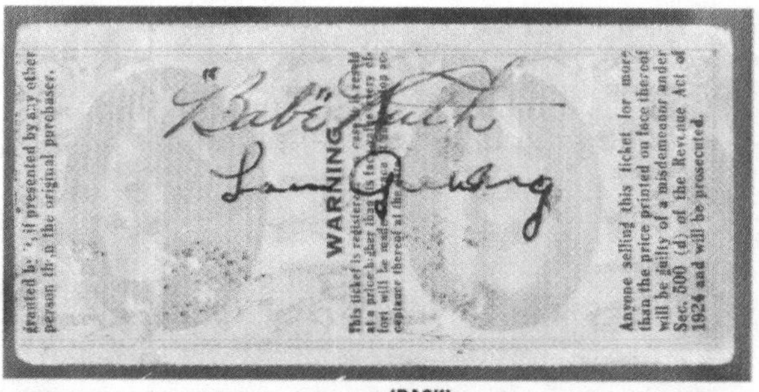

(BACK)

(FRONT)

Ticket stub, 1926 game four of the World Series, autographed across the back by Babe Ruth & Lou Gehrig in black fountain pen, the front w/printed seat information & an owner-penned inscription "Babe Ruth hit 3 home-runs - Oct. 6th 1926 - New York vs St Louis," actual game date was October 7th, rare, 2 x 4 1/4" (ILLUS. of front & back) **$3,335**

If you find an antique or collectible priced significantly less than normal, consider the possibilities. The dealer may not know the fair market value of the item, or it may not be his specialty. The dealer may have acquired the item at an unusually low price. The dealer may have had the item for a long time and wants to be rid of it. It may be damaged or not in top condition. An extremely low price is an indicator that the item might be a reproduction or fake.

Tobacco silk, No. S110, a large white square printed in color w/five images of period baseball players in action, a baseball diamond & equipment around the center, early 20th c., overall excellent condition, framed, 27 x 28" **$3,557**

BASKETS

The American Indians were the first basket weavers on this continent and, of necessity, the early Colonial settlers and their descendants pursued this artistic handicraft to provide essential containers for berries, eggs and endless other items to be carried or stored. Rye straw, split willow and reeds are but a few of the wide variety of materials used. Nantucket baskets, plainly and sturdily constructed, along with those made by specialized groups, would seem to draw the greatest attention to this area of collecting.

Bobbin basket, woven splints or caning, hanging-type w/three tiers of projecting rectangular baskets, arched hanging loop at the top, decorated w/alternating bands of green, red & natural, the bottom pocket w/a herringbone weave across the bottom, good original surface w/some splint breaks, attributed to Native Americans, 9 1/2 x 13", 41 1/2" h. **$978**

Nantucket basket, finely woven splint, oval w/ deep sides & a bentwood wrapped rim, a center squared bentwood swing handle, oval wood bottom, base w/label reading "Made by Mitchel Ray, Nantuckeet, Mass.," nice old patina, four section of edge wrap missing, 20th c., 11 1/2 x 14 1/2", w/handle 13" h.... **$4,025**

Picnic basket, woven splint, square bottom w/tall flaring sides w/a round rim fitted w/ a flat cover, high D-shaped bentwood fixed handle, interior w/wood support shelves for a removable basketweave shelf & two basketry cup holders, 14" d., overall 14 1/2" h. **$81**

Shaker basket, finely woven splint, wide round shape w/wrapped rim & carved arched flat rim handles, turned round wood base, probably Canterbury, New Hampshire, late 19th c., few minor breaks in the weaves, 20 1/2" d., 14 1/2" h. (ILLUS. inside larger Shaker basket) **$705**

Shaker basket, woven splint, deep rectangular shape w/flat bottom, wrapped rim & carved arched rim handles, leather-lined, the number "20" inscribed twice in ink on the base, probably New Hampshire or Maine, 19th c., wear, 16 1/4 x 22 1/4", 12 5/8" h. **$353**

Shaker basket, woven splint, deep round sides w/wrapped rim & high arched carved handle w/ letters "OLS" pyrographically pricked into both ends, Mount Lebanon, New York, late 19th c., some losses, 11 1/4" d., 14 1/4" h. **$206**

Utility basket, heavy wooden splint, deep gently tapering round sides w/a bentwood rim band & high bentwood riveted handle, two crossed tin bands woven into the sides & across the base for stability, old red paint w/good patina & dry surface, 19th c., 14 1/2" d., w/handle 18 1/4" h......................... **$431**

Storage basket, woven splint, deep rectangular sides w/wrapped rim & center swing bentwood handle, yellow bands w/blue potato print designs, 15 1/2 x 23", 10 3/4" h. (minor damage) **$275**

Utility basket, woven splint, round w/wrapped rim & small bentwood rim handles, good detail, traces of old yellow varnish, 14 1/2" d., 4 1/2" h. plus handles (minor damage) **$385**

Utility basket, woven splint, deep rounded rectangular form w/ wrapped rim & bentwood swing handle, old greyish patina, 9 1/2 x 13", 8 1/4" h. plus handle (wear, damage) **$138**

The Shakers, known for their superb baskets, learned their skills from Native American basket-makers.

To prevent excessive moisture loss and possible cracking of splints and cane, do not display baskets near heat sources such as fireplaces, furnace vents, or radiators.

BOTTLES

Bitters

(Numbers with some listings below refer to those used in Carlyn Ring's For Bitters Only.)

Brown's Celebrated Indian Herb Bitters - Patented Feb. 11, 1868, figural Indian queen, inward rolled mouth, smooth base, unusual coloring w/arms & upper body in yellow w/a hint of green, headdress & lower portion in yellowish amber, highlighted by old red & yellow paint, 12 1/8" h. **$1,792**

Carter's - Liver Bitters - C.M. Co. New York, oval, rounded shoulder, smooth base, tooled mouth, ca. 1890-1900, amber, 8 1/4" h. (ILLUS. front & back).. **$448**

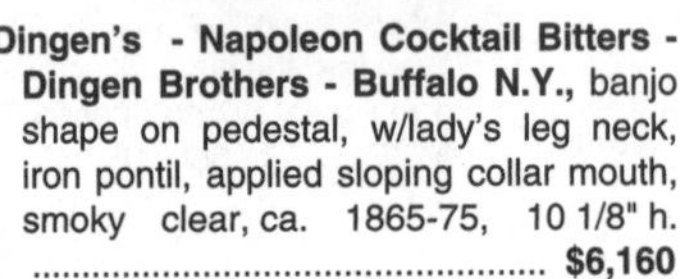

Dingen's - Napoleon Cocktail Bitters - Dingen Brothers - Buffalo N.Y., banjo shape on pedestal, w/lady's leg neck, iron pontil, applied sloping collar mouth, smoky clear, ca. 1865-75, 10 1/8" h. **$6,160**

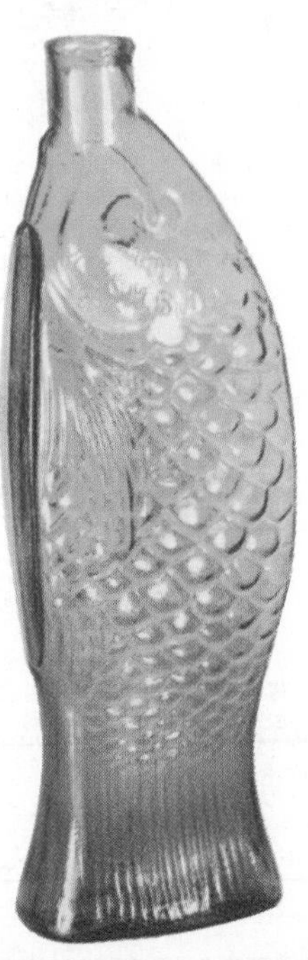

Fish (The) Bitters - W.H. Ware, Patented 1866, figural fish, "W.H. Ware Patent 1866" on bottom, applied small round collared mouth, smooth base, ca. 1866-1875, yellow w/faint amber & olive tones, 11 5/8" h. **$1,456**

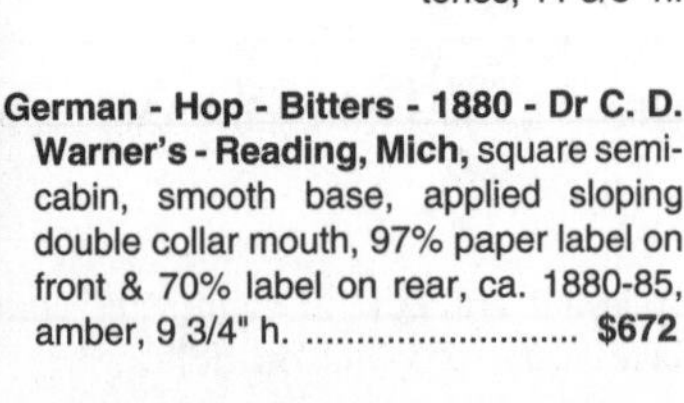

German - Hop - Bitters - 1880 - Dr C. D. Warner's - Reading, Mich, square semi-cabin, smooth base, applied sloping double collar mouth, 97% paper label on front & 70% label on rear, ca. 1880-85, amber, 9 3/4" h. **$672**

Greeley's Bourbon Bitters, barrel-shaped, ten rings above & below center band, applied mouth, smooth base, ca. 1860-75, smoky copper topaz, 9 1/4" h. **$476**

Hertrichs Bitter, Einziger Fabrikant, Hans Hertrich Hof Gesetzlich Geschutzt, footed ball-shaped w/tall ringed neck, applied double collar mouth, smooth base, Germany, ca. 1880-1900, yellowish olive green, 9 1/4" h. **$336**

Holtzermann's Patent Stomach Bitters (on roof), cabin-shaped, two-roof, smooth logs, applied sloping collar mouth, smooth base, ca. 1865-75, amber, smoothed out chip on one log, tiny faint iridescent bruise on one roof, 9 3/8" h. **$784**

National Bitters, figural ear of corn, "Patent 1867" on base, applied sloping collared mouth w/ring, smooth base, medium golden yellowish amber, ca. 1867-75, 12 1/2" h.... **$840**

Nibol Kidney and Liver Bitters - The Best Tonic Laxative & Blood Purifier, square, smooth base, tooled lip, w/98 percent original front & back labels & contents, medium amber, 9 1/2" h. (ILLUS. of two sides) **$728**

Bitters

Old Sachem Bitters and Wigwam Tonic, barrel-shaped, ten-rib, pontil scarred base, applied mouth, deep bluish aqua w/patch of olive in area of embossing, ca. 1855-70, 10 1/4" h. **$5,040**

Pineapple figural, embossed diamond-shaped panel, applied top, smooth base, ca. 1865-75, medium amber, 9" h. **$308**

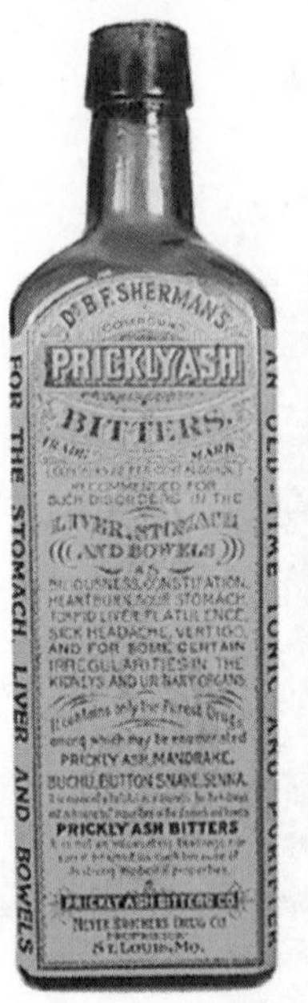

Prickly Ash Bitters, square, smooth base, ABM lip, w/99 percent original label on three sides & contents, made by Meyer Brothers Drug. Co., St. Louis, Missouri, medium amber, ca. 1910-15, 9 1/4" h. (ILLUS. of two sides) **$258**

Thads. Waterman - Warsaw - Stomach Bitters, octagonal, smooth base, applied sloping double collar mouth, many seed bubbles, medium golden amber, ca. 1865-75, 10 1/2" h. **$3,920**

Travellers Bitters, rectangular w/rounded side panels, cabin-like shoulder, front panel embossed w/a figure of a man walking w/a cane (Robert E. Lee), applied sloping collared mouth, smooth base, golden amber, 1860-80, small flat chip on base, pinpoint bruise to right of figure, minor exterior wear & scratches, rare, 10 1/2" h. **$5,320**

Tippecanoe (birch bark & canoe design), H.H. Warner & Co., cylindrical, "Patent Nov. 20. 83 - Rochester - N.Y." on smooth base, applied disc mouth, ca. 1880-95, yellowish amber, 9" h. **$168**

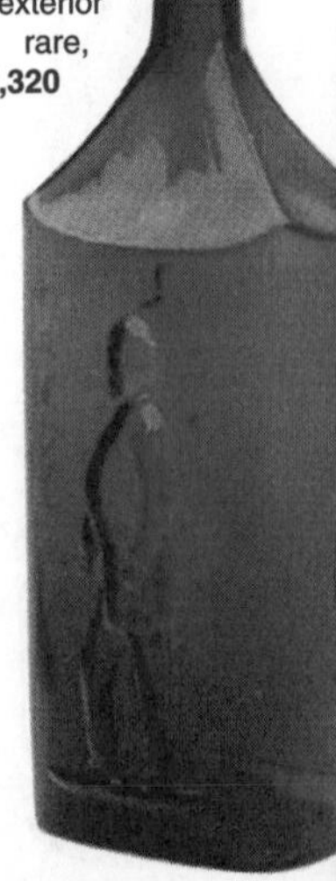

Figurals

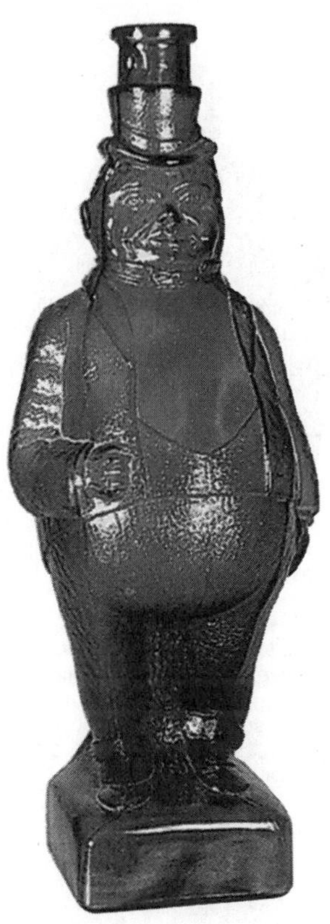

"Big Bill," stout man in three-piece suit, top hat, standing on square smooth base, tooled lip (similar to figure pictured on label of Big Bill's Best Bitters bottles), medium amber, ca. 1890-1910, 11 5/8" h. **$784**

Egyptian Pharaoh seated on throne, black milk glass w/traces of original paint, smooth base, sheared & ground lip, "DEP" embossed on rear indented panel edge, very rare, probably France, ca. 1890-1920, 13 1/8" h. **$896**

Hot air balloon, cobalt blue, diamond lattice design w/"Ballon Captif - 1878," pontiled base w/"Depose," France, ca. 1878, missing original stopper, 9" h. **$7,840**

Keep an inventory of your antiques and collectibles. It will be easier to maintain using a computer and a program like Excel, but if necessary, use index cards or a notebook. List the name of the item and description, including size, markings, date acquired, and price paid. When selling, update the listing with date sold and price. Also, take a photo of every item you own. This will document the information you need to file a police report or insurance claim if they are stolen or lost in a fire, flood, earthquake, or other natural disaster. Keep a copy of the inventory in a safe deposit box or other safe place.

Flasks

GI-14 - Washington bust below "General Washington" - American eagle w/shield w/seven bars on breast, head turned to right, "E Pluribus Unum" in semicircle above, vertically ribbed edges, w/"Adams & Jefferson July 4. A.D. 1776" & "Kensington Glassworks rich green, pt. **$7,280**

GI-21 - Washington bust (facing right) below "Fells," "Point" below bust - Washington Monument in Baltimore without statue above "BALTo," tooled mouth, pontil, greenish aqua, qt................ **$179**

GI-34 - Washington bust portrait obverse - Jackson bust portrait reverse, Coventry, Connecticut Glass Works, sheared mouth, pontil scar, yellowish amber, 1/2 pt.) **$448**

GI-38 - Washington bust below "The Father of His Country" - Taylor bust, "Gen. Taylor Never Surrenders, Dyottville Glass Works, Philada.," sheared mouth, smooth edges, pontil scar, medium bluish green, pt. **$364**

GI-40a - Washington bust below "The Father of His Country" - Taylor bust below "Gen Taylor Never Surrenders," smooth edges, sheared mouth, pontil scar, deep cobalt blue, tiny spot of roughness on interior of lip, pt........... **$5,040**

GI-54 - Washington bust without queue - Taylor bust in uniform, open pontil, applied sloping double collar mouth, light apple green, few spots of stain inside, qt. **$202**

GII-67 - American eagle standing on laurel wreath below nine five-pointed stars - large anchor w/"New London" in banner above & "Glass Works" in banner below, smooth base, applied double collar mouth, smooth base, orange amber, very minor open shoulder bubble, 1/2 pt. **$1,680**

GIII-1 - Cornucopia w/produce surrounded by oval beaded panel - Large circular beaded medallion enclosing star-shaped design w/six ribbed points & small eight-petaled rosette center, above symmetrical palm motif, edges w/ horizontal beading, pontil scarred base, inward rolled lip, aqua, 1/2 pt. **$5,600**

GIII-17 - Cornucopia with Produce - Urn, pontil scarred base, applied double collar mouth, medium blue green, pt. **$616**

GIV-1a - Masonic arch - American eagle w/ribbon above "I P" in oval, pontil scarred base, sheared & tooled lip, medium blue green, pt. **$364**

GIV-8a - Masonic arch - American eagle above oval containing pinwheel, pontil scarred base, sheared & tooled lip, deep yellow olive, extremely rare mold in unlisted color, possibly unique, two minor sliver-type chips off one rib, pt. **$2,800**

GIX-10 - Scroll w/two eight-point stars obverse & reverse, applied collar, iron pontil, golden amber, pt. **$1,650**

GIX-2 - Scroll w/two six-point stars obverse & reverse, vertical medial rib, long neck, pontil scarred base, sheared & tooled lip, medium cobalt blue, qt. **$3,080**

GV-4 - "Success to the Railroad" around embossed horse pulling cart, reverse identically embossed, pontil scarred base, sheared & tooled lip, yellowish olive amber, pt. **$672**

GVI-4 - "Baltimore" below monument - "Corn for the World" in semicircle above ear of corn, smooth edges, smooth base, applied double collar mouth, yellow w/olive tone, 1/4" open bubble near base, qt. **$2,128**

GVIII-5a - Sunburst w/twenty-four rounded rays obverse & reverse, horizontal corrugated edges, pontil scarred base, sheared & tooled lip, yellow olive, pt. **$4,200**

GX-15 - "Summer" over tree in circle - "Winter" over tree in circle, smooth base, applied double collar mouth, yellowish topaz w/subtle puce striations, pt. **$3,640**

GXI-22 - "For Pike's Peak" above prospector w/tools standing on oblong frame - American eagle, smooth base, applied ringed mouth, amber, pt. **$3,920**

GXII-7 - Clasped hands above oval, all inside large shield under "Union" - American eagle w/banner & "No. 2," smooth base, applied ringed mouth, olive yellow, shallow flake off side near mold seam, qt. **$1,456**

GXIII-8 - Sailor dancing a hornpipe on an eight-board hatch cover, above a long rectangular bar - Banjo player sitting on a long bench, smooth edges, smooth base, applied double collar mouth, yellow w/amber tone, 1/2 pt. **$560**

GXIII-4 - Hunter facing left wearing flat-top stovepipe hat, short coat & full trousers, game bag hanging at left side, firing gun at two birds flying upward at left, large puff of smoke from muzzle, two dogs running to left toward section of rail fence, "Dr. Taylor's Olive Branch Bitters" painted in gold - Fisherman standing on shore near large rock, wearing round-top stovepipe hat, V-neck jacket, full trousers, fishing rod held in left hand w/end resting on ground, right hand holding large fish, creel below left arm, mill w/bushes & tree in left background, calabash, edges w/wide flutes, iron pontil, applied mouth, salmon puce, 9 1/4" h. **$1,680**

GXIII-48 - Anchor between fork-ended pennants inscribed "Baltimore" & "Glass Works" - Sheaf of grain w/crossed rake & pitchfork, yellowish orange, qt. **$1,904**

Pattern molded, flattened oblong form w/tiny flared & tooled mouth, twenty-four vertical ribs, brilliant sapphire blue, probably Germany, 1775-1825, 4 7/8" w., 7 1/2" h. **$1,232**

←

Nailsea, ovoid lobed shape, yellow amber w/white loop pattern, pontil scarred base, tooled mouth, England, ca. 1820-50, 5 3/8" h. **$308**

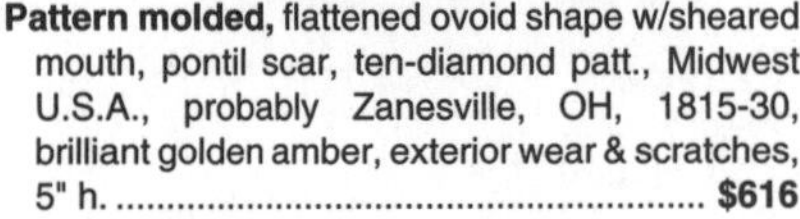

Pattern molded, flattened ovoid shape w/sheared mouth, pontil scar, ten-diamond patt., Midwest U.S.A., probably Zanesville, OH, 1815-30, brilliant golden amber, exterior wear & scratches, 5" h. **$616**

Pitkin, thirty-six ribs swirled to the left, open pontil, sheared & tooled lip, blown in the German half-post method, golden amber, America, ca. 1815, 6" h. **$1,008**

Pitkin, thirty-six ribs swirled to the right, sheared mouth, pontil scar, possibly Pitkin Glass Works, East Hartford, Connecticut, 1783-1830, brilliant forest green, 5" h. **$1,064**

While bubbles in glass add interesting visual effects and evidence that a bottle has been hand blown, they do not of themselves raise the value of a bottle. In fact, they are considered flaws and can lower the value of bottles.

Be aware of what's in the bottles you are buying and selling, as some bottles may contain their original contents of liquor, cocaine, opium, or poison. All can be dangerous and/or illegal to sell.

Inks

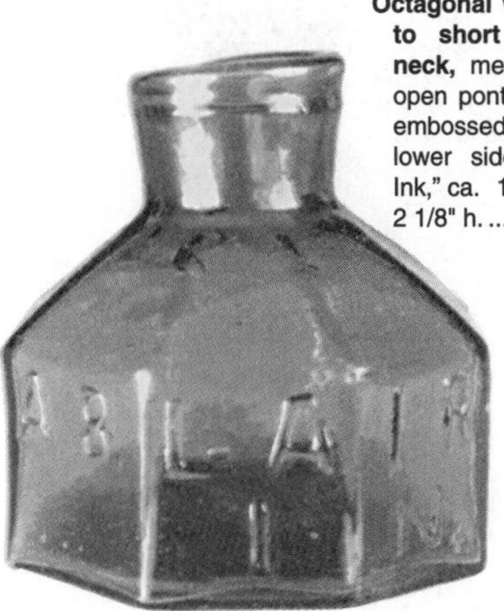

Octagonal w/angled shoulder to short wide cylindrical neck, medium bluish green, open pontil, inward rolled lip, embossed around paneled lower sides "A.B. Laird's - Ink," ca. 1840-60, very rare, 2 1/8" h. **$4,480**

Double-font teakettle-type fountain inkwell w/neck extending up at angle from base, medium emerald green, tapering octagonal body below the upper squatty octagonal font, rough sheared lips, smooth base, minor lip slivers, ca. 1875-95, 3 1/2" h. **$960**

Teakettle, clear, ground lip, minor stain, 3 1/4" h.................... **$88**

Octagonal, bluish aqua, short squatty shape w/central neck w/sheared & rolled lip, pontil scar, some very light inside haze, ca. 1840-60, 1 3/4" h. **$202**

Teakettle-type fountain inkwell w/neck extending up at angle from base, cobalt blue cut glass, sheared & ground lip, polished pontil, original metal neck ring & hinged cap, some tiny flakes on paneled edges, ca. 1875-95, 2 1/4" h. **$224**

Teakettle-type fountain inkwell w/neck extending up at angle from base, bright lime green, squatty bulbous finely ribbed body w/a domed lobed top, ground lip w/original brass neck ring & hinged cap, smooth base, rare, ca. 1875-95, 2 3/8" h... **$1,456**

Umbrella-type (8-panel cone shape), apricot-amber, rolled lip, open tubular pontil, 95 percent intact label reads "Sheppard - Allen's Writing Fluid Manufactured at Albany NY," 2 3/4" h. **$550**

Umbrella-type (8-panel cone shape), brilliant light olive yellow, inward-rolled mouth, pontil scar, professionally cleaned, 1840-80, 2 3/8" h. **$1,140**

Umbrella-type (8-panel cone shape), light to medium green, embossed in panel "M & P - New York," inward rolled mouth, tubular pontil, 1840-60, 2 3/4" h. ... **$728**

Umbrella-type (8-panel cone shape), yellow olive green, short neck w/tooled mouth, smooth base, w/97 percent original label reading "Unoco Fast Black Writing Ink," ca. 1870-85, 2 3/4" h. **$532**

An interesting label can significantly add to the value of an antique bottle. The more color and design, the better, but condition is also important too. In an auction listing, the amount of the original label remaining is typically listed in a percentage of the total.

Umbrella-type (8-panel cone shape), cobalt blue, inward rolled mouth, tubular pontil, minor exterior high point wear, some internal ink residue, ca. 1830-60, 2 7/8" h. **$5,320**

Medicines

Buckhout's (E.A.) Dutch Liniment (design of standing man) - Prepared at Mechanicville Saratoga Co. N.Y., flattened rectangle w/rounded shoulders & rolled lip, open pontil scar, ca. 1840-60, bluish aqua, 4 3/4" h. **$560**

Carter's Spanish Mixture, cylindrical, applied sloping double collar mouth, pontil, 95% original paper label, ca. 1845-55, medium olive green, 8 1/4" h.......... **$1,456**

Gargling Oil, Lockport, N.Y., rectangular w/arched side panels & arched shoulder, short neck w/applied sloping collared neck, smooth base, ca. 1865-75, medium emerald green, larger size, 7 3/8" h........................ **$202**

Jacob's - Cholera & - Dysentery - Cordial, square shape w/applied mouth, open pontil, number of seed bubbles, aqua, ca. 1840-60, 6 3/4" h. **$134**

Kidder (Mrs. E.) Dysentery Cordial Balsam, cylindrical w/rounded shoulder, applied top, open pontil, light green, 8 1/4" h. **$2,090**

Embossing is the raised lettering on a bottle formed by plate inserts added to the bottle mold. The embossing is made more interesting by occasional misspellings or backward letters.

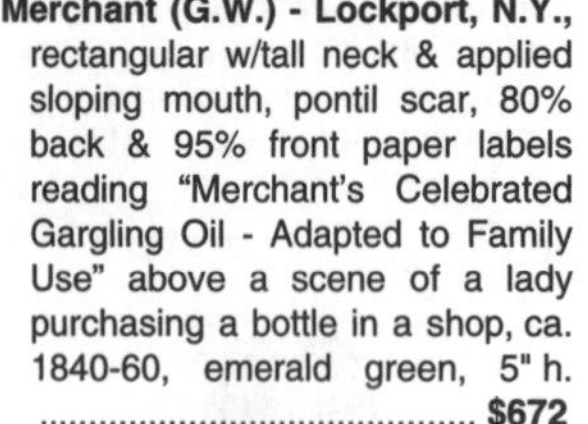

Merchant (G.W.) - Lockport, N.Y., rectangular w/tall neck & applied sloping mouth, pontil scar, 80% back & 95% front paper labels reading "Merchant's Celebrated Gargling Oil - Adapted to Family Use" above a scene of a lady purchasing a bottle in a shop, ca. 1840-60, emerald green, 5" h. **$672**

Miner's Damiana and Celery Compound [above image of woman standing amid boxes] - For the Cure of All Nervous Diseases Manufactured by H.C. Miner New York, rectangular w/ sloping shoulder, smooth base, tooled mouth, one of only two known to exist, medium amber, ca. 1885-95, 8 3/4" h. **$7,280**

Rohrer's Expectoral + Wild Cherry Tonic Lancaster, Pa., tapering rectangular form w/rounded corners decorated w/rope twist design, smooth base, applied mouth, yellow w/amber tone, ca. 1865-75, 10 3/8" h. **$504**

Swaim's - Panacea - Philada, cylindrical w/rounded shoulder & paneled sides, pontil scarred base, applied sloping collar mouth, deep apple green, ca. 1840-60, 8 1/8" h. **$728**

St. Andrew's Wine of Life Root, rectangular w/paneled sides & tooled mouth, smooth base, 99% original paper label, amber, ca. 1890-1900, 9" h. (ILLUS. of front & label)....................... **$168**

Mineral Waters, Sodas & Sarsaparillas

Bear Lithia Water - Bear Lithia Water (embossed on walking bear) - Trade Mark - Near Elkton, VA. - E.H.E. Co., wide cylindrical body w/a wide rounded shoulder & short neck w/tooled mouth, smooth base, ca. 1880-1900, greenish aqua, 10" h. **$280**

Boardman (John) - Mineral Waters - New York, eight-sided shape, electric cobalt blue, applied blob mouth, iron pontil, ca. 1840-60, faint inside haze, 7 1/4" h. ... **$616**

Central Springs - Green & Co. - Sheldon, VT., wide cylindrical body w/a tall neck & applied double collar mouth, smooth base, ca. 1865-75, deep bluish green, qt. **$8,400**

Clarke (John) around shoulder, cylindrical w/rounded shoulder & tall neck w/applied sloping collared mouth w/ring, smooth base, forest green, ca. 1860-70, rare, qt. **$560**

Beware of fake labels attached to genuine but plain, low-value antique bottles. Modern high quality photocopiers and offset printers can produce convincing replicas.

Cox (A.R.) Norristown, cylindrical form w/long neck, deep blue green, applied double collar mouth, iron pontil, ca. 1840-60, 7 1/8" h. **$179**

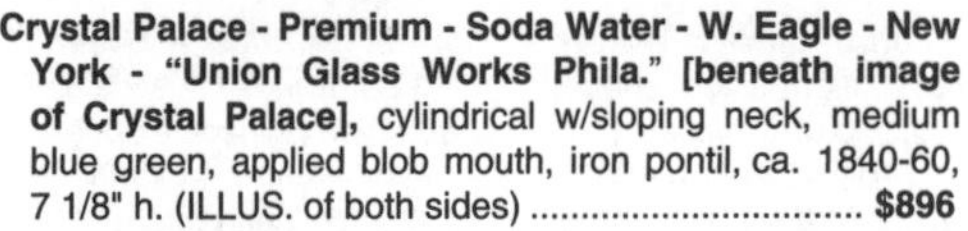

Crystal Palace - Premium - Soda Water - W. Eagle - New York - "Union Glass Works Phila." [beneath image of Crystal Palace], cylindrical w/sloping neck, medium blue green, applied blob mouth, iron pontil, ca. 1840-60, 7 1/8" h. (ILLUS. of both sides) **$896**

Davison (J.C.) Chester, Pa., squat cylindrical form w/long neck, medium teal blue, applied mouth w/original lightning-type closure, smooth base, ca. 1870-80, 7 1/8" h. **$179**

Dearborn (J. & A.) - New York - Mineral Waters, eight-sided shape, deep cobalt blue, applied blob mouth, iron pontil, ca. 1840-60, 7" h. **$392**

Dowdall (J.) - Avondale - The - Excelsior, eight-sided shape, blue green, iron pontil, applied blob mouth, extremely rare, ca. 1840-60, minor scratching, 7 3/8" h. **$3,920**

Haddock & Sons, modified ten pin-form soda water, crudely applied collared mouth, pontil scar, attributed to the Coventry Glassworks, Coventry, Connecticut, 1830-48, light yellowish olive, 1/2 pt., 7" h. **$1,792**

Harris (J.W.) Soda New Haven, Conn., octagonal w/slender neck & heavy applied collared mouth, iron pontil, sapphire blue, ca. 1845-60, professionally cleaned, some small chips & small burst bubble on one plain panel, 1/2 pt. **$364**

Iodine Spring Water - L - South Hero. VT, cylindrical w/tall cylindrical neck w/applied double collar mouth, smooth base, ca. 1875-75, deep old amber, qt. **$1,568**

Old Dr. - J. Townsend's - Sarsaparilla - New York, rectangular w/beveled sides, blue green or teal, iron pontil, applied sloping collar mouth, ca. 1845-60, tiny flake off shoulder edge on label panel, 9 5/8" h. **$1,568**

Pickle Bottles & Jars

Citron, figural, model of a lighthouse, embossed ring trademark reading "Skilton Foote & Co.'s - Bunker Hill Pickle," tooled sloping collared mouth, smooth base, 1870-90, minor interior stain spots, 11" h.............. **$3,080**

Deep bluish aqua, four-sided Cathedral-type, Wellington-style w/a pendant star at the top of each arch, outward folded lip, pontil, ca. 1850-60, rare form, 13 1/4" h. **$3,080**

Deep bluish aqua, six-sided Cathedral-type, rolled lip, smooth base, ca. 1855-75, 13 1/4" h. **$179**

Light bluish green, four-sided cathedral-type w/Gothic windows, outward rolled mouth, iron pontil, ca. 1845-60, 11 1/2" h. **$1,008**

Medium green, four-sided cathedral-type w/fancy Gothic windows, outward rolled mouth, smooth base, ca. 1860-80, 11 3/8" h. **$1,120**

Reddish amber, octofoil upright lobed design w/a tapering shoulder & flaring neck w/flattened rim, smooth base, Stoddard, New Hampshire, 1860-70, 8 1/8" h. **$1,008**

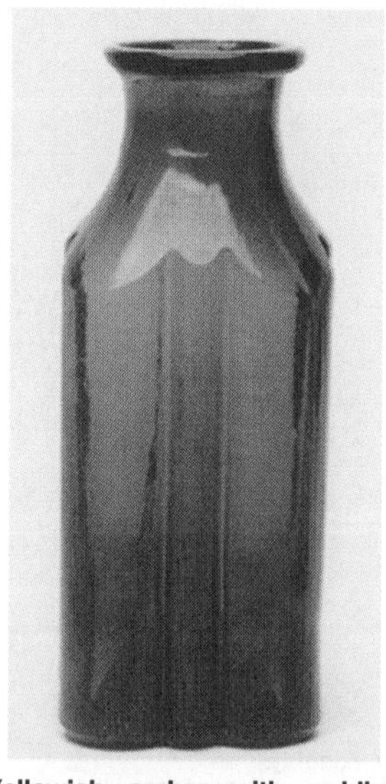

Yellowish amber with reddish tone, squared upright cloverleaf-form, outward rolled mouth, smooth base, from Stoddard, New Hampshire, ca. 1860-70, 7 3/4" h. **$1,568**

Yellowish olive amber, octofoil upright lobed sides tapering to an outward rolled mouth, smooth base, Stoddard, New Hampshire, ca. 1860-70, 8" h. **$1,064**

Poisons

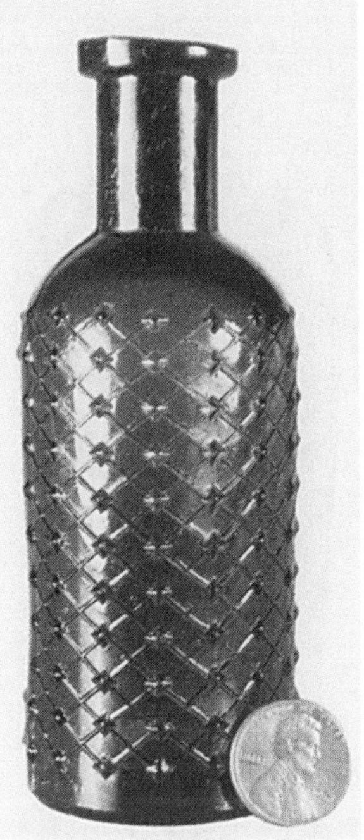

Smoky bluish green, cylindrical w/overall embossed diamond lattice design, tooled lip, smooth base, ca. 1890-1910, some very faint inside haze, 4 5/8" h. ... **$308**

Whiskey & Other Spirits

Beer, "Bay View Brewing Co Seattle Wash.," "NOT TO BE SOLD" on reverse, cylindrical, moss green, pt. **$303**

Beer, "Dallas Brewery - Malt Wein - Dallas, Texas," smooth base, tooled mouth, medium amber, ca. 1890-1900, 8 1/4" h. **$78**

Beer, "Dr. Cronk - R.McCoun," cylindrical 10-paneled sides w/ sloping shoulder to an applied mouth, iron pontil, ca. 1845-60, deep cobalt blue, 8 1/4" h. **$2,464**

Beer, "M. Richardson," cylindrical w/sloping shoulder to an applied mouth, smooth base, ca. 1845-60, yellowish emerald green, shallow sliver chip off underside of neck collar, 9 3/4" h. **$1,680**

Beer, "Property of Frey & Co San Rafael," cylindrical, w/original stopper, medium amber **$55**

Case gin, medium yellowish olive amber, square tapering shape w/applied mouth & open pontil, Holland, ca. 1770-90, 10 1/8" h. **$134**

Gin, "Bininger (A.M.) & Co. - N.Y.," square w/beveled corners & applied flared mouth, iron pontil, medium bluish green, 9 3/8" h. **$2,352**

Gin, case gin form, "Royal - T.M.W. - Champion," smooth base, applied mouth, blue-green, ca. 1870-80, 8 7/8" h. **$102**

Spirits, mold-blown seal-type w/ cylindrical body & tall tapering neck w/applied mouth, pontil scar, deep olive amber, seal molded "Wine - P.C. Brooks - 1820," England, ca. 1820, 9 7/8" h. **$3,360**

Spirits, mold-blown seal-type w/cylindrical body & tall tapering neck w/applied string lip, pontil scar, medium olive green, seal molded "1770 - James Oakes - Bury," England, ca. 1770, faint long stress crack, 10" h. **$960**

Whiskey, "Bininger's Old Dominion Wheat Tonic - A.M. Bininger & C0., No. 338 Broadway, N.Y.," square w/beveled corners, applied sloping mouth, smooth base, ca. 1855-70, yellowish olive, pinhead flake on base edge, 9 3/4" h. **$616**

Whiskey, "Booz's (E.G.) Old Cabin Whiskey - 120 Walnut St. Philadelphia" on roof, "1840 - E.G. Booz's Old Cabin Whiskey" on sides, cabin-shaped w/beveled roof ends, applied sloping collar mouth, smooth base, ca. 1865-75, deep root beer amber, 7 7/8" h. **$3,920**

Whiskey, "Chestnut Grove Whiskey, C.W. (on applied seal)," chestnut flask-shaped w/applied neck handle, applied mouth, ca. 1855-75, tobacco amber, 9" h. **$280**

Whiskey, "Chestnut Grove Whiskey, C.W. (on applied seal)," chestnut flask-shaped w/applied neck handle, applied mouth, pontil, ca. 1865-75, medium amber, 8" h. **$392**

Whiskey, "Griffith Hyatt & Co. - Baltimore," arched panel on front, bulbous ovoid shape tapering to neck w/applied mouth & applied handle, open pontil, probably Baltimore Glassworks, Baltimore, Maryland, 1840-60, yellowish amber, 7" h. **$1,008**

Whiskey, "Iron Front (steer's head) - Neff & Duff - Austin, Texas," flattened round flask-form w/an overall cobweb embossed design, tooled mouth, smooth base, clear w/amethystine tint, ca. 1879-81, some light stain, 6 5/8" h. **$5,320**

Whiskey, "J.F.T. & Co. - Philad." embossed in circular seal on the shoulder, mold-blown pear shape w/twenty-six vertical ribs, applied double collared mouth & applied handle w/fancy rigaree at base, pontil scar, light yellowish amber, American, 1840-60, 7" h... **$2,016**

Whiskey, "Perrine's - Apple - Ginger - Phila" on roof, "Perrine's (design of apple) Ginger," cabin-shaped w/ropetwist corners, applied mouth, smooth base, ca. 1875-85, pinhead flake off one corner, amber, 10" h. **$392**

Whiskey, "Wharton's Whisky (sic) 1850 Chestnut Grove (all inside a linked chain," flask-shaped w/short neck w/applied mouth, smooth base, ca. 1855-75, cobalt blue, 5 1/8" h. **$728**

Whiskey, elephant figure molded on one side, "Pint" embossed on the other, flattened chestnut form w/ solid applied strap handle, applied mouth w/ring, large rectangular iron pontil, bright bubbly deep golden amber, ca. 1845-60, small potstone w/iridescent bruise in pinhead-sized mouth flake, 6" h. **$1,792**

Whiskey, label-under-glass flask, clear w/large round colorful label w/a spread-winged American eagle above the crossed flags of Cuba & the United States over an American shield & crossed cannons w/a banner reading "E. Pluribus Unum," ground lip w/ original metal screw cap & strap wire handles at the shoulder, smooth base, label marked along bottom edge "C. Packman Jr. & Co. Baltimore, Md.," ca. 1898, 5" h. **$952**

BOXES

Band box, cov., deep oval sides w/fitted flat cover, the sides w/wallpaper block-printed w/designs of buildings w/peaked roofs & steeples in brown & white w/green trees, old printed book pages on interior, edge damage & splits, first half 19th c., 14 1/2 x 18", 12" h. **$575**

Band box, cov., deep oval sides w/fitted flat cover, the top of the cover w/a block-printed design of Castle Garden in New York City on a dark blue ground, the sides decorated w/a Rustic Bridge patt., features mounted horsemen, hunters & dogs in yellow, white, red & black on a blue ground, ca. 1830-40, wear, repairs, tears in cover rim, 15 1/2 x 19 1/2", 14 1/2" h. **$705**

Band box, cov., deep oval sides w/fitted flat cover, the top of the cover w/a block-printed design a spread-winged American eagle perched on a branch w/flowers, foliage & a cluster of grapes, the sides printed w/continuous scenes of the "Grand Canal" (Erie Canal) including the arched bridge at Little Falls, New York, on the Mohawk River, canal boats & figures in shades of brown, red & white varnish on a creamy yellow background, ca. 1830, fading, rim separation on cover **$382**

Bentwood box, cov., round bent maple sides fastened w/a single seam of iron tacks, fitted pine cover & bottom, 19th c., 10 1/4" d., 6" h. **$118**

Federal era box, inlaid mahogany veneer & cherry, rectangular w/flat hinged cover, raised on front French feet joined by a serpentine apron, banded border inlay & a shield-shape inlaid keyhole escutcheon, the interior divided into three compartments, early 19th c., age split in bottom, 5 3/8 x 10", 5 1/4" h. (ILLUS. bottom with curly maple box) **$2,415**

←

CANDLESTICKS & CANDLEHOLDERS

Candelabra, gilt-bronze, seven-light, each w/ a long slender arched bar fitted w/short C-scrolls fitted w/a squatty round candle socket, the bar supported by long open scrolls joined to the central double-knop shaft above the heavily scroll-cast three-sided base w/paw feet, each side cast in relief w/a small bust portrait of Jesus, Mary or Joseph, 19th c., 20" w., 19 1/4" h., pr. **$441**

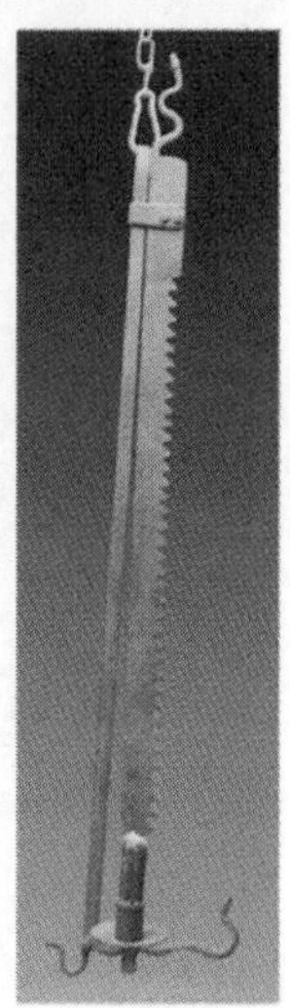

Candleholder, wrought-iron trammel-type, a long vertical flat bar w/serrations along the outside joined to a narrow back bar, fitted at the bottom w/a single candle cup w/drip pan set on a looped support w/a curled handle the adjusts up the trammel, probably late 18th or early 19th c., some rust & pitting, adjusts from 36" to 48" h. **$288**

Candleholder, wrought-iron, double tray-type, a shallow rectangular pan fitted w/a tall & short cylindrical candle socket, one end w/a curved iron fitting w/a simple turned wood handle, probably 19th c., 3 1/2" w., 14" l. **$173**

Candlestick, brass, high ringed cone-shaped base below the four-knob slender standard supporting the tall ringed cylindrical socket w/side hole for removing candle stub, probably Europe, possible Dutch, 18th c., 6 1/4" d., 10 1/2" h. . **$230**

Candlestick, brass, Queen Anne style, a square stepped base tapering to the ring- and baluster-turned shaft below the tall flaring socket, 6" h. **$115**

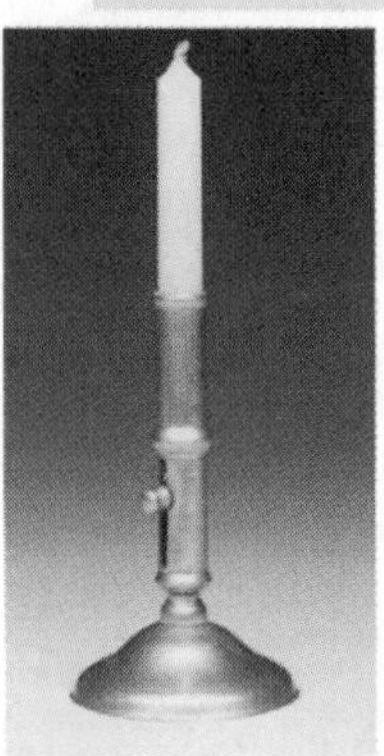

Candlestick, brass, Queen Anne-Style, round domical foot supporting a tall cylindrical shaft w/center ring above the slide ejector knob, 19th c., 7" h. .. **$115**

Candlestick-rush holder, wrought iron & wood, a heavy turned burl wood domed base supporting an upright wrought-iron clip mechanism for holding a piece of rush, the upturned arm topped by a cylindrical candle socket, jaws locks, 19th c., overall 9 1/2" h. **$288**

Candlesticks, brass, "King of Diamonds" patt., square foot w/ beveled corners below the stepped base & ring-turned shaft w/a large diamond-cast center knob, tall socket w/flaring rim, bases marked, push-ups present, England, late 19th - early 20th c., 12 1/4" h. pr. **$460**

Candlesticks, brass, Federal style, a square stepped base tapering sides to the tall plain square & slightly flaring standard w/a flared, ringed top supporting a tall ringed bell-form socket w/a wide rolled rim, American, ca. 1790-1815, 10" h., pr. **$690**

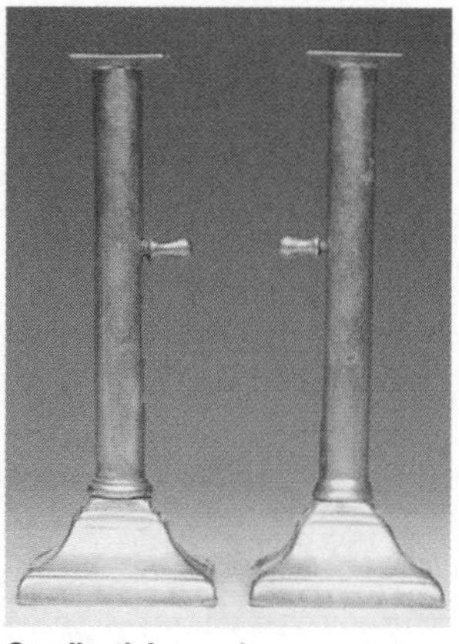

Candlesticks, brass, square tapering base supporting a tall slender cylindrical standard w/a flattened wide rim, long knob ejector handle on the side, late 18th - early 19th c., 9 1/2" h. **$230**

Candlesticks, brass, rectangular stepped base tapering to a ring-turned cylindrical shaft w/ejector slide knob, flat flaring rim, bottoms filled & marked "Turner & Co.," 19th c., 5 1/2" h., pr. **$201**

Candlesticks, bronze, two-socket, a squared footed platform base mounted w/the upright slender body of a detailed dragon arching at the top w/the two upper claws grasping pearl-like balls forming candle sockets, unsigned, Japan, Meiji Period, 10" h., pr. **$500**

Candlesticks, gilt- and black-patinated bronze, a low silhouette form on a rectangular base w/ rounded corners & a cast scroll band supporting a leaping griffin & scrolled branch below the oblong flaring leafy cap centered by a tall pierced scroll & leaf-cast socket, France, late 19th c., electrified, 12 1/2" h., pr. **$690**

Candlesticks, gilt- and patinated-bronze, a round ringed foot supporting the columnar standard w/ cast acanthus leaves, a slender ringed connector to a collar ring composed of large scrolled acanthus leaves, each suspending a cut crystal prism, a ringed beehive-form candlesocket w/a flat flaring rim, Regency Era, England, ca. 1825, 9" h., pr. **$1,093**

Candlesticks, pewter, round tapering ringed foot below a wide squatty bulbous base centered by the ring- and knob-turned shaft w/a cylindrical socket, Europe, 17th c., one shaft slightly bent, unmarked, base 5" d., 7 1/2" h., pr. **$1,200**

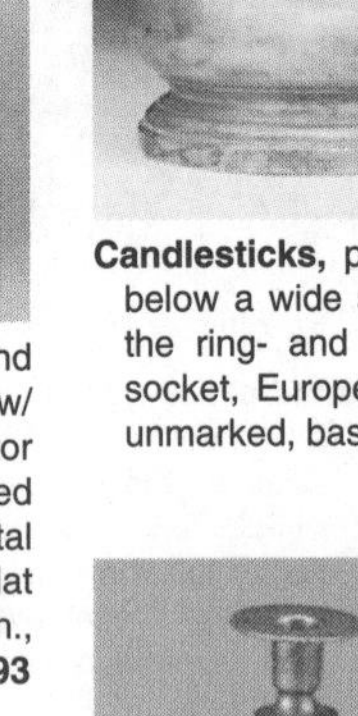

Candlesticks, pewter, wide domed & dished footed base centered by a ring- and knob-turned stem below the cylindrical socket, Europe, probably 17th - 18th c., 7" h., pr. **$1,495**

Candlesticks, silver plate, round foot tapering to a slightly flaring cylindrical shaft below the socket w/a wide flattened rim, band of stylized pine cone silver overlay near the top, overall acid-etched silver finish, Silver Crest mark of Smith Metal Arts Co., Buffalo, New York, ca. 1920s, minor dent to one bobeche & minor dent to rim of other, 9 3/4" h., pr. **$230**

Candlesticks, stamped brass, altar-type, a tall tapering triangular base on three paw feet decorated w/geometric panels & stamped leaves below a tall waisted & squared standard decorated as paneled & swag-trimmed column below the large urn-form socket w/rolled & gadrooned rim, 19th c., 22" h., pr. **$805**

Candlesticks, steel, hog scrapper-style, a wide round & slightly domed base & cylindrical shaft w/a push-up ejector, flattened rim w/thin curved finger grip, possibly Shaker-made, 19th c., 5 1/2" h., pr. **$345**

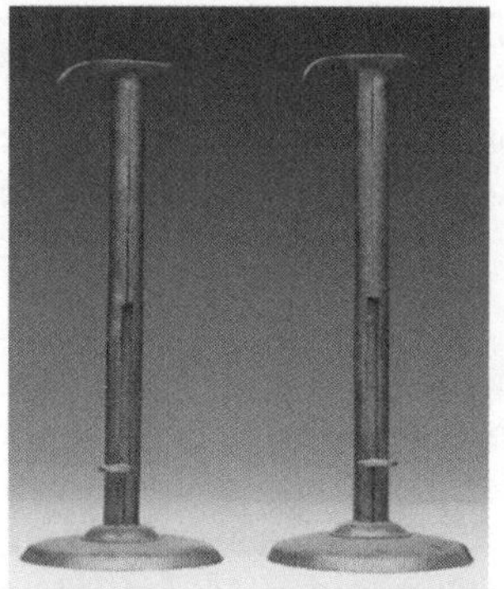

Candlesticks, steel, hog scrapper-type, a round foot centered by a very tall slender cylindrical shaft w/a tab-handled ejector, flattened & flared top w/small curved finger grip, early 19th c., overall 11 3/4" h., pr. **$1,610**

Candlesticks, sterling silver, an oval ornately scroll-cast rococo-style foot below the knopped & lobed ovoid crosshatch-etched standard below the matching ovoid socket w/wide rolled & scroll-cast rim, base engraved w/an egret w/a fish in its mouth next to a rampant lion w/a branch above a banner w/an engraved Latin inscription, weighted base, Frank Smith Silver Co., one w/repair where base meets shaft, late 19th - early 20th c., 10 1/4" h., set of 4 ..... **$3,163**

Chamberstick, copper, Arts & Crafts style, shallow dished base w/an arched riveted strap handle from the rim to the cylindrical center socket, stamped Jarvie mark, some cleaning to patina, early 20th c., 5 3/4" d., 3" h. **$633**

Chamberstick, copper, Arts & Crafts style, three-sided base w/cutout feet, scrolled strap handle, bobeche w/ upturned sides, the base decorated w/stylized flowers in green, red & black, stamp marked for Buffalo Art Craft Shop, 4 1/2" **$489**

Chamberstick, copper, hand-hammered Arts & Crafts style, trumpet-form base w/riveted angular handle, cupped socket, medium patina, either Onondaga or Benedict, recent mark on base, early 20th c., 6 1/2" h. **$345**

Robert Jarvie is considered the finest craftsman and designer of chambersticks in the Arts & Crafts style. Born in upstate New York, he moved to Chicago near the end of the Civil War, where he took a government job. He believed he could create better candlesticks than those being commercially produced, so he taught himself metalworking. After finding success, he retired from his government job to pursue his craft full time.

CERAMICS MARKET REPORT

Jack Becklund, of Pottery Nuts (www.potterynuts.com) in Bingham, Maine, said "the ceramics market continues to be soft, except for really good pieces. High-end pottery like Tiffany and George Ohr sell well, but the middle and low end of the market is slow."

Small Roseville pieces—4, 5, and 6 inches high—of late floral lines, for example, are stagnant. Bigger pieces are moving better, but there's not much markup available for them. People with deep pockets, though, always want to buy the best and are willing to pay handsomely for them. Becklund, like most dealers, has found it difficult to find and purchase high-end pieces at a price at which he can make a profit.

He attributes the slump to a number of factors. Although the economy has seen a modest improvement, unemployment is still high, and there's no sign of a dramatic improvement any time soon. People are making tough choices about how they spend their money. Also, since demand for pottery is down, the supply remains high, depressing the prices. On a positive note, this is an excellent time to buy. For collectors who have been waiting to find certain pieces or find them at the right price, it should be easier to purchase them now than it has been in the past.

Becklund relies heavily on online sales. He joined Ruby Lane in spring of 2010 and is pleased with the results he is getting. His Web site and Ruby Lane make up about 70 percent of his sales with the remaining 30 percent coming from shows and his brick and mortar shop. His online store allows him to sell to a much broader national and international market, including Canada and Australia. International customers comprise about 5 percent of his sales. A former newspaper reporter, he has been writing articles on Ruby Lane, which brings hundreds of visitors to his store.

His physical store is in a rural area, and much of that traffic is seasonal, coming from summer tourists. He travels across the country frequently, buying at various shops and venues and selling at shows. He regularly sets up at the Florida Mt. Dora show in the winter.

Becklund estimates that 50 percent of his customers are collectors, while 25 percent buy for resale, and 25 percent for decorating. He sees relatively little increase in purchases at Christmas mainly because people have such individual tastes that it's hard to buy a piece of pottery for someone else.

He hasn't seen a big change in demographics in recent years, but noted that the advent of the Internet has changed the market the most over the years. As more pieces were offered on eBay and other online sites, it became apparent that there was a much larger supply than previously believed. Plus, the Internet leveled the regional playing field. Prices became more uniform nationally as buyers became more aware of what was taking place in other parts of the country.

Becklund isn't sure what to expect in the future, but said, "I'm an optimist, who always sees the glass half full." Meanwhile, he is hard at work updating his Web site and expanding his Ruby Lane listings to take full advantage of online opportunities.

Belleek

The name Belleek refers to an industrious village in County Fermanagh, Northern Ireland, on the banks of the River Erne, and to the lustrous porcelain wares produced there.

In 1849, John Caldwell Bloomfield inherited a large estate near Belleek. Interested in ceramics, and having discovered rich deposits of feldspar and kaolin (china clay) on his lands, he soon envisioned a pottery that would make use of these materials, local craftspeople and water power of the River Erne. He was also anxious to enhance Ireland's prestige with superior porcelain products.

Bloomfield had a chance meeting with Robert Williams Armstrong who had established a substantial architectural business building potteries. Keenly interested in the manufacturing process, he agreed to design, build, and manage the new factory for Bloomfield. The factory was to be located on Rose Isle on a bend in the River Erne.

Bloomfield and Armstrong then approached David McBirney, a highly successful merchant and director of railway companies, and enticed him to provide financing. Impressed by the plans, he agreed to raise funds for the enterprise. As agreed, the factory was named McBirney and Armstrong, then later D. McBirney and Company.

Although 1857 is given as the founding date of the pottery, it is recorded that the pottery's foundation stone was laid by Mrs. J.C. Bloomfield on Nov. 18, 1858. Although not completed until 1860, the pottery was producing earthenware from its inception.

With the arrival of ceramic experts from the (William Henry) Goss Pottery in England, principally William Bromley, Sr. and William Wood Gallimore, Parian ware was perfected and, by 1863, the wares we associate with Belleek today were in production.

With Belleek Pottery workers and others emigrating to the United States in the late 1800s and early 1900s, Belleek-style china manufacture, known as American Belleek, commenced at several American firms, including Ceramic Art Company, Colombian Art Pottery, Lenox Inc., Ott & Brewer, and Willets Manufacturing Co.

Throughout its Parian production, Belleek Pottery marked its items with an Irish harp and wolfhound and the Devenish Tower. The 1st Period mark of 1863 through 1890 is shown below. Its 2nd Period began with the advent of the McKinley Tariff Act of 1891 and the (revised) British Merchandise Act as Belleek added the ribbon "Co. FERMANAGH IRELAND" beneath its mark in 1891. Both the 1st and 2nd period marks were black, although they occasionally appeared in burnt orange, green, blue or brown, especially on earthenware items. Its 3rd Period begin in 1926, when it added a Celtic emblem under the 2nd Period mark as well as the government trademark "Reg No 0857," which was granted in 1884. The Celtic emblem was registered by the Irish Industrial Development Association in 1906 and reads "Deanta in Eirinn," and means "Made in Ireland." The pottery is now utilizing its 13th mark, following a succession of three black marks, three green marks, a gold mark, two blue marks and three green. The final green mark was used only a single year, in 2007, to commemorate its 150th anniversary. In 2008, Belleek changed its mark to brown. Early earthenware was often marked in the same color as the majority of its surface decoration. Early basketware has Parian strips applied to its base with the impressed verbiage "BELLEEK" and later on, additionally "Co FERMANAGH" with or without "IRELAND." Current basketware carries the same mark as its Parian counterpart.

The item identification scheme is that followed within the works by Richard K. Degenhardt: Belleek The Complete Collector's Guide and Illustrated Reference (both first and second edition). Additional information, as well as a thorough discussion of the early marks, is located in these works as well as on the Internet at Del E. Domke's Web site: http://home.comcast.net/~belleek_website.

The prices given are for items in excellent condition, i.e., no chips, cracks, crazing or repairs. On flowered items, however, minimal chips to the flowering are acceptable, to the extent of the purchaser's tolerance. Earthenware items often exhibit varying degrees of crazing due to the primitive bottle kilns originally utilized at the pottery.

All Irish Belleek photographs used with permission, Rod Kearns, photographer, rkearns bak.rr.com.

American Belleek

Marks:

American Art China Works - R&E, 1891-95

AAC (superimposed), 1891-95

American Belleek Company - Company name, banner & globe

Ceramic Art Company - CAC palette, 1889-1906

Colombian Art Pottery - CAP, 1893-1902

Cook Pottery - Three feathers w/"CHC," 1894-1904

Coxon Belleek Pottery - "Coxon Belleek" in a shield, 1926-1930

Gordon Belleek - "Gordon Belleek," 1920-28

Knowles, Taylor & Knowles - "Lotusware" in a circle w/a crown, 1891-96

Lenox China - Palette mark, 1906-1924

Ott & Brewer - crown & shield, 1883-1893

Perlee - "P" in a wreath, 1925-1930

Willets Manufacturing Company - Serpent mark, 1880-1909

Cook Pottery - Three feathers w/"CHC"

Plates and Platters

Ceramic Art Company, plate, 10 1/2" d., finely h.p. in the center w/a bust portrait of a young maiden holding a closed book & a stylus, wearing a white wrap on her head, a white gown & red shawl, wide claret border band decorated w/an ornate gilt swag band w/foliate scrolls & flower garlands, gilt rim band, artist-signed, ca. 1905 .... **$2,880**

Irish Belleek

Comports & Centerpieces

Comport, Trihorse Comport, impressed "Belleek Co. Fermanagh," D37-I **$3,400**

The Ceramic Art Company was founded by Walter Scott Lenox in Trenton, New Jersey, in 1889. The firm began as a studio rather than a factory, producing high-end, handpainted wares. Its works were of such high quality that within ten years The Smithsonian was displaying examples of its products. In 1906, the company's name was changed to Lenox. Lenox porcelain was chosen for use at the White House by five U.S. presidents: Wilson, Truman, Reagan, Clinton and George W. Bush. It has also been used in more than 300 U.S. embassies and more than half of the governor's mansions and remains one of the oldest and most respected potteries in the world.

Figurines

Boy and Shell, 9" h., D9-II.......... **$3,000**

Tea Ware - Museum Display Patterns (Artichoke, Chinese, Finner, Five O'Clock, Lace, Ring Handle Ivory, Set #36 & Victoria)

Muffin dish, cov., Artichoke Tea Ware, gilt trim, D720-I............... **$2,000**

Plate, Ring Handle Ivory Ware plate, h.p. Irish scene, unsigned but from the School of Eugene Sheerin, 7 1/2" d., D823-II **$1,800**

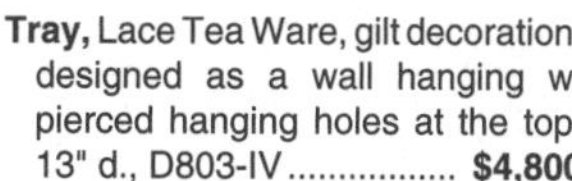

Tray, Lace Tea Ware, gilt decoration, designed as a wall hanging w/ pierced hanging holes at the top, 13" d., D803-IV **$4,800**

Tea Ware - Rare Patterns (Aberdeen, Blarney, Celtic (low & tall), Cone, Erne, Fan, Institute, Ivy, Lily (high & low), Scroll, Sydney, Thistle & Thorn)

Celtic Candlestick, Low, painted & gilt, 4 3/4" h., D1511-VI **$340**

Celtic Design bread plate, Celtic Design tea ware, multicolored & gilt, D1425-III **$600**

Celtic Design creamer, Celtic Design tea ware, tall shape, multi-colored, ('mystery' mark, 1st Period over Celtic Scroll, probably a transition from 1st to 2nd period), 4 1/2" h., D1442-II **$400**

Replacement value and actual cash value are not the same. Replacement value is the cost required to purchase a comparable item at retail value. Actual cash value is replacement value minus depreciation. Depreciation is a loss in value due to wear and tear. Depreciation is typically calculated by using a depreciation schedule, which mathematically calculates the loss in value according to the number of years the item has been in existence.

Tea Wares - Miscellaneous

Celtic bowl of roses, h.p. colors of dark pink, yellow & green, D1510-VII **$2,600**

Plate, scenic center of Irish peasant homes w/ornate gilt scroll border, h.p. by former pottery manager Cyril Arnold, artist-signed & w/what appears to be "15 PA" following the signature, 8 1/2" d., D1527-IV **$1,200**

Plate, pottery, Scenic Celtic Commemorative Plate, painted & gilded, D1553-V **$800**

Wedding cup, three-handled, Shamrock patt., h.p. trim, D2105-II.. **$640**

Collectors are conscious of the idea of antiques as investments, but it should never be the driving force. The greatest benefit of collecting should be enjoyment, from the thrill of the hunt to learning more about their history. Acquire the highest quality pieces you can afford, learn as much as you can, stay focused, and someday your diligence may be rewarded.

Bennington

Bennington wares, which ranged from stoneware to parian and porcelain, were made in Bennington, Vermont, primarily in two potteries, one in which Captain John Norton and his descendants were principals, and the other in which Christopher Webber Fenton (also once associated with the Nortons) was a principal. Various marks are found on the wares made in the two major potteries, including J. & E. Norton, E. & L. P. Norton, L. Norton & Co., Norton & Fenton, Edward Norton, Lyman Fenton & Co., Fenton's Works, United States Pottery Co., U.S.P. and others.

The popular pottery with the mottled brown on yellowware glaze was also produced in Bennington, but such wares should be referred to as "Rockingham" or "Bennington-type" unless they can be specifically attributed to a Bennington, Vermont factory.

Book flask, binding marked "Departed Spirits G," Flint Enamel glaze, 5 1/2" h. **$532**

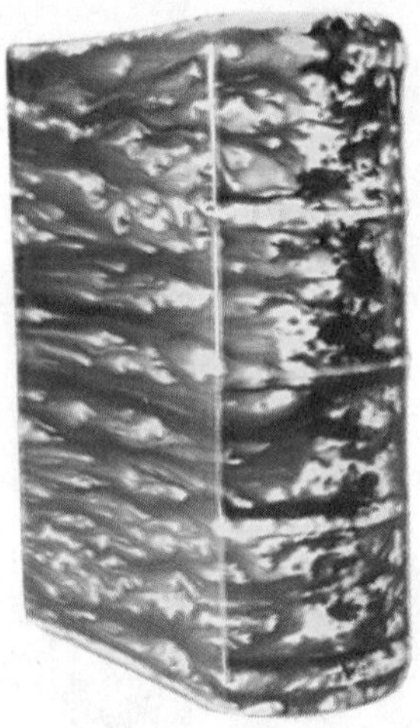

Book flask, noting lettering on binding, mottled brown & cream Rockingham glaze, 5 3/4" h. **$392**

Picture frame, oval w/wide ringed rounded sides, overall mottled Rockingham glaze, few underside flakes, mid-19th c., 8 3/4 x 9 3/4" **$489**

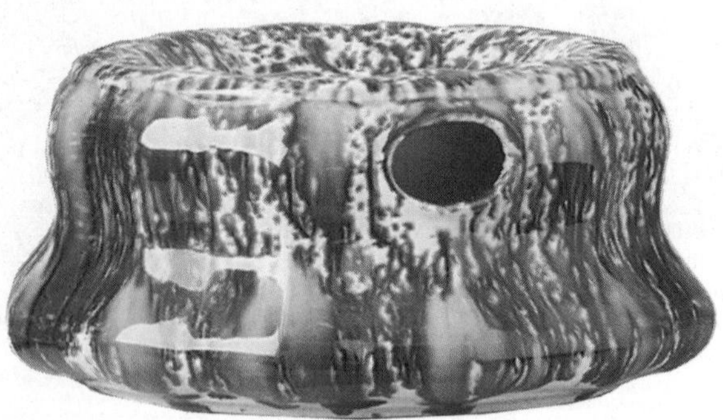

Cuspidor, short round waisted shape w/side hole, Flint Enamel glaze, Type A impress mark on base, mid-19th c., 8" d., 3 3/4" h. **$144**

Toby pitcher, figural seated Mr. Toby, dark brown mottled Rockingham glaze, unmarked, 6" h. **$259**

Berlin (KPM)

The mark KPM was used at Meissen from 1724 to 1725, and was later adopted by the Royal Factory, Konigliche Porzellan Manufaktur, in Berlin. At various periods it has been incorporated with the Brandenburg scepter, the Prussian eagle or the crowned globe. The same letters were also adopted by other factories in Germany in the late 19th and early 20th centuries. With the end of the German monarchy in 1918, the name of the firm was changed to Staatliche Porzellan Manufaktur and though production was halted during World War II, the factory was rebuilt and is still in business. The exquisite paintings on porcelain were produced at the close of the 19th century and are eagerly sought by collectors today.

Centerpiece, in the Vienna style, a deep oval bowl w/serpentine sides pierced at the rim & flanked by large gold scrolling loop handles, the front finely painted w/a Classical view representing the Arts in a garden setting & the reverse depicting Neptune as a child riding a dolphin w/other putti, a gold bead band around the base of the bowl & raised on a deep maroon pedestal w/gilt scroll decoration & an oblong gold foot w/block feet alternating w/dolphin mask feet between gold knobs, titled in German on the bottom, blue sceptre mark, late 19th c., 15" l. **$4,183**

Model of a squirrel, seated animal in dark brick red holding a brown acorn, on a green & brown stump molded w/acorns & oak leaves, some gold wear, second half 19th c., 10" h. **$1,150**

Charger, pate-sur-pate, round w/a wide dished rim band in white decorated w/ornate gold Art Nouveau floral looping panels w/small forget-me-nots & roses, the wide center w/a celadon green ground painted & hand-tooled in white slip w/a scene of a diaphanously clad Bacchante pouring a vessel of wine into Pan's lips as he kneels beside a tree stump, blue sceptre & iron-red orb marks, ca. 1895, 13 3/4" d. **$5,378**

Charger, round, the wide border band w/a cobalt blue ground very ornately painted in gold w/alternating panels of a wreath & crown & scrolls in pointed arcs, the center painted in color w/a bust portrait of a 16th c. lady w/a fancy headdress, signed by Wagner, in a deep square giltwood shadowbox frame lined in red velvet, late 19th c., 16" d. **$2,185**

Plaque, oval, decorated w/a bust portrait of a lovely young woman w/a red flower in her long flowing brown hair, a deep yellow off-the-shoulder shawl, in an ornately molded oval gilt-plaster frame, KPM mark on the back, late 19th c., plaque 8 1/2 x 10 1/2", overall 15 x 18" **$11,155**

Plaque, oval, decorated w/a color copy of "The Sistine Madonna" after Raphael, mounted in an elaborate rectangular giltwood pierce-carved frame composed of scrolling acanthus leaves w/a red velvet liner, fitted in a glazed rectangular shadowbox frame, impressed sceptre & KPM marks, late 19th c., plaque 13 1/2 x 17" ... **$4,025**

Plaque, oval, titled "Meditation," bust-length portrait of a brunette beauty w/a red flower in her hair, diaphonous white & pale blue drapery around her shoulders, artist-signed, impressed monogram & sceptre marks, late 19th - early 20th c., unframed, 6 5/8 x 8 7/8" **$7,800**

Plaque, rectangular, a long classical scene depicting the goddess Aurora & her attendants, after a painting by Guido Reni, inscribed & titled on the back along w/a label reading "Painted for Mermood and Jaccurd Jewelry Co., St. Louis," impressed KPM & other marks, artist-signed, mounted in an elaborate reticulated giltwood framed, plaque 8 x 13" **$10,638**

In Roman mythology, Aurora is the goddess of the dawn. Each morning she crosses the sky to precede and announce the arrival of the sun. In Greek mythology, Aurora is known as Eos. According to legend, Aurora fell in love with the human Tithonus, who, would someday face death, unlike the immortal Aurora. Aurora asked Zeus to grant Tithonus eternal life, and the wish was granted, but while he was given eternal life, he was not granted eternal youth.

Plaque, rectangular, finely painted w/the portrait of an exotic raven-haired beauty playing a lyre carved as the head of an Egyptian pharaoh, a brazier at her feet, impressed monogram & sceptre mark, titled on the back, late 19th - early 20th c., mounted in giltwood frame, 6 1/4 x 9 3/8" **$4,183**

Plaque, rectangular, painted w/a winter scene of an elderly grandfather just outside a cottage door & standing holding a small baby w/his little granddaughter nearby, titled "The First Snowfall," impressed sceptre & KPM marks, artist-signed, in a fancy acanthus leaf-carved wooden frame, late 19th c., plaque 7 1/2 x 10" **$4,370**

Plaque, rectangular, scene of two young women w/long flowing hair & wearing diaphanous gowns holding floral garland above their heads, reverse impressed "KPM" w/scepter, in very ornate gilt wood frame of pierced scroll decoration, 19th c., 7 1/2 x 10" **$4,830**

Plaque, rectangular, three-quarter length portrait of a young girl seated in a woodland setting winding thread for her embroidery, impressed monogram & sceptre mark, late 19th - early 20th c., in giltwood frame, 8 3/4 x 10 3/4" **$7,200**

Plaque, rectangular, titled "Bonheur Maternal," depicting an interior scene w/two young women rocking a child in a hammock accented in gold, impressed monogram & sceptre mark, early 20th c., in giltwood frame, 7 1/2 x 10" **$6,000**

Plaque, rectangular, titled "Fruhling," a bust-length portrait of a dark haired beauty w/white blossoms in her hair in a wooden background of blossoming trees, wearing diaphanous white draped gown, artist-signed, impressed monogram & sceptre mark, late 19th - early 20th c., in giltwood frame, 10 1/4 x 12 3/8" **$12,000**

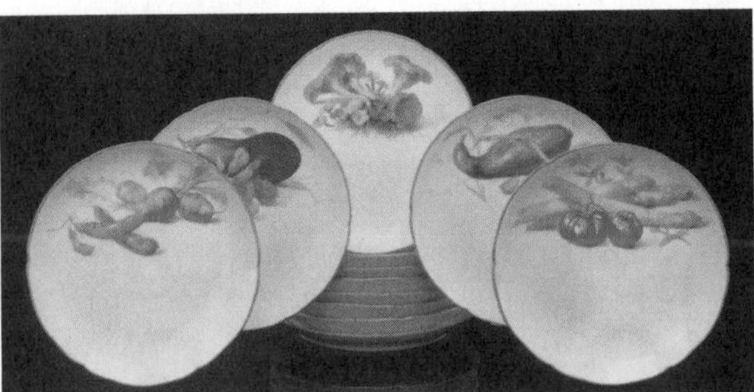

Plates, salad, 8 1/2" d., each finely painted at the top w/a still-life of vegetables, herbs & grains, titled in German on the back, the lobed rim trimmed in gold, blue sceptre & iron-red orb marks, late 19th c., set of 12 (ILLUS. of part) **$60,000**

Urn, octagonal stepped base below ringed pedestal supporting baluster-form body w/trumpet neck, two gilt coiled snake-form handles, front w/h.p. decoration of winged cherub among floral bouquet, reverse w/butterflies & florals, marked w/red orb & blue underglaze circle, late 19th c., 18 3/4" h. **$3,680**

Some show promoters charge an early buyer fee for admission to their show a few hours before opening the gates to the public. Customers must decide if the fee, which can be $20 or more, is worth the expense. Even with the advantage of shopping before the public arrives, the show may have been picked clean of bargains by dealers during the show setup. On the other hand, the savings realized by just one good purchase may more than cover the early buyer fee.

Buffalo Pottery

Incorporated in 1901 as a wholly owned subsidiary of the Larkin Soap Company, founded by John D. Larkin of Buffalo, New York, in 1875, the Buffalo Pottery was a manufactory built to produce premium wares to be included with purchases of Larkin's chief product, soap. In October 1903, the first kiln was fired and Buffalo Pottery became the only pottery in the world run entirely by electricity.

In 1904 Larkin offered its first premium produced by the pottery. This concept of using premiums caused sales to skyrocket and, in 1905, the first Blue Willow pattern pottery made in the United States was introduced as a premium.

The Buffalo Pottery administrative building, built in 1904 to house 1,800 clerical workers, was the creation of a 32-year-old architect, Frank Lloyd Wright. The building was demolished in 1953, but many critics considered it to be Wright's masterpiece.

By 1910 annual soap production peaked and the number of premiums offered in the catalogs exceeded 600. By 1915 this number had grown to 1,500. The first catalog of premiums was issued in 1893 and continued to appear through the late 1930s.

John D. Larkin died in 1926, and during the Great Depression the firm suffered severe losses, going into bankruptcy in 1940. After World War II the pottery resumed production under new management, but its vitreous wares were generally limited to mass-produced china for the institutional market.

Among the pottery lines produced during Buffalo's heyday were Gaudy Willow, Deldare, Abino Ware, historical and commemorative plates, and unique handpainted jugs and pitchers. In the 1920s and 1930s the firm concentrated on personalized wares for commercial clients including hotels, clubs, railroads, and restaurants. In 1983 Oneida Silversmiths bought the pottery, an ironic twist since, years before, Oneida silver had been featured in Larkin catalogs. The pottery has now ceased all domestic production of ceramics. - Phillip M. Sullivan.

Blue Willow Pattern (1905-1916)

Pitcher, wash-type **$750**

Deldare Ware (1908-1909, 1923-1925)

Charger, "An Evening at Ye Lion Inn," decorated by W. Forster, 1908, some superficial scratches, 13 1/2" d. **$403**

Old Sears catalogs can be used as antiques identification guides. Like price guides, they list features, colors, and measurements. While the illustrations are black and white, rather than color, they do show good detail. And antique Sears catalogs are collectors items in their own right.

Chocolate set: tall tapering hexagonal covered chocolate pot w/serpentine handle decorated w/"Ye Village Street" scene & two tapering conical chocolate cups, artist-signed, 1909, small rim repairs on cups, chocolate pot 10 1/2" h., the set .. **$1,500-3,000**

Jardiniere & garden seat pedestal base, "Ye Lion Inn" scenes on jardiniere, two "Ye Olden Days" scenes on base, 1908, jardiniere 9" h., base 13 1/2" h., the set **$12,000**

Plates, 9 1/4" d., "The Fallow Field Hunt - The Start," artist-signed, set of 4, each **$300**

Emerald Deldare (1911)

Coffee/chocolate pot, cov., tall tapering hexagonal form w/pinched spout & angled D-form handle, inset lid w/blossom finial, stylized symmetrical designs highlighted w/white flowers on body & lid, band just under spout w/stylized moths & large butterfly, decorated by L. Newman, ca. 1911, artist's name in green slip, ink stamp logo & "7," 10 1/2" h. **$3,000**

Pitcher, 8 3/4" h., octagonal, angled handle, color scene of "Dr. Syntax Setting Out to the Lakes," signed by M. Gerhardt, dated 1911 .... **$2,000**

Plate, 7 1/4" d., h.p. floral border & center scene, "Dr. Syntax Soliloquizing," by E. Missel, marked w/Emerald Deldare logo, "1911" & "4" **$1,400**

Gaudy Willow (1905-1916)

Author's Note: Pieces dated 1905 and marked "First Old Willow Ware Manufactured in America" are worth double the prices shown here. This line is generally priced five times higher than the Blue Willow line.

Jugs and Pitchers (1906-1909)

Pitcher, "Gloriana," blue on white, ca. 1908, 9" h. **$900**

Plates - Commemorative (1906-1912)

B. & M. Smelter, and the largest smokestack in the world. Great Falls, Montana, deep green, ca. 1909, 7 1/2" d. **$150**

Niagara Falls, dark blue w/Bonrea pattern border, ca. 1907, 7 1/2" d. **$150**

Miscellaneous Pieces

Christmas Plate, 1950, first of a series of annual plates ending in 1962, 9 1/2" d. **$75**

Feeding dish, child's, alphabet border, Dutch children at play in center, ca. 1916, 7 3/4" d. **$125**

Pitcher, York patt., white body w/blue & red flowers, 1910, rare, 7 1/2" h. **$650**

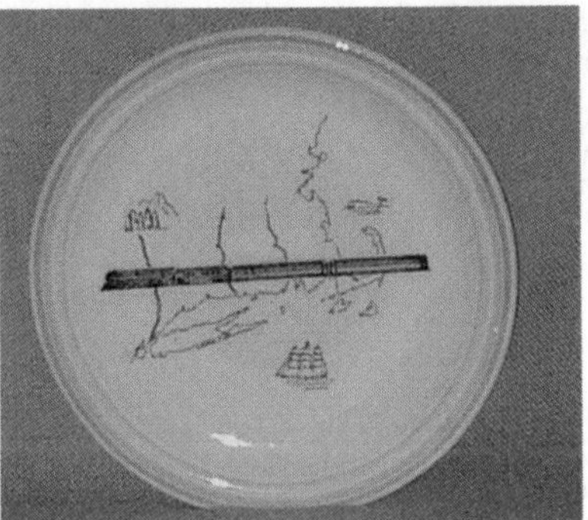

Plate, 6 3/8" d., bread & butter, made for the New York, New Haven & Hartford Railroad, ca. 1935 .... **$95**

Platter, 11 x 14", rectangular w/rounded corners & gently scalloped edges, dark teal blue-green wide border around a transfer-printed central scene of a Native American buffalo hunt, ca. 1910 .... **$288**

Platter, 13 1/4 x 18 1/2", Turkey patt., large colorful turkey in landscape in center, fall landscape border scenes, Colorido Ware, 1937, Buffalo China .... **$3,200+**

Canton

This ware has been decorated for nearly two centuries in factories near Canton, China. Intended for export sale, much of it was originally inexpensive blue-and-white hand-decorated ware. Late-18th- and early-19th-century pieces are superior to later ones and fetch higher prices.

Bowl, 10 1/2" w., 4 3/4" h., squared w/cut corners, simple island landscape in the center bottom, 19th c. **$881**

Bowl, 10" d., 2 1/4" h., wide shallow shape w/a flaring scalloped rim, orange peel glaze bottom, 19th c. **$460**

Bowl, 9" d., 4 1/2" h., serpentine four-lobed rim, 19th c. **$1,035**

Candlesticks, slender tapering cylindrical form w/flattened socket rim, 19th c., rim chip, 7 1/2" h., pr. **$2,233**

Charger, wide round shape w/dished rim, large round central landscape, small edge fleck, 19th c., 14 3/4" d. **$403**

Plates, 7 1/4" d., shallow dished shape, 19th c., one w/a repaired edge, set of 7 .... **$316**

Plates, 8 1/2" d., shallow dished shape, 19th c., two w/small chips, one w/spider cracks, one w/very old tight hairline, set of 10 .... **$575**

Platter, 10 1/4 x 13", rectangular w/cut corners, large Chinese landscape in the center, decorative floral & scroll border band, first half 19th c. **$863**

Platter, 16 1/2 x 20", oblong w/cut-corners, deep curved sides, 19th c. **$748**

Platter, 16 x 18 3/4", oblong w/angled corners, 19th c. **$1,150**

Punch bowl, narrow footring below deep rounded sides, early 19th c., 13 1/4" d., 5 1/2" h. **$3,055**

Serving dish, cov., rectangular foot w/rectangular flaring sides w/rounded corners, high domed cover w/a pine cone finial, 19th c., 10 x 11", 6" h. **$633**

Soup tureen, cov., flared base band below the deep oval canted sides w/figural boar head end handles, long low domed cover w/figural helmet finial, 19th c., 8 3/4 x 12", 9" h. **$1,265**

Teapot, cov., tapering cylindrical lighthouse-shape, straight spout, double strap handle, domed cover w/ snail-like finial, small spout nick & tip of finial, 19th c., 8 1/2" h. **$690**

Tureen, cov., footed deep oblong base w/boar's head end handles, low domed cover w/large center handle & a butterfly design edge band, 19th c., 9 1/2 x 11 1/2", 9" h. **$550**

Tureen, cover & undertray, oblong w/beveled corners, molded boar's head handles on base & molded stem handle on the cover, 19th c., overall 12 5/8" l., 9" h., the set **$1,998**

Warming dish, cov., shallow oblong base w/angled corners & filling hole at one end, domed cover w/nut-like finial, 19th c., 9 3/4 x 15" **$1,265**

Warming platter, oval w/flanged rim, small tab handle at one end & filling hole at other end, 19th c., 15 3/4" l., 2 1/2" h. **$441**

Chinese Export

Large quantities of porcelain have been made in China for export to America from the 1780s, much of it shipped from the ports of Canton and Nanking. A major source of this porcelain was Ching-te-Chen in the Kiangsi province, but the wares were also made elsewhere. The largest quantities were blue and white. Prices fluctuate considerably depending on age, condition, decoration, etc.

Creamer, helmet-shaped, armorial-type, blue band decoration & h.p. blue, red & gold crest below the spout, ca. 1790, 6 3/4" l., 5 1/2" h. **$500**

Dish, squared shape w/lobed corners, decorated w/a h.p. central scene depicting a master w/concubines & servants, floral & butterfly border band, late 18th - early 19th c., 9" w. **$863**

Pitcher, 6 1/2" h., Famille Rose palette, slightly swelled cylindrical shape w/a deeply scalloped rim & pointed rim spout, jagged arched handle, the sides decorated w/ large colorful panels of flowers, minor rim chips, 19th c. **$863**

Dishes, round, armorial-type, decorated w/two dark blue overglazed bands centering the colorful arms of Oliphant impaling Browne, minor decoration wear, ca. 1790, 6 1/8" d., 1 1/4" h., pr. (ILLUS. of one) **$920**

Plate, 8 3/4" d., armorial-type, wide fancy floral-decorated rim in underglaze-blue, the center painted w/a the large arms of Godfrey w/a Latin motto, hairline in bottom, ca. 1725 .... **$1,093**

Plate, 9" d., famille rose palette, wide rim painted w/sepia cartouches on a pale rose honeycomb background, centering a scene of a tall vase, table & flowering branch, roughness to glaze on half the rim, minor rim flakes & two small hairlines, ca. 1750 .... **$403**

Plates, 10" d., green Fitzhugh patt., ca. 1800, pr. (ILLUS. of one) **$1,150**

Plates, 9 3/4" d., blue Fitzhugh patt., early 19th c., pr. **$575**

Platter, 13 1/4 x 16 3/4" oval, well & tree-type, Famille Rose palette, the top decorated w/six large triangular panels of colorful florals, some minor gold loss, mid-19th c. **$978**

Sauce tureen, cov., Rose Mandarin design, a deep flaring foot supporting the squatty bulbous oblong body w/double loop end handles, the high domed & stepped cover w/a large gold flower finial, 19th c., 8" l., 6" h. **$1,265**

Famille Rose is Chinese export ware incorporating pink, a color foreign to traditional Chinese pottery and introduced by Europeans. The pink was used only for export and not for domestic Chinese production.

Rose Mandarin is a design similar to Rose Medallion and Rose Canton, except that Rose Mandarin has only people in the panels. Rose Medallion shows a peony or bird in the central medallion, and its panels show people and birds. Rose Canton shows no birds or people.

Tea set: cov. teapot, cov. tea caddy, helmet-shaped creamer, cov. cream pot & handleless cup; the oval teapot w/upright sides & a tapering shoulder to the inset cover w/berry finial, the bulbous tapering cream pot w/domed cover, upright flat-sided rectangular tea caddy w/arched shoulder, short neck & domed cap, each piece h.p. on the side in sepia, orange & gold w/a spread-winged American eagle w/shield, made for the American market, late 18th c., teapot 8 1/2" l., the set **$5,175**

Tea set: tall tapering cov. teapot, short oval cov. teapot, helmet-shaped creamer, cov. sugar bowl, upright rectangular cov. tea caddy, cake plate & two handleless cups & saucers; each piece h.p. w/a sepia & orange spread-winged eagle & shield, gilt trim, late 18th c., tall teapot 10" h., the set **$8,338**

Because tea leaves float, teapot spouts have traditionally emerged from the base of the teapot to prevent tea leaves from being poured out with the tea. Since coffee grounds sink, coffeepot spouts normally emerge from the top of the coffeepot to prevent the grounds from being poured out with the coffee.

Tea set: tall tapering cylindrical cov. teapot, short oval cov. teapot & undertray, upright rectangular cov. tea caddy, serving plate, two large handleless tea cups, one smaller tea cup & saucer; each piece h.p. w/an orange & black spread-winged eagle w/an oval medallion decorated w/the initials "SSD," made for the American market, late 18th - early 19th c., tall teapot 9 1/2" h., the set **$5,000**

Teapot, a footed spherical double-walled style w/ the outer layer pierced overall w/ a delicate green vine w/orange blossoms, a light blue shoulder band & the matched domed & pierced cover w/a button finial, a C-form handle & a straight angled silver spout, unmarked, late 18th - early 19th c., chips & repairs on cover, small chip on base rim, 6" h. **$230**

Teapot, a round foot below a low flaring base below a wide slightly concave body band below a wide slightly rounded shoulder centering a short gold neck, a serpentine spout & C-scroll handle, the high domed cover w/a gold ball finial above a scene of a woman & a cartouche of a man above a band of flowers & birds, the wide shoulder painted overall w/colorful birds, flowers & butterflies, the body band decorated w/continuous scenes of Chinese ladies, ca. 1840, restoration to rim & spout, chip at pot mouth, wear to cover gilt, 9" h. **$690**

Teapot, cov., Rose Medallion patt., a round flaring foot supporting a wide urn-form body w/a serpentine spout & C-scroll handle, the high domed cover w/a gold ball finial, the cover, shoulder & body all decorated w/h.p. cartouches featuring birds, flowers & butterflies or Chinese figures, gold trim, ca. 1860, 11" l., 10 1/2" h. **$920**

Teapot, Famille rose palette, footed squatty spherical body w/straight spout & C-form handle, domed flanged cover w/pointed knob finial, h.p. w/Chinese figures in a landscape, 19th c., 5 1/2" h. **$288**

Teapot, tall tapering cylindrical body w/a straight angled spout & twisted strap handle, the flanged domed cover w/a knob finial, decorated for the American market w/a rusty orange design of an American eagle w/ floral-decoratedshield, similar to a design used by the Nichols Family of Salem, Massachusetts, late 18th - early 19th c., two small hairlines w/dings, overall 10" h. **$920**

Tureen, cov., armorial-type, famille rose palette, footed squatty bulbous oval body w/gilt twisted branch end handles, domed cover w/gilt artichoke finial, decorated w/continuous scenes of Chinese figures in a landscape on the cover, the base painted w/the arms of Grant w/family mottoes, a rim band decorated w/flowers, butterflies & birds, the sides w/a continuous scene of Chinese figures on balconies & in gardens, portions of interior cover rim restored, gilt wear, glaze flaws, ca. 1810, 13 1/2" l., 9" h. **$4,140**

Umbrella stand, Famille Rose palette in a Mandarin design, the tall cylindrical ribbed body decorated up the sides w/three bands containing alternating figural & floral panels, 19th c., 24 3/4" h. **$4,025**

Never hire an appraiser who offers to exchange his services for an antique or who charges based on a percentage of the appraisal. This is unethical because it gives an incentive for the appraiser to inflate values. Appraisers should only charge by the hour or by a predetermined fee for the job.

Urn, cov., wide baluster-form body w/foo dog head & ring shoulder handles, domed cover w/figural foo lion finial, famille rose palette, the sides painted w/large reserves w/festival scenes & crowds of Chinese figures, floral background & wide geometric base band, cover finial w/broken tail, second half 19th c., 21" h. **$403**

Clarice Cliff Designs

FANTASQUE
HAND PAINTED
Bizarre
by
Clarice Cliff
NEWPORT POTTERY
ENGLAND

Clarice Cliff was a designer for A.J. Wilkinson, Ltd., Royal Staffordshire Pottery, Burslem, England when it acquired the adjoining Newport Pottery Company, whose warehouses were filled with undecorated bowls and vases. In about 1925 her flair with the Art Deco style was incorporated into designs appropriately named "Bizarre" and "Fantasque" and the warehouse stockpile was decorated in vivid colors. These hand-painted earthenwares, all bearing the printed signature of designer Clarice Cliff, were produced until World War II and are now finding enormous favor with collectors.

Note: Reproductions of the Clarice Cliff "Bizarre" marking have been appearing on the market recently.

Bowl, 16 3/8" d., a wide flat bottom & wide flaring sides, Latona patt., decorated around the exterior w/a polychrome scene of stylized trees in shades of red, orange, green, blue, black & cream, printed Bizarre Ware backstamp, surface wear to interior center, ca. 1930 .... **$1,645**

Candlesticks, slender baluster-form shaft above a disk foot & w/a wide flattened rim, painted w/bold geometric designs in blue, orange & green, Delicia Citrus patt., brightly painted fruits on a cream ground pr. **$2,500**

Charger, large round dished form, Crest patt., three large Japanese-style crests in gold, blue, rust red, black & green on a mottled green ground **$12,000**

Pitcher, 11 5/8" h., jug-form, the ovoid ribbed body tapering to a flat rim, decorated in the Fantasque Blue Chintz patt. in shades of blue, rose red, greens & cream, cream-colored handle, printed Bizarre Ware backstamp, ca. 1930 .... **$1,880**

Pitcher, 12" h., "Bizarre" ware, Lotus shape, ringed ovoid body tapering to a wide cylindrical neck, heavy loop handle, Delicia Citrus patt., large stylized red, yellow & orange fruits around the top w/ green leaves & streaky green on a cream ground **$2,200**

Plates, 7 1/2" d., "Bizarre" ware, Crocus patt. in orange, dark blue, purple & green, black Clarice Cliff logo, slight surface wear, pr. **$115**

Tumbler, Bizarre Ware, slightly flaring cylindrical form, half-round stylized large blossoms along edge of rim in orange, pale green & yellow w/matching narrow bands around the inner rim, minor glaze nicks, 3 5/8" h. **$115**

Vase, 8" h., "Bizarre" ware, Shape No. 386, swelled cylindrical base below the angled shoulder & tall gently flaring neck, Crocus patt., a yellow rim band & brown bottom section below a cluster of colorful crocus blossoms on a cream ground **$1,000**

Vase, 9 3/4" h., simple ovoid form tapering to a wide flat rim, decorated in color in the Patina Country patt. in shades of green, purple, red, yellow & blue on a mottled light yellow ground, printed Bizarre Ware backstamp, ca. 1930 .... **$1,293**

Disreputable auctioneers who have difficulty getting an opening bid may resort to fabricating a first bid, figuring certainly someone will come in with a second bid. He may continue the charade by pulling additional bids out of the air. Your best defense as a buyer is to leave and never patronize the auctioneer again.

Delft

In the early 17th century, Italian potters settled in Holland and began producing tin-glazed earthenwares, often decorated with pseudo-Oriental designs based on Chinese porcelain wares. The city of Delft became the center of this pottery production and several firms produced the wares throughout the 17th and early 18th century. A majority of the pieces featured blue on white designs, but polychrome wares were also made. The Dutch Delftwares were also shipped to England, where eventually the English copied them at potteries in such cities as Bristol, Lambeth and Liverpool. Although still produced today, Delft peaked in popularity by the mid-18th century.

Bowl, 8 5/8" d., 2" h., scalloped rim on low lobed body, h.p. w/blue stylized flowers on a powder blue ground, England, mid-18th c., minor rim chips & glaze wear **$470**

Charger, round shallow dished form w/a narrow flanged rim, the center w/a large rounded panel-sided reserve h.p. w/leafy scrolls around a round center w/a stylized leafy blossom, the border band decorated w/small oval reserves decorated w/scrolls & squiggles, a blue initial or X under the bottom, various glaze & rim chips, Holland, 18th c., 13 3/4" d. **$460**

Plate, 8 3/4" d., shallow dished form w/a wide flanged rim, the center h.p. in dark blue w/a large urn filled w/fruit & fanned & feathery leaves & flowers, the border h.p. in dark blue w/wide half-leaves alternating w/squiggle bands, Holland, 18th c., tight hairline from rim nearly to center, small rim chip **$230**

Tile, rectangular, decorated in blue & white w/a seaside scene w/women standing on the shore & sailing ships heading out to sea, after a painting by Hendrik Willem Mesdag, marked w/Delft & other painted & impressed marks, late 19th - early 20th c., 7 7/8 x 10" **$500**

Doulton & Royal Doulton

Doulton & Co., Ltd., was founded in Lambeth, London, in about 1858. It was operated there until 1956 and often incorporated the words "Doulton" and "Lambeth" in its marks. Pinder, Bourne & Co., Burslem was purchased by the Doultons in 1878 and in 1882 became Doulton & Co., Ltd. It added porcelain to its earthenware production in 1884. The "Royal Doulton" mark has been used since 1902 by this factory, which is still in operation. Character jugs and figurines are commanding great attention from collectors at the present time.

John Doulton, the founder, was born in 1793. He became an apprentice at the age of 12 to a potter in south London. Five years later he was employed in another small pottery near Lambeth. His two sons, John and Henry, subsequently joined their father in 1830 in a partnership he had formed with the name of Doulton & Watts. Watts retired in 1864 and the partnership was dissolved. Henry formed a new company that traded as Doulton & Co.

In the early 1870s the proprietor of the Pinder Bourne Co., located in Burslem, Staffordshire, offered Henry a partnership. The Pinder Bourne Co. was purchased by Henry in 1878 and became part of Doulton & Co. in 1882.

With the passage of time the demand for the Lambeth industrial and decorative stoneware declined whereas demand for the Burslem manufactured and decorated bone china wares increased.

Doulton & Co. was incorporated as a limited liability company in 1899. In 1901 the company was allowed to use the word "Royal" on its trademarks by Royal Charter. The well known "lion on crown" logo came into use in 1902. In 2000 the logo was changed on the company's advertising literature to one showing a more stylized lion's head in profile.

Today Royal Doulton is one of the world's leading manufacturers and distributors of premium grade ceramic tabletop wares and collectibles. The Doulton Group comprises Minton, Royal Albert, Caithness Glass, Holland Studio Craft and Royal Doulton. Royal Crown Derby was part of the group from 1971 until 2000 when it became an independent company. These companies market collectibles using their own brand names.

Animals & Birds

Cat, Persian Cat, seated, black & white, HN 999, 1930-85, 5" h. **$115**

Dog, Bull Terrier, K 14, lying, white, 1940-59, 1 1/4 x 2 3/4" **$325**

Dog, Alsatian, "Benign of Picardy," dark brown, HN 1117, 1937-68, 4 1/2" **$250**

Dog, Boxer, Champion "Warlord of Mazelaine," golden brown coat w/white bib, HN 2643, 1952-85, 6 1/2" h. **$145**

Bird, Bullfinch, blue & pale blue feathers, red breast, HN 2551, 1941-46, 5 1/2" h. **$80**

Dog, Airedale Terrier, Ch. "Cotsford Topsail," standing, dark brown & black, light brown underbody, HN 1024, 1931-68, 4" h. **$275**

Dog, Bulldog, HN 1044, brown & white, 1931-68, 3 1/4" h....... **$250**

Dog, Bulldog Puppy, K 2, seated, tan w/brown patches, 1931-77, 2" **$85**

Dog, Cocker Spaniel, Ch. "Lucky Star of Ware," black coat w/grey markings, HN 1021, 1931-68, 3 1/2" h. **$195**

Dog, Cocker Spaniel w/pheasant, seated, white coat w/black markings, HN 1137, 1937-66, 6 1/2 x 7 3/4" **$375**

Dog, Collie, Ch. "Ashstead Applause," dark & light brown coat, white chest, shoulder & feet, HN 1057, 1931-60, 7 1/2" h. **$750**

Duck, Drake, standing, green, brown & white, HN 807, 1923-77, 2 1/2" h. **$105**

Dog, English Setter, Ch. "Maesydd Mustard," off-white coat w/black highlights, HN 1051, 1931-68, 4" h. **$215**

Dog, Fox Terrier, K 8, seated, white w/brown & black patches, 1931-77, 2 1/2" **$90**

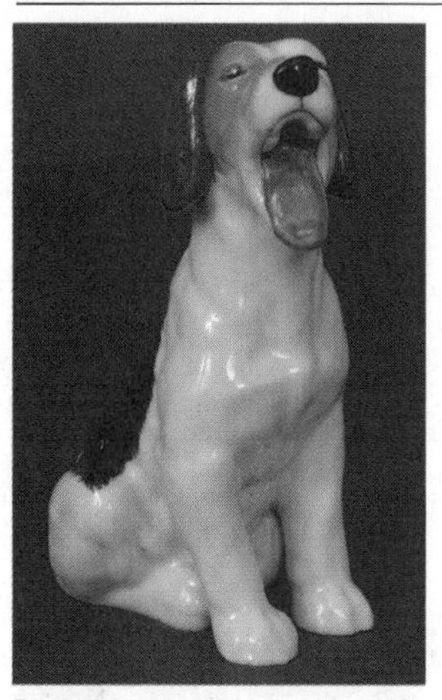

Dog, character dog yawning, white w/brown patches over ears & eyes, black patches on back, HN 1099, 1934-85, 4" h. **$75**

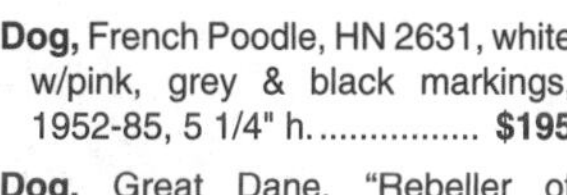

Dog, French Poodle, HN 2631, white w/pink, grey & black markings, 1952-85, 5 1/4" h. **$195**

Dog, Great Dane, "Rebeller of Ouborough," light brown, HN 2562, 191-52, 4 1/2" **$725**

Dog, Greyhound, standing, golden brown w/dark brown markings, cream chest & feet, HN 1065, 1931-55, 8 1/2" h. **$1,150**

Dog, Irish Setter, Ch. "Pat O'Moy," HN 1056, 1931-68, 6" l., 4" h. **$225**

Dog, Springer Spaniel, white w/ black markings, HN 1078, 1932-68, 3" **$150**

Dog, Springer Spaniel, "Dry Toast," white coat w/brown markings, HN 2517, 1938-55, 3 3/4" **$175**

Horse, Punch Peon, Chestnut Shire, bay w/white markings on legs, HN 2623, 1950-60, 7 1/2" h. **$750**

Horses, Chestnut Mare and Foal, chestnut mare w/white stockings, fawn-colored foal w/white stockings, HN 2522, 1938-60, 6 1/2" h. **$695**

Kitten, sleeping, brown & white, HN 2581, 1941-85, 1 1/2" **$75**

Kitten, on hind legs, light brown & black on white, HN 2582, 1941-85, 2 3/4" **$75**

Monkey, Langur Monkey, long-haired brown & white coat, HN 2657, 1960-69, 4 1/2" h. **$255**

Penguin, grey & white w/black tips, K 22, 1940-68, 1 3/4".......... **$195**

Dog, Chow (Shibu Ino), K 15, golden, 1940-77, 2 1/2" **$135**

Dog, Doberman Pinscher, Ch. "Rancho Dobe's Storm," black w/ brown feet & chin, HN 2645, 1955-85, 6 1/4" **$165**

Dog, Labrador, "Bumblikite of Mansergh," black, HN 2667, 1967-85, 5 1/4" **$145**

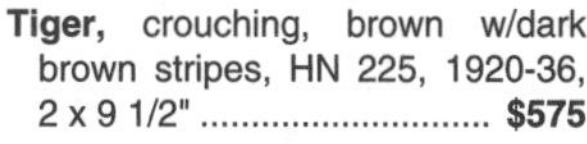

Tiger, crouching, brown w/dark brown stripes, HN 225, 1920-36, 2 x 9 1/2" **$575**

Dog, Dalmatian, "Goworth Victor," white w/black spots, black ears, HN 1113, 1937-85, 5 1/2" ... **$225**

Dog, Foxhound, K 7, seated, white w/brown & black patches, 1931-77, 2 1/2" **$110**

Dog, Rough-haired Terrier, Ch. "Crackley Startler," white w/black & brown markings, HN 1014, 1931-85, 3 3/4" h. **$125**

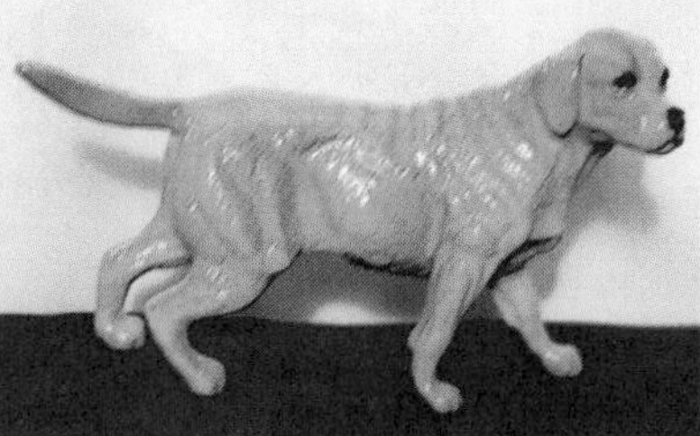

Dog, Labrador, standing, golden, DA 145, 1990-present, 5" h. **$55**

Dog, Pekinese, Ch. "Biddee of Ifield," golden w/black highlights, HN 1012, 1931-85, 3" **$95**

Dog, St. Bernard, lying, brown & cream, K 19, 1940-77, 1 1/2 x 2 1/2" **$105**

Dog, Scottish Terrier, Ch. "Albourne Arthur," black, HN 1015, 1931-60, 5" **$315**

Dog, Sealyham, Ch. "Scotia Stylist," white, HN 1031, 1931-55, 4" **$425**

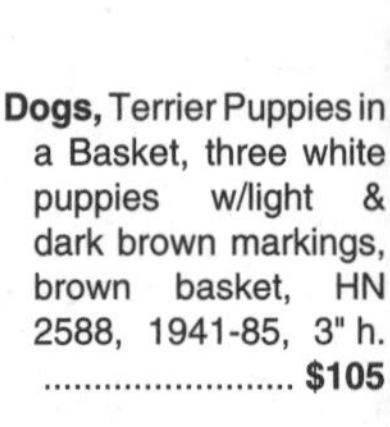

Dogs, Terrier Puppies in a Basket, three white puppies w/light & dark brown markings, brown basket, HN 2588, 1941-85, 3" h. **$105**

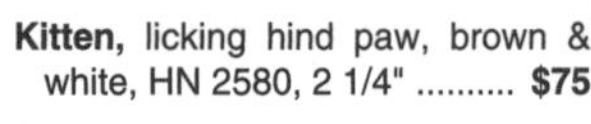

Kitten, licking hind paw, brown & white, HN 2580, 2 1/4" **$75**

Elephant, trunk in salute, grey w/ black, HN 2644, 1952-85, 4 1/4" **$175**

Pony, Shetland Pony (woolly Shetland mare), glossy brown, DA 47, 1989 to present, 5 3/4" ... **$45**

Bunnykins Figurines

Australian Digger, DB 248, brown, yellow webbing, edition limited to 2001 .... **$125**

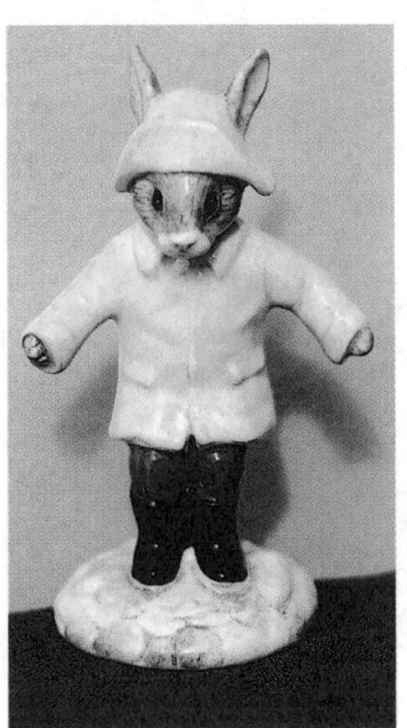

Rainy Day, DB 147, yellow coat & hat, blue trousers, black boots, 1994-97 .... **$40**

Santa, DB 17, red, white & brown, 1981-96 .... **$45**

Ace, DB 42, white & blue, 1986-89 .... **$250**

Astro, DB 20, white, red & blue, 1983-88 .... **$155**

Basketball Players, DB 208, limited edition of 2,500, the set (sold only in set of 5)............................ **$625**

Bedtime, DB 55, blue & white striped pajamas, 1987-98...... **$40**

Billie Bunnykins Cooling Off, DB 3, burgundy, yellow & greenish grey, 1972-87 .... **$185**

Boy Skater, second variation, DB 187, blue jacket, white trousers, red boots, 1998, limited edition of 2,500 .... **$55**

Business Man, DB 203, 1999, limited edition of 5,000 .... **$85**

Cheerleader, DB 142, second variation, yellow, 1994, limited edition of 1,000.................... **$225**

Cymbals, DB 88, blue coat, 1990, limited edition of 250 .... **$525**

Doctor, DB 181, white lab coat & shirt, dark blue trousers, black shoes, white & blue striped tie, 1998-2000 .... **$45**

Dollie Bunnykins Playtime, DB 80, white & yellow, 1988, by Strawbridge & Clothier, limited edition of 250....................... **$225**

Double Bass Player, DB 185, green & yellow striped trousers, 1999, limited edition of 2,500 .... **$125**

Lawyer, DB 214, black robe, white wig, 2000, RDICC exclusive **$60**

Magician, DB 126, black suit, yellow shirt, yellow table cloth, 1992, limited edition of 1,500 .... **$375**

Mary, Mary, Quite Contrary, DB 247, pink, 2002..................... **$55**

Morris Dancer, DB 204, multicolored, 1999, limited edition of 2,000 .... **$45**

Mountie, Sergeant, DB 136, red coat w/yellow stripes on sleeve, blue & brown, 1993, limited edition of 250 .... **$1,500**

Mr. Bunnybeat Strumming, Music Box, DB 38, pink, white, yellow, 1987-89 .... **$355**

Mrs. Bunnykins Clean Sweep, DB 6, blue & white, 1972-91........ **$75**

New Baby, DB 158, blue dress w/white trim, white cradle, pink pillow, yellow blanket, 1995-99 .... **$45**

Scotsman (The), DB 180, dark blue jacket & hat, red & yellow kilt, white shirt, sporran & socks, black shoes, 1998, limited edition of 2,500 .... **$185**

Soccer Player, DB 123, dark blue & white, 1991, limited edition of 250 .... **$650**

Storytime, DB 9, white dress w/ blue design & pink dress, 1972-97 .... **$45**

Stopwatch, DB 253, green & yellow, produced only in 2002........... **$55**

Sweetheart, DB 130, yellow sweater, blue trousers, red heart, 1992-97 .... **$50**

Tyrolean Dancer, DB 246, black & white, 2001 .... **$60**

Waltzing Matilda, DB 236, yellow, red jacket, brown hat, 2001, limited edition of 2,001 .... **$225**

Burslem Wares

Charger, round w/flanged rim, Hunting - Morland Series, central scene of a lady riding horse sidesaddle w/hound racing alongside, in yellow, brown, green, black & white, border band of dark green stylized grapevine, marked "George Morland #1784," 14" d. **$100-200**

Urn, cov., tall slender ovoid body raised on a ribbed & gadrooned gold & Kelly green pedestal base w/square foot & flanked by long gold full-length handles, tapering to a ringed & ribbed cylindrical neck w/flaring rim fitted w/a high Gothic spire-form cover, finely h.p. w/a colorful scene of highland cattle against a purplish mountain backdrop, glossy glaze, artist-signed by S. Kelsall, small professional repair to handle & pedestal, ca. 1910, 32" h. **$2,500**

Cabinet plates, 10 1/4" d., each w/a different English garden view within a narrow acid-etched gilt border, transfer-printed & painted by J. Price, ca. 1928, artist-signed, green printed lion, crown & circle mark, impressed year letters, painted pattern numbers "H3587," set of 12 .... **$2,750**

Chocolate set: 8" h. cov. chocolate pot, 6 1/2" h. cov. water pot, creamer, sugar bowl & eight cups & saucers; bone china, each enamel decorated w/relief-molded fox in various poses, crop-form handles, 20th c., England, the set **$650**

Fish plates, 10" d., each transfer-printed in blue & white w/a different fish, late 19th c., set of 12 ... **$400**

Lamp base, slender ovoid ceramic body w/a tapering neck supporting electric lamp fittings, base decorated w/daffodils in greens, blue, white & yellow, fine brass round base mount w/a ring on the backs of four tiny figural turtles resting on a round disk on small ball feet, early 20th c., overall 28 1/2" h. (minor damage to body) **$325**

Mug, stoneware, tall slender & slightly tapering sides w/a sterling silver rim band, the upper third w/a dark brown glaze, the lower section w/a tan glaze, the upper band molded in relief w/a large scrolling ribbon band reading "Speed Wheel," the lower sides w/three white relief groups of bicycle racers each titled either "Path," "Military," or "Road," base incised "1957," late 19th c., 6" h. **$275**

Pitcher, 5 1/2" h., brightly colored rose design on a salmon pink background, angled handle, mottling on the collar & base rim, gold trim, Doulton, Burslem, artist-signed **$150**

Pitcher, 11" h., Poplars at Sunset patt. **$175**

Plates, dessert, 8 3/4" d., raised gilt enamel scrolls, floral & diapered cartouches, on a pale blue ground, ca. 1920, set of 15 .... **$1,300**

Plates, 9" d., each h.p. w/different type of game bird including ducks, pheasant & quail, gold encrusted rims, artist signed "S. Wilson," purple stamped label w/impressed "Doulton," set of 6 .... **$425**

Plates, 9" d., slightly dished w/ scalloped rim, gilt-trimmed rim w/ polychrome leafy vines bordering brown enameled Shakespearean sites, retailed by Theodore B. Starr, New York City, Doulton, Burslem, late 19th c., set of 12 .... **$450**

Plate, 9 1/8" d., Peony patt., dark blue floral center w/rectangular panels around the border, trimmed w/reddish rust & beige, ca. 1900 .... **$65**

Plates, 10 1/4" d., each w/a central rosette, the border elaborately gilded & enameled in the Art Nouveau style w/displaying peacocks, spade ornaments & trailing berried branches, the outer paneled blue border gilded w/beaded flowers, dated 1902, retailed by Tiffany & Co., New York, set of 4 .... **$1,500**

Plate, 10 1/2" d., Cypress Series, overall decoration of Aesthetic Movement florals in green & blue, marked w/lion & crown, "Royal Doulton, England, Cyprus" **$75**

Platter, 17 1/2" l., oval, Imari patt., ca. 1860s................ **$1,000**

Tureens, cov., earthenware sauce tureens, Raby patt., w/cobalt floral motif & gilt accents, each w/small matching ladle, ca. 1900, 6" h., 8 3/4" l., pr. **$225**

Character Jugs

'Ard of' Earing, large, D 6588, 7 1/2" h. **$1,250**

'Arriet, large, D 6208, 6 1/2" h. **$65**

Anne Boleyn, large, D 6644, 7 1/4" h. **$85**

Bacchus, large, D 6499, 7" h. **$60**

Beefeater, large, D 6206, 6 1/2" h. **$125**

Capt. Henry Morgan, large, 6 3/4" h. **$115**

'Arry, tiny, D 6255, 1 1/2" h.... **$150**

Antony & Cleopatra, large, D 6728, 7 1/4" h. **$95**

Aramis, miniature, D 6508, 2 1/2" h. **$45**

Athos, small, D 6452, 3 3/4" h. **$50**

Baseball Player, small, D 6878, 4 1/4" h. **$115**

Ben Franklin, small, D 6695, 4" h. **$90**

Bootmaker, small, D 6579, 4" h. **$65**

Buzfuz, small, D 5838, 4" h. **$55**

Capt. Ahab, large, D 6500, 7" h. **$90**

Cardinal (The), small, D 6033, 3 1/2" h. **$60**

Cavalier (The), small, D 6173, 3 1/4" h. **$50**

Capt. Hook, large, D 6597, 7 1/4" h. **$500**

Catherine Howard, large, D 6645, 7" h. **$115**

Catherine Parr, large, D 6664, 6 3/4" h. **$220**

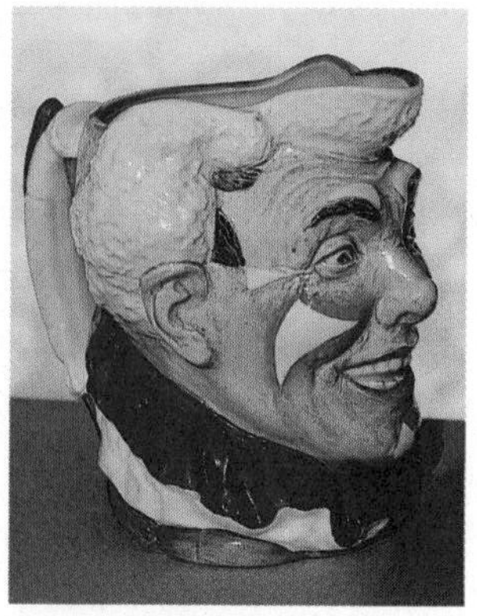

Clown w/white hair (The), large, D 6322, 7 1/2" h. **$1,000**

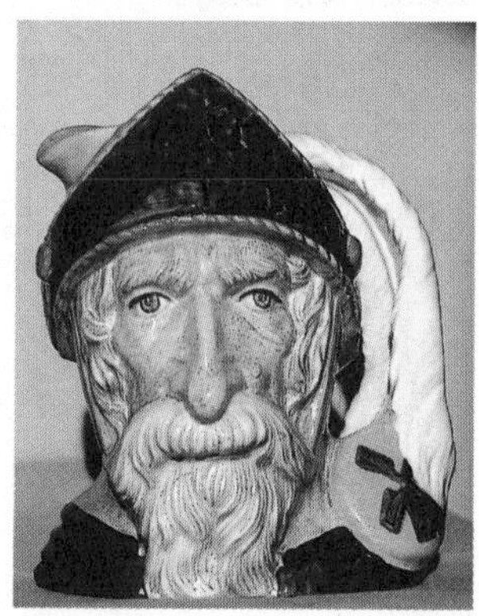

Don Quixote, large, D 6455, 7 1/4" h. **$60**

Falstaff, large, D 6287, 6" h. ... **$65**

Fortune Teller (The), large, D 6497, 6 3/4" h. **$550**

Gardener (The), large, D 6630, 7 3/4" h. **$115**

Gladiator, large, D 6650, 7 3/4" h. **$600**

Groucho Marx, large, D 6710, 7" h. **$155**

Cliff Cornell, large, variation 2, dark blue suit, red tie w/cream polka dots, 9" h. **$250**

Clown w/red hair (The), large, D 5610, 7 1/2" h. **$2,750**

Collector (The), large, D 6796, 7" h. **$165**

Davy Crockett & Santa Anna, large, D 6729, 7" h.............. **$150**

Dick Turpin, pistol handle, small, D 5618, 3 1/2" h. **$35**

Dick Whittington, large, D 6375, 6 1/2" h. **$350**

Falconer (The), small, D 6540, 3 3/4" h. **$50**

Friar Tuck, large, D 6321, 7" h. **$450**

Gaoler, small, D 6577, 3 3/4" h. **$55**

Genie, large, D 6892, 7" h...... **$175**

Gulliver, large, D 6560, 7 1/2" h. **$700**

Henry VIII, large, D 6642, 6 1/2" h. **$105**

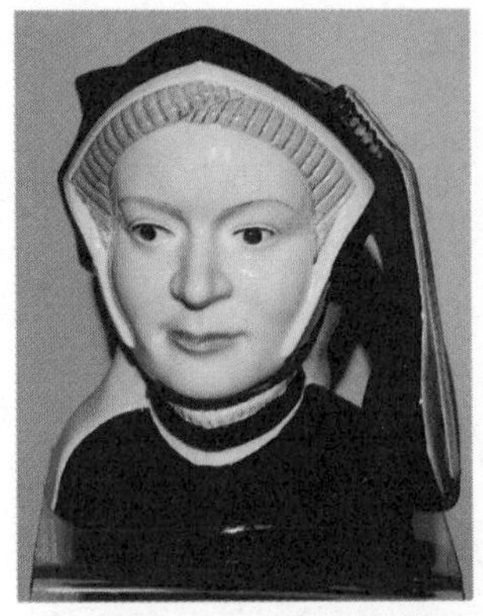

Jane Seymour, large, D 6646, 7 1/4" h. **$100**

Johnny Appleseed, large, D 6372, 6" h. **$325**

Louis Armstrong, large, D 6707, 7 1/2" h. **$185**

Lumberjack, large, D 6610, 7 1/4" h. **$90**

George Washington, large, D 6669, 7 1/2" h. **$145**

Granny, large, D 5521, 6 1/4" h. **$55**

Gunsmith, small, D 6580, 3 1/2" h. **$80**

Happy John "A," large, D 6031, 8 1/2" h. **$85**

Jester, seated, medium, D 6910, 5" h. **$145**

Jockey, large, D 6625, 7 3/4" h. **$150**

Juggler (The), large, D 6835, 6 1/2" h. **$125**

Leprechaun, large, D 6847, 7 1/2" h. **$125**

Mark Twain, small, D 6694, 4" h. **$65**

North American Indian, small, D 6614, 4 1/4" h. **$45**

Mad Hatter, large, D 6598, 7 1/4" h. **$165**

Old Salt, large, D 6551, 7 1/2" h. **$125**

Pied Piper, large, D 6403, 7" h. **$75**

Merlin, large, D 6529, 7 1/4" h. **$85**

Night Watchman, large, D 6569, 7" h. **$130**

Ringmaster (The), large, D 6863, 7 1/2" h. **$150**

Rip Van Winkle, large, D 6438, 6 1/2" h. **$115**

Robin Hood, 2nd version, large, D 6527, 7 1/2" h. **$65**

Robinson Crusoe, large, D 6532, 7 1/2" h. **$140**

Santa Claus, doll & drum handle, large, D 6668, 7 1/2" h. **$145**

William Shakespeare, large, D 6689, 7 3/4" h. **$125**

St. George, large, D 6618, 7 1/2" h. **$175**

Yachtsman, large, D 6626, 8" h. **$145**

Punch & Judy Man, large, D 6590, 7" h. **$675**

Queen Victoria, small, D 6913, 3 1/2" h. **$165**

Robin Hood, 2nd version, small, D 6234, 3 1/4" h. **$55**

Town Crier, large, D 6530, 7" h. **$175**

Winston Churchill, style 1, large, D 6907, Union Jack & bulldog handle, 7" h. **$325**

Figurines

Abdullah, HN 2104, multicolored, 1953-62 .... **$425**

Afternoon Tea, HN 1747, pink & blue, 1935-82 .... **$475**

Anna, HN 2802, purple & white, Kate Greenaway Series, 1976-82 .... **$225**

Anne Boleyn, HN 3232, red & grey, 1990, limited edition of 9,500 .... **$550**

Artful Dodger, M 55, black & brown, Dickens Miniatures Series, 1932-83 .... **$75**

Ascot, HN 2356, green dress w/ yellow shawl, 1968-95 .... **$200**

Babie, HN 1679, green dress, 1935-92 .... **$70**

Ballerina, HN 2116, lavender, 1953-73 .... **$425**

Balloon Seller (The), HN 583, green shawl, cream dress, 1923-49 .... **$950**

Basket Weaver (The), HN 2245, pale blue & yellow, 1959-62 .... **$450**

Beachcomber, HN 2487, matte, purple & grey, 1973-76 .... **$215**

Blacksmith of Williamsburg, HN 2240, white shirt, brown hat, 1960-83 .... **$225**

Bluebeard, HN 2105, purple, green & brown, 1953-92 .... **$450**

Bo Peep, HN 1811, orange dress, green hat, 1937-95 .... **$115**

Bride (The), HN 2166, pale pink dress, 1956-76 .... **$175**

Bridesmaid (The Little), M 12, multicolor gown, 1932-45 .... **$425**

Broken Lance (The), HN 2041, blue, red & yellow, 1949-75 .... **$450**

Bunny's Bedtime, HN 3370, pale blue, pink ribbon, 1991, RDICC Series, limited edition of 9,500 .... **$175**

Captain Cook, HN 2889, black & cream, 1980-84 .... **$425**

Carpet Seller (The), HN 1464 (hand open), green & orange, 1929-? **$275**

Cavalier, HN 2716, brown & green, 1976-82 .... **$265**

Centurian, HN 2726, grey & purple, 1982-84 .... **$225**

Chief (The), HN 2892, gold, 1979-88 .... **$225**

Auctioneer (The), HN 2988, black, grey & brown, 1986, R.D.I.C.C. Series **$195**

Christmas Parcels, HN 2851, black, 1978-82 .... **$225**

Sleeping Beauty, HN 3079, green 1987-89 .... **$225**

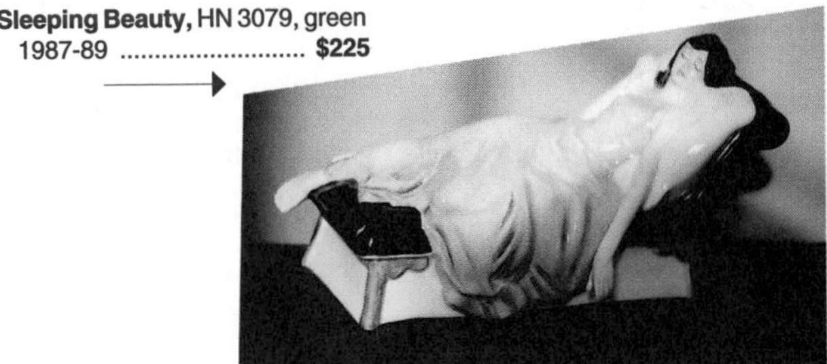

China Repairer, HN 2943, blue, white & tan, 1983-88 .... **$205**

Christmas Morn, HN 1992, red & white, 1947-96 .... **$175**

Coachman, HN 2282, purple, grey & blue, 1963-71 .... **$575**

Country Lass (A), HN 1991A, blue, brown & white, 1975-81 .... **$210**

Daffy Down Dilly, HN 1712, green dress, 1935-75 .... **$375**

David Copperfield, M 88, black & tan, Dickens Miniatures Series, 1949-83 .... **$65**

Embroidering, HN 2855, grey dress, 1980-90 .... **$275**

Ermine Coat (The), HN 1981, white & red, 1945-67 .... **$365**

Eventide, HN 2814, blue, white, red, yellow & green, 1977-91 ...... **$275**

Fagin, M 49, brown, 1932-83 ... **$65**

Fair Lady, HN 2193, green, 1963-96 .... **$125**

Farmer's Wife, HN 2069, red, green & brown, 1951-55 .... **$250**

French Peasant, HN 2075, brown & green, 1951-55 .... **$575**

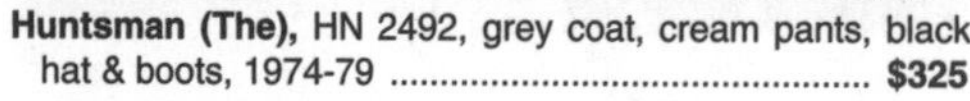

Huntsman (The), HN 2492, grey coat, cream pants, black hat & boots, 1974-79 .... **$325**

Shepherd (The), HN 1975, light brown, 1945-75 .... **$205**

> Always keep the original boxes and tags that collectibles came with. They add significant value to the resale value of the collectibles. Collectibles retain their greatest value when unopened. The great debate, however, is whether collectibles should be displayed and enjoyed, or packed away to retain maximum value. This, of course, is for the collector to decide.

Friar Tuck, HN 2143, brown, 1954-65 .... **$595**

Foaming Quart (The), HN 2162, brown, 1955-92 .... **$125**

Gandalf, HN 2911, green & white, Middle Earth Series, 1980-84 .... **$275**

Genie (The), HN 2989, blue, 1983-90 .... **$185**

Good King Wenceslas, HN 2118, brown & purple, 1953-76 .... **$275**

Gypsy Dance, HN 2230, lavender dress, 1959-71 .... **$275**

Happy Anniversary, HN 3097, style one, purple & white, 1987-93 .... **$205**

Harlequin, HN 2186, blue, 1957-69 .... **$425**

Joker (The), HN 2252, white, 1990-92 .... **$250**

Judge (The), HN 2443, red & white, 1972-76 .... **$250**

La Sylphide, HN 2138, white dress, 1954-65 .... **$475**

Oliver Twist, M 89, black & tan, Dickens Miniatures Series, 1949-83 .... **$65**

Omar Khayyam, HN 2247, brown, 1965-83 .... **$195**

Parisian, HN 2445, blue & grey, matte glaze,1972-75............ **$150**

Puppetmaker, HN 2253, green, brown & red, 1962-73.......... **$475**

Sir Edward, HN 2370, red & grey, 1979, limited edition of 500 .... **$550**

Skater (The), HN 3439, red, 1992-97 .... **$250**

Southern Belle, HN 2229, red & cream, 1958-97 .... **$350**

Stop Press, HN 2683, brown, blue & white, 1977-81 .... **$175**

Tiny Tim, HN 539, black, brown & blue, 1922-32 .... **$75**

This Little Pig, HN 1793, red robe, 1936-95 .... **$85**

Town Crier, HN 2119, 1953-76 .... **$275**

Toymaker (The), HN 2250, brown & red, 1959-73........................ **$425**

Flambé Glazes

Animals & Birds

Dog, Dog of Fo, Rouge Flambé, RDICC, Model 2957, 1981, 5 1/4" h. **$215**

Miscellaneous Pieces

Humidor, cov., Sung Ware, flambé glaze, figural elephant finial, artist-initialed **$2,400**

Jar, cov., Rouge Flambé, footed squatty bulbous body w/a wide low-domed cover, scattered black splotches on crimson red ground, by Noke, fully stamped, 3 1/4" d., 2 3/4" h. **$358**

Vase, 9 5/8" h., Rouge Flambé glaze, small footring under a spherical body tapering to a short stick neck, red "flambé" glaze w/ veined design **$175**

Vase, 7" h., 4 1/4" d., Rouge Flambé glaze, footed ovoid body w/the wide shoulder tapering to a small, short rolled neck, black silhouetted desert landscape against the crimson red ground, shallow scratch, stamped "ROYAL DOULTON - FLAMB... - MADE IN ENGLAND" **$250**

Kingsware

Pitcher, jug-form, "Memories" design w/twelve faces shown, ca. 1920 .... **$600**

Vase, 10 3/4" h., cylindrical w/raised scene of Dr. Johnson in a tavern scene, verse on the back **$300**

Whiskey jug w/figural stopper, bulbous ovoid body w/a loop shoulder handle, the body in overall dark brown, the stopper in the shape of a stout 18th c. man wearing a tricorn hat & painted in polychrome, 8 1/4" h............ **$135**

Lambeth Art Wares

Ewers, Carrara Ware, bulbous body w/a tan ground decorated w/life-sized pink wild roses w/ enameled white highlights, gold molded leaf & florals, grey rim & ornate handle, marked "Doulton Carrara Lambeth," 11 1/2" h., pr. **$375**

Loving cup, stoneware, cylindrical body w/low tapering base & wide short flaring rim, the wide tooled central band in band w/enameled floral designs in white & green flanked by thin brown stripes, three applied ear-form loop handles, handles, top & base in blue, marked "Doulton Lambeth," 6 1/8" h. **$275**

Loving cup, stoneware, three-handled cylindrical form w/a sterling silver rim band, a dark brown glaze band below the rim, most of the body w/a tan glaze, molded around the sides w/three white relief groups of bicycle riders, each titled either "Path," "Military," or "Road," late 19th c., base incised "8238," 5 1/2" h. **$275**

Lambeth Art Wares (cont)

Pitcher, 5 1/2" h., stoneware, bulbous form, the tan ground incised w/playful cats, the shoulder & neck glazed w/cobalt blue strap work, decorated by Hannah Barlow, impressed Doulton Lambeth mark, late 19th c... **$750**

Pitcher, 9" h., stoneware, bulbous ovoid body tapering to a cylindrical neck w/pinched spout, C-form handle, the upper half w/a dark brown glaze over a tan glaze on the lower half, lower half applied w/white relief designs including a windmill, dogs chasing deer, men drinking, etc., Model No. 6859, Doulton, Lambeth mark, late 19th c... **$125**

Vase, 5 1/4" h., 3 1/8" d., stoneware, footed ovoid body w/short tapering neck, grey ground w/an incised design of pointed panels framing stylized leafy scrolls in brown, green & light blue, artist-signed by Arthur Beeve, Doulton, Lambeth **$175**

Soap dish, stoneware, oblong w/large brown & lavender flying insect molded along one side of the dark blue glazed dish, impressed markings on base for Wright's Coal Tar Soap, 4 1/4 x 5 3/4", 1 1/2" h. **$150**

Tyg, waisted cylindrical shape decorated w/applied figures & animals in relief, Sheffield silver rim band marked "Maypin and Webb," Doulton, Lambeth, late 19th - early 20th c., 4 3/4" d., 6 1/2" h. **$175**

Vase, 7 3/4" h., Art Deco style baluster-form decorated w/ alternating vertical green & black panels, horizontal black & white panels on shoulder, impressed "Royal Doulton Lambeth England," "8190" w/"S" in black slip, artist's monogram incised in bottom **$400**

Vase, 11" h., baluster form, the shoulder tapering to a tall wide cylindrical neck w/flat rim, the center w/sgraffito continuous scene depicting eight deer in blue, black or brown, by Hannah Barlow, the dark brown neck & shoulder decorated w/raised scrolled designs in gold & swags of white beads, beaded bands flanking the center scene, the dark brown base w/raised gold lines, impressed "Doulton - Lambeth - England" & incised artist's initials........ **$1,250**

Vase, 11 1/4" h., tall slender baluster-form w/flaring domed foot & waisted short widely flaring neck, the neck & foot in cobalt w/lacy gilt decoration, the body w/a creamy ground decorated w/scattered clusters of colorful flowers, Doulton-Burslem mark & incised "Lambeth - Doulton - Faience L6339," ca. 1882 .... **$225**

Planter, stoneware, ovoid form w/flat rim, short foot, decorated w/design of ferns or oak leaves on tan ground, Lambethware style & colors, Doulton Archives series, limited edition of 100, 2002 .... **$800**

Pitcher, jug-form, 8 3/4" h., Lambethware style & color, Doulton Archives series, blue tracery on tan body, limited edition of 100, 2002 .... **$1,000**

Pitcher, 11" h., Hannah Barlow Doulton Lambethware, design of hounds chasing fox, 1875, vertical hairline crack **$1,250**

Series Wares

Bowl, 8" d., English Old Scenes Series, The Gleaners scene **$185**

Bowl, 8 1/2" h., Gallent Fishers Series **$200**

Candlestick, Old Moreton Series, low flaring round foot & slightly swelled cylindrical shaft below widely flaring flattened socket rim, color transfer of 16th c. gentleman titled "Old Moreton," impressed "7277," 6 3/8" h. **$80**

Charger, Shakespeare Plays Series, scene from "A Midsummer Night's Dream," 12 5/8" d. **$65**

Chop plate, round w/flanged rim, Old Moreton Series, black transfer-printed design decorated in polychrome, a large center interior scene titled "Queen Elizabeth at Old Moreton 1589," early 20th c., 12 3/4" d. **$85**

Cracker jar, cov., Gallant Fisher Series, Isaac Walton Ware, signed "NOKE" **$175**

Dish, oval, English Old Scenes Series, The Gleaners scene, 9 x 11 1/4, 2 1/8" h. **$55**

Pitcher, 5 1/2" h., Jackdaw of Rheims Series **$150**

Pitcher, 9 1/4" h., Shakespeare Characters Series, standing portrait of Sir John Falstaff, tall waisted cylindrical form w/high arched spout, printed around the bottom border "A Tapster is a Good Trade," early 20th c. **$150**

Plate, 7 1/2" sq., Under the Greenwood Tree Series, Friar Tuck Joins Robin Hood, natural-colored scene of Robin Hood & Friar Tuck standing & talking under large tree **$85**

Pitcher, Shakespeare Characters Series, Juliet, scene from Shakespeare's Romeo & Juliet **$150**

Plate, 9 1/2" d., Gallant Fishers Series, Izaac Walton Ware, signed "NOKE" **$75**

Plate, 10 1/4" d., English Old Scenes Series, The Gipsies (sic) scene **$65**

Plate, 10 1/4" d., English Old Scenes Series, The Gleaners scene.. **$65**

Plate, 10 1/4" d., Golfers Series, Bradley Golfers, "All Fools Are Not Knaves...," **$150**

Plates, 10 1/4" d., Nautical History Series, color transfer-printed scenes on a tan speckled ground, one titled "The Battle," the other "The Press Gang," pr........... **$150**

Plate, 10 1/2" d., Shakespeare Characters Series, blue transfer w/center portrait of Shakespeare, border w/twelve characters from his plays **$75**

Plate, 10 3/4" d., Bobby Burns Series, blue transfer w/Burns portrait in center, border shows characters such as Tam-O-Shanter, Highland Mary & others **$75**

Teapot, cov., Night Watchman Series, night watchman scene **$125**

Teapot, cov., Old Moreton Series, Queen Elizabeth at Moreton Hall scene **$125**

Blue Children - Babes in Wood Series

Vase, 6" h., bulbous base, short slightly bulbous neck w/flat rim, decorated w/blue & white scene of young woman at snowy gate, printed green mark, early 20th c. (ILLUS. front row, left w/other Seriesware vases) **$450-500**

Vase, 17" h., slightly ovoid cylindrical body w/ring foot & rim, decorated w/blue & white scene of woman looking back at child, who is holding the train of her cloak, printed green mark, early 20th c. (ILLUS. back row, center w/other Seriesware vases).. **$1,380**

Vase, 6 1/2" h., tapering rectangular arched shape w/rounded edges, gilt flat rim & foot, gilt angular handles, decorated w/blue & white winter scene of woman carrying basket, printed green mark, early 20th c. (ILLUS. front row, center w/other Seriesware vases) **$690**

Vase, 8 1/2" h., ovoid form w/short slender cylindrical neck w/slightly flaring rim, decorated w/blue & white scene of little girl carrying basket, printed green mark, early 20th c. (ILLUS. back row, second from right w/other Seriesware vases)... **$431**

Vase, 6 1/2" h., ovoid form tapering to ring foot & flaring rim, decorated w/blue & white scene of woman w/basket at snowy gate, printed green mark, early 20th c. (ILLUS. front row, right w/other Seriesware vases) **$633**

Vase, 7" h., cylindrical shape w/slightly flaring rim, ruffled foot & small gilt angled handles near base, decorated w/blue & white scene of bonneted woman & child holding basket, printed green mark, early 20th c. (ILLUS. back row, right w/other Seriesware vases) **$748**

Vases, 13 1/4" h., tapering ovoid body, tapering shoulder, ruffled foot, short flaring cylindrical neck, slender gilt handles, decorated w/blue & white winter scene of young woman & child walking along path, printed green mark, early 20th c., pr. (ILLUS. of both, back row, far left w/other Seriesware vases).. **$2,070**

Tray, oblong, flattened diamond shape w/rounded corners, center design of woman followed by girl holding woman's cloak, 13 1/2" l. **$1,000**

Vase, 11 1/2" h., tall slender baluster-form w/cylindrical neck & flat rim, design of woman sheltering child in wintry landscape, color variation **$750**

Coaching Days Series

Bowl, 9" d., 4 1/8" h., street scenes.............. **$125**

Plates, 8" d., includes three scenes, "Boarding the Coach," "The Journey" & "Farewell," polychrome transfer decoration, early 20th c., set of 12 .... **$413**

Dickens Ware Series

Plate, 10 1/2" d., blue transfer w/central portrait of Dickens, border w/eleven of the Doulton characters used on various wares, unmarked **$75**

Fiesta (Homer Laughlin China Co. -HLC)

Fiesta dinnerware was made by the Homer Laughlin China Company of Newell, West Virginia, from the 1930s until the early 1970s. The brilliant colors of this inexpensive pottery have attracted numerous collectors. On February 28, 1986, Laughlin reintroduced the popular Fiesta line with minor changes in the shapes of a few pieces and a contemporary color range. The effect of this new production on the Fiesta collecting market is yet to be determined.

For additional information on Fiesta Ware see Warman's Fiesta Ware Identification & Price Guide by Mark F. Moran (Krause Publications, 2004).

Ashtray grey **$80-90**

Ashtray medium green ... **$200-230**

Ashtray yellow **$35-45**

Bowl, cream soup cobalt blue **$50-70**

Bowl, cream soup forest green **$50-70**

Bowl, cream soup ivory **$50-70**

Bowl, fruit, 11 3/4" d. cobalt blue **$300-350**

Bowl, fruit, 11 3/4" d. ivory **$300-350**

Bowl, fruit, 11 3/4" d. light green **$300-350**

Bowl, fruit, 11 3/4" d. yellow **$300-350**

Bowl, individual fruit, 4 3/4" d. chartreuse **$25-35**

Bowl, individual fruit, 4 3/4" d. forest green **$25-35**

Bowl, individual fruit, 4 3/4" d. grey **$25-35**

Bowl, individual fruit, 4 3/4" d., medium green **$650-700**

Bowl, individual fruit, 4 3/4" d. red **$25-35**

Bowl, individual fruit, 5 1/2" d. light green........................ **$25-40**

Bowl, individual fruit, 5 1/2" d. red **$25-40**

Bowl, individual fruit, 5 1/2" d. turquoise......................... **$25-40**

Bowl, individual fruit, 5 1/2" d. grey **$25-40**

Bowl, individual salad, 7 1/2" d. medium green **$100-150**

Bowl, individual salad, 7 1/2" d. turquoise...................... **$100-150**

Bowl, individual salad, 7 1/2" d. yellow **$100-150**

Bowl, dessert, 6" d. chartreuse **$35-50**

Bowl, dessert, 6" d. light green **$35-50**

Bowl, dessert, 6" d. rose ... **$35-50**

Bowl, dessert, 6" d. turquoise **$35-50**

Ashtray cobalt blue **$50-60**

Bowl, individual fruit, 5 1/2" d. rose **$25-40**

Bowl, dessert, 6" d. medium green **$700-800**

Candleholders, bulb-type, pr. turquoise ... **$90-125**

Carafe, cov. light green **$225-325**

Bowl, nappy, 9 1/2" d. turquoise **$55-70**

Bowl, nappy, 9 1/2" d. yellow **$55-70**

Bowl, nappy, 8 1/2" d. medium green **$150-175**

Bowl, nappy, 9 1/2" d. cobalt blue **$55-70**

Bowl, nappy, 9 1/2" d. forest green **$55-70**

Bowl, nappy, 9 1/2" d. ivory **$55-70**

Bowl, nappy, 9 1/2" d. light green **$55-70**

Bowl, nappy, 9 1/2" d. grey **$55-70**

Bowl, nappy, 8 1/2" d. chartreuse **$40-65**

Bowl, nappy, 8 1/2" d. cobalt blue **$40-65**

Bowl, nappy, 8 1/2" d. forest green **$40-65**

Bowl, nappy, 8 1/2" d. grey **$40-65**

Bowl, salad, large, footed, 11 3/8" d., cobalt blue **$550-625**

Bowl, salad, large, footed, 11 3/8" d., light green **$550-625**

Bowl, salad, large, footed, 11 3/8" d., red **$550-625**

Bowl, salad, large, footed, 11 3/8" d., yellow **$550-625**

Bowl, salad, large, footed, 11 3/8" d., turquoise **$550-625**

Cake plate, 10 3/8" d. cobalt blue **$950-1,050**

Cake plate, 10" d. ivory .. **$850-900**

Cake plate, 10" d. light green **$900-950**

Cake plate, 10" d. red ...... **$1,500+**

Calendar plate, 10" d., 1954 ivory **$40-50**

Calendar plate, 10" d., 1955 light green **$40-50**

Calendar plate, 10" d., 1955 ivory **$40-50**

Calendar plate, 10" d., 1955 yellow **$40-50**

Candleholders, bulb-type, pr. cobalt blue **$120**

Candleholders, bulb-type, pr. ivory **$120**

Candleholders, bulb-type, pr. red **$120**

Candleholders, bulb-type, pr. yellow **$90-125**

Candleholders, tripod-type, pr. cobalt blue **$650-700**

Candleholders, tripod-type, pr. red **$675-725**

Candleholders, tripod-type, pr. turquoise....................... **$675-725**

Candleholders, tripod-type, pr. ivory............................. **$600-650**

Candleholders, tripod-type, pr. light green.................... **$475-525**

Candleholders, tripod-type, pr. yellow **$400-425**

Carafe, cov. cobalt blue **$225-325**

Carafe, cov. ivory........... **$225-325**

Carafe, cov. red............. **$225-325**

Carafe, cov. turquoise **$250**

Carafe, cov. yellow **$250**

Casserole, cov., two-handled, 9 3/4" d. chartreuse,..... **$300-325**

Casserole, cov., two-handled, 9 3/4" d. cobalt blue **$250-275**

Casserole, cov., two-handled, 9 3/4" d. forest green ... **$300-325**

Casserole, cov., two-handled, 9 3/4" d. grey................ **$300-325**

Casserole, cov., two-handled, 9 3/4" d. ivory **$250-300**

Casserole, cov., two-handled, 9 3/4" d. light green...... **$150-175**

Casserole, cov., two-handled, 9 3/4" d. medium green **$1,600-1,700**

Casserole, cov., two-handled, 9 3/4" d. red **$250-300**

Casserole, cov., two-handled, 9 3/4" d. rose................ **$300-325**

Casserole, cov., two-handled, 9 3/4" d. turquoise........ **$160-180**

Casserole, cov., two-handled, 9 3/4" d. yellow.................... **$150**

Coffeepot, cov. chartreuse **$325-350**

Coffeepot, cov. cobalt blue **$250-300**

Coffeepot, cov. forest green $325-350

Coffeepot, cov. grey....... $675-725

Coffeepot, cov. ivory............. $230

Coffeepot, cov. light green $225-250

Coffeepot, cov. red $275-325

Coffeepot, cov. rose....... $375-425

Coffeepot, cov. turquoise...... $180

Coffeepot, cov. yellow $200-250

Coffeepot, cov., demitasse, stick handle cobalt blue $600-625

Coffeepot, cov., demitasse, stick handle ivory $625-650

Coffeepot, cov., demitasse, stick handle light green $675-725

Coffeepot, cov., demitasse, stick handle turquoise $700-725

Coffeepot, cov., demitasse, stick handle yellow...................... $400

Compote, 12" d., low, footed cobalt blue.................... $200-225

Compote, 12" d., low, footed ivory $200-225

Compote, 12" d., low, footed light green $150-175

Compote, 12" d., low, footed red $700-725

Compote, 12" d., low, footed turquoise...................... $700-725

Compote, 12" d., low, footed yellow $400-425

Compote, sweetmeat, high stand cobalt blue $75-100

Compote, sweetmeat, high stand light green...................... $75-110

Compote, sweetmeat, high stand turquoise.............................. $95

Creamer, stick handle cobalt blue $60-65

Creamer, stick handle light green $35-45

Creamer, stick handle turquoise $100-125

Creamer, stick handle yellow $35-45

Creamer, ring-handled, chartreuse $25-40

Creamer, ring-handled, cobalt blue....................................... $25

Creamer forest green.......... $25-40

Creamer, ring-handled, grey $25-40

Creamer, ring-handled, light green $25-40

Coffeepot, cov., demitasse, stick handle red $700-725

Gravy boat yellow $45-65

Creamer, ring-handled, medium green $125-150

Creamer red............................ $25

Creamer yellow.................. $25-40

Creamer & cov. sugar bowl, individual size, on figure-8 tray, yellow on cobalt tray, the set $700-750

Cup & saucer, demitasse, stick handle chartreuse........ $500-550

Cup & saucer, demitasse, stick handle forest green...... $400-450

Cup & saucer, demitasse, stick handle ivory $95

Cup & saucer, demitasse, stick handle red................... $100-125

Cup & saucer, demitasse, stick handle rose................. $400-450

Cup & saucer, ring handle chartreuse $30-45

Cup & saucer, ring handle grey $30-45

Cup & saucer, ring handle light green $30-45

Cup & saucer, ring handle medium green $70

Cup & saucer, ring handle rose $30-45

Egg cup chartreuse $125-175

Egg cup forest green...... $125-175

Egg cup grey $500-550

Egg cup light green............. $70-80

Egg cup rose $400-450

French casserole, cov., stick handle cobalt blue $3,550-3,650

French casserole, cov., stick handle ivory $525-575

French casserole, cov., stick handle light green $575-625

French casserole, cov., stick handle yellow............... $275-325

Fork (Kitchen Kraft) yellow... $150

Fork (Kitchen Kraft) cobalt blue $150

Fork (Kitchen Kraft) red........ $150

Gravy boat chartreuse........ $70-80

Gravy boat grey.................. $70-80

Gravy boat light green........ $45-65

Gravy boat rose.................. $70-80

Marmalade jar, cov. cobalt blue $365

Marmalade jar, cov. ivory...... $365

Marmalade jar, cov. light green $300-400

Mixing bowl, nest-type, size No. 1, 5" d. cobalt blue $275

Mixing bowl, nest-type, size No. 1, 5" d. light green........... $250-325

Mixing bowl, nest-type, size No. 1, 5" d. turquoise............. $250-325

Mixing bowl, nest-type, size No. 2, 6" d. yellow.................. $110-160

Mixing bowl, nest-type, size No. 3, 7" d. cobalt blue $135-170

Mixing bowl, nest-type, size No. 2, 6" d. cobalt blue $125

Mixing bowl, nest-type, size No. 2, 6" d. light green........... $110-160

Mixing bowl, nest-type, size No. 3, 7" d. light green........... $135-170

Mixing bowl, nest-type, size No. 4, 8" d. cobalt blue $200-225

Mixing bowl, nest-type, size No. 4, 8" d. light green........... $100-120

Mixing bowl, nest-type, size No. 4, 8" d. turquoise............. $150-175

Mixing bowl, nest-type, size No. 5, 9" d. cobalt blue $225-270

Mixing bowl, nest-type, size No. 5, 9" d. light green........... $225-270

Mixing bowl, nest-type, size No. 5, 9" d. turquoise............. $225-270

Mixing bowl, nest-type, size No. 5, 9" d. yellow.................. $225-270

Mixing bowl, nest-type, size No. 6, 10" d. ivory.................. $300-375

Mixing bowl, nest-type, size No. 6, 10" d. light green.......... $300-375

Mixing bowl, nest-type, size No. 7, 11 1/2" d. cobalt blue ... $550-650

Mixing bowl, nest-type, size No. 7, 11 1/2" d. light green.... $550-650

Mixing bowl, nest-type, size No. 7, 11 1/2" d. turquoise...... $550-650

Mug, chartreuse $80-90

Mug, cobalt blue.................. $80-90

Mug, forest green................ $75-85

Mug, grey $70-80

Mug, ivory........................... $65-75

Mug red.............................. $70-80

Mug, light green $55-65

Mug, medium green $115-125

Mug, rose $75-85

Mug, turquoise $40-50

Onion soup bowl, cov. turquoise $8,000

Plate, 9" d. medium green $70-80

Mug, yellow $40-50

Mustard jar, cov. ivory ... $300-375

Mustard jar, cov. red...... $300-375

Mustard jar, cov. yellow $300-375

Onion soup bowl, cov. cobalt blue $700-750

Onion soup bowl, cov. ivory $700-750

Onion soup bowl, cov. light green $700-750

Onion soup bowl, cov. medium green $700-750

Onion soup bowl, cov. red $700-750

Onion soup bowl, cov. yellow $700-750

Plate, 6" d. chartreuse $5-10

Plate, 6" d. forest green........ $5-10

Plate, 6" d. grey $5-10

Plate, 6" d. medium green .. $25-35

Plate, 6" d. rose $5-10

Plate, 7" d. chartreuse $8-12

Plate, 7" d. forest green........ $8-12

Plate, 7" d. grey $8-12

Plate, 7" d. medium green .. $50-60

Plate, 7" d. rose $8-12

Plate, 9" d. chartreuse $15-25

Plate, 9" d. forest green...... $15-25

Plate, 9" d. light green $15-25

Plate, 9" d. red $15

Plate, 9" d. rose $15-25

Plate, 10" d. chartreuse $40-50

Plate, 10" d. forest green.... $40-50

Plate, 10" d. grey $40-50

Plate, 10" d. medium green $150-200

Plate, 10" d. rose $40-50

Plate, 10" d. turquoise $40-50

Pitcher, juice, disc-type, 30 oz. red $600-700

Pitcher, juice, disc-type, 30 oz. turquoise...................... $10,000+

Pitcher, juice, disc-type, 30 oz. yellow $40-50

Pitcher, water, disc-type chartreuse $250-300

Pitcher, water, disc-type forest green $250-300

Pitcher, water, disc-type light green $100-125

Pie server (Kitchen Kraft) cobalt blue................................. $150

Pie server (Kitchen Kraft) light green **$150**

Pie server (Kitchen Kraft) yellow **$150**

Pitcher, jug-type, 2 pt. ivory **$100-125**

Pitcher, jug-type, 2 pt. light green **$75-85**

Pitcher, jug-type, 2 pt. rose **$125-150**

Pitcher, jug-type, 2 pt. turquoise **$75-85**

Pitcher, jug-type, 2 pt. yellow **$75-85**

Pitcher, juice, disc-type, 30 oz. grey .... **$3,000+**

Pitcher, jug-type, 2 pt. cobalt blue **$100-125**

Pitcher, jug-type, 2 pt. grey **$125-150**

Pitcher, water, disc-type rose **$275-375**

Pitcher, water, disc-type yellow **$110-140**

Pitcher, w/ice lip, globular, 2 qt. ivory **$125-150**

Pitcher, w/ice lip, globular, 2 qt. red **$125-150**

Plate, chop, 13" d. chartreuse **$80-100**

Plate, chop, 13" d. cobalt blue **$45**

Plate, chop, 13" d. forest green **$80-100**

Plate, chop, 13" d. grey ... **$80-100**

Plate, chop, 13" d. light green **$40-60**

Plate, chop, 13" d. medium green **$600-700**

Plate, chop, 13" d. rose ... **$80-100**

Plate, chop, 13" d. yellow .. **$40-60**

Plate, chop, 15" d. cobalt blue **$90**

Plate, chop, 15" d. forest green **$150-175**

Plate, chop, 15" d. grey **$150-175**

Plate, chop, 15" d. light green **$150-175**

Plate, chop, 15" d. red **$80-110**

Plate, chop, 15" d. rose **$150-175**

Plate, 9" d. yellow **$15-25**

Plate, 10" d., cobalt blue..... **$40-50**

Plate, 10" d., forest green... **$40-50**

Plate, 10" d., medium green **$150-200**

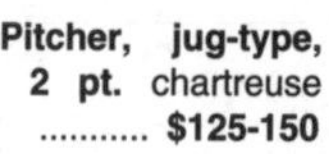

Pitcher, jug-type, 2 pt. chartreuse **$125-150**

Salt & pepper shakers, pr. cobalt blue ... **$25**

Plate, 10" d., light green **$40-50**

Plate, 10" d., red................ **$40-50**

Plate, 10" d., turquoise **$40-50**

Plate, grill, 10 1/2" d. chartreuse **$70-80**

Plate, grill, 10 1/2" d. cobalt blue **$40**

Plate, grill, 10 1/2" d. forest green **$70-80**

Plate, grill, 10 1/2" d. light green **$35-50**

Plate, grill, 10 1/2" d. turquoise **$35**

Plate, grill, 10 1/2" d. yellow ... **$35**

Plate, grill, 12" d. cobalt blue **$50-70**

Plate, grill, 12" d. ivory....... **$50-70**

Plate, grill, 12" d. red **$50-70**

Plate, grill, 12" d. yellow **$50-70**

Platter, 12" oval chartreuse **$45-65**

Platter, 12" oval grey **$45-65**

Platter, 12" oval light green **$45-65**

Platter, 12" oval medium green **$200-225**

Platter, 12" oval red **$50**

Platter, 12" oval yellow **$45-65**

Relish tray w/five inserts multicolored **$300-375**

Relish tray w/five inserts cobalt blue.................................... **$355**

Relish tray w/five inserts light green **$300-375**

Salt & pepper shakers, pr. forest green **$25-45**

Salt & pepper shakers, pr. grey **$25-45**

Salt & pepper shakers, pr. chartreuse **$25-45**

Salt & pepper shakers, pr. light green **$25-45**

Salt & pepper shakers, pr. medium green **$225-250**

Salt & pepper shakers, pr. red **$25**

Salt & pepper shakers, pr. rose **$25-45**

Salt & pepper shakers, pr. yellow **$25-45**

Soup plate, rimmed, 8 3/8" d. cobalt blue **$40-65**

Soup plate, rimmed, 8 3/8" d. red **$50**

Soup plate, rimmed, 8 3/8" d. yellow **$40-65**

Spoon (Kitchen Kraft) light green **$125-140**

Spoon (Kitchen Kraft) red **$140-150**

Soup plate, rimmed, 8 3/8" d., chartreuse **$40-65**

Soup plate, rimmed, 8 3/8" d. forest green, ... **$40-65**

Soup plate, rimmed, 8 3/8" d. rose **$40-65**

Soup plate, rimmed, 8 3/8" d. medium green **$125-150**

Sugar bowl, cov. chartreuse **$60-70**

Sugar bowl, cov. forest green **$60-70**

Sugar bowl, cov. grey........ **$60-70**

Sugar bowl, cov. light green **$45-60**

Sugar bowl, cov. red.......... **$60-70**

Sugar bowl, cov. rose........ **$60-70**

Syrup pitcher w/original lid, cobalt blue.............................. **$350-450**

Syrup pitcher w/original lid, ivory **$350-450**

Syrup pitcher w/original lid, light green **$350-450**

Syrup pitcher w/original lid, red **$350-450**

Syrup pitcher w/original lid, yellow **$350-450**

Teapot, cov., medium size (6 cup), forest green **$250-300**

Teapot, cov., medium size (6 cup), grey **$425-475**

Teapot, cov., medium size (6 cup), light green.............. **$1,600-1,700**

Teapot, cov., large size (8 cup), cobalt blue **$300-400**

Teapot, cov., large size (8 cup), light green.................... **$300-400**

Teapot, cov., large size (8 cup), red **$300-400**

Teapot, cov., medium size (6 cup), yellow **$150-175**

Tumbler, juice, 5 oz. cobalt blue **$45-60**

Tumbler, juice, 5 oz. grey **$225-275**

Tumbler, juice, 5 oz. ivory.. **$45-60**

Tumbler, juice, 5 oz. chartreuse **$550-600**

Tumbler, juice, 5 oz. forest green **$400-500**

Tumbler, juice, 5 oz. red.... **$45-60**

Tumbler, juice, 5 oz. turquoise **$45-60**

Tumbler, water, 10 oz. cobalt blue **$80**

Tumbler, water, 10 oz. ivory **$70-90**

Tumbler, water, 10 oz. turquoise **$70-90**

Utility tray, 10 1/2" l. cobalt blue **$45**

Utility tray, 10 1/2" l. light green **$40-55**

Teapot, cov., medium size (6 cup), medium green **$1,600-1,700**

Utility tray, 10 1/2" l. red......... **$45**

Utility tray, 10 /2" l., yellow **$40-55**

Vase, bud, 6 1/2" h. light green **$100-150**

Vase, bud, 6 1/2" h. red **$100**

Vase, bud, 6 1/2" h. yellow **$100-150**

Vase, 8" h. cobalt blue........... **$650**

Vase, 8" h. red....................... **$650**

Vase, 8" h. yellow **$650-800**

Vase, 10" h. cobalt blue...... **$1,050**

Vase, 10" h. ivory...... **$1,000-1,300**

Vase, 10" h. turquoise **$1,000-1,300**

Vase, 10" h. yellow ... **$1,000-1,300**

Vase, 12" h. ivory...... **$1,100-1,500**

Vase, 12" h. red........ **$1,850-2,000**

Vase, 12" h. turquoise **$1,500-1,600**

Anyone selling antiques at a garage sale should not expect to receive price-guide prices. Garage sale shoppers want bargain prices. When selling to dealers, expect to get 40 to 60 percent of retail prices. To receive top prices, avoid the middleman and sell directly to other collectors.

Joining a collecwtor's club is an excellent way to further your experience and meet other collectors in your field. For nominal dues, collectors with similar interests meet and trade at annual conventions. Often a club sponsors an antique show that is open to the public. Many clubs publish newsletters and membership directories. Some major clubs have regional chapters, which also sponsor shows.

Flow Blue

Flow Blue ironstone and semi-porcelain was manufactured mainly in England during the second half of the 19th century. The early ironstone was produced by many of the well known English potters and was either transfer-printed or hand-painted (brush stroke). The bulk of the ware was exported to the United States or Canada.

The "flow" or running quality of the cobalt blue designs was the result of introducing certain chemicals into the kiln during the final firing. Some patterns are so "flown" that it is difficult to ascertain the design. The transfers were of several types: Asian, Scenic, Marble or Floral.

The earliest Flow Blue ironstone patterns were produced during the period between about 1840 and 1860. After the Civil War, Flow Blue went out of style for some years but was again manufactured and exported to the United States beginning about the 1880s and continuing through the turn of the century. These later Flow Blue designs are on a semi-porcelain body rather than heavier ironstone and the designs are mainly florals. Also see Antique Trader Pottery & Porcelain Ceramics Price Guide, 6th Edition.

AMOY (Davenport, ca. 1844)

Teapot, cov., Octagon body shape, ca. 1850 .... **$650**

Teapot, cov., Amoy patt., Squat Sixteen Panel Fluted body shape, ca. 1850 .... **$950**

ANEMONE (Cumberlidge, Humphreys & Hele, ca. 1889-93)

Biscuit jar, cov., 6 1/2" h. **$175**

ARABESQUE (T. J. & J. Mayer)

Teapot, cov., Long Octagon body shape, ca. 1845 .... **$650**

BOUQUET (Henry Alcock & Co., ca. 1895)

Vegetable dish, cov., footed, 12" l. **$225**

BRAZIL (W.H. Grindley & Company, ca. 1891)

Sugar bowl, cov., 5" h. **$175**

BRITISH SCENERY (Davenport & Co., ca. 1856)

Platter, 19" l. **$350**

CALICO (Warwick China Co., American, ca. 1887-1910, aka Daisy Chain)

Pitcher, 7 1/2" h., 9" w. **$350**

CAMBRIDGE (Alfred Meakin, ca. 1891)

Plate, luncheon, 9" d. **$85**

CANNISTER (maker unknown, marked "Germany," ca. 1891) - Miscellaneous (These canisters, spice jars & kitchen items were made for export. They arrived without the name of the intended contents i.e. "Tea."

Box for pickled herring, very unusual, 6 x 14", 6" h. **$250**

CANNISTER (continued)

Canister, cov., marked "Sugar," 6" d., 8" h. **$145**

Salt box, hanging type, 5 x 7", 8 1/2" h. **$145**

CARLTON (Samuel Alcock & Co., ca. 1850)

Sauce tureen, cov., rosebud finial, 7 1/2" handle to handle, 8 1/2" d. underplate **$575**

Teapot, cov., Broad Shoulder body shape, ca. 1850, each (ILLUS. of two size variations) **$950**

CASHMERE (Francis Morley, ca. 1850)

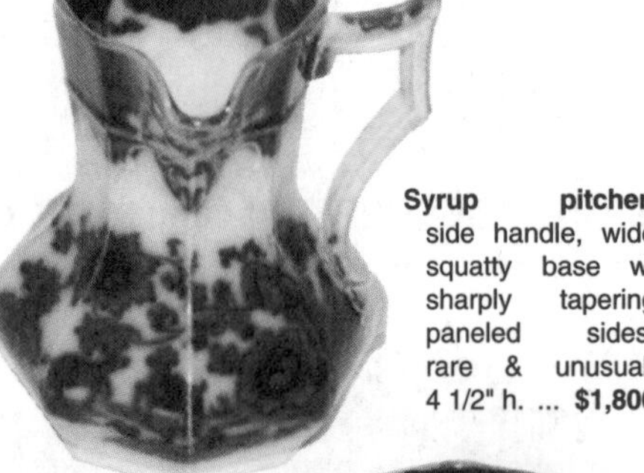

Syrup pitcher, side handle, wide squatty base w/ sharply tapering paneled sides, rare & unusual, 4 1/2" h. ... **$1,800**

Teapot, cov., Classic Gothic body shape, ca. 1850, each (ILLUS. of two size variations) **$950**

Teapot, cov., Split Panel Primary body shape, ca. 1850, each (ILLUS. of two size variations)..... **$1,200**

CHAPOO (John Wedge Wood - aka Wedgwood, ca. 1850)

Teapot, cov., Tall No Line Primary body shape **$1,200**

Teapot, cov., Double Line Primary body shape, ca. 1850 .... **$550**

CHEN-SI (John Meir, ca. 1835)

Teapot, cov., Eight Sided Primary Belted body shape **$650**

CLARENCE (W.H. Grindley & Co., ca. 1900)

Platter, 16" l. **$250**

CHINESE (T. Dimmock, ca. 1845)

Teapot, cov. **$800**

CLAYTON (Johnson Bros., ca. 1902)

Soup plate w/flanged rim, luncheon, 9" d. **$85**

CHINESE (Thomas Dimmock & Co., ca. 1845)

Drainer, 10 x 14" **$575**

CONWAY (New Wharf Pottery & Co., ca. 1891)

Vegetable bowl, open, round, 9 1/2" d. **$85**

DAISY (Burgess & Leigh, ca. 1897)

Soup plate w/flanged rim, 9" d. **$65**

EBOR (Ridgways, ca. 1910)

Plate, 10" d. **$75**

DELAMERE (Henry Alcock & Co., ca. 1900)

Bowl, soup, franged edge rim, 10" d. **$115**

GOTHIC (Jacob Furnival & Co., ca. 1850)

Pitcher & bowl set, 13 1/2" h. pitcher, 14" d. bowl, the set.. **$1,800**

DEVON (Alfred Meakin, ca. 1907)

Dinner service: thirteen 9 3/4" d. dinner plates, twelve 7 1/2" d. soup plates, twelve bread & butter plates, eleven dessert plates, twelve dessert bowls, seventeen saucers-underplates, eight coffee cups & four saucers, eight teacups & four saucers, one gravy boat, open sugar bowl, creamer, 8 1/2" d. vegetable dish, small oval relish dish, two open oval vegetable dishes, one two-handled cov. vegetable tureen, oval chop platter & matching 16" l. roasted meats platter & cov. butter dish, the set **$3,220**

GRAPE (unknown maker, ca. 1840)

Teapot, cov., free-hand Gaudy Ironstone, Ten Panel Primary shape **$650**

GRAPES (Unknown, ca. 1850s, brush-stroke painted)

Plate, 9" d., scalloped, reticulated **$175**

GRENADA (Henry Alcock & Co., ca. 1891)

Plate, 10" d. **$75**

HEATH'S FLOWER (Thomas Heath, ca. 1850)

Teapot, cov., free-hand, Full Panel Gothic body shape **$650**

Teapot, cov., free-hand, Gothic Decagon body shape **$650**

Teapot, cov., free-hand, Six Sided Gothic (Lantern) body shape **$650**

HONG KONG (Charles Meigh, ca. 1845)

Teapot, cov., Ridged Square body shape **$750**

Teapot, cov., Long Octagon body shape **$850**

Teapot, cov., Vertical Panel Gothic body shape **$750**

Teapot, cov., Twelve Panel Fluted body shape ... **$950**

LEAF & BERRY (Unknown, ca. 1860s, brush-stroke painted)

Relish mitten, marked w/impressed "Real Ironstone," a mark that G.L. Ashworth & Bros. impressed on their pieces ca. 1862, 8 1/2" w. **$225**

LEAF & SWAG (Unknown, probably 1850s, brush-stroke painted)

Plate, 8 1/2" d. ... **$150**

LEON (J. & G. Meakin, ca. 1890)

Platter, 16" l. $400

LESBURY (Armstrong & Co., marked "Cetemware," ca. 1906)

Sauce tureen, cov. $175

LILY (Thomas Dimmock & Co., ca. 1844)

Pitcher, 8" h. $325

LOIS (New Wharf Pottery & Co., ca. 1891)

Soup bowl, flanged edge, 10" d. $75

LONSDALE (Ridgways, ca. 1910)

Platter, 14 x 17" $350

MANHATTAN (Henry Alcock & Co., ca. 1900)

Teapot, cov., footed deeply waisted ruffled unnamed body shape $450

Teapot, cov., unnamed body shape **$450**

MARECHAL NEIL (W.H. Grindley & Co., ca. 1895)

Teapot, cov., deeply waisted & lobed unnamed body shape **$450**

MARGUERITE (W.H. Grindley & Co., ca. 1891)

Platter, 18" l. **$525**

MARQUIS, The (Also See Marquis II) (W. H. Grindley & Co., ca. 1906)

Tea cup & saucer **$65**

MEISSEN (Brown-Westhead, Moore & Co., ca. 1895)

Cake plate, tab handles, 10" d. **$175**

MENTONE (Johnson Bros., ca. 1900)

Teapot, cov., embossed squatty bulbous body **$150**

MOREA (J. Goodwin, ca. 1878)

Plate, 8 1/2" d. $100

OLYMPIA (Johnson Bros., ca. 1890)

Pitcher, 7" h. $150

MORNING GLORY (Unknown, ca. 1850s, brush-stroke, gaudy)

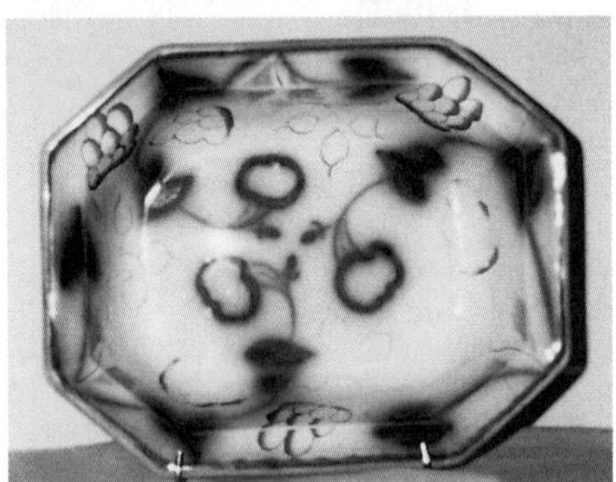

Vegetable dish, open, 7 x 8 1/2" $200

OLYMPIA (W. H. Grindley & Co., ca. 1894)

Soup tureen, cov., round $300

NON PAREIL (Burgess & Leigh - Middleport Potteries, ca. 1891)

Teapot, cov., oblong boat-shaped body $650

Vegetable dish, open, oval, 10" d. $175

OREGON (T. J. and J. Mayer, ca. 1845)

Teapot, cov., Classic Gothic body shape **$650**

ORIENTAL (Ridgways, ca. 1891)

Fruit compote, footed, two handles, 10" d., 6" h. **$750**

PASTORAL (J. & T. Furnival, ca. 1843)

Teapot, cov., Tall Primary Single Line body shape **$1,200**

Cobalt oxide was used to produce Flow Blue because it could survive the intense heat needed to glaze the pieces. Adding lime or ammonia chloride enhanced the blur, which conveniently hid defects in the blanks.

OVANDO (Alfred Meakin, ca. 1891)

Dinner service: nine 9" d. dessert plates, nine 6" d. saucers, seven bread & butter plates, six soup plates, six dessert bowls, one 8 1/2" l. oval relish dish, 9 3/4" l. oval vegetable dish, sauceboat, 12 1/2" l. oval meat platter, 16" l. oval meat platter, two-handled oval cov. vegetable dish, two-handled round cov. vegetable dish, handled sugar bowl w/no cover & handles repaired, the set **$1,840**

PEKING (unknown maker, ca. 1845)

Teapot, cov., Six Sided Primary Belted body shape $600

PENANG (Wm. Ridgway, ca. 1840)

Teapot, cov., Twelve Panel Fluted shape $750

PELEW (Edward Challinor, ca. 1840)

Teapot, cov., Long Decagon body shape $1,400

ROYSTON (Johnson Bros., ca. 1891)

Platter, 14" l. $175

Teapot, cov., Grape Octagon body shape, each (ILLUS. in two size variations).. $650

The Chinese perfected blue glazed pottery long before the Europeans, but Englishman Josiah Wedgwood is generally given credit for developing the blurred effects of Flow Blue.

Originally, Flow Blue designs were inspired by Chinese patterns. Later, more European designs were adopted and became widespread.

SAVOY (Johnson Bros., ca. 1900)

Platter, 18" l. **$300**

SCINDE (J. & G. Alcock, ca. 1840)

Teapot, Double Line Primary body shape (ILLUS. right with child's teapot)... **$600**

Teapot, cov., Eight Panel Pumpkin shape body **$650**

Teapot, cov., tall ovoid demitasse pot **$450**

SEAWEED (Wm. Ridgway, ca. 1856)

Rim soup bowl, flanged edge, 10" d. **$100**

SHANGHAE (Jacob Furnival & Co., ca. 1860)

Plate, 9" d., 14-sided **$150**

SHANGHAI (W. H. Grindley & Co., ca. 1898)

Teapot, cov., footed wide squat body **$450**

SHUSAN (F. & R. Pratt & Co., ca. 1855)

Teapot **$525**

SINGA (Cork, Edge & Malkin, ca. 1865)

Loving cup/tyg, two-handled, 5" h., 4 3/4" d., 8 1/4" w. from handle to handle **$350**

WALDORF (New Wharf Pottery & Co., ca. 1892)

Plate, 10" d. **$95**

SNOWFLAKE (unknown maker, ca. 1840)

Teapot, cov., Plain Round body shape, also found in purple or a combination of blue & purple, each (ILLUS. of two sizes) **$750**

Franciscan Ware

A product of Gladding, McBean & Company of Glendale and Los Angeles, California, Franciscan Ware was one of a number of lines produced by that firm over its long history. Introduced in 1934 as a pottery dinnerware, Franciscan Ware was produced in many patterns including "Desert Rose," introduced in 1941 and reportedly the most popular dinnerware pattern ever made in this country. Beginning in 1942 some vitrified china patterns were also produced under the Franciscan name.

After a merger in 1963 the company name was changed to Interpace Corporation and in 1979 Josiah Wedgwood & Sons purchased the Gladding, McBean & Co. plant from Interpace. American production ceased in 1984.

Coffee & tea service: cov. coffeepot, cov. teapot, round serving plate, creamer & cov. sugar; Fine China, Westwood patt., the set **$165**

Coffee server, El Patio tableware, red/orange glossy glaze **$40**

Plate, dinner, 10 1/2" d., Desert Rose patt. **$23**

Plate, luncheon, 9 1/2" d., Coronado Table Ware, matt ivory glaze **$8**

Teapot, cov., Desert Rose patt., ca. 1960 .... **$100**

Frankoma

John Frank started his pottery company in 1933 in Norman, Oklahoma. However, when he moved the business to Sapulpa, Oklahoma, in 1938, he felt he was home. Still, Mr. Frank could not know the horrendous storms and trials that would follow him. Just after his move, on November 11, 1938, a fire destroyed the entire operation, which included the pot and leopard mark he had created in 1935. Then, in 1942, the war effort needed men and materials so Frankoma could not survive. In 1943, John and Grace Lee Frank bought the plant as junk salvage and began again.

The time in Norman had produced some of the finest art ware that John would ever create and most of the items were marked either "Frank Potteries," "Frank Pottery," or to a lesser degree, the "pot and leopard" mark. Today these marks are avidly and enthusiastically sought by collectors. Another elusive mark wanted by collectors shows "Firsts Kiln Sapulpa 6-7-38." The mark was used for one day only and denotes the first firing in Sapulpa. It has been estimated that perhaps 50 to 75 pieces were fired on that day.

The clay Frankoma used is helpful to collectors in determining when an items was made. Creamy beige clay know as "Ada" clay was in use until 1953. Then a red brick shale was found in Sapulpa and used until about 1985 when, by the addition of an additive, the clay became a reddish pink.

Rutile glazes were used early in Frankoma's history. Glazes with rutile have caused more confusion among collectors than any other glazes. For example, a Prairie Green piece shows a lot of green and it also has some brown. The same is true for the Desert Gold glaze; the piece shows a sandy-beige glaze with some amount of brown. Generally speaking, Prairie Green, Desert Gold, White Sand, and Woodland Moss are the most puzzling to collectors.

In 1970 the government closed the rutile mines in America and Frankoma had to buy it from Australia. It was not the same so the results were different. Values are higher for the glazes with rutile. Also, the pre-Australian Woodland Moss glaze is more desirable than that created after 1970.

After John Frank died in 1973, his daughter Joniece Frank, a ceramic designer at the pottery, became president of the company. In 1983 another fire destroyed everything Frankoma had worked so hard to create. They rebuilt but in 1990, after the IRS shut the doors for nonpayment, Joniece, true to the Frank legacy, filed for Chapter 11 (instead of bankruptcy) so she could reopen and continue the work she loved. In 1991 Richard Bernstein purchased the pottery and the name was changed to Frankoma Industries.

The company was sold again in 2006. The new buyers are concentrating mostly on dinnerware, none of which is like the old Frankoma. They have a "Collectors Series," "Souvenir & State Items," and "Heartwarming Trivets." None of these is anything like what Frankoma originally created. The company is doing some Frankoma miniatures such as a dolphin on a wave, a fish, a wolf, a bear, etc. These, too, do not resemble Frankoma miniatures, and all their glazes are new.

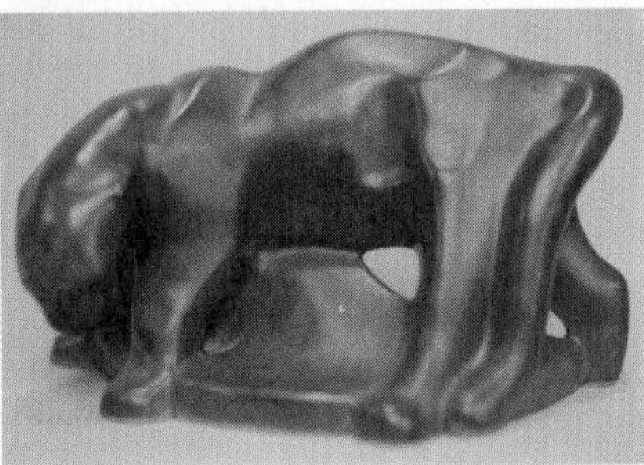

Book ends, model of leopard, Pompeian Bronze glaze, Model No. 431, 9" l., 5 1/2" h., pr. **$1,800**

←

Book ends, Walking Ocelot on a two-tiered oblong base, black high glaze, Model No. 424, signed on reverse of tiered base "Taylor" denoting designer Joseph Taylor, pot & leopard mark on bottom, 7" l., 3" h., pr. **$1,900**

↓

Bowl, 5 3/4" d., shallow form, advertising "Oklahoma Gas Company - Golden Anniversary," 1956, Desert Gold, marked "Frankoma" **$186**

Mortar & pestle, advertising "Schreibers Drug Store," White Sand, marked "Frankoma," 3 1/4" **$145**

Sign, dealer teepee, Prairie Green, 1940s, marked "Frankoma," 6 1/2" h. **$725**

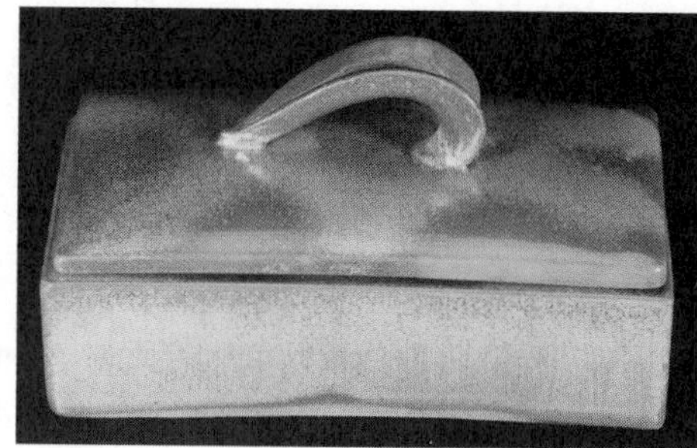

Cigarette box, cov., rectangular, cover w/single raised & hard-to-find curved leaf handle, Bronze Green glaze, Ada clay, marked "Frankoma," 4 x 6 3/4", 3 1/2" h. **$175**

Ornament, "The ABCs of life," gift w/purchase from Tulsa shopping mall, 1987, white background w/ sketch of three children, 3 1/2" d. **$69**

Teapot, cov., Wagon Wheel patt., Desert Gold glaze, Sapulpa, Oklahoma, ca. 1942 .... **$25**

Fulper Pottery

The Fulper Pottery was founded in Flemington, New Jersey, in 1805 and operated until 1935, although operations were curtailed in 1929 when its main plant was destroyed by fire. The name was changed in 1929 to Stangl Pottery, which continued in operation until July of 1978, when Pfaltzgraff, a division of Susquehanna Broadcasting Company of York, Pennsylvania, purchased the assets of the Stangl Pottery, including the name.

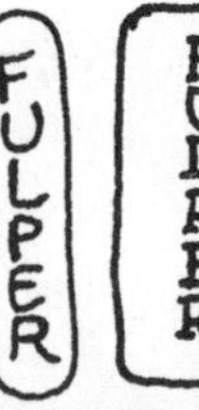

Flower frog, figural, model of a large oval scarab beetle, nice matte green glaze, unmarked, 3 1/4" l., 1 1/2" h. **$150**

Jug, bulbous ovoid body w/ a wide shoulder centered by a short cylindrical neck, a high arched handle from base of neck to edge of shoulder, Copper Dust Crystalline glaze, small in-the-making grinding chip on base, incised racetrack mark, 7 3/4" d., overall 11 1/2" h. **$2,760**

Lamp, table model, a wide pottery mushroom-shaped shade w/a fine Leopard Skin Crystalline glaze, the border pierced w/clusters of small openings centered by a large triangular opening, all inset w/leaded slag glass pieces, on a widely flaring matching pottery pedestal base, original sockets & switch, hairline in a ceramic bridge between the two pieces of slag glass, rectangular ink mark on both pieces, shade 15 1/4" d., overall 18 1/2" h. **$10,925**

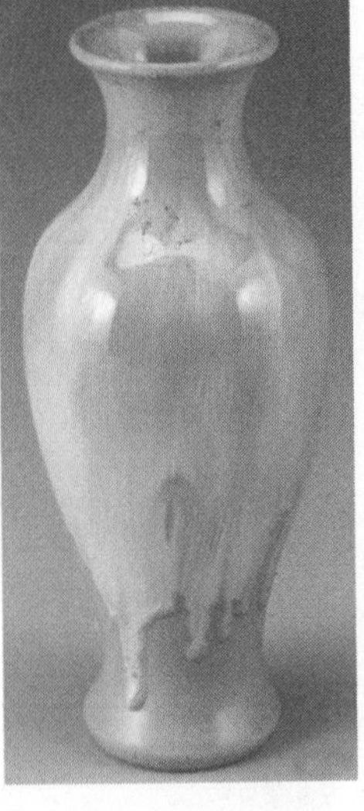

Vase, 10 1/2" h., 4 1/2" d., simple tall baluster-form body, Ivory Flambé glaze dripping over a mustard yellow matte ground, ink racetrack mark **$805**

In the early 1900s, Fulper's most well known product was its "germ-proof filter" developed by William Fulpter for its crockware water coolers. The filter was a welcome feature at a time when public water supplies were not treated as they are today.

Vase, 11 1/2" h., 9" d., footed baluster-form body w/flaring rim, molded w/vertical low ribs forming panels up the sides, fine mirrored Cat's-eye Flambé glaze, raised racetrack mark **$4,025**

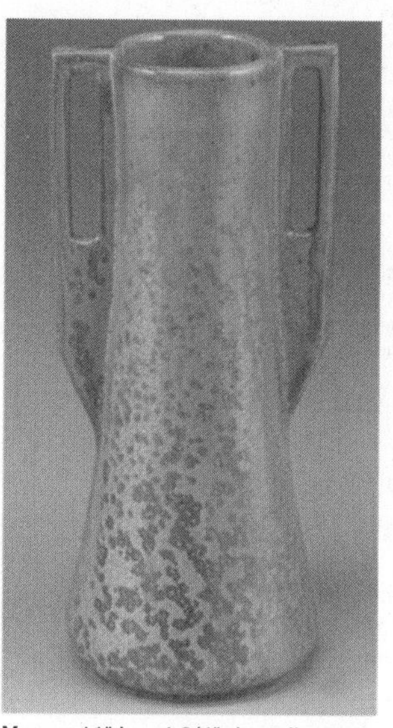

Vase, 11" h., 4 3/4" d., tall gently tapering cylindrical body w/a flat mouth flanked by long squared buttressed handles, fine Leopard Skin Crystalline glaze, rectangular ink mark **$1,093**

Vase, 12 3/4" h., 4 3/4" d., "Cattail" patt., tall cylindrical form molded overall w/cattails, Leopard Skin crystalline glaze, minor burst bubble at rim, rectangular ink mark **$4,025**

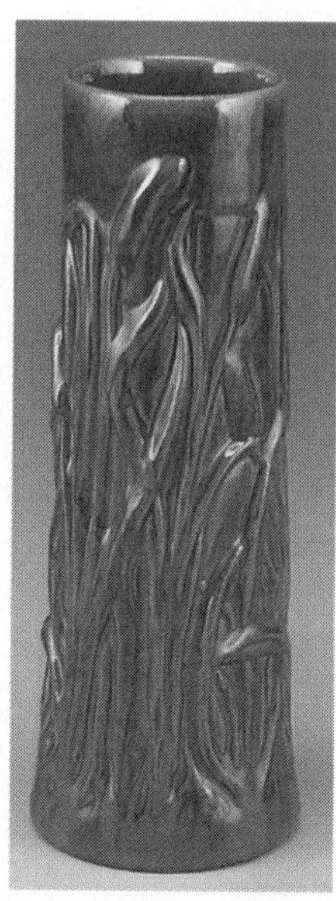

Vase, 13" h., 4 3/4" d., tall slightly tapering cylindrical body molded in relief overall in cattails, glossy bluish grey & Moss Flambé glaze, rectangular ink mark **$4,313**

Vase, 4 3/4" h., 5 3/4" d., wide low squatty lower body w/a wide tapering shoulder to the wide flat mouth flanked by squared scroll handles, Copper Dust Crystalline glaze, incised racetrack mark **$575**

Vase, 5 1/2" h., 5" d., bulbous ovoid body tapering to a low wide molded mouth, Copper Dust Crystalline glaze, raised racetrack mark **$1,035**

Vase, 6" h., 8 1/2" d., footed wide squatty bulbous body w/a short wide cylindrical neck surrounded by three short loop handles, Cucumber Crystalline glaze, raised racetrack mark **$1,150**

Vase, 7 1/2" h., 4" d., corseted cylindrical body, dripping frothy ivory, blue & mahogany Flambé glaze, rectangular ink mark **$1,035**

Vase, 7 1/2" h., 6" d., bulbous ovoid gourd-form body w/a slightly tapering cylindrical neck flanked by curved handles to the shoulder, blue & amber Crystalline glaze, incised racetrack mark **$546**

Vase, 7" h., 9 1/2" d., wide squatty bulbous tapering form w/a flat closed rim flanked by square buttressed handles, cafe-au-lait glaze, rectangular ink mark **$748**

Fulper is famous for its beautiful glazes. The firm used nearly 100 glazes during its production of art pottery.

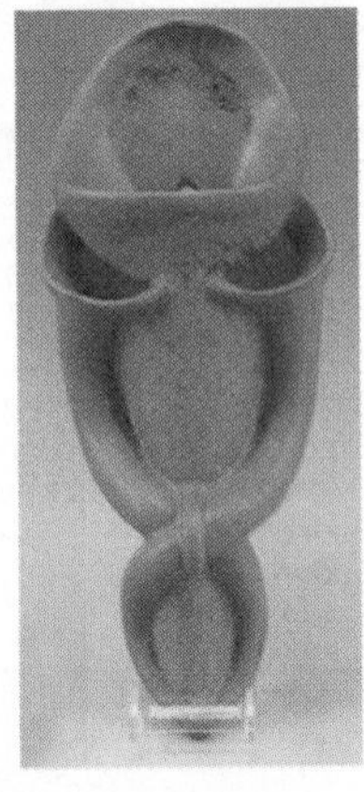

Wall pocket, triple, a central tapering cone w/a high upturned back rim flanked down the sides w/smaller entwined open-topped cones, matte blue glaze, remnant of rectangular ink mark, 11 1/2" h. **$374**

Gallè Pottery

Fine pottery was made by Emile Gallè, the multitalented French designer and artisan who is also famous for his glass and furniture. The pottery is relatively scarce.

Basket, the flaring body composed of ribbed feather-like panels resting on large knobs w/tiny ball feet, the high arched handle formed by two facing fish w/their tails curving up to the top, glazed in steaky glazes in shades of red, green, orange & blue, accent w/overall gold spatter, signed "Emile Gallè - Nancy Dèposè," professionally repaired handle, ca. 1890, 8 1/2" h. **$1,410**

Ewer, a squatty bulbous body centered by a tall slender stick neck, a long flat handle from near the top of the neck to the shoulder, a crimson glazed decorated w/ gold-trimmed dark blackish green foliage & a praying mantis, white blossoms around the neck, accented w/gold spatter, signed in black enamel w/the Cross of Lorraine & "E & G dèposè - E. Gallè Nancy," ca. 1890, 9 3/4" h. **$1,880**

Ewer, footed wide squatty bulbous low body centered by a tall flaring & swelled neck w/a pinched spout & long angled handle from top to shoulder, a mottled glossy purple glaze decorated w/sponged gold & enameled w/a large & gangly praying mantis about to land on white spider mums on leafy stems below, all outlined in gold, base stamped in black "E+G dèposè - E. Gallè" & a possibly obscured "Nancy," footring w/a few flat chips, 7 1/4" h. **$1,725**

While Emile Galle's faience (tin glazed earthenware) was commercially successful, he is better known for his spectacular glass.

Ewer, squatty bulbous body centering a very tall slender cylindrical neck, a long curved handle from the rim to the side of the shoulder, one side decorated w/a modeled mushroom-shaped flower, the opposite decorated w/a great raised blue & brown grasshopper, background w/splashes of blue, yellow, gold, rust & brown, signed on the bottom "E G Dèposè" & signed "E Gallè Nancy," some very minor crazing to glaze, 9 1/4" h. **$1,495**

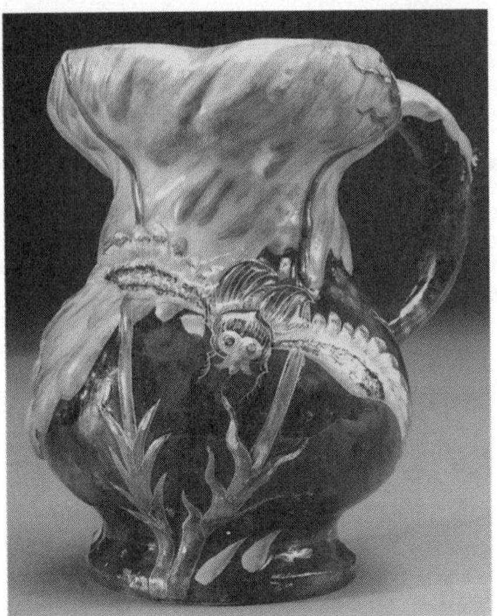

Pitcher, 7 1/2" h., footed squatty bulbous body tapering to a cylindrical section & widely flaring cupped rim, applied strap handle, the upper half w/a thick drippy light blue glaze w/gold trim above a mottled brown lower half, enameled w/a large flying insect above long leaved plant, stamped in the glaze "Emile Galle Nancy Dèposè" & the E & G monogram, short hairline in bottom, ca. 1890 .... **$3,760**

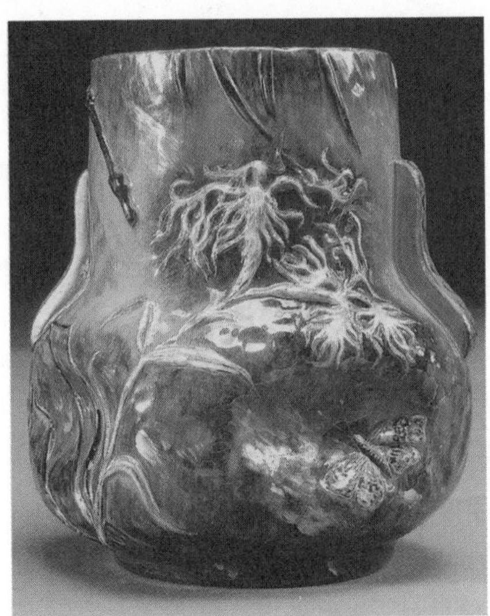

Vase, 7 1/2" h., a footed bulbous lower body w/deeply pinched-in sides, tapering to a wide cylindrical upper body, glazed in mottled shades of dark mustard brown & black, enameled w/ naturalistic flowers & two polychrome butterflies, small low curved side handles trimmed in blue, stamped w/the Cross of Lorraine & "Emilè Gallè - Nancy Dèposè" **$2,350**

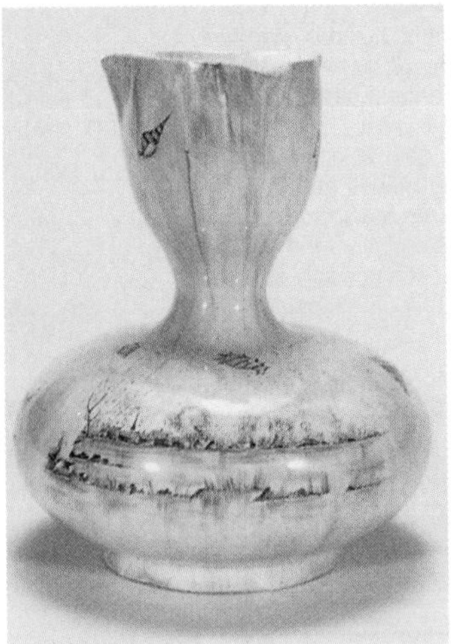

Vase, 7 1/8" h., footed wide squatty bulbous body centered by a tall upright gently flaring & deeply crimped neck, overall flowing pink & blue glaze, the base h.p. w/a scene of a quiet inlet village painted in sepia tones, various sea shells painted around the neck & shoulder, base signed "E. Gallè Fayencerie Nancy," crazed inside & out **$1,093**

Vase, 7" h., 4 1/2 x 11 1/2", long flat-sided oval form w/a long rectangular mouth flanked by lion heads w/ring handles, raised on four scroll feet, one side h.p. w/a colorful scene of a hen & rooster w/four chicks & a ladder, the other side w/a scene of a chicken w/wheelbarrow & broom on hay, base impressed w/lozenge mark "E.G.," mold number 244, artist-signed, late 19th c. **$518**

Wall pocket, round w/a large relief-molded crescent man-in-the-moon face around the border, the background h.p. Italianate seascape, signed "E. Gallè à Nancy 195" & molded "EG" w/a Cross of Lorraine & "Mode... et dècor dèp...," ca. 1890s, 14" w., 13 1/2" h. **$5,736**

Grueby

Some fine art pottery was produced by the Grueby Faience and Tile Company, established in Boston in 1891. Choice pieces were created with molded designs on a semi-porcelain body. The ware is marked and often bears the initials of the decorators. The pottery closed in 1907.

GRUEBY

Bowl, 3" d., 4 1/4" h., a small footring supporting the deep vertical & slightly uneven sides, wide flat rim, dappled green matte glaze, impressed mark, two pinhead-sized glaze pops **$805**

Bowl, 5 3/8" d., 1 7/8" h., wide low rounded sides & a wide flat molded rim, overall medium-dark blue matte glaze, impressed mark **$345**

Candlestick, a wide flat dished base w/low vertical sides, centered by a tapering ringed shaft w/an ovoid socket w/a flattened flared rim, mottled yellow & brown matte glaze, circular tulip-style insignia, No. 227, glazed-over chip at top rim, 5 3/8" h. **$460**

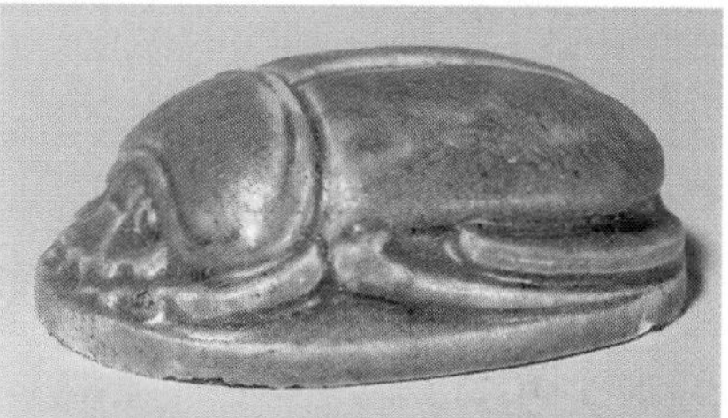

Paperweight, model of a scarab beetle, oval, matte blue glaze, impressed circular mark, some small glaze chips at base, 3 7/8" l. **$196**

Paperweight, model of a scarab beetle, oval, matte oatmeal glaze, impressed circular mark, glaze peppering, 3 7/8" l. **$345**

Grueby's excellence was recognized at the Paris Exhibition in 1900, where it was awarded two gold medals and one silver medal.

Plaque, rectangular, architectural-type, carved & modeled w/a family of elephants in black against a bluish grey ground, mounted in a black box frame, two firing lines in body, restoration to one, small chip to one corner, stamped mark, 14 x 23" **$9,775**

Tile, square, a large white rabbit crouched behind a small stylized leafy shrub in white, both outlined in dark blue against a pale blue ground, impressed tulip-style mark, burst glaze bubbles, some small edge nicks, 3 7/8" w. **$690**

Vase, 12 1/2" h., 8 1/4" d., rare large form w/bulbous body centered by a flaring cylindrical neck, tooled & applied w/large wide pointed overlapping leaves, fine organic matte green glaze, couple of very minor edge nicks, by Marie Seaman, stamped round mark **$11,500**

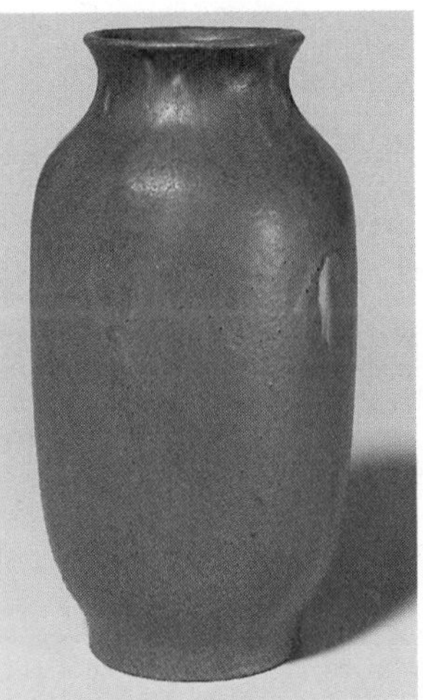

Vase, 12 1/2" h., swelled cylindrical body tapering to a short flared neck, matte green glaze w/a number of pinhead burst bubbles, area of thin glaze on side **$1,265**

William Henry Grueby, the owner and founder of the Grueby firm, gained fame for his matte glaze. His mastery of glazes did not begin with art pottery, however, but with the experience and training he received working with tile for the J. & J.G. Low Art Tile Works.

Vase, 5 1/2" h., 4 1/2" d., bulbous ovoid body w/a wide rolled rim, crisply tooled w/broad leaves up the sides, covered in a leathery dark green glaze, some highpoint nicks, circular mark **$2,875**

Vase, 6 1/4" h., squatty bulbous form w/a wide flat mouth, molded around the shoulder w/seven flower buds alternating w/seven wide leaves down the sides, mottled matte yellow glaze, unmarked, restoration to center of base, ca. 1908 .... **$5,288**

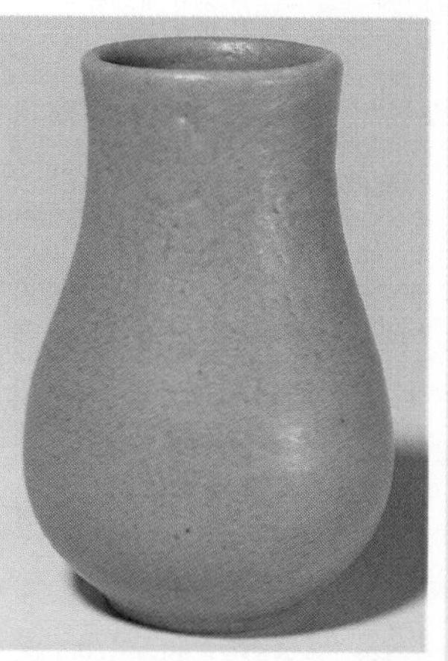

Vase, 6 3/4" h., footed simple ovoid body tapering to a flat mouth, textured matte blue glaze, impressed Grueby mark **$690**

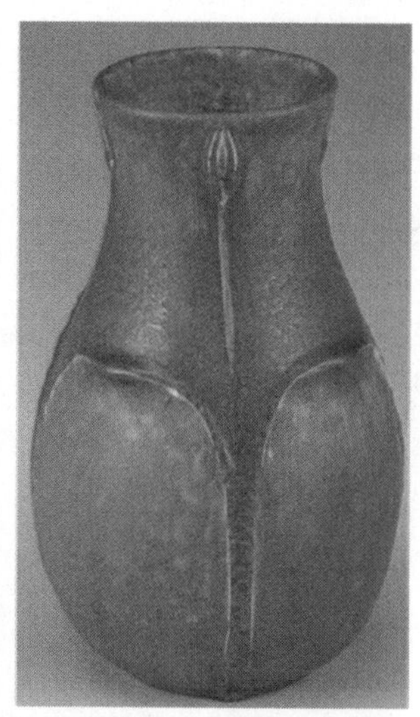

Vase, 7 1/2" h., 4 1/2" d., ovoid body tapering to a wide gently flaring neck, tooled & applied w/rounded leaves around the lower half w/four buds up the sides, medium matte green glaze, small nick to one leaf edge, mark obscured by glaze **$2,875**

Vase, 7 3/4" h., squatty bulbous base w/an angled shoulder to the tall gently flaring neck, tooled floral designs, dark matte green glaze, impressed tulip mark **$1,610**

Vase, 9 1/2" h., footed squatty bulbous lower body tapering to a wide cylindrical neck w/a molded rim, dark green matte glaze **$1,265**

Hall China

Founded in 1903 in East Liverpool, Ohio, this still-operating company at first produced mostly utilitarian wares. It was in 1911 that Robert T. Hall, son of the company founder, developed a special single-fire, lead-free glaze that proved to be strong, hard and nonporous. In the 1920s the firm became well known for its extensive line of teapots (still a major product), and in 1932 it introduced kitchenwares, followed by dinnerwares in 1936 and refrigerator wares in 1938.

The imaginative designs and wide range of glaze colors and decal decorations have led to the growing appeal of Hall wares with collectors, especially people who like Art Deco and Art Moderne design. One of the firm's most famous patterns was the "Autumn Leaf" line, produced as premiums for the Jewel Tea Company. For listings of this ware see "Jewel Tea Autumn Leaf."

HALL CHINA

Helpful books on Hall include *The Collector's Guide to Hall China* by Margaret & Kenn Whitmyer, and *Superior Quality Hall China - A Guide for Collectors* by Harvey Duke (An ELO Book, 1977).

Batter bowl, Five Band shape, Chinese Red **$95**

Bean pot, cov., Sani-Grid (Pert) shape, Chinese Red **$100**

Casserole w/inverted pie dish lid, Radiance shape, No. 488, 6 1/2" d., 4" h. **$60**

Casserole, cov., Art Deco w/chrome reticulated handled base **$55**

Coffeepot, cov., Terrace shape, Crocus patt. **$80**

Cookie jar, cov., Five Band shape, Meadow Flower patt. **$325**

Cookie jar, cov., Flareware **$65**

Creamer, Radiance shape, Autumn Leaf patt. **$45**

Humidor, cov., Indian Decal, walnut lid **$55**

Leftover, cov., Zephyr shape, Chinese Red **$110**

Mug, Irish coffee, footed, commemorative, "Hall China Convention 2000" **$40**

Pitcher, ball shape, Autumn Leaf patt., 1978, w/box **$65**

Pitchers, Sani-Grid (Pert) shape, Chinese Red, three sizes (ILLUS. of three) **$35-55**

Salt & pepper shakers, Sani-Grid (Pert) shape, Chinese Red, pr. **$35**

Teapot, cov., Adele shape, Art Deco style, Olive Green **$200**

Teapot, cov., Aladdin shape, round opening for cover & insert, Gold Swag decoration **$70-75**

Teapot, cov., Aladdin shape, round opening w/ insert, Marine Blue **$65-75**

Teapot, cov., Aladdin shape, round opening w/ insert, Maroon **$65-75**

Teapot, cov., Aladdin shape, w/infuser, Serenade patt. **$350**

Teapot, cov., Aladdin shape, Wildfire patt., w/oval infuser, 1950s **$75**

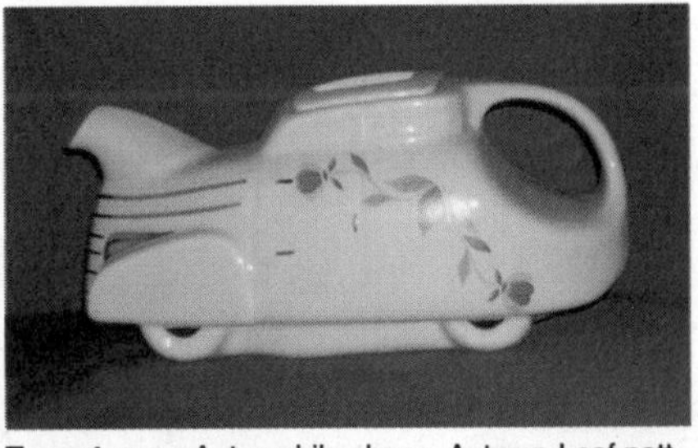

Teapot, cov., Automobile shape, Autumn Leaf patt., reissue for China Specialties w/commemorative stamp on the bottom, 1993 .... **$175**

Do not store antiques and collectibles wrapped in newspaper, as it has a high-acid content and the ink can rub off, causing permanent stains. Also, don't store antiques and collectibles in rental storage units for long periods because the temperature and humidity can vary greatly.

Teapot, cov., Birdcage shape, Canary Yellow w/"Gold Special" decoration **$450**

Teapot, cov., Donut shape, Orange Poppy patt. **$450**

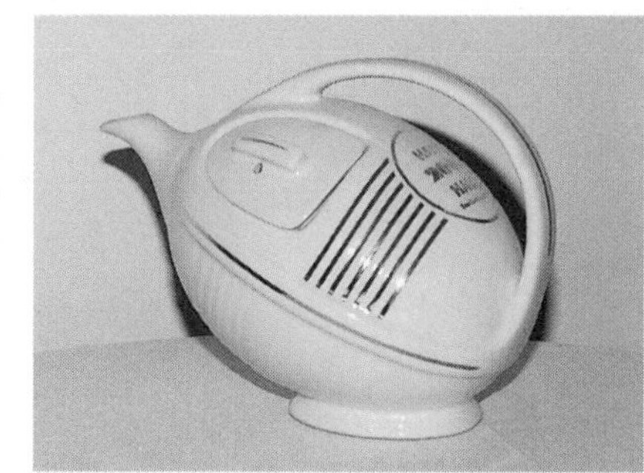

Teapot, cov., Football shape, commemorative, "Hall 2000 Haul, East Liverpool, Ohio" Ivory **$125**

Teapot, cov., Hook Cover shape, Cameo Rose patt., part of a limited edition produced exclusively for China Specialties, Strongsville, Ohio, fewer than 500 made **$95**

Teapot, cov., Hook Cover shape, Chinese Red **$250**

Teapot, cov., Illinois shape, Maroon w/gold decoration **$225**

Teapot, cov., Lipton Tea shape, Mustard Yellow **$40**

Teapot, cov., Morning Set shape, Blue Garden patt. **$350**

Teapot, cov., Philadelphia shape, Chinese Red **$250**

Teapot, cov., Radiance shape, Acacia patt. **$225**

Teapot, cov., Rutherford shape, ribbed, Chinese Red **$300**

Teapot, cov., Star shape, Turquoise w/gold decoration **$100-125**

Teapot, cov., Streamline shape, Fantasy patt. **$400**

Teapot, cov., Sundial shape, Blue Blossom patt. **$300**

Teapot, cov., Tea-for-Two shape, Pink w/ gold decoration **$150**

Harris Strong Designs

Harris Strong (1920-2006) is so identified with the decorative tiles produced by his company during the 1950s and 1960s that even unsigned tiles of that era are often attributed to him although the style may be markedly different.

Born in Wisconsin, Strong studied ceramics and chemical engineering at North Carolina State University. In 1947, after working for Kelby Originals, a Brooklyn pottery, Strong and co-worker Robert Krasner founded Potters of Wall Street. Their new firm specialized in ceramic lamps, ashtrays and other decorative pieces, including tiles.

The tiles for which Strong became famous were actually a secondary focus of his, created primarily to test glazes. However, their novelty, whether used as individual accent pieces or grouped together to form a tile "painting," caught on with the public. Buoyed by this success, Strong opened his own firm in the Bronx in the early 1950s.

Strong's tile scenes, framed or mounted on burnished wood backings, proved popular with architects, interior decorators and consumers seeking contemporary wall art at affordable prices. Themes included portraits, abstracts and exotic locales as well as medieval and other period depictions. Strong's tile plaques are noted for their vibrant color combinations, three-dimensionality of the figures and scenes, and attention to detail. Color and form are filtered through the precise parameters of ceramic tile as well as through Strong's own visual sense that encompasses both the primitive and the contemporary.

The sheer size of many Harris Strong plaques made them especially well suited to corporate, hotel, and restaurant decor where they made arresting focal points in the interior. In essence, Strong created the early 1950s market for tile-based decorative wall hangings, adapting his designs for nearly every location: ship's lounges, office building facades, elevator interiors and even bowling alleys. One particularly challenging commission was the massive "Cathedral Wall" divider created for New York's Waldorf-Astoria Hotel, which spanned the entire interior of the hotel's Marco Polo Club.

Attribution of Harris works has often been haphazard since paper labels were used on the back of his plaques rather than a permanent signature. In the absence of a label, one reliable indicator of a Strong plaque is the heart-shaped hooks used for hanging.

Harris G. Strong, Inc. relocated to Maine in 1970 and eventually phased out tile production, focusing instead on paintings, collages, and other types of wall decor. For the company's 40th anniversary in 1992, a series of commemorative tiles were produced. The company ceased all production in 1999.

In looking back on his career, Mr. Strong said, "Nobody ever handled tiles the way we did because we regarded them as a piece of pottery; A lot of us worked together to achieve our goal. What I provided, I hope, was the continuing thread that went through all the years — of quality, workmanship, and good design. If I did that, then that's enough."

Advisor for this category, Donald-Brian Johnson, is an author and lecturer specializing in Mid-Twentieth century design. Photos are by his frequent collaborator, Leslie Pina.

Ashtray, rectangular, #C-35, a reclining man w/a bird in black on turquoise, 9" l. (ILLUS. back with smaller ashtray) **$75-100**

Dish, triangular, #B-75, stylized female musicians, 9 1/2" l. **$175-200**

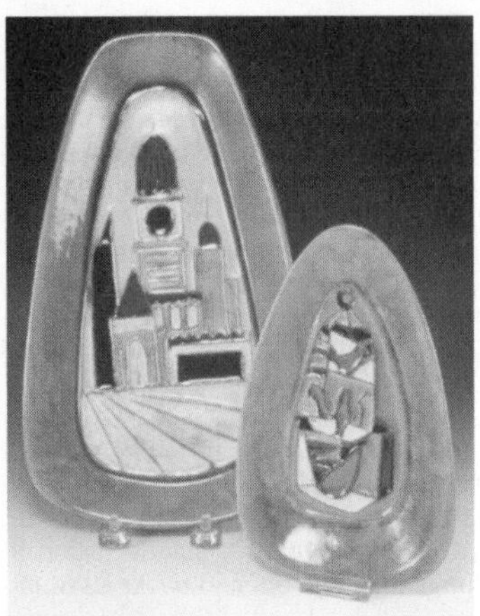

Dish, triangular, #B-77, red-domed building on a yellow ground within a green border, 11 3/4" l. (ILLUS. left with smaller dish) **$125-150**

Shadowbox, the central tile depicting dancing stick figures, 12 1/4" square **$175-200**

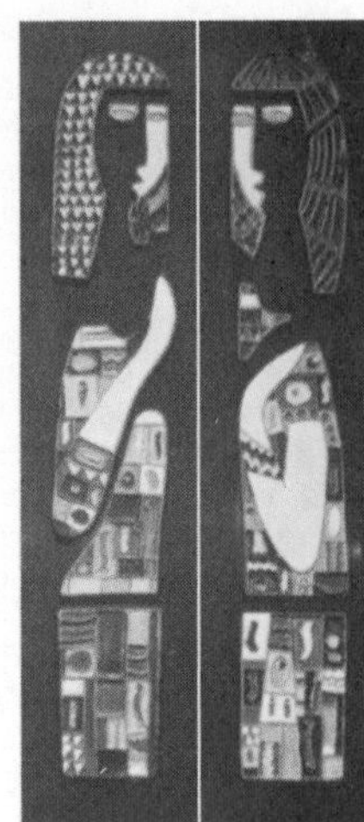

Tile picture on leather, rectangular, #L-101, a tall slender stylized image of an Egyptian woman in shades of brown, 11" w., 42 1/2" h. (ILLUS. left with Egyptian man picture) **$400-500**

Tile picture, rectangular, No. 141, a landscape w/sailboats in a bay & mountains beyond, composed of six tiles, framed, 15 1/2" w., 21 1/2" h. **$300-400**

Tile picture, rectangular, #1503, fifteen square tiles in dark blue & black forming a scene of alpacas & Machu Picchu, framed, 1960, 24 x 36" **$600-700**

Tile picture, rectangular, #313, a long industrial scene showing a line of buildings in various colors, composed of three tiles, signed "Strong" on the front, framed, 10 x 22" **$200-300**

Tile plaque, rectangular, "Harlequin," P-15, half-length stylized portrait, a Marvin Waller design, 9" w., 14" h. **$800-900**

Tile, #A-43, a stylized design of native dancers wearing ceremonial masks in browns on a black ground, linen mat & white oak frame, 10 3/4" sq. **$150-175**

Tile, design of a ram figure in dark blue on a light blue ground, framed, 11" sq. **$150-175**

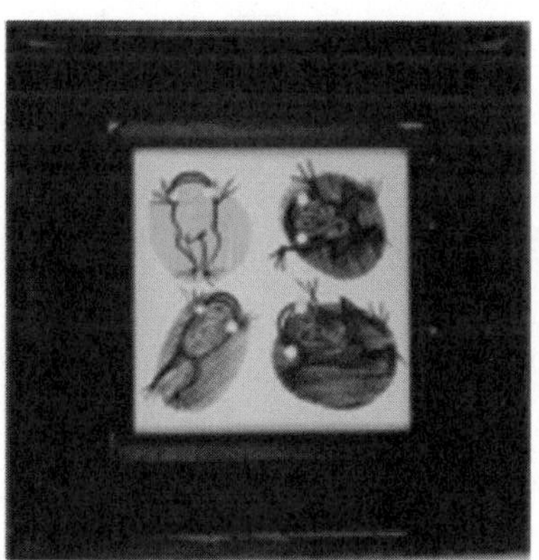

Tile, No. E-32, stylized design of swimming frogs, framed, 10 3/4" sq. **$150-175**

Tile, No. E-78, two stylized fish, framed, 10 3/4" sq. **$150-175**

When a bidder does not wish to increase the bid by a full increment, he may signal his intentions to the auctioneer to increase the bid by a half increment. This is done by the bidder placing the fingertips of one hand to the palm of the other hand, similar to the "time-out" signal in basketball, or by moving one hand horizontally across his throat. If the auctioneer recognizes and accepts the bid, the competing bidder or bidders will be afforded the same consideration.

Much like a preemptive bid, jumping the bid by more than the increment is a way of gaining the upper hand and discouraging competitors. When two bidders are competing by increments of $25, one may say, "three-hundred," when the auctioneer was calling for $225. The sudden jump may discourage the competitor from continuing and anyone else from joining the bidding.

Haviland

Haviland porcelain was originated by Americans in Limoges, France, shortly before the mid-19th century and continues in production. Some Haviland was made by Theodore Haviland in the United States during the last World War. Numerous other factories also made china in Limoges.

Chocolate set: tall tapering pot & six tall cups & saucers; Albany patt., white w/narrow floral rim bands & gold trim, late 19th - early 20th c., the set **$450-650**

Comport, pedestal on three feet w/ornate gold shell design, top w/reticulated edge, peach & gold design around base & top, 9" d. **$595**

Cups & saucers, Papillon butterfly handles w/Meadow Visitors decoration, six sets (ILLUS. of one set) **$900**

Dinner service: service for eight w/five-piece place settings & additional bowls, pitcher, gravy boat & other pieces; mostly Blank No. 5 w/delicate pink floral decoration, late 19th - early 20th c., 54 pcs. (ILLUS. of part) **$2,500**

Dinner service: twelve 8-piece place settings w/additional open & cov. vegetable dishes & oval platter; Albany patt., white w/narrow floral rim bands & gold trim, late 19th - early 20th c., the set **$2,700**

Fish set: 22" l. oval platter & twelve 8 1/2" d. plates; each piece w/a different fish in the center, the border in two shades of green design w/gold trim, h.p. scenes by L. Martin, mark of Theodore Haviland, 13 pcs. (ILLUS. of plate) **$2,750**

Hair receiver, cov., squatty round body on three gold feet, h.p. overall w/small flowers in blues & greens w/gold trim, mark of Charles Field Haviland **$225**

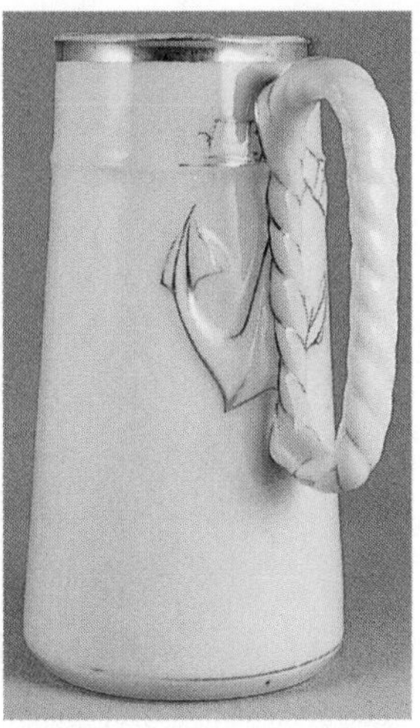

Pitcher, 7" h., milk-type, tankard style w/tapering cylindrical white body w/a large relief-molded anchor under the heavy rope-twist loop handle, bright gold trim, old Haviland & Co. mark **$175**

Pitcher, 9" h., lemonade-type, Schleiger 1026B variation, Blank 117, decorated w/ lavender flowers & brushed gold trim, Theodore Haviland **$250**

Pitcher, 9" h., tankard-shaped lemonade-type, Ranson blank, delicate floral band around the upper body trimmed in gold, gold handle & trim bands, factory-decorated, Haviland & Co. mark **$250**

Plate, bread & butter, 6 1/2" d., Paisley patt., smooth blanks w/gold edge, brownish red ground w/flowers in yellow, bright blue, green & white border design w/yellow flowers & bright blue leaves, turquoise scroll trim, Haviland & Co. mark **$28**

The Haviland empire in France came about through a chance encounter between David Haviland and one of his customers in the Haviland china importing shop in New York City. The customer gave Haviland a broken china cup that he wanted replaced, but the cup had no mark so Haviland could not identify it. Intriqued by the superb craftsmanship of the cup, Haviland doggedly tracked the cup to its manufacturer in Limoges, France. Haviland eventually opened a factory in Limoges, thus beginning a world-renowned dynasty.

Pennsylvania Hospital, Philadelphia platter, flowers within medallions border, Beauties of America series, dark blue, Ridgway, few minor scratches, 14 1/8 x 18 3/8" **$1,880**

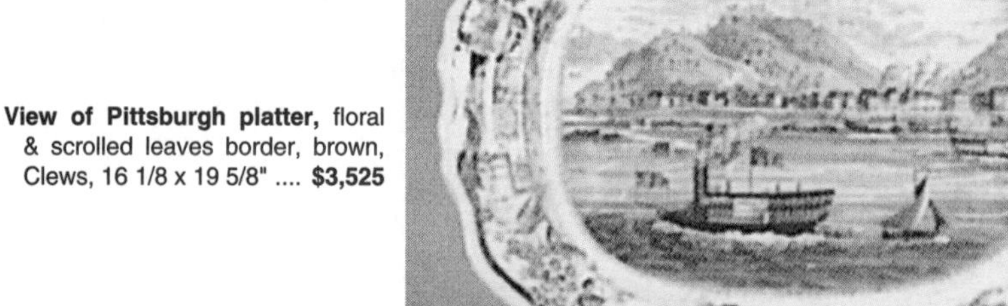

View of Pittsburgh platter, floral & scrolled leaves border, brown, Clews, 16 1/8 x 19 5/8" **$3,525**

While David Haviland had great success producing china in Limoges, France, for export to the United States, his early efforts were met with great resistance from local French artists who protested his break from tradition. Haviland's designs incorporated American styles and shapes, as the French were too ornate for American tastes. The protests became so intense that Haviland employees had to travel in groups to avoid being attacked. Eventually, though, the hostility subsided. Americans immediately embraced Haviland's quality and design, and exports rapidly increased. The Limoges facilities expanded to meet demand and Haviland continued to innovate. In 1880, Haviland produced a dinner service for the White House under the Rutherford B. Hayes administration. The service is currently housed at the Smithsonian.

Hull

In 1905 Addis E. Hull purchased the Acme Pottery Company in Crooksville, Ohio. In 1917 the A.E. Hull Pottery Company began to make a line of art pottery for florists and gift shops. The company also made novelties, kitchenware and stoneware.

Hull's Little Red Riding Hood kitchenware was manufactured between 1943 and 1957 and is a favorite of collectors, as are the beautiful matte glaze vases it produced.

In 1950 the factory was destroyed by a flood and fire, but by 1952 it was back in production. Hull added its newer glossy glazed pottery plus pieces sold in flower shops under the names Regal and Floraline. Hull's brown dinnerware lines achieved great popularity and were the main lines being produced prior to the plant's closing in 1986.

Hull U.S.A

H

References on Hull Pottery include: *Hull, The Heavenly Pottery*, 7th Edition, 2001 and *Hull, The Heavenly Pottery Shirt Pocket Price Guide*, 4th Edition, 1999, by Joan Hull. Also *The Dinnerwares Lines* by Barbara Loveless Click-Burke (Collector Books 1993) and *Robert's Ultimate Encyclopedia of Hull Pottery* by Brenda Roberts (Walsworth Publishing Co., 1992). -- Joan Hull, Advisor.

Basket, Tokay patt., No. 6, overhead branch handle, white ground, 8" h. **$95**

Bell, Sun-Glow patt., No. 87, closed or open handle, dark yellow or dark pink ground, 6 1/2" h., each (ILLUS. of two) **$100-200**

Bowl, 8" d., 4 1/2" h., House 'N Garden line, pour spout, Mirror Brown glaze w/ivory foam trim, marked "8 Lip Oven Proof U.S.A." ... **$18**

Casserole, cov., Sun-Glow patt., No. 51-7 1/2", 7 1/2" d. **$50**

Cookie jar, cov., figural Ginger Bread Man, No. 123, grey Flint Ridge line, 1980s, 12" h. (ILLUS. right with sand colored cookie jar) **$150**

Cookie jar, cov., Little Red Riding Hood patt., many design variations, each **$400-1,000**

Pitcher, 4 1/2" h., Early Utility ware, vertical ribs from base to bottom of handle, white thin horizontal line, wider dark brown line & a second thin white line directly below shoulder, marked "107 - H" in a circle & "36" below it **$78**

Teapot, cov., Magnolia Gloss patt., H-20-6 1/2", 1947-48 .... **$65**

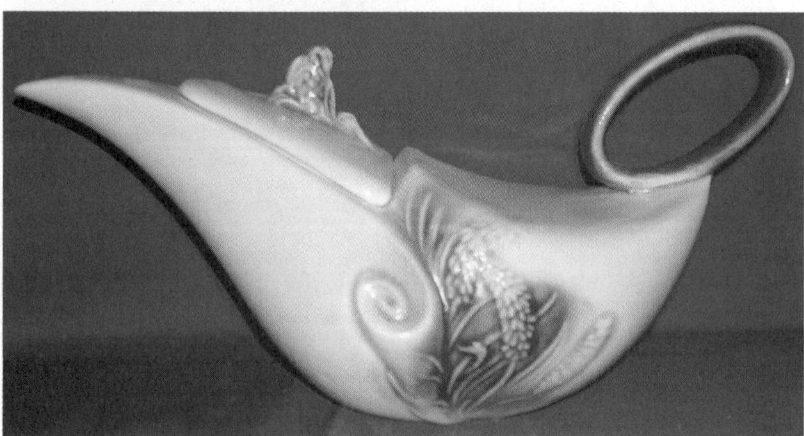

Teapot, cov., Parchment & Pine patt., S-11 .... **$105**

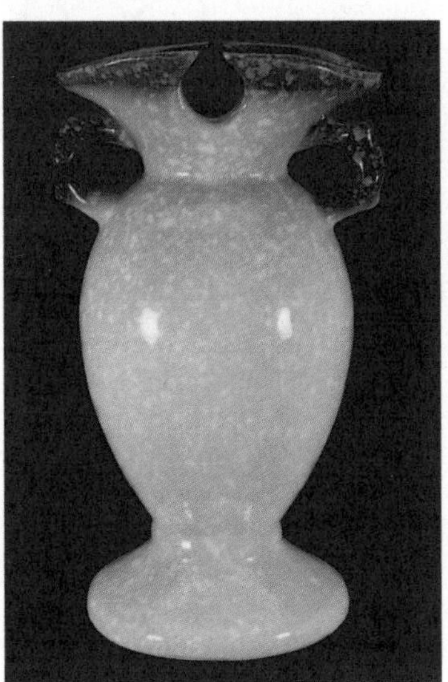

Vase, 6 1/2" h., Royal Woodland patt., pale turquoise w/white overall splotching, darker handles & rim, marked "Hull W4-6 1/2 U.S.A." **$38**

Vase, 6 1/2" h., Thistle patt., blue ground, No. 55 .... **$150**

Vase, 8 1/2" h., Open Rose (Camellia) patt., No. 126, hand & fan design **$325**

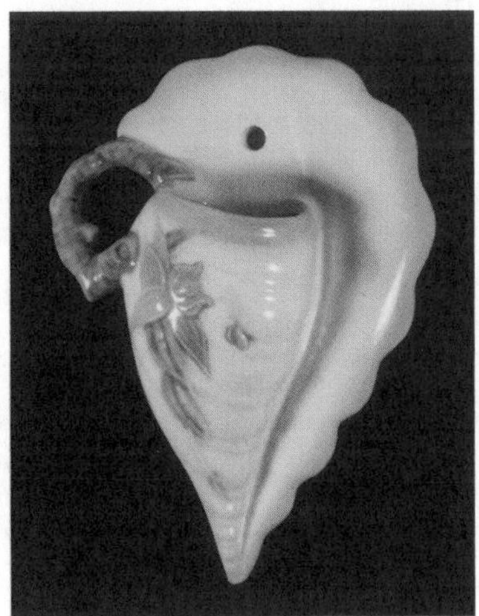

Wall pocket, Woodland Gloss patt., conch shell shape, No. W13-7 1/2", 7 1/2" l. ... **$95**

Because auctioneers usually attempt to start bidding at the value of the item they are selling, it's probably not wise to enter the bidding at that point. When no one opens the bidding at that level, the auctioneer will quickly seek a lower starting bid and work up to the sale price.

Hummel Figurines & Collectibles

The Goebel Company of Oeslau, Germany, first produced these porcelain figurines in 1934, having obtained the rights to adapt the beautiful pastel sketches of children by Sister Maria Innocentia (Berta) Hummel. Every design by the Goebel artisans was approved by the nun until her death in 1946. Although not antique, these figurines with the "M.I. Hummel" signature, especially those bearing the Goebel Company factory mark used from 1934 and into the early 1940s, are being sought by collectors, although interest may have peaked some years ago. A good reference is *Luckey's Hummel Figurines & Plates, Identification and Value Guide* by Carl F. Luckey (Krause Publications). Trademarks: TMK 1 - Crown - 1934-1950; TMK 2 - Full Bee 1940-1959; TMK 3 - Stylized Bee - 1958-1972; TMK 4 - Three Line Mark - 1964-1972; TMK 5 - Last Bee - 1970-1980; TMK 6 - Missing Bee - 1979-1991; TMK 7 - Hummel Mark - 1991-1999; TMK 8 - Goebel Bee - 2000-

A Fair Measure, #345, 4 3/4" h., new style, Trademark 5 .... **$350-450**

A Stitch in Time, #255, 6 3/4" h., Trademark 3 .... **$550-800**

Accordion boy, #185, 5 1/2" h., Trademark 2 .... **$425**

Adoration, #23/I, 6 1/4" h., Trademark 2 .... **$600-800**

Adoration, #23/I, 6 1/4" h., Trademark 6 .... **$430**

Advent Boy with Horse candleholder, #117, 3 1/2" h., Trademark 4 .... **$100-125**

Advent Girl with Fir Tree candlestick, #116, 3 1/2" h., Trademark 2 .... **$150-200**

Adventure Bound, #347, 7 1/4 x 8", Trademark 5 .... **$5,000-6,000**

Angel at Prayer font, #91/A, 4 3/4" h., Trademark 2 .... **$200-260**

Angel Cloud font, #206, 2 1/4 x 4 3/4", Trademark 2 .... **$250-350**

Angel Duet font, #146, 2 x 4 3/4", Trademark 3 .... **$250-275**

Angel Duet, #261, 5" h., Trademark 5 .... **$270**

Angel Lights candleholder, #241, 8 1/3 x 10 1/3", Trademark 5 .... **$400-500**

Angel Serenade, #214D (angel standing), color decoration, part of Nativity set, 3" h., Trademark 2 .... **$125-145**

Angel Serenade with lamb, #83, 5 1/2" h, Trademark 5 .... **$240**

Angel with Accordion, #238/B, 2 1/2" h., Trademark 4 .... **$125**

Angel with Lute candleholder, #III/38/I, 2 1/2" h., Trademark 2 .... **$250-300**

Angel with Trumpet, #238/C, 2 1/2" h., Trademark 4 .... **$125**

Angelic Song, #144, 4" h., Trademark 1 .... **$550**

Apple Tree Boy & Apple Tree Girl book ends, 5 1/4" h., Trademark 3, pr. **$425**

Apple Tree Boy, #142/I, 6" h., Trademark 5 .... **$400-450**

Apple Tree Boy table lamp, #230, 7 1/2" h., Trademark 3 .... **$375-400**

Apple Tree Boy, #142/3/0, 4" h., Trademark 2 .... **$300-350**

Apple Tree Boy, #142, 6" h., Trademark 2 .... **$600-700**

Apple Tree Girl table lamp, #229, 7 1/2" h., Trademark 2 .... **$900-1,000**

Apple Tree Girl, #141/3/0, 4 1/4" h., Trademark 6 .... **$150**

Artist (The), #304, 5 1/2" h., Trademark 3 .... **$2,000-3,000**

Auf Wiedersehen, #153/0, 5 3/4" h., Trademark 6 .... **$255**

Autumn Harvest, #355, 4 3/4" h., Trademark 6 .... **$250**

Ba-Bee Rings plaques, #30A & #30B, boy & girl, 5" d., Trademark 2, pr. **$250-350**

Ba-Bee Ring plaque, #30/B, boy, 5" d., Trademark 2 .... **$350-450**

Baker, #128, 4 3/4" h., Trademark 5 .... **$245**

Band Leader, #129, 4 1/4", Trademark 2 .... **$425**

Barnyard Hero, #195, 4" h., Trademark 5 .... **$200**

Bashful, #377, 4 3/4" h., Trademark 5 .... **$400-600**

Be Patient, #197/I, 6 1/4" h., Trademark 2 .... **$550-650**

Be Patient, #197/2/0, 4 1/4" h., Trademark 2 .... **$400-500**

Begging His Share, #9, 5 1/2" h., Trademark 1 .... **$750-900**

A Stitch in Time, #255, 6 3/4" h., Trademark 6 .... **$300**

Big Housecleaning, #363, 4" h., Trademark 4 .... **$1,500-2,500**

Bird Duet, #169, 4" h., Trademark 4 .... **$225-250**

Bird Watcher, #300, 5" h., Trademark 5 .... **$255**

Birthday Serenade, #218/2/0, reverse mold, 4 1/4" h., Trademark 3 .... **$400-450**

Birthday Serenade, #218/2/0, 4" h., Trademark 6 .... **$185**

Blessed Child (Infant of Krumbad), #78/III, 5 1/4" h., Trademark 3 .... **$75-100**

Blessed Event, #333, 5 1/2" h., Trademark 6 .... **$365**

Botanist (The), #351, 4 1/4" h., Trademark 6 .... **$200**

Boy with Toothache, #217, 5 1/2" h., Trademark 2 .. **$400-600**

Boy with Toothache, #217, 5 1/2" h., Trademark 6 .... **$225**

Book Worm, #3/III, 9 1/2" h., Trademark 3 .... **$1,600-1,800**

Book Worm, #3/I, 5 1/2" h., Trademark 3 .... **$600-700**

Call to Glory (Fahnentager), #739/I, 5 3/4" h., first issue 1994, three flags included **$265**

Carnival, #328, 5 3/4" h., Trademark 6 .... **$235**

Celestial Musician, #188, 7" h., Trademark 2 .... **$850-1,100**

Chef, Hello, #124/0, 6" h., Trademark 6 .... **$240**

Chick Girl, #57/0, 3 1/2" h., Trademark 2 .... **$310-375**

Chick Girl candy dish, #III/57, 5 1/4" h., Trademark 2.. **$580-650**

Chick Girl candy dish, #57/III, old style, 5 1/4" h., Trademark 3 .... **$300-350**

Chicken Licken, #385, 4 3/4" h., Trademark 5 .... **$350-400**

Child in Bed plaque, #137/B, 2 3/4" d., Trademark 2 .... **$250-350**

Chimney Sweep, #12/1, 6 1/2" h., Trademark 2 .... **$475**

Christmas Song, #343, 6 1/2" h., Trademark 6 .... **$240**

Cinderella, #337, new style, eyes closed, 5 1/2" h., Trademark 5 .... **$250-300**

Close Harmony, #336, 5 1/2" h., Trademark 5 .... **$365-395**

Coffee Break, #409, 4 1/4" h., 1984, exclusive special edition No. 8 for Members of the Goebel Collectors' Club **$300**

Confidentially, #314, 5 1/2" h., Trademark 3 .... **$1,000-1,500**

Congratulations, #17/0, early version, no socks, 6" h., Trademark 2 .... **$450-550**

Congratulations, #17/0, newer version, w/socks, 6 1/4" h., Trademark 3 .... **$250-300**

Coquettes, #179, 5" h., Trademark 6 .... **$325**

Cow (Ox), #214/K, Nativity set piece, 6 1/2" l., Trademark 2 .... **$160**

Crossroads, #331, 6 3/4" h., Trademark 2 .... **$4,000-5,000**

Culprits, #56A, 6 1/4" h., Trademark 2 .... **$375-425**

Daddy's Girl, #371, 4 3/4" h., Trademark 6 .... **$250**

Dealer display plaque, #187 (Moon Top), 4 x 5 1/2", Trademark 4 .... **$375-475**

Doctor, #127, 4 3/4" h., Trademark 2 .... **$300-350**

Doll Bath, #319, 5 1/4" h., Trademark 3 .... **$750-1,000**

Doll Mother, #67, 4 3/4" h., Trademark 2 .... **$600-700**

Duet, #130, 5 1/4" h., Trademark 3 .... **$450-475**

Easter Greetings, #378, 5" h., Trademark 5 .... **$245**

Evening Prayer (Abengebet), #495, 4" h., first issue 1992 .... **$110**

Eventide, #99, 4 3/4" h., Trademark5 .... **$400-500**

Fair Measure, #345, 6" h., Trademark 5 .... **$365**

Farm Boy, #66, 5 1/4" h., Trademark 3 .... **$300-325**

Farewell, #65/I, 4 3/4" h., Trademark 3 .... **$350-450**

Favorite Pet, #361, 4 1/2" h., Trademark 6 .... **$320**

Feathered Friends, #344, 4 3/4" h., Trademark 5 .... **$350-400**

Feeding Time, #199/0, 4 1/4" h., Trademark 3 .... **$300-350**

Feeding Time, #199, 5 3/4" h., Trademark 2 .... **$525-625**

Festival Harmony, #172/II, angel w/mandolin, 11" h., Trademark 3 .... **$700-800**

Festival Harmony, #173/0, 8", Trademark 6 .... **$355**

Flitting Butterfly plaque, #139, 2 1/2 x 2 1/2", Trademark 1 .... **$350-550**

Flower Madonna, #10/I, white, 9 1/2" h., Trademark 1 .... **$500-600**

Flower Vender, #381, 5 1/4" h., Trademark 6 .... **$275**

Follow the Leader, #369, 7" h., Trademark 4 .... **$1,350-1,400**

For Father, #87, 5 1/2" h., Trademark 2 .... **$400-530**

For Father, #87, 5 1/2" h., Trademark 4 .... **$325-350**

For Mother, #257, 5 1/4" h., Trademark 3 .... **$700-800**

For Mother, #257, 5 1/4" h., Trademark 6 .... **$225**

Forest Shrine, #183, 9" h., Trademark 6 .... **$625**

Friends, #136/1, 5 3/8" h., Trademark 6 .... **$225**

Friends, #136/V, 10 3/4" h., Trademark 2 .... **$2,000-3,000**

Gift from a Friend (Aus Nachbars Garten), #485, 5 1/4" h., exclusive edition 1991/92 M.I. Hummel Club, original box **$275**

Girl with Doll, #239B, 3 1/2" h., Trademark 4 .... **$100-200**

Flower Madonna, #10/I, color, 8 1/4" h., Trademark 3 .... **$575-675**

Globe Trotter, #79, 5" h., Trademark 1 .... **$500-750**

Globe Trotter, #79, 5" h., Trademark 2 .... **$350-450**

Going to Grandma's, #52/0, 4 3/4" h., Trademark 1 .... **$750-1,000**

Going to Grandma's, #52/I, 6" h., Trademark 2 .... **$550-650**

Good Friends table lamp, #228, 7 1/2" h., Trademark 3 .... **$550-650**

Good Friends, 4" h., Trademark 4 .... **$350-400**

Good Shepherd, #42/0, 6 1/4" h., Trademark 2 .... **$500-550**

Goose Girl, #47/II, 7 1/2" h., Trademark 2 .... **$700-900**

Goose Girl, #47/3/0, 4" h., Trademark 3 .... **$250-350**

Goose Girl, #47/II, 7 12/" h., Trademark 5 .... **$450-500**

Goose Girl, #47/3/0, 4 1/4" h., Trademark 6 .... **$185**

Good Hunting, #307, 5 1/4" h., Trademark 6 .... **$300-325**

Happiness, #86, 4 3/4" h., Trademark 1 .... **$400-500**

Happy Birthday, #176, 5 1/3" h., Trademark 1 .... **$1,150**

Happy Days, #150/0, 5 1/4" h., Trademark 5 .... **$325-350**

Happy Pastime, #69, 3 1/2" h., Trademark 3 .... **$350-450**

Happy Traveler, #109/0, 5" h., Trademark 2 .... **$275-350**

Hear Ye, Hear Ye, #15/0, 5" h., Trademark 5 .... **$225**

Hear Ye, Hear Ye, #15/I, 6" h., Trademark 1 .... **$1,600-1,700**

Heavenly Lullaby, #262, 3 1/2 x 5", Trademark 4 .... **$600-700**

Heavenly Protection, #88, 9 1/4" h., Trademark 2 .... **$1,300-1,600**

Heavenly Protection, #88/II, 9 1/4" h., Trademark 3 .... **$1,000-1,200**

Home From Market, #198/I, 5 3/4" h., Trademark 4 .... **$375-400**

I'm Carefree, #633, 4 3/4" h., signature on back, first issue 1994 .... **$875**

Joyful, #53, 4" h., Trademark 1 .... **$350-450**

Joyful candy box, #III/53, 6 1/4" h., Trademark 2 .... **$475-500**

Joyous News, #27/3, 4 1/4 x 4 3/4", Trademark 1 .... **$2,000**

Jubilee, #416, 6 1/4" h., 1980, 50 years, M.I. Hummel Figurines 1935-1985, "The Love Lives On" **$475**

Just Resting, #112/I, 5" h., Trademark 2 .... **$400-600**

Just Resting table lamp, #II/112, 7 1/2" h., Trademark 3 .... **$375-525**

Kiss Me, w/socks, 6" h., Trademark 4 .... **$400-450**

Knit One, Purl One, #432, 3" h., Trademark 5 .... **$130**

Knitting Lesson, #256, 7 1/2" h., Trademark 5 .... **$550-650**

Latest News, #184, inscribed "Munchener Presse," 5 1/4" h., Trademark 3 .... **$425-500**

Let's Sing ashtray, #114, 3 1/2 x 6 3/4", Trademark 4 .... **$250-350**

Little Bookkeeper, #306, 4 3/4" h., Trademark 3 .... **$1,000+**

Little Bookkeeper, #306, 4 3/4" h., Trademark 4 .... **$425**

Little Drummer, #240, 4 1/4" h., Trademark 3 .... **$245-260**

Little Fiddler, #2/0, 6" h., Trademark 3 .... **$350-400**

Little Gabriel, #32/0, 5" h., Trademark 3 .... **$250-300**

Little Goat Herder, #200/I, 5 1/2" h, Trademark 5 .... **$275**

Little Hiker, #16/2/0, 4 1/4" h., Trademark 2 .... **$250-350**

Little Nurse, #376, 4" h., Trademark 6 .... **$270**

Little Pharmacist, #322, 6" h., Trademark 6 .... **$265**

Lost Sheep, #68/0, 5 1/2" h., Trademark 2 .... **$325-350**

Little Sleeper, #171/4/0, 3" h., Trademark 6 .... **$115**

Little Sweeper, #171, 4 1/2" h., Trademark 5 .... **$200-250**

Madonna plaque, #48/II, 4 3/4 x 6", Trademark 2 .... **$375-525**

Make a Wish (Die Pusteblume), #475, 4 1/2" h., Trademark 6 .... **$225**

Max & Moritz, #123, 5 1/4" h., Trademark 5 .... **$265**

Merry Wanderer, #11/2/0, 4 1/4" h., Trademark 1 .... **$450-550**

Merry Wanderer plaque, #92, 4 3/4 x 5 1/8", Trademark 3 .... **$250-350**

Mischief Maker, #342, 5" h., Trademark 5 .... **$345**

Mother's Helper, #133, 5" h., Trademark 4 .... **$275**

Mountaineer, #315, 5 1/4" h., Trademark 4 .... **$400-450**

On Holiday, #350, 4 1/4" h., Trademark 6 .... **$165**

Out of Danger, #56/B, 6 1/2" h., Trademark 6 .... **$335**

Photographer (The), #178, 4 3/4" h., Trademark 5 .... **$345-370**

Pigtails, #2052, 3 1/4" h., M.I. Hummel Club Membership Year, 1999/2000, original box **$75**

Playmates, #58/I, 4 1/2" h., Trademark 3 .... **$400-500**

Postman, #119, 5" h., Trademark 3 .... **$300**

Prayer Before Battle, #20, 4 1/4" h., Trademark 1 .... **$650**

Puppy Love, #1, 5" h., Trademark 6 .... **$325**

Retreat to Safety plaque, #126, 4 3/4 x 5", Trademark 3 .... **$250-350**

Ring Around the Rosie, #348, 6 3/4" h., Trademark 5...... **$3,200**

Ride into Christmas, #396, 5 3/4" h., Trademark 4 .... **$2,000-2,500**

Ride into Christmas, #396, 5 3/4" h., Trademark 6......... **$525**

Saint George, #55, 6 3/4" h., Trademark 6 .... **$350**

School Boy, #82/2/0, 4" h., Trademark 2 .... **$400-500**

School Boy, #82/II, 7 1/2" h., Trademark 5 .... **$550-650**

School Girls, #177, 9 1/2" h., Trademark 2 .... **$3,000-4,000**

School Girl, #81/0, 5 1/4" h., Trademark 5 .... **$300-400**

Sensitive Hunter, #6, 4 3/4" h., Trademark†1 .... **$850-1,000**

Sensitive Hunter, #6/0, 4 3/4" h., Trademark 3 .... **$350-450**

Serenade, #85/0, 4 3/4" h., Trademark 3 .... **$200**

She Loves Me, She Loves Me Not!, #174, 4 1/4" h., Trademark 6 .... **$225**

Shepherd's Boy, #64, 5 1/2" h., Trademark 2 .... **$450-550**

Shining Light, #358, 2 3/4" h., Trademark 5 .... **$100**

Signs of Spring, #203/2/0, 4" h., Trademark 4 .... **$425-525**

Silent Night candleholder, #54, 5 1/2" l., 4 3/4" h., Trademark 1 .... **$1,100**

Sing Along (Auf los geht's los), #433, 4 1/2" h., Trademark 6 .... **$315**

Singing Lesson, #63, 2 3/4" h., Trademark 3 .... **$200-300**

Sister, #98/2/0, 4 3/4" h., Trademark 6 .... **$155**

Skier, #59, 5 1/4" h., Trademark 3 .... **$400-500**

Sleep Tight (Schlaf gut), #424, 4 3/4" h., Trademark 6......... **$240**

Smart Little Sister, #436, 4 3/4" h., Trademark 4 .... **$400-500**

Strolling Along, #5, 4 3/4" h., Trademark 2 .... **$750-950**

Star Gazer, #132, 4 3/4" h., Trademark 3 .... **$350**

Stormy Weather, 71, 6 1/4" h., Trademark 3 .... **$900-1,000**

Soldier Boy, #332, red cap, 6" h., Trademark 4 .... **$650**

Soloist, #135, 4 3/4" h., Trademark 2 .... **$325**

Sound of the Trumpet, #457, 3" h., Trademark 6 .... **$110**

Spring Cheer, #72, 5" h., Trademark 5 .... **$250-300**

Spring Dance, #353/0, 5 1/2" h., Trademark 6 .... **$365**

St. George, #55, 6 3/4" h., Trademark 5 .... **$400-450**

Standing Boy plaque, #168, 4 1/8 x 5 1/2", Trademark 2 .... **$800-900**

Storybook Time (Marchenstude), #458, 5" h., First Issue 1992 .... **$445**

Street Singer, #131, 5 1/2" h., Trademark 3 .... **$325**

Strolling Along, #5, 4 3/4" h., Trademark 2 .... **$750-950**

Supreme Protection, #364, 9 1/4" h., 1984, "1909-1984, In Celebration of the 75th Anniversary of the Birth of Sister M.I. Hummel" **$375**

Surprise, #94/I, 5 1/2" h., Trademark 3 .... **$450-550**

Sweet Greetings, #352, 4 1/4" h., Trademark 6 .... **$200**

Telling Her Secret, #196/0, 5 1/4" h., Trademark 5 .... **$365**

To Market, #49/3/0, 4" h., Trademark 1 .... **$500-650**

To Market, 6 1/4" h., Trademark 1 .... **$1,400-1,700**

Trumpet Boy, #97, 4 3/4" h., Trademark 2 .... **$300-400**

Trumpet Boy, #97, 4 3/4" h., Trademark 6 .... **$145**

Tuneful Goodnight plaque, #180, 4 3/4 x 5", Trademark 3 .... **$300-400**

Two Hands, One Treat (Rechts oder links?), #493, 4" h., 1991-99, M.I. Hummel Club **$125**

Umbrella Boy, #152, 8" h., Trademark 2 .... **$2,400-2,900**

Umbrella Boy, #152/0 A, 5" h., Trademark 3 .... **$1,000-1,200**

Umbrella Girl, #152/B, 8" h., Trademark 2 .... **$2,200-2,700**

Valentine Gift, #387, 5 3/4" h., 1972, exclusive special edition No. 1 for members of the Goebel Collectors' Club **$575**

Village Boy, #51/3/0, 4" h., Trademark 1 .... **$350-450**

Village Boy, #51/I, 7 1/4" h., Trademark 3 .... **$550-650**

Visiting an Invalid, #382, 5" h., Trademark 4 .... **$1,000-1,500**

Volunteers, #50/0, 5 1/2" h., Trademark 3 .... **$455-480**

Waiter, #154/0, 6" h., Trademark 2 .... **$375-475**

Wash Day, #321, 5 3/4" h., Trademark 3 .... **$750-1,000**

Watchful Angel, #194, 6 1/2" h., Trademark 3 .... **$600-700**

Wayside Devotion, #28/II, 7 1/2" h., Trademark 1 .... **$1,500**

Wayside Devotion, #28/III, 8 3/4" h., Trademark 2 .... **$1,000-1,200**

Wayside Harmony, #111/3/0, 3 3/4" h., Trademark 3 .... **$200-300**

Weary Wanderer, #204, 6" h., Trademark 4 .... **$400-500**

We Congratulate, #220/2/0, 4" h., Trademark 2 .... **$475-575**

What Now?, #422, 5 3/4" h., 1983, exclusive special edition No. 7 for members of the Goebel Collectors' Club **$375**

Whitsuntide, #163, 7 1/4" h., Trademark 1 .... **$1,000-1,200**

Whitsuntide, #163, 6 1/2" h., Trademark 6 .... **$325**

Worship, #84, 5" h., Trademark 1 .... **$475-625**

Worship, #84/V, 13" h., Trademark 4 .... **$1,250-1,350**

Hummel mini glossary:

Open Edition: Figurine currently in production.

Closed Edition: Figurine no longer manufactured.

Limited Edition: Figurine produced for a specific time period or in a limited quantity.

Members' Exclusive Edition: Figurine created only for Hummel club members.

Expired Edition: Hummel club exclusive figurine that is no longer available.

Ironstone

The first successful ironstone was patented in 1813 by C.J. Mason in England. The body contains iron slag incorporated with the clay. Other potters imitated Mason's ware, and today much hard, thick ware is lumped under the term ironstone. Earlier it was called by various names, including graniteware. Both plain white and decorated wares were made throughout the 19th century. Tea Leaf Lustre ironstone was made by several firms.

General

Chamber pot, cov., Atlantic shape, all-white, T. & R. Boote **$125-150**

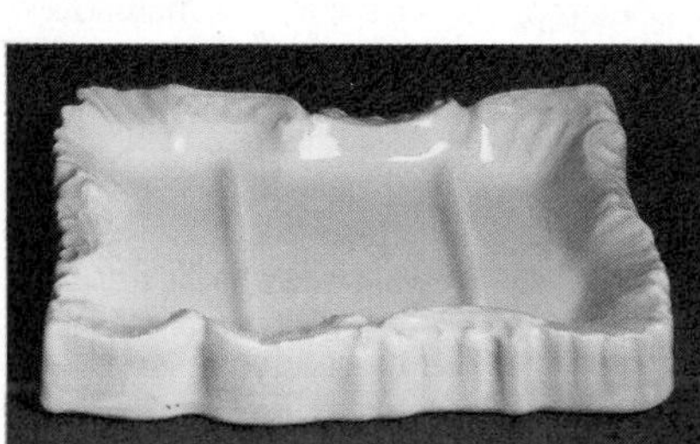

Soap slab, rectangular w/molded scroll edges, all-white, marked "ELO" [East Liverpool, Ohio] **$20-30**

Sugar bowl, cov., Four Square Wheat shape, all-white, unmarked **$80**

Compote, open, oval, President shape, all-white, John Edwards **$350-400**

Soup tureen, cover & undertray, Gothic Octagon shape, all-white, Wedgwood & Co., 3 pcs. **$900**

Syllabub cup, Hyacinth shape, all-white, Wedgwood & Co., ca. 1865 .... **$45**

Teapot, cov., all-white, Plain Seashore shape, molded dolphin on handle & finial, by W. & E. Corn, ca. 1885 .... **$125-150**

Teapot, cov., Full Paneled Gothic shape, all-white, John Alcock, ca. 1850 .... **$275-300**

Vegetable tureen, cov., Sydenham shape, all-white, T. & R. Boote, 1853 .... **$190-240**

Tea Leaf Ironstone

Butter dish, cover & insert, Chelsea patt., Alfred Meakin, the set (minor flaws) **$60**

Butter dish, cover & insert. Brocade patt., Alfred Meakin, flanks inside base, chip on insert **$110**

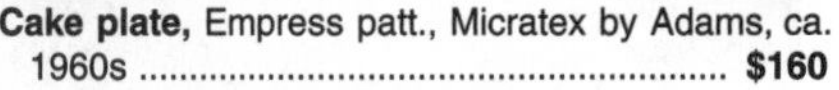

Cake plate, Empress patt., Micratex by Adams, ca. 1960s **$160**

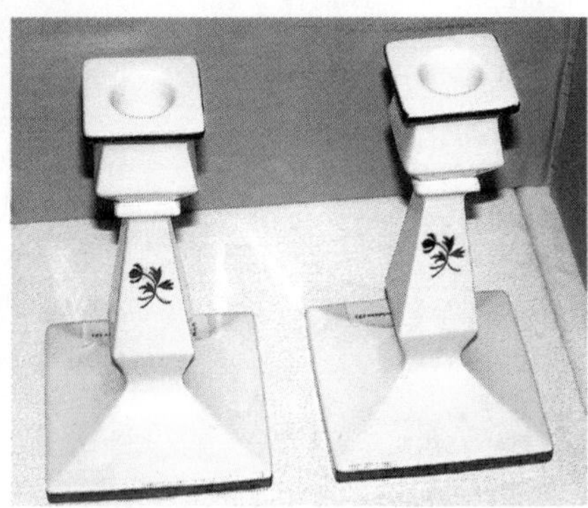

Candlesticks, square, Red Cliff, ca. 1970, pr. **$360**

Chamber pot, cov., Cable shape, Anthony Shaw **$175**

Compote, open, square w/rounded corners, pedestal base, H. Burgess **$185**

Creamer & cov. sugar bowl, child's, slant-sided shape, Mellor Taylor, pr. **$100**

Creamer, Chinese shape, Anthony Shaw **$410**

Chamber pot, open, King Charles patt., Mayer **$100**

The tea leaf decoration probably orginated from a superstition that finding a complete open tea leaf at the bottom of a tea cup would bring good luck.

Coffeepot, cov., Woodland patt., W. & E. Corn, minor flaws **$60**

Creamer, Maidenhair Fern patt., T. Wilkinson **$150**

Gravy boat with attached undertray, Empress patt., Micratex by Adams, ca. 1960 .... **$80**

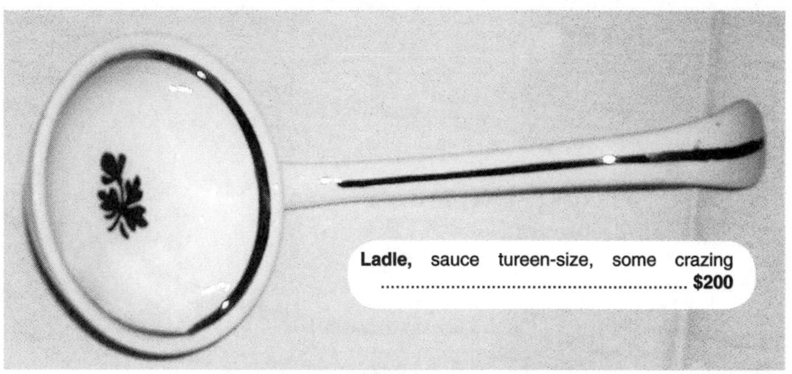

Ladle, sauce tureen-size, some crazing **$200**

Mustache cup & saucer, Edge Malkin, professional rim repair **$500**

Pitcher, 8" h., Blanket Stitch shape, Alcock **$140**

Pitcher, 8" h., Square Ridged shape, Wedgwood **$50**

Pitcher, water, Cable shape, Anthony Shaw, rare **$1,200**

Punch bowl, Cable shape, Anthony Shaw **$400**

Teapot, cov., Scroll shape, Alfred Meakin **$160**

Toothbrush vase, cylindrical w/ molded handles near pedestal base, drain holes, no underplate, possibly by Shaw **$850**

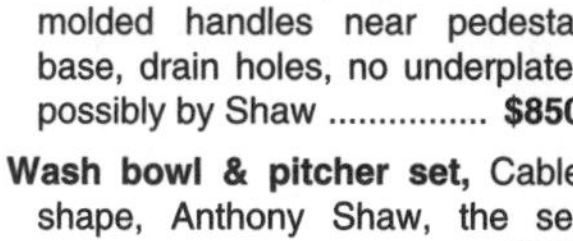

Wash bowl & pitcher set, Cable shape, Anthony Shaw, the set **$225**

Platter, oval, Fleur-de-Lis Chain patt., Wedgwood & Co., large **$50**

Vegetable dish, cov., Bullet patt., A. Shaw, minor flaws **$65**

Salt & pepper shakers, Empress patt., Micratex by Adams, ca. 1960s, pr. **$130**

Ironstone can darken with age, but it should never be cleaned with chlorine bleach, as it will destroy the glaze.

Teapot, cov., Ginger Jar patt., unmarked, repair to spout **$60**

Vegetable dish, cov., oval, Edge Malkin $325

Wash bowl & pitcher set, Chrysanthemum patt., H. Burgess, the set $575

Tea Leaf Variants

Chamber pot, cov., Pre-Tea Leaf patt., Niagara shape, E. Walley $1,050

Coffeepot, cov., Wheat in Meadow shape, lustre band trim, Powell & Bishop $325

Creamer, Wrapped Sydenham shape, lustre bands & pinstripes, Edward Walley $260

Cup & saucer, handleless, Pre-Tea Leaf patt., Niagara shape, E. Walley $90

Gravy boat, Scallops patt., Sydenham shape, E. Walley $250

Chamber pot, cov., Grape Octagon shape, lustre band trim, E. Walley, minor flaws .. $150

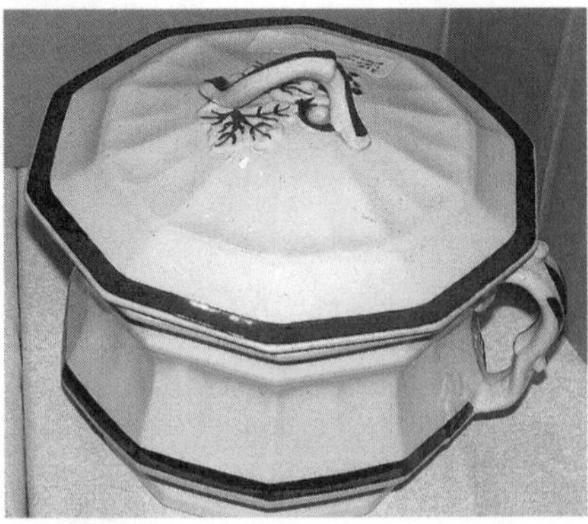

Traditional tea leaf ironstone consists of a tea leaf motif with three leaves and a bud in a copper or gold lustre created by adding copper or gold oxide to the glaze. Current collectors, however, tend to consider any lustre on ironstone to be tea leaf ironstone regardless of the actual motif used.

Coffeepot, cov., Pinwheel patt., Grape Octagon shape, E. Walley, slight crazing on cover **$230**

Pitcher, 7 3/4" h., Laurel Wreath patt., lustre trim, Elsmore & Forster, minor flaws **$325**

Vegetable dish, cov., Reverse Teaberry patt., Portland shape, Elsmore & Forster **$380**

Teapot, cov., Teaberry patt., Ring O' Hearts shape, J. Furnival **$650**

Mug, Gothic shape, paneled sides, lustre band, Livesley & Powell **$100**

Posset cup, Tobacco Leaf patt., Tulip shape, Elsmore & Forster **$325**

Sauce tureen, cov., Gothic Cameo shape, lustre band trim, Edward Walley **$250**

Sauce tureen, cover, undertray & ladle, Moss Rose patt., H. Burgess, the set **$375**

Soap dish, cover & insert, Lily of the Valley shape, lustre band trim, chip inside lip, Anthony Shaw, the set **$205**

Sugar bowl, cov., Quartered Rose shape, copper lustre bands & cobalt blue plumes, minor flaws, J. Furnival **$180**

Syrup pitcher w/hinged metal lid, Moss Rose patt., George Scott **$325**

Teapot, cov., Moss Rose patt. **$100**

Teapot, cov., Quartered Rose shape, copper lustre bands & cobalt blue plumes, possibly J. Furnival **$225**

Vegetable dish, cov., Quartered Rose shape, copper lustre bands & trim & cobalt blue plumes, slight flaws **$250**

Waste bowl, Gothic shape, Chelsea Grape patt., minor flaws **$35**

Toothbrush vase, Teaberry patt., Heavy Square shape, Clementson Bros., slight flaws **$1,350**

Lefton China

The Lefton China Company was the creation of Mr. George Zoltan Lefton who migrated to the United States from Hungary in 1939. In 1941 he embarked on a new career and began shaping a business that sprang from his passion for collecting fine china and porcelains. Though his funds were very limited, his vision was to develop a source from which to obtain fine porcelains by reviving the postwar Japanese ceramic industry, which dated back to antiquity. As a trailblazer, George Zoltan Lefton soon earned the reputation as "The China King".

Counted among the most desirable and sought after collectibles of today, Lefton items such as Bluebirds, Miss Priss, Angels, all types of dinnerware and tea-related items are eagerly acquired by collectors. As is true with any antique or collectible, prices may vary, depending on location, condition and availability.

For additional information on the history of Lefton China, its factories, marks, products and values, readers should consult *Collector's Encyclopedia of Lefton China*, Books I and II and *The Lefton Price Guide* by Loretta DeLozier.

Tea set: cov. teapot, cov. sugar bowl & creamer; Elegant Rose patt., oval upright cylindrical ribbed bodies, decorated w/clusters of large red roses & green leaves on a white ground, sponged gold trim, ca. 1955-65 .... **$200-250**

Teapot, cov., figural Dutch Girl, blonde hair, wide white apron & dark blue dress, No. 2699 .... **$225-250**

Teapot, cov., footed squatty bulbous lobed body w/ serpentine spout, ring handle & cover finial, Rose Chintz patt., ca. 1970s **$35**

Teapot, cov., individual size, Rose Chintz patt., ca. 1960s **$20**

Lenox

The Ceramic Art Company was established at Trenton, New Jersey, in 1889 by Jonathan Coxon and Walter Scott Lenox. In addition to true porcelain, it also made a Belleek-type ware. Renamed Lenox Company in 1906, it is still in operation today.

Game plates, 9" d., ivory ground, h.p. in the center w/a vignette w/a different game bird perched or in flight, narrow gilt border band, artist-signed, green printed marks, ca. 1925, set of 12 (ILLUS. flanking the equestrian fox hunt plate) **$5,040**

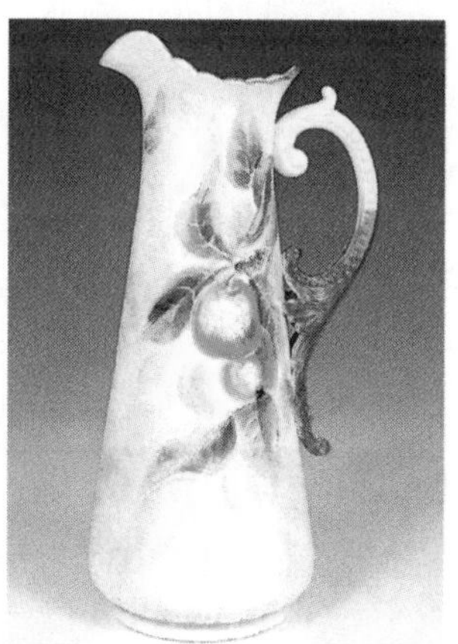

Pitcher, 13" h., tankard-type, footed tall gently tapering cylindrical sides w/a scalloped rim & large arched rim spout, fancy C- scroll handle, h.p. w/large red cherry on a leafy branch, pale yellow to brick-red handle, artist-signed, early 20th c. **$196**

Plate, 10 3/8" d., cabinet-type, a wide maroon rim band decorated w/ornate gilt floral swags & scrolls, the center h.p. w/a bust portrait of a lovely maiden w/long brown hair holding a cluster of pink roses, Ceramic Art Company monogram & Lenox wreath mark, artist-signed, ca. 1903-07 .... **$1,434**

Plates, 10 1/2" d., each finely h.p. w/a different species of pheasant in their natural habitat, wide gold rim band w/a rinceau scroll within seeded bands, green printed marks, artist-signed, ca. 125, set of 12 (ILLUS. of part) **$4,560**

Service plates, round w/slightly scalloped rim, an ivory center decorated in the middle w/a small flower-filled urn within a floral ring, the wide border decorated w/pale blue panels centered by floral urns & separated by narrow floral bars, base marked "Made Expressly for Ovington Bros. New York - 1445/A.326," 10 1/2" d., set of 10 .... **$1,200**

Tea set: 6" h. cov. teapot, 3 3/4" h. cov. sugar bowl & 4" h. creamer; each of bulbous ovoid form wrapped around the body w/slender scrolls & starburst designs in sterling silver, each w/the green laurel leaf mark, the set **$288**

Teapot, cov., Butler's Pantry Series, Sunday Brunch design, tapering cylindrical ruffled form, undecorated, modern **$45**

Teapot, cov., Butler's Pantry Series, tapering cylindrical form w/molded V-shaped panels, undecorated, modern **$45**

Teapot, cov., Summer Enchantment patt., footed squatty spherical body w/serpentine spout, C-form handle & domed cover w/figural butterfly finial, colorful butterfly & vine decoration, modern **$75**

Limoges

Charger, large rounded shape w/an ornate scroll-molded gold border, h. p. w/a scene of two battling brown stags against a shaded ground w/ leaves in shades of yellow, green & lavender, 13" d. **$201**

Fish set: 11 x 24" oval fish tray, twelve matching 9 1/2" d. plates & a 7 1/4" l. sauceboat & underplate; each piece w/a gently scalloped rim & paneled sides & each h.p. w/a different game fish, a lake landscape & a flower, bases marked "B.B. H. Limoges, France," the set **$1,668**

Pitcher, 14 1/2" h., tankard-type, a gold & brown ringed base below the slightly tapering cylindrical body w/a reddish brown D-form handle, h.p. w/a friar seated at a tavern table, artist-signed **$518**

Punch set: punch bowl, base & ten champagne-style stems; the footed bowl w/deep rounded & flaring sides h.p. around the sides w/large gold leafy grapevines on stems against a pale blue shaded to white ground, on a matching base w/large gold paw feet, the saucer-shaped matching stems w/a wide shallow round bowl on a simple stem, mark of Tressemann & Vogt, Limoges, late 19th - early 20th c., bowl 16" d., 7" h., base 3 1/2" h., stems each 3 1/2" h., some rubbing to gold, the set **$1,035**

Teapot, cov., wide squatty bulbous body w/low domed cover & knob finial, C-form handle, serpentine spout, white w/gold bands on the spout, rim & handle, marks of Tressemann & Vogt, Limoges, France, ca. 1907-1919, four-cup size **$150**

Tea set: one-cup cov. teapot, open sugar, creamer & oblong tray; each piece painted w/colorful roses, a gold wave scroll band around the teapot & creamer neck, gold loop handles & teapot finial, marks of Gèrard, Dufraisseix & Abbot, Limoges, France, ca. 1900-41, the set **$900**

Lladro

Spain's famed Lladro porcelain manufactory creates both limited- and non-limited-edition figurines as well as other porcelains. The classic simple beauty of the figures and their subdued coloring make them readily recognizable and they have an enthusiastic following.

"Chit Chat", No. 5466, 1988 to present, 7 3/4" h. **$140**

A Stitch in Time, No. 5344, 1986 to present, 9" h. **$475**

Aerobics Scissor Figure, No. 5336, 6" h., 1985 to present **$200**

Afghan, No. 1069, 1969-85, 11 1/2" h. **$450**

All Aboard, No. 7619, 5 1/4" h., LCS limited edition, 1992-93 .... **$312**

Allegory of Liberty, No. 5819, 20 1/2" h., 1991 to present **$1,250**

Andean Fluteplayer, No. 2174, 1987-90, 11 1/2" h. **$275**

Angel Tree Topper, No. 5831, 1991, 7 1/4" h. **$120**

Angel with Violin, No. 1324, artist-signed, 12 1/4" h., 1976-85 .... **$200**

Angela, No. 5211, 7" h., 1984 to present **$165**

Angelic Cymbalist, No. 5876, artist-signed, limited edition, 1992, 7 1/4" h., ... **$200**

Angelic Melody, No. 5963, 1993 to present, 7 1/4" h. **$160**

Angelic Voice, No. 5724, 1990 to present, 6 1/4" h. **$84**

Angels Group, No. 4542, 1969 to present, 6 1/2" h. **$121**

At the Ball, No. 5859, 6 1/4" h., 1992 to present **$215**

Autumn, No. 5218, 1984 to present, 7 3/4" h. **$160**

Avoiding the Goose, No. 5033, 1979-93, 9 3/4" h. **$295**

Baby Jesus, No. 1388, 1981 to present, 3 1/4" h. **$150**

Barnyard Scene, No. 5659, 1990 to present, 9 1/2" h. **$160**

Barrow of Fun (A), No. 5460, 1988 to present, 8 1/4" h. **$390**

Bashful Bather, No. 5455, 1988 to present, 5" h. **$120**

Basket of Love, NO. 7622, 1994 to present, LCS Special limited edition, 9 1/2" h.................... **$350**

Beagle Puppy, No. 1072,, 1969 to present, 2 1/4" h. **$200**

Bear Seated, No. 1206, 1972-8, 3" h. **$100**

Best Friend, No. 7620, signed, 1993 to present, 6 1/2" h. **$298**

Beth, No. 1358, 1978-93, 7 1/2" h. **$188**

Big Sister, No. 5735, 1991 to present, 6 3/4" h. **$550**

Bird Watcher, No. 4730, 1970-85, 6 1/4" h. **$225**

Black Angel, No. 4537, 4 1/2" h., 1969 to present **$75**

Black Bride (The), No. 5439, 1987 to present, 11 3/4" h. **$295**

Blustery Day, No. 5588, 1989-93, 6" h. **$175**

Bongo Beat, No. 5157, 1982 to present, 9" h. **$154**

Bowing Crane, No. 1613, 1989 to present, 7 3/4" h. **$279**

Boy Awaking, No. 4870, 1974 to present, 8 1/2" h. **$44**

Boy Meets Girl, No. 1188, 1972-89, 8 1/2" h. **$295**

Boy Thinking, No. 4876, 8 1/2" h., 1974-93 .... **$65**

Boy with Dog, No. 4522, 1970 to present, 7 1/2" h. **$143**

Boy with Goat, No. 4506, 1969-85, 10 1/2" h. **$200**

Boy with Guitar, No. 4614, 7 1/2" h., 1969-79 .... **$150**

Boy with Smoking Jacket, No. 4900, 1974-83, 7 3/4" h....... **$195**

Bridal Portrait, No. 5742, 1991 to present, 13 1/4" h. **$425**

Budding Blossoms, No. 1416, 1982 to present, 10 1/4" h. **$198**

Butterfly Girl, No. 1403, 1982-88, 6" h. **$475**

Can I Play?, No. 7610, 1990, LCS Special Edition, 8 1/4" h. **$463**

Car in Trouble, No. 1375, limited edition of 1,500, 1978, 16 3/4" h. **$6,500**

Carnival Couple, No. 4882, 1974 to present, 10 1/4" h. **$300**

Cart (The), No. 1245, 1973-81, 8 1/2" h. **$450**

Cat, No. 5113, 1982 to present, 5 1/4" h. **$55**

Cathy and Her Doll, No. 1380, 1978-8, 12 1/4" h. **$450**

Centaur Boy, No. 1013, 1969-89, 8 1/4" h. **$325**

Centaur Girl, No. 1012, 1969-89, 9 1/2" h. **$200**

Chinese Angel, No. 4536, 1969 to present, 5 1/2" h. **$75**

Chrysanthemum, No. 4990, 1978 to present, 11 1/2" h. **$180**

Cinderella, No. 4828, 1972 to present, 9 3/4" h. **$150**

Circus Magic, No. 5892, 1992 to present, 10 1/2" h. **$450**

Circus Sam, No. 5472, 1988 to present, 8 1/2" h. **$130**

Claudette, No. 5755, 1991-93, 14 1/4" h. **$285**

Clean Up Time, No. 4838, 1973-93, 7 1/2" h. **$75**

Clown with Clock, No. 5056, 1980-85, 11 3/4" h. **$640**

Clown with Concertina, No. 1027, 1969-93, 17 3/4" h. **$650**

Clown's Head with Bowler Hat, No. 5130, 1982 to present, 9 3/4" h. **$325**

Comforting Her Friend, No. 1326, 1976-81, 11" h. **$500**

Cook in Trouble, No. 4608, 1969-85, 9 1/2" h. **$625**

Coy, No. 5011, 1978 to present, 10 1/4" h. **$78**

Dancing Crane, No. 1614, 1989 to present, 11 1/2" h. **$279**

Death of the Swan, No. 4855, 5" h., 1973 to present **$225**

Debbie and Her Doll, No. 1379, 1978-85, 10 1/2" h. **$700**

Demure Centaur Girl, No. 5320, 1985-90, 5" h. **$325**

Dog and Cat, No. 5032, 1979 to present, 6 3/4" h. **$140**

Dog and Snail, No. 1139, 1971-81, 6" h. **$680**

Dog in the Basket, No. 1128, 1971-85, 7 1/2" h. **$340**

Dogs - Bust, No. 2067, 1977-79, 7" h. **$950**

Doncel with Roses, No. 4757, 1971-79, 10 1/2" h. **$600**

Dress Rehearsal, No. 5497, 1988 to present, 7 1/2" h. **$255**

Dressmaker, No. 4700, 1970-93, 14 1/4" h. **$363**

Dutch Girl, No. 4860, 1974-85, 10 1/4" h. **$300**

Dutchgirl with Braids, No. 5063, 1980-85, 9 3/4" h. **$395**

Elephant Promenade, No. 5802, 1991 to present, 15 1/4" h... **$479**

Elephants Walking, No. 1150, 1971 to present, 14 1/2" h. **$358**

Embroiderer, No. 4865, 1974 to present, 11" h. **$425**

English Lady, No. 5324, 1985 to present, 10 1/4" h. **$249**

Eskimo Riders, No. 5353, 1986 to present, 6 1/2" h. **$173**

Exquisite Scent, No. 1313, 1974-90, 11" h. **$400**

Fall Clean-Up, No. 5286, 1985 to present, 13" h. **$385**

Feeding the Ducks, No. 4849, 1973 to present, 6 1/2" h. **$235**

Feeding the Pigeons, No. 5428, 1987-90, 9" h. **$590**

Fisher Boy, No. 4809, 1972 to present, 8 1/2" h. **$115**

Fishing with Grandpa, No. 5215, 1984 to present, 18" h. **$538**

Flower Song, No. 7607, 1988 LCS limited edition, 7" h. **$498**

Flowers of the Season, No. 1454, 1983 to present, 11" h. **$1,750**

Follow Me, No. 5722, 1990 to present, 4 1/2" h. **$96**

Following Her Cats, No. 1309, 9 1/2" h., 1974 to present **$195**

Full Moon, No. 1438, 1983-88, 7 1/2" h. **$610**

Garden Classic, No. 7617, 1991, LCS limited edition, 9" h. **$600**

Garden Song, No. 7618, 1992 LCS limited edition, 8 3/4" H........ **$280**

Garden Treasure, No. 5591, 1989-93, 4 3/4" h. **$175**

Geisha, No. 4807, 1972-93, 12 1/4" h. **$400**

Giddy Up, No. 5664, 1990 to present, 4 1/4" h. **$129**

Gift of Beauty, No. 5775, 1991 to present, 8 3/4" h. **$550**

Girl and Sparrow, No. 4738, 1971-79, 11 1/2" h. **$600**

Girl Kneeling and Tulips, No. 5041, 1980-81, 4 1/4" h. **$525**

Girl Manicuring, No. 1082, 1969-85, 7 1/2" h. **$188**

Girl Shampooing, No. 1148, 1971-85, 8 1/2" h. **$300**

Girl with Doll, No. 1211, 1972-93, 8 1/2" h. **$370**

Girl with Goose and Dog, No. 4866, 1974-93, 10 1/2" h..... **$225**

Girl with Goose, No. 1052, 1969 to present, 9" h. **$125**

Girl with Goose, No. 4815, 1972-91, 12 1/4" h. **$295**

Girl with Heart, No. 1028, 1969-70, 13" h. **$450**

Girl with Lamb, No. 1010, 1969-93, 8 1/2" h. **$200**

Girl with Lamb, No. 4584, 1969-93, 10 1/2" h. **$150**

Girl with Lantern, No. 4910, 1974-90, 8 1/2" h. **$275**

Girl with Mother's Shoe, No. 1084, 1969-85, 7 1/2" h. **$225**

Girl with Pig, No. 1011, 1969 to present, 7" h. **$90**

Girl with Pigeons, No. 4915, 1974-9, 8 1/2" h. **$300**

Goddess and the Unicorn (The), No. 6007, 1993 to present, 10 3/4" h. **$899**

Golfing Couple, No. 1453, 1983 to present, 13 1/4" h. **$325**

Good Bear, No. 1205, 1972-89, 4 3/4" h. **$100**

Goya Lady, No. 5125, 1982-90, 12 1/2" h. **$250**

Graceful Offering, No. 5773, 1991 to present, 12" h. **$550**

Gymnast Balancing Ball, No. 5332, 1985-88, 6 1/4" h. **$200**

Heather, No. 1359, 1978-93, 5" h. **$195**

Heavenly Chimes, No. 5723, 1990 to present, 3" h. **$67**

Hebrew Student, No. 4684, 1970-85, 11 1/4" h. **$500**

Henry VIII, No. 1384, 1978-93, 12 1/4" h. **$800**

Here Comes the Bride, No. 1446, 1983 to present, 13 3/4" h... **$650**

High Society, No. 1430, 1982-93, 14 1/4" h. **$360**

Horse's Group White, No. 1022, 1969 to present, 17 1/4" h. **$1,000**

Horseman, No. 1037, 1969-70, 16" h. **$1,775**

Horses Galloping, No. 4655, 1969 to present, 11 1/2" h. **$399**

How You've Grown, No. 5474, 1988 to present, 6 1/4" h. **$153**

I Love You Truly, No. 1528, 1987 to present, 14 1/2" h. **$420**

In Full Relave, No. 5815, 1991 to present, 11 3/4" h. **$600**

In the Garden, No. 4978, 1977-81, 11" h. **$800**

In the Gondola, No. 1350, 1978 to present, 17 3/4" l. **$2,900**

Ingenue, No. 5487, 1988 to present, 8" h. **$79**

Island Girl, No. 2171, 1987-90, 9 1/2" h. **$170**

Japanese Girl Flower Decorating, No. 4840, 1973 to present, 7 1/2" h. **$250**

Jazz Horn, No. 5832, 1991 to present, 8 3/4" h. **$175**

Jester's Serenade, No. 5932, 1993 to present, 14 1/2" h. **$1,098**

JKiyoko, No. 1450, 1983 to present, 7" h. **$275**

La Tarentela, No. 1123, 1971-75, 16" h. **$2,100**

Lady from Majorca, No. 5240, 1984-90, 11 1/2" h. **$250**

Laura, No. 1360, 1978-93, 9" h. **$180**

Lawyer, No. 1089, 1971-73, 11" h. **$383**

Lehua, No. 1532, 1987-90, 11" h. **$345**

Lesson Shared (A), No. 5475, 1988 to present, 6" h. **$117**

Let's Make Up, No. 5555, 1989 to present, 7 3/4" h. **$214**

Litter of Fun, No. 5364, 1986 to present, 8 1/2" h. **$311**

Little Bo Peep, No. 1312, 1974-85, 6 1/2" h. **$250**

Little Boy Bullfighter, No. 5116, 1982-85, 10 1/4" h. **$400**

Little Boy Bullfighter, No. 5117, 1982-85, 9 3/4" h. **$400**

Little Dogs on Hip, No. 1311, 1974 to present, 9 3/4" h. **$195**

Little Dreamers, No. 5772, 1991 to present, 3 1/2" h. **$145**

Little Eagle Owl, No. 2020, 1975-85, 6 1/4" h. **$375**

Little Friends, No. 6129, 1994 to present, signed, 9 1/2" h...... **$250**

Little Gardener, No. 4726, 1970-78, 9 3/4" h. **$295**

Little Girl with Slippers, No. 4523, 1969-93, 5 1/2" h. **$78**

Little Jester, No. 5203, 1984-93, 7 3/4" h. **$135**

Little League, Catcher, No. 5290, 1985-90, 6 1/2" h. **$400**

Little Pals, No. 7600, 1985, LCS limited edition, 8 3/4" h. **$2,500**

Little Pals, No. 7600, 1985, limited edition, 8 3/4" h. **$1,800**

Little Traveler, No. 7602, 1986 LCS limited edition, 8 1/2" h. **$899**

Little Troubador, No. 1314, 1974-79, 13" h. **$1,200**

Lonely, No. 2076, 1978 to present, 8 1/4" h. **$80**

Looking for Refuge, No. 4891, 1974-79, 11 1/2" h. **$2,500**

Love Letters, Rockwell (RL-400) **$763**

Lovers in the Park, No. 1274, 1974-93, 11 3/4" h. **$1,050**

Madame Butterfly, No. 4991, 1978 to present, 11 3/4" h. **$175**

Madonna Head, No. 4649, 1969 to present, 8 1/4" h. **$140**

Maja Head, No. 4668, 1969-85, 12 1/4" h. **$750**

Mariko, No. 1421, 1982 to present, 16" h. **$900**

Mayumi, No. 1449, 1983 to present, 9 1/2" h. **$275**

Michiko, No. 1447, 1983 to present, 8 1/4" h. **$275**

Milanese Lady, No. 5323, 1985 to present, 10 1/4" h. **$228**

Mimi, No. 4985, 1978-80, 10 1/2" h. **$513**

Mini Seal Family, No. 5318, 1985-90, 5 1/2" h. **$225**

Miniature Angels Ornaments, No. 1604, 1988, limited edition, 2" h., set of 3............................... **$375**

Moon Glow, No. 1436, 1983-88, 7" h. **$550**

Mother with Child & Lamb, No. 5299, 9 1/2" h., 1985-88...... **$365**

Motherhood, No. 4575, 1969 to present, 13" h. **$150**

Music Time, No. 5430, 7 1/2" h., 1987-90 .... **$495**

My Best Friend, No. 5401, 6 1/2" h., 1987- **$195**

My Buddy, No. 7609, 1989, LCS limited edition, 8" h. **$390**

My New Pet, No. 5549, 1989-, 8 1/4" h. **$125**

My Wedding Day, No. 1494, 15 1/2" h., 1986- **$975**

Naptime, No. 5448, 1987 to present, 4 3/4" h. **$149**

Nature's Gifts, No. 5774, 1991 to present, 13 1/4" h. **$575**

Naughty Dog, No. 4982, 1978 to present, 7 3/4" h. **$250**

New Playmates, No. 5456, 4 3/4" h., 1988 to present **$159**

New Shepherdess, No. 4576, 1969-85, 9 1/2" h. **$149**

Nippon Lady, No. 5327, 1985 to present, 9" h. **$325**

Nostalgia, No. 5071, 1980-93, 6 1/4" h. **$310**

Nothing to Do, No. 5649, 1990 to present, 6" h. **$126**

Obstetrician, No. 4763, 16 1/2" h., 1971-73 .... **$250**

Old Man with Violin, No. 4622, 1969-82, 13" h. **$369**

On the Farm, No. 1306, 1974-90, 9 3/4" h. **$240**

One More Try, No. 5997, 1993 to present, 10" h. **$750**

Oriental Music, No. 1491, 1986, limited edition, 11 3/4" h. **$1,500**

Oriental Spring, No. 4988, 1978 to present, 11 1/2" h. **$209**

Ox, No. 1390.30, 1983-85, 5 1/4" h. **$220**

Papillon Dog, No. 4857, 1974-79, 7 1/2" h. **$500**

Parisian Lady, No. 5321, 1985 to present, 9 3/4" h. **$218**

Pekingese Sitting, No. 4641, 1969-85, 6" h. **$323**

Penguin, No. 5247, 1984-88, 6 1/2" h. **$170**

Penguin, No. 5248, 1984-88, 5 1/2" h. **$168**

Penguin, No. 5249, 1984-88, 6" h. **$200**

Peter Pan, No. 7529, 1993, limited edition, 9 1/2" h.................... **$850**

Pharmacist, No. 4844, 12 1/2" h., 1973-85 .... **$1,250**

Pick of the Litter, No. 7621... **$425**

Picture Perfect, No. 7612, LSC Special edition, 1991, 8 1/2" h. **$475**

Poodle, No. 1259, 1974-85, 5 1/2" h. **$280**

Practice Makes Perfect, No. RL-402 .... **$600**

Preening Crane, No. 1616, 1989 to present, 7 1/2" h. **$279**

Pretty Pickings, No. 5222, 1984 to present, 7" h. **$100**

Pretty Pose, No. 5589, 1989-93, 3 1/2" h. **$175**

Lady Swinging Golf Club, No. 6689, 14 1/2" h. **$115**

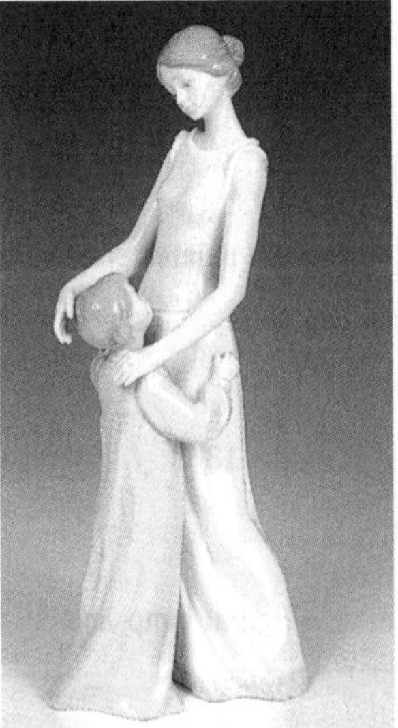

Mother & child, tall slender mother looking down at her child wearing a blue nightgown, 14" h. **$316**

Princess and Unicorn, No. 1755, 1991 limited edition, 11" h. **$2,267**

Pulling Doll's Carriage, No. 5044, 1980 to present, 11" h. **$150**

Pupper Painter (The), No. 5396, 1986 to present, 9 1/2" h. **$700**

Mother & infant, matte finish, a young mother wearing a long mottled blue robe & holding her infant close to her face, No. 2429, 18 1/4" h. **$259**

Resting Nude, No. 3025, 1991-92, limited edition, 8 1/2" h. **$725**

Rhino, No. 5437, 1987-90, 2" h. **$99**

Roaring 20s, No. 5174, 1982-93, 13" h. **$195**

Rosalinda, No. 4836, 1973-83, 8 1/4" h. **$250**

Saint Nicholas, No. 5427, 1987-91, 15 1/2" h. **$578**

Sayonara, No. 4989, 1978 to present, 10 1/4" h. **$175**

Scarecrow and Lady, No. 5385, 1986 to present, 9 3/4" h. **$500**

School Chums, No. 5237, 1984 to present, 8 1/2" h. **$475**

School Days, No. 7604, 1988 LCS Special edition, 8 1/4" h....... **$350**

Sea Breeze, No. 4922, 13 3/4" h., 1974- **$230**

Sea Captain, No. 4621, 1969-93, 14 1/2" h. **$199**

Seated Torero, No. 1162, 1971-73, 11 3/4" h. **$485**

See Saw, No. 4867, 1974 to present, 7 3/4" h. **$303**

Shepherd Sleeping, No. 1104, 1971-78, 14" h. **$1,625**

Shepherdess with Basket, No. 4591, 1969-93, 9 3/4" h. **$100**

Shepherdess with Basket, No. 4678, 1969 to present, 8 1/2" h. **$80**

Shepherdess with Dog, No. 1034, 10 1/2" h., 1969-91 .... **$195**

Shepherdess with Rooster, No. 4677, 1969 to present, 7 3/4" h. **$80**

Skier Puppet, No. 4970, 7" h., 1977-83 .... **$500**

Skye Terrier, No. 4643, 1969-85, 6" h. **$350**

Snow White with Apple, No. 5067, 1980-83, 10 1/2" h., ... **$950**

Soldier with Gun, No. 1164, 1971-78, 12 1/4" h. **$295**

Sorrowful Mother, No. 5849, 12 3/4" h., limited edition of 1,500, 1992 .... **$995**

Spring Bouquets, No. 7603, 1987, L.C.S. limited edition, 8 1/4" h. **$599**

Spring Breeze, No. 5590, 1989-93, 7" h. **$175**

Spring Is Here, No. 5223, 1984 to present, 6 1/2" h. **$87**

Spring, No. 5217, 1984 to present, 7 1/2" h. **$115**

Springtime in Japan, No. 1445, 1983 to present, 11 3/4" h. **$1,100**

St. Joseph, No. 1386, 1981 to present, 13" h. **$435**

Stepping Out, No. 1537, 13 1/4" h., 1968- **$250**

Summer on the Farm, No. 5285, 1985 to present, 9 1/2" h. **$323**

Summer Stock, RL-401......... **$600**

Summer Stroll, No. 7611, 1991-92, limited edition, 9" h. **$438**

Sunning, No. 1481, 1985-88, 8 1/2" h. **$395**

Suzy and Her Doll, No. 1378, 1978-85, 11" h. **$475**

Swan Ballet, No. 5920, 6 1/4" h., 1992- **$145**

Sweety, No. 1248, 7 1/2" h., 1974-90 .... **$500**

Talk of the Town, No. 5788, 1991 to present, 10 1/4" h. **$135**

Teruko, No. 1451, 1983 to present, 10 1/4" h. **$275**

Thai Couple, No. 2058, 1974 to present, signed, 20" h....... **$1,900**

Thai Dancer, No. 2069, 1977 to present, 17" h. **$425**

Time to Rest, No. 5399, 1987-93, 4 3/4" h. **$295**

Tinkerbell, No. 7518, 1992 limited edition, 7" h............ **$1,900-2,225**

Trimming the Tree, No. 5897, 12 3/4" h., 1982- **$750**

Valencian Beauty, No. 5670, 1990-93, 6" h. **$138**

Valencian Boy, No. 1400, 11 1/2" h., 1982-88 .... **$475**

Valencian Children, No. 1489, 11" h., 1986- **$825**

Viennese Lady, No. 5322, 1985 to present, 10 1/4" h. **$198**

Virgin Mary, No. 1387, 1981 to present, 9 3/4" h. **$420**

Voyage of Columbus (The), No. 5847, 9" h., limited edition of 7,500, 1992 .... **$1,049**

Wishing on a Star, No. 1475, 1985-88, 6 1/2" h. **$385**

Wistful Centaur Girl, No. 5319, 1985-90, 5 1/2" h. **$325**

Young Madonna No. 2149, 1985-88, 14 1/2" h. **$900**

Young Mozart, No. 5915, 1962, limited edition, 1992-, 6 3/4" h. **$1,400**

Youth, No. 3538, 1983 limited edition, 23 1/2" h............... **$1,500**

Yuki, No. 1448, 1983 to present, 7 1/2" h. **$325**

Repairing valuable ceramics should be left to professionals who can do the job expertly and minimize loss of value to the piece. Of course, the cost of the repair should be weighed against the value of the piece. But keep in mind that poorly done, do-it-yourself repairs generally can not be undone and will permanently lower a piece's value.

Lotus Ware - Knowles, Taylor & Knowles (KT&K)

Knowles, Taylor & Knowles made Lotus Ware (bone china) for a very short time. Reference books differ on the starting date but it ranges between 1889 and 1892. There is agreement that production of the ware ceased sometime in 1896. KT&K tried to make Lotus Ware again in 1904 but it proved too costly and was soon abandoned. Many pieces of this ware were hand-painted and hand-decorated. Lotus rivaled some of the finest European decorated bone china in quality and refinement of decoration and artwork. KT&K employed skilled artists, whose work is highly prized to this day by knowledgeable collectors. Photos courtesy of Nancy Wetzel, East Liverpool, Ohio.

Bowl, 10" w., Shell design, rough sheel embossing on the outsides w/blue & pink blush trim, smooth shell interior, red along inside edge, blue & pink blush, h.p. scene in the bottom of a sailing ship & gulls on rough seas crashing on a rocky shoreline **$600-800**

Bowl, 6 1/2" d., 4 1/2" h., Columbia design, pinched ovoid shaped w/applied flowers & filigreed medallions on the sides (ILLUS. left with two other Columbia bowls) **$300-450**

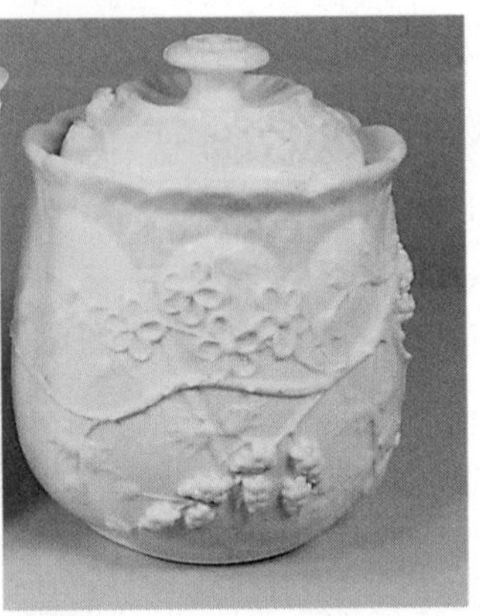

Cracker jar, cov., all-white, barrel-shaped body w/a low flared & scalloped rim, domed inset cover w/button finial, applied w/flowers, branches, vines & berries, 6 1/2" h. **$200-350**

Creamer, Chestnut design, all-white w/ twig handle, 3 1/2" h. (ILLUS. left with other Chestnut creamer) **$150-200**

Cup & saucer, after-dinner style, Mecca design, all-white, cylindrical cup w/angled handle, lightly molded matching saucer, saucer 3" d., cup 2 3/8" h., the set **$75-125**

Cup & saucer, cylindrical cup w/ruffled rim, decorated in color w/a scene of a frog seated under an umbrella & fishing, titled, "Oregon Webfoot," w/ a lotus pad-shaped saucer, saucer 4 3/4" d., cup 2 1/4" d., 1 5/8" h. **$125-150**

Cup & saucer, Star design, all-white, cup 3 1/2" d., 1 5/8" h. **$75-100**

Cup, after-dinner style, cylindrical cup w/a green transfer design titled "Holyrood Castle," 2 3/4" h. **$75-100**

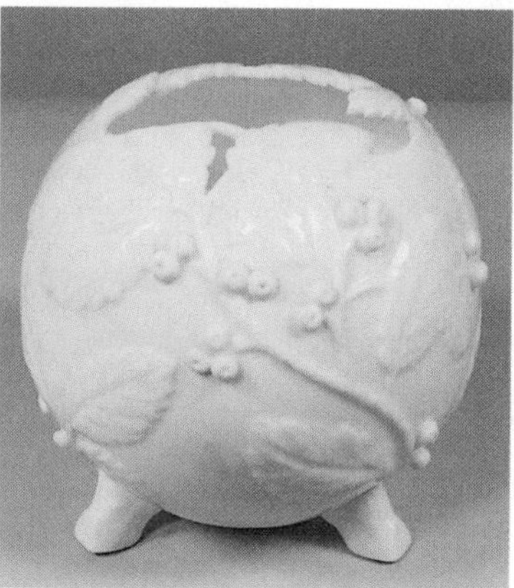

Flower bowl, footed spherical form w/a pierced closed rim, applied w/berries & leaves around the sides, 3 3/4" d., 4 1/2" h. **$250-300**

Jar, cov., Deccan Jar (a.k.a. Luxor Jar), all-white footed bulbous body decorated w/four filigreed medallions & applied teardrops & beaded strings, matching pierced cover **$400-600**

Jar, Ivica Jar, footed bulbous ovoid body w/a closed rim, large gold beads around the foot & rim, h.p. pink & white flowers & green leaves around the sides, missing the cover, 4 5/8" h. ... **$250-350**

Covers for jars are often broken, which makes them scarcer than the jars. If you find a lone cover for a bargain, it may be a good investment. You may be able to resell it to a collector looking for a replacement.

Nappy, scalloped oblong four-lobed all-white shape, twig feet, 4 x 5 1/8" (ILLUS. right with larger nappy & salt dip) **$100-125**

Pitcher, 3 1/8" h., 4 1/4" d., jug-style, Globe design, squatty bulbous body w/a wide low rim & spout, gold forked handle, bisque finish, the sides h.p. w/pink & yellow flowers & blue & green leaves all outlined in gold **$125-150**

Pitcher, 6 1/4" h., 7 1/2" d., jug-style, Leaf design, all-white, squatty bulbous body lightly embossed w/a leaf design, made from a Lotus Ware mold but not bone china **$45-60**

Sugar bowl, cov., squatty bulbous body w/a domed cover & button finial, angled handle, molded gadroon body design, highlightover overall w/gold, 6" l., 4" h. **$100-125**

Tea set: cov. teapot, open sugar bowl & creamer; Venice design, oblong bodies w/lightly molded designs, gold banding, creamer 4" l., 3" h., sugar 5 1/2" l., 3" h., teapot 7" w., 4 1/4" h., the set **$375-475**

Tea set: cov. teapot, cov. sugar bowl & creamer; Valinciennes design, each piece h.p. w/violets in panels between light purple applied fishnet, twig handles, creamer (some damage) 4" l., 3 1/8" h., sugar 5 1/2" l., 3 3/4" h., teapot 7" l., 4 1/4" h., the set **$475-600**

Tea set: cov. teapot, cov. sugar bowl & creamer; Valinciennes design, each piece h.p. w/violets, twig handles, creamer (some damage) 4" l., 3 1/8" h., sugar 5 1/2" l., 3 3/4" h., teapot 7" l., 4 1/4" h., the set **$300-400**

Teapot, cov., squatty bulbous body w/swirled ribbing, domed cover w/knob finial, short spout & angled handle, blue blush ground h.p. w/pink & blue flowers on a brown transfer, gold-sponged throat & cover, from a Lotus Ware mold but not bone china, 7 1/2" l., 5" h. **$75-85**

Tray, shell-shaped, raised base, white ground w/a delicate brown vine decoration & gilt trim, 4 3/8" w., 4" h. **$100-125**

Majolica

Majolica, a tin-enameled glazed pottery, has been produced for centuries. It originally took its name from the island of Majorca, a source of figurine (potter's clay). Subsequently it was widely produced in England, Europe and the United States. Etruscan majolica, now avidly sought, was made by Griffen, Smith & Hill, Phoenixville, Pa., in the last quarter of the 19th century. Most majolica advertised today is 19th or 20th century. Once scorned by most collectors, interest in this colorful ware so popular during the Victorian era has now revived and prices have risen dramatically in the past few years.

Etruscan

Basket, Begonia Leaf patt., wicker-form forked overhead handle, wicker strap border band, 11 1/2" l. **$1,120**

Sardine box, cov., Water Lily patt., rectangular base w/molded white water lilies & green leaves on a pink ground w/a brown ropetwist border band, the rectangular flat-topped cover w/matching decor & a figural swan finial, professional restorations, 2 pcs. **$825**

Teapot, cov., Cauliflower patt., the body molded as a head of cauliflower in creamy white & dark green, green spout & handle, marked on bottom, Griffin, Smith & Hill, Phoenixville, Pennsylvania, late 19th c., minor roughness on interior rim, interior rim chip on cover, 5 1/2" h. **$374**

Teapot, cov., Shell & Seaweed patt., spherical body molded as large shells trimmed w/seaweed, mottled green coral-form handle & spout, mottled pink, brown & green cover w/shell finial, Griffin, Smith & Hill, Phoenixville, Pennsylvania, late 19th c., 10" l., 6 1/2" h. **$525-575**

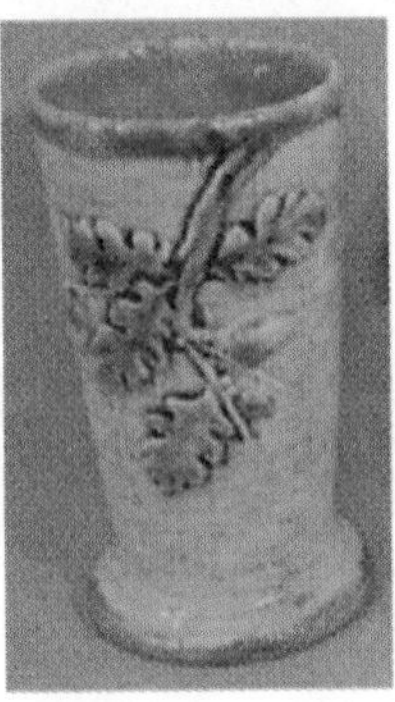

Vase, 5" h., Oak Leaf, Acorn & Basketweave patt., yellow ground, scarce, hairline **$700**

General

Bowl, 11" w., 7 1/2" h., the small rounded foot molded as coral & seaweed in white, green, yellow & brown supporting the very large shell-shaped bowl w/a cobalt blue exterior & pale blue interior, George Jones, minor professional repair **$1,540**

Bust of a young boy, the realistically modeled and colored bust show the smiling youth wearing a brown cockade hat w/purple bow, a shirt w/a large ruffled white collar, blue inner jacket & lavender outer jacket trimmed along the edge w/ball-shaped tassels, Brothers Urbach, Germany, 19th c., minor glaze loss, 19" h. **$748**

Centerpiece, figural, modeled as two large mermaids supporting a massive seashell between their backs, raised on an oblong shell-formed base, designed by Minton for international exhibitions, 40" w., 24" h. **$16,500**

Centerpiece, Rabbits Under Cabbage patt., designed w/the top bowl in the form of a large bluish green cabbage leaf raised on the backs of small white & black rabbits sitting among green foliage, Minton, date code for 1870, 9 1/2" w., 4 1/2" h. **$10,450**

Cheese keeper, cov., Argenta Primrose patt., by Wedgwood, 9 1/2" h. **$440**

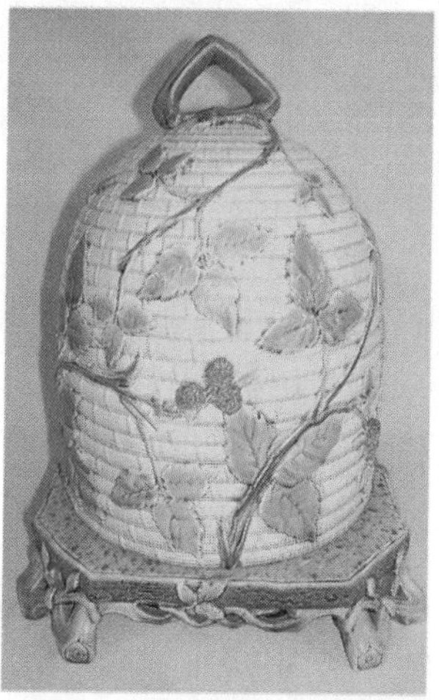

Cheese keeper, cov., Beehive & Blackberry patt., modeled as a large straw beehive w/a vine loop top handle & blackberry vines wrapping around the sides, the base a square platform w/ cut-corners raised on vine legs, Minton, England, ca. 1880s, hairline in base, very rare, 13" h. **$35,200**

Cheese keeper, cov., Blackberry patt., by Holdcroft, professional rim repairs, 9 1/2" h. **$1,100**

Cheese keeper, cov., Fern patt., tall cylindrical cover w/a flat top, the sides molded w/large green fern leaves on a brown ground, the cover w/water lily pads & a blossom finial, base w/green ferns on the flanged rim, France, late 19th c., minor nicks to cover finial, rim chip on cover, 11 1/2" h. **$880**

Smart buying at auctions takes self-control. Establish a maximum amount you are willing to pay for a particular lot in advance and do not exceed it.

Cheese keeper, cov., Pansy patt., wide cylindrical cover w/flat top, pink blossoms on green leafy vines around the sides against a cobalt blue ground, George Jones, England, late 19th c., professional repair to cover handle, base 10 1/4" d., overall 7 1/2" h. **$3,850**

Compote, open, 9 1/4" h., 10 1/2" d., the wide shallow dished top composed of large overlapping green leaves raised on a tall green stem framed by three standing storks w/their heads bent down touching their breasts & glazed in mottled yellow to dark brown, on a mottled brown & bluish green tripartite base, unmarked **$518**

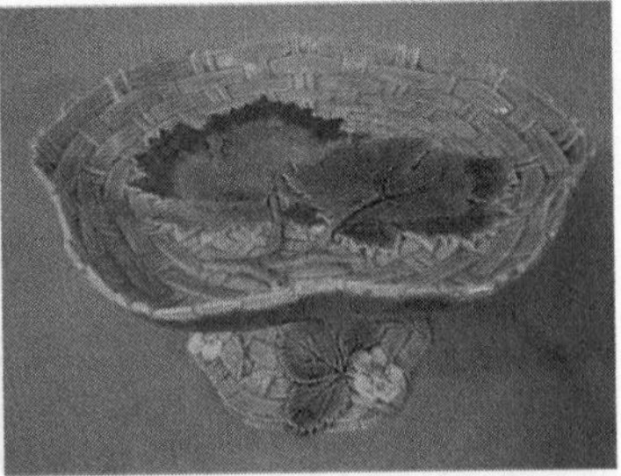

Compote, open, 9" d., 5" h., Basketweave & Maple Leaf patt., wide gently fluted shallow bowl w/a turquoise basketweave design & large brown & green leaves, turquoise basketweave pedestal w/green leaves & white blossoms, Victoria Pottery Co. **$605**

Compotes, 12 1/4" d., a round flaring foot tapering to a ringed pedestal supporting the wide brown basketweave bowl bordered around the rim w/a band of white primrose blossoms & leaftips, by Wedgwood, date code for 1872, pr. **$2,629**

Creambowls, figural, a large naturalistic nautilus shell bowl supported on a pedestal composed of entwined dolphins & green seaweed, on a round disk-form gadrooned green oval foot, Minton, England, Model No. 902, date code for 1862, overall 9" h., pr. **$3,824**

Dresser tray, oval, Butterfly & Iris patt., the flowers molded in high-relief, by George Jones, 11" l. **$3,300**

Game dish, cov., the oval tapering basketweave base trimmed w/ green oak leaves, the domed cover molded in high-relief w/ realistic dead game, w/the liner, by Minton, date code for 1870, chip to wing of bird, 14" l. **$2,200**

Jardiniere & pedestal, the large bulbous jardiniere w/a widely flaring scrolling & rolled rim above scroll-molded sides in deep red & dark blue framing a large reserve h.p. w/a wooded landscape, the matching pedestal w/a round brick red top band above a dark blue molded band & a baluster-form pedestal molded w/further scrolls & a full-relief mermaid wrapping down one side beside a large h.p. landscape reserve, the dark blue domed base molded w/leafy scrolls in dark brown & white, probably Europe, late 19th c., jardiniere 17" d., 40" h., pedestal 29" h., the set **$2,522**

Egg basket, the oval basket w/vertical sides molded in relief w/blackberries on leafy blossoming vines against a yellow basketweave ground, cobalt blue upper border, double bamboo-form arched handle from side to side, the interior fitted w/six holes to support eggs, Brownfield, England, late 19th c., 11 1/2" l., 6 1/2" h. **$990**

Garden seat, figural, Blackamoor patt., three mottled green & brown bun feet supporting a base w/a cobalt blue border band supporting a brown mound issuing the figural pedestal composed of a full-figure Blackamoor youth seated among green & brown cattails, the top composed of a flattened cobalt blue cushion-form seat w/yellow ropetwist border, professional restoration to the seat, Holdcroft, England, late 19th c., overall 17 1/2" h. **$6,050**

Fish platter, oblong w/slightly serpentine rim, molded in the center w/a large grey fish on a bed of green ferns & leaves, by Wedgwood, 25 1/2" l. **$2,750**

Fish platter, oval w/pointed ends, molded in the center w/a large dark grey & brown fish against a pale blue ground trimmed w/ cattails, supported on four cattail feet, by Holdcroft, 26" l. ... **$2,750**

Garden seat, the wide squatty round tapering top centered by a cluster of three openwork white flowers forming a handle, the sides of the top in cobalt blue molded w/large notched green leaves alternating w/pendent white & yellow lily-like blossoms, three wide flattened & tapering legs decorated w/white & yellow petals on a cobalt blue ground, each ending in a tight scroll & raised on a tripartite foot, George Jones, repairs to legs & base, 18 1/2" h. **$3,300**

Jardiniere, deep oval form w/gently flaring paneled & scalloped sides, cobalt blue ground decorated on the sides w/oblong green scroll-framed panels enclosing colorful scenes of Classical figures & Cupids, Shape No. 1087, Minton, England, ca. 1880s, professional rim repair, 17 1/2" l., 7 3/4" h. **$3,300**

Jardiniere, Oak Leaf & Acorn patt., the rectangular deep container w/molded branch edges, each side molded w/vining oak leaf branches w/acorns, minor nicks, 10 x 14 1/2", 13" h. **$358**

Jardiniere-stand, figural, a model of a very tall stork in grey, black, white & gold standing holding a fish in its beak, a flaring cylindrical container behind it formed as a cluster of cattails & leaves, Hugo Lonitz, late 19th c., repairs to stork body & beak & tips of cattails, fine detail **$8,800**

Marmalade pot, cov., Apple Blossom patt., the high domed top w/spoon opening molded w/a brown branch handle & pink blossoms & green leaves on a turquoise ground, the base w/a turquoise ground banded w/brown wicker design & a flanged rim w/further blossoms & leaves, George Jones, England, late 19th c., interior rim chips on rim of cover, 5" h. **$2,475**

Patè box, cover & undertray, the deep oval box molded w/a band of upright green leaves on a cobalt blue ground, the cobalt blue domed cover molded in high relief w/a red lobster & seaweed, the matching undertray in cobalt blue trimmed w/green seaweed, Holdcroft, 7 1/2" l., the set **$3,850**

Pitcher, 8 1/2" h., Egyptian Lotus patt., the four sides each molded w/a tall pointed arch enclosing a large pink lotus blossoms & green leaves, a square flared neck w/a palmette at each corner, fancy scroll handle, Copeland **$3,025**

Pitcher, 8" h., Water Lily & Iris patt., the sides molded in high-relief w/water lilies, iris & green leaves on a lavender ground, yellow base & rim band, brown vine-wrapped handle, George Jones, professional rim repair **$4,950**

Plaque, oblong, molded in high-relief w/a scene of three putti frolicking in a forest, one holding lovebirds, the other two crowning each other w/wreaths of roses, marked w/monogram of the painter Thomas Sergent, France, ca. 1870, 30" l. **$1,195**

Tea set: Basketweave & Floral patt., cov. teapot, cov. sugar bowl, creamer, two cups & saucers & oblong handled tray; serving pieces w/tapering ovoid bodies molded around the bottom w/bands of tan basketweave below a cobalt blue upper body molded w/branches of pink blossoms & green leaves, domed covers w/arched twig handles, brown branch handles & spout, George Jones, England, late 19th c., professional repair to sugar cover rim, one cup & saucer repaired, teapot cover not perfect fit, tray 19 1/2" l., teapot 7" h., the set **$3,640**

Tea set: Bird & Fan patt., cov. teapot, cov. sugar bowl & creamer; spherical bodies molded w/colorful fans, each w/a flying bird against a pebbled pale yellow background, brown branch handles & spout, probably England, late 19th c., minor spout chip on teapot, the set **$308**

Tea set: Cauliflower patt., cov. teapot, cov. sugar bowl & creamer; each piece modeled as a white head of cauliflower w/wide green leaves, Josiah Wedgwood, England, late 19th c., minor spout nicks on teapot, teapot 6" h., the set **$924**

Tea set: cov. teapot, cov. sugar bowl & creamer; Shell & Seaweed patt., in mottled shades of grey, pink & brown w/green sea plants, late 19th c., some roughness to creamer rim, teapot 5 1/2" h., the set **$374**

Tea set: Daisy patt., cov. teapot, cov. sugar bowl & creamer; each piece w/a hexagonal body in dark brown, the panels molded w/large white & yellow daisy blossoms & green leaves, angled green branch handles & spout, figural flower cover finials, mark of the Victoria Pottery Company, late 19th c., professional spout repair on creamer, the set **$784**

Tea set: Drum patt., cov. teapot, cov. sugar bowl & creamer; each piece w/a spherical body designed as a round drum w/wide cobalt blue bands separated by narrow brown bands joined by interwoven rope bands w/ buckles, strap & buckle handles & a drum stick spout, very rare design, George Jones, England, late 19th c., teapot 6" h., the set **$12,320**

Tea set: Floral Branch patt., cov. teapot, cov. sugar bowl & creamer; wide cylindrical bodies w/narrow shoulder bands, pale blue background molded w/a large branch w/green leaves & a stylized pink & white blossom, brown branch handles, covers w/flower bud finials, probably England, late 19th c., hairline in creamer, the set **$364**

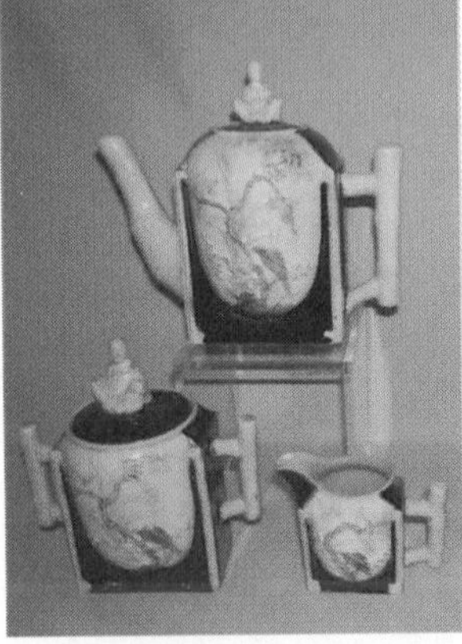

Tea set: Oriental patt., cov. teapot, cov. sugar & creamer; each piece w/an upright square body w/ swelled panels on the sides, each corner w/a pale yellow molded band, cobalt blue ground w/shaded pale green & white swelled panels molded w/an Oriental slender tree w/green leaves & pink blossoms & a perched brown bird, squared pale yellow bamboo handles & a bamboo spout, the low domed covers w/a seated Oriental man forming the finial, probably England, late 19th c., repair to teapot cover finial, teapot 7" h., the set **$364**

Teapot, cov., Chinaman patt., figural, model of a large brown melon w/green stem spout & handle, the figure of a Chinese man climbing on the side, wearing a dark blue robe, cream-colored pants & black shoes, Holdcroft, England, third quarter 19th c., 9 1/2" l., 7" h. **$4,400**

Teapot, cov., figural Chinaman patt., produced by Minton, based on Victorian original, limited edition of 2,500, introduced in 2000 .... **$650**

Teapot, cov., figural Cockerel patt., produced by Minton, based on Victorian original, limited edition of 2,500, introduced in 2000 .... **$700**

Teapot, cov., figural Monkey model, made by Minton, reissue of Victorian original, limited edition of 1,793, introduced in 1993 ... **$850**

Teapot, cov., figural Fish patt., produced by Minton, based on Victorian original, limited edition of 2,500, introduced in 2000 .... **$750**

Teapot, cov., Japonisme style, a flattened demi-lune form in turquoise blue, the flat cover w/a small squared finial, straight angled spout & simple C-form handle, the shoulder molded w/a stylized fret design, the sides molded w/an Oriental figure preparing tea in a garden & a large stylized blossom on a leafy stem, England, possibly by Joseph Holdcroft or Samuel Lear, ca. 1880, 9 3/4" l. ... **$2,271**

Teapot, cov., Lemon patt., model of a large yellow lemon w/molded green leaves around the sides & forming the base, green stem spout & handle, cover modeled as an inverted mushroom, Mintons, England, date code for 1873, Shape No. 643, 7" l., 4 1/2" h. **$8,800**

Teapot, cov., Monkey & Coconut patt., the body modeled as a large mustard yellow coconut w/the figure of a seated brown monkey at one end grasping the nut, wearing a black jacket w/dark red blossoms & green leaves, the grey head w/pale green knob finial forming the cover, molded green leaves below the curved brown bamboo-form spout, the tail of the monkey forming the handle, Mintons, England, third quarter 19th c., minor hairline in spout, 8 1/2" l., 6" h. **$6,440**

Teapot, cov., Monkey & Coconut patt., the bulbous body modeled as a seated grey monkey wearing a dark blue outfit w/large pink polka dots, its arms & legs wrapped around a large mustard yellow coconut w/green leaves, the stem forming the spout, the monkey's head & shoulders forming the cover w/a blue knob finial, Model No. 1844, Mintons, England, date letter for 1874, 9" h. **$8,225**

Teapot, cov., Mushroom patt., designed by Gordon Brooks, produced by Minton, limited edition of 1,000, introduced in 2002 .... **$750**

Teapot, cov., oblong sad iron-shaped body w/a short spout, high arched fixed handle, the cobalt blue body molded w/a band decorated w/alternating grey mouse & pink blossom, the top of the handle molded w/the figure of a curled up white cat looking down at a grey mouse & carrot forming the finial of the flat cover, Mintons, England, possibly designed by Christopher Dresser, Model No. 622, date letter for 1876, 7 1/2" h. **$47,000**

Teapot, cov., Putto Rowing Boat patt., wide low squatty rounded body on three scroll feet, the body in cobalt blue w/a straight brown spout & C-form brown handle, the top modeled w/the figure of a winged putto seated in a model of a tan rowboat w/pale green interior & green oars, Holdcroft, England, third quarter 19th c., very rare, professional repair to arm of figure, 8" l., 6" h. **$15,680**

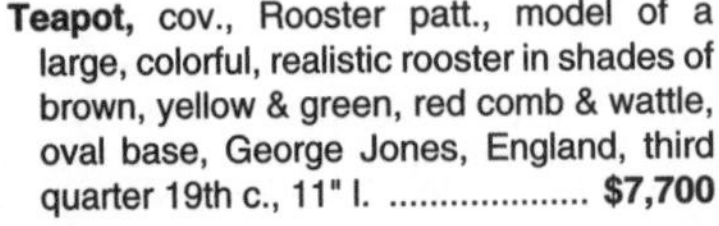

Teapot, cov., Rooster patt., model of a large, colorful, realistic rooster in shades of brown, yellow & green, red comb & wattle, oval base, George Jones, England, third quarter 19th c., 11" l. **$7,700**

Teapot, cov., Spikey Fish patt., the body modeled as a large grey & green bulbous fish raised on green waves, a large branch of brown seaweed w/a shell thumbrest forming the handle, angled brown straight spout emerging from the mouth, the small cover w/an arched spiky fin handle, Mintons, third quarter 19th c., extremely rare, professional repair to spout, base rim & rim of cover, 9 1/2" l., 7" h. **$29,120**

Teapot, cov., Tortoise patt., produced by Minton, limited edition of 2,500, introduced in 1999 .... **$750**

Tray, 13 3/4" l., oval, Palissy Ware, the center molded in high-relief w/a realistic fish on a bed of leaves & water, the thick border molded w/realistic seaweed & sea creatures on a dark blue ground **$3,025**

Teapot, cov., Vulture & Snake patt., an elaborately modeled design w/a large standing vulture w/a yellow & black body & pink neck & head grasping the head & body of a large writhing green snake, both on a rockwork base, Model No. 1851, designed by H.H. Crealock, Mintons, England, dated ca. 1872, 8 3/8" h. **$89,625**

Umbrella stand, Banana Plant design, tall upright triangular form, the front sides molded in bold relief w/a cluster of tall wide green & yellow leaves & leafy branches w/molded bulbous brown fruit, turquoise blue background & a bark-textured pale greenish brown band at the rim & base, Joseph Holdcroft, England, ca. 1880, overall 21 1/4" h. **$3,346**

Tray, oblong shallow form w/a yellow border surrounding large molded leaves & blossoms, one end molded in full-relief w/a monkey seated on a tree branch, attributed to George Jones, 10" l., 5" h. **$550**

Vase, 6 3/4" h., footed wide bulbous ovoid body tapering to a short flaring cylindrical neck w/a gold rim band flanked by loop handles, molded w/clusters of white & yellow daisy-like flowers on the sides above a yellow basketweave band around the base, Minton, England, No. 1316, second half 19th c., minor nicks on flowers **$770**

McCoy

Collectors are now seeking the art wares of two McCoy potteries. One was founded in Roseville, Ohio, in the late 19th century as the J.W. McCoy Pottery, subsequently becoming Brush-McCoy Pottery Co., later Brush Pottery. The other was also founded in Roseville in 1910 as Nelson McCoy Sanitary Stoneware Co., later becoming Nelson McCoy Pottery. In 1967 the pottery was sold to D.T. Chase of the Mount Clemens Pottery Co., who sold his interest to the Lancaster Colony Corp. in 1974. The pottery shop closed in 1985. Cookie jars are especially collectible today.

McCoy

A helpful reference book is *The Collector's Encyclopedia of McCoy Pottery*, by the Huxfords (Collector Books), and *McCoy Cookie Jars From the First to the Latest*, by Harold Nichols (Nichols Publishing, 1987).

Cookie jar, Bunch of Bananas, ca. 1948 .... **$150-250**

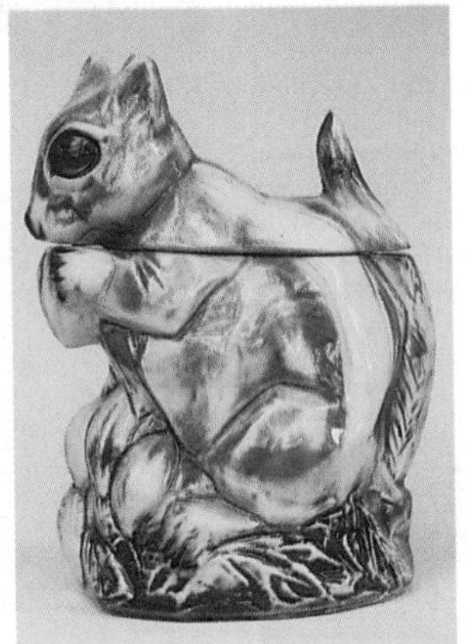

Cookie jar, Chipmunk, ca. 1960 .... **$100-125**

Cookie jar, Christmas Tree, ca. 1959 .... **$1,000+**

Cookie jar, Indian Head, ca. 1954 .... **$633**

Cookie jar, Yellow Mouse, ca. 1978 .... **$35-45**

Jardiniere & pedestal base, Leaves & Berries design, ca. 1930s, overall 21" h., 2 pcs. **$250-350**

Lamp w/original shade, model of pair of cowboy boots base, original shade, ca. 1956 .... **$150-200**

Model of angelfish, aqua, ca. early 1940s, Cope design, 6" h. **$300-400**

Porch jar, wide tapering cylindrical body w/ribbed base, embossed leaf & berry decoration below rim, green, marked "NM," ca. 1940s, 9 1/2 x 11" **$200-250**

Planter, figural, Madonna, white, ca. 1960s, rare, 6" h. **$200-250**

Planter, model of fish, green, ca. 1955, 7 x 12" **$1,000-1,200**

TV lamp, model of fireplace, ca. 1950s, 6 x 9" **$75-100**

Umbrella stand, cylindrical w/applied handles, ribbed panels alternating w/ embossed leaf design panels, glossy brown glaze, ca. 1940s, 19" h. **$250-350**

Meissen

The secret of true hard paste porcelain, known long before to the Chinese, was "discovered" accidentally in Meissen, Germany by J.F. Bottger, an alchemist working with E.W. Tschirnhausen. The first European true porcelain was made in the Meissen Porcelain Works, organized about 1709. Meissen marks have been widely copied by other factories.

Centerpiece, allegorical, the flaring reticulated oblong top base w/open end handles decorated overall w/encrusted colorful flowers & green leaves among gilt-trimmed scrolls, raised on an ornate flower-encrusted pedestal w/a flower-painted scrolled cartouche above a group of children representing the Four Seasons around the scrolled base, blue crossed-swords mark, modeled by Leuteritz, ca. 1880, overall 17 3/8" h. **$7,768**

Figure group, a young mother in 18th c. costume seated holding her bare-bottomed toddler across her lap w/a switch to spank it in her other hand, her young daughter pulling at her arm to dissuade her, on a round molded & gilt-trimmed base, blue crossed-swords mark, late 19th c., 10 1/4" h. **$3,585**

Dinner service: ten 10" d. dinner plates, nine cups & saucers, eight cream soup bowls & eight underplates; Blue Onion patt., all marked w/the blue crossed swords, 19th c., the set (ILLUS. of part)................................ **$1,725**

Teapot, cov., nearly spherical slightly tapering body decorated w/a robin's-egg blue ground, the flat cover w/a gold knob finial, short curved shoulder spout & pointed arch handle, each side centered by a h.p. color scene of merchants haggling at quayside within a gold border, the cover w/two smaller views, "Indianische Blumen" design under spout & on handle, blue crossed-swords mark, 1735-40, overall 4 1/4" l., 4 1/4" h. **$4,780**

Urn, a flaring gadrooned foot joined by a white-beaded disk to the large ovoid urn-form body w/gold gadrooning around the lower portion below the wide white central band h.p. w/a large bouquet of colorful flowers, the tapering neck in deep pink below the heavy gold rolled & gadrooned rim, white & gold entwined serpent handles at each side, blue crossed-swords mark, late 19th c., 11" h. **$518**

←

Vase, 6 5/8" h., footed bottle-form body tapering to a ringed neck w/a widely flaring rim, cobalt blue ground enameled in white in the Limoges style w/a pair of amorous putti sitting on a leafy branch, one extending a floral wreath to a third in flight releasing a dove, gold banding at the foot, neck ring & rim, blue crossed-swords mark, probably designed by E.A. Leuteritz, ca. 1880 .... **$2,868**

Vase, 15 1/2" h., classic baluster-form, a fluted flaring base & pedestal w/rings supporting the ovoid body w/a band of flutes below the wide cobalt blue body band decorated w/large gilt & silver florals, ringed shoulder & short flaring neck w/incurved molded rim flanked by long looped snake handles from rim to shoulder, gilt trim on base & body & new gilt trim on handles, late 19th c. **$2,300**

Vases, 19" h., baluster form w/entwined snake handles, cobalt blue ground, the mouth, collar & foot molded & trimmed w/gilt, late 19th - early 20th c., blue crossed swords marks & incised & impressed numbers, mounted as lamps, pr. **$2,990**

Mettlach

Ceramics with the name Mettlach were produced by Villeroy & Boch and other potteries in the Mettlach area of Germany. Villeroy and Boch's finest years of production are thought to be from about 1890 to 1910. Also see STEINS.

Drinking set: tall tapering cylindrical tankard pitcher w/hinged pewter cover & twelve cylindrical beakers; paint-under-glaze decoration, the pitcher decorated w/tan bands at the top & base, a large black Prussian eagle at the front w/bands featuring the crests of various German cities above & below, each beaker decorated w/a different German city crest below a border band naming the city, pitcher No. 2893-1200 & beakers No. 2327-1200, beakers 1/4 L , pitcher 3 1/4 L, the set **$1,811**

Jardiniere, Aesthetic Movement-style, the round disk foot w/a molded leaftip band supporting the wide compressed rounded lower body decorated w/oblong panels w/stylized flowers below wide slightly tapering sides below the low rounded leaftip rim, leafy C-scroll handles at the lower body each mounted by a figure of a putto playing a mandolin, the sides decorated w/a continuous frieze of Renaissance era beauties in a garden among fruiting trees all painted in shades of blue & brown, No. 1355, ca. 1880, signed by Warth, 16 3/8" d., 23" h. **$4,183**

Jardiniere, Phanolith type, a wide disk foot supporting the wide cylindrical body w/a flared rim, dark blue ground decorated w/ applied white relief mythological figures & pale green florals around the sides, incised mark, 8" h. **$690**

A putto (from the Latin "putus," meaning little man) is portrayed as a chubby human baby, often having wings. The plural of putto is "putti." The putto comes from Greek and Roman mythology and is, therefore secular, whereas cherubs come from the Bible and are considered sacred figures.

Mantel garniture: clock in urn & pair of matching side urns; the large baluster-form central urn w/a mosaic design of stylized floral & leaf panels in alternating cream w/green & tan & rust red w/tan, brown & green, the flared neck w/tan ground & floral swags, raised on a high gilt-metal plinth w/a scroll-cast footed base, gilt-metal serpent-form shoulder handles & a scalloped metal rim band & gadrooned domed cover w/leaf bud finial, a clock set into one side within a brass bezel, the matching shorter urns w/similar gilt-metal details, shorter urns 15 1/2", tallest urn 19" h., the set **$3,565**

Pilsner beaker, a flaring foot supporting a tall gently flaring bowl, the sides decorated in color w/a scene of the Munich Child framed by brick red & deep yellow bands on a creamy ground, No. 2775-1014, 1/2 L **$432**

Pitcher, 5 1/2" h., bulbous octagonal lower body tapering to tall cylindrical sides w/a wide long angled spout & angled handle, stylized Art Nouveau decorated in deep gold & dark blue w/stylized fruiting trees up the sides & geometric panels around the lower body, marked "Mettlach Reg. US Pat. Off. - Made in Germany," ca. 1920s **$115**

Planter, Art Nouveau-style, oblong scrolling base band below the squatty bulbous body tapering to a scalloped gadrooned rim w/six C-scroll handles curving down from the rim to the shoulder, the body in dark blue etched & decorated overall w/stylized six- petaled dark & light blue flowers w/brown centers, the border bands in pale green & dark brown, No. 2417, 10 x 16 1/2", 8" h. **$1,150**

Plaque, an etched color scene of Snow White & the Seven Dwarfs against a dark blue ground, decorated by H. Schlitt, minor gold wear, No. 2148, 17" d. **$1,116**

Plaque, Art Nouveau design, a large etched bust portrait of an Art Nouveau woman on the left sniffing large tan roses on dark green leafy stems, tan border band decorated w/dark green & rust red leaf devices, No. 2544, pierced to hang, 20" d. **$863**

Plaque, phanolith, a dark green ground decorated in white relief w/three seminude classical water nymphs & flying birds, No. 7043, pierced to hang, 21" d. **$719**

Punch bowl, cover & underplate, a footed bulbous squatty bowl w/a short wide cylindrical neck & low domed cover w/leaf loop finial, large loop shoulder handles w/satyr mask terminals, red foot, body & neck bands, the body band decorated w/a continuous white relief scene of dancing peasants, the background body in a putty color, No. 2087, 8 L, the set **$1,208**

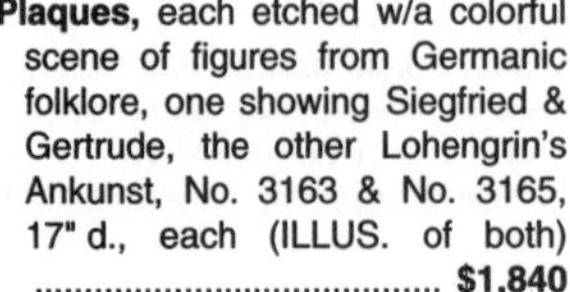

Plaques, each etched w/a colorful scene of figures from Germanic folklore, one showing Siegfried & Gertrude, the other Lohengrin's Ankunst, No. 3163 & No. 3165, 17" d., each (ILLUS. of both) **$1,840**

Newcomb College

This pottery was established in the art department of Newcomb College, New Orleans, Louisiana, in 1897. Each piece was hand-thrown and bore the potter's mark & decorator's monogram on the base. It was always a studio business and never operated as a factory. Its pieces are, therefore, scarce, with the early wares being eagerly sought. The pottery closed in 1940.

Bowl, 2 1/2" h., wide squatty flat-bottomed form tapering to a wide flat rim, dark blue ground molded w/a band of light blue spaced blossoms around the shoulder, decorated by Sadie Irvine, potted by Joseph Meyer, 1926 .... **$1,610**

Bowl, 5 1/4" d., 2 7/8" h., footed wide low compressed lower body below a wide steeply tapering shoulder to the wide flat mouth, the shoulder decorated w/clusters of pale pink blossoms below leafy green stems against a dark blue ground, the lower body in medium blue, decorated by Henrietta Bailey, potted by Joseph Meyer, dated 1920 .... **$1,840**

Jar, cov., wide bulbous ovoid body tapering to a flat mouth flanked by large thick loop shoulder handles in dark blue, flattened inside cover w/a dark blue knob finial, decorated around the sides w/groups of tall slender trees in dark blue w/a leafy canopy at the top, impressed logo, date code for 1910, unobtrusive overall crazing, tiny nick on lower edge of cover, 4 7/8" h. **$3,680**

Even a tiny amount of damage can significantly decrease an item's desirability and resale value, so be sure to inspect thoroughly before purchasing.

Jar, cov., wide bulbous ovoid body tapering to a flat rim w/a low domed cover w/disk finial, carved decoration of live oaks & Spanish moss in dark blue & pale green on a denim blue ground, matte glaze, decorated by A.F. Simpson, 1929, original paper label, 4 1/2" d., 5" h. **$8,625**

Mugs, tankard-type, tapering cylindrical form w/thick angled handle in dark blue, painted w/large stylized saracena blossoms & undulating leaves in brushed light blue over white against a dark blue ground, incised base rings, decorated by Marie de Hoa LeBlanc, potted by Joseph Meyer, glossy glaze, 1901, 5 1/4" h., set of 4 .... **$9,488**

Pitcher, 7 1/2" h., 5 1/2" d., tankard-type, tapering cylindrical body w/a rim spout & long angled dark blue handle, decorated w/large open medium blue tulip blossoms on tall green leafy stems, dark blue top band, panels of tiny dark blue horizontal striping between each set of leaves, glossy glaze, painted by Elizabeth Rogers, potted by Joseph Meyer, ca. 1900 .... **$5,750**

Teapot, cov., "Solitaire," wide squatty bulbous body w/a short angled spout, low slightly tapering cover w/knob finial, C-form handle, rare early high-glaze shaded green, potted by Joseph Fortune Meyer, decorated by Irene Borden Keep, fully signed & numbered, 1901, 4" h. **$2,300**

Tyg (three-handled mug), motto-type, wide tapering cylindrical body flanked by three long C-form handles, each panel modeled w/grape clusters & vines in shaded blue, a continuous band around the base w/phrase "Till Love and Life Are One - Live and Love," glossy glaze, decorated by Sadie Irvine, potted by Joseph Meyer, dated 1909, 6" d., 4 3/4" h. **$5,865**

Vase, 4 3/4" h., footed wide squatty bulbous body tapering to a short tapering cylindrical neck, incised around the wide shoulder w/a continuous band of large white blossoms & green leaves against the mottled dark blue matte ground, decorated by Anna Frances Simpson, dated 1916 .... **$2,645**

Vase, 4" h., wide flat-bottomed bulbous ovoid form tapering to a wide low molded rim, dark blue Spanish moss in oaks decoration against a pale blue sky w/a pale yellow full moon, decorated by Sadie Irvine, potted by Kenneth Smith, dated 1933 .... **$2,875**

Vase, miniature, 3 1/4" h., glossy glaze, bulbous nearly spherical body w/the creamy yellow sides incised w/vertical stripes, the shoulder incised w/overlapping cobalt blue scales outlined in pale green, a short wide cobalt blue rim, decorated by Sadie Irvine, potted by Kenneth Smith, dated 1933 .... **$2,070**

Vase, miniature, 3 7/8" h., flat-bottomed wide ovoid body w/a wide short cylindrical neck, a very dark blue & green Spanish moss in oak trees design against a pink ground, decorated by Sadie Irvine, potted by Jonathan Hunt, dated 1929 .... **$2,300**

Vase, 4" h., 2 3/4" d., gently tapering ovoid body w/ closed rim, decorated w/white bell-shaped flowers against a cobalt & light green ground, by Sadie Irvine, 1914, impressed "NC - SI - JM - C - 51 - GN52" **$935**

Vase, 4 1/4" h., 2 3/4" d., tapering ovoid body w/a wide closed rim, modeled & surface-painted trees in blue & green against a pink sky, by Sadie Irvine, 1918, impressed "NC - JM - SI - JO-3"..................... **$1,435**

Vase, 4 1/2" h., 3 1/2" d., slightly ovoid body tapering gently to a wide flat rim, molded around the top w/ stylized white & yellow flowers & green leaves w/ stems down the sides against a soft blue ground, Sadie Irvine, 1928, impressed "NC - SI - JM - 25 - QS100".. **$990**

Vase, 4 1/2" h., 4 3/4" d., spherical form on cylindrical rim w/short flat rim, carved matte decorations of pink & yellow blossoms on a green branch, against a cobalt blue ground, impressed "NC - SI- JM - W22 - 271," by S. Irvine, 1920 .... **$1,760**

When shopping for antiques, bring the tools necessary to spot repairs and fakes. Bring a book on marks. Use a blacklight to detect fluorescing modern glues that have been used to repair cracks. Bring a tape measure and antique references to verify that measurements match those of authentic pieces. Use a magnet to discern between ferrous and non-ferrous metals. A magnifying glass will help you see the dot matrix of a modern print and the brush strokes of a painting.

Nippon

"Nippon" is a term used to describe a wide range of porcelain wares produced in Japan from the late 19th century until about 1921. It was in 1891 that the United States implemented the McKinley Tariff Act, which required that all wares exported to the United States carry a marking indicating their country of origin. The Japanese chose to use "Nippon," their name for Japan. In 1921 the import laws were revised and the words "Made in" had to be added to the markings. Japan was also required to replace the "Nippon" with the English name "Japan" on all wares sent to the United States.

Many Japanese factories produced Nippon porcelain, much of it hand-painted with ornate floral or landscape decoration and heavy gold decoration, applied beading and slip-trailed designs referred to as "moriage." We indicate the specific marking used on a piece, when known, at the end of each listing. Be aware that a number of Nippon markings have been reproduced and used on new porcelain wares.

Important reference books on Nippon include: *The Collector's Encyclopedia of Nippon Porcelain, Series One through Three*, by Joan F. Van Patten (Collector Books, Paducah, Kentucky) and *The Wonderful World of Nippon Porcelain, 1891-1921* by Kathy Wojciechowski (Schiffer Publishing, Ltd., Atglen, Pennsylvania).

Humidor, cov., three square block feet supporting the wide slightly tapering cylindrical body w/a slightly tapering cover w/large mushroom finial, the body decorated w/a landscape of a man in a canoe w/a stag in green bushes on the shore, dark yellow to pale cream ground, the feet & top rim decorated w/geometric decorative bands w/stylized symbols, matching band around the cover, 7" h. **$575**

Vase, 5 3/4" h., bulbous ovoid body tapering to a short flaring neck trimmed in gold & flanked by arched gold shoulder handles, the body centered by a large gold oval reserve painted w/a full-length portrait of an exotic young woman standing in front of a peacock, surrounded by an overall gold lattice & pink rose decoration on the white ground, green Maple Leaf mark, minor gold wear **$432**

Vase, 7 1/8" h., "sharkskin" technique, slender slightly tapering cylindrical body w/ a narrow shoulder centered by a short neck w/widely flaring mouth, arched & pierced-loop gold shoulder handles, the sides h.p. w/a stylized landscape w/tall trees in the foreground & small houses & a lake in the distance, done in pastel shades of blue, yellow, green, lavender & orange, purple Cherry Blossom mark, tiny glaze nick in the base **$230**

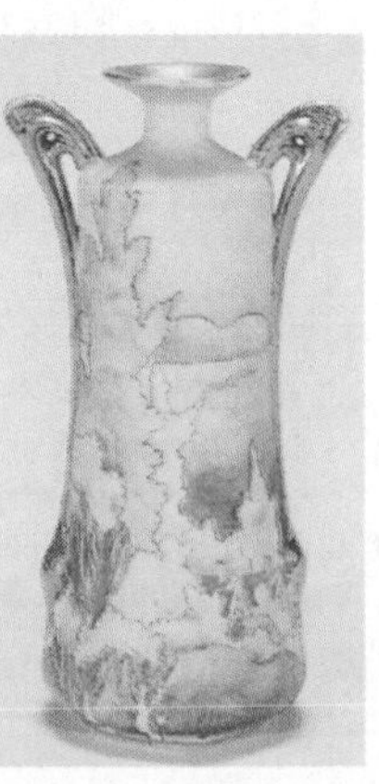

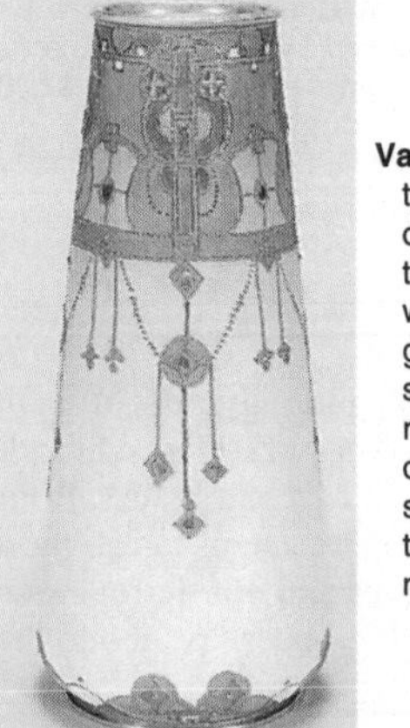

Vase, 9 1/2" h., tapestry-type, tall gently tapering cylindrical body w/a flat rim, the upper body decorated w/a wide band of stylized geometric designs in shades of green, blue, rose red & gold & faux jewels, delicate gold beaded swags suspended down the sides, blue Maple Leaf mark **$1,150**

Noritake

Noritake china, still in production in Japan, has been exported in large quantities to this country since early in the last century. Although the Noritake Company first registered in 1904, it did not use "Noritake" as part of its backstamp until 1918. Interest in Noritake has escalated as collectors now seek out pieces made between the "Nippon" era and World War II (1921-41). The Azalea pattern is also popular with collectors.

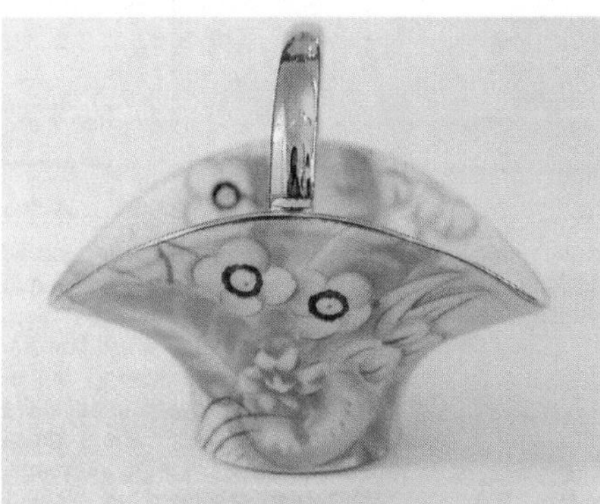

Basket, short form w/extremely flaring sides, decorated inside & out in/floral motif in peach, pearl grey & black, silvered rim & center handle, 4 1/2" d., 6 1/2" h. **$188**

Breakfast set: cov. teapot, teacup, sugar, creamer, tray; tray w/ruffled sides & four depressions to hold teapot, cup & creamer, all w/yellow C-form handles & decorated w/pastoral scene of woman in ruffled yellow dress & wide brimmed yellow bonnet standing under tree & holding flowers, the cylindrical sugar w/scene of tree & flowers, all w/gilt line trim at rims, tray 8 1/2 x 10 1/2", the set **$293**

Calendar holder, narrow rectangular base w/an upright oblong holder at one end & a flattened figural rabbit at the other end, iridized orange & green w/stylized purple & blue blossoms, 5 1/4" l., 2" h. **$720**

If you haven't seen an item of interest that is about to be auctioned, ask a ring man to allow you to inspect it immediately. The auctioneer will note your interest and hold the bidding momentarily while you decide. Inspections are better made during the preview, however.

Chip & dip, cov., round, the attached plate & dip container & lid decorated w/ blue ribbons around their rims, the plate & lid w/red, orange, pink, lavender & yellow flowers, the lid's handle in the form of a seated/kneeling black-haired woman in blue, overall 4 1/2" h., plate 9 1/2" d. **$945**

Chocolate pot, cov., decorated w/ figure of black-haired girl in purple knee-length dress w/wide skirt, the hem decorated w/red flowers, a matching sash flowing out at each side, yellow-trimmed white petticoats showing where dress appears to be billowing in breeze, the waist decorated w/yellow & red flowers, a large green floppy-brimmed hat w/floral trim obscuring one eye, one hand reaching up toward hanging flowers in yellow, red & caramel w/green leaves, a purple bird flying by, all on caramel ground, the lid w/handle in the form of a perched bird in red, blue, brown, green & yellow, C-scroll side handle, 9" h. **$650**

Cigarette holder, footed, figural swan, orange lustre w/black neck & head, black outlining on wing feathers & tail, 3" w., 4 1/2" h. **$310**

Creamer & sugar, the sugar container a round shallow form w/gilt scroll side handles, slight depression in center to hold creamer, the creamer a cylindrical form w/angled gilt trimmed handle & slightly arched spout, both pieces decorated in alternating black & white panels, the black w/white & gilt oval designs, the white w/stylized floral designs in deep red/orange, black & white, both pieces w/gilt trim, 5 1/2" d., the set **$153**

Dish, cov., caramel colored bowl & lid, the lid w/embossed daisy-like flowers, the handle in the form of a seated black-haired masked Pierrot-type figure dressed in pearl-grey, black & white w/caramel ruff, holding one leg up to chest, 7" h., 7 1/8" d. **$2,890**

Jam server, cov., three-legged round container on disk base, the lid w/opening just big enough for handle of serving spoon, in pink, deep orange & black w/green leaf decorations, orange knob handle on lid, white spoon, 4 1/4" w., 5 1/4" h., the set **$203**

Jug, slender ovoid form w/cut-out handle at top & short cylindrical spout set in body at an angle, the top a deep cyan w/black line trim, the rest of the body a deep red ground decorated w/scene of an 18th-c. woman w/powdered hair & wearing a blue off- the-shoulder top & full white skirt holding a songbird on one outstretched finger, the birdcage open in front of her, all against a background of shade trees & arbor vitae, the foreground w/yellow roses, 3 1/2 x 4 1/4", 7 1/2" h. **$325**

Pin tray, round, mauve tray decorated w/ applied image of seated dog in caramel & black, 2" h., 2 3/5" d. **$65**

Plate, 6 1/4" d., caramel ground w/figure of woman wearing elaborate powdered coiffure or wig bedecked w/yellow, deep pink, mauve & apricot flowers w/green leaves & black ribbons, dressed in blue sleeveless gown w/full skirt trimmed in yellow, one hand fingering green bead necklace, the other holding a black mask **$740**

←

Potpourri pot, cov., ovoid form, the flat lid white w/black line trim & black & white knob handle, the body decorated w/figure of Oriental woman in deep red kimono holding green flower-decorated fan in one hand, a sprig of cherry blossoms in the other, standing beneath branches of cherry trees in bloom, all against a caramel ground, 4" d., 5" h. **$395**

Originally, potpourri was made by allowing herbs and flowers to ferment and mold ("pourri" means "rotten" in French.)

Powder box, cov., round, in the form of a woman in full-skirted off-the-shoulder dress in coral-pink decorated w/light pink roses & green leaves, the bottom of the skirt making up the powder container, the top of the skirt the lid, the handle formed by the figure of a fan-holding woman w/powdered hair & a beauty mark, 3 1/2" d., 6 1/4" h. $875

Powder puff box, cov., round, the lid decorated w/figure of woman sitting w/back to viewer, wearing dark green & cream-colored dress w/full skirt, dark green bodice, festooned w/lavender ribbons at waist & shoulders & pink & yellow flowers decorating skirt, two dark curls escaping from back of the yellow & green flower-bedecked bonnet that hides her face, all on caramel ground, 1 3/4" h., 4 1/4" d. $420

Powder puff box, cov., squat circular shape, pale mauve w/black line trim, the cover w/caramel top upon which perches a blue, red, yellow & black bird, 1" h., 4" d. $434

Sandwich serving plate, round, w/gilt angular handle in middle, the plate decorated w/scene of pink-clad figures on rolling green ground gathering red fruit from large tree, a line of shrubs in the background, all against a pink & green ground, 9 1/2" d. $385

Tea set: cov. teapot, creamer, cov. sugar, tray; the teapot, creamer & sugar w/ gold angled loop handles, the 6 x 11" tray w/tab side handles, all in vivid deep orange w/gold & black trim, decorated w/desert scene of robed, turbaned figure against backdrop of palm trees & a tower, the set $395

Vase, 6 7/8" h., U-form double vase, the two receptacles joined by double bars, the top one serving as roost for tropical bird in vivid orange, dark blue, green, yellow & pink, the double vases in pale mauve decorated w/deep orange & yellow/gold flowers & green leaves, the scalloped rims w/gilt trim, flared base **$261**

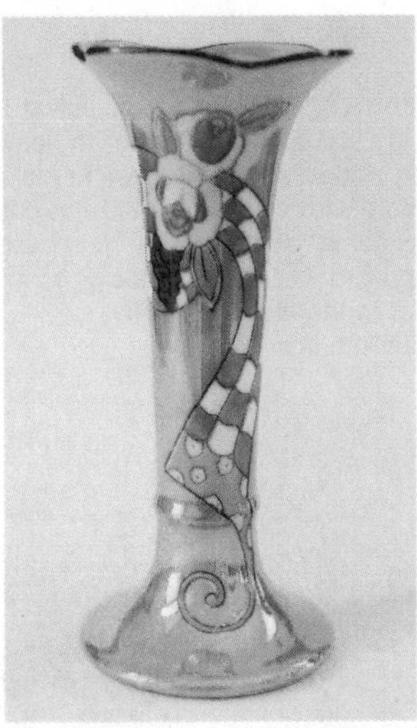

Vase, 6" h., trumpet form w/wavy black-trimmed rim & flared base, the ringed body decorated w/green & white checked sash & rose-like flowers in shades of pink & yellow, all on a caramel ground **$171**

Vase, 8 1/4" h., ovoid shape tapering out to scalloped rim, C-scroll handles, the bottoms of which are applied to the top of vase, w/the tops of the handles unconnected to vase, pale mauve disk base, the body decorated w/ ornate flower in deep red, grape, yellow, pink & blue/grey colors & black dots, green leaves, against caramel ground w/pale mauve & brown trim **$156**

Vase, 8" h., squatty form w/tapering shoulder & high pointed arch handle at top, caramel ground w/black trim on handle & short pink neck, the body decorated w/figure of young woman in powdered hair adorned w/a single red rose, wearing black full-skirted gown trimmed w/red roses, one hand holding a decorative fan **$615**

Wall pocket, trumpet form in caramel w/black rim, decorated w/figure of lute-playing musician dress in black w/extravagant white & red ruff & cuffs, 2 7/8" w. x 6" h. **$505**

Ohr (George) Pottery

George Ohr, the eccentric potter of Biloxi, Mississippi, worked from about 1883 to 1906. Some think him to be one of the most expert throwers the craft will ever see. The majority of his works were hand-thrown, exceedingly thin-walled items, some of which have a crushed or folded appearance. He considered himself the foremost potter in the world and declined to sell much of his production, instead accumulating a great horde to leave as a legacy to his children. In 1972 this collection was purchased for resale by an antiques dealer.

Bowl-vase, footed squatty body w/deeply indented & folded sides below a flattened rounded shoulder, bisque red clay, script signature, 5" d., 3 3/4" h. **$2,875**

Pitcher, 2 1/2" h., 4 1/4" l., a round foot below the body pulled & pinched into a large spout opposite a thin, pointed fin-form handle, rolled rim, speckled gunmetal glaze, repairs to handle & rim edge, stamped "G.E. OHR - Biloxi, Miss." **$5,463**

Pitcher, 5 1/2" h., 3 3/4" d., footed spherical lower body w/a small waist below the deep cupped upper body w/ a flaring rim & wide folded rim spout, arched loop handle, mirror black & eggplant glazed, stamped "G.E. OHR - Biloxi, Miss." **$6,325**

Teapot, cov., a cylindrical slightly waisted body w/ a flattened shoulder centering a short cylindrical neck, serpentine spout & long C-form handle, small inset cover w/large mushroom knop, covered overall in a green speckled glossy glaze, stamped "GEO. E. OHR/BILOXI, MISS.," minor restoration to spout, rim & cover, 6 1/2" l., 4 1/4" h. .. **$5,581**

Teapot, cov., a large size pot w/a footring supporting the wide squatty bulbous body tapering to a cupped neck w/inset flat cover, long serpentine spout & simple C-form handle, covered in a spectacular white, red & pink glaze sponged on an amber ground, stamped "G.E. OHR/ Biloxi, Miss.," late 19th - early 20th c., 12 1/2" l., 5 1/2" h. **$55,813**

Vase, 3 1/4" h., 3" d., wide domed base w/medial ring below the trumpet-form neck w/pinched & twisted rim, overall raspberry & amber glossy glaze, stamped "GEO. E. OHR," tight line in the base **$1,955**

Vase, 3 3/4" h., 4" d., bulbous squatty form w/a deep in-body twist around the center, bisque red clay fired to a dark brown sheen, stamped "GEO. OHR" **$2,760**

Vase, 4 3/4" h., 3 3/4" d., wide squatty bulbous lower body centered by a cylindrical deeply twisted neck w/a bulbed top w/a flaring crimped rim, gunmetal black glaze, stamped "GEO. E. OHR - Biloxi, Miss.," minute rim nick & small kiln kiss **$5,463**

George Ohr is known as "the mad potter of Biloxi" because of his eccentric personality.

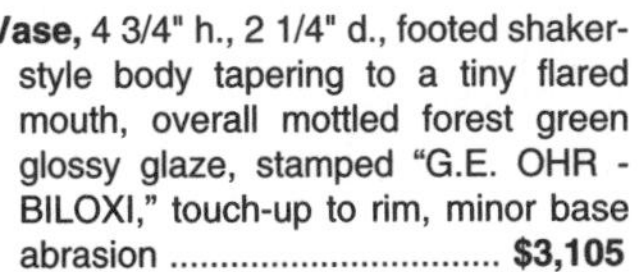

Vase, 4 3/4" h., 2 1/4" d., footed shaker-style body tapering to a tiny flared mouth, overall mottled forest green glossy glaze, stamped "G.E. OHR - BILOXI," touch-up to rim, minor base abrasion **$3,105**

Vase, 6" h., 2 3/4" d., bulbous ovoid lower body tapering to a waisted neck w/cylindrical top, overall unusual raspberry & white volcanic glaze on a glossy blue ground, stamped "G.E. OHR - Biloxi, Miss.," underglaze firing line inside neck **$14,950**

Paul Revere Pottery

This pottery was established in Boston, Massachusetts, in 1906, by a group of philanthropists seeking to establish better conditions for underprivileged young girls of the area. Edith Brown served as supervisor of the small "Saturday Evening Girls Club" pottery operation, which was moved, in 1912, to a house close to the Old North Church where Paul Revere's signal lanterns had been placed. The wares were mostly hand decorated in mineral colors, and both sgraffito and molded decorations were employed. Although it became popular, it was never a profitable operation and always depended on financial contributions to operate. After the death of Edith Brown in 1932, the pottery foundered and finally closed in 1942.

Bowl, 4 1/4" d., bulbous ovoid body w/a wide flat mouth, decorated around the top w/a yellow band accented by flying scarabs in light green, streaky pale blue glaze, marked "S.E.G. - 05-1-14," crazing, 1914 .... **$1,093**

Bowl, 6" d., 3" h., deep rounded sides w/a wide flat rim, brown semi-matte ground decorated around the rim w/a cuerda seca band of Greek key in taupe & ivory on white, signed "SEG - 10.12 - FL" **$1,116**

Breakfast set: child's, 7 1/2" d. plate & 3 5/8" h. mug; each h.p. w/a circle enclosing a picture of a white rabbit lying on a green grassy mound, white & blue outer bands, initialed by the artist, early 20th c., the set **$1,116**

Jardiniere, wide bulbous squatty body w/a closed rim, yellow ground w/a wide rim band in cuerda seca w/black-outlined white lotus blossoms trimmed w/yellow, stamped mark, firing lines around rim & base, two restored rim chips, 9" d., 7" h. **$1,495**

Plate, dinner, 10" d., dark greyish blue ground decorated around the rim in cuerda seca w/a band of stylized white lotus blossoms, signed "SEG - AM - 11-14," rim bruise, small chips to footring **$646**

Plates, 8 1/2" d., luncheon, creamy white w/a dark blue border band decorated w/stylized white lotus blossoms, Saturday Evening Girls mark & dated 1910, set of 12 .... **$2,645**

Tea set: cov. bulbous 4 3/4" h. teapot, 4 1/4" h. cylindrical creamer, 4" h. cylindrical cov. sugar bowl & 5 1/4" w. square tea tile; each decorated w/ a dark blue glaze w/a border band of stylized white lotus blossoms, all marked w/the Saturday Evening Girls mark & dated 1910, teapot cover cracked, glued chip on inner rim of teapot, the set **$1,955**

Vase, 6 1/4" h., 3 3/4" d., simple ovoid body w/a wide flat rim, dark bluish grey lower body, a wide shoulder band in cuerda seca decorated w/a band of stylized oak leaves & acorns in green, brown & pale blue, inkstamped "SEG - AM - 12-17," 1917 .... **$4,025**

High-end antique shows sometimes begin with a preview party the evening before the event opens to the public. Food and drinks are served. Proceeds from the party usually go to a charity. A preview party is a good opportunity to become acquainted with many of the top dealers in the trade and to scout out your favorite items at the show. Because dealers are typically anxious to get off to a good start, they may be willing to offer an attractive price on a choice piece.

Peters & Reed

In 1897 John D. Peters and Adam Reed formed a partnership to produce flowerpots in Zanesville, Ohio. Formally incorporated as Peters and Reed in 1901, this type of production was the mainstay until after 1907, when they gradually expanded into the art pottery field. Frank Ferrell, a former designer at the Weller Pottery, developed the "Moss Aztec" line while associated with Peters and Reed, and other art lines followed. Although unmarked, attribution is not difficult once familiar with the various lines. In 1921, Peters and Reed became Zane Pottery, which continued in production until 1941.

ZANEWARE
MADE IN U.S.A.

Vase, 10" h., Marbleized line, flaring base tapering to a trumpet-form body, streaky bands of black & yellow on the brown ground, glossy glaze, unmarked, overall crazing **$127**

Vase, 4 3/4" h., Landsun line, baluster-form body w/a dark blue upper band above the mottled & streaked blackish brown, tan & yellow green lower body, unmarked, some burst glaze bubbles near base **$104**

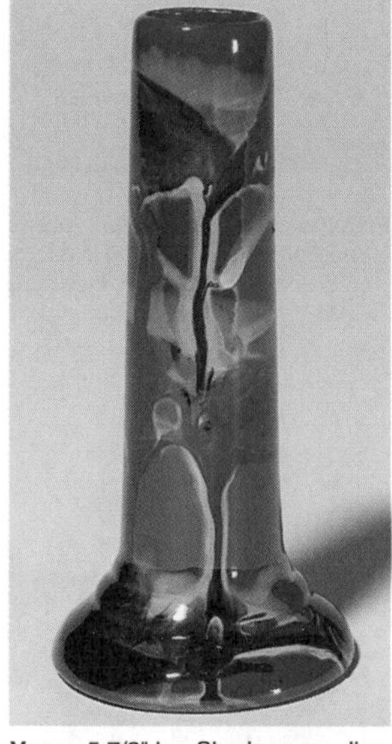

Vase, 5 7/8" h., Shadowware line, flaring foot tapering to tall slender cylindrical body, swirled blue & yellow over a dark blue ground, unmarked **$127**

Vase, 5" h., Landsun line, flared foot & widely flaring trumpet-form body, decorated w/a band of upright swirled & pointed dark brown leaf-like devices around the bottom overlapping a band of transparent brown leaves over a dark green & yellow ground, unmarked, some small base chips **$81**

Vase, 6 3/4" h., Shadowware line, baluster-form body w/a short flared neck, streaky dripping dark blues & pale green over a tan background, unmarked, few tiny underglaze inclusions **$150**

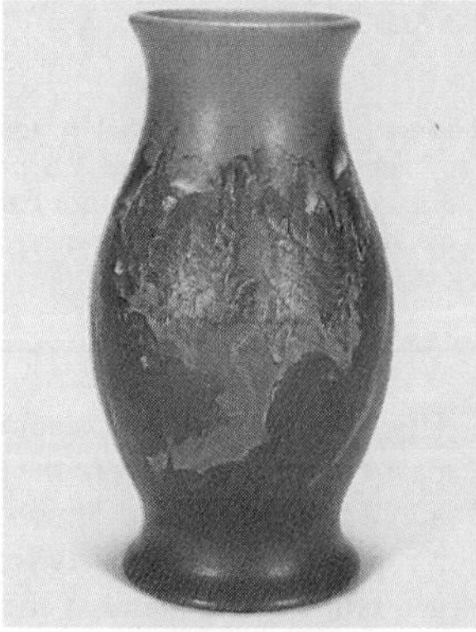

Vase, 7 1/2" h., Shadow Ware, footed flaring trumpet-form body below the angled shoulder centered by a short molded neck, drippy streaks of blue, black & yellow down over a caramel ground, unmarked, overall crazing **$460**

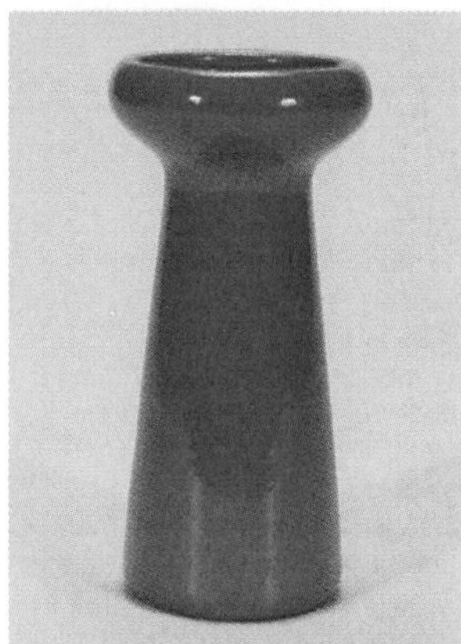

Vase, 7 1/4" h., Wilse line, gently tapering cylindrical body w/a wide cupped top, overall speckled glossy blue glaze, impressed Zane Ware mark **$69**

Vase, 8 7/8" h., Shadowware line, cylindrical body below a squatty compressed top w/a wide flat mouth, streaky & drippy dark blue & brown over a tan ground, impressed mark, crazing **$230**

Vase, 9" h., Shadow Ware, simple ovoid body w/a short wide flaring mouth, black, blue & yellow dripping streaks down the sides against the creamy yellow glossy glaze, unmarked, overall crazing **$219**

Vase, 7 5/8" h., Landsun Ware, footed gently swelled cylindrical body w/a flaring molded rim, mottled matt green & dark blue on a tan ground, unmarked **$259**

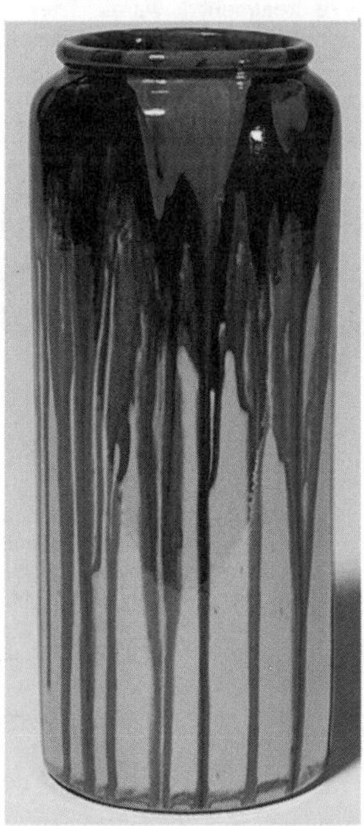

Vase, 8 7/8" h., Shadowware line, cylindrical body w/a molded rim, streaky dripping dark blues & browns over a tan ground, faintly marked w/Zane Pottery logo, crazing **$259**

Vase, 8 5/8" h., Shadowware line, simple ovoid body w/a low flaring neck, mottled & swirled blue & olive green on a dark blue ground, unmarked **$374**

Vase, 8" h., Landsun line, flared foot & swelled cylindrical body w/a wide ringed & molded wide flat mouth, overlapping angled streaky blue & brown bands around the sides against the pale green ground, impressed Zane Ware logo **$195**

Vase, 9 3/4" h., Landsun Ware, conical base tapering to a tall slender cylindrical body, overall mottled & streaky dark blue & brown on a pale blue & yellow ground, unmarked, crazing **$115**

Pierce (Howard) Porcelains

Howard Pierce was born in Chicago, Illinois in 1912. He attended the university there and also the Chicago Art Institute but by 1935 he wanted a change and came to California. That move would alter his life forever. He settled in Claremont and attended the Pomona College. William Manker, a well-known ceramist, hired Mr. Pierce in 1936 to work for him. That liaison lasted about three years. After leaving Manker's employment Howard opened a small studio in Laverne, California and, not wishing to be in competition with Manker, began by creating miniature animal figures, some of which he made into jewelry. In 1941, he married Ellen Voorhees who was living in National City, California. In the 1950s, Mr. Pierce had national representation through the N.S. Gustin Company. Polyurethane animals are high on collectors lists as Howard, after creating in the early years only a few pieces using this material, realized he was allergic to it and had to discontinue its use. Pierce was a man of many talents and a great deal of curiosity. He experimented with various mediums such as a Wedgwood Jasper Ware type body, then went into porcelain bisque animals and plants that he put close to or in open areas of high-gloss vases. When Mt. St. Helens volcano erupted, Pierce was one of the first to experiment with adding the ash to his silica which produced a rough-textured glaze. Lava, while volcano associated, was a glaze treatment unrelated to Mt. St. Helens. Howard described Lava as "...bubbling up from the bottom..." Pierce also created some pieces in gold leaf which are harder to find than the gold treatment he formulated in the 1950s for Sears. They had ordered a large number of pieces and wanted all of them produced in the gold treatment. Many of these pieces are not marked. Howard also did what he termed 'tipping' in relation to glazes. A piece would be high-gloss overall but, then the tops, bottoms, sides, etc. would be brushed, speckled or mottled with a different glaze, most often brown, black or grey. For example, a set of three fish made in the late 1950s or early 1960s were on individual bases that were 'tipped' as were the fins with the bodies being a solid brown or black. Toward the late 1970s, Mr. Pierce began putting formula numbers on his pieces and recording the materials used to create certain glazes. In November 1992, because of health problems, Howard and Ellen Pierce destroyed all the molds they had created over the years. Mr. Pierce began working on a limited basis producing miniature versions of past porcelain wares. These pieces are simply stamped "Pierce." Howard Pierce passed away in February, 1994.

Pierce

HOWARD PIERCE

HP

Howard Pierce
Claremont, Calif

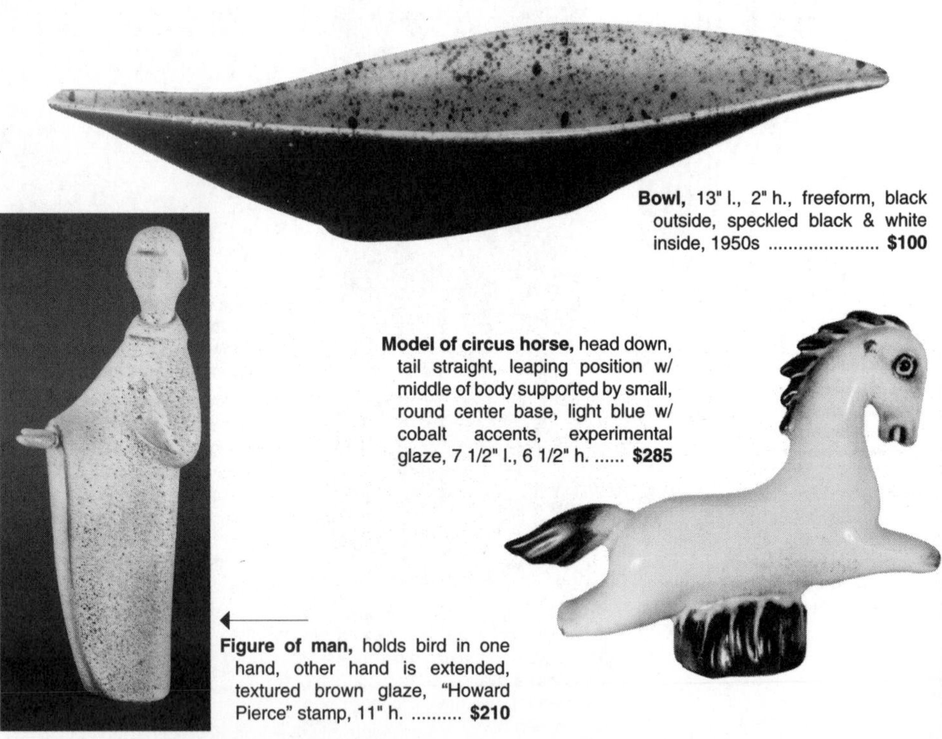

Bowl, 13" l., 2" h., freeform, black outside, speckled black & white inside, 1950s **$100**

Model of circus horse, head down, tail straight, leaping position w/ middle of body supported by small, round center base, light blue w/ cobalt accents, experimental glaze, 7 1/2" l., 6 1/2" h. **$285**

Figure of man, holds bird in one hand, other hand is extended, textured brown glaze, "Howard Pierce" stamp, 11" h. **$210**

Model of mouse, pink & ivory high glaze, "Howard Pierce Porcelain" stamp, 2" h., 3 1/4" l. **$390**

Model of skunk, rough textured matte glaze, 6" h. **$220**

Models of dogs w/drooping ears, dark & light brown, 8" h., & 6" h., pr. **$220**

Sugar bowl, open, Wedgwood-type white bisque lamb motif, pale blue matte handle & outer edges, produced in 1950s, 2 3/4" h. **$105**

Models of fish, each on a half-circle base, dark blue bodies w/speckled bases & fins, large fish, 6" h., medium fish, 4 3/4" h., small fish, 3" h., the set......................... **$365**

Quimper

This French earthenware pottery has been made in France since the end of the 17th century and is still in production today. Because the colorful decoration on this ware, predominantly of Breton peasant figures, is all hand-painted and each piece is unique, it has become increasingly popular with collectors in recent years. Most pieces offered today date from about the mid- 19th century to the present. Modern potteries continue to operate today, with contemporary examples available in gift shops.

HB HENRIOT QUIMPER

The standard reference in this field is Quimper Pottery A French Folk Art Faience by Sandra V. Bondhus (privately printed, 1981).

Coffee set: 9 1/4" h. cov. coffeepot, creamer & cov. sugar; each decorated w/different Breton musician & very richly ornamented "Rouenesque" border, "HB Quimper 15," excellent, the set **$525**

Dish, divided, double bagpipe shape, "decor riche" patt., bow & twisted knot handles, each division featuring peasant couple standing beneath sprigs of Breton wildflowers, 13 1/2" l., 11" w., excellent **$550**

Inkwell, cov., in the form of a Breton hat, w/original inset & lid w/acorn finial, scene on lid of seated woman w/basket of eggs at her side, "HenRiot Quimper France 72," 5 1/2" w., mint **$175**

Jardiniere, cradle shape on four tiny feet, double knobs at four upper corners, w/scene of peasant couple executed in the "demi- fantasie" style, back panel displaying full-blown red & yellow rose set in flower branch, "HR Quimper," 7 1/4" l., mint **$675**

Jardiniere, octagonal shape w/country French geometric patt., blue sponged ropetwist handles, unsigned, 19th c., excellent, 12" l. **$300**

Jardiniere, oval w/scalloped rim, footed, flat ring handles, "decor riche" patt., image of seated musician on front, "HB Quimper 128," 9" l., mint **$325**

Liquor set: 7" d. tray, 6" h. cov. decanter & four 1" h. handleless cups; figure of traditional peasant woman adorning decanter, a bold daisy patt. covering the tray, each cup w/flower spray on front, "HenRiot Quimper France 75," mint, the set **$175**

Plate, 9 1/2" d., First Period Porquier Beau, "Botanique" patt., decorated w/spray of yellow narcissus & snail, signed w/intersecting "PB" mark in blue, mint **$1,150**

Plates, 7 1/2" d., pale blue sponged ruffled rims, center display of seated peasant man on one, seated peasant woman on other, "HB" mark only, 19th c., mint, pr. **$300**

Platter, 12" l., 8 1/2" w., oval, "decor riche" patt., center showing courting scene of young Breton couple seated beneath canopy of trees, "HB Quimper," excellent **$550**

Platter, 14 1/2" l., 11" w., oval, scene of peasant couple & "a la touche" flower garland band, "HB" mark only, 19th c., mint **$175**

Platter, 19" l., 8 1/2" w., oblong shape in Modern Movement Celtic style, center depicting wedding procession walking on path from building in distance, "HenRiot Quimper 72," pierced for hanging, mint **$425**

Tray, yellow glaze w/multicolor ropetwist handles, center featuring a pitcher-toting woman wearing the headdress of Cherbourg flanked by floral designs, HenRiot made-on-commission example, signed only "Cherbourg," 12 x 8", mint **$175**

Vase, 9" h., "Decor Riche," donut shape divided at top center w/ separate openings on each side of division, four short outcurved feet, "decor riche" patt., decorated w/cartouches featuring woman holding basket & man playing flute flanking one w/view of the city of Quimper reflected in the Odet River, reverse side decorated w/ multicolor flower garland, dragon-like side handles, mint **$1,800**

Red Wing

Various potteries operated in Red Wing, Minnesota, from 1868, the most successful being the Red Wing Stoneware Co., organized in 1877. Merged with other local potteries through the years, it became known as Red Wing Union Stoneware Co. in 1906, and was one of the largest producers of utilitarian stoneware items in the United States. After a decline in the popularity of stoneware products, an art pottery line was introduced to compensate for the loss. This was reflected in a new name for the company, Red Wing Potteries, Inc., in 1936. Stoneware production ceased entirely in 1947, but vases, planters, cookie jars and dinnerwares of art pottery quality continued in production until 1967, when the pottery ceased operation altogether.

Art Pottery

Bowl, 7 5/8" d., 5" h., deep rounded sides, white exterior & black interior, on a black rectangular plinth base, impressed "Red Wing U.S.A. 1333" **$259**

Bowl, 8 3/8" l., 5 1/2" h., stylized gondola-shaped body tapering to arched rolled ends, white exterior & black interior, on a rectangular black plinth, impressed "1370" **$150**

Cookie jar, cov., barrel-shaped w/molded rim & wide cover w/disk finial, molded in relief w/cattails & the word "Cookies" against a stippled ground, dark brown bands at the rim & base w/tan center **$250-300**

Cruet w/original stopper, Nokomis Line, footed ovoid body w/an integral upright slender long spout joined w/a flat brace to the cylindrical ringed neck, curved handle from neck to shoulder, original cap-form stopper, overall mottled & drippy glaze in shades of green & brown, blue ink label, 8 3/4" h. **$633**

Jug, Nokomis Line, bulbous ovoid body tapering to a cylindrical neck w/flared rim, small angled handle from rim to shoulder, overall mottled & drippy glaze in shades of green & brown, Shape No. 204, blue company ink stamp mark, 9 1/2" h. **$460**

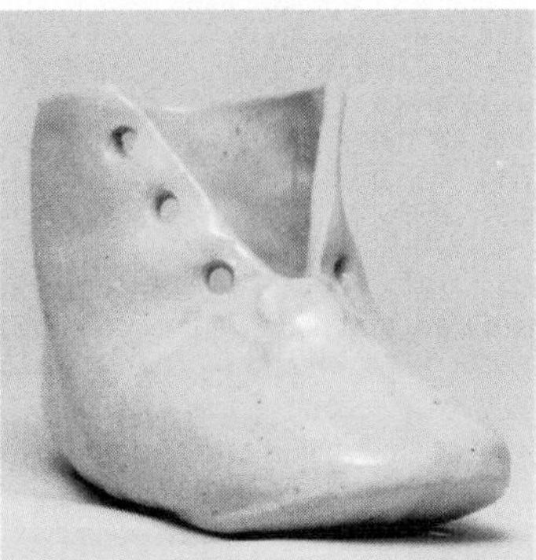

Model of a baby shoe, miniature, overall white glaze **$450-550**

Model of a dog, miniature, Staffordshire-style seated spaniel, white glaze w/blue eyes, 3" h............... **$250-300**

Planter, modernistic upright flattened domed shape w/a recessed arching panel, dark brown glaze, No. B1418 .... **$41**

Vase, 10 1/4" h., Nokomis Line, simple ovoid body w/a short wide cylindrical neck, overall mottled & drippy glaze in shades of green & brown, Shape No. 203 .... **$690**

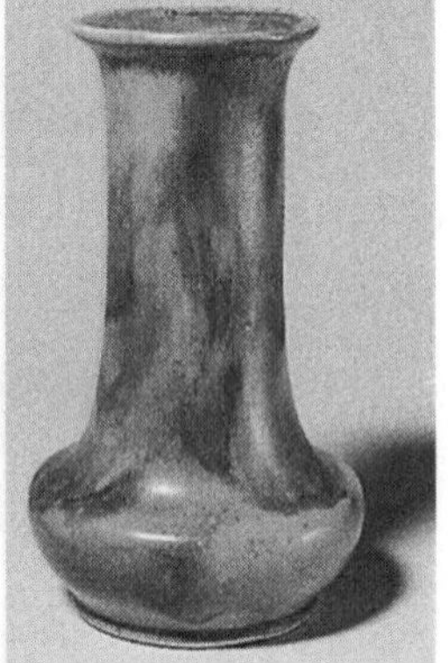

Vase, 10 1/8" h., Nokomis Line, footed squatty cushion-form base tapering to a tall cylindrical neck w/a flaring rim, overall mottled & drippy glaze in shades of green & brown, Shape No. 196, Red Wing blue stamp mark **$345**

Vase, 10 3/8" h., Nokomis Line, swelled cylindrical body w/a narrow shoulder & wide tapering neck w/a flat mouth, overall mottled & drippy glaze in shades of green & brown, blue Red Wing ink mark, Shape 208 .... **$575**

Vase, 7 1/4" h., Nokomis Line, simple ovoid body tapering to a small flat mouth, overall mottled streaky brown, green & blue glaze, Shape No. 206, round inkstamp mark, various tiny pinprick depressions in the glaze **$230**

Vase, advertising florist-type, cylindrical w/flared base & molded flat rim, white glaze trimmed w/blue bands & blue rectangle enclosing "Alpha Floral Co.," early 20th c. **$1,000-1,200**

Brushed & Glazed Wares

Vase, 7 1/2" h., Lion patt., bulbous ovoid body w/a wide round shoulder to the short wide flaring neck, lightly molded around the sides w/walking lions, overall mottled drippy glossy ochre-green & brown glaze above a matte lower body, No. 164S, ca. 1931, couple of tiny base chips **$127**

Don't pass up a deal on an antique when you are traveling because you don't want to have to transport it. Dealers may be willing to pack and ship it for you to make a sale.

Dinnerwares & Novelties

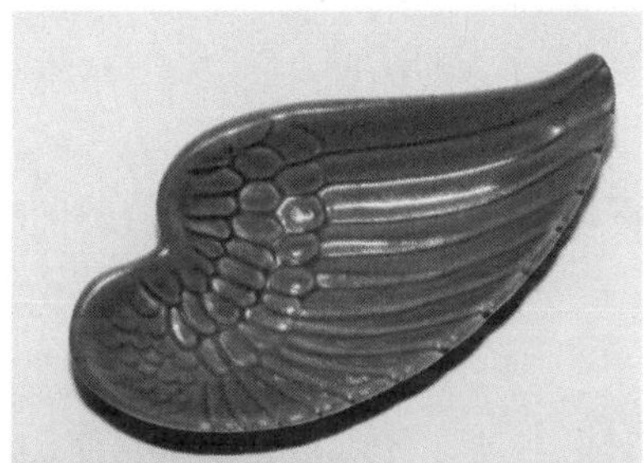

Ashtray, earthenware, model of a wing w/a deep red glaze, bottom marked earthenware, "Red Wing Potteries" **$50-60**

Teapot, cov., Bob White patt., cream ground h.p. w/stylized quails, ca. 1956, 7 1/2" h. **$125**

Stoneware & Utility Wares

Baking dish, advertis ing-type, wide flat bottom w/deep sides w/molded graduating bands, overall glossy maroon glaze, dark blue printed advertising on inside bottom (ILLUS. of two views) **$375-425**

Beater jar, advertising-type, cylindrical w/molded flat rim, white-glazed w/blue bands & blue advertising reading "Red Wing Beater Jar - Eggs - Cream - Salad Dressing" **$125-150**

Bowl, 11" d., deep rounded paneled sides & a wide molded rim, overall red & blue sponging on white **$325-350**

Bowl, 5" d., deep rounded paneled sides & a wide molded rim, overall red & blue sponging on white **$550-650**

Bowl, nappie-style, Saffron ware, ribbed sides below the wide flat rim decorated w/a white band flanked by thin brown bands **$250-300**

Butter churn, cov., miniature, advertising- and commemorative-type, swelled cylindrical body w/a flared rim, eared handles & original cover w/wooden dasher, white-glazed w/blue script number above a pair of printed birch leaves above a printed oval w/advertising, also marked "Iowa Chapter Red Wing Collectors Society 2nd Annual Conf. 1994," 4" h. ... **$127**

Butter churn, cov., tapering cylindrical body w/molded rim & inset cover, white-glazed w/a large blue printed size number above a 4" red wing mark & the blue oval Red Wing Union Stoneware mark, 2 gal. **$475-525**

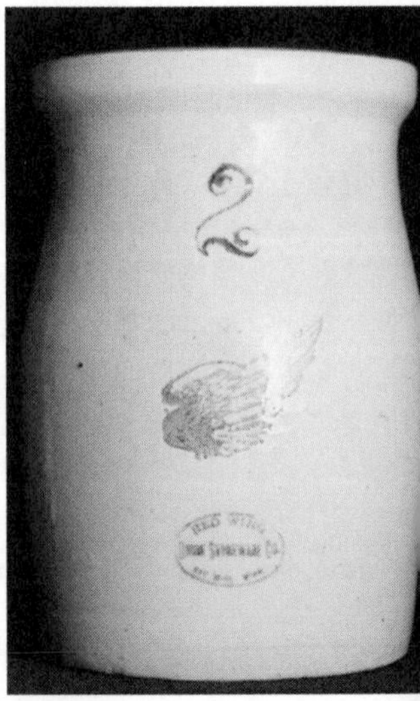

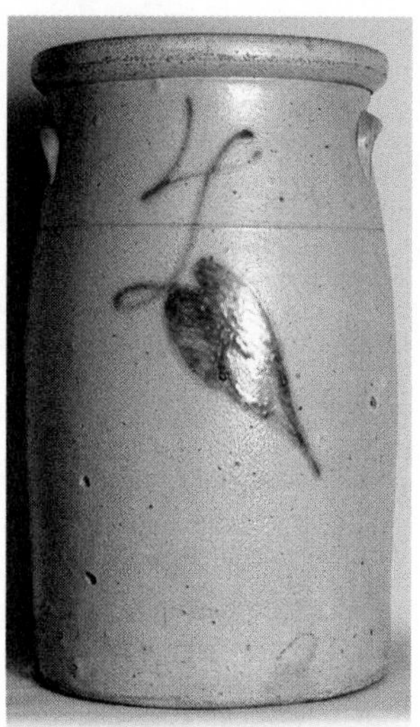

Butter churn, tall slightly tapering cylindrical salt-glazed body w/ thick molded rim & eared handles, cobalt blue slip-quilled "4" above a large leaf, impressed Red Wing Stoneware mark on the side, 4 gal. **$3,000-3,500**

Butter crock, wide cylindrical body w/molded rim, white-glazed, printed w/a large dark blue rectangle w/"20 lbs." above a 4" red wing mark, 20 lb. **$1,000-1,200**

Crock, advertising-type, cylindrical w/molded rim, white glaze printed in black w/a script "2" above an oval enclosing Nebraska advertising, 2 gal. **$2,000-2,500**

Crock, advertising-type, cylindrical w/molded rim, white glaze printed in black w/an oval enclosing Wisconsin honey advertising, 1/2 gal. **$200-250**

Crock, cylindrical w/molded rim & eared handle, white glaze w/fancy printed blue marking "Fresh Oysters," 6 gal. **$4,000-4,500**

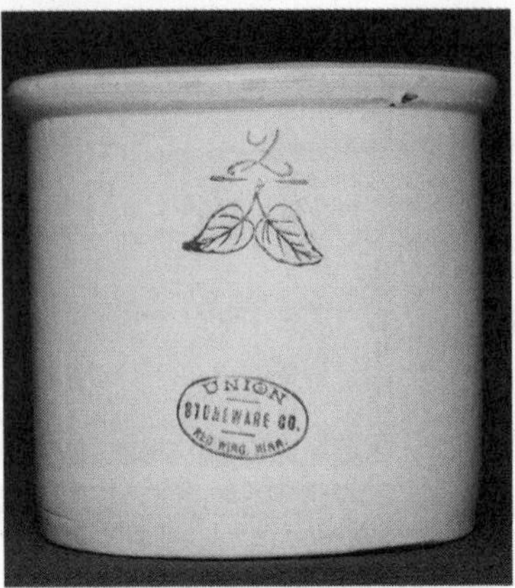

Crock, cylindrical w/molded rim, white glaze printed in black w/a script "2" above two elephant ear leaves & an oval Minnesota Stoneware Company mark, 2 gal. **$125-150**

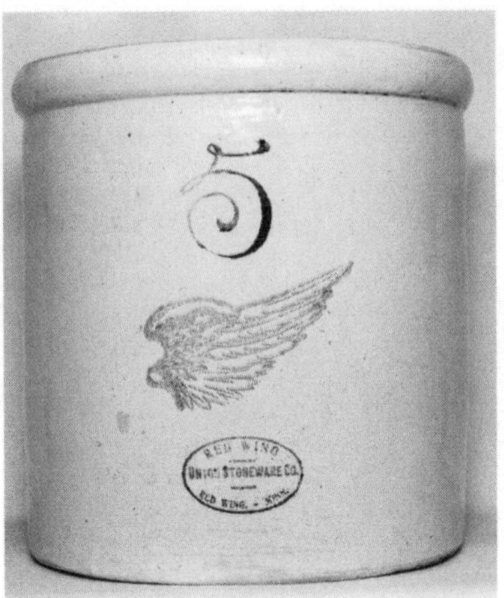

Crock, cylindrical w/molded rim, white glaze printed w/a large blue size number, large red wing logo & the oval mark of the Red Wing Union Stoneware Company, 5 gal. **$175-200**

Crock, cylindrical w/molded rim, white glaze printed w/the large 4" red wing logo, 1 gal. **$500-600**

Fruit (or canning) jar, dome-top style, twist-on metal lid, printed blue shield logo of the Red Wing Union Stoneware Company, 1 gal. **$4,500-5,500**

Jug, beehive-shaped, advertising-type, white glaze, printed blue birch leaves mark & an oval panel w/Kansas advertising **$3,500-4,000**

Jug, miniature, beehive-shaped, overall dark brown glaze, original yellow paper label for the Minnesota Stoneware Company on the base, 1/8 pt. (ILLUS. of side & bottom)................ **$1,000-1,200**

Pitcher, 9 1/4" h., embossed Cherry Band patt., advertising-type, white glaze w/large blue rectangle w/ unique printed image of a two-story store above advertising dated 1914 .... **$3,000-3,500**

Jug, miniature, fancy-style, white base & brown shoulder, printed in blue "Minnesota - Michigan," 1/8 pt. **$275-325**

Refrigerator jar, advertising-type, short cylindrical stacking-type w/molded rim, white glaze decorated w/blue band & printed w/advertising for a Nebraska merchant, early 20th c. **$500-600**

Pitcher, 9 1/4" h., tall cylindrical hall-boy style w/molded rings, overall red & blue sponging **$3,500-4,000**

Spittoon, deep cylindrical salt-glazed form w/top opening & oval side drain opening, double-stamped on the side "Red Wing Stoneware Company" **$3,000-3,500**

Rockingham Wares

The Marquis of Rockingham first established an earthenware pottery in the Yorkshire district of England around 1745, and it was occupied afterwards by various potters. The well-known mottled brown Rockingham glaze was introduced about 1788 by the Brameld Brothers and became immediately popular. It was during the 1820s that the production of true porcelain began at the factory, and it continued to be made until the firm closed in 1842. Since that time the so-called Rockingham glaze has been used by various potters in England and the United States, including some famous wares produced in Bennington, Vermont. Very similar glazes were also used by potteries in other areas of the United States including Ohio and Indiana, but only wares specifically attributed to Bennington should use that name. The following listings will include mainly wares featuring the dark brown mottled glaze produced at various sites here and abroad.

Creamer, tapering ovoid body w/an undulating rim & wide arched spout, C-scroll handle, yellowware w/overall mottled dark brown Rockingham glaze, 19th c., 5 1/2" h. **$44**

Flask, figural Mermaid design, dark brown glaze, ca. 1860, 8" h. **$187**

Flask, flattened ovoid body w/ small neck, yellowware molded in relief w/an oval reserve enclosing a half-length portrait of a man snorting snuff on each side, overall dark mottled brown Rockingham glaze, possibly Bennington, Vermont, or East Liverpool, Ohio, excellent condition, first half 19th c., 7 1/2" h. **$248**

Inkwell, figural, modeled as a woman reclining asleep on an oblong rockwork base, yellowware w/overall mottled dark brown Rockingham glaze, several old edge chips, reportedly made by the Larkin Bros. Company, Newell, West Virginia, ca. 1850-80, 3 7/8" h. **$101**

Flask, flattened ovoid shape tapering to a fluted neck & ringed mouth, molded on one side w/the American Eagle & on the other w/ a morning glory vine, dark brown Rockingham glaze, No. G11-19, several old glaze chips, ca. 1840-60, pt. **$308**

Foot warmer, wide flattened half-round form w/two molded indentations on the top for feet, a small spout at the top end, overall mottled brown glaze, American-made, ca. 1860, underside crazing, small flakes in the glaze, 7" w., 10" h. **$230**

Jug, advertising-type, figural, model of a walking pig, impressed on the rear "Bieler's Ronny Club," yellowware w/a mottled brown Rockingham glaze, original white porcelain stopper marked "Brookfield Rye Bieler," reportedly from Cincinnati, Ohio, ca. 1880- 1900, 9 1/2" l., 5 1/4" h. **$1,232**

Model of a lion, recumbent animal raised on a deep rectangular base, mottled dark brown glaze, restoration to minor surface roughness along base, ca. 1860, 6 3/4 x 9" **$303**

Pitcher, 6 1/2" h., hound-handled, flat-bottomed swelled cylindrical body w/a flattened shoulder to the neck w/a wide arched spout, the body molded in relief w/a continuous hound & deer hunting scene, molded vine band around the neck, yellowware w/overall dark brown Rockingham glaze, possibly West Troy Factory, Troy, New York, ca. 1860, excellent condition **$275**

Pitcher, 6 1/2" h., hound-handled, wide bulbous body w/a flattened shoulder to the wide flared neck & wide arched spout, relief- molded w/ stag hunting scene, overall very dark brown glaze, possibly Bennington, Vermont, ca. 1850 .... **$144**

←

Pitcher, 9 1/2" h., yellowware w/overall mottled dark brown glaze, molded hound handle, wide baluster form shape molded in relief w/eight panels of hanging game & fowl, a molded eagle under the wide spout, minor hairline in bottom, minor glaze wear, ca. 1850 .... **$121**

Teapot, cov., footed ovoid body w/swan's-neck spout & C-form handle, domed cover w/bud-form finial, mottled brown glaze w/relief-molded scene of Rebecca at the well, early 20th c., Ohio, 8 1/2" h........................ **$200**

Tobacco jar, cov., wide molded base below the paneled body w/a large Gothic arch in each panel, wide rolled rim & inset cover w/knob handle, molded leaf scroll side handles, overall dark brown mottled glaze, attributed to Bennington, Vermont, ca. 1847- 58, some nicks on top rim, cover replaced, 8" w., 8 1/2" h. **$288**

Rookwood

Considered America's foremost art pottery, the Rookwood Pottery Company was established in Cincinnati, Ohio, in 1880 by Mrs. Maria Nichols Longworth Storer. To accurately record its development, each piece carried the Rookwood insignia or mark, was dated, and, if individually decorated, was usually signed by the artist. The pottery remained in Cincinnati until 1959, when it was sold to Herschede Hall Clock Company and moved to Starkville, Mississippi, where it continued in operation until 1967.

A private company is now producing a limited variety of pieces using original Rookwood molds.

Basket, squatty rounded shape w/the sides folded up and the ends pulled out, a broad peaked handle from side to side, Standard glaze decorated w/ yellow flowers & buds & large green leaves against a shaded dark to light brown ground, decorated w/silver overlay in a leafy scroll design around the ends, rim & handle, silver marked by the Gorham Mfg. Co., breaks & losses to silver, 1893, Harriet Wilcox, 7 x 10 1/2" **$2,185**

Humidor, cov., Limoges-style decoration, round foot below the four-sided rounded body w/a flattened domed cover, painted w/an overall design of spiders & bats on a mottled tan, rust, blue & white ground, glaze bubble under outer lid, 1882, Maria Longworth Nichols, 6" w., 6" h. **$2,185**

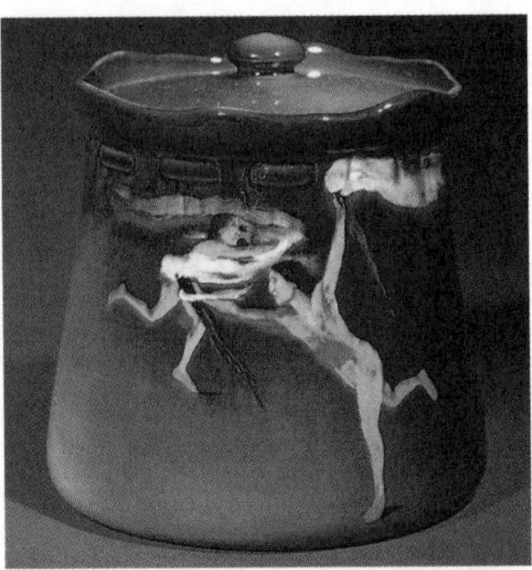

Humidor, cov., wide gently tapering cylindrical body w/a low flaring serpentine rim & inside flat cover w/ knob finial, Standard glaze, decorated w/a scene of two Native American dancers against a dark brown to brownish green ground, 1893, Harriet Wilcox, 6 1/2" d., 6 1/2" h. **$1,115**

Humidor, cov., wide slightly tapering cylindrical form w/a low cupped rim around the inset flattened cover w/a button finial, Standard glaze, decorated around the sides w/orange nicotiana blossoms & green leaves against a shaded gold to moss green ground, hairline inside cover, 1893, Bruce Horsfall, 6" d., 6 1/4" h. **$575**

Mug, tankard-type, base band & tall tapering cylindrical sides w/an angled handle, Standard glaze, decorated w/a three-quarters length portrait of a Native American, Chief Mountain (Big Brave) - Blackfeet, against a dark green to golden yellow ground, 1899, Grace Young, 6 1/2" d., 7 1/2" h. **$4,600**

Pitcher, 10" h., 5" d., tankard-type, a base band below the tall tapering slender body w/a small rim spout & squared handle, Standard glaze decorated w/a school of green fish against a shaded yellow to orange ground, further decorated w/silver overlay pierced scrolls around the base & a grapevine around the rim, a silver-clad handle, silver marked by the Gorham Mfg. Co., 1894, Matthew Daly **$3,335**

Plaque, long horizontal rectangular form, decorated w/a misty lakeside landscape w/trees in the foreground, in shades of dark & light green, blue, grey & lavender, in a wide flat oak frame, 1922, E. Timothy Hurley, glaze miss, plaque 4 x 8" **$4,313**

Plaque, rectangular, Vellum glaze, a verdant landscape w/a large meadow in the foreground & a small river & trees in the distance, shades of green, grey, blue & white, original wide flat oak frame, 1915, Kate Van Horn, 8 3/4 x 11" **$6,325**

Vase, 11" h., 7 1/2" d., footed cylindrical form w/a rounded base & shoulder centered by a flat mouth, Jewel Porcelain, decorated w/smeary branches of large pink & grey magnolia blossoms on an ivory ground, No. 2581, 1923, William Hentschel **$4,025**

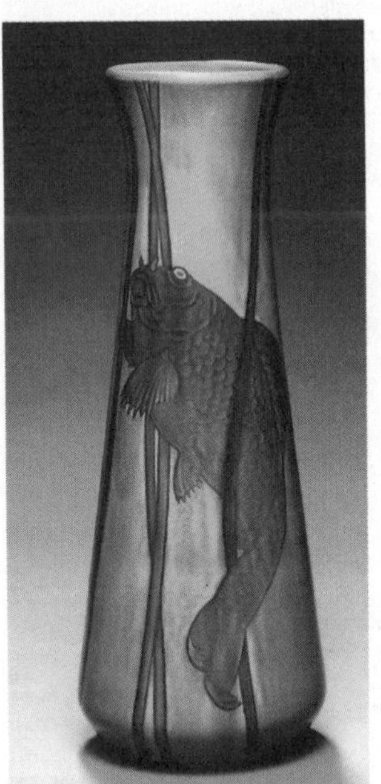

Vase, 12 7/8" h., slender tapering cylindrical form w/a flaring rim, Sea Green glaze, decorated w/a large fish swimming among sea grass, in shades of green against a pale yellow ground, 1899, Albert Valentien **$17,925**

Vase, 16" h., 15" w., pillow-type, wide flattened & rounded form w/a narrow pinched-in rim, Standard glaze, decorated w/a large bust portrait of the Native American Chief Hollow Horn Bear - Sioux, against a shaded dark brown to orange & green ground, 1900, Matthew Daley **$74,750**

Vase, 23 1/2" h., 11" d., broad ovoid body tapering to a wide cylindrical neck w/a flared rim, Limoges-style, the body decorated w/a continuous Japanese-inspired scene of birds perched on blossoming branches against a tan ground highlighted w/brown & white, the neck in dark green w/a gold rim, 1883, Albert Valentien **$5,750**

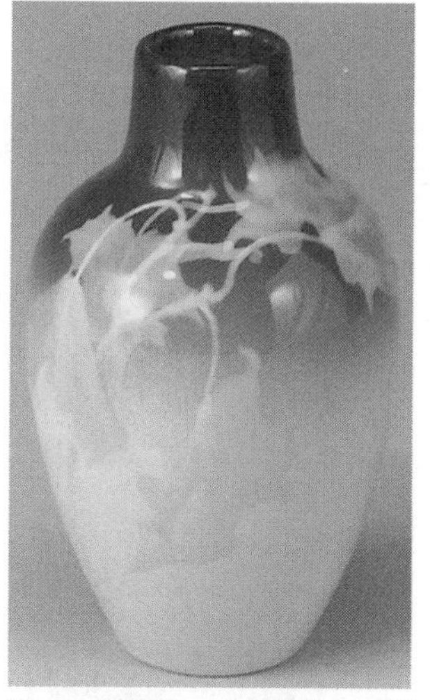

Vase, 6 1/2" h., 3 3/4" d., ovoid body tapering to a short cylindrical neck, Iris glaze, decorated w/ yellowish amber maple leaves against a dark grey shaded to pale yellow ground, overall crazing, No. 1905E, 1903, Irene Bishop **$1,725**

Vase, 6 3/4" h., 5" d., ovoid body tapering to a wide flat mouth flanked by small loop handles, Sea Green glaze, decorated w/ large brown & cream flowers on dark green stems against a dark blue to green ground, No. 604D, 1902, Sallie Toohey **$3,738**

Vase, 7 1/2" h., 3 1/2" d., cylindrical w/incurved flat wide mouth, Vellum glaze, scenic design elegantly painted w/flying Canada geese above stalks of bamboo against a dark blue to cream to green ground, no crazing, 1911, No. 952E, Kataro Shirayamadani **$8,625**

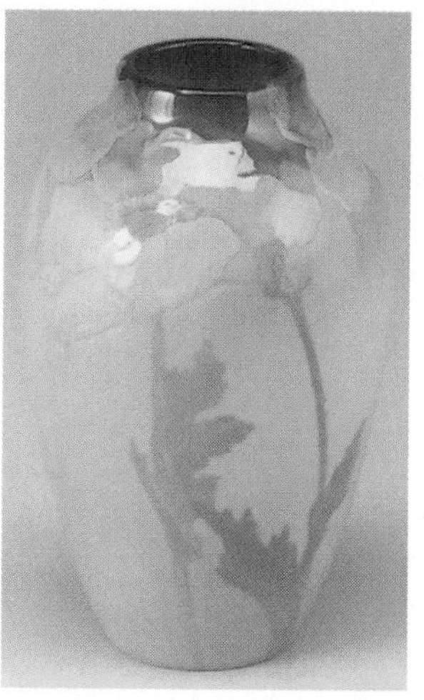

Vase, 9 1/2" h., 6" d., simple ovoid body tapering to a flat rim, Iris glaze, decorated w/large mauve poppies w/yellow centers on pale green leafy stems against a shaded mauve to pale yellowish green ground, Pan American Exposition paper label, No. 900B, 1900, O.G. Reed **$9,775**

Rookwood Pottery won the gold and silver medal at the Pan American Exhibition World's Fair, which was held in Buffalo, New York, from May 1, 1901 to November 2, 1901. The Exposition was known for showcasing technology as well art. For instance, it used AC electricity developed by Nikola Tesla and generated by Niagara Falls for lighting its buildings. It was also here that the X-ray machine was unveiled to the world. But tragically, the Exposition is best known as the site where President William McKinley was assassinated by anarchist Leon Czolgosz.

Roseville

Roseville Pottery Company operated in Zanesville, Ohio, from 1898 to 1954, having been in business for six years prior to that in Muskingum County, Ohio. Art wares similar to those of Owens and Weller Potteries were produced. Items listed here are by patterns or lines.

Apple Blossom (1948)

Jardiniere, wide bulbous body w/a molded flat mouth flanked by small twig handles, pink ground, No. 300-4", 4" h. **$69**

Vase, 10" h., swelled cylindrical body w/shaped rim, disk base w/handles up the sides, green ground, No. 389-10" **$184**

Vase, 10" h., swelled cylindrical body w/shaped rim, disk base w/ handles up the sides, pink ground, No. 389-10" **$140-180**

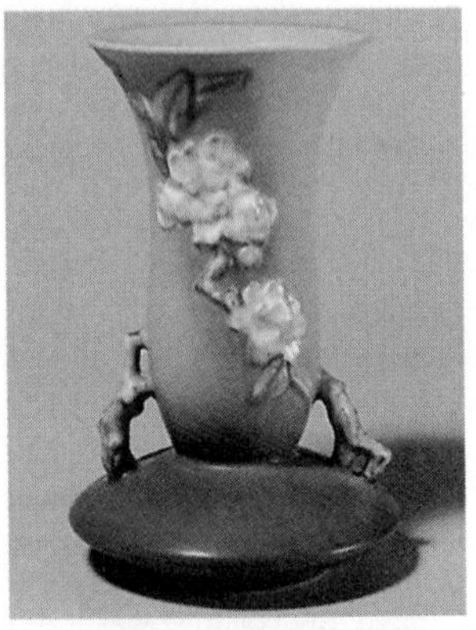

Vase, 10" h., wide flaring foot w/ base handles, trumpet-form body, blue ground, No. 388-10" ... **$184**

Vase, 15" h., floor type, double base handles, short globular base, long cylindrical neck, blue ground, No. 392-15" **$518**

Vase, 9 1/2" h., 5" d., asymmetrical handles, cylindrical w/disc base, green ground, No. 387-9" ... **$184**

Carnelian II (1915-31)

Vase, 10" h., compressed globular base w/trumpet form neck, ornate angled handles from base to midsection, mottled blue & green glaze, No. 323-10" **$518**

Vase, 7" h., footed, bulbous base tapering to wide cylindrical neck w/rolled rim, ornate handles from shoulder to below rim, mottled rose, grey & green glaze, No. 311-7" **$317**

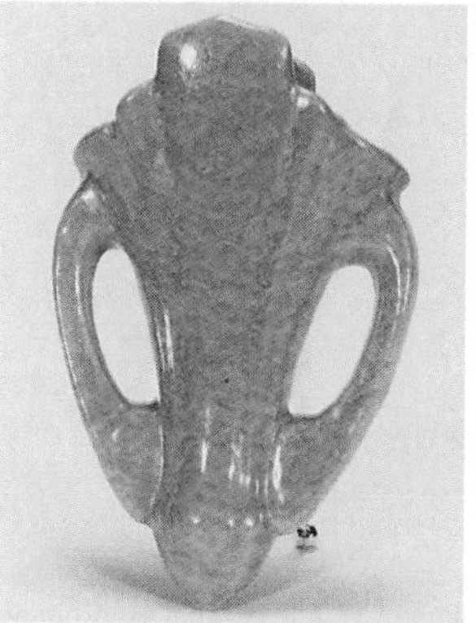

Wall pocket, wide arched & fanned top w/panels down the sides, heavy loop side handles from under rim to near base, mottled blue & green glaze, No. 1252-8", 8" l. **$460**

Cherry Blossom (1933)

Vase, 5" h., bulbous ovoid body tapering to a small molded mouth flanked by small loop handles, pink & blue ground, No. 618- 5" **$431**

Vase, 5" h., bulbous ovoid body tapering to a small molded mouth flanked by small loop handles, terra cotta ground, No. 618-5" **$288**

Vase, 5" h., wide ovoid body tapering to a wide slightly rolled mouth flanked by small loop handles, terra cotta ground, No. 619- 5" **$259**

Vase, 5" h., wide ovoid body tapering to a wide, slightly rolled mouth flanked by small loop handles, pink & blue ground, No. 619- 5" **$375-400**

Vase, 6" h., bulbous body, shoulder tapering to wide molded mouth, small loop shoulder handles, terra cotta ground, unmarked, No. 621-6" **$259**

> Advertisements for "antiques wanted" that offer free house calls should be ignored. Do not let any stranger into your home. The fewer people who know what you have in your home, the more secure you are.

Cosmos (1940)

Vase, 12 1/2" h., footed ovoid w/ large loop handles from sides of short paneled neck to sides of shoulders, blue ground, No. 956-12" **$260**

Dahlrose (1924-28)

Jardiniere, footed spherical body w/ a wide low rolled neck flanked by small pointed handles, No. 614-4", 4 1/4" h. **$173**

Jardiniere, footed, bulbous form w/ a thick molded rim flanked by tiny squared rim handles, No. 614-6", 6" h. **$161**

Vase, 6 1/8" h., square flared foot below the slightly tapering square body w/a wide sharply flaring neck, black paper label, No. 372-6" **$748**

Vase, 6" h., 8" l., flattened pillow-type, tall upright rectangular form w/small angled handles at the top ends, black paper label, No. 358-8" **$489**

Vase, 6" h., squatty bulbous body tapering to wide rolled rim, tiny angled handles from shoulder to rim, No. 364-6" **$288**

Donatello (1915)

Vase, 12 1/2" h., tall waisted cylindrical body w/a wide flat mouth, long serpentine angled handles down the sides, restoration to rim & handles, rare shape **$375**

Noting a point of condition on an item when negotiating a price is acceptable if done in a polite manner. However, berating the merchandise to get a rock-bottom price will only anger the dealer.

Freesia (1945)

Tea set: cov. teapot No. T, creamer No.6-C & open sugar bowl No.6-C; bulbous tapering shapes, green ground, No. 6, 3 pcs. **$250-300**

Vase, 6 1/4" h., footed, squatty, bulbous base w/wide cylindrical neck, large angled base handles, blue ground, No. 118-6" **$104**

Vase, 6" h., baluster-form w/flat mouth & pointed angled handles, blue ground, No. 117-6" **$150**

Vase, 7" h., footed disk-form base w/angular base handles below the tall cylindrical neck, blue ground, No. 119-7" **$115**

Vase, 8" h., footed, ovoid body flanked by D-form handles, blue ground, No. 121-8" **$115**

Vase, 9 1/2" h., a short ringed pedestal base supporting a flaring half-round body w/an angled shoulder tapering slightly to a tall, wide cylindrical neck, down-curved angled loop handles from center of neck to rim of lower shoulder, blue ground, No. 123-9 .... **$115**

Vase, bud, 7" h., handles rising from compressed globular base, long slender tapering neck, blue ground, No. 195-7" **$115**

Fuchsia (1939)

Vase, 6" h., footed ovoid w/handles rising from shoulder to short cylindrical neck rim, overall crazing, green ground, No. 892-6" **$104**

To help prevent breakage, loss, or theft of items you have purchased at an antique show, don't carry more than one bag at a time. Consolidate packages into one bag. Many people carry a canvas tote bag for this reason.

Iris (1938)

Jardiniere, two-handled, footed squatty bulbous body w/a wide short cylindrical mouth, blue ground, No. 647-3", 3 1/2" h. **$92**

Vase, 15 1/2" h., footed large ovoid body tapering to a paneled & scalloped neck flanked by loop handles, blue ground, No. 929- 15" **$518**

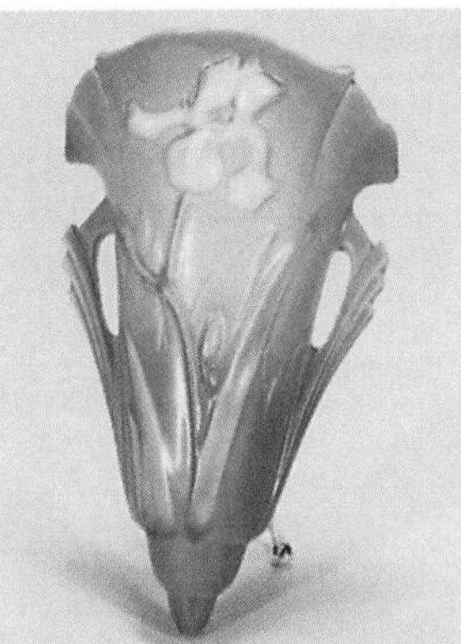

Wall pocket, two handles rising from base to below flaring rim, blue ground, No. 1284-8", 8" h. **$432**

Ixia (1930s)

Vase, 12" h., cylindrical, closed upright shoulder handles, yellow ground, No. 864-12" **$200-300**

Luffa (1934)

Jardiniere, large squatty bulbous body w/a wide flat rim flanked by tiny squared shoulder handles, brown ground, No. 631-7", 7" **$288**

Morning Glory (1935)

Urn-vase, bulbous nearly spherical body tapering to a wide flat mouth, squared shoulder handles, green ground, No. 269-6, 6" h. **$575**

Vase, 14 1/4" h., tapering cylindrical body w/flared rim, angled handles from shoulder to mid-section, green ground, No. 732-14" **$920**

Moss (1930s)

Vase, 8 1/2" h., urn-form, flared foot, bulbous body w/pointed side handles & wide flaring rim, pink shading to blue ground, No. 779-8" **$288**

> With more people selling antiques and collectibles on the Internet, the perception of what is rare has changed. Some items once thought to be rare are now considered scarce after more examples have surfaced.

Mostique (1915)

Jardiniere, wide bulbous body w/a very wide flat rim, geometric designs in dark yellow, brown & blues alternating w/long dark & medium blue vertical leaf-like geometric designs on a light tan ground, No. 740-8", 8" d., 7" h. **$210**

Panel (Rosecraft Panel 1920)

Wall pocket, cylindrical w/rounded end, curved asymmetrical rim, long tan trailing leaves & berries down the front on a dark brown ground, 9" h. **$260**

Pine Cone (1935 & 1953)

Basket, wide flaring foot & trumpet-form body w/an overhead branch handle, green ground, some glaze crazing, No. 338-10", 10" h. **$260**

Mug, footed, brown ground, No. 960-4", 4" h.......................... **$316**

Jardiniere, footed wide squatty bulbous body w/a wide flat mouth, small asymmetrical twig handles, brown ground, No. 632-4", 4" h. **$259**

Pitcher, 9 1/2" h., ovoid body tapering to a small neck w/ pinched rim, small branch handle, brown ground, very slight glaze peppering, No. 708-9" **$633**

Mug, footed, blue ground, few minor glaze puckers, No. 960-4", 4" h. **$316**

Planter, a deep cup-shaped bowl set off-center on an oval foot w/a pine cone & pine needle handle extending from base to rim, another sprig on pine needles molded into the lower body, blue ground, No. 124-5", 5" h. **$288**

Planter, deep cup-shaped bowl set off-center on an oval foot w/a pine cone & pine needle handle extending from base to rim, another sprig on pine needles molded into the lower body, green ground, No. 124-5", 5" h. **$173**

Planter, oval upright sides w/ flaring arched serpentine rim, an openwork pine needle & cone handle at one end & a small twig handle at the other, some glaze discoloration, few pinpoint glaze dimples, brown ground, No. 457-7", 4 1/2" h. **$207**

Vase, 6 1/2" h., wide cylindrical body w/flaring rim, asymmetrical handles, brown ground, No. 838-6" **$259**

Vase, 6" h., footed bulbous base w/wide cylindrical neck, handles from shoulder to midsection of neck, blue ground, No. 839-6" **$316**

Vase, 6" h., footed bulbous base w/wide cylindrical neck, handles from shoulder to mid-section of neck, brown ground, No. 839- 6" **$230**

Vase, 7 1/2" h., footed wide cylinder w/flat rim & small asymmetrical twig handles, green ground, No. 704-7" **$196**

Vase, 7 1/4" h., long oval base supporting a tall flattened & fanned body w/asymmetrical twig handles & a large molded pine cone & needle sprigs across the front, brown ground, No. 121-7" **$345**

→

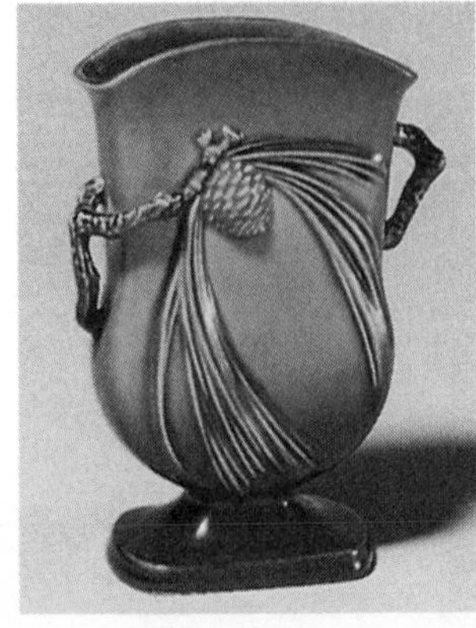

←

Vase, 7 1/2" h., footed wide cylinder w/flat rim & small asymmetrical twig handles, silver foil label, minor glaze inconsistencies, brown ground, No. 704-7" **$288**

Vase, 7 1/4" h., long oval base supporting a tall flattened & fanned body w/asymmetrical twig handles & a large molded pine cone & needle sprigs across the front, green ground, No. 121-7" ... **$207**

Vase, 7" h., footed gently flaring cylindrical body w/a flaring wide rim flanked by large angular branch handles, blue ground, No. 907-7" **$316**

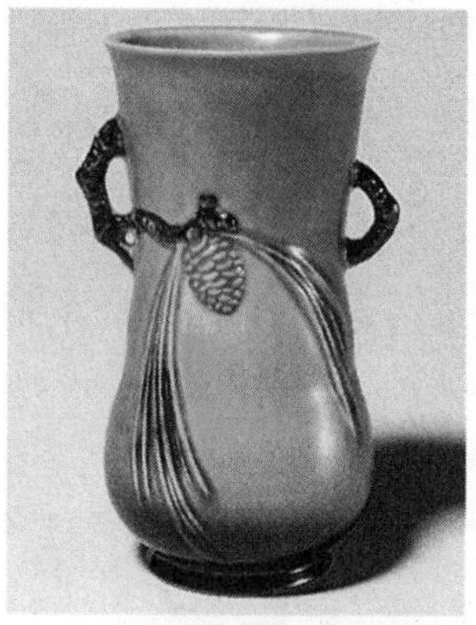

Vase, 7" h., footed waisted cylindrical body tapering to slightly flaring rim, asymmetrical twig handles, brown ground, minor glaze inclusions, No. 840-7" **$219**

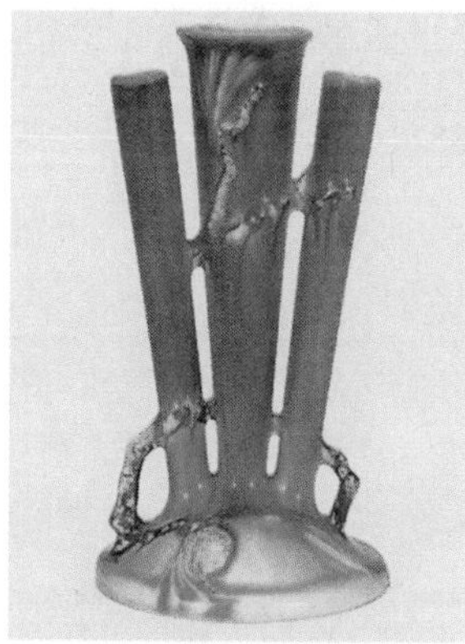

Vase, 8" h., triple bud, domed foot w/ twig handles w/a slender trumpet-form central vase flanked by angled smaller cylindrical vases, green ground, No. 113-8" ... **$317**

Vase, bud, 7 3/4" h., round disk foot w/upright slender ovoid body w/ sprig handle from side to foot, blue ground, No. 479-7", 1950s version of No. 112-7" **$403**

Vase, bud, 7 3/4" h., round disk foot w/upright slender ovoid body w/sprig handle from side to foot, brown ground, No. 479-7", 1950s version of No. 112-7" **$259**

Poppy (1930s)

Vase, 8" h., footed, wide cylindrical form w/C-form handles, green ground, No. 871-8" **$115**

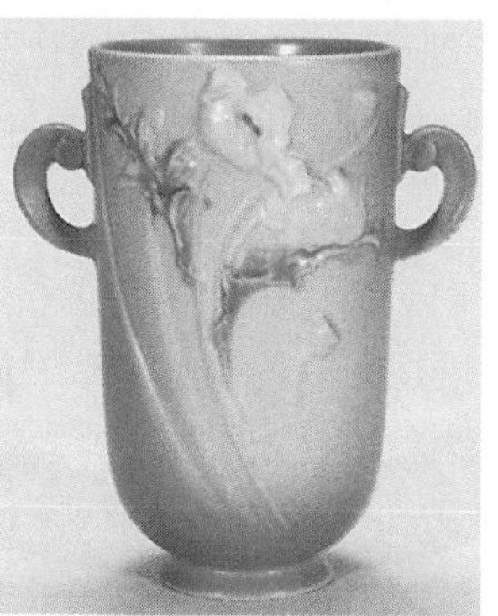

With few exceptions, collectors should not attempt to repair antiques. In many cases, any repairs, even professional, will lower value. In some cases, repairs can increase value, but should be done by an expert. Research carefully before having any work performed.

Primrose (1932)

Vase, 14 5/8" h., footed tall ovoid body w/a wide flat mouth, low pointed angled handles at center of sides, blue ground, No. 772-14", silver foil sticker & original retailer sticker **$432**

Rozane (1900)

Vase, 7 3/4" h., bulbous ovoid body tapering to a tall slender neck w/ widely flaring rim, h.p. with a large yellow & deep red iris & green leaves on a shaded dark brown to green ground, impressed mark "Rozane 838 5," overall crazing **$173**

Snowberry (1946)

Vase, 10" h., footed, bulbous lower body below a wide, cylindrical neck w/flaring rim, pointed handles from middle of neck to shoulder, shaded rose ground, No. 1V2-10" **$161**

Vase, 12 1/2" h., footed, tall, baluster-form body w/flaring rim, pointed angled handles at sides, shaded rose ground, No. IVI-12" **$200-300**

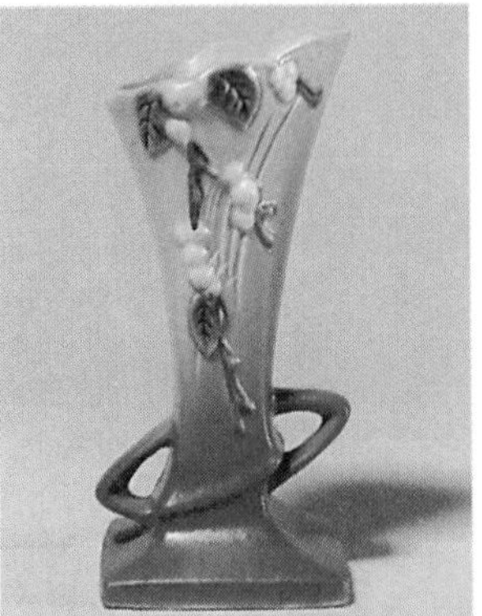

Vase, 7 1/2" h., bud, rectangular foot tapering to a tall, slender, flaring body w/angled rim, asymmetrical pointed loop handles at the base, shaded rose ground, No. 1V1-7" **$104**

Vase, 7 1/2" h., bulbous base w/tall cylindrical neck, pointed shoulder handles, shaded blue ground, No. 1V2-7" **$104**

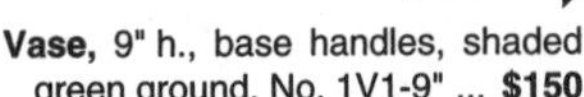

Vase, 9" h., base handles, shaded green ground, No. 1V1-9" ... **$150**

Sunflower (1930)

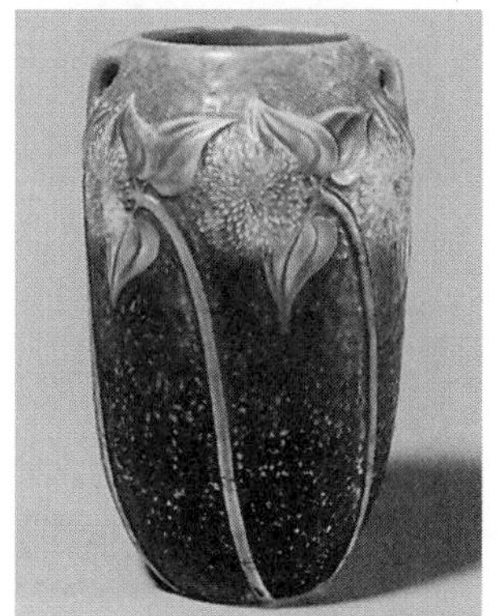

Vase, 10" h., swelled cylindrical body w/tiny shoulder handles, No. 492-10" **$920**

Vase, 5" h., wide, flat base w/ gently flaring cylindrical sides & a rounded shoulder to the wide closed mouth, No. 486-5" ... **$863**

Vase, 6 1/4" h., slightly swelled & flaring cylindrical body w/a wide, short, slightly flaring neck flanked by tiny loop handles, No. 494-6" **$575**

Vase, 6" h., bulbous, nearly spherical body, wide shoulder tapering to a short cylindrical neck, No. 488-6" **$900-1,000**

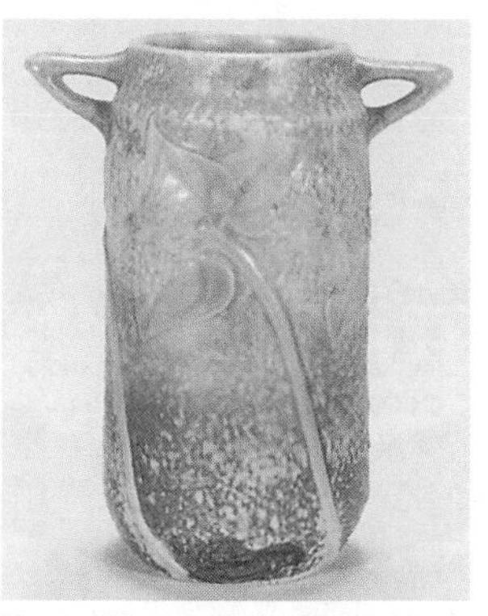

Vase, 6" h., swelled cylindrical body w/short cylindrical neck flanked by small loop handles, No. 485-6" **$547**

Vase, 8 1/4" h., ovoid body w/a widely flaring rim flanked by small loop handles, No. 491-8" **$1,035**

Vase, 8" h., bulbous base, wide tapering cylindrical neck, No. 490-8" **$1,093**

Sylvan (1918)

←

Jardiniere, wide tapering ovoid form w/a wide flat mouth, light green band of hunting dogs decoration against a light brown tree bark ground, some very small glaze nicks, No. 568, 10" h. **$375**

Tourmaline (1933)

Candlesticks, flared ribbed base, flaring nozzle, mottled blue ground, gold labels, No. 1089-4 1/2", 4 1/2" h., pr. **$127**

Urn, footed globular body w/ embossed lines around shoulder interrupted w/some vertical bands, mottled gold, No. 238-5", 5 1/2" h. **$81**

Vase, 6" h., footed nearly spherical body w/a wide band of narrow rings just below the wide rolled rim, mottled blue, No. 611-6" **$115**

Vase, 6" h., footed nearly spherical body w/a wide band of narrow rings just below the wide rolled rim, mottled pink, No. 611-6" **$81**

Vase, 6" h., rectangular pillow-type w/horizontally ribbed lower half flanked by small scroll handles, mottled blue w/drippy green upper band, No. A-65-6" **$92**

Vase, 6" h., rectangular pillow-type w/horizontally ribbed lower half flanked by small scroll handles, mottled pink w/pale blue upper band, gold foil sticker, No. A-65-6" **$69**

Vase, 7" h., footed swelled cylindrical body tapering to a short wide neck w/flared rim, mottled blue, No. A-308-7" **$159**

Vase, 8 1/4" h., footed flating cylindrical body w/a ringed base, tapering pointed tab handles at lower sides, the body molded in low-relief w/narrow ribbed strips joined around the top by a molded leaf band, mottled blue **$184**

Vase, 9 1/2" h., footed gently flaring square form w/a narrow molded herringbone band below the flared rim, mottled blue ground, No. 615-9" **$260**

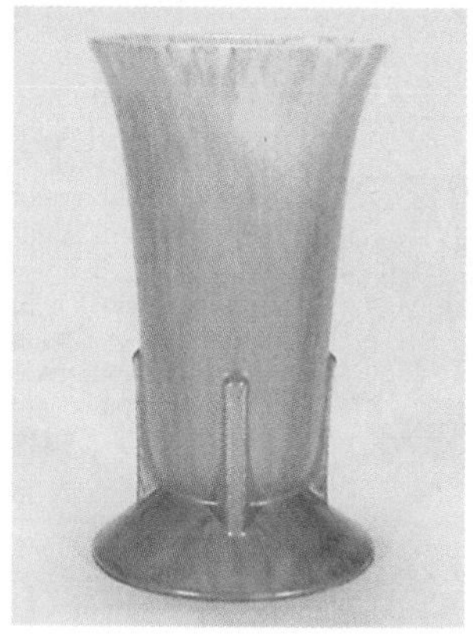

Vase, 9" h., flared foot below buttressed base, trumpet-form body, mottled blue glaze, No. A-429-9" **$317**

Before the arrival of the Internet, only the largest auction houses had an international following. To get top prices on important items, sellers had to sell through the major houses. Now regional auction houses using the World Wide Web can attract international bidders.

Tuscany (1928)

Vase, 4" h., 6 1/2" w., bowl-form, footed widely flaring trumpet-form w/open handles from under rim to the foot, mottled turquoise, No. 67-4" **$92**

Wall pocket, conical w/wide flaring half-round ringed rim, loop handles at sides molded w/small purple grape clusters & pale green leaves, pink, No. 1254-7", 7" h. **$288**

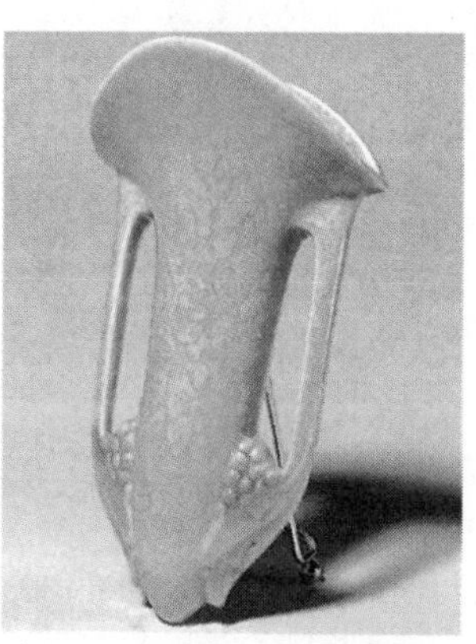

Wall pocket, long open handles, rounded rim, mottled pink glaze, paper label, short hairline from mounting hole to rim, No. 1255- 8", 8" h. **$173**

Vista (1920s)

Vase, 12" h., 4 3/4" d., footed, bulbous base tapering to tall wide cylindrical neck w/flat rim, No. 125-12" **$978**

If you want a discount greater than the typical 10 percent at an antique mall, ask the manager to call the owner of the merchandise so you can make an offer directly. Make a reasonable offer. Do not make an offer so low that the dealer is insulted and believes you are wasting his time.

Water Lily (1943)

Model of a conch shell, shaded blue ground, No. 438-8", 8" l. **$150-200**

Tea set: cov. teapot No. 5, open sugar bowl No. 5-S & creamer No. 5-C; squatty bulbous forms, shaded blue ground, the set **$345**

Vase, 10 1/4" h., low foot below the widely flaring flattened lower body tapering to a tall waisted neck w/ flaring rim, large angled handles from center of neck to edge of lower body, tan shading to brown ground, No. 80-10" **$200-300**

Vase, 8 1/4" h., footed, bulbous, ovoid body w/a short, wide, cylindrical neck flanked by angular handles, pale blue ground, No. 77-8" **$175-225**

Vase, 9" h., footed, ovoid body w/wide, flat mouth, the sides w/pointed down swept handles, pale blue ground, No. 78-9" **$175-250**

Vase, 9" h., footed, ovoid body w/wide, flat mouth, the sides w/ pointed downswept handles, pink shaded to green ground, No. 78-9" **$250-350**

White Rose (1940s)

Jardiniere, spherical w/wide notched rim flanked by small shoulder loop handles, blended blue ground, No. 653-10", 10" h. **$200-250**

Urn-vase, pedestal base below the wide, bulbous, ovoid body w/a wide cylindrical neck w/a notched rim, curved handles from rim to shoulder, brown shaded to green ground, No. 147-8", 8" h. **$150-175**

Wisteria (1933)

Vase, 10" h., cylindrical body w/closed rim, angled shoulder handles, brown shaded to yellow & green ground, silver foil sticker, No. 639-10" **$500**

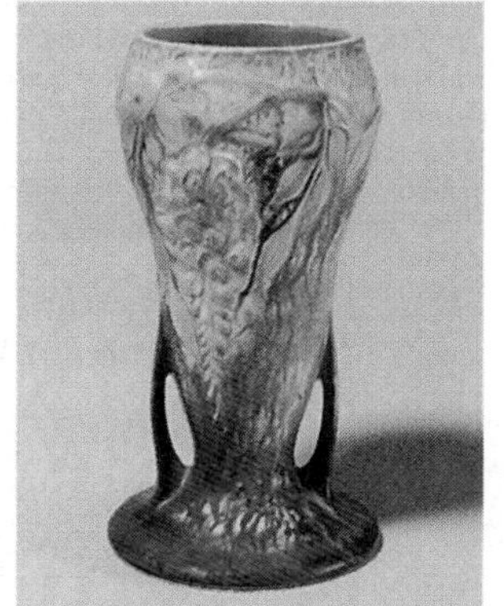

Vase, 8 1/2" h., flaring foot tapering to the gently flaring body bulging slightly below the flat rim, short handles from lower body to foot, brown shading to yellow & green ground, gold foil label, blue ground, No. 635-8" **$1,035**

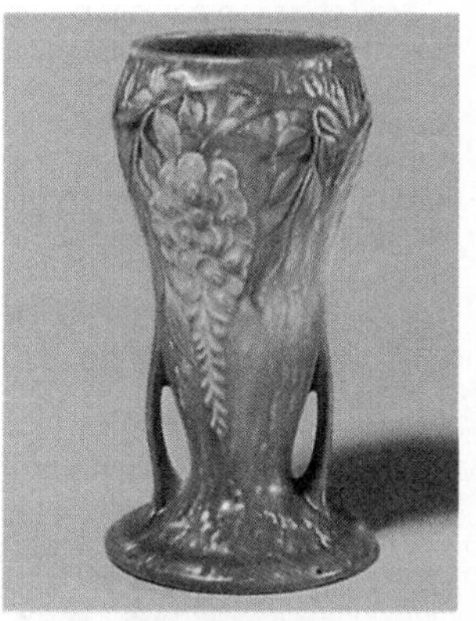

Vase, 8 1/2" h., flaring foot tapering to the gently flaring body bulging slightly below the flat rim, short handles from lower body to foot, brown shading to yellow & green ground, No. 635-8" **$575**

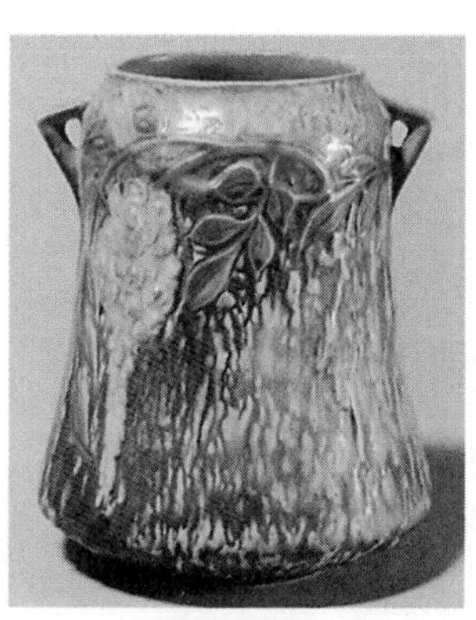

Vase, 8" h., 6 1/2" d., wide, tapering, cylindrical body w/small angled handles flanking the flat rim, blue ground, No. 633-8" **$1,265**

Vase, 9 1/2" h., cylindrical ovoid body w/angular handles rising from shoulder to midsection of slender cylindrical neck, brown shaded to yellow & green ground, No. 638-9" **$690**

Zephyr Lily (1946)

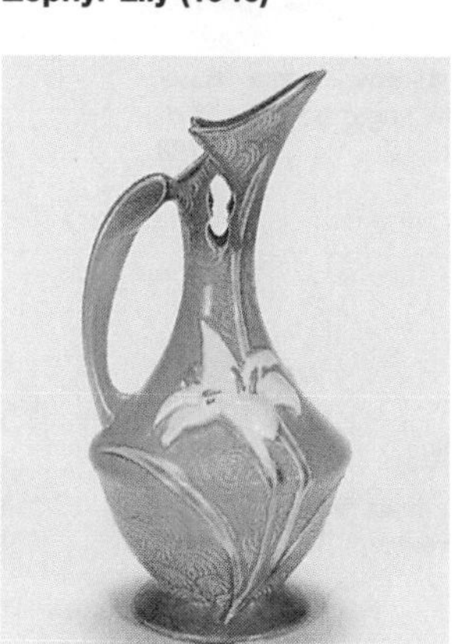

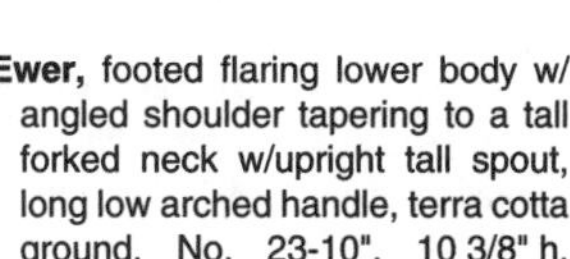

Ewer, footed flaring lower body w/ angled shoulder tapering to a tall forked neck w/upright tall spout, long low arched handle, terra cotta ground, No. 23-10", 10 3/8" h. **$127**

Flowerpot w/saucer, terra cotta ground, No. 672-5", 5" h. **$150-175**

Royal Bayreuth

Good china in numerous patterns and designs has been made at the Royal Bayreuth factory in Tettau, Germany since 1794. Listings below are by the company's lines, plus miscellaneous pieces. Interest in this china remains at a peak and prices continue to rise. Pieces listed carry the company's blue mark except where noted otherwise.

Among the important reference books in this field are Royal Bayreuth - A Collectors' Guide and Royal Bayreuth - A Collectors' Guide - Book II by Mary McCaslin (see Special Contributors list).

Devil & Cards

Candy dish, shallow paneled dish composed of playing cards w/a figural seated devil handle, 6 1/2" w. **$288**

Mother-of-Pearl

Creamer, figural Spiky Shell patt., pale lavender & pink highlights **$81**

Rose Tapestry

Dresser set: 10" rectangular tray & cov. hair receiver; three-color roses decoration, blue marks, the set **$460**

Tomato Items

Tomato creamer & cov. sugar bowl, creamer 3" d., 3" h., sugar bowl 3 1/2" d., 4" h., pr. **$75-100**

Miscellaneous

Berry set: 9 3/4" d. bowl & five 5" d. sauce dishes; Peasant Musicians decoration, 6 pcs. **$350-450**

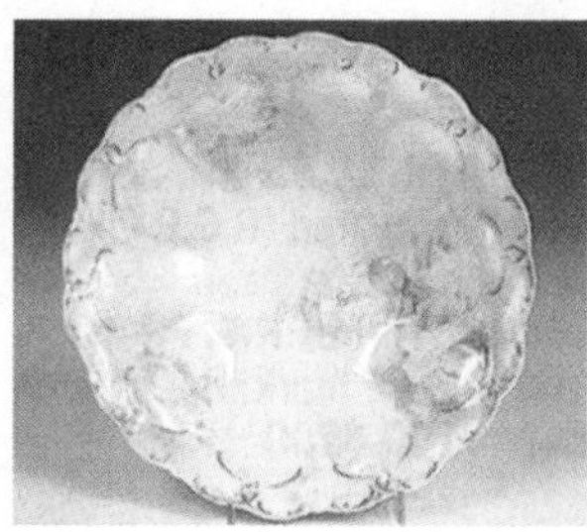

Bowl, 10 1/2" d., scalloped rim & molded interior lobes, decorated w/scattered pink roses & green leaves w/a satin finish, blue mark **$115**

Charger, round w/lightly scalloped rim stenciled w/gilt sprigs, decorated w/large clusters of deep red & green grapes on a shaded pale green to white ground, blue mark, 13" d. **$92**

Ewer, squatty bulbous form w/a flat cylindrical body band & wide flattened shoulder centered by a short cylindrical neck w/angled handle, green shoulder & lower body, side band decorated w/a continuous scene of cows in a landscape in shades of rust, green, brown & black, blue mark, 5" h. **$104**

Pitcher, water, 6" h., figural apple **$500-700**

Pitcher, water, 7" h., figural elk **$500-700**

Tea set: cov. teapot, cov. sugar bowl & creamer; each w/a squatty bulbous body & gold handles, "Tapestry" decoration of white mums & purple violets on a pale blue ground, blue mark, Germany, early 20th c., teapot 7" l., the set **$460**

Tea set: child's, cov. teapot, cov. sugar, creamer, two plates, & two cups & saucers; ovoid bodies, each piece decorated w/a scene of children playing, the set **$700-800**

Tea set: cov. teapot, cov. sugar bowl & creamer; ovoid bodies, the sugar & creamer w/C-scroll handles, the teapot w/ overhead fixed handle & serpentine spout, each piece decorated w/a colorful fairy tale scene, the set **$350-400**

Vase, 4 1/2" h., footed ovoid body tapering to a short flaring neck, decoration of cows watering w/mountains in the distance, in shades of purple, lavender, green, orange, brown & black, blue mark **$92**

Vase, 7" h., footed cylindrical form w/trumpet-form rim, central color band w/Skiff with Sail decoration, gold band borders trimmed w/ delicate gilt stencil bands & gilt floral stencils around the lower body, a pale blue ground & shaded brown foot, blue mark **$92**

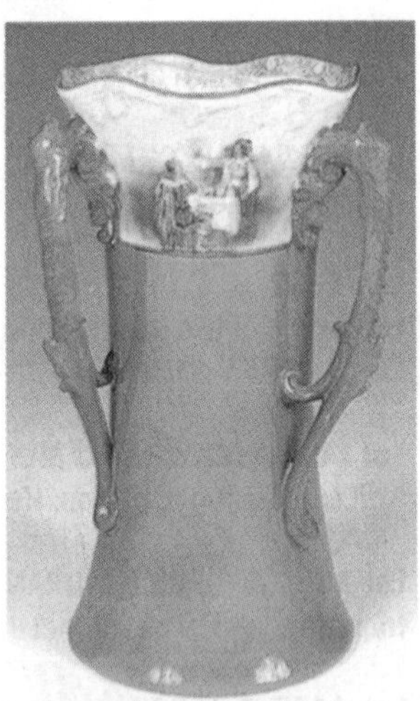

Vase, 9" h., tall waisted cylindrical shape w/a flaring ruffled rim, three angular green scrolled branch handles around the sides, the main body in dark green, a color top band in the Toasting Cavalier design, blue mark **$184**

Vase, 9" h., tall, slender, waisted, cylindrical body w/a gently scalloped flaring rim, three long green scroll & bead loop handles down the sides, the top body w/a band decorated w/ a toasting Cavaliers scene in color on one side & "Ye Old Bell" scene on the other, the lower body all in dark green, ca. 1902 .... **$200-325**

Vase, 9" h., tall, slender, waisted, cylindrical body w/a gently scalloped flaring rim, three long green scroll & bead loop handles down the sides, the top body w/ a band decorated w/a toasting Cavaliers scene in color on one side & "Ye Old Bell" scene on the other, the lower body all in dark green, ca. 1902 .... **$500-600**

Vase, 2 3/4" h., 2 1/4" d., nearly spherical body on three tiny feet, small cylindrical gold mouth, blue, yellow & green ground decorated w/a color scene of an Arab horseback rider in the foreground & another horse in the background............................ **$75**

Royal Bonn & Bonn

Bonn and subsequently Royal Bonn china were produced in Bonn, Germany, in a manufactory established in 1755. Later wares made there are often marked "Mehlem" or bear the initials "FM" or a castle mark. Most wares were of the hand-painted type. Clock cases were also made in Bonn.

Vase, miniature, 3 3/4" h., Old Dutch Line, spherical body w/a small trumpet neck, decorated around the shoulder w/a band of colorful stylized blossoms in pink, white & brick red on a dark green & blue ground, white & yellow leafy stems up from the lower body against a dark brown ground, marked "Royal Bonn - Old Dutch - 7 3091/3 319," late 19th c. **$115**

Vase, miniature, 3 3/4" h., Old Dutch Line, spherical body w/a small trumpet neck, decorated w/a wide central band featuring an undulating thin green-striped ribbon entwined w/matching arches, against a dark brown ground w/deep purple leaf clusters, the shoulder w/a band of repeating arches in brown, yellow & dark blue below a thin dark blue band & the dark green & yellow neck, a matching arched band around the base, marked "Royal Bonn - Germany - Old Dutch - D60," late 19th c. **$100-150**

Vases, 11 1/2" h., ovoid form w/ short neck & flaring lobed rim, studio decorated in the round w/ h.p. scenes of cattle standing in shallow stream, w/trees & foliage in background & foreground, low hills in the distance, artist signed "J. Sticher," marked "Royal Bonn," Germany, late 19th c., pr. **$2,300**

Vases, 14" h., cylindrical form tapering out to rounded shoulder w/short flaring neck, each w/h.p. scene of young woman w/flowing brown hair picking flowers in meadow w/trees & distant hills in background, one wearing green skirt & pink & white blouse, the other a white sleeveless dress w/green apron, the meadow in shades of yellow & light yellow-green, the base & neck of each turquoise w/gilt decoration, artist signed indistinguishably, printed marks, Germany, early 20th c., pr. **$1,725**

←

Vases, 15 3/4" h., small tapering cylindrical foot supporting the bulbous ovoid body tapering to a tall slender trumpet neck flanked by wide squared gold handles, gold neck & gold base band on the foot, the creamy body h.p. on the front w/a large colorful parrot on entwined branches w/fan-shaped green leaves, the reverse w/a flying butterfly among the branches, heavy gold trim, marked on the base, late 19th c., pr. **$400-600**

Vase, 8 1/2" h., tapering cylindrical body w/a short flaring neck, overall sand tapestry decoration, four tall arch-topped narrow panels w/a cream ground decorated w/multicolored scrolls & blossoms, dividing bands in dark maroon w/gold trim & patterned gold around the shoulder & neck, a narrow & white chain band around the base, one in gold on maroon, the other w/maroon on green, marked, ca. 1890 .... **$330**

Royal Copenhagen

This porcelain has been made in Copenhagen, Denmark, since 1715. The ware is hard paste. Although the Royal Copenhagen factory in Denmark has been in business for over 200 years, very little has been written about it. That is not to say the very beautiful porcelain it produces is not easily recognizable. Besides producing gorgeous dinnerware, such as "Blue Fluted" and "Flora Danica," it produced - and still does - wonderful figurines depicting animals and people. The company employs talented artists as both modelers and painters. Once you become familiar with the colors, glazes and beauty of these figurines, you will have no trouble recognizing them at a glance.

Collecting these magnificent figurines seems as popular now as in the past. As with most objects, and certainly true of these figurines, value will depend on the complexity, size, age and rarity of the piece. There is other Danish porcelain on the market today, but the Royal Copenhagen figurines can readily be recognized by the mark on the bottom with the three dark blue wavy lines. Accept no imitations!

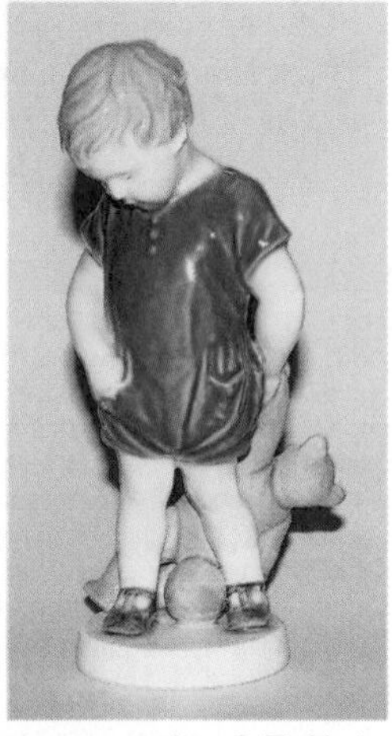

Figure group, boy & Teddy bear, toddler standing wearing blue romper, holding tan bear behind him, No. 3468, 3 1/2" w., 7" h. **$150**

Figure group, girl feeding calf, a farm girl bending over to feed a calf from a pail, green oblong base, No. 779, 6 1/2" l., 6 1/2" h. **$250**

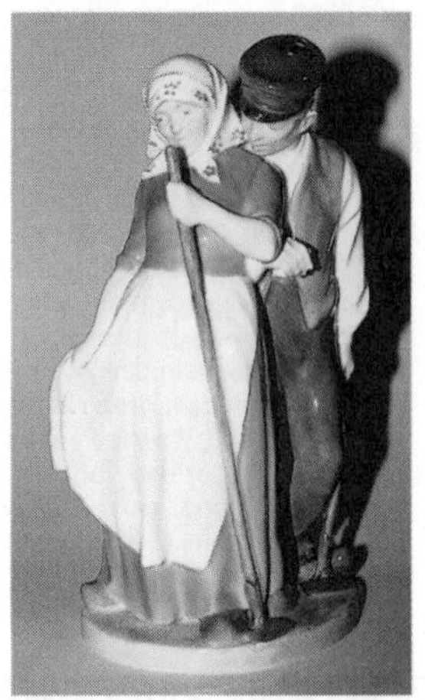

Figure group, Harvest Group, young farmer & farm girl standing close together, each leaning on a hoe, No. 1300, small, 4" w., 7 1/2" h. **$250**

Figure group, shepherd boy w/dog, standing boy wearing cap & long blanket cloak, No. 782, 3 1/2" w., 7 1/2" h. **$175**

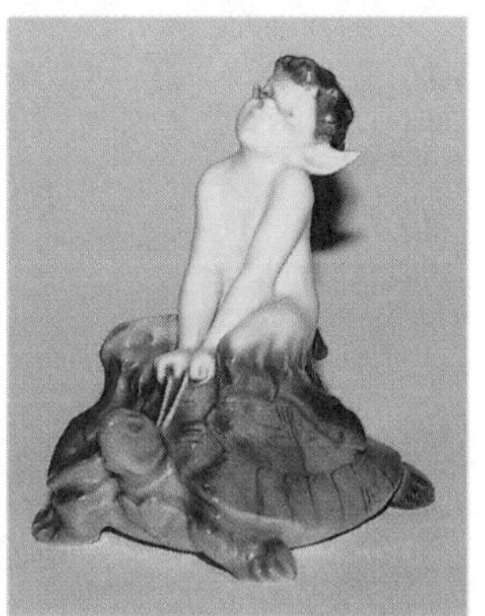

Figure group, young faun seated astride a large tortoise, No. 858, 3 1/2" l., 4" h. **$145**

Figure group, young girl & boy hugging brown puppy, No. 707, 5 1/2" l., 5 3/4" h. **$250**

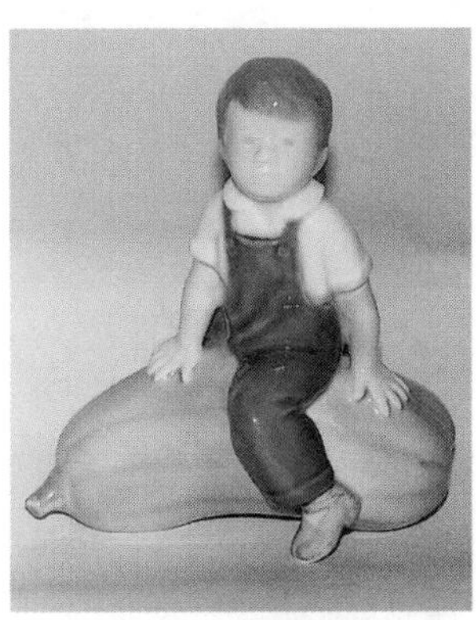

Figure of boy on gourd, young barefoot boy wearing white shirt & blue overalls seated astride a large green gourd, No. 4539, 4 1/4 x 4 1/2" **$75**

Figure of boy, Sandman (Wee-Willie-Winkie), standing on white square stepped base & leaning on an umbrella, holding another, dressed in grey, No. 1145, 6" h. **$75**

Figure of boy, Sandman (Wee-Willie-Winkie,) standing wearing a long white nightgown & pointed blue cap, a closed umbrella under one arm, opening a brown vial in his hands, No. 1145, 6 3/4" h. **$75**

Figure of young man eating lunch, reclining position, eating from a lunch box, No. 865, 7" l., 4" h. **$150**

Model of bird, Fat Robin, rounded baby robin in blue, white & rust red, No. 2266, 3" h. **$55**

Model of bird, Grebe, handsome swimming bird w/blue crest & grey & white body, No. 3263, 7" l., 4" h. **$95**

Model of bird, Icelandic Falcon, large bird w/speckled bluish grey & white feathers, No. 263, 8 1/2" l., 11" h. **$350**

Model of birds, pair of blue, white & grey finches perched close together, No. 1189, 5" l., 2" h. .. **$45**

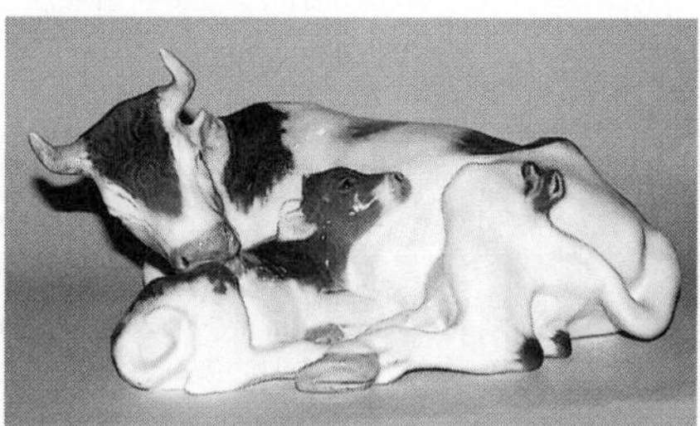

Model of cow & calf, Mother cow licking calf nestled against her, white w/shaded grey & black spots, No. 800, 5 x 11" **$250**

Model of dog, Great Dane, large recumbent dog in tan w/black striping, No. 1679, 9" l., 4" h. **$175**

Model of elephant, walking w/head & trunk raised & mouth open, No. 2998, small size, 6" l., 5" h. **$65**

Model of elk, (moose), reclining position, shaded grey & white w/white antlers, No. 2813, 9 x 10" **$300**

Model of lioness, recumbent animal, No. 804, 12" l., 6 1/2" h. **$200**

Before going to an antiques market, take along a few small items you no longer wish to keep. You may be able to find a dealer willing to take them in trade toward the purchase of something of greater value. Look for dealers who carry similar types of antiques and collectibles. If one dealer is not interested in your items, he may direct you to someone who might be.

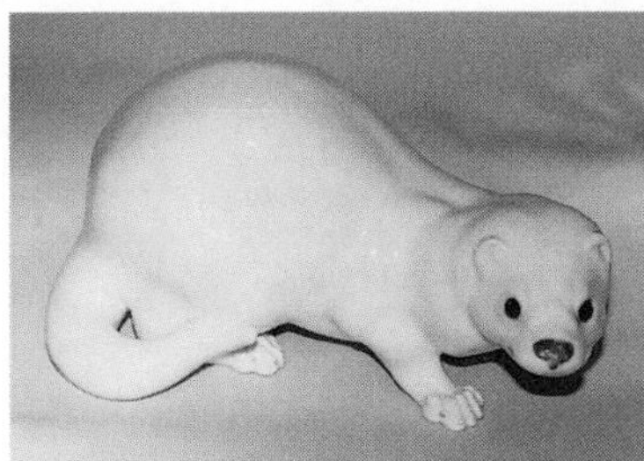

Model of mink, white w/black eyes & brown nose, No. 4654, 3 3/4 x 7" **$175**

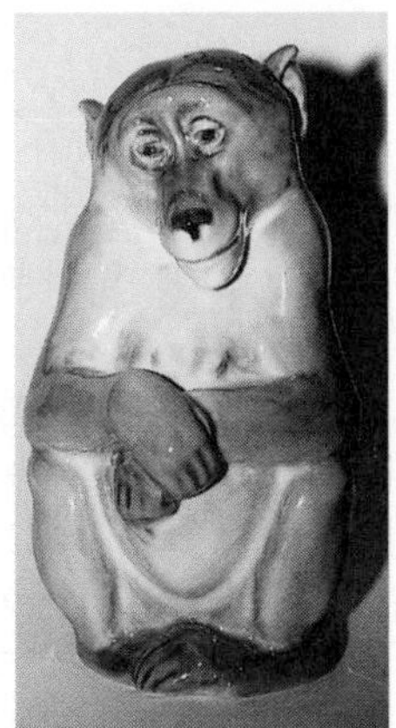

Model of monkey, seated animal w/ head tilted to side, No. 1444, 3" w., 5" h. **$95**

Model of mouse, white & pink mouse perched on an ear of brown corn, No. 512, 5" l., 2" h. **$48**

Model of panda, seated eating bamboo, No. 662, 5 1/2" w., 7" h. **$175**

Model of penguins, two birds seated side by side, No. 1190, 4" h. **$75**

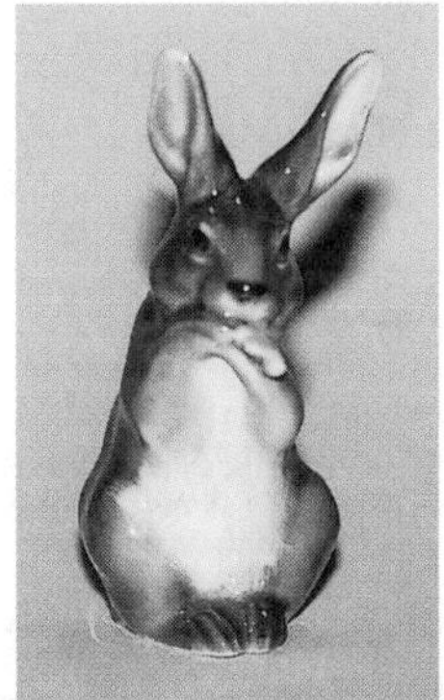

Model of rabbit, seated upright eating leaf, No. 1019, small size, 3 1/2" h. **$48**

Model of sea lion, head raised, shades of tan & grey, No. 265, 7 x 12" **$275**

Rose bowl, squatty spherical form w/ wide flat mouth, dark blue ground painted w/large white blossoms & green leaves, No. 424, 8" d., 6" h. **$125**

Careless handling at auction previews can quickly degrade the condition of many antiques and collectibles. When items are placed on tables where anyone, even children, can pick things up, damage can easily occur. Use great care when examining items and be sure to re-examine your purchases after winning them to make sure no damage took place during inspection.

Royal Vienna

The second factory in Europe to make hard paste porcelain was established in Vienna in 1719 by Claud Innocentius de Paquier. The factory underwent various changes of administration through the years and finally closed in 1865. Since then, however, the porcelain has been reproduced by various factories in Austria and Germany, many of which have also reproduced the early beehive mark. Early pieces, naturally, bring far higher prices than the later ones or the reproductions.

Charger, round, h.p. w/a romantic mythological scene of a pretty maiden seated on a garden bench beside a fountain & playfully scolding Cupid who has broken his bow, an orb at her feet, artist-signed, within a pink velvet & giltwood frame, early 20th c., 11" d. **$2,400**

Plate, 9 1/2" d., cabinet-type, a central color bust portrait of Marie Antoinette, signed by Wagner, the cobalt blue border band ornately decorated w/gold panels, scrolls & florals **$1,150**

Plate, 9 1/2" d., cabinet-type, the center w/a finely painted bust portrait of a Renaissance era noblewoman w/a feathered headdress, the cobalt blue border band ornately decorated w/undulating panels of fancy florals, mounted in a deep giltwood shadowbox frame lined in deep red velvet, overall 16" sq. **$1,725**

Urn, cover & stand, the domed stand on shaped gold tab feet & a gold border, the cobalt blue ground ornately decorated w/overall bands of delicate floral vines centering a round reserve h.p. in color w/a scene of a Greek god & goddess, the urn w/ a tapering pedestal below the wide urn-form body, cobalt blue ground decorated overall w/gold bands & ornate delicate leafy vines, a large central oval reserve h.p. in color w/ a group of Greek gods & goddesses, long angled gold handles flanking the shoulder & the tapering domed cover w/a pointed gold finial & h.p. w/another color reserve, late 19th - early 20th c., overall 21 1/4" h., the set **$5,581**

Vase, 10" h., tapering cylindrical body w/an angled shoulder to the small flaring neck, iridescent lavender ground w/a tall oval reserve decorated w/an allegorical scene of Love, a winged Cupid arranging roses in the dark hair of a standing classical young woman in a garden setting, the sides & shoulder ornately decorated w/ delicate beaded gold trellis & leafy scroll designs, blue Beehive mark, artist-signed, titled on the bottom, late 19th - early 20th c. **$2,640**

Vase, 15" h., small domed foot & tall ovoid body tapering to a tall trumpet neck, iridescent amethyst ground decorated on one side w/a large oval reserve h.p. w/a scene of a classical maiden seated in a wooded landscape, a book in her lap, gold border trimmed w/raised gilt bouquets & C-scrolls, the back w/an oval reserve of white "jeweled" radiating foliate design among trellis & leaves within gilt rims, blue Beehive mark, artist-signed, late 19th - early 20th c. **$2,880**

Vase, 22" h., a low cylindrical base attached to a short ringed pedestal supporting the wide bulbous urn-form body w/a short rolled neck flanked by bold leafy scroll handles from the rim to the side of the body, burgundy ground w/the body centered by a large reserve h.p. w/a shoulder-length portrait of an auburn haired beauty within a raised gilt floral border, edged by trellis & foliate scrolls, the back in gilt w/a trellis arabesque design, the base h.p. w/gold rectangular panels flanked by gold leafy scrolls, delicate gold lacy bands around the shoulder & neck, blue Beehive mark, artist-signed, ca. 1880 .... **$8,400**

Vase, 5" h., ovoid body tapering to a slender neck w/a flaring rim, gilt openwork vine-like gold handles from the center neck to shoulder, a large gold oval enclosing a color portrait of a young maiden w/brown hair, background in pale shaded green w/ornate gilt decoration, artist-signed, marked on the base "Germany - Sincerity - 3666," tiny flat nick on the rim **$575**

Vase, 7" h., footed bulbous base tapering to a tall slender cylindrical body w/a bulbed forked mouth, gold ruffled loop handles on center of the blue neck trimmed w/gilt florals & a Greek key band, the main body decorated w/a color scene of a young maiden seated looking at a pair of doves w/a cherub by her side, artist-signed, blue Beehive mark on the base **$863**

Vases, 7 5/8" h., tall slightly tapering squared body w/a rounded shoulder & short cylindrical neck w/rolled rim, short gold scroll handles from rim to shoulder, ruby ground, each centered by an oval reserve h.p. w/a color bust portrait of Napoleon or Josephine, each within a raised gold border below a trellis & diaper cartouche, the back decorated w/an octagonal turquoise 'jeweled' panel of scrolling leaves above ribbon-tied floral garlands, red Beehive mark, early 20th c., pr. **$3,360**

Rozart Pottery

George and Rose Rydings were aspiring Kansas City (Missouri) potters who, in the late 1960s, began to produce a line of fine underglaze pottery. An inheritance of vintage American-made artware gave the Rydings inspiration to recreate old ceramic masters' techniques. Some design influence also came from Fred Radford, grandson of well-known Ohio artist Albert Radford (ca. 1890s-1904). Experimenting with Radford's formula for Jasperware and sharing ideas with Fred about glazing techniques and ceramic chemistry led the Rydings to a look reminiscent of the ware made by turn-of-the-century American art pottery masters such as Weller and Rookwood. The result of their work became Rozart, the name of the Rydings' pottery.

Many lines have been created since Rozart's beginning. Twainware, Sylvan, Cameoware, Rozart Royal, Rusticware, Deko, Krakatoa, Koma and Sateen are a few. It is rare to find a piece of Rozart that is not marked in some way. The earliest mark is "Rozart" at the top of a circle with "Handmade" in the center and "K.C.M.O." (Kansas City, Missouri) at the bottom. Other marks followed over the years, including a seal that was used extensively. Along with artist initials, collectors will find a date code (either two digits representing the year or a month separated by a slash followed by a two-digit year). George signs his pieces "GMR," "GR," or "RG" (with a backwards "R"). Working on Twainware, Jasperware and Cameoware in the early years, George has many wheel-thrown pieces to his credit. Rose, who is very knowledgeable about Native Americans, does scenics and portraits. Her mark is either "RR" or "Rydings." Four of the seven Rydings children have worked in the pottery as well. Anne Rydings White (mark is "Anne" or "AR" or "ARW") designed and executed many original pieces in addition to her work on the original Twainware line. Susan Rydings Ubert (mark is "S" over "R") has specialized in Sylvan pieces and is an accomplished sculptor and mold maker. Susan's daughter Maureen does female figures in the Art Deco style. Becky (mark is "B" over "R"), now a commercial artist, designed lines such as Fleamarket, Nature's Jewels, and Animals. Cindy Rydings Cushing (mark is "C" over "R" or "CRC") developed the very popular Kittypots line. Mark Rydings is the Rozart mold maker. The Rozart Pottery is still active today. Pottery enthusiasts are taking notice of the family history, high quality and reminiscent beauty of Rozart. Its affordability may soon cease as Rozart's popularity and recognition are on the rise.

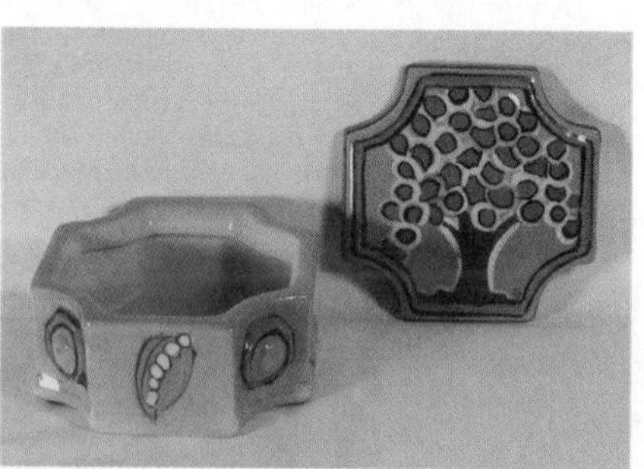

Box w/lid, Arts & Crafts style, quatrefoil shape w/image of tree painted on lid and various decorations about sides of box, George Rydings, 6" w. **$212**

Ewer, sgraffito mouse design, Rose Rydings, 10" h. **$255**

Mugs, w/various incised Native American designs, signed "RR," 5" h., each (ILLUS. of seven) **$120**

Tankard, Rusticware, decorated in various motifs, George Rydings, 50 made **$425**

Tile, frog & leaf design, in wood frame, Copperverde glaze, Susan Ubert, 8" sq. **$175**

Vase, 15" h., Rozart Royal, w/eagle in landing position on front, Rose Rydings **$345**

Vase, 7 1/2" h., pillow shape w/bird on branch on front, Cindy Cushing **$150**

In cataloged auctions, bidding increments are often stated in the conditions of the sale. Otherwise, auctioneers set bidding increments as they sell each item. When there is keen interest in a lot, the auctioneer may choose to increase the increment as the bidding progresses, e.g. upping the bid by $100 instead of raising it $50 each time.

R.S. Prussia & Related Wares

Ornately decorated china marked "R.S. Prussia" and "R.S. Germany" continues to grow in popularity. According to the Third Series of Mary Frank Gaston's Encyclopedia of R.S. Prussia (Collector Books, Paducah, Kentucky), these marks were used by the Reinhold Schlegelmilch porcelain factories located in Suhl in the Germanic regions known as "Prussia" prior to World War I, and in Tillowitz, Silesia, which became part of Poland after World War II. Other marks sought by collectors include "R.S. Suhl," "R.S." steeple or church marks, and "R.S. Poland."

The Suhl factory was founded by Reinhold Schlegelmilch in 1869 and closed in 1917. The Tillowitz factory was established in 1895 by Erhard Schlegelmilch, Reinhold's son. This china customarily bears the phrase "R.S. Germany" and "R.S. Tillowitz." The Tillowitz factory closed in 1945, but it was reopened for a few years under Polish administration.

Prices are high and collectors should beware of the forgeries that sometimes find their way onto the market. Mold names and numbers are taken from Mary Frank Gaston's books on R.S. Prussia.

The "Prussia" and "R.S. Suhl" marks have been reproduced, so buy with care. Later copies of these marks are well done, but quality of porcelain is inferior to the production in the 1890-1920 era.

Collectors are also interested in the porcelain products made by the Erdmann Schlegelmilch factory. This factory was founded by three brothers in Suhl in 1861. They named the factory in honor of their father, Erdmann Schlegelmilch. A variety of marks incorporating the "E.S." initials were used. The factory closed circa 1935. The Erdmann Schlegelmilch factory was an earlier and entirely separate business from the Reinhold Schlegelmilch factory. The two were not related to each other.

R.S. Germany

Chocolate set: cov. 10" pot & six cups & saucers; Art Deco-style mold, transfer decoration of pink roses on ivory ground w/etched gilt trim, marked "R.S. Germany," early 20th c., the set (ILLUS. second from left w/other R.S. Germany chocolate sets) **$800-1,200**

Cheese server, a slightly dished round plate centered by a short pedestal supporting a small dished plate, each section decorated w/large blossoms joined by green tendrils on a shaded ground, 8 1/2" d. **$39**

Cup & saucer, decorated w/blue, black & white bands on beige lustre ground, cup w/center silhouette of Art Deco woman in blue dancing w/ blue scarf, cup 3 1/2" d., 2 1/4" h., saucer 5 3/4" d. **$160-175**

Cracker jar, cov., Mold 540a, beige satin ground w/floral decoration in orchid, yellow & gold, 9 1/2" w. handle to handle, overall 5 1/2" h. **$300-350**

R.S. Prussia

Berry set: 11" d. master bowl & five 4" d. sauce dishes; Mold 155, each decorated w/a Sheepherder landscape scene w/cottage & flowering trees & shrubs, the set.... **$1,400-1,800**

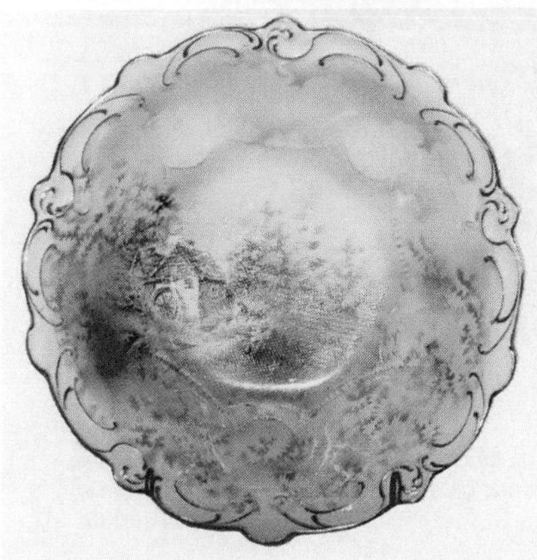

Bowl, 10 3/4" d., Mold 217, "tapestry" center mill scene, gilt scroll border **$1,200-1,500**

Bowl, 10" d., Mold 85, Summer Season portrait w/ mill scene in background **$2,500-3,000**

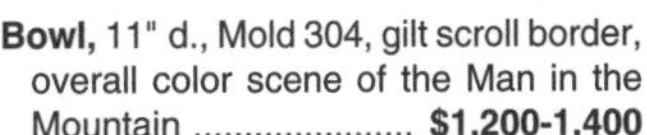

Bowl, 11" d., Mold 304, gilt scroll border, overall color scene of the Man in the Mountain **$1,200-1,400**

Cake plate, open-handled, Ribbon & Jewel mold (Mold 18), heavy gold border around florals framing the keyhole scene of Dice Players, 9" d. **$1,200-1,400**

Pitcher, tankard, 12 1/4" h., Mold 569, very rare Bird of Paradise decoration w/shaded gold & light green in the lower half, white above, gold trim, only one known **$13,00-17,000**

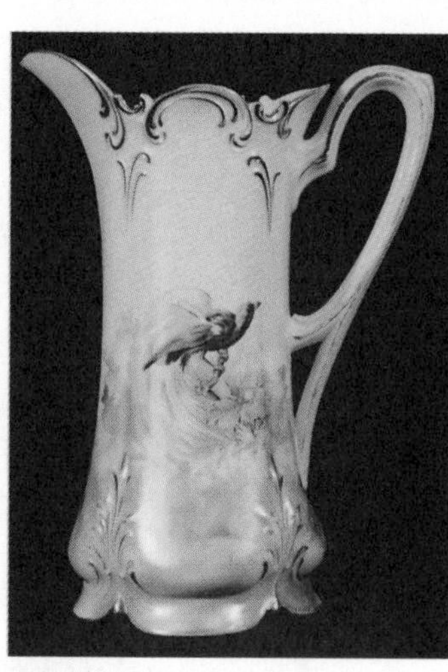

Pitcher, tankard, 13" h., Carnation mold (Mold 526), decorated w/ clusters of dark pink & creamy white roses w/a shaded dark green ground & pale green molded blossoms **$1,000-1,200**

Plate, 12" d., Lily mold (Mold 29), Madame Recamier portrait, dark blue Tiffany bronze finish in border panels **$2,000- 4,000**

Plate, 9" d., Mold 343, Spring figural scenic decoration in keyhole medallion, iridescent Tiffany purple finish at base of figure, heavy gold around portrait decoration w/small pink roses against a deep red ground **$1,800-2,100**

Vase, two-handled, tall, slender, ovoid body w/colorful scene of two parrots, shaded brown foliage, unmarked $1,800- 2,000

Vases, 11 3/4" h., Mold 901, footed, slightly tapering cylindrical bodies w/high, flaring, cupped, deeply fluted necks w/jewels, beading & jewels around the shoulders & feet, ornate scrolled gilt handles, Melon Eaters decoration against shaded dark green ground, each (ILLUS. of pair) $1,600-2,000

Other Marks

Coffee set, cov. coffeepot, cov. sugar bowl, creamer & six cups & saucers; the tall ovoid pot w/a long swan's-neck spout, domed cover w/flame finial & ornate scrolled handle, each piece decorated w/an oval color central reserve w/a classical scene based on Angelica Kauffmann, borders in dark burgundy & green on white w/scattered delicate gold trim, coffeepot 9" h., R.S. Suhl, the set $1,800-2,000

If you don't like the risk of selling an item at an auction, consider consigning it to an antique shop or mall. If there is space available and your item is accepted, expect to pay at least 25 percent commission when it sells.

Vase, 9" h., 3" d., tall, slender, ovoid body tapering to a tall, slender trumpet neck, a wide band around the body decorated w/a colored scene of The Melon Eaters between narrow gold & white bands, the neck & lower body in deep rose decorated w/gilt leaf sprigs, R.S. Suhl $800-1,000

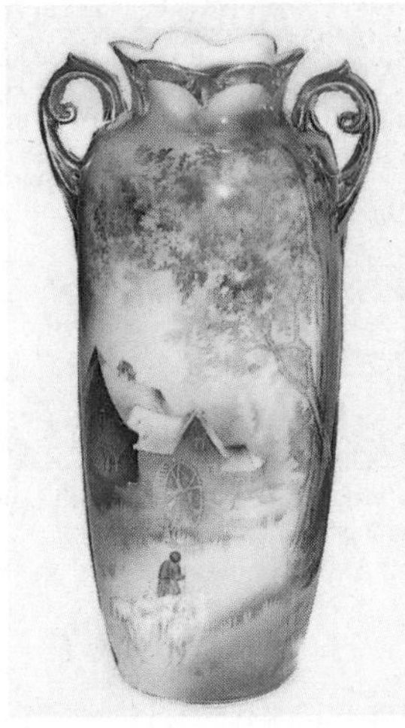

Vases, 10" h., gently swelled body tapering to narrow rounded shoulders & a short, flaring, scalloped neck, ornate C-scroll gilt shoulder handles, gold neck band, the body decorated w/a colored scene of a sheepherder leading his flock toward a mill in the background, trees overhead, the second identical except w/a cottage scene, R.S. Poland, pr. (ILLUS. of one) $1,350-1,400

Russel Wright Designs

The innovative dinnerware designed by Russel Wright and produced by various companies beginning in the late 1930s was an immediate success with a society that was turning to a more casual and informal lifestyle. His designs, with their flowing lines and unconventional shapes, were produced in many different colors, which allowed a hostess to arrange creative tables.

Although not antique, these designs, which we list here by line and manufacturer, are highly collectible. In addition to dinnerwares, Wright was also known as a trendsetter in the design of furniture, glassware, lamps, fabric and a multitude of other household goods.

American Modern (Steubenville Pottery Co.)

Bowl, fruit, lug handle, chartreuse (ILLUS. left) .. **$20**

Casual China (Iroquois China Co.)

Coffeepot, cov., oyster grey (ILLUS. right with creamer and pitcher) **$225**

Creamer & cov. sugar bowl, redesigned, mustard gold (color produced only one year), the set **$100**

Mug, original design, ice blue (ILLUS. center with two other mugs) **$60-85**

Knowles Esquire Line (Edwin M. Knowles China Co.)

Pitcher, water, Grass patt., pink, unusual .... **$225+**

Residential Pattern (Plastic tablewares by Northern)

Tumbler, red or blue, each (ILLUS. of two)..................................... **$50**

Sterling Line (Sterling China Co.)

Creamer, gray **$50**

Sascha Brastoff

Sascha Brastoff dedicated his life to creating works with a flair all his own. He was a costume designer for major movie studios, a dancer, a window dresser and a talented painter. The creator in Sascha put him on the path to ceramics early in life, when he was awarded a scholarship to the Cleveland Art School; however, he also worked with watercolors, charcoals, pastels, resin, fabrics, ceramics, metal sculptures, and enamels. Nelson Rockefeller, Brastoff's friend, understood the uniqueness of his talents and, in 1953, he built a complex in Los Angeles, California, to house the many creations Sascha was able to produce.

A full line of handpainted china with names such as Allegro, La Jolla, Roman Coin and Night Song was created. Surf Ballet was a popular dinnerware line with a look achieved by dipping pieces of blue, pink or yellow into real gold or platinum. Also highly popular was Sascha's line of enamels on copper. Many collectors do not know that Sascha dabbled in textiles. A yard of cloth in good condition might command several hundred dollars on today's market. His artware items included patterns such as Star Steed, a leaping-fantasy horse, and Rooftops, a series of houses where the roofs were the prominent feature. These pieces were - and continue to be - two of the most highly collectible Sascha artware patterns.

Sascha Brastoff also created a line of Alaskan-motif items. Many collectors confuse Matthew Adams pieces with those of Sascha. Even though Adams worked for Brastoff for a period of time, his pieces are not nearly as sought after as those that Sascha created.

Sascha B.
Sascha Brastoff

Brastoff's crystal ball served him well during his lifetime. In the late 1940s and early 1950s he created a series of Western-motif cache pots that excite any collector when found today. Almost a decade before the poodle craze in the 1950s, Sascha created a line of poodle products. In the 1950s, cigarette smoking was at an all-time high and Sascha was there with smoking accessories.

From 1947 to 1952 pieces were signed "Sascha B." or with the full signature, "Sascha Brastoff." After 1953 and before 1962, during the years of his factory-studio, pieces done by his employees showed "Sascha B." and, more often than not, also included the Chanticleer back stamp. Caution should be taken to understand that the Chanticleer with the full name "Sascha Brastoff" below it is not the "full signature" mark that elevates pieces to substantial prices. The Chanticleer mark is usually in gold and will incorporate Sascha's work name in the same color. Sascha's personal full signature is the one commanding the high prices.

Health problems forced Sascha to leave his company in 1963. After 1962 pieces were marked "Sascha B." and also included the "R" in a circle trademark. Ten years later the business closed.

Sascha Brastoff died on February 4, 1993. The passing of this flamboyant artist, whose special character was well reflected in his work, means that similar creations will probably never be achieved again.

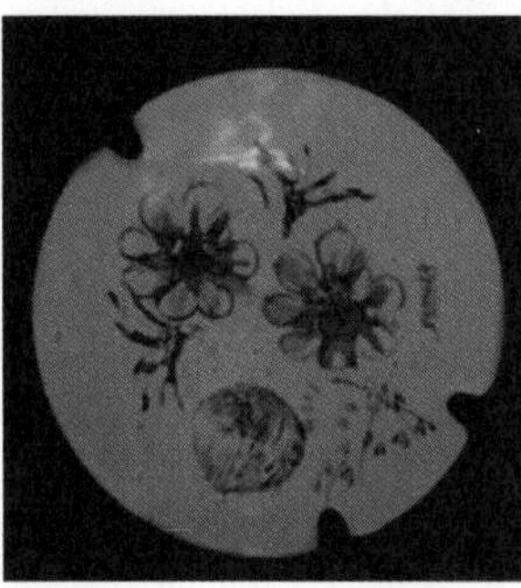

Ashtray, enamel, floral design on white, 5 1/2" d. **$30**

Ashtray, fish-shaped, multicolored glaze, 6 1/4" d. **$75-100**

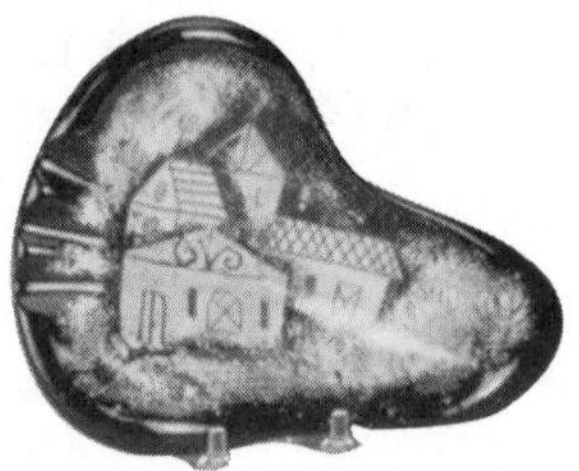

Ashtray, free-form, No. F 2, Rooftops patt., 8 1/2" w. **$70-80**

Ashtray, low domed shape, No. H 1, black & orange glaze, 6" d. (ILLUS. front left with two hooded ashtrays)................................. **$25-35**

Ashtray, No. O 16, Poodle patt., 11" d. (ILLUS. back row with bowls, Alaska cigarette container, Star Steed dish & Alaska egg- shaped box).. **$65-75**

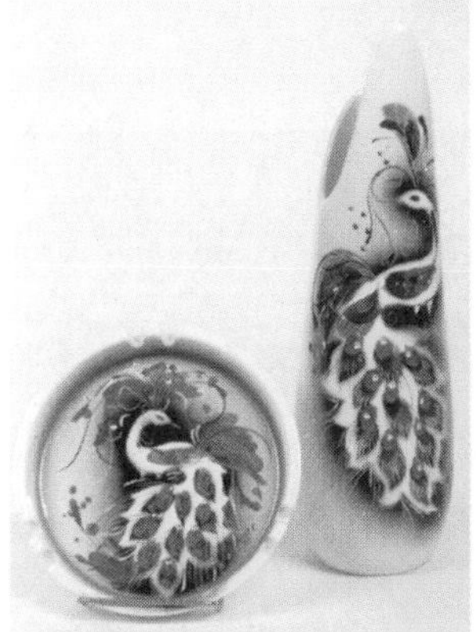

Ashtray, round, Jeweled Peacock patt., 7" d. (ILLUS. left with Jeweled Peacock vase).... **$65-75**

Ashtray, rounded freeform, No. F-33, Aztec-Mayan patt., 13" w. (ILLUS. back row right with Aztec-Mayan bowl, Aztec-Mayan box, Aztec-Mayan egg & Aztec-Mayan ewer) **$60-70**

Bowl, 13" d., footed, decorated w/grapes & leaves on a black background **$200-225**

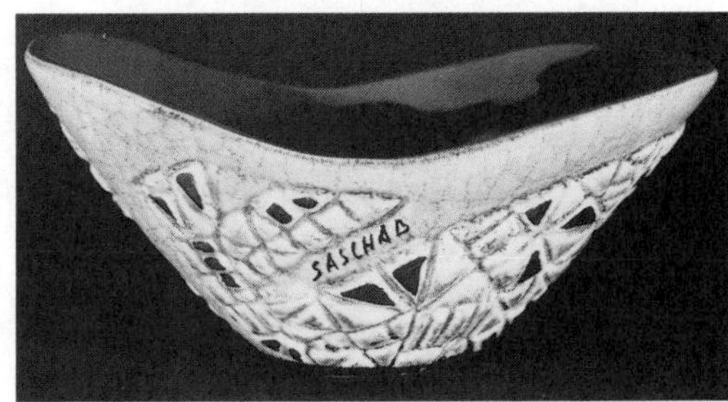

Bowl, banana shape, Mosaic design outside, solid color inside **$65-75**

Box, cov., rectangular, "Rooftops" patt., No. 021, 5 x 8" **$50-75**

Candleholder, resin, yellow w/incised diamond design, 6" h. (ILLUS. left with red resin candleholder) **$25-50**

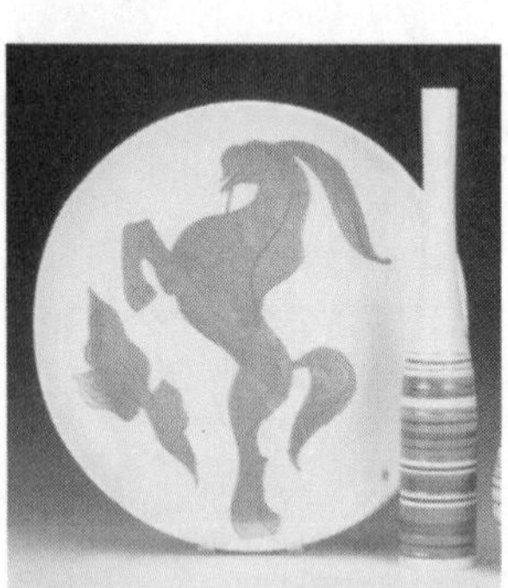

Chop plate, Aztec-Mayan patt., 16 1/2" d. (ILLUS. left with Abstract Originals vase) **$175-200**

Cigar tray, oblong, No. 78, Persian patt., 17 3/4" l. (ILLUS. back with two other Persian pieces) **$90-100**

Pipe, sinuous shape, abstract design w/gold accents, 4" l. **$84**

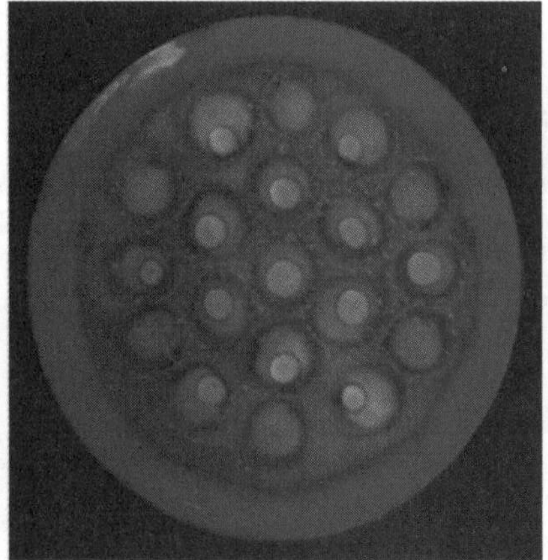

Plate, 11 1/2" d., enamel, orange & gold abstract design, factory hanger on back **$100**

Schoop (Hedi) Art Creations

By far one of the most talented artists working in California in the 1940s and 1950s was Hedi Schoop. She designed and modeled almost every piece in her line. She began her business in 1940 in Hollywood, California. Barker Brothers department store in Los Angeles discovered Schoop's work which encouraged her to open the small Hollywood studio. Shortly after a move to larger quarters, financed by her mother, Hedi began calling her business Hedi Schoop Art Creations. It would remain under that name throughout Schoop's career which was ended when a fire destroyed the operation in 1958. At that time, Hedi decided to free-lance for other companies (see: Cleminson Clay). Probably one of the most imitated artists of the time, other people began businesses using Schoop's designs and techniques. Hedi Schoop decided to sue in court and the results were settled in Schoop's favor. Among those imitators were Kim Ward, and Ynez and Yona. Hedi Schoop saw forms differently than other artists and, therefore, was able to create with ease and in different media. While Hedi made shapely women with skirts that flared out to create bowls as well as women with arms over their heads holding planters, she also produced charming bulky looking women with thick arms and legs. When TV lamps became popular, Hedi was able to easily add her talents to creating those designs with roosters, tragedy and comedy joined together in an Art Deco fashion, and elegant women in various poses. A variety of marks were used by Schoop including her signature (incised or stamped) which also, on occasion, shows "Hollywood, Cal." or "California," and there was also a sticker used but such pieces are hard to find.

Hedi Schoop left Germany in 1930, then immigrated to Hollywood, California, in 1933. She began producing ceramics of her own designs in 1940. Schoop turned out as many as 30,000 pieces per year once her production was running smoothly. A fire destroyed the pottery in 1958, and Hedi did freelance work for several California companies. She retired from working full-time in the early 1960s, but her talents would not let her quit completely. She died in 1996 and had painted, although sparingly, until then.

Hedi Schoop
HOLLYWOOD CAL.

There were a variety of marks ranging from the stamped or incised Schoop signature to the hard-to-find Hedi Schoop sticker. The words "Hollywood, Cal." or "California" can also be found in conjunction with the Hedi Schoop name. You can find items with a production number, artists' names or initials.

Schoop was imitated by many artists, especially some decorators who opened businesses of their own after working with Schoop. Mac and Yona Lippen owned Yona Ceramics, and Katherine Schueftan owned Kim Ward Studio. They used many of Schoop's designs and today have their own following among collectors. There were others, but Schueftan lost a lawsuit Hedi had brought against her in 1942 for design infringements. It is important to buy pieces marked "Hedi Schoop" or buy from a reputable dealer if you want to be sure you have the real thing.

Considering the number of products created, it would be easy to assume that Schoop pieces are plentiful. This would be an erroneous assumption. Collectors will indeed be fortunate to find any Schoop figurines for less than $100, and to amass many of her products takes dedication and determination.

Ashtray, in the shape of a butterfly w/spread wings, yellow w/gold trim & "eyes" on wings, inkstamp overglaze, 5 1/2" w. **$66**

Ashtray, model of a bird, 7 1/2" l., 5 1/4" h. .. **$50-75**

Console set: "Young China Musicians," Chinese boy & Chinese girl w/ rectangular planter; planter 11" l., girl 10 1/4" h., boy 10 3/4" h., the set **$300-350**

Figural group, cowboy & woman dancing, bisque faces & hands, cowboy wears hat & kerchief, woman wears black top & ruffled yellow full-length skirt, cowboy has one hand around woman's waist, woman holds skirt out w/one hand, incised unglazed mark "Hedi Schoop, California," 11" h. **$400**

Figure of Chinese woman, standing on a round black base, white floor-length skirt, black, white & green blouse w/long sleeves flaring at wrists, a white flower in black hair above each ear, right fingers bent to hold a pot w/black cloth handle & in same colors as blouse, right leg bent at knee, woman 9" h., pot 2 1/2" h., 2 pcs. **$215**

Figures, "Lantern Girls," squatting Chinese girls each holding a stick suspending a lantern, accompanying figures for the "Young China Musicians" console set, in red, 8 1/2" h., each **$100-125**

Figure of woman, in 19th-c. mint-green off-the-shoulder dress decorated w/h.p. pink flowers on bodice & skirt, light hair w/gold hair bow & curls cascading down one side, holds parasol in one hand, other hand holds skirt, inkstamp underglaze "Hedi Schoop, Hollywood, Cal.," 13" h. **$258**

Figure of woman, standing on one foot & holding large basket above her head w/both hands, dressed in yellow top & full yellow skirt w/blue & green stripes, on yellow oval base, incised overglaze "Hedi Schoop Design, California U.S.A.," 14" h. **$395**

Figures, Oriental couple each holding a basket, black & gold shirts & white pants, woman 11 1/2" h., man 12 1/2" h., pr. **$275-300**

Flower holder, figure of kneeling woman, short light textured hair, white dirndl-type dress w/blue trim & h.p. flowers on skirt, one hand holds apron out for holding flowers, on light blue oval base, inkstamp underglaze "Hedi Schoop, Hollywood, Cal.," 8 1/2" h. .. **$125**

Vase, 9" h. at highest point, 4 1/2" h., at lowest point, 9" l., seashell-form, footed oval base, fluted edge rising from the low end to the higher end, dark green base w/dark green & gold fading to light green, rim trimmed in gold, transparent textured glossy glaze, marked w/a silver label w/red block letters, "Hedi Schoop Hollywood, Calif." on two lines **$110**

Flower holder, figure of woman w/long light hair & a wide picture-style hat, dressed in ruffled teal off-the-shoulder long-sleeved full-length dress & teal picture hat w/scalloped rim, hands clasped in front holding matching basket, all w/applied pink flowers, inkstamp underglaze "Hedi Schoop, Hollywood, Cal.," 11" h. **$245**

Figure of girl, standing on cobalt blue-glazed round base, legs slightly apart, arms stretched out to sides, hands folded to hold jump rope, rough textured black hair w/pigtails out to sides & held in place w/cobalt blue glossy ties, light blue long sleeved shirt, cobalt blue overblouse w/straps, rough textured cobalt blue short skirt & socks, inkstamp on unglazed bottom, "Hedi Schoop Hollywood, Cal.," 8 1/2" h........................ **$240**

Figural group, cowboy & woman dancing, bisque faces & hands, cowboy wears hat & kerchief, woman wears black top & ruffled yellow full-length skirt, cowboy has one hand around woman's waist, woman holds skirt out w/ one hand, incised unglazed mark "Hedi Schoop, California," 11" h. **$400**

Jardiniere, cylindrical, incised stylized design of a kneeling Chinese woman w/Ming trees & animals, base & design in gold glaze on a light green body, 7" h. **$148**

Planter, model of a horse, rough textured mane & tail, white glossy glazed body w/mint green face accents, saddle, bows in assorted areas & scalloped edging at the base, inkstamp mark "Hedi Schoop," 7 1/2" h................. **$126**

Tray, figural, divided w/irregular leaf-shaped raised edges, the rim mounted w/the figure of a cherub on her knees, arms outstretched beside her, head tilted, beige & gold tray interior, beige w/pink-tinged cherub, gold wings, rose on left wrist, belt of roses around her waist w/rose-glazed bowl exterior & rose hair, bottom of tray also in a glossy rose, incised "Hedi Schoop," 11 1/2" l., overall 6" h. **$268**

Sèvres & Sèvres-Style

Some of the most desirable porcelain ever produced was made at the Sèvres factory, originally established at Vincennes, France, and transferred, through permission of Madame de Pompadour, to Sèvres as the Royal Manufactory about the middle of the 18th century. King Louis XV took sole responsibility for the works in 1759, when production of hard paste wares began. Between 1850 and 1900, many biscuit and soft-paste pieces were made again. Fine early pieces are scarce and high-priced. Many of those available today are late productions. The various Sèvres marks have been copied, and pieces listed as "Sèvres- Style" are similar to actual Sèvres wares but not necessarily from that factory. Three of the many Sèvres marks are illustrated here.

Box, cov., casket-form, the low rectangular serpentine sides supported on ornate gold scrolled corner legs, the dark blue sides h.p. w/ oval reserves w/colorful florals framed by ornate gilt scrolls, the hinged & low domed cover also in dark blue w/a large white reserve w/floral clusters & vines framing a central panel decorated w/a couple in 18th c. costume, pseudo-Sèvres marks, late 19th c., 6 1/2" h. **$3,220**

Center bowl, Sèvres-style, gilt-bronze mounted, the long oval shallow bowl w/a dark blue exterior centering a large oval reserve w/a color scene of 18th c. lovers in a landscape, framed by ornate gold leafy vines, the white interiors decorated w/floral designs, a beaded gilt-brown rim band & slender inward-scrolled end handles connecting to the pedestal base w/scrolls raised on an oblong platform w/scroll feet, late 19th c., overall 20" l. **$2,875**

Centerpiece bowl, in the Louis XVI taste, a celeste blue wide border w/gilt floral sprig band around the center painted w/a colorful scene of 18th c. peasant figures, mounted in a gilt-brass framework w/scroll handles & scroll feet joined by floral swags, pseudo-Sevres interlaced Ls mark on base, late 19th c., 16 1/2" w., 6" h. **$690**

Garniture set: centerpiece & a pair of cov. vases; the vases w/ovoid bodies w/flaring necks ending in flattened dome lids w/pinecone finials, on slender ringed flaring pedestals on gilt bronze rectangular plinths w/bracket feet, the necks w/pierced gilt decorative band joined to gilt scroll handles mounted to shoulders, the body decorated w/h.p. romantic scenes in pastel shades on emerald green ground framed in raised gilt scroll & bead design, the wide bowl-form centerpiece w/matching pierced gilt rim & handles attached at rim & scrolling to base of bowl, bowl w/matching decoration & raised on a matching pedestal base, artist signed "Poylet," lids marked "Chateau de Longpre" w/"S" in diamond & "France," ca. 1900, centerpiece 17" w., vases 18" h., the set **$3,450**

Jardiniere, Sèvres-style, gilt bronze-mounted, a wide low squatty bowl decorated w/upper & lower dark blue bands w/gilt stripes & floral clusters, a white central band h.p. w/playful putti alternating w/lion face masks, metal rim band joining arched scroll handles continuing down to the ornate scrolled metal platform raised on claw feet, ca. 1870, 11 1/2 x 26 1/2", 13 1/2" h. **$1,725**

Jardinieres, Sèvres-style, gilt bronze-mounted, a footed wide cylindrical body w/a dark blue ground, one side h.p. w/ a large rectangular reserve of 18th c. figures in a woodland, the other side w/a large floral reserve, gold borders & lacy scrolls, metal rim band joined to lion mask & ring side handles continuing to the round base on ornate scrolled feet, blue interlaced "L"s mark, late 19th c., 10 1/2" d., 10 1/2" h., pr. **$5,060**

Tea set: cov. teapot, cov. sugar bowl, creamer & one cup & saucer; dark Blue Nouveau ground, the serving pieces w/bulbous ovoid bodies, each piece decorated w/gilt leaf band around the base & a band of stylized blossoms & leaves around the shoulder, further leaf band & gilt line decoration on each piece, various decorator & potter marks, France, mid-19th c., teapot 6 1/4" h., the set **$2,271**

Teapot, cov., cylindrical body w/flat shoulder centering a short neck & low domed cover w/pointed knob finial, curved rim spout & C-scroll handle, turquoise blue ground decorated on one side w/a vignette in color of a barefoot boy playing the flute w/a dog at his feet, the other side w/a colorful bouquet of flowers within a gilt scroll border, teapot 18th c., the decoration added later, spurious blue Sevres interlaced Ls mark, 5" h. **$598**

"In the style of," or "-style" means that a piece imitates the design of another maker. Such a piece was not necessarily manufactured to deceive, but a seller should describe the piece accurately.

Urn, cov., Sèvres-style, gilt bronze-mounted, a gilt-bronze notch-cornered foot below the cobalt blue ringed pedestal w/ornate gilt scrolls below the tall urn-form body supported on gilt-bronze leaves, the main body h.p. w/a continuous color scene of a semi- nude maiden frolicking w/putti in a garden setting, the shoulder cast w/a narrow metal band w/ one side featuring frolicking putti, the other side w/a putto drawing a sword, the tapering cobalt blue neck & domed cover w/ornate gilt scrolling, upright gilt-bronze scroll shoulder handles & a gilt-bronze flame finial on the cover, late 19th c., overall 25 1/4" h. .. **$3,346**

Vases, 13 1/8" h., simple ovoid body tapering to a tall trumpet neck, decorated in the Japanese taste to resemble cloisonnè, the dark blue ground h.p. w/large purple peonies & rust-colored leafy stems, delicate white blossoms & stems around the neck, Sèvres factory marks, ca. 1875-80, pr. (ILLUS. of one) **$4,780**

Spatterware

This ceramic ware takes its name from the "spattered" decoration, in various colors, generally used to trim pieces handpainted with rustic center designs of flowers, birds, houses, etc. Popular in the early 19th century, most was imported from England.

Related wares, called "stick spatter," had freehand designs applied with pieces of cut sponge attached to sticks, hence the name. Examples date from the 19th and early 20th century and were produced in England, Europe and America.

Some early spatter-decorated wares were marked by the manufacturers, but not many. Twentieth century reproductions are also sometimes marked, including those produced by Boleslaw Cybis.

Tea set: child's size, two cov. teapots, two cov. sugar bowls, two creamers, four handleless cups & one saucer; Peafowl patt., teapots & sugars w/ footed squatty bulbous bodies w/flaring necks & inset domed covers w/pointed knob finials, each piece decorated w/a green spatter center band decorated w/a yellow, red & blue peafowl, similar designs w/slightly varying colors, England, ca. 1830, some damage & repair, teapots 4 1/4" h., the set (ILLUS. of part) **$1,610**

Tea set: child's, cov. teapot, cov. sugar bowl, two handleless cups & saucers; Fort patt., the teapot & sugar w/footed squatty bulbous bodies w/wide tapering paneled shoulders supporting domed covers w/button finials, teapot w/serpentine spout & C- scroll handle, sugar w/rolled tab handles, each piece w/a blue spatter ground centered by a painted fort building in black & brown w/green trees, England, ca. 1830, spout & rim flake on teapot, hairline on base of sugar, one cup w/repaired rim, teapot 4 3/8" h., the set **$825**

Teapot, cov., Thistle patt., a flared base tapering to a wide bulbous ovoid body tapering to a cylindrical neck w/flat rim, serpentine spout & C-form handle, low domed cover w/button finial, bright yellow spatter ground centered by a large red & green thistle design, end of spout damaged, English-made, ca. 1830, 7" h. **$4,140**

Spongeware

Spongeware's designs were spattered, sponged or daubed on in colors, sometimes with a piece of cloth. Blue on white was the most common type, but mottled tans, browns and greens on yellowware were also popular. Spongeware generally has an overall pattern with a coarser look than Spatterware, to which it is loosely related. These wares were extensively produced in England and America well into the 20th century.

Bowl, 8 3/4" d., 3 1/2" h., three bands of blue on white sponging alternating w/two narrow white bands, minor surface wear, late 19th - early 20th c. **$88**

Butter crock, wide flat-bottomed cylindrical form, overall dark blue sponging on white w/the printed word "Butter," excellent condition, 6 1/2" d., 4 1/4" h. **$143**

Canister, cov., cylindrical w/molded rim & inset flat cover, light blue fine overall sponging on cream, very tight hairline through bottom, stack mark on cover, late 19th - early 20th c., 7" h. **$303**

Chamber pot, miniature, cream w/overall light blue sponging, ca. 1900, 1 1/2" h. **$88**

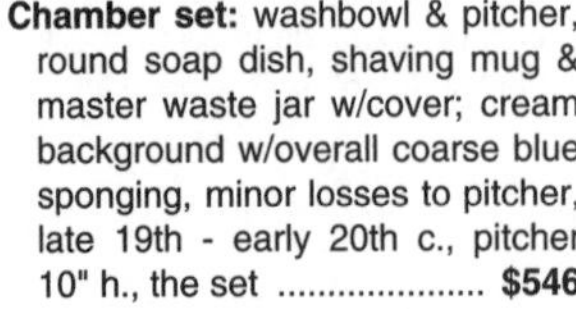

Chamber set: washbowl & pitcher, round soap dish, shaving mug & master waste jar w/cover; cream background w/overall coarse blue sponging, minor losses to pitcher, late 19th - early 20th c., pitcher 10" h., the set **$546**

Charger, round dished form w/ overall dark blue sponging on white, minor wear, late 19th c., 10 1/8" d. **$173**

Creamer, bulbous wide body tapering to a wide cylindrical neck w/wide spout & loop handle w/pointed thumb rest, the lower body molded in relief w/a scene of a heron holding a snake in its beak in a garden setting, dark blue overall sponging on white, late 19th - early 20th c., 5 1/2" h. **$495**

Pitcher, 6 1/2" h., cylindrical body w/molded rim & pointed rim spout, pointed scroll loop handle, overall dark blue sponging on white, minor interior stains, late 19th - early 20th c. **$201**

Harvest jug, beehive-shaped w/high arched handle across the top above the short angled shoulder spout & round raised back shoulder opening, overall heavy blue sponging on white w/the incised & blue-tinted name "A. Noland," long U-shaped glued crack on the back, rare, ca. 1860, 13" h. **$688**

Pitcher, 9 1/2" h., bulbous ovoid body tapering to a cylindrical neck, pinched spout & long C-form handle, overall medium blue sponging on white, marked on the base by the Uhl Pottery Co., Huntingburg, Indiana, early 20th c., excellent condition **$303**

Attending an antique show or market is often more fun when done with friends. Save on gas by carpooling, but take a large vehicle so everyone's purchases will fit. It's fine to split up at the market, just meet at agreed places and times. Allow time to shop at antique shops on the way home.

Pitcher, 9" h., cylindrical body w/a flat rim & large pointed spout, small C-form handle, overall coarse banded blue sponging on white, early 20th c. **$403**

Pitcher, 9" h., cylindrical body w/flat rim & pointed spout, squared loop handle, overall fine medium blue sponging on white, flake on base, early 20th c. **$288**

Pitcher, 9" h., slightly tapering cylindrical body w/pointed rim spout & small C-form handle, dark overall navy blue on white wavy design, hairline from rim near handle, late 19th - early 20th c. **$176**

Pitcher, 9" h., slightly tapering cylindrical body w/pointed rim spout & small C-form handle, overall blue on white "chicken wire" design, tight T-shaped hairline in bottom rim up into the sides, late 19th - early 20th c. **$165**

Pitcher, 9" h., swelled bottom below the cylindrical body w/a pointed rim spout & angled loop handle, overall blue sponging on white, minor glaze flake at spout, late 19th - early 20th c. **$303**

Pitcher, 9" h., cylindrical w/rim spout & C-form handle, medium blue repeating wavyvertical bands of sponging on white, interior rim flake near spout **$275**

Pitcher, 9" h., paneled cylindrical form w/rim spout & C-form handle, all over scattered large blue dot sponging on white, professional restoration to a large chip at spout & a couple of interior glaze flakes at rim, overall glaze crazing, late 19th - early 20th c. (ILLUS. second from left with three larger sponged pitchers).. **$143**

Pitcher, 9" h., tall slightly tapering cylindrical body w/a molded rim w/pointed spout, C-form long handle, overall bold blue sponging on white, minor crazing in glaze, late 19th - early 20th c. **$303**

Salt & pepper shaker, one-piece, ovoid body divided into two halves w/two short spouts w/metal caps, overall blue & brown sponging on white, some small cap dents, excellent condition, early 20th c., 3" h. **$154**

Spittoon, footed bulbous rounded body tapering to a widely flaring rim, grey ground w/molded overall basketweave design decorated w/ scattered bold dark blue sponging, few glaze flakes, small tight hairline at rim, 8" d., 5" h. **$66**

Syrup jug, advertising-type, bulbous beehive-shaped w/short rim spout & wire bail handle w/black turned wood grip, overall blue sponging w/lower oval reserve stenciled "Grandmother's Maple Syrup of 50 Years Ago," relief-molded vine design around top half, bottom molded in relief "Mfg'd by N. Weeks - Style XXX Pat. Pending - Akron, O.," surface chips on spout, late 19th - early 20th c., 5 1/4" h. **$495**

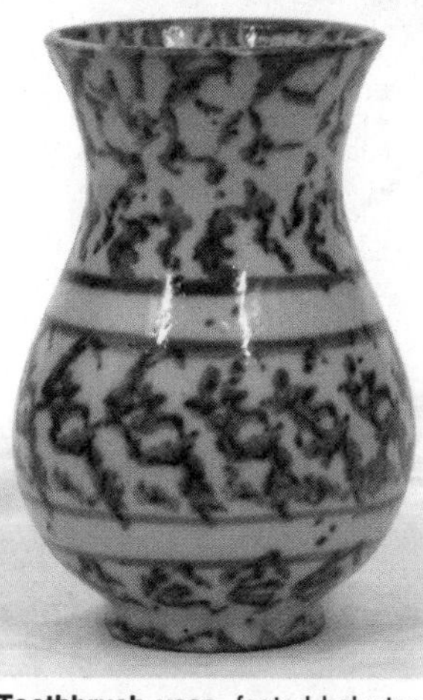

Toothbrush vase, footed baluster-form, wide dark blue on white sponged bands alternating w/two narrow white bands, excellent condition, late 19th - early 20th c., 5" h. **$440**

Washbowl & pitcher, bulbous ovoid pitcher tapering to a wide flaring neck, C-scroll handle, matching bowl w/rolled rim, the pitcher w/overall coarse blue sponging on white w/a wide band in blue & white around the bottom, sponged rim & base bands on the bowl flank the wide blue & white bands, attributed to Red Wing, Minnesota, early 20th c., minor hairline & glaze flake on pitcher, pitcher 12" h. **$633**

Whimsey, model of a standing pig, white Bristol glaze w/scattered blue spots, some surface chipping, ca. 1990, 5" l. **$303**

Blue is one of the most common and popular colors for glazing partly because it is less susceptible to color changes than bright colors like red.

Staffordshire Figures

Small figures and groups made of pottery were produced by the majority of the Staffordshire, England potters in the 19th century and were used as mantel decorations or "chimney ornaments," as they were sometimes called. Pairs of dogs were favorites and were turned out by the carload, and 19th-century pieces are still available. Well-painted reproductions also abound, and collectors are urged to exercise caution before investing.

Cats, seated facing viewer, on a flaring rectangular blue pillow w/gilt trim, each white w/sponged black & yellow spots, a yellow neck ribbons & painted facial features, 19th c., 7 1/2" h., pr. **$431**

Dogs, Spaniels in a seated pose w/head facing the viewer, white w/a rust-red spotted curly coat, h.p. head details & painted collar & chain, England, late 19th c., 10" h., pr. **$570**

Dogs, Spaniels in a seated pose w/head facing the viewer, white w/a yellow eyes & gilt chains & fur trim, England, late 19th c., gilt wear, one w/scuff mark, 14 5/8" h., pr. **$431**

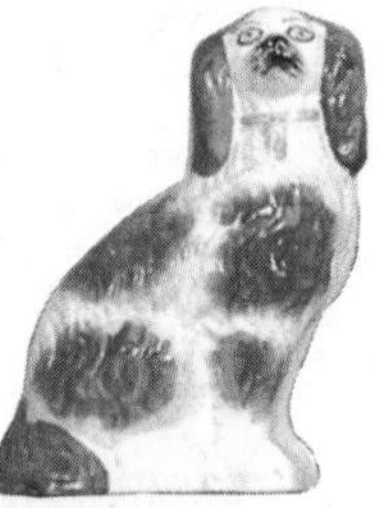

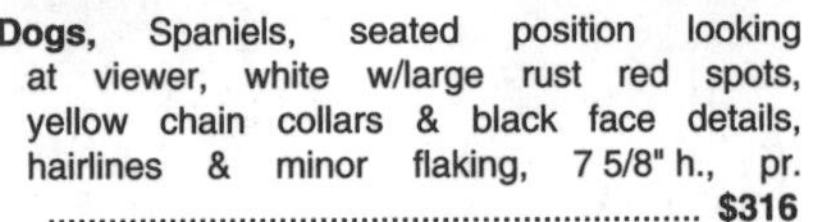

Dogs, Spaniels, seated position looking at viewer, white w/large rust red spots, yellow chain collars & black face details, hairlines & minor flaking, 7 5/8" h., pr. **$316**

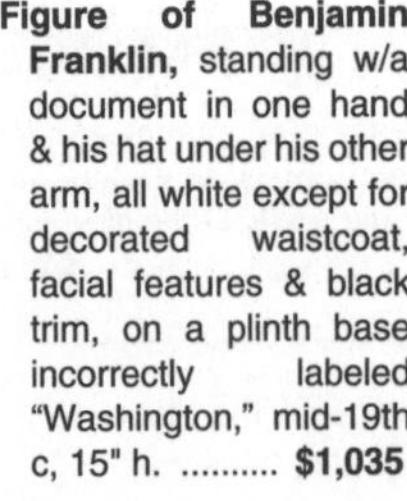

Figure of Benjamin Franklin, standing w/a document in one hand & his hat under his other arm, all white except for decorated waistcoat, facial features & black trim, on a plinth base incorrectly labeled "Washington," mid-19th c, 15" h. **$1,035**

Pastille burner, modeled as a two-part cottage w/two sheep under a open pillar in front, trimmed in blue, black, yellow, green & orange, chimney w/a hold for the smoke, some loss to paint, small chip on base w/small crack, 9" w., 8" h. **$489**

Staffordshire Transfer Wares

The process of transfer-printing designs on earthenwares developed in England in the late 18th century, and by the mid-19th century most common ceramic wares were decorated in this manner, most often with romantic European or Oriental landscape scenes, animals or flowers. The earliest such wares were printed in dark blue, but a little later light blue, pink, purple, red, black, green and brown were used. A majority of these wares were produced at various English potteries right up until the turn of the 20th century, but French and other European firms also made similar pieces and all are quite collectible. The best reference on this area is Petra Williams' book Staffordshire Romantic Transfer Patterns - Cup Plates and Early Victorian China (Fountain House East, 1978).

Bowl, 10" d., 4 3/4" h., a footed deep round form w/molded shell-form rim handles, dark blue & white, the interior printed w/a central romantic landscape w/two fishermen in the foreground & a tower & forest in the background framed by a wide parrot & flower border, the exterior printed w/ a scene of a shepherd among Gothic ruins, edge wear, ca. 1820s **$633**

Bowl, 7 1/2" d., 1 1/2" h., dark blue, marked "The Valentine - From Wilkies Designs," by Clews, rare form **$288**

Cup plate, Moral Maxim patt., red, two border reserves, minor edge wear, 4 1/8" d. **$121**

Plates, 9" d., dark blue, marked "The Valentine - From Wilkies Designs," by Clews, pr. **$345**

Platter, 15 1/4 x 18 1/4" oval, the oval center decorated w/a large cluster of fruit, the wide body band decorated w/ large clusters of flowers alternating w/ scrolled panels, early deep blue, back marked "Stubbs #18," first quarter 19th c. **$1,150**

Platter, 16 1/2 x 21", oval, titled on back "Italian Scenes, Turin," dark blue landscape w/town in the distance across a lake, figures in the foreground framed by tall arching leafy trees, ca. 1830, hairline, small firing imperfection **$575**

Platter, 16 3/4 x 21", oval w/angled corners, a large central rural landscape w/a castle bridge w/moat, figures & cattle, scrolled floral border w/ fleur-de-lis, impressed Clews mark, dark blue, minor knife scratches **$633**

Platter, 16 x 20 3/4" oval, well-and-tree style, the interior decorated w/a large exotic Far Eastern landscape w/large castle & temple ruins, the wide naturalistic border band w/leafy trees & flowers, deep blue on white, impressed mark of Rogers & Son or J. & G. Rogers, England, ca. 1830 .... **$1,438**

Platter, 17 1/2" l., octagonal, the center w/a large exotic mountainous landscape, the border band w/scroll-bordered panels of large roses, dark greyish mulberry on white, Vdina patt., Joseph Clementson, ca. 1845-64 .... **$460**

Platter, 20 1/2" l., oval, dark blue, Seashells patt., Longport, ca. 1830 .... **$1,955**

Platter, 6 1/2 x 19 3/4" oval, gently scalloped rim, large central landscape scene w/a large mansion in a pastoral wooded landscape, wide border band w/four large scroll-bordered floral sections alternating w/small oblong bird-decorated panels, printed in green & brown, England, ca. 1840, some light stain **$690**

Soup plates, round, Aesthetic Movement style, a Japonesque design w/a large fan w/ribbons in the center, the border band w/arched panels of Oriental motifs, dark blue on white, Browne-Westhead, Moore & Co., England, ca. 1875, 10" d., set of 9 .... **$230**

Tea set: cov. teapot, cov. sugar bowl, creamer, two handled cups & saucers & a large undertray; each serving piece of upright diamond shape, each wide side panel decorated w/overall small salmon-colored flowers separated by a narrow panel decorated w/stylized black cranes, blue & black floral neck border, mark of Powell & Bishop, England, second half 19th c., minor gilt wear, small flake on teapot spout, tray 14 x 21 1/2", teapot 5" h., the set **$330**

Stangl Pottery

Johann Martin Stangl, who first came to work for the Fulper Pottery in 1910 as a ceramic chemist and plant superintendent, acquired a financial interest and became president of the company in 1926. The name of the firm was changed to Stangl Pottery in 1929 and at that time much of the production was devoted to a high grade dinnerware to enable the company to survive the Depression years. One of the earliest solid-color dinnerware patterns was its Colonial line, introduced in 1926. In the 1930s it was joined by the Americana pattern. After 1942 these early patterns were followed by a wide range of hand-decorated patterns featuring flowers and fruits, with a few decorated with animals or human figures.

Around 1940 a very limited edition of porcelain birds, patterned after the illustrations in John James Audubon's "Birds of America," was issued. Stangl subsequently began production of less expensive ceramic birds, which proved to be popular during the war years 1940-46. Each bird was handpainted and well marked with impressed, painted or stamped numerals indicating the species and the size.

STANGL POTTERY BIRDS

All operations ceased at the Trenton, New Jersey, plant in 1978.

Two reference books collectors will find helpful are The Collectors Handbook of Stangl Pottery by Norma Rehl (The Democrat Press, 1979), and Stangl Pottery by Harvey Duke (Wallace-Homestead, 1994).

Birds

Cockatoos, large, colorful decoration, No. 3584, 11 3/8" h., pr. **$460**

Pheasant Cock, No. 3492, 11" l., the set (ILLUS. of two)................. **$250-300**

Red-Headed Woodpeckers, double, ornate leaf & blossom branches on a white oval base, one reglued leaf, more ornate than usual model, 7 1/2" w., 7 1/2" h. **$4,406**

Other Wares

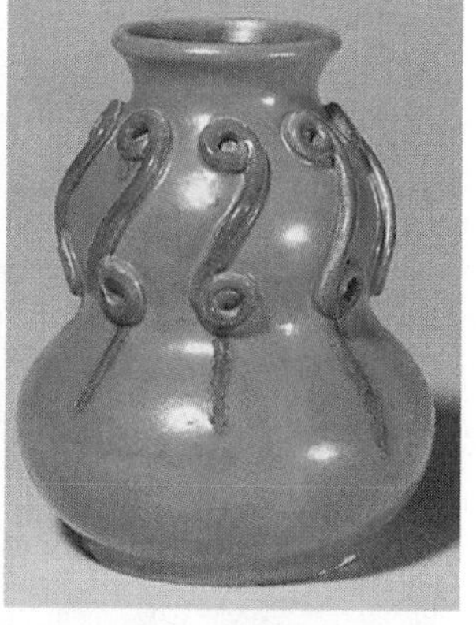

Vase, 7 1/4" h., bulbous double-gourd form w/flared neck, deep orange ground applied around the sides w/blue S-scrolls, Tropical Ware line, ca. 1935, Shape 2024-7", impressed mark **$345**

Vase, 4 7/8" h., squatty bulbous form tapering to a short flared neck flanked by shoulder handles, tangerine glaze h.p. w/green leaves & black seed pods, ca. 1931, small glaze nick on handles **$115**

Charger, round, h.p. in the Pennsylvania Dutch style w/a large stylized yellow, brown & green tulip, pale green & yellow banded border, marked, No. 3319, 14 1/2" d. **$100-200**

A charger is a large decorative underplate used to hold the various smaller dishes and plates on which food is served.

Stoneware

Stoneware is essentially a vitreous pottery, impervious to water even in its unglazed state, that has been produced by potteries all over the world for centuries. Utilitarian wares such as crocks, jugs, churns and the like were the most common productions in the numerous potteries that sprang into existence in the United States during the 19th century. These items were often enhanced by the application of a cobalt blue oxide decoration. In addition to the coarse, primarily salt-glazed stonewares, there are other categories of stoneware known by such special names as basalt, jasper and others.

Crock, bulbous ovoid body w/a wide slightly flared mouth flanked by eared handles, large brushed cobalt blue tulip design below the impressed mark of C. Hart & Co., Ogdensburg, New York, & impressed number, some glaze spider cracks & crazing on back, ca. 1855, 2 gal., 10" h. **$220**

Jug, cylindrical body tapering to a small molded mouth & strap handle, cobalt blue slip-quilled long parrot perched on a vertical leafy sprig below the impressed mark "F.B. Norton and Co. - Worcester, Mass. - 2," excellent condition, ca. 1870, 2 gal., 13 1/2" h. **$1,485**

Jug, cylindrical body w/rounded shoulder tapering to a molded mouth, applied strap handle, unusual bold slip-quilled cobalt blue four-petal starburst w/arrows & dots design, impressed mark of Cortland, New York, minor glaze wear, surface chip on back base, ca. 1860, 1 gal., 11" h. **$578**

Jug, flat-bottomed beehive shape w/small mouth & strap handle, advertising-type w/brushed cobalt blue inscription reading "R.H. Gilgallon - Scranton - Pa" & "2," made by Co-operative Pottery Co., Lyons, New York, cinnamon clay color in the making & some staining from use, ca. 1890, 2 gal., 12 1/2" h. **$275**

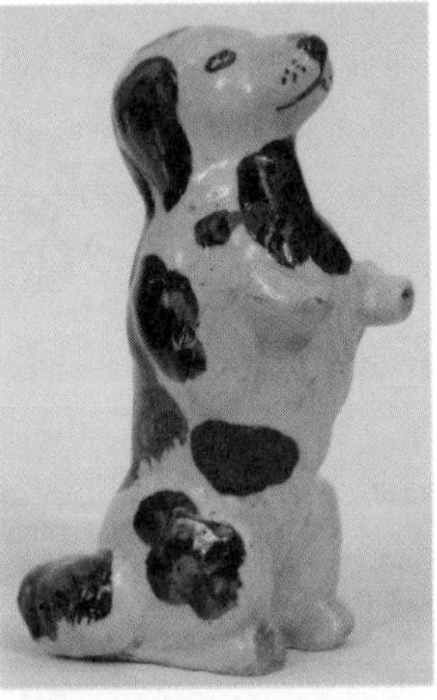

Model of a dog, seated begging spaniel in cream w/dark bluish green applied accents under the Bristol glaze, probably from Ohio, possibly early 20th c., minor surface wear, 5 1/2" h. **$495**

Water cooler, disk foot supporting tapering urn-form body w/loop shoulder handles, incised birds trimmed in cobalt blue, mark of the Somerset Potters Works, Massachusetts, kiln burn on front, glued crack on front, in-the-making chip out of bung hole frame, ca. 1870, 3 gal., 15" h. **$3,960**

Teco Pottery

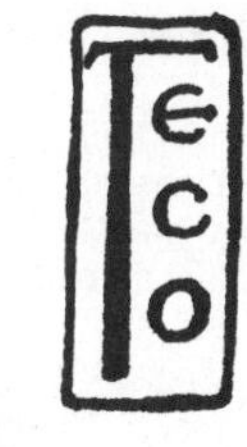

Teco Pottery was actually the line of art pottery introduced by the American Terra Cotta and Ceramic Company of Terra Cotta (Crystal Lake), Illinois, in 1902. Founded by William D. Gates in 1881, American Terra Cotta originally produced only bricks and drain tile. Because of superior facilities for experimentation, including a chemical laboratory, the company was able to develop an art pottery line, favoring a matte green glaze in the earlier years but eventually achieving a wide range of colors including a metallic lustre glaze and a crystalline glaze. Although some hand-thrown pottery was made, Gates favored a molded ware because it was less expensive to produce. By 1923, Teco Pottery was no longer being made, and in 1930 American Terra Cotta and Ceramic Company was sold. A book on the topic is Teco: Art Pottery of the Prairie School, by Sharon S. Darling (Erie Art Museum, 1990).

Vase, 11 1/4" h., footed bulbous bottle-form body w/tall gently flaring neck, glossy crystalline glaze in swirled deep reds & black, unmarked, tiny stilt pull on base **$748**

Vase, 9 3/8" h., ovoid lower body w/ a rounded shoulder to the tapering cylindrical neck, long handles from the edge of the rim to the shoulder, nicely charcoaled crystalline green glaze, Shape No. 283, designed by Fritz Albert, two impressed marks on the base **$1,115**

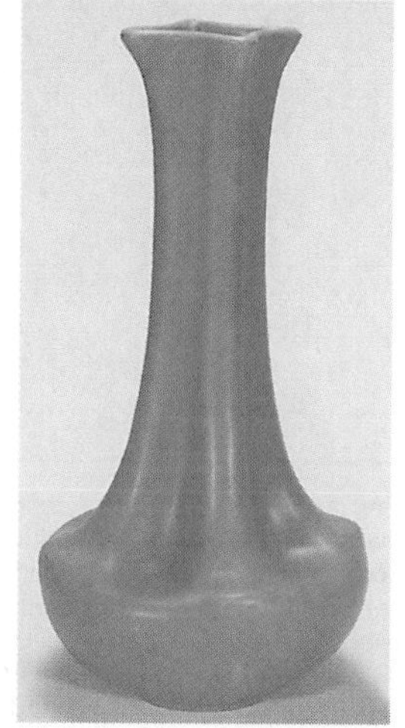

Vase, 15 3/4" h., squatty bulbous base below the slender tall squared four-column sides w/a flared mouth, nicely charcoaled green matte glaze, designed by W.D. Gates & Fritz Albert, two impressed marks on base **$2,645**

Vase, 6 3/4" h., 5 1/2" d., bulbous double-gourd body w/four heavy curved & squared handles from the base to the wide flat mouth, designed by W.B. Mundie, charcoal matte green glaze, stamped mark **$4,313**

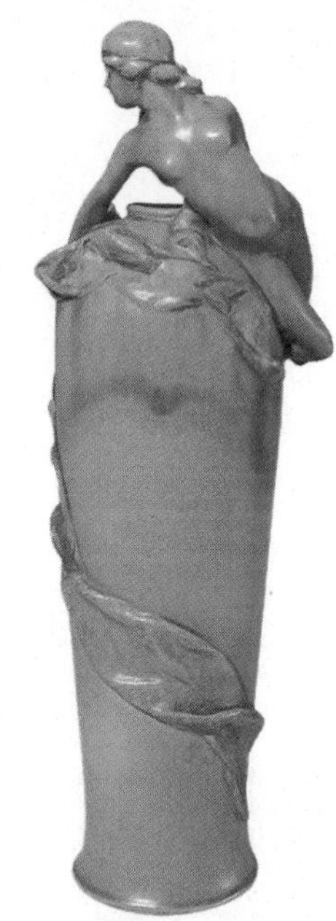

Vase, 22 5/8" h., rare design reminiscent of Van Briggle's "Lorelei" vase, the top mounted by a finely modeled nude wrapping backward around the small opening, the tall slender slightly swelled cylindrical body also molded w/a leafy vine down around the sides, all w/a mottled green glaze, stamped mark & No. 228, figure & one large leaf at top broken off & professionally restored **$24,150**

Vase, 5 1/2" h., 8 1/2" l., squatty bulbous oblong form w/the sides pulled up to form integral loop handles flowing into the widely flaring rim of the short flaring neck, overall smooth matte green glaze, stamped mark **$1,998**

Tiffany Pottery

In 1902 Louis C. Tiffany expanded Tiffany Studios to include ceramics, enamels, gold, silver and gemstones. Tiffany pottery was usually molded rather than wheel-thrown, but it was carefully finished by hand. A limited amount was produced until about 1914. It is scarce.

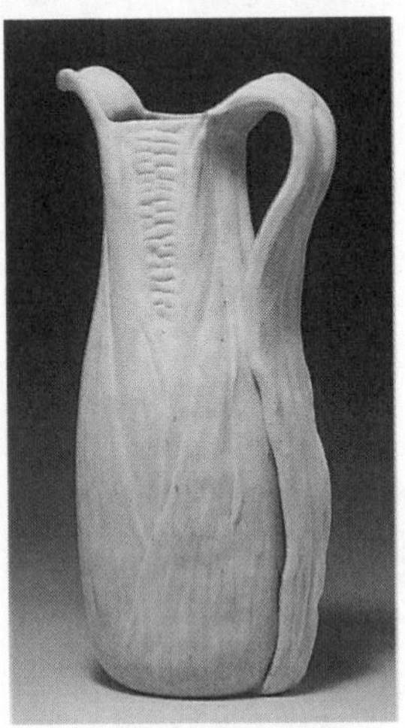

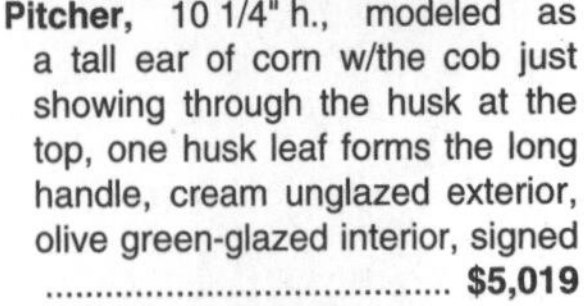

Pitcher, 10 1/4" h., modeled as a tall ear of corn w/the cob just showing through the husk at the top, one husk leaf forms the long handle, cream unglazed exterior, olive green-glazed interior, signed **$5,019**

Vase, 15" h., a round foot below the large wide flaring cylindrical body w/a wide angled shoulder centering a wide low mouth, overall mottled green glaze, signed "L.C.T. 7 - Pottery," hairline & possible restoration **$1,610**

Vase, 3 1/2" h., flaring base & cylindrical sides molded in relief w/mushrooms, unglazed cream-color exterior & green-glazed interior, signed on base, slight discoloration on side of base **$1,725**

Vase, 14 1/2" h., stepped disk foot supporting a bulbous ovoid body tapering to a wide cylindrical neck w/flat rim, decorated w/raised narcissus & leaves swirling around the body under a fading brown, dark blue & khaki matte glaze, chip on base, inscribed "LCT" **$1,380**

Vase, 9 1/2" h., base w/an Art Nouveau design consisting of four long relief-molded lobes, the body swelling slightly at the top w/an undulating rim, covered in an unusual glossy metallic black & green finish, incised "LCT" **$7,700**

←

Vase, 6 3/4" h., Favrile bronze pottery type, cylindrical shape w/ molded flowers & stems in relief, signed on bottom "LCT" conjoined & "BP197" w/"L," ca. 1910-14 .... **$2,358**

Vase, 8 3/4" h., cylindrical body w/ flared foot & slightly swelled top, decorated w/molded & reticulated arrowhead plants under blue & green lustered glaze, irregular rim formed by leaftips & blossoms, three very short, very tight hairlines from rim, incised "LCT - acid-etched L.C. Tiffany - Favrile Pottery" **$15,400**

Vase, 6 5/8" h., wide gently waisted cylindrical form, molded up the sides w/long pointed leaves w/ three leaf stems forming arched loop handles down the sides, streaky light & dark blue glaze, signed "LCT - Tiffany Favrile Pottery - P 412" (chip to rim) **$4,800**

Vase, 10" h., tall cylindrical form w/ scalloped rim, glossy pale green glaze on white clay w/a molded organic design of fiddleback fern heads around the top above full-length stems, center base inscribed w/"LCT" monogram (glaze crazing, some interior water stain)................................ **$2,875**

Van Briggle

The Van Briggle Pottery was established by Artus Van Briggle, who formerly worked for Rookwood Pottery, in Colorado Springs, Colorado, at the turn of the century. He died in 1904, but the pottery was carried on by his widow and others. From 1900 until 1920, the pieces were dated. It remains in production today, specializing in Art Pottery.

Bookends, figural, a plump seated puppy on a rectangular block base, deep mulberry matte glaze w/dark blue on the puppy, marked, pr. **$345**

Bust of Native American Chief, finely detailed, wearing a large feathered headdress, dark turquoise blue matte glaze, company logo on base w/"Van Briggle Colo. Springs Co. - Chief Two Moons - Cheyenne - Limited Edition No. 186 - 1979," 11 1/2" h. **$196**

Candlestick, a round foot tapering to a tall slender cylindrical shaft supporting a wide cupped socket, overall mottled dark brown matte glaze, dated 1914, small grinding chips off the base, 8 5/8" h. **$546**

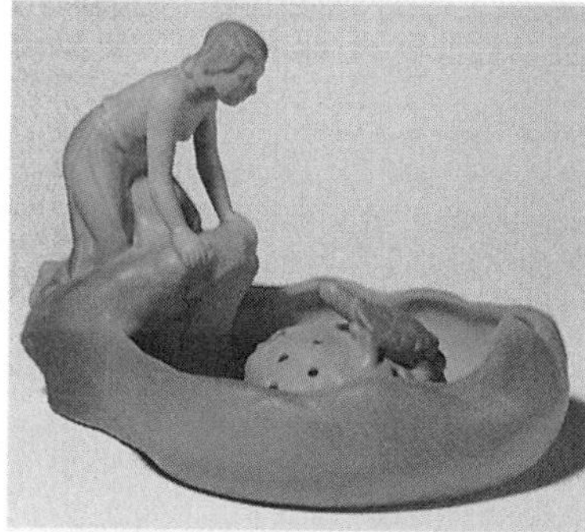

Console bowl & flower frog, "Lady of the Lake" design, a low undulating oblong bowl w/incurved sides, one end w/an angled rockwork ledge mounted w/the kneeling figure of a maiden looking down into the bowl, a round flower frog inside mounted w/the model of a turtle, shaded blue & turquoise blue matte glaze, each piece marked, some interior staining, bowl 9 7/8 x 14 3/4", 2 pcs. **$690**

Console bowl & flower frog, "Siren of the Sea" design, turquoise blue matte glaze, a low footed & rounded shell-shaped bowl w/a full-length figure of a mermaid wrapping around the sides, a shell-form flower frog inside, frog 6" d., 2 3/4" h., bowl 8 x 13", 2 pcs. **$460**

Bowl-vase, spherical form w/ hexagonal paneled sides & closed rim, embossed around the rim w/peacock feathers, matte brown glaze, Shape No. 851, dated 1905, 6" d., 5 1/2" h.................... **$1,540**

Bowl-vase, wide rounded squatty lower body below a wide angled & sloping shoulder to the wide flat mouth, molded w/large, wide pointed leaves around the sides, overall maroon & blue matte glaze, post-1920s, 9 1/2" d., 5" h. ... **$330**

Bowl-vase, wide bulbous body w/molded rim, covered in a fine matte green glaze, incised "AA - VAN BRIGGLE - Colo. Spgs. - 1910," 1910, 4 x 5 1/2" **$440**

Lamp, table-type, "Damsel of Damascus" design, a kneeling peasant woman holding an urn on one shoulder, urn holding electric fittings, on a domed rockwork base, overall black matte glaze, signed on base, w/newer shade not shown, base 10 5/8" h. . **$196**

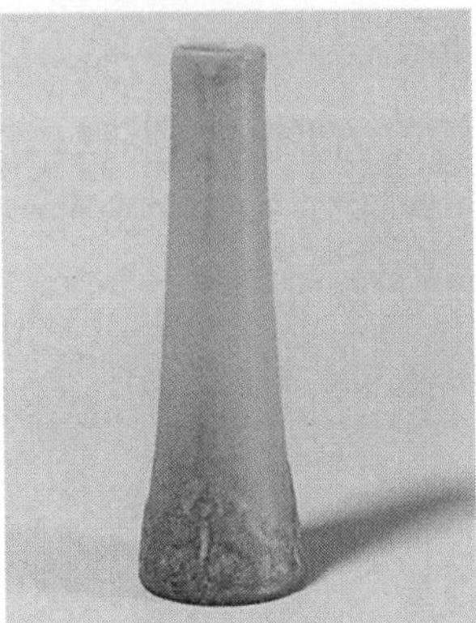

Vase, 10 3/4" h., a tall very slender tapering cylindrical form, molded around the base w/scrolling leaves, slender stems up the sides w/tiny blossoms at the rim, shaded dark blue to pale green matte glaze, dated 1914, fine overall crazing **$690**

Vase, 13 1/2" h., 5" d., a low swelled base below the slightly tapering cylindrical sides w/a small flat mouth, crisply molded w/tall irises & leaves, periwinkle blue leathery matte glaze, buff clay showing through, dated 1903, Shape No. 133 .... **$10,350**

Vase, 4 1/4" h., squatty bulbous lower body tapering to a wide cylindrical neck w/a flat mouth, molded around the bottom w/ large rounded leaves w/swirled stems up the sides, Mountain Craig Brown glaze w/green leaves **$104**

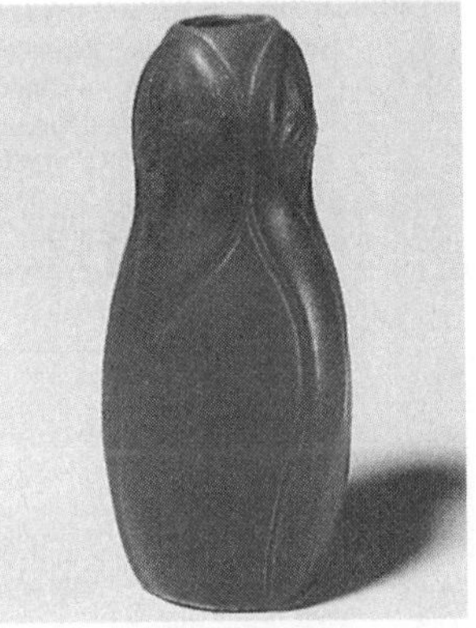

Vase, 6" h., ovoid corseted form w/ a small flat mouth, lightly molded around the top w/stylized three-petaled flowers in undulating panels, dark blue flowers against a dark mulberry matte ground, marked **$173**

Vase, 7 1/2" h., 4 3/4" d., "Dos Cabezas," ovoid body molded around the top w/two Art Nouveau maidens, unusual mustard yellow matte glaze, small flat chip in one fold, ca. 1908-11 .... **$6,900**

→

Vase, 8 1/2" h., 7 1/2" d., tapering bulbous body w/a wide cupped rim w/a flat mouth, molded w/ dandelion blossoms glazed in red w/leafy stems around the sides all on a chartreuse matte ground, dated 1904, Shape No. 137 .... **$6,325**

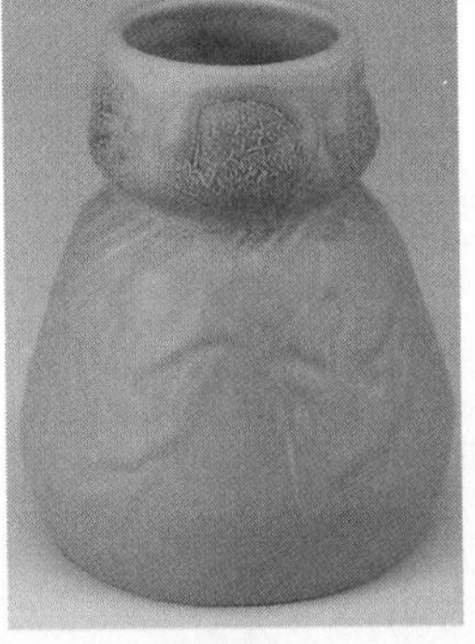

Vase, 9 5/8" h., flat-bottomed completely smooth ovoid body tapering to a slender tall trumpet neck, overall deep mulberry matte glaze **$115**

Vase, 9 1/4" h., 4" d., "Lorelei," swelled cylindrical form w/a figure of a maiden draped around the rim, cobalt blue over a dark mulberry matte glaze, 1920-25, marked, overall crazing **$978**

Wedgwood

WEDGWOOD

Reference here is to the famous pottery established by Josiah Wedgwood in 1759 in England. Numerous types of wares have been produced through the years to the present.

Basalt

Ewer, Classical urn-form body on a square foot & ringed & reeded pedestal, the body w/a fluted lower body & narrow molded band below large molded grapevine swags, the angled shoulder w/a cylindrical neck & high arched spout w/the figure of a crouching satyr reaching around the base of the spout to grasp the horns of a goat mask below the spout, the loop handle issuing from the shoulders of the satyr, 19th c., 15 1/2" h. **$863**

Figure of a nude male, standing w/legs crossed & playing a flute, leaning against a tall tree trunk w/his cloak pinned at one shoulder & draping down around the stump, 19th c., 17 1/4" h. **$920**

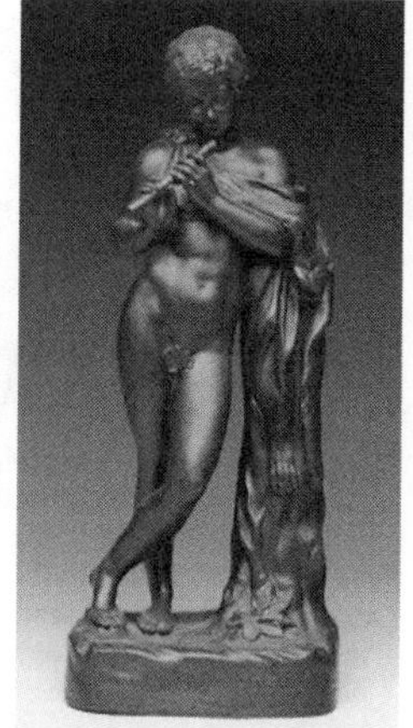

Miscellaneous

Boston cup, Fairyland Lustre, a low cylindrical footring supporting the wide rounded bowl, the exterior decorated w/the Leaping Elves patt., yellowish brown upper sides decorated w/fairing w/transparent gold wing frolicking on a green & blue ground w/mushroom, the upper section sprinkled w/printed gold stars; the interior decorated w/the Elves on a Branch patt. w/two small elves perched on a prickly branch w/black bat & bird around the leafy rim, base w/the Portland Vase mark & "ZXXXX," 5 1/4" d. **$1,725**

Bowl, 10 3/4" d., 4 3/4" h., Fairyland Lustre, a narrow footring supports the deep rounded sides, exterior Poplar Tree patt. decorated w/a fanciful landscape of stylized trees against a midnight blue lustre ground, interior decorated w/the Woodland Elves V, Woodland Bridge patt., some minor scratches on the interior **$5,175**

Bowl, 11" d., Fairyland Lustre, wide rounded shape, the interior decorated w/the Garden of Paradise (Variation I) patt. w/daylight lustre, the arch in the design is missing but the black pillars remain against a mother-of-pearl sky, two different idol figures appear in violet & the dancing beetle faces the opposite way, the green "Cake" tree w/ a companion tree w/a curvaceious black trunk & copper brown foliage, the exterior w/the Flight of Birds patt. printed in gold outline on a very dark green & blue lustre ground encircling the sides, the under rim & foot decorated w/gold pebble & grass border, signed on the base, Pattern No. Z4968 (ILLUS. of interior) **$4,600**

Bowl, 8 1/2" d., 4" h., Fairyland Lustre, Woodland Elves VI patt., a narrow footring supports the octagonal bowl, the exterior w/a continuous design of tree trunks in dark bluish green & all the elves in brown on a flame lustre background of orange over crimson, the interior w/the Ship & Mermaid patt. w/a flame lustre center, Pattern No. Z5360 .... **$7,475**

Lustreware features an iridescent metallic glaze intended to imitate the appearance of gold and silver. It was popular among the middle class, who wanted to emulate the wealthy.

Bowl, 13" d., 5 1/4" h., Fairyland Lustre, Daventry patt., a low pedestal round foot supporting the wide bowl w/sharply flaring sides, the interior w/a design in four panels done in bluish lavender lustre over-printed w/a crimson lustre thorn diamond, border flower inserts covered w/orange lustre & the narrow surrounding the panels in green, the panel designs & center design in brown outlined in gold, the exterior decorated w/a ground of orange lustre over-printed w/a crimson or brown pheasant eye diaper & a wide band w/an Oriental landscape in solid brown outlined in gold **$4,600**

Bowl, 8" w., Fairyland Lustre, footed octagonal form, the exterior in the Woodland Elves VI patt., the Fiddler in Tree against a midnight blue lustre background, the interior decorated w/the Ship & Mermaid patt. against a white lustre ground, some minor scratches to interior bottom **$4,600**

Bowl, 8" w., Fairyland Lustre, footed deep octagonal shape decorated in the Willow patt., the exterior in Coral & Bronze decorated w/a printed gold Willow Ware style decoration, the interior w/a Willow patt. in the bottom & a blue leafy band around the rim, Portland Vase mark & "Z5406" **$3,450**

Bowl, 9 3/8" w., 4 1/2" h., Fairyland Lustre, footed octagonal shape, Fairy in a Cage patt., the exterior w/each side w/a lacy gold border enclosing a landscape scene, the interior decorated w/fantastic creatures in an exotic landscape, No. Z5125 .... **$3,450**

Bowl, miniature, 2 1/4" w., Lustre Ware, footed octagonal shape, the exterior w/a mottled orange lustre glaze decorated w/ various gold mythological beasts between gold rim & base bands, the dark blue mottled interior decorated w/a stylized spider **$260**

It is possible to sense high quality and a good value even though you can't immediately identify the manufacturer, craftsman, or artist. If the price is right, savvy buyers will take a chance on an unknown item.

Plates, 11" d., Lustre decoration, octagonal w/eight alternating panels of gold geometric designs alternating w/panels showing Oriental men, the figures in gold against a dark blue lustre ground, Portland Vase mark & retailer mark for William H. Plummer & Co., New York, set of 12 .... **$900**

Jar, cov., Fairyland Lustre, malfrey pot Shape No. 2312, bulbous ovoid body fitted w/a domed cover, the exterior includes various patterns including Demon Tree, Roc Bird, Bat in the Demon Tree, Black Toad & Dwarf, Red Monkeys & the Scorpion w/a long yellow tail & spines, a narrow dragon bead border around the base & rim of the collar, inside of collar decorated in the Pan-Fei border, the cover decorated w/Owls of Wisdom w/purple bodies & bright copper-colored faces, blue eyes & red pupils, the cover w/a Red Fei border band & the Scorpion, cover also w/a Pan-Fei border around the inside surrounding Elves on a branch in the center, Pattern No. Z-4968, very light wear to gold cover trim, 14" h. **$57,500**

Punch bowl, Fairyland Lustre, wide flaring foot supporting the wide deep rounded bowl, exterior decorated w/the Lahore patt. featuring swags of brilliant colors & hanging lanterns, the interior decorated w/three elephants, two of which have riders, a camel, a war horse w/lancer & a flying goose in the center, all figures in black mother-of-pearl outlined in gold against a yellow lustre ground, Pattern Z5266, 11" d., 5 5/8" h. **$8,625**

Vase, 11" h., Fairyland Lustre, Serpent Tree patt., a flaring base tapering to a tall cylindrical body w/a flaring rim, the abstract tree & landscape design in bright colors against a flame lustre sky, base signed, Pattern No. Z4968 .... **$7,475**

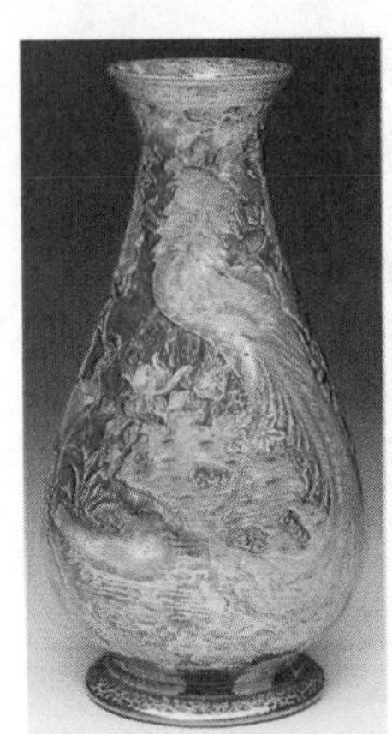

Vase, 12" h., Fairyland Lustre, Argus shape, Chinese Pheasant patt., footed bulbous baluster-form body w/a flaring rim, decorated w/ a large strutting Chinese pheasant in crimson & pink w/gold-trimmed feathers on both the front & back, birds surrounded by other water & shorebirds & is standing on a green grassy round w/leafy flowers in red & pink, foot & rim surrounded w/a gold dragon border, base marked "Wedgwood - Made in England Argus" **$6,325**

Vase, 12" h., Fairyland Lustre, Tree Serpent patt., tall simple ovoid body tapering to a short cylindrical neck w/a flared rim, a full- length scene of the tree, which hides the initials "SMJ," in a bazaar landscape w/the baby done in white resting on green grass on both sides, green Imps walking across a bridge below a large flying bat on one side, Shape No. 3150, Pattern No. Z5360 .... **$17,250**

Vase, 17" h., Fairyland Lustre, footed squatty bulbed base band below the tall slightly flaring cylindrical body, decorated w/daylight lustre background w/crimson & violet Imps crossing a red bridge w/a light yellow top against green bushes, the sky in reddish pink & the river in deep blue w/a yellow canoe, the bubbles boy & bat are black & the Roc bird is vermilion, the base band w/a blue lustre background w/a green flaming wheel border, the treehouse above the bridge w/a green roof w/yellow, red & black walls, signed on the base & numbered "Z4968" **$43,125**

Vase, 8 1/2" h., Fairyland Lustre, Willow patt., baluster-form body w/a short flaring neck, finely decorated w/violet tree trunks & flower spikes, green leaves & lanterns of red & yellow w/orange lustre that are surrounded by a view of sky & water of blue lustre over a rich bluish green shade, the houses in black w/torches of crimson & the conventional "Candle Lighthouse" on the bridge reflected in orange ripples, a group of violet gnomes shelter under black toadstool umbrellas at the base, the chestnut leaflets not hatched in gold print but have both Flame & Moonlight Fairyland Lustre, Pattern No. Z5228 .... **$6,900**

Weller

WELLER
Weller
Pottery

This pottery was made from 1872 to 1945 at a pottery established originally by Samuel A. Weller at Fultonham, Ohio, and moved in 1882 to Zanesville. Numerous lines were produced, and listings below are by pattern or line.

Reference books on Weller include The Collectors Encyclopedia of Weller Pottery by Sharon & Bob Huxford (Collector Books, 1979) and All About Weller by Ann Gilbert McDonald (Antique Publications, 1989).

Aurelian (1898-1910)

Ewer, a thin widely flaring disk-form base tapering sharply to a tall slender neck w/a tri-lobed flaring mouth, long S-scroll handle from the top rim to the base, shaded dark to light brown ground h.p. w/ large yellow roses & green leaves around the lower body, decorated by Marie Rauchfuss, Aurelian-Weller mark, 9" h. **$374**

Jug, footed squatty bulbous body w/a short small rolled neck & C-form shoulder handle, h.p. golden grapes & dark green leaves on a shaded gold to black ground, impressed mark, initials of artist Helen Windle, 5" h. **$345**

Mug, flared ringed base below the tall slightly tapering sides, large C-form handle, h.p. large deep orange fruits & green leaves against a mottled gold & dark green & brown ground, decorated by Charles Chilcote, 6 1/2" h. **$173**

Vase, 4 1/4" h., three flared knob feet supporting the squatty bulbous body tapering to a low three-lobed rolled rim, h.p. yellow carnations & green leaves on a dark blackish brown ground, Aurelian mark, some dry crazing **$184**

Whiskey jug, footed nearly spherical body w/ a short round shoulder spout & large arched handle across the top, h.p. w/large dark purple grapes & green leaves on a mottled yellow, dark brown & black ground, initialed by artist Frank Ferrell, 6 1/8" h. **$259**

Blue Louwelsa (ca. 1905)

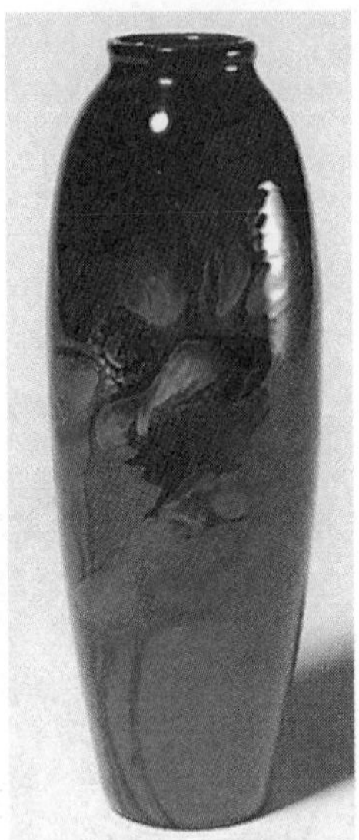

Vase, 11 1/2" h., tall slender ovoid form tapering to a small molded flat mouth, dark blue shaded to lighter blue ground h.p. w/large stylized black, dark blue & light blue blossoms up the sides, repair to the rim **$690**

Vase, 5 1/8" h., simple cylindrical form, a dark blue ground h. p. w/large pansy-like blossoms in lavender, dark blue & black, impressed mark, glaze inclusion on back **$431**

Burnt Wood (1908)

Vase, 15 1/2" h., a sharply tapering conical body below a wide shallow squared cupped rim supported on a winged scarab design, the body design showing the Three Wise Men on camelback following the Christmas star, some glaze misses inside the rim & some background unevenness **$805**

Coppertone (late 1920s)

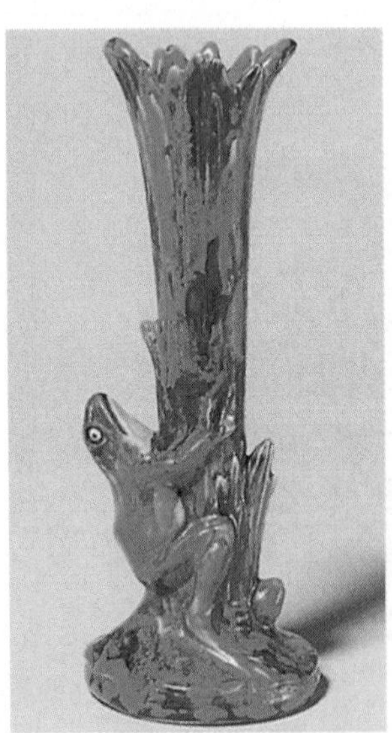

Vase, bud, 9" h., 3 1/4" d., slender body w/flaring irregular rim, frog crawling up the side, mottled green & brown glaze **$920**

Dickensware 2nd Line (early 1900s)

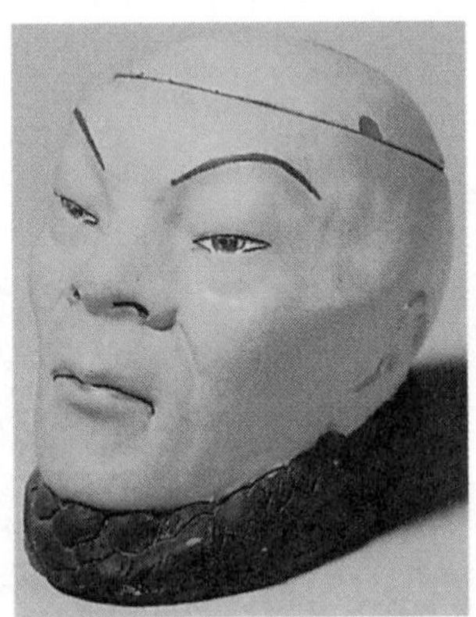

Humidor, cov., figural, model of a Chinese man's head, realistic coloring, two chips on edge of cover, 5 1/2" h. **$431**

Vase, 10 1/8" h., cylindrical w/a narrow angled shoulder to the flat low rounded rim, incised & colored portrait of a monk playing a flute, decorated by Anna Best, minor surface rubs **$288**

Dresden (ca. 1907)

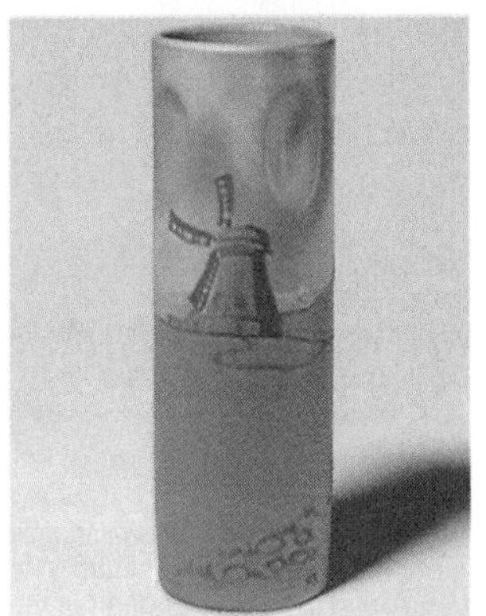

Vase, 10" h., simple cylindrical form, decorated w/a landscape with a Dutch windmill against a mottled blue over dark green ground, decorated by Levi Burgess, barely visible glaze line down from rim **$575**

> The popularity of antiques and collectibles goes in cycles, but the cycle times are not uniform. Catalysts like exposure in one or more life-style magazines often trigger an upward cycle.

Vase, 7 1/8" h., flaring cylindrical body w/a wide rounded shoulder tapering to a short molded neck, h. p. w/a large pale yellow rose & green leaves atop long thorny stems down the sides, on a dark greyish blue to pale blue ground, initialed by the artist **$345**

Eocean and Eocean Rose (1898-1925)

Lamp base, tall baluster form w/a cushion base, h.p. w/a pale tan crabapple bough w/pink & white blossoms descending from the rim & supporting two bluebirds against a shaded black body band, cast hole in base, Arthur Powell mark on base, slight overall crazing w/small glaze skip near base & rim, great color & composition, 15 1/4" h. **$1,610**

Vase, 7 7/8" h., a cushion foot tapering to a tall ovoid body w/a wide low flared mouth, a black shaded down to grey ground painted w/a tall cluster of yellow irises accented w/pink & green leaves, unmarked **$259**

Pitcher, 6 1/4" h., a footed low wide cylindrical lower section w/a deep indented band joining it to the wide slightly tapering cylindrical upper body w/a wide rim spout & squared inverted D-form heavy handle from the side of the top to the side of the base, very dark green shaded to lighter green ground painted on the upper body w/dark red cherries & green leaves, marked, minor firing separations **$230**

Wine carafe, footed wide cylindrical body w/a narrow shoulder tapering to a wide cylindrical neck surrounded by six short integrated arched handles from the rim to the shoulder, dark green shaded to pale green ground, h.p. w/a large bunch of purple & green grapes w/leafy stems, decorated by Frank Ferrell, marked on base, missing the cover, 11 1/2" h. **$575**

Etched Floral (ca. 1905)

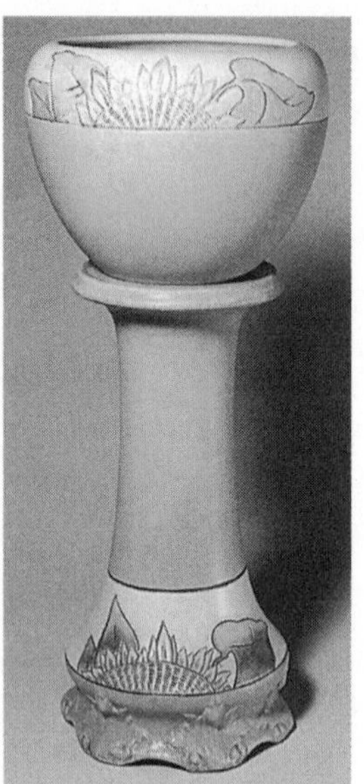

Jardiniere & pedestal, the wide bulbous ovoid body w/a wide flat closed mouth, decorated w/a wide incised rim band of half- round sunflowers & large green leaves above the pale yellow body, the matching tall waisted pedestal w/a flaring base w/a leaf- molded ruffled foot, a matching sunflower band above the foot, signed by Frank Ferrell, small chip on inside of jardiniere & some interior staining, overall 31 1/4" h., 2 pcs. **$2,070**

Etna (1906)

Vase, 10" h., a slightly tapering cylindrical body w/a bulbous top centered by a short rolled neck, dark green shaded to pale green ground painted w/a large pink poppy blossom at the top w/green stems & leaves down the sides, marked, few underglaze color spots **$219**

Vase, 5 1/2" h., a wide low squatty round base tapering sharply to a flaring neck, very dark green shaded to pale green ground painted w/dark maroon wild roses & dark green leaves, impressed Weller & Etna marks **$150**

Vase, 9 3/4" h., slightly tapering cylindrical body flaring at the top, a black top shading down to dark grey & pale grey, painted w/large pink blossoms at the top & base joined by a slender green stem, Weller & Etna marks **$219**

Flemish (mid-teens to 1928)

Towel bar, narrow oblong back plate molded in relief w/a pair of bluebirds at the top center w/pale green vines around the edges & a cluster of deep red blossoms at the lower edge, a long round curve-ended bar from end to end, tiny handle nick, 12" l., 6" h. **$1,610**

Forest (mid-teens to 1928)

Pitcher, 5 1/2" h., cylindrical w/ small rim spout & branch handle, overall molded forest scene in color, chip at top of handle, marked on base **$173**

Vase, 12" h., tall gently flaring waisted shape, woodland path through trees scene, some old glaze chips at rim **$230**

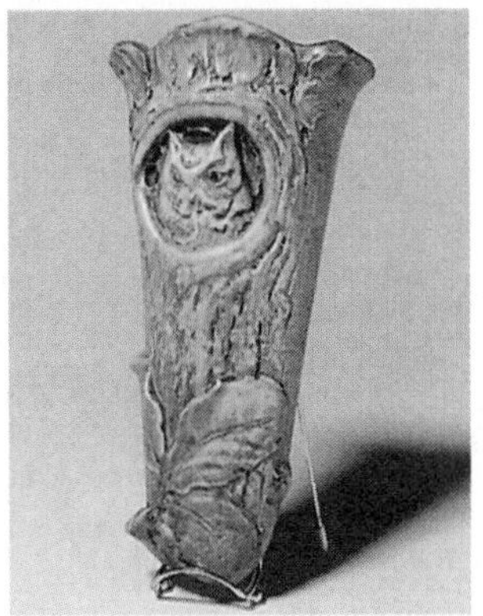

Wall pocket, conical w/owl peering out of tree trunk, die-stamped twice "Weller," chips on back edge of top & back edge of hanging hole, some glaze skips, 5 1/2 x 11" **$207**

Fudzi (ca. 1905)

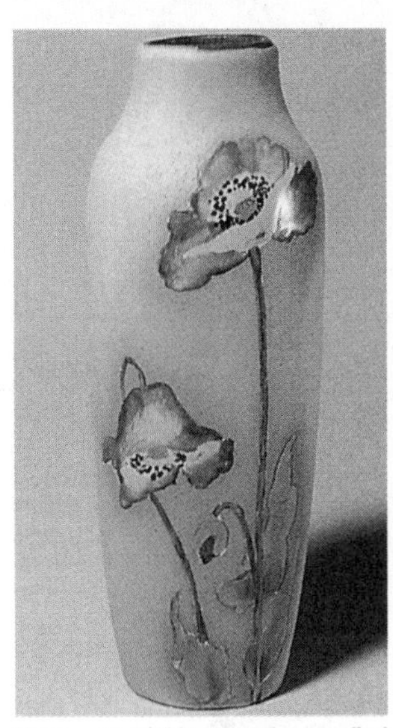

Vase, 11 3/4" h., gently swelled cylindrical body tapering gently at the shoulder to a flat mouth, a tan shaded to pale blue ground incised w/large maroon & pale green poppy blossoms up the sides w/green leaves & buds near the base, unmarked **$2,185**

Garden Wares & Related Items

Basket, hanging-type, a wide rounded bowl form w/a narrow angled rim fitted w/hanging chains, all molded to resemble glossy green rockwork, four round holes spaced around the sides w/a model of a yellow & black goldfinch applied below each, tail repair to each bird, stress lines at each round hole, 9 1/2" d., 4 3/4" h. **$460**

Greenbriar (early 1930s)

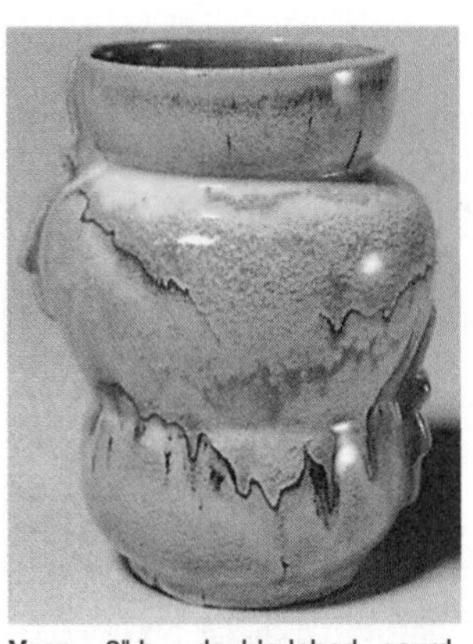

Vase, 8" h., double-lobed gourd-form graduated body w/a short wide gently flaring neck, some short firing separations at base **$104**

Hudson (1917-34)

Bowl-vase, 3 5/8" h., wide squatty bulbous body tapering to a wide flat mouth, a pale green to yellow ground decorated w/large yellow & white rose blossoms & green leaves, marked **$173**

Vase, 12" h., simple ovoid body tapering to a low widely flared neck, light blue shaded to pale pink ground h.p. w/a large cluster of pale pink, white & blue poppy-like blossoms on leafy stems, signed by Hester Pillsbury, drill hole in base removed part of the mark, few minor glaze inclusions **$920**

Vase, 7 3/4" h., footed bulbous ovoid body tapering to a cylindrical neck w/molded rim flanked by small angular shoulder handles, a deep tan shading to pale yellow ground decorated around the neck & shoulder w/black prunus branches w/white blossoms, decorated by Mae Timberlake, Weller mark **$431**

Vase, 7 3/4" h., footed ovoid body tapering to a wide short cylindrical neck w/molded rim flanked by angled handles from rim to shoulder, dark blue to pale yellow ground decorated w/a large white & green water lily w/a golden center & large lily pad leaves, signed by Mae Timberlake on side, some roughness at base **$690**

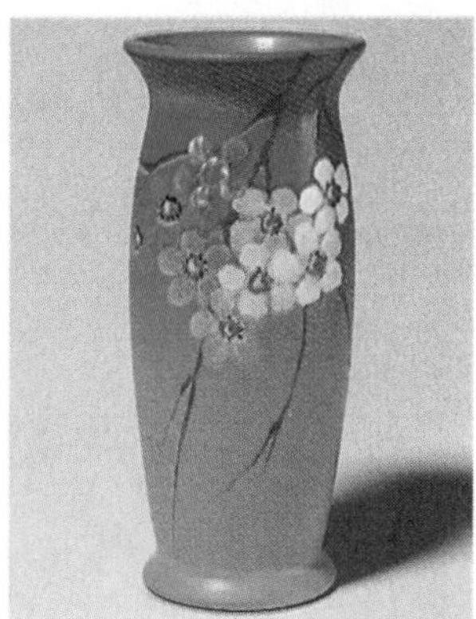

Vase, 7" h., narrow flared foot supporting the swelled cylindrical body w/a widely flaring rim, dark blue shaded to lighter blue ground h.p. w/a cluster of five-petal white, pink, purple & blue blossoms on slender green stems, Weller mark & mark of artist Ruth Axline, small glaze miss at base **$374**

Vase, 8" h., simple swelled cylindrical form tapering to a wide flat mouth, shaded dark blue to dark grey ground decorated w/ large blue & white morning glories on green leafy vines, decorated by Hester Pillsbury, marked on base **$1,150**

Hunter (before 1910)

Mug, wide ringed base below the tall slightly tapering cylindrical sides w/ a flat mouth & large C-form handle, decorated w/a swimming brown & white duck against a mottled light green & brown shading to dark green ground, Hunter mark, roughness to rim, 6" h. **$259**

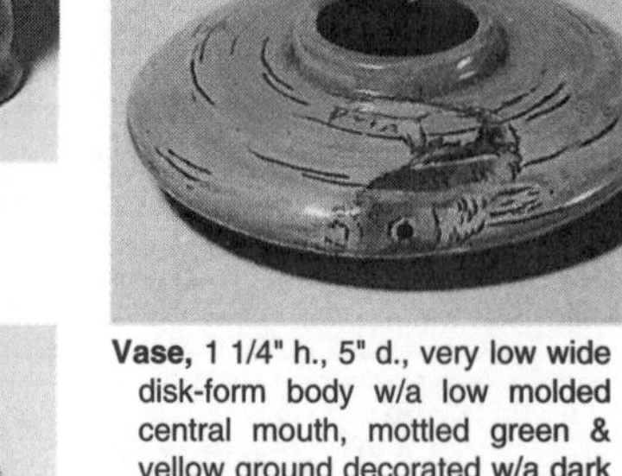

Vase, 1 1/4" h., 5" d., very low wide disk-form body w/a low molded central mouth, mottled green & yellow ground decorated w/a dark green & brown swimming fish, decorated by Edwin L. Pickens, Hunter mark on base, minor glaze inclusion & several pinpoint glaze pimples **$748**

Vase, 5 1/4" h., pillow-type, a flattened bulbous oblong body tapering to a narrow flared oval mouth, decorated w/a large soaring duck in brown & white below a band of dark green stripes around the top, a shaded dark golden yellow to mottled green background, Hunter mark, some very minor glaze rubs on back **$518**

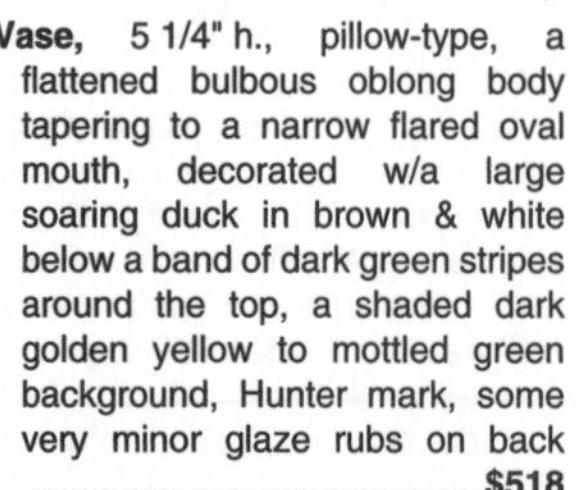

Jap Birdimal (1904)

Umbrella stand, gently swelled cylindrical form w/a swelling band below the wide low flaring neck, decorated w/slip-quilled landscape of tall dark blue trees in the foreground & smaller trees in the distance, all on a shaded medium to light blue ground w/a pale yellow moon, marked .. **$920**

Juneau (ca. 1933)

Vase, 10 1/4" h., footed bulbous ovoid body tapering to a wide cylindrical neck flanked by angled handles from the top rim to the shoulder, mottled deep red, pink & maroon drip glaze, marked, few tiny glaze indentations **$207**

Kenova (1920)

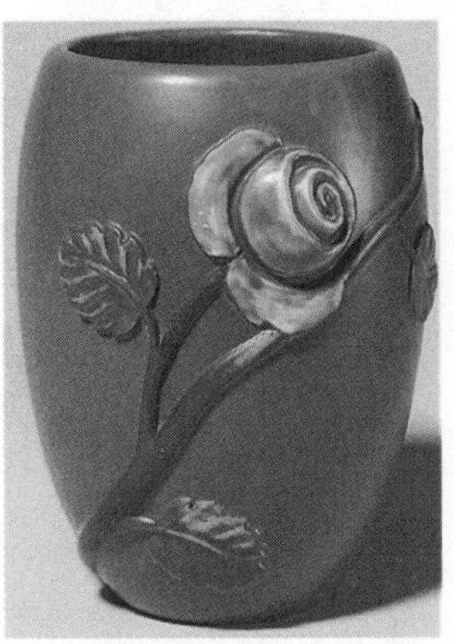

Vase, 8" h., simple wide ovoid shape w/a wide flat mouth, molded w/a large red rose on a leafy green vine wrapping around the sides, Weller mark, museum label on the base, very rare **$1,150**

L'Art Nouveau (1903-04)

Lorbeek (mid-1920s - 28)

Console set: 13 3/4" w. console bowl, 5" w. flower frog & a pair of low 2 1/2" h. candleholders; all w/a white glaze, some minor chips on bowl, the set **$259**

←

Vase, 13 3/4" h., a compressed bulbous lower body w/tapering cylindrical sides up to a band of molded high-relief pink poppy blossoms below a small top band, shaded pale green background, impressed Weller mark, minor surface rubs **$690**

Louwelsa (1896-1924)

Mug, tall slightly tapering cylindrical body w/a thick D-form handle, decorated w/dark red cherries & green leaves against a dark background, Louwelsa Weller logo & number 562, several glaze scratches, 5 3/4" h. **$127**

Pitcher, 10" h., jug-type, footed bulbous ovoid body tapering to a wide curved stove pipe-style cylindrical neck w/a second small cylindrical spout at the back of the neck above the C-form strap handle, decorated w/yellow cherries & green leaves w/some goldtone effect on a dark ground, Weller Louwelsa mark & "3 8," some minor in-the-making glaze flaws **$230**

Pitcher, 16 3/4" h., tankard-type, stepped ringed foot below the tall slightly tapering cylindrical body w/small rim spout & large C-form handle, h.p. bust portrait of a Native American warrior against a black to gold ground, decorated by Marie Rauchfuss, subject identified on the base as High Bear, Sioux Chief w/Weller Louwelsa marks, some restoration to sides, ca. 1905 .... **$920**

Pitcher, 5" d., three-footed wide squatty low body tapering to a short neck w/a wide arched spout & round loop handle, h.p. pink & deep red wild roses & green leaves on a shaded dark green ground, Louwelsa mark, some areas of dry glazing **$161**

Vase, 13 1/2" h., tall slender swelled cylindrical body tapering to a short cylindrical neck, dark blackish brown shaded to green ground, h. p. w/large orange trumpet vine flowers on leafy stems, decorated by Amelia Brown Sprague, Weller Louwelsa mark on base, some small glaze bubbles **$460**

Vase, 14 1/8" h., tall cylindrical body w/a thin shoulder & low rolled mouth, dark brown shaded to tan & pale green ground, h.p. w/large green & orange clematis-like blossoms on leafy vines, decorated by Anna Fulton Best, impressed marks, tight hairline at the rim, some dry crazing ... **$230**

Vase, 4" h., footed wide low squatty lower body tapering sharply to a tall widely flaring trumpet neck, decorated w/red & yellow wild roses & dark green leaves on a dark background, numbered "239-1" & artist-initialed for Lillie Mitchell, tiny base nick **$127**

Quality trumps quantity. Novice collectors who start by buying indiscriminately will spend years and much more money upgrading their collections than those who buy only the best examples from the start.

Marengo (1926)

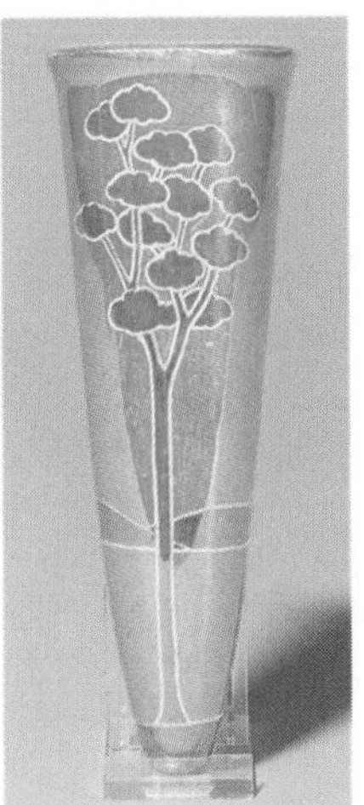

Wall pocket, long conical shape in deep orange lustre decorated w/tall stylized trees & distant hills in dark reddish brown outlined w/ white, 8 3/4" l. **$259**

Muskota (1915 - late 1920s)

Fish bowl base, figural, a low oblong woodgrained base w/two short stumps rising from one end, one stump w/a white & blue Kingfisher perched on it, impressed Weller mark, repairs to beak & tail, 13 1/2" l., 11" h. **$500**

Flower frog, model of two white ducks, one standing on the rim, the other below it swimming, pale green base, few minor glaze flakes, 5 1/2" h. **$288**

Flower frog, model of a green turtle w/a lily pad & white blossom on its back, impressed mark, small chip on side of lily pad, 9 1/2" l., 4 1/4" h. ... **$330**

Matt Green (ca. 1904)

Vase, 10 1/4" h., slightly waisted cylindrical body w/a flat rim, a repeating band of stylized looped scrolls around the top, the sides w/ overall molded swirling stylized Art Nouveau florals, impressed mark **$316**

Paragon (1934)

Bowl, 4 1/2" h., bulbous nearly spherical form w/ a wide flat mouth, dark magenta glaze, Weller script mark **$127**

Art Nouveau, French for "New Art," is a highly stylized form especially popular from around 1890 to 1905. It is characterized by flowing organic forms, especially flowers, and curving lines. The German form of Art Nouveau is known as Jugendstil, after *Jugend*, a youth magazine that championed the style.

Perfecto (early 1900s)

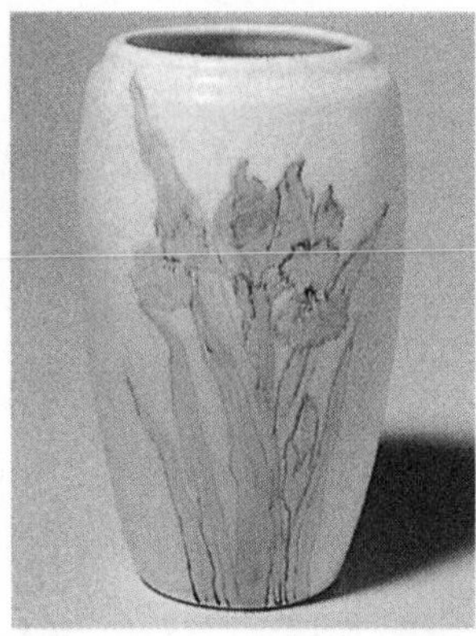

Vase, 7 1/4" h., gently swelled cylindrical body w/a narrow shoulder to the wide flat mouth, the pale blue ground decorated w/a tall cluster of dark blue & lavender irises & tall pale green leaves, painted by Dorothy England, impressed Weller mark, chip- bruise on rim **$345**

Scandia

Vases, 7 5/8" h., gently swelled cylindrical body w/flat rim, tight hairline from rim of one, pr. **$138**

Do not overload glass display shelves, especially top shelves, as a collapsing top shelf can create a domino effect on lower shelves.

Sicardo (1902-07)

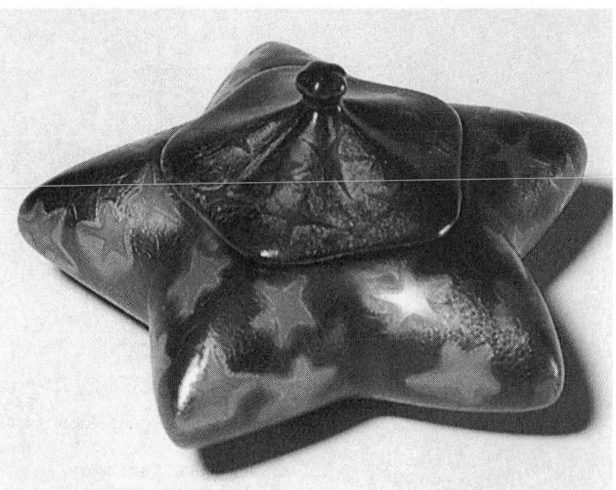

Box, cov., shaped as a five-pointed star w/a conforming cover w/ knob finial, overall iridescent design of small stars, unmarked, cover restoration, some grinding chips on base, 2 1/2" w. **$403**

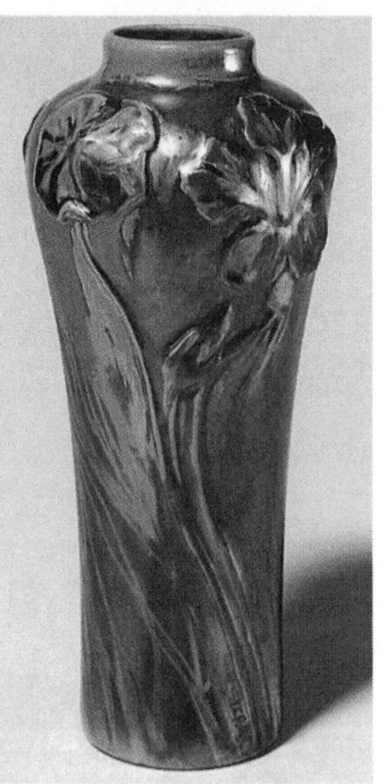

Vase, 11" h., tall cylindrical lower body w/a bulbous shoulder centered by a small, short cylindrical neck, large relief-molded nasturtium blossoms & leaves around the shoulder w/stems & buds down the sides, colorful iridescent glaze, signed on the side, rare form **$10,350**

Vase, 6 3/4" h., squatty tapering four-part melon-lobed lower body below the wide squatty lobed top, small pointed loop handles from upper lobes to lower sides, overall iridescent sunflowers & leaves design in shades of red, blue & green, impressed Weller mark & signed on the side **$2,645**

Vase, 4 3/8" h., inverted pear-shaped body w/flat rim, decorated w/relief-molded arrowroot leaves, iridescent glaze in shades of green, burgundy & gold, marked "Weller Sicard" on side **$660**

Vase, 9 3/4" h., cylindrical w/a narrow rounded shoulder to the low flared mouth, overall design of stylized spider mums in tones of gold, green, red & blue, signed on the side **$1,840**

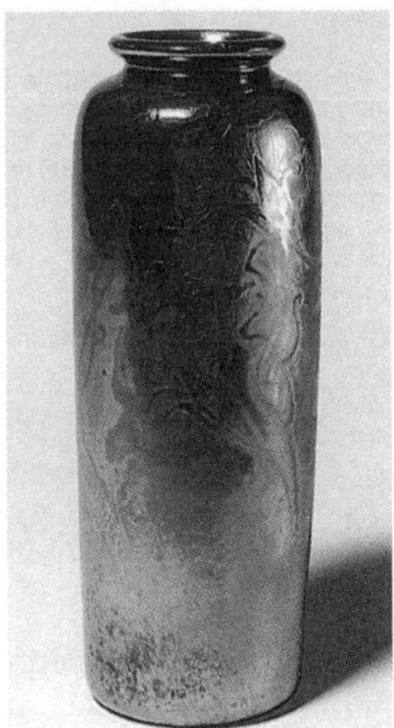

Vase, 9 5/8" h., cylindrical w/a narrow rounded shoulder to the low flared mouth, overall design of stylized nasturtium blossoms & leaves in tones of gold, green, red & blue, some open pinpoint glaze bubbles in one area, signed on the side **$1,265**

Souevo (1907-10)

Vase, 5 3/8" h., flat-bottomed wide bulbous ovoid body w/a rounded shoulder to the low molded rim band, black rim above a thin scalloped band, the body decorated w/a wide white band painted w/large black Native American-style geometric designs, some staining **$150**

Woodcraft (1917)

Planter, wide low cylindrical log form w/three small embossed foxes peeking out on front, flat rim, short tight hairline at rim, 7 1/2" d., 4 1/4" h. **$250**

Velvetone (late 1920s)

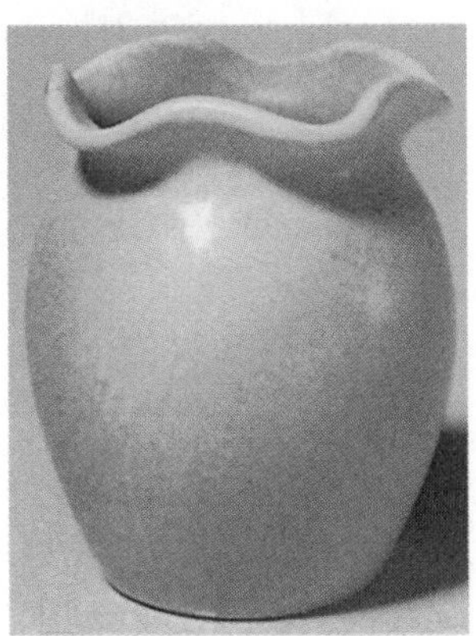

Vase, 4 3/4" h., bulbous ovoid body tapering to a widely flaring ruffled rim, pale pink shaded to light green, incised mark **$69**

White & Decorated Hudson (1917-34)

Vase, 8 7/8" h., simple tall ovoid body w/a low rolled mouth, creamy ground h.p. w/continuous curving black branches w/small purple blossoms & pale green leaves, impressed mark, pinpoint rim nick **$316**

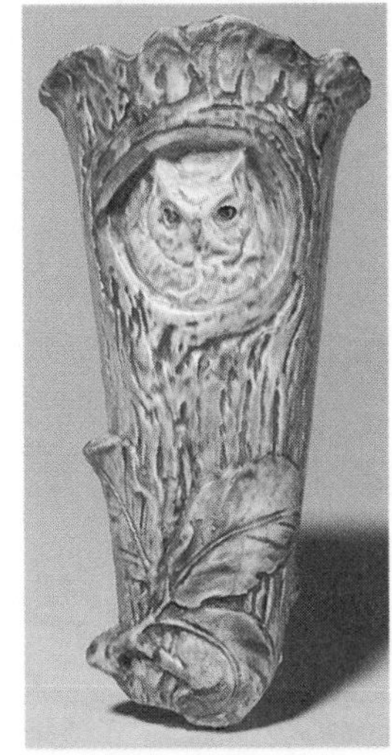

Wall pocket, long flattened trumpet form molded as a tree trunk w/molded leaves near the base & a round opening showing the head of an owl near the top, 11" l. **$250-350**

Willow Wares

This pseudo-Chinese pattern has been used by numerous firms throughout the years. The original design is attributed to Thomas Minton about 1780, and Thomas Turner is believed to have first produced the ware during his tenure at the Caughley works. The blue underglaze transfer print pattern has never been out of production since that time. An Oriental landscape incorporating a bridge, pagoda, trees, figures and birds supposedly tells the story of lovers fleeing a cruel father who wished to prevent their marriage. The gods, having pity on them, changed them into birds, enabling them to fly away and seek their happiness together.

Blue

Bone dish, Buffalo Pottery, 6 1/2" l. **$60-70**

Canister, labeled "Coffee," marked "Willow," Australia, ca. 1920s, 5 3/4" h. **$35-40**

Cheese stand, J. Meir & Sons, England, 8 1/2" d. **$150-175**

Creamer w/original stopper, figural cow standing on oval base, mouth forms spout & tail forms handle, ca. 1850, unmarked, England, 7" l., 5" h. **$500-600**

Creamer, cow-shaped, W. Kent, England, 1950s **$250-300**

Cracker jar, cov., silver lid & handle, Minton, England, 5" h. **$150-175**

Gravy boat, ca. 1890, unmarked, England, 7" l. **$45-50**

Ladle, pearlware, pattern inside & outside bowl, unmarked, England, 6" l. **$125-150**

Mug, barrel-shaped mold, Granger & Worcester, England, ca. 1850, 4 1/4" h. **$200-250**

Mug, Maling, England, 4 1/2" h. **$50**

Mustard pot, cov., ca. 1870, unmarked, England, 3" h. **$90-100**

Nut dish, scalloped shape, ca. 1900, 7" l. **$75-85**

Pepper pot, ca. 1870, England, 4" h., each (ILLUS. of four different styles) **$90-100**

Pepper shaker, figural Toby, "Prestopan," unmarked, Scotland, 5 1/4" h. **$225-250**

Pitcher, 5 1/2" h., Ridgways, England **$50-75**

Pitcher, 7" h., "Chicago Jug," ca. 1907, Buffalo Pottery, 3 pt. **$150-175**

Pitcher, cov., 5 1/2" h., Buffalo Pottery **$150-175**

Place card holder, unmarked, England, ca. 1870s, 2 1/2" d. **$85-100**

Plate, dinner, Buffalo Pottery, 1911 .... **$30-35**

Platter, 11 x 14" l., rectangular, ca. 1880s, unmarked, England ... **$100-150**

Platter, 9 x 11" l., rectangular, Wedgwood & Co., England **$100-125**

Relish dish, leaf-shaped, ca. 1870, England **$100-125**

Salt box, cov., ca. 1960, wooden lid, Japan, 5 x 5" **$125-150**

Punch cup, pedestal foot, unmarked, England, ca. 1900, 3 1/2" h. **$30-40**

Sauce tureen, cov., England, ca. 1880s, 5" h. **$100-125**

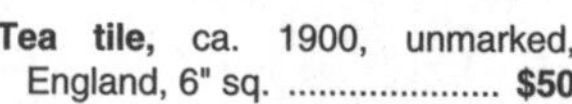

Tea tile, ca. 1900, unmarked, England, 6" sq. **$50**

Sugar barrel, cov., silver lid & handle, unmarked, England, ca. 1880s, 5" h. **$175**

Salt dip, master, pedestal base, unmarked, England, 2" h. **$100-125**

Teapot, cov., miniature, lobed ovoid body, domed inset cover w/finial, C-scroll handle, serpentine spout, gold line decoration on handle, spout, rim & finial, Windsor China, England, modern, 3 3/4" h. **$15-20**

Teapot, cov., six-paneled squatty bulbous body on short feet, flat hexagonal neck & cover topped w/figural gold lion finial, gold beaded C-form handle, serpentine spout, embellished w/gold line decoration on feet, spout & lid, the sides of the neck reading "We'll take a cup o' kindness yet, for days o' auld lang syne" in blue, made for Tiffany & Co., New York by Copeland China, England, ca. 1870s **$200**

Teapot, cov., squatty bulbous body tapering to flaring asymmetrical neck, slightly domed cover w/trefoil finial, C-scroll handle, slightly serpentine spout, dark blue handle, spout & finial, Mintons, England, ca. 1900 .... **$175-200**

Teapot, cov., squatty ovoid body on short foot, flattened dome cover w/button finial, C-form handle, gently serpentine spout, dark blue spout, handle & finial, gold highlights, Royal Corona Ware, S. Hancock & Sons, England, early 20th c. **$225-250**

Teapot, cov., squatty ovoid body on short foot, incurved neck, C-scroll handle, slightly serpentine spout, inset cover tapering to peaked circular finial, decorated w/bands of gold beading at shoulder & on cover, gold decoration on rim, handle, spout & finial, Hammersley & Co., England, ca. 1912-39 .... **$150-175**

Teapot, cov., squatty ovoid body tapering in at shoulder to gently peaked cover w/knob finial, straight spout, C-scroll handle, Royal Worcester porcelain, England, ca. 1920s **$150-175**

Teapot, cov., squatty ovoid body tapering in at shoulder to short cylindrical neck, slightly tapering inset cover w/disk finial, angled handle, slightly curved spout, shoulder reads "We'll take a cup o' kindness yet, for days o' auld lang syne," Doulton & Co., England, ca. 1882-91 .... **$200**

Teapot, cover & trivet, spherical body on short tapering foot, short neck w/inset cover w/button finial, C-scroll handle, serpentine spout, on matching round trivet, Grimwades, England, early 20th c., teapot 6" h., 2 pcs. .. **$250-275**

Teapot, cov., squatty ovoid body tapering in at shoulder to short neck, C-scroll handle, slightly serpentine spout, tapering cover w/disk finial, embellished w/silver line decoration & band of silver grapevine decoration at shoulder & on cover, Miles Mason, England, ca. 1807-13 .... **$300-350**

Tip tray, "Schweppes Lemon Squash," England, 4 1/2" d. **$30-40**

Tip tray, "Yorkshire Relish," England, 4" d. **$40-50**

Toby jug, w/Blue Willow jacket, unmarked, England, 6" h. **$250-300**

Wash pitcher & bowl, Royal Doulton, the set **$400-500**

Zeisel (Eva) Designs

One of the most influential ceramic artists and designers of the 20th century, Eva Zeisel began her career in Europe as a young woman, eventually immigrating to the United States, where her unique, streamlined designs met with great success. Since the 1940s her work has been at the forefront of commercial ceramic design, and in recent decades she has designed in other media. Now in her ninth decade, she continues to be active and involved in the world of art and design.

Hall China Company - Kitchenware

Cookie jar, cov., Golden Clover **$65**

Teapot, cov., 6-cup, Tri-tone, ca. 1954 .... **$150**

Teapot, cov., Tri-Tone side-handle model **$95**

Hallcraft - Century Dinnerware

Vegetable bowl, 10 1/2" d., White **$80**

Hallcraft by Hall China Co. - Tomorrow's Classic Shape

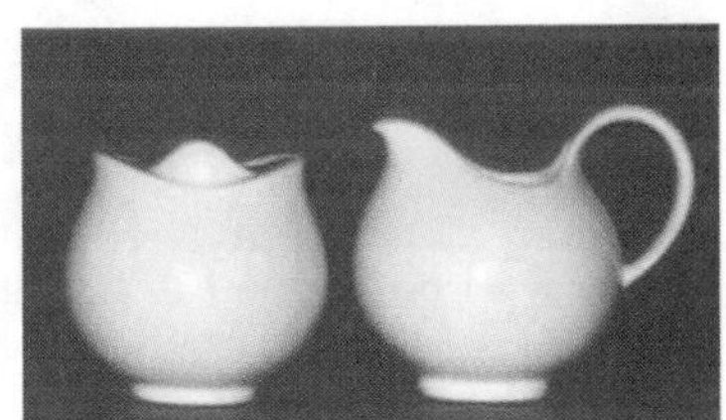

Creamer & sugar, White, the set **$50-75**

Hollydale

Chop plate, 14" l., brown **$80**

Hyalyn "Z Ware"

Coffee server, cov., satin black w/ white lid **$150**

Klein Reed

Teapot, cov., wide squatty bulbous body on small base, woven wicker bail handle, 2002 .... **$200**

Monmouth Dinnerware

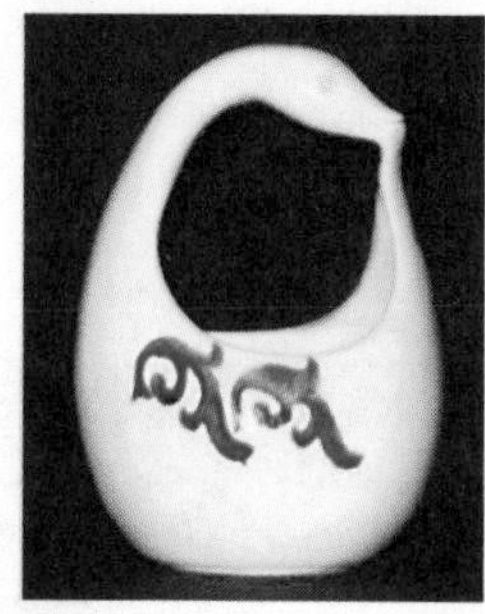

Gravy boat, goose shape, Lacey Wings **$175**

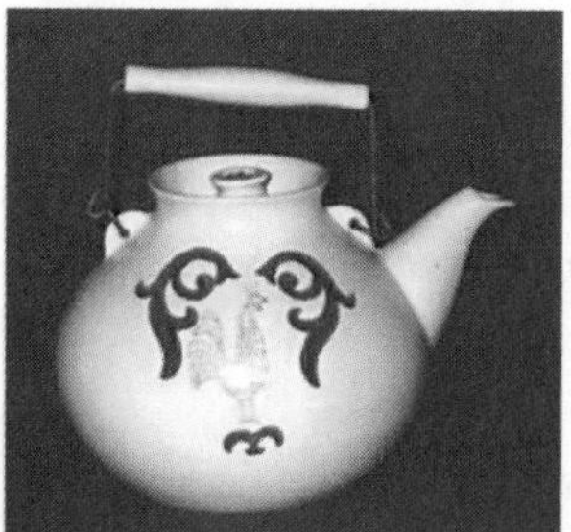

Teapot, cov., Lacey Wings patt., wire handle w/ceramic grip, Prairie Hen, w/bird decoration, ca. 1952 .... **$300**

Riverside

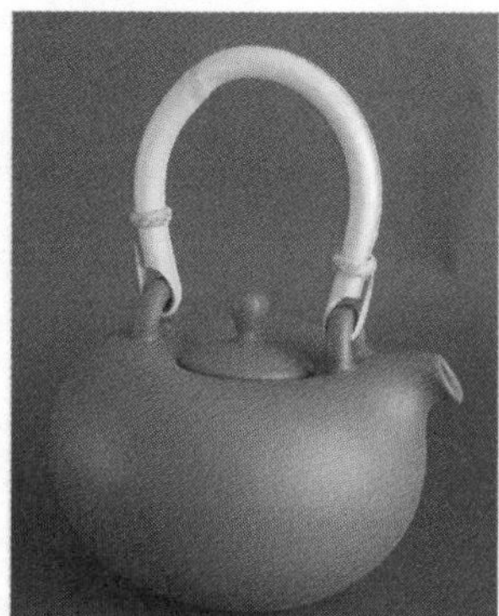

Teapot, cov., design reissue, distributed by The Orange Chicken, made by World of Ceramics, 2002 .... **$200**

Norleans Dinnerware by Meito

Gravy boat w/underliner, Livonia **$65**

Vegetable bowl, 12" oval, Livonia **$65**

Schmid Dinnerware

Coffeepot, cov., Lacey Wings/ Rosette **$250**

Teapot, cov., bird-shaped w/woven wicker bail handle, Lyric patt., 1965 .... **$225**

Teapot, cov., bird-shaped, rattan handle, Lacey Wings, 1950s **$150**

Consider combining a vacation with your collecting interests. Attend antique shows such as ones in Atlantic City, N.J., Brimfield, Mass., or Round Top, Texas, or even Aloha Flea Market at the Aloha Stadium in Honolulu. These destinations will provide sightseeing as well as shopping opportunities.

Schramberg

Ashtray, triangular, Gobelin 13 .... **$160**

Jar, cov., terraced, Mondrian, 5" **$1,000**

Teapot, cov., footed tapering bulbous body decorated w/ colorful polka dots, No. 3356, Pattern 3369, Germany, ca. 1930 .... **$1,200**

Teapot, cov., Gobelin 13 patt., Germany, 1930s **$900**

Teapot, cov., wide low cylindrical shape w/polka dot decoration, reissue of a 1929 design, Pattern 3366, produced for the Metropolitan Museum of Art, 2000 .... **$125**

Stratoware

Candlestick, brown trim **$120**

Refrigerator jar, cov., blue & beige **$200**

Sugar, cov., gold & beige **$100**

Town and Country Dinnerware - for Red Wing Potteries

Creamer, "yawn," bronze **$70**

Lazy Susan relish set w/mustard jar **$600**

Mixing bowl color??? gray??? **$175**

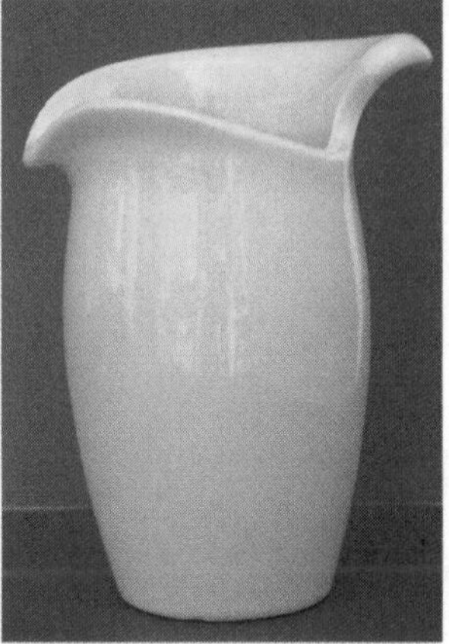

Pitcher, syrup, chartreuse **$135**

Platter, 15" l., comma shape **$85-100**

Shaker, large "schmoo," Ming green (ILLUS. right w/small "schmoo" shaker) **$75**

Teapot, cov., ca. 1947, blue **$200-225**

Tureen, cov., soup, sand **$850**

Watt Pottery

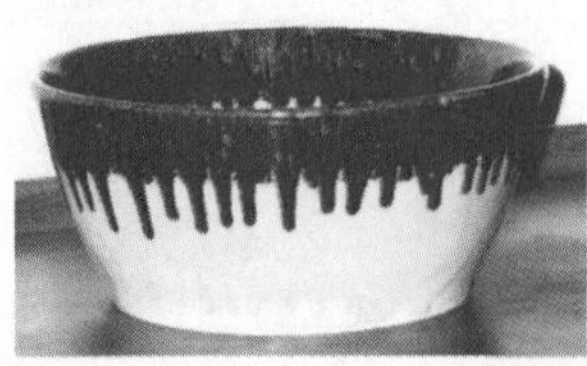

Bowl, 8 1/4" d., blue drip glaze **$25**

CLOCKS

Anniversary clock, Le Coultre, upright rectangular gilt-bronze footed frame w/glass sides, a large white dial w/Arabic numerals w/the works visible behind, France, ca. 1955, 9 3/4" h. **$518**

Banjo clock, Grant (William) attribution, Boston, Massachusetts, a round bell mounted at the very top above the round painted dial w/Roman numerals enclosed by a brass bezel & convex glass cover, dial signed by the maker, a tall tapering throat, reverse- painted stylized leaves & scrolls on a white ground & flanked by tall narrow openwork brass brackets above the rectangular pendulum box w/a reverse-painted panel decorated in color w/a rural landscape, eight-day weight-driven alarm movement, imperfections, ca. 1820, 32" h. (ILLUS. second from right with other banjo clocks & the mirror clock) **$2,468**

Bedside clock, Caldwell (J.E.) & Co., Philadelphia, Art Deco style, an upright square pink quartz block w/beveled edges inset w/ a square glass-covered dial w/ Arabic numerals & an eight-day Swiss movement, a rectangular black onyx base w/molded edges, key-wound base, running, 3 x 3" **$748**

Bracket clock, Linden, Germany, mahogany case w/a domed top & metal loop handle, the square glass front w/molding over a dial w/Roman numerals & applied gilded spandrels, stepped bottom molded on flat tab feet, eight-day time & triple chime movement, ca. 1940s, 7 1/2 x 11", 14 1/2" h. **$350**

Bracket clock, Thomas (Seth) Clock Co., Thomaston, Connecticut, walnut case w/a domed top & brass loop handle, brass & enamel dial w/Roman numerals, based on an 18th c. English design, eight-day time & strike movement w/floating balance, ca. 1950s, 3 3/4 x 7 1/2", 10 1/2" h. **$180**

Preserve any labels found on a clock case, as they may give important horological and historical information that may increase the value of your clock.

Establish a regular schedule to wind your clock. Use your normal routine as a reminder. For example, you might want to wind your clock at the beginning of a weekly TV show.

Calendar desk clock, DuBois & Fils, Switzerland, tall silver case w/round top dial section w/notched rim & topped by spread- winged eagle finial, a white porcelain time dial w/Arabic numerals framed by a/polychrome scene at top showing a man holding dog & looking toward draped columns, two subsidiary dials for date & days of the week, raised on a flattened waisted support w/a bulbous lower body w/applied flower decoration, all supported by two figural satyrs standing on a rectangular stepped base w/bands of notched decoration & leaf & bead trim, keywind calendar movement, chain fusèe movement w/monometallic balance just visible behind the fancy gilt cock that fits in dial, both dial & movement signed, replaced crystal, ca. 1830, 7" h. **$1,960**

Calendar shelf or mantel clock, Ithaca Calendar Clock Co., Ithaca, New York, upright walnut case w/ebonized trim, the top section w/an arched & pierced leaf-carved crest above columns flanking the round bezel & paper dial w/Roman numerals, the slightly stepped-out deep lower case enclosing a large glass calendar dial exposing the crystal gridiron pendulum & date roles, molded base, eight-day time & strike movement, second half 19th c., 20 1/4" h. **$3,600**

Crystal regulator, Ansonia Clock Company, New York, New York, ornate upright gilt-bronze case w/the domed top centered by a swag-draped urn above the floral-cast rounded scroll corners, ornate leafy scroll frame enclosing glass sides & front panel below the round dial w/Roman numerals & an open escapement surrounded by a brass bezel, a squared flaring scroll-cast base w/projecting scroll feet, late 19th c., 16 1/2" h. **$1,380**

Crystal regulator, gold-painted cast-spelter upright case w/an arched top w/five flower basket finials, an egg-and-dart cornice over a scroll-cast panel above the long beveled glass door & sides, porcelain dial w/Arabic numerals & decorated w/flower swags, glass tube pendulum, rectangular platform base cast w/a scroll & floret band on flat tab feet, eight-day time & strike movement, early 20th c., 5 3/4 x 8 3/8", 15" h. **$600-650**

←

Cuckoo wall clock, American Cuckoo Clock Co., Philadelphia, Pennsylvania, fumed oak Neo-Gothic Arts & Crafts case, stepped flat top above Gothic arched & flat pilasters flanking the cuckoo door & brass dial w/Arabic numerals, eight-day weight- driven movement, time & strike, oak pendulum bob in a wheel design, tall obelisk-shaped iron weights, early 20th c., 5 1/4 x 9 1/4", 12 3/4" h. plus chain & weights (ILLUS. disassembled) **$200-250**

Desk clock, clock-inkstand combination, cast-brass, Rococo style, the small clock w/a round dial w/Roman numerals framed by ornate pierced scrolls in an upright case above a rectangular inkstand w/ornate scroll trim & fitted w/two inkwells w/domed covers, on small peg feet, 30-hour movement, probably French, late 19th - early 20th c., 6 x 10 1/2", 8 1/8" h. **$180- 200**

Grandfather, Herschede Clock Co. (attributed), Cincinnati, Ohio, the dark mahogany case w/an arched & molded cornice & frieze panel above the tall arched door, the upper arched glass panel over the ornate dial w/silvered metal chapter ring on the gilt face w/ Arabic numerals & a h.p. moon dial w/ship scene, the long lower glass door panel showing the nine tube chimes & cylindrical weights & pendulum, the door flanked by round columns, glass sides, flat molded base, ca. 1910, 88" h. **$2,300**

Grandfather, Reynolds (John), Hagerstown, Maryland, Federal-style inlaid mahogany case, a broken-scroll pediment w/inlaid rosettes & an inlaid paterae centered by an urn-form finial above a shell-inlaid frieze panel above the arched top door flanked by colonettes & opening to a painted dial w/Roman numerals & a moon phase dial, the body of the case fitted w/a tall narrow door w/small leaf inlays at each corner & a central shell inlay, the stepped-out lower base w/an inlaid square band w/inlaid leaf corners & an oval reserve inlaid w/ a spread-winged American eagle, a serpentine apron & short French feet, 1797-1814, restorations to feet & tympanum, 104 1/2" h. **$23,900**

Grandfather, Phillips & Sons (James), Bristol, England, ornately carved Chippendale Revival mahogany case, the inlaid broken-scroll pediment topped w/ball spiked finials above an arched molded cornice above an arched leaf-carved glazed door flanked by heavy carved corner scrolls, opening to the ornate silvered metal dial w/Arabic numerals & enhanced w/chased & engraved pierced gilt-bronze surround, a molded flaring molding above the tall waist section w/a tall glazed door w/delicate scrolling & lattice-carved wood overlay & flanked by heavy carved corner scrolls, the door showing the large pendulum & chime tubes, another flaring molding above the bottom section centered by a shell-and-scroll carved raised panel enclosing an inlaid leafy scroll panel surrounding a basket of flowers, carved scrolls at the corners, all resting on a heavy molded base w/stepped flattened block feet, the movement playing bow bells, St. Michael, Westminster & Withington chimes, ca. 1892, 18 1/2 x 29", 111" h. **$37,950**

Novelty shelf or mantel clock, Haddon Clock Co., electric motion clock, "Home Sweet Home," model of a house in plastic & composition, a square large window over the dial on the left, a window on the right w/a scene of an old woman in a rocker, when plugged in woman rocks & fire shimmers, 20th c., 3 1/2 x 12 1/4", 7 3/8" h. **$185**

Novelty shelf or mantel clock, Mastercrafter electric motion clock, the brown plastic case designed to resemble an open stage w/ railing showing a boy & girl who sit on moving swings, the large round top centering a steel dial w/Arabic numerals & a sweep seconds hand, ca. 1950s, 5 x 7 1/4", 10 3/4" h. **$180**

Shelf or mantel clock, Ansonia Clock Co., Ansonia, Connecticut, "Opera" model cast-metal case, the tapering rectangular base w/sawtooth apron & cast-metal scroll feet supporting a large cast-metal figure of a seated classical woman on an elaborate stool & holding a wreath w/a lyre at the side, the ornate upright cast-metal clock case to one side enclosing a brass bezel around the porcelain face w/Roman numerals, eight-day movement, time & strike, open escapement, minor surface wear, ca. 1885-95, 8 x 21", 16 1/4" h. **$800-1,000**

Shelf or mantel clock, Ansonia Clock Co., Ansonia, Connecticut, black marble temple-style case, thin flat rectangular top above the blocked front w/a central brass bezel around the dial w/Roman numerals, the side panels w/incised scrolls & small inset blocks of tan marble, deep rectangular flat base w/inset tan marble trim, eight-day movement, time & strike, open escapement, ca. 1890, 7 x 17 1/2", 10 1/4" h. **$400-450**

Shelf or mantel clock, Ansonia Clock Co., Ansonia, Connecticut, ornate Royal Bonn "La Mine" model china case, the tall upright arched case w/ waisted sides molded at the top w/a central shell flanked by long open scrolls w/further scrolls down the sides & across the base w/incurved scroll feet, painted a deep magenta at the top w/pale yellow in the center shading to dark green at the base, decorated on the front w/large h.p. white & magenta blossoms & green leaves, the large brass bezel around the porcelain dial, Arabic numerals, open escapement, eight-day movement, time & strike, ca. 1900, 6 1/4 x 11", 13 1/2" h. **$1,000-1,200**

Shelf or mantel clock, Ansonia Clock Co., Ansonia, Connecticut, black cast-iron "Irving" model case, two full fluted green columns on the front w/applied gilt ornaments, enameled dial w/Roman numerals, eight-day movement, time & strike, ca. 1910, 5 x 11 3/8", 12" h. **$595**

Shelf or mantel clock, Ansonia Clock Co., Ansonia, Connecticut, gilt-metal, seated figure of a 17th c. writer or poet beside the upright ornately scroll-cast case surrounding the porcelain dial w/Arabic numerals, long ornate scrolling base on scroll feet, eight-day movement, time & strike, case repainted, ca. 1890, 7 x 14 1/4"., 11 1/4" h. **$600-700**

Shelf or mantel clock, Ansonia Clock Co., Ansonia, Connecticut, simple dark hardwood case w/veneering removed, upright rectangular case w/a two-pane door, the large upper pane over the large faded dial w/Roman numerals & gilt trim above a narrow rectangular glass panel reverse-painted black w/geometric gilt loops, deep molded base, time & strike, second half 19th c., 4 x 8 1/2", 11 3/4" h. **$90**

Shelf or mantel clock, Ansonia Clock Co., Ansonia, Connecticut, Victorian walnut Renaissance Revival style case w/a high scroll-carved crest centered by a classical head over the arched, molded cornice w/urn-form finials above an arched glass door w/ gilt stencil decoration of cupids & ferns, white dial w/Roman numerals, the door flanked by tall narrow angled mirrors backing gilt-metal standing cupid figures, base w/curved, molded sides flanking a front panel w/gilt-metal scroll boss, eight-day movement, time & strike, third-quarter 19th c., 5 1/2 x 16 1/2", 24 1/4" h. **$750-800**

Shelf or mantel clock, Ansonia Clock Co., New York, New York, "La Charny" model, Royal Bonn china case, the upright arched case molded at the top w/a grotesque mask & scrolls continuing down the sides flanked at each corner by a stylized figure of a seated griffin, the borders in gold & brown shaded to golden yellow & green & decorated w/large red & yellow iris-like flowers, brass door & bezel around the porcelain dial w/Roman numerals, eight-day movement, time & strike, ca. 1900, 5 1/2 x 11 1/4", 11 3/4" h. **$700-800**

Shelf or mantel clock, Brewster & Ingrahams, Bristol, Connecticut, Kirk's patent movement, beehive form rosewood case w/molded frame & round molding around the round white signed dial w/black Roman numerals, the lower pane reverse-painted w/an image of Ballston Springs, eight-day time & strike rack & snail movement w/ original brass springs, age cracks to dial paint, key escutcheon repaired, pendulum a later Seth Thomas type, hands are old but incorrect for this model, ca. 1845, 19" h. **$560**

Shelf or mantel clock, cast spelter, figural case, a large spread-winged eagle atop a rockwork base enclosing a round brass bezel & small dial w/Arabic numerals, Germany, late 19th - early 20th c., 6 x 8 3/4", 13 1/2" h. ... **$250-300**

Shelf or mantel clock, figural "Bonapart's Son" model, high stepped ormolu case w/a figure of a seated boy on the top w/his elbow resting on a draped table holding world map & books (one a "Memorial" of Napoleon, the other titled "Code Napoleon"), the table enclosing the round dial w/ patterned gilt bezel & black Roman numerals, all on rectangular stepped base w/panels of scroll, floral & shell decoration, notched design & ribbing, waveform feet & corner decorations, engine-turned time & strike movement, dial w/a stress fracture, ca. 1870, 17" h. **$1,232**

Shelf or mantel clock, Gilbert (Wm. L.) Clock Co., Winsted, Connecticut, "Acheron" model, walnut case w/fan-carved crest & line-incised scrolls above the arched molded glazed door opening to a dial w/Roman numerals, the lower door w/original silver stenciled leaves, flowers & a checkerboard design, deep flared platform base, paper label inside, late 19th c., 4 1/2 x 13", 19 1/4" h. **$200-250**

Shelf or mantel clock, Forestville Mfg. Co., Bristol, Connecticut, tall upright "column & cornice" case in crotch-grained mahogany veneer, a deep ogee molded blocked cornice over tall half-round columns w/ringed capitals & bases flanking a two- pane door, the upper pane over the polychrome wooden dial w/ spandrels, black Roman numerals, open escapement & marked "Forestvill [sic], Manufacturing Co. - Bristol, CT. U.S.A.," the lower pane w/an original Wm. B. Fenn monochromatic silver-colored decoration of a vase w/floral stems, bottom ogee-front block feet flank another glass pane w/an original Wm. B. Fenn monochromatic silver-colored decoration of a bird on limb, good label, hand-colored lithograph of Saturday night scene on backboard, time & strike movement, ca. 1850, 34" h. **$1,456**

Shelf or mantel clock, Gilbert (Wm. L.) Clock Co., Winsted, Connecticut, walnut "Necho" model, a pointed scroll-carved pediment above scroll-cut & line-incised cornice above the rounded & reeded glazed door w/ornate silver stenciled drapery design over the large dial w/Roman numerals & a brass pendulum w/applied grape leaves, scroll cutouts at the lower sides above the flaring stepped base, eight-day movement, time, strike & alarm, ca. 1890, 5 x 13 1/4", 20 3/4" h. **$300-350**

Shelf or mantel clock, French Victorian Renaissance Revival-style, gilt-bronze case w/a large swag-draped urn finial on the upright case topped w/ornate scrolls & grape clusters above the round gilt-trimmed enameled dial w/Roman numerals flanked by caryatids, the blocked rectangular base w/leafy scrolls & grapes flanking the case & decorated w/ scroll bands & florets, pinwheel movement, third quarter 19th c. **$5,200**

Dedicated clock collectors usually keep their clocks running if possible. The parts will not wear out. In fact, keeping the moving parts running will help preserve them and maintain the clock's accuracy.

Shelf or mantel clock, Gilbert (Wm. L.) Clock Co., Winsted, Connecticut, walnut kitchen-style case, Victorian Eastlake design, the sawtooth-cut central cornice flanked by tall corner blocks w/ knob finials above reeded sides flanking the tall glazed door w/ ornate silver stenciled arches below the dial w/Roman numerals, brass pendulum w/applied grape leaves, molded & blocked base w/line-incised decoration, original varnish, eight-day movement, time & strike, ca. 1885, 4 x 12 1/4", 21 1/4" h. **$450-550**

Shelf or mantel clock, Gilbert (Wm. L.), Winsted, Connecticut, miniature steeple-type clock, walnut case w/pointed pediment flanked by turned finials above the pointed two-pane glazed door, the upper pane opening to the white metal dial w/Roman numerals & painted spandrels, the lower panel w/a reverse-painted windmill scene, flat base, possibly a salesman's sample, eight-day time & strike movement, mid-19th c., 4 1/2 x 6 1/2", 10 3/4" h. **$250**

Shelf or mantel clock, Jennings Bros. Mfg. Co., Bridgeport, Connecticut, gilt spelter, the tall Art Nouveau design case bulbous at the top & tapering down to a wide serpentine foot, openwork leaves & cherries at the top & down the front w/loop side handles, the round dial w/Arabic numerals, ca. 1900, 4 3/4 x 5 1/4", 12" h. **$200**

Shelf or mantel clock, Ingraham Company, Bristol, Connecticut, temple-style, black enamel over wood, the long, high rectangular case w/ applied stamped metal columns & cast-metal paw feet, metal lion head mask end handles, top panels on the front inset w/slag glass framed by metal simulating curtained windows, eight-day movement, time & strike, ca. 1900, 5 1/2 x 20", 10 7/8" h. **$300-400**

Shelf or mantel clock, Kieninger, Germany, skeleton movement in an upright walnut case w/beveled glass front door & back, open ring steel dial w/Roman numerals, brass movement & bell, eight-day movement, 7 3/4 x 10 7/8" d., 16" h. overall ... **$600**

If your clock runs too fast or slow, you can adjust its timing by up to five minutes a week by raising or lowering the pendulum bob or adjusting its weights.

Shelf or mantel clock, Lux Clock Mfg. Co., Waterbury, Connecticut, miniature domed celluloid case, dial w/Arabic numerals, flat molded base, early 20th c., 2 1/4 x 6 1/4", 3 1/4" h. **$40**

Shelf or mantel clock, music box clock, fruit wood case w/domed top w/ring-turned finial & crosshatch & scroll carving w/matching corner finials above the stepped flaring cornice, a large brass bezel around the white dial w/Arabic numerals & scrolled brass spandrels flanked by ring-turned finials at each corner, flaring stepped base on small bun feet, eight-day movement, Germany, ca. 1930s, 4 1/4 x 7 1/4", 13" h. **$250-300**

Shelf or mantel clock, New Haven Clock Co., New Haven, Connecticut (attributed), Victorian Neo-Gothic style walnut case, a steeply pointed top w/Gothic scroll cutout border & trefoil finial flanked by sunburst side finials on thin blocks over roundels & shaped side panels w/incised scrolls, the tall steeply pointed door w/heavy molding around the glass decorated w/a fancy gilt stencil border band w/Oriental motifs, the dial w/a brass bezel & Roman numerals printed w/ patent date "Feb. 11, 1879," brass pendulum w/unique inset compensating needle indicator, deep rectangular platform base w/incised scrolls, original finish, eight- day movement, time & strike, 4 3/4 x 14 5/8", 22 1/4" h. **$350-400**

Shelf or mantel clock, Thomas (Seth) Clock Co., Plymouth, Connecticut, Classical Revival tall case, mahogany veneer, the deep ogee cornice w/blocked corners above a pair of gilt columns flanking the two-pane door, the large upper pane over the worn painted metal dial w/Roman numerals, clear lower pane, the lower section w/ogee corner blocks flanking a panel w/a small round pendulum window, eight-day movement, time & strike, some veneer damage, last quarter 19th c., 4 1/2 x 8 1/2", 16" h. **$225**

Shelf or mantel clock, Thomas (Seth) Clock Co., Plymouth, Connecticut, Classical-style ogee rosewood veneer case, the front w/rounded molding around the two-pane long door w/rounded molding, the upper pane over the painted metal dial w/Roman numerals, the lower pane showing the pendulum & works, eight-day movement, time, strike & alarm, face wear, ca. 1880, 4 x 10 3/4", 16 1/2" h. **$200-250**

> The phrase "lower, slower; higher, sprier" provides a good way to remember how to adjust a pendulum clock. Raising the bob on the pendulum rod shortens the swing so the clock goes faster. Lowering the bob make the arc longer, which slows the clock.

Shelf or mantel clock, Thomas (Seth) Clock Co., Plymouth, Connecticut, Classical-style two-deck decorated mahogany veneer case, the deep ogee blocked top above large gilt-decorated half-round columns flanking the tall two-pane door, the upper pane over the dial w/ Roman numerals, the lower pane decorated w/elaborate reverse-painted gilt decor of a scalloped frame enclosing lattice centered by a colored urn of flowers, the deep lower case w/heavy ogee scrolls flanking a small glazed door reverse- painted w/further gilt stencil decoration centering a diamond & bowl of colored flowers, flat base, dated 1863, eight-day movement, time & strike, original finish, 5 1/8 x 18 1/2", 32 1/2" **$1,200-1,500**

Shelf or mantel clock, Thomas (Seth) Clock Co., Plymouth, Connecticut, mahogany, the angled domed case top above a conforming glazed door opening to a dial w/Roman numerals above a brass & silvered metal pendulum w/inset brass star, rectangular stepped base, paper label inside, eight-day movement, time & strike, 1850-80, 4 3/4 x 10 3/8", 16" h. **$150**

Shelf or mantel clock, Thomas (Seth) Clock Co., Plymouth, Connecticut, round-topped rosewood veneer case, the front forms a door w/a molded ring around the dial w/Roman numerals, eight-day movement, time & strike, ca. 1865, 4 x 8 3/8", 12 1/4" h. **$200**

Shelf or mantel clock, Thomas (Seth) Clock Co., Plymouth, Connecticut, temple-style case, beige marbleized wood w/cast-metal scroll feet & lion heads at each end, flat rectangular top w/a stepped cornice over the blocked center w/an ornate brass bezel & dial flanked by stepped-back side panels w/applied gilt-metal scroll cartouches, a deep molded flat base, eight-day movement, time & strike, ca. 1890, 7 x 16 1/2", 10 3/4" h. **$250-300**

Shelf or mantel clock, Thomas (Seth) Clock Co., Plymouth, Connecticut, simulated adamantine wood finish on temple-style case, gently arched top w/flat cornice above the blocked case centering a brass-framed glass door over the porcelain dial w/Arabic numerals, deep platform base on tiny brass knob feet, eight-day movement, time & strike w/Sonora chimes, early 20th c., 7 x 15 1/4", 13 1/2" h. **$700-800**

Shelf or mantel clock, Thomas (Seth) ogee-case clock, mahogany veneer w/tall two-part door, the upper section over the dial w/Roman numerals, a clear lower pane showing the printed label inside, time-and-strike movement, ca. 1850-70 ...... **$175**

Shelf or mantel clock, Welch, Spring & Co., Forestville, Connecticut, Classical Revival rosewood veneer case, the paneled arched top above conforming molding framing a round molding around the dial w/Roman numerals & two roundels over a trapezoidal glass panel showing the pendulum, rectangular base w/ogee border, label inside, ca. 1880, 5 x 11 1/4", 16 1/4" h. **$200-250**

Shelf or mantel clock, Waterbury Clock Co., Waterbury, Connecticut, mahogany veneer "steeple" clock, pointed top flanked by turned tapering finials above a pointed two-pane glazed door, the top pane over the dial w/Roman numerals, the replaced pane w/a frosty & etched leafy vine design, half-round columns down the sides, stepped base, one finial replaced, eight-day movement, strike & alarm, ca. 1860-80, 4 3/8 x 11 1/4", 19 1/4" h. **$250-300**

Shelf or mantel clock, Waterbury Clock Co., Waterbury, Connecticut, round-top walnut case, an arched top molding continuing to tapering gilt spear points at the front flanking the tall glazed door w/gilt scroll decoration & opening to the replaced dial face w/Roman numerals, rectangular molded base, eight-day movement, strike & alarm, adjustable mercury pendulum, late 19th c., 4 3/4 x 11 1/4", 17 1/4" h. **$200-300**

Shelf or mantel, Ansonia Clock Co., New York, New York, gingerbread-style kitchen shelf clock, the stamped oak case w/a high arched & scroll-cut crest molded w/overall ornate scrolling leaf & shell-like design above the arched panel w/ tall glazed door opening to a metal dial w/Roman numerals, the lower door decorated w/gilt-stenciled swag design, smaller tapering scroll- stamped wings flanking the lower door, molded flat flaring base, late 19th c., 22" h. **$184**

Shelf or mantel, Art Deco-style, walnut & rosewood veneer, the long gently arched case w/fine veneered designs centering a domed glass round door w/brass bezel opening to a yellow chapter ring w/silvered Arabic numerals, ca. 1920s, 18 1/2" l. **$81**

Shelf or mantel, Atkins Clock Mfg., Bristol, Connecticut, upright stepped rosewood veneer case, a flat top w/ blocked front corners above an upper case w/canted corner panels flanking a glazed door over the painted dial w/ Roman numerals & gilt- stenciled on black border, a mid-molding w/canted corners stepped out slightly above canted paneled front corners flanking a short, long rectangular mirrored door opening to an iron & brass patent equalizing lever spring thirty-day movement, labeled on the back of the case, ca. 1855-58, 17 3/4" h... **$3,525**

Shelf or mantel, Birge & Fuller, Bristol, Connecticut, Gothic Revival double-steeple style mahogany veneer case, the pointed upper case w/pointed corner steeple finials above the pointed two-part glazed door, the upper panel showing the painted dial w/Roman numerals & an open escapement, the short lower panel reverse-painted w/a green border surrounding a silver, white & red diamond design, the stepped-out lower case w/two pointed corner steeple finials above a case w/a long low rectangular glazed door reverse-painted w/a blue border around a design w/a large oval in white on grey reverse-painted w/stylized red & white blossoms & leaves, flat base, thirty-hour movement marked "J. Ives Patent Accelerating Lever Spring Movement," ca. 1845, 24 1/4" h. **$3,290**

Shelf or mantel, Classical-style, mahogany veneer & stenciled case, the arched crestrail w/a gilt-stenciled basket of flowers on black flanked by mahogany corner blocks, the tall case w/half-round turned columns in black w/gilt stenciled designs flanking the tall two-part glazed door, the upper glass panel showing the floral-painted white dial w/Roman numerals, the taller lower panel w/a reverse-painted gilt-stenciled black border around the reverse-painted bust portrait of General Lafayette, probably produced about the time of his death in 1831, missing weights & pendulum, minor damage to case, unmarked, 33" h. **$1,115**

Shelf or mantel, commemorative-type, the flat upright bronzed-metal case front w/scrolled sides topped by a wreath enclosing a bust portrait of Admiral Dewey, hero of the 1898 Spanish-American War, "Dewey - Manila" cast below the bust & above the round dial w/a brass bezel & Arabic numerals, the lower case cast w/cannon, weapons & an American shield, non-working, ca. 1898, 9 1/2" h. **$348**

Shelf or mantel, gilt-bronze & gilt-brass, figural Troubadour-style, the metal Gothic Revival upright rectangular base decorated w/ the figure of an angel across the apron & Gothic figures at the front corners centered by figural panels & the small metal dial w/Roman numerals, the top mounted by a large figure of an angel musician guarding the arts of the past & leaning upon a square pedestal inscribed "Francois I - Raphael - Leonardo da Vinci," France, second quarter 19th c., 22 1/2" h. **$1,150**

Shelf or mantel, Knox (Archibald) for Liberty & Co., London, England, pewter & enamel, Art Nouveau style, the upright rectangular pewter case w/the cut-out front face panel cast w/leaves & berries, the large dial w/Arabic numerals enameled w/a mottled purple & green ground & centered by a red dot & gilt scroll design, ca. 1902-05, 8 1/8" h. **$17,925**

Shelf or mantel, Louis XVI-Style, gilt-metal porcelain-mounted case, a tall upright case topped w/an ornate gilt-metal urn w/a porcelain body painted in dark blue around a reserve of birds & flowers, the arched main case w/ cast ribbons & flower finials above sides w/cast corner busts, rosettes & leafy fruiting vines, a large round porcelain dial w/blue outlining white blocks w/Roman numerals centered by a ring of painted florals, a large open porcelain panel below the dial h.p. w/a color scene of peasant lovers resting beneath a large tree, the wide rounded & stepped lower case raised on ornate outswept scroll feet joined by a fruit-and-leaf-cast apron, France, ca. 1890, missing pendulum, 16 1/2" h. **$805**

Shelf or mantel, Parian & gilt-bronze, figural, the oval base w/small gilt-bronze feet & a gilt-bronze band topped by a Parian figure group forming the clock case, a young girl wearing a bonnet leaning against one side & looking into a nest of small birds, a flowering rose vine up the other side, all centering a brass bezel & domed glass door opening to a porcelain dial w/Roman numerals, incised mark of the Sevres factory, France, second half 19th c., 10" h. **$345**

Shelf or mantel, polished slate & green marble, the long rectangular slate base w/a serpentine apron banded around the top w/green marble, the top fitted w/a pair of heavy slate scrolls w/small oval marble insets supporting a large cylindrical slate case w/a marble ring front enclosing the dial w/a porcelain chapter ring w/Roman numerals around the open escapement movement, Europe, ca. 1900, 17" h. **$288**

Shelf or mantel, Terry (Eli) & Sons, Plymouth, Connecticut, Federal era Pillar & Scroll clock, mahogany veneer case, a broken-scroll pediment centered by a brass urn-form finial & flanked by matching corner finials, the case w/slender colonettes flanking the two-part door, the large upper glazed panel showing the painted dial w/Arabic numerals, the short rectangular lower glass door panel reverse-painted w/a landscape w/river & mansion, a thin molded base w/serpentine apron & thin French feet, labeled inside, ca. 1820, 31 1/2" h. **$4,140**

Shelf or mantel, Thomas (Seth) Clock Co., Plymouth, Connecticut, fancy walnut gingerbread-style case, the very tall scrolled & arched crest mounted at the center w/an arched plaque w/roundel & matching roundels at the corner wings, overall line-incised vines, the arched panel door opening to a white dial w/Roman numerals, the lower door gilt-stenciled w/ stylized ferns, blossoms & scrolls, pointed scroll wings flanking the lower door, on a flaring molded base, late 19th c., 22 3/4" h. **$207**

Shelf or mantel, Victorian Renaissance Revival walnut & burl walnut gingerbread-style, the high upper case topped w/a peaked & pierced crestrail w/blocks above a flaring molded flat cornice over a line-incised frieze band & a tall scroll-cut glazed door opening to a painted metal dial w/Roman numerals & an open escapement, the lower door stenciled in silver w/stylized florals & exposing the fancy brass pendulum set w/a white on black cameo, deep molded base w/incised lines, a center roundel & small burl panels, time-and-strike movement, late quarter 19th c., 21" h. **$173**

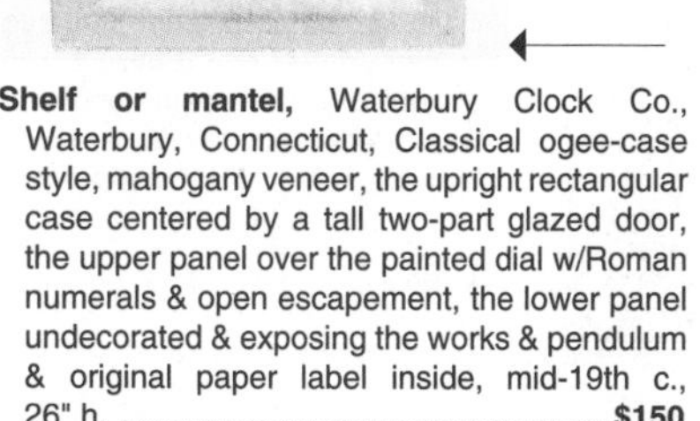

Shelf or mantel, Waterbury Clock Co., Waterbury, Connecticut, Classical ogee-case style, mahogany veneer, the upright rectangular case centered by a tall two-part glazed door, the upper panel over the painted dial w/Roman numerals & open escapement, the lower panel undecorated & exposing the works & pendulum & original paper label inside, mid-19th c., 26" h. **$150**

Shelf or mantel, Welch (E.N.) Manufacturing Co., Bristol, Connecticut, Classical style mahogany veneer case, tall upright form w/a flat peaked crestrail flanked by corner blocks above flat side pilasters flanking the tall two-part glazed door, the upper panel w/gilt-stenciled spandrels around the large white dial w/Roman numerals, the lower glass panel w/ a gilt-stenciled design of flowers & twigs framing a central oval reserve showing a scene of ships in a harbor, flat molded base, second-half 19th c., 26 1/2" h. **$259**

Swinging arm clock, bronzed white metal, a round plinth base supporting a tall cast-metal figure of a Classical maiden painted in natural colors, one arm to her chin, the other raised to support the swinging clock movement composed of a large gilt-metal ball mounted w/Arabic numerals & enclosing the clock movement & attached to the swinging open bar pendulum w/a heavy ball base drop, late 19th c., 28" h. .. **$1,064**

Wall clock, Atkins Clock Co., Bristol, Connecticut, rosewood veneer cottage-style, arched paneled top over a conforming door w/two glass panes, upper pane over the original painted dial w/Roman numerals, lower pane w/original gilt-stenciled rose & wreath decor, interior label coming loose, 30-hour movement, time & alarm, ca. 1865, 10 1/4" h. **$252**

Well-made and maintained clocks are valuable and in constant demand. If you prepare your clock for sale properly and ask a fair price, you should have little difficulty selling it.

Wall clock, Black Forest-type, ornate carved walnut case w/a large carved crest of a spread-winged eagle attacking a mountain goat, the wide sides of the rounded case finely carved w/ evergreen trees & roots entwining around the round black glass dial w/white Roman numerals, two further carved goats at the bottom of the case, eight-day movement, Germany, late 19th - early 20th c., dial possibly replaced, overall 47" h. **$3,600**

Wall clock, Bourgis-Chevalier, Billom, France, brass, the top case front composed of a large rectangular stamped brass plate topped by scrolls w/fruits & flowers around the sides & bottom all enclosing a large white enameled dial w/Roman numerals & signed by the maker, a long openwork wire pendulum w/a large brass lyre-topped pendulum bob, 19th c., 13" w., 54 3/4" h. **$805**

Wall clock, Junghans, Germany, mahogany-finished hardwood box-style, arched pediment w/ applied brass classical wreath & swags above top corner blocks w/similar brass trim flanking the two-pane glass front, the top pane over the celluloid dial w/Arabic numerals, the lower long pane w/slender brass wire overlay showing the pendulum & large brass bob, half-round base apron w/applied brass wreath, eight-day time & strike movement, ca. 1920, 12" w., 33" h. **$900-1,000**

Wall clock, Kroeber (Frederick J.) Clock Co., New York, New York, Model No. 46, Victorian Neo-Gothic style walnut case, the pointed pediment w/blossom finial flanked by matching corner finials above shaped sides w/applied half-round bobbins flanking the rounded tall glass door opening to the dial w/Roman numerals & pendulum w/large brass bob, deep base drop w/Gothic-style curved bracket trim, eight-day movement, time & strike, original finish, ca. 1890, 4 3/4 x 9 1/2", 33 1/2" h. **$800-1,000**

Wall clock, Mauthe Clock Co., Germany, Berliner style, walnut & softwood case, a cast-metal spread-winged eagle finial atop the high stepped pediment w/shell carving flanked by corner blocks w/urn-turned finials over the stepped flat cornice above boldly ring-and-baluster-turned half-columns flanking the dial panel w/leaf carvings in each corner around the wide brass bezel enclosing the celluloid chapter ring w/Arabic numerals centered by an embossed brass Art Nouveau floral center disk, turned drop finials at the front base corners backed by a large, long scroll-cut board behind the free-hanging ornate floral-stamped pendulum bob, eight-hour time & strike movement w/hour & half hour gong strike, ca. 1895-1910, 15" w., 36" h. **$1,200-1,500**

Wall clock, Sessions Clock Co., Bristol, Connecticut, miniature "Aztec" model Mission Oak case, a square molded frame enclosing the square wood dial face w/ applied brass Arabic numerals, the free-hanging pendulum w/ brass bob backed by a lattice framework, eight-day time & strike movement, ca. 1915-20, 10" w., 19" h. **$500-600**

Wall clock, Thomas (Seth) Clock Co., Plymouth, Connecticut, "World" model, oak case w/a large octagonal top framing the brass bezel enclosing the dial w/Roman numerals & sweep seconds hand, the long pointed drop base enclosing a pointed glass door over the pendulum w/a brass bob, double spring 15-day movement w/Graham dead beat escapement, ca. 1905-15, 17" w., 32" h. **$1,500-1,750**

Wall clock, novelty movement, hand-carved landscape w/a waterwheel & stream, trees & an onion-dome church w/the clock dial set in the tower, framed, eight-day seven-jewel movement, string on reverse runs from waterwheel to clock & is wound by turning the wheel, Germany, ca. 1950s, 15 x 31" **$300**

Wall clock, Waterbury Clock Co., Waterbury, Connecticut, "Galesburg" model, long oak case, the molded arched crest centered by a block w/turned urn finial flanked by turned corner finials, short reeded columns & turned drops flank the top sides above the tall arched & glazed door, a wood molding encloses the brass bezel & original paper dial w/ Roman numerals, the long lower pane shows the pendulum & large brass bob, short reeded columns & finials flank the bottom of the door, a long stepped & tapering base drop w/a turned finial, two drop finials at the bottom case corners, original finish, late 19th - early 20th c., eight-day time & strike movement w/half-hour gong strike, 52" h. **$1,069**

Wall clock, Waterbury Clock Co., Waterbury, Connecticut, Classical Revival style rosewood veneer case, the flat stepped cornice over an ogee panel flanked by end blocks above half-round maple columns w/gilt capitals & bases flanking the two-pane door, the large upper pane over the painted tin face w/Roman numerals & green-stenciled leaves, the lower door pane reverse- painted w/a bluebird in a gilt ring surrounded by flowers on a tan ground, deep blocked ogee base, open escapement, paper label inside, ca. 1890, 4 3/8 x 14 3/4", 24 3/4" h. **$600-700**

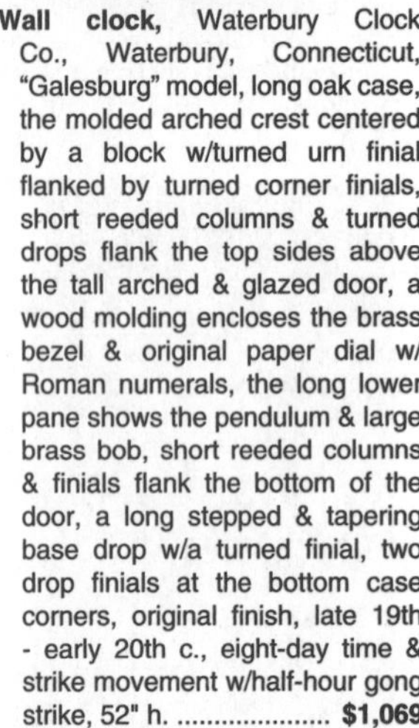

Wall clock, Welch (E.N.) Mfg. Co., Bristol, Connecticut (attributed), hanging oak kitchen-style, the high arched crest w/a carved shell above scrolls & blocked corners above carved scrolls & notch-cut sides flanking the angled arched door w/beaded edging & ornate gilt stencil decoration, dial w/Roman numerals, flat built-in shelf above a scroll-stamped apron centered by an inset level above the pointed scallop-cut drop, eight-day movement, strike & alarm, old case refinish, late 19th c., 4 1/2 x 14 3/8", 27 3/4" h. **$350-400**

Wall clock, Waterbury Clock Co., Waterbury, Connecticut, short-drop salesman's sample, stained softwood, dial w/Arabic numerals, eight-day movement, time-only, ca. 1920, 4 3/8 x 8", 12 1/2" h. **$200-300**

Wall clock, Welch (E.N.) Mfg. Co., Bristol, Connecticut, octagonal drop wall case, original dark varnish finish, the stepped octagonal top w/a large brass bezel enclosing the dial w/Roman numerals, sweep seconds hands & an outer day-of-the-month band, the short pointed drop case w/a small glass door w/gilt trim, eight-day movement, time, strike & calendar, open escapement, minor wear on face, ca. 1890, 4 1/2 x 17", 22" h. **$350-400**

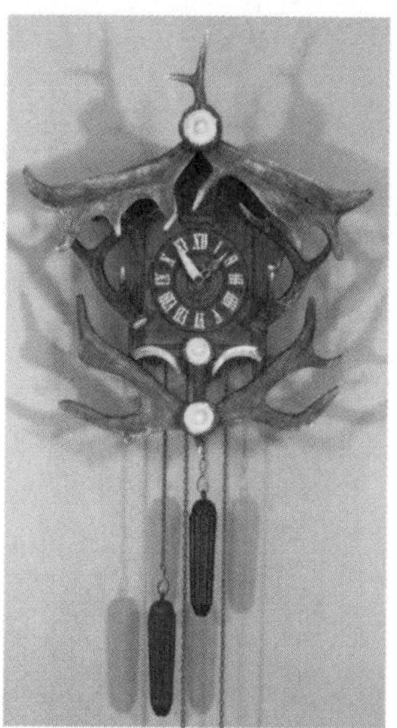

Wall cuckoo clock, antler-mounted carved lindenwood, the small central wooden case centered w/ a chapter ring mounted w/carved bone Roman numerals & handles, suspending long chains w/long weights, the clock case enclosed by a pair of peaked carved & polished antlers joined by a carved roundel, a smaller pair of antlers below the case forming the pendulum counterweight, Schwarzwald region of Germany, late 19th c., lower antler counterweight broken & spliced, one bone hand replaced w/an aluminum one, 18" w., 21" h. **$201**

Wall mirror-clock, Classical style, large rectangular frame in gilt & black w/corner blocks w/metal florettes joined by half-round ring- & rod-turned spindles, the deep pine case hinged to open, the top panel of the front reverse-painted w/a brown ground & gold, black & reddish-brown leaves framing a clear round center showing the clock dial w/Roman numerals above the long rectangular mirror, the case holding the brass works w/weight, pendulum & key, dial signed "B. Morrill, Boscawen," New Hampshire, first half 19th c., some edge damage & touch-up, hinges & reverse-painted panel replaced, 18 1/4 x 38 1/4" **$1,265**

←

Wall regulator clock, Ingraham & Co., Bristol, Connecticut, "Western Union" model, long oak case w/ a flat rectangular top w/a wide cornice lightly carved & centered by a fan device above the flat case molding enclosing the tall, wide two-pane glazed door, the upper pane w/black corners centered by the large brass bezel & dial w/ Roman numerals, the lower pane w/a gilt Greek key border band & the word "Regulator" over the pendulum & large brass bob, short base brackets flank the scroll-cut & carved drop backboard, late 19th - early 20th c., 37" h. .. **$338**

Wall regulator clock, Ansonia Clock Co., Ansonia, Connecticut, "Regulator A" model, walnut veneer case w/a large octagonal top section w/molded black ring around the brass bezel enclosing the paper dial w/Roman numerals & an outer calendar date ring w/ Arabic numerals, the long drop case w/a pointed bottom w/conforming molding framing the glazed door printed w/"Regulator A," pendulum w/large brass bob, eight-day time & strike movement, ca. 1900-10, 17" w., 32" h. **$900- 1,000**

Wall regulator clock, oak, a simple arched paneled crestrail above a narrow molded cornice above a case w/a long paneled door, the upper wood panel around a brass bezel & enameled dial w/Roman numerals, the lower door panel composed of geometric beveled glass sections, flat base above a pair of quarter-round brackets & an arched drop backboard, Germany, early 20th c., 33" h. **$316**

Wall regulator clock, Sessions Clock Co., Bristol, Connecticut, "Regular E" model, pressed oak case, a large wide octagonal top w/molded bands around the brass bezel enclosing the original paper dial w/Roman numerals & outer calendar date band w/ Arabic numerals, the pointed drop case w/stamped molding on the glazed door printed w/"Regulator," pendulum w/large brass bob, eight-day time & strike movement, ca. 1915, 16 1/2" w. top, 38" h. **$850-950**

Wall regulator clock, Sessions Clock Co., Bristol, Connecticut, oak case w/wide flaring flat cornice above the large two-pane door, the top pane reverse-painted in black w/a gold ring over the paper dial w/Arabic numerals, the lower pane banded in gold & printed "Regulator," showing the pendulum w/brass bob, molded base above cutout side scallops & a scroll-cut backboard w/stamped designs, eight-day movement, time-only, original finish, foxing on paper dial, ca. 1900, 5 1/8 x 17 3/4", 36" h. **$700-800**

Wall regulator clock, tall rectangular mahogany case w/a long glazed door w/small carved scrolls flanking the arched top, a wide brass bezel enclosing the porcelain dial w/Roman numerals, a long gridiron brass pendulum w/harp design over the large brass disk bob, eight-day time-only pinwheel movement, France, late 19th - early 20th c., 61" h. **$2,138**

Wall regulator clock, Thomas (Seth) Clock Co., Plymouth, Connecticut, "No. 2" model, tall oak case w/a large molded round top enclosing the brass bezel & painted dial w/Roman numerals & sweep seconds hand, the long rectangular drop base w/a tall rectangular molding enclosing a glass pane over the cylindrical brass weight & large brass pendulum bob, ca. 1890-1900, 17" w., 36" h. **$1,800-2,000**

Wall Vienna Regulator clock, fancy carved walnut case, a high crest w/a flat top molding above a scroll-carved & pierced panel fitted w/pairs of small turned spindles flanking half-round spindles centered by a carved classical face, the corner blocks w/urn- form finials, the tall arched glass front showing the white enamel dial w/Roman numerals & large brass pendulum, the case sides w/ring-turned columns resting on blocks on a flat base above turned round corner droops & a curved & blocked central drop w/ knob finial drop, Europe, late 19th c., 31" h. **$259**

COCA-COLA MARKET REPORT

Pharmacist Dr. John Stith Pemberton created Coca-Cola as a medicinal drink in Atlanta, Georgia, in 1886. Within a few years after purchasing full rights to the company in 1888, Asa Candler began an advertising campaign for the product that has endured for nearly 140 years and is responsible for Coca-Cola being the most globally recognizable and available product in history. As a result, a vast amount of Coca-Cola memorabilia exists. However, most of the items that appreciate in value were made before about 1970. Made-for-collector items produced since that time have not generally appreciated significantly.

Hot Areas of Coca-Cola Collecting

Vintage (pre-1970) signs, calendars, and trays are some of the most popular collectibles as they are especially colorful and suited for display. Some early pieces can sell for $10,000 or more, depending on rarity and condition. Fortunately, later pieces are much more affordable and there are pieces that will fit any collector's budget. Other common collectibles include bottles, paper items, and toys. Lesser known items include Coca-Cola candy and gum. Original Coca-Cola art, a narrow specialty primarily for high-end collectors, can sell for $100,000 or more if the artwork is by a famous artist like Norman Rockwell or Haddon Sundblum.

The Role of Condition

With Coca-Cola collecting, as with all antiques and collectibles, condition is everything. As noted Coca-Cola authority Allan Petretti stated in *Petretti's Coca-Cola Collectibles*, 12th Ed., "In the beginning of organized Coca-Cola collecting, when prices were relatively low, collectors were willing to buy a piece in less than desirable condition with the intent to upgrade to a better piece later. But, as prices rose, many collectors opted to wait to find a piece in perfect or near perfect condition, eliminating the entire upgrade method of collecting. Over time, it became more difficult to sell medium or lesser grade pieces." It is perhaps even more difficult to find perfect early Coca-Cola items than other collectibles because Coca-Cola items date back to the 1880s, which is far earlier than many others. Also, a large percentage of Coca-Cola items were made of paper, which were intended to be ephemera. Plus, many of the paper items that did survive the early 20th century didn't make it past World War II, as they were donated to paper drives to support the war effort.

Fakes, Fantasy and Reproductions

The Coca-Cola collectibles field has been hit by a glut of fakes and reproductions, but most are perpetrated by those who are careless and want to make a quick buck off the naive and unsuspecting. Their work is usually crude, as they don't want to invest time and effort in making their wares accurate. So fakes are generally fairly easy to detect if you know what the genuine item looks like. In some cases, counterfeiters create fantasies, supposed originals of items that never existed in the first place.

Because the Coca-Cola market is so vast, it is a good idea to specialize, so you can develop your expertise and so your collection has a theme, which will help increase its marketability and value.

COCA-COLA ITEMS

Coca-Cola promotion has been achieved through the issuance of scores of small objects through the years. These, together with trays, signs and other articles bearing the name of this soft drink, are now sought by many collectors. The major reference in this field is Petretti's Coca-Cola Collectibles Price Guide, 12th Edition, by Allan Petretti (Krause Publications). An asterisk (*) indicates a piece which has been reproduced.

Calendar, 1921, roll-down type, color illustration of young woman wearing dark blue & white outfit & hat sitting in garden setting amid pink & yellow flowers & holding glass of Coke, metal band at top, portion of calendar pad for November at bottom, framed, 16 1/2 x 36" **$900**

Calendar, perpetual type, metal frame w/red button at top reading "Drink Coca-Cola in Bottles" in white lettering, the lower portion white w/gold trim, panel reading "Have a Coke" in red above paper calendar pages, the top showing date of Friday, March 27, 1953, 8 w. x 19" h. **$431**

Cooler, rectangular, red embossed tin advertising panels on all four sides, legs that have been cut down just above lower case storage rack, metal tag reads "The Coca-Cola Company Cooler Patented March 4, 1930. Mfg. by Glascock Bros. Mfg. Co. Muncie, IN," no top, 23 1/2 x 31 1/2", 31 3/4" h. **$374**

Clock counter sign, light-up type, brass colored metal, square clock w/white face & dark green number panel w/gold Arabic numerals, attached at side to panel reading "Drink Coca-Cola" in white lettering on red ground, all on base w/white front edge reading "Have a Coke" in green lettering, a Price Makers decal on back, 19 1/2" l., 8 1/2" h. **$840**

Counter sign, light-up type, aluminum frame holding rectangular panel reading "Drink Coca-Cola" in white lettering on red ground, marquee at top reading "Please Pay When Served" in green lettering on white, back marked "Price Bros. Chicago and New York," rare, 19" w., 9" h. **$575**

Beware of the vast amount of fake, reproduction, and fantasy Coca-Cola items on the market. This collectible category is one of the most heavily reproduced in the antiques and collectibles field.

Counter sign, light-up type, brass colored frame, square panel w/ silver textured ball in reverse & "Pause and Refresh" bisecting ball in gold lettering on dark green ground, attached at side to panel reading "Drink Coca-Cola in Bottles" in white lettering on red ground, all on base w/ white front edge reading "Have a Coke" in green lettering, Price Manufacturing label on rear, rare, 19 1/2" l., 9" h. **$1,840**

Counter sign, light-up type, metal frame, square panel w/textured glass dial reading "Pause" in yellow, attached at side to panel reading "Drink Coca-Cola in Bottles" in white lettering on red ground, all on base w/white front edge reading "Please Pay When Served" in green lettering, ca. 1950, corrosion to housing, glass dial cracked, not operational, 20" l., 9" h. **$431**

Counter sign, reverse printed transfer on glass in wooden base, rectangular, reads "Drink Coca-Cola" in white lettering on bright red ground, the rear w/original paper decal reading "Price Bros. The Sign of Quality Chicago, NY," the wooden base w/attached white panel reading "Coke" in red, 5 x 12" **$460**

Counter sign, light-up waterfall type, brass colored frame, square panel w/waterfall effect reading "Pause and Refresh" in gold on black ground w/green top & bottom borders, attached at side to panel reading "Drink Coca-Cola" in white lettering on red ground, all on base w/white front edge reading "Please Pay When Served" in green lettering, Price Manufacturing label on rear, rare, 19 1/2" l., 9" h. **$1,898**

Salesman's sample cooler, open-front version, red w/"Drink Coca-Cola" in white on front, comes w/carrying case, ring binder pages on inside of lid labeled "A Business Builder," & Cellotex insulation insert, 1939, paint touchups, exterior has been clear-coated, 7 1/4 x 12 1/4", 10 1/4" h. **$3,220**

Sign, wood, scroll sign spelling out "Drink Coca-Cola" in red atop fluted base, tail of first "C" marked "Trade Mark, Reg. U.S. Pat. Off.," by Kay of Austria Displays Inc., New York, 1930s, 6 3/4 x 20 1/4" **$1,380**

Thermometer, round, red center w/gold outline of Coke bottle & "Drink Coca-Cola" in white lettering, surrounded by green border w/black degree marks & numerals, black hand for indicating temperature, marked at bottom "Pam Clock Co. Mt. Vernon, New York 48," 12" d. **$518**

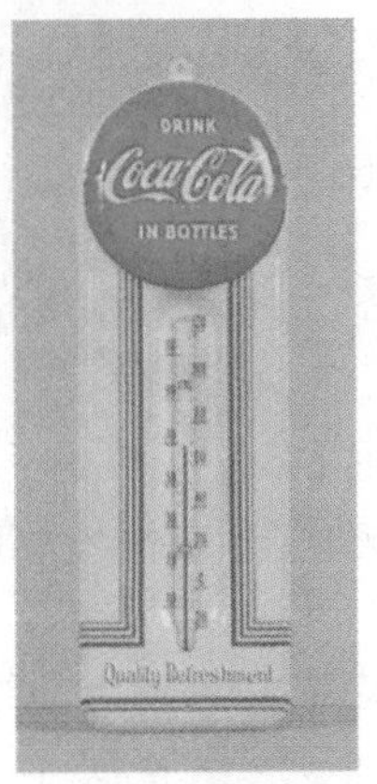

Thermometer, enameled tin litho, red button at top reads "Drink Coca-Cola in Bottles" in white lettering, thermometer flanked by black geometrical line decoration, bottom w/ more line decoration & reading "Quality Refreshment" in red, all on white ground, 9 1/2" h. **$230**

Tray, 1916, serving, rounded rectangular shape, center w/ color illustration of young woman wearing wide-brimmed hat & cream- colored dress seated under a tree near pink cut roses while holding a glass of Coke & looking back over her shoulder at viewer, "Drink Coca-Cola" in light blue letters at top, decorated gilt rim, edge wear, 8 1/2 x 19" **$220**

Tray, 1922, serving, tin litho, rounded rectangular shape, center panel w/ close-up color illustration of dark-haired young woman wearing peach dress & wide-brimmed hat w/pale blue ribbon holding flared glass of Coke & looking back over her shoulder toward viewer, "Coca-Cola" at top of gilt-trimmed dark border w/rolled rim, mottled finish, light surface pitting, paint chips to rolled rim, 10 1/2 x 13 1/2" .. **$460**

Tray, 1937, serving, tin litho, rounded rectangular shape, center panel w/color illustration of fair-haired young woman wearing bathing suit running on beach toward viewer & holding a bottle of Coke in each hand, a cape-like cover-up flowing behind her, the gilt-trimmed rim w/"Drink Coca-Cola" in yellow lettering on red ground at both top & bottom, American Art Works, 10 1/2 x 13 1/4" **$237**

Tray, 1939, serving, tin litho, rounded rectangular shape, center panel w/color illustration of young woman wearing white bathing suit & sandals sitting on towel on red-striped diving board & holding bottle of Coke, a rectangular red panel at top reading "Drink Coca-Cola - Delicious and Refreshing" in grey lettering, red rim w/ silver-grey trim, 10 1/2 x 13 1/2" **$259**

COMIC BOOK MARKET REPORT

Brent Frankenhoff, editor of Krause Publications' *Comics Buyers Guide* (www.CBGxtra.com), said that one of the major developments of 2010 is the move by Marvel, DC, and other publishers to produce comics in digital form for the iPad and other formats. They are creating both re-releases of back issues and same-day releases of new issues to increase lagging revenue caused by the recession and rising prices of print comics. Print editions now average between $3 and $4 each.

Frankenhoff also said that trade paperback compilations of comic book series are seeing increased sales. "The reason for their growing popularity," he explained, "is that in some cases the compilations are cheaper than buying individual issues. Other readers like to wait because they want to have a substantial chunk of reading."

On the auction front, rare, top grade comics have been blazing hot in 2010, smashing previous records in quick succession. For the first time this year, a comic has broken the seven-figure mark. On February 22, 2010, ComicConnect.com auctioned an Action Comics #1 (first Superman comic) for $1,000,000. The Certified Guaranty Company (www.cgccomics.com), the industry's most prominent independent comic authenticator and grader, assigned the comic a condition grade of 8.0 on a scale of 1 to 10. The significance of this sale is highlighted by the fact that just a year earlier, on March 13, 2009, an Action Comics #1 CGC 6.0 sold for $317,000, at the time the highest price ever paid for a comic, and that was with nearly 90 bidders competing for it.

Just three days later after the February 22 million-dollar sale, Heritage Auctions sold a copy of Detective Comics #27 (first appearance of Batman), CGC 8.0, for $1,075,500, indicating that the million dollar price tag wasn't just a fluke, but the beginning of a trend.

A month later, on March 29, 2010, ComicConnect.com, stunned the comics world with another record-breaking sale, this time of an Action Comics #1, CGC 8.5, for $1,500,000, upping the record by nearly a half million dollars in a single month. It is one of approximately 100 copies of the comic. This particular copy, however, was previously unknown, but in especially good condition, as it had been found tucked in a pile of magazines that protected it through the intervening decades since it was released in 1938.

Another example of the skyrocketing values of rare comics is the spectacular increase in value of a 1960 Green Lantern #1 (inaugural Green Lantern comic), CGC graded 9.5. In 2003, the comic sold for $18,975. In 2010, however, it sold for $50,787.50, more than ten times its 2003 price guide value.

Original comic art is on fire too. (These original artworks are the actual pieces that the artists created, rather than the reproductions made from them). For example, Charles Schulz's *Peanuts* comic strip panel that ran Sunday, July 31, 1966, featuring Snoopy vs. The Red Baron, sold for $101,575.

While it is difficult to predict the comics market with certainty, it seems likely that high-end comics will continue to break records. And regardless of their collector value, no doubt readers will continue to enjoy comics for their colorful art and entertaining stories.

COMIC BOOKS

Comic books, especially first or early issues of a series, are avidly collected today. Prices for some of the scarce ones have reached extremely high levels. Prices listed below show a range for copies from "Good" to "Mint" condition.

All Great Jungle Adventures, unnumbered, Fox Giant, 1949 .... **$300-1,200**

Attack on Planet Mars, Avon, 1951, dramatic spaceship battle cover scene **$350-1,100**

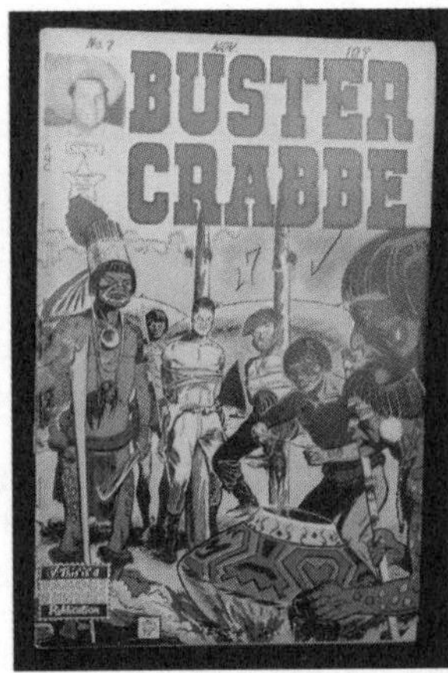

Buster Crabbe, #7, Famous Funnies Publications, 1952, Frazetta advertisement inside **$100-250**

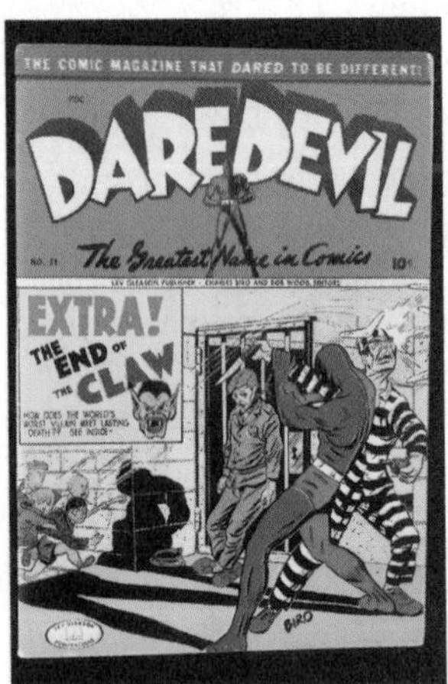

Daredevil, #31, Lev Gleason Publications, features the death of the Claw, 1940s **$400-1,200**

Doctor Fate and Hourman, #55, DC Comics, origins of the title characters w/the Green Lantern & Soloman Grundy, 1965 .. **$100-500**

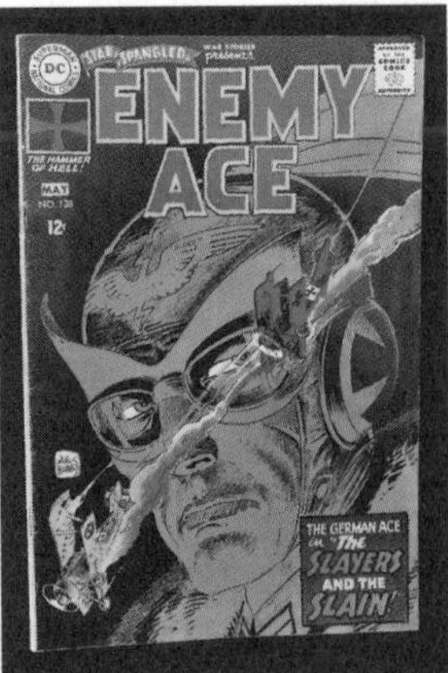

Enemy Ace, DC#138, Star Spangled War Stories, Joe Kubert, 1968 .... **$30-150**

To get the most money for a high-value comic book, have it condition-graded by a third-party grading service, such as the Certified Guaranty Company. The service will carefully inspect the comics for flaws, assign a grade, and seal it in transparent tamperproof case. This impartial grading gives buyers confidence that they are paying for an accurately described comic, which in turn, encourages higher prices.

Evel Knievel, Marvel Comics/Ideal toy Corp., unnumbered give-away, 1974 .... **$20-60**

Fantastic Four (The), #4, Marvel Comics, first Sub-Mariner appearance, 1962 .... **$1,200-6,000**

Fat Freddy's Comics & Stories, #1, Gilbert Shelton, 1970s **$6-15**

Ghosts, #1, DC Comics, 1971 .... **$50-250**

Hate, #1, Fantagraphics, 1990 .... **$10-30**

Iron Man and Sub-Mariner, #1, Marvel, one-shot, predates their individual #1 issues, 1968 .... **$75-300**

Jason vs Leatherface, #2, Topps Comics, Nancy Collins story, low print run, 1995 .... **$10-25**

←

→

Journey Into Mystery, #85, first appearance of Loki & Helmdall, 1960s **$800-2,000**

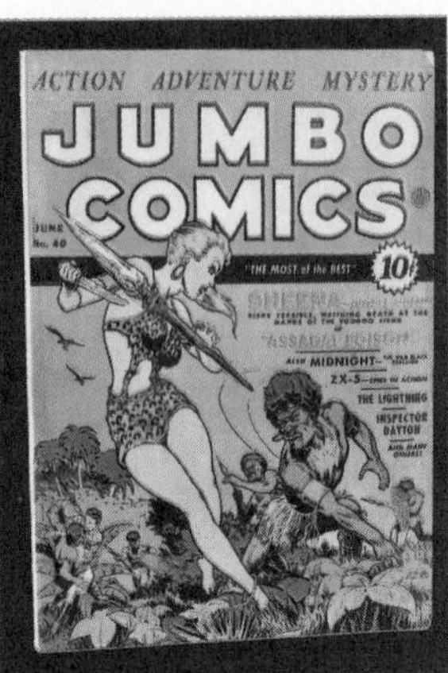

Jumbo Comics, #40, Fiction House Magazines, features Sheena, Jungle Queen, 1942 .... **$200-700**

Sabotage?, Crusader Comics #11, by Jack T. Chick, Christian warnings, 1979 .... **$5-15**

Secret Squirrel, #1, Gold Key, Hanna-Barbera comic, 1966 .... **$60-225**

Silver Surfer (The), #1, Marvel Comics, features origin story, 1960s **$600-1,500**

Suspense Comics, #8, Continental Magazines, L.B. Cole spider cover, mid-1940s **$1,500-6,000**

Teen Titans, #1, DC Comics, features Robin, Wonder Girl, Kid Flash & Aqualad, 1966 .... **$120-500**

The Challenger, #2, Interfaith Publications/TC Comics, anti-Fascist theme, 1945 .... **$100-450**

←

→

Weird Tales of Terror, Blue Bolt #111, L.B. Cole cover art **$200-600**

CURRIER & IVES PRINTS

This lithographic firm was founded in 1835 by Nathaniel Currier, with James M. Ives becoming a partner in 1857. Current events of the day were portrayed in the early days, and the prints were hand-colored. Landscapes, vessels, sport and hunting scenes of the West all became popular subjects. The firm was in existence until 1906. All prints listed are hand-colored unless otherwise noted. Numbers at the end of the listings refer to those used in Currier & Ives Prints - An Illustrated Checklist, by Frederick A. Conningham (Crown Publishers).

A Good Chance, large folio, 1863, framed, 2424, mat stain, subtle toning, minor foxing, repaired tear in corner edge, old tape residue on face edges & back **$4,700**

American Field Sports: Flush'd, large folio, 1857, framed, 149, hinged at top, mat stain, small loss on lower corner **$3,173**

American Winter Scenes - Evening, large folio, 1854, framed, 207, hinged at top, several repaired tears, minor toning **$3,408**

American Country Life - October Afternoon, large folio, N. Currier, 1855, framed, 122, margins trimmed, stains & small tears framed **$2,070**

American Forest Scene - Maple Sugaring, large folio, 1856, N. Currier, framed, 157, mat staining, toning, staining on back **$19,975**

Common Currier & Ives Print Sizes:

Trading Card: 3" x 5" or less

Very Small: Up to 7" x 9"

Small: 8-3/4" x 12-3/4"

Medium: 9" x 14" to 14" x 20"

Large: More than 14" x 20"

American Winter Sports - Deer Shooting "On the Shattagee," large folio, N. Currier, 1855, framed, 209, several repaired tears, some into image, light toning & stains **$3,055**

American Winter Sports - Trout Fishing "On Chateaugay Lake," large folio, 1856, N. Currier, framed, 210, light mat stains, minor tears, loss on margin edge **$4,994**

Camping Out "Some of the Right Sort," large folio, 1856, framed, 777, small loss in upper right corner **$3,408**

Cares of a Family (The), large folio, 1856, N. Currier, framed, 814, repaired margin tear, light toning, mat stains, framed **$2,468**

Catching a Trout, large folio, after Arthur Tait, 1854, framed, minor foxing & corner staining **$3,819**

Celebrated Horse Lexington (The), large folio, 1855, framed, 887, toning, light stains, hinged at top **$2,233**

Central Park, Winter. The Skating Carnival, small folio, undated, framed, 953, repaired tear in lower margin **$3,173**

City of New York (The), large folio, 1870, bird's-eye view looking north, framed, 1105, bands of pale staining, repaired tears at lower margin, minor margin damage & repairs **$8,963**

Clipper Ship "Nightingale," large folio, 1854, framed, 1159, scattered light spotty stains & few light vertical streaks **$2,938**

Clipper Ship "Red Jacket," large folio, 1855, framed, 1165, hinged at top, toning, light stains, few fox marks **$4,994**

Clipper Ship Dreadnought Off Tuskar Light, large folio, 1856, N. Currier, framed, 1144, toning, vertical light brown stains, scattered black stains in margins, faded inscriptions **$2,350**

General Tom Thumb...Now Performing with Barnum's Travelling Museum and Menagerie, small folio, 1849, N. Currier, standing on chair w/six small views up each side, evenly toned, framed **$231**

Grand Drive (The) - Central Park, N.Y., large folio, 1869, framed, 2481, light stains in lower margin, light toning **$4,700**

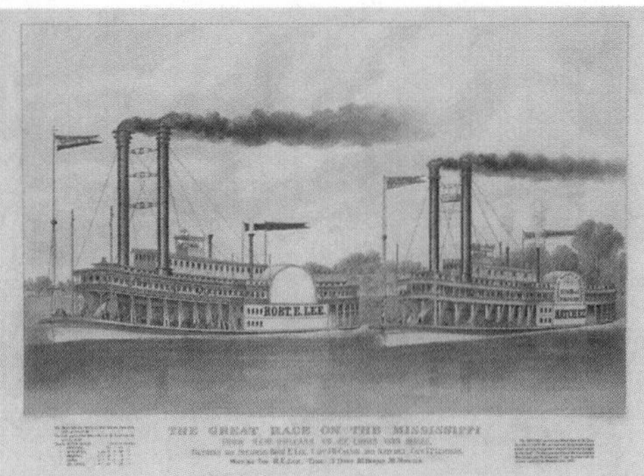

Great Race on the Mississippi from New Orleans to St. Louis (The), large folio, 1870, unframed **$3,738**

Hunter's Shanty (The), large folio, 1861, in a narrow modern frame, overall toning & foxing, No. 2993 .... **$1,035**

Landscape, Fruit and Flowers, large folio, 1862, 3440, framed, top corners reinforced, minor toning **$2,820**

Life of a Hunter (The) - A Tight Fix, large folio, 1861, 3522, repair to margin, framed **$44,063**

Life on the Prairie - The Buffalo Hunt, large folio, 1862, framed, 3527, several repaired tears, subtle toning, retouch to sky & margins **$5,288**

"Lightning Express Trains" (The) - Leaving the Junction, large folio, 1863, framed, 3535, tear left corner, toning, old ink inscription on back **$25,850**

Midnight Race on the Mississippi (A), large folio, 1860, 4116, margins reinforced, touch-up to scratch, repaired corners, framed **$11,163**

Mill-Dam at "Sleepy Hollow" (The), large folio, undated, framed, 4124, margins cut off, repaired, light toning **$823**

Mink Trapping - Prime, large folio, 1862, framed, 4139, tears in right edge, repaired tear in upper right edge, old tape remaining on back, light mat staining & minor foxing **$15,275**

Peytona and Fashion. In Their Great Match for $20,000, large folio, undated, N. Currier, ca. 1845, framed, 4763, several repaired tears, subtle toning **$4,700**

Preparing for Market, large folio, 1856, framed, 4870, repaired margin tears, light toning & stains, framed **$3,055**

Rail Shooting. On The Delaware, large folio, 1852, framed, 5054, light toning & mat stain, five repaired tears in margin edges, small surface abrasions **$2,703**

Ready For the Trot - "Bring Up Your Horses," large folio, 1877, framed, 5085, hinged at top, repaired tears to upper corner, light stains & toning **$1,998**

Splendid Naval Triumph on the Mississippi, April 24, 1862 (The), large folio, 1862, framed, 5659, repaired tear in margin, slight abrasions, part of bottom title trimmed **$1,058**

Western Farmer's Home (The), small folio, 1871, framed, 6619, some staining, ... **$161**

Whale Fishery, (The) - Sperm Whale "In a Flurry," large folio, 1852, 6627, repaired tear in margin, light staining **$8,813**

Winter in the Country - The Old Grist Mill, large folio, 1864, framed, repaired tear in lower title, light mat stain **$8,813**

DECOYS

Decoys have been used for years to lure flying water fowl into target range. They have been made of carved and turned wood, papier-mâché, canvas and metal. Some are in the category of outstanding folk art and command high prices.

Bluewing Teal drake, carved & painted wood, Mason factory, Challenge grade, original paint w/minor to moderate flaking & wear, several tiny dents & shot marks, branded "DWH" **$8,250**

Canada goose, Ben Schmidt, Detroit, Michigan, good feather carving detail, hollowed out from underside, detachable head w/ small metal plate at neck seam, original paint, crack in tail, second quarter 20th c. **$5,500**

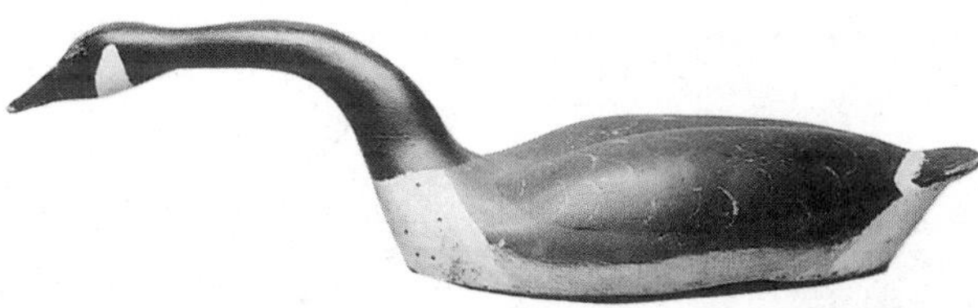

Canada goose, Marcel Dufour, Verdun, Quebec, Canada, swimming position, head turned slightly, original paint, shot marks **$1,100**

Canada goose, Sam Soper, Barnegat, New Jersey, swimming pose, hollow-carved w/good feather detail, original paint w/ good patina, minor wear, repair to crack in neck, early **$2,200**

Canvasback drake, Lee Dudley, Knott's Island, North Carolina, humpback "classic" style w/"V" wing carving, original paint w/ some overpaint removed, branded "ELM" for E.L. Mayer, vice president of Morse Point Gunning Club & Pocahontas Fowling Club, very rare, professional repair to bill, ca. 1900 .... **$25,300**

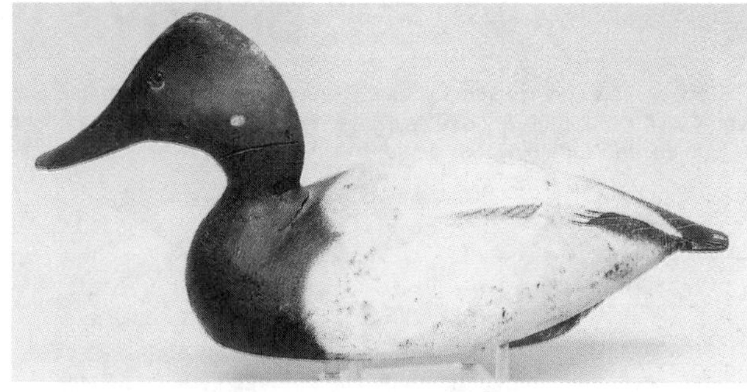

Canvasback drake, Ward Brothers, Crisfield, Maryland, 1932-36 model, original paint **$10,450**

Canvasback hen & drake, Ken Anger, Dunnville, Ontario, Canada, original paint, pr. **$4,620**

Goldeneye drake, Ward Brothers, Crisfield, Maryland, "Fat Jaw" model, head turned approximately 20 degrees & lifted slightly, dry original paint w/alligatored surface, old replaced glass eyes, ca. 1918 (ILLUS. left) **$28,600**

Gull, standing position, relief wing carving w/crossed wing tips, old black overpaint removed to show original paint, Long Island, New York, ca. 1900 .... **$12,650**

Merganser drake, carved & painted wood, Mason factory, Challenge grade, taken down to original paint w/minor wear, numerous dents & shot marks, some old neck filler replaced, first quarter 20th c. **$3,575**

Merganser drake, George Huey, Friendship, Maine, large red-breasted body w/slightly turned inlet head attached to body w/small wooden dowel, carved eyes, "G R HUEY" carved in underside, original paint, second quarter 20th c., professional repair to bill **$11,275**

Old squaw, Gus Wilson, South Portland, Maine, w/ characteristic carved eyes & raised shoulder & wings, dry original paint, swivel heads, rare, second quarter 20th c., pr. **$5,500**

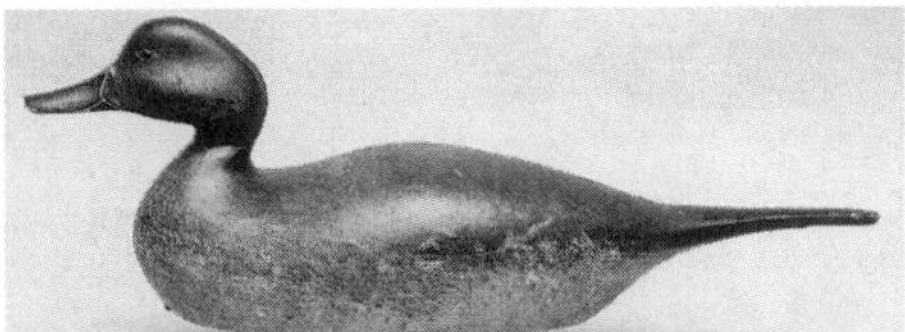

Pintail drake, Mason Factory, Detroit, Michigan, hollow body, original paint w/crazed & crackled surface, original feathering still visible, thin crack in tail secured from bottom w/two small nails, first quarter 20th c. **$9,900**

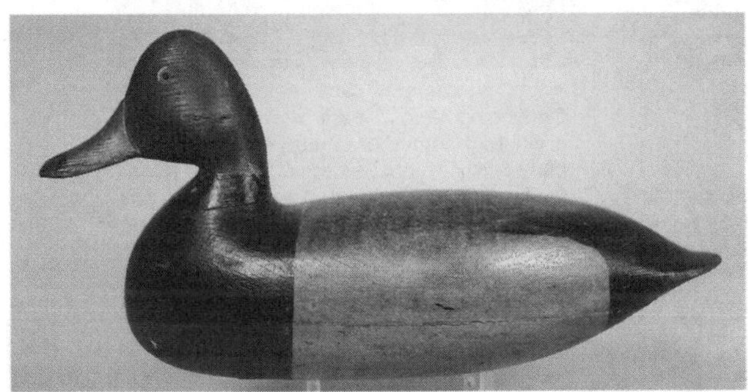

Redhead drake, Harry V. Shourds, Tuckerton, New Jersey, carved & painted wood w/original paint & minor wear, slight roughness on bill edge, some tiny dents, last quarter 19th c. **$1,540**

Trout, metal fins & tail, original paint, Lake Chautauqua, New York, 6 1/4" l. **$2,420**

Wood drake & hen, carved & painted wood, glass eyes & highly detailed bill carving, both were used as stick-ups & floaters, each w/painted initials "GRW" on the bottom, original paint w/fine patina & very minor wear, slight roughness on hen's tail & tiny chip under her bill, very small chip on top of drake's tail, both lightly hit by short, only five of these are known, Ontario, Canada, ca. 1900, pr. **$110,558**

DISNEY COLLECTIBLES

Alice in Wonderland movie cel, the White Rabbit running, shown in profile, gouache on celluloid, 1951, 3 x 4" **$239**

Disney characters card set, "Walt Disney Cartooning Cards," each w/a color picture of a different Disney character including Dumbo, Lady & the Tramp, Pinocchio & Mickey Mouse, the back of each w/instructions on how to draw the character, 1959, complete set of 18 cards (ILLUS. of part).. **$278**

Donald Duck & Goofy toy, windup tin, Donald & Goofy Duet, large Goofy standing on a large drum w/a small Donald on a drum in front of him, 1946, Marx, Goofy missing one arm, replaced ears, 10 1/4" h. **$201**

The paint on tin toys can easily be scratched by dust wiped across the surface, so be sure to wash carefully with a damp cloth. Even better, store a tin toy in a ventilated display case to prevent dust from accumulating.

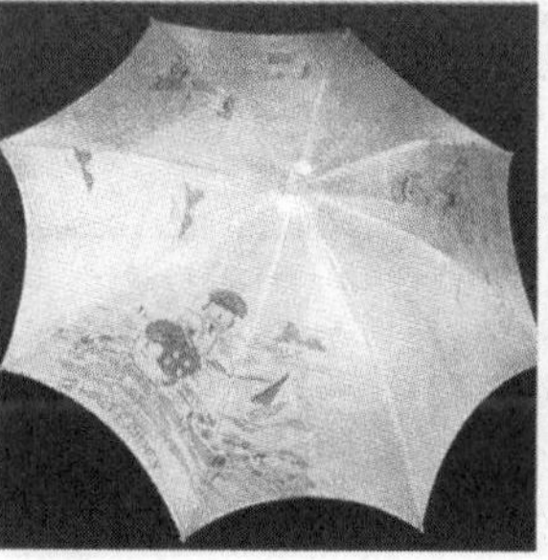

Donald Duck parasol, child's, white fabric printed around top w/three different color vignettes of the early long-billed Donald, wooden handle, 1930s, excellent condition, 20" d. open, 19 1/2" l. (ILLUS. of two views) **$276**

Donald Duck toy, windup tin, Donald Duck walker, by Schuco, original colorful box w/one inside flap missing, ca. 1950s, 6" h. **$480**

Donald Duck toy, windup tin, Donald the Drummer, Donald sways back & forth & nods & drums, Line-Mar, Japan, 6" h. **$210**

Dwarf Dopey movie cel, half-length portrait of Dopey wearing an oversized jacket, applied to a wood veneer background, original descriptive label on the back, 1937, cel 3" w., overall 5 1/2 x 6" **$1,793**

Dwarfs Doc & Dopey movie cel, Dopey & Doc looking at diamonds, applied to a wood veneer background, original sticker on the back, minor chipping & some wrinkling on the cel, 1937, cel 4" sq., overall 7 x 9" **$3,346**

Fantasia movie premier program, large format souvenir-type printed on the cover w/a large black title panel surrounded by colored sketches of various characters from the movie, virtually mint, 1940, 9 1/2 x 12 1/2" **$225**

Fantasia pre-production sketch, pastel on paper, a scene of two centaurettes frolicking, in shades of green, yellow & blue, 1940, matted & framed, 7 x 11" **$1,315**

Ferdinand the Bull toy, windup tin, Ferdinand & the matador, each figure on a platform joined by a wheeled base, Louis Marx & Co., 1938, working, 7" l. **$240**

Ferdinand the Bull toy, key-wind tin, walking Ferdinand w/fabric flowers in his mouth, marked "Japan - Walt Disney Productions," 1938, all original w/box, 5 1/2" l., 4" h. **$360**

Mickey Mouse & Pluto toy, windup tin & celluloid, celluloid figure of Mickey standing on two-wheeled platform joined by a wire to a larger wheeled platform w/a figure of Pluto running, Japan, 1930s, original paint, missing string reins, working, overall 8" l. **$2,990**

Mickey Mouse bank, cast pot metal, a standing pie-eyed Mickey w/his arms spread beside a spherical bank marked "Delaware Water Gap," on a thin rectangular base, base marked "Germany," original paint & miniature padlock on the bank, 1930s, base 3 1/4" l., Mickey 3 1/2" h. ... **$1,553**

Mickey Mouse figure, celluloid nodder, flattened standing figure of Mickey w/a nodding head, holding a square banjo, on a blue round base, excellent original paint & rare paper label reading "Mickey Mouse Copt. 1928, 1930 by Walter E. Disney," made in Japan, 7" h. **$805**

Mickey Mouse game, "Pin The Tail On 'Mickey'," a large cloth banner printed in red, black & white w/a rear few of Mickey, comes w/original cloth tails & original cardboard box, Marks Bros., Boston, apparently never used, early 1930s, box 9 x 10 1/2", banner 17 x 21", the set **$604**

Mickey Mouse pencil sharpener, celluloid, rounded upright figure of Mickey w/sharpener in the base, 1930s, original paint, slight rim damage at back, 3" h. **$98**

Mickey Mouse poster, for a color cartoon, a bright yellow background printed w/a large image of Mickey & colorful wording reading "now in Technicolor - Walt Disney's Mickey Mouse - Released thru United Artists," one-sheet, 1935, linen-backed, 27 x 41" ... **$14,350**

Mickey Mouse toy, windup tin, "Jazz Drummer," plunger causes a lithographed two-dimensional Mickey to play the drum, by Nifty, Germany, ca. 1931, 6 3/4" h., good working condition **$2,100**

Mickey Mouse toy, windup tin, Mickey Mouse Ferris Wheel, colorful printing w/the head of Mickey at the side of the base, other Disney characters on the baskets, by Chein, mechanism replaced, other restoration, 17" h. **$230**

Minnie Mouse toy, windup tin, "Minnie Mouse Knitter," Minnie sitting in rocking chair knitting, colorful, Line Mar, Japan, 1950s, mechanism works but skips, 6 1/2" h. **$288**

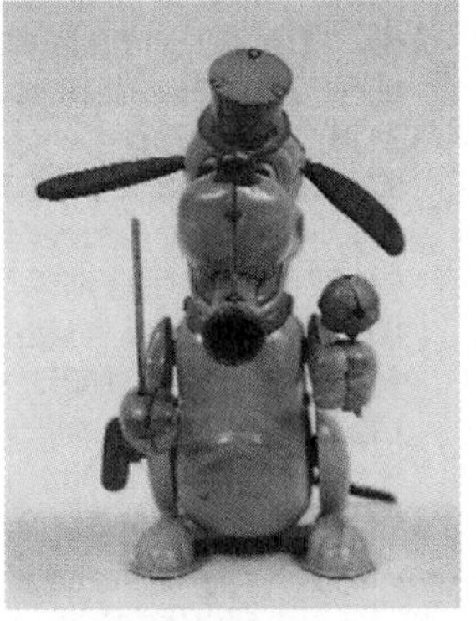

Pluto toy, windup tin, "Drum Major," seated Pluto holding a horn, cane & bell, Line Mar, Japan, replaced ears, 5 1/2" h. **$201**

Pluto toy, pull-type w/bell, lithographed paper on wood figure of a racing Pluto pulling a four-wheeled platform w/bell, three small lithographed cardboard figures of Mickey Mouse are detached from the platform & one is missing, early 1930s, overall 20 1/2" l. **$1,898**

Sleeping Beauty movie cel, a forest landscape w/a small figure of Briar Rose walking w/her basket, gouache on celluloid applied to an airbrushed background, 1959, 1 1/2 x 3" **$837**

Snow White & the Seven Dwarfs candy containers, hand-painted papier-mâché, many w/original tags marked "© W.D.P. Container made in Germany," four w/fixed heads, 1930s, large 5 1/2" h., the set **$180**

Snow White & the Seven Dwarfs dolls, Snow White in stockinet w/painted features, black mohair wig & wearing a velvet & silk dress w/ the hem silk screened w/images of the Dwarfs, made by Ideal, the seven Dwarfs in jointed composition w/molded shoes & felt outfits & hats w/their names, made by Knickerbocker, 1930s, Dwarfs 9" h., Snow White 15 1/2" h., the set **$1,610**

Snow White & the Seven Dwarfs lawn ornaments, cast cement, small airbrushed & hand-painted figures of each Dwarf & a reclining Snow White, minor chipping & fading, Doc missing right arm, break in right elbow of Snow white, largest 9 1/4" h., the set **$230**

Snow White & the Seven Dwarfs movie cel, scene of Snow White gazing down into the wishing well w/eight doves perched around the rim, gouache on celluloid applied to an airbrushed background, vintage matte board w/handwritten pencil notation, also marked on the back & w/copyright stickers, 1937, 4 x 5 1/2" **$4,541**

Walt Disney photograph, black & white image signed by Walt Disney, framed & mounted on an 8 x 10" mat board, photo 7 x 9" **$3,123**

Traditional movie animation, such as was used to produce Disney's *Snow White and the Seven Dwarfs*, relied on multiplane cameras. The cameras took photographs of layers of animation cels moving at various distances and speeds to produce the illusion of movement and depth.

DOLLS

A.M. (Armand Marseille) bisque socket head toddler, marked "1894 - A.M. 3/0 DEP," set blue eyes, single-stroke brows, open mouth w/four upper teeth, original blonde mohair wig, jointed wood & composition body, wearing all original outfit of light blue lace-trimmed print dress, lace-trimmed bonnet, underclothing, black cotton socks w/garters attached to chemise, original handmade shoes, minor repair on neck socket, 11" **$400**

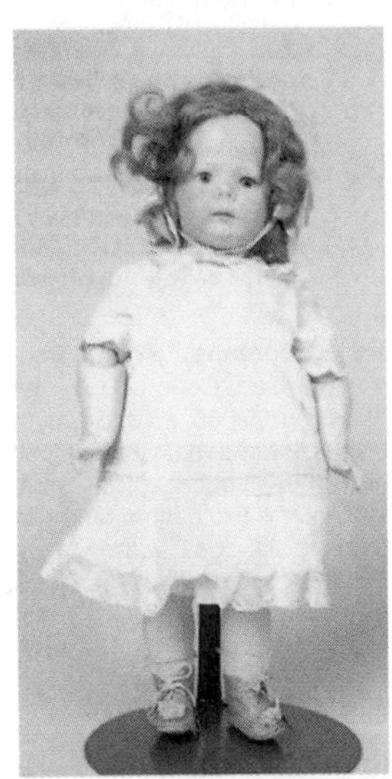

A.M. bisque head "Fany" girl, marked "AM Fany 231," blue sleep eyes, closed mouth, blonde mohair wig, composition ball-jointed child's body w/straight wrists, wearing white dress, white bonnet w/blue ribbon, socks & shoes, pinkie missing on right hand, 15 1/2" **$5,175**

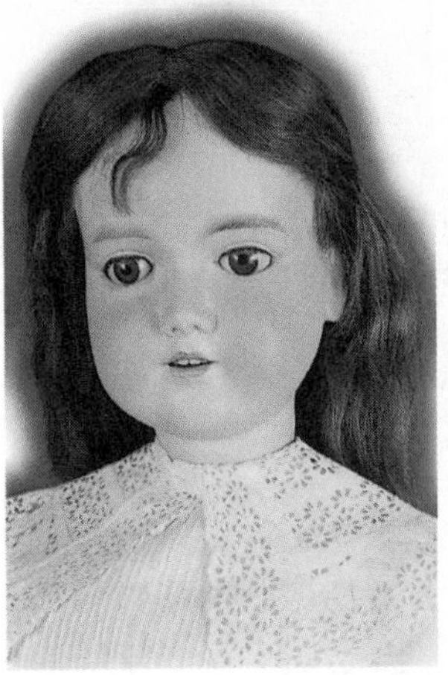

A.M. bisque socket head girl, marked "A. 18 M." on back of head, bisque socket head w/blue sleep eyes, molded & feathered brows, painted lashes, open mouth w/four upper teeth, long brown h. h. (human hair) wig, jointed wood & composition body, wearing antique child's dress w/eyelet trim & many tucks, underclothing, knit socks, black leather shoes, missing real lashes, some repair on body, minor cracks in finish, 39" **$1,200**

A.M. Googlies, marked "Germany - 323 - A. 11/0 M." on back of heads, bisque socket heads w/blue sleep side-glancing eyes, single-stroke brows, painted lashes, closed smiling mouths, original blond mohair wigs, crude five-piece bodies w/unfinished carton torsos, molded & painted socks & shoes, wearing ethnic-type costumes, the boy in black pants, red wool vest front w/gold buttons, black velvet jacket w/red embroidery & black silk top hat, the girl in black dress w/blue embroidered apron w/yarn flower decorations, black neck scarf, original underclothing, replaced bow in hair, 7", pr. **$1,800**

Alexander (Madame) Dionne Quintuplets, marked "Dionne - Alexander" on heads, "Alexander" on backs, composition heads w/painted brown eyes to side, single-stroke brows, painted upper lashes, closed mouths, molded & painted hair, composition baby bodies, all wearing white flannel diapers & short white baby dresses, all in one wood & wicker cradle w/pink flannel blanket, some crazing, 7 1/2", the set **$850**

Alexander (Madame) Jacqueline, marked "Alexander - 19©61" on head, "'Jacqueline' - by Madame Alexander" on tag on seam of slip, vinyl head w/brown sleep eyes w/blue shadow, real lashes, feathered brows, closed mouth, pierced ears, rooted hair, hard plastic body jointed at hips & knees, vinyl arms w/jointed elbows, adult figure, high heel feet, wearing original white satin gown w/matching cape, taffeta slip & panties, stockings, high heeled shoes, "diamond" bracelet & ring, pearl necklace, purse & earrings w/pearls & "diamond," some stains, one pearl missing from right earring, 21" **$450**

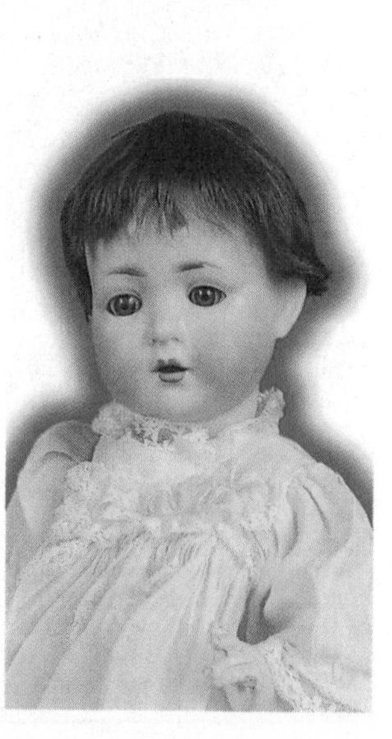

Averill (Georgene) "Bonnie Babe" doll, marked "Copr. by Georgene Averill 7005/365 2/0, Germany," bisque head w/painted hair, blue glass eyes, open smiling mouth w/tongue & two bottom teeth, five-piece cloth body w/swivel arms & legs, composition arms, 13" **$518**

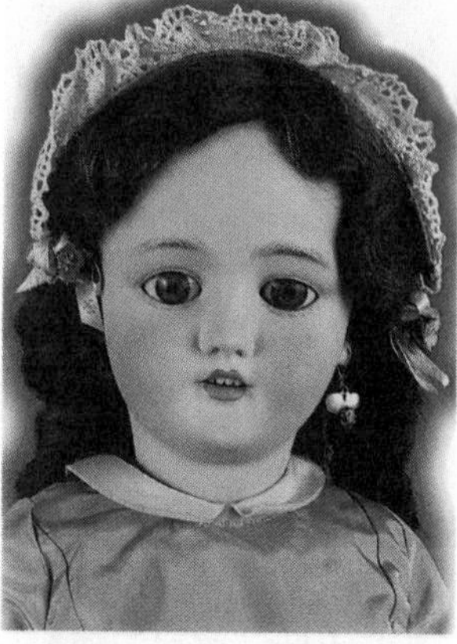

Bergmann (C.M.) bisque socket head girl, marked "C.M. Bergmann - Simon & Halbig - 13 1/2" on back of head, blue sleep eyes, molded & feathered brows, painted lashes, open mouth w/four upper teeth, pierced ears, original h. h. brunette wig, jointed wood & composition body, wearing pale green taffeta dress, lace bonnet, antique underclothing, socks & center-snap leatherette shoes, repair at neck socket of body, 29" **$500**

Babyland Rag, unmarked, cloth head w/flat face, h.p. features, blushed cheeks, strip of human hair sewn across forehead at bonnet line for bangs, cloth body stitch jointed at shoulders, elbows, hips & knees, stitched fingers, wearing antique, possibly original faded blue dress w/lace-trimmed bodice, matching bonnet, antique underclothing, pale blue cotton socks, black leather doll shoes w/buckles, hole on outside of left foot, 1 1/2" split on seam of torso, fingers missing some stitches, 30" **$1,850**

Belton-type bisque socket head girl, marked "183, 15," set brown eyes w/heavily feathered brows, painted upper & lower lashes, closed mouth, pierced ears, h.h. wig, antique white blouse, maroon wool jumper w/matching coat & hat 24" **$275**

Bergmann (C.M.) bisque socket girl, marked "Simon & Halbig, C.M. Bergmann, 1," blue sleep eyes w/feathered brows, painted upper & lower lashes, open mouth w/four upper teeth, original mohair wig, antique knit dress w/ ribbon trim, 22" **$400**

> Dolls with original clothing, especially with full wardrobes and accessories, command premium prices.

Bahr & Proschild bisque socket head baby, marked "678 - 7 - BP [in heart] - Made in - Germany" on back of head, stamped "Made in Germany" in red on lower back, blue sleep eyes, feathered brows, painted lashes, open mouth w/two upper teeth, antique mohair wig, composition bent limb baby body, wearing pale pink baby dress, new underclothing, socks & shoes, missing tip of left little finger, 15" **$275**

Bisque head lady w/wardrobe, unmarked, dark blue stationary eyes, closed mouth, cup & saucer neck, original light blonde braided mohair wig, kid body w/ball-jointed knees, bisque lower arms, 18", w/red leatherette trunk w/tray & variety of clothing including cream-colored dress w/green trim, black silk jacket, black & grey striped silk princess dress, pink cotton skirt, purple wool bodice w/black & white trim, skirts, jacket, undergarments, rubberized overshoes, hair accessories & jewelry, original high button leather boots, France, ca. 1870 .... **$9,400**

Bisque shoulder head lady, unmarked, white bisque w/blue glass eyes, closed mouth, pierced ears, elaborate molded cafe au lait hair w/molded flower decoration, new cloth body, wearing purple velvet dress, drop earrings & necklace, evidence of repair on shoulder plate, redressed, 21" **$201**

Look for identifying marks on a doll at the base of the back of the head. To ensure the entire mark is visible, the hair may need to be pulled out of the way.

Bisque socket head lady, body stamped "Rohmer," attributed to Alexandre Dehors, heart-shaped face w/blue stationary eyes, feathered brows, smiling closed mouth, double chin, pierced ears, original ash blonde mohair wig, shoulder plate w/molded bosom, kid body, wearing old gold silk taffeta gown w/train, France, ca. 1870s, small chip to front of shoulder plate, small finger of right hand broken, left ring finger broken, middle finger cracked, sides of body restitched, 18" **$15,275**

Bru bisque head girl, marked w/ impressed "3" at crown, shoes marked w/"B" in script in oval & "2," brown paperweight eyes, open closed mouth w/painted upper & lower teeth, blonde skin wig, fully articulated wooden baby body w/mortise & tenon joints, wearing white cotton undergarments, pink silk satin & faille dress, ribbon festooned straw hat & cream leather ankle-strap shoes, France, ca. 1880, 19" (ILLUS. center w/Jumeau dolls) **$18,800**

Bru bisque socket head girl, impressed "Bru Jne 1" mark, brown paperweight eyes, closed mouth w/tongue tip, pierced ears, blonde wig, bisque shoulder plate w/molded bosom & scalloped kid trim, full kid body w/bisque lower arms, wearing original deep maroon silk dress w/brocaded anemone pattern, matching hat, small maroon silk & lace-trimmed parasol, red net stockings & brown leather shoes marked "BRU JNE" in oval, ca. 1880, some wear to clothing, 11 1/4" **$24,675**

China head man, unmarked, painted blue eyes w/molded lids, single-stroke brows, closed mouth, molded & painted curly side- parted hair, new cloth body w/china lower arms, green leather boots, redressed in white shirt, black pants, gold jacket w/dark velvet collar & silk tie in antique fabrics, 21" **$1,500**

China shoulder head lady, marked in red inside shoulder plate, pressed china shoulder head w/ painted blue eyes, single-stroke brows, closed mouth, molded black hair showing under molded hat trimmed in yellow, white & green feathers & molded red decoration, cloth body jointed at shoulders, hips & knees, no indication of hands, fingers or toes, wearing antique white skirt, gathered top, chemise, half slip & pantalets, cotton socks & leather shoes, 1 1/2" hairline through left back sew hole, light soil, 19" **$15,000**

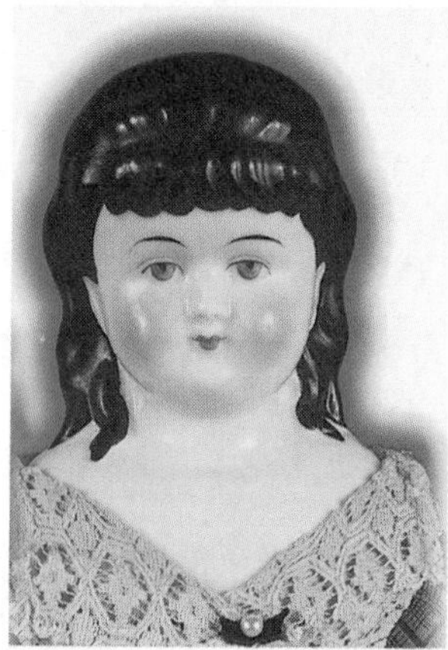

China shoulder head lady, so-called "Currier & Ives" style, marked "5" on back of shoulder plate, stamped "Made - in - Germany" on left front of torso, painted blue eyes, single-stroke brows, closed mouth, molded black hair w/short wavy bangs & long curls worn behind ears & falling to shoulders, pink cloth body w/china lower arms & lower legs, molded black boots w/blue tassels, wearing old red & black plaid dress w/white lace bodice, underclothing, repair to left ankle, 17" **$500**

Dolley Madison china shoulder head lady, unmarked, painted blue eyes, brown single-stroke brows, closed mouth, heavily rouged cheeks, pierced ears, molded & painted blonde hair w/molded blue ribbon & bow, cloth body w/leather lower arms, striped lower legs w/leather boots, wearing black velvet two-piece outfit w/lace trim, antique underclothing, torso re-covered, arms replaced, right boot patched & repaired, leather on left boot deteriorating, 24" **$725**

Effanbee "Patsy Ruth," marked "Effanbee - Patsy Ruth" on head, "Effanbee - Durable - Dolls" on tag on dress & on metal heart bracelet, composition head w/ brown sleep eyes w/real lashes, feathered brows, closed "rosebud" mouth, original h.h. wig, five- piece composition body wearing original peach silk dress, matching romper, socks & leatherette T-strap shoes, eyes cloudy, dress very fragile & deteriorating on bodice, 26" **$800**

Closed mouth dolls can be significantly more valuable than open-mouthed dolls.

Effanbee Cowardly Lion doll, vinyl, from the Effanbee Storybook Collection, posable heads w/sleep eyes, mint in box **$25**

Gaultier (Francois) bisque Poupee Peau, marked "4" on back of head, "F.G." on left shoulder, bisque socket head on bisque shoulder plate, blue paperweight eyes, heavy feathered brows, painted lashes, closed mouth, pierced ears, replaced mohair wig, kid body w/gussets at elbows, hips & knees, individually stitched fingers, redressed in pale green plaid two-piece outfit of antique fabric, antique underclothing, new socks & lace boots, floral headpiece, small repair at each earring hole **$1,400**

Gutta percha head lady, painted features, black pupil-less eyes, lower lashes angling outward, upper lashes angling toward center of face, slightly smiling closed mouth, molded dark hair falling into curls behind exposed ears onto shoulder plate, suggestion of wire at lower edge as on mystery linen head dolls, cloth body, kid arms w/ separate fingers, wearing red wool princess-line dress w/pleated hem & black buttons down back, early kid slippers, probably America, ca. 1840s, breaks to hands, 18 1/2" (ILLUS. front right w/papier-mâchè & metal head dolls)........... **$2,350**

Handwerck (Heinrich) bisque socket head girl, marked "Germany - Heinrich - Handwerck - Simon & Halbig - 7" on head, "Heinrich Handwerck - Germany - 7" stamped in red on back, blue sleep eyes, molded & feathered brows, open mouth w/accented lips & four upper teeth, pierced ears, original brown h.h. wig, jointed wood & composition Handwerck body, wearing antique white child's dress, antique underclothing, cotton socks, black patent leather shoes, left knee ball replaced, 32 1/2" **$1,025**

Hallmark Susan B. Anthony doll, stuffed cloth, wearing a long blue dress & a red, white & blue sash reading "Votes," house- form box cover includes the story of Susan B. Anthony, sold in Hallmark stores, 1979, in original box, doll 6 1/2" h. **$7**

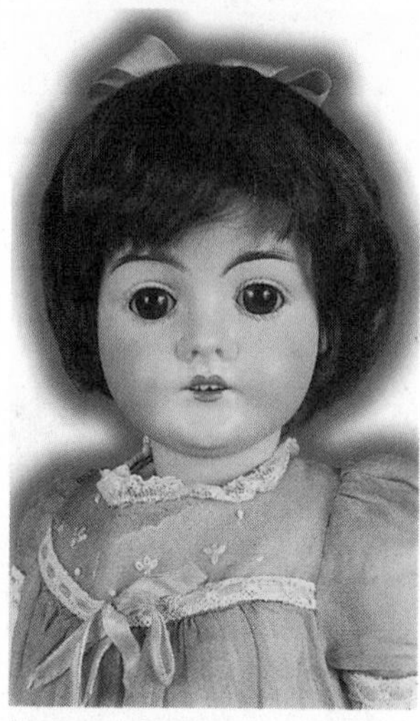

Hartman (Karl) bisque socket head girl, marked "28.5 - K/0" inside large "H" on back of head, brown sleep eyes, heavy feathered brows, painted lashes, open mouth w/four upper teeth, replaced mohair wig, jointed wood & composition body, wearing blue lace-trimmed organdy dress, underclothing, socks & replaced shoes, small chips, size of body may be slightly large for head, 22 1/2" **$200**

Huret bisque socket head character girl, impressed "MA" & "HURET" on head, dark blue stationary glass eyes, closed mouth, pink cheeks, long blonde wig, composition & wood child body, wearing ribbed aqua silk dress & bonnet, France, late 19th - early 20th c., paint flaking on hands, tiny chip at neck hole, 16" (ILLUS. right w/Huret character lady)................................ **$7,638**

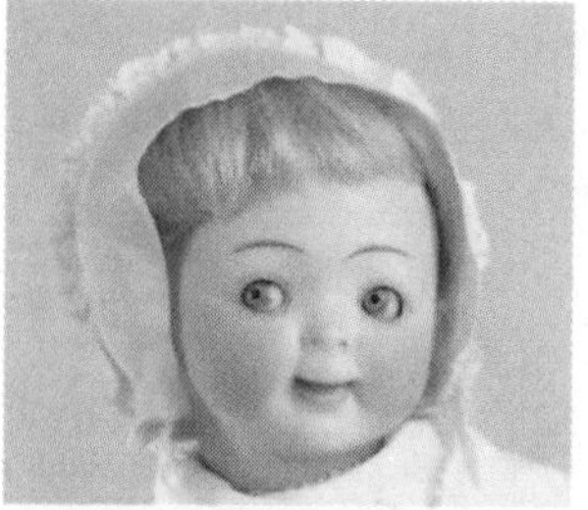

Hertel & Schwab bisque head googlie, marked "165/4," blue set googlie eyes, single-stroke brows, open closed smiling mouth, pink cheeks, replacement blonde wig, jointed composition baby body, wearing older baby clothes & bonnet, comes w/remainder of original wig, small hairline to rear of head, 13" **$1,783**

Heubach (Gebruder) twins, marked "1 - Germany - 72 Heubach [in square] 46 - 16" on backs of heads, bisque socket heads w/blue sleep eyes, single stroke brows, painted lashes, closed pouty mouths, original mohair wigs, jointed wood & composition bodies w/jointed wrists, wearing completely original factory outfits, the boy in two-piece wool outfit of short pants & belted tunic- style top w/silk-covered buttons, felt cap w/tassel, original socks & shoes, the girl in blue wool drop-waist dress w/silk-covered buttons, straw hat w/pompom trim, factory underclothing, socks & shoes, minor cracks & hairlines, wooden upper arms & legs split & glued on each, 11", pr. **$2,650**

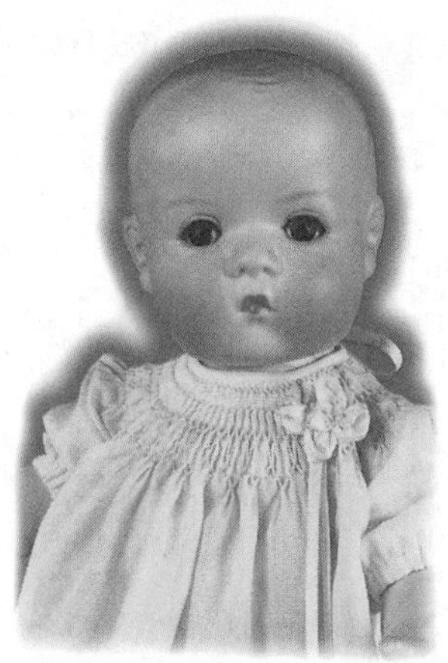

Hertel, Schwab & Co. "Patsy" baby, no visible marks, solid dome bisque head w/brown sleep eyes w/real lashes, soft brows that match molded & painted baby-type hair, closed "rosebud" mouth, five-piece composition toddler body, wearing baby-style smocked dress, matching panties, socks & shoes, body repainted, 18" **$1,400**

Heubach (Ernst) bisque socket head girl, marked "Heubach Koppelsdorf - 417 8/0 - Germany" on back of head, blue sleep eyes to side, feathered brows, tiny painted upper lashes, open mouth w/two upper teeth, antique mohair wig, five-piece composition body w/unfinished torso, wearing blue blouse w/white dots, matching bonnet, white pinafore, underclothing, original socks & leatherette shoes w/pompoms, 12" **$975**

Ideal "Toni," marked "P-91 - Ideal Doll - Made in U.S.A." on head, "Ideal Doll - P-91" on back, "Genuine Toni Doll - with nylon wig - Made by Ideal Novelty & Toy Co." on dress tag, hard plastic head w/blue sleep eyes w/real lashes, single-stroke brows, closed mouth, original wig, five-piece hard plastic body wearing tagged red & yellow pique dress w/embroidery, attached half slip w/matching panties, socks, original red center-snap shoes, hair repinned & w/net, 15" **$235**

Ideal Shirley Temple, marked "11 - Shirley Temple" on head, "Shirley Temple - 11" on back, "Genuine - Shirley Temple - Doll - Registered - [illegible]" on dress tag, composition head w/blue sleep eyes w/real lashes, feathered brows, open mouth w/six teeth, original mohair wig, five-piece composition child body wearing original red & white organdy coin dot dress from movie "Stand Up and Cheer," underwear combination, rayon socks, center-snap leatherette shoes, tiny crack over left eye, minor crazing, socks replaced, 11" **$575**

Jenny Lind china head lady, marked "6" on front edge of shoulderplate, china shoulder head w/painted blue eyes, single-stroke brows, closed mouth, molded & painted black hair w/full rolls on sides flowing back to bun, cloth body jointed at shoulders, hips & knees, leather lower arms, red & white striped lower legs w/leather boots, wearing antique two-piece outfit & antique underclothing, some rubs & flaking, torso re-covered, lower arms replaced, lower legs reattached, boots worn, 19 1/2" **$1,050**

←

Jumeau bisque head "long face" girl, blue paperweight eyes, feathered brows, closed mouth, blonde wig, composition body, wearing fancy ivory colored dress, buff-colored shoes marked "12" & socks, comes w/pale blue bonnet, blue silk dress w/ivory cape & bonnet, parasol, wire rimmed hat & white shoes marked "12," plaster has been added to eyes, slight repair to body at neck, 26" **$13,225**

Jumeau bisque head 1st series portrait doll, marked "2/0" on head, hazel almond-shaped eyes, feathered brows, closed mouth, pierced ears, honey-colored replacement wig, repainted original eight ball jointed body, newer replacement clothes, 14 1/2" **$8,625**

Jumeau bisque socket head portrait lady, large blue paperweight eyes, feathered brows, closed mouth, large applied ears, slightly double chin, brown wig, fully articulated wooden body, wearing aubergine silk satin dress & ribbon-trimmed peaked hat, brown leather shoes marked "Jumeau," model associated w/Jumeau production for 1876 exhibition, 27" **$22,325**

K [star] R (Kammer & Reinhardt) bisque socket head character girl, marked "K [star] R - 114 - 23," painted blue eyes, single-stroke brows, closed pouty mouth, mohair wig in coiled braids, five-piece composition body w/molded & painted white socks & brown two-strap shoes, wearing original factory chemise trimmed w/red embroidery, 8 1/2" **$1,175**

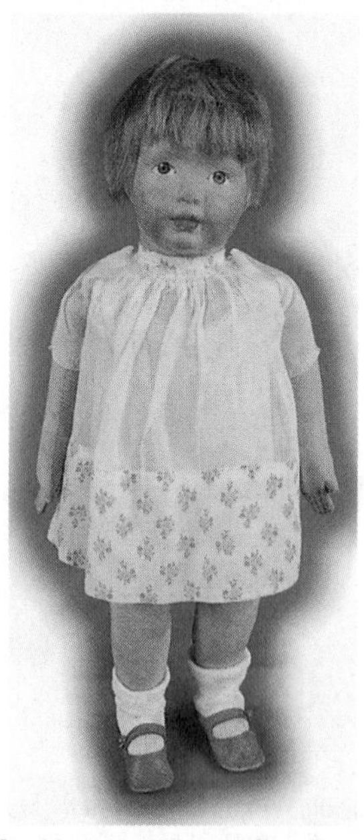

Kamkins doll w/wardrobe, unmarked, oil painted cloth swivel head w/painted blue eyes, single-stroke brows, closed mouth, original mohair wig, cloth body tab jointed at shoulders, stitch jointed at hips, stitched fingers & separate thumb, wearing original organdy dress w/flower print trim along bottom, matching teddy w/flower print trim, orange wool coat w/black curly mohair collar, matching hat w/black ribbon reading "US Navy," replaced rayon socks, original brown leather shoes w/button strap, 18"; comes w/extra original Kamkins orange, gold, black & white striped dress w/orange trim, matching teddy & orange hat, white pique dress w/pleated print skirt, matching print coat & hat, red mohair jacket w/beige trim & matching hat, extra pair of shoes, knit sweater, skirt & matching hat, flannel pajamas, black felt buckle boots, some paint missing from face, rust stains on back from non-working crier (ILLUS. of doll without coat & hat)............ **$5,700**

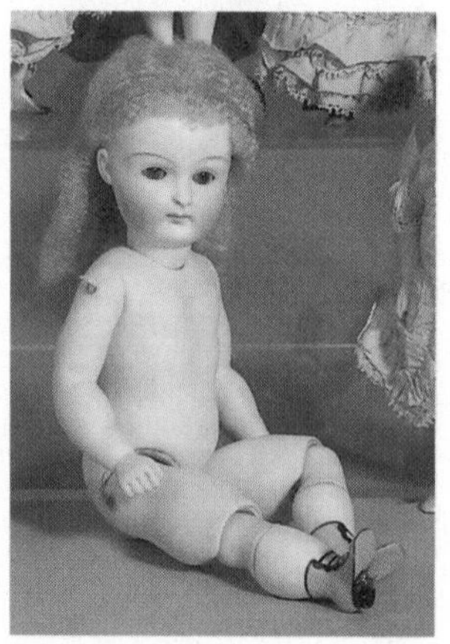

←

Kestner (J. D.) bisque socket head girl, impressed "111" on upper torso & back of upper legs, brown sleep eyes, closed mouth, rosy cheeks, original blonde curly mohair wig w/blue hair ribbon, kid-lined swivel neck, peg-jointed limbs, the right hand molded in closed fist, left hand open, wearing molded pink high-heeled boots w/ four straps, green banded ribbed stockings w/lacy imprint at top, ca. 1880, 8 1/2" **$8,225**

Kestner (J.D.) all-bisque child, marked "3/0" on back of head & below neck opening of body, swivel head w/blue sleep eyes, feathered brows, painted lashes, open mouth w/two square upper teeth, original mohair wig, body jointed at shoulders & hips, black boots w/blue tassels, wearing off-white dress w/embroidered decoration, probably child-made, large chip at top of left hip, small chip on left toes touched up, 5" **$1,300**

Kestner (J.D.) bisque socket head girl, marked "(?) made in - Germany 0 - 143," brown sleep eyes, feathered brows, open mouth w/four upper teeth, original auburn mohair wig, composition Kestner body w/straight arms, jointed at shoulders, hips & knees, wearing possibly original white dress trimmed w/tucks & lace, original underclothing, white cotton socks, white leather shoes, lace-trimmed bonnet, arms have been restrung w/elastic through composition at shoulders, 8 3/4" **$825**

Kestner Kewpie, marked "Ges. gesch. - O'Neill. J.D.K. - 10" on back of head, solid dome bisque socket head w/topknot, oversized brown glass eyes set to side, dash brows, painted lashes, closed smiling mouth, five-piece chubby composition body w/"starfish" hands, wearing old white underwear w/crocheted trim, peach organdy dress w/new blue silk ribbon trim, front of torso & bottom of left foot repainted, touchups to both heels, right shoulder, left fingers, toes worn, 10" **$4,600**

←

Kling bisque shoulder head lady, marked "144-9" on back of shoulder plate, painted blue eyes, single-stroke brown brows, closed mouth, pierced ears, elaborate molded blonde hair w/ black comb, molded lace collar w/decorative trim, cloth body jointed at shoulders, hips & knees, leather lower arms, printed lower legs, leather boots, redressed in gown of antique fabric, antique underclothing, repairs on leather arms, edges of boots & toe of left boot worn, 24" **$1,100**

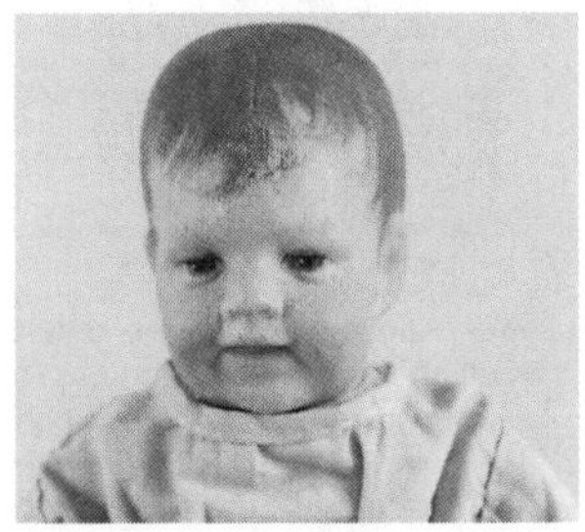

Kruse (Kathe) "Schlenkerchen" baby, cloth head w/painted features & hair, brown eyes, smiling open closed mouth, brown hair, wearing period clothing, rare smiling model, 13" **$7,475**

Largo Scarecrow doll, stuffed cloth, from The Wizard of Oz series, mint in original box **$30**

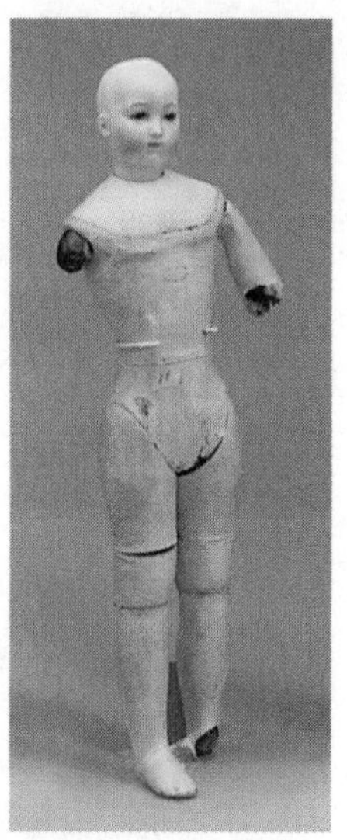

Leverd (Alexandre) bisque socket head character lady, impressed "SGDG" on head, torso stamped "E. Leverd Cie PARIS Brevete S.G.D.G.," narrow dark blue glass eyes, open closed mouth, deeply sculpted facial modeling, recessed hairline area for application of wig as patented in 1869, bisque shoulder plate, jointed body of kid over gutta percha, France, ca. 1870, missing right arm, left forearm & left foot, small damage to joints, 19" **$10,575**

Lenci "400 D" girl, illegible mark on bottom of right foot, marked "Lenci Turin - (Italy) - Di E. Scavini - Made in Italy - 400/D - Pat. Sept. 8-1921 - Pat. N. 142433 - Bte S.G.D.G. X87395 - Brevetto 501-178" on paper tag, pressed felt swivel head w/painted brown eyes to side, single-stroke brows, painted upper lashes, closed mouth, applied ears, original long mohair wig, cloth torso w/felt arms & legs, individually stitched fingers w/middle fingers together, stitched & tinted toes, wearing light green felt dress, original underclothing, silk stockings to hips, black leather shoes, blue-green felt cape-coat & matching hat, some soil & fading, 16" **$850**

Lenci Series 110 felt socket head girl, marked "Lenci" on bottom of left foot, painted features of brown side-glancing eyes, pouty closed mouth, blonde wig, wearing peach dress w/applied felt flowers & matching pink & yellow wide-brimmed hat & pink shoes, Italy, ca. 1930s, head loose in socket, small moth hole to shoe, 23" **$805**

Loews Dorothy & Toto dolls, vinyl, from The Wizard of Oz series, Dorothy w/long brown hair, wearing a blue checked jumper & white blouse, by Turner Entertainment, ca. 1988, in original box **$12**

←

Morimora Bros. bisque head baby, marked w/two parts of "Morimora Bros." emblem & "Japan" & "3," brown sleep eyes, open mouth w/two upper teeth, five-piece composition bent-leg body, skull cut for voice box, which is present but not working, 11" **$144**

"Mascotte" bisque head girl, marked "Mascotte" & "Bebe Mascotte Paris" on body, amber paperweight eyes, closed mouth, possibly original brown h.h. wig on cork pate, ball-jointed body, wearing antique shoes, replacement clothing, France, minor wear to fingertips & joints, 29" **$2,645**

Parian shoulder head lady, pressed parian-type bisque w/ blue painted eyes, closed smiling mouth, brown molded hair pulled back into a bun w/defined widow's peak, wispy tendrils at ears, cloth body, Germany, ca. 1850, 15 1/2" **$5,288**

Papier-mâchè shoulder head milliner's model, unmarked, painted blue eyes, single-stroke brows, closed mouth, molded & painted hair w/long side curls to shoulders, braided bun in back, kid body w/wooden lower arms & legs, painted orange shoes, wearing original black silk dress w/lace trim, original underclothing, 8 1/4" **$500**

Petterssen (Ronnaug) Norwegian ethnic dolls, marked "Made in Norway - Vare-Marke - Ronnaug Petterssen" on paper tags on clothing, celluloid socket heads w/painted blue eyes, single-stroke brows, closed mouths, original h. h. blond wigs, five-piece celluloid bodies, wearing original wool & felt Norwegian ethnic costumes, the girl in red felt skirt, white cotton blouse w/lace trim, black felt jacket, red felt bodice w/gold decorative pins & beading, red felt ribbons w/ embroidery, underclothing, black stockings & black felt shoes, a gold crown w/red felt backing on her head, the boy in white cotton shirt w/gold decorative pin at neck, black wool pants w/embroidery, red wool jacket edged in green w/ decorative buttons, black felt top hat, white stockings & black felt shoes, some small moth holes on girl's skirt, girl's right cuff missing, 17", pr. **$1,000**

←

"Queen Anne" wooden doll, painted features, black pupil-less eyes, stylized line & dot brows, dots for lashes, closed mouth, carved ears, nailed-on woven dark brown h.h. wig, wooden upper arms & upper legs, carved hands & feet, wearing cream- colored silk flowered Watteau-style gown of period fabric w/coral-colored stomacher, long silk stockings, silk slippers from dress fabric, England, ca. 1780, 17 1/2" **$5,875**

Schmitt wax over papier-mâché socket head baby, Schmitt shield stamp on bottom, pale blue paperweight eyes, closed mouth, fully articulated eight-ball composition body, France, late 19th c., extensive repainting, 14" **$705**

Simon & Halbig Oriental bisque head child, marked "S & H 1329," brown sleep eyes, feathered brows, open mouth w/teeth, black wig, ball jointed composition body, wearing original kimono, 18" **$1,380**

French and German dolls of the 19th and early 20th century are prized for their superb artistry.

Schoenhut character girl, all painted wood, brown eyes, closed mouth, original ash brown wig, jointed body, wearing original shoes & older replacement clothing, some crazing on face, 15" **$1,035**

Steiner bisque head girl, marked "Fre A 17 Steiner," blue paperweight eyes, closed mouth, replacement brunette wig w/long curls, straight-wristed body, body repainted, later clothing, 24" **$2,013**

→

Thullier (A.) bisque head girl, marked "A. 14 T" on head, large blue paperweight eyes, feathered brows, closed mouth w/protruding upper lip, light brown h.h. wig, original jointed composition body, wearing antique blue mariner's outfit of pleated skirt & sailor-style top & hat & antique shoes marked "Bebe Jumeau 12," body repainted, 30" **$21,275**

Simon & Halbig bisque socket head Oriental lady, marked "1129 - S&H - DEP - 0 - Germany," set brown eyes, feathered brows, open mouth w/four upper teeth, pierced ears, original black mohair wig w/original queue, five-piece composition body w/molded & painted socks & shoes, wearing original red crepe kimono, 9" **$1,275**

DOLL FURNITURE & ACCESSORIES

←

Bed & doll, mahogany low-poster bed w/turned head- and footposts fitted w/turned whalebone finials, fitted w/original tiny bisque head doll, mattress, linens & patchwork quilt, made by Captain David Folger for Lydia N. Folger, Nantucket, Massachusetts, ca. 1850, bed 9 1/2 x 15 1/2", 11 1/2" h., the set **$8,365**

Bedroom set: double bed, chest of drawers w/mirror, commode, rocking chair without arms & side chair; each painted red w/ gold pinstriping, all made for Catherine Bell Black by her father, late 19th c., includes a 1930s photo of the owner as a grandmother, the set **$184**

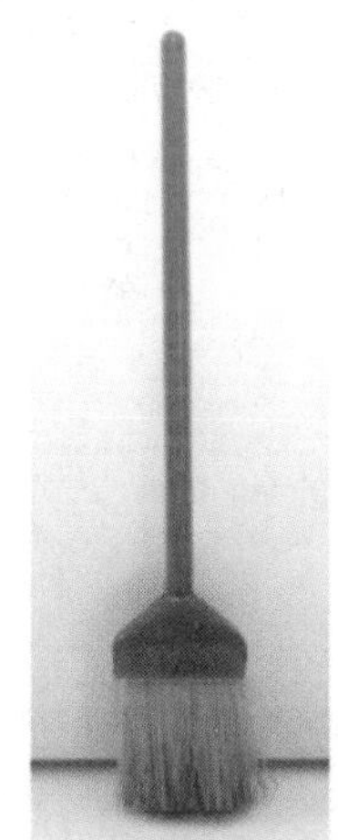

Broom, dollhouse-type, green plastic handle, Renwal, 1950s, rare, 5" l. **$150**

Bedroom set: high-backed double bed, chest of drawers w/tall mirror, settee, commode, round-topped side table, armchair, rocking chair & side chair; each of delicately pierce-carved hardwood, mid-19th c., bed 13" l., the set **$224**

→

Chair, painted & decorated wood, Federal "fancy" style, the flat, slightly curved & tapering stiles flanking a flat top stretcher w/a gilt stenciled globe w/crossed arrows flanked by leaves on the original red & black-grained ground, a center stepped stretcher w/gilt-stenciled acanthus leaves above a thin lower stretcher w/a gilt band, the rest of the chair also w/the grained background & highlighted overall w/gilt stenciled leaves & banding, woven rush yellow-painted seat, ca. 1830, minor wear & edge damage to front seatrail, overall 13 3/4" h. **$1,840**

Chest-on-chest, dollhouse-type, creamy molded plastic, two long drawers in the lower section & five drawers in the upper section, Louis Marx & Co., New York, New York, 1950s (ILLUS. second from left with other pieces of Marx dollhouse furniture).................. **$3**

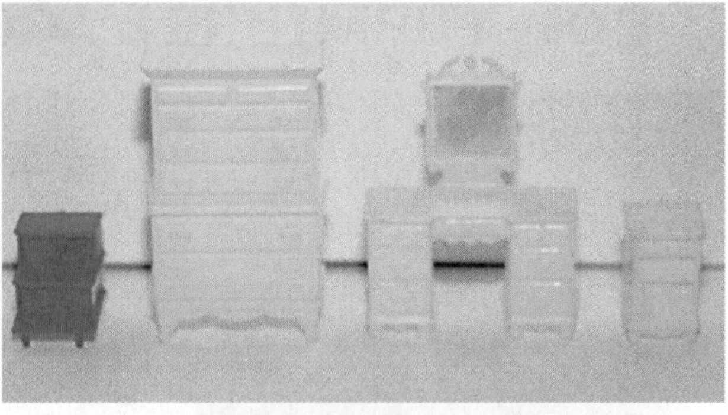

Dining table, dollhouse-type, brown molded plastic, by Dulev, 1950s, 4" l., 2" h. **$15**

Doll carriage, tightly woven wicker, half-round body & hinged hood in natural wicker w/a printed green diamond design, wire handle, wire-spoked wheels, early 20th c., slight losses to wicker, 27" l., 27" h. **$115**

Doll carriage, wood & iron, the shallow wooden body painted black w/red trim & burgundy satin upholstered seat w/a pierced cast-iron seat back, wire upright for the fringed canopy of burgundy satin, tall upright wooden push handle, two large wooden rear wheels w/two smaller front wheels, second half 19th c., some minor paint wear, 10 1/2 x 24", 25 1/2" h. **$891**

Wicker is valued for its durability, water resistance, and light weight, making it ideal for outdoors items that need to be moved often.

Doll cradle, painted poplar, hooded-type, the angle-topped hood on the raised ends of the gently canted sideboards w/ square nail construction joining them to the canted end boards, raised on long low rockers, old dark finish, mid-19th c., 25" l., 12 1/2" h. **$345**

Dollhouse & original furnishings, "Jolly Twins" two-story traditional-style lithographed metal seven-room dollhouse w/a red & black roof, includes furnishings in original boxes for the nursery, bedroom, dining room (damaged), living room, bathroom, kitchen & Little Red Schoolhouse, overall good played-with condition, colorful boxes, about 60 pieces of furniture, Renwal, the set **$604**

Dollhouse, painted & decorated wood, in the Victorian Queen Anne style, a pedimented shingled roof & turret & paneled sides & back, glazed double-hung working windows, the rear open to reveal a floored interior w/some traces of old wallpaper, late 19th c., America, 20 1/2 x 32", 46" h. **$3,585**

Dollhouse, color-printed metal, two-story traditional style w/siding over brick lower half, front bay window, end garage area replaced w/a fallout shelter, back open to show the rooms w/printed wall & floor decoration, Marx Toys, New York, 1959, excellent condition **$200**

Dresser, dollhouse-type, molded brown plastic, a long rectangular top above a case molded w/ drawers & doors & an arched center apron, Dulev, 1950s, 4" l., 2 1/2" h. **$15**

Firehouse, color-lithographed paper on wood, Bliss Fire Station #2, two-story Victorian structure w/opening double front doors, a balcony & windows in the upper story, paper overall quite bright & largely intact, possibly missing a dormer above the second story window, one door hinge missing, late 19th c. **$403**

Lithography (from Greek: lithos, "stone" and grapho, "writing" literally means stone writing. In traditional lithography, a stone or metal plate is engraved with a design, and the incised lines are filled with ink. Paper is then pressed on the surface, transferring the design to the paper.

Furniture set: dining table, two side chairs, crib, chest of drawers, wardrobe, outside patio table & chairs; fine light hardwood, set No. 144, Strom-Becker Mfg. Co., Moline, Illinois, ca. 1954, complete in original box, the set (ILLUS. of the dining set) **$45**

Highchair, wood, the wide back w/rounded edges decorated w/a lithographed paper picture of a small baby framed by red & blue gold-trimmed panels, turned back stiles & open arms flanking the plank seat, on tall canted slender square legs w/a footrest & slender rungs, made by Bliss-Whitney Reed, late 19th c., minor wear, 27" h. **$345**

Ladder, dollhouse-type, green plastic, opens up, five steps & support to hold tiny paint tray, Renwal, 1950s, 4 1/2" h. **$45**

Sideboard, carved walnut, a back superstructure w/arched crest & serpentine shelf supported on ring-turned posts, the rectangular top w/ serpentine sides above a case w/a long curved drawer above a pair of glazed cupboard doors opening to a mirrored back & flanked by turned columns, flat molded base, bottom board cracks, mid-19th c., 7 3/4 x 12 1/2", 17" h. **$431**

Picnic table, dollhouse-type, molded red plastic, No. 1-1001, Ideal Toy Company, 1950s, 4 1/2" l. **$15**

DRUGSTORE & PHARMACY ITEMS

The old-time corner drugstore, once a familiar part of every American town, has now given way to a modern, efficient pharmacy. With the streamlining and modernization of this trade, many of the early tools and store adjuncts have been outdated and now fall in the realm of "collectibles." Listed here are some of the tools, bottles, display pieces and other emphemera once closely associated with the druggiest's trade.

Apothecary jar w/fitted lid, cobalt blue-glazed pottery, cylindrical w/waisted neck, wide gold banner printed in black "Pulv. Lapis P.," probably English, ca. 1860-80, 6 5/8" h. **$448**

Apothecary show bottle, blown bulbous ovoid ruby glass body w/ tapering cylindrical neck & flaring rim, raised on an applied clear pedestal & round foot, original clear hollow-blown stopper, probably American, ca. 1870-90, 10" h. **$504**

Apothecary show globe w/original stopper, Art Deco style, a large clear glass teardrop-shaped globe w/a stepped shoulder, short cylindrical neck & tall oblong stopper, fitted in cast- and polished aluminum three-footed stand, American, ca. 1920-35, 18 1/8" h. **$420**

Apothecary storage jar, cov., free-blown clear cylindrical jar w/two applied cobalt blue bands around the body, high domed clear cover w/cobalt blue rim band & hollow blown knob finial, pontil scar, ca. 1850, 11" h. **$532**

Apothecary storage jar, earthenware, wide baluster-form body w/a flaring round foot, fluted band around the lower body & short flaring neck w/flattened inset cover w/small pierced holes & knob finial, leaf-molded loop shoulder handles, sea green at the bottom & top w/the white center area h. p. w/leafy scrolls & a large sea green banner decorated in gold w/the word "Leeches," impressed "Alcock" mark, England, some damage on lid, late 19th - early 20th c., 13 1/2" h. **$8,625**

Apothecary storage jar, porcelain, cylindrical w/ringed white base & rim, domed cover w/ small air holes & button finial, the sides & cover in dark moss green, the base h.p. w/ a gilt crown & scrolls above a red-bordered white banner reading "Leeches," early, 9 1/2" h. **$5,980**

Apothecary storage jar, pottery, wide baluster-form body w/flattened disk cover w/small pierced holes & knob finial, deep cobalt blue glaze w/an arched red-bordered gold banner reading "Leeches," impressed "Royal Doulton England," label probably repainted, late 19th - early 20th c., 9 1/2" h. **$8,625**

Drug bottle, narrow rectangular w/beveled sides, embossed "Maximo M. Dia - Druggist - Ybor City, Fla.," tooled lip, "W.T. & Co. U.S.A." on smooth base, ca. 1890-1910, cobalt blue, 5 1/8" h. **$190**

Balance scales, brass, central shaft w/the balance arm suspending a fixed tray on one side & a suspended small tray on the other, on a rectangular wooden base, w/five weights, crossbar marked "W & T Avery Lt. - To Weigh 2 lb.," minor scuffing, 19th c., 10 3/4 x 20", 22" h. **$259**

Countertop display jar, square tall clear glass w/a wide mouth w/fitted mushroom-style stopper, the front w/a large rectangular label-under-glass reading "Dr. D. Jayne's Sanative Pills for Constipation, Biliousness, Sick Headache, Etc. - Sugar-Coated - 25 Cents," ca. 1880-95, 8" h. **$1,456**

Drug bottle, "C.W. Snow & Co., Druggists (design of eagle w/shield & mortar & pestle), Syracuse, N.Y.," square w/tooled lip, ca. 1885-95, deep cobalt blue, 8 1/4" h. **$468**

Drug bottle, "Jacob's Pharmacy (motif of eagle on mortar & pestle) Atlanta GA," tooled mouth, "W.T. Co. U.S.A." on smooth base, 70% original label for "Strychnine Sulphate," ca. 1885-1910, amber, 2 1/2" h............... **$77**

Drug bottle, rectangular w/sloping shoulder, embossed "Jozeau" & "Pharmacien" on opposite ends, rolled lip, pontil-scarred base, ca. 1840-1855, deep olive green, 4 1/2" h. **$165**

Pill roller, walnut device on a brass base w/a star stamp & a separate two-handled device which glides along top, 19th c., 12" h. **$220**

FIREARMS

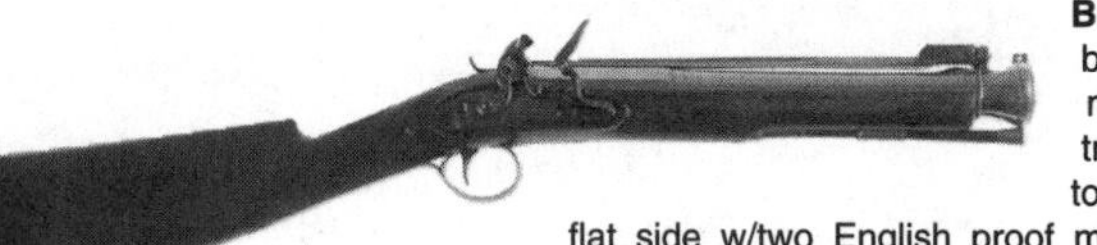

Blunderbuss, Noyes flintlock model, brass barrel octagonal to round w/cannon muzzle, a 12 1/2" l. spring-loaded triangular bayonet mounted to the top, top of barrel marked "Warminster" & left flat side w/two English proof marks, well made lock marked "Noyes," reinforced hammer & safety w/roller frizzen w/boat-shaped waterproof pan, mounted in a one-piece walnut stock w/brass furniture consisting of a ramrod guide & nose pipe containing the original brass-tipped rammer w/worm on small end, trigger guard flared wide in middle & engraved w/a long nicely detailed pineapple finial, buttplate w/narrow engraved tang, fine checkered wrist & the barrel secured w/two wedges through the forestock without escutcheons, bayonet w/brazed repair, stock w/stress crack on right side & hairline in front of trigger guard, barrel 13 1/2" l. **$3,680**

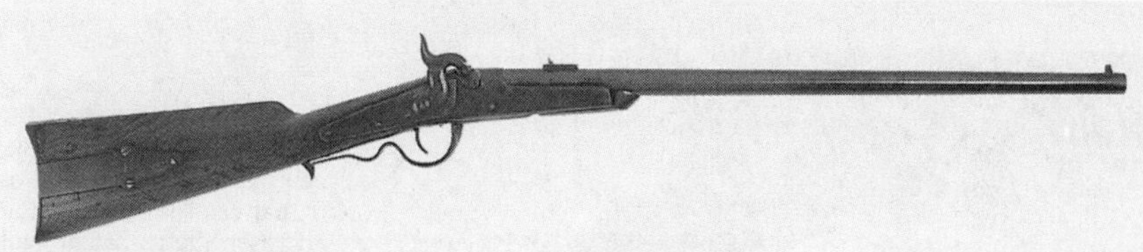

Carbine, Gallager Civil War standard percussion model, .54 cal., pinched front sight & two-position flip rear sight, straight grip walnut stock w/smooth steel carbine buttplate, sling bar & ring on left side of wrist, patchbox containing a spare nipple on right side of butt, round 22 1/2" l. round barrel **$2,415**

Carbine, Maynard Second Model Civil War percussion model, martially-marked, .50 cal., pinched front sight, two-leaf three- position rear sight, stock without patchbox, date 1865, barrel w/90% bluing, buttstock w/several small crude scratched drawings, octagonal to round 20" barrel **$2,645**

Carbine, Sharps & Hankins Model 1862, .52 cal., walnut stock, Serial No. 6340, 24" l. barrel, ca. 1859, fair condition, pitting & bruises to metal, nicks & separation to stock, overall 39" l. **$748**

Carbine, Sharps & Hankins saddle ring model, .52 cal., missing sights, the lever catch & a chunk of the stock, also missing sling swivel on stock, main spring broken, round barrel 19" l. **$690**

Carbine, Spencer Model 1865 model, .50 cal., "ESA" cartouche on left side of stock behind sling ring bar, traces of finish, round barrel 20" l. **$2,128**

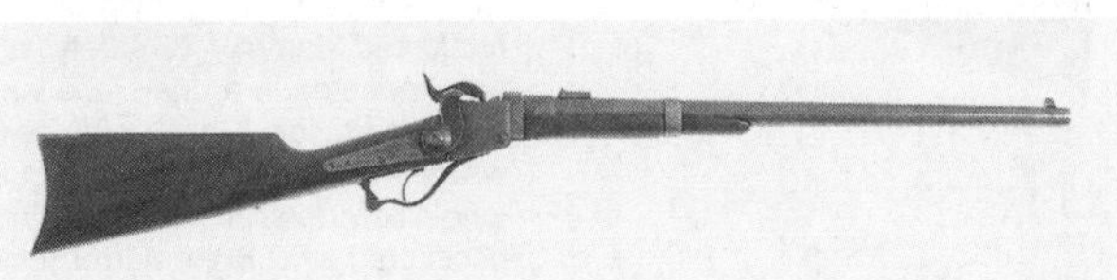

Carbine, Starr Civil War percussion model, .54 cal., unusual configuration w/a stepped round barrel w/blade front side & two-position flip rear sight, small forearm w/straight stock & semi-crescent carbine brass buttplate, usual markings on lockplate & top tang, no original finish, barrel 20 3/4" l. **$2,013**

Derringer, Sharps Model 3B, .32 cal. rim fire, four barrels, cluster of barrels w/Sharps & Hankins address, Sharps patent markings on right side of frame, button barrel release & the barrels without extractor, smooth rosewood grip panels, barrels w/95 percent glossy bluing, Serial No. 11399, barrels 3 1/2" l. **$1,725**

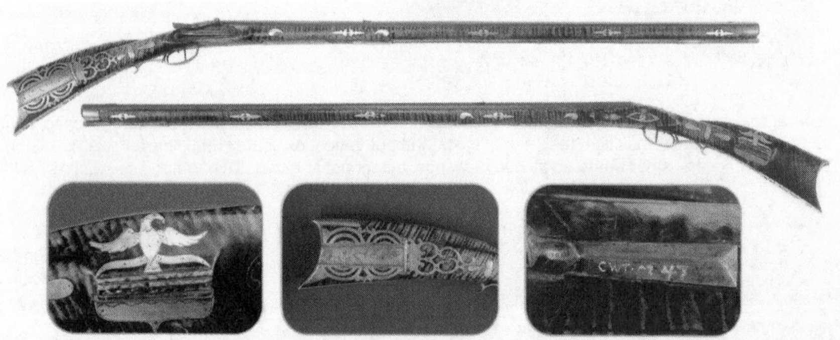

Long rifle, Morrison (Samuel) side hammer model, .50 cal., highly decorated w/an octagonal barrel, fine brass front sight & wide fixed rear sight w/lightly engraved decorations, muzzle decorated w/stars & dots, the top flat signed in script "JM" separated by an engraved star, full-length maple stock w/applied striping & brass furniture, a plain nose cap w/two long faceted guides & a long plain nose pipe, also a 6" l. narrow brass wear plate on the bottom of the stock, typical simple trigger guard, brass buttplate w/a faceted top tang & filigree toeplate w/four cut-outs & a ball finial, the roach-back comb w/a long, thin decorative brass plate attached w/iron pins, lockplate screws passing through brass escutcheons, one of which is an elliptical-shaped filigree w/two cut- outs, forestock & buttstock w/22 sterling silver inlays in various designs, some quite elaborate & the most elaborate being a fine spread-winged American eagle w/light engraving mounted on the small cheek piece, unusual brass shield-shaped inlay w/pick slot below, right side of buttstock w/an extremely fancy & delicate four-piece brass filigree patchbox w/a lightly engraved lid, dbl. set triggers, left side of buttstock, between the cheek piece & buttpiece, lightly incised in arabesque designs, the forestock w/an incised line by the ramrod channel, pictured in the book "The Kentucky Rifle" by John G.W. Dillin, overall very fine condition, barrel 40 1/4" l. **$14,375**

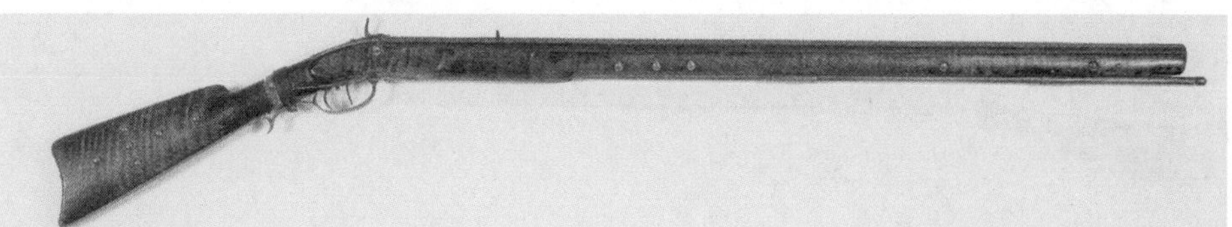

Long rifle, percussion-type w/tiger stripe maple full stock, left-handed side-action lock set w/multiple brass dome-head tacks, first half 19th c., barrel 36" l. **$661**

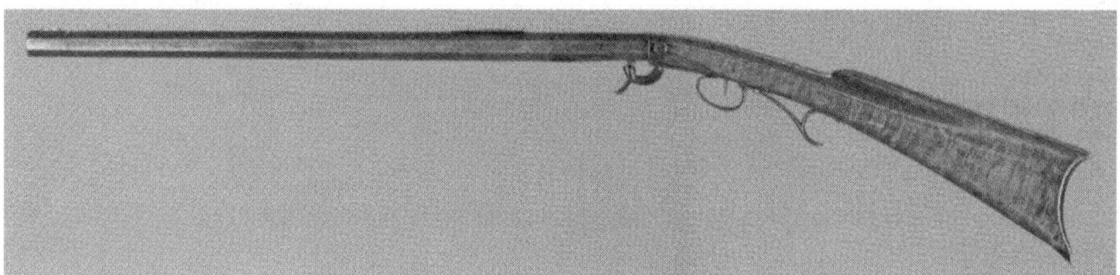

Long rifle, underhammer percussion-type made by Nicanor Kendall, .50 cal., tiger strip maple stock, Windsor, Vermont, ca. 1850, octagonal barrel 23 2/3" l. **$2,875**

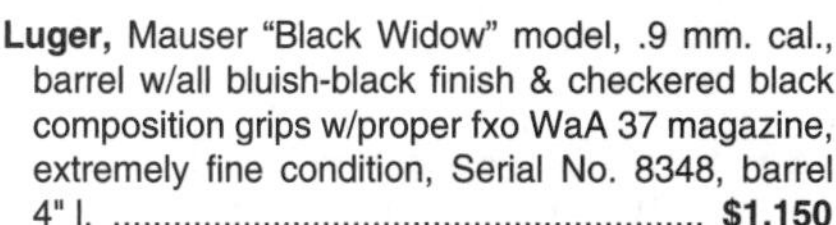

Luger, Mauser "Black Widow" model, .9 mm. cal., barrel w/all bluish-black finish & checkered black composition grips w/proper fxo WaA 37 magazine, extremely fine condition, Serial No. 8348, barrel 4" l. **$1,150**

Luger, S/42 1937 Model, .9mm cal., standard type w/all bluish-black finish w/full checkered wood grips & an aluminum based magazine w/no. 373n, British proofs on various parts, 95 percent original dark finish, right grip severely bruised, Serial No. 2278, barrel 4" l. **$978**

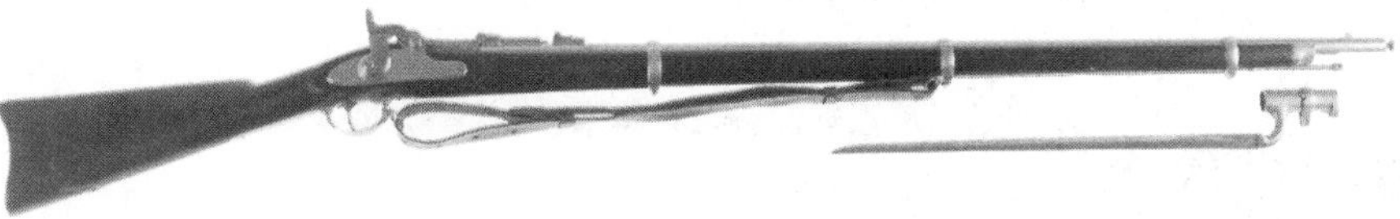

Musket, Berdan conversion Colt Model 1861 Special model, .58 cal. centerfire, original barrel w/square base front sight/bayonet lug, three bands w/two-blade musket rear sight, mounted in original one-piece walnut stock w/musket buttplate & a small metal tag on the toe w/number "7," converted by cutting away about 3" of rear of barrel & fitting a lifting breechlock, muzzle counterbored about 5/8", w/a small brass & leather tampion w/patent date in 1863, very fine condition, only known example extant, barrel 40" l. **$5,750**

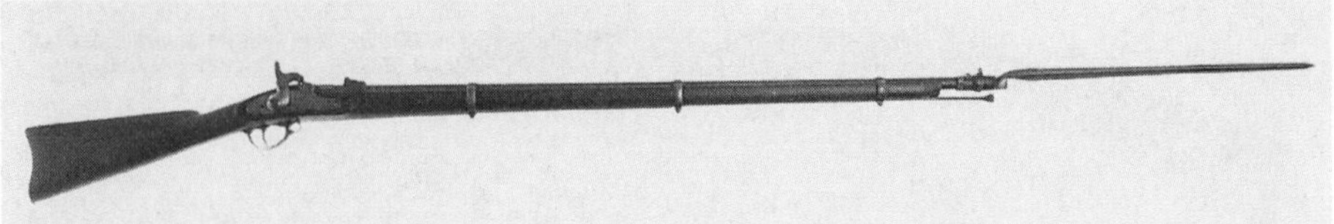

Musket, Colt Special Model 1861, .58 cal., dated 1863 on lockplate, overall rust brown patina, w/bayonet w/broken locking ring, partially octagonal barrel 40" l. **$1,323**

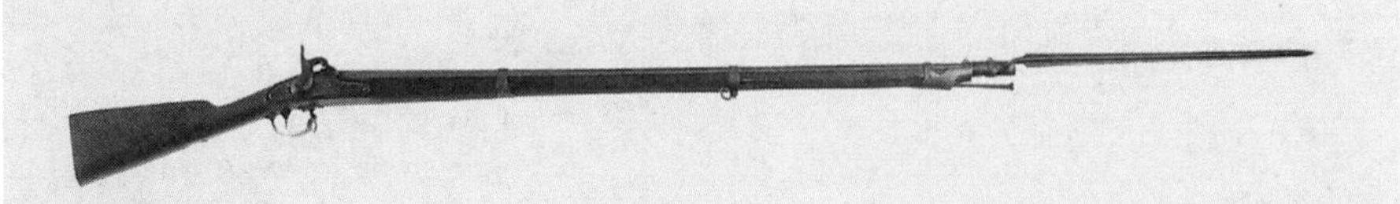

Musket, Harpers Ferry Model 1842, .69 cal., barrel dated 1852, faint inspector mark, overall grey patina, w/ bayonet, barrel 42" l. **$978**

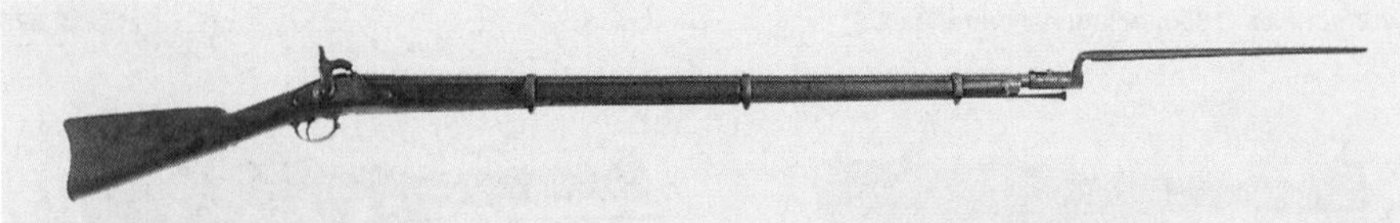

Musket, Mason Model 1863, .58 cal., barrel dated 1863 on the lock, nipple welded into place, rear side & swing swivels missing, ramrod & bayonet replacements, moderate to heavy pitting, stock repaired, barrel 48" l. **$633**

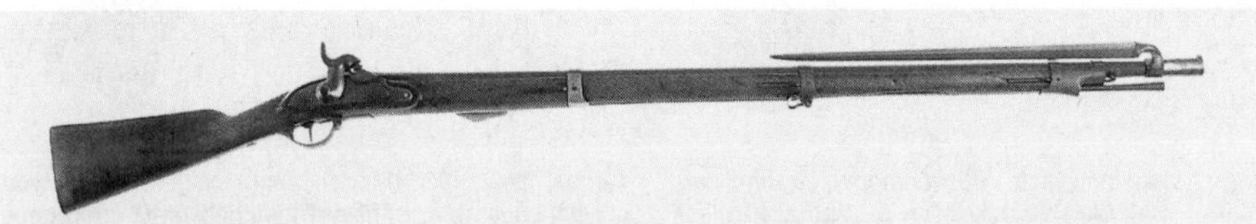

Musket, Ohio surcharge German model, .74 cal., barrel dated 1831, lockplate engraved "Saarn." & "OHIO" stamped at the wrist & left side of stock, correct 18 3/4" l. bayonet, rear sling swivel missing, rust brown patina on barrel, bayonet rusted, partially octagonal barrel 41 1/4" l. **$1,158**

Musket, Savage Model 1861 rifle model, .58 cal., standard Civil War era rifle musket w/long barrel, square base front sight/bayonet lug w/two-leaf, three-position musket rear sight, usual barrel & lock markings dated 1863, walnut stock w/a crisp cartouche, cleaned & stock restored, minor damage on stock, barrel 40" l. **$2,358**

Pistol, Colt 1911A1 Military Model, .45 cal. ACP, barrel w/fixed sights, short trigger & short wide hammer spur w/long grip safety & arched main spring housing, greyish-green parkerized finish w/full checkered brown plastic grips, Serial No. 744948, most original finish, barrel 5" l. **$1,380**

Pistol, Manton (Joseph) double-barreled flintlock model, .20 cal., barrels mounted in nicely figured one-piece walnut stock w/raised side panels around the lockplate w/a smooth round grip w/knob at the bottom, a decorative nosepipe for the iron-tipped rammer & an urn finial on the plain trigger guard, lock plates & gooseneck hammers w/ light engraving & the maker's name & "London" on each side, locks slightly curved w/stepped ends without teats & roller frizzens w/separate pans & platinum flash holes, barrel secured in stock w/two wedges, stock w/crack in front of each lock, fine medium patina, barrels 10 1/8" l. **$1,380**

Pistol, Model 1816 flintlock relic model, .54 cal., no visible markings except "US" proof on breech end of barrel, all-iron furniture w/brass upward-tilting pan, severely pitted, wooden grip also eroded, top jaw appears to be replacement, stock w/crack, overall 15 1/2" l. **$633**

Pistol, Model 1842 EIG Army percussion-type, .65 cal., heavy military type w/round barrel, fixed sights, front action lock, nickeled brass furniture w/captive rammer & a sling loop in the button, lock dated 1867 - Burningham w/a large cartouche on the left flat that is also marked "Woodward & Sons," very fine w/95 percent original bluing, barrel 8" l. **$1,150**

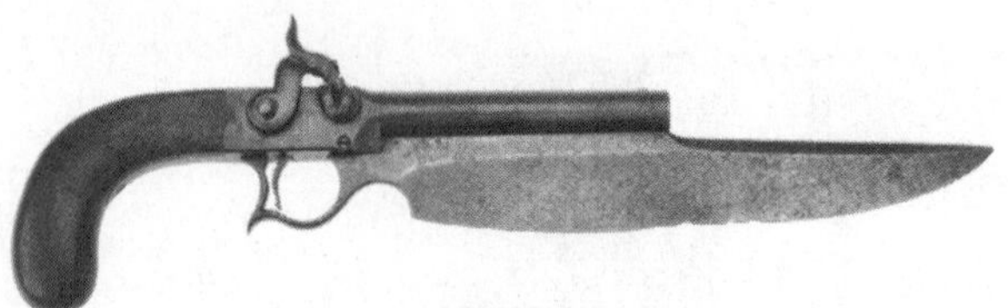

Pistol, Morrill Elgin small-frame cutlass model, .36 cal., authentic w/9 3/8" l. blade w/an integral trigger guard, attached to a small frame box lock side hammer pistol w/a one-piece bag-shaped walnut grip, blade w/etched panels on both sides w/spread-winged early American eagles, left side eagle w/banner in beak reading "Liberty" & 17 stars above & inscription of maker in Amherst, Massachusetts below, right side of blade w/eagle & another inscription & spray of flowers, barrel w/thin half-moon sight w/a fixed rear sight, blade dovetailed into bottom of barrel & held w/a screw, rare, Serial No. 42, barrel 4" l. **$11,500**

Revolver, Allen & Wheelock belt model percussion model, 36 cal., side hammer w/4 3/4" l. octagonal barrel w/German silver front sight & two-piece walnut grips, cylinder engraved w/a forest scene w/deer, dogs & birds, good condition, no original finish remains, medium brown patina, broken nipples, Serial Number 301 .... **$518**

Revolver, Allen & Wheelock belt percussion model, .36 cal., two-piece walnut grips, side hammer w/octagonal barrel w/German silver front sight, cylinder w/an engraved forest scene w/deer, dogs & birds, no original finish, Serial No. 84, barrel 5 3/4" l. **$920**

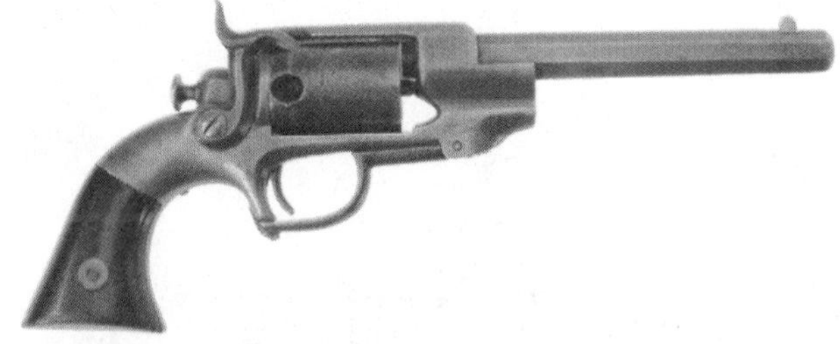

Revolver, Colt 1851 Navy model, .36 cal., standard Navy w/7 1/2" l. octagonal barrel, tiny brass front sight, blue- and case- colored w/one-piece walnut grips, in a modern red-lined, compartmented case containing a ball bullet mold, a modern flask, & a tin of modern caps, very fine condition, Serial No. 143416, the set **$949**

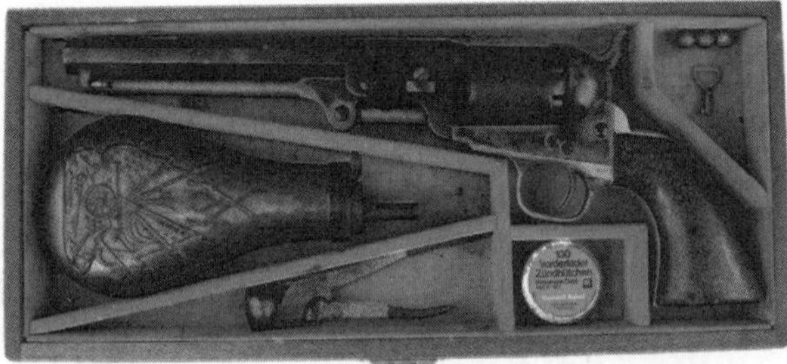

Revolver, Colt early martially-marked single-action model, .45 cal., very rare Samuel B. Lewis-inspected cavalry Colt, barrel slightly reduced in length, original front sight modified, one-piece walnut grips, barrel nickel-plated, barrel w/slant one-line address w/daggers at each end, small "L" proofs on various parts, original bull's-eye ejector rod head, Serial No. 16293, barrel 7 5/16" l. **$8,338**

Revolver, Colt Model 1849 pocket type, .31 cal., one-piece walnut grip, octagonal barrel w/two-line New York address marking, small brass front sight, silver plated trigger guard & back strap, fine condition, Serial No. 24484, barrel 4" l. **$1,035**

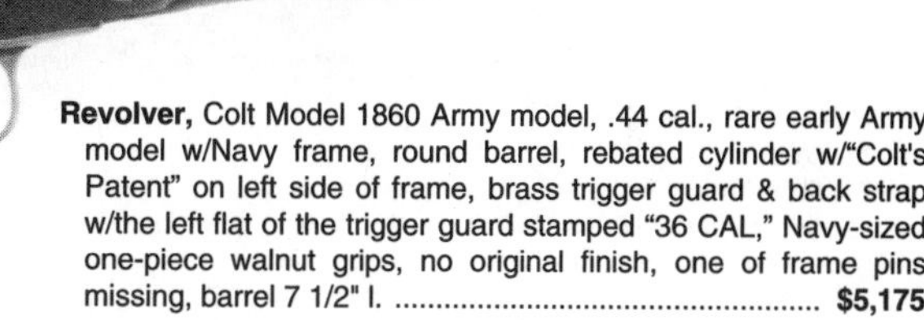

Revolver, Colt Model 1860 Army model, .44 cal., rare early Army model w/Navy frame, round barrel, rebated cylinder w/"Colt's Patent" on left side of frame, brass trigger guard & back strap w/the left flat of the trigger guard stamped "36 CAL," Navy-sized one-piece walnut grips, no original finish, one of frame pins missing, barrel 7 1/2" l. **$5,175**

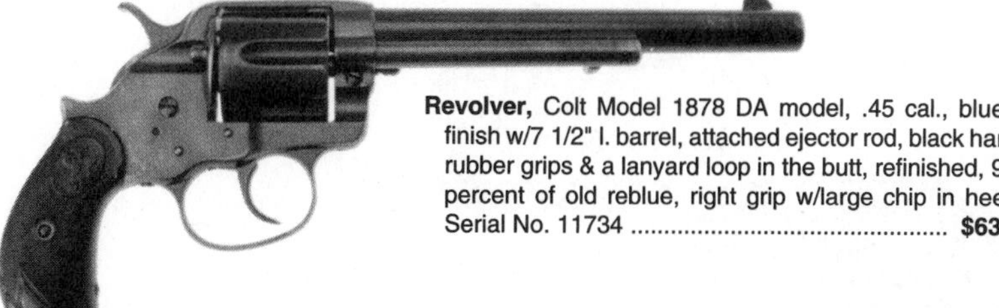

Revolver, Colt Model 1878 DA model, .45 cal., blued finish w/7 1/2" l. barrel, attached ejector rod, black hard rubber grips & a lanyard loop in the butt, refinished, 90 percent of old reblue, right grip w/large chip in heel, Serial No. 11734 .... **$633**

Revolver, Colt single-action, handle w/ applied bone plaques, one side carved w/a steer head, produced in 1891, 10 1/8" l. **$1,725**

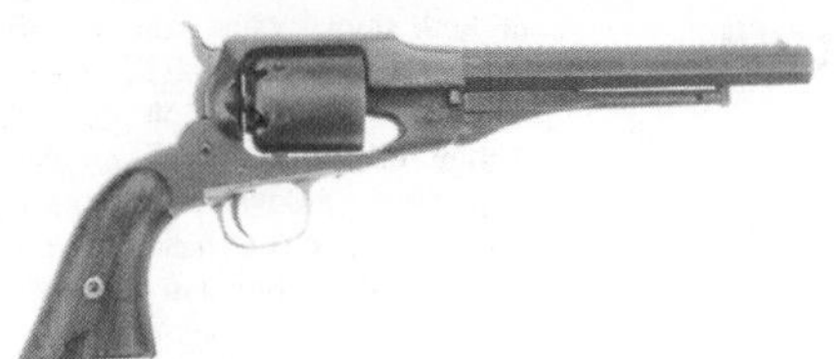

Revolver, Remington Beals Army model, .44 cal., standard Beals Army w/octagonal barrel, dovetailed cone German silver front sight w/two-piece walnut grips, usual markings on top of barrel, brass trigger guard, one of only 1900 produced, worn but legible markings, replaced rammer screw, missing large chip from right side, barrel 8" l. **$2,128**

Revolver, Remington New Model Army, .44 cal., martially marked w/blue finish, two-piece walnut grips, outline of a cartouche on the left grip & small inspector initials on various parts, overall good condition, brass trigger guard w/inspector initial from a smaller frame Navy revolver, cylindrical pin stamped "24," barrel 8" l. **$1,265**

Revolver, Rogers & Spencer percussion model, .44 cal., octagonal barrel, cone front sight, reproduction two-piece walnut grips, small "B" inspector mark on various parts, Serial No. 2738, barrel 7 1/2" l. **$1,093**

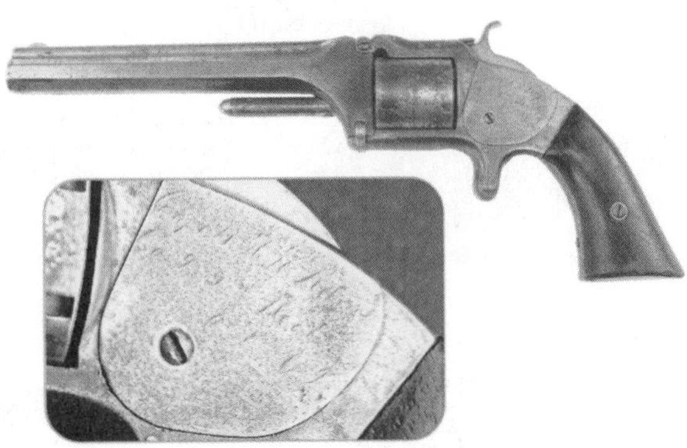

Revolver, Smith & Wesson No. 2 Army model, .32 cal. rim-fire, keyhole barrel, half-moon front sight, unfluted cylinder w/two-piece rosewood grips, Civil War-era inscription for Union officer from Kentucky, about 25 percent original nickel-plating, dark patina, grips w/chipped toes, Serial No. 8215, barrel 6" l. **$3,738**

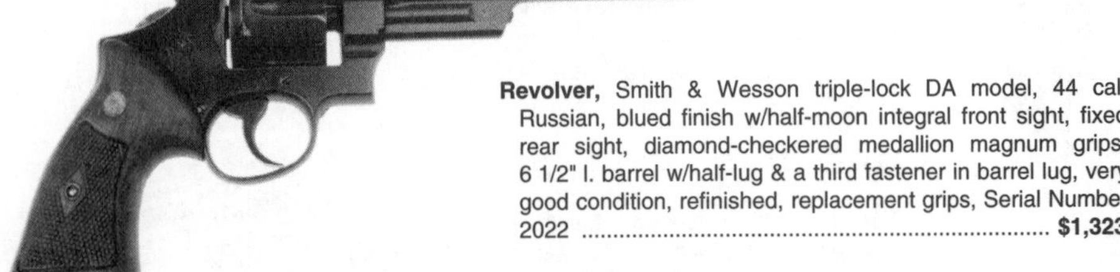

Revolver, Smith & Wesson triple-lock DA model, 44 cal. Russian, blued finish w/half-moon integral front sight, fixed rear sight, diamond-checkered medallion magnum grips, 6 1/2" l. barrel w/half-lug & a third fastener in barrel lug, very good condition, refinished, replacement grips, Serial Number 2022 .... **$1,323**

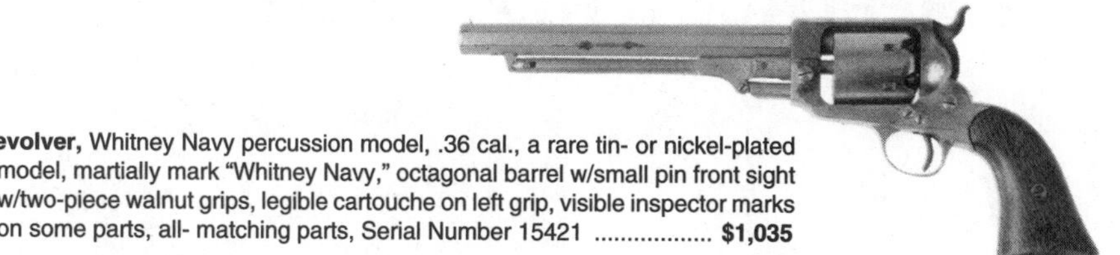

Revolver, Whitney Navy percussion model, .36 cal., a rare tin- or nickel-plated model, martially mark "Whitney Navy," octagonal barrel w/small pin front sight w/two-piece walnut grips, legible cartouche on left grip, visible inspector marks on some parts, all- matching parts, Serial Number 15421 .... **$1,035**

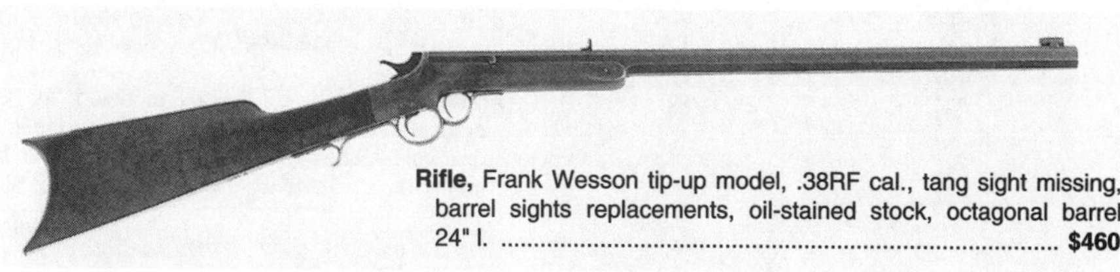

Rifle, Frank Wesson tip-up model, .38RF cal., tang sight missing, barrel sights replacements, oil-stained stock, octagonal barrel 24" l. **$460**

Rifle, Maynard Model 1873 Improved Hunters No. 8 single-shot model, .35-30 cal., blued finish, pinched front sights w/two position V-notch rear sight, straight stock w/carbine-type smooth steel buttplate, octagonal to round 26" barrel **$1,035**

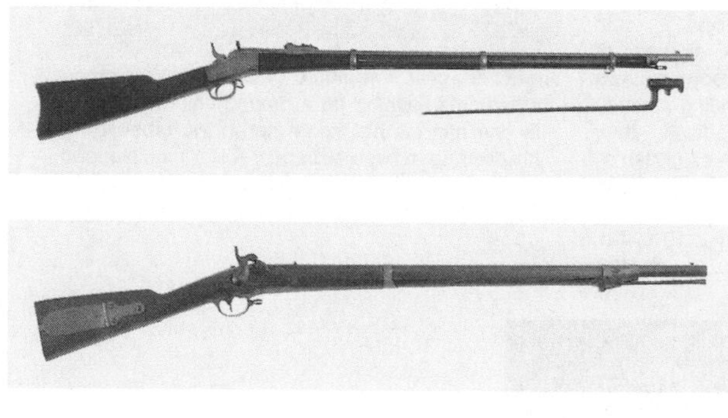

Rifle, Remington rolling-block military model, .50/70 cal., standard markings on upper tang, action w/the New York safety but no markings, bayonet & ramrod replaced, round barrel 36" l. **$518**

Rifle, Robbins, Kendall & Lawrence Model 1842 Mississippi, .54 cal. dated 1847 on the lockplate, "WAT" cartouche on left side of stock, spare nipple in patchbox, overall greyish brown patina, round barrel 33" l. **$1,955**

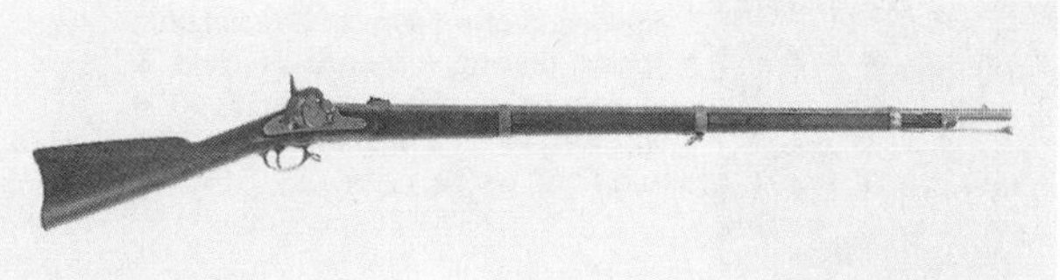

Rifle, Springfield Model 1855 Cadet model, .60 bored out cal., barrel & lock dated 1869, overall grey patina, ramrod a short replacement, stock including forearm tip 49 1/2" l. **$1,438**

FIREPLACE & HEARTH ITEMS

Andirons, brass & iron, Federal style, each w/an urn-form finial w/bright-cut & punchwork swag & pendant designs w/beaded borders supported on a tapered column embellished w/spiraling vines, stepped square plinth w/engraved shield & punchwork chevron border, over a shaped skirt w/conforming swag & pendant design, further supported on arched spurred cabriole legs w/claw-and-ball feet, attributed to Daniel King, Philadelphia, 1790-1810, 13 1/4 x 25 1/2", 30 1/2" h. **$41,125**

Andirons, cast iron, figures of cowboy outlaws standing ready to draw their six-shooters, back bar log support, very rusty, 19 1/4" h. **$1,495**

Andirons, cast iron, figural, modeled as facing crescent-shaped man-in-the-moon faces w/ dramatic features, double-step half- round base, latter 19th c., 9 1/2" w., 14 1/4" h., pr. **$5,175**

Andirons, cast iron, figure of George Washington standing & leaning on a draped column, a book in one hand & his tricorn hat in the other, on a tall plinth-form base w/drapery & star trim, stepped block feet, repainted, 19th c., 9 1/4 x 14 1/4", 21 1/2" h. **$633**

Andirons, ormolu, Regence-Style, each composed of a figure of a recumbent sphinx draped w/fleur-de-lis cloth & resting on a large cartouche on a volute-shaped base, France, late 19th c., 14 1/2" w., 19" h., pr. **$5,975**

Fireplace fender, gilt- and patinated bronze, Regency style, modeled as a stylized long honeysuckle flowerhead-and-scroll bar surmounting a patinated bronze stepped molded base, England, first quarter 19th c., 40 1/2" l., 8 1/2" h. **$1,840**

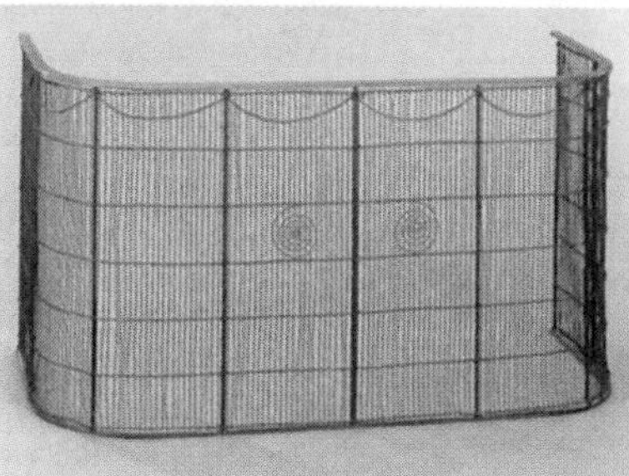

Fireplace screen, brass & wire, Federal style, tall U-form screen w/a brass top support band, fine wire banding highlighted w/swags along the top & small central spirals, early 19th c., 34" l. **$717**

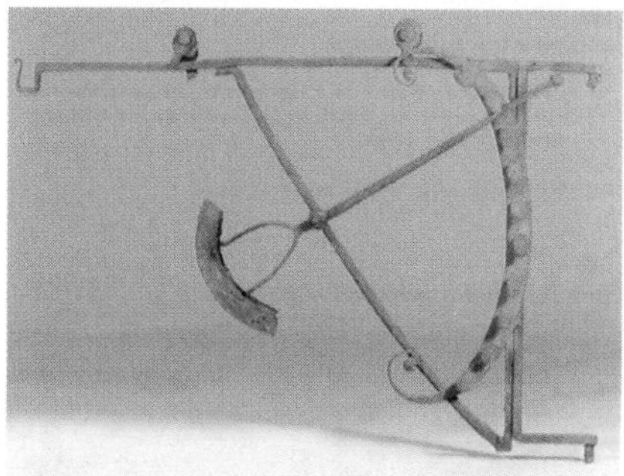

Hearth crane, wrought iron, a large L-bracket w/C-form adjusting mechanism & support bar w/adjusting bar arm, Pennsylvania, 18th c., 47 1/2" w., 34" h. **$2,990**

Hearth broom, horse hair bristles fitted in a small board w/a long center slender turned handle, original red paint w/black, yellow & gold striping & stenciled & free-hand floral decoration in brown powder & black, 28" l. (wear, some paint flaking) **$248**

Hearth trivet, wrought iron, three tall slender legs supporting a horseshoe-shaped trivet top w/spade & scroll openwork designs, carved wooden handle extending from top, American, early 19th c., 14 1/2" l., 7 5/8" h. (corrosion, holes) **$316**

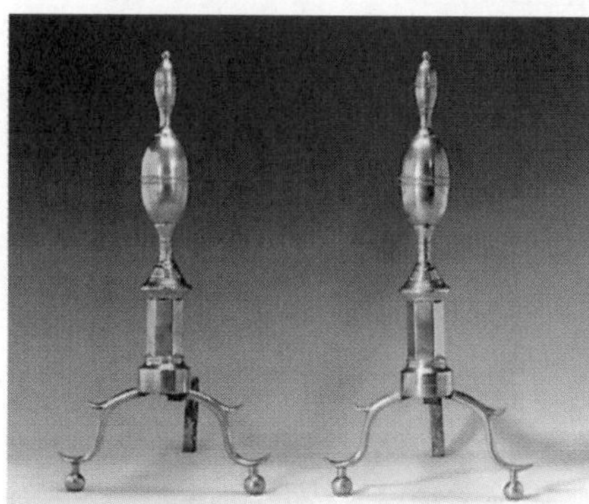

Fireplace tool set, brass, Federal style, the ring-turned oval top w/a matching finial, above a hexagonal support on arching spurred cabriole legs on ball feet, together w/a matching pair of tongs & a shovel, New York, New York, ca. 1800-20, andirons 21 1/2" h., the set (ILLUS. of andirons only) **$2,868**

Fireboard, painted & decorated, diamond & rosette border framing three recessed geometric carved panels centering foliate scrolled designs painted in black, dark green, maroon & yellow, possibly New England, last quarter 19th c., 38 x 39" (minor imperfections) **$863**

Fireplace fender, brass & wire, Federal style, long low form w/curved ends, a brass top rail above scroll-decorated vertical wirework screening, America or England, late 18th - early 19th c., 15 x 49 1/2", 10" h. **$2,875**

Fireplace tender, brass & wire, a narrow brass upper rail w/square corners & a bowed center section above wire side composed of thin vertical bands, iron base plate, America or England, late 18th - early 19th c., 14 1/2 x 29 3/4", 9 1/2" h. **$1,495**

Fireplace tool set, gilt-bronze, Egyptian Revival style, andirons w/a female Egyptian bust wearing a flaring headdress w/serpent finial above an lotus blossom & columnar block shaft above a winged scarab above the front feet cast w/Egyptian masks, King Tut-style figural Egyptian busts at the ends of the log rests, a set of matching tools in a rack topped by an Egyptian pharaoh bust & ending in a tray w/early Egyptian designs, late 19th or early 20th c., the set **$2,760**

FRAKTUR

Fraktur paintings are decorative birth and marriage certificates of the 18th and 19th centuries and also include family registers and similar documents. Illuminated family documents, birth and baptismal certificates, religious texts and rewards of merit, in a particular style, are known as "fraktur" because of the similarity to the 16th century typeface of that name. Gay watercolor borders, frequently incorporating stylized birds, often frame the hand-lettered documents, which were executed by local ministers, schoolmasters or itinerant penmen. Most are of Pennsylvania Dutch origin.

Birth & baptism certificate, pen & ink & watercolor on paper, features the figures of two standing woman flanking a columned arcade topped by two large urns & inscribed across the top "Certificate of Birth & Baptism," the opening between the columns w/information on the birth of Jacob William Lutz, 1850, in Clinton County, Pennsylvania, attributed to the Reverend Henry Young, bright colors of blue, yellow & orange, light staining & creases, later wood frame, 13 5/8 x 16 1/4" **$6,038**

Birth & baptism record, pen & ink & watercolor on paper, recording the birth of a child in 1823, a wide border h.p. w/ tall serpentined flowering stems & large birds at the sides & hex signs & flowers & vines at the top & bottom, a central bordered square w/the information printed in Gothic script, Pennsylvania school, 8 x 10" **$1,673**

Birth & baptismal fraktur (Geburts und Taufschein), pen & ink & watercolor, recording the birth of George Stober in York County, Pennsylvania in November 1800, large rectangular form w/the German inscriptions in a central square formed by pale green bands w/an angel head w/ long wings at the center top & a spread-winged American eagle at the center bottom, the side panels each decorated w/a three-towered castle-like building w/arched windows above pairs of stylized crowned lions w/human faces, painted in green & salmon pink by Christian Mertel, a school master in Dauphin County, Pennsylvania, in a modern molded frame, 14 5/8 x 18 5/8" **$2,990**

Birth certificate, pen & ink & watercolor on paper, commemorating the birth of Leah Tiefenbachen, Columbia County, Pennsylvania, flying eagles in the top corners flanking a title box over a flowering sprig over a large text box flanked by tall flowering plants in urns resting atop text boxes, a pair of birds on flowering plants in the bottom center, in dark yellow, red, green & black, dated March 24, 1825, by Fredrich Kusler, 12 x 15 1/2" **$2,400**

Bookplate, pen & ink & watercolor on paper, colorful design centered w/a tall leafy stem w/pairs of red tulip flowers flanking a fanned yellow flowers, a slender black & yellow bird flank the stem above further tulips & other flowers, on laid paper, w/note recording purchase at a Pennsylvania sale, in a worn gilt shadowbox frame, some stains & edge damage, early 19th c., 6 1/2 x 8 1/4" **$2,990**

Drawing, watercolor on paper, stylized portrait of a lady on horseback, wearing a long spotted dress & a crown-form cap, flanked by stylized tulip blossoms & w/smaller flowers below, inscribed to Elizabeth Mayerin below the horse, in shades of red, yellow, black & brown, ca. 1784, by Frederick Krebes, Pennsylvania, framed, picture 12 1/4 x 15" **$6,000**

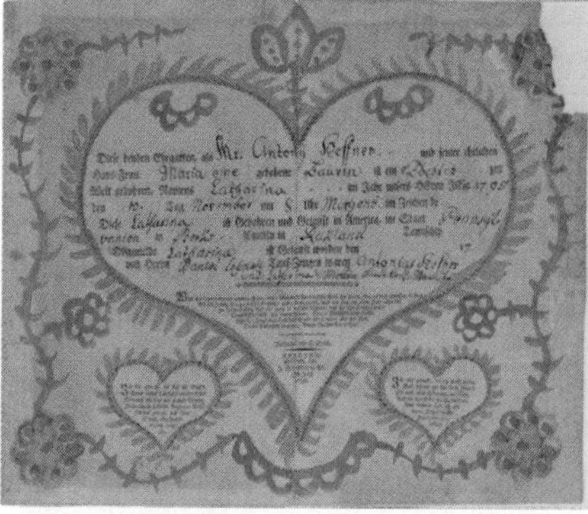

Marriage certificate, pen & ink & watercolor on paper, celebrating the marriage of Mr. Anthony Beffner & Maria Laurin Bochler, centered by a large heart in pale green enclosing black script & trimmed w/orange loops w/two small script-filled hearts below & a top tulip blossom, a meandering orange vine around the sides & bottom w/scalloped round orange & pale green blossoms, marriage dated 1795, paper print date in lower left corner 1798, Pennsylvania, 13 1/4 x 16" **$600**

FURNITURE MARKET REPORT

"Business is better than expected, given current conditions," said furniture dealer Charles Pharr, who owns and operates Aadvark-Antiques and Estate Liquidations (www.aardvark-antiques.com) in Oakwood, Georgia. Pharr's shop specializes in traditional early American and early English furniture.

He attributes his success in part to his online presence. Many people are very comfortable with buying online, examining their prospective purchases solely through photos. These shoppers are so experienced with the Internet that they don't hesitate to search through online pages, pay electronically, and have their merchandise delivered directly to their door.

Pharr estimates that 50 percent of his business is to out-of-state-customers, primarily in urban and suburban areas. He also sells to customers in Europe, but they generally purchase smaller items. He recently sold a $10,000 table and set of chairs to a customer in the Dominican Republic, however.

"Shoppers are becoming savvy," Pharr commented, but noted that people who have a lot of money are still eager to buy top-notch furnishings. People are not using interior decorators as much now, so they apparently trust their instincts to select their decor themselves.

He sells a wide variety of furniture and it runs the gamut in style and function. He noted, though, that his customers tend to prefer darker woods—the brownish reds of mahogany and cherry to the lighter woods of oak and maple.

According to Pharr, "sales of art and rugs have slowed way down," although the rest of his inventory has sold steadily. His strongest sales are in long dining room tables, other dining room pieces, and bedroom furniture. While these pieces are relatively large, heavy, and bulky, the logistics in shipping them has not been a problem, and he has been able to arrange good deals on shipping costs.

Pharr said his integrity and honesty are also essential to his success and helps bring in repeat customers—not only twice but three and four times, in some cases. He explained that he offers a good product for a good price and believes antique furniture is a much better value than brand new because of its superior quality, especially in relation to its cost.

Pharr acquires his inventory by buying the contents of entire estates and by purchasing large pieces of furniture that people no longer have room for because they are downsizing. This creates an opportunity for customers to buy high quality furniture at a bargain. He also sells quite a few long dining tables to businesses. Corporate buyers find his store when they type in the key words "conference table" in their online searches. Office equipment stores don't offer antiques, so his store is ideal for companies who prefer the look of an antique conference table to a new one.

While furniture is one of the more challenged antique categories, Pharr has demonstrated that with the right business model, dealers can still do well.

FURNITURE

Furniture made in the United States during the 18th and 19th centuries is coveted by collectors. American antique furniture has a European background, primarily English, since the influence of the Continent usually found its way to America by way of England. If the style did not originate in England, it came to America by way of England. For this reason, some American furniture styles carry the name of an English monarch or an English designer. However, we must realize that, until recently, little research has been conducted and even less published on the Spanish and French influences in the area of the California missions and New Orleans.

After the American revolution, cabinetmakers in the United States shunned the prevailing styles in England and chose to bring the French styles of Napoleon's Empire to the United States and we have the uniquely named "American Empire" (Classical) style of furniture in a country that never had an emperor.

During the Victorian period, quality furniture began to be mass-produced in this country with its rapidly growing population. So much walnut furniture was manufactured that the vast supply of walnut was virtually depleted and it was of necessity that oak furniture became fashionable as the 19th century drew to a close.

For our purposes, the general guidelines for dating will be: Pilgrim Century - 1620-85; William & Mary - 1685-1720; Queen Anne - 1720-50; Chippendale - 1750-85; Federal - 1785-1820; Hepplewhite - 1785-1820; Sheraton - 1800-20; American Empire (Classical) - 1815-40; Victorian - 1840-1900; Early Victorian - 1840-50; Gothic Revival - 1840-90; Rococo (Louis XV) - 1845-70; Renaissance - 1860-85; Louis XVI - 1865-75; Eastlake - 1870-95; Jacobean & Turkish Revival - 1870-95; Aesthetic Movement - 1880-1900; Art Nouveau - 1890-1918; Turn-of-the-Century - 1895-1910; Mission (Arts & Crafts movement) - 1900-15; Art Deco - 1925-40

All furniture included in this listing is American unless otherwise noted.

Beds

Arts & Crafts, oak, three-quarters size, the headboard composed of two pairs of vertical slats flanking a wide central slat between rails joined to the tapering square corner posts, the slightly shorter footboard of matching design, mattress slats & original side boards, good original finish, one broken peg, decal label of L. & J.G. Stickley, early 20th c., 50 3/4 x 80", 46" h. **$2,300**

Classical "sleigh" bed, mahogany, double-size, the even upright S-scroll head- and footboards joined by shaped side rails on flat rounded feet, ca. 1830-40, 57 1/2 x 75", 41 1/2" h. **$1,160**

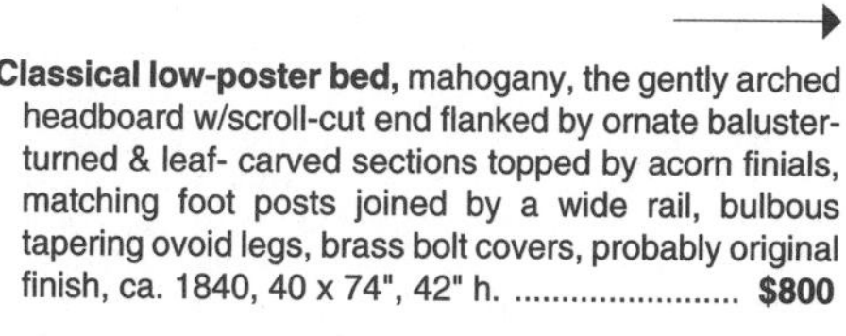

Classical low-poster bed, mahogany, the gently arched headboard w/scroll-cut end flanked by ornate baluster-turned & leaf- carved sections topped by acorn finials, matching foot posts joined by a wide rail, bulbous tapering ovoid legs, brass bolt covers, probably original finish, ca. 1840, 40 x 74", 42" h. **$800**

Classical tall-poster bed, mahogany, the arched & scroll-carved headboard over two large rectangular flame veneer panels flanked by tall knob-, ring- and acanthus leaf-carved tall posts w/ knob finials, matching foot posts, short baluster-turned legs, original brass bolt covers, original dark finish, ca. 1835, 58 x 80", 7' h. **$5,500**

Classical low-poster bed, mahogany, the wide arched & scroll-carved headboard flanked by paneled posts topped by leaf- carved baluster-and-ring-turned finials, heavy tapering ring-turned legs, original dark finish, ca. 1830s, 58 x 78", 5' h. **$1,000**

Classical Revival tall-poster bed, mahogany, the wide headboard w/ a broken-scroll crestrail centered by a pointed knob finial & flanked by rope-twist-turned posts w/knob-turned finials, the slightly shorter foot posts joined by a ropetwist-, knob- and ring- turned rail above a wide scroll-ended lower rail, short knob-turned feet, refinished, early 20th c., 58 x 78", 5' h. **$850**

Classical tall-poster bed, mahogany, the high paneled headboard w/notched corners flanked by tall slender baluster-and-ring- turned posts w/acanthus leaf carving & baluster-form finials w/knobs, matching foot posts joined by a rail, brass-capped casters, ca. 1835, refinished, 60 x 80", 7' 6" h. **$7,500**

Classical Revival tall-poster bed, mahogany, each post w/ring-turned segments alternating w/reeded segments & carved pineapple designs, the narrow cut-out headboard w/a carved crest bar w/rosette ends, on pineapple-and paw-carved legs, late 19th c., 52 x 79", 96" h. **$3,680**

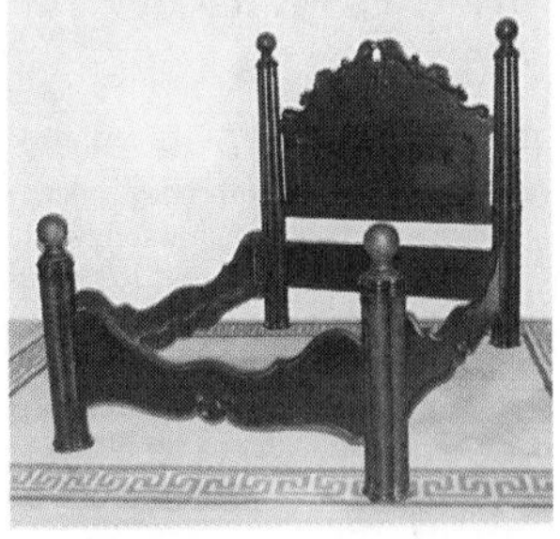

Classical-Rococo transitional tall-poster bed, mahogany, the high arched headboard w/ornate carved scrolls flanked by tall posts formed by a cluster of four columns topped w/a ball finial, shorter matching foot posts, serpentine scroll-trimmed siderails & footrails, possibly original finish, ca. 1845, 66 x 84", 6' h. **$4,500**

Colonial Revival tall-poster canopy bed, mahogany w/stenciled decoration, the rectangular cove-molded canopy frame raised on tall baluster-, ring- and rod-turned posts, a high scroll-cut arched headboard w/carved center shell above an arched stenciled panel, wide side rails & foot rail w/carved scrolls & beaded base band, on short Spanish feet, original dark finish, full-sized, ca. 1920s, 60 x 80", 6' 8" h. **$1,500**

Empire-Style bed, ormolu-mounted mahogany, the high flat-topped headboard w/a rounded crestrail fitted w/ a small figural ormolu boss over an arched panel w/ corner bosses flanked by free-standing side columns w/ ormolu capitals, the matching lower footboard trimmed w/ormolu bar mounts & a large wreath, on short, square tapering legs, France, ca. 1900, 59 1/2 x 81", 4' 4" h. **$1,265**

→

Federal tall-poster canopy bed, red-stained maple, a delicate arched canopy frame raised on baluster-, ring- and urn-turned reeded posts above corner blocks & baluster- and ring-turned legs ending in peg feet, the simple arched headboard between plain turned & tapering headposts, old surface, minor imperfections, New England, ca. 1815, 51 x 70", 6' 8" h. **$4,994**

Country-style child's rope bed, painted, the wide peaked headboard between block-and-rod-turned spots w/large button finials & on baluster-turned lower legs, a matching lower footboard, original side rails, original black paint, mid-19th c., 36 x 68 1/2" **$460**

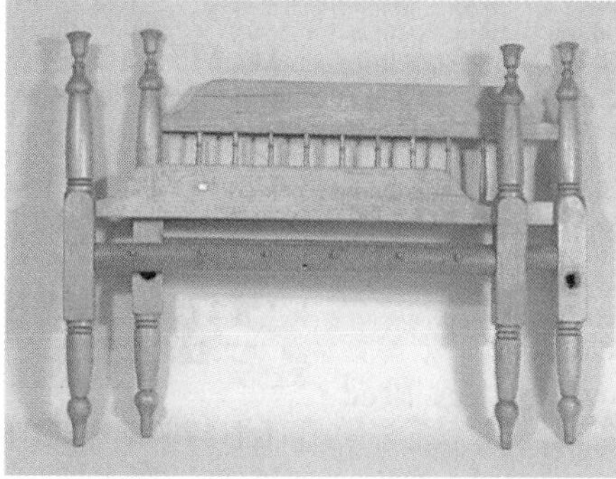

Country-style low-poster rope bed, three-quarters size, maple, the headboard w/a long arched crestrail above a row of slender turned spindles between the block-, rod- and ring-turned headposts w/flared turned finials, the footboard w/a single arched rail above the end rail between footposts matching the headposts, refinished, mid-19th c., 54" w., 40" h. **$138**

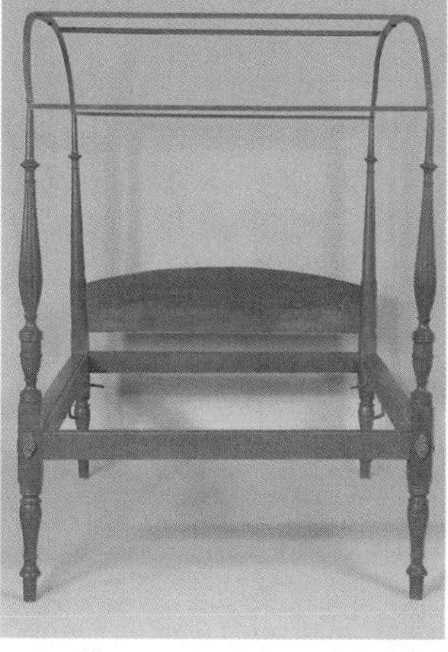

Federal Revival tall-poster twin-sized canopy beds, mahogany, a rectangular molded canopy rail above tall baluster ring- turned & leaf-carved posts w/pineapple finials, the headboard carved across the top w/a spread-winged eagle, the similar footboard w/ shell & scroll carving, tall tapering baluster-turned legs on knob feet, original finish, ca. 1920s, 48 x 76", 8' h., pr. (ILLUS. of one) ... **$5,000**

Louis Philippe bed, mahogany, the even headboards & footboards w/ arched scroll-carved crests above plain panels flanked by paneled stiles w/turned button finials, deep shaped siderails, heavy tapering ring- and knob-turned legs, France, mid-19th c., 40 1/2 x 74", 39" h. **$805**

Victorian Eastlake substyle bed, highback-style frame, walnut & burl walnut, the tall headboard w/a stepped crown-form cornice composed of a low gallery rail between small turned finials projecting above a long narrow floral-carved panel above a grouping of three floral-carved solid panels flanked by bobbin-turned lattice panels between the blocked back styles, a long plain horizontal burl panel above a plain panel in the lower headboard, the low footboard w/a flat crestrail above a narrow floral-carved panel above a long rectangular burl panel, original side rails, ca. 1880, 57 x 74", 6' 7 1/2" h. **$546**

Oriental canopy bed, rosewood, the rectangular canopy top pierce-carved w/rectangular panels & raised on six slender tapering posts above the platform base enclosed by a three-quarters gallery pierce-carved w/squares & quatrefoils, raised on high incurved blocked legs, the top w/overall subtle low-relief carved foliage sprays, China, late 19th c., 59 x 87", 94" h. **$3,450**

Victorian Renaissance Revival substyle bed, walnut & burl walnut, highback-style, the tall headboard w/a large central carved fleur-de-lis form cartouche centered by the relief-carved face of a maiden w/flowing hair, steeply angled crest molding on each side above a very large oval composed of concentric rings w/a large central burl panel, the square side posts w/large urn-form finials & a pendant band of fleur-de-lis down each sides, the low arched footboard w/a curved raised burl band w/central carved sprig above a banded burl oval panel, the curved low corner posts carved w/a fanned shell device above a bold oblong scroll cartouche, shaped siderails w/raised molding trim, attributed to Mitchell & Rammelsberg, ca. 1870s, 80 x 88", 7' 3" h. **$9,775**

Victorian Rococo bed, carved rosewood, the high headboard w/a tall broken-arch crest composed of ornate carved scrolls & pierced scroll panels centered by a turned urn finial, the arched crestrail above a simple paneled board flanked by matching turned urn corner finials, the lower arched footboard w/matching turned finials, wide sideboards, probably New York City, ca. 1855, original finish, 60 x 80", 6' h. **$2,800**

Victorian Rococo bed, chestnut & walnut, the high headboard w/an arched, stepped crestrail topped by a scroll-carved cartouche finial above a central scroll-carved cartouche over an oval raised band, blocked top corners w/knob-turned finials, the matching low footboard w/curved leg panels, refinished, ca. 1860, 58 x 78", 5' h. **$950**

Victorian Rococo half-tester bed, mahogany, the top half-tester frame w/serpentine sides w/a button- and scroll-carved front crest & reeded urn-turned corner finials, the arched headboard w/a shell- and rondel-carved crest & scroll-carved stepped crestrails above a burled panel flanked by tapering posts, shaped & scroll-carved siderails & footboard flanked by short columns w/arched panels & ring- and knob-turned pointed finials, attributed to Charles Lee, Manchester, Massachusetts, ca. 1860, 74 1/2 x 88 1/2", headboard 113" h. **$19,550**

Victorian Rococo tall-poster bed, mahogany, the high arched & scroll-carved headboard centered by a shell-carved crest & flanked by tall tapering octagonal posts, wide serpentine side & foot rails, matching tall tapering octagonal foot posts, mid-19th c., missing canopy tester, 66 x 90", 8' 5" h. **$5,060**

Benches

Arts & Crafts hall bench, oak, the wide concave crestrail above three shaped back splats between slender stiles w/curved corner ears, sharply tapering flat open arms above incurved flat supports forming the front legs, hinged plank seat, early 20th c., 16 x 40", 41" h. **$633**

Bucket (or water) bench, country-style, painted pine, a narrow rectangular top shelf atop wide board upright ends w/bootjack feet & chamfered at the top over two open dovetailed medial shelves, original deep red paint, attributed to Ohio, mid-19th c., good patina, minor age splits & wear, 13 x 43", 41 1/2" h. **$2,760**

Bucket (or water) bench, country-style, painted poplar, the narrow rectangular top above a narrow stepped-back enclosed shelf & chamfered one-board ends w/bootjack feet flanking two lower open shelves, old red wash, 19th c., wear to back corners of lower shelves, 12 x 43 1/4", 47" h. **$1,093**

Bucket (or water) bench, country-style, pine w/old red wash & traces of blue paint, a narrow top shelf above one-board sides incurved at the top flanking an upper shelf w/a narrow back brace & front apron above a deeper bottom shelf on a flat apron, old splits w/small notches out of lower front corners, early square nail construction, 13 x 43 1/2", 42" h. **$2,070**

Charles II bench, oak, long narrow rectangular seat cushion on a conforming frame raised on six block- and knob-turned legs joined by barley-twist turned rails, last quarter 17th c. or later, England, 22 x 60", 18 1/2" h. **$2,070**

Classical window bench, parcel-gilt carved mahogany, the deep upright upholstered S-scroll end arms faced w/carved gilt- trimmed dolphins, a flat molded seatrail raised on ornate gilded scrolled dolphin legs, America, early 19th c., 19 x 50", 32" h. **$8,625**

European upholstered bench, walnut, the deep rectangular seat upholstered in a figural tapestry w/a floral background & edged in tassels, the knob- and ring-turned legs & stretchers joined by corner blocks on bun feet, Flemish, late 18th c., 18 x 24", 13" h. **$1,265**

Louis XVI-Style bench, polychrome-painted wood, the long oval top w/a separate cushion above a beaded apron & raised on four turned tapering fluted legs headed by leaf clusters & joined by an H-stretcher centered by a turned knob & ending w/incurved end rungs, simple baluster-turned feet, creamy white w/other colors, France, early 20th c., 14 1/2 x 35", 20" h. **$978**

Modern-style bench, hardwood, the long narrow rectangular top divided into two sections composed of closely spaced slats in natural wood, raised on ebonized box-style legs, designed by George Nelson for Herman Miller Furniture Co., 18 1/2 x 48", 14" h. **$633**

Regency curule bench, carved, rosewood-grained & parcel-gilt wood, flaring U-form outswept upper rails raised on inverted U-form legs ending in giltwood paw feet, seat upholstered in green velvet w/brass tack trim, England, first quarter 19th c., 28 1/4" w., 29" h. **$4,370**

←

Regency-Style window bench, giltwood, long slender U-shaped outswept rails enclosing upholstered arms & seat, raised on tapering reeded & leaf-carved turned legs, England, ca. 1900, 19 x 43", 35" h. **$1,725**

Regency-Style window benches, ebonized giltwood, long reeded inwardly scrolled top raised & joined at the ends by baluster- turned cross-rails, long upholstered cushion seat on long slender reeded arched legs joined by baluster-turned cross-rails, England, late 19th - early 20th c., 20 x 48 1/2", 26" h. **$1,725**

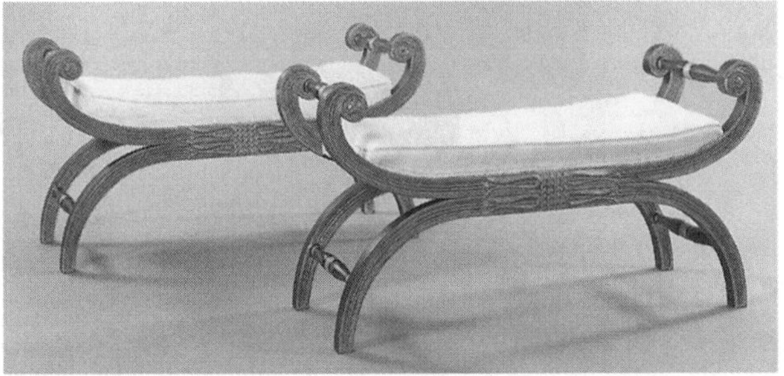

William IV bench, mahogany, rectangular padded & upholstered top raised on heavily reeded short legs raised on brass caps & casters, England, mid-19th c., 24 x 54", 15" h. **$1,380**

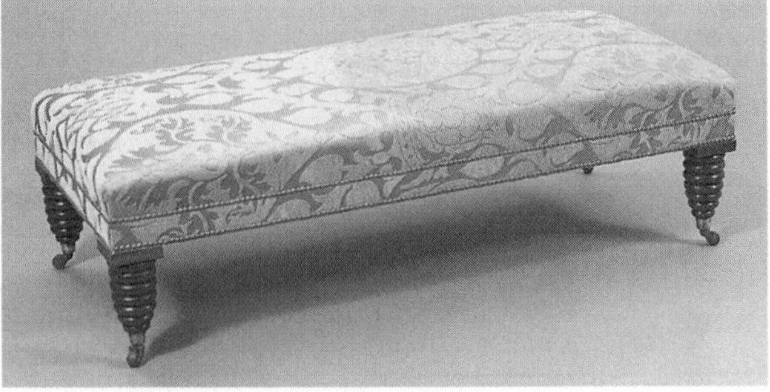

Chairs

Art Deco club chairs, leather & mahogany, the rectangular russet leather back above deep squared arms & a deep cushion seat, on short wooden block feet, France, ca. 1930, 30" h., pr. **$1,955**

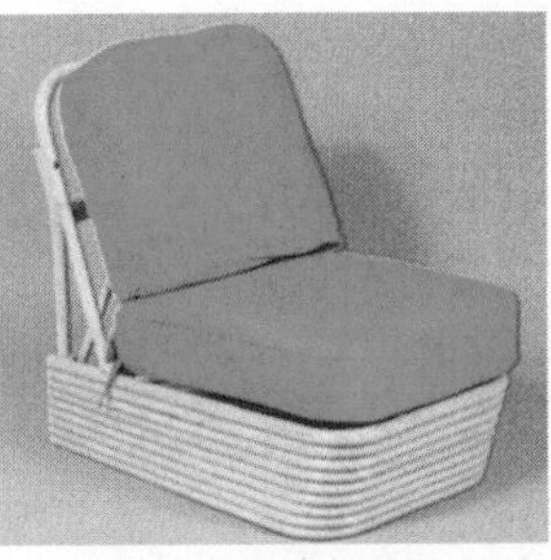

Art Deco lounge chair, bent bamboo, the elongated base platform composed of long curved strips of bamboo w/an adjustable bent bamboo back cushion support, red cushions, ca. 1935-50, 30" h. **$144**

Art Deco side chairs, Cuillernic-style, Macassar ebony, each w/a simple arched barrel-form upholstered back above the over- upholstered seat, square tapering front legs w/brass feet, squared & canted rear legs, designed by Jacques-Emile Ruhlmann, France, ca. 1925, 35" h., pr. **$35,850**

Art Nouveau side chair, giltwood, the asymmetrical back composed of ornate scrolls enclosing a long fan-shaped caned panel above the wide caned seat, slender cabriole front legs w/scroll-carved knees & seatrail, Europe, late 19th c., 35" h. **$575**

Arts & Crafts "Morris" armchair, carved oak, the adjustable slatted back above a pair of flat shaped arms above five square curved spindles, the flat wide shaped arm supports continuing into large carved claw-and-ball front feet, a deep serpentine front apron, on casters, old finish, minor wear, ca. 1900 .... **$518**

The Morris armchair, named after Arts & Crafts designer William Morris, is characterized by its adjustable back, a precursor to the modern recliner.

Arts & Crafts side chair, oak, the tall back w/a wide flat crest above multiple narrow slats continuing down behind the upholstered slip seat, square legs joined by an H-stretcher, designed by Frank Lloyd Wright for the Peter A. Beachy House, Oak Park, Illinois, ca. 1906, 36 1/4" h. **$15,535**

Baroque Revival side chair, oak, the very tall back completely pierce-carved w/elaborate designs, the arched crestrail topped by plumes above scrolls & a cartouche over the tall wide splat completely carved w/scrolls, ribbons, shells & banding all between the slender ring-turned reeded stiles, the back raised above the wide over-upholstered seat w/a front drop, the block-and-ring- turned legs joined by box stretchers w/a pierced, arched scroll-carved front stretcher, on knob feet, Europe, second half 19th c., old dark finish, some upholstery damage, overall 49 1/2" h. **$403**

Baroque-Style armchair, oak, the wide arched & scroll-carved crestrail flanked by scroll-carved ears above the rectangular leather-upholstered back panel raised above the leather seat & flanked by open shaped arms, square legs w/a wide arched & ornate scroll-carved front stretcher & small carved side stretchers, Italian, possibly Tuscan, late 19th c., 47" h. **$518**

Chippendale country-style side chair, mahogany, openwork splat, scrolled crestrail & ears, drop-in seat w/later upholstery, original glue blocks & hand-wrought nails, America, probably Virginia, late 18th c., damage & repair to top of crestrail, 37" h. **$1,760**

Chippendale country-style side chair, painted mahogany, the serpentine crestrail, outswept stiles & pierced vasiform splat all painted w/a finely alligatored design of green & yellow vining w/red flowers on a black ground, paper rush seat, square legs w/ molded edges, late 18th c. w/later paint, 36" h. **$518**

Chippendale country-style side chairs, cherry, pierced scroll, diamond & heart back splat w/ serpentine crest & shaped ears, square legs w/beaded edges & cross stretchers, molded seat frame w/two-tone brown or tan upholstery, America, attributed to Massachusetts, one slip seat damaged, a few later pegs & glued splits, seats 17 1/2" h., overall 38 1/2" h., set of 4 (ILLUS. of one w/two-tone brown upholstery) **$4,600**

Chippendale side chair, cherry, the oxbow crestrail w/outswept ears above the pierced vasiform splat between the raked stiles, trapezoidal slip seat within a beaded frame above cabriole front legs w/arris knees & ending in raised pad feet, chamfered raked rear legs, refinished, minor imperfections, Connecticut, late 18th c., 38" h. **$2,115**

Chippendale side chairs, carved walnut, the shaped crestrail above a pierced Gothic-style splat between raked stiles above the trapezoidal slip seat w/a molded & valanced frame joining front cabriole legs ending in stockinged trifid feet, outward flaring rear legs, refinished, Pennsylvania, ca. 1870, 39" h., pr. (ILLUS. of one) **$3,290**

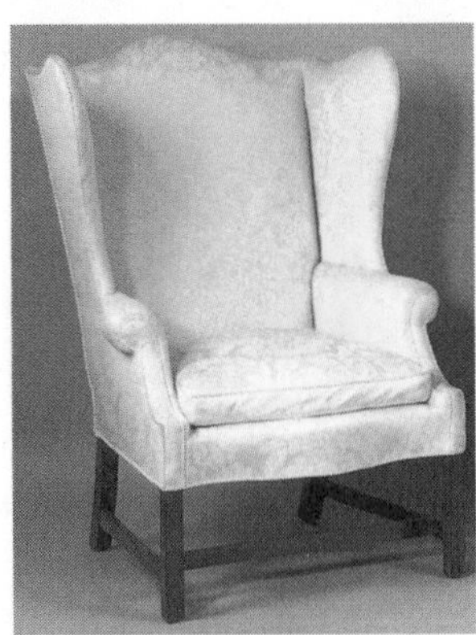

Chippendale wing chair, mahogany, the high arched upholstered back flanked by canted & rounded upholstered wings above rolled upholstered arms above the cushion seat, raised on square molded Marlborough front legs joined by flat stretchers to the chamfered canted rear legs, refinished, probably New England, late 18th c., 45 1/4" h. **$4,700**

Chippendale Revival dining chairs, mahogany, an ox-yoke crestrail w/ears above slightly canted stiles flanking a pierced scroll-carved vasiform splat, wide upholstered seat, cabriole front legs w/leaf-carved knees & ending in ball-and-claw feet, original finish, new upholstery, ca. 1900, 38" h., set of 6 .... **$15,000**

Chippendale legs were made in six basic forms: the lion's paw, the ball and claw, the late Chippendale, the Marlborough, the spade, and the club.

Chippendale Revival dining chairs, walnut, simple ox-yoke crest above solid vasiform splat over a woven rush seat, cabriole front legs ending in claw-and-ball feet, legs joined by turned H-stretcher, two chairs w/shaped open arms, original finish, five side chairs & two armchairs, 42" h., set of 7 .... **$1,750**

Chippendale-Style "lolling" armchair, mahogany, the tall upholstered rectangular back flanked by shaped open arms w/ incurved arm supports above the wide upholstered seat, square reeded legs joined by H-stretchers, early 20th c., 42" h. **$316**

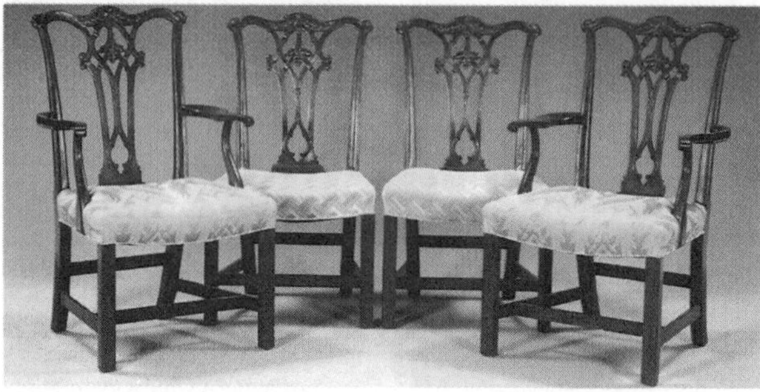

Chippendale-Style chairs: two armchairs & two side chairs; mahogany, openwork splats & carved crestrails, square front legs w/chamfered interior corners & stretcher bases, upholstered shaped seats, late 19th or early 20th c., wear, scratches & minor chips, 40" h., set of 4 .... **$1,430**

Chippendale-Style "lolling" armchairs, mahogany, the tall & wide arched upholstered back flanked by padded open arms w/molded incurved arm supports above the wide over-upholstered seat, molded square front legs joined by an H-stretcher to the rear legs, Hickory Chair Co., 20th c., 40" h., pr. (ILLUS. of one) **$805**

Chippendale-Style side chair, mahogany, the serpentine crestrail above an ornately pierced splat above the wide upholstered seat, square legs joined by an H-stretcher, England, late 19th c., 37 1/4" h. **$173**

Chippendale-Style side chairs, mahogany, the back composed of four pierced ribbon rails between the canted reeded stiles over the slip seat, square legs joined by an H-stretcher, America, late 19th - early 20th c., 39" h., set of six (ILLUS. of one) **$1,208**

Chippendale-Style side chairs, mahogany, the double-arch crestrail w/fancy notch carving & scroll-carved ears above an elaborate pierce-carved splat composed of ribbons & scrolls & flanked by scroll-carved S-form stiles, the wide upholstered seat on a scalloped scroll-carved seatrail & boldly carved front cabriole legs ending in scroll feet, England, late 19th c., 35" h., set of 12 (ILLUS. of one) **$5,750**

Chippendale-Style side chairs, mahogany, the serpentine carved crest above a pierced Gothic style splat over the upholstered slip seat, a shell-carved front seatrail raised on cabriole legs w/scroll-carved knees & ending in claw-and-ball feet, one w/loose joints, other w/ small glued crest split, early 20th c., 39 3/4" h., pr. (ILLUS. of one) **$460**

Chippendale-Style side chairs, mahogany, the serpentine crest w/carved scrolls above the ornate pierced & scroll-carved splat, upholstered slip seat, plain seatrail on heavy cabriole front legs ending in claw-and-ball feet, old finish, early 20th c., 37 1/4" h., set of four (ILLUS. of one) **$1,265**

Chippendale-Style side chairs, mahogany, the serpentine pierced crestrail above a delicate & ornately pierced splat above the upholstered seat, square molded front legs w/corner blocks & ending in pad feet, England, late 19th c., 39" h., set of 14 (ILLUS. of one) **$4,370**

Chippendale-Style wing chairs, mahogany, tan upholstery w/ woven gold colored outdoor scenes including couples dancing, rolled arms w/serpentine wings, molded front legs, stretcher base, early 20th c., light edge wear & stains, seats 18" h., overall 43" h., pr. (ILLUS. of one).............. **$920**

Classical armchair, carved mahogany, the flat rolled crestrail atop backswept serpentine stiles w/carved acanthus leaf trim above the wide upholstered back flanked by padded open arms w/fine C-form scroll-carved arm supports joined to the wide gently curved siderails, a narrow blocked front apron above flute- and ring-turned front legs raised on brass sockets & casters, the serpentine canted rear legs also w/brass casters, remnants of original paper label of William Hancock, Boston, ca. 1820-30, very rare **$97,990**

Classical side chairs, carved mahogany, the flat gently bowed crestrail above a lower pierce-carved rail w/a spread-winged eagle over cornucopia, the molded backswept stiles carved at the top w/acanthus leaf & continuing to form the rails around the caned seat, reeded front seatrail above reeded front sabre legs, outswept rear legs, possibly by Ernest Hagan in the manner of Duncan Phyfe, 31" h., pr. (ILLUS. of one) **$2,760**

Early American child's country-style rocking chair, ash & hickory, turned elements w/later hickory bark seat by Hunter Maney, North Carolina, two splats, backs w/drawknife marks, old red paint w/minor chips & losses, 21" h. **$99**

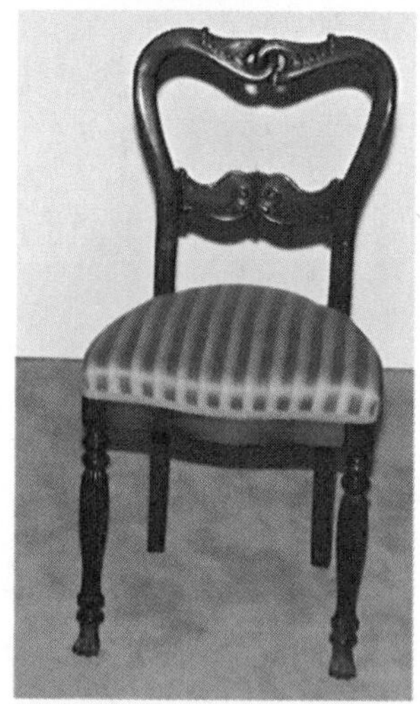

Classical-Victorian transitional side chairs, mahogany, open balloon-back w/a pierced scroll-carved crestrail & scroll-carved lower rail above the wide over upholstered seat, serpentine seatrail over baluster-and-ring-turned front legs on small paw feet, refinished, later upholstery, ca. 1840s, 32" h., pr. (ILLUS. of one) **$600**

Early American country-style highchair, birch, the tall turned canted back legs forming the back stiles w/small knob finials & flanking three arched slats above simple rod arms joining the canted front legs, woven splint seat, traces of red stain, from the Alfred, Maine, Shaker colony, 19th c., 37" h. **$1,725**

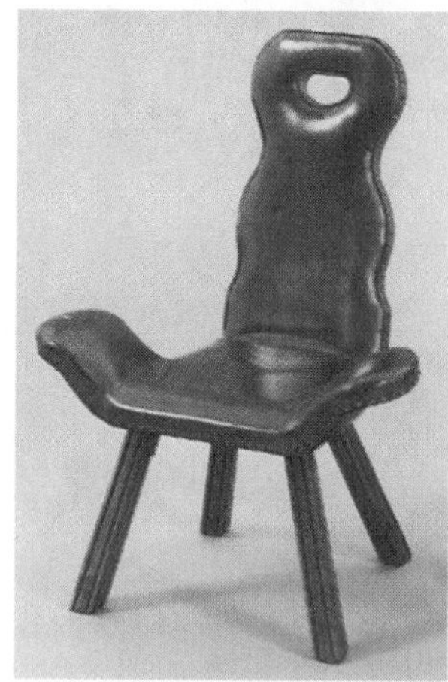

Cock-fighting chairs, mahogany, tall, narrow, oblong & serpentine leather-upholstered back w/pierced hand hole above the leather-upholstered seat w/outswept low sides, raised on canted square molded legs, England, early 20th c., 32" h., pr. **$3,450**

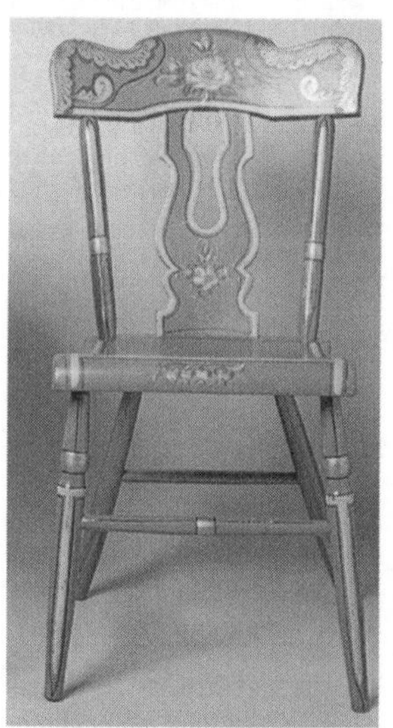

Country-style side chairs, a wide arched crestrail in green decorated in yellow, black, red & dark green w/scrolls & a central rose blossoms above the vase-form bootjack splat w/a rose & yellow banding between the turned stiles, the shaped saddle seat raised on turned front legs trimmed in yellow & gold bands & joined w/box stretchers to the ear legs, first-half 19th c., one back split, 33 1/4" h., set of 6 (ILLUS. of one) **$1,035**

Early American country-style rocking chair w/arms, pine & maple, a stepped oblong crestrail above four tall simple spindles flanked by twisted serpentine stiles, simple rod arms on baluster-and-ring-turned arm supports over the S-roll seat, canted baluster-turned legs joined by stretchers, carpet-cutter rockers, old refinish, ca. 1840, 44" h. **$300**

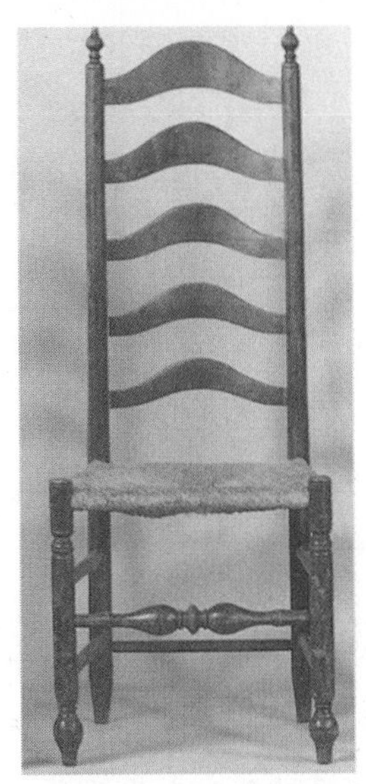

Early American ladder-back side chair, turned maple, very tall turned stiles w/pointed knob finials joining five reverse- graduated arched slats above the woven rush seat, rod- and ring-turned front legs w/pointed knob feet joined by a baluster- and ring-turned front stretcher, side & rear box stretchers, old surface, Delaware River Valley, late 18th c., 45 1/2" h. **$4,113**

Early American-Style "ladder-back" chair, walnut & hickory, five arched splats, ice cream cone finials, corn-shuck seat, double stretchers, peg feet, Shadrick Mace, North Carolina, 1930s-1950s, scattered chips & flakes, 46" h. **$358**

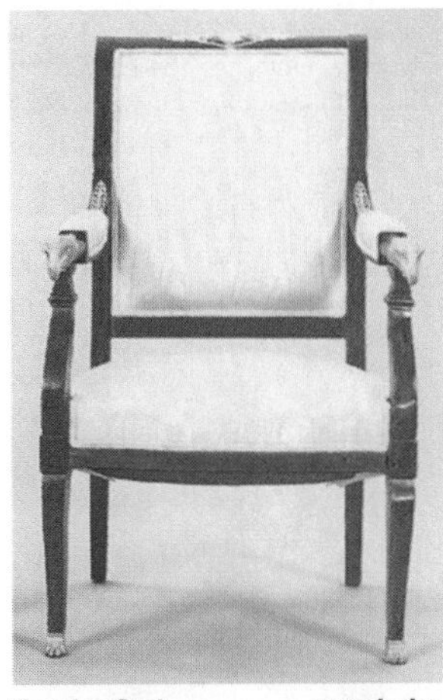

Empire-Style armchairs, mahogany, a square upholstered back w/a back-scrolled frame w/ormolu mounts above padded open arms ending in ormolu eagle head handrests above incurved arm supports, the wide over upholstered seat on a narrow seatrail, shaped tapering squared front legs ending in ormolu paws, France, mid-19th c., 40" h., pr. **$4,830**

Empire-Style bergeres, mahogany, the squared back rail around the wide upholstered back & continuing above the arms over the cushion seat, each arm support w/a classical female term & rosette, a curved front seatrail, square arm supports continuing into the front legs ending in gilt-brass paw caps, France, early 20th c., 37 1/2" h., pr. **$1,840**

Federal "fancy" side chairs, painted & decorated, a crestrail fitted on stiles joined by three slender lower rails above the balloon-form woven rush seat, tapering ring- and rod-turned front legs joined by turned stretchers, black on red paint simulating rosewood, the crestrail w/gold & red shell & acanthus leaf decoration, further gilt trim, probably New York state, ca. 1820, 33" h., pr. (ILLUS. of one) **$546**

Federal "fancy" side chairs, painted & decorated, a slightly serpentine crestrail stenciled w/ gold scrolls above a lower shaped rail w/ornate gilt leaf and roundel stenciling, shaped stiles above the woven rush seat w/ring-turned seatrail, gilt-line decorated front sabre legs joined by a flattened gilt-trimmed front stretcher, rosewood-grained background, probably New York City, first quarter 19th c., 33" h., pr. ... **$920**

Federal country-style side chair, pine & maple, a flat curved crestrail tapering at each end between tapering curved stiles flanking three arrow slats, wide plank seat over ring-turned front legs joined by a shaped stretcher, painted & stenciled decoration w/roses & leaves on the crestrail & bands of leaves down the slats & stiles, ca. 1830, 32" h. **$200**

Federal "fancy" side chairs, red-painted & decorated, the narrow stepped crestrail decorated w/a gold harp & flowers above a pierced central splat carved & painted as a cluster of ribbon-tied musical instruments, the splat flanked by a slender turned colonnette, the flat back stiles w/gold banding above the woven rush seat within a narrow decorated seatrail, knob-and rod- turned front legs joined by a flattened front stretcher, simple turned box stretchers, one w/rush damage & replaced front stretcher, both slightly loose, some wear, New England, ca. 1800, 35" h., pr. (ILLUS. of one) **$3,910**

→

Federal side chairs, inlaid mahogany, the delicate looped heart-shaped back w/molded framing, the central open oval w/ central slender splat w/a pierced fan at the top & inlaid fans & a paterae down the front, the back raised on reeded curved uprights above the wide over-upholstered seat w/a serpentine front & raised on squared tapering legs ending in spade feet, the front of each leg w/ fine line inlay enclosing bellflower pendants, canted rounded rear legs, refinished, repairs, probably Norfolk, Virginia, ca. 1800, 38 3/4" h., pr. **$27,025**

Federal country-style "fancy" side chair, painted & decorated, the wide slightly curved crestrail over a lower rail & three short arrow slats all between the backswept tapering stiles, shaped plank seat on ring-turned tapering legs joined by slender turned stretchers, original mustard yellow paint w/ black & green foliate decoration on the back rails, branded mark under seat for S. Saiter of Marion County, Ohio, ca. 1840-50, 36" h. **$863**

Federal-Style child's wing chair, mahogany, the high flat-topped upholstered back flanked by shallow wings above the rolled upholstered arms over the upholstered seat, 20th c., faded upholstery, 29" h. **$604**

George III-Style armchairs, mahogany, the domed backrail above a pierced wheel-form splat, shaped open arms on incurved arm supports above the padded seat, square paneled tapering legs ending in spade feet & joined by an H-stretcher, England, late 19th c., 38" h., pr. (ILLUS. of one) **$1,955**

Georgian-Style wingchairs, upholstered mahogany, the high back & shaped back wings tufted & padded w/leather upholstery continuing to the outscrolled arms above the cushion seat & apron, molded square legs joined by an H-stretcher, England, Edwardian period, ca. 1905, 47" h., pr. **$4,830**

Louis XV fauteuil, fruitwood, the squared upholstered back w/ molded serpentine framing raised above the wide upholstered seat & flanked by padded molded arms w/incurved arm supports, the serpentine seatrail centered by a carved blossom, cabriole front legs w/floral-carved knees & ending in scrolled toes, France, mid-18th c., 32" h. **$1,610**

Louis XVI-Style bergere avec orielles (wingchair), polychromed wood, the tall upholstered back w/an arched leaf-carved crestrail centered by a floral crest & continuing around the incurved upholstered back wings down to the low padded closed arms flanking the wide cushion seat, the seatrail carved w/leaf bands flanking a floral-carved reserve above the turned tapering fluted legs ending in peg feet, France, first half 19th c., 46 1/4" h. **$4,830**

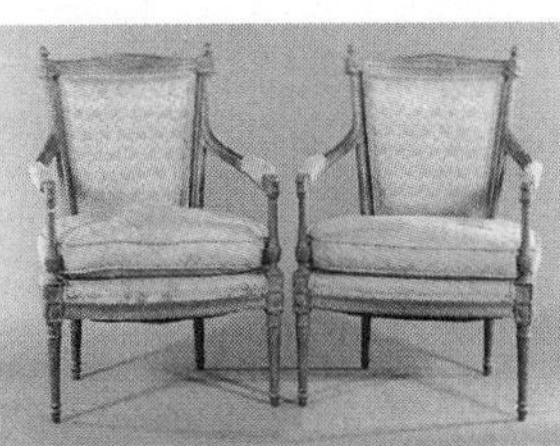

Louis XVI-Style fauteuils, giltwood, the peaked & curved crestrail w/bellflower decoration & artichoke finials above the squared upholstered back, padded open arms on urn-shaped arm supports, cushion seat above turned beechwood legs, old cotton upholstery, label for "Flint & Horner," early 20th c., upholstery faded & soiled, 37" h., pr. **$2,090**

A fauteuil is an upholstered armchair with open arms, as a space exists between the arm rest and the seat cushion. A bergere, on the other hand, is an upholstered armchair with closed arms.

Louis XVI-Style tub chair, mahogany, the U-form molded bellflower band-carved crestrail above the upholstered back curving down to form the shaped outscrolled closed arms w/ incurved leaf-carved arm supports, a cushion seat above the dentil-carved seatrail over baluster- and ring-turned front legs ending in peg feet, England, ca. 1900, 35" h. **$1,093**

Louis XV-Style bergeres (closed-arm armchairs), giltwood, the tall upholstered back w/a gently arched crestrail continuing around the shaped upholstered wings that taper to the padded closed arms, wide cushion seat, molded serpentine seatrail centered by carved florals & continuing into short front cabriole legs w/floral-carved knees & ending in scrolled toes, France, late 19th c., 44" h., pr. (ILLUS. of one)............ **$2,990**

Louis XV-Style fauteuil (open-arm armchair), giltwood, the wide caned back w/an arched crestrail centered by a pierce-carved scroll crest, scroll-carved stiles above the padded, molded open arms above the wide cushion seat, molded serpentine seatrail centered by a scroll-carved reserve & continuing to cabriole legs w/shell-carved knees & ending in scrolled toes, France, late 19th c., 43" h. **$1,265**

Modern style Eames armchair & ottoman, laminated wood & leather, the high wide back w/a padded black leather curved upper panel above a lower panel flanked by rolled upholstered arms & wide upholstered seat, all within a laminated wood framework, raised & swiveling on a metal pedestal supported on a star-shaped metal base, produced by Herman Miller & w/original paper label, mid-20th c., worn original leather, armchair 32" h., 2 pcs. (ILLUS. of chair only)................................. **$1,265**

Modernist style armchair, ebonized & painted wood, "Billet Chair," the tall flat rectangular back slightly swept back, flanked by rod-form cross supports & stiles w/projecting flat rectangular arms, the rectangular seat canted back toward the back panel & supported on front cross rods joined to simple turned rod legs w/ rod stretchers, designed by Gerrit Thomas Rietveld, executed by G. van de Groenekan, 1923 or 1924, 33" h. **$83,650**

Modernist style armchair, molded & painted plywood, the wide U-form back supported by wide side uprights w/bent-over tops, braced under the wide inverted U-form seat raised on flat tapering legs, painted white, designed by Gerrit Thomas Rietveld, ca. 1950, 23 5/8" h. **$38,240**

Modernist style side chairs, molded laminated birch, DCW-style, a wide curved back rest supported on a flat upright above the wide dished & rolled seat, on four flat outswept legs, designed by Ray & Charles Eames for Herman Miller, camel-colored finish, unmarked, ca. 1950s, 29" h., pr. **$460**

Moroccan armchairs, inlaid & marquetry fruitwood, the stepped & blocked crestrail w/ornate mother-of-pearl & marquetry inlay above the low angular inlaid arms & a paneled & inlaid central back panel flanked by turned spindles & side panels, wide tapering ornately inlaid seat raised on deep arched & ornately inlaid base panels between the square line-incised legs ending in turned disk feet, Morocco, late 19th c., 33 1/2" h., pr. **$920**

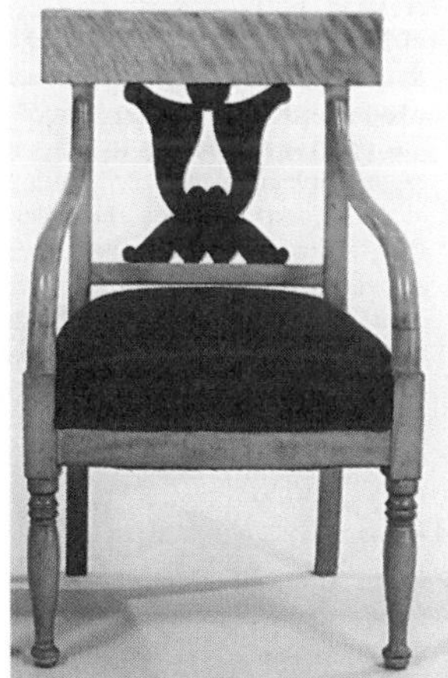

Neoclassical armchairs, birch, the long gently curved rectangular tiger-grained crestrail raised on a squared frame enclosing a pierced & ebonized scroll-carved splat, turned rounded arms above the upholstered seat, flat seatrail raised on baluster- and ring-turned front legs ending in button feet, Baltic region, mid-19th c., 36" h., pr. (ILLUS. of one)............ **$2,070**

Nutting-signed "comb-back" Windsor armchair, mixed woods w/golden brown finish, the slender serpentine crestrail w/curled ears raised on nine slender spindles continuing through the U-form mid-rail that forms the flat arms w/scrolled hand grips on canted, baluster-turned arm supports, wide shaped saddle seat, canted bold baluster- and ring-turned legs joined by a swelled H-stretcher, branded Wallace Nutting signature beneath seat, seat 18" h., overall 44" h. **$1,955**

> Windsor chairs feature backs formed by vertical spindles. They were first made in the 1600s and are named after the town of Windsor in Berkshire, England.

Oriental armchair, carved mahogany, the elaborately carved back composed of two small entwined dragons centered atop the curling tails of large dragons curving around to form the open arms, their heads holding large pearls forming the ends of the arms, the wide flat seat w/a central carved reserve above a deep serpentine seatrail w/ornate floral carving continuing into the cabriole legs w/scroll feet, China, early 20th c., 23" h. **$460**

Oriental armchair, carved rosewood, the arched back ornately pierce-carved w/entwined dragon bodies & scrolls continuing into the arms formed by the dragon body & ending in dragon heads & raised on ornately carved arm supports, the wide seat w/a serpentine molded seatrail w/a pierced scroll carving & continuing into the heavy cabriole front legs ending in scroll feet, China, ca. 1900, 36" h. **$863**

Oriental armchair, carved teakwood, a wide arched crestrail ornately pierce-carved w/iris & leaves above a shaped solid iris-carved splat flanked by iris-carved stiles, the open arms terminating in carved dragon heads on incurved arm supports, the wide seat w/molded border above scroll-carved arms & cabriole front legs w/bat-carved knees & ending in scroll feet, old dark reddish brown finish, China, late 19th - early 20th c., 44" h. **$546**

Oriental armchair, carved teakwood, the high arched crestrail pierce-carved w/a pair of facing dragons among clouds above the wide solid back panel carved w/a large coiling dragon, the open arms ending in dragon heads holding pearls on reeded incurved arm supports, the wide seat w/a serpentine molded front above a pierce-carved seatrail over the cabriole front legs w/large winged bats carved at the knees & ending in scroll feet, old reddish brown finish, China, late 19th - early 20th c., 44 1/2" h. **$575**

Persian side chair, carved & inlaid hardwood, the tall rectangular back formed by a series of interlocking spindles & balls & framed by mother-of-pearl-inlaid stiles w/urn-form finials, the upholstered seat above a similarly formed apron between square inlaid legs ending in pad feet, an inscription under the seat in an archaic Persian dialect, late 19th c., 41" h. .. **$805**

←

Pilgrim Century side chair, red oak & maple, the low rectangular back panel of tack-trimmed leather between the square stiles continuing to form the back legs, the lower leather-upholstered seat raised on block- and knob-turned front legs joined by a block- and-bobbin-turned stretcher, box side & back stretchers, 19th c. leather, imperfections, Essex County, Massachusetts, 1665-95, 36" h. **$34,075**

People sometimes naively claim that a piece of their furniture came to America on the Mayflower. No pieces from the Mayflower have been documented, and given the cramped quarters on the ship, and the need for transporting essential survival items like food, tools, and other supplies, it's unlikely that any furniture made the trip.

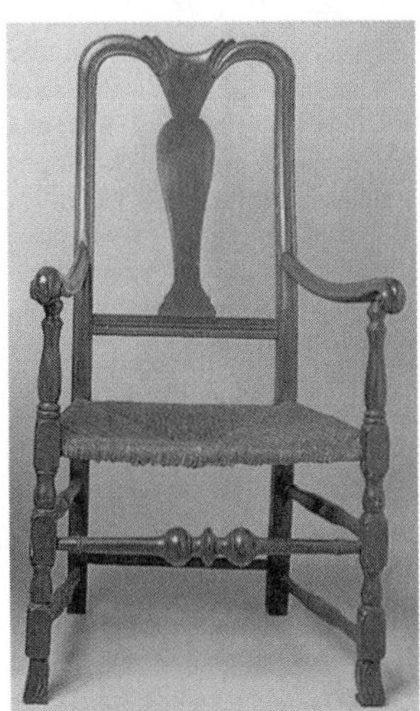

Queen Anne country-style armchair, painted wood, the shaped & arched crestrail above a simple vasiform splat raised on a lower rail between the shaped & molded stiles, long shaped open arms w/scrolled grips raised on baluster-turned arm supports above the woven rush seat, the block-and-knob-turned front legs joined by a turned double-knob & disk stretcher, simple box side & rear stretchers, old dark red repaint over earlier black, restorations to front legs, back feet ended out, late 18th c., 44" h. **$1,783**

Queen Anne-Style side chairs, mahogany, the ox-yoke crestrail above a tall vasiform splat, the upholstered slip seat in a plain seatrail raised on cabriole front legs ending in pad feet, glued split at top of one leg, America, early 20th c., 41" h., pr. (ILLUS. of one) **$173**

Queen Anne side chair, carved walnut, the shaped crestrail centered by a scrolled shell above a raked vasiform splat flanked by shaped stiles, the upholstered compass slip seat in a conforming apron raised on cabriole front legs w/a shell-carved knee & ball-and-claw feet, jointed by swelled stretchers, refinished, restoration, Boston, ca. 1740-60, 39" h. **$29,375**

Regency armchairs, painted & decorated, the backswept & knob-turned back stiles flanking a half-round caned panel w/a small polychrome painted tablet above two thin rails, squared open arms raised on incurved arm supports above the wide caned seat, raised on knob-turned slightly curved front legs, overall black paint w/gilt highlights, England, first quarter 19th c., 33 1/2" h., pr. **$4,140**

Queen Anne side chair, mahogany, the shaped crest above a solid vasiform splat flanked by shaped stiles above the upholstered balloon slip seat, cabriole front legs w/shell-carved knees ending in pad feet, turned & raked rear legs w/pad feet, two seat returns replaced, old refinishing, England, 18th c., 39 1/2" h. **$1,610**

Regency armchair, painted & decorated wood, the flat crestrail w/a pair of white-painted incised panels flanking a lion mask boss, the lower pierced rail also centered by a lion mask boss, serpentine back stiles & scrolled open arms raised on turned tapering post supports above the wide caned seat, flat fluted & gilt-trimmed seatrail, square tapering & slightly outswept fluted front legs, overall rosewood graining & white trim, England, first quarter 19th c., 36" h. **$1,495**

Restauration armchairs, mahogany, the tall upholstered back framed by backswept molding above the padded open arms on incurved scroll-carved arm supports, the wide upholstered seat above a plain seatrail raised on heavy S-scroll carved front legs, France, second quarter 19th c., 40 1/4" h., pr. (ILLUS. of one) **$2,300**

Rustic style folk art twig chair, rectangular back formed by crossed bent twigs, single-twig low arms slope to front legs, cross- stretcher base, chip-carved surface w/green paint, Blowing Rock, North Carolina, or East Tennessee, early 20th c., paint w/losses & chips, 47" h. **$770**

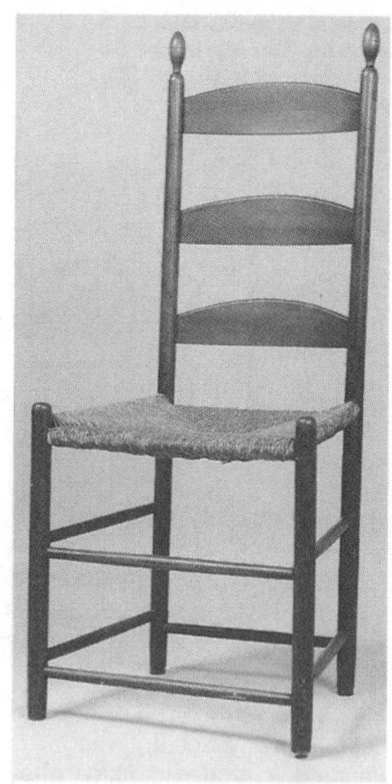

Shaker "ladder-back" side chair, birch, three arched slats between turned stiles w/oval finials above the woven rush seat, slender legs & posts w/wooden tilters on back feet, double stretchers on front & sides, attributed to Enfield, New Hampshire, seat 18" h., overall 41" h. **$2,070**

Victorian "patent" folding armchair, walnut, the needlepoint upholstered back & seat featuring ecclesiastical designs of a communion chalice & flowers, fitted on a folding bamboo-turned frame w/large knob finials & bamboo-turned stretchers, incised stamp mark & label of George Hunzinger, New York City, ca. 1880, 37" h. **$1,035**

Victorian "patent" rocking chair w/arms, walnut, a tall flaring upholstered back w/top corner knob finials flanked by long angled ring-turned rails mounted w/ padded ring-turned angular arms flanking the upholstered seat, ring-turned front stretcher w/two short spindles, patented by George Hunzinger Co., New York, New York, ca. 1870s, original finish, newer upholstery, 32" h. **$400**

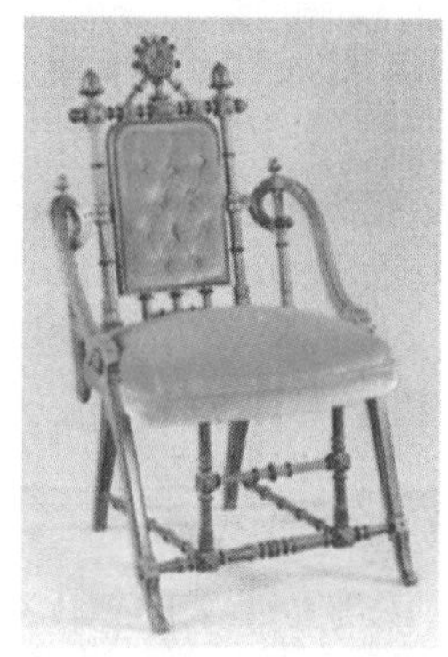

Victorian "patent" side chair, walnut, the back composed of ring-turned stiles w/acorn finials joined by a turned crest bar topped by a fancy sunburst finial above the arched tufted upholstered back panel, scrolled half-arms joined to upright rods at the back of the wide upholstered seat, canted front legs joined by a turned cross stretcher below a turned H-stretcher & joined to the canted rear legs w/ slender turned stretchers, signed by the George Hunzinger firm, ca. 1880s, old repairs to arms, break in top crest, 34 1/2" h. **$489**

Victorian Aesthetic Movement side chair, Louis XV inspiration, giltwood, the wide ornately scroll-carved & pierced crestrail w/a small inset marquetry panel above an upholstered D-form back panel over a pierced scroll-carved & spindled panel, the wide over-upholstered spring seat above a shaped seatrail centered by another small marquetry panel, on scroll-carved front cabriole legs ending in peg feet, England or America, late 19th c., 32" h. **$546**

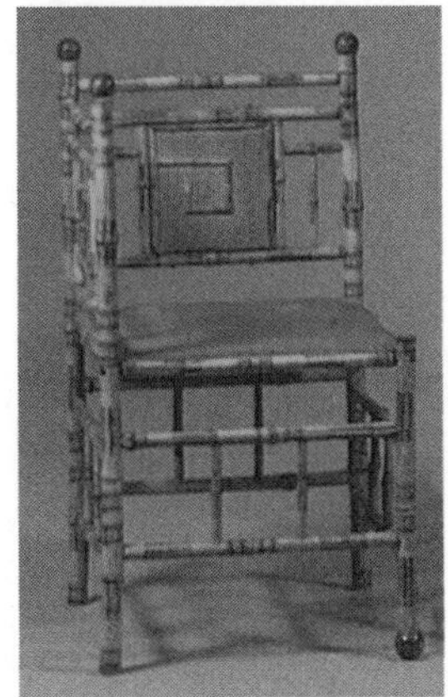

Victorian bamboo corner chair, the rectangular openwork back panels composed of bamboo lattice centered by a tightly woven panel, a tightly woven seat above the legs joined by lattice-form stretchers, some wear, late 19th c., 32 1/4" h. **$259**

Victorian Baroque Revival side chairs, oak, the high rectangular upholstered back raised above the wide spring cushion upholstered seat w/a molded seatrail centered by a scroll-carved front drop, raised on ring- and rod-turned legs joined by an H- stretcher w/scroll-carved trim, Italy, mid-19th c., 38 1/2" h., set of 4 .... **$1,725**

Victorian Renaissance Revival dining chairs, walnut, an arched & ornately scroll-carved crestrail centered by a shell above a pierced leaf-sprig-carved & lunette-carved splat above a lower arched rail, molded straight stiles above the over-upholstered seat, line-incised seatrail above tapering ring-turned legs w/peg feet, original finish, old vinyl upholstery, ca. 1870s, 36" h., set of 4 .... **$800**

Victorian Renaissance Revival dining chairs, walnut, arched & scalloped line-incised crestrail w/eared corners above a reeded splat centered by a large roundel, square stiles w/S-scroll skirt-guards flanked by upholstered seats, simple ring-turned front legs joined by double ring-and-rod-turned stretchers, probably originally had caned seats, original finish, ca. 1875, 34" h., set of 6 .... **$600**

Victorian Renaissance Revival fixed-back recliner armchair, walnut & burl walnut, the backswept serpentine upholstered back w/molded stiles continuing down to low upholstered arms w/ large carved feathered scrolls & rondel sides above scrolled & burl-paneled side seat rails flanking the wide upholstered seat, a turned side column above the widely outswept scrolled & paneled front & rear legs, ca. 1875 .... **$489**

Victorian Rococo armchair, carved & laminated rosewood, the high balloon back centered by an upholstered oval panel surrounded by a pierce-carved frame, the arched scroll crestrail topped by a floral-carved crest & continuing into the scroll- and leaf-carved serpentine sides above the shaped open arms w/incurved arm supports, a serpentine front seatrail centered by a carved floral cluster, demi-cabriole front legs w/floral-carved knees, "Fountain Elms" pattern by John H. Belter, New York City, ca. 1855, arm restorations, 43" h. **$10,925**

Victorian Renaissance Revival side chair, walnut & burl walnut, the gently flaring squared back w/a gently arched crestrail w/ narrow burl panels centered by a small sunburst crest above carved scrolls & a rondel, shaped corner ear above the molded stiles & lower rail enclosing the upholstered back panel, concave skirt guards at the sides of the wide spring-cushioned upholstered seat w/a narrow burl-paneled seatrail w/a central carved drop, ring- and rod-turned tapering front legs w/peg feet raised on casters, squared outswept rear legs, ca. 1875 .... **$150-200**

Victorian Rococo "barrel-back" armchair, mahogany, the simple molded & scroll-carved arched crestrail above the tufted upholstered back continuing down to form the low upholstered arms flanking the upholstered spring seat, molded serpentine seatrail, molded demi-cabriole front legs, ca. 1860-70, 38" h. .. **$2,530**

Victorian Renaissance Revival substyle child's armchair, gilt-incised & ebonized walnut, the arched crestrail centered by a raised platform & demi-lune crest & w/roundel-set ears above a pierced urn-form splat, the squared open arms on trumpet-turned arm supports above the wide upholstered seat, the gently curved seatrail w/a center drop & cross-incised corner blocks above the trumpet-turned front legs w/peg feet, America, ca. 1875, 26 1/2" h. **$633**

Victorian Rococo armchair, carved & laminated rosewood, the balloon-form back w/an arched flower-carved crestrail continuing down to enclose the back panel, open serpentine arms on incurved arm supports, wide seat w/a serpentine seatrail carved w/floral scrolls flanked by demi-cabriole front legs w/flower-carved knees, "Rosalie with Grapes" patt., John H. Belter, New York, New York, ca. 1885, 44" h. **$6,000**

Victorian Rococo armchair, carved rosewood, the large oval back w/an ornate pierce-carved scroll crestrail continuing to form the oval molding enclosing the upholstered back panel, padded serpentine open arms on incurved scroll-carved arm supports flanking the wide upholstered seat w/a serpentine fruit-and-leaf-carved seatrail above demi-cabriole front legs on casters, attributed to Alexander Roux, New York City, ca. 1860, refinished, new upholstery, 45" h. **$2,500**

Victorian Rococo armchairs, carved rosewood, the shaped balloon-back w/an arched crestrail carved w/fanned scrolls & continuing to form the serpentine frame around the tufted upholstered back panels, shaped padded open arms on incurved arm supports over the wide upholstered seat w/a serpentine seatrail centered by a carved cartouche, demi-cabriole front legs ending in scroll feet on casters, refinished, ca. 1860, 36" h., pr. (ILLUS. of one).... **$950**

Victorian Rococo armchair, pierced & laminated rosewood, the high balloon back w/a tufted upholstered oblong center panel enclosed by an ornately pierce-carved frame topped by a high arched crestrail centered by a scroll-carved crest above a floral cluster, the serpentine sides w/further pierced scrolls, shaped padded open arms on incurved arm supports above the wide shaped upholstered spring seat w/a serpentine molded seatrail centered by a carved cartouche, demi-cabriole front legs on casters, in the "Henry Ford" pattern by J. & J.W. Meeks, New York City, ca. 1855, 48" h. **$6,900**

Victorian Rococo chairs, laminated rosewood, arched crestrail w/elaborately carved fruit & flower crest above the shaped upholstered back w/green velvet upholstery, shaped upholstered seat w/serpentine seatrail carved w/further florals, on cabriole front legs on brass casters; the armchair probably "Rosalie" patt., w/shield-shape back, scrolled arms, probably original casters & surface, 40" h.; the side chair w/double-scrolled supports, probably original surface, 37" h., John Henry Belter, New York City, ca. 1850s, small chips & losses to carving, pr. **$3,520**

Victorian Rococo armchair, pierced & laminated rosewood, the tall corseted balloon back w/an upholstered panel framed by an arched crestrail w/an arched grape-and-leaf-carved crest above pierce-carved fruit vines continuing down the sides & flanked by open padded arms on incurved arm supports, wide upholstered spring seat on a serpentine seatrail, a floral-carved reserve flanked by carved leafy scrolls & continuing to the incurved carved cabriole front legs ending in scroll feet on casters, attributed to John H. Belter, New York City, ca. 1855, 47" h. **$8,625**

Victorian Rococo parlor chairs, walnut, an armchair & side chair, each w/a wide balloon back w/an oblong tufted upholstered panel enclosed by a molded frame, the armchair w/padded open arms on incurved arm supports, both w/wide upholstered spring seats on molded serpentine seatrails continuing into demi-cabriole front legs ending in casters, ca. 1870, armchair 40" h., pr. **$518**

Victorian Rococo side chairs, carved & laminated rosewood, a tall back w/an ornate pierced & scroll-carved framework w/a pair of cornucopia forming the crest above the tall rounded & serpentine-sided upholstered back panel, rounded upholstered seat w/an ornately carved serpentine seatrail & carved S-scroll front legs on casters, new red upholstery, attributed to John H. Belter, New York City, ca. 1855, 38" h. pr. **$5,520**

Victorian Rococo side chairs, pierced & laminated rosewood, the tall balloon back centered by an oval upholstered panel enclosed by an ornately pierce-carved frame, the arched crestrail centered by a high arched floral-carved crest & continuing to form the pierced vine- and scroll-carved sides, the rounded upholstered spring seat on a conforming seatrail centered by a carved floral cluster, on demi-cabriole front legs on casters, the "Fountain Elms" pattern, ca. 1855, 38" h., pr. (ILLUS. of one) **$15,525**

Victorian Rococo side chairs, walnut, simple balloon back w/molded railing centered by a cartouche-carved crest above the original horsehair-upholstered back panel, curved skirt guards flank the rounded horsehair-upholstered seat w/a serpentine seatrail above simple cabriole front legs, refinished, ca. 1865, 34" h., set of 4 .... **$800**

←

Victorian Rococo slipper chairs, carved walnut, the tall back w/an oblong upholstered panel below the high arched & pierced crestrail carved w/scrolls & floral clusters & raised on baluster- and ring-turned free-standing back stiles above a scalloped lower back raise, S-scroll skirt guards flanking the wide round upholstered seat & conforming seatrail carved w/ scrolls & raised on ring- turned tapering front legs on casters, ca. 1870, 40 3/4" h., pr. (ILLUS. of one) **$920**

Victorian Rococo substyle side chair, carved laminated rosewood, the ornate back w/an outer frame composed of C-scrolls, an arched top crest of carved roses & flowers & the central long oval upholstered back panel surrounded by finely pierce-carved vines of grapes & acorns, the wide over-upholstered needlework seat w/a serpentine seatrail carved w/a cluster of roses framed by leafy vines, molded cabriole front legs ending in scrolls on casters, canted rear legs, attributed to John Henry Belter, New York, New York, ca. 1855, old break in side carving, 35 1/2" h. **$1,725**

William IV hall chairs, mahogany, the tall back w/a fanned & fluted crest above large S-scrolls framing the back panel centered by a large rosette, the solid trapezoidal seat above ring-turned tapering front legs w/disk feet, England, second quarter 19th c., 35" h., pr. (ILLUS. of one) **$2,990**

Windsor "comb-back" rocker, hardwood w/old dark refinishing, curved crestrail over seven spindles continuing through the U-form mid-rail & continuing to form scrolled arms over two spindles & a canted baluster-turned arm support, "D"-shape seat w/incised edging, canted baluster- and ring-turned legs joined by a swelled H-stretcher & mortised into shaped rockers, attributed to Philadelphia, Pennsylvania, arms missing bottoms of knuckle scrolls, replaced crest, restorations, seat 14" h., overall 37" h. **$863**

Windsor "birdcage" side chairs, hardwood w/old mustard paint, seven-spindle back, shield-shape seats w/incised detail around spindles & fronts, bamboo turned legs & rungs, glued split in seat of one chair, another w/wear, seats 17" h., overall 33 1/4" h., set of 4 (ILLUS. of one) **$1,955**

←

Windsor "comb-back" rocking chair w/arms, painted & decorated wood, the small back comb w/a rectangular crest raised on four small spindles above the flat crestrail over seven bamboo-turned spindles flanked by backswept tapering stiles, shaped arms over a turned spindle & arm supports, wide shaped plank seat raised on canted bamboo-turned legs joined by turned box stretchers & mortised into rockers, old dark green paint, restored split where comb meets crest, America, ca. 1830, 38 1/4" h. **$345**

When seeking an auctioneer to conduct your sale, consider hiring a full-time, full-service professional. Read all the fine print and compare terms, as terms vary widely. Ask questions to clarify any points of uncertainty. Before deciding, ask for references and check on their satisfaction.

Windsor "fan-back" armchair, elm & maple, the tall back w/a serpentine crestrail above an upper vasiform splat flanked by three spindles on each side over a U-form medial rail forming the flat arms & raised on another splat & spindles w/five spindles under each arm & an incurved arm support, wide shaped seat on canted rear legs & cabriole front legs ending in pad feet, joined by a turned H-stretcher, England, ca. 1800, 42" h. **$1,725**

Windsor "writing-arm" armchair, birch & poplar, the back w/a stepped crestrail above squared stiles flanking six spindles, one shaped arm w/a canted baluster-turned support & two spindles, the other arm mounted w/a wide curved teardrop- shaped writing surface w/old oilcloth covering above a wide shallow drawer, the wide plank seat raised on heavy tapering canted legs joined by a ring-turned front stretcher & plain box stretchers, old documents in drawer give history of the piece, ca. 1770s, Massachusetts, glued split on writing arm, 45" h. .. **$863**

Windsor "rabbit ear" side chairs, hardwood w/reddish brown refinishing, flat slightly curved crestrail over five turned spindles between the curved & tapered styles, rounded plank seat, bamboo turned legs reinforced underneath w/shims, incised shield- shape seats, glued spindle restorations, one seat w/repaired split, seats 15 3/4" h., overall 32" h., set of 4 (ILLUS. of one) **$518**

Windsor "sack-back" highchair, painted hardwood, the bowed crestrail over seven turned spindles continuing through a medial rail forming the flat shaped arms raised on a short spindle & a canted baluster- and knob-turned arm support, the wide shaped saddle seat raised on tall canted baluster-, ring- and rod-turned legs joined by a swelled H-stretcher, old black paint, split on one arm, overall 32 1/2" h. **$8,625**

Windsor tall-backed rocking chair w/arms, painted & decorated, the wide rectangular crestrail raised on seven slender turned spindles flanked by turned stiles, serpentine arms over two turned spindles & a canted turned arm support, wide shaped plank seat raised on bamboo-turned canted legs joined by box stretchers & mortised into rockers, original yellow paint w/ gold & black line edging & fruit & scrolls in dark green & gold on the crestrail, walnut arms w/old brown finish, stamped mark under seat appears to read "E.R. Norman," New England, ca. 1830, 46 1/2" h. **$1,265**

Occasionally an auctioneer misses a bid and hammers down a lot to another bidder. To prevent this from happening, make sure you don't wait unitl the last second to make a bid and be sure your bid can be seen or heard.

Chests & Chests of Drawers

Adam Revival chest of drawers, brass-mounted & polychromed satinwood, the rectangular yellow & brown marble top w/a narrow stepped-out front section above a conforming case w/four long, graduated drawers, the front decorated overall w/continuous polychrome leafy vines & floral garlands, the third drawer centered by an oval reserve w/a black ground painted w/a shaded gold neoclassical figural scene, black banding w/further neoclassical designs framing the case, molded base raised on turned disk & peg feet, in the 18th c. style of Robert Adam, England, ca. 1900, 23 x 51", 36" h. **$4,025**

Altar chest, Oriental, pine, the long narrow plain top above a case w/ a row of paneled & lotus-carved drawers above a row of four plain panels, heavy square legs w/long carved front brackets, scroll-cut long brackets down the sides of the case, China, late 19th c., 17 1/2 x 76 1/2", 33" h. **$1,035**

Arts & Crafts chest of drawers, oak, the rectangular top w/a molded cornice above a pair of cupboard doors w/wide frames enclosing h. p. stylized landscapes in shades of green & yellow, the lower case w/a pair of drawers above two long drawers all w/simple bail pulls, simple bracket feet, paneled ends, from The Byrdcliffe Arts & Crafts Colony, 1904, branded mark & date, 23 3/4 x 57", 5' h. **$273,500**

Blanket chest, Chippendale country-style, pine w/old blue paint & faded bittersweet trim, single-board molded top w/iron strap hinges over dovetailed case w/covered till, molded base w/shaped bracket feet, restorations, 20 1/2 x 49 1/2", 26" h. **$1,150**

Blanket chest, Chippendale country-style, pine, the hinged rectangular top opening to a deep well, the front facade composed of two large cross-band panels flanking two small square center raised panels, molded base raised on shaped bracket feet, Eastern Shore of Maryland or Virginia, 18th c., 52" l., 36" h. ... **$14,340**

Blanket chest, early American country-style, pine w/ old blue paint, single board scalloped ends, the lid w/ molded edge, the interior w/unusual till w/reeded lid & dovetailed drawer below, New England, end battens of lid have screws added, lock escutcheon missing, edge wear, chip, 17 x 48", 24" h. **$1,495**

Blanket chest, Federal, walnut, the top w/applied molding, the interior w/lidded till & dovetailed drawer, top of front inlaid w/extensive tassel, vine, turnip & teardrop designs, sides w/shaped skirt & barberpole inlay, original French feet w/shaped skirt w/extensive fan, barberpole & tassel inlay, original glue blocks, Tennessee, first quarter 19th c., lid hinges repaired, some veneer losses, old refinishing, scattered scratches & dents, feet w/repaired tips, 17 3/4 x 38", 20 1/2" h. **$46,200**

Blanket chest, inlaid walnut, the rectangular top opening to a dovetailed well, a molded base on shaped bracket feet, line-inlaid panels on the front & sides w/fans within the front panels & graduated inverted flowers below the diamond-shaped inlaid lock escutcheon, Southern United States, refinished, glued restoration on back foot, replaced strap hinges, small pierced repairs, late 18th - early 19th c., 19 1/4 x 42 1/2", 24 1/2" h. **$1,495**

Blanket chest, poplar, pine & chestnut, the rectangular top lifting above a well w/a lidded till, a pair of molded drawers at the bottom, molded base on bracket feet, black over red painted spiral decoration, strong gold-stenciled initials "N.H." on the front w/a ghost image of the date "1904," black-painted detail on feet & moldings, floral decals on case & drawers, nailed drawers w/ white porcelain pulls, Soap Hollow type, attributed to the Sala Brothers of Pennsylvania, 20 3/4 x 48", 25" h. **$7,475**

Blanket chest, painted poplar, the rectangular top w/a molded edge opening to a well w/a covered till, a dovetailed case w/narrow base molding & turned bun feet, old dark mustard yellow paint, mid-19th c., 18 x 38", 22" h. **$460**

Chippendale "Chinese style" chest of drawers, walnut, four graduated dovetailed drawers w/ scribed borders, original brass pulls & inlaid kite escutcheons, vertical backboards w/cut nails, bracket feet, Virginia, last quarter 18th c., old refinishing, replaced feet, added drawer runners, repairs, 20 x 42", 36" h. **$4,400**

Chippendale chest of drawers, maple & birch, one-board top above a case of four graduated beaded drawers w/replaced batwing brasses & escutcheons, molded base on ogee bracket feet, refinished, feet & base moldings old replacements, one baseboard missing, initialed inside "H.T.," late 18th - early 19th c., 20 1/2 x 40 3/4", 35 1/2" h. **$1,093**

Chippendale "block-front" chest of drawers, mahogany, the rectangular top w/blocked front & molded edge above a conforming case fitted w/ four long graduated drawers, a molded base w/ central drop on scrolled bracket feet, appears to retain original brasses, Boston, Massachusetts, 1760-80, 20 x 36", 30 1/2" h. **$53,775**

Chippendale chest-on-chest, curly maple, two-part dovetailed construction: the upper section w/cove molded cornice above five graduated drawers; the bottom section w/three drawers; all w/ beaded trim & original brass pulls, molded waist & base, high bracket feet w/scalloped returns, a couple splits to foot facings w/section of one back facing missing, 37 1/2 x 20", 6' 5" h. **$23,000**

Chippendale chest-on-chest, tiger stripe maple, two-part construction: the upper section w/a rectangular top w/a flaring stepped cornice above a case w/five long thumb-molded graduated drawers w/butterfly brasses & keyhole escutcheons; the lower w/ a mid-molding above a case w/four long graduated drawers w/matching brasses, molded base on ogee scroll-cut bracket feet, original brasses, old refinish, southwestern New England, late 18th c., 19 x 37 3/4", overall 6' 3" h. **$24,675**

Chippendale tall chest of drawers, maple, the rectangular top w/a molded cornice above a case w/a pair of narrow drawers above a stack of six long graduated thumb-molded drawers each w/butterfly brasses & keyhole escutcheons, molded base on scroll-cut bracket feet, brasses appear to be original, old red-stained surface, minor imperfections, probably Massachusetts, last half 18th c., 18 1/2 x 36", 4' 9" h. **$8,813**

Classical "bow-front" chest of drawers, mahogany & mahogany veneer, a rectangular top w/a gently bowed front flanked by projecting ovolo corners above spiral-turned columns flanking the bowed case of four long graduated drawers w/ round brass pulls, a scalloped apron & ring-turned legs w/peg feet, probably Salem, Massachusetts, early 19th c., 20 x 44", 42" h. **$1,955**

Classical chest of drawers with mirror, mahogany & mahogany veneer, a long rectangular framed mirror swiveling between tall large S-scroll uprights raised atop a long narrow rectangular framework enclosing six thin drawers all set back on the rectangular top of the main case, the main case w/a long narrow ogee-front drawer projecting over two long graduated lower drawers w/lion mask & ring pulls flanked by heavy side columns, flat apron, raised on heavy carved paw front feet, ca. 1820s, 22 1/2 x 42", overall 5' 6" h. **$1,380**

Classical chest of drawers, mahogany & mahogany veneer, the rectangular top above a case w/a long top drawer w/an inset arch projecting over three long deep drawers w/original pressed glass pulls flanked by ring-turned & leaf-carved half-columns, raised on heavy carved front paw feet, top w/old refinishing, remainder w/original dark finish, age split in top, ca. 1840, 21 1/4 x 47", 49" h. **$460**

Classical country-style butler's chest of drawers, curly maple, central pull-out top drawer w/ eight dovetailed graduated & cockbeaded drawers, central prospect door w/two drawers behind, six cubbyholes, three long drawers flanked by beaded pilasters, turned & reeded legs, bottom of fall-front pull-out drawer w/chalk inscription, possibly initials, faint pencil inscription on back of top graduated drawer, Tennessee, early 19th c., old refinishing, some separation to top, 46 x 43 x 23" **$2,310**

Classical country-style chest of drawers, hardwood w/old mustard paint, three set-back drawers on the rectangular top, over four dovetailed drawers w/original embossed brass pulls, turned feet, New England, evidence of later red paint, 18 x 39 1/2", 41 1/2" h. **$1,610**

Coffer chest, Louis XIV Provincial, carved oak, long rectangular hinged top opening to a well, the case front heavily carved w/bands of shallow geometric designs & scrolls, heavy stile legs, back of plank construction, restorations, France, late 17th c., 22 x 67 1/2", 27 1/2" h. **$1,725**

Federal "bow-front" chest of drawers, inlaid mahogany & mahogany veneer, the rectangular top w/a gently bowed front above a conforming case of four long graduated drawers each w/ banded inlay panels & original oval brasses w/a running dog design, serpentine apron & tall French feet, old refinishing, early backboards possibly replacements, replaced base & feet, late 18th - early 19th c., 21 1/4 x 38 3/4", 33" h. **$1,380**

The Federal period in the United Sates was a time of patriotism and anti-British sentiment after the Revolution. Consequently, French styles were preferred.

Federal "bow-front" chest of drawers, mahogany & mahogany veneer, the rectangular top w/a bowed front & ovolu projecting corners above a conforming case w/four long graduated drawers w/replaced batwing brasses, ring- and spiral-turned columns down the side, scalloped apron, raised on baluster- and ring-turned legs w/peg feet, originally had a small case on top w/bonnet drawers, New England, ca. 1820, 19 x 40", 39 1/2" h. **$920**

Federal "swell-front" chest of drawers, mahogany & cherry veneer, rectangular top over four graduated dovetailed & cockbeaded drawers w/brass pulls, probably original, w/inlaid diamond escutcheons, the top drawer w/compartments, original skirt w/cherry veneer, feet facings w/V joints, horizontal backboards, Kentucky, scratches, small dents, one escutcheon off but present, replaced glue blocks & rear returns, old refinishing, 22 x 39 5/8", 38 1/2" h. .. **$15,400**

Federal chest of drawers, bow-front chest w/light wood corner inlay, four graduated dovetailed & cockbeaded drawers w/string & oval inlay, fancy book-matched walnut veneer drawer facings, top drawer w/compartments & ratchet for lift-up dressing mirror w/single-line inlay, inlaid pointed oval escutcheons, skirt w/light inlay & demi-lune fan apron, shaped French feet, includes box of parts, mostly interior compartment sections & supports, Tennessee, 1800-1819, repairs, veneer chips, stains, minor separations, base missing original glue blocks, one rear glue block replaced, most of missing inlay on front present but not attached, 23 3/4 x 44", 39 1/2" h. **$33,000**

Federal butler's chest of drawers, mahogany & cherry, the rectangular top above a row of three narrow drawers over a deep drawer w/fold-down front forming a writing surface & enclosing small compartments above three long graduated drawers, batwing brasses, molded base on incurved bracket feet, late 18th c., 20 3/4 x 48", 46" h. **$4,370**

Federal chest of drawers, inlaid cherry, rectangular top above a case w/a long deep drawer over three long graduated drawers, each w/line border inlay & original oval brasses, serpentine apron above tall bracket feet, band inlay on the top, refinished, glued split, restoration to drawer edges, late 18th - early 19th c., 20 1/2 x 42", 41 1/2" h. **$1,840**

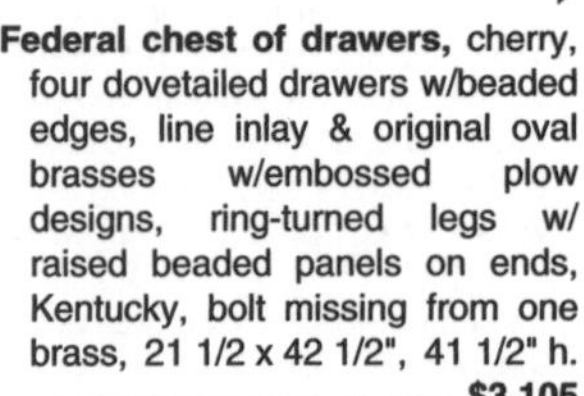

→

Federal chest of drawers, cherry, four dovetailed drawers w/beaded edges, line inlay & original oval brasses w/embossed plow designs, ring-turned legs w/ raised beaded panels on ends, Kentucky, bolt missing from one brass, 21 1/2 x 42 1/2", 41 1/2" h. **$3,105**

Federal chest of drawers with mirror, mahogany w/tiger stripe & bird's-eye maple veneer, a superstructure w/an upright rectangular mirror w/a narrow frame & arched crest swiveling between slender uprights flanked by fancy long C-scroll brackets & set above a narrow compartment w/three small drawers faced in bird's-eye maple & w/round ring pulls, the stepped-out rectangular case top w/ovolo corners above reeded columns flanking the case w/a pair of drawers over two long drawers, all w/bird's-eye maple & round ring pulls, all raised on tapering reeded legs w/a ring-turned top segment, ending in peg feet, attributed to John & Thomas Seymour, Boston, ca. 1820, replaced pulls, old finish, minor imperfections, 20 1/2 x 36", overall 6' h. **$38,188**

Federal chest of drawers, walnut, rectangular top above a case w/ two over three dovetailed drawers decorated w/string inlay w/canted corners & teardrop inlay at original brass pulls, triple-line inlay on edge of top & at base, base w/ original skirt & French feet, vertical backboards, hand-wrought nails, American South, feet & glue blocks probable replacements, triple-line inlay possibly not original, stains, separations & scattered small repairs, 20 x 42", 37" h. ... **$3,520**

George III chest-on-chest, mahogany, two-part construction: the upper section w/a flaring stepped cornice above a pair of drawers over a stack of three long graduated drawers; the lower section w/a mid-molding over three long graduated drawers, molded base w/scroll-cut bracket feet, batwing brasses, England, ca. 1800, 21 x 44", 5' 8 1/2" h. **$1,610**

Federal chest-on-chest, cherry, two-part construction: the upper section w/a rectangular top w/a coved cornice above a row of three small drawers above a stack of four long graduated drawers flanked by quarter-round reeded columns; the lower section w/a mid-molding above a case w/three long graduated drawers, original oval brasses, molded base on tall French feet, old refinish, glued splits on foot facings, late 18th - early 19th c., 22 x 40 1/2", 6' 2 1/4" h. **$13,513**

Federal country-style chest of drawers, walnut, the rectangular top w/light-wood corner inlay, the case w/two over three dovetailed drawers w/triple dark & light string inlay, original brass pulls & inlaid kite escutcheons, shaped skirt w/French feet, yellow pine vertical backboards w/cut nails, original glue blocks for skirt & feet, American South, patches to foot, refinished, 21 1/2 x 42", 39 1/2" h. **$990**

Federal country-style chest of drawers, cherry, double-line inlaid top over four graduated dovetailed & cockbeaded drawers w/double-string inlay, chamfered corners w/line inlay, shaped feet & skirt, chalk inscription inside at bottom of proper right side reads "Amos Downey (?)," interior bottom of top drawer w/painting of three figures including woman w/curly black hair, Kentucky, feet & skirt probably replacements, separation, splits & old paint, two backboards missing, repair to runners, replaced brass pulls, locks missing, old refinishing, 19 1/2 x 39", 39 1/2" h. **$2,970**

Louis Philippe chest of drawers, walnut & burl walnut, the rectangular charcoal marble top overhanging a case w/canted front corners & a paneled long frieze drawer over three long drawers, deep molded base on low block feet, wreath-form ring pulls & pierced brass keyhole escutcheons, France, second quarter 19th c., 22 x 49 1/2", 39 1/2" h. **$3,450**

The brass escutcheons around keyholes are not only decorative; they protect the wood from scratches made by poorly aimed keys.

Jacobean Revival chest of drawers, black-lacquered & decorated wood, the rectangular top w/brass corner caps above a case w/a pair of drawers over two small drawers flanking a deep square drawer over a small drawer, all above a pair of bottom drawers, heavy bun feet, decorated overall w/ polychrome Oriental figures & landscapes, small ring pulls, England, first quarter 19th c., 19 1/2 x 40 1/4", 33" h. **$4,140**

Mission-style (Arts & Crafts movement) tall chest of drawers with mirror, the top w/a square-framed mirror swiveling between flat braced uprights atop the rectangular top over a case w/a pair of small drawers above four long graduated drawers all w/ turned wood knobs, flat apron & simple tapered front bracket feet, original finish, Quaint metal tag mark of the Stickley Brothers, veneer lifting on bottom, early 20th c., 21 x 36", overall 5' 7 1/2" h. **$2,185**

Mule chest (box chest w/one or more drawers below a storage compartment), Chippendale country-style, painted pine, a rectangular one-board top w/ molded edges & wrought-iron staple hinges opening to a deep well w/an old large brass batwing escutcheon at the top front above a long dovetailed base drawer w/replaced wood knob pulls, molded base on shaped bracket feet, rosehead nail construction, old reddish brown paint, split in one front foot, interior lid lock & drawer escutcheon missing, New England, 18th c., 19 1/2 x 42 3/4", 33 1/4" h. **$2,530**

Mule chest (box chest w/one or more drawers below a storage compartment), Chippendale country-style, the top w/molded edges opening to a well faced by two false drawer fronts, two drawers below, molded base on scroll-carved bracket feet, old replaced batwing brasses & keyhole escutcheons, hand-painted inscription on back reads "R. Hathaway, Hudson, Mich.," old reddish brown finish, attributed to New England, late 18th - early 19th c., 18 1/2 x 40 3/4", 42 1/4" h. **$1,610**

Mule chest (box chest w/one or more drawers below a storage compartment), country-style, painted & decorated pine & poplar, the rectangular top opening to a deep well above a single long drawer w/old walnut pulls, deeply scalloped apron & short bracket feet, original reddish brown flame graining on a tan ground, top w/later sponge decoration on interior, age splits, New England, first half 19th c., 18 1/4 x 36 3/4", 31 1/2" h. **$1,265**

Good buys can sometimes be found in the last hours of a show from a dealer who hasn't had strong sales or doesn't want to haul a large item home.

Mule chest (box chest w/one or more drawers below a storage compartment), country-style, painted & decorated pine, the thick rectangular top opening to a deep well fitted w/a covered till & small drawer, the lower case w/two long graduated drawers w/original turned wood knobs, decorated overall in original brown over yellow sponging on the front panels w/dark red over brown on the rest of the case, slight loss to height, pad added to one rear foot, first half 19th c., 20 x 37", 37 3/4" h. **$2,415**

Mule chest (box chest w/one or more drawers below a storage compartment), country-style, painted pine, the rectangular one-board top w/molded edges opening to a deep well above two long dovetailed drawers w/old wooden pulls, single-board sides w/bootjack legs & a base molding, rosehead nail construction, old dark red paint, New England, small molding around upper front missing sections, edge chips to feet & top, 18th c., 17 1/2 x 38", 38 1/2" h. **$1,035**

Oriental chest-on-chest, pine, three-part construction: the top section w/a rectangular top w/ flaring stepped cornice above a pair of large raised-panel doors beside a small raised panel door over a small drawer; the center & lower sections each w/two long drawers, deep molded flat base, original door brasses & simple pail drawer pulls, China, first half 20th c., 19 x 47", 5' 7" h. **$690**

Neoclassical chests of drawers, walnut & walnut veneer, a rectangular top over a case w/a long overhanging drawer above three long graduated drawers flanked by engaged columns w/carved giltwood caryatid capitals & acanthus leaf bases, on square tapering feet, the frieze drawer fitted as a secretary drawer, Austria, first quarter 19th c., 23 1/2 x 48 1/4", 39" h., pr. **$10,063**

Queen Anne chest of drawers, walnut & burl walnut veneer, rectangular top w/molded edges above a case w/a row of three drawers over three long graduated drawers w/butterfly brasses & keyhole escutcheons, molded base raised on large bun feet, England, ca. 1720, 38" w., 38" h. **$2,875**

Museums sometimes sell items they no longer need in their collections to raise money for purchasing other objects. Items sold by a museum are known as "deaccessioned" pieces.

Pilgrim Century chest, carved & painted red oak, the rectangular thumb-molded & cleated top opening to a deep well w/covered till, the lid decorated w/punchwork & carved "MF 1696," the front w/a narrow serrated band above the three-panel front composed of four pairs of black-painted split spindles separating the three large molded diamonds enclosing a cross design composed of four oval buttons, a lower rail above a pair of narrow drawers w/raised rectangular molding & separated by three pairs of short half-round turned spindles, long rounded base molding, flat stile front feet, paneled ends & five-panel back, black & red paint shows some touch-up, wooden pulls appear original, some replacements, South Scituate, Massachusetts area, 21 1/4 x 54 1/2", 34 1/2" h. **$25,850**

Queen Anne chest-on-frame, maple, rectangular top w/a flaring molded cornice above a case w/a pair of narrow drawers above four long graduated drawers w/butterfly brasses & keyhole escutcheons, set on a base w/a molded edge above the deeply scalloped apron raised on short cabriole legs ending in pad feet on platforms, brasses appear to be original old refinish, Massachusetts or New Hampshire, mid-18th c., imperfections, 16 3/4 x 35 3/4", 4' 1 1/4" h. **$6,463**

Queen Anne chest-on-frame, walnut, two-part construction: the upper section w/a rectangular top w/a coved corner over a row of three small drawers above a pair of drawers & a stack of three long drawers, old replaced batwing brasses; the lower section w/a mid-molding over a deep scalloped apron on cabriole legs ending in pad feet, old refinishing, base a well done replacement, 18th c., 24 1/2 x 46 1/2", 4' 11" h. **$2,300**

Queen Anne-Style chest of drawers, inlaid walnut & burl walnut veneer, the rectangular top w/molded edges above a case w/a pair of drawers w/ banded inlay above three long graduated drawers w/pairs of rectangular inlay bands, the bottom drawer centered by a starburst inlay, molded base on bun feet, small ring pulls, partially composed of antique elements, England, late 19th - early 20th c., 21 1/2 x 37 1/2", 34" h. **$1,955**

Queen Anne-Style chest of drawers, walnut & burl walnut, the rectangular top w/molded edges above a row of three small drawers over three long graduated drawers, deep molded base on short ogee bracket feet, pierced batwing brasses & keyhole escutcheons, partially composed of antique elements, England, late 19th - early 20th c., 21 1/2 x 39 1/2", 35" h. **$1,265**

Renaissance-Style, walnut, the long rectangular hinged top w/carved gadrooned edge opening to a deep well, the front formed of a pair of smaller vertical heavily molded panels enclosing two half-round & an oval panel, a large horizontal panel w/matching design across the center front, stepped & molded flat base, Italy, late 19th c., worn finish, 22 x 68", 22 1/2" h. **$1,380**

Spice chest, Chippendale style, cherry & walnut, cove molded top over single raised paneled door & ten interior dovetailed drawers w/old brass pulls, molded base w/shaped bracket feet, inscription on drawer reads "Presented to Margaret Worthington by her mother May 20th, 1836 it being the property formerly of her great grandmother Anne Strode," restorations w/replacements, wood refinished, comes w/book Thomas Worthington by Alfred Byron Sears, 11 3/4 x 19 1/4", 23 3/4" h. **$7,475**

Sugar or blanket chest, cherry, breadboard lift top over open compartment w/dovetailed drawer below, turned feet, two locks, probably Kentucky, first half 19th c., 26 1/2 x 34 x 18 1/2" ... **$2,750**

Sugar chest, cherry, dovetailed construction, lift top w/ breadboard ends, interior w/three compartments, original lock, dovetailed drawer w/original wooden pulls, turned legs, first half 19th c., top w/old separation, old refinishing, chips, light scratches, 40 x 28 x 20" **$8,800**

Sugar chest, country-style, cherry, a rectangular hinged top opening to a deep interior, the front w/a diamond-shaped ivory keyhole & two small drawers across the bottom, double-knob turned feet, Kentucky or Tennessee, ca. 1820, 20 x 36", 29" h. **$3,738**

Rococo-Style chest of drawers, pine, shaped top over three dovetailed drawers w/brass pulls & mounted w/side runners, vertically bowed front, shaped skirt, curved feet, Italy, 19th or 20th c., drawers rebuilt, replaced pulls, old black paint, repairs to runners, new supports under top, 34 x 40 x 21" **$2,750**

Victorian Aesthetic Movement chest of drawers with mirror, inlaid mahogany, the superstructure w/a wide flat cornice band decorated w/ festoons of garlands inlaid in mixed metal & mother-of-pearl above simple uprights flanking the large rectangular mirror swiveling above the rectangular top w/molded edges, the case w/a pair of drawers ornately carved & decorated to match the top cornice above two long molded drawers w/ simple bail pulls, flat base raised on short stile feet, attributed to Gottlieb Vollmer, Philadelphia, ca. 1880s, 22 x 53", overall 6' 9" h. **$1,150**

Victorian Eastlake substyle child's chest of drawers, birch, the tall superstructure w/a pierced serpentine crestrail above a panel w/stylized floral & roundel incised designs above a long swiveling rectangular beveled mirror all flanked by blocks & line- incised stiles above the rectangular top w/molded edges, the case w/three long graduated drawers w/line-incised leaf spring & stamped brass pulls, original wooden casters, refinished, ca. 1890, 14 x 26", 4' 8" h. **$600**

Victorian Golden Oak chest of drawers w/mirror, a large irregular rectangular beveled mirror in a conforming frame w/leafy scrolls across the top & swiveling between tall serpentine uprights flanking an arched lower back panel decorated w/fancy carved scrolls all on the rectangular top w/a bowed front above a case w/a pair of matching bowed drawers above two long flat-fronted drawers all w/pierced brass pulls, thin serpentine apron, short legs on new casters, ca. 1900, 44" w., overall 6' 2" h. **$259**

Victorian Renaissance Revival chest of drawers with mirror, walnut & burl walnut, the tall superstructure w/a very tall arched crest w/an ornate scroll & cartouche design above curved panels above the tall round mirror swiveling between the side frames mounted w/small candleshelves above two small thin hanky drawers on the rectangular white marble top, the case w/three long graduated drawers w/raised oval banding, round wooden knobs & small carved drop scrolls at the top of the chamfered front corners, deep molded flat base, ca. 1875, 19 x 41", overall 7' 11" **$748**

Victorian Eastlake tall chest of drawers, mahogany & burl walnut, a rectangular top w/molded cornice above a case w/a pair of drawers w/fine burl veneer & simple pulls above a stack of five matching long graduated drawers, ca. 1885, 20 x 43 1/8", 5' 4 1/8" h. **$863**

Victorian Renaissance Revival chest of drawers, walnut & burl walnut, the rectangular top above a long top drawer w/a pair of raised shaped burl panels w/rectangular plate & ring brass pulls centering a shield-shaped raised burl panel, projecting above two matching long drawers flanked by turned columns above a forth matching long projecting bottom drawer, deep plinth base, ca. 1875, 17 x 40", 41" h. **$259**

Victorian Renaissance Revival chest of drawers, walnut, the top fitted w/a pair of small drawers w/a raised panel front & pairs of small wooden knobs joined by a shaped back crest, the case composed of four graduated drawers each w turned wood knobs, shaped bracket feet, ca. 1875, 43" w., 42" h. **$259**

Victorian Rococo "wig" chest of drawers, rosewood, the tall superstructure centered by a period oblong mirror in a molded frame raised between two tall narrow cupboards w/Gothic arch panels in the doors & joined at the top by a pair of scrolls w/anthemion carving, the cupboard bases w/small drawers w/cyma-curve fronts, all resting on the rectangular top above a pair of projecting ogee-front drawers above two long drawers, serpentine scroll-carved apron & bracket feet on casters, original pulls, attributed to the New Orleans warerooms of William & James McCracken, ca. 1850, 22 x 47", overall 7' 4" h. $2,070

→

Victorian Rococo chest of drawers, walnut & feather-grained walnut veneer, the tall oblong mirror in a shaped frame swiveling below a high arched & pierced scroll-carved crest centered by a cartouche supported on reeded columnar uprights raised on large scroll-carved brackets, the rectangular white marble top w/ molded edges & a serpentine front above a conforming case w/three long feather-grained veneered serpentine drawers above the serpentine scroll-cut apron above bun feet on casters, refinished, ca. 1860, 22 x 44", overall 7' 2" h. $1,800

Victorian Rococo chest of drawers, mahogany & mahogany veneer, a large oval beveled mirror w/a scroll-carved crest swiveling between an ornately scroll-carved wishbone bracket terminating in carved swans' heads, between two small handkerchief drawers on the rectangular top w/rounded front corners above a case w/a pair of large plain drawers w/beaded edge molding slightly projecting above three long drawers w/scroll-carved ends, beaded band above the scroll-carved apron w/bracket feet, turned wood pulls, old refinish, ca. 1860, 21 x 38", overall 6' h. $850

Victorian Rococo chest of drawers, walnut & feather-grained walnut veneer, the superstructure w/a high arched molded frame w/floral- and scroll-carved crest enclosing a large arched mirror flanked by small arched side panels below small half-round candleshelves & resting on very thin handkerchief drawers on the half-round top w/a wide flat central section, the flat center over three long paneled feather-grained drawers w/scroll-carved pulls flanked by scroll-carved pilasters, quarter-round side sections w/a curved veneer panel above two open rounded shelves w/pierced scroll-cut back brackets, deep conforming molded base, Philadelphia, ca. 1855, refinished, 18 x 44", overall 7' 2" h. ... $3,500

William & Mary "mule" chest (box chest w/one or more drawers below a storage compartment), painted pine, the rectangular one-board top w/molded edges, opening to a deep well w/the front composed of a pair of false drawers over two long false drawers above two long real drawers at the bottom, simple butterfly brasses & escutcheons, flaring molded base, raised on large turned bulb feet, rosehead nail construction, old bluish green paint over earlier red, areas of touch-up, base a replacement, pieced restorations & some replaced moldings, early 18th c., 18 x 36" $2,070

Desks

Art Deco desk & chair, rosewood & chromed metal, the desk w/a white leather top slightly raised in the center above a pair of small drawers, the narrow side sections in rosewood each w/an open compartment above two small drawers above a flared rectangular base, the chair w/a wide gently curved rosewood back above a squared cushion seat, on squared tapering & slightly curved legs, France, ca. 1925, desk 19 x 40 1/4", 28 1/4" h., chair 31 1/4" h., pr. **$11,950**

Art Nouveau desk & chair, walnut, the desk w/a low superstructure w/an undulating pierced crestrail over two shaped side drawers & a central shelf raised above the rectangular quarter-veneered top w/serpentine molded edges above an apron fitted w/two side drawers flanking the kneehole opening & a center drawer, rounded bottom on lower drawers continues into the cabriole legs ending in peg feet, w/a matching balloon-back side chair, Europe, late 19th c., desk 32 x 55 1/2", 42" h., the set **$2,070**

Art Nouveau desk, gilt-bronze mounted mahogany, "Aux Nenuphars" patt., the rectangular top w/raised undulating back corners mounted w/water lilies & pads in gilt-bronze continuing down the forked rear legs & ending in pad leaf feet, the leather-inset top above an apron w/two drawers w/looped vine & bud pulls above the outswept front legs mounted w/gilt-bronze pond lily buds, vines & leaves, designed by Louise Majorelle, France, ca. 1900, 27 1/4 x 48", 32 1/2" h. .. **$47,800**

Baroque Revival style, walnut-finished hardwood, the superstructure w/a scroll-carved crest centered by a carved full-figure putto above an arcaded shelf w/three scroll-carved openings above a deep molding & carved platform behind a central slant top finely carved w/frolicking putti above a pull-out working surface projecting above deep curved brackets carved w/full-figure grotesque beasts & backed by a panel carved w/a grotesque mask, Italy, late 19th c., 31 1/2 x 47", 5' 2" h. **$3,450**

Biedermeier desk, ash, in the Gothic taste, the modified kidney-shaped top banded & w/an inlaid leather writing surface above a conforming quatrefoil inlaid frieze fitted w/a single drawer, raised on two paneled bow-front cupboards w/inlaid arches flanking a central recessed cupboard door, raised on plinth bases, Europe, early 19th c., 24 x 44", 31 1/2" h. **$3,680**

Chippendale "block-front" kneehole desk, carved mahogany, the rectangular top w/molded edges & round-fronted blocks above a conforming case w/ a long central drawer w/the interior fitted w/dividers above a central recessed & paneled door opening to a shelved interior, flanked by three curved block-front drawers all raised on a molded base & serpentine aprons on tall bracket feet, apparently original butterfly brasses, Massachusetts, ca. 1760-80, 18 1/2 x 32 1/2", 30" h. **$65,725**

Chippendale "oxbow-front" slant-front desk, mahogany, a narrow rectangular top above a hinged slant lid centered by a large carved fan & opening to an interior fitted w/drawers & pigeonholes, the double-swelled "oxbow-front" case w/four long graduated drawers w/batwing brasses & keyhole escutcheons, a molded base w/central drop & short cabriole legs w/carved returns ending in claw-and-ball feet, Boston, late 18th c., 23 x 42 1/2", 44" h. **$15,525**

Chippendale country-style slant-front desk, inlaid birch, dovetailed construction, the narrow rectangular top above a hinged slant front w/mitered corners opening to an interior w/eight drawers & six cubbyholes flanking prospect door w/single drawer, the lower case w/three graduated drawers w/oval pulls, Virginia, late 18th - early 19th c., two front feet ended out 3", front skirt & foot facings replaced, 2" of side facings replaced, brasses replaced, slant front faded, 22 x 42", 4' 1" h. **$2,310**

Chippendale slant-front desk, bird's-eye maple, birch & pine, dovetailed construction, a narrow top above a hinged slant front opening to an interior w/six dovetailed drawers & three horizontal letter slots w/some alterations at center section, the base w/four dovetailed drawers w/molded edges & old replaced oval brass pulls, finely scalloped bracket base, late 18th - early 19th c., 17 1/4 x 35 1/2", 41 3/4" h. **$2,070**

Chippendale slant-front desk, mahogany, a narrow rectangular top above a wide hinged slant front opening to an unusual interior w/a total of twenty dovetailed drawers, also pigeonholes & a hinged center door w/ tombstone panel & additional hidden compartments & shelves, the lower case w/four long graduated beaded drawers w/old replaced batwing brasses, molded base on ogee bracket feet, refinished, feet expertly replaced, some other minor restorations, late 18th c., 24 x 43 1/2", 31 1/2" h. **$3,450**

Chippendale-Style library desk, steel-mounted mahogany, the rectangular top w/serpentine molded edges centering an inset gilt-tooled leather top, the front apron fitted w/pairs of small serpentine drawers w/gadrooned bottom edges flanking a single long flat central drawer w/an arched kneehole opening, the opposite side w/blind drawers, raised on cabriole legs w/acanthus-carved knees & ending in scroll feet, England, ca. 1900, 37 1/2 x 64", 30 1/2" h. **$1,840**

Chippendale-Style partner's desk, mahogany, the shaped rectangular top w/three inset leather sections, the two large pedestals carved w/large lion mask corner pilasters & carved swag & wreath designs, opening to reveal folio compartments below shallow drawers, a central drawer above the kneehole opening, facsimile of the renowned Thomas Chippendale model from Nostell Priory, England, late 19th - early 20th c., 39 x 72", 32 1/4" h. **$6,900**

Colonial Revival partner's desk, mahogany, the wide rectangular top w/molded edges above a case fitted on each side w/a scroll-carved central drawer over the arched kneehole opening flanked on one side by a large square cupboard door carved w/ornate scrolls centering a cartouche & on the other side by two scroll-carved small drawers, large lion heads carved at each corner above large wing-form brackets over the cabriole legs w/leaf-carved knees & large paw feet, ornately scroll-carved side panels, attributed to Horner of New York City, original dark finish, ca. 1880s, 30 x 60", 30" h. **$7,500**

Colonial Revival slant-front bombè desk, mahogany veneer, a narrow rectangular top above the wide hinged slant front opening to a fitted interior above a pair of small square pullouts over the wide bombè case fitted w/three long drawers, serpentine apron & short curved legs w/claw-and-ball feet, original finish, ca. 1900, 20 x 42", 40" h. **$1,800**

Colonial Revival slant-front desk, mahogany, an arched & scroll-carved crestrail flanked by brass rail ends on the narrow rectangular top over the wide hinged slant front boldly carved w/rounded panels of leafy scrolls above a case w/three long graduated drawers w/ornate stamped brass pulls, narrow rounded apron above leaf-carved ogee bracket feet, old refinish, ca. 1890s, 22 x 38", 42" h. **$1,000**

Country-style plantation desk, yellow pine, two-part construction: the top fitted w/a three-quarters gallery above two paneled doors opening to an interior w/14 compartments & two drawers; the lower section w/a slant front opening to a well, tapered ring-turned legs, drawers w/original leather pulls, cut nails throughout, old refinishing, possibly a marriage, top & bottom w/traces of old green paint, some rebuilding, Southern U.S., 19th c., 24 x 37", 5' 4" h. **$1,100**

Country-style schoolmaster's desk, walnut, two-part construction: the upper section w/a rectangular top w/a deep ogee cornice above a tall arrangement of twelve pigeonholes above a drawer on the left centered by larger open compartments & w/a group of tall letter slots over a drawer on the right; the lower section w/a wide fixed slant top writing surface above an apron w/a row of three drawers, raised on heavy ball-, ring- and baluster-turned legs on ball feet, ca. 1850-1880, 50" w., 5' 3" h. **$748**

Country-style slant-front desk, walnut, a small rectangular slant top w/molded edges opening to an interior well above a casinet w/ a single door paneled w/a raised diamond-lattice design, plinth base on bun feet, Italy, mid-18th c., 17 x 24", 42" h. **$1,035**

Federal country-style plantation desk, walnut, two-part construction: the upper section w/a rectangular top w/a wide coved cornice above a pair of tall 6-pane glazed doors opening to two shelves above two shallow drawers w/turned wood knobs; the projecting lower section w/a pair of drawers w/turned wood knobs, raised on ring- and baluster-turned tapering legs ending in peg feet, old finish, age splits, mid-19th c., 23 1/2 x 46 1/2", overall 6' 2" h. **$1,840**

Davenport desk, mahogany, a low brass gallery on the narrow rectangular raised top above the wide hinged leather-lined slant- top writing surface opening to compartments for stationery in the bird's-eye maple interior, one side of the case fitted w/ four pigeonholes opposite four dummy drawer fronts w/pairs of turned wood knobs, plinth base w/extended disk feet on casters, stress cracks, new hinges on slant top, England, mid-19th c., 21 x 21", 33 1/2" h. **$1,093**

George III kneehole desk, mahogany, the rectangular top w/ molded edges above a long fold-down drawer opening to reveal a writing surface supported by corner pilasters that extend w/the drawer, a central kneehole w/a recessed cupboard flanked by two ranks of four small drawers each, simple brass bail pulls, molded base w/pairs of arched bracket feet, England, ca. 1800, 24 1/2 x 42", 33" h. **$3,450**

Federal "bow-front" slant-front desk, inlaid mahogany & cherry, a narrow rectangular top above a wide hinged slant front centered by an inlaid satinwood diamond panel bordered by rosewood crossbanding & stringing opening to an interior fitted w/eight drawers & seven valanced compartments, the lower bowed case w/a stack of four long graduated cockbeaded drawers bordered by crossbanding above a curved inlaid molded base w/a serpentine apron & tall French feet, replaced butterfly brasses, old refinish, minor imperfections, possibly Worcester County, Massachusetts, ca. 1800, 21 x 38 3/4", 44" h. **$4,406**

George III slant-front desk, inlaid oak, a narrow top above a hinged slant top w/banded inlay opening to a gilt-tooled leather writing surface & small drawers & pigeonholes flanking a central banded door, the case w/four graduated & inlay-banded drawers w/pierced batwing brasses, molded base on ogee bracket feet, England, late 18th c., 22 x 48", 46" h. ... **$1,840**

Distressing is the natural wear and tear that appears on furniture surfaces. It occurs naturally over the life of the piece through everyday use. It adds to its charm and helps authenticate that a piece is genuinely old.

Georgian-Style slant-front desk, inlaid mahogany, a narrow rectangular top above the hinged slant front opening to two small hand-dovetailed & cockbeaded drawers flanking prospect door w/ six cubbyholes, the case w/three long graduated drawers w/oval brasses, molded base on scroll-cut bracket feet, original brass hinges & pulls, full dust panels, England, probably late 19th or early 20th c., 20 1/2 x 36", 41 1/2" h. **$990**

Louis XVI-Style lady's writing desk, rosewood, the top w/a two-tiered open gallery w/shelves w/a delicate pierced-scroll crest & slender turned supports, the highly figured hinged slant front opening to an inset felt-work surface & small compartments, the apron w/a narrow full-width crossbanded drawer, raised on slender tapering foliate-carved & fluted legs ending in peg feet, restored original finish, New York City, ca. 1870, 18 1/2 x 30 1/2", overall 4' 5 1/4" h. **$2,760**

Jacobean-Style pedestal desk, oak, the rectangular top w/an inset leather writing surface above a frieze fitted w/three drawers each w/pairs of raised-molding panels, a long center drawer above the kneehole opening, each side pedestal composed of three double-paneled drawers, brass teardrop pulls & brass keyhole escutcheons, molded bases on large bun feet, England, ca. 1900, 29 1/2 x 52", 31" h. **$1,265**

Modern-style desk & chair, birch w/wheat finish, the desk w/a rectangular top above a long top drawer over the kneehole opening flanked by curve-fronted stacks of three drawers each w/a long narrow curved pull, on short block feet, the matching chair w/two horizontal slats in the back above the upholstered slip seat on squared legs, by Heywood-Wakefield, ca. 1955, desk 24 x 50", 30" h., the set **$661**

Louis XVI-Style Provincial writing desk, fruitwood, the rectangular top widely overhanging an apron fitted w/two fluted drawers w/simple bail pulls, raised on knob- and ring-turned legs centered by fluted columns & ending in knob feet, France, late 19th c., 27 1/2 x 57", 29" h. **$748**

Oriental writing desk, stained rosewood, the superstructure w/an ornately pierce-carved crestrail above two projecting compartments, one fitted w/three small carved drawers & the other w/a carved paneled door, backed by a delicate pierce-carved panel above a short carved panel, the projecting writing surface over a pair of elaborately carved drawers, raised on cabriole legs w/carved bats at the knees & ornately pierce-carved returns, ending in claw-and-ball feet, China, ca. 1900, 25 x 38 1/2", 46 1/2" h. **$1,150**

Mission-style (Arts & Crafts movement) fall-front desk, oak, the rectangular top w/a low three-quarters gallery w/gently arched sides w/ through mortises above a wide hinged fall front opening to a fitted interior, the lower case w/a pair of narrow drawers above three long graduated drawers all w/hammered brass plate & bail pulls, flat front apron & low arched side cut-outs, fine new finish, unmarked Gustav Stickley, Model 729, early 20th c., 15 x 36 1/2", 45" h. **$3,738**

Victorian Elizabethan Revival lady's desk, mahogany, two-part construction: the top supporting a recessed pair of two-over- two shallow drawers w/the shelf above supported by S-scroll brackets above a low pierced back gallery; the lower section w/a felt-lined projecting writing surface over a pair of drawers supported by a trestle base w/spiral-twist supports & cross stretcher, mid-19th c. **$805**

Victorian Aesthetic Movement partner's desk, cherry, the rectangular top w/inset leather writing surface & gadroon-carved edges above matching case arrangements, each side w/a long narrow central drawer over the kneehole opening fitted w/an inner arcaded shelf & flanked on each side by one small working drawer & one false drawer each above a square cabinet door carved in relief w/the tools of various professions, tapering ring-turned legs joined by heavy square stretchers, metal casters, original finish, ca. 1880s, 30 x 60", 30" h. **$3,500**

Victorian Gold Oak rolltop desk, oak, narrow rectangular top above the paneled S-roll top opening to an interior fitted w/numerous pigeonholes & two small drawers, the case w/a single central drawer over the kneehole opening flanked by a stack of three drawers on one side & four drawers on the other, plinth base, ca. 1900-10, 50" **$805**

Victorian Golden Oak lady's slant-front writing desk, Colonial Revival style, oak, a narrow serpentine top crestrail w/carved scrolls above a wide rectangular hinged paneled slant front decorated w/stamped brass decorative border bands above an apron w/a single long drawer, raised on tall slender cabriole legs w/stamped brass mounts at the knees & feet, ca. 1900, 44" w., 32" h. **$259**

Victorian Renaissance Revival substyle plantation-type desk, walnut, two-part construction: the upper section w/an angular cut-out crown-form crest decorated w/a narrow raised band w/central rondel & leaftip ends above a long narrow shelf over a long molded rectangular panel flanked by cut-out ends above another shelf over the wide flat fold-down front opening to a lined writing surface & a large interior fitted w/drawers, cubby holes & letter slots; the lower section w/a molded edge above an apron w/a pair of drawers raised on turned tapering rod- and ring-turned legs, ca. 1875, 39" w., overall 7' 7" h. **$863**

Victorian Renaissance Revival substyle pedestal desk, walnut & burl walnut, the rectangular leather-lined top w/a wide molded edge above a long central drawer w/fine burl, gilt incised lines & a cartouche flanked by raised panels, the two side pedestals each w/an ornate projecting top drawer above a pair of ornately carved & gilt-trimmed columns flanking a stack of three burl-paneled drawers, the sides w/finely paneled upper panels above pairs of large burl panels, the reverse composed of matching blind drawer facings, on bold toupie feet, ca. 1875, 33 1/2 x 62", 29" h. **$4,888**

William IV writing desk, mahogany, the rectangular top w/rounded corners inset w/a gilt-tooled leather writing surface, the apron fitted w/three drawers w/wooden knobs, raised on knob-turned & reeded tapering legs ending in trumpet feet on brass casters, England, second quarter 19th c., 37 x 60", 30" h. **$4,600**

Antique purists want furniture in as-found condition, with no restoration done. Others prefer to have furniture repaired, refinished, and ready for use in their home. If restoration is done on a valuable piece of furniture, it should be performed by an expert who can minimize loss in value.

Highboys & Lowboys

Highboys

Queen Anne "bonnet-top" highboy, cherry, two-part construction: the top section w/ swan's-neck pediment w/three urn finials above a row of three drawers, the center one fan-carved, above four long graduated lipped & dovetailed drawers; the base w/a long narrow drawer above a row of three drawers, the center one fan-carved, a scalloped skirt above cabriole legs ending in pad feet, original batwing brass pulls & keyhole escutcheons, horizontal backboards, original hand-wrought nails, America, 18th c., old refinishing, feet & legs repaired w/possible replacements, one finial w/repaired tip, 22 x 38 1/2", 6' 1/2" h. **$9,350**

Queen Anne "bonnet-top" highboy, walnut & walnut flame veneer, mortised, two-part construction: the upper section w/ a broken-scroll pediment centered by an urn- and spiral-turned finial on a platform w/matching corner finials above a frieze centered by a deep shell-carved drawer over a pair of banded drawers over three long graduated drawers; the lower section w/a mid-molding over a long narrow banded drawer above a row of three drawers over a serpentine apron centered by a carved shell, finely shaped cabriole legs ending in pad feet, America, 18th c., mellow refinishing & thin coat of old varnish, replaced brasses, lower shell an old addition, backboards of upper case are replacements, pieced restorations to case & old alterations to aprons & bonnet, 20 1/2 x 42", 7' h. **$17,250**

Queen Anne "bonnet-top" highboy, walnut, two-part construction: the upper section w/ a broken-scroll crest centered by an urn & flame finial w/matching corner finials above a pair of small drawers flanking a deep fan-carved drawer above a stack of three long graduated drawers; the lower section w/a mid-molding above a long drawer over a row of three drawers, the center one fan-carved, the scalloped apron fitted w/two long acorn drops, cabriole legs ending in pad feet, glued splits & pieced restoration, later finials, 18th c., 22 x 42", 7' 4 1/4" h. **$14,375**

Queen Anne flat-top highboy, cherry, two-part construction: the upper section w/a rectangular flat top w/a deep covered cornice above a case w/a pair of drawers over four long graduated drawers all w/brass butterfly pulls; the lower married section w/a medial rail above a case w/a single long narrow drawer above two deep square drawers flanking a wide center deep drawer w/a fan-carved front, shaped front apron w/two turned drops, cabriole legs ending in raised pad feet, New England, 18th c., restored, top left cornice missing section of back, base 19 1/2 x 38 1/8", overall 78" h. **$4,025**

Queen Anne flat-top highboy, tiger stripe maple & cherry, two-part construction: the top section w/a rectangular top w/a deep flaring stepped cornice above a case w/five long graduated drawers w/brass butterfly pulls & keyhole escutcheons; the married lower section w/a medial molding above a case w/two deep square drawers flanking a short central drawer above a high serpentine apron w/two turned drops, simple cabriole legs ending in pad feet, replaced brasses, New England, late 18th c., base 17 3/4 x 39", overall 76" h. **$2,300**

Queen Anne "flat-top" highboy, maple w/fancy crotch-figure walnut drawer fronts, dovetailed, two-part construction: the rectangular top w/a cove-molded cornice above two drawers over three long, graduated dovetailed & band-inlaid drawers; the lower section w/a long narrow drawer above a row of three band-inlaid drawers, the scalloped apron above cabriole legs ending in pad feet, original brass pulls & escutcheons, original iron locks throughout, chamfered & lap-jointed vertical backboards, Boston area, 1730-60, backboards w/some added nails, several drawer runners flipped, old refinishing, 23 x 40", 5' 7" h. **$16,500**

Queen Anne flat-top highboy, walnut & burl walnut, two-part construction: the upper section w/a flat top w/a narrow cornice above a pair of drawers over three long graduated drawers; the lower section w/a wide flared molding above a narrow center drawer flanked by deep side drawers all w/butterfly pulls & round keyhole escutcheons, arched & serpentine apron raised on cabriole legs ending in raised pointed pad feet, replaced hardware, England, ca. 1720, 40" w., 5' 3" h. **$8,050**

A "married" piece of furniture is one in which the top and bottom are from different original pieces. Highboys are some of the most commonly married pieces. While not desirable, this practice is acceptable as long as the seller accurately describes the piece as married. A careful comparison of the types of wood, construction, and comparable wear of the two pieces can help detect married sections.

Lowboys

Queen Anne lowboy, fruitwood, the rectangular top w/molded edges overhanging a case w/a shallow drawer flanked by deep drawers all above the deeply arched apron, on straight cabriole legs ending in pad feet, Europe, mid-18th c., 21 x 34", 27 1/2" h. **$2,530**

Love Seats, Sofas & Settees

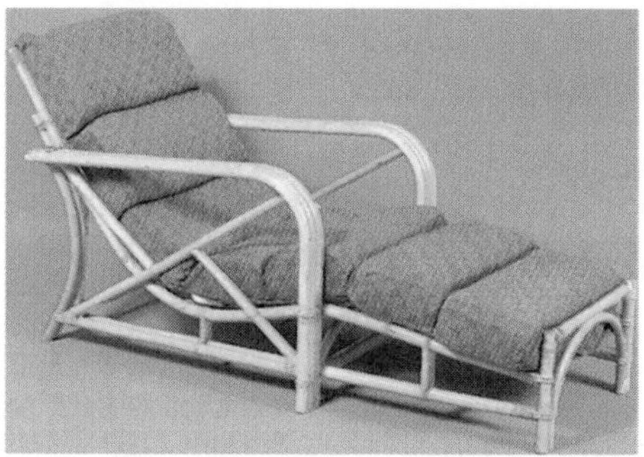

Chaise lounge, Modernist style, a bent bamboo frame w/long curved back & seatrail flanked by round-fronted arms, bamboo rod framing, ca. 1940s-50s, w/upholstered cushion, 64" l. **$144**

Daybed, Louis XVI-Style, polychromed wood & cane, the matching headboards & footboards w/rolled crestrails above wide caned panels flanked by baluster-turned columns on blocks above the baluster-turned legs, joined by molded side rails, France, early 20th c., 34 x 80", 34" h. **$920**

Daybed, Louis XVI-Style, polychromed wood, the matching head- and footboard w/arched crests flanked by small pineapple finials over currently velvet-upholstered panels, joined by molded polychrome rails, France, late 19th c., 32 x 75", 35" h. **$2,530**

Daybed, Louis XVI-Style, upholstered beechwood, the matching head- and footboard w/ an arched molded crestrail & sides enclosing upholstered panels, the flat seatrails centered by small carved panels, raised on short tapering fluted legs, France, late 19th c., 39 x 78", 38" h. ... **$1,610**

Daybed, Louis XV-Style, parcel-giltwood, each end w/an upright scrolling crestrail continuing to scrolling stiles & upholstered sides above a scalloped floral and molded apron continuing to cabriole legs w/scrolling toes, the scalloped siderails also upholstered in a rose & white floral & ribbon velvet fabric, France, late 19th c., 36 x 75", 36" h. **$633**

Duchesse, Louis XV style, carved beechwood, one end w/an arched upholstered back enclosed by a serpentine carved frame flanked by padded open arms & raised above the very long upholstered seat w/a molded serpentine seatrail, raised on six cabriole legs ending in peg feet, signed "H. Amand" (Henri Amand, master in 1749), France, mid-18th c., 64" l., 35" h. **$2,530**

Meridienne, Victorian Rococo substyle, carved & laminated rosewood, the high arched back w/an ornate floral-carved crest atop undulating rails that taper down to form one arm & a partial back section above the long upholstered seat w/a rounded end & serpentine molded seatrails, raised on demi-cabriole legs, the "Rosalie without Grapes" pattern by John H. Belter, New York City, ca. 1855, 36 1/2" h. . **$3,910**

Meridienne, Classical style, rosewood-banded mahogany, an upright upholstered end w/heavy S-scroll uprights above the long rectangular upholstered seat on the deep crotch-veneered apron w/rosewood crossbanding, raised on heavy tapering squared & carved feet on casters, first quarter 19th c., 23 x 48", 26" h. **$2,530**

Meridiennes, Victorian Rococo substyle, carved & laminated rosewood, the high arched upholstered side & back at one end topped by an ornately carved crestrail w/a floral crest above an inverted C-scroll enclosing shell carving, the crestrail composed of C- and S-scrolls continuing down around the tufted back & end arm, long oval upholstered seat w/a molded serpentine seatrail raised on demi-cabriole legs ending in scroll feet on casters, Henry Clay patt., attributed to John Henry Belter, New York, ca. 1855, 26 x 38", 36 1/2" h., pr. .. **$11,500**

Rècamier, Classical style, carved mahogany, the long stepped serpentine backrail carved w/a foliate design & w/a C-scroll above the low upholstered back, one end w/a high S-scroll upholstered arm w/a bolster & a carved reeded & leaf-carved arm support continuing down to the long rounded flat seatrail terminating in a lower outswept S-scroll end arm, raised on ornately carved scrolling figural dolphin front legs, an upholstered cushion seat, possibly by Anthony Quervelle, Philadelphia, ca. 1820-30, 22 x 72", 31" h. **$4,183**

Settee, Art Deco, upholstered Macassar ebony, the long gently arched wooden crestrail above a tufted back flanked by rolled upholstered arms w/flat heavily grained front supports continuing into simple shaped front legs, the scalloped seatrail connected by four flat front legs, long cushion seat, made by Sue et Mare, France, ca. 1925, 27 x 75", 37 1/2" h. **$71,700**

Settee, Art Nouveau style, mahogany marquetry, the simple narrow crestrail above a three-section back composed of narrow loop stiles alternating w/ tapering serpentine splats decorated w/ornate leafy marquetry designs, shaped molded open arms above the long upholstered seat on a flat seatrail & square tapering legs joined by a high slender H-stretcher, designed by Louis Majorelle, France, ca. 1905, 19 x 42 1/2", 38" h. **$5,378**

Settee, Arts & Crafts style, oak, the tall back w/a wide flat crestrail carved w/the motto "Rest Ye And Thankful Be" above a solid back panel flanked by raised side arms w/small arched rests flanking the seat w/a hinged lid over a storage compartment, paneled ends w/stiles forming the legs, early 20th c., 18 x 42", 43" h. **$949**

The Arts & Crafts movement was in vogue between roughly 1880 and 1910. It opposed the mass production of the Industrial Revolution and restore the ideals of quality and pride in handcraftsmanship. Arts & Crafts furniture featured straight, clean lines and relied heavily on oak. Famous designers included William Morris, Elbert Hubbard, and Gustave Stickley.

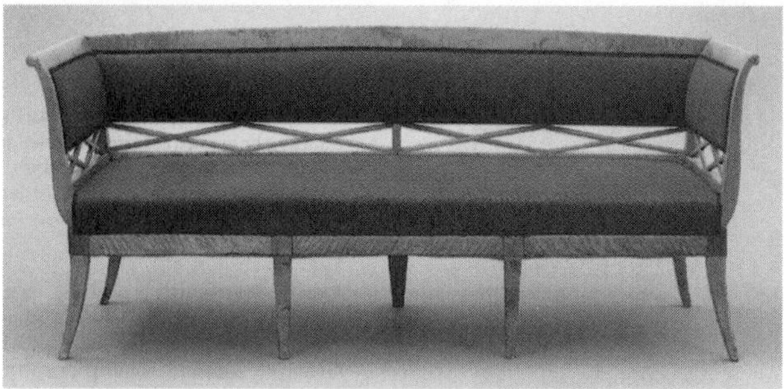

Settee, Biedermeier style, blonde fruitwood, a long narrow crestrail flanked by even outscrolled arms all above upholstered panels over slender pierced diamond-form stretchers, the long upholstered seat on square tapering & slightly splayed legs, Europe, second quarter 19th c., 28 x 81", 34" h. **$3,220**

Settee, George III-Style, mahogany, triple-chairback style, the crestrail composed of three turned bars above three sets of rails flanking narrow horizontal diamonds over smaller vertical diamond lattice-pierced panels, the curved back stiles joined to serpentine open arms on baluster-turned arm supports flanking the long upholstered seat, three baluster- and ring-turned front legs ending in peg feet, England, late 19th c., 24 x 54", 37" h. **$690**

Settee, Modern style, laminated & bent birch, the rectangular upholstered & slightly angled back above the rolled upholstered seat flanked by arched & undulating flat birch one-piece legs & arms, after Alvar Alto, made by Thonet, New York, ca. 1950s, 60" l., 30" h. **$201**

Settee, Oriental style, carved & stained hardwood, the high arched back elaborately carved & pierced w/entwined large birds & serpents w/two serpents continuing to form the end arms above the pierce-carved seat w/a serpentine seatrail above a pierced bat-carved seatrail raised on five cabriole legs w/ scroll feet, China, ca. 1880, minor losses, 26 x 57", 44 1/2" h. **$2,875**

Settee, Oriental, carved softwood, the long back centered by a raised carved crest w/scrolled ends enclosing a narrow carved panel above a row of three carved rectangular panels flanked by solid carved-panel arms, the deep seat above a deep apron fitted w/a row of three drawers above two small drawers flanking two larger drawers, square stile legs w/horse-hoof feet, China, 19th c., 23 x 43 1/2", 39" h. **$690**

Settee, Queen Anne Style, the wide high & gently arched upholstered back flanked by flared wings above rolled arms flanking a two-cushion seat above the upholstered seatrail, raised on simple front cabriole legs w/snake feet, flat canted rear legs, some fabric wear, early 20th c., 51" l. **$173**

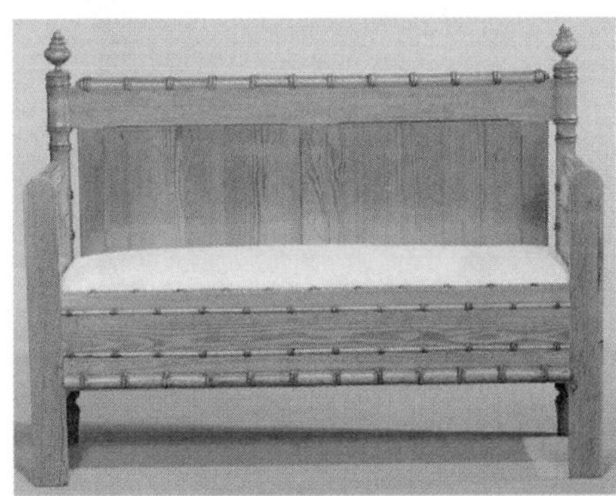

Settee, Victorian country-style, pine, the long back w/a bamboo-turned crestrail rod above the two-panel solid back flanked by heavy bamboo-turned back stiles w/bulbous ring-turned finials, the closed side arms w/turned faux bamboo trims flanking the padded seat w/a deep front seatrail trimmed w/half-round bamboo-turned rods, flat front stile armrests & legs, England, late 19th c., 20 x 50", 39" h. **$1,955**

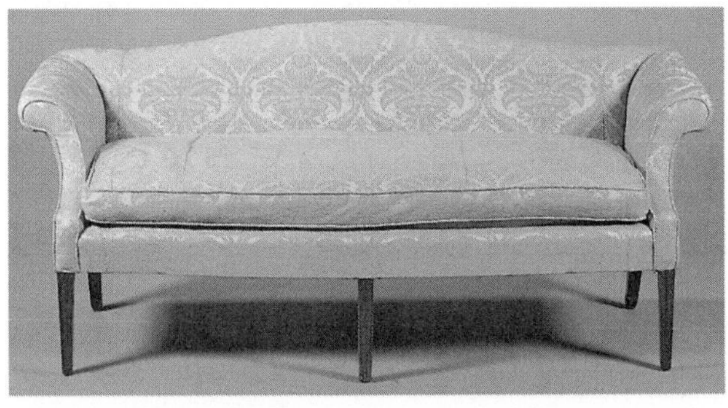

Sofa, Chippendale Style, mahogany, the long serpentine upholstered back flanked by high upholstered scrolled arms above the long cushion seat & upholstered seatrail, raised on six square tapering legs, old repair to one rear leg, restorations & alterations, late 19th c., 73 1/2" l., 33 1/2" h. **$1,265**

Sofa, Chippendale-Style, the long arched & upholstered camel back flanked by outscrolled upholstered arms above the long over-upholstered seat, raised on four square bead-trimmed front legs joined by serpentine box stretchers, England, late 19th c., the base w/several loose joints, side stretchers repaired, upholstery from several sources w/scattered losses & worn areas, 39 x 40", 8' 1" l. **$4,400**

Sofa, Classical Transitional style, mahogany, the triple-serpentine crestrail centered by three leaf-and-fruit-carved crests above the low upholstered back, heavy outscrolled arms w/scroll-carved supports on scroll-carved blocks flanking the deep ogee seatrail, on scroll-carved front feet, original finish, ca. 1850, 28 x 80", 34" h. **$800**

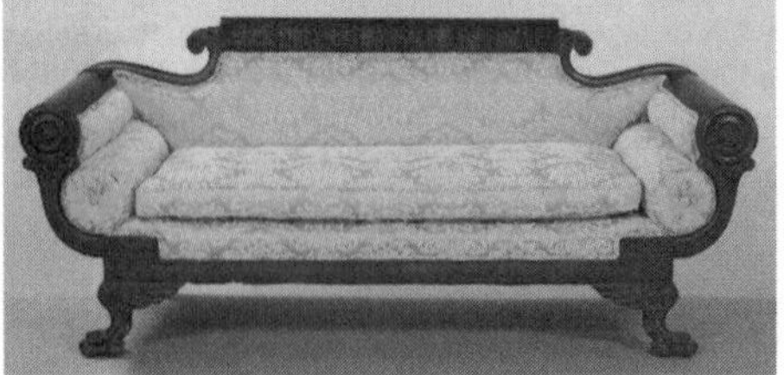

Sofa, Classical Revival style, mahogany, a flat central back crestrail flanked by long S-scroll rails above the long upholstered back flanked by cylindrical arms on forked curved front arm supports flanking bolsters & a long cushion seat, the flat molded seatrail raised on carved winged-paw front legs, America, late 19th c., 27 x 78", 33" h. **$1,265**

Sofa, Classical, carved mahogany & mahogany veneer, the rounded scrolling raised central back crestrail continuing above the shaped upholstered back flanked by incurved upholstered scrolling arms ending in molded terminals & w/bolsters, the half-round straight seatrail ending in blocked ends raised on outswept leaf-carved legs ending in paw feet on casters, some veneer chips, arm joints slightly loose, ca. 1835, 84 1/2" l., 38" h. **$1,150**

Sofa, Classical, mahogany & mahogany veneer, a raised flat central crestrail flanked by scrolling leaf-carved rails above the low upholstered back flanked by rolled upholstered arms w/bolsters supported by leaf-carved scroll supports, the long upholstered seat on a narrow rounded seatrail centered by a leaf-carved reserve & raised on carved cornucopia legs ending in paw feet, old red velvet upholstery, ca. 1830, 23 x 95", 36" h. **$1,955**

Sofa, Classical, mahogany, the long flat crestrail flanked by leaf-carved scrolls over the upholstered back flanked by high scrolled arms w/leaf-carved supports continuing down to form the flat seatrail, on carved paw feet w/large wing-carved returns, on casters, refinished, new upholstery, ca. 1840s, 24 x 72", 36" h. **$950**

It's remarkable how many people turn in lost bid card numbers at auctions. A dishonest person with someone's lost bid card could cause havoc. Keep hold of your bid card at all times and do not turn it in to the cashier when paying your bill; take it with you when you leave.

Sofa, Federal, mahogany & mahogany veneer, the long narrow gently arched veneered crestrail above the upholstered back continuing into shaped reeded arm framing above upholstered arms & ending in baluster-turned reeded columns above bird's- eye maple veneer panels flanking the long cushion seat & upholstered seatrail, raised on four ring- and rod-turned tapering reeded front legs w/peg feet, canted squared rear legs, old refinish, feet repairs, Massachusetts or New Hampshire, early 19th c., 32 1/4" h. **$2,820**

Sofa, Louis XV-Style Provincial type, fruitwood, the long upholstered back w/a serpentine floral-carved crestrail continuing to form the back frame flanked by padded open arms w/incurved arm supports, the long upholstered seat w/a serpentine three- section floral-carved seatrail raised on four cabriole front legs ending in scroll feet on pegs, France, late 19th c., 25 x 74", 42" h. **$2,760**

Sofa, Victorian Knole-type, upholstered, the high flat back upholstered w/three pads flanked by high flat upholstered arms all topped by large pairs of bamboo-turned corner finials, a three-cushion seat over a deep upholstered fringe-trimmed apron, England, late 19th c., 31 x 67", 35" h. **$2,530**

Sofa, Victorian Rococo style, carved & laminated rosewood, finely carved crestrail w/scrolls topped by floral-carved crests above the upholstered back, crestrail continuing down to form closed arms w/ incurved arm supports, the long upholstered seat w/ serpentine seatrail centered by carved florals, demi-cabriole front legs on casters, probably “Rosalie” patt., John H. Belter, New York City, ca. 1855, one rear leg repaired, 34 x 42", 5' 2" l. **$3,740**

Sofa, Victorian Rococo style, carved & laminated rosewood, the high serpentine crestrail pierce-carved overall w/leafy scrolls & grape clusters & centered by a high flower- and shell-carved crest, the crestrail curving down around the high tufted upholstered back to the closed rolled arms w/incurved arm supports, a long upholstered seat w/serpentine molded seatrail centered by a scroll-carved cluster, on demi-cabriole legs on casters, the “Hawkins” pattern by J. & J.W. Meeks, New York City, ca. 1855, 40 x 65", 50" h. **$10,925**

Sofa, Victorian Rococo style, carved & laminated rosewood, the ornate arched & pierce-carved crestrail centered by a pointed rose crest over gadrooned bands & open scrolls continuing to curved pierce-carved corners continuing down & flanking the high tufted upholstered back, closed arms w/incurved carved arm supports continuing to the serpentine finger-carved seatrail & demi- cabriole front legs on casters, "Henry Ford" patt. attributed to J. & J.W. Meeks, ca. 1855 .... **$13,200**

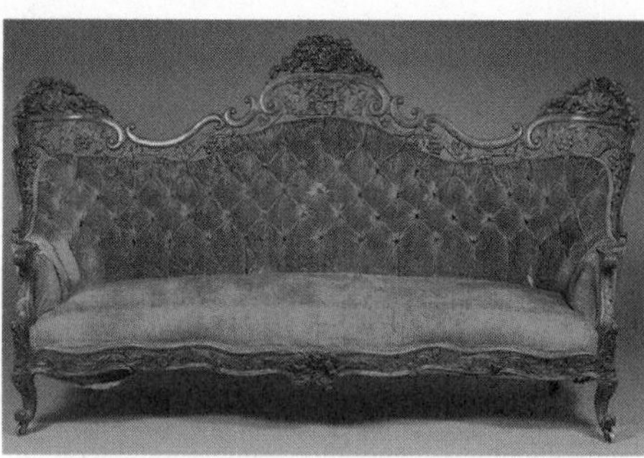

Sofa, Victorian Rococo style, carved & laminated rosewood, the very long serpentine crest topped by a very ornate high pierced & carved crestrail, the highest central arch w/an ornate flower-carved crest above a long C-scroll & fruit-and-leaf carving, continuous S- and C-scrolls across the top w/high flower-carved crests at each end & continuing down & around to the half-length upholstered arms w/incurved arm supports, the long serpentine-front seat w/conforming seatrail carved w/ornate leafy scrolls & a central flower cluster, demi-cabriole front legs on casters, attributed to John H. Belter, New York City, similar to the "Tuthill King" patt., ca. 1855, 30 x 89 1/2", 4' 1 1/2" h. **$49,450**

Sofa, Victorian Rococo style, carved rosewood, triple-back style, a large oblong upholstered center section w/an arched rose- carved crest & scroll-carved side brackets to the flanking oval upholstered sections w/smaller rose-carved crests, padded open arms on incurved arm supports, long serpentine seat above a deep conforming seatrail carved w/leafy scrolls, on demi-cabriole front legs, original dark finish, later upholstery, ca. 1860, 26 x 66", 42" h. **$2,500**

Sofa, Victorian Rococo style, carved rosewood, triple-back style, the high curved end sections w/boldly carved C- and S-scrolls topped by large carved cornucopias, the rails continuing to the arched lower center section w/C-scroll & fruit-carved crest all above the tufted upholstered back, closed half-arms w/incurved arm supports flanking the long serpentine-fronted seat w/a conforming seatrail carved w/scrolls & a central fruit cluster, demi-cabriole front legs on casters, attributed to John H. Belter, New York City, ca. 1855, related to "Cornucopia" patt., 31 x 72", 41 1/2" h. **$20,125**

Sofa, Victorian Rococo style, mahogany, an unusual ornate back w/an oval balloon panel at one end enclosed by a wide looping pierce-carved frame beside a low arched & boldly pierced leafy scroll-carved central section connecting to the simple high arched molding around a high tufted back section, a rolled closed upholstered arm at one end & an open padded arm at the other, incurved arm supports flanking the long serpentine-fronted seat w/a conforming seatrail centered by a carved flower, on demi- cabriole front legs on casters, refinished, ca. 1855, 24 x 68", 36" h. **$2,500**

Sofa, Victorian Rococo style, mahogany, double-chair-back style w/tufted upholstery, two high balloon-shaped end sections w/high pierced & scroll-carved crestrails continuing down to the low arched center section w/another high pierced & scroll-carved crest, low upholstered half-arms on incurved arm supports, long serpentine seat w/simple conforming seatrail, on demi-cabriole front legs on casters, old refinish, older upholstery, ca. 1850s, 26 x 62", 40" h. **$1,600**

Sofa, Victorian Rococo style, walnut, the long pierce-carved crestrail centered by a pair of facing birds w/nest of eggs & flowering leafy scrolls curving down around the tufted upholstered back, open padded arms w/incurved arm supports, long upholstered seat w/a deep scalloped scroll-carved apron on semi-cabriole front legs, refinished, ca. 1850s, 31 x 71", 41" h. **$3,500**

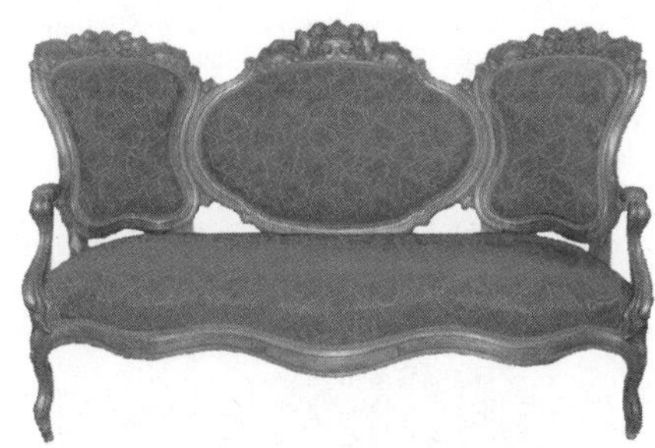

Sofa, Victorian Rococo style, walnut, triple-back style, a large upholstered central oval medallion within a molded frame topped by a fruit-and-scroll-carved crest & flanked by matching waisted balloon-form upholstered panels w/further fruit-and-scroll-carved crests, open padded arms on incurved arm supports, the long double-serpentine seat w/a conforming seatrail, raised on demi- cabriole front legs on casters, refinished, ca. 1860, 30 x 72", 38" h. **$1,800**

Wagon seat, country-style, hardwood w/old mustard paint over an earlier red, two-part back w/double arched slats, tapered round legs w/large round post at center between the two old woven splint seats w/grey paint, turned arms, wafer finials, 19th c., old gesso filler in some areas, 6 x 33 1/2", 29" h. **$431**

Wagon seat, country-style, painted pine, double-back style, each ladder-back back section w/three graduated slats & flanked by a flat shaped open arm on a ring-and baluster-turned front support continuing into the turned front leg, woven rush seat w/front tacked rail, triple turned front & side stretchers, original red paint w/blue medallions on the crestrail & a lady w/parasol, yellow line borders, edge wear, one arm w/glued split, mid-19th c., 16 1/2 x 34 1/2", 34 1/2" h. **$1,495**

Shelves

Apothecary shelves, walnut & pine, dovetailed case at top w/twelve dovetailed drawers w/old brass pulls, a shelf at base, single-board end panels w/scalloped bases & re-shaped arched top & heart cutouts, late black over red sponged decoration, 10 1/2 x 39", 37" h. **$1,725**

Floor shelves, oak, elaborate corner posts having scalloped bracket bases & applied floral vining w/ open twist columns at centers, relief carved urn finials on front, shell & grape finials on back, three shelves w/carved center aprons, old refinishing, Europe, one center apron missing, one back finial chipped, 23 1/2 x 67 1/2", 5' 10" h. **$1,725**

Magazine shelf, hanging folding-type, carved walnut, the wide pointed backboard w/florets above a finely carved panel of daisy- like flowers among leaves, the fold-out front board held by a side chain & also finely carved w/a design of trumpet flowers, Cincinnati Art Club, ca. 1880s, 16" w., 16" h. **$345**

Plate shelves, hanging-type, painted wood, dovetailed construction, three shelves, the narrow rectangular top above graduated sides flanking two upper shelves each w/a front cross rail, a short narrow bottom shelf, old blue paint, some stains, 19th c., 8 1/2" to 4 1/2", 41" w., 32" h. **$460**

Wall shelf, carved wood, a wide rectangular shelf w/rounded front corners & an arch-carved border supported atop the large carved stylized head of a man w/curly hair & a heavy mustache, the large eyes painted white, original black paint, repaired splits in shelf, 19th c., 9 x 10 7/8", 8" h. plus hangers **$978**

If the item at auction is a desirable piece and the opening price asked for by the auctioneer is fair, a bidder can sometimes be successful by bidding that amount immediately. Known as a preemptive bid, the strategy is to shut out competing bidders, especially those who were hoping for a bargain.

Wall shelf, lacquered & parcel-gilt wood, folding-type, the large oblong backboard w/a fancy scroll-cut border, fitted w/a half-round shelf on a swing-out brace support, the backboard in black lacquer decorated overall in color w/various Chinese figures, England, second quarter 19th c., 5 1/2 x 9 3/4", 14 1/4" h. **$690**

Wall shelves, carved giltwood, each w/a rectangular platform top w/a fruit & floral-carved edge supported atop a large spread- winged eagle w/head slightly bent down & perched on rockwork, probably Boston, ca. 1815, 12 1/2" h., pr. **$28,680**

Wall shelves, corner-style, painted & decorated, tall tapering backboard w/serpentine edges flanking three quarter-round shelves, painted bright yellow w/Chinese style florals, the bottom shelf above a quarter-round two-door cabinet opening to a shelf, painted deep red w/each door decorated w/a Chinese landscape w/figures, flat base, some wear & paint loss, one shelf w/old repaint & scattered insect holes, probably Europe, 19th c., 18" w., 36" h. **$210**

Wall shelves, early American country-style, painted pine, whale-end style, a narrow rectangular top shelf above tapering rounded & scroll-cut sides flanking three narrow graduated shelves joined by a back slat, original black & red decoration & old varnishing, attributed to New England, early 19th c., minor wear, 8 1/4 x 32 7/8", 39 1/2" h. **$1,840**

Wall shelves, maple, whale-end style, three narrow graduated open shelves fitted between serpentine shaped sides, old brown wash, 19th c., nails of various ages & some empty nail holes, minor chips, 26" w., 25 3/4" h. **$345**

Appraisers cannot ethically buy from clients. To do so is a conflict of interest, as this gives them an incentive to give a low appraisal.

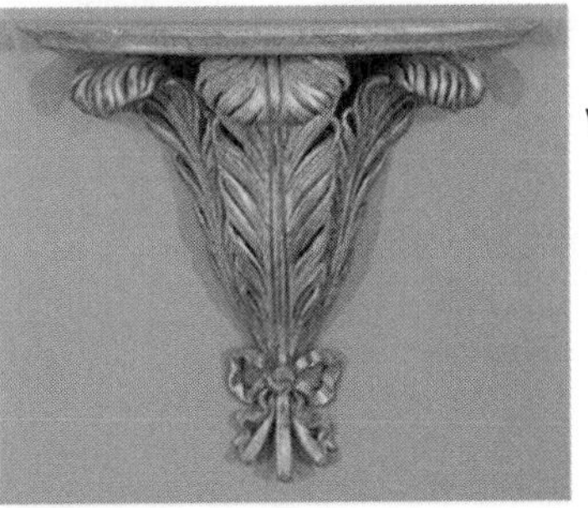

Wall shelves, giltwood, a half-round top shelf w/molded edge supported on tall carved Prince of Wales plumes tied at the base w/a bow & ribbons, England, early 19th c., 8 x 16 1/2", 15" h., pr. (ILLUS. of one) **$431**

Wall shelves, painted & decorated pine, a high top backrail w/a flat center crest & rounded corners above two large hanging holes, decorated w/the original red & black graining & further painted w/a pair of large pink & white blossoms & green leaves, three open graduated shelves each w/slightly canted scallop-cut aprons w/further graining & blossoms & supported by scallop- cut bowed supports, gold banding, one side near crest w/minor damage & touch-up, Maine, first half 19th c., 4 1/2 x 15 1/2", 22 1/2" h. ... **$7,130**

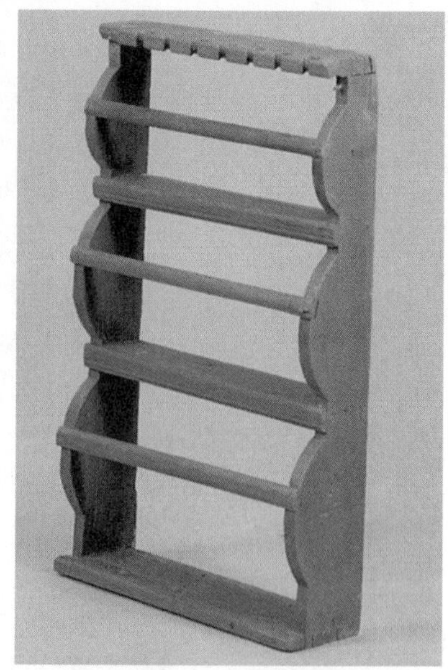

Wall shelves, painted maple, the narrow top board carved as a spoon rack above triple-scalloped graduated sides flanking three shelves each w/a narrow front cross rail, yellowish brown finish, 18th c., 21" h. **$777**

Wall shelves, painted walnut & pine, a rectangular top w/a dentil-carved cornice above a single open shelf above the molded base w/dentil band, old mellow brown finish, some empty nail holes on the sides, found in Maine, 19th c., 9 x 20 3/4", 29 1/2" h. **$575**

Wall shelves, poplar, a three-arch crestrail above a narrow top shelf above three graduated open shelves fitted into the scalloped sides, old refinishing, square nail construction, 19th c., 27 1/2" w., 44 3/4" h. **$546**

Sideboards

Art Deco sideboard, calamander, the rectangular top w/a slightly bowed front inset w/marble above a case fitted w/two wide cabinet doors opening to a fitted bar, joined by stepped side supports above a plinth base, probably France, ca. 1930s, 21 x 65 1/2", 42 3/4" h. **$6,325**

Art Deco sideboard, mother-of-pearl & ebony-inlaid rosewood, the rectangular top w/a molded edge above a deep case w/a pair of wide tapering doors in a basketweave design further inlaid across the front w/a black & white bouquet of flowers & small scattered blossoms, rounded front corner stile w/small gilt-bronze inset bands continuing to the tapering legs w/gilt-bronze feet, wide curved apron, tag of Jules & Andre Leleu, France, ca. 1946, 16 x 53 1/4", 34" h. **$17,925**

Art Nouveau sideboard, carved oak & marquetry, "Chicoree" patt., the wide arched & molded crestrail centered by a large carved blossom above a wide back panel w/a scale design centered by a lower open shelf on leaf-carved corner brackets flanked on each side by an upright glass-door display cabinet w/a single glass shelf all on the long rectangular top overhanging a lower case w/a pair of central drawers over a pair of large paneled doors decorated w/a marquetry floral design, two open shelves at each end w/a serpentine leaf-carved front bracket, stepped & molded plinth base, designed by Louis Majorelle, France, ca. 1905, original label on the back, 23 x 89 1/2", 6' 6 1/8" h. **$16,730**

Classical country-style sideboard, cherry, shaped top w/four conforming central dovetailed drawers flanked by two drawers w/chamfered fronts above two paneled doors, double split-spindle columns on front, turned feet, inlaid diamond escutcheons, back w/frame-&-panel construction w/ cut nails, possibly Catawba Valley, North Carolina, missing locks, old refinishing w/surface chips, scattered old repairs, separations, losses, possibly missing splash panel, 24 x 48", 48" h. **$4,840**

Classical server, mahogany & mahogany veneer, the high arched & scroll-cut backsplash on the rectangular top above a case w/a long veneered drawer w/round brass pulls overhanging another long drawer over a deep center drawer flanked by deep bottle drawers, spiral-turned freestanding columns at each side, on heavy baluster-turned legs, refinished, replaced pulls, ca. 1830, 22 x 46", 4' h. **$650**

Classical sideboard, cherry w/mahogany veneer, the stepped flat upright crest board divided by four flat blocks above the rectangular top above a case w/a long bevel-edged drawer flanked by smaller bevel-edged drawers projecting above a pair of central paneled doors flanked by single paneled doors, all separated by a set of four heavy turned & leaf-carved columns on the plinth base raised on four heavy scroll-carved paw feet, old pressed glass drawer pulls, ca. 1840, 23 x 72", 4' 5 1/2" h. **$1,725**

> Primary woods are those used in the most visible areas of antique furniture. They are usually the more expensive and beautiful woods, whereas secondary woods are generally the more abundant and affordable woods used for the hidden areas of structural support. Primary and secondary woods varied over time and among various countries and geographical areas depending on prevailing styles, and relative cost of the wood based on their scarcity or abundance.

Classical sideboard, mahogany & mahogany veneer, a drop-well rectangular top w/an upright back composed of a pair of large finely carved cornucopias flanking the marble-topped drop well fitted w/ a high central rectangular mirror w/a classical pediment & turned columns, the side sections w/a round-fronted drawer above a tall paneled door flanked by classical free-standing columns, the central section w/two long narrow drawers over a pair of paneled cupboard doors, the blocked base on leaf-carved trumpet-form front legs, early pressed glass pulls on the drawers, attributed to Anthony Quervelle, Philadelphia, ca. 1835, veneer restorations, 23 1/4 x 67", 4' 11" h. **$3,163**

Classical sideboard, mahogany & mahogany veneer, a high broken-scroll backboard centered by a large block & urn finial & w/small urn finials on each end above the rectangular top fitted w/spindled end galleries above slide-out work shelves, the main case w/a long central drawer flanked by shorter drawers above a central pair of paneled cupboard doors flanked by single paneled doors, the drawers & doors separated by reeded pilasters, raised on tapering ring- and rod-turned legs w/peg feet, New York City, ca. 1820s, 25 1/4 x 66 1/4", 5' 4" h.. **$5,175**

Classical sideboard, mahogany & mahogany veneer, the rectangular top above pair of long round-fronted drawers w/round brass pulls flanked by carved corner blocks & slightly projecting over two tall turned & tapering freestanding side columns flanking an arrangement of two deep center drawers over two paneled cupboard doors flanked on each side by a stack of three tall narrow drawers all w/round brass pulls, flat apron, short front legs w/acanthus leaf-carved knees over heavy paw feet on casters, refinished, ca. 1830s, 22 x 50", 4' h. **$1,800**

←

Classical sideboard, mahogany & mahogany veneer, the top w/a crossbanded gallery w/scrolled-end returns above a projecting section w/a pair of small drawers at each end centered by a long false drawer folding down to a writing surface, the stepped-back lower case w/a row of four paneled cupboard doors separated by four freestanding ring-turned columns on blocks above the four beehive-turned legs, round brass pulls, mid-Atlantic states, ca. 1830, 24 x 71", 4' 2" h. **$3,910**

Country-style sideboard, maple, a low arched back crest flanked by short end blocks w/button-turned finials above the long rectangular top above a narrow zigzag-carved frieze band above a row of three drawers w/pairs of turned wood pulls over three- section front w/zigzag-carved stiles, the central section w/a drawer above an arched panel door, each side section w/a stack of three drawers w/pairs of turned wood pulls, simple block feet, old dark surface, attributed to Georgia, 19th c., 21 1/2 x 60", 4' 3/4" h. **$1,725**

Federal server, mahogany, the rectangular top w/a three-quarters gallery w/scrolled ends above a case w/a long deep drawer decorated by a recessed arch, raised on ring- and rod-turned supports joined by a medial shelf w/an incurved front & corner blocks on tapering ring-turned feet, restorations, ca. 1825, 20 x 41 1/2", 38 1/2" h. **$3,450**

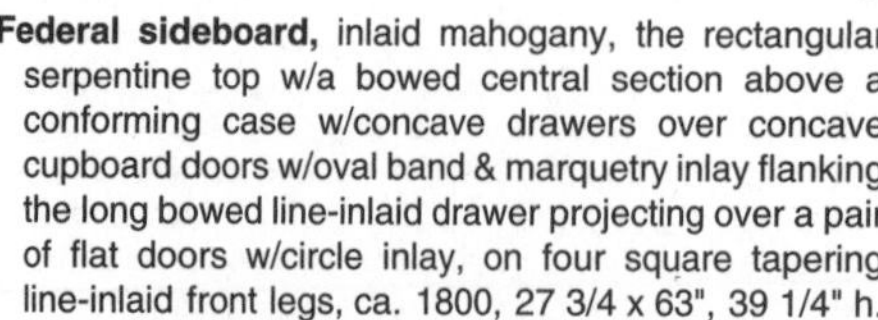

Federal sideboard, inlaid mahogany, the rectangular serpentine top w/a bowed central section above a conforming case w/concave drawers over concave cupboard doors w/oval band & marquetry inlay flanking the long bowed line-inlaid drawer projecting over a pair of flat doors w/circle inlay, on four square tapering line-inlaid front legs, ca. 1800, 27 3/4 x 63", 39 1/4" h. **$4,370**

Federal serpentine-front sideboard, inlaid mahogany, the rectangular top w/a serpentine front above a case w/a conforming long central drawer over a double-arched apron & flanked by doors, all w/oval inlaid banding & inlaid border trim & panels, on square tapering legs, round brasses, very minor shrinkage cracks in top & one side panel, Maryland or Virginia, ca. 1810, 22 3/4 x 72 1/2", 41 1/4" h. **$13,800**

Federal sideboard, cherry, rounded central section w/two conforming drawers above bay w/two doors, flanked by small drawers above cellaret drawer flanked by reeded pilasters & two swell-front drawers w/conforming doors below, dovetailed & cockbeaded drawers, six tapered & reeded legs, frame-and-panel sides, drawer faces w/fancy cherry veneer & mahogany banding, swell- front doors & drawers of stacked-block construction, old, possibly original uneven finish, brass pulls possibly original, Tennessee or Kentucky, early 19th c., some drawer surfaces replaned, possibly missing splash panel, most locks replaced, cellaret drawers missing interior dividers, several minor scratches, veneer losses & separations throughout, 25 x 44", 6' 5" h. **$15,400**

Federal sideboard, mahogany & mahogany veneer, the rectangular top w/a serpentine front above a case w/two small bow- front drawers & a bow-front door on each side flanking the concave center section w/a long drawer over a pair of cupboard doors flanked on each side by a short & deep drawer, arched central apron, raised on four ring-turned tapering & reeded front legs w/peg feet, ca. 1820, old refinish, probably old replacement pulls, 22 x 70", 40" h. **$2,000**

George III-Style sideboard, mahogany, the rectangular top w/a serpentine front above a conforming case w/ two concave drawers flanking a bowed central drawer above an arched opening, on square tapering legs ending in spade feet, England, mid- 19th c., 21 x 53", 35" h. **$4,600**

Jacobean-Style server, carved oak, a high peaked backboard centered by a large carved rosette above the rectangular top over an apron carved w/a band of arched leaves & supported on heavy turned front supports above two more open shelves each w/a carved apron & flanked by two heavy turned supports, short heavy cylinder & disk front legs, old dark finish, England, 19th c., reconstruction & pieced repair, 16 x 46", 4' 4" h. **$1,150**

Jacobean-Style sideboard, oak, the rectangular top above a case w/a pair of deep drawers each carved w/ pairs of squared panels & flanked by knob-turned half-spindles, a molded apron raised on baluster- and ring-turned front legs joined to the square back legs w/box stretchers, partially composed of antique elements, England, 19th c., 21 x 52 1/2", 34" h. **$1,150**

Louis XV-Style Provincial server, fruitwood, the rectangular top w/rounded corners above a conforming case w/notched front corners flanking a pair of arched paneled cupboard doors w/long brass latch mounts above the molded serpentine apron & short bracket feet, France, first half 19th c., 24 x 48 3/4", 44 3/4" h. **$3,450**

Louis XV-Style Provincial sideboard, pearwood, the rectangular top w/molded edges above a case w/a pair of long scroll- carved drawers w/long pierced-brass mounts centering a carved sunburst above a pair of long cupboard doors w/arched & scroll- carved panels & long pierced-brass hardware flanking a central caduceus-carved panel, the serpentine scroll-carved apron centered by a carved wreath enclosing the date "1831," on short scroll-carved front legs, France, 22 1/2 x 53 1/2", 37 1/2" h. **$3,450**

Mission-style (Arts & Crafts movement) server, oak, the back w/a low plate rail above the rectangular top overhanging an apron w/a single long drawer w/ squared hammered copper pulls & an arched apron, flanked by through-tenon side stiles, the square legs joined by a lower medial shelf w/an incurved front & a narrow rear rail, original finish, some foot wear, delamination on back panel, branded mark of the Charles Limbert company, early 20th c., 17 1/4 x 40", 40 1/2" h. **$2,185**

Louis XV-Style Provincial sideboard, walnut, three-piece construction, the top w/ornate carved pediment above door w/20 beveled panes flanked by two carved side doors; the base w/two drawers above two large bay doors, cabriole legs w/carved scroll feet, panels w/ detailed carving throughout, carved & paneled central backboard, France, 24 x 59", 9' h. **$3,080**

Mission-style (Arts & Crafts movement) sideboard, oak, the top w/a wide plate rail above the long rectangular top above a case w/a stack of three central drawers flanked by flat doors all w/copper plate & ring pulls, a long drawer across the bottom, square stile legs, good original finish, branded mark of L. & J.G. Stickley, early 20th c., 20 x 48", 44" h. **$4,600**

Renaissance Revival sideboard, walnut, three-part construction, the top w/beveled mirror glass at the back of the pie shelf & inside the top; the middle section w/ relief-carved arched center crest w/glass interior shelf; the base w/grey, brown & white marble top, flat front w/bowed ends, two doors w/relief carving on raised panels w/two dovetailed drawers above, short turned wafer feet, Europe, 21 x 59 1/2", 6' 7 1/2" h. ... **$1,265**

Victorian Aesthetic Movement sideboard, mahogany, the upper section w/a rectangular top w/a flaring cornice over a gadrooned frieze band projecting over a long rectangular beveled mirror & supported by reeded columnar front supports on a lower shelf projecting above a panel-backed section w/incurved end brackets, all above the rectangular top on the lower case composed of a long drawer above a pair of cupboard doors w/oblong floral-carved panels on one side & a stack of three drawers above a short open compartment w/a serpentine border on the other side, looped hammered brass pulls, molded base on thin bun feet, original dark finish, late 19th - early 20th c., 24 x 77", 6' h. **$1,610**

Victorian Baroque Revival sideboard, carved oak, two-part construction: the upper section w/a rectangular blocked top fitted w/a high arched & scrolling pierce-carved crest w/a central cartouche flanked by small turned corner finials above the deep flaring cornice w/a scroll-carved frieze band over a pair of tall cupboard doors w/rounded panels w/raised molding enclosing ornately carved game trophies flanked by pierce-carved scrolling brackets & two small shelves above a recessed paneled compartment flanked by ornately carved brackets; the lower section w/a wide rectangular top w/a molded edge over a pair of narrow paneled drawers carved w/grapevines above a pair of paneled cupboard doors w/raised molding enclosing finely carved clusters of fruits, three slender turned columns resting on projecting blocks separate & flank the doors, on compressed bun feet, refinished, Europe, late 19th c., 24 x 60", 9' h. **$5,500**

Victorian Baroque Revival sideboard, oak, a tall splashback w/an ornately carved crestrail w/a basket of fruit flanked by reclining dragons all above a plain recessed panel, raised block corners over carved lion masks, the long rectangular top w/blocked corners above a case w/a row of three drawers carved w/leafy scrolls & each separated by a block carved w/a stylized blossom head all above a row of three large doors w/ oval carved panels, the central door w/a large scrolled cartouche framed by leafy scrolls & the matching outer doors carved w/large urns of fruit over scrolls, the central door flanked by vertical herringbone-carved blocks above the blocked apron, each outside edge w/ a large barley twist-carved column, raised on bulbous squatty feet, ca. 1890, American-made, refinished, 26 x 76", 5' h. **$3,500**

Victorian Golden Oak server, quarter-sawn oak, a serpentine crestrail supported on seated winged lion brackets above a conforming long beveled mirror over the rectangular top, the case w/a pair of long slightly projecting drawers over a long deeper drawer above a pair of flat cupboard doors centered by a scroll-carved panel, front animal legs ending in paw feet, on wooden casters, refinished, ca. 1900, 22 x 48", 5' h. **$950**

Victorian Baroque Revival sideboard, oak, the tall canopied superstructure w/a raised rectangular top over a deep coved band carved w/long leafy vines above the flaring cornice over a scroll-carved frieze band & serpentine apron centered by a carved lion mask all supported on tall columns w/large leaf-carved knobs, the tall back centered by a tall rectangular beveled mirror flanked by large scroll-carved panels centered by a carved lion mask & a quarter-round open shelf over a small rectangular beveled mirror, the rectangular top on the case w/a wide egg-and-dart-carved border & scroll-carved frieze band above a case fitted w/a pair of four-panel cupboard doors centered by a diamond flanking two scroll-carved drawers w/lion mask pulls over an open compartment w/scroll-carved side brackets, narrow scroll-carved bands down the sides above the large bulbous bun feet, Europe, ca. 1890, refinished, 24 x 59", 7' 8" h. **$3,200**

Antique shop owners face a stigma when it comes to liquidating their inventory at auction. Antiques that have been offered in a shop tend to sell for less than normal prices at auction. That's good news for customers who have admired something offered in a shop, but at a price they felt they could not afford. If the dealer, however, was widely known and highly regarded for finding great items, the inventory could sell at a premium price.

Victorian Golden Oak server, quarter-sawn oak, a shaped beveled mirror within a pierced & scroll-carved frame above the rectangular top over a pair of drawers above a pair of long rectangular leaded glass doors, a long scroll-carved drawer across the bottom, on tall slender squared legs on casters, original hardware, refinished, ca. 1895, 18 x 40", 4' 6" h. **$1,750**

Victorian Golden Oak sideboard, a high rectangular beveled mirror w/a wide flat frame & top scroll-carved center crest enclosing a long beveled mirror, the rectangular top w/molded edges over a pair of flat cupboard doors w/arched tops flanking a long bowed central geometrically glazed cupboard door above a long drawer at the bottom w/scroll-carved trim & scalloped apron, squared outswept front legs w/paw feet, original brasses & dark finish, ca. 1910, 20 x 48", 5' h. **$1,600**

Victorian Renaissance Revival server, walnut & burl walnut, the superstructure w/a peaked pediment centered by a large fleur-de-lis finial & small raised burl panels above a flaring molding above a wide panel w/incurved sides centered by a large round raised burl panel w/a carved sunburst & shaped raised burl panels over a long narrow rectangular shelf w/rounded corners & flanked by small turned finials, the shelf supported on high pierced & scroll-cut brackets flanking a wide panel centered by a raised oval banding enclosing burl veneer, all atop the rectangular white marble top w/rounded front corners over a conforming case, the case w/a pair of drawers w/oval burl panels above a pair of cupboard doors w/large oval sunken panels w/ burl veneer, deep molded flat base on casters, original finish, ca. 1875, 20 x 42", 7' 4" h. **$2,600**

Victorian Renaissance Revival sideboard, carved oak, the tall superstructure w/a high arched & ornately scroll-carved crestrail centered by a large carved realistic stag head above a long half-round shelf supported on baluster-turned supports on a lower open shelf w/a closed paneled back flanked by pierced scrolls, the lower shelf supported by large projecting brackets w/fruit carving resting on the long white marble top & flanked by further pierced scrolls at the sides, the lower case w/a pair of paneled drawers w/fruit- and nut-carved pulls above a pair of arched panel doors centered by large relief-carved clusters of dead game, the beveled front corners trimmed w/carved scrolls, on a plinth base, related in style to an Alexander Roux example, ca. 1870, 23 1/2 x 59", 7' 6" h. **$4,140**

Victorian Renaissance Revival sideboard, chestnut, walnut & walnut veneer, the tall superstructure topped by a wide peaked scroll-carved crest w/a fan-carved finial above an arched molding above a long arched burl panel flanked by side scrolls & narrow burl panels over a long rectangular shelf w/rounded corners supported on tall blocked brackets w/turned drop finials above a long narrow rectangular mirror & scrolled side brackets, the long rectangular white marble top w/rounded front corners above a conforming case, the case w/a central stack of five small molded drawers flanked at each side w/a burled drawer w/brass ring pulls over large cupboard doors w/a rectangular raised burl panel & notch-carved dark border molding, flat molded base, original finish, 1870s, 22 x 52", 8' h. **$2,400**

Victorian Renaissance Revival sideboard, oak, the high superstructure topped by a tall arched crest carved w/large scrolls flanking a carved cluster of fruit above a narrow rounded shelf w/a sawtooth-cut narrow apron supported on bold scroll-carved brackets flanking a long narrow raised scroll-carved panel & scrolled side brackets above a matching longer shelf on matching brackets flanking another raised panel w/carving of a cluster of fruit all resting on the long rectangular top w/a deep flared apron w/carved scrolls at the sides & w/two long scroll-carved drawers at the front separated by three blocks w/a lion mask carved in relief, a pair of large paneled cupboard doors below each centered by relief-carved decoration of game birds, three long dividing columns down the front each carved in bold relief w/bands of fruit & leaves, blocks & scroll-carved flat base band, Europe, ca. 1875, refinished, 22 x 50", 7' 8" h. **$2,800**

Victorian Renaissance Revival sideboard, walnut & burl walnut w/ebonized trim, the tall superstructure w/a high scroll-carved crestrail w/an arched raised center crest w/a carved cartouche above a carved fruit cluster, a long narrow top shelf raised on four ring-, rod- and knob-turned spindles resting on another shelf supported on matching spindles, both shelves in front of a large rectangular beveled mirror w/an ebonized border, the rectangular ebonized top on a case w/a pair of long narrow burl drawers w/ebonized borders flanked by small reeded blocks, a medial molding above a pair of large paneled doors w/burl & rectangular ebonized molding forming a panel centered by a large cluster of carved fruit, deep molded flat base on turned bun front feet, original finish, Europe, ca. 1875, 20 x 46", 6' 8" h. **$1,600**

Victorian Renaissance Revival sideboard, walnut & burl walnut, massive size, the tall & wide superstructure w/a high arched central section w/a long pierced crest centered by a carved palmette & scrolls above further carved scrolls & an arched molding, the matching broken-scroll side crest above tall & wide carved & burl-veneered side panels w/large half-round candle shelves flanking the large arched mirror which rests above narrow burl-paneled drawers on the long rectangular white marble top w/blocked corners & projecting center section, a conforming case w/a large stepped-out center paneled door w/burl veneer & a carved oblong medallion flanked by blocked side pilasters, each side section w/a paneled drawer over a smaller cupboard door w/burl veneer & a large raised diamond-shaped panel, blocked pilasters at the outside corners, wide blocked flat base band, original dark finish, ca. 1875, 24 x 68", 8' 6" h. **$6,500**

Victorian Renaissance Revival sideboard, walnut & burl walnut, the superstructure w/a serpentine crestrail w/a high arched central section w/full-relief carving of a cluster of fruit flanked by small raised burl panels, small turned finials at the corners above a narrow long shelf supported on large scroll brackets above a long narrow raised burl panel above another long narrow shelf supported on scroll brackets above a larger long raised burl panel flanked by scallop-cut quarter-round outside corner brackets over the long rectangular top w/inset white marble, the case w/two long narrow drawers each w/two raised burl panels & black pear-shaped pulls flanked by burl corner blocks above a pair of large cupboard doors each centered by a large square raised burl panel enclosed by carved scrolls, the inner door molding ebonized, blocked raised burl panels at each side of the case above the flat molded base w/an ebonized band, old refinish, ca. 1875, 22 x 54", 7' h. **$2,400**

Victorian Renaissance Revival sideboard, walnut, burl & figured walnut, the tall superstructure topped by a high broken-scroll pediment w/an arched crest on the center section above a full-relief carved bust of Robin Hood above a wide rectangular shelf w/rounded corners supported on scroll-cut brackets above a molded narrow rectangular panel w/figured walnut & a long narrow shaped raised burl panel over another slightly longer shelf on brackets above a larger figured walnut panel w/a large raised burl panel all flanked by scroll-cut side brackets, a half-round grey marble top w/a flattened front section above a conforming case w/a long narrow center drawer w/narrow raised burl panels flanked by curved matching swing-out trays at the sides all above three large paneled doors each centered by a large carved cartouche, deep molded base band on wafer feet, refinished, 1870s, 22 x 60", 8' 5" h. **$7,500**

Victorian Rococo sideboard, carved oak, two-part construction: the tall superstructure w/a high arched & boldly scroll-carved crest centered by a figural stag head above a long half-round top shelf raised on columnar front supports & w/a paneled back flanked by openwork side S-scrolls all above a matching lower shelf supported by fancy carved supports featuring hound heads; the lower section w/a rectangular white marble top over a case w/a pair of narrow paneled drawers w/nut-carved pulls above a pair of arch-paneled doors, one centered by a boldly carved cluster of fish, eels & lobsters, the other w/a cluster of game including rabbits & fowl, the canted front corners w/carved top corner drops, deep plinth base, attributed to Alexander Roux, New York, New York, ca. 1860, 23 1/2 x 59", 7' 6" h. **$4,600**

William IV sideboard, mahogany, tall upright crestboard w/rounded corners above the rectangular top w/projecting ends above a conforming case w/end pedestal sections each w/ a drawer over a paneled cupboard door flanking a center drawer, molded bases, England, second quarter 19th c., 23 1/2 x 78", 4' 2" h. **$1,380**

Victorian Rococo sideboard, carved rosewood & marquetry, the long white marble top w/a serpentine bowed front above a conforming case w/three front sections, each w/a boldly scrolling leaf-carved band above a wide central bowed door flanked by smaller concave side doors, each door w/panels outlined w/scrolled molding enclosing floral marquetry bouquets, scrolling leaf- carved base bands, the three front sections separated by very large & boldly carved leafy scroll pilasters ending in shell-form feet, ca. 1850s, 23 1/2 x 73", 38" h. **$6,900**

Victorian Rococo sideboard, chestnut, the tall superstructure w/an arched & stepped crestrail over a panel centered by a large relief-carved cluster of fruits & nuts above two long narrow tiered half-round open shelves supported by scrolling uprights w/fruit carving, the shaped outside edges carved in bold C-scroll & fruit decoration, all resting on a half-round white marble top w/a flat projecting center section above a conforming case w/a pair of paneled central drawers flanked by curved end drawers, two flat paneled front doors w/carved fruit clusters & corner roundels w/plain curved & paneled end doors, conforming molded flat base, attributed to Alexander Roux, New York City, ca. 1855-60, original finish, 22 x 70", 6' 2" h. **$5,500**

Victorian Rococo sideboard, figured walnut, the high superstructure w/an arched pediment w/a large scroll finial flanked by delicate pierced scrolls over a panel w/shaped raised panels flanking a circle of carved fruit above a long narrow shelf w/rounded corners supported w/turned & reeded spindles on another long shelf backed by a long narrow shaped mirror flanked by incurved scroll-carved sides & raised on scroll-cut brackets flanking another matching mirror & flanked at each side by asymmetrical recessed burl panels & ornate pierced C-scrolls at the outer edges, on a long half-round white marble top w/a flattened center section, the conforming case w/a pair of paneled drawers flanked by curved swing-out side storage trays above four large cupboard doors, the center two w/flat fronts w/arched panels centering oval banding enclosing a large relief-carved cluster of fruit, the curved side doors w/similar molding but centered by large scroll-carved cartouches, flat molded base, original polished finish, marked by Mitchell and Rammelsberg Co., Cincinnati, Ohio, ca. 1855, 22 x 66", 8' 6" h. **$10,000**

→

Victorian Rococo sideboard, walnut & burl walnut, the tall, wide superstructure w/a large arched & molded pediment centered by a fruit-carved finial over a wide smooth panel topped by a pendent carved fruit cluster, scroll-carved flaring sides down to a long narrow open shelf w/a serpentine front supported on slender turned spindles resting on small half-round side shelves on scroll-cut brackets all backed by pairs of carved scrolls centering a long oval mirror, the rectangular white marble top above a conforming case w/a pair of paneled drawers w/scroll-carved pulls over three cupboard doors each w/a large recessed oval burl panel framed at each corner by small triangular raised burl panels, deep molded flat base on casters, refinished, ca. 1860, 22 x 54", 7' 8" h. **$3,500**

Victorian Rococo sideboard, walnut & burl walnut, the superstructure w/a low pierced & scroll-carved back crest on the long narrow top shelf supported on large ornate S-scroll front supports joined by a lower shelf & a solid back, the rectangular white marble top above a case w/a row of three ogee-front drawers above a beaded molding over three cupboard doors w/raised carved rectangular panels separated by vertical beaded moldings, a beaded base molding on the serpentine scroll-carved apron, scroll-carved bracket feet, attributed to the New Orleans warerooms of William McCracken, ca. 1850s, 22 1/4 x 54 1/2", 5' 11" h. **$2,760**

Tables

Art Deco center table, clear & frosted glass, "Cactus" patt., the wide round top overhanging the frosted glass base composed of eight gently arched cactus stems issuing from a frosted clear round base, Marc Lalique, 1989, engraved "25-5-1989 No. 15," & "1-82," 64" d., 28 1/2" h. ... **$26,290**

Art Deco cocktail table, blond mahogany, in the Chinese taste, the round top w/a rounded apron raised on five square legs on blocked feet & small corner blocks, w/an applied metal tag marked "Gouffè," France, ca. 1930, 35" d., 17 1/2" h. **$288**

Art Deco cocktail table, glass-topped rosewood, the rectangular glass top w/rounded corners raised on two faux ivory & brass-tipped Islamic crescents set upon the ends of H-form rosewood plinth base, France, ca. 1930, 23 x 48", 20" h. **$1,093**

Art Deco side table, ivory-inlaid Macassar ebony, the round top w/a radiating wood grain design edged w/a band of small ivory dots, on three flattened & arched legs, designed by Jacques-Emile Ruhlmann, ca. 1925, France, 19 7/8" d., 25 1/2" h. **$77,675**

Baroque-Style guard room table, oak, the long rectangular planked top raised on heavy serpentine end supports joined by stretchers & w/long slender scrolled iron brackets under the top, Spain, ca. 1900, 39 x 87", 29 1/2" h. **$2,760**

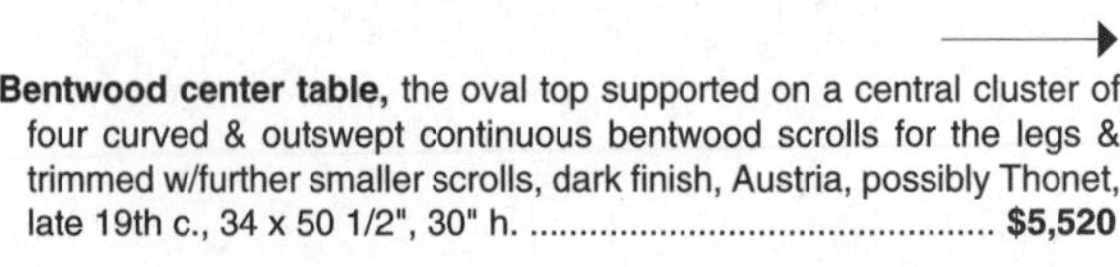

Bentwood center table, the oval top supported on a central cluster of four curved & outswept continuous bentwood scrolls for the legs & trimmed w/further smaller scrolls, dark finish, Austria, possibly Thonet, late 19th c., 34 x 50 1/2", 30" h. **$5,520**

Biedermeier center table, cherry, the nearly square top overhanging an apron fitted w/one long drawer, on simple cabriole legs, good wood figure, Europe, first-half 19th c., 29 1/4 x 30 1/2", 30" h. **$1,495**

Biedermeier side tables, blond wood, a round top raised on a round upper column joined by an ebonized ring to a paneled lower column w/ anotherebonized ring, resting on a tripartite base, Europe, first half 19th c., 20" d., 28" h., pr. (ILLUS. of one) **$1,610**

Biedermeier-Style drop-leaf breakfast table, figured maple veneer, rectangular top w/dovetailed drawer on one side w/raised front, false front on opposite side, thick round column on platform base w/carved paw feet, Europe, 20th c., some reconstruction, 28 x 33" w. plus 9" leaves, 29 3/4" h. **$978**

Chippendale dining table, mahogany, the rectangular top flanked by deep rectangular drop leaves, an arched apron supported on swing-out cabriole legs w/ claw-and-ball feet, New York state, late 18th c., open 48 1/4 x 57", 28 3/4" h. (ILLUS. closed) **$4,600**

Chippendale furniture with Chinese influence, such as the ball-and-claw foot, is known as Chinese Chippendale.

Chippendale tea table, mahogany, carved Chippendale borders, "birdcage" & tilt-top mechanism, spiral-carved urn pedestal w/flower-carved band at base, three legs w/fine acanthus-carved knees w/ball-and-claw feet w/articulated talons, original iron spider & brass latch, England or America, 18th c., top w/several patches, battens probably reset, old refinishing, 33 1/8 x 34 1/8", 28 " h. **$10,450**

Chippendale tea table, mahogany, circular dished top w/ piecrust border tilting on figured mahogany "birdcage" above the ring- & urn-turned pedestal above tripod base, pad feet, original iron spider, original spindles & plate, batten & latch appear to be original & untouched, probably original surface, Virginia family history, 18th c., stains, losses, cracks, chips & separations, 26 1/8 x 26 3/4", 27 1/4" h. **$19,800**

Chippendale Revival tea table, mahogany & mahogany veneer, the large scalloped round top w/carved shells along the border tilting above a turned pedestal on a tripod base w/three outstretched cabriole legs w/leaf-carved knees & ending in pad feet, original dark finish, ca. 1920s, 24" d., closed 4' h. **$700**

Chippendale-Style coffee table, mahogany & mahogany veneer, the rectangular mirrored tray top w/low scalloped upright sides & cut-out hand holes resting in a molded frame above square legs w/block feet & Chinese-style lattice corner brackets, old finish, early 20th c., 19 x 30", 19 1/2" h. **$1,208**

Chippendale-Style dressing table, mahogany & yellow pine, frieze drawer above three dovetailed drawers, central drawer w/carved fan, cabriole legs w/ball-and-claw feet, some cut nails on drawer runners, composed of parts from various pieces of furniture, probably late 19th c., small drawer is reduced, refinishing, scratches & minor separations, 19 x 27", 39" h. **$1,540**

Technically, there are no antique coffee tables, as they weren't in use until the 1920s, and thus aren't 100 years old, the official definition of antique.

Chippendale-Style tea table, lacquered & decorated wood, the scalloped round top decorated w/gilt & gesso Oriental landscape, on a turned tapering pedestal above a tripod base w/cabriole legs w/acanthus leaf-carved knees & ending in ball- and-claw feet, England, third quarter 19th c., 19 1/2" , 28" h. **$805**

Classical card table, mahogany & mahogany veneer, the rectangular fold-over top w/concave edges above a deep ogee-form apron w/a serrated edge raised on a heavy scroll-carved U-form pedestal atop a rectangular platform w/heavy outswept scroll- cut legs on casters, minor veneer chips, probably New York, ca. 1845, 18 x 34 1/2", 29" h. **$345**

Classical card table, mahogany, rectangular fold-over top w/rounded corners, on a scroll-tipped apron raised on a heavy ring- and acanthus-carved center post above four arched & splayed legs w/acanthus-carved knees & ending in brass hairy-paw foot caps on casters, probably made in Boston, ca. 1830, 37 1/2 x 38", 30" h. **$1,955**

Classical center table, carved rosewood, the inset white marble rectangular top w/serpentine sides within a conforming deep apron w/a gadrooned border band above foliate & floral clusters centered on each side over a thin beaded bottom edge band, all raised on heavy S-scroll legs w/acanthus leaf carving at the top & joined by an arched cross-stretcher w/a fan-carved crest, in the manner of J. & J.W. Meeks, New York, New York, ca. 1840, 26 x 41", 29 1/2" h. **$2,070**

Classical dining table, mahogany & mahogany veneer, two-pedestal extension-type, each wide half-round top section w/a wide inside drop leaf, the deep apron w/a turned drop at each corner, each pedestal w/a bulbous acanthus leaf-carved post raised on four outswept leaf-carved legs ending in large paw feet on casters, original finish, replaced casters, ca. 1830s, open 54 x 100", 30" h. (ILLUS. open)............... **$4,500**

Classical dressing table, carved mahogany, the superstructure composed of a tall rectangular beveled framed mirror swiveling between large leafy scroll carved uprights w/brass mounts, the rectangular top over an apron w/a single long drawer w/round brass pulls flanked by brass anthemion mounts above reeded & leaf-carved front columns & incurved sides to an incurved lower shelf & back centered by a large brass mount, front corner blocks w/brass rosettes above the fluted disk front legs & simple turned rear legs on brass casters, attributed to Emmons and Archibald, Boston, 1815-25, base 18 x 34", overall 5' 5 1/2" h. .. **$15,535**

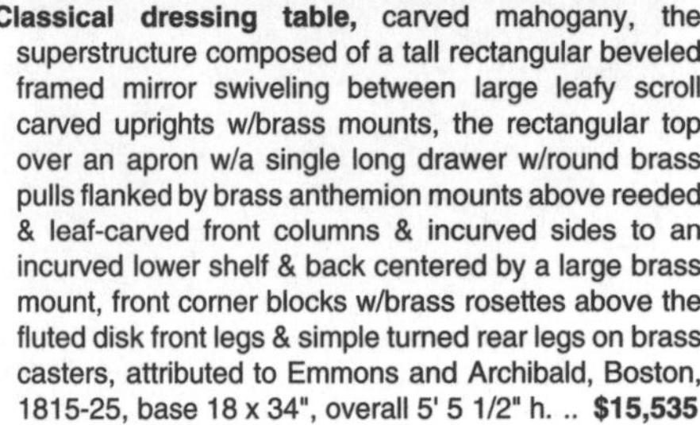

Classical games table, mahogany & mahogany veneer, the rectangular fold-over top w/rounded corners opening to a matching top over a deep crotch-grain veneered apron w/a scroll-carved border, raised on a a flattened scrolled support w/a cut-out center enclosing a scroll-carved finial, resting on a long quadripartite platform base w/outswept scroll feet, original finish, ca. 1850, 18 x 38", 30" h. **$750**

Classical games table, mahogany & mahogany veneer, the rectangular fold-over top w/rounded corners above a conforming top over a deep ogee apron, raised on a widely flaring forked scroll-cut support raised on a stepped flaring platform base w/small ogee bracket feet, original finish, ca. 1845, 18 x 36", 30" h. **$600**

Classical games table, mahogany & mahogany veneer, the rectangular fold-over top w/rounded corners opening to a conforming top over a flat ogee front apron, raised on a flat flared center support atop a large flattened oval disk resting at the center of a resting platform base w/arched shoe feet, probably Boston, ca. 1840, original dark finish, 16 x 32", 30" h. **$500**

Classical games table, mahogany & mahogany veneer, the rectangular serpentine-edged fold-over top above a conforming veneered apron, raised on a flattened lyre-form pedestal above a deep rectangular coved apron & platform raised on pierced scroll-cut feet, Boston, ca. 1830, original finish, 18 x 36", 30" h. (ILLUS. half open)...... **$650**

Classical pier table with vitrine, ormolu-mounted mahogany & mahogany veneer, the rectangular white marble top above an apron mounted in the center w/a long pierced scrolling ormolu mount w/smaller mounts at the front corners & at the sides, the front raised on tall columns w/ormolu capitals & bases that flank a pair of large glazed cabinet doors, glazed side panels, on a thick plinth base, first quarter 19th c., 17 x 39 3/4", 35 3/4" h. **$2,070**

Classical pier table, mahogany & mahogany veneer, the rectangular white marble top w/canted front corners above a conforming deep ogee apron, supported at the front by long heavy S-scrolls & at the back by a framed rectangular mirror all joined by a half-round lower platform on projecting C-scroll front legs, ca. 1830-40, 21 x 41", 37 1/2" h. **$2,530**

Classical pier table, rosewood, faux bois, marble & giltwood, the rectangular white marble top above a gilt-stenciled apron featuring a central cluster of shaded fruit & flowers, the white marble corner columns headed by giltwood Ionia capitals, the back supports designed as marble pilasters flanking a rectangular mirror, the concave bottom shelf bordered w/a geometric stenciled design, the gilt heavy front paw feet w/large giltwood heavy cornucopia brackets, New York City, ca. 1830, 20 1/2 x 44 1/2", 37 1/2" h. **$16,100**

Classical work table, mahogany & mahogany veneer, rectangular top over a deep case w/two drawers w/brass ring pulls & inlaid brass keyholes, small turned drops at each corner, raised on a bulbous acanthus leaf-carved short pedestal above four outswept leaf-carved legs ending in hairy paw feet, original finish, replaced hardware, ca. 1830, 15 x 20", 28" h. **$1,250**

Classical work table, mahogany & mahogany veneer, the rectangular top above a case w/two ogee-fronted drawers raised on a heavy scroll-carved lyre pedestal atop a stepped rectangular platform w/ ogee bracket feet on casters, ca. 1830, 22" l., 28 1/2" h. **$863**

Classical work table, mahogany & mahogany veneer, the rectangular top above a deep case w/two veneered drawers w/turned wood knobs, raised on a tapering turned & reeded pedestal atop a quadripartite platform w/scroll-carved paw feet on casters, probably Southern United States, ca. 1830, 17 1/4 x 21 1/2", 31 3/4" h. **$575**

Classical work table, mahogany & mahogany veneer, the rectangular top flanked by rectangular drop leaves w/rounded corners flanking the deep case w/two shallow drawers over a deep yarn drawer supported by a vasiform trestle base w/outswept scroll legs on casters, ca. 1840, closed 19 x 20 3/4", 28 1/2" h. **$805**

Classical-Rococo transitional center table, rosewood, the rectangular white marble-inset top w/serpentine sides w/a gadrooned border above a serpentine apron carved at the center of each side w/leaf & blossom clusters, raised on heavy S-scroll legs w/leaf-carved knees & forming a trestle base w/an arched, shell-carved cross-stretcher, ca. 1850, 25 3/4 x 42 1/2", 29 1/4" h. **$1,265**

←

Classical-Style breakfast table, mahogany, the rectangular top flanked by deep drop leaves w/notched rounded corners, the apron w/a round-fronted drawer at each end, raised on a heavy acanthus-carved pedestal on a quadripartite platform on outswept heavy carved paw feet on casters, late 19th c., open 38 x 52 1/2", 29" h. (ILLUS. closed) **$863**

Classical-Style dining table, mahogany, extension-type, the round top w/a scroll-carved border band raised on a large ring- turned split pedestal w/a bulbous reeded lower section issuing heavy acanthus-carved shaped legs ending in large paw feet, late 19th c., w/four leaves, closed 54" d., 29 1/4" h. (ILLUS. extended) **$3,220**

Classical-Style dressing table, mahogany, a large horizontal oval mirror swiveling between long outswept dolphin-carved supports above the rectangular top above a case w/a pair of round-fronted drawers flanking a leaf-carved panel over a long round-fronted drawer above a gadroon-carved apron band, the case supported by four S-scroll carved dolphin supports joining a rectangular serpentine-sided platform raised on outswept dolphin-carved legs, late 19th c., 20 3/4 x 27", overall 5' 6 1/2" h. **$2,300**

Colonial Revival coffee table, walnut, the oval glass tray lift-off top w/molded edges & end handles above an oval top carved in the center w/a nude figure, raised on four carved cabriole legs ending in scroll & peg feet, ca. 1920s, 27" l., 19" h. **$219**

Country-style chair-table, painted pine, the large round four-board top w/a scrubbed top tilting above simple turned arms & a rectangular seat base w/a lift-top compartment on simple turned legs, old red paint on base, late 18th - early 19th c., 49 1/2" d., 29" h. **$4,485**

Country-style dining table, mahogany & marquetry, the rectangular top w/ornate floral marquetry flanked by wide rectangular drop leaves w/further marquetry in an urn & vining flower design, the apron & square legs w/further marquetry vines, on casters, Holland, third quarter 19th c., open 48 x 63", 29 1/2" h. (ILLUS. closed) **$2,760**

In addition to collectors clubs devoted to a single type of antique or collectible, another type is the antique study group. These local groups usually meet monthly for members to share and explore their interests. Meetings usually feature a guest speaker. Some groups sponsor annual antique shows.

Country-style tavern table, chestnut, rectangular board top w/rounded corners overhanging an apron w/a single long drawer w/a turned knob & a scalloped shallow skirt, raised on ring- and block-turned legs joined by molded stretchers above knob feet, separation cracks, old inset damage, America, 17th c., 20 3/4 x 30 3/4", 28 1/2" h. **$1,955**

Country-style work table, heart pine, the large square plank top overhanging an apron w/a long drawer w/two turned wood knobs on each side, simple tapering octagonal legs, nicks, scuff & separations in top, Southern U.S., ca. 1790, 48" w., 32 1/2" h. **$1,093**

Country-style work table, yellow pine, two-board top w/cut nails, four turned legs w/mortise-and-tenon construction, 19th c., old refinishing, separations, two legs ended out, 30 1/2 x 123", 29 1/2" h. **$2,200**

Early American country-style work table, walnut, the large rectangular three-board top widely overhanging the deep apron w/two deep drawers w/wooden pulls, raised on three turned & tapering legs ending in knob-and-peg feet, old finish, early 19th c., reconstruction to base & drawers, 33 x 60", 30" h. **$1,725**

Empire-Style center table, mahogany, the round top above a paneled ormolu-mounted apron raised on turned & tapering legs joined by a lower shelf w/ concave sides, on short splayed feet, France, ca. 1900, 33" d., 29 1/2" h. **$1,610**

Federal card table, inlaid mahogany, the hinged half-round top w/pointed front corners & delicate chain-inlaid edge lifting above a matching top over a conforming apron w/line-inlaid panels centering a light-colored rectangular panel enclosing an oval, a band of chain inlay along the bottom edge, raised on knob-turned & spiraled acanthus leaf-carved legs on casters, old refinish, ca. 1820s, 19 x 38", 30" h. **$1,500**

Federal card table, inlaid mahogany, the rectangular hinged top w/wide rounded corners above a matching top above the conforming apron centered by narrow bands of inlay, tall slender reeded tapering legs topped by a ring-turned section & ending in double-knob feet, top refinished, ca. 1820, 20 x 38", 30" h. **$1,100**

Federal country-style dressing table, curly maple, rectangular top w/serpentine three-quarters gallery over a single long drawer, turned tapering legs w/peg feet, some family history written inside drawer, ca. 1850, feet have been ended out, gallery is old replacement, 17 x 34 1/2", 34 3/4" h. **$1,495**

Federal country-style tilt-top tea table, cherry, two-board top w/small wooden pegs & some figure, ring-turned column, cabriole legs w/raised panels at tops & ending in tripod snake feet, decorated w/incised vining down the legs & around the top w/small fans at the corners of top, cleats w/mix of rose head & square cut nails & some later screws, attributed to Connecticut, old refinishing, 26 x 26 1/4", 27" h. **$2,128**

Federal dining table, mahogany, two-part, each section w/a D-form top above a conforming apron & w/a back drop-leaf supported by a swing-out leg, spiral-turned legs w/knob feet on casters, ca. 1825, open, 45 x 92", 30 1/2" h. **$1,495**

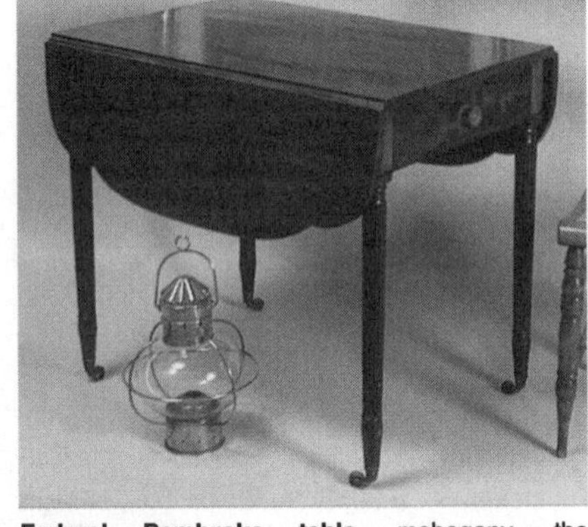

Federal Pembroke table, mahogany, the rectangular top flanked by shaped half-round drop leaves above an apron w/a drawer w/a replaced brass pull at one end, raised on turned reeded legs ending in peg feet on casters, refinished, one foot ended out, first quarter 19th c., 20 3/4 x 32" plus 10 3/8" w. leaves, 27 3/4" h. **$1,380**

Federal Pembroke table, cherry, rounded leaves, tapered legs, dovetailed drawer, hand-wrought nails, probably original brass pull, pivoting drop-leaf supports, original glue blocks, possibly Virginia, early 19th c., top reset w/some new screws, old refinishing, some insect damage, 1/2" hole, 21 x 34", opens to 43", 29" h. **$1,430**

Federal sofa table, mahogany & mahogany veneer, the long rectangular top above an apron w/a pair of drawers flanked by half- round drop leaves, raised on a square center pedestal carved w/a band of acanthus leaves & resting on a quadripartite platform supported by outswept acanthus leaf-carved legs ending in brass paws on casters, attributed to New York City, ca. 1820, 21 x 30 1/2" plus 11" leaves, 29" h. **$18,400**

Federal work table, bird's-eye maple & oak veneer, the rectangular top flanked by two D-shaped drop leaves above a deep apron w/a narrow & deep veneered & string inlaid drawer on the front & matching faux fronts on the back, raised on four ring- and baluster-turned supports on a trestle-style base w/outscrolled legs joined by block- and baluster-turned end stretchers & long double baluster- and ring-turned cross stretchers, old refinish, Middle Atlantic states, ca. 1815-25, imperfections, 17 1/4 x 18", 28 1/4" h. **$2,703**

Federal work table, mahogany & mahogany veneer, square top over a thin pull-out writing shelf above a drawer w/two brass knobs, acanthus leaf carving at each corner above similarly carved supports on a square medial shelf, slender ring-turned & leaf- carved legs on original brass casters, original finish, early 19th c., 18" w., 30" h. **$650**

Federal work table, mahogany & mahogany veneer, square top flanked by hinged drop leaves w/rounded corners above a case of three shallow drawers w/round brass pulls, on ring-turned & spiral-carved legs ending in disk-and-peg feet, old finish, ca. 1820s, 16 x 30" open, 30" h. (ILLUS. half open) **$600**

Federal-Style card table, inlaid mahogany, the half-round serpentine fold-over top above a conforming apron inlaid at the front center by an oval enclosing an American eagle, beaded edge inlay, on square tapering legs w/bellflower inlay on the front legs, early 20th c., open 35 1/2 x 36 1/2", 29 1/2" h. (ILLUS. closed) **$1,093**

Antique hand-cut veneer is significantly thicker and less uniform than the paper thin, perfectly uniform modern machine-cut veneer. The difference between the two can easily be seen by comparing the front edge of an antique and modern drawer.

French Provincial refectory table, walnut, the rectangular top above draw leaves fastened w/wrought-iron hasps, the paneled apron inlaid w/the initials "M.S.," "AM.IH," & numbers "1751," heavy baluster- and ring-turned legs headed by marquetry tulips, the flattened stretchers raised on bun feet, France, mid-18th c., 25 x 66", 31" h. **$7,188**

George III dining table, mahogany, the rectangular top flanked by wide rectangular top leaves, on square tapering legs, England, early 19th c., open 53 x 67", 27" h. (ILLUS. closed) **$575**

George III games table, mahogany, the rectangular fold-over top w/shaped & rounded projecting corners above an apron raised on cabriole legs w/ leaf-carved knees & ending in claw-and-ball feet, England, late 18th c., 34" l., 30 1/2" h. **$2,990**

George III side table, mahogany, the rectangular top flanked by gadroon-edged drop leaves w/ rounded corners, the apron w/two drawers at one end & two false drawers at the other, raised on square tapering legs w/spade feet, joined by arched & pierced cross-stretcher, England, late 18th c., 20 x 29", 23 1/2" h. **$1,610**

George III-Style center table, polychromed & gilded wood, the rectangular top inset w/a specimen multicolored marble top above an apron w/a gilt Greek key band above serpentine scroll-carved edges centered by a large shell carving, the cabriole legs topped by carved gilt eagle heads above scroll-carved knees & ending in claw-and-ball feet, England, 19th c., 23 1/2 x 51 1/2", 33 1/2" h. **$1,840**

George III-Style dining table, mahogany, extension-type, rounded top raised on two turned pedestals on tripod bases w/cabriole legs ending in pad feet, w/ original Kittinger paper label, w/one 24" w. leaf, 20th c., 48 x 92" open, 28 1/2" h. (ILLUS. open)..... **$1,725**

Gothic Revival library table, carved rosewood, the rectangular top inset w/variegated white marble over a wide apron w/a band of quatrefoil cutouts, raised on angled naturalistic animal legs w/scrolled hair at the top & ending in cloven hoof feet, mid-19th c., 25 1/4 x 43 1/2", 28" h. **$16,675**

George III-Style dumbwaiter, mahogany, two graduated scalloped piecrust shelves joined by an urn-turned post & raised on a turned pedestal above a tripod base w/acanthus-carved knees ending in leaf-carved pad feet, England, ca. 1900, 23 1/2" d., 28" h. **$374**

Louis XVI-Style side table, giltwood, the oval top inset w/ cream & rose marble above a ribbon-carved apron supported on six turned & fluted legs joined by two large oval caned lower shelves, on peg feet, France, mid-19th c., 19 x 31", 31" h. ... **$1,495**

Louis XVI-Style side table, giltwood, the round top inset w/ white marble framed by a molded edge on the fluted apron w/florette blocks above the fluted turned & tapering legs joined by a cross-stretcher, France, ca. 1900, 21" d., 24" h. **$863**

Hutch (or chair) table, poplar w/old green paint over earlier brown, two-board top w/old dark scrubbed surface, single-board tapered ends w/high arched cutouts at base, square nail & mortised construction, late 18th - early 19th c., top is warped, 31 x 40", 28 3/4" h. **$1,150**

←

Louis XVI-Style side table, mahogany, the oval top inset w/white onyx bordered by a low pierced brass gallery above the paneled apron w/a brass-bound drawer & side panels raised on square supports to the kidney-shaped lower shelf on square simple cabriole legs, France, late 19th c., 19" w., 31" h. **$1,093**

Mission-style (Arts & Crafts movement) dining table, oak, extension-type, the round divided top raised on a five-post divided pedestal w/blocked shoe feet, includes four 12" leaves in a storage rack, good original finish, decal label of L. & J.G. Stickley, early 20th c., closed 48" d., 29" h. **$3,450**

Modern-style chess table, ebonized plywood, the nearly square top w/serpentine sides in black w/small plastic inserts forming the chess board, raised on a cast aluminum tray above the base w/four wide flat tapering & arched legs, designed by Isamu Noguchi for Herman Miller, ca. 1947, 24 3/4 x 26 1/4", 19 3/4" h. **$83,650**

Modern-style coffee table, walnut, the long tapering naturalistic board top raised on a canted post at one end & a wide rectangular upright board at the other, joined by a long base stretcher board, inscribed w/the name of the client & designer George Nakashima, 1975, 23 x 62", 15" h. **$17,925**

Napoleon III parlor center table, Rococo-style, gilt-brass-mounted ebonized fruitwood & marquetry, the rectangular serpentine- sided top decorated overall w/ very ornate floral scrolling marquetry above the deep serpentine apron w/ormolu-banded marquetry panels centered by large ormolu mount of a putto carrying a lute, the cabriole legs mounted w/large ormolu caryatids at the knees & fitted w/brass feet, France, third quarter 19th c., 30 x 49 1/2", 30 1/2" h. ... **$4,370**

←

Modern-style side table, iron & marble, the round top in white marble inset w/a pale golden starburst centered by a black dot, a ropetwist metal rim band, raised on a pedestal base composed of waisted iron loops joined at the center by a ropetwist band, Model No. 1483, designed by Gilbert Poillerat, ca. 1953, two paper labels under the top reading "Made in France" & "X169/91," 21 1/2" d., 24 3/4" h. **$19,120**

Some auction houses reserve seats for customers who request them. If they don't arrive during the first hour, however, the auctioneer will usually invite anyone standing to take those seats down front.

Neoclassical console tables, polychromed wood, the long demi-lune top w/carved palmetto banding decorated in the center w/a colorful landscape medallion flanked by mermaids & a variety of colorful swag & putti designs, all on a cream background, the narrow matching apron raised on four square tapering legs w/similar decoration & ending in tapering square peg feet, Italy, early 19th c., 58" l., 34" h., pr. . **$5,290**

Oriental side table, carved rosewood, the rounded top w/a beaded edge inset w/red marble, the deep scalloped apron pierce- carved w/leafy florals, raised on short cabriole legs w/carved knees & paw feet, China, late 19th c., 12" d., 13 1/2" h. (ILLUS. right w/ Oriental rosewood side table)...................... **$150-300**

Queen Anne country-style tavern table, maple w/old dark brown paint over earlier red, one-board rectangular top w/worn molded edge, dovetailed drawer w/original turned wooden pull, turned legs w/beaded stretchers & aprons, top edge has early patched knot hole, 17 1/2 x 27 3/4", 26" h. .. **$21,850**

Queen Anne country-style tavern table, maple w/old red paint, pegged construction, single-board oval top, splayed & tapered legs w/pad feet, top slightly warped, age splits, pegged restorations to one leg, minor repairs to pads of two feet, 24 x 29 1/4", 27 1/2" h. **$6,038**

Queen Anne tavern table, figured maple, the oval top overhanging a deeply scalloped apron raised on turned slightly canted legs ending in raised pad feet, New England, 1740-70, 26 1/2 x 35 1/2", 27 1/2" h. **$7,170**

Queen Anne dining table, mahogany, a long narrow rectangular top flanked by wide rectangular drop leaves, shaped apron, block-and-turned legs ending in pad feet, old refinish, Rhode Island, mid-to-late 18th c., repaired, open 50 3/4 x 51 1/2", 27 1/4" h. (ILLUS. closed).. **$3,525**

Queen Anne-Style dining table, mahogany, narrow rectangular top w/rounded ends flanked by wide half-round drop leaves above an apron w/slender ring-turned blocked legs & swing-out support legs joined by simple stretchers, on small pad feet, dark finish, England, early 20th c., small pieced restorations under top near hinges, 18 1/4 x 40" plus 19 3/4" w. leaves, 29 1/2" h. **$863**

Queen Anne dressing table, walnut, the rectangular top w/molded edges & shaped corners overhanging a case w/a cockbeaded long drawer over a row of three deep drawers, the central one fan-carved, the valanced shaped apron continuing into four cabriole legs w/arris knees & ending in raised pad feet, some old brasses, old refinish, probably Massachusetts, ca. 1740-60, imperfections, 20 1/4 x 29 3/4", 29" h. **$22,325**

Queen Anne-Style games table, red-lacquered wood, the fold-over shaped top w/a polychromed & gilt scene in the chinoiserie style, opening to a baize-lined interior, the back gatelegs supporting the open top, raised on heavily turned & paneled tapering legs joined by a shaped box stretcher & ending in bun feet, the whole w/chinoiserie gilt trim, England, third quarter 19th c., open 13 1/2 x 31 1/2", 30 1/2" h. (ILLUS. open) **$3,680**

Regency console table, mahogany, the long rectangular top w/recessed central section on a deep flaring cornice w/a beaded edge, raised on four heavy scrolling front supports ending in large paw feet resting on rectangular plinths, pairs of flat rear supports, England, first quarter 19th c. or later, 27 x 78", 37 1/2" h. **$4,140**

Regency sofa table, mahogany, the long rectangular top flanked by short half-round drop leaves, the apron w/a pair of long paneled drawers w/knobs, a trestle-form base w/a pair of slender baluster- and ring-turned supports at each end resting on cross stretchers over outswept legs w/brass paw caps on casters, a long slender baluster-turned stretcher from end to end, polished original finish, England, ca. 1820, 22 x 46", 30" h. **$1,400**

Regency dining table, mahogany, extension-type, the oval top above a deep plain apron raised on baluster- and ring-turned legs on peg feet w/brass cap casters, England, second quarter 19th c., 34 x 47", 30" h. **$431**

Regency sofa table, rosewood, the long rectangular top flanked by half-round banded inlay drop leaves, the long apron fitted in the front w/two long banded inlay drawers w/round brass pulls, the back w/two false drawers, raised on a tiered turned pedestal above a quadripartite platform w/incurved sides resting on four outswept legs ending in brass leaf-cast caps on casters, England, first quarter 19th c., 27 1/4 x 36 1/4, 57 1/2" l. open, 29 1/2" h. (ILLUS. closed) **$1,840**

Rococo Revival side table, inlaid mahogany, the round top centered by a large inlaid star-shaped dark panel centered by a light circle & bordered by inlaid swags, the molded edge above the deep serpentine apron pierce-carved w/leafy scrolls, raised on four incurved slender square legs ending in paw feet & joined at the center w/a serpentine-sided shelf pierce-carved w/acanthus leaves, original finish, ca. 1920s, 22" d., 30" h. **$500**

Rococo Revival side table, carved mahogany, the round top over a shaped apron carved w/pairs of scrolls, raised on bulbous turned knobs atop S-scroll legs carved at the top w/an acanthus leaf & ending in a scroll foot raised on a bun, joined by a scrolled & arched cross stretcher centered by a turned urn finial, refinished, late 19th c., 24" d., 30" h. **$450**

Rococo-Style games table, mahogany & marquetry, the rectangular fold-over top w/large projecting rounded corners, decorated w/an elaborate inlay of putti & scrolling designs, opening to a similarly inlaid interior, the ornately inlaid apron fitted w/one drawer, on inlaid cabriole legs ending in square feet, the drawer w/paper label for Giovannia Bacci - Oggetti D'arte - Anticui E. Moderni - Via della Vigna Nuova St. - Firenze, Italy, mid-19th c., 33 1/2" l., 29" h. **$2,760**

Victorian Aesthetic Movement parlor table, mahogany, the square top inset w/tiles forming a border band around a cluster of stylized blossoms all framed by a low brass edge gallery & a narrow brass band along the outer edges, raised on four canted ring-turned & reeded tapering legs w/brass bands near the top & supports on brass claw feet w/glass balls, joined by a lower square shelf w/a brass gallery, probably England, ca. 1900, original finish, 20" w., 32" h. **$600**

Victorian Baroque Revival dining table, carved mahogany, extension-type, the square top w/rounded corners above a deep apron w/carved ropetwist border, raised on six legs composed of blocks, a reeded egg-shaped knob over a large leafy scroll, all joined by angled wide scroll-carved solid panels centered by large carved grotesque faces, original finish, w/six leaves, ca. 1890s, 60" w. closed, 30" h. **$5,000**

Victorian Baroque Revival dining table, oak, extension-type, the round top w/a gadrooned edge over an apron w/a thin knob- carved rim raised on a bulbous rosette-carved column on a heavy post issuing four outswept leafy scroll-carved legs ending in scroll feet carved on top w/clusters of fruit, on casters, original finish, ca. 1890, w/four leaves, 48" d., 30" h. **$2,000**

Victorian Baroque Revival dining table, carved oak, extension-type, the round top over a lappet-carved apron, a fixed center support w/a cluster of four reeded columns w/a cross stretcher, four traveling legs at the corners, each carved in full-relief as winged griffins on block bases, ca. 1890, refinished, w/extra leaves, 60" d. closed, 30" h. (ILLUS. extended) **$7,500**

Victorian Baroque Revival dining table, oak, extension-type, the round top w/loop-carved border above a plain apron, raised on a heavy bulbous line-incised column on four outswept legs each carved at the top w/a figural fox head holding fruit it its mouth, crude paw feet on casters, Europe, late 19th c., w/two leaves, sold refinished, 48" d., 30" h. **$1,200**

Victorian Baroque Revival dining table, carved oak, extension-type, the wide square top w/a lappet-carved apron, raised on a large spiral-carved center post & four corner posts resting on the heads of carved full-figure reclining lions on the cross-form base w/carved paw feet, ca. 1890, w/six leaves, sold refinished, 60" w., 30" h. (ILLUS. with the leaves stacked on top) **$4,500**

Victorian Baroque Revival dining table, quarter-sawn oak, extension-type, square top w/plain apron raised on six columnar legs w/reeded bun feet, two fixed center legs, outer legs pull out to extend table & are joined by a high arched & scroll-caved panel, w/four leaves, refinished, ca. 1900, 60" w., 30" h. (ILLUS. with leaves on top) **$2,800**

Victorian Baroque Revival dining table, quarter-sawn oak, extension-type, the round top w/a gadroon-carved apron, raised on four heavy cabriole legs each topped by a carved lion head & ending in a paw foot on a caster, a central split column w/a leaf- carved band, refinished, original label of the Horner Furniture Co., New York City, w/five leaves, refinished, ca. 1890, 58" d., 30" h. **$4,000**

Victorian Baroque Revival dining table, quarter-sawn oak, extension-type, the round top w/a gadrooned edge over the plain apron, raised on a massive center column w/a gadrooned disk over a paneled post issuing outswept legs, each leg carved w/a large head of a roaring lion & ending in a large paw foot, original dark finish, w/five leaves, ca. 1895, 54" d., 30" h. (ILLUS. with the leaves on the top) **$3,500**

Victorian Baroque Revival library table, carved mahogany, partner's-type, wide rectangular top w/a wide scroll-carved border band over a deep rounded apron carved overall w/scrolls & fitted on each side w/ a long drawer, raised on four large full-figure seated winged griffins at the corners on projecting platforms extending from a serpentine central shelf stretcher, on four thin bun feet, attributed to the Horner Furniture Co., New York City, late 19th c., 30 x 48", 30" h. **$4,500**

Victorian Baroque Revival library table, carved oak, the rectangular top covered overall w/ornate floral scrolls above a deep floral scroll-carved apron w/a relief-carved female mask at each corner above a turned drop, on a trestle-form base w/three columns at each end carved w/spiraling vines & raised on wide platforms carved at each end w/a figural sphinx, a heavy flat base stretcher centered by another carved column, fumed oak finish, late 19th c., 26 x 48", 30" h. **$1,400**

Victorian Baroque Revival library table, oak, the rectangular top w/an oval center panel framed by ornately carved scrolls & scallop-carved edge, the deep apron carved w/large scrolls flanking a grotesque mask between leaf-carved corner blocks, raised on four large full-figure seated winged griffins at each corner resting on projecting platforms joined to a flat center stretcher centered by a baluster- and knob-turned column w/carved leaves, late 19th c. .. **$2,800**

Victorian Baroque Revival parlor table, quarter-sawn oak, a narrow rectangular top w/rounded ends flanked by wide half- round drop leaves, raised on a heavy fluted column above four outswept heavy scroll-carved feet, old refinish, ca. 1895, 36 x 46" open, 30" h. (ILLUS. closed) **$950**

Victorian Eastlake style dining table, walnut, extension-type, the square top w/rounded corners above a deep apron w/leaf- incised blocks supported on a heavy squared center pedestal flanked by wide flat pierce-carved panels w/a diamond motif resting on platforms joining the four corner legs, each ring- and bulbous knob-turned leg resting on a stepped block foot, original finish, w/six leaves, ca. 1880s, closed 48" w., 30" h. **$3,000**

Victorian Baroque Revival parlor table, quarter-sawn oak, the round top w/a bead-carved edge raised on four columnar legs resting on large bun feet, the legs joined by a heavy cross stretcher topped by large heavy pierced & scroll-carved brackets, refinished, ca. 1890s, 28" d., 30" h. **$700**

Victorian Eastlake-style parlor table, walnut, a rectangular pink marble top above a line-incised apron w/stepped brackets & small turned corner drops, raised on four flat outswept legs joined by wide arched stretchers composed of cross-stretchers & turned knobs joined to a central round post, on casters, ca. 1880, one corner of marble top chipped, 19 1/2 x 27 3/8", 30 1/4" h. **$200-300**

Victorian country-style dining table, pine, the rectangular top flanked by narrow drop leaves, raised on rod- and ring-turned legs, second half 19th c., 39" l., 28" h. **$161**

Victorian Golden Oak dining table, quarter-sawn oak, extension-type, round top w/ plain apron raised on a heavy octagonal split pedestal resting on a cross-form base w/C-scroll feet on casters, refinished, w/four leaves, ca. 1900, 60" d., 30" h. **$1,200**

Victorian Golden Oak dining table, quarter-sawn oak, extension-type, round top w/scallop-incised rim above an apron w/angled blocks above a cluster of five large reeded columns on a platform base w/scroll-carved feet, w/six leaves, refinished, ca. 1895, 60" d., 30" h. **$4,200**

Victorian novelty side table, inlaid mixed wood, the square top ornately inlaid w/a large central checkerboard surrounded by a wide inlaid band decorated w/fan-inlaid corners & various geometric designs above the shaped apron inlaid w/rectangular panels & diamond & small stars, fitted w/a single drawer w/a black pear-shaped rope pull, large baluster-, ring- and tapering rod-turned legs composed of stacked multicolored woods, original finish, ca. 1890, 26" w., 30" h. .. **$750**

Victorian Renaissance Revival dining table, walnut & burl walnut, extension-type, round top above a deep apron w/narrow burl bands separated by small roundels, raised on a heavy squared split pedestal on a cross-form platform base fitted w/large scroll-carved legs w/ebonized trim, refinished, ca. 1870s, w/four leaves, 48" d., 30" h. **$2,500**

Victorian novelty side table, walnut & cast iron, the large walnut top w/a narrow edge over a pair of tiny drawers w/wide hinged drop leaf pivoting & telescoping above the tapering columnar cast-iron pedestal on a tripod base w/flat cabriole legs ending in knob feet on casters, base w/stenciled classical decoration, marked w/a stenciled label reading "Designed and manufactured at the Washburn Machine Shop connected with the Institute of Industrial Science Worcester, Mass...Patented Nov. 19, 1872," 26 x 29", 31" h. **$1,150**

Victorian Renaissance Revival dining table, walnut, extension-type, the round top w/molded apron raised on a heavy split pedestal w/scroll-carved projecting legs mounted w/roundels & raised on casters, holds four 12"-wide leaves, ca. 1875, open 45 x 93", 30 1/2" h. (ILLUS. open).................................. **$1,150**

Victorian Renaissance Revival library table, walnut, rectangular top w/chamfered corners above a conforming apron w/each side centered by a scroll-carved block cartouche, a long drawer on one side, raised block angled corners w/turned drops, raised on a trestle-style base w/a central ring-, knob- and rod-turned post flanked by flat legs w/scroll-carved brackets all raised on a slightly arched shoe base, joined by a long ring- and rod-turned stretcher w/an urn-turned finial, ca. 1875, refinished, 24 x 42", 30" h. **$1,600**

GLASS MARKET REPORT

According to Jeffrey S. Evans, co-owner and auctioneer at Jeffrey S. Evans & Associates in Mt. Crawford, Virginia, the glass market is recovering from tough market conditions. "Over the last year, glass fared about the same as other areas of antiques. Prices of smalls were off 20 to 40 percent because of the recession," he said. "Like the real estate market, glass experienced a bubble of unrealistically high prices. The higher a bubble goes without a correction, the farther down it goes before it stabilizes."

While the recession slowed the glass market, it certainly didn't destroy it. "People still want to collect," Evans commented. But the glass market relies on discretionary income, so it is price sensitive. As prices have dropped to a more realistic level, auction sales have increased and there has been a substantial pickup in sales at shows, although there are fewer shows. Evans doesn't think the drop in the number of shows is necessarily a bad thing as long as total sales are increasing. The trend could be beneficial, as fewer shows mean lower expenses and less time on the road for both dealers and collectors.

Evans was surprised that he didn't see dumping of collections during the recession. Apparently most collectors had enough of a financial reserve that they weren't forced to liquidate. The lower volume of auction consignments throughout the antiques industry over the last year reinforces the general view that collectors are holding their collections until prices are more favorable. Further evidence of this trend is that when Evans sees complete collections come to auction, they are a result of natural attrition due to collectors dying or retiring from their hobby, not frantic collectors selling to pay off debts.

The average age of glass collectors continues to increase. According to Evans, glass collectors typically begin collecting after their children leave home, when they have more time and disposable income. Because people are having children later, they begin collecting later. "We don't see many 45- or 50-year-olds that have large collections or extensive knowledge and experience," he said.

Younger collectors tend to gravitate toward blown glass and bottles while older collectors favor pressed and pattern glass. Those who buy to decorate look for pieces that go with their furniture or make good accent pieces. Some who buy glass to use only become collectors after they stumble across a piece they like and then begin adding more pieces to complete a set. Cake stands are popular pieces for both using and decorating.

Evans doesn't see any particularly dominant decorating trends, probably because today's collectors tend to be eclectic and decorate according to their own individual tastes.

Glass collecting is less regional than it used to be. While New England and the upper Midwest dominated the glass market in past decades, interest in glass collecting has spread more evenly across the country, primarily because of the Internet and the much broader exposure it gives glass. Much of the antique glass being sold online from collectors who are downsizing or dying off is being sold in the South and on the West Coast, creating a more even distribution nationally.

Fakes and reproductions are still a concern in the glass-collecting field, but there haven't been any especially new or major increases, perhaps because the recession has made it less profitable. Even irradiated purple glass, probably the most significant counterfeit in recent years, has seen a decline. Purple glass is very desirable and can bring high prices, so counterfeiters developed a technique to turn glass from clear to purple by exposing it to radiation.

Natural sun-purpled glass (also known as sun-colored amethyst or SCA) and irradiated glass are similar, but sun-purpled glass changes color gradually over a long period of time and is fairly light in color, sometimes just a strong tint. Irradiated purple, on the other hand, is much deeper in color and the color change occurs as soon as the object is zapped. In both instances, the molecules of the manganese or selenium (substances used to render glass colorless) are affected by radiation: small doses from the sun and large doses in a radiation chamber.

Both irradiated glass and sun-purpled glass can be turned back to colorless by heating it in a kiln-type oven (household ovens can't produce enough heat). Sun-colored glass is easy to spot because the light amethyst color is not a tone originally produced by glassmakers. The darker irradiated purple, however, is very close to the original amethyst color, which is where the big problem arises. The amount of irradiated glass being introduced into the market has decreased, but a large amount is still circulating, so collectors need to be alert for these fakes.

According to Evans, "reattributions" have significantly impacted the glass market in the 21st century. As more accurate historical information has emerged, researchers have been able to correct previously incorrect descriptions. The ages have generally been accurate, but the place of manufacture is sometimes wrong. Typically, a piece that was thought to have been manufactured in the United States has been determined to have been made in Europe. Unlike fakes, which are intended to deceive, the original attributions were simply sincere errors based on incomplete information.

Evans gets quite a bit of business from collectors outside the United States. Canadians, for example, buy a lot of goblets and colored candleholders. He has other buyers from Australia, Germany, and Israel, many of whom are repeat customers. The foreign market seems to be driven by the availability of certain items not found in their markets and by attractive prices of pieces not in demand here. For example, some foreign customers like clear, pattern glass whale oil lamps that Americans have little interest in.

Evans believes the glass market will continue a slow but steady re-emergence from the recession, and he is optimistic about its future. He agrees, though, with the prevailing advice that collectors should buy the best quality they can afford and that they should buy what they like rather than buying for investment. That way they will enjoy what they own regardless of what the economy does. No one can be sure what the long-term trends will be are any more than investors can predict the stock market with certainty. One thing is sure, though: glass can add a touch of beauty and elegance to anyone's home and bring years of pleasure to their owners.

GLASS

Art Glass Baskets

Popular novelties in the late Victorian era, these ornate baskets of glass were usually hand-crafted of free-blown or mold-blown glass. They were made in a wide spectrum of colors and shapes. Pieces were highlighted with tall applied handles and often applied feet; however, fancier ones might also carry additional appliquéd trim.

Bluerina, round foot below the widely flaring, flattened Hobnail patt. rim w/two sides pulled up, tall applied clear twisted thorn handle, 9 1/2" h. **$633**

Cased, bulbous rounded form tapering to a lobed rim, deep pink interior cased in alternating stripes of pulled-up dark red & white and yellow & white, applied clear double entwined overhead handle, raised on four clear applied peg feet, attributed to Northwood, England, 11 3/4" d., 12" h. .. **$863**

Cranberry, bulbous cranberry body w/a widely flaring crimped & ruffled applied opalescent rim, applied clear sharply pointed handle, 4 3/4" d., 6 3/4 h. **$66**

Mother-of-pearl satin, shaded pink Herringbone patt., a round foot below the deep rounded bowl w/ deeply folded & crimped flaring rim, applied pointed frosted clear thorny branch handle, interior cased in bright pale green, Mt. Washington Glass Co., museum exhibit label from the New Bedford Whaling Museum, 11" d., 9" h. **$570**

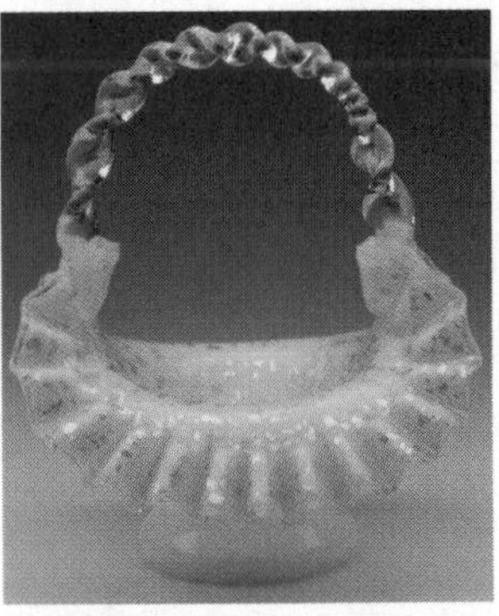

Spangled, bulbous body w/two sides folded down & Grimped, white exterior & butterscotch-cased interior w/overall mica flecks, applied clear twist handle, 6 1/2" h. **$66**

Spangled, deep bulbous lobed body w/a flaring ruffled rim, colorful spatter & silver mica fleck exterior cased in white, applied lightly reeded clear looped handle, 6 3/4" h. **$66**

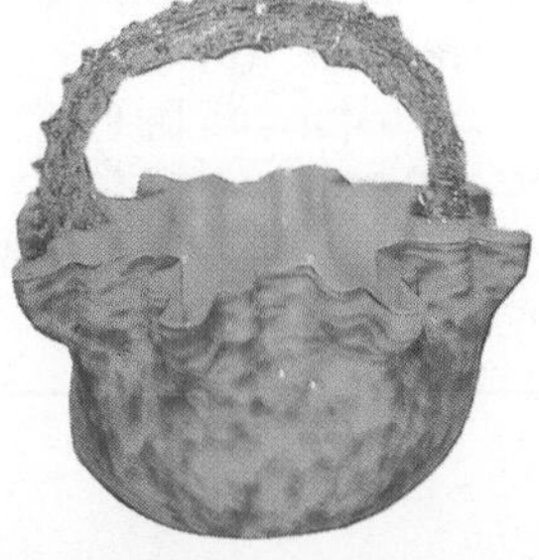

Spatter, rounded body w/flaring crimped rim pulled into points, arched applied clear thorn handle, yellow & pink spatter, white lining, 6" d., 6" h. **$165-185**

Spatter glass is made by adding chips of colored crushed glass to the surface of molten glass and rolling it smooth.

Baccarat

Baccarat glass has been made by Cristalleries de Baccarat, France, since 1765. The firm has produced various glassware of excellent quality as well as paperweights. Baccarat's Rose Tiente is often referred to as Baccarat's Amberina.

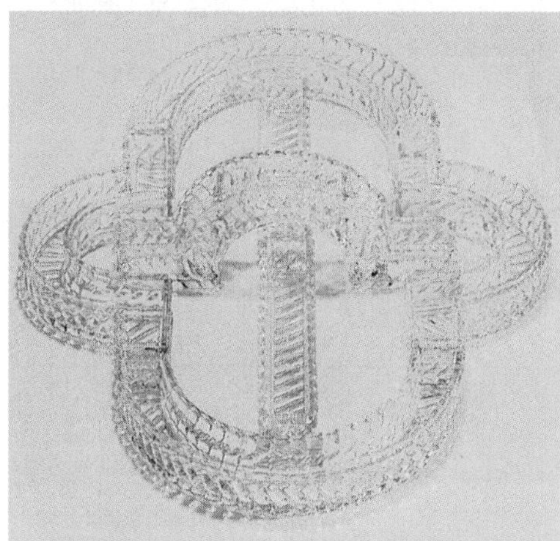

Centerpiece, colorless crystal, seven-part, the long open oval design composed of bowed side tray sections, two rectangular center tray sections & a bridged center tray section, marked, one piece w/rim nick, early 20th c., 18 x 24", the set **$633**

Ewer, yellow cased over white, footed bulbous body tapering to a tall cylindrical neck, large applied yellow handle, decorated in the Japanese taste w/ two overlapping round reserves highlighted w/a pair of brick red & brown birds perched on long blossoming branches, ca. 1880, 8 1/8" h. **$956**

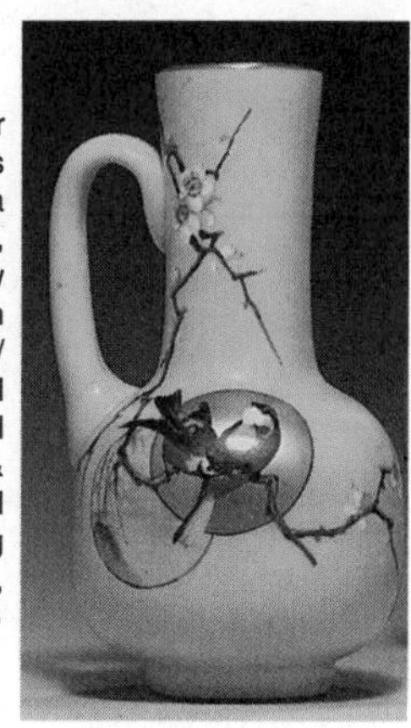

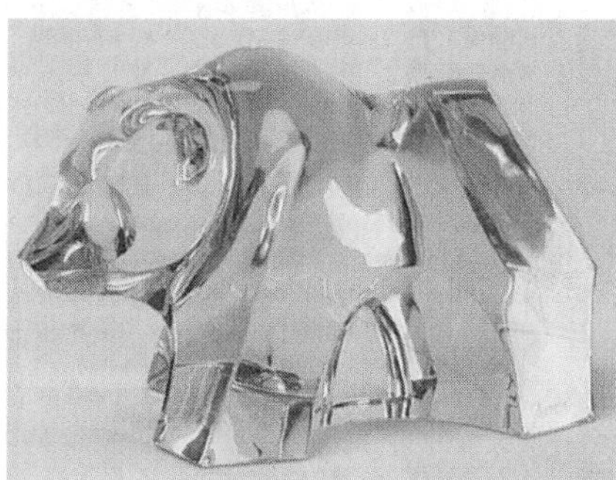

Model of a bear, colorless crystal, a stylized walking animal, signed on the bottom & side, 11" l. **$2,300**

Pitcher, 9 1/4" h., 6 3/4" d., Rose Tiente Swirl patt., spherical body tapering to a cylindrical neck w/pinched spout, applied clear handle **$300-325**

Vases, 7 1/4" h., Art Nouveau style, the wide flattened colorless crystal urn-shaped body fitted on an openwork rectangular bronze base issuing stylized leafy vines behind the vase, vases signed, holders marked on the bottom "E. Enot Paris," gh ca. 1900, pr. **$2,280**

Bride's Baskets & Bowls

These berry or fruit bowls were popular late Victorian wedding gifts, hence the name. They were produced in a variety of quality art glasswares and sometimes were fitted in ornate silver plate holders.

Amethyst opalescent, the plain bowl w/two sides curled up & inward, enameled on the interior w/ white flowers, in an ornate footed brass frame w/ropetwist scrolls & a large, tall arched ropetwist handle, late 19th c., overall 10 1/2" h. **$323**

Butterscotch to yellow, widely flaring ruffled & crimped edges w/overall swirled ribbing & V-form ribs at the rim flutes, 9 5/8" d., 3 1/4" h. **$92**

Cased bowl, apricot shaded to white interior w/a fancy tri-ruffled & fluted rim, white exterior, fitted in a fancy silver plate frame marked by the Rockford Silver Plate Co., small size, bowl 5 1/2" d., overall 5 1/2" h. **$161**

Cased bowl, green cased w/translucent peach on the interior, white opaque exterior, the deep ribbed bowl w/a wide rolled & finely notched & scalloped rim in green decorated w/tiny enameled blossoms & gilt scrolls, in a very ornate silver plate frame by Barbour, overall 14" l. (ILLUS. top row, center, with other five bride's baskets & bowls) **$920**

Cased bowl, pink shaded to white interior, white exterior, deeply ruffled & crimped rim, in a fancy footed silver plate frame w/ overhead bail handle, ca.1900, overall 12" h. **$235**

Satin shaded blue, the wide shallow shaded blue bowl w/a ruffled & crimped rim, molded interior draped pattern, attached atop a silver plate pedestal foot, late 19th c., bowl 10" d. **$147**

Cased bowl, turquoise blue interior & deep shaded pink exterior, wide cylindrical body w/a squared crimped & ruffled rim, fitted in a fancy silver plate frame w/figural cherries applied to the high arched handle, marked by Meriden, two leaves missing on frame, ca. 1890s, bowl 4" h., overall 10 1/2" h. **$345**

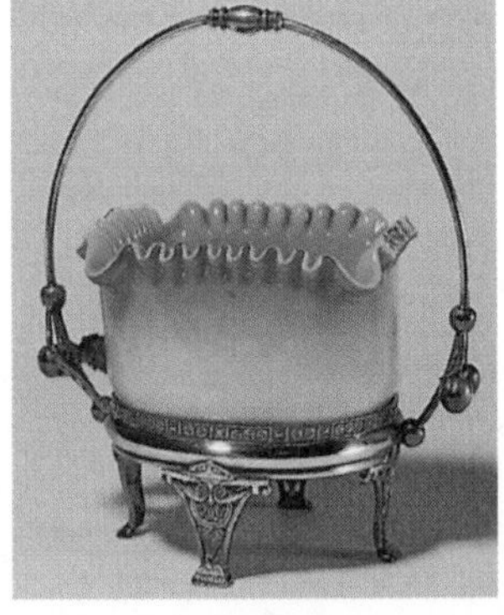

Cambridge

The Cambridge Glass Company was founded in Ohio in 1901. Numerous pieces are now sought, especially those designed by Arthur J. Bennett, including Crown Tuscan. Other productions included crystal animals, "Black Amethyst," "blanc opaque," and other types of colored glass. The firm was finally closed in 1954. It should not be confused with the New England Glass Co., Cambridge, Massachusetts.

Caprice Pattern

Bowl, 8" d., salad, four-footed, pressed Caprice patt., No. 49, Moonlight Blue **$110**

Candy dish, cov., three-footed, pressed Caprice patt., No. 165, Moonlight Blue, 6" d. **$155**

Cruet w/original stopper, pressed Caprice patt., oil, No. 117, clear, 3 oz. **$42**

Cup & saucer, pressed Caprice patt., Moonlight, pr. **$42**

Rose bowl, pressed Caprice patt., No. 236; Moonlight Blue, 6" d. **$145**

Vase, 8 1/2" h., ball-shaped, pressed Caprice patt., No. 339, pattern on the neck, Amber **$175-195**

Salt & pepper shakers, all-glass ball, individual, pressed Caprice patt., Crystal, pr. **$45**

Candleholder, three-light, No. 74, 9 1/2" l., 4 1/4" h. **$35**

Crown Tuscan Line

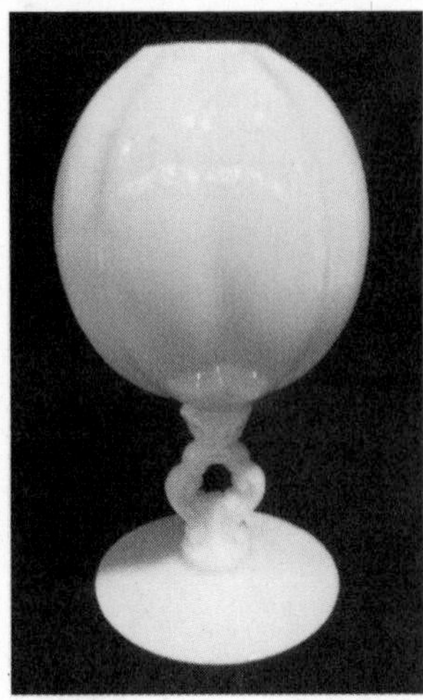

Ivy ball, keyhole stem, No. 1236, 7 1/2" h. **$175**

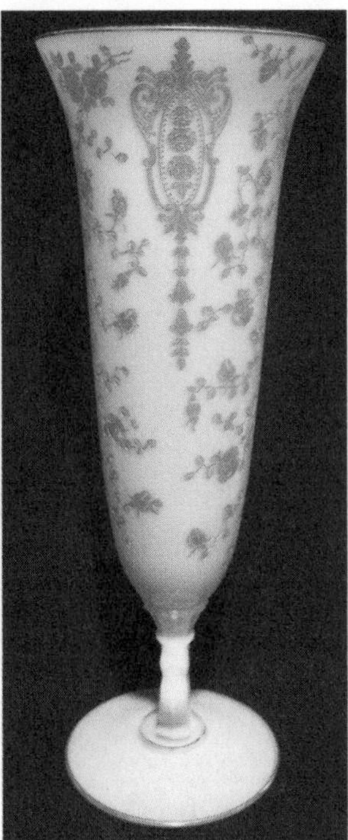

Vase, 12" h., footed, keyhole stem, tall trumpet-form bowl w/gold-encrusted etched Rosepoint patt. **$350**

Vase, 7" h., footed, crimped square form, No. 3500 Gadroon patt. **$100**

Vase, 7" h., Sea Shell line, No. 46 .... **$185**

Etched Rose Point Pattern

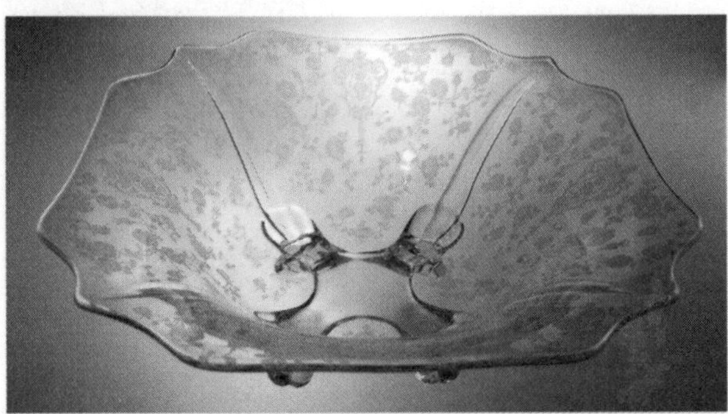

Bowl, 12" w., 4-footed, flared squared sides, No. 3400/4, Crystal **$90**

Dinner service: six round 8" d. plates, 17 3/4" d. round serving platter, small plates & small serving dishes, salt & pepper shakers, clear, set of 15 pcs. (ILLUS. of part) **$403**

Candlestick, two-light, keyhole stem, No. 3400/647, Crystal, 5 3/4" h., pr. **$125**

Compote, No. 3900/136, Crystal, 5 1/2" d., 5 1/2" h. **$85**

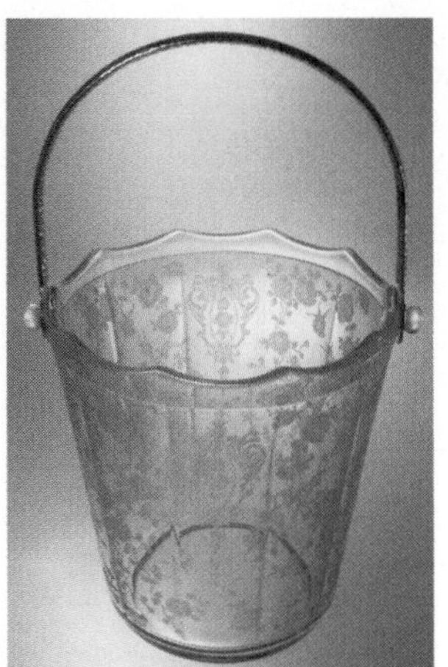

Ice bucket, No. 3900/671, Crystal w/chrome handle, scalloped top, 5 3/4" h. **$170**

Statuesque Line

Cocktails, clear bowl, Ebony Nude Lady stem, 6 1/2" h., set of 9 .... **$1,064**

Miscellaneous Patterns

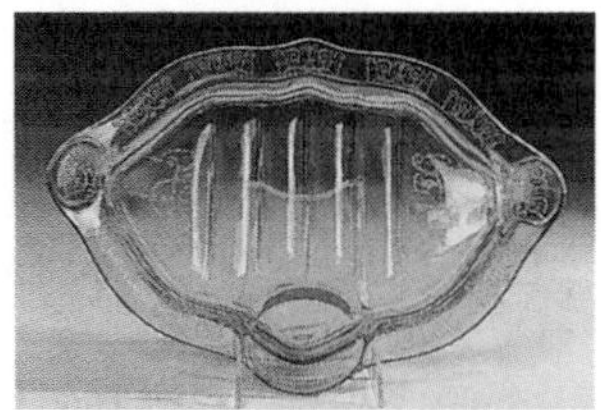

Asparagus platter, almond-shaped w/a molded round rim section & molded bars down the center, etched Cleo patt., Emerald (medium green), chip on the base, 14 1/2" l. **$138**

Beverage set: ball-form pitcher & nine tumblers; Optic Swirl design, Moonlight Blue, the set (ILLUS. of part) **$150-200**

Bowl, 9" d., three-footed, Seashell patt., Amber **$68**

Bowl, 9 1/2" d., shallow flared shape, Honeycomb patt., "sponge" acid etching, Rubina **$375**

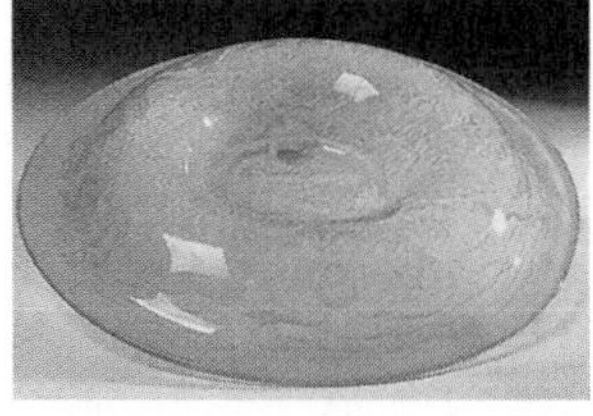

Center bowl, round w/domed & widely flaring sides, Mold No. 1125 molded on the underside w/a continuous buffalo hunt scene w/ figures on horseback, Mystic Blue, 16" d. **$150**

Cocktail, Statuesque line, Nude Lady stem, Carmen bowl, 3 oz. **$220**

Console set: 11" d. console bowl w/etched gold border band & a pair of matching square tapering 8" h. candlesticks, Azurite (blue opaque), the set **$196**

Creamer & open sugar bowl, individual size, Gadroon (No. 3500 line), Crystal, pr. **$19**

Pitcher w/ice lip, bulbous ovoid body, Gyro Optic patt., No. 3900/115, Mandarin Gold, 76 oz. **$67**

Decanter w/crystal stopper, Mt. Vernon line, Amber, 40 oz. ... **$60**

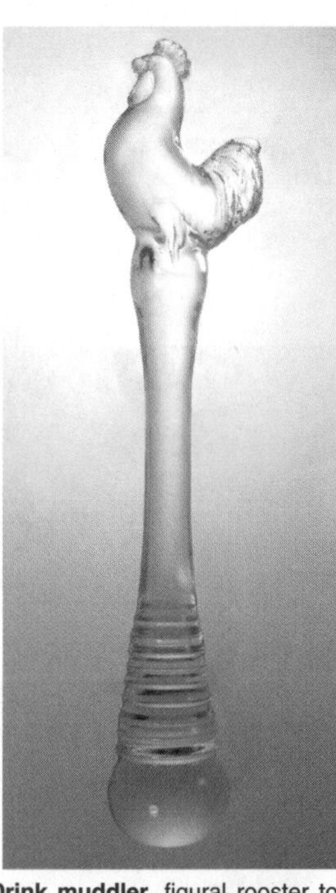

Drink muddler, figural rooster top, clear, 5 1/2" l. **$25**

Salt, open, oval urn-form w/two handles, Mt. Vernon line, Carmen, 2 1/2" l. **$48**

Model of a swan, table centerpiece, Ebony, 13" l. **$795**

Vase, 8" h., ivy ball-style w/keyhole stem, optic ribbed spherical pale green bowl **$75**

Central Glass Works

From the 1890s until its closing in 1939, the Central Glass Works of Wheeling, West Virginia, produced colorless and colored handmade glass in all the styles then popular. Decorations from etchings with acid to hand-painted enamels were used.

The popular "Depression" era colors of black, pink, green, light blue, ruby red and others were all produced. Two of its 1920s etchings are still familiar today, one named for the then President of the United States and the other for the Governor of West Virginia - these are the Harding and Morgan patterns.

From high end Art glass to mass-produced plain barware tumblers, Central was a major glass producer throughout the period.

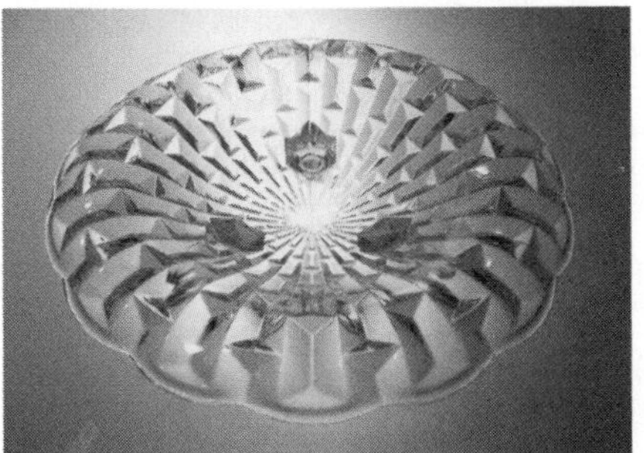

Bowl, 10 1/2" d., 3-footed, rolled edge, Frances patt., pink **$48**

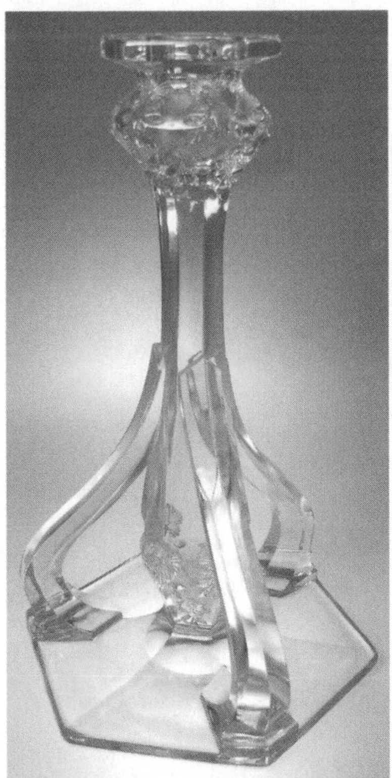

Candlestick, Chippendale patt., three-handled, clear w/cutting, 8 1/2" h. **$77**

Candleholders, one-light, Brocade etching, No. 2000, green, pr. (ILLUS. of one).................. **$95**

Sherbet, low footed, No. 1450 stem, black base w/clear bowl **$10**

Cigarette jar, round ashtray foot, clear optic bowl on amber foot, gold-encrusted Dunn's Parrot etching **$65**

Cracker plate, octagonal w/a center indentation, Morgan etching, pink, 9 1/2" w. **$75**

Creamer, Roses brocade etching, Pattern #1450, amber **$48**

Vase, 8" h., flip-style w/wide tapering cylindrical body, Roses brocade etching, green **$120**

Consolidated

The Consolidated Lamp and Glass Company of Coraopolis, Pennsylvania, was founded in 1894. For a number of years it was noted for its lighting wares but also produced popular lines of pressed and blown tablewares. Highly collectible glass patterns of this early era include the Cone, Cosmos, Florette and Guttate lines.

Lamps and shades continued to be good sellers, but in 1926 a new "art" line of molded decorative wares was introduced. This "Martelè" line was developed as a direct imitation of the fine glasswares being produced by Renè Lalique of France, and many Consolidated patterns resembled their French counterparts. Other popular lines produced during the 1920s and 1930s were "Dancing Nymph," the delightfully Art Deco "Ruba Rombic," introduced in 1928, and the "Catalonian" line, which debuted in 1927 and imitated 17th-century Spanish glass.

Although the factory closed in 1933, it was reopened under new management in 1936 and prospered through the 1940s. It finally closed in 1967. Collectors should note that many later Consolidated patterns closely resemble wares of other competing firms, especially the Phoenix Glass Company. Careful study is needed to determine the maker of pieces from the 1920-40 era.

A book that will be of help to collectors is Phoenix & Consolidated Art Glass, 1926-1980, by Jack D. Wilson (Antique Publications, 1989).

Cone

Sugar shaker, w/original top, cylindrical, cased blue, glossy finish **$143**

Sugar shaker, w/original top, cylindrical, cased pale pink, glossy finish **$143**

Guttate

Pitcher, 9 1/2" h., cased pink, glossy finish **$325**

Pitcher, water, 9 1/4" h., opaque white w/overall gold flecks, applied white handle **$198**

Florette

Cracker jar, cov., barrel-shaped, cased pink satin, silver plate rim, cover & bail handle not secured, 5 1/2" h. **$121**

Pitcher, 7 1/4" h., bulbous w/applied frosted clear handle, cased pink satin **$132**

Later Lines

Bowl, 10" w., deep rounded shape w/a flat rim, blue Vine patt. (Line 700), Martelè Line, mounted w/a ormolu rim band & high arched open floral scroll handles continuing down the sides, raised on a pierced ormolu base w/ winged paw feet **$323**

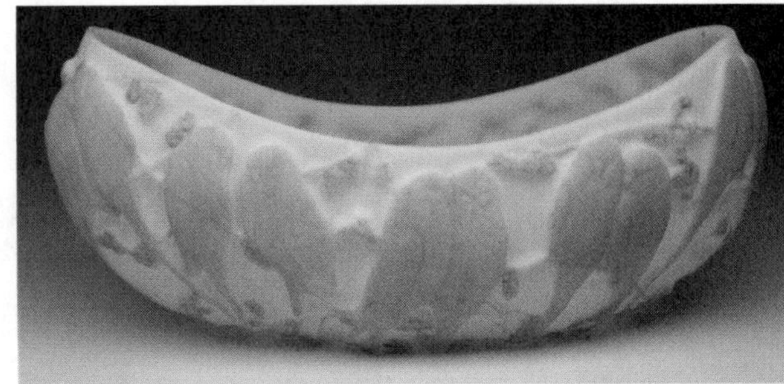

Bowl, boat-shaped, 7 1/2 x 13 1/4", 6 1/4" h., Love Birds patt., Martelè line, pale blue birds on custard ground **$154**

Candleholder, one-light, footed bulbous ovoid shape, custard ground w/molded flowers & leaves painted in pink & blue, undocumented pattern, 3 1/2" h. **$130**

Cup & saucer, Dancing Nymph line, frosted pink, pr. **$150**

Lamp, table model, Pine Cone patt., Martelè line, bulbous ovoid body w/brass fittings, custard ground w/blue pine cones design, made from a vase, 6 1/2" h. **$160**

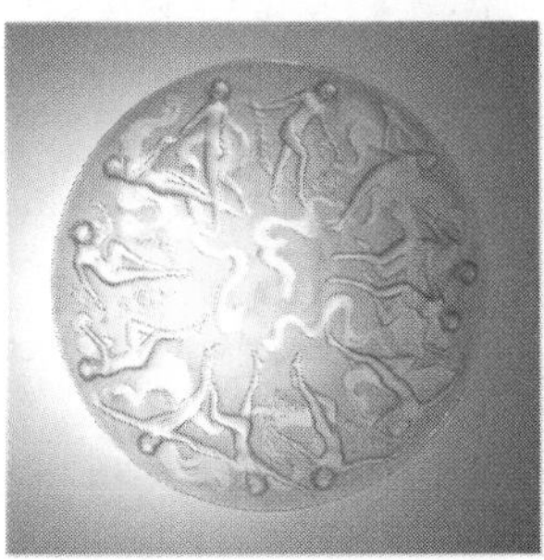

Plate, 8" d., Dancing Nymph line, clear w/brown wash............. **$145**

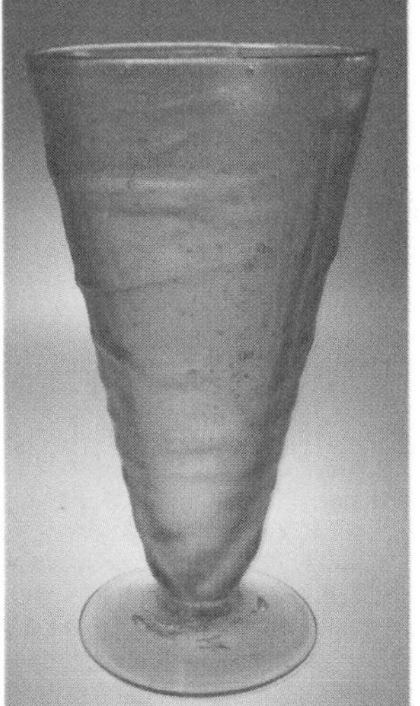

Tumbler, iced tea, footed, Catalonian line, honey color **$28**

Tumbler, Catalonian line, wide tapering cylindrical sides w/a flat bottom, emerald green, 9 oz. **$18**

Vase, 11 1/2" h., Dancing Girls patt., tall ovoid body, girls & Pan relief-molded & colored in deep rose & tan on a creamy custard ground **$518**

Cranberry

Gold was added to glass batches to give this glass its color on reheating. It has been made by numerous glasshouses for years and is currently being reproduced. Both blown and molded articles were produced. A less expensive type of cranberry was made with the substitution of copper for gold.

Bell, large cranberry bell w/tall applied clear handle, possibly English, late 19th c., 10 1/2" h. **$275-325**

Decanter w/original stopper, bulbous ovoid body tapering to a cylindrical neck w/flared rim, clear pointed bubble stopper, applied clear angled handle, ornate gold enameling of cherry blossoms on branches, Bohemia, early 20th c., 10" h. (ILLUS. bottom row, second from right)........ **$100-200**

Pitcher, 10 1/2" h., tankard-type, footed bulbous Optic Ribbed body tapering to a tall neck w/a flaring hexagonal crimped rim, decorated w/enameled white daisies & scattered blue flowers, applied clear handle, light outside residue **$121**

Pitcher, 11 1/4" h., tankard-type, a small cylindrical base flaring to a wide bulbous ovoid body below a tall ringed neck w/a high wide spout, decorated around the body & neck w/polychrome enamel flowers & leaves w/traces of gold, clear applied handle **$110**

Pitcher, 8 1/2" h., ovoid body tapering to a cylindrical neck w/ slightly flared crimped rim, Inverted Thumbprint patt., applied clear handle, engraved presentation "Mrs. M. Goodspeed - Saratoga 1894" **$154**

Pitcher, 8 1/4" h., tankard-type, tall cylindrical body w/a small pinched spout, decorated in white enamel w/a garden scene of flowers & grasses, an applied twisted rope handle splitting at the base terminal w/two pressed daisy prunts, an applied ropetwist band around the neck **$553**

Pitcher, 8" h., ovoid body tapering to a squared neck, Inverted Thumbprint patt., applied clear handle w/pressed fan design at upper terminal, minor flaws **$231**

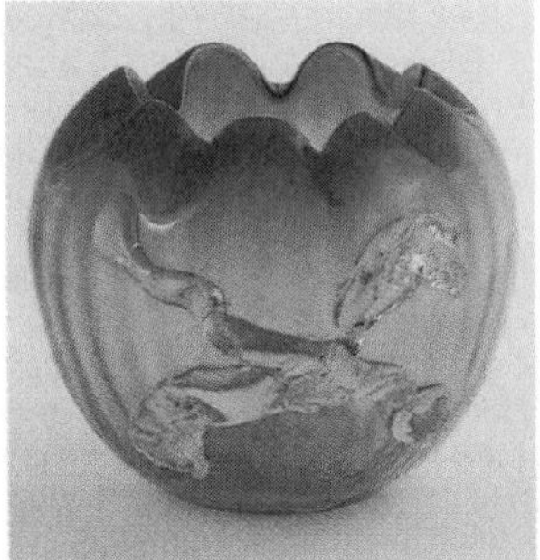

Rose bowl, shaded optic-ribbed bowl w/eight-crimped rim, applied on the side w/clear branch decoration, 4 1/2" d., 3 1/2" h. **$125-150**

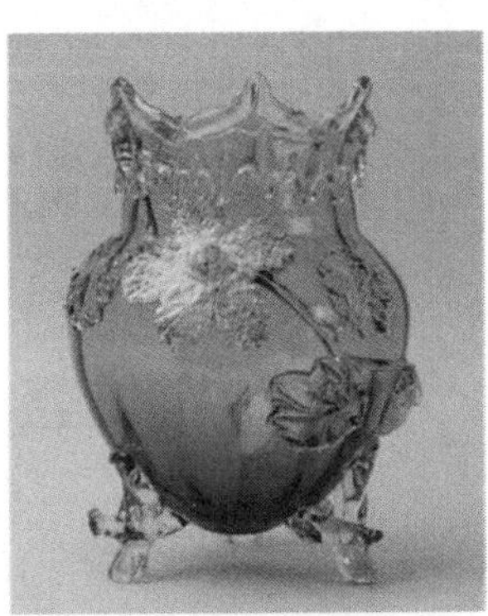

Vase, 11 1/4" h., a bulbous ovoid optic ribbed body tapering to a wide neck w/an appliqued clear icicle-style border band pulled into point, raised on three applied clear thorn feet, the side applied w/a large five-petal pink & white flowers on a clear leafy stem **$288**

Vase, 11 3/4" h., footed bottle-form shape w/a squatty bulbous body tapering to a tall stick neck, decorated overall w/ornate white enameled floral clusters, swags, arches & bands, base marked "Lace Art Cameo," late 19th c. **$375**

Vase, 8" h., 3 1/2" d., footed tapering ovoid body w/a short cylindrical neck, decorated w/large enameled blossom-form white reserve w/a worn scene framed w/gold-trim maroon scallops & flanked by leafy branches w/large blue, white & yellow blossoms, late 19th c. **$175-200**

Glass has been known to crack after being removed from a heated building in freezing weather. To avoid this, pack the glass in bubble wrap and several layers of paper. Don't place the package on the floor of the car where the heater will blow warm air on it. Back home, don't unwrap the item until it has returned to room temperature.

Custard

"Custard glass," as collectors call it today, came on the American scene in the 1890s, more than a decade after similar colors were made in Europe and England. The Sowerby firm of Gateshead-on-Tyne, England had marketed its patented "Queen's Ivory Ware" quite successfully in the late 1870s and early 1880s.

There were many glass tableware factories operating in Pennsylvania and Ohio in the 1890s and early 1900s, and the competition among them was keen. Each company sought to capture the public's favor with distinctive colors and, often, hand-painted decoration. That is when "Custard glass" appeared on the American scene.

The opaque yellow color of this glass varies from a rich, vivid yellow to a lustrous light yellow. Regardless of intensity, the hue was originally called "ivory" by several glass manufacturers then who also used superlative sounding terms such as "Ivorina Verde" and "Carnelian." Most Custard glass contains uranium, so it will "glow" under a black light.

The most important producer of Custard glass was certainly Harry Northwood, who first made it at his plants in Indiana, Pennsylvania, in the late 1890s and, later, in his Wheeling, West Virginia, factory. Northwood marked some of his most famous patterns, but much early Custard is unmarked. Other key manufacturers include the Heisey Glass Co., Newark, Ohio; the Jefferson Glass Co., Steubenville, Ohio; the Tarentum Glass Co., Tarentum, Pennsylvania; and the Fenton Art Glass Co., Williamstown, West Virginia.

Northwood

Custard glass fanciers are particular about condition and generally insist on pristine quality decorations free from fading or wear. Souvenir Custard pieces with events, places and dates on them usually bring the best prices in the areas commemorated on them rather than from the specialist collector. Also, collectors who specialize in pieces such as cruets, syrups or salt and pepper shakers will often pay higher prices for these pieces than would a Custard collector

Key reference sources include William Heacock's Custard Glass from A to Z, published in 1976 but not out of print, and the book Harry Northwood: The Early Years, available from Glass Press. Heisey's Custard is discussed in Shirley Dunbar's Heisey Glass: The Early Years (Krause Publications, 2000), and Coudersport's production is well-documented in Tulla Majot's book Coudersport's Glass 1900-1904 (Glass Press, 1999). The recently formed Custard Glass Society holds a yearly convention and maintains a web site: www.homestead.com/custardsociety.

- James Measell.

Beaded Circle (Northwood at Indiana, Pa., ca. late 1890s)

Butter dish, cov. **$500**

Berry set, master bowl & 5 sauce dishes; 6 pcs. **$495**

Tumbler, polychrome & gilt decoration............................ **$175**

Water set, pitcher & 3 tumblers, 4 pcs....................................... **$845**

Water set, pitcher & 4 tumblers, 5 pcs....................................... **$850**

Grape & Cable, Northwood Grape, or Grape & Thumbprint (Northwood at Wheeling, ca. 1913-15)

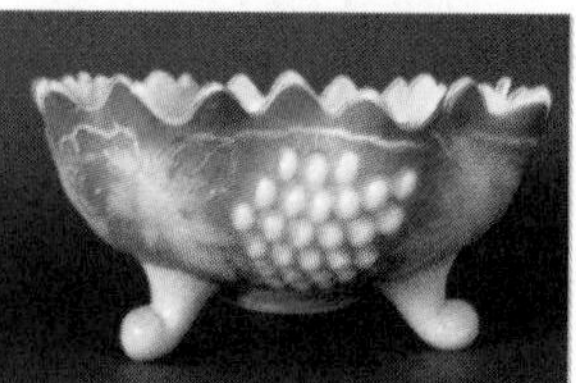

Bowl, master berry, blue stain **$450-550**

Sauce dish, flat **$45-60**

Pitcher, water **$400-550**

Tumbler **$75-85**

Intaglio (Northwood at Indiana, Pa., ca. 1899)

Pitcher, water **$450-500**

Berry set, pitcher & 6 tumblers, green & gold trim, 7 pcs. **$600-700**

Berry set, 9" d. footed compote & 6 sauce dishes, w/green decoration, 7 pcs. **$393**

Table set, cov. sugar bowl, creamer & spooner, 3 pcs. **$180**

Tumblers, blue & gold trim, set of 4 .... **$225**

Water set, pitcher & 6 tumblers, green & gold trim, 7 pcs. **$575**

Inverted Fan & Feather (Northwood at Indiana, Pa., ca. 1900)

Bowl, master berry **$200-225**

Bowl, master berry or fruit, 10" d., 5 1/2" h., four-footed............ **$225**

Berry set, master bowl & 6 sauce dishes, 7 pcs. **$650**

Berry set, master bowl & 2 sauce dishes, 3 pcs. **$340**

Sugar bowl, cov. **$275-300**

> To determine if a piece of reputed custard glass is genuine, shine a black light on it. Real custard glass will produce a greenish glow under the light because it was made with uranium salts. Although the glass emits little radiation and is considered safe, understandably, little was made after the detonation of the atomic bomb in World War II.

Pagoda or Chrysanthemum Sprig (Northwood at Indiana, Pa., ca. 1899)

Cruet w/original stopper (ILLUS. center with other pieces) **$350-450**

Condiment set, four-footed tray, cruet w/original stopper & salt & pepper shakers w/original tops; 4 pcs. **$950-1,000**

Table set, cov. sugar bowl, creamer, cov. butter dish & spooner, 4 pcs. **$740**

Pitcher .. **$550-650**

Tumbler **$80-125**

Peacock and Urn (Northwood at Wheeling, WV, ca. 1913-15)

Ice cream bowl, master w/nutmeg stain, 9 3/4" d. $300-375

Trailing Vine or Endless Vine (Bastow, ca. 1903-04)

Sauce dish $90

Wild Bouquet (Northwood at Indiana, Pa., ca. 1899)

Spooner $200-300

Miscellaneous Pieces

Bowl, Poinsettia Lattice patt., ruffled rim, Northwood $90

Bowl, shallow w/paneled sides, iridized finish w/black edge trim, Northwood $250

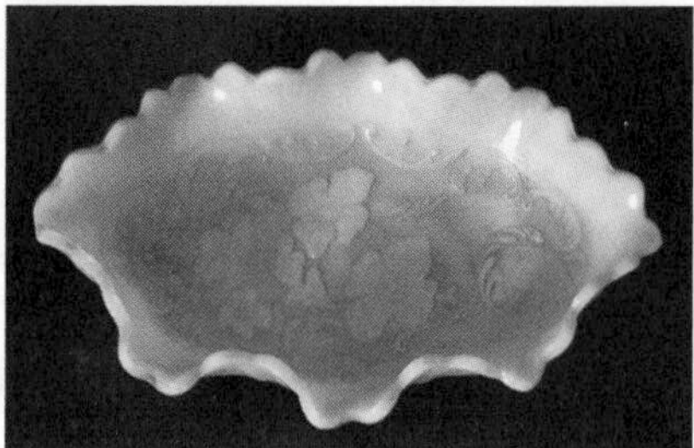

Pickle dish, oval, Poppy patt., Northwood ... $100

Visit antique shops, malls, shows and museums to study antiques in person and learn to recognize quality. Your experience will reward you later in spotting overlooked deals and avoiding fakes and reproductions.

Cut

Cut glass most eagerly sought by collectors is American glass produced during the so-called "Brilliant Period" from 1880 to about 1915. Pieces listed below are by type of article in alphabetical order.

Baskets

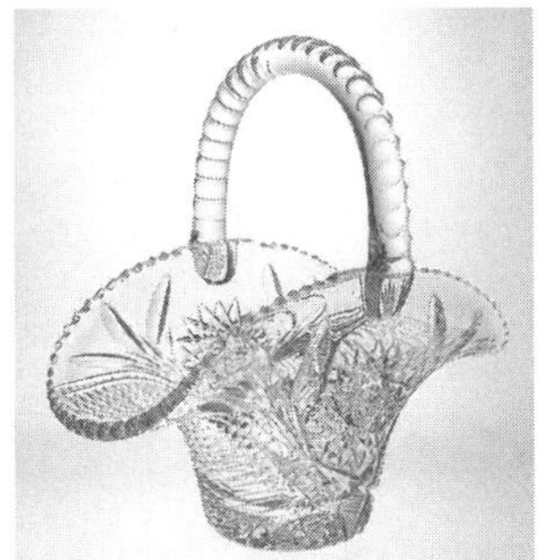

Pairpoint, "Cactus," 12" h. **$1,595**

Boxes

Dresser, rectangular w/hinged cover w/original metal hardware & key, cranberry cut to clear w/an overall button & rayed button pattern, 4 3/4 x 9 3/4", 5 1/4" h. **$3,450**

Bowls

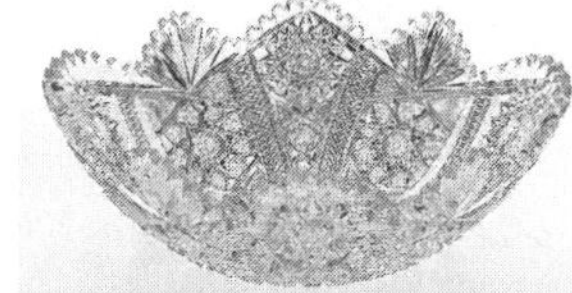

Blackmer, orange bowl, Columbia patt., 8 x 11 1/2", 4 1/2" h. .. **$775**

Clark, 14" d., Mercedes patt. **$2,750**

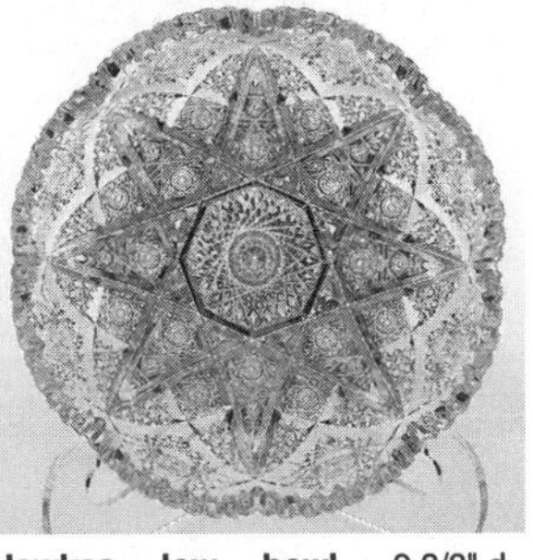

Hawkes low bowl, 9 3/8" d., Kensington patt. **$1,275**

Hawkes, 11 3/4" x 8 1/4" oval, "Kohinoor," clear **$2,700**

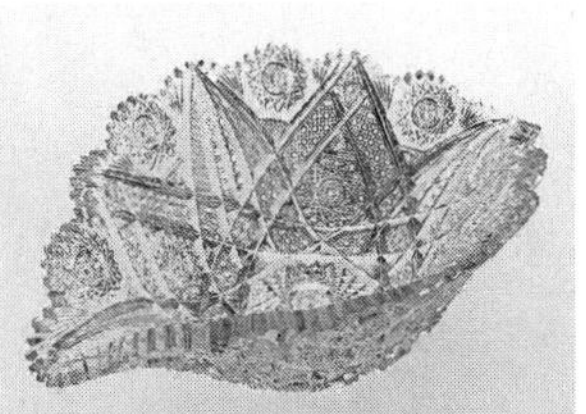

Hoare (J.) & Co., Napoleon's hat fruit bowl, "Carolyn," clear, 9 x 13 1/2", 4" h. **$1,650**

Jewel Cut Glass Co., 8" d., 3 1/2" h., Margaret patt. **$495**

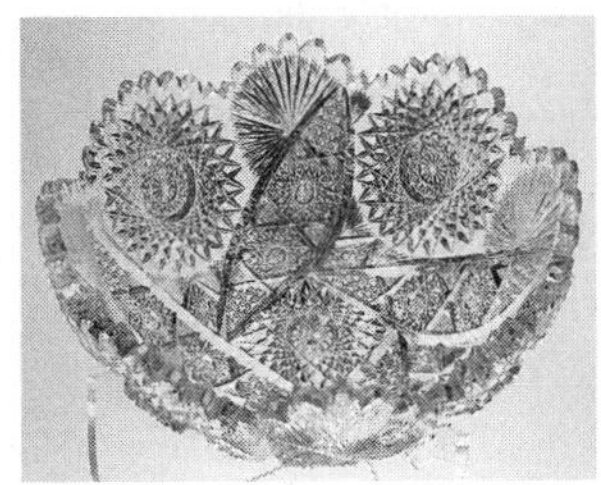

Pitkin & Brooks, 9" d., 4" h., Cypress patt. **$395**

Champagnes, Cordials & Wines

Wines, Dorflinger Russian Cut hock wines in cranberry cut to clear, facet-cut knob stems w/a controlled bubble, each 4 3/4" h., set of 9 .... **$3,450**

Compotes

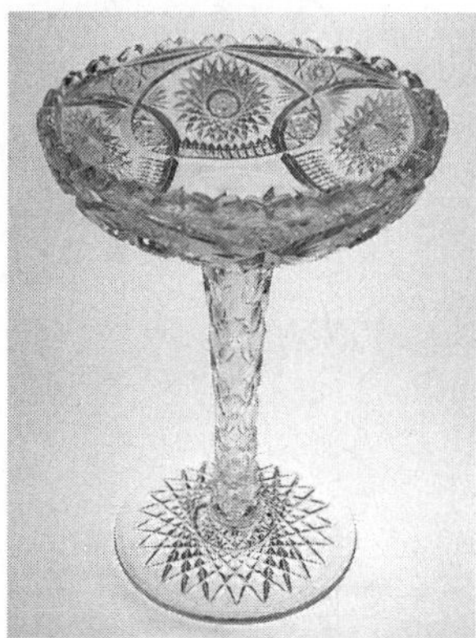

Monroe, Tempt patt., 8 x 11" **$795**

Ice Tubs

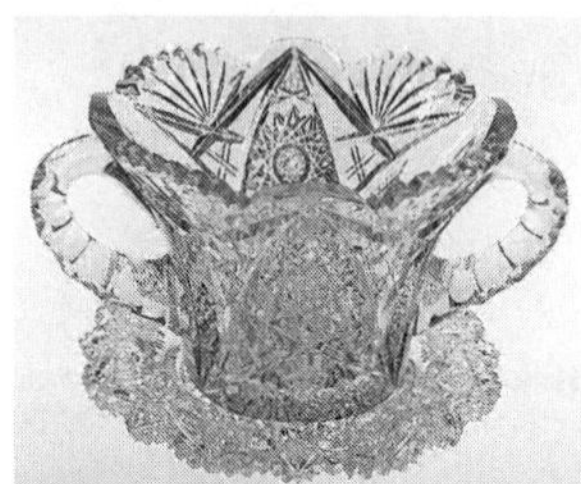

Blackmer, Crescent patt., handled tub w/underplate, 6" h. **$1,450**

Miscellaneous

Finger bowl, Dorflinger, American patt., 4 3/4" d., 2 1/4" h. **$145**

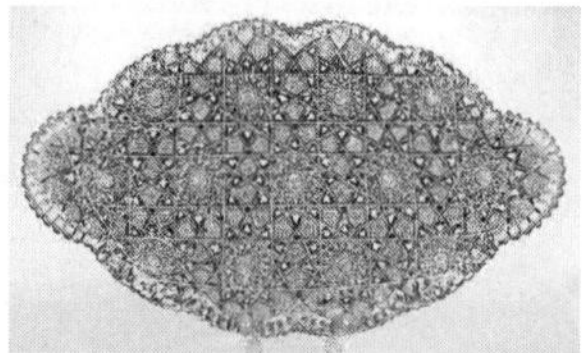

Ice cream tray, Empire, Seneca patt., 18" l. **$1,775**

Decanters

Clark (T.B.) & Co., whiskey decanter, Lakewood patt., 10" h., signed **$795**

Flower center, Pairpoint, Sillsbee patt., 9 1/2" h. **$1,350**

Olive dish, Straus, Imperial patt., 7 1/8" l. **$195**

Hawkes, ship's decanter, Flutes patt. **$575**

Libbey, Harvard patt., 15 1/2" h. **$975**

Stevens & Williams, baluster shape with teardrop stopper, amethyst with clear decoration, the body with floral and scrolling designs, a band of cross-cut diamonds on the base & the foot with a single band of beads, rare, 9" h. **$6,500**

Perfumes & Colognes

Dorflinger, Belmont patt., square shape, 9" h. **$495**

Pitchers & Jugs

Libbey jug, Harvard patt., 8" h. **$395**

Plates

8 1/4" d., Alexandrite-type coloring w/strawberry diamond & fan cutting, possibly America, late 19th c. **$2,013**

Punch bowls

Clark, Mercedes patt., 14" d., 11 1/2" h., signed **$4,950**

Hoare (J.) & Co., Rookwood patt., two-piece **$4,450**

Ohio Cut Glass Co., Fern patt., two-piece, 12" h., 12" d. ... **$4,250**

Rose Bowls

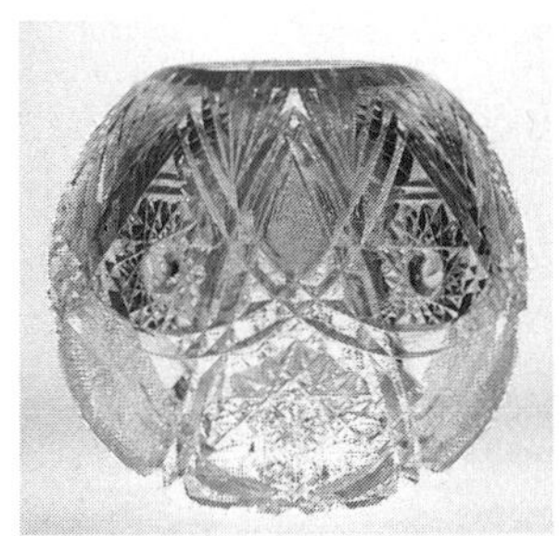

Clark, Baker's Gothic patt., 7" **$650**

Trays

Blackmer, Estelle patt., 14" d. **$4,450**

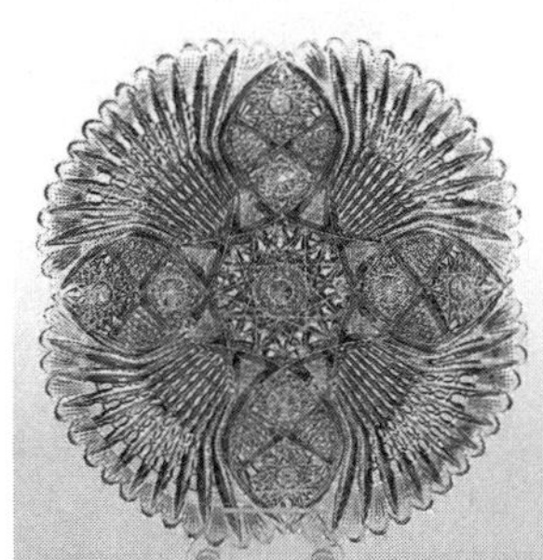

Blackmer, Princess patt., 12" d. **$1,750**

Vases

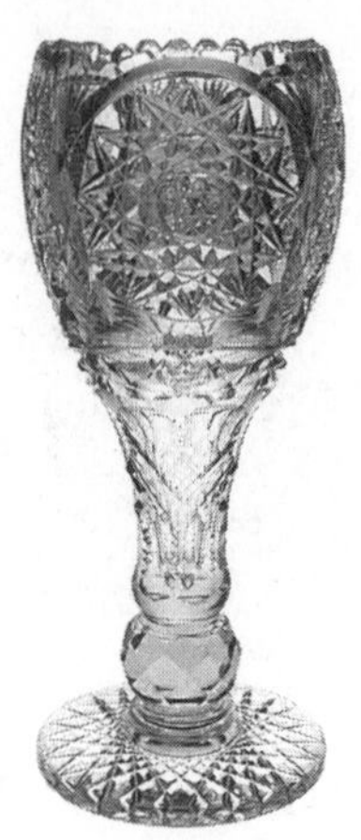

Bergen (J.D.) Co., 12" h., chalice form, Sheldon patt. **$975**

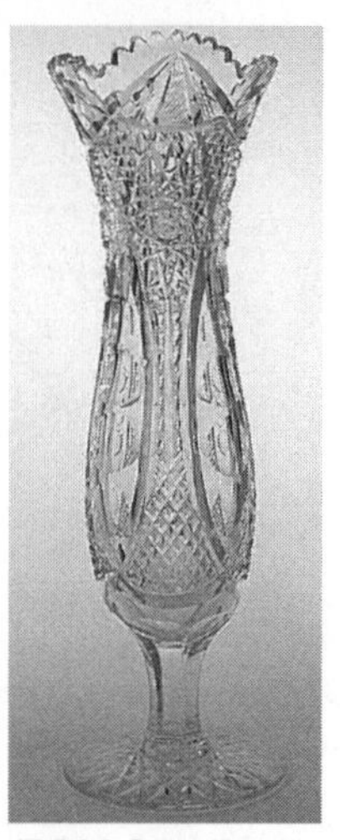

Clark (T.B.) & Co., 14" h., "American Beauty," clear **$795**

Cranberry cut to clear, 4" h., footed waisted cylindrical body cut w/vertical flutes, applied clear loop side handles, applied flaring silver rim band **$1,323**

Cranberry cut to clear, 9 1/2" h., chalice-form bowl on a hollow blown lapidary-cut applied stem w/applied cut foot **$1,955**

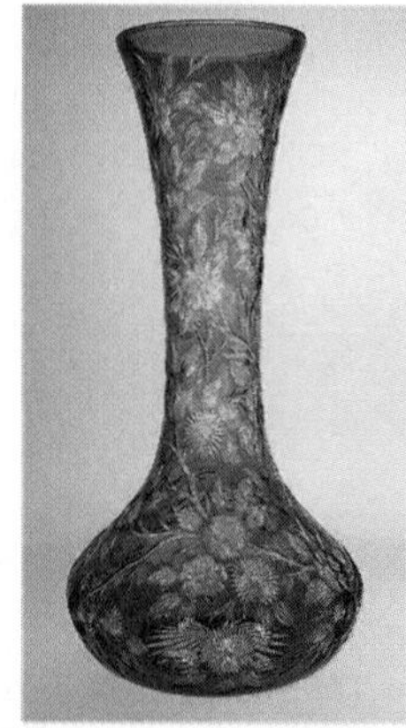

Dorflinger, 12 5/8" h., green cut to clear, tall form with bulbous base and long, thin neck flaring slightly at rim, decorated overall w/engraved floral & leaf designs **$4,850**

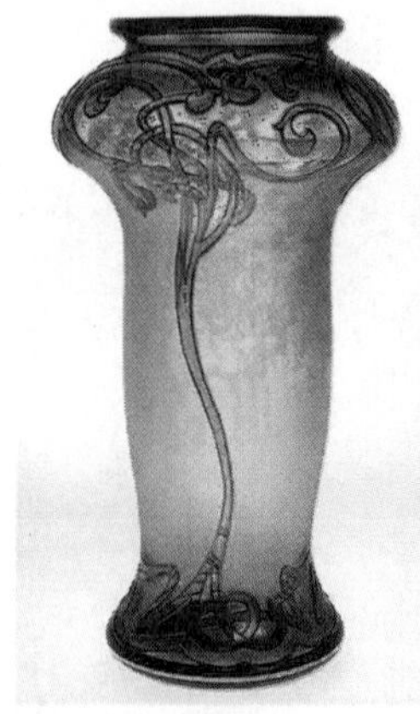

Dorflinger, 8" h., "Honesdale," sinuous shape w/Art Nouveau-style whiplash design **$1,475**

Hawkes, 14" h., "Navarre" variation, clear **$595**

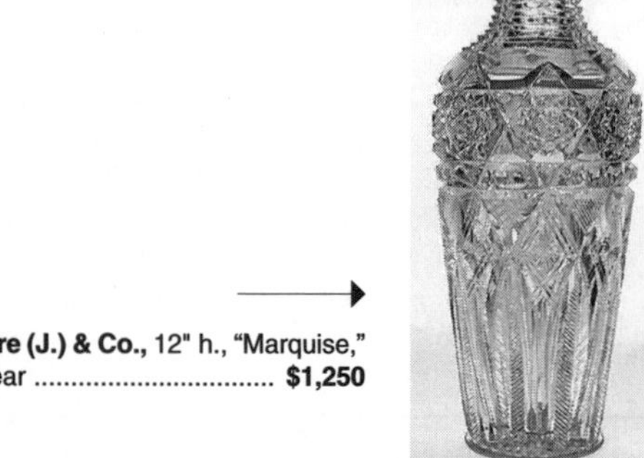

Hoare (J.) & Co., 12" h., "Marquise," clear **$1,250**

Czechoslovakian

The country of Czechoslovakia, including the glassmaking region of Bohemia, was not founded as an independent republic until after the close of World War I in 1918. The new country soon developed a large export industry, including a wide range of brightly colored and hand-painted glasswares such as vases, tablewares and perfume bottles. Fine quality cut crystal or Bohemian-type etched wares were also produced for the American market. Some Bohemian glass carries faint acid-etched markings on the base.

With the breakup of Czechoslovakia into two republics, the wares produced between World War I and II should gain added collector appeal.

Bowl, 7" d., deep bulbous tapering body w/closed rim in the Inverted Thumbprint patt., pale blue w/ applied yellow rigaree bands & prunts **$81**

Cameo vase, 10 1/4" h., 10" d., footed bulbous ovoid body w/a short rolled neck, pearl overlaid w/orange & brown & etched w/large orange flowers & brown leaves, signed in cameo "Leopal," ca. 1920s **$1,438**

Dresser set: round hand mirror, oval 11" l. hair brush & 6 1/4" l. clothes brush; Malachite glass inserts, each piece w/a gilt-metal frame, the long handles w/delicate pierced scrolling designs, Malachite w/a pressed putti design, Schlevogt factory, ca. 1935, the set (ILLUS. with vases) **$891**

Vase, 5 1/4" h., 7 1/2" d., footed squatty bulbous body w/a wide shoulder tapering to a wide flat rim w/a deeply rolled-out flaring rim, overall gold iridescence w/flashes of purple, blue & green, signed **$300**

> Careless handling at auction previews can quickly degrade the condition of many antiques and collectibles. When items are placed on tables where anyone, even children, can pick things up, damage can easily happen. Use great care when examining items and be sure to re-examine your purchases after winning them to make sure no damage took place during inspection.

Daum Nancy

This fine glass, much of it cameo, was made by Auguste and Antonin Daum, who founded a factory in 1875 in Nancy, France. Most of their cameo and enameled glass was made from the 1890s into the early 20th century.

Cameo bowl, 8" d., wide w/low sides incurved & crimped into a four-lobe rim, mottled yellow & amethyst overlaid w/vitrified green, red & yellow powders & cameo-cut w/a continuous design of red berries on leafy stems, signed in cameo, ca. 1900 .... **$2,760**

Cameo box, cov., oval w/upright sides, mottled yellow base cameo carved w/rose leaves & stems, low domed cover in mottled white cased in mottled green & pink & carved w/rose blossoms & leaves, two small filled rim chips, engraved signature, 5 3/8" l., 3 1/8" h. **$5,175**

Cameo box, cov., round, squatty bulbous base in pale mottled blue over yellow cameo-carved & enameled w/small purple blossoms on green stems, mottled blue cover w/matching blossoms, base rim polished, nicks in cover rim, 4" d., 2 1/2" h. **$2,645**

Cameo creamer, footed squatty bulbous body tapering to a wide angled rim w/spout, light amber ground overlaid in dark brown & cameo-cut w/a landscape of trees along a lake, applied angled amber handle, signed on base, 3 3/4" h. **$1,179**

Cameo creamer, small round foot & knop stem below the widely flaring trumpet-form body w/cupped top & pinched spout, applied frosted clear handle, frosted white to amber ground cameo-carved & enameled w/small blue flowers, a dragonfly, leaves & stems, signed on the base in gold script, 4 1/2" h. **$5,060**

Cameo glass is made by carving into multiple layers of colored glass to create a design in relief. Cameo glass is at least as old as the Romans, who produced the famous Portland Vase.

Cameo tumbler, miniature, cylindrical, cameo-etched w/a winter landscape of leafless trees enameled in brown, black & white against the mottled yellow & orange background, signed on the bottom, 1 7/8" h. **$1,035**

Cameo vase, 12" h., Art Deco style, clear ground w/a textured surface overlaid in black & etched around the middle w/two bands of stylized birds perched on two bands of arches, sawtooth rim & base bands, wheel-carved mark, ca. 1925 .... **$13,145**

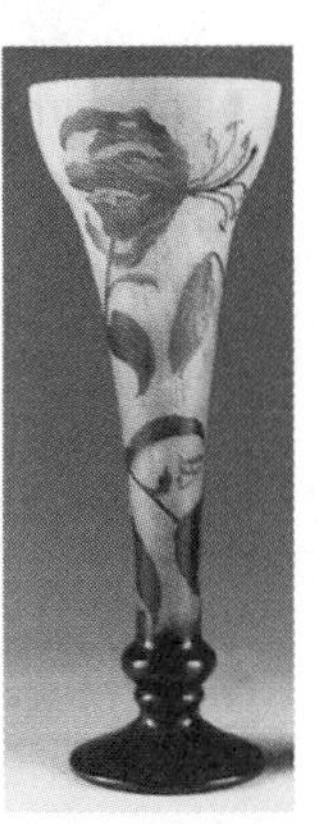

Cameo vase, 10" h., a swelled base band & tall flaring cylindrical body w/an angled shoulder to the short cupped neck, grey, yellow & turquoise mottled ground overlaid in dark green & etched w/long stemmed cockscomb & grasses, the eyes of the plants in deep cobalt blue framed by robin's-eye blue, incised mark, ca. 1910 .... **$5,520**

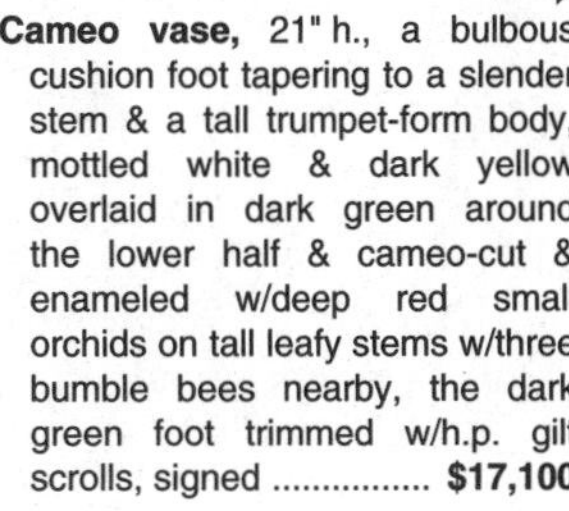

Cameo vase, 21" h., a bulbous cushion foot tapering to a slender stem & a tall trumpet-form body, mottled white & dark yellow overlaid in dark green around the lower half & cameo-cut & enameled w/deep red small orchids on tall leafy stems w/three bumble bees nearby, the dark green foot trimmed w/h.p. gilt scrolls, signed **$17,100**

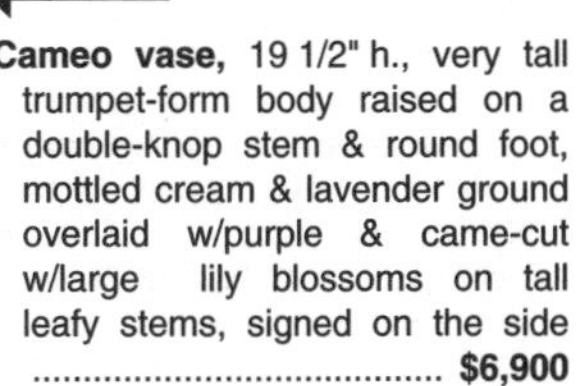

Cameo vase, 19 1/2" h., very tall trumpet-form body raised on a double-knop stem & round foot, mottled cream & lavender ground overlaid w/purple & came-cut w/large lily blossoms on tall leafy stems, signed on the side **$6,900**

Cameo vase, 15 1/2" h., a pale blue round foot & double-knop stem supporting a tall ovoid body w/a flared flat rim, mottled dark & light blue, yellow, white & green w/a wheel-carved finish & overlaid in muted brownish-green & dark blue & cameo-carved w/a design of large leaves & daisies on tall stems, carved signature on foot **$15,525**

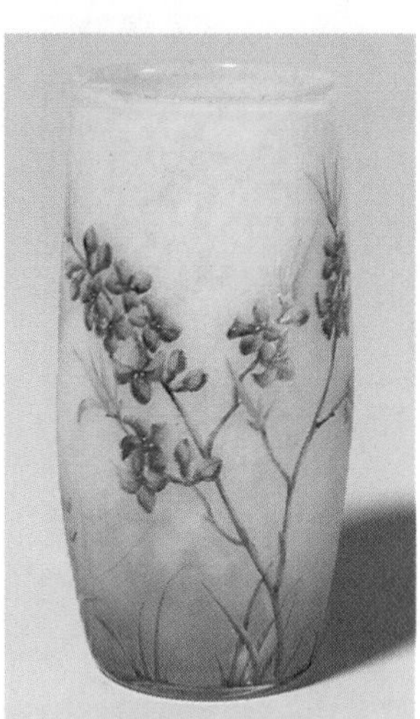

Cameo vase, 4 3/4" h., slightly swelled cylindrical form, mottled pale blue shading to lime green, cameo-cut & enameled w/purplish red blossoms on tall thin green leafy stems, cameo signature & monogram in enamel **$1,725**

Cameo vase, 6 1/4" h., flared foot & gently flaring cylindrical sides w/an angled shoulder to the short flaring neck, mottled dark orange & deep yellow ground overlaid deep maroon shading to reddish orange & cameo-cut w/a design of nicotana flowers on leafy stems, signed **$1,560**

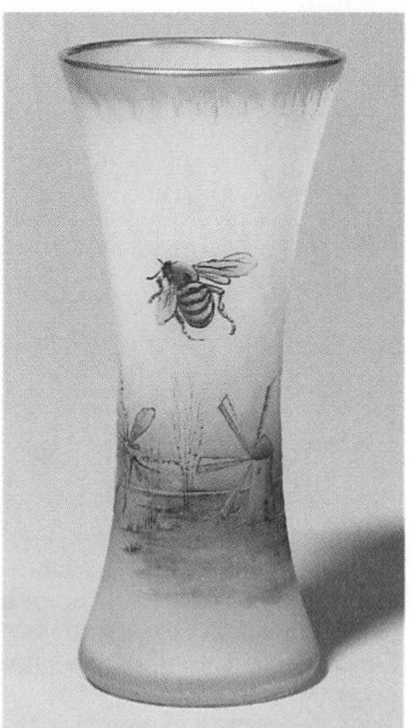

Cameo vase, 6 1/8" h., slender waisted form, frosted white cameo-carved & enameled w/a scene of a bumble bee & damselfly above a winter landscape of Dutch windmills in black & green, gold rim bands, unsigned **$2,990**

Cameo vase, 9 1/4" h., a cushion foot supporting the flaring cylindrical body w/a tapering shoulder to the wide flat mouth, mottled orange & yellow background finely etched w/a snowy winter landscape w/ barren trees enameled in shades of charcoal, frosty white & dark grey, signed in black enamel, ca. 1900 .... **$4,370**

Cameo vase, 9 1/4" h., a wide round foot & squatty knop supporting the tall flaring cylindrical body w/an incurved wide flat rim, grey mottled w/light blue, dark blue & white & overlaid in dark maroon & white & etched w/a design of white blossoms atop tall slender leafy stems, intaglio signature, ca. 1900 .... **$10,350**

Cameo vase, 9 3/4" h., 4 3/4" d., a flattened cushion base tapering to a cylindrical body w/a swelled ring around the flat rim, mottled & streaking red & orange ground overlaid in dark maroon & cameo-carved w/slender trees in the foreground, cameo signature, ca. 1910 .... **$2,160**

Decanter w/original hollow blown stopper, clear cylindrical panel-cut body tapering to a tall cylindrical neck w/a small rim spout, applied handle & rim trimmed in gold, facet-cut bulbous stopper, signed in gilt, 10" h. **$345**

Teacup & saucer, each in crystal, the tapering round cup enameled in black & white w/a tiny winter landscape trimmed w/small blue flowers & dragonflies & trimmed in gold, applied clear C-scroll handle, the lightly optic-ribbed saucer w/a lightly scalloped rim, also enameled w/a small landscape panel & further floral & dragonfly designs, signed, saucer 4 1/2" d., cup 2" h., pr. **$805**

Do not display fragile items too close together, as one falling piece could knock over and damage others.

Vase, 1 5/8" h., miniature, ovoid body tapering to a cylindrical neck w/an uneven rolled rim, milky white ground enameled in dark blue & black w/a Dutch winter scene w/a windmill near boats in a harbor, acid-etched background, signed on the bottom **$780**

Vase, 3 1/4" h., miniature, flattened swelled form in frosted milky white enameled in color w/the figure of a young girl holding four geese on leashes, signed on the bottom **$1,610**

Englishman John Lockwood inspired a revival of cameo glass in 1876 when he created a reproduction of the renowned Roman Portland Vase.

Vase, 4" h., 4 1/8 x 6 7/8", narrow oblong foot & conforming gently flaring sides, mottled frosted clear over mottled maroon, yellow & green at the bottom acid-etched w/swirling autumn leaves enameled in shades of yellow, cameo signature, ca. 1910 .... **$2,880**

Vase, 7 1/2" h., 6" d., footed bulbous nearly spherical body tapering to a short flaring neck, iridescent greyish blue ground etched & gilt-decorated w/ seagulls & a rising sun, also carved w/ tortoises rising from the sea, signed in gilt on the bottom **$8,625**

Duncan & Miller

Duncan & Miller Glass Company, a successor firm to George A. Duncan & Sons Company, produced a wide range of pressed wares and novelty pieces during the late 19th century and into the early 20th century. During the Depression era and after, they continued making a wide variety of more modern patterns, including mold-blown types, and also introduced a number of etched and engraved patterns. Many colors, including opalescent hues, were produced during this era, and especially popular today are the graceful swan dishes they produced in the Pall Mall and Sylvan patterns.

The numbers after the pattern name indicate the original factory pattern number. The Duncan factory was closed in 1955.

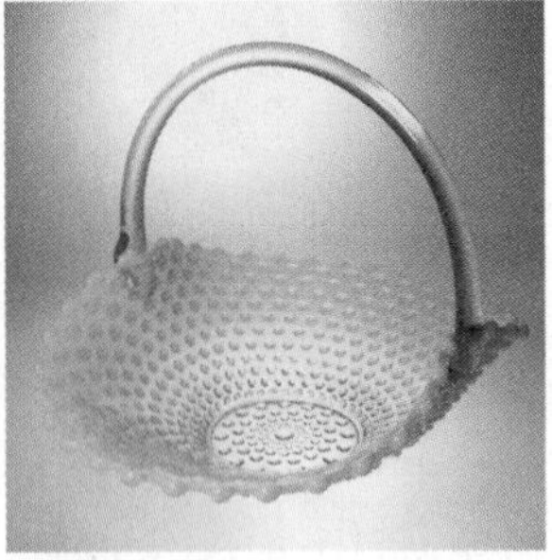

Basket, Hobnail patt., applied handle, blue opalescent, 9 x 14" **$200**

Bowl, 11 1/2" d., Early American Sandwich patt., flared & ruffled rim, clear **$50**

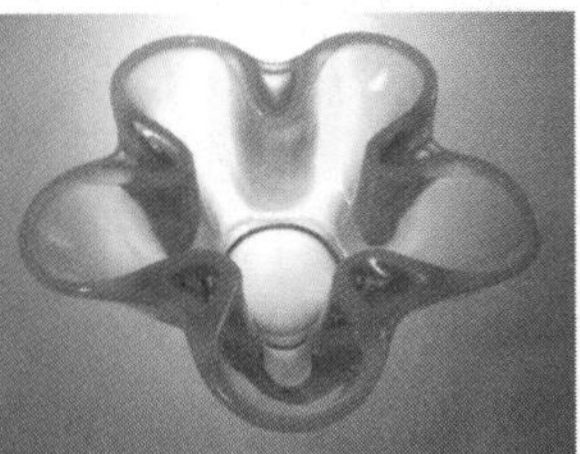

Bowl, 6" d., garden-type w/five deep lobes, blue opalescent.......... **$68**

An epergne is a table centerpiece used to hold food, candles or flowers.

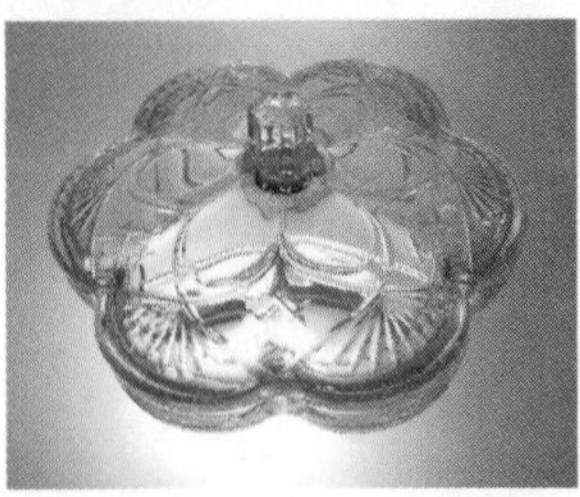

Candy dish, cov., three-part, Canterbury patt., clear w/cutting, 7" d. **$45**

Coaster-ashtray, green, 4 1/4 x 6" **$25**

Epergne, one-lily, three-piece, fruit & flower-type, a tall English Hobnail patt. lily above the wide Early American Sandwich patt. dish, raised on a pedestal base w/swirled foot, clear, 15" h. **$165**

Honey jug, miniature, Mardi Gras patt., clear, 2 1/2" h. **$28**

Plate, 8 1/2" d., pressed Ship patt. in center, amber **$16**

Relish dish, Sylvan patt., two-part, milk white w/green handle, 8 1/2" l. **$125**

Rose bowl, Canterbury patt., Jasmine, yellow opalescent, 6" **$125**

Rose bowls are designed to hold fresh flower petals to release a perfume-like fragrance.

Vase, 10" h., tall trumpet-form body on a short stem & round foot, Early American Sandwich patt., #108, clear **$78**

Salt dip, individual, footed, No. 63 Homestead patt., clear, 2" h. **$18**

Vase, 5 1/2" h., deep flaring sides pulled into six ruffles, clear ... **$24**

Vase, 5" h., Early American Sandwich patt., fanned shape, clear **$49**

Vase, 5" h., 6" d., Hobnail patt., pink opalescent **$65**

Vase, 8" h., Canterbury patt. (No. 115), crimpted, straight sided, clear....................................... **$35**

Vase, 10 1/2" h., footed, Venetian No. 126 patt., ruby **$225**

Vase, 6" h., footed trumpet form, Spiral Flutes patt., green **$20**

Vase, 8" h., cornucopia-shaped, Three Feather patt., clear w/ cutting.................................... **$55**

Vase, 5" h., Early American Sandwich patt., crimped rim, footed, clear............................ **$45**

Vase, 8 3/4" h., Spiral Flutes patt., green **$25**

Vase, 9" h., Caribbean patt., ruffled rim, footed, blue.................... **$200**

In an auction that is not cataloged the auctioneer will usually announce the order of the sale beforehand while discussing terms and conditions. The order may change depending on the how sale progresses. Don't miss out on an item you want by going to the lunch at the wrong moment. Stay close to the auction ring.

Fenton

Fenton Art Glass Company began producing glass at Williamstown, West Virginia, in January 1907. Organized by Frank L. and John W. Fenton, the company began operations in a newly built glass factory with an experienced master glass craftsman, Jacob Rosenthal, as their factory manager. Fenton has produced a wide variety of collectible glassware through the years, including Carnival. Still in production today, its current productions may be found at finer gift shops across the country.

William Heacock's three-volume set on Fenton, published by Antique Publications, is the standard reference in this field.

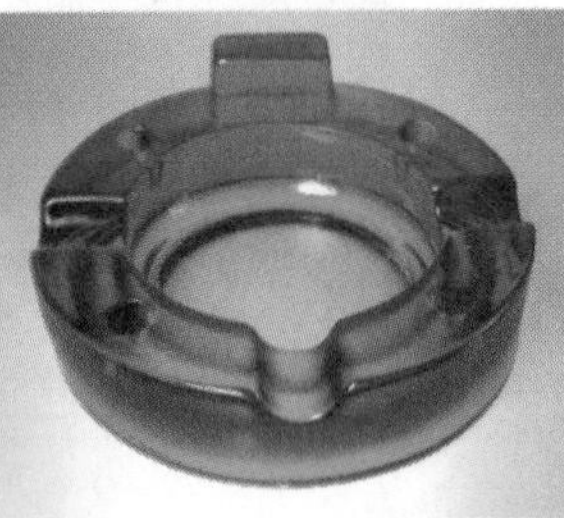

Ashtray, round w/four cigarette indentations on the rim, Celeste Blue stretch glass, Pattern #202, 5" d. **$72**

Bowl, 10" d., 3 1/2" h., cranberry opalescent Diamont Optic patt., flaring ruffled & crimpled rim, marked "Fenton" **$165**

Candleholders, squatty bulbous finger-style w/applied clear handle, Hobnail patt., cranberry opalescent, 3 1/4" h., pr. **$145**

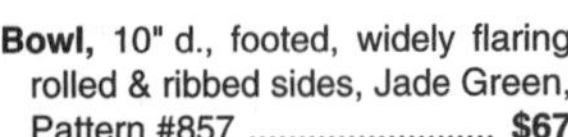

Bowl, 10" d., footed, widely flaring rolled & ribbed sides, Jade Green, Pattern #857 .... **$67**

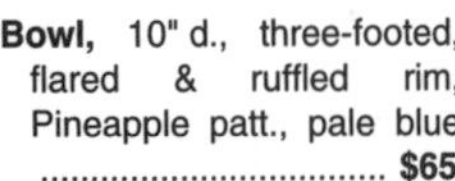

Bowl, 10" d., three-footed, flared & ruffled rim, Pineapple patt., pale blue **$65**

Candlesticks, one-light, short style w/round base pressed w/ leaves on the underside, bulbous candle socket supported by two dolphin-shaped handles, ruby red, 3 1/2" h., pr. **$55**

Console set: 10" d. bowl w/flaring crimped & ruffled rim & a pair of double-knop 5" h. candlesticks; Peach Crest, candlesticks Pattern #1523, the set **$120**

Ewer, footed Melon lobed body tapering to a tall ringed neck w/high arched & ruffled spout & rim, applied notched blue handle, cased blue body, Pattern #192A, 9" h. **$55**

Lamp, Victorian-style, squatty bulbous base w/applied clear handle, brass electric fitting & chimsey-style shade, Hobnail patt., French Opalescent **$165**

Mug, tall waisted shape w/D-form handle, Chocolate glass, pressed Bicentennial design, 6 3/4" h. **$24**

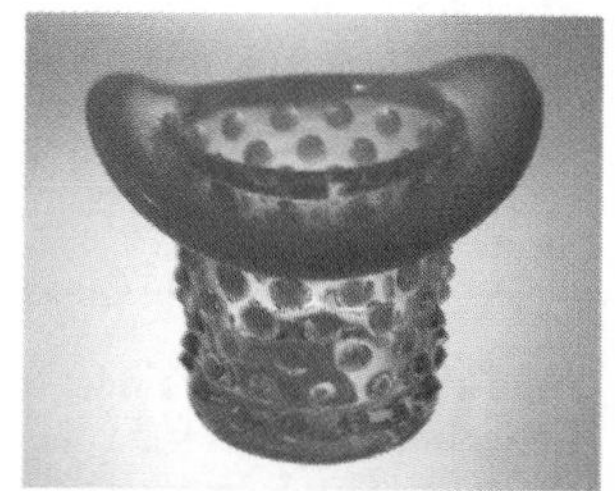

Model of a top hat, Hobnail patt., blue opalescent, 2 1/2" h. **$24**

Vase, 1 3/4" h., miniature, footed & ringed cylindrical body w/a flaring & turned up crimped rim, blue opalescent **$55**

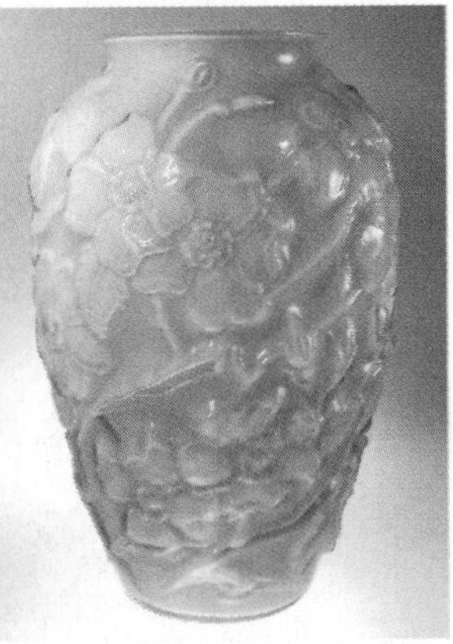

Vase, 10" h., tall ovoid body w/a low rolled rim, molded Dogwood patt. made from a Consolidated mold, pink cased in milk glass, ca. 1980 .... **$125**

Vase, 13" h., swung-type, tall waisted form w/flaring rim, Shape #1530, Jade Green **$82**

Vase, 4" h., footed bulbous squatty body w/a widely flaring crimped & ruffled rim, Shape #203, Coin Dot patt., cranberry opalescent ... **$44**

Vase, 5" h., footed squatty shape w/ widely flaring lower body w/a wide flattened shoulder tapering to a short four-lobed rolled neck, white opaque cased in dark yellow, Pattern #3001 .... **$34**

Vase, 9" h., footed Melon-lobed body w/a tall ringed neck w/a widely flaring crimped & ruffled rim, Peach Crest, Shape #192A **$45**

Vase, 6" h., footed bulbous lower body w/flared upper body ending in a widely flaring crimped & ruffled rim, Shape #1925, Coin Dot patt., cranberry opalescent **$78**

The worst spot for a bidder to stand at an auction is behind the auctioneer. If he cannot see you without turning his head, he won't know you're bidding. Even if he hears your loud, "Yeah," he'll have to turn around to see who said it. That pause will slow his pace, which he won't like.

Fostoria

Fostoria Glass company, founded in 1887, produced numerous types of fine glassware over the years. Its factory in Moundsville, West Virginia, closed in 1986.

Almond dish, square foot, flaring bowl, No. 4020, Wisteria, 2 3/4" d. **$32**

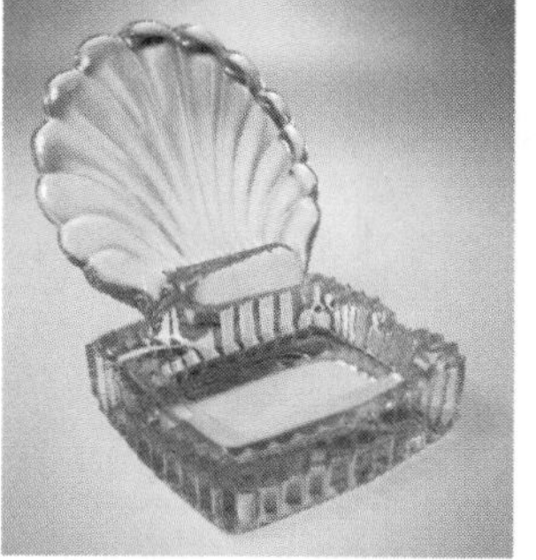

Ashtray/place card holder, rectangular w/low fluted sides & upright shell-shaped back, Azure Blue, Pattern #2538, 3" h. **$22**

Beverage set: 48 oz. 10" h. pitcher & 11 footed & handled tumblers; Priscilla patt., amber, the set (ILLUS. of part) **$250-300**

Bonbon, low ribbed swan-like shape w/arched end handle, ruby, Pattern #2517, 4 1/2" l. **$16**

Bowl, 5 1/2" w., ice cream-type, square, Colony patt., clear ... **$28**

Bowl-vase, footed wide squatty bulbous heavy body w/a thick rolled rim, crystal iridescent, Designer Collection "Impressions" patt., ca. 1970s, 8 1/2" d., 5" h. **$120**

Candle lamp, three-part, American patt. footed base, clear blown bell-shaped shade, clear **$100**

Candleholder, three-light, Baroque patt., clear **$29**

Candleholder, three-light, Pattern #2383, Rose, 4" h. **$38**

Candleholders, one-light, Onyx Lustre, No. 2324, 3" h., pr. (ILLUS. of one) **$425**

Candlesticks, one-light, Coin patt., Emerald Green, 4 1/2" h., pr. 4 3/4" h. **$65**

Candlesticks, one-light, Navarre etching, Baroque blank, No. 2496, clear, 4" h., pr. (ILLUS. of one) **$45**

Champagne, Pattern #5099, clear stem & Wisteria flaring bowl, 6 1/4" h. **$47**

Cigarette holder with ashtray foot, Pattern #2349, green, 3 1/4" h. **$35**

Cocktail, No. 5099, Azure Blue, 3 oz. **$22**

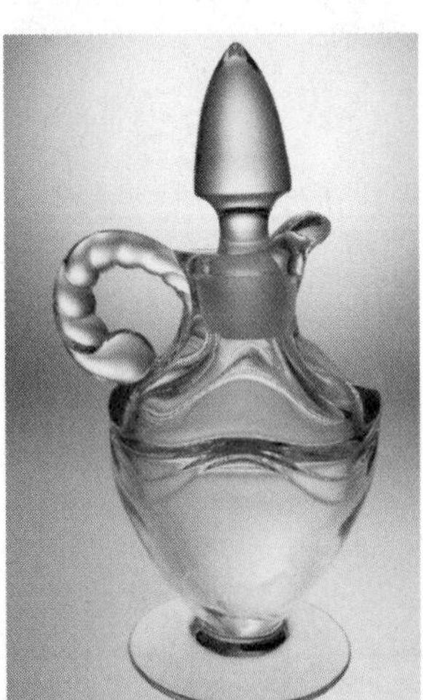

Cruet w/original stopper, oil-type, Sunray patt., clear, 3 0z. **$32**

Cruet w/original stopper, oil-type, footed, Coronet patt., clear, 3 0z. **$37**

Cup & saucer, Lafayette patt., translucent Jade green, rare color **$150**

The word "cruet "comes from the French word "crue," meaning "earthen pot."

Goblet, American Lady patt., Amethyst bowl, 10 oz. water, 6 1/8" h. **$36**

Ice bucket w/arched metal swing handle, tapering cylindrical form, Versailles etching, Rose, 6" h. **$135**

Mayonnaise bowl w/two ladles, American patt., divided, clear, 3 1/4" d., 6 1/4" h., 3 pcs. **$65**

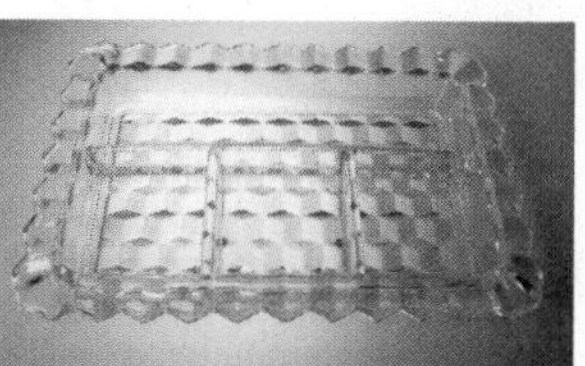

Relish dish, American patt., four-part, rectangular, clear, 6 1/4 x 9" **$42**

Salt & pepper shakers w/original tops on tray, individual size, Colony patt., clear, the set **$45**

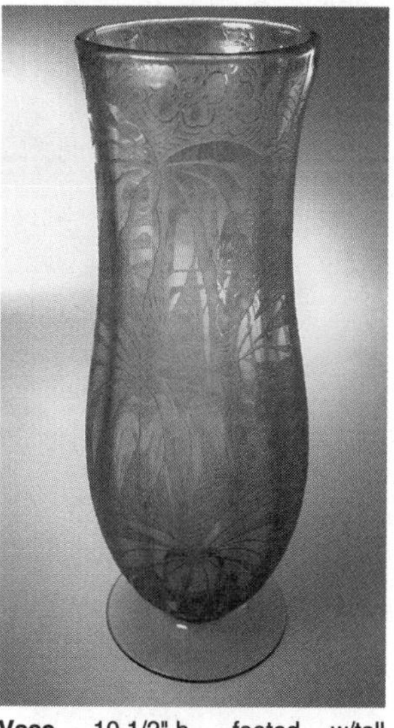

Vase, 10 1/2" h., footed w/tall slender waisted bowl, etched Brocade Palm Leaf patt., green **$450**

Vase, 6" h., footed bulbous ovoid optic-ribbed body tapering to a low cylindrical neck, Pattern #4108, Rose **$49**

Vase, bud, 6" h., clear foot & tall trumpet-form Empire Green body tapering to a wide low neck, Pattern #6102, original company sticker **$32**

Vase, 9" h., pitcher-style, Heirloom patt., ruby **$90**

Gallè

Gallè glass was made in Nancy, France, by Emile Gallè, a founder of the Nancy School and a leader in the Art Nouveau movement in France. Much of his glass, both enameled and cameo, is decorated with naturalistic motifs. The finest pieces were made in the last two decades of the 19th century and the opening years of the 20th.

Pieces marked with a star preceding the name were made between 1904, the year of Gallè's death, and 1914.

Gallé Nancy Déposé

Cameo bowl, 4 1/4" d., 3 1/8" h., low squatty bulbous form tapering to a low four-lobed neck, "Verre Parlant" (speaking glass), internally decorated in pale yellowish green w/thin swirled bands of color granules overlaid in a deep mauve & etched w/an underwater scene of an octopus among seaweed, cameo etched around the neck "L'Etoile du Matin et L'Etoile du Soir - Victor Hugo" (The Morning Star and The Evening Star - Victor Hugo), cameo signature, ca. 1895 (ILLUS. center with two internally decorated & etched cameo vases) **$8,365**

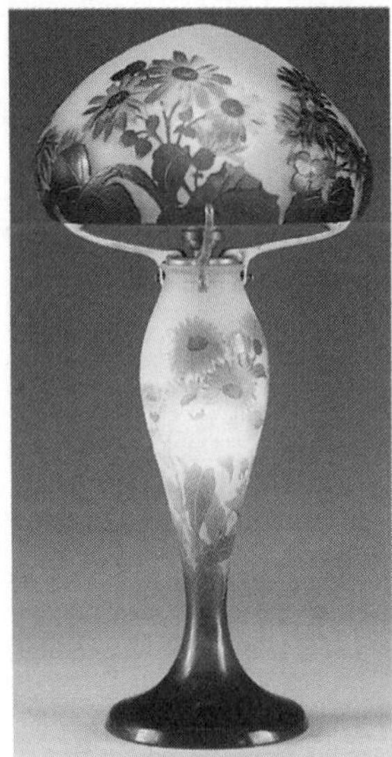

Cameo lamp, the base w/a wide round dark purple foot tapering to a slender ovoid body in pale shaded yellow & overlaid in light blue & olive green & cameo-cut w/a cluster of blue daisy-like flowers above green leafy stems, the peaked mushroom-form shade w/matching decoration, base & shade signed in cameo, shade 8" d., overall 17 1/2" h. .. **$10,350**

Cameo perfume lamp, bulbous body in frosted deep yellow cased in dark maroon shaded to red & cameo- cut w/fuschia blossoms & leaves, signed in cameo, the neck fitted w/a cylindrical brass lamp collar, also w/paper label reading "Gallè Nancy Paris," & the brass collar marked "Made in France," 6" h. **$2,160**

Cameo scent bottle w/original stopper, footed flaring cylindrical body w/a wide rounded shoulder centering a small cylindrical neck w/a pointed stopper, pale green & opalescent white ground overlaid in green & cameo-cut w/stylized Queen Anne's lace blossoms trimmed in white & green leafy stems, cameo-signed, 6 1/2" h. **$1,323**

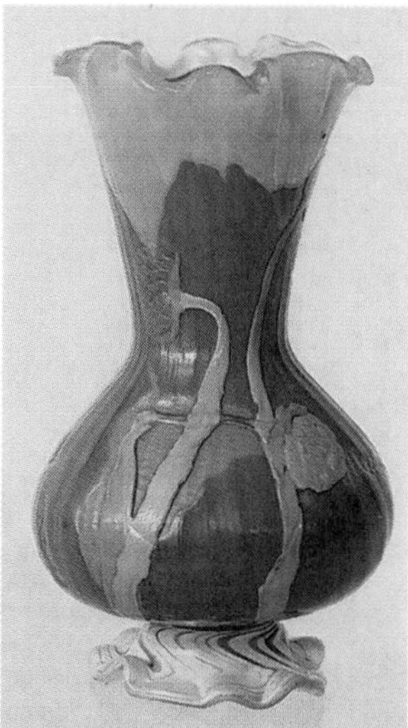

Cameo vase, 10 1/2" h., Marquetry-style, the round ruffled foot supporting a squatty bulbous body tapering to a tall trumpet neck w/a crimped & ruffled rim, mottled creamy white ground overlaid w/brown further overlaid w/white & finely wheelcarved w/ large blossoms on tall leafy stems, engraved signature "Gallè 1900" **$39,675**

Cameo vase, 11" h., wide ovoid body tapering to a short rolled mouth, frosted grey overlaid in amethyst, yellow & blue & cameo-etched w/a continuous landscape of Lake Como w/trees in the foreground, a castle in the mid-ground & the lake & mountains in the distance, cameo signed, ca. 1900 .... **$8,625**

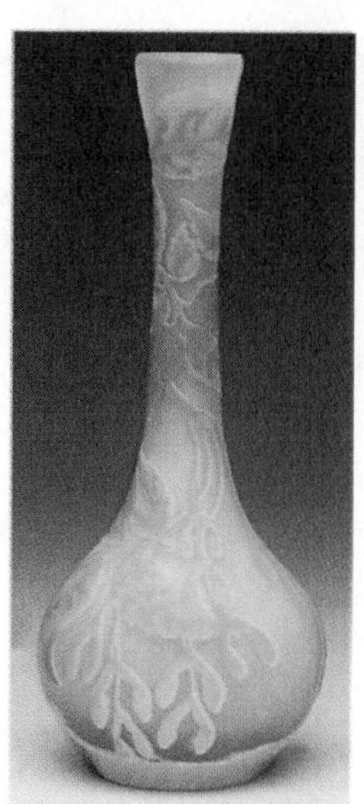

Cameo vase, 15" h., flat-bottomed bulbous spherical lower body tapering sharply to a very tall gently flaring cylindrical neck, mottled salmon pink & frosted white ground overlaid in green & chartreuse & cameo-cut w/long leafy stems & seed pods, signed in cameo on the side **$2,185**

Cameo vase, 17 1/4" h., large ovoid body tapering to a small trumpet neck, clear frosted & peach overlaid w/shades of turquoise & dark blue & etched w/a landscape w/tall trees in the foreground w/a lake & mountains in the distance, cameo signed, ca. 1900 **$10,120**

Cameo vase, 6 3/4" h., banjo-style, bulbous flattened base tapering to a tall slender stick neck w/small cupped rim, frosted pale yellow shaded to dark blue ground overlaid in dark purple & cameo cut around the lower body w/a landscape w/large leafy trees in the foreground & a river & mountains in the distance, cameo signature on the back **$1,725**

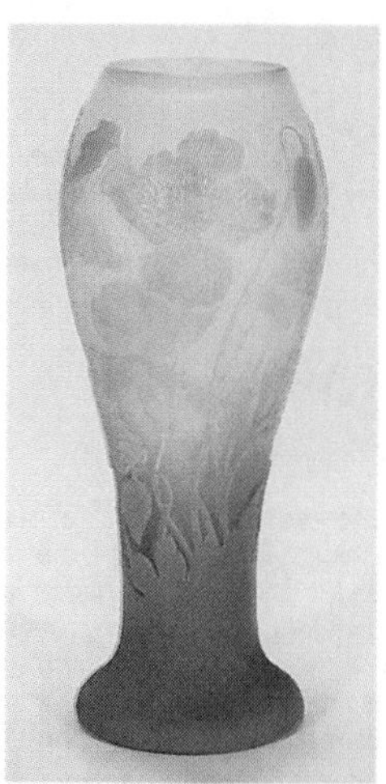

Cameo vase, 7 1/2" h., cushion foot tapering to a large ovoid body w/a flat mouth, frosted white shaded to dark blue ground overlaid in orange, pink & dark green & cameo cut w/a design of large pink poppies above green leafy stems, cameo signature w/star on the side **$1,610**

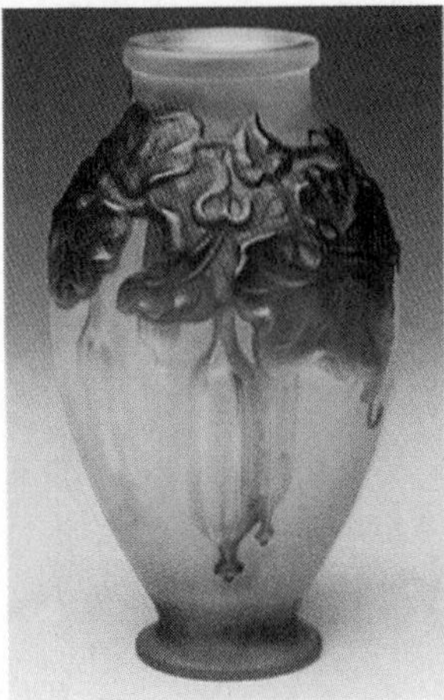

Cameo vase, 7" h., round foot below the ovoid body tapering slightly to the molded flat mouth, mottled citrine yellow & frosted ground w/an applied blown-out design of deep purple leaves suspending long pale pods, molded signature **$5,405**

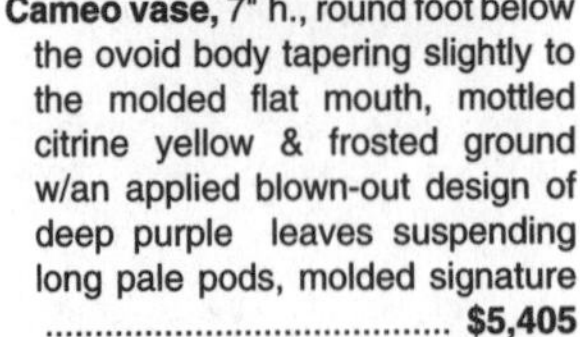

Cameo vase, 7" h., wide swelled & slightly tapering cylindrical body w/ a thin rolled rim, yellow shaded to frosted white background overlaid in brown & green & deeply cameo-cut w/a stylized forest landscape w/ large leafy trees in the foreground, cameo signature on the side **$2,990**

Cameo vase, 8 1/4" h., a round ringed cushion foot supporting a very wide bulbous ovoid body tapering to a short flaring neck, mottled amber & frosted white ground overlaid in dark brown & pale green & cameo-cut w/a landscape of leafy trees around a lake, etched signature on side **$2,300**

Cameo vase, 8 1/8" h., a round cushion foot below the tall slender stick body, shaded pink to white frosted ground overlaid in amethyst & cameo cut w/a cascading wisteria vine, cameo signature on top of the foot **$740**

Cups, clear flat-based cylindrical shape w/an applied twisted rope handle, overall enameled decoration of fleurs-de-lis w/a gilded rim, engraved "E. Gallè Nancy," late 19th c., 2" h., pr. **$345**

Vase, 12" h., "Lion of Lorraine" design, rum-colored blown tapering ovoid body w/a flaring flat rim, raised on three applied rum-colored peg feet & w/two large rigaree bands of rum up the sides & around the rim, finely enameled overall w/scattered flowers in gold, maroon & blue & w/a dark blue griffin near the bottom, signed "E. Gallè Nancy Dèposè" **$2,588**

Pitcher, 9 3/4" h., Marquetry-style, a low squatty round lower body tapering to bell-shaped sides below the high cylindrical neck w/rim spout, marquetry-carved body decorated w/ stylized pink magnolia flowers & green leaves against a lightly martelè clear to white mottled background, long applied peach-stained handle, engraved signature in one of the leaves **$18,400**

Heisey

Numerous types of fine glass were made by A.H. Heisey & Co., Newark, Ohio, from 1895. The company's trademark, an H enclosed within a diamond, has become known to most glass collectors. The company's name and molds were acquired by Imperial Glass Co., Bellaire, Ohio, in 1958, and some pieces have been reissued. The glass listed below consists of miscellaneous pieces and types.

Basket, fruit-type, No. 466, round w/high, arched handle, crystal w/ cutting, 7 1/4" d., 9 1/2" h. .. **$275**

Bell, Victorian Belle, hollow figure of girl made into bell, crystal satin, 4" h. **$98**

Candleholder-vase, one-light, two-piece, Ipswich patt., square foot, flaring rim hung w/twelve prisms, clear, 10" h. **$155**

Candlesticks, toy-size, one-light, Patrician patt., clear, 4 1/2" h., pr....... **$85**

Cruet w/original stopper, Double Rib & Panel patt., low squatty body & squared handle, No. 417, clear, 3 0z. **$52**

Depending on the venue, prices on antiques are seldom firm. Most dealers will not be offended if you ask, "Can you give me a better price on this?" The key is being tactful. Don't expect a dealer to be receptive to an offer of one-fourth of the marked price.

Cruet w/original stopper, oil-type, Yeoman patt., Moongleam, 2 oz. **$80**

Crushed fruit jar, cov., Colonial Pattern No. 352, clear, 10" h. **$295**

Cornucopia-Vase, Crystolite patt., ornate Calcutta overall cutting, notching & crosshatching, signed, 9" h., pr. **$650**

Plate, 8" d., Minuet etching, luncheon, clear **$28**

Punch bowl, spherical, Ridgeleigh patt., clear, 11" d. **$225**

Syrup pitcher, cov., Colonial Panel patt., No. 331, clear w/clear applied handle, marked, 5 1/2" h. **$28**

Consider arriving at an antique market before it opens and get in line. Do a quick walk-through, looking for items that are highest on your want list. After viewing the market quickly the first time, go through again at a deliberate pace. Rather than beginning again from the start, do an about face and view the show back to front. From a different vantage point, you might view something you didn't see the first time.

Dresser set: two 4 oz. cologne bottles & stoppers & a 2 3/4 x 4" rectangular covered box; Ridgeleigh patt., each piece in clear w/ fancy brass filigree mounts, the set **$225**

Punch set, 9 qt. Dr. Johnson punch bowl, six cups & ladle; Plantation patt., clear, 8 pcs. **$1,100**

Toothpick holder, Pineapple & Fan patt., green **$295**

Vase, 5" h., cornucopia-shaped, Warwick patt., clear (ILLUS. front with larger Warwick vase) **$48**

Water set: 63 oz. pitcher & four tumblers; Renaissance etching, clear, tumblers 3 3/4" h., pitcher 7 1/2" h., the set (ILLUS. of pitcher) **$250-300**

Higgins Glass

Fused glass, an "old craft for modern tastes" enjoyed a mid-20th century revival through the work of Chicago-based artists Frances and Michael Higgins of the Higgins Glass Studio. Although known for thousands of years, fusing had, by the 1940s, been abandoned in favor of glassblowing. A meticulous craft, fusing can best be described as the creation of a "glass sandwich." A design is either drawn with colored enamels or pieced with glass segments on a piece of enamel-coated glass. Another piece of enameled glass is placed over this. The "sandwich" is then placed on a mold and heated in a kiln, with the glass "slumping" to the shape of the mold. When complete, the interior design is fused between the outer glass layers. Additional layers are often utilized, accentuating the visual depth. Sensing that fused glass was a marketable commodity, the Higginses opened their studio in 1948 and applied the fusing technique to a wide variety of items: tableware such as bowls, plates, and servers; housewares, ranging from clocks and lamps to ashtrays and candleholders; and purely decorative items, such as mobiles and jewelry. With its arresting mix of geometric and curved lines and bold use of color, Higgins glass transformed the ordinary into decor accent pieces both vibrant and exciting.

Unlike many of their contemporaries, the Higginses received national exposure thanks to an association with Chicago industrial manufacturer Dearborn Glass Company. This collaboration, lasting from 1957 through 1964, resulted in the mass marketing of "higginsware" worldwide. Since nearly every piece carried the lower-case signature "higgins," name recognition was both immediate and enduring.

The Dearborn demand for new Higgins pieces resulted in more than 75 identifiable production patterns with such buyer-enticing names as "Stardust," "Arabesque," and "Barbaric Jewels." Objects created in these patterns included ashtrays of every size (4" "Dinner Dwarfs" to 15" jumbo models), "rondelay" room dividers and an extensive line of tableware. (As evidenced by Dearborn promotional postcards, complete dining tables could literally be set with Higgins glass).

In 1965, the Higginses briefly moved their base of operations to Haeger Potteries before opening their own studio in Riverside, Illinois, where it has been located since 1966. Although Michael Higgins died in 1999 and Frances Higgins in 2004, the Studio today continues under the leadership of longtime artistic associates Louise and Jonathan Wimmer. New pieces celebrate and expand on the traditions and techniques of the past. Higgins pieces created from 1948 until 1957 are engraved on the reverse with the signature "higgins" or the artist's complete name. A raised "dancing man" logo was added in 1951. Pieces created at Dearborn or Haeger (1957-65) bear a gold "higgins" signature on the surface or a signature in the colorway. The marking since 1966 has been an engraved "higgins" on the reverse of an object, with the occasional addition of the artist's name. Pieces produced since the death of Frances Higgins are signed "higgins studio."

Once heralded as "an exclamation point in your decorating scheme," Higgins glass continues, nearly 60 years since its inception, to enchant collectors with its zest and variety.

References on Higgins glass include the Schiffer books Higgins: Poetry in Glass (2005), and Higgins: Adventures in Glass (1997), both by Donald-Brian Johnson and Leslie Pina. Photos for this category are by Dr. Pina.

The Higgins Glass Studio is located at 33 East Quincy Street, Riverside, IL 60546 (708-447-2787), www.higginsglass.com.

Price ranges given are general estimates covering all available patterns produced at Dearborn Glass Company and Haeger Potteries (1957-1965). The low end of the scale applies to the most commonly found patterns (e.g., "Mandarin," "Siamese Purple"), the upper end to those found less frequently (e.g., "Gemspread," "Carousel").

Ashtray, circular, scalloped edge, Stardust patt. only, 11 1/2" d. **$150-200**

Candleholders, Petal patt., 4 1/2" h., pr. **$150-225**

Watch for bargains. A dealer who specializes in a particular category may underprice an item in a different category.

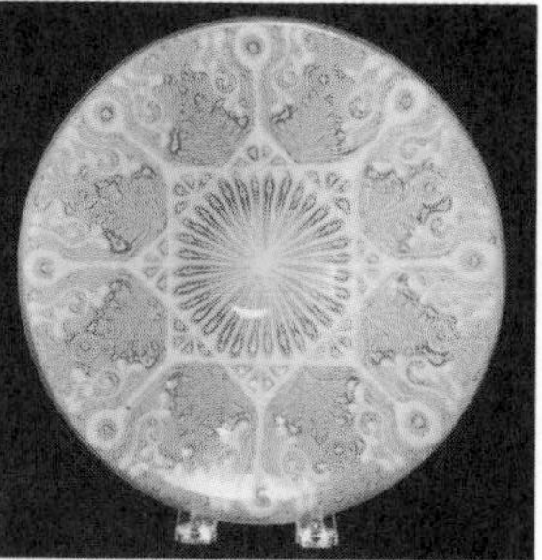

Bowl, 9" d., round, controlled bubble pattern, green & yellow, by Frances Higgins **$700-750**

Clock, wall or table, gold & black, General Electric, 1954, 8" d. **$900-1,000**

Jewelry set: necklace & earrings; coral glass nuggets & brass spirals, the set **$900-1,000**

Plaque, oblong, "Green-Eyed Snowy," cat face design, by Frances Higgins, 4 1/2 x 7" **$350-400**

Plaque, rectangular, "Ugly Duchess A" patt., by Michael Higgins, framed, 12 x 20" **$3,500-3,750**

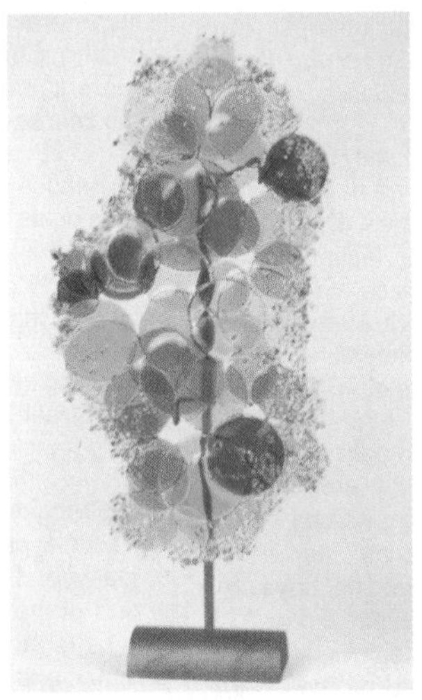

Sculpture, "Bubbles" patt., multi-colored glass circles & chipped glass, brass stem, by Frances Higgins, 13" h. **$1,500-1,700**

Vase, 11" h., 14" d., oversized dropout style, multicolored **$1,500-1,750**

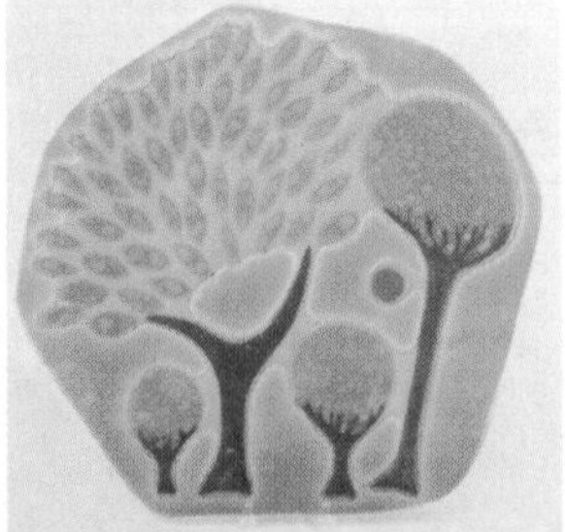

Platter, 15" l., irregular shape, "Summer Trees" patt., by Frances Higgins **$3,500-3,750**

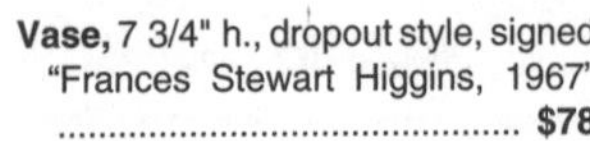

Vase, 7 3/4" h., dropout style, signed "Frances Stewart Higgins, 1967" **$78**

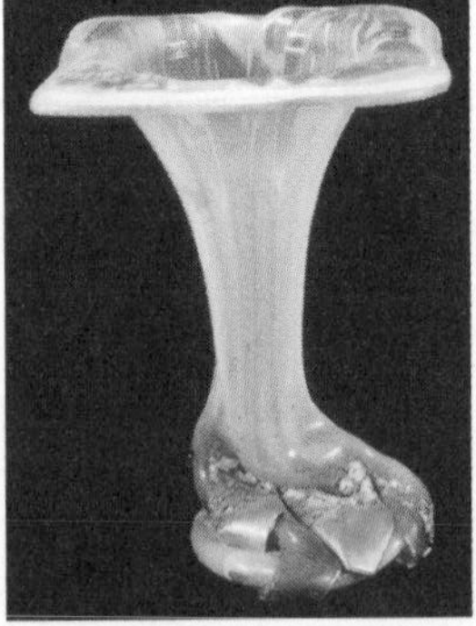

Imperial

From 1902 until 1984 Imperial Glass of Bellaire, Ohio, produced hand made glass. Early pressed glass production often imitated cut glass and may bear the raised "NUCUT" mark in the interior center. In the second decade of the 1900s Imperial was one of the dominant manufacturers of iridescent or Carnival glass. When glass collecting gained popularity in the 1970s, Imperial again produced Carnival and a line of multicolored slag glass. Imperial purchased molds from closing glass houses and continued many lines popularized by others including Central, Heisey and Cambridge. These reissues may cause confusion but they were often marked.

Candlewick

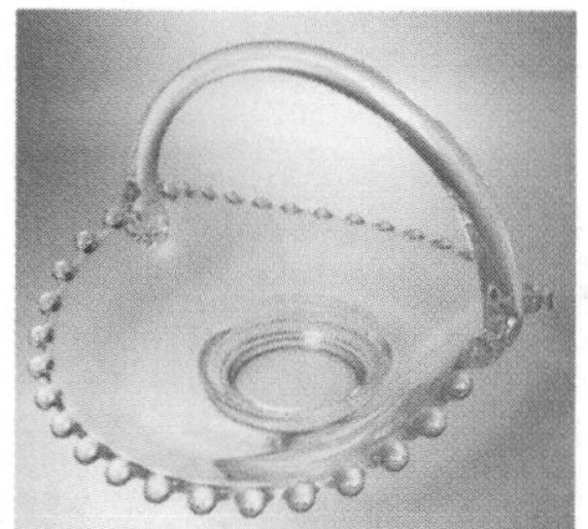

Basket, No. 400/40/0, clear, 6 1/2" l., 4 1/2" h. **$38**

Cake stand & dome cover, No. 400/10D, beaded stem, cover made by West Virginia Glass Specialty & sold w/the stand, cover 10" d., stand 11" d., 2 pcs. **$135**

Compote, 10" h., crimped, three-bead stem, No. 400/103, clear w/h.p. pink roses & blue ribbons **$260**

Compotes are footed bowls with stems used to serve fruit, nuts, etc. They are also known as comports.

Cruet w/stopper, No. 400/274, flat, bulbous bottom, clear, 4 oz. **$52**

Candleholder, No. 400/40C, flower-type w/crimped rim, clear, 5" h. **$47**

Jam set: oval tray w/two cov. marmalade jars w/ladles; No. 400/1589, clear, 5 pcs. **$125**

Punch set, punch bowl, underplate, 12 cups & ladle; No. 400/20, bowl & cups w/cut Mallard patt., 15 pcs. **$650**

Vase, two open beaded arms, crimped top, clear **$38**

Cream soup bowl wi/underplate, two-handled, No. 400/50, clear, 5" d. bowl & 6 3/4" d. underplate, 2 pcs. **$75**

Relish dish, three-part, three-toed, No. 400/208, clear, 9" l. **$98**

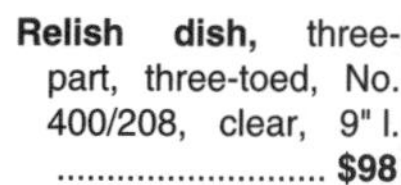

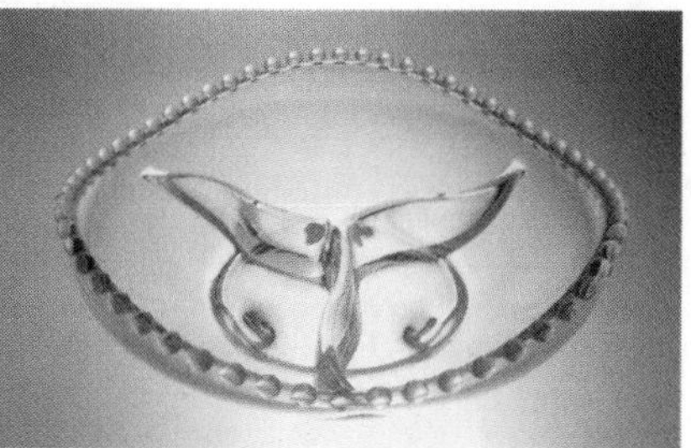

Cape Cod

Candlestick, two-light, No. 160/100, crystal **$85**

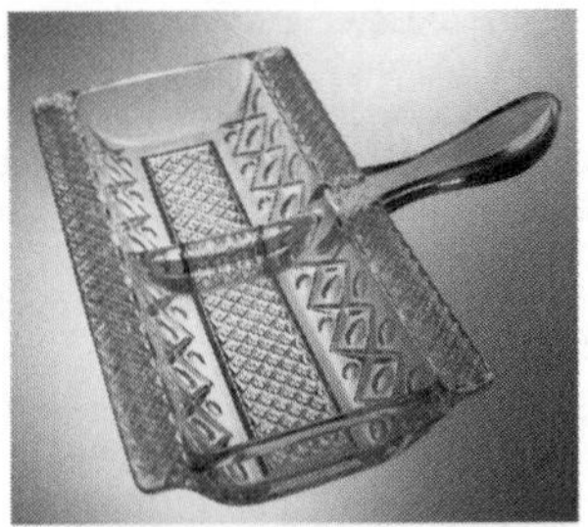

Cigarette server/relish, handled, two-part, No. 160/223, clear, 8 1/2" l. **$40**

Finger bowl, No. 1604 1/2A, ruby, 4 1/2" d. **$24**

Goblet, dinner, ball stem, Azalea Pink, 11 oz. **$17**

Pepper mill & salt shaker, chrome base & covers, No. 16/236 & 160/238, clear, pr. **$55**

Pitcher w/ice lip, No. 160/24, clear, 60 oz., 2 qt............................ **$92**

Pitcher, No. 160/239, clear, 60 oz. **$95**

Plate, 16" d., cupped, No. 160/20V, clear....................................... **$50**

Punch set: punch bowl, underplate & twelve cups; clear, 1 gal., 14 pcs. **$220**

Salt & pepper shakers w/original tops, original factory label, No. 160/251, clear, pr. **$20**

Sherbet, tall, No. 1602, Verde green, 6 oz. **$15**

Sundae, No. 1602, ball stem, clear, 4" h. **$7**

Tumbler, ced tea, No. 1602, amber, 6" h. **$15**

Tom & Jerry punchbowl, footed, No. 160/200, clear **$290**

Wine carafe & stopper, footed, handled, No. 160/185, crystal **$220**

Free-Hand Ware

Lamp, electric, cast metal foot & cap, tapering ovoid glass body in iridescent orange w/cobalt blue Hanging Hearts patt., 10" h. **$1,650**

Vase, 8" h., flat flaring foot & tall slender gently flaring cylindrical body, iridescent cobalt blue exterior & orange interior **$235**

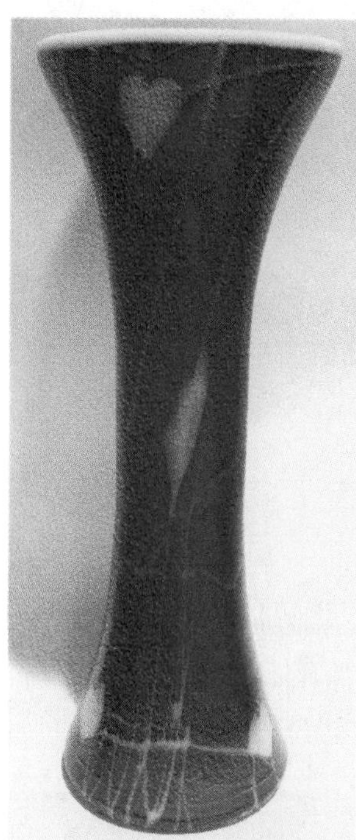

Vase, 10 1/2" h., tall slender waisted shape w/flaring top, iridescent cobalt blue exterior w/ white Hanging Heart decoration **$1,175**

Miscellaneous Patterns & Lines

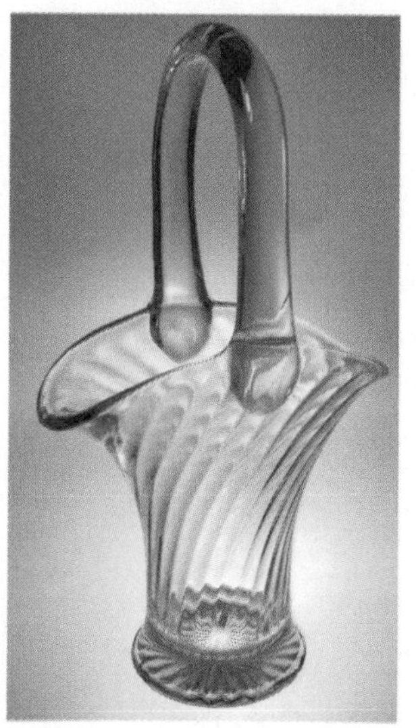

Basket, Twisted Optic patt., pale blue, 10" h. **$85**

Cake plate, hexagonal w/two open handles, Brocaded Daffodils etching, green, 7" w. **$49**

Open handles have an open space that allow fingers to wrap around to provide a better grip. Closed handles are solid and have no place for fingers to wrap around the handle.

Candlestick, single-light, Cathay Line, figural Candle Servant (female), No. 5035, clear satin **$195**

Decanter w/crystal mushroom stopper, No. 451, spherical body w/ringed foot & cylindrical neck, ruby **$120**

Tumbler, footed, Parisian Provincial patt., milk glass stem & foot & amethyst bowl, 7 oz. **$22**

Epergne, one-lily, two-piece, Pattern #1950/196, Doeskin (milk glass), 9" d., 11" h. **$78**

Goblet, water, Chroma patt. No. 123, Burgandy, 5 1/2" h. **$24**

Plate, 8" w., Beaded Block patt., pink **$20**

Pitcher, Reeded patt., No. 701, green w/clear applied handle **$80**

Punch bowl & base, Broken Arches patt., No. 733, clear, 12 1/2" d., 10 1/2" h. **$65**

Vase, 8" h., pressed, trumpet-shaped, Pattern #G 505, gold on crystal **$28**

Lalique

R. Lalique France No. 3152

R LALIQUE
FRANCE

R. LALIQUE
FRANCE

Fine glass, which includes numerous extraordinary molded articles, has been made by the glasshouse established by Renè Lalique early in the 20th century in France. The firm was carried on by his son, Marc, until his death in 1977 and is now headed by Marc's daughter, Marie-Claude. All Lalique glass is marked, usually on or near the bottom, with either an engraved or molded signature. Unless otherwise noted, we list only those pieces marked "R. Lalique," produced before the death of Renè Lalique in 1945.

Bowl, 14 1/4" d., "Martigues," wide flattened shallow form molded w/ a wide band of curved swimming fish, clear opalescent, molded "R. Lalique" **$2,868**

Lamp, table model, "Poisson" patt., the frosted clear upright disk-form base molded w/a pair of large fish framed in chrome on a rectangular chrome foot, a long narrow rectangular arched & reeded half-round frosted clear shade, introduced in 1931, etched mark "R. Lalique France," 15 1/8" w., 12 1/2" h. **$42,000**

Plates, 8 1/4" d., clear w/a flanged rim, the center molded w/a wide frosted stylized leaf, signed "Lalique France," mid-20th c., set of 12 .... **$323**

Vase, 10 1/4" h., "Archers," wide ovoid body in opalescent cased in butterscotch yellow, molded in relief w/archers shooting at flying birds, short neck, introduced in 1921, marked "R. Lalique" in script & molded **$21,600**

Vase, 10" h., "Perruches," wide ovoid body tapering to a low molded neck, molded overall w/pairs of lovebirds perched on blossoming branches, electric blue, introduced in 1919, engraved R. Lalique mark **$13,145**

Vase, 8 3/4" h., "Languedoc," footed squatty bulbous form w/a wide low flat molded mouth, molded overall w/a bold design of overlapping pointed scales, frosted green, introduced in 1929, engraved R. Lalique mark **$21,510**

Vase, 9 1/2" h., "Bacchantes," wide tapering cylindrical body molded in high-relief w/a continuous band of nude maidens in various poses, textured clear ground w/ amber patination, signed in block letters "R. LALIQUE - France" **$8,338**

Vase, 9 1/4" h., "Damiers," footed widely flaring trumpet-form body, clear etched w/a heavily textured background & raised concentric rings composed of small squares enameled in black, introduced in 1935, stenciled R. Lalique mark .. **$5,975**

Vase, 9 3/8" h., "Poissons," footed spherical body topped by a short cylindrical neck w/a flattened rim, molded overall w/large swimming fish, introduced in 1921, frosted orange, engraved & "R. Lalique France No. 925" & also w/molded mark .. **$11,353**

Vase, 10" d., "Nemours," thick deep rounded frosted & enameled sides molded on the exterior w/graduated bands of stylized inset flowerheads, each w/a glossy black enameled center, inscribed "Lalique - France," reissued model after 1945 .... **$632**

Vase, 8 1/4" h., "Ronsard," frosted clear spherical body w/a small rolled neck flanked by applied ringed shoulder handles each molded in the center w/a nude seated woman supporting the wreath ring, traces of original greyish patine, molded mark, introduced in 1926 (rim chip)......... **$1,610**

Vase, 6 1/2" h., "Ormeaux," frosted deep amber spherical body w/a small trumpet neck, molded overall w/a design of overlapping leaves, traces of white patine, inscribed "R. Lalique France No. 984," small rim chip, ca. 1926................ **$1,265**

Vase, 7 1/8" h., "Soucis," ovoid body molded in medium- and low-relief w/ stylized flowers & leaves growing from a meandering vine, on a low tapering circular foot, flaring inverted conical neck, frosted blue, etched "R. LALIQUE," inscribed "France," introduced in 1930 (two rim chips) **$3,220**

Libbey

In 1878, William L. Libbey obtained a lease on the New England Glass Company of Cambridge, Massachusetts, changing the name to the New England Glass Works, W.L. Libbey and Son, Proprietors. After his death in 1883, his son, Edward D. Libbey, continued to operate the company at Cambridge until 1888, when the factory was closed. Edward Libbey moved to Toledo, Ohio, and set up the company subsequently known as Libbey Glass Co. During the 1880s, the firm's master technician, Joseph Locke, developed the now much desired colored art glass lines of Agata, Amberina, Peach Blow and Pomona. Renowned for its cut glass of the Brilliant Period (see CUT GLASS), the company continues in operation today as Libbey Glassware, a division of Owens-Illinois, Inc.

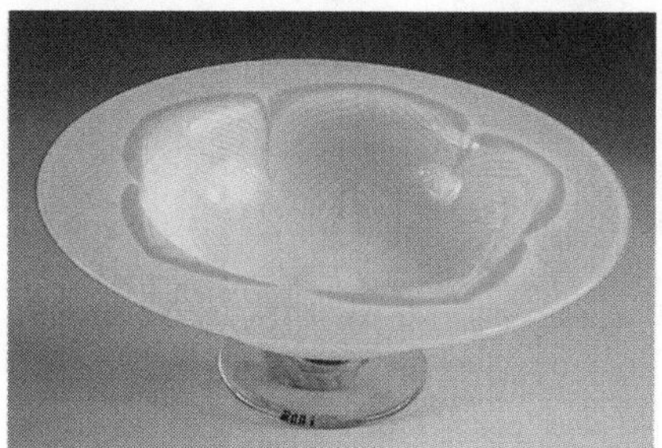

Bowl, 12" d., 4 1/4" h., a wide shallow bowl w/a flattened rim, white ground decorated in the center w/a lime green pulled feather design, raised on an applied clear pedestal foot, signed **$210**

Champagnes, a wide flaring bowl on a slender tapering stem & round foot, wheel-cut & polished crystal in the "Patrician" patt., each w/Libbey mark, early 20th c., 6" h., set of eight (ILLUS. of part) **$300-500**

Cocktails, Silhouette patt., clear bowl on a moonstone figural kangaroo stem, ca. 1930s, one w/very slight rim chip, 6" h., set of four **$288**

Maize bowl, 7 3/4" d., 3 5/8" h., iridized clear w/ light blue-stained leaves, minor inner rim flakes **$165**

In 1903, Libbey employee Michael Owen invented a glass making machine that dramatically increased Libbey's production and profits.

Maize cruet w/original stopper, tall ovoid body w/tricorner rim, applied clear handle, pale iridescent ground w/pale blue husks, pointed corn-molded stopper w/shallow chip at tip, 7" h. **$605**

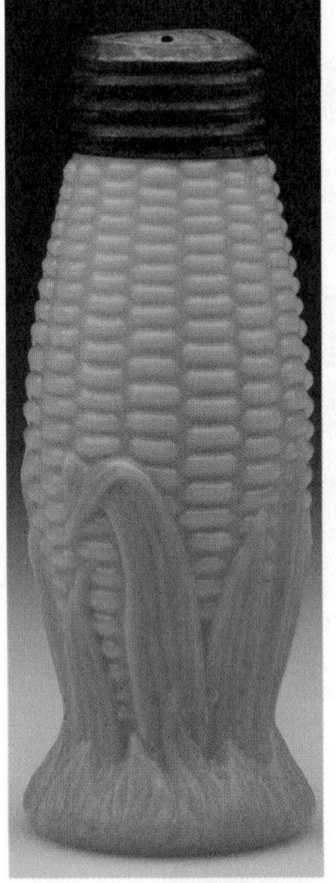

Maize salt shaker, original top, creamy opaque w/yellow husks, slight damage to metal top, 4" h. **$143**

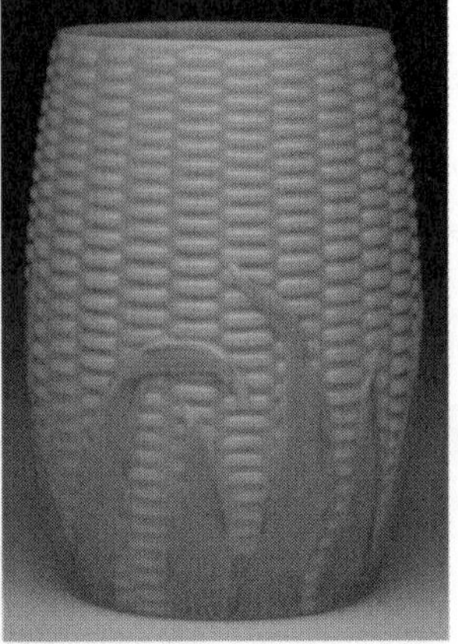

Maize spooner, creamy opaque w/ yellow husks, 4 1/4" h. **$132**

Punch cup, pressed clear petal-form marked "World's Fair 1893," impressed "Libbey Glass Co., Toledo, Ohio - World's Fair" inside **$75**

Stemware set, two champagnes, nine red wines, a water goblet, eight white wines, seven highballs & one liqueur; Art Deco design, clear w/a drawn ovoid bowl, fluted rectangular stem & circular foot, etched Libbey mark, the group **$2,645**

Maize toothpick holder, creamy opaque w/yellow leaves trimmed in gold, 2 1/4" h. **$345**

Table service, six wine goblets w/ polar bear stems, four candlesticks w/camel stems, one compote w/giraffe stem; Silhouette patt., opalescent stems on colorless glassware, each piece stamped "Libbey," designed by Nash, compote 7" h., the group ... **$2,300**

Vase, 10" h., trumpet-form, clear ribbed body w/green "zipper" design, stamped "Libbey" **$165**

Toothpick holder, Little Lobe patt., opaque white w/pink shaded rim & enameled floral decoration, satin finish, 2 1/4" h. **$110**

Vase, 8 1/2" h., footed gently flaring cylindrical crystal body w/internal optic thumbprints alternating w/ fronds of laurel leaves, the exterior decorated w/thin lilac threading down the sides, Nash design, acid-stamped mark on base............ **$374**

Mary Gregory

Glass enameled in white with silhouette-type figures, primarily of children, is now termed "Mary Gregory" and was attributed to the Boston and Sandwich Glass Company. However, recent research has proven conclusively that this was not decorated by Mary Gregory, nor was it made at the Sandwich plant. Miss Gregory was employed by Boston and Sandwich Glass Company as a decorator; however, records show her assignment was the painting of naturalistic landscape scenes on larger items such as lamps and shades, but never the charming children for which her name has become synonymous. Further, in the inspection of fragments from the factory site, no paintings of children were found.

It is now known that all wares collectors call "Mary Gregory" originated in Bohemia beginning in the late 19th century and were extensively exported to England and the United States well into this century.

For further information, see The Glass Industry in Sandwich, Volume #4 by Raymond E. Barlow and Joan E. Kaiser, and the book Mary Gregory Glassware, 1880-1900 by R. & D. Truitt.

Dress box w/hinged cover, squatty bulbous Prussian blue optic-ribbed base decorated w/a band of white enamel dots, the rim & cover w/brass fittings, the low domed cover decorated w/a white enamel scene of a young Victorian boy in a garden holding a butterfly net, colored enamel face & hands, late 19th c., 4 1/4" d., 2 3/8" h. **$138**

Pitcher, 11" h., tankard-type, gently tapering cylindrical green body w/an arched rim & pinched spout, applied long clear handle, decorated across the front in white enamel w/the standing figure of a Victorian girl in a garden, late 19th c. **$125-150**

Vases, 17 1/2" h., cranberry body w/a flaring scalloped rim, each decorated w/the white enamel portrait of a Victorian lady standing in a garden, band of white beads around the neck, attributed to Mulhaus, Bohemia, ca. 1885, facing pr. ... **$2,070**

Vases, 8" h., cylindrical ring-type, mottled white & clear cased in light blue, white enameled figure of a Victorian girl in a garden, Muhlhausfactory, Bohemia, late 19th c., facing pr. **$431**

McKee

McKee

The McKee name has been associated with glass production since 1834, first producing window glass and later bottles. In the 1850s a new factory was established in Pittsburgh, Pennsylvania, for production of flint and pressed glass. The plant was relocated in Jeanette, Pennsylvania, in 1888 and operated there as an independent company almost continuously until 1951, when it sold out to Thatcher Glass Manufacturing Company. Many types of collectible glass were produced by McKee through the years including Depression, Pattern, Milk Glass and a variety of utility kitchenwares. See these categories for additional listings.

Kitchenwares

Flour shaker w/original metal lid, Skokie Green **$75**

Flour shaker, original metal cover, Seville Yellow **$37**

Measuring cup, Custard, four-cup **$55**

Reamer, butterscotch, embossed "SUNKIST," marked "Pat. No. 18764 Made in USA," 6" d. **$850**

Rock Crystal Pattern

Bowl, 8 1/2" d., center handle, cupped, plain edge, ruby **$195**

Bowl, 10 1/2" d., salad, scalloped edge, pink **$55**

Candleholders, two-light, cobalt blue, pr. **$345**

Candlesticks, clear, 8 1/2" h., pr. **$45**

Candy dish, cov., green, 7" d. **$85**

Candleholders, orange slag, 5" d., pr. **$375**

Candlestick, one-light tall, amber, 8 1/4" h. **$62**

Cup & saucer, scalloped edge on saucer, ruby, pr. (ILLUS. w/plate) **$90**

Miscellaneous Patterns & Pieces

Creamer & sugar, child's, French Ivory, Laurel patt. **$45-55**

Clock, Tambour Art-style, blue, 14" l. **$550**

Mayonnaise set: footed bowl, ladle & underplate; Brocade etching, pink, 3 pcs. **$75**

Sherbet, Clico patt., green bowl on square black base **$38**

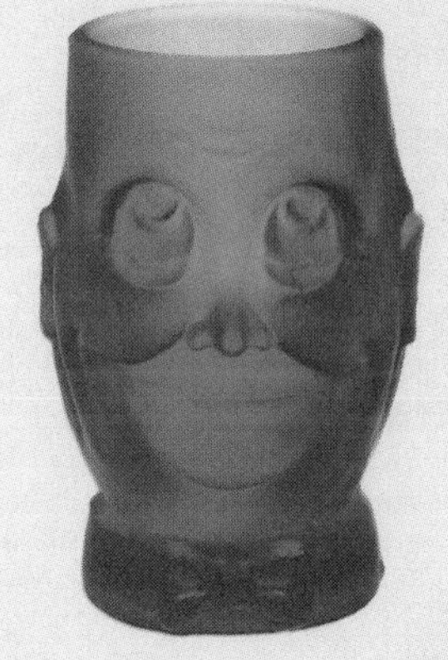

Tumbler, "Jolly Golfer," missing cap, green, 4" h. **$48**

One way to distinguish antique glass from reproductions is by color. Generally colors in new glass are harsher than the old, which are mellow.

Vase, 8" h., Art Deco-style triangular "Art Nude" design, Skokie Green **$375**

Whiskey set: "Jolly Golfer," figural decanter in the form of a stocky male golfer wearing knickers & cap & grasping a golf club, cap form the stopper, together w/four matching head-shaped glasses w/cap-shaped lids, frosted pink, marked "Pat. Applied For" on smooth base of decanter, some tiny checks & bruise, late 1930s, decanter 11 5/8" h., the set **$616**

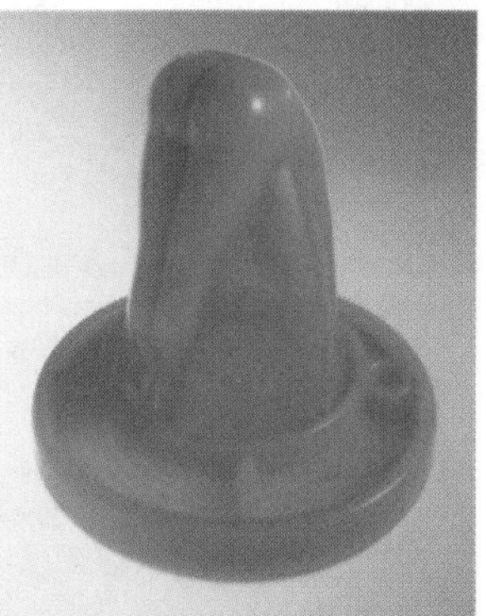

Whiskey tumbler & base, Bottoms-Up patt., Skokie Green, satin finish, 2 pcs. **$275**

Milk Glass

Opaque white glass, or "opal," has been called "milk-white glass," perhaps to distinguish it from transparent or "clear-white glass." Resembling fine white porcelain, it was viewed as an inexpensive substitute. Opacity is obtained by adding bone ash or oxide of tin to clear molten glass. By the addition of various coloring agents, the opaque mixture can be turned into blue milk glass, or pink, yellow, green, caramel, even black milk glass. Collectors of milk glass now accept not only the white variety but virtually any opaque color and color mixtures, including slag or marbled glass. It has been made in numerous forms and shapes in this country and abroad from about the first quarter of the 19th century. Many of the items listed here were also made in colored opaque glass, which collectors call blue or green or black "milk glass." It is still being produced, and there are many reproductions of earlier pieces. Pieces here are all-white unless otherwise noted.

Animal covered dish, Boar seated on basketweave base, 4 1/2" h. **$468**

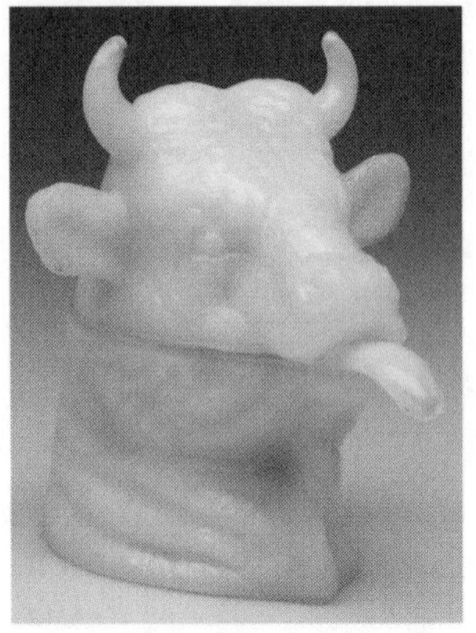

Animal covered dish, Bull's Head mustard jar, w/separate tongue spoon, no paint, Atterbury .. **$132**

Animal covered dish, Bull's Head mustard jar, w/separate tongue spoon, one original glass eye, blue opaque, rim chip on lid, Atterbury, 4 1/4" h. **$187**

Animal covered dish, Cat on lacy base, original blue glass eyes, Atterbury, 1880s **$176**

Animal covered dish, Cow on oval barrel-type base w/end tab handles, probably French, 5 1/4" l. **$176**

Animal covered dish, Cow on split-ribbed base, 5 1/2" l. **$231**

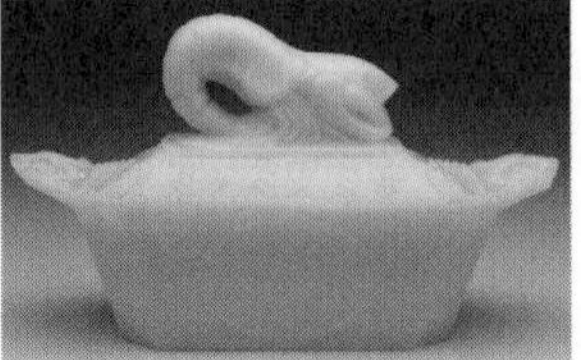

Animal covered dish, Crawfish on two-handled oblong base, Westmoreland Specialty Co., flake on one bead, overall 7 1/2" l. **$88**

Animal covered dish, Deer on fallen tree base, marked by Flaccus, flake on base rim, 6 3/4" l. **$88**

Animal covered dish, Dog (Chow) on split rib base, McKee, 4" h. **$99**

Animal covered dish, Dove on split-ribbed base, signed "McKee," one flake & annealing lines on rim of base, 5 1/4" l. **$220**

Cake stand, domed ribbed foot & figural lady's hand stem supporting a round starburst-decorated plate, 11 1/2" d., 6 1/4" h. **$55**

Covered dish, Fainting Couch, good green & brown paint, very good, 5" l. **$165**

Jar, cov., tall Owl, original glass eyes, Atterbury, 7" h. ... **$125-130**

Animal covered dish, Swan w/ raised wings & replaced glass eyes on lacy-edged base, Atterbury, 9 1/2" l. **$143**

Covered dish, Dewey on Battleship base, 5 1/2" l. **$88**

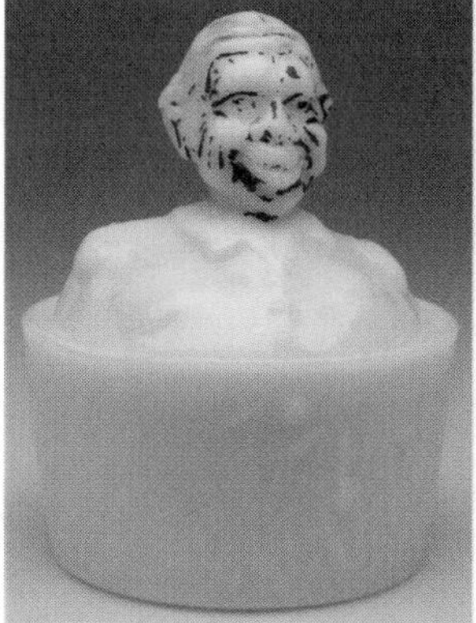

Covered dish, Mammy Head on round rush base, remnants of black paint on head, very minor flaws, 4" d., 4 3/4" h. **$523**

Models of dogs, Mantel Dogs, recumbent animal on an oval serrated base, attributed to England, 7" l., 5" h., pr....... **$1,700**

Plate, 7 1/2" d., Three Owls patt., looped border halfway around plate, Westmoreland Specialty Company, ca. 1901 .... **$48**

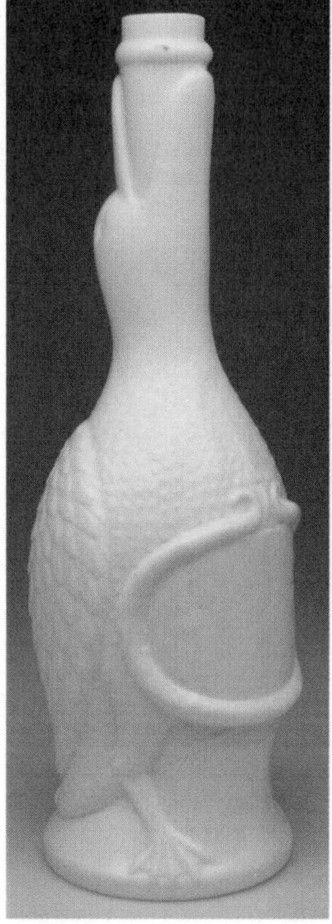

Bottle, Duck, upright bird w/oval panel on the breast, Atterbury patent, sliver flake on lip, 11 1/2" h. **$143**

Water set: tankard-type pitcher & six tumblers; blue opaque, Scroll patt., Challinor, Taylor & Company, 1880s, 7 pcs. **$187**

Morgantown (Old Morgantown)

Morgantown, West Virginia, was the site where a glass firm named the Morgantown Glass Works began in the late 19th century, but the company reorganized in 1903 to become the Economy Tumbler Company, a name it retained until 1929. By the 1920s the firm was producing a wider range of better quality and colorful glass tablewares; to reflect this fact, it resumed its earlier name, Morgantown Glass Works, in 1929. Today its many quality wares of the Depression era are growing in collector demand.

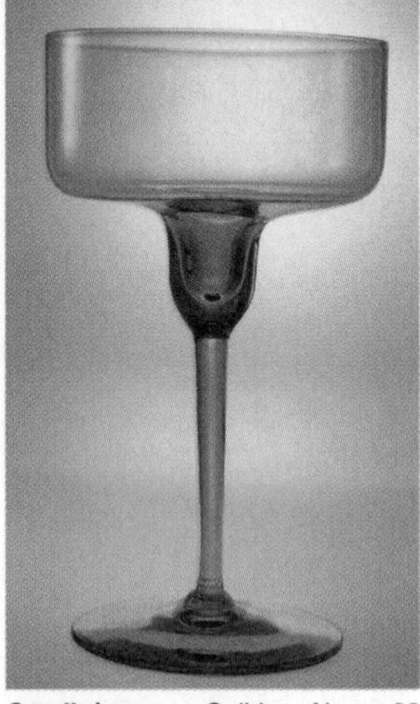

Candle/vase, Guild, No. 83 Patrician, Pineapple (deep yellow), 8" h. **$36**

Candlestick, No. 7640 Art Moderne, one-light, clear stem & foot, Ritz Blue socket, 4 1/4" h............ **$200**

Compote, cov., 4 7/8" h., No. 7801 Cumberland, Ebony w/green foot & finial **$475**

Goblet, Tiburon (No. 7634) blank w/ Westchester Rose cutting, water, Anna Rose color, 9 oz. **$48**

Goblet, water, Queen Anne shape, Sunrise Medallion etching, crystal **$72**

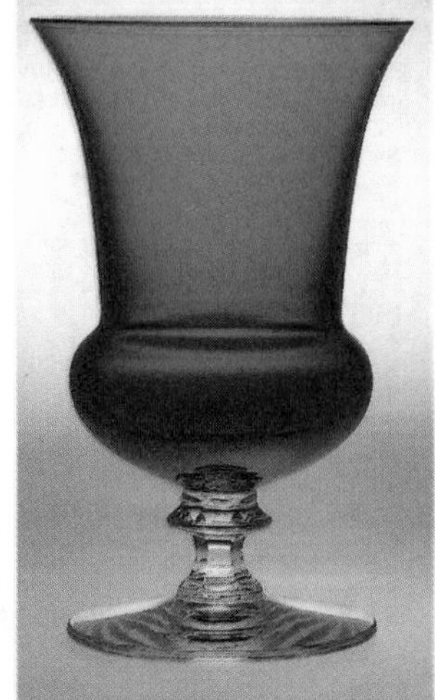

Tumbler, No. 7682 Ramona, footed iced tea, Stiegel Green **$45**

Mt. Washington

A wide diversity of glass was made by the Mt. Washington Glass Company of New Bedford, Massachusetts, between 1869 and 1900. It was succeeded in 1900 by the Pairpoint Corporation. Miscellaneous types are listed below.

Bowl, miniature, 2 3/4" d., 2 1/4" h., squatty melon-lobed shape w/a flat rim, satin opal w/shaded pink rim, decorated w/simple polychrome florals, enamel-beaded rim **$50-75**

Box w/hinged cover, molded colorless round swirled form decorated in the Royal Flemish manner w/ dancing flamingos, gilt-metal hinged rims, 7" d., 4" h. (wear, soiled lining) **$3,450**

Cameo compote, 4 7/8" d., 3 3/4" h., round gold-banded alabaster white foot & baluster-form stem supporting the wide shallow bowl in alabaster white cased on the interior in pink & carved w/a leafy scroll rim band & cluster of central stylized blossoms, gilt rim band, slight gold wear **$259**

Cracker jar w/silver plate rim, cover & bail handle, "Colonial Ware," the squatty bulbous white opaque body decorated at the front w/an oblong reserve of a Colonial couple dancing, framed by gold scrolls, pale cream background, metal fittings marked "MW 4419," base numbered "520," 6" h. **$316**

Cracker jar, cov., barrel-shaped, shaded pink & creamy white ground decorated w/delicate flowering branches, silver plate rim w/crimped edge, domed cover & arched bail swing handle, silver w/Pairpoint logo, slight wear to silver plate, 7" h. **$345**

Cracker jar w/silver plate rim, cover & bail handle, mold-blown squatty tapering round base w/ small scrolls around the bottom, pale yellow background h.p. w/ large pink & white blossoms & green leaves, gold-washed metal fittings marked "MW 4436," base marked "3930/230," 5 3/4" h. **$345**

Cracker jar, cov., barrel-shaped, cased rose satin exterior decorated overall w/pale blue blossoms outlined in yellow enamel, white interior, silver plate rim, floral-embossed domed cover & twisted rope bail handle, 7 1/2" h...... **$523**

Cracker jar w/silver plate rim, cover & bail handle, barrel-shaped, satin fired-on pale pink to white ground decorated w/ color enameled pansies, silver plate mounts marked "MW - 4404," base marked "3926," 6" h. **$468**

Rose bowl, eight-crimp rim, spherical, fired-on Burmese-like ground w/satin finish enameled w/yellow, pink & white chrysanthemums, pontil marked w/No. 617, 6 1/4" d., 5" h. **$231**

Rose bowl, eight-crimp rim, spherical, peach to white ground w/a satin finish, enameled w/scattered small blue violets, polished pontil w/No. 616, 7" d., 6" h. **$154**

Sugar shaker w/original silver plate cap, egg-shaped, unfired Burmese h.p. w/white & yellow daisies on green leaves & stems, 4" h. **$575**

Sugar shaker w/original silver plate cap, fig-shaped, unfired Burmese w/an overall h.p. decoration of tiny blue, pink & yellow blossoms, 4" h. **$2,185**

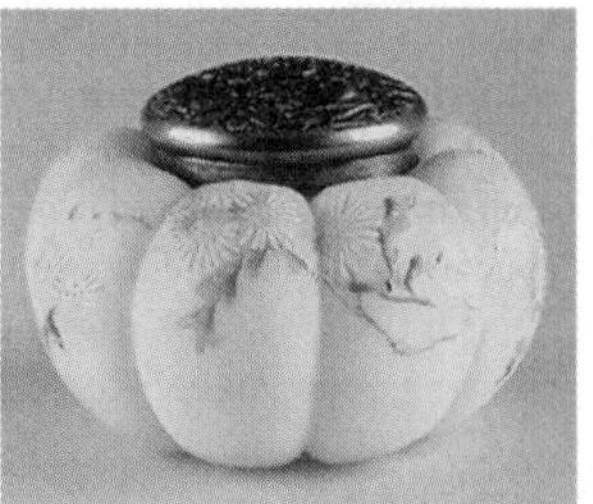

Sugar shaker w/original silver plate cap, tomato-shaped, opaque white w/a pink band around the top & delicate h.p. floral sprigs, 4" d., 2 1/4" h. **$480**

Scent bottle w/original stopper, milk white ground w/an overall decoration of color enameled florals, acid-etched on the base "Trademark of Mt. Washington Glass Co.," late 19th c., 9" h. **$116**

Toothpick holder, transfer-printed scene of three Brownies in a group on front & a Brownie dressed as an Indian w/hatchet on the reverse, light blue shaded to white (very minor flake on rim)................**$250**

Tumbler, cylindrical, Colonial Ware line w/a white glossy ground decorated around the body w/two raised gold bows suspending garlands of assorted flowers, crown & wreath mark on bottom, 3 3/4" h. **$550**

Tazza, cornflower blue bowl w/ engraved floral decoration, silver plate pedestal base w/three dolphin-shaped feet, signed **$450**

Vase, 8" h., eight-ribbed body w/a flared rim, colored base w/green thistle decoration outlined in gold in the Verona manner........... **$201**

A tazza is a shallow cup or bowl on a classical pedestal.

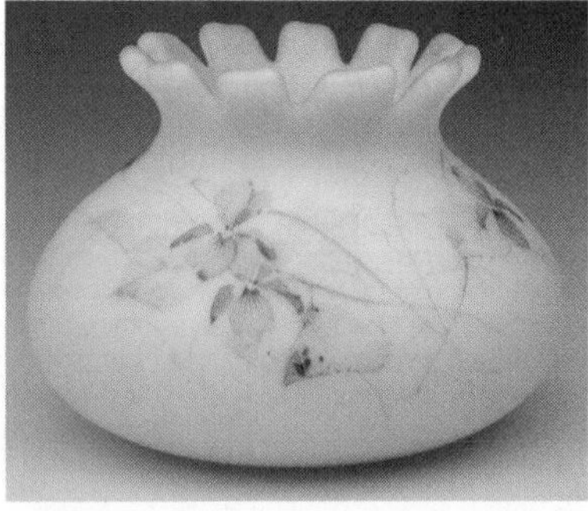

Vase, miniature, 2 3/4" h., 3 3/4" d., squatty bulbous body tapering to a short fluted neck, satin opal ground w/a pale blue rim band, enameled w/scattered violets **$176**

Nailsea

Nailsea was another glassmaking center in England where a variety of wares similar to those from Bristol, England were produced between 1788 and 1873. Today most collectors think of Nailsea primarily as a glass featuring swirls and loopings, usually white, on a clear or colored ground. This style of glass decoration, however, was not restricted to Nailsea and was produced in many other glasshouses, including some in America.

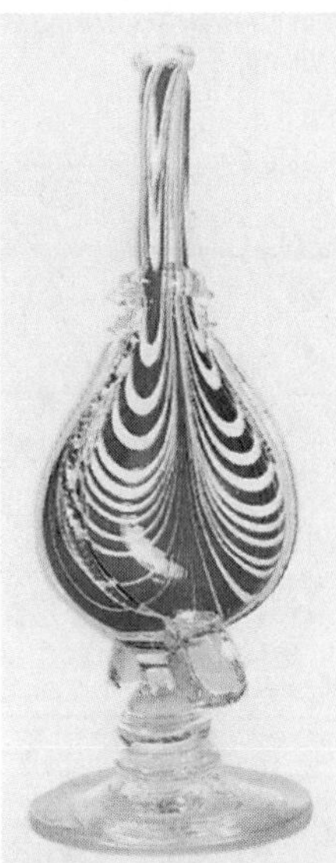

Bellows on pedestal cranberry red body w/white loop pattern throughout & applied clear glass rigaree, pedestal & foot, pontil scarred foot, applied mouth & neck rings, America or England, ca. 1860-90, 8 3/4" h. **$420**

Sugar bowl base, clear heavy disk foot & short ringed pedestal supporting a bulbous bowl w/a tooled rim in milk white decorated overall w/dark blue looping, pontil scar, Pittsburgh district, ca. 1840-60, some white casing lost in manufacture, 5 3/4" h. **$504**

Vase & witch ball, 12" h., free-blown vase w/a flaring funnel pedestal base supporting a squatty bulbous body below the tall widely flaring trumpet neck, milk glass decorated overall w/ cranberry looping, supporting a round matching ball, American, possibly New England, ca. 1850-70, 2 pcs. **$2,240**

Wine glass, free-blown w/an aqua cup-shaped bowl w/white looping, applied to a simple aqua pedestal base, probably South Jersey, ca.1840-60, 3 1/8" h. **$448**

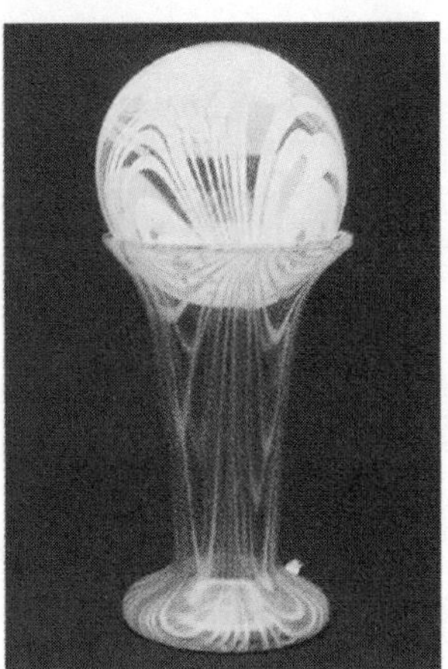

Witchball on stand, round ball w/ white loopings on clear, matching trumpet-form base w/cushion foot, New Jersey, 1850-70, overall 12 1/4" h., 2 pcs. **$952**

Vase, 11 1/2" h., bulbous lower body w/a tall cylindrical neck w/a widely rolled rim, clear w/heavy white looping down the sides, on an applied clear short pedestal foot w/ pontil, probably Pittsburgh (some interior residue & cloudiness) **$605**

Vase & witch ball, 13 1/2" h., free-blown vase of trumpet form w/cushion foot, clear w/white loopings, supporting a round clear ball w/white loopings, probably New Jersey, ca. 1850-70, 2 pcs. **$840**

Vase w/witch ball, clear w/white & fiery opalescent looping, the tall slender trumpet-form vase w/a swelled base on an applied clear foot, the large witch ball sitting atop the flared rim, probably South Jersey, vase 11" h., overall 16 1/2" h., 2 pcs............... **$4,290**

New Martinsville

The New Martinsville Glass Mfg. Co. opened in New Martinsville, West Virginia, in 1901 and during its first period of production came out with a number of colored opaque pressed glass patterns. Also developed was an art glass line named "Muranese," which collectors refer to as "New Martinsville Peach Blow." The factory burned in 1907 but reopened later that year and began focusing on production of various clear pressed glass patterns, many of which were then decorated with gold or ruby staining or enameled decoration. After going through receivership in 1937, the factory again changed the focus of its production to more contemporary glass lines and figural animals. The firm was purchased in 1944 by The Viking Glass Company (later Dalzell-Viking).

Ashtray, figural, model of a wheelbarrow, clear, 4 x 5 1/2" **$24**

Basket, oval w/flaring sides & high applied handle, Janice patt., light blue, 9" h. **$120**

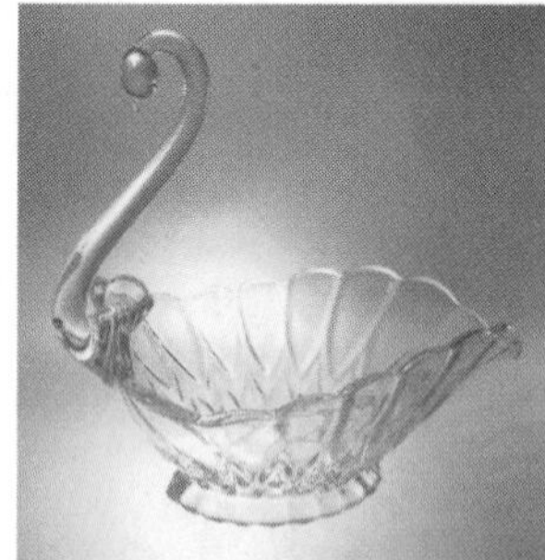

Bowl, 9" l., swan-shaped, Janice patt., clear **$58**

Bowl, 9 1/2" d., shallow w/lightly scalloped rim, Princess patt., Prelude etching, clear **$42**

Cordial, Moondrops patt., ruby, 3/4 oz. **$32**

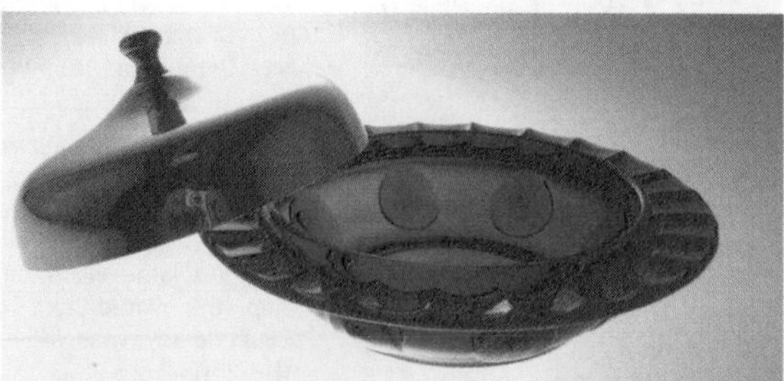

Butter dish w/chrome lid, round, Moondrops patt., cobalt blue, 6" d. **$120**

Opalescent

Presently, this is one of the most popular areas of glass collecting. The opalescent effect was attained by adding bone ash chemicals to areas of an item while still hot and refiring the object at tremendous heat. Both pressed and mold-blown patterns are available to collectors and we distinguish the types in our listing below. Opalescent Glass from A to Z by the late William Heacock is the definitive reference book for collectors.

Arabian Nights (possibly Beaumont)

Pitcher, 9" h., bulbous ovoid body, short cylindrical ringed neck w/ ruffled rim & arched spout, applied handle, blue w/applied blue handle **$990**

Water set: 9" h., pitcher & four tumblers; blue w/applied blue handle, tumblers w/rim flakes, rim flake on pitcher, the set **$880**

Pitcher, 9" h., bulbous ovoid body, short cylindrical ringed neck w/ ruffled rim & arched spout, applied handle, cranberry w/clear applied handle **$2,000-3,000**

An applied handle is formed separately from the body then attached to the body while still molten.

Beatty Rib

Sugar shaker w/original metal lid, blue, 5" h. **$248**

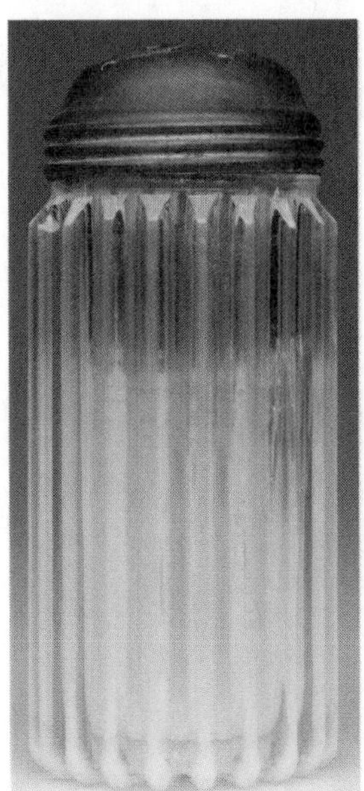

Sugar shaker w/original metal lid, clear, chip to top of one rib, 5" h. **$110**

Buttons & Braids (Jefferson & Fenton)

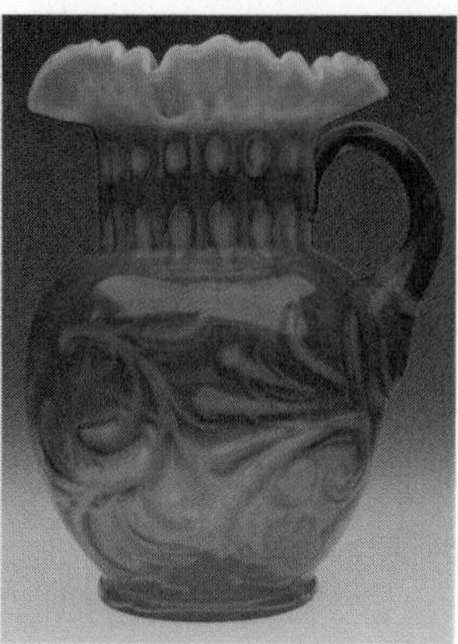

Pitcher, 9 1/2" h., footed bulbous body w/a cylindrical neck & round flaring crimped rim, blue w/applied blue handle **$250-300**

Pitcher, 9 1/2" h., footed bulbous body w/a cylindrical neck & round flaring crimped rim, clear w/applied clear handle **$132**

Pitcher, 9 1/2" h., footed bulbous body w/a cylindrical neck & round flaring crimped rim, cranberry w/ applied clear handle **$1,430**

Pitcher, 9 1/2" h., footed bulbous body w/a cylindrical neck & round flaring crimped rim, green w/ applied green handle ... **$200-225**

One strategy at an auction is to not start the bidding or come in as the first opposing bidder. Instead wait until the initial bidding has stopped, then bid. This will surprise and discourage the previous high bidder who anticipated succeeding. The strategy changes, however, if a second person does not enter into the bidding. You must jump into the fray before the auctioneer knocks the item down to the opening bidder.

Tumbler, blown, blue Jefferson **$80-100**

Tumbler, pressed, green, Fenton **$65-80**

Tumbler, pressed, green, Fenton **$50-60**

Water set, pitcher & eight tumblers; blue, 9 pcs. **$450**

Water set, pitcher & six tumblers, blue, 7 pcs. **$800-900**

Water set, 9 3/4" h. pitcher & four tumblers; pitcher w/bulbous ovoid body, short cylindrical neck & flaring ruffled rim, tumblers w/ cylindrical shape tapering out slightly at rim, blue, 5 pcs. (rim chip to one tumbler).............. **$550**

Christmas Snowflake (Northwood/National & Dugan)

Pitcher, 9" h., ribbed mold, clear w/ applied clear handle ... **$400-600**

←

Pitcher, 9" h., slightly ovoid body w/ tapering shoulder, cylindrical neck & ruffled rim, cranberry w/clear applied handle **$2,400**

Pitcher, water, bulbous, cranberry w/applied clear twisted handle **$3,000-3,500**

Pitcher, 9" h., ribbed mold, cranberry w/applied clear handle....... **$2,400**

Sugar shaker w/original top, cobalt, 4 3/4" h.................. **$2,400**

Tumbler, cranberry (open bubble on rim) **$170**

Tumbler, blue.......................... **$160**

Coinspot

Pitcher, 11" h., three-tier mold, Northwood Glass Co., green w/ applied green handle **$358**

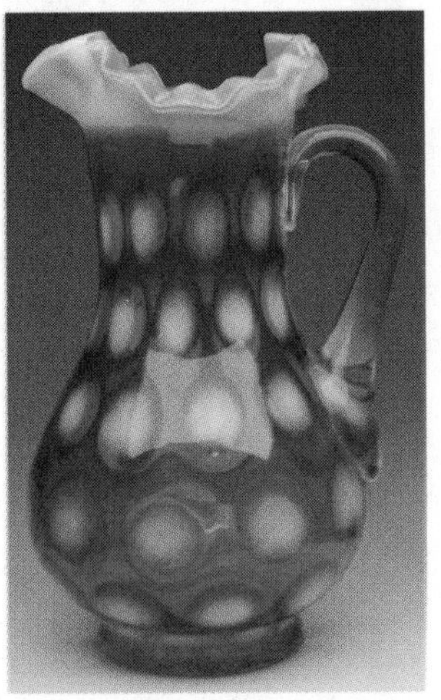

Pitcher, 11" h., footed bulbous lower body tapering to a tall cylindrical neck a/tri-corner ruffled rim, Jefferson Glass Co., cranberry w/ applied clear handle **$660**

Pitcher, 10" h., baluster-form body w/a wide neck & tall upright ruffled rim, Northwood Glass Co., signed in the base, blue w/applied blue handle **$385**

Pitcher, 8 1/2" h., bulbous ovoid body tapering to a cylindrical neck w/round flaring & crimped rim, cranberry w/applied clear handle **$200-300**

Salt & pepper shakers w/original lids, cranberry, pr. **$375**

Sugar shaker w/original lid, nine-panel mold, cranberry........... **$265**

Sugar shaker w/original lid, nine-panel mold, cranberry........... **$165**

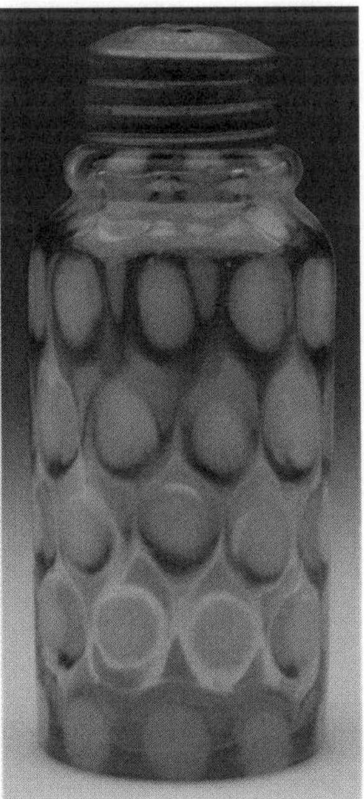

Salt shaker w/old metal lid, cylindrical ring-neck mold, blue, minute flake near base, 4" h. **$88**

Daisy & Fern (Northwood, various locations)

Pitcher, 8 3/4" h., bulbous body tapering to a flaring upright squared & ruffled neck, applied clear handle, cranberry **$400-550**

Sugar shaker w/original lid, ring-neck mold **$150**

Sugar shaker w/original lid, nine-panel, Jefferson variant, cranberry **$295**

Syrup pitcher w/original metal lid, blue...................................... **$145**

Pitcher, 9 1/4" h., footed shoulder-shape mold, triangular ruffled rim, blue, applied blue reeded handle **$250-300**

Pitcher, 9" h., bulbous body tapering to a flaring upright squared neck w/ crimped rim, applied clear handle, clear **$150-175**

Sugar shaker w/original lid, Apple Blossom mold, blue **$358**

Sugar shaker w/original lid, Apple Blossom mold, clear **$176**

Northwood/National, Indiana, Pa., ca. 1899-1901

Pitcher, 12" h., ribbon tie mold, tankard-style, green w/applied green handle **$200-300**

Pitcher, 8 1/2" h., squat mold, wide cylindrical body tapering to cylindrical neck w/upright flaring & ruffled rim, blue w/applied blue handle **$600**

Pitcher, 11 1/2" h., nine-panel mold tankard-style, green w/green applied handle **$1,000-1,500**

Pitcher, 11 1/2" h., nine-panel mold tankard-style, clear w/clear applied handle **$300-500**

Pitcher, 9 1/2" h., tall ovoid body, ruffled rim, blue w/blue applied handle **$500**

Pitcher, 9 3/4" h., ovoid body tapering to a cylindrical neck w/a tri-corner crimped rim, clear w/ applied clear handle **$100-150**

Pitcher, 9 3/4" h., tall ovoid body tapering to a tri-corner ruffled rim, applied clear handle, cranberry **$1,250-1750**

Sugar shaker w/original lid, ribbon tie mold, canary, minor damage, 3 1/4" h. **$231**

Sugar shaker w/original lid, wide waist mold, clear, 4 3/4" h. **$132**

Ribbed Opal Lattice

Pitcher, water, 10" h., tankard-type, blue w/translucent blue applied handle **$1,430**

Pitcher, water, 10" h., tankard-type, clear w/clear applied handle **$660**

Pitcher, water, 10" h., tankard-type, cranberry w/clear applied handle **$1,500-1,700**

Salt shaker w/early metal lid, cranberry **$88**

Sugar shaker w/period lid, clear, 4 1/4" h. **$99**

Stripe

Pitcher, 8 3/4" h., bulbous ovoid body tapering to neck, flared crimped rim, light blue w/ translucent blue applied handle **$300-500**

Pitcher, 9 1/2" h., footed nearly spherical body w/a cylindrical neck & squared flaring crimped rim, clear w/applied clear handle **$75-125**

Pitcher, 9 1/4" h., ring-neck mold, blue w/applied blue handle **$400-600**

Pitcher, 9" h., ring-neck mold, tapering ovoid body, ruffled rim, cranberry w/clear applied handle **$1,600**

Pitcher, 9" h., ring-neck mold, tapering ovoid body, ruffled rim, cranberry w/clear applied handle **$600**

Pitcher, 9 1/2" h., spherical body, short cylindrical neck w/tricorner rim, canary w/translucent canary applied ribbed handle w/unique faint opalescent striping within **$800**

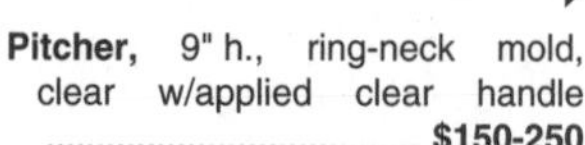

Pitcher, 9" h., ring-neck mold, clear w/applied clear handle **$150-250**

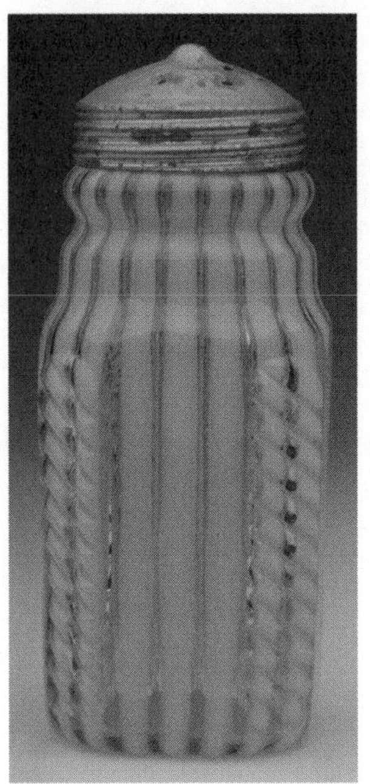

Salt shaker w/original lid, cylindrical w/narrow molded rings & a tapering ringed shoulder, pale canary, Belmont Glass, 4 1/4" h. **$99**

Salt shaker w/original lid, six-lobed mold, blue, 3" h. **$50-75**

Sugar shaker w/original lid, footed tapering cylindrical body w/ringed neck, blue, possibly Buckeye, 5" h. **$660**

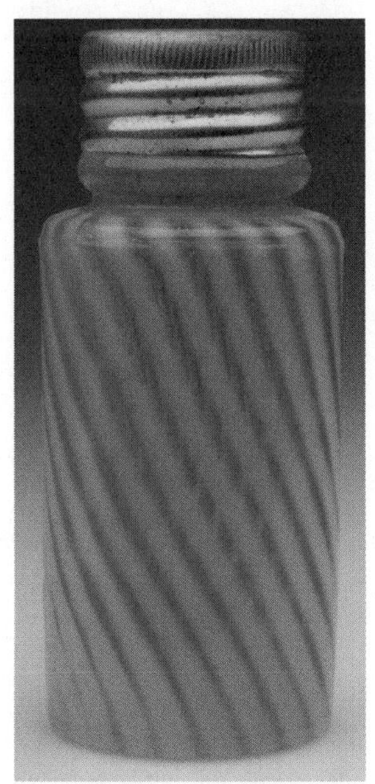

Salt shaker w/original lid, cylindrical, cranberry, 3 3/4" h. **$99**

Swirl

Pitcher, 8 1/2" h., bulbous ovoid body tapering to a cylindrical neck w/squared rim, cranberry w/ applied clear handle **$605**

Pitcher, 8 3/4" h., bulbous ovoid body tapering to neck, flared squared rim, blue w/translucent blue applied handle w/pressed fan design at upper terminal **$385**

Pitcher, 11" h., footed bulbous lower body tapering to a tall cylindrical neck w/a tri-corner ruffled rim, Jefferson Glass Co., blue w/ applied blue handle **$400-600**

Pairpoint

Originally organized in New Bedford, Massachusetts, in 1880 as the Pairpoint Manufacturing Company on land adjacent to the famed Mount Washington Glass Company, this company first manufactured silver and plated wares. In 1894, the two famous factories merged as the Pairpoint Corporation and enjoyed great success for more than forty years. The company was sold in 1939 to a group of local businessmen and eventually bought out by one of the group who turned the management over to Robert M. Gundersen. Subsequently, it operated as the Gundersen Glass Works until 1952 when, after Gundersen's death, the name was changed to Gundersen-Pairpoint. The factory closed in 1956. Subsequently, Robert Bryden took charge of this glassworks, at first producing glass for Pairpoint abroad and eventually, in 1970, beginning glass production in Sagamore, Massachusetts. Today the Pairpoint Crystal Glass Company is owned by Robert and June Bancroft. They continue to manufacture fine quality blown and pressed glass.

Candlesticks, a round foot & disk stem supporting a tall hollow baluster-form stem below the applied cylindrical candle socket w/a flattened rim, sulfur yellow, the stem & base engraved w/lush pods on a vine w/florets scattered around the sockets, 10 1/8" h., pr. **$633**

Compote, open, 6" d., cut overlay, Lincoln patt., a shallow wide round bowl in cobalt blue cut to clear, on a tapering facet-cut stem & star-cut round foot **$650-750**

Candlesticks, tall blown baluster-form w/a cylindrical socket & flattened rim, clear optic ribbed design w/dark blue swirls, 12" h., pr. **$1,200-1,800**

Tazza, Fine Arts line, a rib-cut cylindrical flaring amber glass bowl mounted in a swag-cast brass-plated metal holder supported by a figural putto standing on a square onyx platform w/a cast brass-plated border, signed, ca. 1920s, 10" h. **$500- 750**

Compote, open, 5" h., 8" d., the widely flaring & gently ruffled bowl w/a wide cobalt blue border around spirals in clear & blue, on an applied clear stem & foot **$780**

Vase, 12 1/2" h., Crown Pairpoint Ware, painted overall w/dark earthtone colors w/a large realistic owl on the front, signed, ca. 1895, rare **$3,500-5,000**

Vase, 12" h., blown chalice-form, the cobalt blue ovoid body w/a flaring rim supported by a clear controlled bubble connector to the cobalt blue foot **$450-650**

Pattern

Though it has never been ascertained whether glass was first pressed in the United States or abroad, the development of the glass pressing machine revolutionized the glass industry in the United States, and this country receives the credit for improving the method to make this process feasible. The first wares pressed were probably small flat plates of the type now referred to as "lacy," the intricacy of the design concealing flaws.

In 1827, both the New England Glass Co., Cambridge, Mass., and Bakewell & Co., Pittsburgh, took out patents for pressing glass furniture knobs; soon other pieces followed. This early pressed glass contained red lead, which made it clear and resonant when tapped (flint.) Made primarily in clear, it is rarer in blue, amethyst, olive green and yellow.

By the 1840s, early simple patterns such as Ashburton, Argus and Excelsior appeared. Ribbed Bellflower seems to have been one of the earliest patterns to have had complete sets. By the 1860s, a wide range of patterns was available.

In 1864, William Leighton of Hobbs, Brockunier & Co., Wheeling, West Virginia, developed a formula for "soda lime" glass that did not require the expensive red lead for clarity. Although "soda lime" glass did not have the brilliance of the earlier flint glass, the formula came into widespread use because glass could be produced cheaply.

An asterisk (*) indicates a piece which has been reproduced.

Bellflower

Creamer, double vine, fine rib, applied handle **$110**

Creamer, single vine, fine rib, applied handle, unpatterned band at rim, star in foot **$660**

Lamp, kerosene-type, all-glass, single vine, fine rib, squatty bulbous font applied to a high waisted & paneled pedestal on a round scalloped foot, 7 1/2" h. **$242**

Broken Column (Irish Column, Notched Rib or Bamboo)

Carafe, water **$143**

Compote, cov., 7 1/2" d., high stand, minor flaking **$88**

Cracker jar, cov., clear **$143**

Pitcher, water, ruby-stained notches **$550**

Sugar shaker w/metal top, clear, minor flaws, 4 3/4" h. **$66**

Cathedral

Cake stand, canary, 10" d. **$143**

Columbian Coin

Mug, beer, handled, gilded coins **$66**

← **Lamp,** kerosene-type, milk white, 10" h. **$187**

Daisy & Button

Bowl, 10" d., 4" h., round w/eight-scallop rim, canary **$110**

Bowl, 9 1/2 x 11 1/2", 2 1/2" h., rectangular w/curved & flared sides, canary **$110**

Gas shade, canary, scallop & point rim, 8 3/4" d. rim **$110**

Gas shade, sapphire blue, flaring octagonal shape w/scalloped rim, 9" d. rim **$77**

Novelty, model of a wheelbarrow w/ pewter front wheel, normal flakes, amber, 5 3/4 x 10" **$187**

Pitcher, 9 3/4" h., 5" d., water, footed ovoid body w/a high arched spout & applied reeded handle, clear **$55**

***Pickle castor,** apple green insert, w/silver plate frame & tongs **$165**

Pitcher, 8 3/4" h., tankard-type, applied handle, canary, minor flaws **$198**

Spoon holder in silver plate frame, horizontal blue oblong bowl in a footed oval silver plate frame w/a high arched end handle, overall 2 1/8 x 6 1/4", 6 1/2" h. **$220**

Daisy & Button - Single Panel (Elrose or Amberette, when amber- stained)

Compote, open, 11" d., 7" h., widely flaring bowl, amber panels **$1,760**

Compote, open, 11" d., 7" h., widely flaring bowl, apple green **$55**

Compote, open, 9 1/2" d., 9 1/2" h., very deep bell-form bowl w/flared & scalloped rim, foot reduced in size, canary **$176**

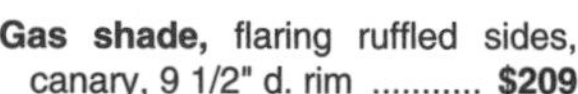

Gas shade, flaring ruffled sides, canary, 9 1/2" d. rim **$209**

Compote, open, 9 1/2" d., 9 1/2" h., very deep bell-form bowl w/flared & scalloped rim, clear **$99**

Salt & pepper shakers w/original tops, amber panels, pr. $176

Table set: cov. sugar, cov. butter dish, creamer & spooner; amber panels, minor nick on sugar, the set $250-350

Water set: water pitcher & two tumblers; amber panels, the set $385

Daisy & Button with Crossbars (Mikado)

Celery vase, canary yellow $40-60

Compote, cov., canary, 8" d., high stand $154

Cruet w/original stopper, canary yellow, minor interior residue, 8" h. $176

Compote, cov., canary, 8" d., low stand.................................. $154

Pitcher, water, canary yellow $121

Sugar bowl, open, individual size, blue.. $35

Syrup pitcher, w/original top $70

Toothpick holder, ruby stained $45

Tumbler, amber $45

Goblets, canary, set of 3 .... **$132**

Wines, canary yellow, set of 6 .... **$154**

Daisy & Button with Thumbprint Panels

Cake stand, four-lobed top & squared pedestal base, minor flaws, canary, 10" w., 7 1/4" h. **$143**

Compote, cov., 5 3/4" w., high stand, blue............................. **$55**

Frosted Lion (Rampant Lion)

***Celery vase** **$75-100**

Cheese dish, cov., rampant lion finial **$300-400**

Compote, cov., 9" d., high stand, lion head finial **$150-250**

***Pitcher,** water **$300-400**

Hobnail

"Hobnail" glass derives its name from the thick nail heads added to the bottom of hobnail boots to increase traction.

Barber bottle, Frances decoration w/an amber-stained neck & frosted clear body, Hobbs, Brockunier & Co., some loss to knobs, 6 5/8" h. **$143**

Carafe, ovoid body tapering to a tall neck w/flared rim, Rubina Verde, ruby neck above yellowish green body, losses to numerous hobs, Hobbs, Brockunier & Co., 8 1/2" h. **$264**

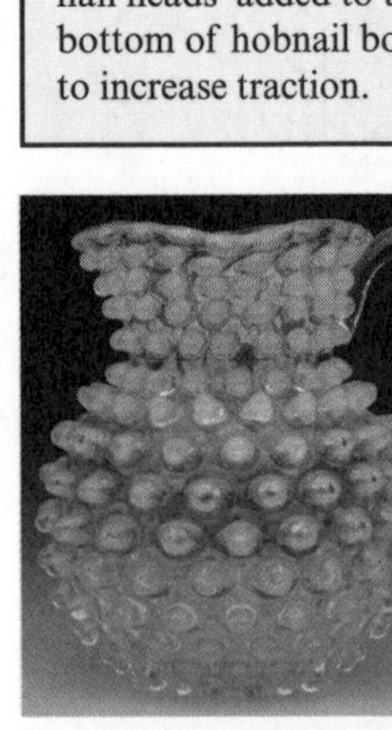

Creamer, bulbous body w/a squared neck, applied clear handle, clear opalescent, Hobbs, Brockunier & Co., 4 1/2" h. **$303**

Pitcher, 7 3/4" h., bulbous body w/a squared neck, applied clear handle, clear opalescent, Hobbs, Brockunier & Co. **$110**

Pitcher, 8 1/4" h., bulbous body tapering to a squared rim, Rubina Verde opalescent, applied canary handle, Hobbs, Brockunier & Co. **$495**

Pitcher, 8" h., bulbous body tapering to a squared rim, applied clear handle, cranberry opalescent, Hobbs, Brockunier & Co. damage to numerous hobs **$209**

Pitcher, 8" h., bulbous body tapering to a squared rim, applied clear handle, Frances decoration in frosted amber above frosted clear, Hobbs, Brockunier & Co., flake on one hob **$143**

Tumblers, cylindrical, Rubina Opalescent, Hobbs, Brockunier & Co., one w/minor flaws, 4" h., pr. **$187**

Horn of Plenty (McKee's Comet)

Butter dish & cover w/Washington's head finial (ILLUS. center with large creamer and celery vase) **$2,600**

Plate, 6 1/4" d., canary **$1,150**

Horseshoe (Good Luck or Prayer Rug)

Cake stand, 8" d., 6 1/2" h. **$75-100**

Cheese dish, cov., w/woman churning butter in base, minor flaws **$100-150**

Compote, open, 9" d., 8 3/4" h., wide flaring shallow bowl on a plain stem w/domed foot **$77**

Goblets, knob stem, minute flakes on some, set of 8 .... **$154**

Pitcher, water, 9" h. **$88**

Small items have a way of getting misplaced at country auctions. If you're interested in a particular item, keep your eye on it. Unscrupulous buyers may try to help themselves by moving items from one box lot to another.

Relish, model of a wheelbarrow, clear, embossed "Pat. Apld. For" on bottom, metal wheel, minor flaws, 4 1/4 x 8" **$77**

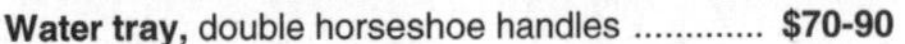

Water tray, double horseshoe handles **$70-90**

Wine **$121**

Magnet & Grape with Frosted Leaf

Celery vase, scalloped rim, 8 1/2" h. **$240-250**

Polar Bear

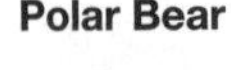

Goblet, flared rim, frosted **$121**

Tray, water, frosted, 16" l. **$300-500**

Waste bowl, clear **$90**

Water set, water pitcher, two goblets, flared waste bowl & oval water tray; frosted & clear, some minor flaws, the set **$300-500**

Water tray, oval, frosted, flakes on interior of table ring, 11 x 15 1/2" **$100-150**

Ruby Thumbprint

Castor set, 4-bottle, in clear glass frame, wire loop center handle, minor flakes on frame, one shaker w/minor pattern flake, 9 1/2" h. **$280**

Berry set: master boat-shaped, engraved bowl & 4 sauce dishes, 5 pcs. **$65**

Goblet, engraved vintage band **$70**

Pitcher, milk, tankard, 8 3/8" h., engraved souvenir inscription dated 1900 .... **$90**

Sunk Honeycomb (Corona)

Cake stand, ruby-stained, 8 1/2" d., 5 1/4" h. **$275**

Cruets, ruby-stained & enameled w/leaves & flowers, 6 1/2" h. **$120**

Decanter, ruby-stained & engraved leaf & vine design, 13 5/8" h. **$160**

Wines, ruby-stained & enameled leaf & flower decoration, 4" h., set of 4 .... **$125**

Shell & Tassel

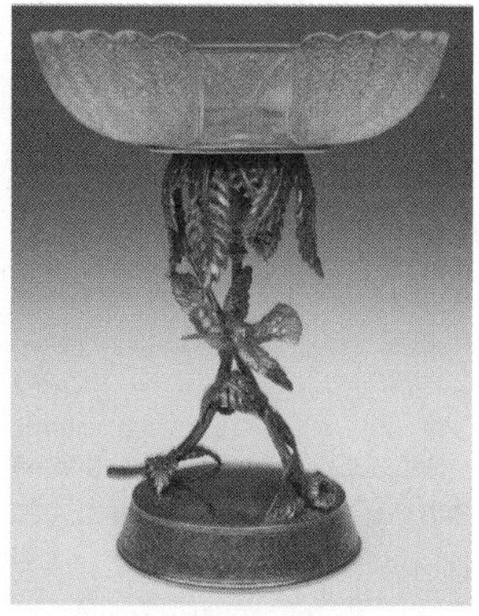

Bride's bowl, a clear squared 8" w. bowl w/pegged base raised on a tall ornate silver plate stand w/twig-like legs trimmed w/a hummingbird & leaves, bowl w/partial loss to one scallop, 10 1/4" h. **$121**

Dish, 5 3/4 x 8" rectangle, blue, light rim flakes **$50-75**

Cake stand, shell corners, 7" sq. **$55**

Pitcher, water, round **$99**

Salt shaker w/original top **$77**

Tumblers, clear, set of 3 .... **$77**

Pattern

U.S. Coin

Goblet, straight top, frosted dimes, 6 1/2" h. **$154**

Lamp, kerosene-type, handled finger style, frosted twenty cent pieces, 5" h. **$660**

Water tray, frosted coins, two interior rim flakes, 10" d. **$400-600**

Lamp, kerosene-type, square font, frosted half dollars & dollars, 10 1/4" h. **$935**

Washington Centennial

Cake stand, 11" d. **$55**

Celery vase, flint.............. **$165-175**

Lamp, kerosene-type, brass stem & marble base............................ **$45**

Pitcher, water **$110**

Relish, bear paw handles, dated 1876 .... **$45**

Salt dip, master size, flat, round, flint.................................... **$35-45**

Salt dip, individual size, flint...... **$20**

Spooner, flint **$29**

Syrup pitcher, w/original metal top, applied handle, milk white **$140**

Syrup pitcher, w/dated pewter top w/tiny figural finial, clear **$165**

Toothpick holder, w/enameled floral decoration....................... **$30**

Whatever you are considering buying, examine it carefully. Hold glassware to the light to look for cracks, which are especially difficult to see in cut glass. Run your fingertips around the around the edges of pressed glass or Depression glass for chips. Feel for differences in the texture of decorations on china, which could be a clue to a restoration.

Peach Blow

Several types of glass lumped together by collectors as Peach Blow were produced by half a dozen glasshouses. Hobbs, Brockunier & Co., Wheeling, West Virginia, made Peach Blow as a plated ware that shaded from red at the top to yellow at the bottom and is referred to as Wheeling Peach Blow. Mt. Washington Glass Works produced an homogeneous Peach Blow shading from a rose color at the top to pale blue in the lower portion. The New England Glass Works' Peach Blow, called Wild Rose, shaded from rose at the top to white. Gundersen-Pairpoint Co. also reproduced some of the Mt. Washington Peach Blow in the early 1950s and some glass of a somewhat similar type was made by Steuben Glass Works, Thomas Webb & Sons and Stevens & Williams of England. New England Peach Blow is one-layered glass and the English is two-layered.

Another single-layered shaded art glass was produced early in the 20th century by the New Martinsville Glass Mfg. Co. Originally called "Muranese," collectors today refer to it as "New Martinsville Peach Blow."

Gundersen - Pairpoint

Compote, open, 7 1/4" d., 6 3/4" h., a round foot & slender baluster-shaped stem below a twisted knop below the wide shallow bowl w/a six-ruffle rim, satin finish **$288**

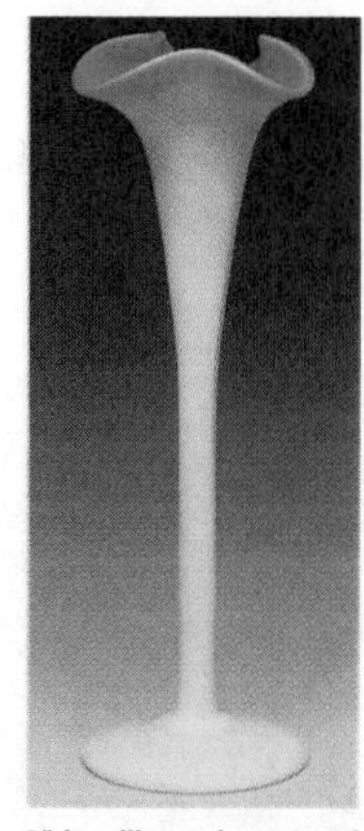

Vase, 9" h., lily-style, round foot & tall very slender stem to the flaring & inwardly-folded tricorner rim, deep rose to white, satin finish **$173**

New England

Creamer, tankard-style slightly tapering cylindrical body, satin finish, applied white reeded handle, crack to tip of upper handle terminal, 2 1/4" d., 4 1/4" h. **$413**

Punch cup, deep rounded bowl w/ applied reeded white handle, satin finish, 2 3/4" h. **$150**

Sugar bowl, open, squatty bulbous form w/lightly molded ribbing & wide flat rim, applied white handles, 4 1/2" w., 2 3/4" h. **$120**

Mt. Washington

Toothpick holder, cylindrical w/ a tricorner rolled-in rim, glossy finish, ca. 1885, 2 1/8" h. **$275**

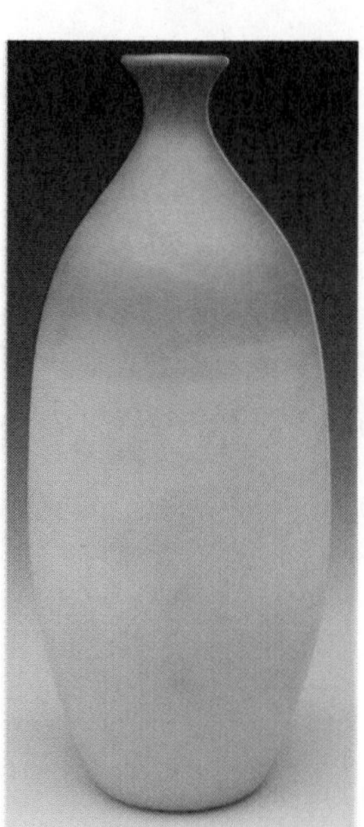

Vase, 9 3/4" h., tall slender ovoid body tapering to a tiny flared neck, satin finish **$935**

Wheeling

Creamer, footed squatty bulbous body in the Drape patt., a flaring squared neck w/in the Drape patt., applied clear reeded handle, glossy finish, 4 1/2" h. **$345**

Cruet w/stopper, ovoid body tapering to small cylindrical neck w/arched spout, applied amber handle, facet-cut stopper, glossy finish, 7" h. **$748**

Cruet w/stopper, tall ovoid body tapering to small cylindrical neck w/arched spout, applied amber reeded handle, rounded facet- cut stopper, glossy finish, 6 3/4" h. **$880**

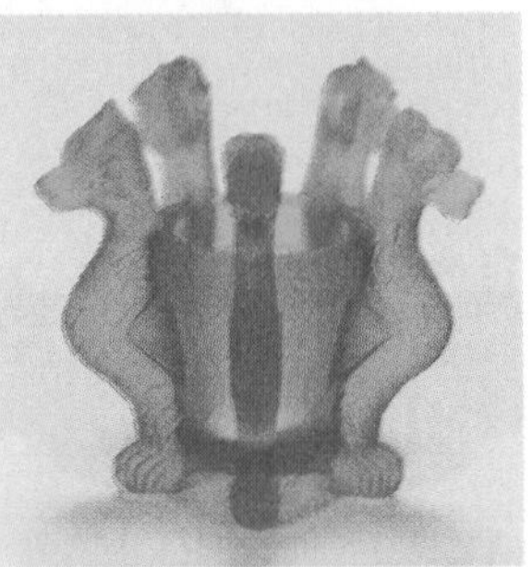

Griffin vase holder, for the Morgan vase, pressed amber glass w/five griffin heads around the cylindrical center, satin finish, chips to interior heads of griffins, 3 1/8" h. **$1,265**

Mustard jar, cov., footed spherical body, now fitted w/a period two-part shaker lid, glossy finish, 2 5/8" h. **$468**

Pitcher, 5 1/2" h., bulbous ovoid body tapering to a flaring squared neck, applied amber handle, glossy finish **$935**

Tumbler, cylindrical, glossy finish, 3 3/4" h. **$253**

Vase, 6 1/4" h., bulbous ovoid body tapering to a short cylindrical neck, glossy finish **$805**

Salt & pepper shakers, spherical body w/original metal lid, glossy finish, 2 1/2" h., pr. **$748**

Quezal

Quezal

In 1901, Martin Bach and Thomas Johnson, who had worked for Louis Tiffany, opened a competing glassworks in Brooklyn, New York. The Quezal Art Glass and Decorating Co. produced wares closely resembling those of Tiffany until the plant's closing in 1925.

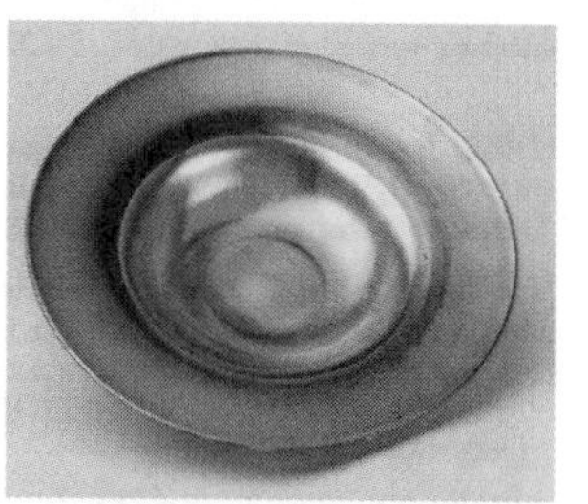

Bowl, 9 1/2" h., a low gold foot supporting the shallow round bowl w/a widely flaring flattened rim, gold w/overall green shading to blue iridescence, unsigned **$748**

Compote, 9 1/2" d., a low flaring round foot supporting the wide shallow bowl w/a widely flaring flattened rim, gold iridescent foot & bowl decorated w/a wide green iridescent rim band, unsigned **$575**

Punch bowl, a wide funnel foot supporting the deep wide rounded bowl w/a widely flaring angled rim, amber w/overall gold iridescence, signed, ca. 1920, 14" d. ... **$1,265**

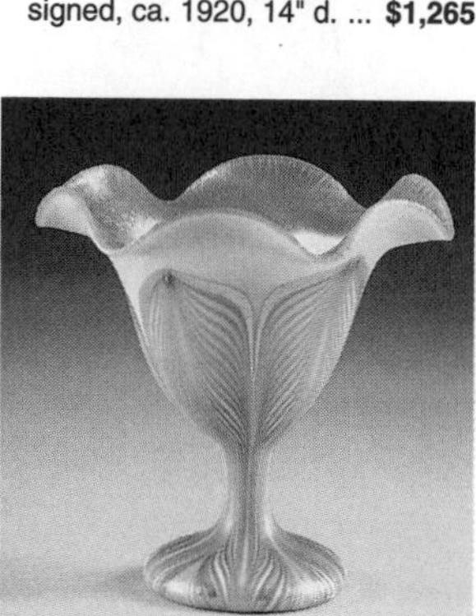

Vase, 5 3/8" h., flower-form, a round cushion foot & slender stem supporting a deep rounded bowl w/a widely flaring six-ruffle rim, the exterior in white w/green & gold pulled-feather decoration up from the foot, iridescent gold interior, signed "Quezal P 413" **$2,160**

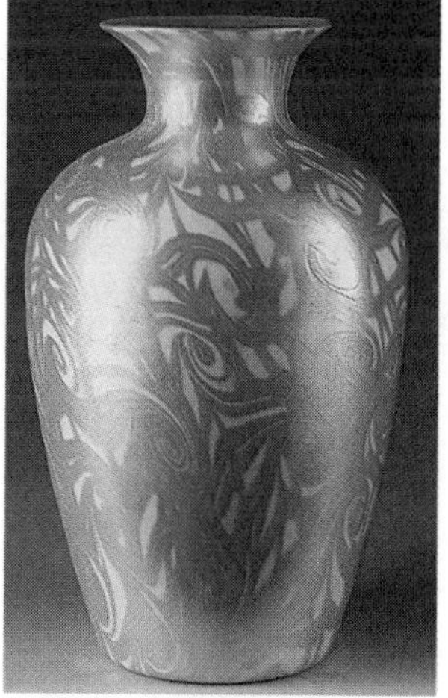

Vase, 12 1/2" h., wide flat-bottomed ovoid body tapering to a short trumpet neck, King Tut design, overall scrolling gold iridescence against a cream background, interior in gold iridescence, signed in the pontil **$2,645**

Vase, 7 5/8" h., wide bulbous tapering ovoid body w/a short widely flaring neck, the exterior decorated w/a dark green double-hooked design under a silver iridescent hooked & feathered decoration, gold banding separates the green from the ivory white shoulder & neck, gold iridescent interior, polished pontil engraved "Quezal 121" **$5,290**

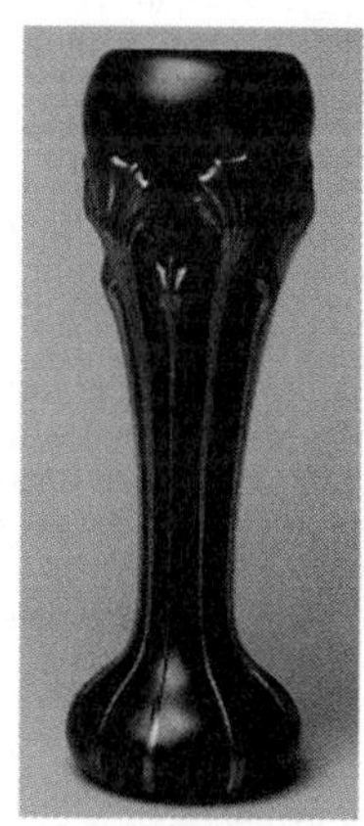

Vase, 14 1/4" h., the bulbous foot tapering to slender flaring cylindrical sides below the bulbous upper body w/a wide flat mouth, dark green iridescent applied up the sides w/ribbed lily pad decoration w/blue & purple iridescence, signed in the pontil **$4,715**

Sandwich

Numerous types of glass were produced at The Boston & Sandwich Glass Works in Sandwich, Massachusetts, on Cape Cod, from 1826 to 1888. Those listed here represent a sampling. Also see BLOWN THREE MOLD, and LACY.

All pieces are pressed glass unless otherwise noted. Numbers after salt dips refer to listings in Pressed Glass Salt Dishes of the Lacy Period, 1825-1850, by Logan W. and Dorothy B. Neal.

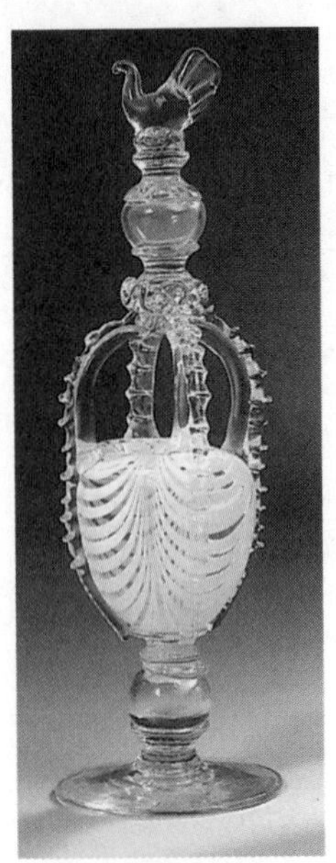

Bank, free-blown, a clear disk base & hollow knob stem supporting the blown ovoid body w/a center opening in clear w/white loopings, applied w/four arching rigaree ribs joined above the body & topped w/a rigaree band supporting a hollow knob applied w/a stylized rooster on a disk in clear, the base & top hollow knob each containing an 1833 American half-dime coin, extremely rare, w/a matching dug fragment, overall 11" h. **$19,975**

Inkstand, pressed flint glass, a squatty round ribbed inkwell w/ metal rim & cap & matching sand shaker, each set on a raised platform on rectangular stand w/peg feet, several edge nicks & small cracks on stand, ca. 1835-55, extremely rare, 6 1/3" l., bottles 2" h., the set **$32,900**

Candlestick, figural dolphin stem w/ petal socket, on a stepped square base, light lavender alabaster-clambroth, minute petal & base nicks, 10" h., pr. **$3,300**

Compote, open, 8 1/4" h., 8 1/4" w., a pressed flaring octagonal pedestal base wafer-joined to the pressed openwork bowl w/16 vertical staves below the 32-point rim & above a 34-point star in sloping base, bright deep amethyst, 1840-55, minor flaws, very rare **$17,600**

Lamp, whale oil-type, hexagonal base & knop below the three-printed block font w/early burner & collar, ca. 1840-60, minor chips on base edge, amethyst, 9" h. **$881**

Lamps, whale oil type, hexagonal base & knopped stem, slender four-printed block font, original pewter collar & camphene burners, base edge chips, canary yellow, 12 7/8" h., pr. **$2,115**

Candlesticks, pressed flint glass, figural dolphin stem w/a petal socket, on a single-step square base, ca. 1845-70, dark blue, minor base roughness, 10 1/4" h., pr. **$9,988**

Decanter w/bar lip, pressed flint glass, Ashburton patt., pewter stopper, ca. 1840-60, canary yellow, small chip on neck ring, light scratches, 11 5/8" h. **$1,410**

Vase, 9 1/2" h., 5" d., pressed flint glass, Twisted Loop patt. top w/ flaring ruffled rim, on wafers above the waisted & paneled standard & round foot, amethyst, ca. 1850, tiny rim nick, very small rough spot on foot rim, some interior residue **$1,760**

Vase, 10 1/4" h., tulip-style, deep amethyst, octagonal base, wafer construction, ca. 1850 ..... **$3,575**

Satin

Satin glass was a popular decorative glass developed in the late 19th century. Most pieces were composed of two layers of glass with the exterior layer usually in a shaded pastel color. The name derives from the soft matte finish, caused by exposure to acid fumes, which gave the surface a "satiny" feel. Mother-of-pearl satin glass was a specialized variety wherein air trapped between the layers of glass provided subtle surface patterns such as Herringbone and Diamond Quilted. A majority of satin glass was produced in England, Bohemia and America, but collectors should be aware that reproductions have been made for many years.

Pitcher, 7 3/4" h., cylindrical body w/ a triangular neck w/a large spout & crimped rim, shaded pink mother-of-pearl Moirè Optic patt., applied frosted clear reeded handle, minor flaws **$198**

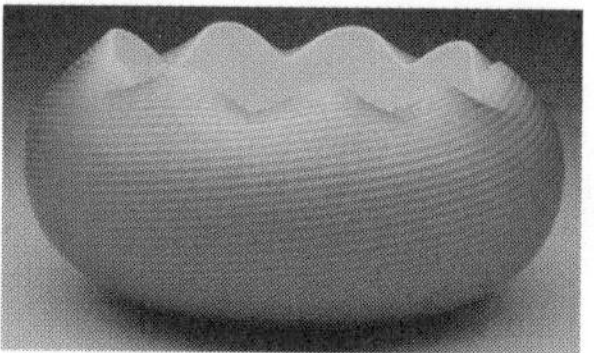

Rose bowl, eight-crimp rim, wide low squatty rounded body in powder blue mother-of-pearl Swirl patt., 6 3/4" d., 3" h. **$143**

Vase, 4 3/4" h., 3 1/2" d., bulbous spherical body w/an upright six-crimp neck, shaded blue mother-of-pearl Basketweave patt. **$121**

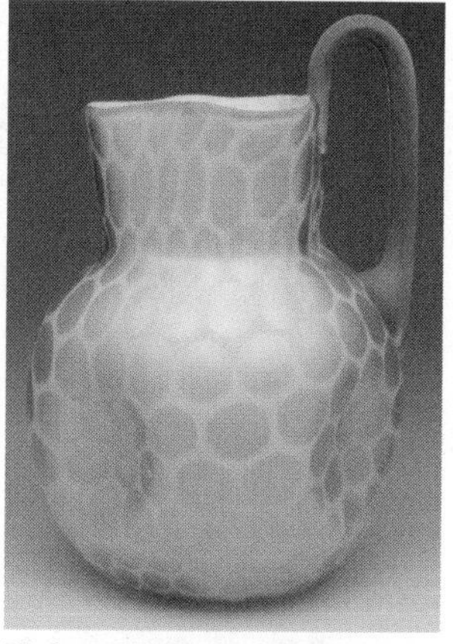

Pitcher, 9" h., bulbous sides w/four large indentations, triangular neck, pale blue & rose striped mother-of-pearl Windows patt., applied high arched clear frosted handle **$385**

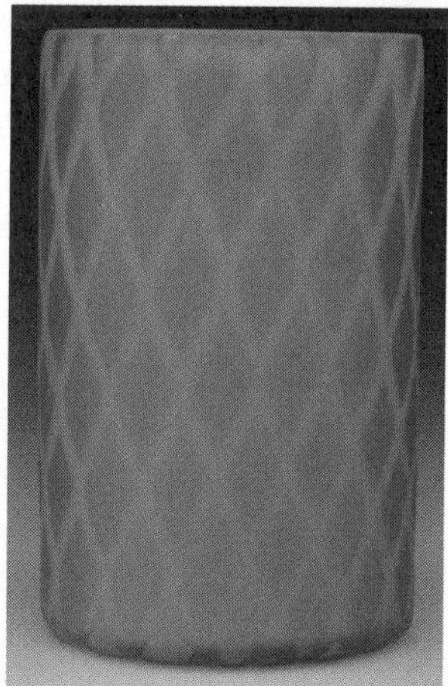

Tumbler, cylindrical, pale blue mother-of-pearl Diamond Quilted patt., 4 1/4" h. **$40-60**

Vase, 6 1/4" h., bulbous ovoid body w/a small short neck below the flaring tri-lobed rim, shaded red to rose mother-of-pearl Stripe patt. **$198**

Rose bowl, eight-crimp rim, spherical form, shaded blue mother-of-pearl Zig-Zag patt., possibly Phoenix Glass Co., 3 3/4" h. **$99**

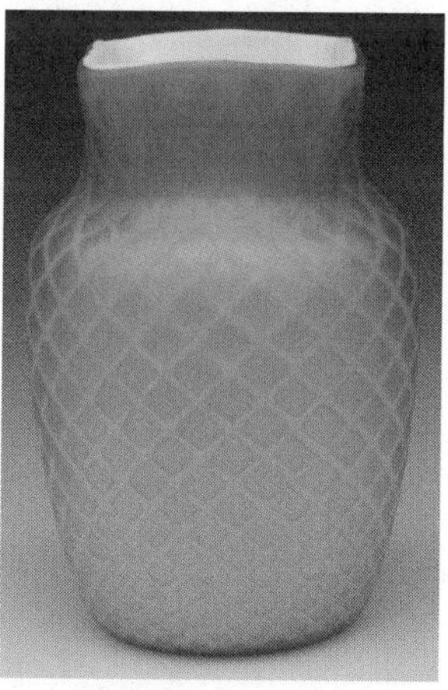

Vase, 4 3/4" h., 2 1/4" d., swelled cylindrical body w/a squared neck, shaded apricot mother-of-pearl Diamond Quilted patt. **$176**

Water set: 7" h. pitcher & one tumbler; yellow shaded to white mother-of-pearl Diamond Quilted patt., one exterior bruise on the pitcher, the set..................... **$110**

Steuben

Most of the Steuben glass listed below was made at the Steuben Glass Works, now a division of Corning Glass, between 1903 and about 1933. The factory was organized by T.G. Hawkes, noted glass designer Frederick Carder, and others. Mr. Carder devised many types of glass and revived many old techniques.

Acid Cut-Back

Jar, cov., ovoid body tapering to a short cylindrical neck w/a fitted domed cover w/pointed knob finial, green Jade cut back to Alabaster in the "Chinese" patt., Shape No. 5000, minor in-the-making roughness on rim of cover, 6 3/8" h. **$2,530**

Lamp, table model, the baluster-form glass body w/a rolled rim in Green Jade cut-back to Alabaster in an overall flowering vine design, mounted on a bronzed metal swag-cast base on scroll feet, early 20th c., body 12" h., overall 28" h. **$863**

Vase 12 1/2" h., wide ovoid body tapering to a flattened rim, Mirror Black cut-back to Green Jade in the Tropic patt., Shape No. 7097, ca. 1928 .... **$9,925**

←

Vase 12" h., a funnel foot supporting the trumpet-form body, light amethyst cut-back to Alabaster in the Birds #2 patt., Shape No. 6034, ca. 1924 .... **$8,626**

Vase, 7" h., wide bulbous nearly spherical body w/a closed rim, Jade green cut to Alabaster w/ an overall stylized floral design w/large flowers on slender leafy branches, shape No. 6078 .... **$1,595**

Vase, 11 3/4" h., footed slender ovoid body tapering to a flaring rim, pink Rosaline cut to Alabaster in the "Mayfair" patt., tall upright flowering leafy branches against the textured ground, glossy applied Alabaster foot, shape No. 7442 .... **$2,090**

Vase 7" h., nearly spherical body w/a wide flat mouth, Rosaline cut-back to Alabaster w/an overall flowering vine design, unsigned **$1,150**

Vase, 4 3/4" h., ovoid body tapering to a short wide cylindrical neck, Roseline overlaid on Alabaster & cut-back w/a wide central band of Oriental designs w/lappet bands around the shoulder & base, shape No. 1500 variant **$1,265**

Aurene

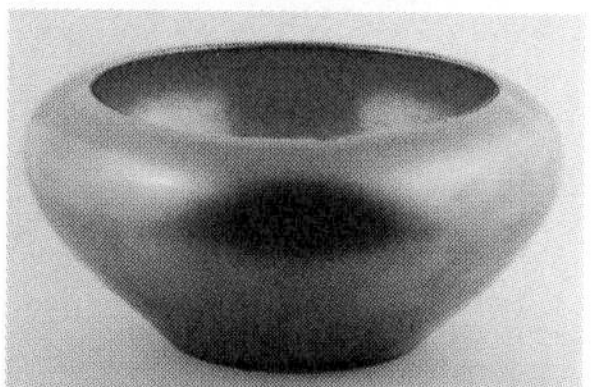

Bowl, 8" d., 3 3/4" h., wide squatty tapering round form w/closed rim, overall golden iridescence, signed **$375-450**

Candleholders, a wide round slightly domed foot below the knopped stem w/tiny applied prunts supporting the tall cylindrical candle socket w/a widely rolled rim, bluish gold iridescence, signed, Shape No. 6384, 3 3/4" h., pr. **$1,265**

Candlestick, a thin round foot below the slender twisted stem & cylindrical flaring socket, all in iridescent blue, signed on the base, Shape No. 686, 8" h. **$920**

Candlesticks, round domed foot supporting the slender ribbed stem entwined w/a slender applied rib leaf, a tapering ribbed bud- form candle socket, brilliant gold iridescence, Shape No. 7613, signed, 11 5/8" h., pr. **$6,613**

Compote, 8" d., 3 1/2" h., a round foot & pedestal in Calcite supporting a widely flaring shallow bowl in Calcite lined w/blue Aurene intaglio etched in a stylized violet design, Shape No. 3234 (ILLUS. of top interior) **$1,380**

Finger bowl & underplate, the deep rounded bowl w/a six-crimp flaring rim, matching ruffled underplate, overall gold iridescence w/ stretcher surface, Shape No. 171, underplate 6 1/4" d., bowl 2 1/2" h., pr. **$500**

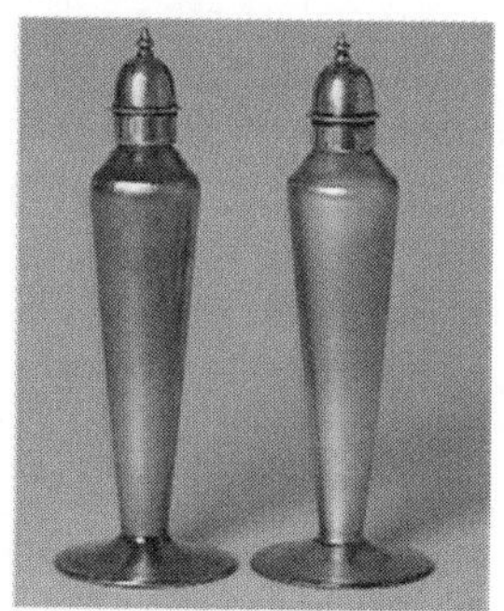

Salt & pepper shakers w/original brass tops, a thin round foot below the flaring cylindrical body in overall gold Aurene, unsigned, 6 3/4" h., pr. **$949**

Vase, 7 1/2" h., bulbous nearly spherical body w/a wide short trumpet neck, overall blue Aurene iridescence decorated w/random threading of leaves & vines in silvery blue, the neck in gold iridescence w/zigzag intarsia bands in white & blue, opal white interior, signed on the base **$25,875**

Vase, 6" h., triple stump-form, overall gold Aurene iridescence, Shape No. 1744, signed **$780**

Vase, 5 3/4" h., urn-form shape, a wide round foot supporting the wide bulbous urn-form body w/a wide shoulder centering a wide flaring neck, three applied upright fleur-de-lis ornaments around the edge of the shoulder, deep blue iridescence, signed, Shape No. 6627 .... **$2,300**

Vase, 10 3/4" h., bulbous ovoid body w/a short flaring neck, overall blue Aurene iridescence, Shape No. 1683, signed on the bottom **$1,800**

Vase, 8 1/2" h., flora-form, a thin round foot & tapering ovoid lobed stem below the trumpet-form bowl w/a deeply ruffled flaring top, overall blue iridescence, Shape No. 2708, signed on base "Steuben Aurene 2708" ... **$3,680**

Cintra

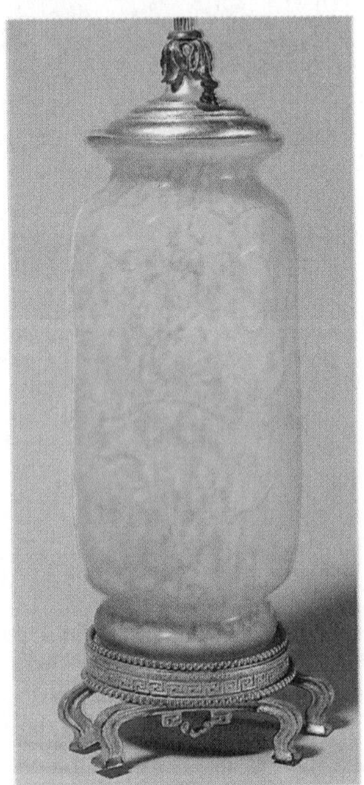

Lamp, table model, a footed swelled cylindrical body w/a short flaring neck, golden yellow acid-cut in the "Sculptured" patt. showing pods of fruit on a meandering leafy vine, mounted on a silvered metal base ring w/a Greek key design & raised on four scroll legs, domed silvered metal top mount, body Shape No. 6375 on base foot bent inward, body 12" h., overall 30 1/2" h. **$2,415**

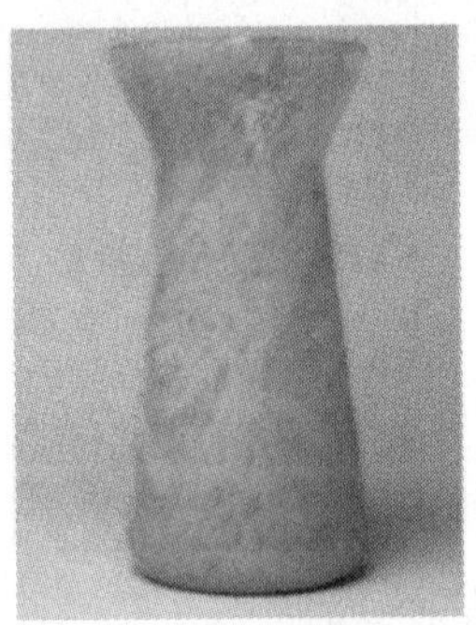

Vase, 12" h., tall slightly tapering cylindrical body w/a flat flaring neck, green Cintra acid cut-back w/a design of stylized flowers & trellis **$4,025**

> While museum employees may be able to help identify and date items that are difficult to research, they are not allowed to estimate values.

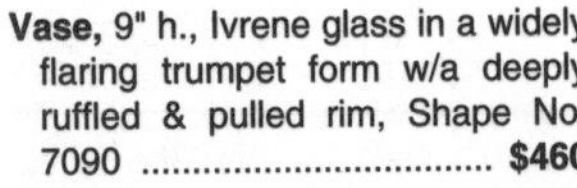

Vase, 9" h., Ivrene glass in a widely flaring trumpet form w/a deeply ruffled & pulled rim, Shape No. 7090 .... **$460**

Grotesque

Vase, 9 1/4" h., Ivrene glass in a trumpet form w/a pulled & ruffled top w/four pinched corners, silver paper Steuben label **$403**

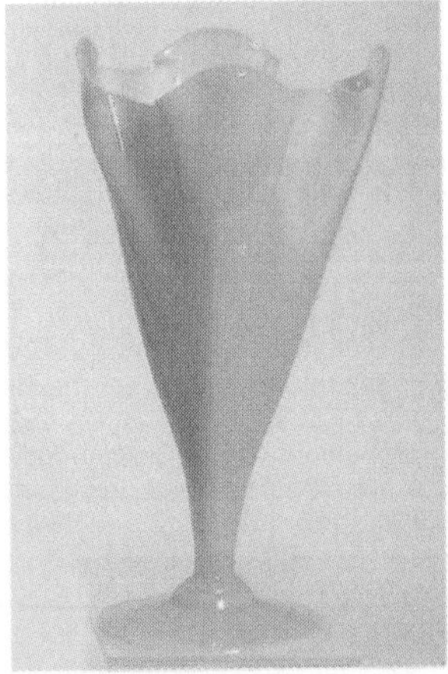

Jade

Candlesticks, Green Jade, a wide flaring round foot supporting a short stem w/four applied Alabaster prunts below the cylindrical socket w/a deeply rolled rim, signed w/the Steuben fleur-de-lis mark, 4" h., pr. **$575**

Donut holder, Green Jade, a wide low domed foot centered by a baluster-form upright w/twisted knob finial, a scratch at the rim & one open bubble, 9" d., 5 1/2" h. **$460**

Vase, 6 1/4" h., Green Jade, wide ovoid shouldered body w/a short cylindrical neck, swirled optic ribbing, Steuben fleur-de-lis mark **$230**

Celeste Blue

Goblet, a blue round foot & swelled clear stem below the flaring optic ribbed bell-form Celeste Blue bowl, signed on the base "F. Carder Steuben," 6" h. **$180**

Topaz

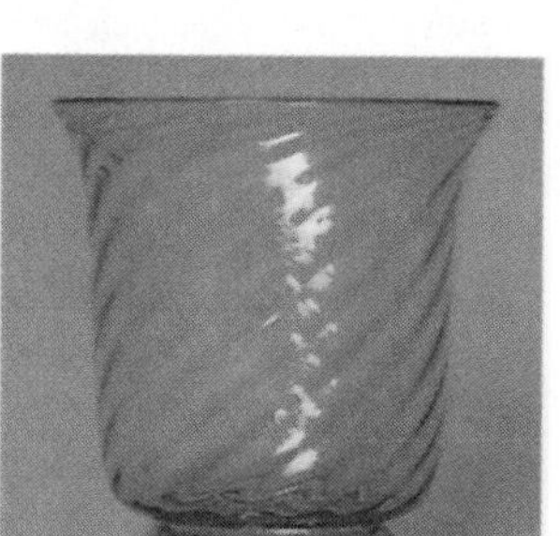

Vase, 7" h., footed wide cylindrical swirled optic ribbed body w/a flared rim, signed w/Steuben fleur-de-lis mark **$230**

Pomona Green

Center bowl, footed oblong shaped shallow Pomona Green bowl w/ applied Topaz loop end handles, signed w/Steuben fleur- de-lis mark, 8 1/4 x 15 3/4", 4 1/2" h. **$403**

Vase, 7" h., footed wide cylindrical swirled optic ribbed body w/a flaring rim, signed w/the Steuben fleur-de-lis mark **$100-200**

Verre de Soie

Basket, cylindrical base w/two widely flaring sides pulled up & joined by a high arched applied handle, large deep maroon blossom w/a pair of green leaves applied at each side of the handle base, similar to Shape No. 453, pontil w/original serrated round paper label, one flower petal professionally repaired, a line within the same blossom, 8" h. **$460**

Perfume bottle w/original stopper, squatty bulbous tapering melon lobed body w/a short neck & flared rim, pointed blown hollow stopper, Shape No. 1455, 2 3/4" d., 4 1/2" h. **$431**

Tiffany

This glassware, covering a wide diversity of types, was produced in glasshouses operated by Louis Comfort Tiffany, America's outstanding glass designer of the Art Nouveau period, from the last quarter of the 19th century until the early 1930s. Tiffany revived early techniques and devised many new ones.

Bottle w/original stopper, bulbous squatty body tapering sharply to a slender gently bent neck fitted w/a silver collar & ball stopper, overall green pulled-feather decoration around the body, may have been a Persian sprinkler form damaged & adapted to this shape, signed on base "L.C. Tiffany Favrile 8530N," 8 1/2" h. **$1,553**

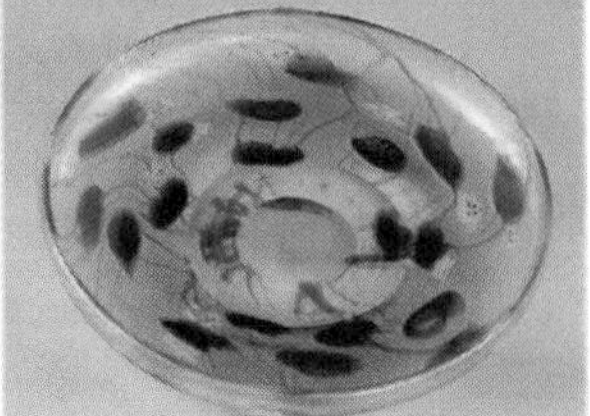

Bowl, 5" d., footed wide flattened shallow form, millefiori-type, large green leaves & vines swirling around w/white & green millefiori flowers scattered, small open bubble on inside, signed on base "L.C.T. R6115" **$1,323**

Bowl, 7 1/4" d., 3 1/2" h., squatty ribbed form w/incurved scalloped rim, overall gold iridescence, signed on the base "L.C.T. Favrile," ca. 1900 .... **$460**

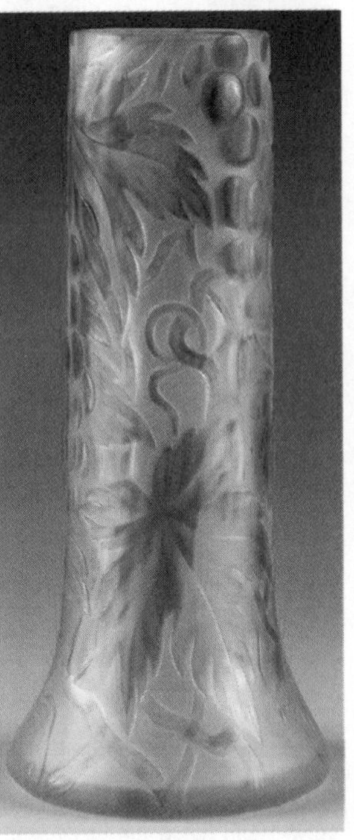

Cameo vase, 10 1/2" h., flaring base tapering to tall cylindrical sides, internally decorated w/areas of rich green shading dark to light, exterior w/wheel-carved large grape vines & clusters against a frosted ground, signed on base "L.C. Tiffany Favrile 6242C," rim slightly reduced **$4,083**

Candlestick lamp, the tapering swirled gold iridescent base w/a flaring rim, fitted w/a Bakelite insert supporting the open-topped domed & ruffled gold iridescent shade, both portions signed, unelectrified, overall 15" h. **$2,520**

Creamer, slightly swelled cylindrical shape w/a flat rim & pinched rim spout, applied angled handle, light greenish iridescent tint shading to blue opalescent w/a dark blue iridescent rim & interior, signed on the base, 3 1/4" h. **$1,035**

Cup & saucer, footed squatty rounded cup w/a flat rim & applied C-form handle, shallow dished matching saucer, gold iridescence intaglio-cut w/grape & leaf band on each piece, cup signed "9776E L.C. Tiffany Favrile," saucer w/ just initials, saucer 5 1/2" d., cup 2 1/2" h. **$1,093**

Flower frog, pinched cylindrical white opalescent center applied w/two bands of clear loops & open loops across the top, signed on base, one loop cracked, 3 5/8" h., 2 1/4" h. **$200-400**

Goblet, pastel type w/an optic ribbed opalescent domed foot & slender stem supporting a stepped & flaring bell-form optic ribbed bowl shading from pearly opalescent to aqua to yellow, signed on the foot "L.C.T. Favrile," 7 1/2" h. ... **$518**

Inkwell w/hinged bronze neck & cap, footed squatty round waisted well in iridescent blue w/silver & blue iridescent pulled- feather decoration, signed on bottom "L.C.T. H205," 5 1/2" h. ... **$6,038**

Loving cup, swelling wide cylindrical body w/three applied long loop handles, overall gold iridescence decorated w/green leaf & vine decoration, signed on base "LC Tiffany - Favrile 5127C" & w/original Tiffany paper label, 7 1/4" h. **$2,588**

Pitcher, 12" h., tall waisted cylindrical shape w/a pinched rim & applied loop handle, overall gold iridescence, signed "Louis C. Tiffany - Favrile" .. **$2,000 - 2,500**

←

Parfait, pastel, a disk foot & tall optic ribbed slightly flaring cylindrical bowl, aqua w/opalescent vertical bands, signed "L.C. Tiffany - Favrile" & original Tiffany paper label, 6 1/4" h. **$604**

←

Salt dip, witch's cauldron-style, wide squatty lower body w/a very wide flaring rim, tiny applied loop handles, overall gold iridescence, signed "LCT - Favrile X621," 1" h. **$345**

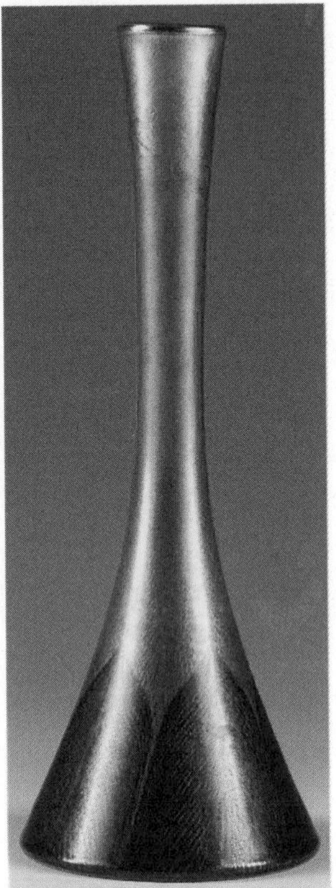

Vase, 10 1/4" h., a wide conical base tapering sharply to a very tall slender & slightly flaring stick neck, overall blue iridescence w/purple & gold highlights, blue pulled feathers around the flaring base, signed "L.C. Tiffany - Favrile - X137 1116 7912K" **$2,990**

Vase, 6" h., 5 1/4" d., wide bulbous ovoid body tapering to a wide flat mouth, gold & platinum iridescent ground applied w/pod & tendril designs in a rare blue, an Art Nouveau hooked design around the mouth, signed "LCT R3291" **$18,400**

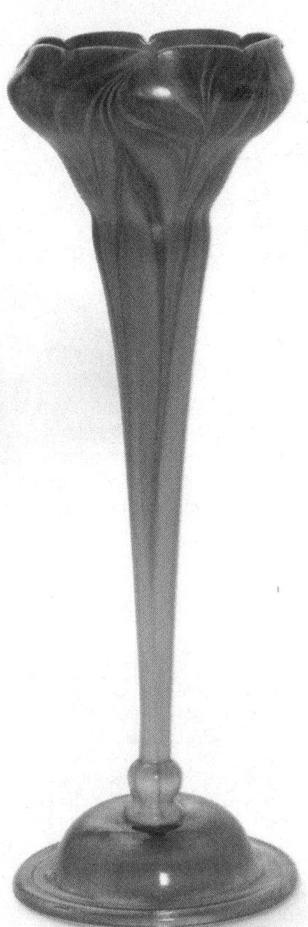

Vase, 15" h., floriform, an amber domed foot w/opalescent edge supports a slender knopped stem continuing into the tall slender bowl w/a widely flaring cupped tulip-form top w/scalloped rim decorated in striated green & amber iridescent feathering, early Corona factory example, ca. 1892 .... **$5,060**

Vase, 2 1/8" h., miniature, round base flaring widely to a squatty rounded shoulder centered by a wide low flared mouth, green iridescent ground w/a scattered Art Nouveau platinum iridescence, signed "LCT - V3785" **$2,040**

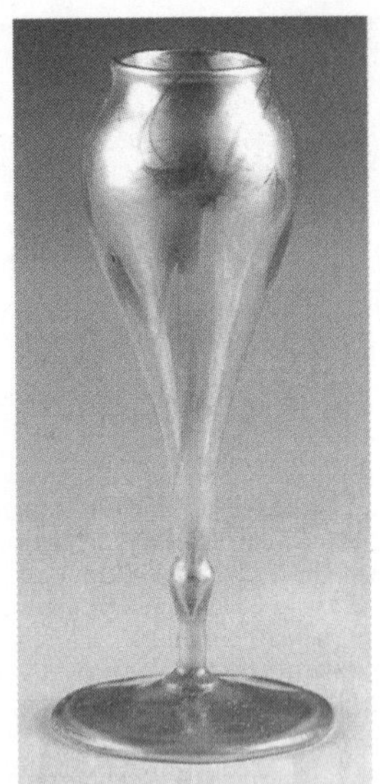

Vase, 6" h., floraform, wide round foot supporting a slender stem flaring to a tall ovoid body w/a flat rim, gold iridescent ground decorated w/green leaves & vines, signed "L. C. Tiffany - Favrile - 7198D" **$2,128**

Vase, 8" h., wide baluster form body w/a cupped round neck, dark green iridescent body, the neck in bronze iridescence w/intertwined zigzag lines in lime green & blue, signed on the base "8745M LC Tiffany Inc. Favrile" **$7,763**

Tiffin

A wide variety of fine glasswares were produced by the Tiffin Glass Company of Tiffin, Ohio. Beginning as a part of the large U.S. Glass Company early in the 20th century, the Tiffin factory continued making a wide range of wares until its final closing in 1984. One popular line is now called "Black Satin" and included various vases with raised floral designs. Many other acid- etched and hand-cut patterns were also produced over the years and are very collectible today. The three "Tiffin Glassmasters" books by Fred Bickenheuser are the standard references for Tiffin collectors.

Ashtray, shallow oval form, molded stag & wolf design, Black Satin, 6" l. **$55**

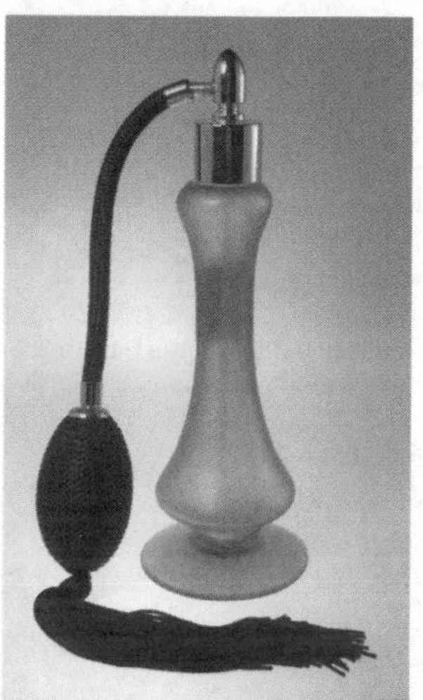

Atomizer, footed tall slender waisted body, blue satin, new atomizer fitting, 7" h. **$120**

Atomizer, round foot & slender stem w/a tall slender ovoid body, amber satin, new atomizer fitting, 7" h. **$115**

Bowl, 9 1/2" w., square w/flaring sides, Velva patt., frosted blue **$87**

> An atomizer relies on the Venturi effect. When the bulb is pressed and released, it creates a vaccuum that pulls perfume up into a chamber where it boils in the low pressure, creating the fine mist that is released into the air.

Candleholder, three-light, Art Deco style Pattern 308, Sky Blue, 7 1/4" w., 6 3/8" h. **$65**

Candleholders, one-light, figural stylized frogs, black satin, 5 1/2" h., pr. **$250**

Candlestick, one-light, floral cut decoration, Royal Blue, pr. (ILLUS. of one) **$160**

Candlestick, one-light, No. 82 w/ Jack Frost decoration, canary, 8 1/2" h., pr. (ILLUS. of one) **$130**

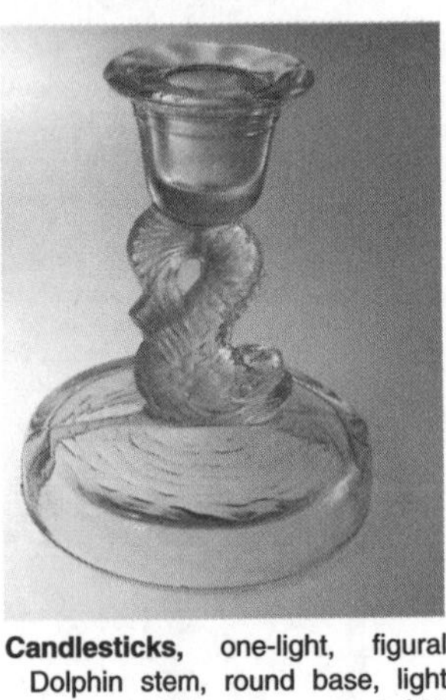

Candlesticks, one-light, figural Dolphin stem, round base, light green, 4 1/4" h., pr. **$68**

Stemware set: 23 - 4 3/4" h. wines, 13 - 6" sherbets, 10 - 10 1/2" goblets, 2 - 5 1/2" tumblers & one cordial; etched Athens-Diana patt., platinum rim bands, the set . **$949**

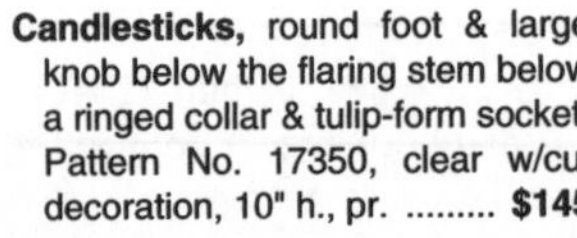

Candlesticks, round foot & large knob below the flaring stem below a ringed collar & tulip-form socket, Pattern No. 17350, clear w/cut decoration, 10" h., pr. **$145**

Candlesticks, one-light, Pattern No. 151, Black Satin w/gold band trim, 8" h., pr. **$85**

Candlesticks, one-light, Velva patt., blue satin, 5 3/4" h., pr. **$115**

Candlesticks, Twist Stem patt., Pattern 315, Amberina, 8 3/4" h., pr. (ILLUS. left & right with Twist Stem compote) **$95**

Candy jar, cov., mold-blown, No. 6106, diamond optic ovoid body tapering to a very slender stem & foot, domed cover w/pointed finial, Plum **$125**

Candy jar, cov., Pattern No. 179, footed widely flaring base & wide pagoda-style cover w/Gold Ship decoration, Black Satin, 6 1/2" d., 7 1/2" h. **$95**

Compote, open, 6 1/4" d., 3" h., wide shallow Killarney Green bowl raised on four applied clear pointed feet, Pattern No. 17430 (ILLUS. right with Killarney Green vase)...................................... **$48**

Console set: footed round bowl & pair of tall candlesticks; bowl No. 8098 & No. 300 candlesticks, Royal Blue w/satin finish, bowl 9 1/2" d., candlesticks 8 1/2" h., the set **$230**

Ivy ball, mold-blown, No. 6120 patt., bulbous diamond optic bowl on a tall faceted stem w/faceted rings on a round foot, original label, Golden Banada **$72**

Sherbet, tall stem & deep rounded bowl, Topaz stretch glass, 4 1/2" h. **$24**

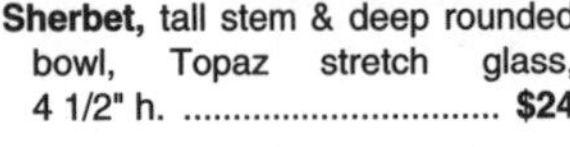

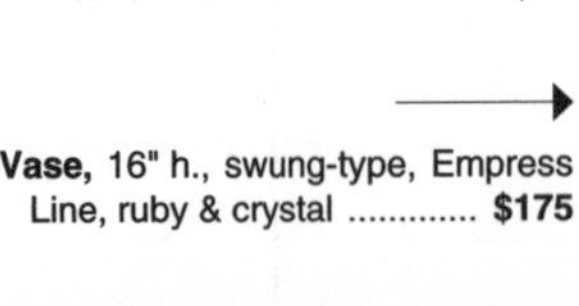

Vase, 16" h., swung-type, Empress Line, ruby & crystal **$175**

Decanter w/original stopper, Pattern No. 17437, a clear applied foot & heavy clear swirled ribs supporting the tall slender ovoid Killarney Green body, tall rounded clear stopper, 12" h. **$140**

Rose bowl, spherical w/wide flat mouth, Killarney Green bowl w/gold Melrose etching, on four applied clear pointed feet, 6 1/4" h. **$250**

Serving tray, flaring open center handle, Pattern No. 15320, Black Satin w/gold border bands, 10 1/2" d. **$58**

Vase, 20" h., swung-type, Green Fantasy Line, green & crystal **$235**

Westmoreland

In 1890 Westmoreland opened in Grapeville, Pennsylvania, and as early as the 1920s was producing colorwares in great variety. Cutting and decorations were many and are generally under appreciated and undervalued. Westmoreland was a leading producer of milk glass in "the antique style." The company closed in 1984 but some of their molds continued in use by others.

Basket, English Hobnail patt., fan-shaped body w/high arched handle, milk glass, 5" w., 10" h. **$30**

Basket, English Hobnail patt., high arched handle, clear, 5" w. ... **$24**

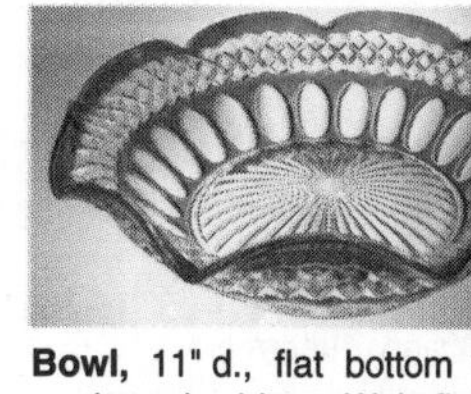

Bowl, 11" d., flat bottom w/flaring crimped sides, Wakefield patt., clear w/ruby stain **$120**

Bowl, 9 1/2" d., scalloped rim, American Hobnail patt., blue opalescent **$50**

Cheese compote, Marguerite patt., No. 700, pink, 4 1/2" d., 2 3/4" h. **$18**

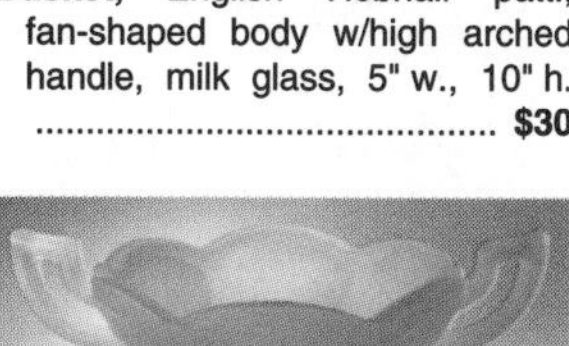

Compote, 5 1/4" w., 6" h., two-handled, tall stem, Colonial patt., Blue Mist **$22**

Compote, 7" d., 7 3/4" h., hexagonal foot & tall figural dolphin stem supporting a wide shallow round bowl, milk glass w/h.p. Charlton Leaf decoration **$85**

Compote, 8" h., sweetmeat-type w/ ball stem, Della Robbia patt., clear w/ruby stain **$125**

Compote, 7 1/2" h., 8" d., ball stem, spray-cased black, amber stain, cut to clear **$150**

Compote, 5 1/2" d., 3 1/2" h., open stem, Lotus patt., Flame red... **$30**

Compote, 8" h., Mother of Pearl Dolphin & Shell line, shell-shaped bowl w/dolphin base, milk white w/mother of pearl finish **$85**

Compote, oval, 6 1/2" l., 4 1/4" h., pressed cut glass-style design, Pattern No. 240, clear **$25**

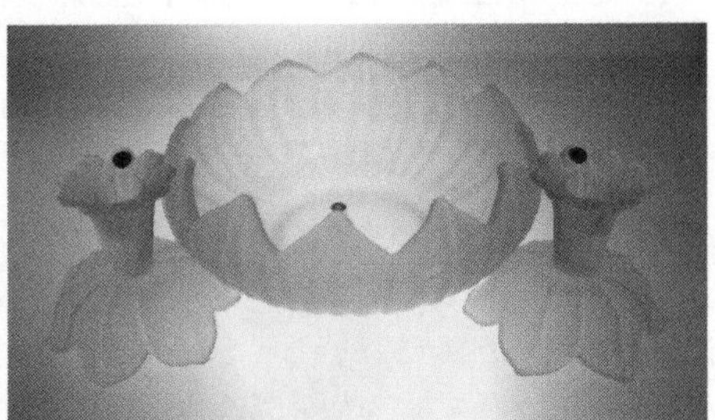

Console set: 9" d. cupped petal-form bowl & pair one-light 4" petal-form candleholders; Lotus patt., original labels, pink satin, the set **$95**

Lamp, table model, hexagonal foot & figural dolphin stem supporting a large flaring cylindrical paneled font, made to resemble an antique lamp, pink, 9 1/4" h. **$200**

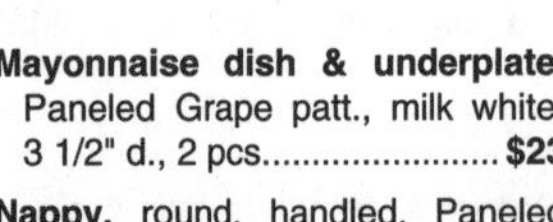

Mayonnaise dish & underplate, Paneled Grape patt., milk white, 3 1/2" d., 2 pcs....................... **$23**

Nappy, round, handled, Paneled Grape patt., milk white, 5" d. .. **$17**

Planter, Paneled Grape patt., square, milk white, 4 1/2" w.... **$40**

Plate, 8" d., openwork Forget-Me-Not patt., black decorated in white enamel w/a scene of a running deer, modern version of an early design **$40**

Vase, 8 1/4" h., Jack-in-the-pulpit style, Corinth patt., Amethyst Carnival **$49**

Tumbler, iced tea, English Hobnail patt., square foot, clear, 11 oz. **$14**

Puff box, cov., Paneled Grape patt., milk white, 4 1/2" d. **$32**

Sweetmeat, cov., Old Quilt patt., high-footed, milk white, 6 1/2" h. **$35**

Tumbler, Beaded Edge patt., No. 64-2 fruit decoration, milk white **$19**

Vase, 9" h., Old Quilt patt., bell-rimmed, footed, milk white...... **$45**

Vase, 11 1/2" h., Paneled Grape patt., bell-rimmed, footed, milk white....................................... **$45**

GLOBE MAPS

Celestial globe, the openwork round framework enclosing an Earth-centered solar system, the octagonal platform frame decorated w/celestial motifs w/ bone edging raised on four square tapering reeded legs ending in gilt paw feet & joined by four square stretchers, Woodward, London, 19th c., 32" d., 51" h. **$4,830**

Celestial globe, table model, a 6" d. globe fitted in a cherry stand w/vertical & horizontal medial rings & raised on three baluster- and ring-turned legs joined by swelled stretchers joined at the center, by Gilman Joslin, United States, ca. 1840 (minor abrasions) **$4,025**

Celestial & terrestrial globes, table models, the terrestrial globe embroidered w/gold silk threads & inscribed w/black ink, the celestial globe similarly decorated w/the addition of watercolor highlights, both on cream silk grounds, & mounted on a wooden baluster-turned stem & circular molded foot, probably Westtown School, Chester County, Pennsylvania, 5" d., 12 1/4" h., pr............ **$8,625**

Celestial & terrestrial globes, miniature, each small globe fitted in a two-part domed manogany case, marked "Malby's Celestial Globe Showing the Principal Stars of each Constellation. Boughton St. London. March 1, 1844," & "Newton's New & Improved Terrestrial Globe Published by Newton & Son 66 Chancery Lane, London," 19th c., globes 3" d., near pr. (abrasions, losses to globes, repairs to cases) ... **$4,312**

Terrestrial globe, large hand-colored globe in a four-legged ebonized fruitwood stand w/ baluster- and ring-turned legs joined by a turned cross-stretcher, w/a medial zodiac ring, Merzback and Falk, Brussels, Belgium, 19th c., 16" d., 18" h. **$546**

Terrestrial globe, paper mat cover a wooden core, round maker mark to the left of North America, D.C. & A. Murdock, West Boylston, Massachusetts, ca. 1835-40, some stains, some rub marks, holes at end for mounting in a stand, 5" d. **$862**

Celestial & terrestrial globes, table models, each globe raised on a foliate-molded cast-iron base, issued by Merriam & Moore, Troy, New York, 1852, 8 3/4" d., 9" h., pr. **$9,775**

Terrestrial globe, floor model, 18" d. globe mounted on a partial gilt Art Nouveau-style metal stand, Geo. F. Cram, United States, ca. 1900 .... **$2,990**

Terrestrial globe, Louis XV-Style, the Provincial style carved & turned oak stand w/cabriole legs joined by three turned stretchers joined by a central drop post, the serpentine apron carved w/ scrolling florals, the globe w/a metal-banded meridian band, France, late 19th c., 23" d., 30" h. **$316**

Terrestrial globe, table model, 12" d. globe mounted within a round ring supported on ebonized baluster- and knob-turned legs joined by stretchers, by W. & T. M. Bardin, England, corrected to 1817, 16" h. to meridian **$1,380**

Terrestrial globe, floor model, mahogany, raised on a baluster standard continuing to sabre legs ending in brass casters, J. W. Carey, Strand, London, early 19th c., 44" h. **$14,950**

Terrestrial globe, mounted in half round ring on ebonized turned wooden stand w/round foot, Strand Publications, England, ca. 1920, 6" d., 11" h................. **$633**

Terrestrial globe, table model, tilted globe raised on a cast-iron base w/ a short ringed pedestal above the circular plinth w/floral decoration on leaf-tip cast feet, globe marked "H. Schedler's - Terrestrial - Globe - 12 In. Diameter - Compiled from the latest and most authentic sources including all the recent Georgr. Discoveries - Containing the Principal Lines of Oceanic Steam Communications & Submarine Telegraphs - Pat No. 24751868 Copyright 1889 - USA," late 19th c., globe 12" d........ **$805**

INDIAN ARTIFACTS MARKET REPORT

Market News

According to Danica Farnand, the Native American specialist at Cowan's Auctions (www.cowansauctions.com) in Cincinnati, Ohio, "interest in Native American art and artifacts remains strong, especially for materials from the Arctic and Northwest regions." Collectors are attracted by the quality of the art and the historical background. Most collectors are in their 50s and are passionate and well informed about traditional Native American culture and history. For those who collect jewelry and clothing accessories, they often love them so much that they buy them to wear rather than just to display—even pieces that cost as much as $25,000.

Farnand explained that those who collect only for investment constitute just a small percentage of her clients. "Most are collectors who love the pieces for art's sake, but virtually all collect with value in mind as well,"she commented. She agrees with the axiom that it's best to buy what you love, rather than only for investment, as future value is impossible to predict with certainty.

A wide variety of artifacts are selling, such as pottery, beadwork, baskets, totem poles, jewelry, blankets, rugs and other textiles. Farnan has not seen any particular form dominate the market but, as in most categories, the high-end of the market is doing the best, with the middle and lower end soft.

She noted that early pieces (1880s and before) are becoming scarce, as much of it is already in museums or private collections. Consequently, items from the 1920s and 30s and later have started to come to the market as owners realize their growing value. Contemporary pottery (1950s and later), especially from the Southwest, is a growing area and has a lot of future potential.

Fakes are a big problem, especially with pottery, beadwork, and wood pieces. Some fakes are clumsy and easy to spot, but certain ones, like wood pieces, are harder to detect. This is in part because genuine pieces were handmade, one-of-a-kind works, so they lack the standardized manufacturing methods and markings of commercially made products that can be used as benchmarks to determine authenticity.

Legal Alert

Just as with firearms and ivory, Native American artifacts are regulated, but provide enormous opportunity. Dealers who are willing to take the time to learn the laws have a great advantage over those who are not. Developing a reputation as an expert, law-abiding dealer can create a larger and more loyal customer base than in other non-regulated categories, as fewer dealers are willing to take the time to learnthe regulations and maintain proper records.

Certain Native American artifacts are covered by federal and state law. Federal laws include the Antiquities Act of 1906, National Historic Preservation Act of 1966, Archaeological Resources Protection Act of 1979, and the Native American Graves Protection and Repatriation Act (NAGPRA) of 1990. For more information visit the National Park Service site covering Archaeology Law and Ethics. (http://bit.ly/aW46dy).

While it's legal to buy and sell many Native American items such as pipes, arrowheads, textiles, etc. recovered from private lands, it's illegal to remove any artifacts from state or federal lands. Depending on the items and circumstances, it may even be illegal to sell items purchased legally before the first federal law was passed in 1906. The laws have been enacted to prevent "pot hunters" from digging up artifacts from federal and state lands, a serious and growing problem across the country, especially in the Southwest. Not only do these illegal diggings desecrate sacred burial grounds, but they also prevent the compilation of historical and archaeological information.

Penalties can be severe. Violators can have their artifacts seized without compensation and can be fined or jailed. In a widely publicized case in the Four Corners area, a Utah antiquities dealer participated in a two-year sting operation in which he secretly recorded transactions with collectors for the FBI that resulted in the arrests of 26 suspects.

Laws are especially specific concerning sacred and cultural items. NAGPRA covers human remains, funerary objects, sacred objects, or objects of cultural patrimony. These items are illegal to own or sell and are required to be returned to lineal descendants or Indian tribes. An example of a sacred item that cannot be bought or sold and must be repatriated is a pot with a "kill hole." Some pots buried with bodies had kill holes added to allow the spirit to go free. While the NAGPRA law has been primarily applied to museums and other organizations, it can be applied to individuals as well.

Another law applies to contemporary Native American arts and crafts. According to the The Indian Arts and Crafts Act of 1990, it is illegal to offer or display for sale, or sell any art or craft product in a manner that falsely suggests it is Indian produced. According to the Act, an Indian is defined as a member of any federally or state recognized Indian tribe, or an individual certified as an Indian artisan by an Indian tribe. The law covers all Indian and Indian-style traditional and contemporary arts and crafts produced after 1935. Typical items often copied by non-Native Americans include jewelry, pottery, clothing, baskets, rugs, kachina dolls, and fetishes.

In addition to federal laws, many states have enacted their own more restrictive laws. (See http://bit.ly/bSD5ko)

To be safe, always buy from a reputable dealer or auction house, who will provide a letter of authenticity documenting an artifact's origin and provenance. This will protect you from legal problems and make it easier to resell the item in the future. Since museums and other official organizations cannot accept or purchase undocumented items, and private collectors may be hesitant, not having the proper documentation can make them harder to resell.

INDIAN ART & ARTIFACTS

Bag, Sioux, quillwork, dark red ground w/yellow diamonds trimmed in purplish blue, rectangular designs along the bottom fringe, brass bells & metal sequins, losses & restoration, ca. 1890, overall 20 1/2" l. **$345**

Ceremonial dance apron, Northern California, buckskin w/fringe cut at bottom, the backskirt doubled over at top & fringed, rows of fringe w/additional black & white beaded drops w/larger trade yellow, blue, aqua, black & veined russet beads along w/fringe, dimes, etc., a row of American dimes borders at the top of the fringe, earliest date 1845, latest date 1873, probably Hupa group, 29 1/2 x 33" **$6,613**

Coat, Sioux, boy's, fine hide w/ elaborate beaded designs on the front & back including a horse, deer, buffalo, pipe & bird in shades of red, yellow, blue, white, black & green, w/a Sioux blue border, red white heart & cut metal bead trim, fringe across the yoke in back, down the sleeves, around the collar & across the bottom, interior lined w/muslin, remnants of silk piping on eges & remnants of quill on rear collar fringe, ca. 1890, width across sleeves 41" (ILLUS. of front & back)............... **$13,225**

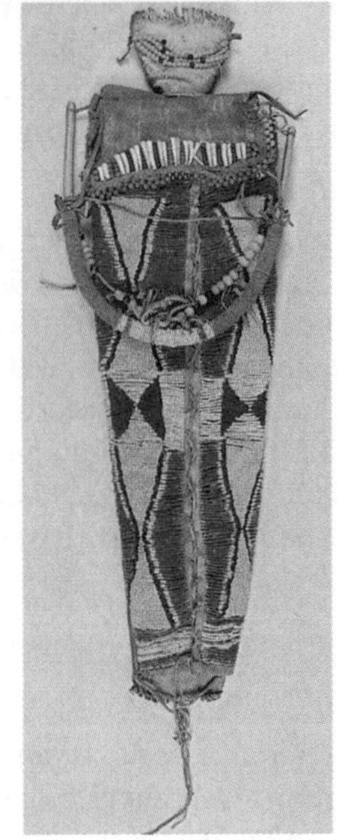

Cradle board, Cheyenne or Arapaho, toy-sized, on brain-tanned leather, elaborate overall geometric beading in Cheyenne pinks & greasy yellow beads, Peking glass, cobalt blue & French brass pony beads & bells, as well as dentillium shell-decorated hood & top crown, wooden board w/additional top frame to support traditional leather flag, back inscribed "Purchased in SW Colorado, 1902," 8 1/2" w., 23" l. **$12,937**

Basket, Eastern Woodland Indian, woven double wall-type, painted w/red & blue swab decoration, 19th c., 17" h. (minor breaks) **$863**

Basket, Apache, woven coiled construction, seventeen female, male & horse figures w/zigzag bands, 18 1/2" d. **$4,600**

Basket, Pima, coiled construction w/a flat base, flaring sides & a rosette center, design of whirling meanders **$3,450**

Bowl, San Ildefonso, pottery, wide squatty rounded black-on-black design of feathers & geometric devices, signed by Maria & Popovi, 8 1/2" d. **$7,475**

Cradle board, Paiute (Mono), woven construction w/the bottom board w/a delicate brown diamond & zigzag design, the arched hood w/a central diamond band & long beaded tassels, black & red yarn lacing, first half 20th c., base 14 1/2" w., 31" l. **$1,150**

Necklace, Navajo, a massive size w/a central fancy drop including two 1921 Morgan silver dollars, two pieces of turquoise & three pieces of red coral, facing claws frame the pieces w/an outside border of silver leaves & & flowers, the three-string necklace composed of large silver beads & six similar attached pendants separated by framed silver dollars, at total of 16 silver dollars dating from 1884 to 1926, signed by John Yellowhorse, two loose claws, 54" l. **$2,875**

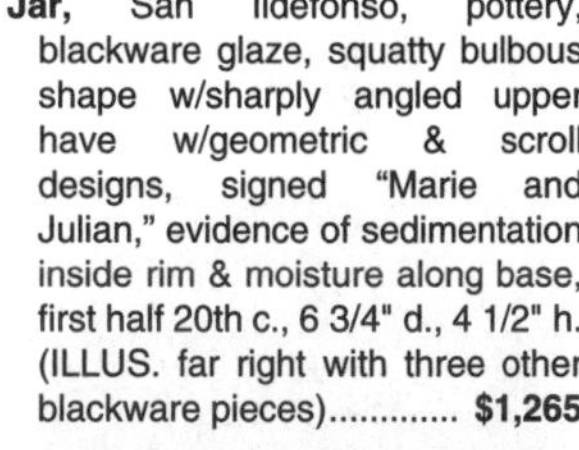

Jar, San Ildefonso, pottery, blackware glaze, squatty bulbous shape w/sharply angled upper have w/geometric & scroll designs, signed "Marie and Julian," evidence of sedimentation inside rim & moisture along base, first half 20th c., 6 3/4" d., 4 1/2" h. (ILLUS. far right with three other blackware pieces)............. **$1,265**

Parfleche envelope, Plains, h.p. hide, the long folded form decorated w/bold geometric triangles & rectangles in dark green, red & yellow outlined in blue, ca. 1890, 14 3/4" w., 25" l. **$1,725**

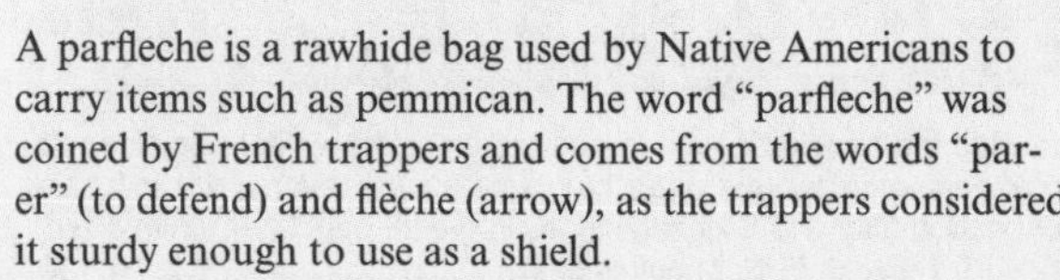

A parfleche is a rawhide bag used by Native Americans to carry items such as pemmican. The word "parfleche" was coined by French trappers and comes from the words "parer" (to defend) and flèche (arrow), as the trappers considered it sturdy enough to use as a shield.

Photograph, cabinet-sized, studio shot of a standing Pawnee Indian in native costume including arm bracelets, shell necklace, peace meddal, apron, fringed leggings, beaded moccasins & wool trade blanket w/beaded blanket strip, photographed by J.H. Taylor, Republic Michigan, reverse inscribed "George Osbornes, Pawnee Indian - Nov. 18th, 1889" **$150**

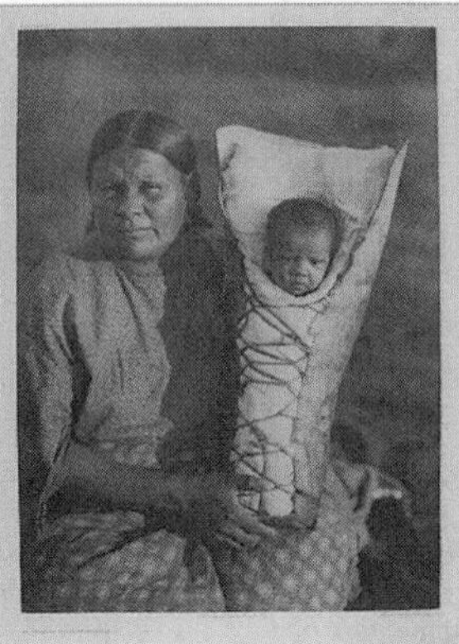

Photographic portfolio, "The North American Indian," by Edward Sherrif Curtis, Portfolio #19, complete set of 36 large-format photogravures after photographs by Curtis, comprising plate numbers 652-687, each photogravure w/a printed caption, plate number, photographer's copyright & printer's credit in the margin, contained loose as issued in a large portfolio w/leather spine & corners, cloth ties w/gilt-impressed number "19," complete w/large-format printed plate list page, 1927, each sheet 18 x 22 1/2", the set (ILLUS. of part) **$16,675**

Pipe bag, Cheyenne, woman's, beaded hide, made from possible bag, a large section covered w/ traditional bar designs of yellow ochre, red white hearts, dark green & greasy yellow, fringe at the bottom, Native repairs, ca. 1875, 28" l. **$1,265**

Plate, San Ildefonso, pottery, black on black, round w/a border design of a snake w/broken arrow coming from mouth, signed "Maria & Santana," some light scratching, 13" d. **$3,480**

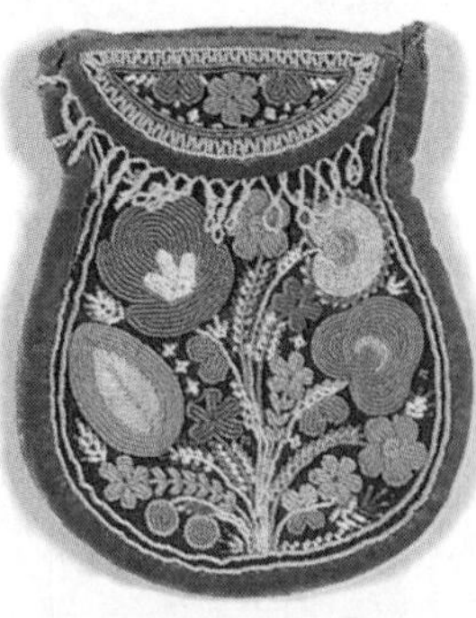

Purse, Maliseet, beaded on black vevlet, overall cluster beadwork forming an overall colorful floral bouquet w/red velvet trim, double flap w/bead fringe & red silk handles, ca. 1880, 6 1/4" l. . **$690**

Purse, Sioux, beaded, brass fittings, swing top handle beaded in dark green, red & white, one side w/a white beaded ground decorated w/bold geometric designs in red, blue & green, the reverse w/a light blue ground decorated w/a narrow center beaded diamond & zigzag stripes in green, dark blue, white & red, matching beaded ends, ca. 1880, 12" l., 9 1/2"h. (ILLUS. of both sides) **$1,150**

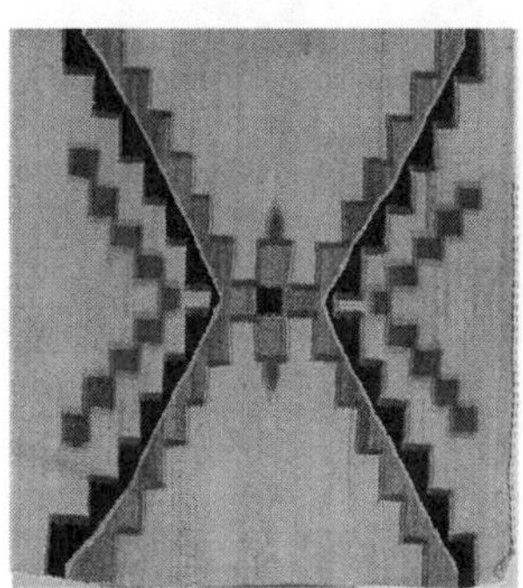

Rug, Navajo, a Storm variant design w/stepped angled bands in rust red, black & grey on a natural ground, ca. 1930, 32 x 39" **$345**

Rug, Navajo, Bright West Reservation area, Eye Dazzler style, bands of pictorial elements of arrows & arrowheads w/serrate bands & multiple borders, in dark red, black, white, yellow & natural, probably Tees Nos Pas, minute color transferal & minor wear, 5' 1" x 7' 8" **$3,795**

Rug, Navajo, early West Reservation, wide central serrate diamond designs surrounded by concentric lightning bands in black & red on a carded grey ground, reciprocal tan, black & white terraced border, spirit line, 3' 1" x 5' 8" **$1,380**

Rug, Navajo, Eye Dazzler-style, dark red ground w/a central small cross within diamonds & angled bars in grey, white, blue & tan, complex ticked border on each end, handspun, aniline dyes, ca. 1890, 57 x 81" **$4,370**

Rug, Navajo, wool, transitional style w/stripes of red, tan, grey & natural along w/a bit of aniline orange at one end, corner tassels, early 20th c., 2' 11" x 4' 4" **$863**

Rug, Navajo, woven wool w/finely carded yarn, chief's style in dark brown w/natural banding in central area w/a blue stripe at center, possibly indigo, corner tassels, Third Phase, ca. 1910-20, 3' 7" x 4' 9" **$2,760**

The Navajo originally made utilitarian blankets with few patterns and colors. Only after they began trading with American setlers did they begin making the more elaborate designs.

Rug, Navajo, woven wool, Western Reservation, early regional weaving w/exceptional carded yarn in a beautiful outlined serrate diamond design overall in complimentary browns, tans, dark red, blue & natural, surrounded by a Tees-Nos-Pas border frame, fine corner fringes, 3' 7" x 5' **$2,415**

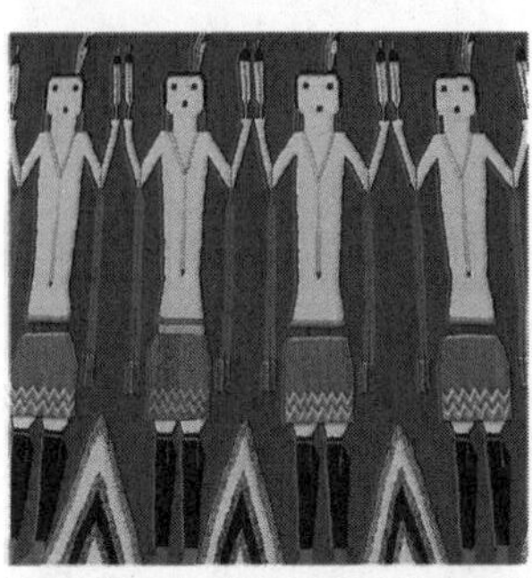

Rug, Navajo, Yei patt. bright red background w/white yei figures in blue kilts & colorful detailing, triangular peak motifs anchor the bottom of the rug between the figures, very large size, 4' 2" x 12' **$4,025**

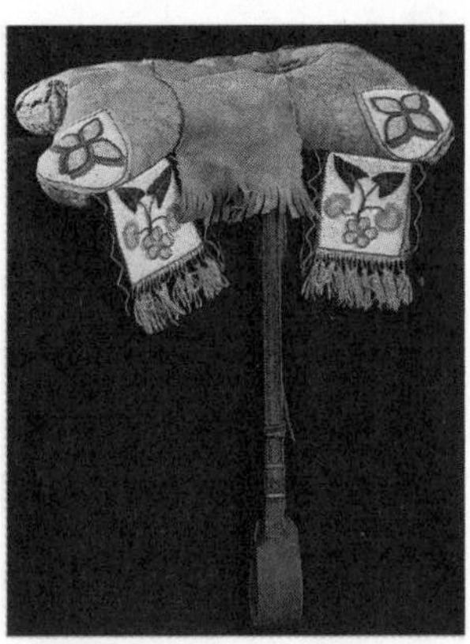

Saddle & stirrups, Cree, pad-type, tanned hide w/floral beaded teardrops at each corner & suspended panels from same w/ floral elements trimmed in stroud border w/coral tassels on bead drops at bottom, commercial stirrups, probably Army issue, & cinch finding of harness leather, ca. 1885, saddle 22 x 29 1/2", stirrups 30" l. **$3,575**

Saddle bags, Sioux, fine hide lazy stitiched w/traditional geometric designs & bars on the sides in shades of green, blue, yellow & red on white, cones w/horsehair tassels, ca. 1880, 13 1/2 x 18 3/4", pr. **$8,338**

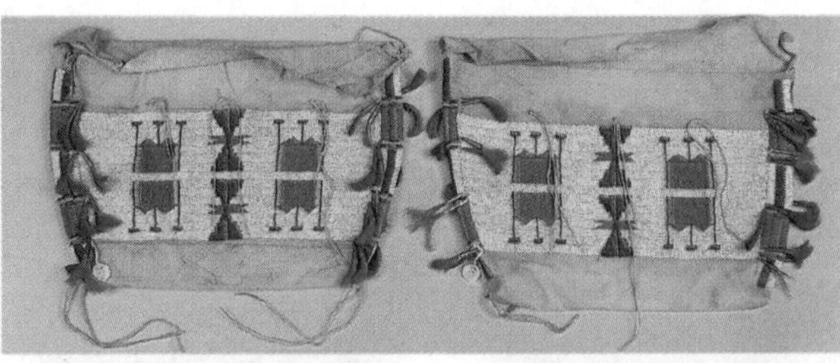

Saddle blanket Navajo, double-type, bold graduated diamond designs in shades of red, dark blue, grey & natural, ca. 1940, 30 x 44" **$345**

Saddle blanket Navajo, double-type, Storm variant design w/ Spiderwoman crosses in the corners, done in red, black & brown on natural, good lazy lines, ca. 1930, 30 x 46" **$431**

Saddle blanket Navajo, pictorial double-type w/a Tree of Life variant patt., done in red, black, brown & natural, ca. 1940, 24 x 48" .. **$460**

Sugar bucket, Woodlands, birchbark, miniature size, rectangular flat base w/tapering sides w/a wrapped rim, a colored trefoil or leaf design on front in red & brown, stitching at sides & top, nice patina, 6 3/4" l., 4 1/2" h. **$201**

Tomahawk, Plains, bronze pipe-form, 19th c. **$2,990**

Tray, Apache, basketry, tightly & finely coiled w/a woven-in concentric design & whirling logs, 8 1/2" d. **$86**

Tray, Hopi, basketry, coiled in the "Crow Mother" design in black, brown & red, 15" d. **$431**

Tray, Northern California Hupa, woven basketry, flattened round ceremonial meal-type, banded geometric & lightning design, 13 3/4" d., 3" h. (minor wear, rim damage) **$165**

Tray, Piaute, Navaho basketry wedding-type, wide shallow coiled form w/bands of serrated rings in colors, ca. 1920, finely woven, 14 3/8" d. (some soiling & damage) **$468**

Tray, Yavapai, basketry, coil construction w/expanding star design in dark martynia & willoa, 7 3/8" d. (one missing stitch) **$880**

Trinket box, cov., Wakashan, basketry, oblong, finely woven Nootka form w/whale boat & bird, fitted cover, small stain, rim split, 5" l., 3" h. **$660**

Trousers, Plains, man's, ringed & beaded hide, decorated w/contour beaded flowers & leaves in red, pink, green, brown & yellow, fringe along entire length of outer seam, ca. 1920s, 38" l. **$288**

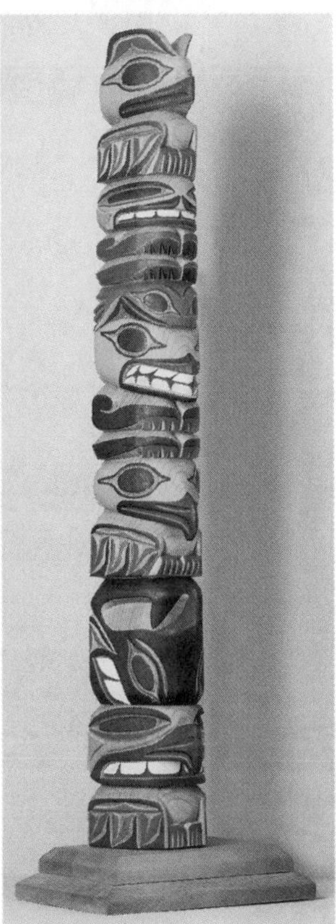

Totem pole, Northwest Coast, carved wood, composed of seven stacked clan figures, each w/ painted details, well-done, typical of work from the Ye Olde Curiosity Shoppe of Seattle, carved & signed by L. Rudick of Vancouver Island, signed in pencil "12- 2-23 Seattle totem," 25 1/2" h. **$863**

Ulu, Northeastern states, 3,000 BC, 6-8" l. **$500-1,000**

Vest, Sioux, man's, fully beaded, pictorial & spiritual markings, front shows headdressed warrior on each side w/crossed flags above, back depicts Indian on horse spearing buffalo, crossed flags in both lower corners & on trim around bottom, white background, leather fringe & front ties **$650**

Tray, Pima, basketry, wide shallow bowl-form w/an expanding whirling design of stepped rectangles, triangles & bands emanating from a dark center of Martynia on a willow body, finely woven, 12 1/4" d. **$1,035**

Vest, Sioux, man's, lazy stitch beaded pictorial type, front panels w/deer, stepped terraces & crosses beaded in greasy yellow & red white hearts on a Sioux blue ground, fringe on back, down shoulders & on sides, ca. 1880, 17 1/2 x 20" **$3,680**

Vest, Eastern Sioux, child's, beaded hide w/a floral & bird stitched design in dark blue, green, red, white & light blue beads, black cotton cloth back w/blue striped cotton lining, 16 x 16" **$1,035**

War club, Plains, skull-cracker, polished stone head encircled w/ band of translucent red, green & opaque yellow beads which is also wrapped around handle above leather end, 27" l. (wear to leather & stone, bead loss)............... **$600**

An ulu is a traditional Inuit knife with a broad curved blade and a handle above the blade so that the weight of the knife is centered above the blade and cuts by rocking back and forth. The position of the handle makes it easier to use one-handed, as the vertical presssure holds the cut item in place.

IVORY

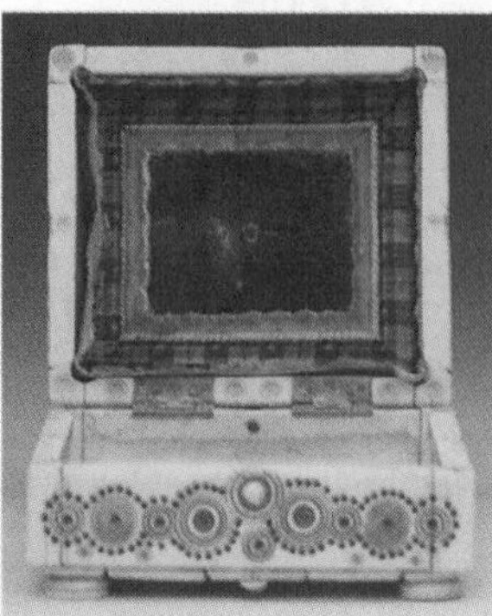

Box w/hinged cover, rectangular, the sides & top composed of thick pieces of ivory incised & drilled w/bands of roundels of various sizes, the interior of the top lined w/a tartan plaid material centered by a rectangular mirror, 19th c., some old age cracks, 4 x 4 1/2", 2 1/4" h. **$978**

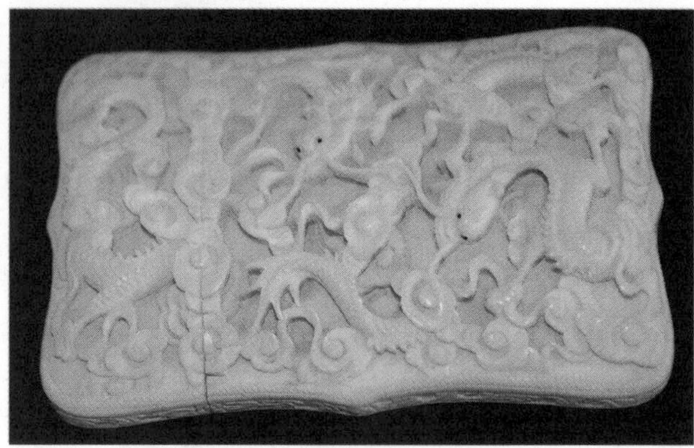

Calling card case, flattened rectangular form w/serpentine edges, ornately carved overall w/entwined Oriental dragons, late 19th c. **$325**

Figure group, a tall slender Chinese mother standing beside her child, flanking a short tree trunk w/a colorful parrot, each figure w/dark polychrome decoration, probably China, late 19th - early 20th c., 5" w., 16" h. **$900**

Figure of a Buddhist Immortal, a tall gently curved tusk carved as the figure of a bearded man w/a high bald head & a bare chest & belly, holding a fan in one hand & prayer beads in the other, on a round black wood base, Oriental, mid-20th c., minor loss, 13 1/2" h. **$489**

Plaque a pointed pediment carved in high-relief w/a spread-winged American eagle above a shield & long leaves, above a long rectangular panel carved in high-relief w/a scene of Washington Crossing the Delaware, in original embossed leather & velvet fitted case, American, late 19th c., 9 3/4" l., 7 1/2" h. **$5,019**

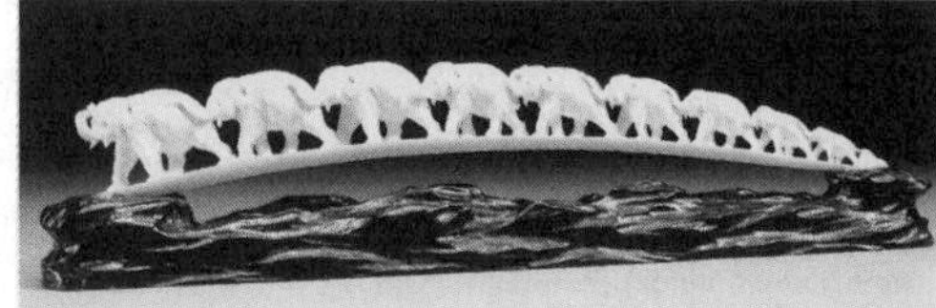

Sculpture, a parade of elephants, each connected & carved in graduated sizes from a single tusk, mounted on a carved wood stand, probably China, 20th c., 21" l. **$575**

JEWELRY MARKET REPORT

According to jewelry collector, dealer, journalist and author Kathy Flood, jewelry is a steadily growing market. "New buyers are coming into the market all the time," she said. "Foreign buyers' interest in American jewelry continues to grow, and American buyers range from newly retired baby boomers to younger collectors interested in making jewelry part of their portfolios."

Flood has a special interest in figural jewelry and owns the Web sites FiguralPins.com and ChristmasTreePins.com. But she keeps a close eye on the full breadth of the jewelry market, covering both fine and costume jewelry.

"In fine jewelry, the passion for colored gems burns on, especially in diamonds, from rare colors to fashiony blacks. Also, while fine jadeite has always sold well in the uppermost echelons of top auction houses, the new wealth of Chinese collectors is driving acquisition even more aggressively, and this is filtering down even to intensified interest in simulated jadeite.

"In costume jewelry, statement necklaces got everyone accustomed to massive size, leading the way to enormous ring styles with two-finger shanks. Earrings are also rather enormous, with chandeliers and shoulder dusters everywhere. Still, if most women could have any pair of earrings in the world, they would be the Colombian emeralds Angelina wore on the red carpet ... what now seems like an eternity ago. But they remain embedded in many visual memories!"

While the economy is still struggling to rebound from the recession, jewelry is doing well, especially top quality pieces. "Auction-house sales are strong, and antiques-mall sales have picked up," Flood commented. "The Internet has tremendous strengths, from eBay to Ruby Lane to privately owned Web sites.

"Because collectors want to be smart and not just amused, they seek jewelry they believe will hold and accrue the most value," she added. "Typically this is in the high-end realm, but collectors won't just plunk down any amount of cash simply because something is 'high end.' If you check sites that sell only high-end jewelry, a lot of great stuff ... sits there. Top designers, rare marks, and scarce categories usually still do very well. But some sales just take time. If it has quality, integrity, cache, great signature, it will sell—unless the price point is insane. Just one reason (among many) I'm a proponent of figural jewelry is that it's not only highly entertaining to collect, but it can sell across the board, low end to high end, because collectors fancy what they don't have in these categories."

Of course, as in all collecting categories, fakes and reproductions are issues to contend with. "More are appearing all the time," she noted. "If something is highly desirable, it's often reproduced or faked. Of special note, because colored gems are extremely popular, composition rubies are deluging the market, as well as coated diamonds treated to achieve 'fancy color.' Sometimes reproductions have the blessing of original design houses, but that can still cause confusion in the market, as in sought-after Mexican silver, with even original family members recreating great vintage works by famous designers."

Flood believes the foreign market has exceptional potential. "American sellers would be wise to cultivate foreign buyers," she noted. "From Toronto to Tasmania, from Montreal to Moscow, our friends beyond our borders are excellent trade partners. They comprise 50 percent or more of my clientele and are almost always people you'd enjoy knowing."

For more information on identification and values of fine and costume jewelry, consult *Warman's Jewelry*, *Warman's Costume Jewelry Figurals*, and *Collecting Costume Jewelry Christmas Tree Pins*.

JEWELRY

Antique (1800-1920)

Bar pin, garnet, diamond & 14k gold, centering a sugarloaf garnet surrounded by rose-cut diamonds, three large garnets at each end & set throughout w/ faceted garnets, French hallmarks, missing one stone $1,058

Bar pin, garnet, diamond & 15k gold, the center set w/a large garnet surrounded by 18 round diamonds flanked by gold bar ends, one diamond replaced, Victorian $413

Bracelet, garnet & silver, gradually tapering band set overall w/prong-set garnets in bands & other patterns, early 20th c., 2 1/2" w. $345

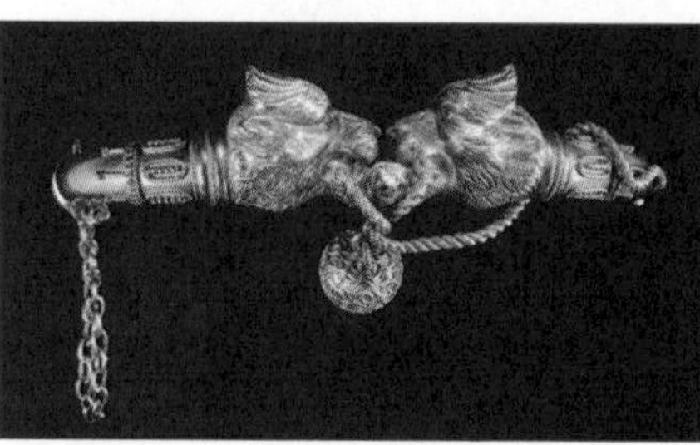

Bracelet, gold (14k yellow), circular tubular form w/ a section of two facing gargoyle heads w/a small diamond six-prong setting above a ball drop, hinged to open, small safety chain, unmarked, Victorian, 2 1/4 x 2 1/2" $2,300

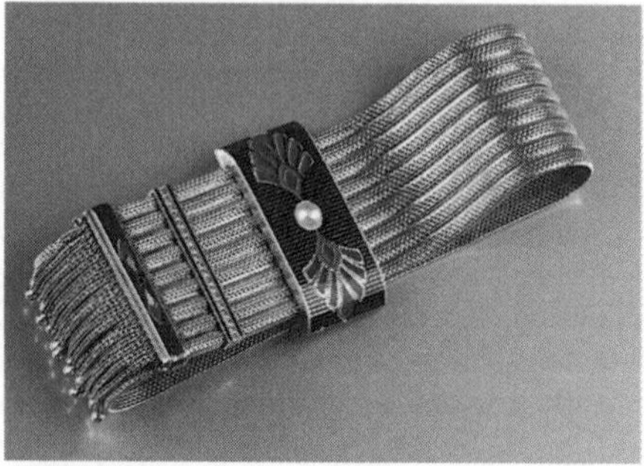

Bracelet, gold (14k) & enamel, slide-type, wide flat adjustable mesh band w/the flat slide enameled w/blue palmettes centered by a pearl on a black-enameled ground, foxtail fringe $1,998

Bracelet, gold (14k), enamel & seed pearl, composed of circular engraved gold links surmounted by blue enamel circles each set w/a seed pearl, one link is a drop, 7 1/2" l. $940

Bracelet, platinum, 14k gold & diamond, designed as a coiled snake w/a platinum & yellow gold mesh body, the head set w/an old European-cut diamond weighing approx. 1.01 cts., rose-cut eyes offset by dark patination, stamped "PD," 11 1/2" l. **$7,050**

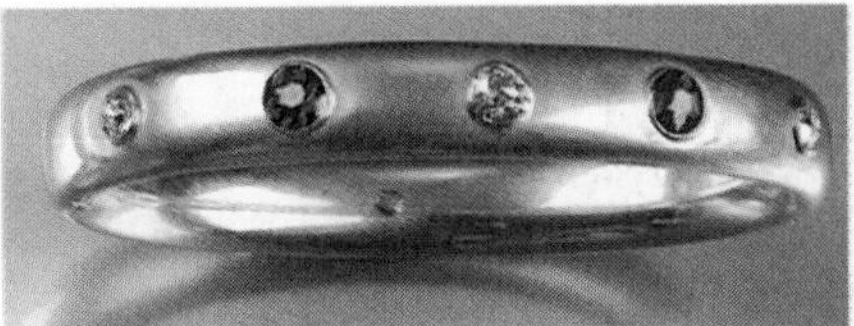

Bracelet, sapphire, diamond & 14k gold, bangle-type, simple hinged gold band bezel-set w/three old European-cut diamonds alternating w/two circular-cut sapphires, Edwardian **$3,525**

Brooch, enamel & diamond, model of butterfly, red, yellow, blue & black base taille enamel wings & old mine-cut diamond body, ruby eyes, rose-cut diamond accents, silver-topped 14k gold mount, Austro-Hungarian hallmarks **$6,463**

Brooch, gold (18k) & plique-à-jour, Art Nouveau-style model of a dragonfly w/a yellow gold body set w/one oval blue sapphire, the shoulder of the wings, mouth, eyes & body set w/small round diamonds, early 20th c. ... **$1,725**

Brooch, micromosaic, a round wide gilt-metal frame w/wirework & bead accents centering a round color design of a butterfly on a white ground **$1,293**

Earrings, amethyst & 14k gold, ornate oblong gold leaf & coiled wirework frame enclosing a large collet-set pear-shaped amethyst w/a smaller amethyst above & below, Victorian, missing tops, pr. **$1,645**

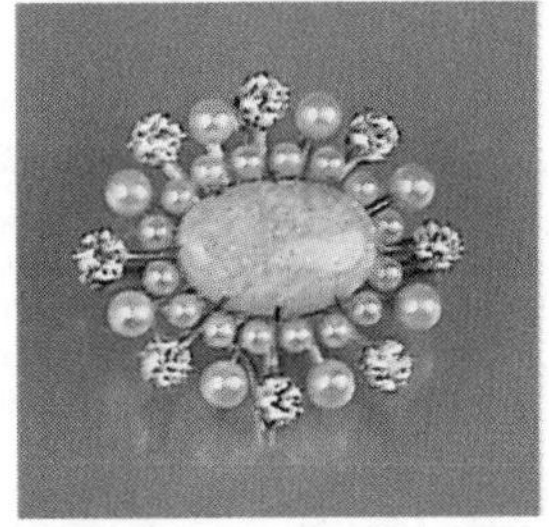

Brooch, opal & diamond, oval opal framed by seed pearls & old European-cut diamonds, 14k gold mount, early 20th c., hallmark for Krementz & Co., w/original Tiffany & Co. box **$1,293**

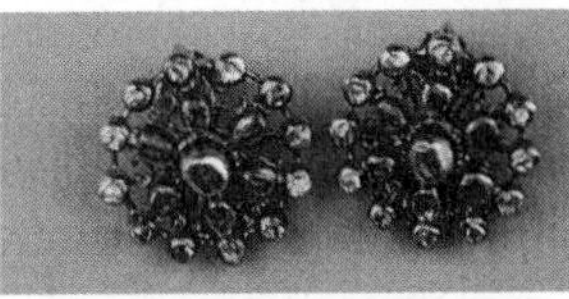

Earrings, ruby, diamond & gold, a round openwork gold frame bezel-set w/rubies surrounded by rose-cut diamonds, one small ruby missing, ca. 1890, pr. **$633**

Locket, gold, pearl & diamond, oval set w/an outer band of pearls around a large stylized flower set w/24 partial-cut diamonds & a central pearl, scrolled top for hanging ring, French hallmarks, 19th c. **$403**

Necklace, diamond & ruby, negligee-style, two rose-cut diamond flower terminals framed by calibrè-cut rubies suspended from knife-edge bar links highlighted by bezel-set full- and rose-cut diamonds, millegrain accents, completed by a fancy link chain, platinum & 18k gold mount, Edwardian, w/original fitted Parisian jeweler's box, 20" l. (ILLUS. of part) **$4,935**

Necklace, garnet, graduated wide form set overall w/faceted garnets in a graduating florette design, gilt-metal mount, Victorian, one stone missing, 14 1/2" l. (ILLUS. of part) **$1,763**

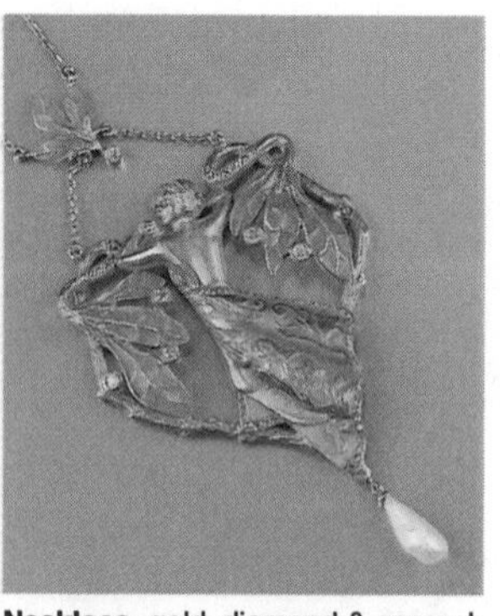

Necklace, gold, diamond & enamel, Art Nouveau style, delicate trace link chain, suspended figure of woman in blue enamel dress, framed by curving branches w/ pink & blue plique-à-jour enamel leaves, bezel-set w/seven old European-cut diamonds & bead-set w/rose-cut diamond highlights, freshwater pearl terminal, 18" l. **$4,935**

Plique-a-jour enameling is similar to stained glass because it has no back, so light can pass through it.

Pendant-brooch, diamond & 18k gold, starburst design, set w/fifty-five old European-cut diamonds, 18k gold mount, signed "Tiffany & Co." **$7,168**

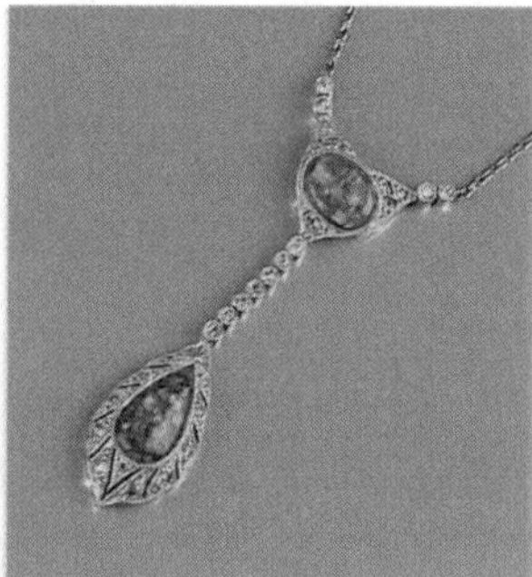

Pendant-brooch, diamond & sapphire, centered by oval sapphire measuring approximately 10.10 x 7.85 x 5.05 mm, surrounded by fifty-eight old mine, old European- and single-cut diamonds, approx. total wt. 5.56 cts., silver-topped 14k gold mount **$8,225**

←

Pendant-necklace, black opal & diamond, delicate trace link chain suspending a pendant w/two bezel-set harlequin black opals & thirty-one bead & bezel-set single-cut diamonds, millegrain accents and pierced gallery, platinum-topped 18k gold mount, platinum chain, 16 1/2" l. **$3,525**

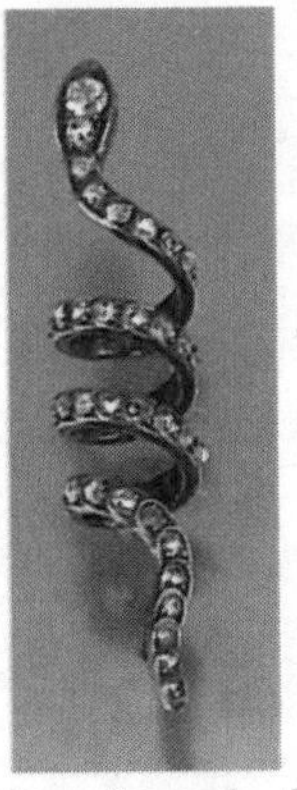

Pin, diamond & ruby, designed as coiled rose-cut diamond serpent w/ruby eyes, silver-topped, 14k gold mount, Austro- Hungarian hallmarks **$1,058**

Pin, diamond & seed pearl, designed as a diamond baton tied w/ribbon, bead-set w/fifty-nine old mine-cut diamonds, seed pearl & millegrain accents, silver-topped 18k gold mount, ... **$646**

Pin, enamel & diamond, a large central round enamel plaque h.p. w/a bust portrait of a costumed lady w/ diamonds inset into her headdress & shoulder, within an outer band of 40 rose-cut diamonds, set in 18k yellow gold **$2,200**

Pin, gold (18k) & diamond, Art Nouveau-style, designed as griffin clutching an old European-cut diamond, rose-cut diamond accents, marker's mark "GC" **$2,350**

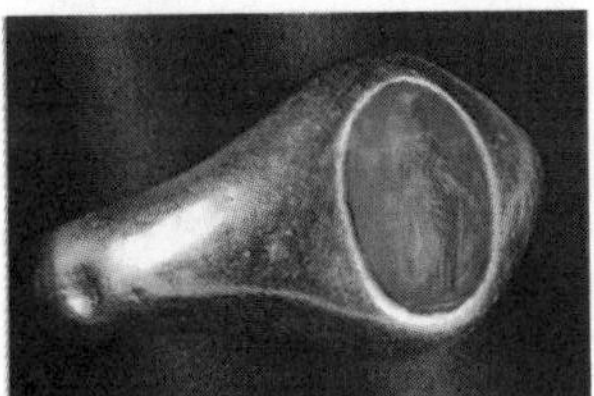

Ring, gold & carnelian, Ancient Roman piece w/a plain hollow gold hoop flat on the interior & rounded on the exterior, expanding at the shoulders, set w/a convex oval carnelian engraved w/a standing draped figure of Fortuna, the goddess holding a cornucopia in one hand & sheaves of wheat & a ship's rudder in the other, ca. 1st century A.D. **$1,035**

Ring, ruby & diamond, a large central cushion-shaped ruby framed by ten old mine-cut diamonds, diamond-set shoulders, platinum-topped 18k gold mount, size 5 .... **$10,575**

In the early Middle Ages, diamond cutting was crude. Diamonds were cut with few facets, and in Medieval paintings, diamonds appear black because they had little sparkle. Consequently, colored gemstones like rubies were preferred.

Ring, diamond, floret composed of nine old mine-cut diamonds weighing approx. 0.89 cts., scrolling openwork white metal & 18k yellow gold mount, English karat stamp, size 2, shank indistinctly inscribed **$764**

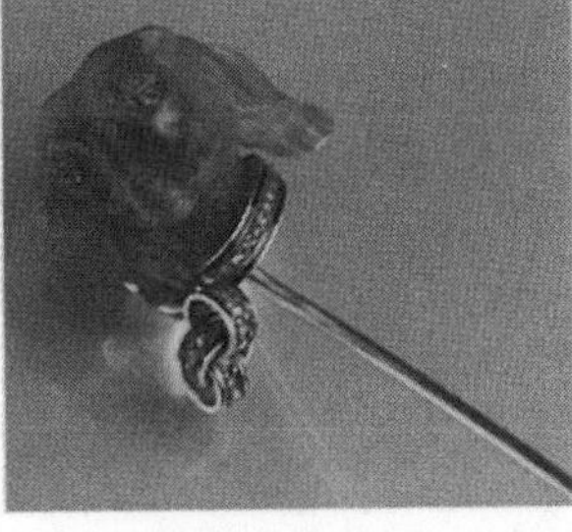

←

Stickpin, gold (18k), amethyst, diamond & enamel, the top w/an amethyst carved as a spaniel head w/a rose-cut diamond collar & chain, hallmarks of Cabrelli, Paris, France **$2,350**

Sets

Brooch & earrings, gold (14k) & amethyst, the brooch designed as a ringed knot set w/a spray of amethyst berries, applied wire- twist decoration, a glass compartment on the back, the earrings of similar design, Victorian, the set **$1,410**

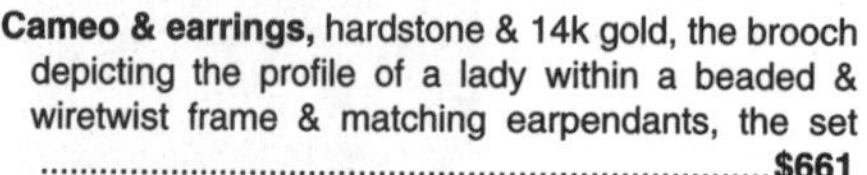

Cameo & earrings, hardstone & 14k gold, the brooch depicting the profile of a lady within a beaded & wiretwist frame & matching earpendants, the set **$661**

Cameo pendant/brooch & earrings, hardstone, depicting a woman in profile within an openwork frame w/gold bead & pearl accents, with matching earrings, 14k yellow gold mounts, Victorian, the set **$1,610**

Cameo pin, necklace, earrings & hair comb, the pin w/four mythological figural oval & round cameos, a tortoiseshell hair comb w/six oval cameos & the necklace of oval cameos, depicting mythological scenes, the frames accented w/green & white enamel & ropetwist accents, 18k yellow gold, in original box together w/pair of cameo earrings, Victorian, the set... **$7,475**

Earrings & pendant, amethyst & diamond, pendant centered by a faceted oval amethyst, flanked by two collet-set old European-cut diamonds, within an openwork foliate frame set w/rose-cut diamonds, 14 1/5" l. 14k yellow gold trace-link chain, together w/ similar earrings set w/oval amethysts, silver-topped 14k yellow gold mounts, Russian hallmarks, the set **$3,220**

Necklace, bracelets & ring: 14k yellow gold, emerald & seed pearls, the necklace & bracelets w/a central knot motif highlighted by seed pearls & emeralds & applied wiretwists w/similar hinged bangle bracelet & ring, Victorian, the set.. **$920**

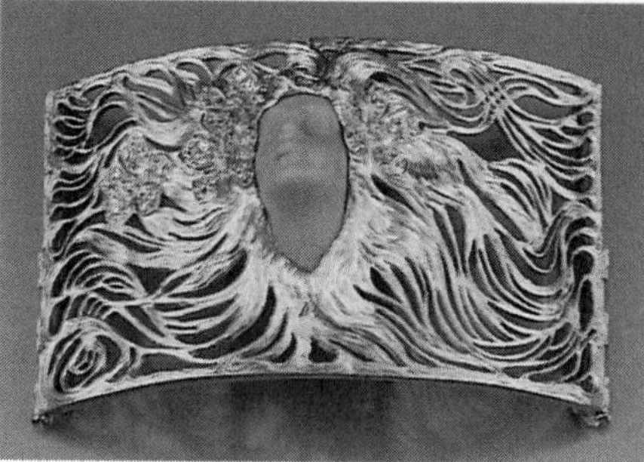

Necklace plaques, gold (18k), diamond & turquoise "Placque de Cou," Art Nouveau design, largest 2 x 7" rectangular curved openwork plaque centered w/ carved turquoise woman's head w/chased flowing gold hair highlighted by old European-cut diamond blossoms, signed "Lalique," similar 2" square plaque also w/carved turquoise head & signed "Lalique," also a pair of smaller openwork plaques set w/diamond blossoms, accompanied by 18k gold flattened baton link chain, 20 1/2" l., two gold satin ribbons, one gold satin cord, & two screwdrivers, may be worn as chokers or necklaces, one plaque w/brooch fitting, the set (ILLUS. of largest plaque)...................... **$49,938**

Pendant & earrings, bi-color coral, the pendant carved as a large finely-petaled flower blossom below a cluster of small carved flowers, matching earrings, gilt-metal mounts, 19th c., one flower bud detached, the set.. **$529**

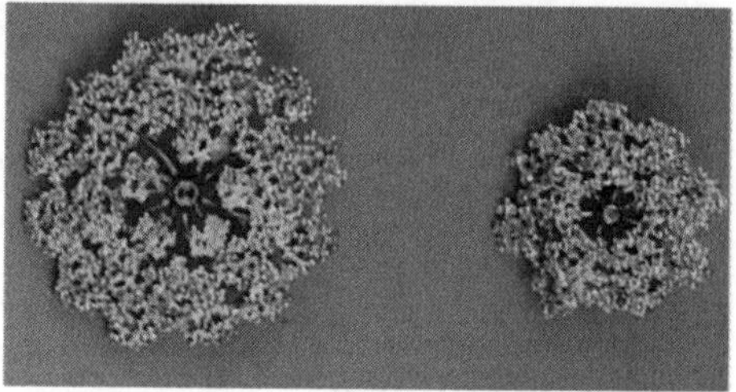

Slides, each designed as a Queen Anne's Lace blossom set w/rose-cut diamonds & demantoid garnets, circular-cut ruby blood spot, platinum-topped 18k gold mounts, w/Tiffany box, unsigned, minor losses, pin stems added, Edwardian, England, early 20th c., pr. **$10,281**

> Before selling your jewelry, get two or three quotes from a jeweler who is a graduate gemologist. If any pieces are antique, take them to an antique dealer or appraiser who specializes in jewelry.

Costume Jewelry (19th & 20th Century)

Belt buckle, steel made in marcasite style, 3 3/4" w., 1 3/4" h. **$25-35**

Bracelet, goldplate, glass, carved oval links in scarab style, each link a different color, 1/2" w. **$45-60**

Bracelet, sterling silver & rhinestone, late Retro style, openwork design of ribbons/scrolls in rectangular panels linked together, entirely set w/clear rhinestones, signed "Unicraft Sterling," 1 3/8" w. **$175-195**

Clip, dress-type, goldtone metal, openwork kite-shaped design studded w/large purple, pink, aqua, yellow, green & clear rhinestones, 1 3/4 x 2 1/4" **$55-75**

Clip, dress-type, gold plate, glass & rhinestone, large spray of three gold bell-shaped flowers w/large center amber crystal centers & pavè clear rhinestone petals & stem, 2 x 3 1/2" **$75-100**

Bracelet, white metal set w/ multicolor agate style glass stones, links style, w/one link hanging as a charm, 6 1/2" l., 3/4" w. **$45-65**

A cabochon is a stone that has been shaped and polished rather than faceted.

Clip, dress-type, goldtone metal, oval openwork design w/large oval red cabochon stone in center surrounded by panel w/leaf decoration & four smaller round multicolored cabochon stones in rope-twist border, an outer panel decorated w/fleur-de-lis & 12 oval multicolored cabochon stones, 2 1/4 x 2 1/2" **$70-90**

Clip, dress-type, rhinestone, three vertically stacked large round black stones framed by slightly smaller clear oval & marquise rhinestones, signed "Doctor Dress," 2 x 2 1/2" **$75-100**

Dress clip, fur-type, goldplated insect motif, green rhinestones eyes, purple center diamond-shaped stone on body, 1 1/2 x 1" **$40-55**

Dress clip, rhinestones, all deep blue marquise stones in openwork design, 2" x 2 3/4" **$55-65**

Dress clip, rhinestones, round flower design set w/red, blue, green, amber petals, 1 3/4" d. **$30-45**

Earrings, goldplate & cabochon, hoop top w/double circle drop w/ blue oval cabochon set stones, drop can be removed so hoop top can be worn alone, signed "Agatha," 2" l., pr. **$45-60**

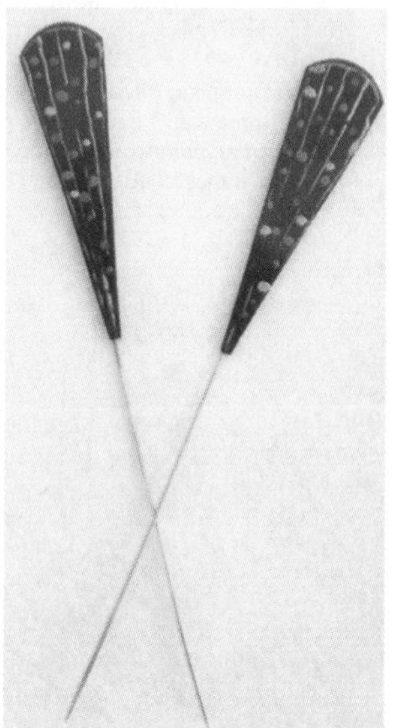

Hatpins, plastic, black flat large heads with h.p. multicolor dots, heads 3 3/8" l. x 1" w., overall 7 1/2" h., pr. **$70-90**

Earrings, goldplate & glass beads, clip-on drop style, three large black glass beads suspended from three chains, 2" l., pr. **$35-50**

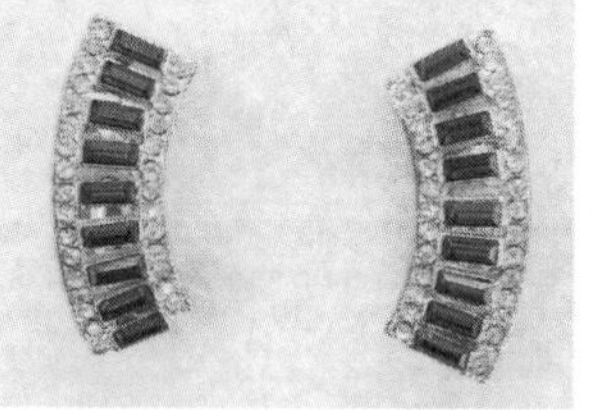

Earrings, rhinestone, slightly curved design w/horizontal rows of red baguette stones inside bordering clear round rhinestones, clip-on style, 1" l., pr. **$40-55**

A baguette is a narrow, rectangular cut gem.

Necklace, glass, beads of various colors & shapes accented w/long cylindrical art glass beads, 38" l. **$65-85**

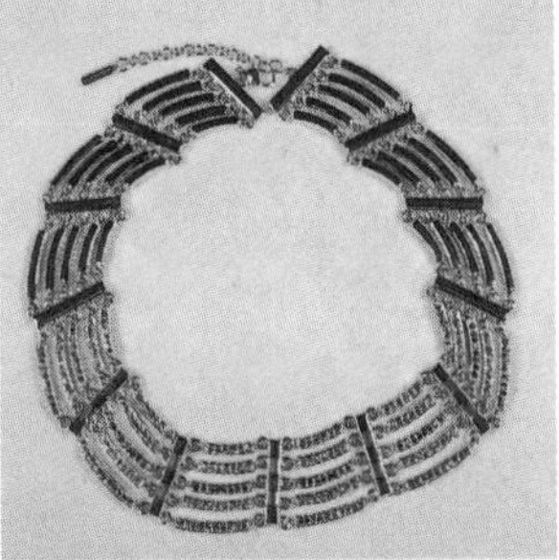

Necklace, goldplate & rhinestone, collar-style, six front panels, each made up of five horizontal rows of pink & red rhinestones, the panels separated by vertical bars of pink & red baguettes; six back panels, each w/six horizontal goldplate bars separated by vertical goldplate bars, all without rhinestones, signed "Napier," 14" adjusts to 16 1/2" **$75-100**

Pendant, goldplate & rhinestone, three dimensional model of kitten w/green rhinestones eyes sitting in rope-twist circle hanging from 24" chain, 2" d. **$55-75**

Pin, goldplate & glass beads, circle entirely covered w/Aurora Borealis hanging glass drops, 1 3/4 x 2 1/2" **$60-85**

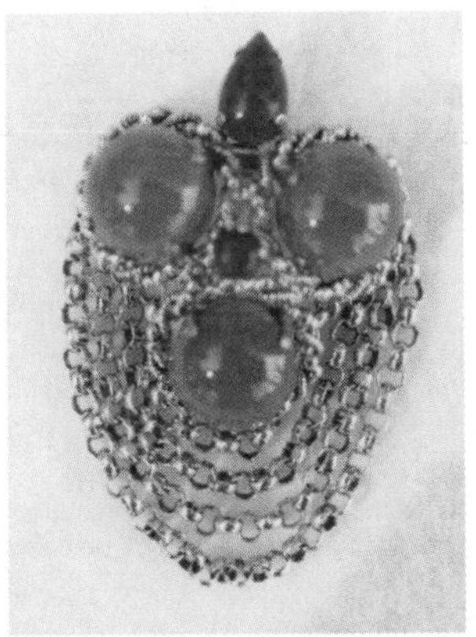

Pin, goldplate & large cabochon purple & blue glass stones, four swag chains on bottom, signed "Christian Dior-Germany," dated "1965," 1 1/2 x 2 1/2" **$75-90**

Pin, goldplate, rhinestones, Christmas ball design set w/ multicolored large & small rhinestones, goldplated holly leaves top, 1 1/2" w., 2 1/4" h. **$25-35**

→

Pin, goldplate & rhinestone, medal-style, three-dimensional sunburst design w/four pear-shaped amber stones & four smaller pear-shaped black stones radiating from large amber center stone framed by eight smaller clear rhinestones, signed "Joan Rivers," 2 1/2" d. **$125-150**

Rhinestone is imitation diamond made from acrylic, glass, or rock crystal. Rhinestones derived their name from the rock crystals collected from the Rhine river in Germany.

Pin, goldplate, rhinestones, enamel, Christmas motif, word "JOY" w/red enamel on the "J" & "Y," center "O" in form of a wreath w/red rhinestones, green enamel, w/original box, 1 1/2 x 2" **$15-25**

Pin, mother-of-pearl & goldplate, butterfly motif w/etched mother-of-pearl wings, unsigned, designer quality, 3 1/4" w., 2" h. **$55-75**

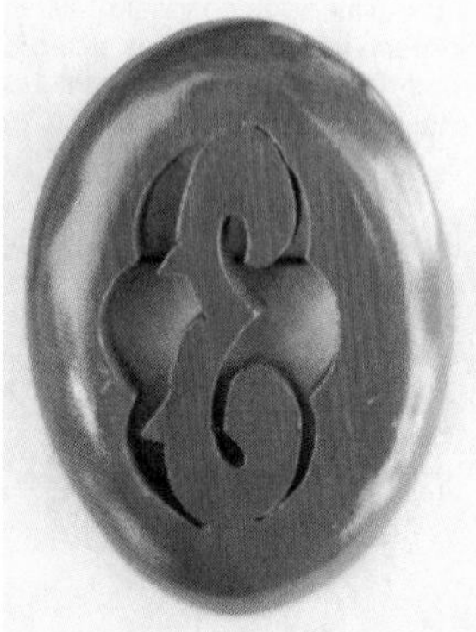

Pin, mahogany, letter "E" carved inside center oval, 2 1/2 x 2" **$25-40**

Pin, rhinestone, enamel & antiqued white metal, model of a coach w/enameled coachman driving four horses, coach & horses set w/blue, green, pink, & clear rhinestones, wheels on coach spin, unsigned, designer quality, 3" w., 1 1/2" h. **$75-95**

Pin, rhinestone, garnet colored marquise stones set in snowflake-style design, unsigned, 1 1/2 x 2" **$60-85**

Pin, white metal & glass, in the form of a snake, large oval purple stones & smaller round light blue stones set as flexible body of snake, fasteners w/antique finish forming its head & tail, unsigned, 7 3/4" l. **$95-120**

Pin-pendant, red enamel stylized heart, made in France, signed "YSL" (Yves St. Laurent), 1 1/2 x 1 1/2" **$45-65**

Sets

Necklace & bracelet, goldplate w/ rhinestone trim, flexible brickwork design, necklace made like a collar, adjustable length, matching bracelet, both pieces signed "Denbe," necklace adjusts to 14", matching bracelet is 6" l., 1" w., the set (ILLUS. of necklace) **$120-145**

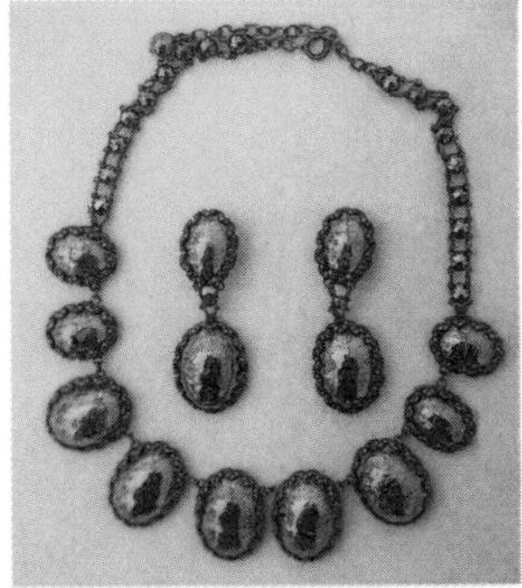

Necklace & earrings, French iridescent glass, marcasite & goldplate, the 16 1/2" necklace made of nine green oval mold-formed cabochons, each w/pontil mark on back, in ornate goldplated settings filling front half of necklace, the back half of necklace a link chain w/18 large marcasites in cup settings; the matching 2 1/8" l. drop earrings each made of two green oval cabochons in ornate settings connected by goldplated links, the set **$250-275**

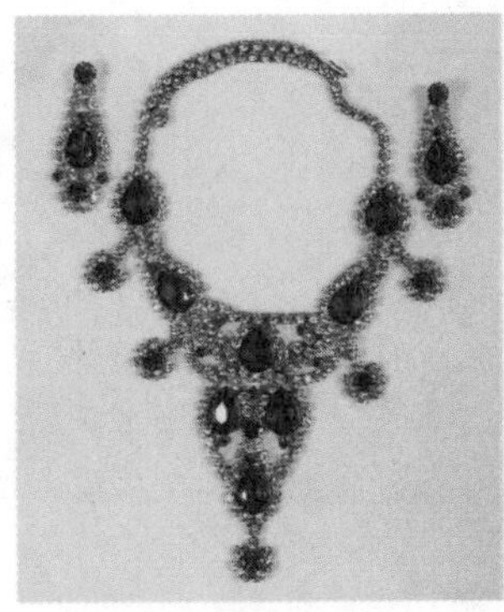

Necklace & earrings, rhinestone, the 16" bib-style necklace w/eight large 3/4" royal blue crystal pear-shaped stones in descending design w/clear floral accents w/ matching blue centers, all on chain made of clear rhinestones; the matching 2 1/4" l. drop earrings w/ blue pear-shaped & smaller blue round stones set in frame of clear rhinestones, unsigned, the set **$325-350**

Necklace & earrings, Venetian art glass, the 17" necklace made of 13 large flat red circular beads w/gold flecks & much smaller cylindrical matching spacers; simple matching 1" d. earrings, the set **$75-100**

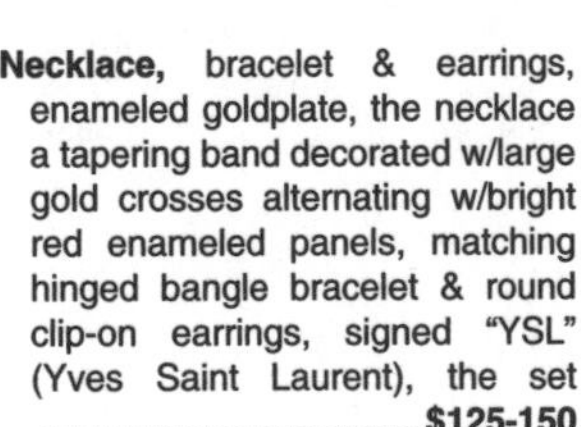

Necklace, bracelet & earrings, enameled goldplate, the necklace a tapering band decorated w/large gold crosses alternating w/bright red enameled panels, matching hinged bangle bracelet & round clip-on earrings, signed "YSL" (Yves Saint Laurent), the set **$125-150**

Pendant & earrings, goldplate & faux opal center stones, flower motif on chain, center opal stone in clear rhinestone frame, 1/2" d., 16" fine chain, matching screw-on earrings, 12" d., the set ... **$50-75**

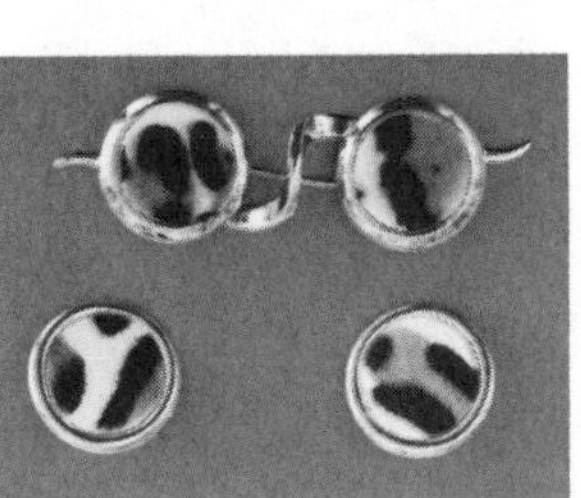

Pin & Earrings, goldplate, w/black, tan & white fur, pin w/two fur-set circles on S-shaped design, 3 1/4" w., clip-on earrings 1" d., the set **$35-50**

Pin & earrings, enamel w/rhinestone trim, curved blue enamel feather motif, matching earrings, signed "Kramer," pin 1 3/4" x 2, mint in original gift box, the set **$150-175**

Pin & necklace, enamel on gold plate, the 2 5/8 x 3" pin w/three open iridescent purple & gold flowers w/clear rhinestone trim on petals in three-dimensional design; the 16" l. necklace w/single row of conforming flowers, chain ends, 1 1/4" w., unsigned, the set **$145-170**

Pin & earrings, rhinestone, ice blue baguettes, ovals in snowflake motif, pin 2" d., screw-on earrings, 3/4" h., the set **$65-80**

Pin & earrings, rhinestone, the 3" d. pin w/large round red crystal center stone surrounded by/row of smaller red rhinestones, a third row made up of blue baguettes radiating from center w/red pear-shaped stones at ends, resembling candles; the matching 1 1/4" d. earrings w/blue center stones & alternating blue & red baguettes radiating from center, the set **$125-150**

Pin & earrings, white metal, faux turquoise, the 5" l. chatelaine-style pin w/two chains ending in white metal blackamoor heads w/filigree trim & round turquoise stones; the matching 1" d. earrings in floral design w/turquoise stone centers, the set **$65-85**

Modern (1920-1950s)

Art Deco

Bar pin, platinum, pink star sapphire & diamond, the narrow mount bezel-set w/six sapphire cabochons alternating w/seven full- cut diamonds **$1,528**

Bar pin, platinum, sapphire & diamond, Art Deco bezel, bead-set throughout w/sixty-six old European, French, baguette & single-cut diamonds, approx. total wt. 1.98 cts., rectangular and triangular-cut sapphire accents, millegrain accents & pierced gallery **$3,055**

Bracelet, platinum & diamond, composed of articulated geometric-form plaques set w/three marquise, four half-moon, ninety baguette, & 394 full- and single-cut diamonds, approx. total wt. 11 cts., 7 1/4" l. **$22,913**

Bracelet, platinum, diamond & carved sapphire & ruby, composed of sapphire & ruby leaves interspersed w/eight old marquise, 16 old mine-cut & 75 single-cut diamonds, completed by interlocking circular single-cut diamond links, approx. 2.28 cts., one diamond & two colored stones missing, 7" l. **$7,050**

Bracelet, platinum, diamond, emerald & onyx, composed of three long flexible plaques spaced by pairs of oblong links, set throughout w/318 old European- and single-cut diamonds, approx. 8.40 cts., highlighted by carved emerald leaves & cabochon onyx, millegrain accents & open gallery, a few nicks & abrasions to emeralds, 7" l. **$14,100**

Bracelet, platinum, sapphire & diamond, bangle-type, the hinged mount set w/43 calibrè-cut sapphires & 173 old European- and single-cut diamonds, approx. 5.55 cts., millegrain accents & engraved sides, probably European hallmark **$6,463**

Bracelet, platinum, sapphire & diamond, composed of semi-flexible plaques bead-set w/176 old European-cut & 44 single-cut diamonds highlighted by a channel-set French-cut sapphire Greek key motif, approx. 7.70 cts., millegrain accents, 7 1/2" l. **$15,275**

Bracelet, platinum, sapphire, & diamond, articulated links w/channel-set calibrè & square step-cut sapphires & bead-set old European-, rose- and single-cut diamonds, approx. total wt. 3.34 cts., 7 1/4" l. **$11,163**

Brooch, diamond & sapphire, bow design, bead-set w/seventy-two old European & old single-cut diamonds weighing approx. 1.60 cts., edged by channel-set rectangular step-cut and calibre-cut sapphires, millegrain accents, platinum mount **$6,463**

Brooch, platinum & diamond, round shape bead-set w/156 old European- and mine-cut diamonds, approx. 7.80 cts., millegrain accents **$8,813**

Brooch, platinum, diamond & onyx, bow-shaped, bead-set w/110 old European & single-cut diamonds, channel-set French-cut onyx & millegrain accents, pierced gallery **$4,230**

Dress clip, pink diamond & ruby, centered w/emerald-cut pink diamond weighing 1.90 cts. framed by square step-cut rubies, further enhanced by bead-set single-cut diamonds & two diamond baguettes weighing approx. 2.26 cts., square step-cut ruby accents, platinum mount, ca. 1930 .... **$35,250**

Dress clips, platinum & diamond, each of palmette form set throughout w/54 old European-cut diamonds, approx. 20.00 cts., further set w/32 French-cut, two baquette & 102 single-cut diamonds, approx. 29.00 cts., 14k white gold findings, ca. 1930 (ILLUS. of one) **$48,175**

Dress clips, sapphire & diamond, bead-set w/seventy-two full- and single-cut diamonds, channel-set, square-, step- and calibrè- cut highlights, millegrain accents, platinum mount, w/brooch conversion, pr. **$3,173**

Necklace, carnelian & enamel, five graduating floral carved & pierced carnelian plaques joined by bow-form celadon green & black enamel links, seed pearl accents, 14k gold mount, partially obliterated hallmark for "Carter Howe & Gough," 16 1/2" l. **$4,700**

Pendant, emerald, diamond & 14k yellow gold, teardrop-shaped lacy mount mounted in the center w/a large 14 ct. pear-shaped emerald surrounded by round-cut diamonds, 4.5 cts., gold mount **$10,350**

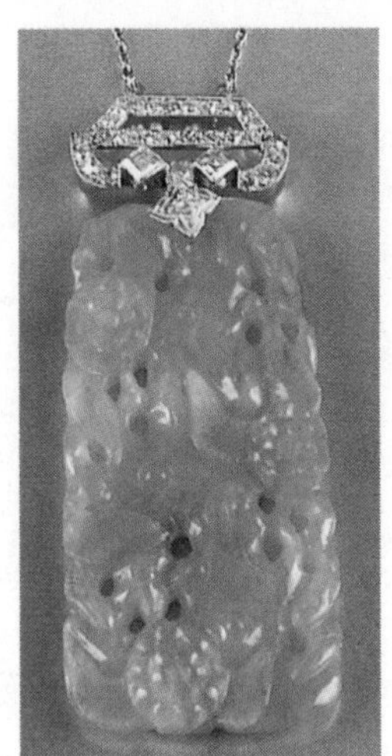

Pendant, platinum, jadeite & diamond, the rectangular green jade plaque pierced & carved w/ stylized florals, the openwork bail set w/diamond mèlèe, suspended from a delicate trace link chain, 17" l. **$2,938**

Pendant-necklace diamond & platinum, detachable pendant centering a flexibly set faceted pear-shaped yellow diamond weighing approx. 9 cts., frame, bail & necklace further bezel & bead-set w/one marquise & 164 old mine- and old European-cut diamonds weighing approx. 5.25 cts., millegrain accents, platinum mount, 16" l. **$193,000**

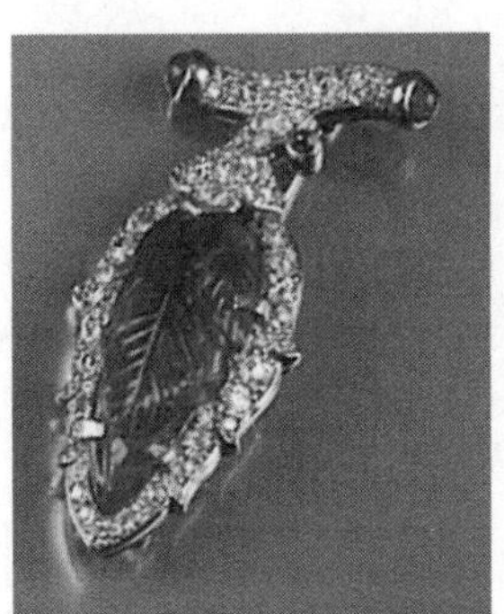

Pin, platinum, diamond & ruby, Mughal design w/a central leaf-carved ruby framed by old mine- and single-cut diamonds on a diamond-set stem accented w/ emerald & ruby cabochons, signed by Cartier **$11,750**

Pin, sapphire & diamond, bezel-set w/one faceted oval & two cushion-cut sapphires, w/forty-six old European- and old mine-cut diamonds, approx. total wt. 1.88 cts., millegrain accents, platinum mount, French hallmark & guarantee stamps **$4,700**

Ring, diamond, set w/a pear-shaped solitaire diamond weighing approx. 2.35 cts. further set w/six straight baguettes, nine single- & six transitional-cut diamonds, platinum mount signed "Shreve & Co., no. B9550," size 8 .. **$17,625**

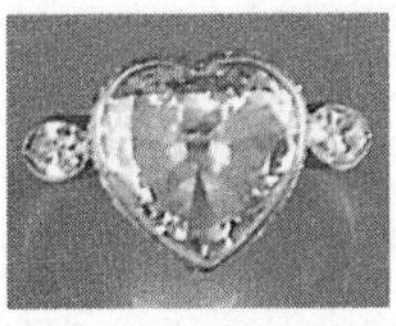

Ring, platinum & diamond solitaire, bezel-set w/a faceted heart-shaped diamond, approx. 2.25 cts., openwork scrolling gallery bead-set w/old single-cut diamonds, bezel-set marquise-cut diamond shoulders, engraved shank, chip to girdle, size 6 1/4 .... **$17,625**

Ring, platinum & diamond, bezel-set w/an old mine-cut diamond approx. 1.00 cts., surrounded by 12 old mine- and European- cut diamonds, approx. 2.34 cts., worn signature of Cartier, ca. 1930s, size 8 3/4 .... **$8,225**

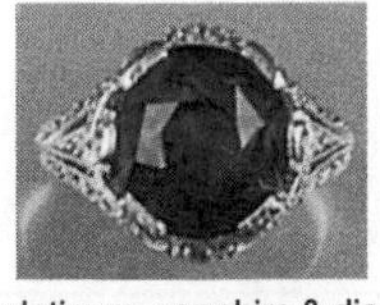

Ring, platinum, sapphire & diamond, prong-set w/a large faceted oval sapphire, the prongs, open gallery & shoulders bead-set w/old European- and single-cut diamond mèlèe, one mèlèe missing, size 4 1/2 .... **$8,225**

Retro Style

Brooch, diamond, synthetic rubies & 14k rose gold, a swirled styled leafy floral design, the center set w/an old European-cut diamond flanked by 38 small diamonds & synthetic rubies, 14k rose gold mount, mid-20th c. **$275**

Miscellaneous Pieces

Brooch, amethyst, ruby, sapphire, blue spinel, spessarite, garnet, green beryl, diamond & 14k gold, a large faceted oval amethyst flowerpot overflows w/leafy gem-set stems & blossoms, silver-topped gilt & 14k gold mount, ca. 1940 .... **$1,058**

Amethyst is a form of quartz. Its name means "not intoxicated." The Greeks and Romans believed that drinking from a vessel made from amethyst would prevent drunkeness.

Necklace, diamond & platinum, a large slender ring-form w/the thin sides graduating to a wider front section composed of two rows of diamond-set bands flanking a long central looping openwork section, set throughout w/92 transitional, old European-, baguette- and rectangular step-cut diamonds, weighing 5.20 cts., ca. 1930, 14 3/4" l. **$17,265**

Pendant, emerald, diamond & 18k gold, designed w/a top prong-set square step-cut diamond weighing 3.00 cts. suspending a flexibly-set large pear-shaped emerald framed by twenty graduated old European-cut diamonds, early 20th c.............................. **$76,375**

Pendant-necklace, faux pearl & glass, composed of swirled glass beads highlighted by paste rondels & faux pearls, joined by multi-strand trace link chain, bicolor gilt-metal mount, designed by Coco Chanel, w/an oval plaque stamped "Chanel," 28" l........ **$823**

Brooch, gem-set & enamel, calibrè-cut buff-top sapphire, emerald & ruby exotic bird & flowers mounted on meandering black enamel branch within circular frame bead-set w/seventy-six old European-cut diamonds weighing approx. 1.33 cts., platinum & gold mount, signed "E. Besson," ca. 1920s **$16,450**

Earrings, gold (14k bi-color) & gem-set earrings, designed as a cluster of yellow & rose gold blossoms, full-cut diamond & garnet accents, 7.4 dwt., pr........................... **$558**

Man's dress set: oval cuff links & two shirt studs; platinum & black diamond, the oval cuff links each bezel-set w/an old European-cut black diamond joined by trace links to an old European-cut black diamond & onyx baguette baton, matching shirt studs, signed by Cartier, New York, w/original fitted box, ca. 1930, the set........ **$9,400**

Ring, diamond, yellow radiant-cut solitaire diamond weighing 1.64 cts. framed by ten faceted half-moon shaped diamonds weighing 2.13 cts., shoulders pavé-set w/twenty full-cut diamond mélée weighing 0.31 cts., custom-made 18k white gold mount, size 7 1/2 .... **$9,106**

Ring, platinum & diamond, centered w/European-cut diamond weighing approx. 1.19 cts., w/single-cut diamond highlights, millegrain accents, pierced gallery, size 6 1/2 .... **$2,585**

Ring, sapphire, diamond & platinum, mounted w/a 5.5 mm round blue sapphire flanked by four old European-cut diamonds in a platinum mount, ca. 1920s, size 6 3/4 .... **$990**

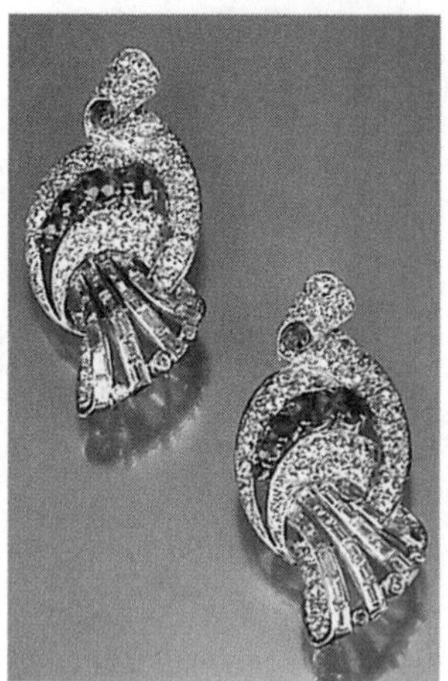

Dress clips, platinum, ruby & diamond, five prong-set circular-cut rubies & sixty-one full-cut and baguette diamonds, approx. total wt. 4.48 cts., w/14k gold brooch attachment **$5,875**

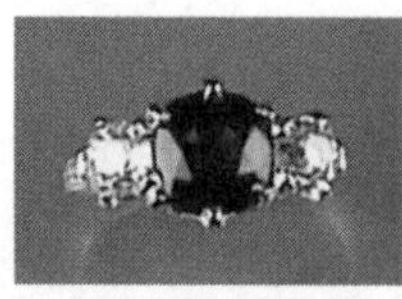

Ring, sapphire, diamond & platinum, prong-set w/cushion-cut sapphire weighing 3.01 cts. flanked by old mine-cut diamonds, approx. total diamond wt. 1 ct., open gallery, size 5 .... **$4,406**

Wedding ring w/ring guards, lady's, diamond & 14k yellow gold, the main band w/a six-prong Tiffany mount holding a European-cut diamond weighing 3.51 cts., the flanking wedding band guards mounted w/a total of 26 straight diamond baguettes, early 20th c. **$14,350**

Wedding ring set: diamond & platinum; the engagement band centered by a large round old European-cut diamond weighing 1.74 cts. flanked by six round full-cut diamonds; the wedding band mounted w/five round full-cut diamonds alternating w/four baguette-cut diamonds w/a total weight of .86 cts., size 7, early 20th c., the pair.................. **$4,481**

Twentieth Century Designer & Fine Estate Jewelry

Bracelet, cultured pearl, diamond & 14k white gold, composed of four strands totaling 80 white cultured pearls w/rose overtones & ranging in size from 7.50 to 7.95 mm., accented w/three gold crossbars & an openwork rectangular clasp w/oval designs all set w/ full-cut diamonds weighing about 2.56 cts., 7 1/2" l. **$1,116**

Bracelet, diamond & 14k gold, bangle-type, the wide hinged band decorated w/ridged swirled bands each set w/five graduating lines of single-cut diamonds **$470**

Bracelet, diamond & 14k white gold, a narrow double band set w/full-cut diamonds centered by pairs of S-scrolls set w/full-cut & baguette diamonds centered a marquise-cut diamond, diamonds weighing about 6.93 cts., formerly a covered watch, adjustable from 6 to 6 1/4" **$1,998**

Bracelet, diamond & 18k white gold, the wide openwork feather-like band decorated overall w/prong- and bead-set full-cut diamond mèlèe, diamonds weighing about 4.36 cts., interior circumference 5 3/4" **$1,763**

Bracelet, diamond & 18k white gold, composed of long rectangular links w/pointed ends & angled loops joined by ring & bar links, pavè & channel-set overall w/full-cut diamond mèlèe & diamond baguettes, 7" l. **$4,113**

Bracelet, diamond & platinum, composed of navette-shaped links set w/baguette diamonds alternating w/ links centered by an emerald-cut diamond flanked by four marquise-cut diamond leaves, diamonds weighing about 9.45 cts., 7" l. **$14,100**

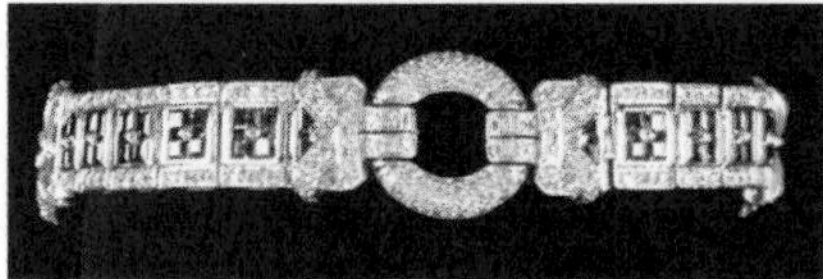

Bracelet, diamond, sapphire & 18k white gold, composed of 14 square links each w/four small square-cut blue sapphires framed by six diamonds interspersed w/ three buckle-type round links each set w/diamonds, marked a lion hallmark & "18k - BM1466," sapphire total weight 6.33 cts., diamond total weight 2.47 cts., 1/2" w., 7 1/4" l. **$4,600**

Bracelet, gem-set 14k gold, composed of six links each set w/a different large cabochon stone including rose quartz, citrine, green beryl, aquamarine & amethyst, 7" l. **$1,116**

Bracelet, gold (18k), a wide finely woven gold band highlighted by smooth leafy serpentine stems, No. 434 AL, Italy, 7" l. **$1,116**

Bracelet, turquoise, diamond & 18k white gold, bangle-type, the wide hinged band prong-set around the center w/a band of large turquoise cabochons surrounded by small turquoise cabochons accented w/full-cut diamonds, interior circumference 6 1/2" **$8,225**

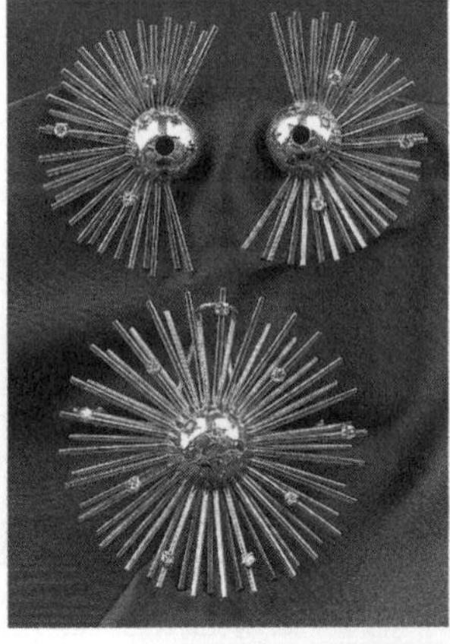

Brooch & earrings, gold (14k), ruby & diamond, the large multi-rayed sunburst w/a solid domed center accented w/ruby mèlèe & a central diamond, small diamond mèlèe scattered on the rays, w/matching clip-on earrings, one earring missing central diamond, brooch 2" d., the set **$646**

Brooch & earrings, bicolor 18k gold, emerald & diamond, the brooch designed as a long curved spray of flowers on a leafy stem, the leaves & flower petals set w/diamonds & each flower center set w/a circular-cut emerald, the matching clip-on earrings composed of three flowers, in original fitted box, the suite **$3,173**

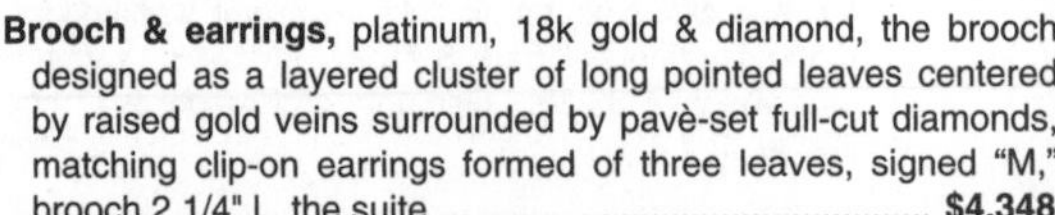

Brooch & earrings, platinum, 18k gold & diamond, the brooch designed as a layered cluster of long pointed leaves centered by raised gold veins surrounded by pavè-set full-cut diamonds, matching clip-on earrings formed of three leaves, signed "M," brooch 2 1/4" l., the suite **$4,348**

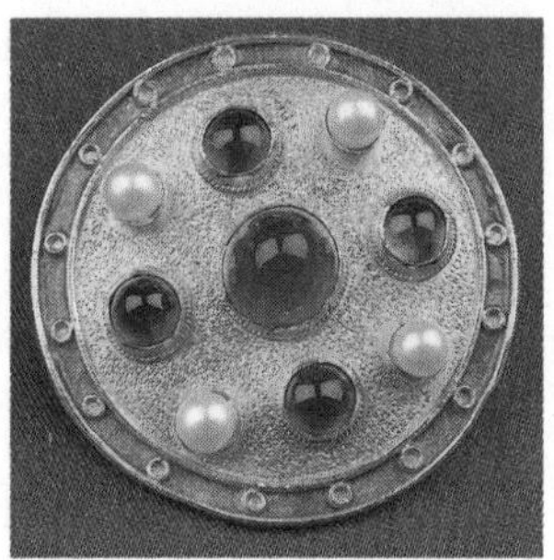

Brooch, amethyst, emerald, cultured pearl & 22k gold, the round flat disk bezel-set w/an arrangement of a central sugarloaf cabochon emerald framed by four cabochon amethysts & pearls, blue enamel border accents, Greek karat stamp, 1 3/8" d. **$353**

Brooch, coral, diamond, hardstone & 18k white gold, designed as a carved green stone leaf above a gold stem suspending a large bunch of coral bead grapes, full-cut diamonds along the stem **$1,175**

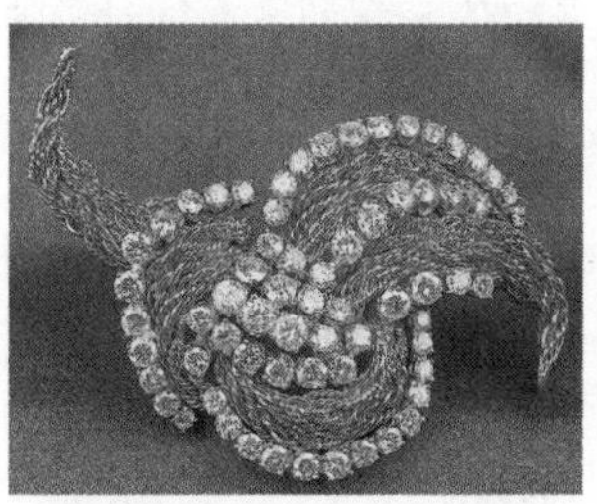

Brooch, diamond & 18k gold, a spiraled knot-form design w/finely woven ropetwist gold bands ending in points, bordered & centered by prong-set full-cut diamonds weighing about 5.00 cts., 2 1/4" l. **$2,468**

Brooch, diamond, 14k gold & frosted glass, a gold diamond-set stem suspending a bunch of frosted green glass grapes **$1,410**

Brooch, enameled & gem-set 18k gold, designed as a comical green-enameled frog grasping a cultured pearl, the body accented w/scattered bezel-set diamonds, cabochon ruby eyes **$705**

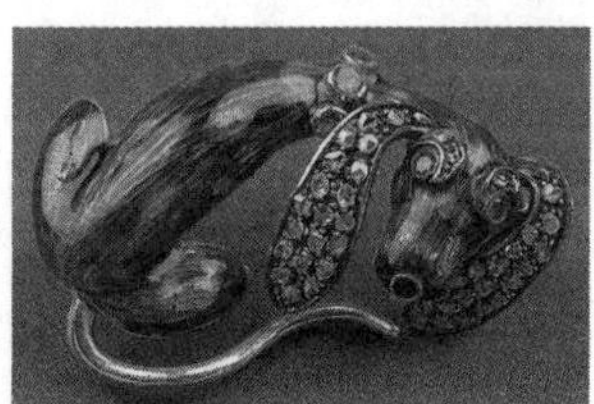

Brooch, enameled & gem-set gold, in the shape of a reclining Dachshund, the body enameled in brown w/a gold tail, the long ears set w/rose-cut diamonds, ruby eyes & an emerald collar, Portuguese guarantee stamps, 1 1/2" l. **$705**

Brooch, enameled gold & diamond, designed as a sailboat w/two full sails, one enameled in dark gold, the other in dark blue, sailing on waves set w/full-cut diamonds & flying a diamond-set pennant, 14k gold mount, 1 1/4 x 1 3/8" **$1,410**

Brooch, gem-set 18k gold, designed as a cluster of three large sunflower-like blossoms above a cluster of four pointed leaves, each blossom prong-set w/either circular-cut ruby, sapphire or emerald mèlèe, 1 3/4" l. **$1,116**

Brooch, gem-set 18k gold, designed as a stylized seated Terrier w/ the body set w/a large cabochon turquoise, tiny ruby eyes, 2" l. **$411**

Brooch, hardstone & 14k gold, designed as a tropical fish w/the body composed of pieces of lapis lazuli, onyx, malachite, coral & mother-of-pearl, signed "OA/G" **$1,058**

Brooch, platinum & diamond, designed as a large stylized spray of three opening flower buds & leaves atop entwined curved stems, prong-, bead- and channel-set set overall w/163 full, 17 marquise- and 27 baguette diamonds, diamonds weighing about 8.47 cts., 2 3/4" l. **$4,700**

Brooch-pendant, diamond & 18k white gold, model of a starfish, the center of each arm prong-set w/a band of brown diamonds surrounded by 163 white diamond mèlèe, diamonds weighing about 8.97 cts., 2" l. **$4,700**

Brooch, lapis lazuli, diamond & gold, in the shape of a turtle w/the domed shell formed by a cabochon lapis bordered by 16 full- cut diamonds, emerald eyes, 1" l. **$1,763**

Brooch, sapphire, diamond & platinum, a wide cross-form design w/short pointed arms between the cross arms, prong-set w/five large cushion-cut blue sapphires & further set overall w/smaller prong-set square-cut & baguette sapphires, the tips of each arm set w/bands of full-cut diamonds, mark of maker, No. 2887, 2" w. **$6,756**

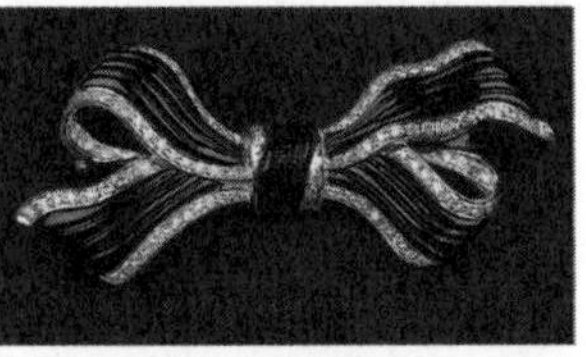

Brooch-pendant, platinum, onyx & diamond, designed as a long wide ribbon bow lined w/bands of ribbed onyx edged by narrow bands of full-cut diamonds, 2 5/16" l. **$1,645**

Brooch, platinum & diamond, designed as a large rose bud atop a long thorny stem fitted w/three leaves, the bud & leaves pavè-set w/full-cut diamonds weighing about 4.50 cts. **$2,468**

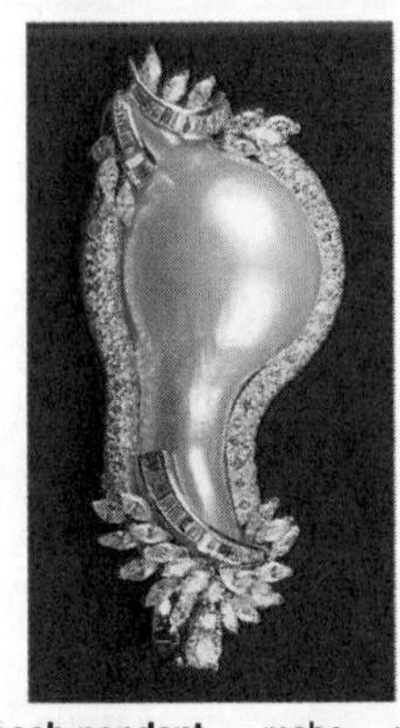

Brooch-pendant, mabe pearl, diamond & 14k white gold, a large bulbous tapering baroque pearl framed along the sides by bands of full-cut diamonds w/scroll & leaf designs at the top & base set w/marquise-cut & baguette diamonds, diamonds weighing about 3.16 cts., 2 1/4" l. ... **$1,763**

Cameo pendant-necklace, opal, enamel & 14k gold, oval opal cameo depicting a lady in Renaissance dress, in an oval frame decorated w/black & green champlève enamel, suspended from a matching enamel baton link chain highlighted by opal beads, 29" l. **$2,115**

Charm bracelet, gold (14k), composed of a double curb-link chain suspending numerous gold charms including a doctor's bag, birthday cake w/retractable candles, scissors, artist palette, jewel casket, mad money & trash can, 6 3/4" l. **$1,175**

Choker, platinum, cultured pearl, diamond & sapphire, composed of a double strand of 85 white pearls w/rose overtones measuring about 7.50 to 8.00 mm, completed by a round clasp pavè-set w/a center cluster of diamonds enclosed by a ring of blue sapphires & an outer ring of diamonds, diamonds weighing about 1.04 cts., 14 3/4" l. **$1,763**

Cuff links, stone-set 14k gold & platinum, a cylindrical waisted bar engraved in a scale design & centered by a ring of step-cut red stones, mark of American maker, 7/8" l., pr. **$499**

Earrings & ring, emerald, diamond & 18k white gold; each piece centered by a rectangular step-cut emerald weighing from 1.32 to 1.56 cts., each emerald surrounded by a mèlèe of round full-cut diamonds, 78 total, 18th white gold mount, the set **$1,434**

Earrings, bicolor 18k gold & diamond, clip-on type, designed as curled stylized fish, the gold bodies w/an openwork lattice design, the snout, fins, tail & body set w/single-cut diamond mèlèe, France, 1 3/8" l., pr. **$1,410**

Earrings, bicolor 18k gold & emerald, clip-on type, each w/double curved gold bars suspending a fringe of faceted emerald beads, French guarantee stamps & mark of the maker, 1 1/4" l., pr. **$3,878**

Earrings, cultured pearl, diamond & 14k white gold, clip-on type, designed as a concave oval shell set overall w/single- and full- cut diamonds & centered by a single white pearl, pr. **$940**

Earrings, diamond & 14k white gold, pendant-type, a top cluster of prong-set pear- and single-cut diamonds suspending two oval loops further set w/diamonds, diamonds weighing about 4.00 cts., 1 3/8" l., pr. **$1,880**

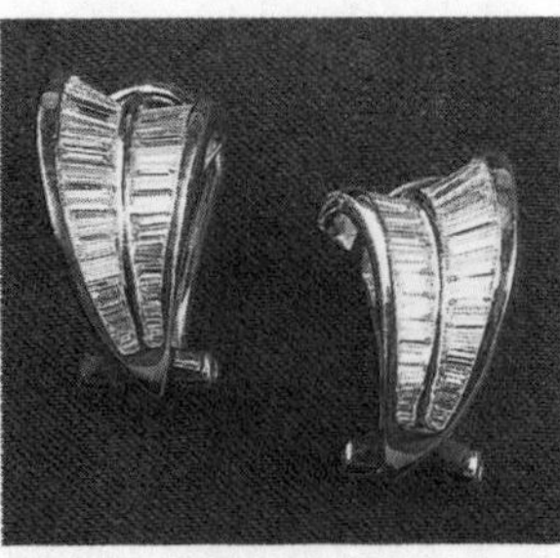

Earrings, diamond & platinum, clip-on type, designed as a double scroll channel-set w/baguette diamonds weighing about 1.89 cts., pr. **$1,410**

Earrings, diamond, cultured pearl & platinum, pendant-type, the top set w/a white pearl above a straight drop of eight full-cut diamonds suspending another pearl, diamonds weighing about 2.10 cts., 1 7/8" l., pr. **$1,528**

Earrings, pink sapphire, diamond & 18k white gold, each designed as an openwork scallop shell bead-set w/full-cut diamond mèlèe & centered by an oval pink sapphire, pr. **$2,115**

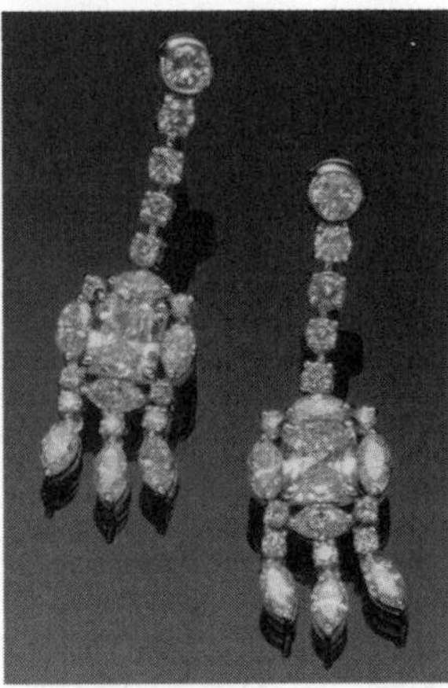

Earrings, diamond & platinum, dangle-style w/friction-style posts & backs, each centered by a cushion-cut diamond, both totaling 1.16 cts., framed by a mèlèe of 14 marquise-cut diamonds & 24 round full-cut diamonds, pr. **$5,975**

Earrings, diamond, pink stone & 14k white gold, pendant-type, each prong-set w/a large pear-cut pink stone framed by a thin band of diamonds & suspended from a thin diamond-set line link, diamonds weighing about .55 cts. 1 1/4" l., pr. **$1,116**

Earrings, platinum & diamond, clip-on type, each in a rounded snowflake design w/each ray prong-set w/an old European-cut or full-cut diamond, diamonds weighing about 2.70 cts., 14k white gold findings, 1" w., pr. **$2,585**

Earrings, diamond & platinum, pendant-type, a full-cut diamond top suspending a flexible line of full-cut diamonds suspending a shaped diamond-set ring surrounding a larger pendant diamond, diamonds weighing about 1.15 cts., pr. **$2,115**

Earrings, diamond, sapphire & 18k bicolor gold, each designed as a five-petal blossom pavè-set w/diamond mèlèe & centered by a cluster of blue sapphires, pr. **$705**

Pavè jewelry features stones set so densely that little of the metal shows.

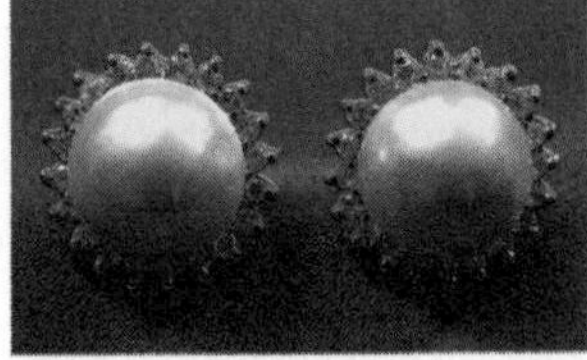

Earrings, mabe pearl & diamond, each silvery blue pearl framed by full-cut diamonds, 14k white gold mounts, pr. **$588**

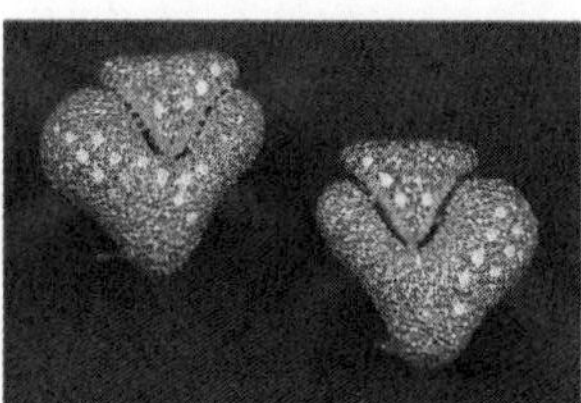

Earrings, platinum & diamond, each of an abstract heart shape pavè-set overall w/full-cut diamonds, diamonds weighing about 3.50 cts., pr. **$1,175**

Earrings, South Sea pearl, diamond & 14k white gold, pendant-type, each topped by a seven-diamond floret suspending a diamond-set leafy vine supporting a large South Sea pearl measuring about 13.50 mm, pr. **$4,406**

Necklace, cultured pearl & sapphire, three strands composed of 153 white pearls graduating in size from 9.50 to 6.15 mm, completed by a 14k gold heart-shaped clasp pavè-set w/blue sapphires, 16 1/4" l. **$823**

Earrings, platinum, 18k gold & diamond, a curled stem set w/ single-cut diamonds above a gold leaf accented w/a single full-cut diamond, pr. **$1,293**

Earrings, star sapphire, diamond & platinum, prong-set w/a large rounded oval star sapphire flanked on two sides by curved bands set w/full-cut & baguette diamonds, size 5 3/4 .... **$2,938**

Necklace, cultured pearl, emerald, diamond & 18k white gold, composed of a triple strand of off-white pearls measuring about 6.20 mm & spaced by thin bars set w/diamonds, completed by a box clasp set w/a large emerald-cut emeralds framed by a rectangular notch-cornered ring of square step-cut diamonds, diamonds weighing about 1.86 cts., 18 3/4" l. (ILLUS. of part)................. **$2,350**

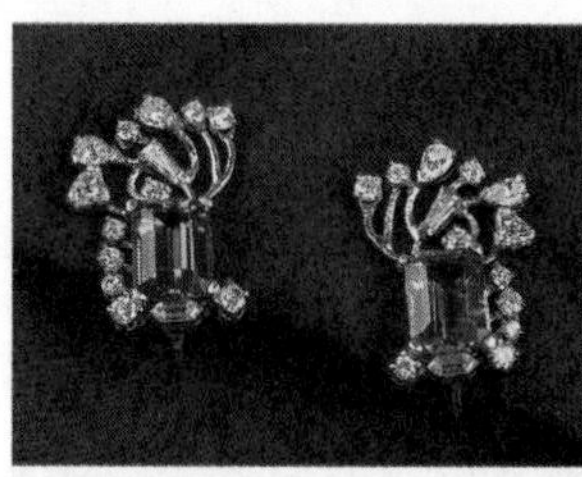

Earrings, platinum, pink tourmaline & diamond, clip-on type, prong-set w/a large rectangular step-cut pink tourmaline framed up one side by a spray of fancy-cut diamonds, 14k white gold finding, pr. **$1,140**

Earrings, turquoise, sapphire & 14k gold, clip-on type, each designed as a group of four blossoms w/ cabochon turquoise petals & a blue sapphire center, pr. **$705**

Necklace, South Sea pearl & diamond, composed of 37 white pearls w/rose overtones graduating from 9.60 to 12.90 mm, completed by a half-spherical platinum clasp pavè-set w/full-cut diamonds, 18 1/4" l. **$2,820**

Necklace, tourmaline, composed of ten strands of tumbled small pink & green oval tourmaline beads, 18k gold hook clasp, 17 1/2" l. **$764**

Pendant, carved tourmaline, the purple tourmaline stone carved in the form of a seated Buddha, suspended from a fancy looping gold link on a fine trace link chain, pendant 1 1/8" l. **$1,293**

Pendant, diamond & 14k gold, designed as a gold sphere pavè-set overall w/full-cut diamonds **$1,293**

Pendant, diamond & 18k gold, designed as a heart pavè-set w/121 full-cut diamond mèlèe, diamonds weighing about 3.00 cts., suspended from a fancy link gold chain, overall 17 1/2" l. **$1,175**

Pin, diamond & 18k gold, a long delicate gold feather centered by narrow bands bead-set w/diamond mèlèe, 2 1/2" l. **$705**

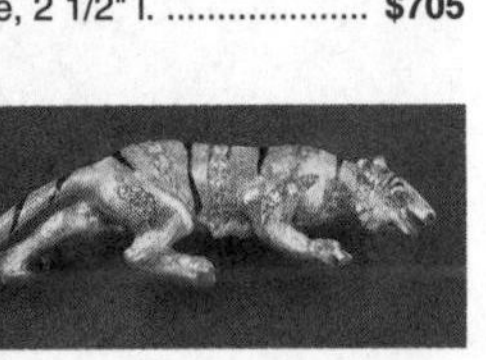

Pin, enameled & gem-set 18k gold, modeled as a crouching tiger, black enamel stripes & single-cut diamond accents, emerald eye, 1 3/4" l. **$499**

Pin, diamond & gem-set 18k gold, modeled as a standing terrier w/ruby eyes & nose playing a diamond-studded flute **$470**

Pin, enameled 18k gold, designed as a racing sulky & driver, driver & horse blanket accented in green, yellow & blue enamel, 1 3/4" l. **$646**

Pin, gem-set 14k gold, in the shape of a winged insect, the body & four-part wings set w/circular-cut emeralds, rubies & diamonds, rose-cut garnet eyes **$646**

Pin, gem-set 18k gold, designed as a seated leopard w/black enamel spots each set w/a single or full-cut diamond, emerald eyes, 1 3/4" l. **$470**

Ring, cultured pearl & enameled 14k gold, the top formed by a pearl cluster mounted w/four tiny enameled pansies each centering a tiny single-cut diamond, size 4 1/2 .... **$353**

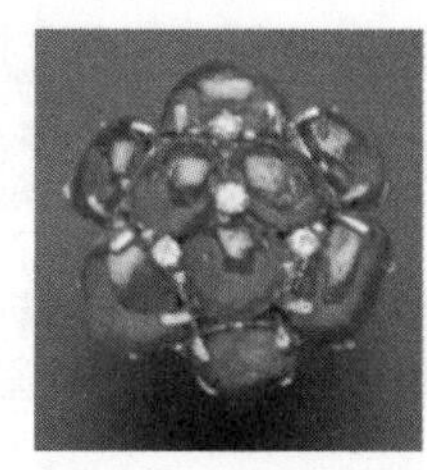

Ring, cabochon ruby, diamond & 14k gold, the domed top composed of a cluster of nine cabochon rubies accented w/scattered full-cut diamonds, gold mount, size 6 1/2 .... **$646**

Ring, coral, diamond & 18k gold, the top center pavè-set w/diamonds flanked by panels of flute-carved pink coral, size 9 1/2 .... **$382**

Ring, diamond & 14k yellow gold, the flat gold band box-set at the top w/a full-cut diamond weighing about 1.10 cts., size 8 ..... **$1,763**

Ring, cat's-eye green tourmaline & platinum, the top pront-set w/a large oval tourmaline cabochon flanked on each side by three small full-cut diamonds, 14k white gold hinged shank **$1,058**

Ring, diamond & 18k gold, designed as a cluster of full-cut diamonds surrounded by gold leaves further set w/diamonds, diamonds weighing about 2.77 cts., w/ring guard, ca. 1960s, size 5 1/2 .... **$1,880**

Ring, diamond & 18k gold, the wide band set overall w/four rows of princess-cut diamonds, diamonds weighing about 3.68 cts., size 5 .... **$1,175**

Ring, diamond & 18k gold, the wide gold band decorated w/scattered inset small diamonds, size 6 3/4 .... **$646**

Ring, diamond & platinum, solitaire-type, the top centered by a large prong-set pear-cut diamond weighing 5.73 cts., flanked by 16 tapered baguette diamonds, size 7 .... **$11,750**

Ring, diamond & platinum, the rectangular top centered by a band of six channel-set baguette diamonds flanked by two narrow rows w/six full-cut diamonds in each, diamonds weighing about 1.40 cts., size 6 1/2 .... **$1,175**

Ring, diamond & platinum, the top prong-set w/three emerald-cut diamonds weighing about 3.75 cts. & flanked on the shoulders w/diamond baguettes, size 6 .... **$11,750**

Ring, diamond solitaire, prong-set w/a round brilliant-cut diamond weighing about 2.01 cts., flanked by narrow bands of small full-cut diamonds, 18k gold & platinum mount, size 5 .... **$23,500**

Ring, diamond, colored diamond & platinum, ballerina-style, the long four-lobed top set w/a wide border of 48 tapering baguette diamonds around an oval band of 16 full-cut diamonds all centered by an orangish brown marquise-cut diamond weighing about 1.50 cts., other diamonds weighing about 2.48 cts., size 6 1/2 .... **$5,581**

Ring, diamond, cultured pearl & 18k white gold, bypass-style, the top tips set w/a white or black pearl, the shoulders set w/full-cut diamond mèlèe, size 7 1/4 .... **$470**

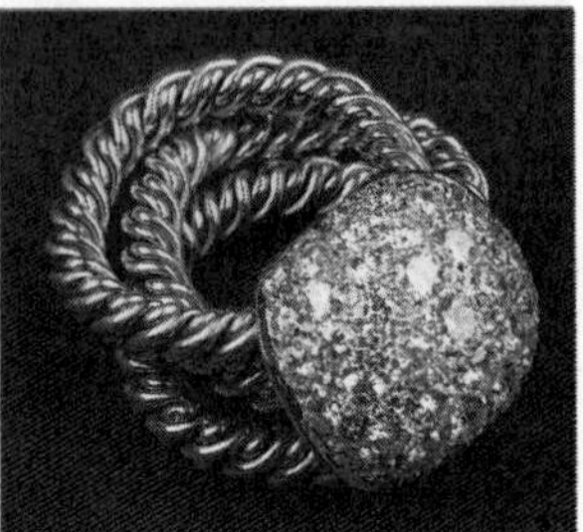

Ring, diamond, platinum & 18k gold, the domed top pavè-set slide on three gold ropetwist bands, diamonds weighing about 5.00 cts., size 7 .... **$6,463**

Ring, diamond, ruby & 18k white gold, the wide band centered by an undulating stripe of pavè-set clear diamonds flanked on one side by a panel of pavè-set small rubies & on the other side by a panel of pavè-set black diamonds, size 6 .... **$1,058**

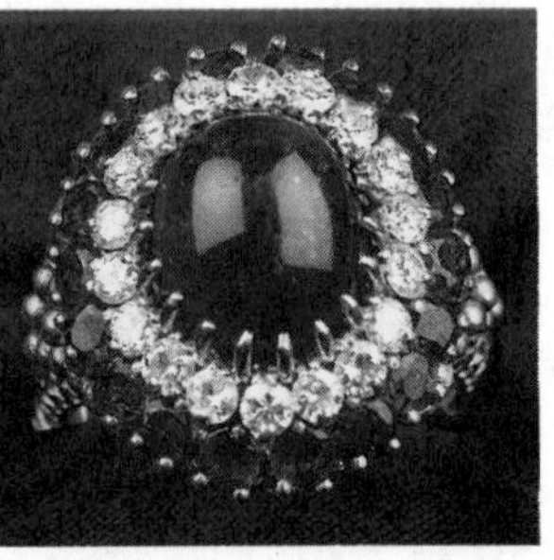

Ring, emerald, diamond & 18k gold, the round top centered by a large emerald cabochon surrounded by a ring of full-cut diamonds & an outer ring of circular-cut emeralds, w/ring guard, size 5 1/2 ... **$1,293**

Ring, enameled 18k gold & diamond, designed as a snarling tiger head w/black & white enameled stripes & a red & black- enameled nose & a red tongue, the upper lips & side of the head set w/single-cut diamonds, the black & white-striped tail curls up at one side, size 5 .... **$499**

Ring, lady's fashion-type, amethyst, diamond & 18k white gold, the top mounted w/a large 4.28 ct. Siberian color square-cut amethyst framed at each corner by a heart-shaped mount accented w/small diamonds, narrow channels of diamonds also along the sides of the shank, stamped mark "18K NI 3794" **$863**

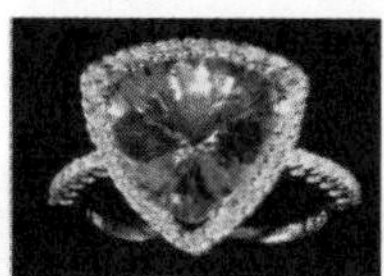

Ring, lady's fashion-type, diamond, pink tourmaline & 14k white gold, the triangular top mounted w/a large 6 ct. pink tourmaline surrounded by 21 small diamonds, the shank w/five small diamonds on each side, maker's mark & "14k BH," size 7 1/2 .... **$920**

Ring, lady's fashion-type, emerald, diamond & 18k white gold, the starburst top centered by one square step-cut emerald weighing .58 cts., surrounded by two bands of 28 round full-cut diamonds, slender band **$418**

Ring, lady's fashion-type, pearl, diamond & 18k yellow gold, the branch-form gold mount supporting four grey baroque-shaped cultured pearls 9.5 mm to 10 mm, also mounted w/four small scattered diamonds, size 11 .... **$448**

Ring, lady's, amethyst, citrine & 14k white gold, the top cushion-set w/a large oblong facet-cut amethyst flanked by two half-moon facet-cut citrines, marked "14k" w/initials of maker "FP," size 7 1/2 .... **$345**

Ring, opal, diamond & 18k white gold, a large oval prong-set opal framed by 25 full-cut diamonds, boxed, size 7 .... **$823**

Ring, opal, ruby, diamond & 14k gold, the wide round top centered by a prong-set round opal framed by a ring of 14 cushion-cut rubies divided by two small bands each set w/two old mine-cut diamonds, size 9 .... **$764**

Ring, peridot & enameled 18k gold, the top bezel-set w/an oval-cut peridot weighing 2.55 cts. flanked by green enameled leaves, w/a hallmark, size 5 3/4 .... **$1,175**

Ring, pink diamond, colorless diamond & 18k gold, the simple rounded mount centered by a fancy intense radiant-cut pink diamond weighing about .76 cts. flanked by round brilliant-cut diamonds weighing .71 cts. and .76 cts., size 5 1/2 .... **$33,000**

Ring, pink tourmaline, green tourmaline, diamond & 18k gold, the wide tapering mount centered at the top by a large bezel-set oval-cut pink tourmaline flanked by small triangular pink tourmalines, the shoulders w/center panels set w/square-cut green tourmalines framed by outer bands of diamonds & buff-top rubies, mark of maker Ste. H.V. & French guarantee stamp, size 6 1/4 .... **$1,175**

Ring, platinum & diamond, the squared top centered by a bezel-set brilliant-cut diamonds w/rounded corners weighing about 1.05 cts., framed by a ring of smaller diamonds, decorative shoulders, size 6 1/4 .... **$5,581**

Ring, ruby, diamond & 18k gold, the four-section oblong top composed of two sections each w/two cabochon rubies alternating w/ openwork ropetwist band section, a cross-form central band set w/full-cut diamonds, diamonds weighing about 1.95 cts., ca. 1960s, size 6 .... **$2,938**

Ring, ruby, diamond & 18k gold, twin-stone style, prong-set w/two rectangular step-cut rubies framed by bands of full-cut diamonds, w/ ring guard, size 2 1/2 .... **$940**

Ring, ruby, diamond & platinum, bypass-style, two side-by-side bands, one bead-set w/tapering lines of rubies & the other set w/diamond baguettes, size 7 .... **$1,645**

Ring, sapphire, diamond & 18k gold, the double band prong-set w/an oval pink & purple sapphire, pavè-set w/56 full-cut diamonds, diamonds weighing about 2.62 cts., size 6 1/4 .... **$1,763**

Ring, sapphire, diamond & 18k white gold, the floret-form top centered by a full-cut diamond surrounded by six circular-cut blue sapphires & bordered by a band of smaller full-cut diamonds, diamonds weighing about 1.84 cts., English hallmarks, size 6 3/4 .... **$588**

Ring, sapphire, diamond & 18k white gold, the wide tapering band bead-set w/dark blue sapphires shading to light blue sapphires shading to diamonds, size 6 1/2 .... **$646**

Sets

Necklace & earrings, enameled high-karat gold & seed pearl, the necklace composed of scalloped flower-form links suspending a large drop pendant w/a wide almond form plaque w/a lower fringe of seed pearls suspending a wide pointed chevron-form plaque also w/an ornate seed pearl & colored stone fringe & central matching drop, the plaques all enameled w/a dark green ground decorated in gold & red w/stylized flowering tree & bird designs, matching pendant-style earrings w/14k gold findings, India, earrings 3 1/4" l., necklace 15" l., the suite **$2,350**

KITCHENWARES

The Vintage Kitchen - 1850-1920

Coffee mills, commonly called grinders, are perfectly collectible for many people. They are appealing to the eye and are frequently coveted by interior decorators and today's coffee-consuming homeowners. Compact, intricate, unique, ornate, and rooted in early Americana, coffee mills are intriguing to everyone and are rich and colorful.

Coffee milling devices have been available for hundreds of years. The Greeks and Romans used rotating millstones for grinding coffee and grain. Turkish coffee mills with their familiar cylindrical brass shells appeared in the 15th century, and perhaps a century or two later came the earliest spice and coffee mills in Europe. Primitive mills were handmade in this country by blacksmiths and carpenters in the late 1700s and the first half of the 19th century. These were followed by a host of commercially produced mills, which included wood-backed side mills and numerous kinds of box mills, many with machined dovetails or finger joints. Characterized by the birth of upright cast-iron coffee mills, so beautiful with their magnificent colors and fly wheels, the period of coffee mill proliferation began around 1870. The next 50 years saw a staggering number of large and small manufacturers struggling to corner the popular home market for box and canister-type coffee mills. After that, the advent of electricity and other major advances in coffee grinding and packaging technology hastened the decline in popularity of small coffee mills.

Value-added features to look for when purchasing old coffee grinders include:

• good working order and no missing, broken, or obviously replaced parts

• original paint

• attractive identifying markings, label or brass emblem

• uncommon mill, rarely seen, or appealing unique characteristics

• high quality restoration, if not original.

—Mike White

Coffee Mills

Box Mills

Box mill, iron cover w/gear opening & crank & sunken hopper, on wooden box w/pull-out drawer in front, Parker National **$100**

Box mill, iron crank & side handle on wooden box w/pull-out drawer in front, 1 lb. capacity, Logan & Strobridge Brighton No. 1180 .... **$150**

Box mill, raised brass hopper & crank, Moravian base & inlaid drawer, signed by maker **$200**

Patina is the natural accumulation of wax and dirt on antique over time. In past generations, patina was considered grime to be removed, and countless items were refinished, forever removing their original finish. Today, patina is valued because it retains the historical significance of the item, helps establish its age, and embues it with a mellow look and individual character.

Box mill, raised iron hopper & crank on tin canister w/picture of woman painted on front, drawer in back, patented Norton **$650**

Box mill, raised iron hopper w/ patented partial cover design & crank on wooden box w/pull-out front drawer, Arcade Favorite No. 357 .... **$100**

Upright Mills

Upright mill, cast iron, L.F. & C. New Britain, Conn. Universal, overall green paint w/gold highlights, hand crank w/wooden grip, slide-out base drawer, mounted on wooden board, all-original & like new, late 19th c., 11 1/2" h. **$320**

Upright two-wheel mill, cast iron, miniature model for children, two 2"-h. wheels, Arcade No. 7, rare, overall about 2 1/2" h. **$350**

Upright two-wheel mill, cast iron, w/17" wheels, pivoting cover on hopper, original red paint, decals & pin striping, 1898 patent date marked on grinding burrs, Enterprise #7 .... **$1,500**

Upright two-wheel mill, cast iron, pivoting lid on hopper, two 12"-h. wheels, Coles No. 4 .... **$950**

Side Mills

Side mill, iron, sliding cover, Kenrick patented, England **$110**

Side mill, tin hopper on wood backing, brass emblem reads "Peck Smith Mfg." **$100**

Upright two-wheel mill, cast iron, single wheel, cup, patented Clawson & Clark No. 1 model **$1,000**

Upright two-wheel mill, cast iron, w/nickel-plated brass hopper, 10 3/4" wheels, Enterprise No. 4 .... $2,000

Wall Canister Mills

Wall-mounted canister mill, cast iron, decorative design based on Ami Clark's 1833 patent, w/ adjusting thumbscrew in back & two-sided grinding burr, only known example $2,500

Wall-mounted canister mill, ceramic w/glass measure, marked on front "Douwe-Egberts Koffie," Europe $140

Wall-mounted canister mill, ceramic, children's model, glass measure, "Cafe" on front, Europe, about 6" h. $420

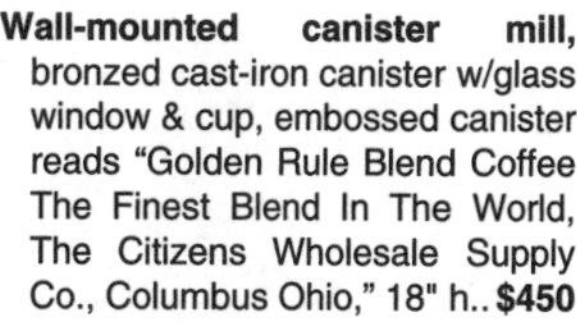

Wall-mounted canister mill, bronzed cast-iron canister w/glass window & cup, embossed canister reads "Golden Rule Blend Coffee The Finest Blend In The World, The Citizens Wholesale Supply Co., Columbus Ohio," 18" h.. $450

Wall-mounted canister mill, tin lithographed canister, pictures a young girl wearing white dress, yellow apron & bonnet, Bronson-Walton Holland Beauty, 13" h. including cup $350

Wall-mounted canister mill, iron & glass, w/2-qt. jar, L.F. & C. Universal No. 24 .... $190

→

Wall-mounted canister mill, iron, clamp-on type, w/pivoting lid, red, rare National Specialty No. 0 .... $310

Egg Beaters

Eggbeaters are pure Americana! No other invention (although apple parers come close) represent America at its best from the mid-19th century to the 1930s or '40s. Eggbeaters tell the unbeatable story of America—the story of demand for a product, competition, success, retreat, failure, faith, and revival.

The mechanical (rotary) eggbeater is an American invention, and ranks up there with motherhood and apple pie, or at least up there where it counts—in the kitchen. American ingenuity produced more than 1,000 patents related to beating eggs, most before the 20th century.

To put it in perspective, try to imagine 1,000 plus ways to beat an egg. Here's a clue, and it's all due to Yankee tinkering: There are rotary cranks, archimedes (up and down) models, hand-helds, squeeze power, and rope and water power—and others. If you ever wanted a different way to beat an egg it was (and is) available.

Today, eggbeaters are a very popular Americana kitchen collectible—a piece of America still available to the collector, although he/she may have to scramble to find the rare ones.

But, beaters are out there, from the mainstay A & J to the cast-iron Dover to the rarer Express and Monroe. There is always an intriguing mix, ranging in price from less than under $10.00 to the hundreds of dollars.

—Don Thornton

A & J, Ecko, wood handle, rotary w/apron marked "A&J USA Ecko," on a two-cup measuring cup marked "A&J" **$35**

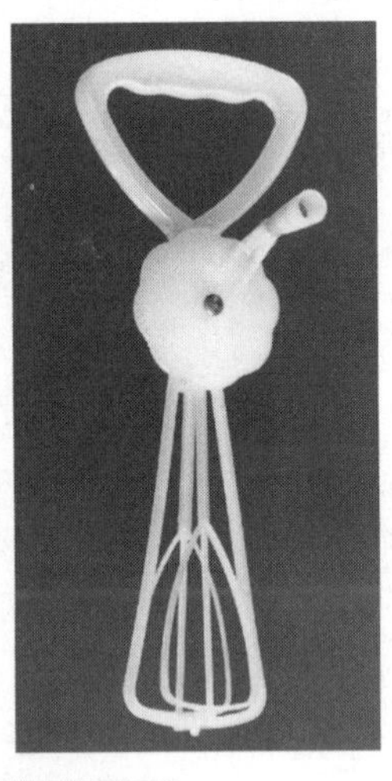

Blisscraft of Hollywood, plastic, rotary, marked "Blisscraft of Hollywood Pat. USA Pend.," scarce, 12" h. **$75**

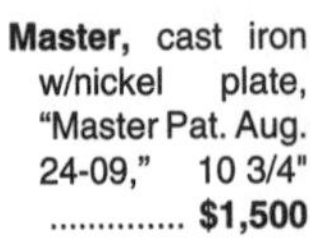

Master, cast iron w/nickel plate, "Master Pat. Aug. 24-09," 10 3/4" **$1,500**

S & S Hutchinson, heavy tin rotary marked "S & S Hutchinson No. 2 New York Pat. Sept. 2, 1913," w/ heavy tin apron on ribbed glass jar embossed "National Indicator Co. No. 2 S & S Trade Mark Long Island City," 9 1/2" h. **$450**

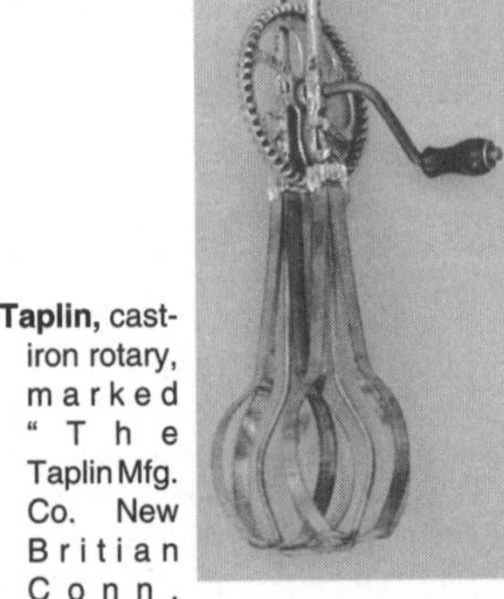

Taplin, cast-iron rotary, marked "The Taplin Mfg. Co. New Britian Conn, U.S.A. Light Running Pat. Nov. 24 '08," 12 1/2" h. **$45**

Miscellaneous

Apple peeler, cast iron, "Wiggin Pat. Aug. 4, 1868" **$1,000**

Basket, wire w/twisted wire center handle, 7" at widest diameter **$85**

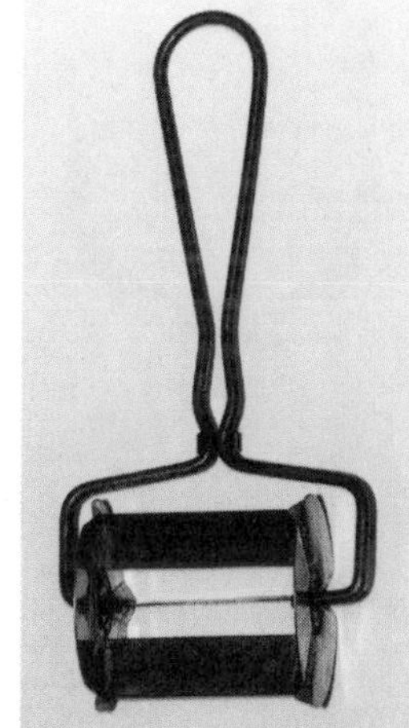

Biscuit cutter, tin, rolls three biscuits at a time, Pat. Sept. 12, 1893 .... **$65**

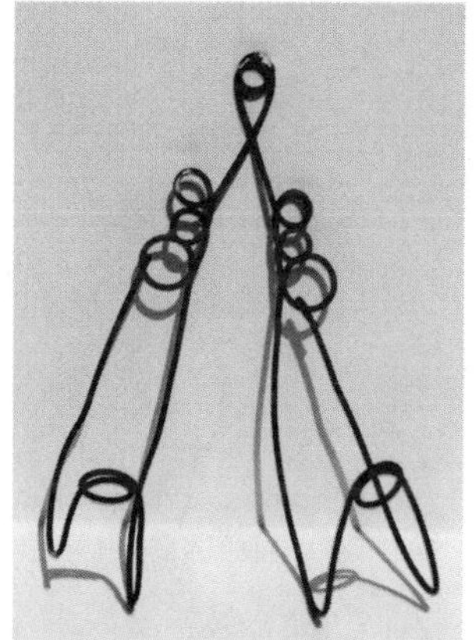

Broom holder, wire, ca. 1890 .... **$65**

Butter churn, table model, tin & cast-iron top w/unmarked glass jar, "The Home Butter Maker, Kohler Die & Specialty Co. Dekalb, Ill USA" **$125**

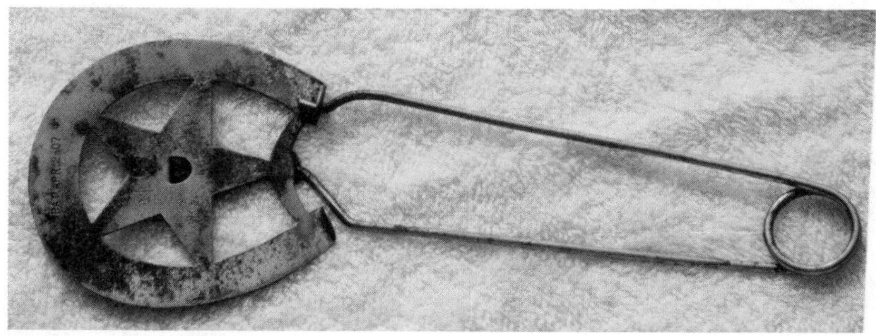

Cake turner, tin, horseshoe-shaped w/star marked "M.C.W. Cake Turner, Pat. Apr. 2. 07," wire handle flips it **$115**

Can opener, cast iron, mounted on board, Williams's Patent of Jan 8, 1878, rare **$275**

Candy kettle, copper, a large half-round form w/a heavy rolled rim & heavy riveted iron loop rim handles, early 20th c., 20" d. **$259**

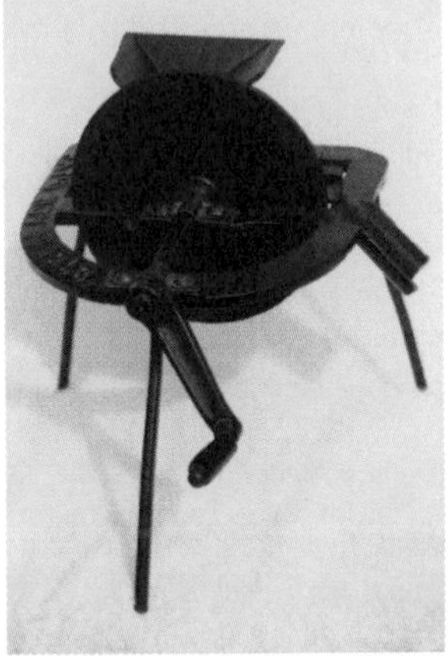

Cherry pitter, cast iron w/three legs, marked "Pat'd Nov. 17, 1863" **$145**

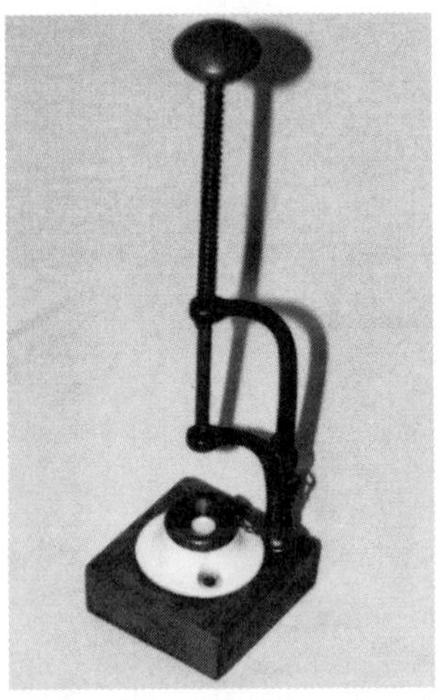

Cherry pitter, wood, porcelain & cast iron, crack-type, unmarked, 10 1/2" **$125**

Chopper, cast iron handle w/two metal blades, handle marked "Pat'd. May 2, 93 No. 20 Croton, NY" **$45**

Dish drainer, tin & wire, wire dish rack fits into rectangular tilted pan **$50**

Dipper, tole, cylindrical bowl w/ tapering strap handle, the bowl decorated w/red & mustard decorative band on black ground, the handle w/mustard & red leaf decoration, bowl 3 1/2" d., 2 1/4" h., 8" w/handle **$480**

Egg scale, metal, platform-style, "Reliable Mfg Co./Los Angeles Calif," 8 3/4" **$75-85**

Flour sifter, tin, mesh screen in bottom, shake handle from side to side for action, marked "The New Shaker Sifter, Center Drive, Prevents Tipping, Pat. Applied For," two-cup size **$35**

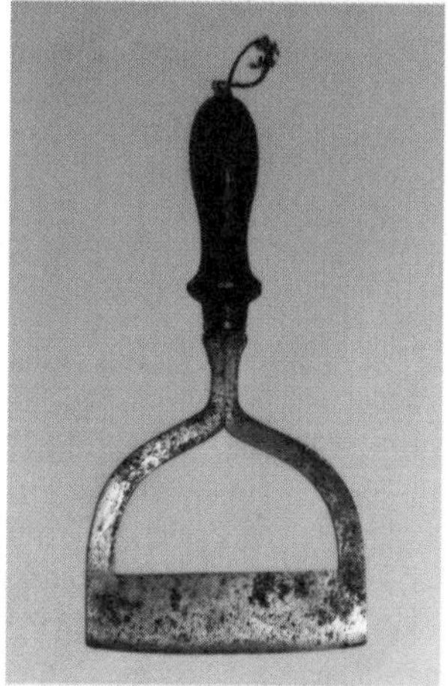

Food chopper, hand-wrought iron, single blade, wood handle, ca. 1850 .... **$30**

Grater, tin, hand-punched, common **$45**

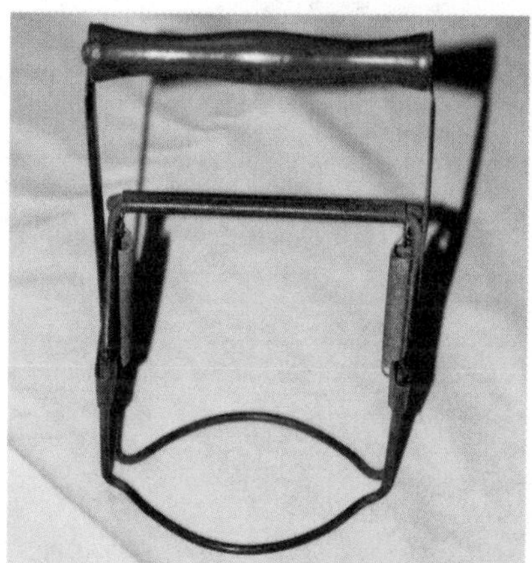

Jar lifter, steel w/turned wood handle, marked "Pat Pend," 8 1/2" h. **$30**

Jar opener, cast iron, very unusual screw clamp mechanism, marked "Pat June 18, 1888," 8 3/4" l. **$150**

Kettle, a deep cylindrical form w/a slightly rounded bottom, the slightly domed hinged cover pierced w/overall decorative holes, iron side rim handle for holding wooden extension, early 19th c., 19" l. **$104**

Kettle stand, brass, the rectangular top w/ a slightly bowed front above a conforming scroll-cut front apron w/front cabriole legs, iron rod back legs, a cast brass handle flanking the top, 19th c., 11 3/4 x 18 3/4", 12" h. **$201**

A pan with a slightly rounded bottom allows food to flow to the center away from the edges where it could burn.

Kraut cutter, a long flat rectangular board inset w/an angled metal cutting blade, the heart-shaped top w/a small hanging hole, well scrubbed & used surface, 7" w., 21 1/2" l. **$345**

Nut grater, tin, half-round w/hanging hole at top, stamped “Acme Nut Grater Rd 114671,” English **$40**

Nutmeg grinder, sterling silver oval cylindrical case w/engine-turned design & hinged cover holding the grater, touch marks for Thomas Hall, Exeter, England, 1855-56, 1 1/4" w., 3" l. **$275**

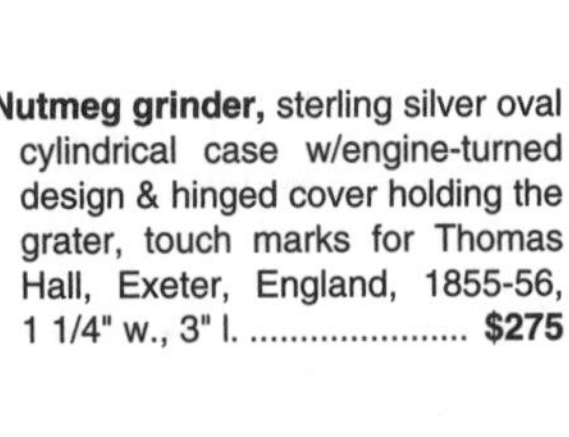

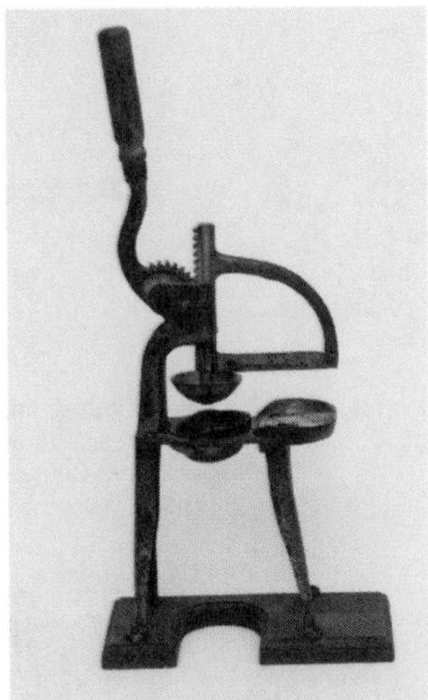

Lemon squeezer/slicer, cast iron, combination cutter & squeezer on wood base w/crank action of handle forcing juice from lemon, inserts often missing, approx. 13" h. **$200-225**

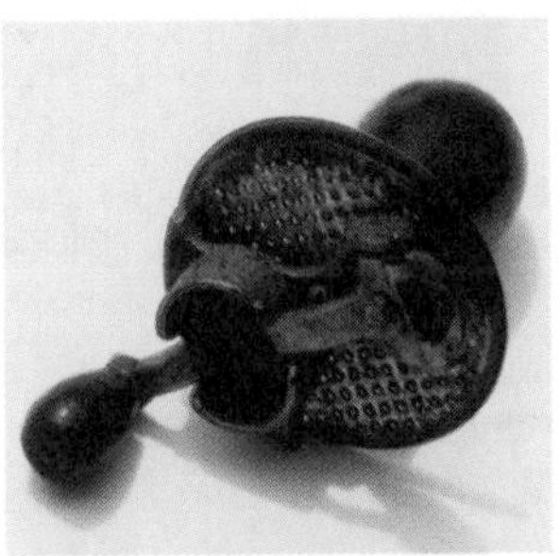

Nutmeg grater, cast iron, tin & wood, “The Gem” **$75-85**

Nut cracker, cast iron, clamp-style for attaching to table edge, clamp-form cracker, marked “Perfection Nut Cracker - Made in Waco, Texas - Patented 1914,” 6 x 6 1/2" **$55-65**

Nutmeg grater, tin, marked “H. Carsley, Patented Nov. 20, 1855, Lynn, Mass,” rare **$975**

Peach stoner, cast iron, “Rollman Mfg. Co. Pat Pend Mount Joy PA U.S.A.,” 8 3/4" **$250**

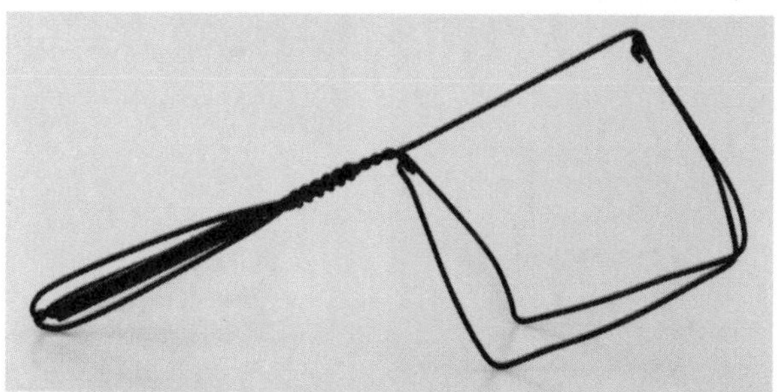

Pie lifter, wire handle w/wood insert, two hinged wings on opposite end which act to grab pan **$95**

Pie pan, tin, pierced star design holes in bottom, used to make crisper crusts **$55**

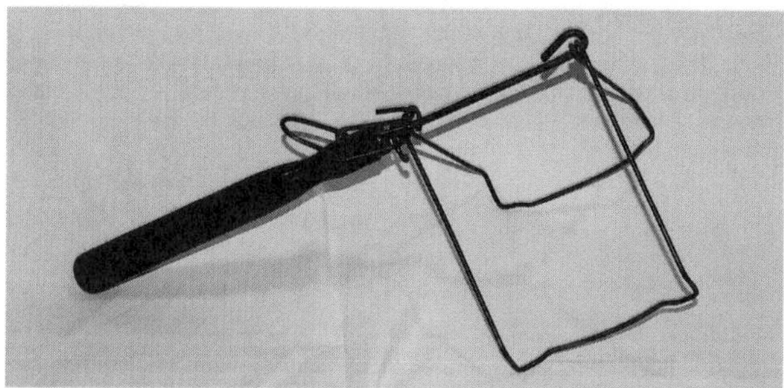

Pie lifter, wire w/long turned black wood handle, an unusual wire lever top opening the wire grips, 12 1/2" l. **$75**

Potato masher, double-spring-action type w/two heavy wire wavy sections, one over the other, turned wooden handle **$45**

Rolling pin, wooden, turned wood handles, the cylinder carved w/20 springerle designs in rows of blocks, early, overall 17" l. **$250-350**

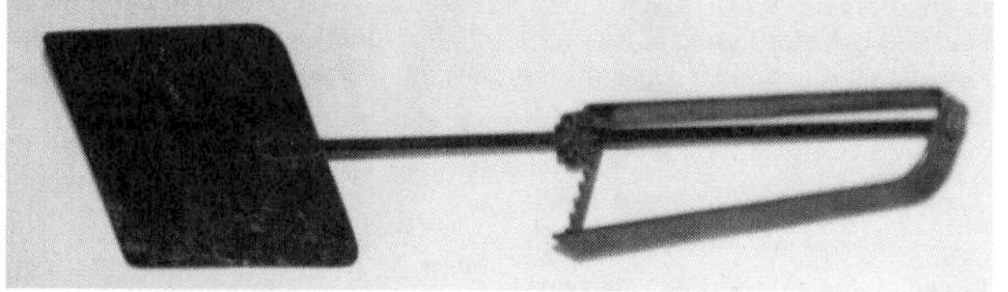

Spatula, tin & cast iron, mechanical, squeezing handle flips end **$75**

Rolling pin, peacock blue blown glass, hollow w/closed handles, rare, 19th c., 14" l. **$400**

Spoon holder, tin, oval shape w/ seven holes & ridge around edge, w/hook, to be placed on side of kettle for drippings from spoon, unmarked **$35**

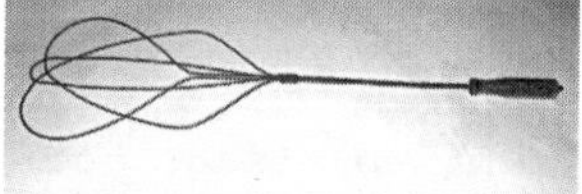

Rug beater, wire w/complex woven design forming three loops of different widths & angles, turned maple handle, late 19th - early 20th c., 9" w., 29" l. **$30-40**

Sugar bucket, cov., stave construction w/three finger lappets w/copper tacks, swing bentwood hickory bail handle, old mustard yellow paint, 19th c., minor wear & edge chips, 13 3/4" h. **$460**

Teakettle, cov., copper, flat-bottomed dovetailed body w/a wide base & tapering sides to a short cylindrical neck w/a fitted low domed cover w/baluster-form finial, angular snake spout, overhead brass strap swing bail handle, stamped number "6," American-made, 19th c., overall 13" l. **$1,208**

Teakettle, cov., copper, oval cylindrical body w/deep sides below the wide angled shoulder, ringed domed cover w/mushroom finial, angular snake spout, fixed tall brass curved supports joined by a bar handle, tin-lined, 19th c., 11" h. **$201**

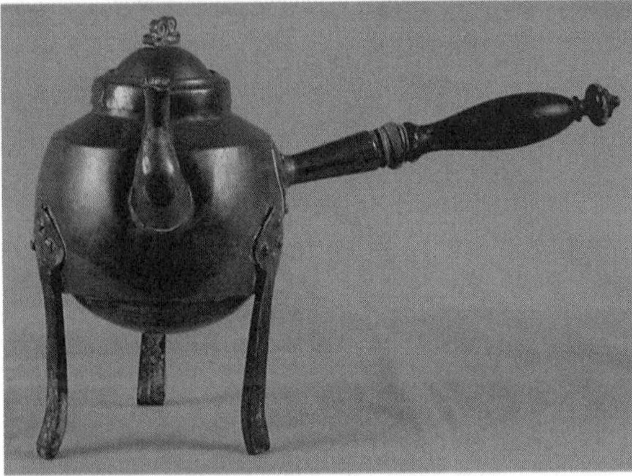

Teapot, cov., copper, bulbous nearly spherical body w/an angled shoulder to a short cylindrical neck w/a fitted domed cover w/scroll finial, tapering cylindrical side handle fitted w/a baluster-turned black wood handle w/pointed terminal, body raised on three straight riveted wrought-iron legs, probably Europe, 19th c., wear, spout pressed in, 8" h. **$125**

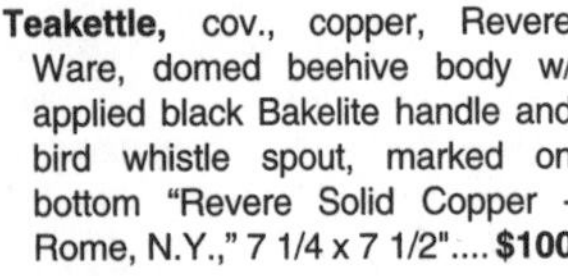

Teakettle, cov., copper, Revere Ware, domed beehive body w/applied black Bakelite handle and bird whistle spout, marked on bottom "Revere Solid Copper - Rome, N.Y.," 7 1/4 x 7 1/2".... **$100**

Toaster, wire w/wood handle, bread was placed between decorative wire, rare **$65**

Toaster, wire w/wood handle, mechanical, lever was pulled to open wire circles to insert bread **$45**

Trivet, wire, rounded starburst design of stamped wire w/double-loop ends & triangles, used as a coffeepot or teapot stand........ **$45**

Trivet, hand-wrought, model of a coiled snake, on three short scroll legs, incised underside, found in Pennsylvania, 19th c., minor surface corrosion, 4 3/4 x 10 1/2", 3 1/4" h. **$978**

Trivet, cast-iron, advertises "C D Kenny Teas, Coffees, Sugars, 60 Stores," 5" l. **$145**

Wafer iron, cast iron, traditional scissor-form w/a pair of hinged round disks on long handles ending in a loop catch, one disk intaglio-cast w/a spread-winged American eagle & shield w/a banner in its beak reading "E Pluribus Unum," Pennsylvania, ca. 1800, overall 29 1/4" l. **$1,610**

Wafer iron, hand-wrought iron, hinged scissor-form w/long slender handles ending in a pair of rectangular plates each incised w/a rectangular zigzag border enclosing a monogram "E.R.D." & heart on one & initials "I.D." & a heart on the other, dated 1763, Pennsylvania, overall 32 1/2" l. **$978**

A wafer iron is like a waffle iron but was used to cook raw dough over an open fire. The dough was placed on one circular iron. Then the iron was closed and the dough cooked over the heat, baking into the dough the design on the iron plates.

The Modern Kitchen - 1920-1980

Kitchen Glassware

Baking dishes, crab-shaped, Glasbake by McKee, manufactured in the 1920s, boxed set of six **$20-24**

Batter bowl, Jadeite, w/spout & angled handle, 3/4" w. rim band, Fire-King **$40-45**

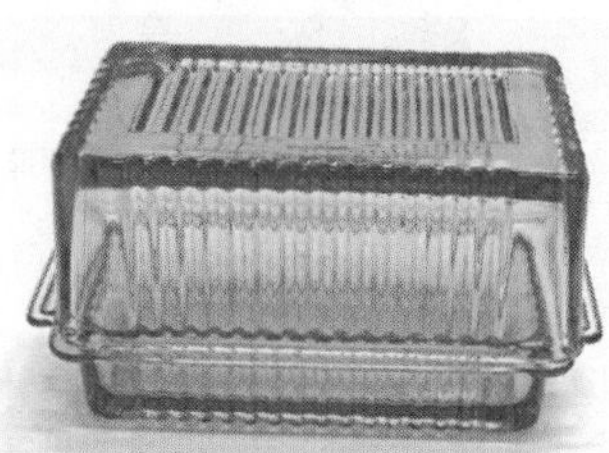

Butter dish, cov., one-pound size, amber rectangular low base w/tab handles & high matching cover, impressed "BOTTOM" on the base, Federal Glass Co., 3 1/4 x 5 1/2" **$45**

Canister, Chalaine Blue, wide cylindrical base & flat fitted cover, McKee, 4 1/2" d., 2 1/2" h. **$75**

Canister w/original screw-on metal lid, milk glass w/Blue Circle decoration & "Sugar," Vitrock line by Hocking, rare, 5 1/4" h. .. **$115**

Canister, clambroth Hoosier-style flour canister, wide cylindrical shaped w/heavy molded rings, flat metal lift-off cover, 7" d., 7 1/2" h. **$125**

Canister, clear w/green silhouette decoration of old men at a table, square w/green metal screw-on cover, Hocking, 4 1/2" w., 6 3/4" h. **$65**

Canister, forest green transparent, upright oval cylindrical shape w/ fine ribbing, "Flour" in a vertical panel up the front, screw-on metal lid, Owens Glass, 8" h. **$65**

Canister, Jadite green fired-on color w/a stylized floral Art Deco decoration & "Tea" in black, black screw-on cover, Hazel-Atlas, 5" h. **$95**

Canisters, Jadite, upright square shape w/flat fitted cover w/inset handle, no label, no sunflower design on the cover, Jeannette, each (ILLUS. of two).............. **$65**

Casserole, cov., clear, part of an embossed set from Glasbake, by McKee Glass Company, two-cup capacity, 6" d. across the top, not counting the tab handles **$10-12**

Casserole, cov., oval, "Arsenic" yellow, Pyrex by Corning Glass **$12-18**

Cottage cheese bowl, footed, milk glass w/green Tulips patt., came in four different colors, stackable, Fire King **$12- 18**

Cream pitcher, cobalt blue, Chevron patt., rectangular top, Hazel-Atlas, gas station giveaway w/matching sugar bowl, small size, 3 " h. **$20-25**

Custard cup, sapphire blue, Philbe patt. "flared" design, Fire King by Anchor Hocking, w/original label **$8-10**

Cobalt blue is one of the most popular glass colors because of its rich, deep hue. It has been a favorite for more than a century and because it coordinates so well with various decorating schemes, will likely remain one of collectors' top choices for the forseeable future.

Drippings jar, cov., cylindrical milk glass base w/flanged rim, wide flat cover w/a black oval enclosing "DRIPPINGS" in black, uncommon, Hazel-Atlas, 4" d. **$95**

Egg cup, double, Chalaine Blue, McKee Glass, 4 1/2" h. **$40**

Egg cup, double, Jade-ite, Fire King, 4" h. **$45**

Flour shaker w/original screw-on metal lid, range-size, cylindrical Jadite ringed shaker w/black block lettering, Jeannette, 5" h. **$75**

Grease jar, cov., ivory w/deep flaring sides, decorated in the Tulips patt., Fire King, 5 3/4" d. **$60**

Grease jar, cov., milk glass Vitrock w/the red Flowerpots design, domed glass cover w/black & red banding, Hocking Glass, 1950s, 6" h. **$45**

Knife, clear, Star patt., in original Vitex-Glass Knife box marked "Pat Pend - Made in USA," 9" l. ... **$35**

Loaf or bread baking pan, sapphire blue, Philbe patt., Fire King, 5 x 9" **$18**

Loaf pan, clear, rectangular ringed sides w/red-painted handles, Glasbake by McKee Glass Co., 5 x 9" **$8-10**

Measuring cup, amber, triple-spout, tapering cylindrical sides w/measurements, no handle, two-cup, Federal Glass, 4 3/8" h. **$50**

Measuring cup, commemorative, clear w/red wording, "Commemorating 50 Years - Fire-King," 1992, 2 cup **$15-18**

Measuring cup, green transparent, footed, measurements on the sides & "Measuring and Mixing" pressed into the bottom, two- cup, Hocking Glass, 3 3/4" h. **$55**

Measuring cup, green transparent, single spout, measurement marking to the rim, arched spout, one cup, Hocking, 3" h. **$48**

Measuring pitcher, footed, Seville Yellow, wet measures on one side, dry on the other, McKee, four-cup, 1930s, 6" h. **$145**

Measuring pitcher, green transparent, tapering cylindrical sides w/measurement markings, four-cup, Hocking, 6" h. **$95**

Mixing bowl set, milk glass w/ flaring sides & abstract dot & scroll designs in red, blue, green & yellow, by Federal, mark is an "F" in a shield, the bowls measure 5" d., 6" d., 7" d., 8" d., & 9" d., five-piece set **$65-75**

Mixing bowl, Jade-ite, Swedish Modern shape by Fire King, smallest size, 5" w. **$65**

Mixing bowl, milk glass w/the Black Flowers patt., accented w/thin red orange & yellow rings, Hazel Atlas, 9" d. **$50**

Mixing bowl, milk glass w/the red Kitchen Aides patt., Splashproof design, shows various kitchen utensils, Fire King, 7 1/2" d. **$100**

Mug, Jade-ite, D-style, Fire King **$18**

Mug, turquoise, D-style, Fire King **$30**

Pepper shaker w/original screw-on metal lid, range-size, cylindrical Delphite blue ringed shaker w/black block lettering, Jeannette, 5" h. **$85**

Pepper shaker w/original screw-on metal lid, range-size, square milk glass decorated w/three small black Scottie dogs w/red bows, red lettering, Hazel-Atlas, 4 3/4" h. **$50**

Pitcher, Jade-ite, milk size, Beads & Bars patt., Fire King by Anchor Hocking, 20 oz. **$125-175**

Pitcher, Jadite, wide spout, angled handle, impressed sunflower in the bottom, Jeannette, 5 1/2" h. **$65-75**

Range set: rectangular milk glass grease jar w/flat red metal cover & matching square salt & pepper shakers, all on a long red metal rectangular tray w/an upright center handle, each piece decorated w/the red & black Flower Basket patt., Tipp City, shakers 2 3/4" h., the set **$175**

Range set: salt & pepper shakers & grease jar; ivory, ringed cylindrical shape w/"Tulip" lids, Fire King by Anchor Hocking, note corrosion of salt lid (difficult to find good condition), the set **$85-95**

Range set: salt & peppers shakers & flour & sugar shakers w/original screw-on metal lids, cylindrical milk glass w/green scroll design above & below "Sugar," "Salt," "Pepper" & "Flour," black metal caps, 3 3/4 to 4 1/2" h., the set **$95**

Refrigerator dish, cov., Delphite blue, square w/flat cover w/inset handle, Jeannette, 4 1/2" w., 2 3/4" h. **$55**

Refrigerator jar, cov., squared shape, "Bluebelle" line in Canadian blue, Pyrex by Corning, scarce, 3 1/2 x 4 3/4" **$20-25**

Roaster pan, cov., Philbe patt., sapphire blue, lid & bottom are same piece, Fire King, 10 3/4" d. **$95**

Salt & pepper shakers w/original screw-on aluminum lids, range-size, milk glass, square, decorated w/blue circles, 3 5/8" h., pr. .. **$45**

Salt & pepper shakers w/original screw-on black metal lids, range-size, milk glass, square, decorated w/red apple & green leaves, 3 1/4" h., each **$20-25**

Salt & pepper shakers w/original screw-on metal lids, range-size, cylindrical milk glass w/Tulips decoration, color decoration of tulips on the metal lids, Fire King, the set **$90**

Salt & pepper shakers w/original screw-on metal lids, range-size, milk glass, square, red & blue design of "Uncle Sam" hats, 3 1/8" h., pr. **$45-55**

Salt box, cov., green transparent, footed round & paneled base w/a center-hinged flat chrome cover, larger of two sizes made, U.S. Glass Co., 5 1/2" d., 3 3/4" h. **$285**

Salt box, Hoosier-type, clear, open round, Triple Skip patt., 4 3/8" d., 3 1/4" h. **$65**

Salt shaker w/original screw-on metal lid, range-size, square Skokie Green w/a small black rectangle & black lettering, McKee, 5" h. **$75**

Spice shakers w/original screw-on red metal lids, milk glass, square w/ beveled corners, each printed w/various blue Dutch scenes on front, paper labels on reverse, red star & name of spice in red letters above scene, 3 1/4" h., each **$12-20**

Sugar bowl, open, cobalt blue, Chevron patt., Hazel-Atlas, gas station give-away w/the matching creamer, large size, 3 1/2" h. **$24-28**

Sugar shaker w/original metal screw-on pour top, clear pear shape w/wide panels & thin ribs, chrome top w/pouring flap, Dripcut Starling Corp., Santa Barbara, California, 5 1/2" h. **$35**

Sugar shaker w/original scew-on metal lid, range-size, square milk glass w/blue & black Dots decoration of oval panel w/"Sugar" in black, Hazel-Atlas, rare, 4 3/4" h. **$175**

Syrup pitcher & cover, green transparent, Mayfair patt., cylindrical body w/rim spout & shaped loop handle, flat cover w/angled loop handle, Fostoria Glass, 6" h. **$125**

Syrup pitcher & cover, green transparent, slightly tapering cylindrical body w/cupped rim w/ spout, fancy hand-etched design of flowers & leaves, applied green threaded handle, inset glass cover w/knob finial, Imperial Glass, 6" h. **$195**

Trivet, green transparent, round w/a wide ring of thick ribs around the top, indented center impressed "Protecto," for hot pans, 5" d. **$25**

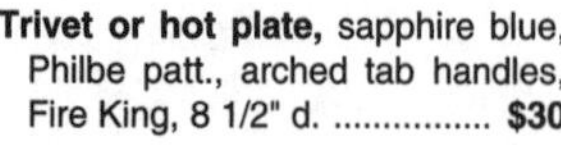

Trivet or hot plate, sapphire blue, Philbe patt., arched tab handles, Fire King, 8 1/2" d. **$30**

Reamers

Reamers are a European invention dating back to the 18th century. Devised to extract citrus juice as a remedy for scurvy, by the 1920s they became a must in every well-equipped American kitchen. Although one can still purchase inexpensive glass, wood, metal and plastic squeezers in today's kitchen and variety stores, it is the pre-1950s models that are so highly sought after today. Whether it's a primitive wood example from the late 1800s or a whimsical figural piece from post-World War II Japan, the reamer is one of the hottest kitchen collectibles in today's marketplace - Bobbie Zucker Bryson

Ceramic, figural Oriental man's head, two-piece, w/collar as base, hat as lid/reamer, light blue w/dark grey highlights, incised "9496," 5 3/4" h. **$125-150**

Ceramic, figure of a clown, two-piece, aqua & white body w/ maroon hands & black feet, maroon, black & white conical reamer hat, marked "Japan," 5 1/2" h. **$55-65**

Ceramic, model of orange, two-piece, realistic w/green leaf spout & brown branch handle, white top & reamer cone, marked "Goebel," Germany, 4 1/2" h. **$65-75**

Ceramic, model of orange, two-piece, w/a green loop handle, marked "Japan" on the base, 3 3/4" h. **$45-55**

Ceramic, model of orchid, two-piece, pink & white w/green handle & bottom, 3" h. **$100-115**

Ceramic, model of orange, two-piece, yellow w/pebbled surface resembling orange peal, white & yellow cone top, front reads "Orange for Baby," marked "Registered Germany," 4" h. **$60-75**

Ceramic, pitcher-shaped, two-piece, tall form w/lip, C-form handle & short out curved base, pale pink ground w/painted floral decoration in pinks, blues, yellows & greens, thin green rim decoration, marked "Pantry Bak-In Ware by Crooksville," 8 1/4" h. .. **$125-175**

Ceramic, pitcher-shaped, two-piece, squat form w/lip & circular handle, white ground w/maroon & yellow flower design, gold trim, marked "Hand Painted Japan," 3 3/4" h. **$75-95**

Ceramic, pitcher-shaped, two-piece, w/C-form handle, basketweave design in dark green w/orange & maroon flowers & light green leaves, yellow top & cone, black trim, marked "Maramotoware Hand Painted Japan," 4" h. **$40-50**

Ceramic, saucer-shaped, one-piece w/lipped spout and shell-form handle, white ground w/pink & magenta flowers, green leaves & gold bead trim, marked "Hand Painted Japan" **$150-175**

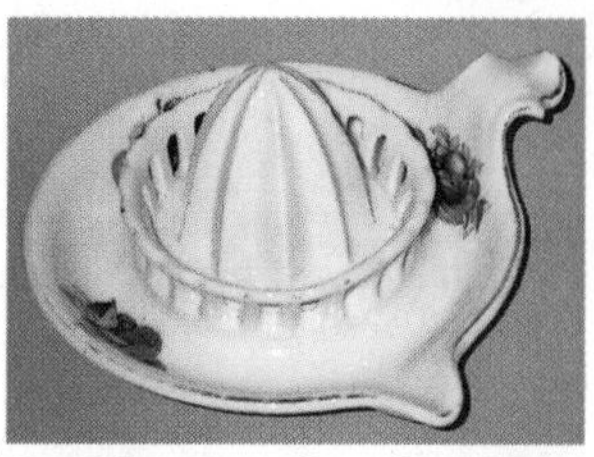

Ceramic, saucer-shaped, one-piece w/spout & side handle, round seed dam w/lattice strainer, white ground w/design of red cherries & green leaves, gold trim, 3" h. **$85-115**

Ceramic, saucer-shaped, one-piece, souvenir-type, w/spout & side handle, blue, rust & cream, w/painted image of Victorian woman w/parasol on one side of bowl & mass of flowers on the other, marked "Made in England, A Present From Dobercourt," 3 1/4" d. **$85-125**

Ceramic, saucer-shaped, one-piece, white w/gold trim, w/figures of tree, swan, butterfly & flowerpot, marked "Made In France - Limoges France," 3 1/2" d. **$75-95**

Ceramic, teapot-shaped, two-piece, earthtones & purple pansy-type flowers on white ground, green lustre trim on handle & rim of body, lid & spout, ribbed lid w/holes for liquid to pass through, reamer in the form of a head with yellow ribbed cone hat, marked "Made in Japan," 6" h. **$75-125**

Glass, dark transparent red, two-piece, paneled base & round reamer top, limited edition by Edna Barnes, marked on the bottom w/a "B" in a circle, 3 1/2" h. **$35-40**

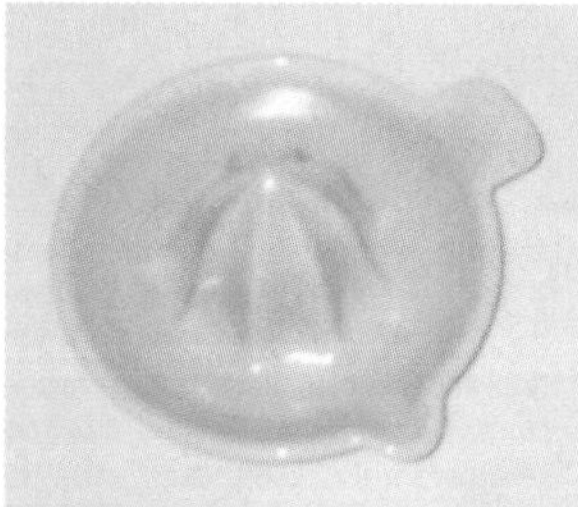

Glass, pale blue opaque, saucer-shaped, limited edition by Edna Barnes, marked on the bottom w/a "B" in a circle, 2 1/2" d. **$15-20**

The words "Made in Japan" were first used in 1921, when a law was passed requiring that all goods imported into the United States be labeled with the words "made in" followed by the importing country's name in English. Before this, from 1891 until 1921, goods made in Japan were marked "Nippon," the Japanese word for Japan.

LIGHTING DEVICES

Early Non-Electric Lamps & Lighting

Lamps, Miscellaneous

Banquet lamp, composite-style, a white metal domed footed base supporting a tall brass stem & embossed brass font w/burner supporting a replaced bulbous frosted & etched clear shade w/ ruffled open top, marked "New Juno" burner, electrified, late 19th c., 26" h. **$288**

Gone-with-the-Wind table lamp, decorated milk glass, the domed pierced cast-metal foot supporting a bulbous squatty font w/blown-out lion heads alternating w/small Egyptian landscapes all on a deep rusty brown ground, brass collar & font insert supporting the matching ball shade, some damage, 22" h. **$403**

Banquet lamp, three-section, milk glass baluster-form standard molded w/acanthus leaves & painted w/pink roses joined to a bulbous matching font w/inset burner supporting the matching tulip-form shade, on a gilt-iron openwork squared foot, Consolidated Lamp & Glass Co., ca. 1890s, overall 35" h. **$1,035**

Cut-overlay table lamp, kerosene-type, the inverted pear-shaped cranberry cut to clear font in a design of clustered circles, joined by a brass connector to a white opaque Baroque variant pattern base, brass collar w/reducer & late HB&H lip burner, Boudoir-style shade ring soldered to burner, a 3 1/4" h. clear engraved & frosted Oregon shade & early lip chimney, ca. 1870, open bubble on side of font, 10 3/4" h. **$440**

←

Gone-with-the-Wind table lamp, milk glass bulbous base & ball shade h.p. w/a dark shaded green ground & clusters of large white mums & small red daisies & green leafy stems, cast-metal scroll-decorated base & brass collar connector, ca. 1890s, electrified, 22" h. **$316**

Hall lamp, blown spherical deep cranberry swirled ribbed shade w/a brass base cap & drop finial, the top w/a brass crown band w/ hanging chains, electrified, 12" h. **$316**

Hall lamp, gas-type, leaded glass & brass, a tall square form w/each side composed of clear leaded segments centered by an amber & red cross design, metal corner finials & four arched top bars & drop center burner joined to hanging cap, ca. 1890s, electrified, 9" w., 24" h. **$633**

Hanging parlor lamp, kerosene-type, frosted & shaded open-topped domed cranberry shade w/a Diamond Quilted patt. fitted on an ornate shade ring suspending facet-cut prisms above a very elaborate brass framework centered on each side by a red jewel, an ornate brass cap & drop framing the matching Diamond Quilted font, ca. 1880s, shade 14" d. **$3,450**

Hanging parlor lamp, kerosene-type, the open-topped domed milk glass shade h.p. w/large deep red & white flowers & green leaves on a tan ground, pierced brass shade ring suspending facet-cut prisms, looping brass frame supporting the bulbous milk glass font w/ decoration matching the shade, complete w/hanging chains, crown & brass smoke bell, solder repair within brass font cup, late 19th c., overall 36" h. **$440**

Parlor table lamps, kerosene-type, mold-blown cranberry glass, each w/a round cushion foot below the large baluster-form ringed body supporting the burner ring & large Diamond Quilted matching tulip-form shades, overall ornate gilt leafy scroll decoration, burner marked "Duplex," some wear & minor flakes, overall 29" h., pr. **$1,610**

Sinumbra table lamp, gilt-lacquered bronze, the cut-and-etched clear tulip-form shade resting on a circular shade ring above a tall reeded vasiform standard w/a pair of foliate-cast handles, on a columnar stand joined to a square plinth base, mid-19th c., America or England, electrified, overall 33" h. **$2,185**

Student lamp, double style, the ornate brass body w/raised design of lion heads surrounded by scrolled designs, central bulbous ringed font flanked by upturned large arms each supporting a ring & ribbed white-cased pink open-topped shade & clear chimney, drilled & electrified, width shade to shade 24", shades 10" d., overall 18" h. **$2,300**

Table lamp, kerosene-type, clear Adams Temple - Applesauce design, round plinth-style base supporting four open columns centered by a glass dome w/ apparently original contents, the squatty bulbous patterned font w/brass shoulder & shade ring fitted w/a frosted Oregon shade, No. 2 burner & chimney, rim below columns molded "Patented March 20 1883 July 25 1882," cork on center dome w/paper label reading "Fruit Bowl Patented Nov. 15 1881 July 25 1882," Ripley, Vogeley & Adams Co., overall 13" h. ... **$880**

Table lamp, "Ripley Marriage lamp," two bulbous translucent blue fonts flanking a central covered match holder & joined on a tapering flange to a threaded brass connector on an opaque milk glass stepped, square pedestal foot, connector dated "1868," lamp marked "D.C. Ripley, Patent Pending," brass font collars w/kerosene burners & shade rings supporting clear tulip-shaped etched chimney shades, one shade cracked, overall 19 3/4" h. **$1,265**

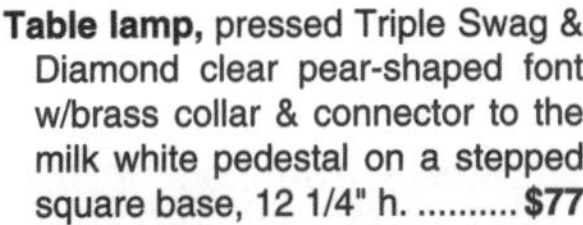

Table lamp, pressed Triple Swag & Diamond clear pear-shaped font w/brass collar & connector to the milk white pedestal on a stepped square base, 12 1/4" h. **$77**

Table lamp, 7 1/2" d. domical open-topped porcelain lithophane shade w/four panels showing different ladies in garden settings, colorful tinted interior, raised on a Meissen porcelain base w/a bulbous basketweave font w/applied gilt-trimmed floral sprigs supported by three standing cupids w/ delicate coloring all on a round mottled brown base, blue Crossed Swords mark, late 19th c., overall 13 1/2" h. **$2,585**

Table lamp, pressed glass, a kerosene burner & brass collar on the squatty ringed onion-form blue opaline glass font above a turned brass connector & flaring ringed pedestal on a square white marble foot, ca. 1860, 9" h. **$61**

Table lamp, Burmese glass, 10" d. domical shade & base handpainted & enameled w/Egyptian decoration of five ibis birds in flight in sunrise sky w/pyramids & palm tree oasis scene, original Burmese glass chimney, gilt metal mounts, not electrified, Mount Washington, late 1890s, 20" h.............. **$10,350**

Table lamp, kerosene-type, blue opalescent Coin Spot squatty bulbous font joined by a brass connector to a "Detroit" style pedestal base composed of swirls of reds, yellow & white, a brass collar w/a No. 2 slip burner & clear chimney, screw connector, one foot flake, ca. 1880s, 9 1/4" h. **$605**

Whale oil lamp, tin & glass, a clear cylindrical glass font w/brass collar & two-wick whale burner flanked by upright tin round frames enclosing bull's-eye focusing lenses, all on a slender cylindrical tin shaft & round disk weighted base, old worn black finish, first half 19th c., 8 1/2" h. (old repairs, one lens chipped)............................... **$248**

Whale oil table lamp, pressed sapphire blue flint glass, the tapering ovoid fonts w/the Arch patt. fitted w/original pewter collar & double burner, fonts joined w/a wafer to an ornate flaring tiered octagonal pedestal base, Pittsburgh, ca. 1830-50, 10 3/8" h., pr. **$7,425**

Electric Lamps & Lighting

Handel Lamps

The Handel Company of Meriden, Connecticut (1885-1936) began as a glass and lamp shade decorating company. It became a major producer of decorative electric lamps which have become very collectible today.

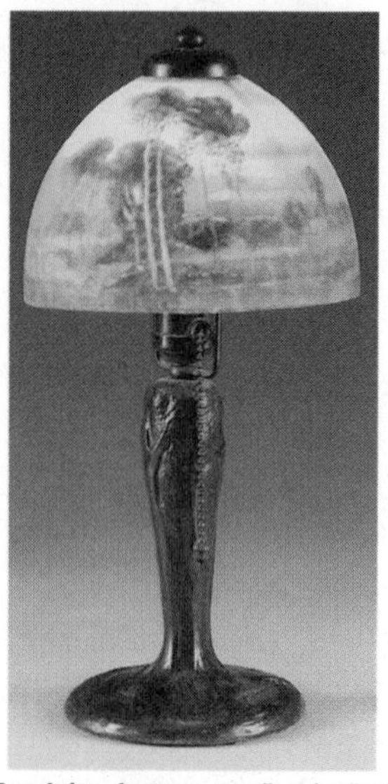

Boudoir lamp, small domical reverse-painted shade decorated w/a continuous meadow landscape w/tall trees at sunset in shades of yellow, brown, tan & green, raised on a bronze base case in low-relief w/tree trunks, shade signed "Handel 6661," 13" h. **$2,300**

Hanging lamp, domical eight-paneled open-topped caramel slag shade, Hawaiian metal filigree design w/a tropical sunset scene w/palm trees & a lagoon in each panel, hanging hardware & three-light bulb socket, signed, 24" w. **$7,475**

Student lamp, the round bronzed metal reticulated foot centered by a tall reeded shaft issuing two adjustable arching arms ending in electric sockets each fitted w/a 10" d. domical green "Mosserine" shade signed "Handel 6047X," unmarked base, 24" h. **$3,525**

Table lamp, 18" d. domical reverse-painted shade in the Bird of Paradise patt., large exotic birds in shades of deep red, lavender, yellow & orange among shaded brown & yellow foliage against a black background, chipped ice exterior, signed "Handel 7026 - Broggi," atop a heavily enameled urn-form three-legged base w/red enameled berries separating the stylized leaf design around the book, hung w/original amber glass drops & matching glass ball finial, base signed w/label on the felt bottom, 24" h. **$18,300**

Table lamp, 18" d. domical reverse-painted shade in the Mt. Fuji patt., a contiuous Oriental landscape w/tall bamboo in the foreground & a lake & Mt. Fuji in the background, the reverse side shows a bay w/Oriental ships & a dock, signed "Handel 6945 - John Bailley," raised on a Handel cast-bronze bamboo-shaped base w/Handel cloth tag under the bottom, base w/some minor pitting, rewired, 23" h. **$7,475**

Moss Lamps

Clock lamp, No. XT 815, deLee Art male figurine "Siamese Dancer," 2' 11" h. **$275-300**

Floor lamp, No. 2293, "Leaning Lena," butterfly Plexiglas angled standard, 4' 7" h. **$275-300**

Floor lamp, No. 2317, marble pattern plexiglass, Decoramic Kilns figurine "Cocktail Girl," 5' h. **$600-625**

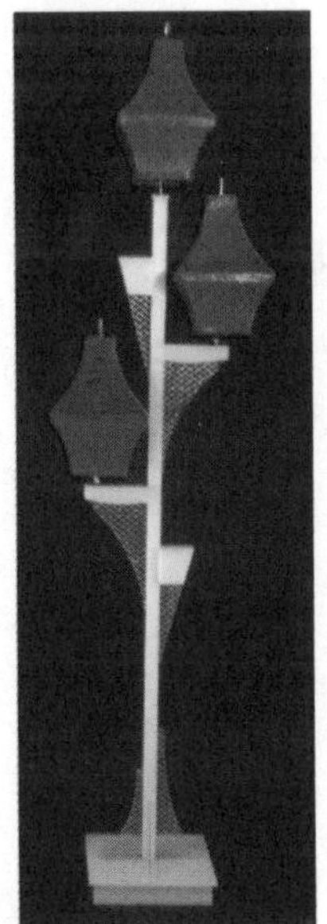

Floor lamp, No. 2328, triple red pagoda-style shade, 6' 5 1/2" h. **$400-425**

Music box lamp, No. T 534, Lefton "Harlequinade Boy & Girl" figurines, 2' 5" h. **$275-300**

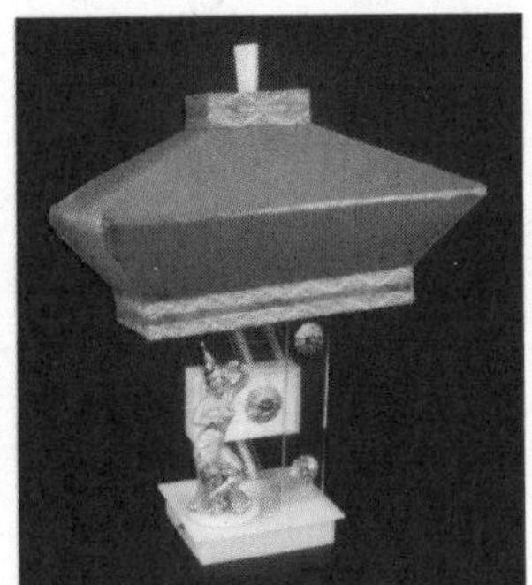

Partner lamp, No. XT 815, no clock, deLee Art female "Siamese Dancer" figurine, 2' 11" h. **$200-225**

Table lamp, No. T 544, corner table-style, triple pod shades, Decoramic Kilns "Bell Girl" figurine, 2' 10" h. **$300-325**

Table lamp, No. T 681, corner table-type, double rectangular shades, Decoramic Kilns "Bali Dancer" figurine, 3'4" h. **$300-325**

Table lamp, No. T 731, Decoramic Kilns "Prom Girl" figurine, 3' 7 1/2" h. **$300-325**

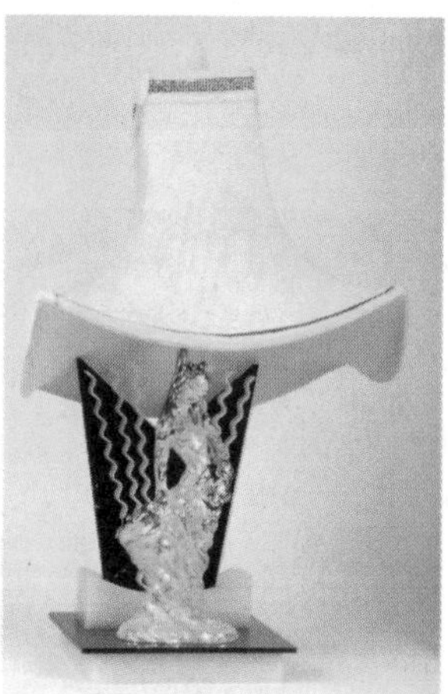

Table lamp, No. XT 807, Hedi Schoop "Phantasy Lady" figurine, 2' 5 1/2" h. **$250-275**

Table lamp, No. XT 821, "Egyptian Woman," 2' 8" h. **$200-225**

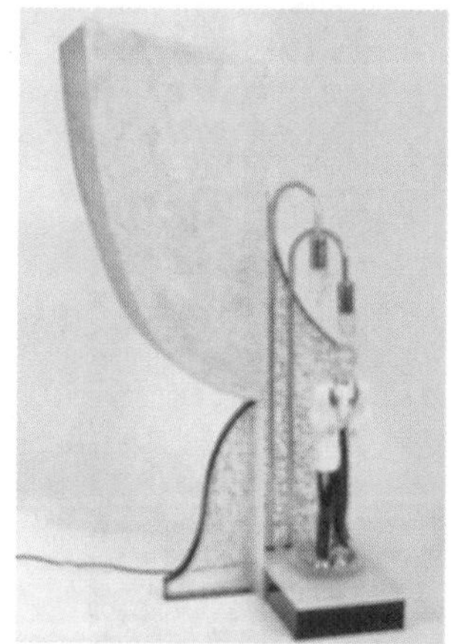

Table lamp, No. XT 827, torchere shade, Decoramic Kilns "Escort" figurine **$375-400**

Table lamp, No. XT 835, Johanna "Black Luster Dancer" figurine, 3' h., each (ILLUS. of two) **$125-150**

Table lamp, No. XT 838, double cone shades, Decoramic Kilns "Mambo" figurine, 4' 4 1/2" h. **$325-350**

Table lamp, No. XT837, "Las Maracas," double pod shades, 3' 8 1/2" h. **$300-325**

Pairpoint Lamps

Well known as a producer of fine Victorian art glass and silver plate wares between 1907 and 1929, the Pairpoint Corporation of New Bedford, Massachusetts, also produced a wide range of decorative lamps.

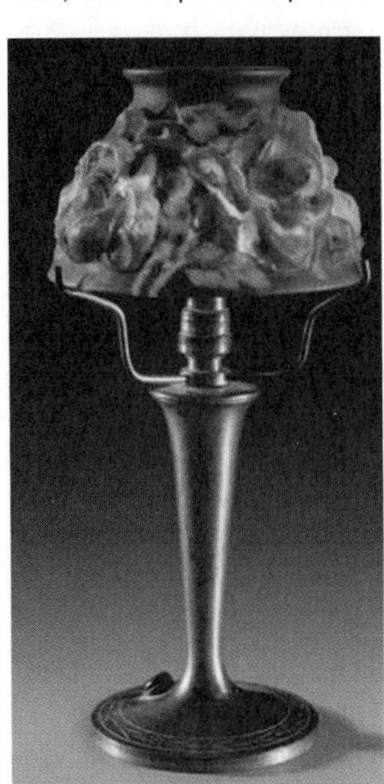

Boudoir lamp, 5 1/4" d., domical "Puffy" reverse-painted "Pansy" shade, open-topped & decorated w/dark red, yellow & purple pansy flowers on a dark green ground, raised on a spider support above the simple bronzed metal candlestick-style marked base, minor bruise to shade rim, small fitter rim flake, 11 1/2" h. .. **$1,528**

Boudoir lamp, 5" d., domical "Puffy" reverse-painted "Rose Bouquet" shade, decorated w/large red & yellow roses & green leaves on a frosted clear blue-striped ground, raised on a green patinated brown Pairpoint tree trunk base, base signed "Pairpoint B 3079," 10 1/2" h. **$6,000**

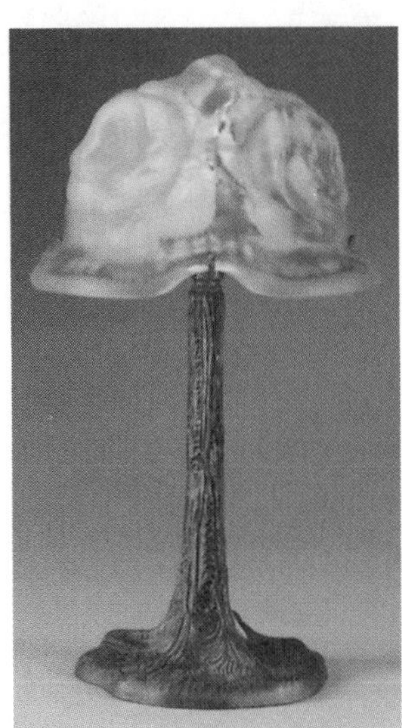

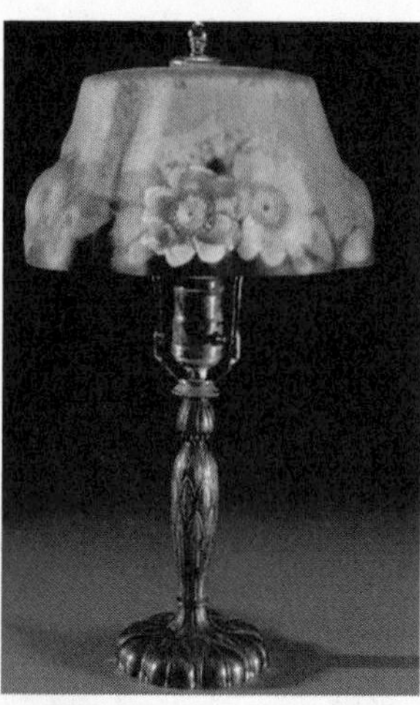

Boudoir lamp, 8 1/2" d., domical "Puffy" reverse-painted "Stratford" shade, flat top & flaring undulating sides decorated around the lower border w/large blue & eyllow dogwood flowers against a pale pink shaded to black ground, signed, raised on a signed slender bronzed metal base w/the swelled shaft cast w/overlapping pointed leaves, the round base w/ribbing, one small flake inside shade rim, 16" h. **$2,350**

Boudoir lamp, 8" d. domical reverse-painted shade decorated w/a nighttime maritime scene of sailing ships in harbor against a green sea & purple sky, marked "Pairpoint Corp. - C. Durand," raised on a slender turned wood urn-form shaft w/an applied openwork brass band, on a wide round foot w/a brass rim band, several small chips to rim of shade, overall 16" h. **$489**

Boudoir lamp, 8" w. domical "Puffy" reverse-painted "Bristol" shade, slightly domed top center above four flaring sides, decorated in each panel w/various flowers including roses, daisies, pansies & poppies, rests on a gilt-bronze Pairpoint base w/a swelled four-sided standard impressed on two sides w/flowers & leaves, on a stepped rectangular foot, base signed "Pairpoint Mfg. Co. B 3050," minor discoloration on base, 15" h. **$4,800**

Table lamp, 12" d. domical reverse-painted "Venice" shade, decorated w/large pink rose blossoms w/ yellow & green leaves against a frosted white scrolling ground, on a slender bronze base w/a square foot marked "Pairpoint B 3003," 21" h. **$4,485**

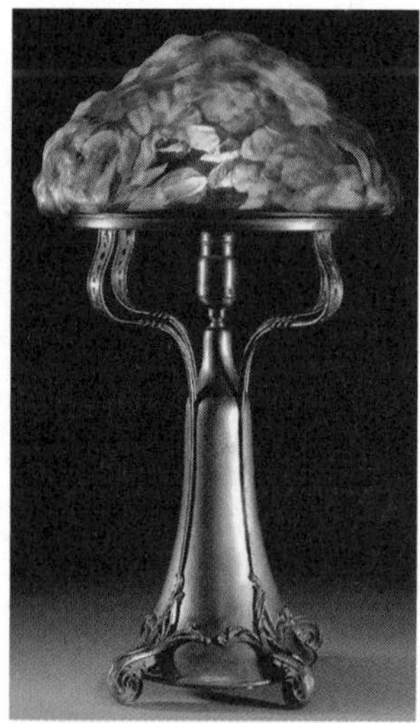

Table lamp, 12" d., domical "Puffy" reverse-painted "Azalea" shade, closed-top design w/the flowers painted in shades of red, pink, white & yellow w/green leaves against a black ground, signed, raised on an antiqued brass base signed "Pairpoint 3035," w/a shade ring supported by four curved & pierced flat arms tapering to the conical base raised on fancy ornate leaf-scroll feet, overall 22" **$12,925**

←

Table lamp, 17" d. hexagonal tapering "Directoire" shade reverse-painted w/a continuous colorful expansive landscaped ground & marked "The Pairpoint Corp'n" on the border, raised on a candelabrum-style base w/three electric candle sockets on short gilt-metal arms w/pointed drops centered by a knob above a cut glass knop on a gilt-metal tapering pedestal & octagonal dark onyx foot, impressed "Pairpoint Mfg. Co. E3001," 27 1/2" h. **$2,645**

Table lamp, 13 1/2" d., domical "Puffy" reverse-painted "Devonshire" shade, closed-top design w/a wide border band of large yellow, white & red roses below a flying hummingbird, all against a background of light & dark green stripes, signed, raised on an antiqued bronze Art Nouveau-style base w/the tapering four-sided shaft decorated w/ slender leafy vines above the wide swelled four-lobed foot w/further vining, base marked & stamped "B3031," 22" h. **$9,400**

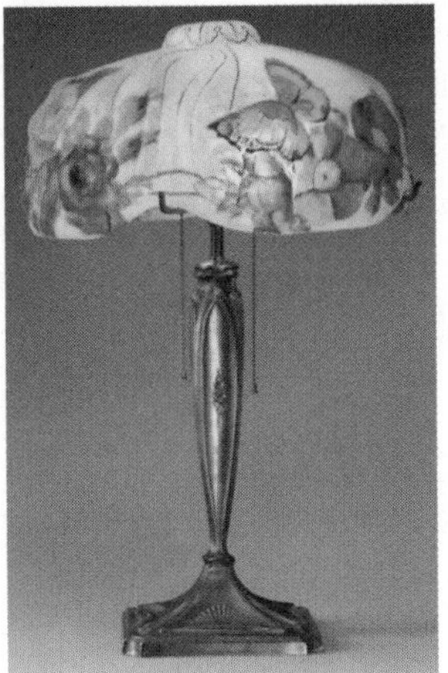

Table lamp, 14" d., domical "Puffy" reverse-painted "Papillion" shade, closed-top design decorated w/ sections of large red, yellow & orange flowers & green leaves below large yellow & orange butterflies, all against a mottled white ground, signed, on an antiqued brass base w/a slender columnar shaft w/tall narrow oval panels centered by tiny floral sprigs above the paneled & squared foot cast w/shell-like devices, base marked "Pairpoint Mfg. Co. B33202," 21" h. **$10,500**

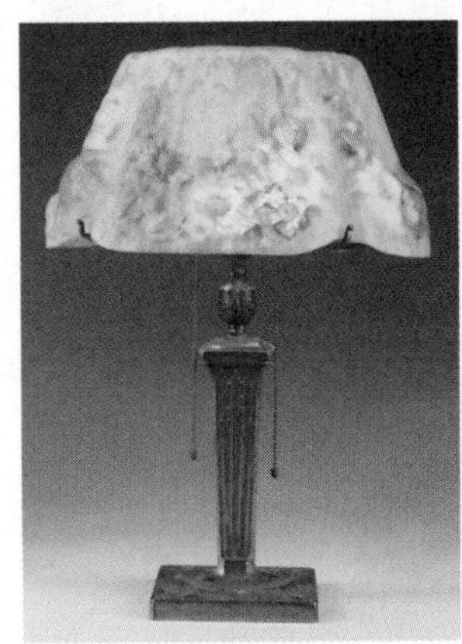

Table lamp, 15 1/2" d., domical "Puffy" reverse-painted "Devonshire" shade, closed-top design decorated on each side w/ garlands of colorful flowers against a pale bluish green ground, riased on a green patinated bronze base w/a tall square slightly tapering fluted column above a rectangular foot, interior of shade w/some darkening from light bulb heat, a couple of tiny rim fleabites, 21 3/4" h. **$9,300**

Tiffany Lamps

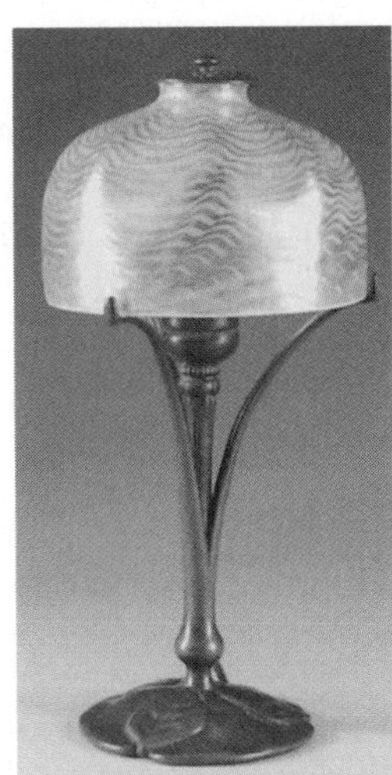

Desk lamp, 7" d. domical open-topped shade w/molded ribbing & decorated w/a continuous wavy golden orange banded design, cased in gold iridescence, supported on a Tiffany bronze three-prong base w/a central shaft resting on a round leaf-cast foot w/a brown patina, shade signed "LCT," base signed "Tiffany Studios - New York 426," chips to fitted rim, minor damage to top cap & socket of base, overall 14" h. **$8,625**

←

→

Desk lamp, Arabian-style, a conical shade decorated w/a gold & platinum iridescent snakeskin design on a butterscotch ground, on a slender baluster-form optic ribbed amber iridescent glass standard on a domed foot, shade & base signed, 13" h. **$4,680**

Desk lamp, counter-balance style, a 7" w. domed shade w/platinum damascene iridescent decoration on an orange & purple ground w/ cased interior, supported atop a high arched counter-balance arm above the domed base trimmed w/a row of teardrop nodules, fine dark patina, shade signed "LCT Favrile," base signed "Tiffany Studios - New York 415," 16" h. **$16,200**

Desk lamp, the shade formed by a large white nautilus shell trimmed in hammered silver & raised on a forked bronze standard above a round domed base w/a ribbed edge & raised on five small ball feet, fine reddish brown patina w/green highlights, base signed "Tiffany Studios - New York 403," 13" h. **$7,763**

Table lamp, "Acorn Border," a 16" d. domical leaded glass shade composed of concentric rows of graduated rectangular tiles in heavily mottled yellow opalescent glass above a medial band of mottled green opalescent glass heart-shaped leaves, w/finial, raised on a gilt-bronze slender three-arm standard w/applied thin reeded bands w/small curled ends above the leaf-cast cushion base on scroll feet, shade signed "Tiffany Studios - New York," base signed "Tiffany Studios - New York - 357 - S171," 22" h. **$17,825**

Table lamp, "Daffodil," 16" d. domical open-topped leaded glass shade composed of tall clusters of yellow daffodils on leafy stems against a mottled white shaded to mottled green ground, shade marked "Tiffany Studios - New York," raised on a tall slender shaft above a cushion base cast w/ rounded teardrops raised on scroll feet, base impressed "Tiffany Studios - New York - 6842," 22 1/2" h. **$37,375**

Table lamp, "Lily," ten-light, the long clambroth & butterscotch optic-ribbed iridescent Favrile glass trumpet-form lily shades on a clustered stem bronze dorè lily pad base, shades signed "L.C. T.," base impressed "Tiffany Studios - N.Y." & numbered, 20" h. **$40,538**

Table lamp, "Geranium," 16 1/8" d. conical leaded glass shade decorated w/mottled red geranium blossoms above, against a mottled pale blue & green ground, among a profusion of varied colored green leaves below, interspersed w/rippled glass leaves, against a mottled & striated pale pink & green ground, bordered by three bands in mottled pale pink, blue & green, the standard cast w/ scrolling tendrils & pods, in rich greenish red patina, tag stamped "TIFFANY STUDIOS - NEW YORK," 23" h.................. **$32,200**

Table lamp, "Linenfold," the 14 1/2" w. twelve-sided slightly tapering shade w/an arrangement of large square amber linenfold panels between smaller amber linenfold borders between amber smooth borders, intaglio finish, shade impressed "TIFFANY STUDIOS - NEW Y0RK - 1950 - PAT. APPLIED FOR," the base impressed "TIFFANY STUDIOS - 442," 24 1/2" h.................. **$5,000**

Other Lighting Devices

Chandeliers

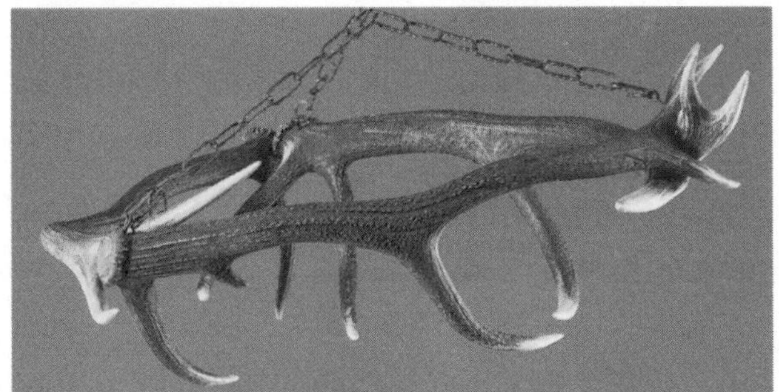

Antler, five-light, composed of two entwined deer antlers drilled for five fixtures, Europe, late 19th c., 31" d., 26" h. **$288**

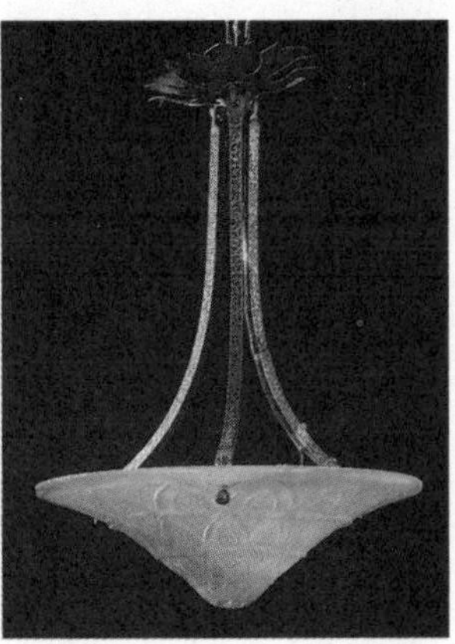

Art Deco, glass & iron, a widely flaring inverted conical molded shade in frosted blue glass w/ an arched geometric design, suspended by a hammered wrought-iron frame, ca. 1925, 16" d., 23" h. **$460**

Art Deco, one-light, frosted clear glass & nickel-plated bronze, a six-lobed frosted glass shade molded w/large stylized flower blossoms suspended in a framework of six curved button-cast scroll arms joined to six long & slender C-scroll arms suspended from the paneled ceiling plate, attributed to Genet-Michon, France, ca. 1930, 25" d., 39" h. **$1,955**

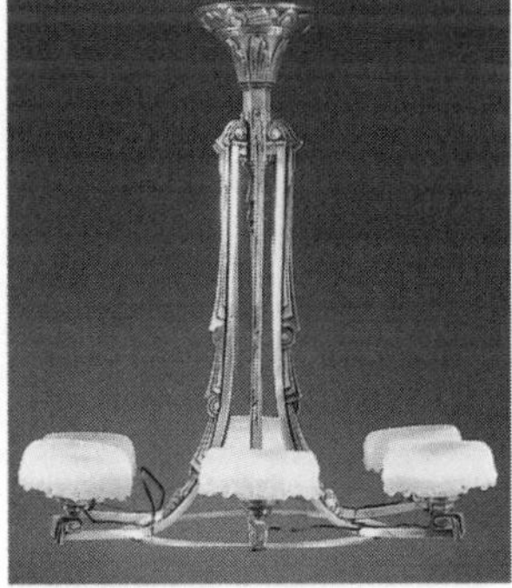

Art Deco, six-light, the tall center nickel-plated bronze framework w/six square drapery-cast arms curving out at the bottom to each support an opalescent glass shade w/a molded drop decoration, ca. 1930, 28" d., overall 29" h. **$2,530**

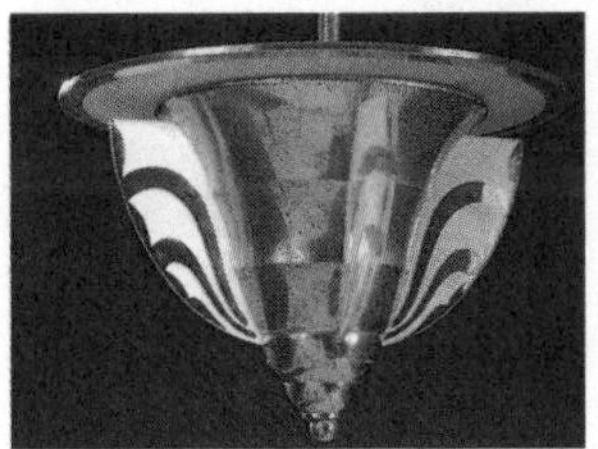

Art Deco, spun copper, a ringed pointed conical copper center w/ four protruding etched pink glass wings, pink etched disk glass top, ca. 1925, 18" d. **$604**

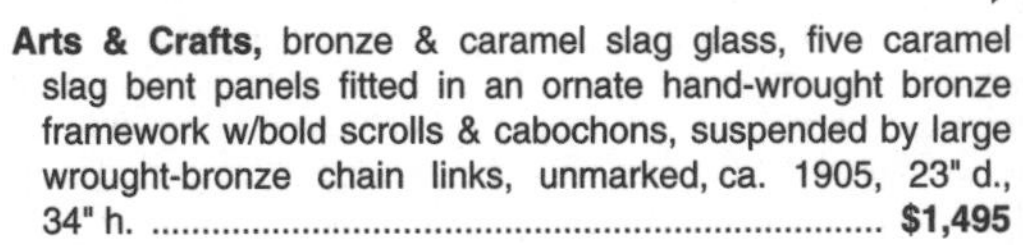

Arts & Crafts, bronze & caramel slag glass, five caramel slag bent panels fitted in an ornate hand-wrought bronze framework w/bold scrolls & cabochons, suspended by large wrought-bronze chain links, unmarked, ca. 1905, 23" d., 34" h. **$1,495**

Art Nouveau, 10-light, bronze & glass, "Chicoree" patt., the long central post w/an upturned leaf ceiling cap above a cluster of scrolling arms w/sockets ending in small blown milky opalescent bell-shaped glass shades above a bottom ball issuing large looping & curling arms suspending four milky opalescent flaring conical ribbed shades, a central rounded matching shade at the center bottom, designed by Louis Majorelle, France, ca. 1905, 37" d., 49" h. **$10,755**

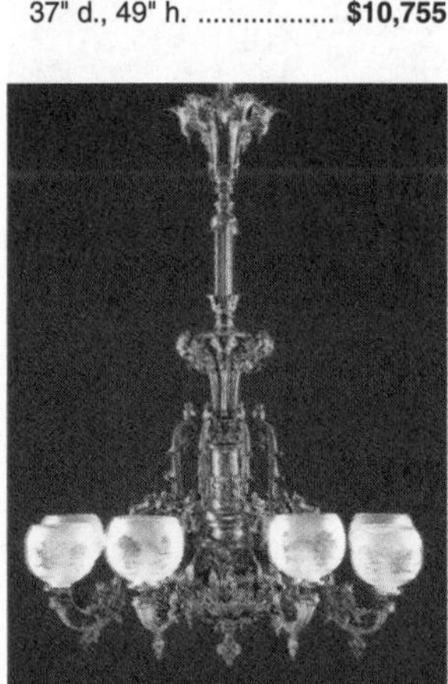

Gilt-brass, Rococo Revival-style gasolier, eight-arm, the large cast arms w/foliate & leaf decor surrounding the central bowl profusely adorned w/rococo mounts & tassels, the fluted shaft w/a large bell canopy w/applied decoration, attributed to Starr, Fellows & Co., New York, New York, ca. 1850, 40" d., overall 58" h. **$27,600**

Brass, five-light gasolier style, a reeded rod leading to a stem of pierced ball shape, supporting five scrolling arms w/turned & fluted finial candle sockets, ornate scrolls from the center to the arms decorated w/large blossoms, America, ca. 1890, electrified, 27" d., 39" h. **$2,070**

Cut glass & gilt-brass, ten-light, Louis XVI-Style, the brass scroll arms elaborately dressed w/glass fleurettes, jewel-cut beaded chains & faceted drops & cut palmette-like leaves, France, late 19th c., 25 1/2" d., 28" h. **$1,610**

Handel, 24" d. domical octagonal slag glass shade, the large tapering upper bent panels in deep mottled reds & oranges above a border panel in mottled yellow & green, the upper panels decorated w/a delicate tropical palm tree metal filigree overlay, the border panels overlaid w/whiplash scroll filigree **$6,325**

Muller Freres, four-light, a wide bowl-form central shade internally decorated in mottled peach, red, green, blue & amethyst, suspended from wrought-iron bars & fitted around the rim w/three metal sockets each suspending a matching tapering cylindrical glass shade, glass etched "Muller Fres - Luneville," France, early 20th c., 18" d., 29" h. **$1,840**

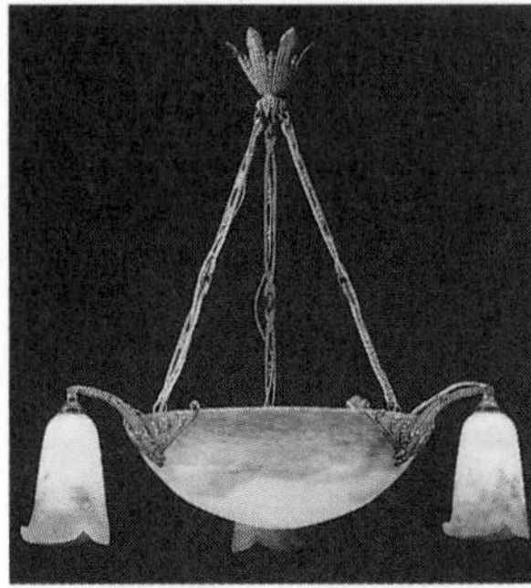

Muller Freres, three-light, a wide bowl-shaped central glass shade in mottled blue, pink, yellow & white supported by three chains w/scrolled gilt-iron rim brackets, each bracket supporting a socket w/a flaring cylindrical matching glass shade, ca. 1920, 22" d., overall 23" h. **$1,495**

Quezal, four-light, a brass central fixture w/a long shaft suspending a wide round deep disk suspending a central metal tassel & fitted around the rim w/squared scrolls each suspending a metal socket fitted w/a signed ribbed flora-form golden iridescent Quezal shade, shades 6" h., overall 31" h. **$2,300**

Slag glass, bent-panel type, six wide tapering slag panels in mottled blue, tan & white fitted into a cast-metal framework w/bands of floral filigree along the bottom of each panel, ca. 1920, 15" d. **$259**

Steuben, four-light, a long brass ceiling shaft suspending a round center disk w/a tapering center drop finial, the rim fitted w/four sockets each fitted w/a signed Steuben bell-form shade in ivory iridescent decorated w/gold iridescent heart-shaped leaves & random threading, shade Shape No. 904, each shade 4 3/4" h., overall 18" d. **$1,265**

Venetian blown glass, eight-light, in the 18th c. taste, the faux candles emanating from large scalloped coupes atop upswept clear glass arms, the whole adorned w/arched & twisting leaves, multicolored flowerheads & strawberries, ca. 1900, electrified, 34" d., 34" d. **$4,140**

Wood & iron, eight-light, a baluster-turned wooden hub painted white, now grey w/age, issuing eight slender serpentine iron arms ending in tin candle sockets, America, late 18th c., imperfections, 29 1/2" d., 15" h. **$2,820**

Wood & tin, twelve-light, country-style, a slender central ring- and rod-turned shaft issuing twelve slender iron wire arched & upturned arms each supporting a tiny candle cup w/crimped edges, 20th c., 24" h. **$550**

Shades

Durand, a wide squatty bulbous stepped shape w/a long pierced leaf-shaped metal center pendant drop, heavily crackled gold iridescent surface, chips to fitter rim, fitter 4" d., 6 1/2" h. **$300**

Jefferson-signed, hexagonal tapering shape, each panel reverse-painted w/an Art Deco design in dark orange & green chevrons, signed on metal fitter rim, ca. 1920s, 14" w., 9" h. **$863**

Lustre Art-signed, trumpet-form w/ swelled band at the top below the connector flange, overall golden orange iridescence w/green hanging leaf design & decorated w/fine gold threading, early 20th c., 5 1/2" h. **$275-325**

Quezal-signed, long tulip-form, blue & gold pulled-feather design on white, iridescent gold interior, 4 7/8" d., 6" h. **$1,438**

Quezal-signed, ribbed trumpet-form, opal decorated w/overall golden iridescent ribbons, gold iridescent interior, 5" h. **$552**

Quezal-signed, tall trumpet form, the exterior w/a platinum zipper pattern over a dark green pulled-feather design in light green, dramatic deep purple & blue iridescence, gold iridescent interior, signed on the fitter rim, fitter rim 3 1/4" d., 8 1/4" h. **$2,703**

Slag glass bent-panel, umbrella-shaped eight-paneled style, each panel in mottled red & green w/pointed crown panels at the top center, a drop border w/ruby panels decorated w/fancy pierced metal filigree, ca. 1925, 22" d. **$230**

Steuben-signed, ribbed trumpet-form, blue iridescent Aurene, 5 1/2" h. **$633**

Steuben-signed, ribbed trumpet-form, green Alabaster, 5 3/4" h. **$518**

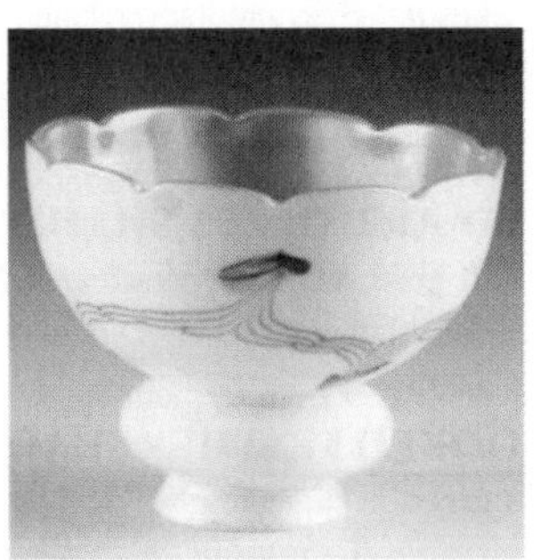

Steuben-signed, small fitter opening above a cushion-form band over the wide umbrella-shaped sides, white Calcite exterior decorated w/ an undulating band of green vining & florettes, iridescent gold interior, 5" d., 4 1/4" h. **$1,150**

Tiffany-signed, domical lightly ribbed open-topped damascene glass w/a rich green ground decorated w/overall wavy gold iridescent band decoration w/ purple & blue highlights, signed w/initials inside the rim, 5 1/2" d. **$5,175**

Tiffany-signed, domical open-topped shape in ribbed opal decorated overall w/a gold damascene decoration, signed, ca. 1900, 10" d. **$8,740**

Tiffany-signed, a simple lightly ribbed tulip form, overall gold iridescence, fitter rim signed "L.C.T.," 5" h. **$840**

Tiffany-signed, domical open-topped form w/a butterscotch iridescent exterior cased in white, signed "L.C.T.," chips to fitter rim, 8" d. (ILLUS. inverted)...... **$1,150**

Tiffany-signed, domical open-topped shape, silver iridescent ground decorated overall w/a green King Tut design, cased in white, signed, two small chips to outside top rim, 10" d. **$7,475**

Tiffany-signed, domical open-topped shape, silver w/overall green iridescent damascene decoration, cased in white, 12" d. **$8,050**

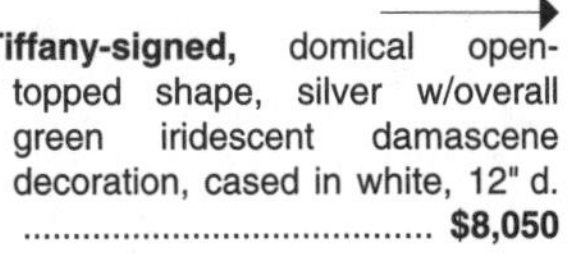

Tiffany-signed, bulbous ovoid ribbed form w/a flat incurved rim, heat reactive glass decorated w/a lemon yellow & red pulled- feather exterior decoration, probably originally a candlestick shade, numbered "X2175," fitter 2 1/8" d., 4 1/2" h. **$1,955**

Tiffany-signed, domical open-topped shape in green w/overall iridescent gold damascene decoration, numbered "56837," ca. 1900, large **$3,450**

Tiffany-signed, leaded glass, wide tapering flat sides composedd of alternating narrow & wide green slag panels swirled w/ blues & orange, the flattened top composed of narrow double slag glass bands around the center opening, signed "Tiffany Studios New York 1587," numerous cracks in the large panels, 11" w. **$2,013**

LIPSTICK TUBES

Forerunners of the lipstick tube as we know it now included lip and rouge pots and lipstick matches. The push-up lipstick tube preceded the swivel lipstick tube. In between the use of the lip and rouge pot and the modern type of lipstick tube, there were many ingenious lipstick tubes were devised with unique mechical devices for raising and lowering the lipstick.

Lipstick tubes have been produced in precious metals, enamel, metal alloys, Bakelite, papier-maché, wood, mother-of-pearl, cord and cardboard. These can be further enhanced with crystals, precious gems, fur, sparkles, colored rhinestones and petit-point. Most lipstick tubes are square or round with a flat base.

Many manufacturers of vintage lipstick tubes also had matching compacts. Costume jewelry and haute couture designers, including Paul Flato, Salvador Dali, Halston and Christian Dior, created delightful lipsticks that are now very coveted by collectors.

My personal favorite lipstick tubes are designed to resemble figurals, dolls, etc., and the gadgetry whimsical lipstick tubes that are combined with a secondary accessory such as a watch, whistle, flashlight, cigarette case, jewelry, a pen or a perfume vial. These dual-purpose collectibles are very desirable and are sought by both lipstick tube collectors and those who collect the various accessory items.

Lipstick tubes, both the vintage and contemporary examples, are beautiful, affordable and fun vanity collectibles.

For additional information on the history and values of lipsticks, consult the book Vintage and Contemporary Purse Accessories by Roselyn Gerson (Collector Books).

Atomette lipstick tube, polished goldtone decorated in relief w/an owl trimmed w/rhinestones, the top w/tiered bands of rhinestones around the flat mirror top **$125**

Leaning Tower of Pisa lipstick tube, a model of the famous tower in vermeil sterling silver trimmed w/cabochon turquoise stones, comes w/a turquoise velvet case decorated w/gold trim, Rome, Italy **$300**

Christian Dior crystal lipstick tube, modeled as an obelisk on a pedestal base, the first lipstick created by Dior in 1956, made as a smaller vesion of his famous perfume bottles **$200**

Revlon lipstick case, designed to resemble a 1920s Flapper, trimmed in gold cloth & wrapped in black velvet **$85**

Revlon lipstick case, figural design of a sphinx-shaped doll complete w/a gold & black headpiece **$225**

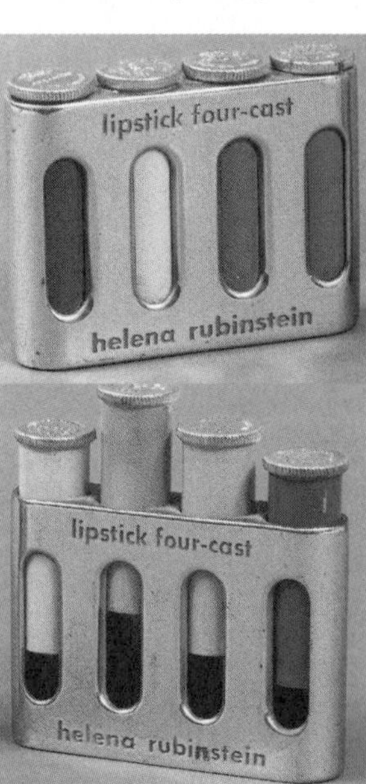

Helena Rubinstein, Four-Case lipsticks, four brightly colored enameled lipstick tubes indicating the shades of lipstick encased in the polished goldtone holder, each (ILLUS. of one open & one closed)................................ **$125**

Papier-machè lipstick dolls, cylindrical w/decorated doll-shaped tops, handcrafted in Mexico, each **$65**

METALS

Brass

Hall lanterns, brass, four-light, Georgian-style, round w/glazed panels between the brass uprights, one panel a hinged door, the upper rim w/beaded swags suspended from ribbons, undulating braces from the top rim to the center shaft which drops down into the center & curves up to end in candle sockets, England, 12 1/2" d., 14 3/4" h., pr. (electrified) **$4,025**

Palace jar, wide bulbous body w/a wide shoulder tapering to a short flaring neck, overall delicate chased designs of various deities within a scrolled field, India, early 20th c., 17" d., 16" h. **$414**

Samovar, a square base on knob feet supporting a two-part pierced pedestal below the large nearly spherical body w/large scroll & bar handles & a large spigot, a gadrooned top band w/large inserted top w/wooden knob handles flanking the tall ringed chimney, Imperial era, Russia, marked, 15" h. .. **$374**

Samovar, tray & bowl, the samovar w/a footed square base & vented pedestal supporting the wide urn-form body w/scroll-and- bar side handles & a large spigot w/a fancy scroll handle, the ringed flaring top fitted w/a stepped & ringed top w/wooden knob handles flanking the flaring vented chimney, w/a shallow widely flaring bowl for under the spigot, both on a conforming shaped undertray, marked, Russia, ca. 1890, overall 18 1/2" h., the set ... **$546**

←

Vase, hand-hammered Arts & Crafts style, shell casing-type w/a slightly tapering cylindrical lower section w/a widely flaring upper section w/a deeply ruffled rim, Dirk Van Erp, early 20th c., impressed "U.M.C. Co.," 6" d., 9 3/4" h. (light wear to patina) **$1,430**

Wall sconces, each w/oval reflector plate decorated w/pair of winged putti flanked by stylized foliage & fruit, centers a convex reserve w/C-scroll embossed surrounds, two removable serpentine projecting candlearms below, cylindrical candle cups w/dished drip plates, 12 1/2" w., 16" h., pr. **$13,800**

Bronze

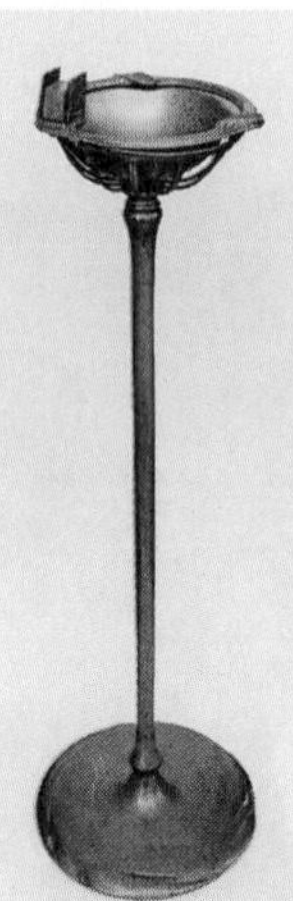

Ashtray, floor model, gold finish, flared base supporting long shaft holding bowl-shaped tray w/hinged top & match holder, marked on base "Tiffany Studios, New York, No. 1649," 9 x 28" .... **$3,000+**

Baby shoes, high-button, worn-looking, 2 1/2 x 4", 6 1/2" l., the pr. **$35**

Jewel casket, eight-sided shape on beveled base, adorned on sides & lid w/Wedgwood blue & white jasper medallions, inside lined w/possibly original purple velvet, inside of lid marked "Tiffany & Co. New York," back edge of base marked "G. Betjemann & Sons Makers London," 6 3/4 x 10", 6 1/2" h. **$2,185**

Medallion, commemorative, honoring labor, rectangular, w/ embossed scene of classically garbed woman w/arm around boy & pointing to distant industrial scene and the word "Labor" radiating from it, 2 x 2 1/4" **$75**

Book ends, cast, copper finish, flat base merging into upright embossed w/heads of Abraham Lincoln & George Washington in profile, 4" h., the pr. (ILLUS. of one) **$195**

Book ends, cast, silver finish, stepped base, arched open Moorish-style upright w/figure of knight in armor holding a shield standing between pillars w/background of embossed vining leaves, marked on reverse "Travelers Convention, Palm Beach, Florida, 1931 - patent pending," 3 x 4 1/2", 8" h., the pr. (ILLUS. of one) **$250**

Vase, wide baluster-form body w/a wide rolled gadroon-cast rim, scrolled foliate handles & raised on a foliate scroll base, the sides cast w/ chrysanthemums in relief, good dark patina, Japan, early 20th c., 15" h. **$201**

→

Copper

Book ends, hammered copper w/brass wash, upright form decorated w/stylized floral motif, marked w/orb & cross, Roycroft, 4 1/2 x 5", pr. **$201**

Book ends, hammered copper w/ brass wash, upright form w/curled & riveted straps, marked w/orb & cross, Roycroft, 2 3/4 x 5", pr. **$201**

Book ends, ovoid upright shapes w/embossed owl motifs & riveted decoration to bases, orb & cross mark, Roycroft, 5 x 5 1/2", pr. **$431**

Card tray, round w/raised rim, hammered copper, orb & cross mark in center, Roycroft, 8" d. **$518**

Coal scuttle, Arts & Crafts style, tapering cylindrical shape, hammered copper w/rèpoussè floral decoration, riveted seams & rolled scalloped rim, some dents & replaced rivets, new patina, 12 x 15" **$633**

Dish, round shape w/scalloped rim, hammered texture, new interior patina, open box mark, Dirk Van Erp, 7 1/2" d., 1 1/2" h. **$633**

Firestarter, hinged can, stone rod & footed square tray, the can embossed w/image of fish, stamped "Cape Cod Shop, Pat. 1916," can 6 1/2" **$288**

Mirror, English Arts & Crafts style, hanging type, oval shape, frame of hammered texture w/rèpoussè vine motif inset w/ ceramic cabochon at top, 23 x 28" **$2,070**

Plate, 9 3/4" d., hammered copper, the raised rim w/stylized quatrefoil designs & rolled borders, die-stamped mark, Karl Kipp **$460**

Tray, hand-hammered, Arts & Crafts style, rectangular w/low flared rim, narrow angled end handles, each corner incised w/peacocks in blue-patinated squares, in the manner of the Roycrofters, unmarked, original patina w/normal wear, early 20th c., 11 3/4 x 16 1/2" **$345**

Tray, oval shape, hammered copper w/riveted wrought end handles, orb & cross mark, Roycroft, some ring stains to enhanced patina, 10 x 20" **$374**

Tray, rectangular shape w/riveted rolled handles, stamped, Drumgold, 12 x 18" **$46**

Tray, rounded shape w/raised lobed rim embossed w/center dots, no patina, stamped "36," Stickley Brothers, 13 1/2" d. **$805**

Vases, 11" h., Jugenstil tapering cylindrical forms w/brass bases, rims & buttressed cutout side handles, polished finish, unmarked, Europe, early 20th c., pr. **$115**

Vessel, Arts & Crafts style, spherical shape w/very short neck, rolled rim & base, 16 1/4" d., 21 1/4" h. **$2,070**

Tray, Arts & Crafts style, hand-hammered, bulbous ribbed form tapering to a scalloped everted rim w/embossed pine cone, scallop & stylized floral decoration, unmarked, early 20th c., 8 1/2" h. (polished patina) **$403**

Umbrella stand, hand-hammered, Arts & Crafts style, flaring round foot riveted to the tall cylindrical riveted body w/a riveted rim band, two loose swing handles at sides, dark patina, America, early 20th c., some wear & discoloration, 11" d., 26 1/2" h. **$288**

Wall plaque, round, raised foliate design around a bust portrait of a woman, impressed diamond w/ bird mark of the W.M.F., Germany, early 20th c., polished, 17" d. **$173**

Wall sconces, candle-type, hand-hammered, Arts & Crafts style, rectangular backplate w/tooled linear edge decoration & a domed panel above the flattened scroll bracket supporting the tall cylindrical candle socket w/a wide dished drip pan, lightly cleaned patina, Karl Kipp, early 20th c., 3" w., 10" h., pr. **$468**

Water bottle, strap-on type, wide, oval, shallow, gently arched shape w/small brass spout & screw-on cap, one strap guide missing, 8 x 12", 3" h. **$79**

Weathervane, gilt-copper model of a running horse, the full-bodied animal w/a copper head & hollow body, no stand, American, late 19th c., gilt wear, minor dent, 41 1/2" l., 21" h.) **$4,113**

Weathervane, molded & gilded model of a steeplechase horse, molded in two parts, the horse w/hole-eyes, notched mouth, windswept, stamped & serrated mane & tail, leaping w/forelegs tucked under & rear legs extended over a stamped sheet metal fence on a vertical rod support, A.L. Jewell, Waltham, Massachusetts, mid-19th c., on modern base, 37" l., 34" h. **$94,600**

Wine urn, cov., a tall urn-form vessel w/a gadrooned pedestal base & a wide ringed shoulder centered by a tall ringed & leaf-engraved neck fitted w/a small domed cover w/an acorn finial, the body w/a lion mask issuing a long brass spigot below a chased reserve w/a crest framed by chased leaf or leafy scroll bands, high looped scroll shoulder handles extending down the sides, nice dark patina, France, early 19th c., 35" h. **$575**

Pewter

Beakers, tall cylindrical form w/flaring rim, touch marks of Boardman & Hart, New York, ca. 1840s, polished w/some battering, 5 1/4" h., pr. (ILLUS. of one, bottom row, second from right at back) **$345**

Frame, Art Nouveau style, flattened rectangular form w/a gently arched top, cast around the sides w/berried ivy-like vines, Archibold Knox for Liberty & Co., England, ca. 1900-05, 6 x 7 5/8" **$5,019**

Teapot, cov., pear-shaped body w/a hinged domed cover w/ turned metal finial, serpentine spout, ornate C-scroll wooden handle, "Lovebird" touch mark, Pennsylvania, ca. 1800, 7" h. **$8,963**

Hot water platter, oblong w/a flattened flanged rim above the deep molded sides raised on small ball feet, scrolled loop end rim handles, marked "Compton, London," wooden hand grips, 20" l. (wear, scratches)......... **$193**

Mold, chocolate, in the shape of four Easter eggs decorated w/lambs, rabbits & chicks, hinged down middle of mold, closed measures 3 x 8 1/4", 10 1/2" h. **$395**

Antique pewter contains tin, copper, antimony, and lead, with tin comprising 85 to 99 percent of the alloy. Modern pewter is made with at least 90 percent tin and only tiny amounts of lead, if any.

Flagon, cov., flaring ringed base tapering to a tall slightly tapering cylindrical body w/a hinged stepped domed cover w/urn-form finial & scrolled thumbrest, short enclosed rim spout, long S-scroll handle, Thomas D. & Sherman Boardman, Hartford, Connecticut, ca. 1815-20, 3 qt., 14" h. **$3,819**

Tureen, cover & ladle, a wide tapering pedestal base supporting a deep rounded bowl w/a domed cover topped by a figural fish finial, figural fish handles at the side rims, the ladle w/a rounded shell-shaped bowl & a cut-out fish handle tip, Old Newbury Pewter, 12" d., 12 1/2" h., the set **$460**

Tankard, cov., slightly tapering body w/banded base & rim, hinged domed cover w/molded thumbrest & overhanging rim, cased S-scroll handle, Peter Young, Albany, New York, ca. 1795, 4 3/4" d., 7" h. **$16,100**

Tankard, cov., communion-type, tapering cylindrical body w/a screw-top opening to a fitted pewter bowl, the body w/a spurred scroll handle, on a molded base, Roswell Gleason, Dorchester, Massachusetts, 1822-71 .... **$1,380**

Tankard, cov., cylindrical ringed body w/a wide flaring ringed foot, cupped rim w/spout, flat hinged cover w/forked thumbrest, strap handle, top dated "1605," stamped "Zanon...Antoine," Switzerland, 8 1/4" h. **$748**

Sheffield Plate

The term "Sheffield Plate" refers to a very specific variety of silver plated ware produced in England during the 18th and early 19th century.

Beginning in the 1740s, manufacturers in the city of Sheffield developed a technique of bonding thin ingots of copper and pure silver using tremendous heat and pressure. These ingots could then be rolled out into very thin sheets of metal that would be used to fashion decorative objects. These pieces appeared identical to sterling silver pieces but could be sold at a fraction of the cost. Any fashionable silver object could be copied in Sheffield plate, including epergnes, coffee- and teapots, candlesticks, serving dishes and trays.

For nearly a century, true Sheffield plate was widely popular with the British and American buying public; however, in the mid-1840s, the development of the process of silver plating through electrolysis soon killed off the Sheffield plate trade. The new form of plating was faster, cheaper and required less pure silver to obtain the same effect.

True Sheffield plate wares were only produced in England and never in the American colonies or the United States. The earliest English Sheffield was not often marked by the manufacturer because the authorities were afraid such markings might mislead the buying public. By the late 18th century, however, some Sheffield platers were allowed to use simple markings that would not be confused with the strictly controlled sterling silver hallmarks.

Because the layer of silver used in Sheffield plate was quite thin, the copper base metal may begin to show through after years of polishing. Serious wear can affect the market value of Sheffield plate pieces, but they should never be replated since this destroys their value as antiques. Also, in the late 19th and early 20th centuries, many silver plating companies began to use the term "Sheffield Plate" as part of their markings. This silver plate ware has no relationship to the original hand-crafted English wares, which were never marked with this phrase."

Candlesticks, an inverted tapering stem gadrooned on the lower half & connected by a gadrooned knop to a circular ogee- domed foot w/ gadrooned banding, the top w/a thistle-form gadrooned socket w/ gadrooned bobeche, some rosing, Matthew Boulton, ca. 1810, 12 1/4" h., pr. **$1,610**

Chambersticks, shallow dished round base w/gadrooned border, a curved side finger handle w/ conical snuffer, the open- centered center shaft w/an urn-form candle socket w/a swirled gadrooned flattened rim, by Matthew Bolton, England, ca. 1785, some copper bleeding through, missing wick trimmers, 7" w., 4 1/4" h., pr. (ILLUS. of one) **$500**

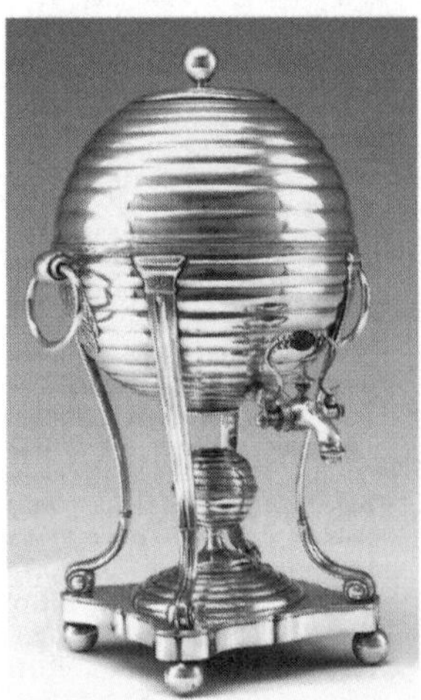

Hot water urn, cov., large spherical beehive-form body raised on four flat columnar legs & scroll feet on a concave square & serpentine-edged base on four ball feet, a spigot w/loop handle at the bottom front, ring handles at the sides, small cover w/knob finial, the base w/a spherical beehive-form covered burner, possibly Roberts, Cadmen & Company, England, ca. 1800, 9" d., 19" h. **$920**

Mirror plateau, the round concave table frame w/an ovolo base border band & a top cast shell & acanthus leaf rim band enclosing the mirror, Creswick mark on hinged mounts, Regency Era, England, ca. 1825, 17 3/4" d., 2 1/4" h. .. **$1,035**

Entree dish, cov., rectangular base w/rounded corners raised on large ball feet, large looped acanthus leaf & cornucopia handles at each end, fitted w/ a liner w/an elaborate gadrooned flanged rim, the conforming domed cover w/a gadrooned band around the top centered by the upright gadrooned loop handle, I. & I. Waterhouse, Sheffield, England, ca. 1835, 10 x 14 1/2", 8 1/2" h. **$489**

Hot water urn, neoclassical urn form, the square base on ball feet & decorated w/a delicate swag border band, the tapering pedestal supporting the tall urn-form body w/another delicate swag band around the top, projecting base spigot w/fanned ebony handle, upright incurved scrolled leaf shoulder handles flanking the very tall slender waisted cover w/ a tiered finial, large area of wear above the spigot, England, ca. 1790, 10 1/2" d., 22" h. **$863**

Tea caddy, cov., Neoclassical style, tall oval & slightly flaring sides inlaid & chased w/silver bands & a crest, the concave curved shoulder around the domed cover w/knob finial, lock on the front, George III Era, England, ca. 1770, unmarked, 6 1/4" h. **$546**

Soup tureen, cov., two-handled, mounted w/leaf-capped reeded handles w/lion's mask terminals, gadrooned rims w/acanthus & shells at intervals, on four shell & acanthus-capped claw feet, Matthew Boulton, London, early 19th c., 15 3/4" l................. **$1,495**

Tea urn, cov., tall urn-form body raised on a slender pedestal above a round domed & ringed base, low domed cover w/an urn-form finial, long arched loop strap side handles, extended spigot near the bottom w/a decorative scroll handle, unmarked, England, ca. 1800, some small dents, 18" h. **$431**

Vegetable dish, cov., squatty bulbous oval base raised on four knob feet topped by acanthus leaf detail, upturned loop end handles w/acanthus leaf terminals, flared gadrooned rim supporting a stepped & domed cover w/a leaf-cast ring handle, early 19th c., 16" l. (minor wear) **$688**

Warming dishes, liners & covers, rectangular, surrounded by gadrooned borders & rims, applied w/reeded foliate handles & knop, raised on scrolled feet headed by foliage, early 19th c., 14 1/4" l., pr. **$1,725**

Wine coolers, campana-form, a knopped stem supporting the urn-form body w/foliate-capped handles & rim, fitted w/a liner & collar, engraved w/a crest, early 19th c., 12" h., pr. **$2,530**

Always wash silver pieces by hand rather than in a dishwasher. Dishwasher water is much too hot and the soap too harsh.

Silver

American (Sterling & Coin)

Basket, shallow oblong form w/a serpentine scroll-trimmed rim, the sides pierced overall w/ delicate scrolls around the oval bottom panel engraved w/a script monogram, Towle Silversmiths, Newburyport, Massachusetts, early 20th c., 9 x 12", 2 3/4" h. **$431**

Berry server, large oblong gilded bowl w/thin enameled scrolls at the top of the bowl & around the oblong handle, Gorham Mfg. Co., Providence, Rhode Island, ca. 1900, 9" l. **$50-100**

Bowl, round w/deep rounded sides w/a flat rim & a thin footring, embossed w/spiral gadrooning separated by a matte band from the milled & applied shell-and-scroll border band, Tiffany & Company, New York, ca. 1884, 8 1/2" d., 3 1/2" h. **$2,185**

Bowl, the lobed circular bowl w/a wide undulating rim decorated in high relief w/scrolls & foliage, bowl center w/an engraved script monogram, Frank W. Smith Silver Co., Gardner, Massachusetts, early 20th c., 11 7/8" d., 2" h. **$316**

Brandy warmer, squatty bulbous bowl tapering to a flaring double-spout rim, baluster-turned wooded side handle, F.B. Rogers Silver Co., Taunton, Massachusetts, ca. 1900, 4 3/4 x 9 3/4", 3 1/4" h. **$100-150**

Bread tray, Art Nouveau style, shallow rounded navette form, the wide everted rim decorated w/deep rèpoussè irises on a matte ground, the center monogrammed, Unger Brothers, New York, ca. 1895, 7 1/2 x 12 1/2" **$403**

Bread tray, oval w/wide rolled & scalloped rim, Francis I patt., Reed & Barton, dated 1949, 7 1/2 x 12" **$690**

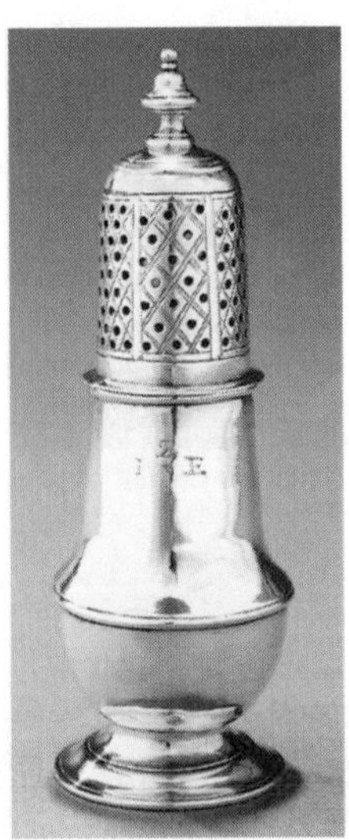

Caster, coin, slender baluster-form w/molded banding, raised on an ogee-domed foot, the cap w/pierced & engraved panels, molded banding & baluster-form finial, marked on the base w/ initials of Zachariah Bridgon of Boston, & a set of wedding initials of a couple, ca. 1760, 1 3/4" d., 5 1/2" h. **$3,738**

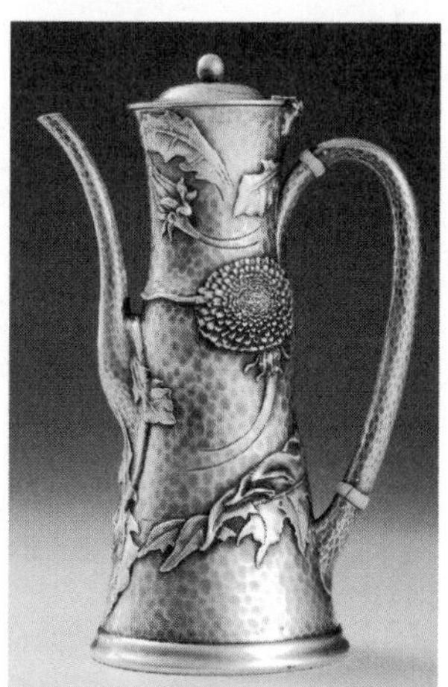

Coffeepot, cov., Aesthetic Movement style, tall slender waisted shape w/a hand-hammered ground, tall slender spout & C-form long handle w/ivory insulators, the sides wrapped w/chased & applied dandelion flowers, buds & leaves, the low domed hinged cover w/ chased curly dandelion stem & ball finial, mark of Tiffany & Co., New York, New York, 1881-91, 7 1/4" h. **$19,120**

Creamer, bulbous shape w/scroll handle & three trifid feet, the front w/crest & "Rand R M 1758," inscription on one side reading "E.S. & S. Rand to Caroline M. Fitch July 4th, 1828" & on other side "Caroline M. Fitch to Mary F. Jenks April 1st, 1882," square hallmark "T.S.," Thomas Barton Simpkins, 3 3/4" h. **$6,900**

Pitcher, Art Nouveau style, footed bulbous baluster-form body w/a wide flared rim w/high arched spout, ornate floral-cast C-scroll handle, the body chased around the top & base w/sprays of intertwining flowers & leaves, engraved foliate monogram on the side, Gorham Mfg. Co., Providence, Rhode Island, 1903, 9 1/2" h. **$5,378**

←

Porringer, round shape, 2 1/2" l. pierced handle, engraved "MR to MF," w/"Simpkins" touch mark, William Simpkins, Boston, 18th c., 5 1/4" d. **$2,875**

Pitcher, Neoclassical style, large urn-form body decorated w/milled swag banding & engraved acanthus scrolls, raised on an ogee-domed foot, a waisted neck w/integral spout, angled loop handle w/scroll finial, monogrammed body, Frank M. Whiting, ca. 1920, 10 1/2" h. (ILLUS. left with platter) **$863**

Sterling silver produced in the U.S. contains at least 92.5 percent pure silver. Coin silver is 90 percent silver and Britannia is 95.8 percent silver.

Tea set: cov. teapot, cov. sugar bowl & creamer; coin, Classical boat-shaped style, round stepped pedestal base supporting bulbous oblong lower body below a wide curved shoulder band w/leafy vine motif below the curved & rounded shoulder & domed hinged cover w/pineapple finial, high arched fancy C-scroll handles, tall serpentine spout on teapot, each piece w/ engraved monogram on the side, mark of Peter Chitry, New York, New York, ca. 1830, teapot 9 3/4" h., the set (ILLUS. of teapot & sugar bowl) **$1,195**

Tea set: cov. teapot, cov. sugar bowl & creamer; Neoclassical style, each piece w/a tall ovoid body raised on three long scroll legs ending in paw feet, domed cover & arched C-scroll handles, narrow shoulder & cover bands of classical designs, each leg headed by a Bacchanalian mask, mark of Tiffany & Co., New York, New York, ca. 1860-64, teapot 9 1/2" h., the set **$2,760**

Tea set: cov. teapot, cov. sugar urn & creamer; coin, Classical style, the oval teapot w/flat sides & a concave shoulder band w/a hinged tapering domed cover w/urn finial, tall helmet-shaped creamer & sugar urn w/tall waisted cover w/urn finial, both on a square foot, each w/bright-cut floral swags centering a cartouche w/drapery mantling, monogram in the cartouche, beaded borders, straight spout on teapot & C-scroll black wood handle, mark of William G. Forbes, New York, New York, ca. 1790, teapot 12 1/2" l., the set **$13,145**

Tea set: cov. teapot, cov. sugar urn & creamer; coin, each of Classical form, the teapot oval w/beaded border at foot & rim & the hinged cover w/urn finial, straight spout, wooden loop handle, the creamer & sugar of vase form on a square base, each engraved w/a monogram within a mantle, teapot 12 3/4" l., John Vernon, New York, New York, ca. 1792, the set ... **$8,365**

Teakettle on stand, cov., coin, the bulbous fluted body w/a ring-banded short neck & hinged domed cover w/flower finial, scroll-trimmed serpentine spout, arched scroll swing handle, raised on a burner base w/four ornate scroll legs ending in shell feet & joined by serpentine straps centered by the burner ring, engraved inscription w/later date, mark of Ball, Tompkins & Black, New York City, ca. 1839-51, no burner, overall 15" h., the set **$1,150**

Teapot, cov., coin, footed spherical body w/a hinged double-domed cover w/baluster-form finial, octagonally faceted straight spout, C-scroll wooden handle w/ octagonally faceted handle joins, base engraved "E*H," base also w/ mark of maker Simeon Soumaine, New York, New York, ca. 1730, overall 10 1/4" l. **$207,500**

When displaying silver, keep in mind that fumes emitted by latex painted shelves and oak furniture can make silver tarnish more quickly.

Teapot, cov., coin, inverted pear-shaped body on a disk foot, domed hinged cover w/pointed finial, serpentine spout w/cast leafy scrolls, C-scroll wooden handle w/scrolled silver terminal & leaf-clad joins, the shoulder engraved w/diaperwork, rocaille scrolls & flowering vines, the edge of the cover engraved w/a scallop band, base engraved w/block initials "H" over "IM," also w/mark of maker John Bayly, Philadelphia, ca. 1765, overall 9 1/4" l. **$71,700**

Teapot, cov., coin, oval upright body w/a flat shoulder centered by a hinged domed cover w/ pineapple finial, straight angled spout, C-scroll wooden handle w/silver joins, the sides engraved w/a drapery cartouche enclosing a monogram, mark on base of Daniel Van Voorhis, New York, New York, ca. 1790, 7 1/8" h. **$4,780**

Teapot, cov., coin, wide bulbous inverted pear-shaped body on a domed foot, domed hinged cover w/a pinecone finial, serpentine spout w/cast shell & scroll decoration, black wooden C-scroll handle w/scroll-decorated joins, the body engraved w/a rococo cartouche enclosing monogram "HPG," the shoulder engraved w/a strapwork bird & mask border, base w/mark of Samuel Casey, South Kingstown, Rhode Island, ca. 1760, overall 10" l. **$47,800**

Tray, coin, round w/a foliate-decorated rim band, the center engraved w/a coat-of-arms, raised on four small cartouche-form feet, marked by John Mood, Charleston, South Carolina, ca. 1825, small dent on side of rim, minor body warping, 9" d., 1 1/4" h. **$3,450**

English & Other

Basket, oval footring w/pierced diamond & star designs below the deep flaring basket pierced overall w/delicate cross, dot & chevron design, serpentine narrow gadrooned rim band, twisted arched swing handle, mark of William Vincent, London, England, 1773-74, 8 3/4" l. **$863**

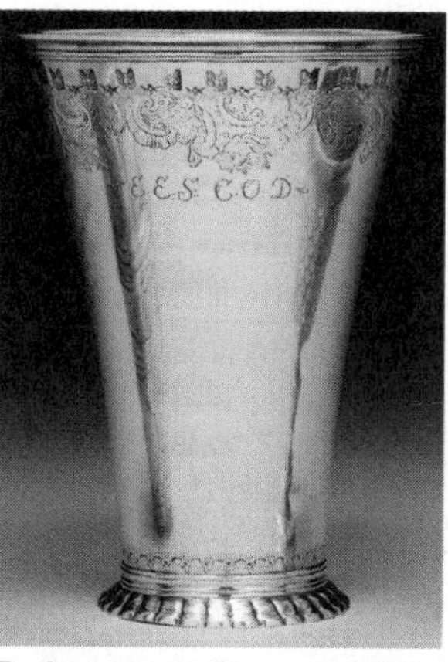

Beaker, parcel-gilt, a narrow flared gadrooned foot below the tall flaring cylindrical body w/the upper rim engraved w/a band of rocaille & flowers against a matted ground, a gilt molded rim, marked under foot by Johan Andersson Starin, Stockholm, Sweden, 1753, 7 5/8" h. **$2,390**

Bowl, round, w/elaborate raised design of scrolls, flowers & leaves along flaring sides, marked "WC" & hallmarks for London, England, 4 3/4" d. **$155**

Cigarette box, cov., rectangular w/ hinged cover, the sides decorated w/rèpoussè flying birds above turbulent seas, the cover decorated w/bold rèpoussè chrysanthemums & leaves, opening to a cedar-lined interior, raised on narrow bracket feet, Japanese Export, ca. 1900, 3 1/2 x 6 1/2", 3" h. **$1,955**

Cup, flared base & cylindrical sides w/high arched loop handle, the body engraved w/Art Nouveau flowers, gold-washed interior, Russian touch marks, 19th c., 3 1/2" h. **$345**

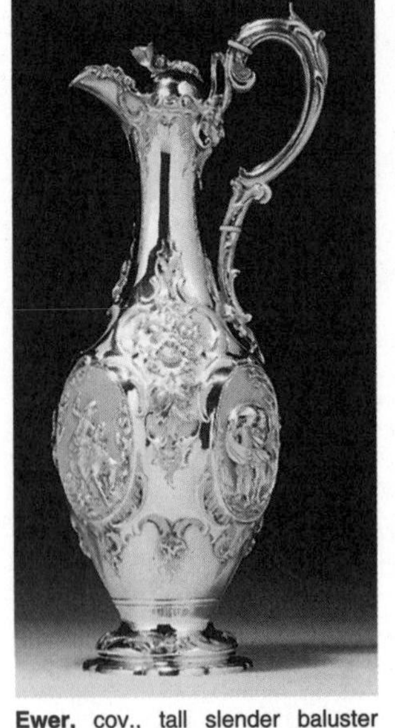

Ewer, cov., tall slender baluster form, a small round flaring foot, the body inset w/four oval plaques decorated w/cast figures representing the Four Seasons, surrounded by large chased flowers & scrolls, the slender neck w/cast scrolls continuing around the high arched spout, hinged domed cover w/flower finial, the ornate C-scroll leaf-clad handle w/ivory insulators, marked by Thomas, James & Nathaniel Creswick, London, England, 1852, 14 1/4" h. **$2,629**

Frame, for carte-de-visite picture, Art Nouveau style, hallmarked "84," Imperial-era Russia, 3 1/4 x 5 5/8" **$295**

Serving spoon, figural relief handle w/a standing figure of Frederick the Great of Prussia, royal emblems at base of handle, chased scrolls in the wide shovel-form bowl, Europe, early 20th c., 11" l. **$595**

19th century Russian silver is prized for its high quality and superb workmanship. Look for marks with the Cyrillic characters of the Russian alphabet.

←

Serving spoon, figural relief handle w/a standing figure of Mary, Queen of Scots, engraved initials in the wreath & swag-trimmed wide shovel-form bowl, back marked "800," Europe, early 20th c., 10 1/2" l. **$645**

Serving spoon, figural relief handle w/a standing figure of Napoleon I above his imperial emblem & his initial & swags in the large shovel-form bowl, Europe, early 20th c., 10 1/2" l. **$550**

Serving spoon, figural relief handle w/a standing lady in Victorian dress, above a section of pierced entwined branches, chased musical instruments & sheet music in the wide oblong handle, marked "800," Europe, early 20th c., 11 1/4" l. **$595**

Serving spoon, the long oval bowl chased & pierced, a central figure of Moses & cherubs, a classical head below, the long flat handle w/ pierced scrolls & masks & pierced griffins at the base, Europe, late 19th - early 20th c., 12" l. **$750**

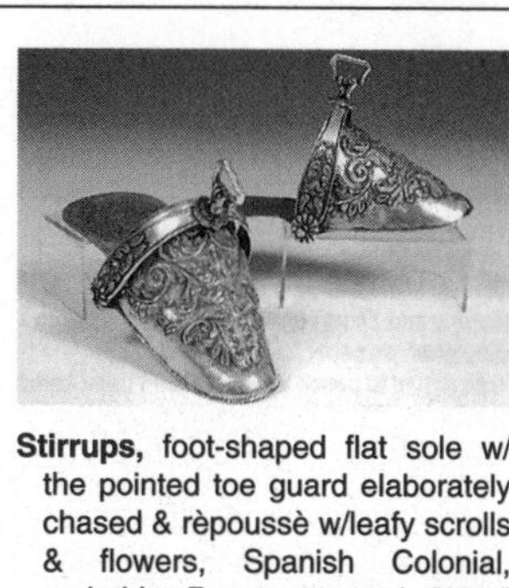

Stirrups, foot-shaped flat sole w/ the pointed toe guard elaborately chased & rèpoussè w/leafy scrolls & flowers, Spanish Colonial, probably Peru, stamped "925," 9" l., pr. **$633**

Sugar bowl, cov., silver-gilt, inverted pear-shaped body raised on a round domed foot, chased w/ rococo floral garlands & centering a vacant cartouche, the domed cover w/matching decoration & a figural spread-winged bird finial, mark of Samuel Taylor, London, England, 1746, 5 3/8" h. .. **$1,673**

Soup tureen, cov., Rococo style, the deep undulating oval base raised on four large pierced rocaille feet, the body rèpoussè & chased w/floral garlands & centering two vacant rocaille cartouches, large leafy scroll end handles, the high domed & stepped cover w/conforming decoration & a cast bird on branch figural finial, mark of Gottfried Bartermann, Augsburg, Germany, 1751- 53, also later French control marks, overall 15 1/2" l. **$28,680**

Tankard, cov., baluster form w/round foot & medial body band, hinged stepped domed cover, a heavy scroll handle w/baluster drop & openwork thumbpiece, initial mark probably of John King, London, England, 1770, 8 3/4" h. **$2,629**

Tea set: cov. teapot, cov. sugar bowl & creamer; each footed piece w/a squatty melon-lobed body, lobed domed covers w/figural flower finials, ornate C-scroll handles, one piece marked "F. Guzman - Mexico," .900 quality, 20th c., the set **$1,150**

Tea set: cov. teapot, cov. sugar bowl, cov. creamer, waste bowl, tongs & oval tray; each piece w/a squatty bulbous boldly lobed shape w/ivory handles & ivory lobed finials, designed by Josef Hoffmann & produced by The Wiener Werkstatte, Austria, ca. 1920s, tray 20 1/2" l., teapot 7 3/4" h., the set **$71,700**

Tea set: cov. teapot, cov. sugar bowl, creamer, teakettle on stand & oval tray; the serving pieces w/upright flat oval bodies w/hinged tapering covers w/brass ball finials, cylindrical rosewood side handles, the kettle on a conforming burner stand w/pierced side holes, designed by Josef Hoffmann, manufactured by The Wiener Werkstatte, tray w/original Wiener Werkstatte lace doily, Austria, ca. 1923, tray 14 1/4" l., teakettle & stand 9 1/2" h., the set **$53,775**

Tea urn, cov., George III era, tall Classical urn-form body w/a tall slender tapering cover w/acorn finial, beaded shoulder band, long arched reeded side handles, a projecting spigot near the base w/a dark ivory handle, raised on a slender flaring pedestal on a square foot, interior fitted w/a heating column, cover engraved w/a crest, the body engraved w/a coat-of-arms, mark of John Wakelin & William Tayler, London, England, 1784, overall 20 1/2" h. **$4,780**

Teakettle on stand, cov., George II era, spherical body w/a flat hinged cover w/wooden knop finial, serpentine spout, overhead swing bail handle w/shaped uprights joined by a baluster-turned black wood grip, the body finely engraved w/a border of brickwork, scrolls, putti & foliate as well as a coat-of-arms, on a round stand raised on three leafy scroll legs w/wooden knob feet joined by shaped braces centered by a deep burner, marks of Peze Pilleau, London, England, 1731, burner dating from 1956, overall 22 1/2" h. **$3,824**

Teapot, cov., George I era, footed spherical body w/small hinged cover w/knop finial, angled faceted straight spout, C-scroll wooden handle, body engraved w/a crest, base engraved w/initials "E.R.," mark of Seth Lofthouse, London, England, 1720, overall 8 1/4" l. **$4,183**

Teapot, cov., George II era, footed spherical body w/a small flat detachable cover w/reeded border & wooden disk finial, curved spout w/stylized petal join, C-scroll wooden handle, marked "RP," English provincial maker, ca. 1740, overall 8 5/8" l. **$3,760**

Teapot, cov., George III era, footed wide inverted pear-shaped body w/domed hinged cover w/pointed knob finial, ribbed serpentine spout, C-scroll handle, the body swirl-fluted & decorated w/rèpoussè & chased rococo floral & scroll designs w/a vacant cartouche, mark of Paul Storr, London, England, 1814, 6 7/8" h.... **$1,610**

Teapot, cov., George III era, oval upright body w/flat shoulder & hinged flat cover w/wooden disk finial, angled straight spout, wooden C-scroll handle, the body engraved around the base & shoulder w/a floral & foliate band, the body engraved w/a coat- of-arms, mark on base of Richard Gardner, London, England, 1774, overall 9" l. **$3,585**

Repoussè is a technique in which silver is pushed up from underneath to create a raised design on the surface. Chasing, on the other hand, is the opposite process, in which metal is pushed down from the top. The two techniques are well suited for silver because it is soft and malleable and only need be stretched to produce three-dimensional shapes, which eliminates the expense of adding more metal.

Tray, footed shell-shaped tray w/elaborate scrollwork & engraved but indistinct initials, England, 9 1/2 x 16" **$995**

SILVERWARE MARKET REPORT

Phil Dreis owner of Antique Cupboard (www.antiquecupboard.com), Waukesha, Wisconsin, and author of *Warman's Sterling Silver Flatware*, 2nd Edition, said "sales of sterling silver flatware have been strong. Because of the recession, museum quality pieces have been coming on the market and are in great demand." Modern designs from the 1950s and 1960s have also become popular. The artists who created those patterns have been recognized in other fields for a long time, but now they are finally becoming known for their silverware designs.

The demographics of the silver market are changing, with younger people buying more silver now, especially the Modern designs. Interest in Victorian patterns, however, which are now more than 100 years old, are dropping off. Dreis explained that this is a typical generational trend, in which nostalgia prompts people to seek designs they remember from their childhood, generally around 50 years ago. Items that reach 100 years are too far in the past for the current generation to appreciate.

New silver is very expensive compared to estate silver. For example, a new four-piece place setting can sell for $450, while an estate set can go for just over $100. The sterling silver flatware industry has seen tremendous changes in the last century. A hundred years ago, there were 2,200 silverware manufacturers in the United States. Twenty years ago there were only around 25. Consolidation has continued, with Wallace buying Gorham, making Wallace the owner of about 20 firms. Only one Wallace competitor—Reed & Barton—remains in the U.S. (Lunt Silversmiths declared bankruptcy in December 2009 and was sold to Reed & Barton in February 2010.) Dreis added that, unfortunately, the sterling silver market has suffered from a lack of artistic innovation over the last 20 years, with almost no new patterns created. On the other hand, because of stainless steel's low material cost and relatively high profit margin, it has experienced a lot of growth in new designs.

Dreis said that high-end sterling silver pieces are selling for $200 to $400 each and that market is solid. The market for middle range pieces, around $27 each, is soft, while the low end of $20 per piece is doing well.

The price of the base silver metal has been volatile over the past year or so, dropping from $20 an ounce to $8, then back up to $18. Dreis predicts silver will continue to rise because of the weakening dollar.

Dreis estimates that only five percent of his customers are shopping for investment, but they account for 40 to 50 percent of sales. According to Dreis, sterling silver flatware, especially museum quality, is an excellent investment.

He advises people not to sell sterling silver at coin shops or jewelry stores because they will get metal value only. He strongly warns against selling to companies that advertise on TV urging people to mail in their valuables for cash. The amount paid is usually extremely low. Dreis recommends selling to a silver matching firm or a respected and trusted dealer, where sellers will be paid for the artistic merit and workmanship and not just the melt value of the metal.

Sterling Silver (Flatware)

Bittersweet patt., dinner service: eight each dinner forks, salad forks, cake forks, tablespoons, soup spoons, teaspoons, dinner knives & butter spreaders; Georg Jensen Silversmithy, Copenhagen, Denmark, 64 pcs. (ILLUS. of three) **$5,750**

Old English patt., dinner service: thirty-six each dinner knives & dinner forks, twenty-four each luncheon knives, luncheon forks & dessert spoons, twelve each fish knives, fish forks, dessert knives, dessert forks, tablespoons & teaspoons, four sauce ladles, pair of salad servers, pair of fish servers, one gravy spoon & four-piece carving set; in fitted oak cabinet w/five drawers & double doors, Francis Higgins, London, England, 1936, 229 pcs. (ILLUS. of three) **$20,700**

Francis I patt., dinner service: forty-two teaspoons, twenty-four each luncheon forks, salad forks, luncheon knives & butter spreaders (twelve w/silver blades), twenty bouillon spoons, twelve each dinner knives, soup spoons, demitasse spoons, coffee spoons, dinner forks, cocktail forks, ice cream forks, eight grapefruit spoons plus fourteen serving pieces, w/two wood cases; Reed & Barton, Taunton, Massachusetts, 20th c., 276 pcs. (ILLUS. of three) **$9,000-10,000**

Arcadia patt., dinner service: twelve each dinner knives, dinner forks, dessert spoons, luncheon forks & salad forks, eleven teaspoons & eight luncheon knives; Georg Jensen Silversmithy, Copenhagen, Denmark, post-1945, 79 pcs. **$3,500-4,500**

Imperial Chrysanthemum patt., dinner service: twenty-four each table forks & dessert forks, twenty-one tablespoons, twelve each dessert spoons, teaspoons, fruit spoons, demitasse spoons, fish forks, cocktail forks, fish knives & butter knives, four condiment spoons & one each fish server, fish slice, serving fork, punch ladle & lobster server plus twenty-four table knives & twelve dessert knives & fruit knives w/stainless steel blades; the terminals chased w/flower heads & leaves, also engraved w/a monogram, in fitted wooden case, 222 pcs. **$6,500-8,000**

Louis XIII Richelieu patt., dinner service: twelve each dinner knives, dinner forks, luncheon knives, luncheon forks, tablespoons, dessert spoons, lobster forks, teaspoons, fish knives, fish forks, demitasse spoons, three butter knives, two serving forks & one each soup ladle, sauce ladle, slice, cake knife & cheese knife; monogrammed, w/rattail bowls, trifid ends & cannon- handled knives w/stainless steel blades, Puiforcat, Paris, France, 20th c., in three fitted trays stamped w/ maker's name, 144 pcs. (ILLUS. of three) **$28,750**

Lap-Over-Edge Etched patt., dinner service: twenty-four each teaspoons & luncheon forks, twelve each dinner knives, luncheon knives, butter spreaders, dinner forks, dessert spoons & dessert knives, ten tablespoons, one sauce ladle & butter knife; etched w/plants, animals & fish, some identified on the back, engraved w/name "Scoville" in script on back, Tiffany & Co., New York, New York, ca. 1885, 132 pcs. **$20,700**

Versailles patt., dinner service: twelve each salad forks, dinner forks, teaspoons, soup spoons, dinner knives & butter spreaders, ten small teaspoons & eight seafood forks; monogrammed, Gorham Mfg. Co., Providence, Rhode Island, 1888, 90 pcs. **$2,300**

Silver Plate (Hollowware)

Ash receiver, figural, a small figure of a chick & wishbone beside a round dished base centered by a stem centered by a fan- shaped cigar trimmer below the tall cup-shaped top match holder w/a hammered dot design, mark of the Derby Silver Co., ca. 1880s, 4 1/2" h. **$127**

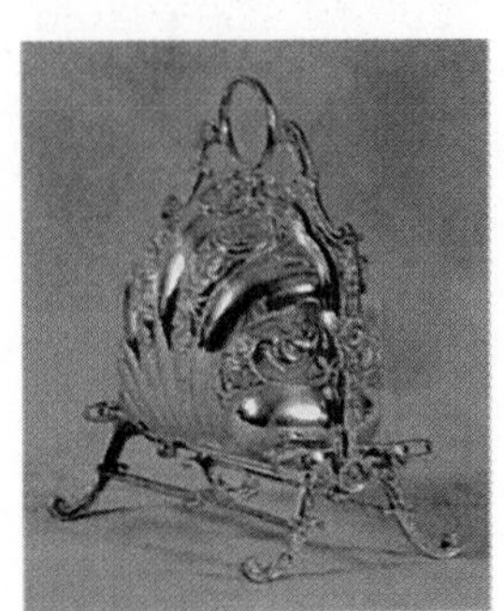

Biscuit box, upright hinged shell shape w/engraved scrolls, an arched scrolling top border w/ center ring handle, raised on a trestle-style base w/outswept scrolled legs, England, early 20th c., 6 x 81 2/", 10" h. **$225**

Breakfast server set, a footed diamond-shaped base w/engraved edge supporting a ring-engraved footed salt cup & matching shaker flanking the central tall arched handle enclosing a napkin ring w/ an ornate pierced finial & resting atop a tiny seated boy & applied leaf, mark of the Meriden Britannia Co., ca. 1880s, overall 7" h. **$403**

Breakfast server set, a shell-shaped tray on ball feet centered by a tall loop handle w/a napkin holder & a side bracket to support a ruffle-rimmed butter pat above a pair of attached small tapering waste cups flanking the bulbous salt & pepper shakers, all decorated w/ floral engraving, impressed mark of the Aurora Silver Plate Mfg. Co., tray 6 3/4" d., overall 7 1/2" h., the set **$633**

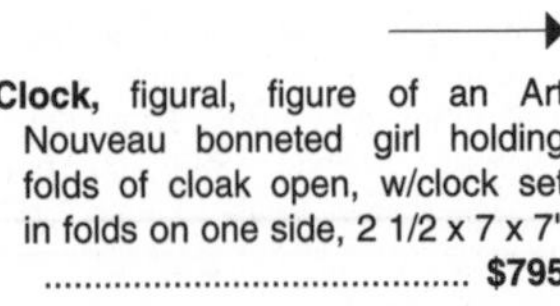

→

Clock, figural, figure of an Art Nouveau bonneted girl holding folds of cloak open, w/clock set in folds on one side, 2 1/2 x 7 x 7" **$795**

Candleholders, a slightly domed round base w/a leaftip band centering an upright short leaf & bud issuing two upturned long slender arms ending in tulip-form sockets, marked "Her Majesty 1847 Rogers Bros. 009056 I.S.," 20th c., 10 7/8" w., 6 3/4" h., pr. (ILLUS. of one) **$200**

Card tray, four-lobed squared-shape tray decorated w/engraved flowers & insects, attached to round base by three legs & two applied leaf & flower supports, maker's name indistinct, 5 7/8 x 6 1/4" **$175**

Silver hollowware is generally made of silver plate (a thin layer of silver over copper) because these serving containers need the added strength and rigidity that copper provides.

Condiment holder, in the form of a woven basket containing three egg-shaped holders for salt & pepper shakers & mustard cup, w/spread-winged baby bird perched on rim, English, indistinct maker's mark on bottom, 5 1/2" h. **$1,295**

Hairbrush, Art Nouveau style, decorated at one end w/the head & shoulders of a woman in profile w/long flowing hair, heavily embossed w/floral & whiplash design, 1 3/4 x 2 1/4 x 7 1/4" **$21**

Jewelry casket, oblong form, the arched top w/two hinged covers flanked by arched sides w/a pierced design of flowers & leaves & raised on four leaf-sprig feet, a slender arched handle from side to side, mark of the Pairpoint Mfg. Co., portions of base reinforced & some leaves missing, 1890s, 6 1/2" l., 9" h. **$633**

Cup, cylinder shape on flared base, repeating panels w/stylized floral design around rim & base, made by Rockford Silver Co., style number 288, 3 x 4 x 4 1/4" ... **$45**

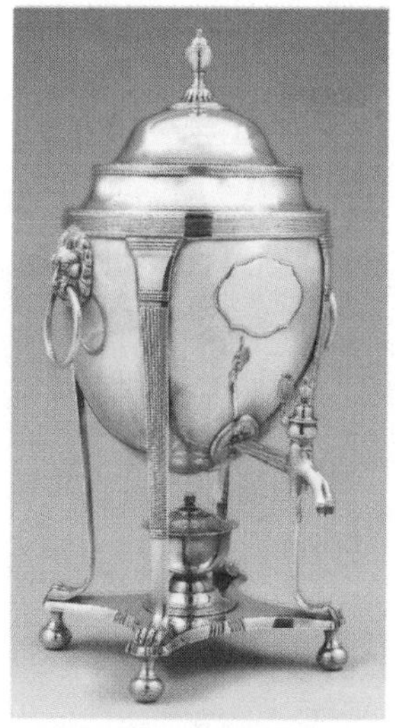

Hot water urn, Neoclassical style, the large ovoid body w/reeded band & concave top w/a domed cover & vasiform finial, the sides w/ringed lion-mask handles, raised on four flat reeded columnar legs ending in paw feet connected by a concave square base centered by a bowl-shaped burner, the whole w/four flattened bun feet, plain downturned spout w/pineapple spigot, England, ca. 1890, 10 1/2" d., overall 20 1/2" h. **$863**

Epergne, model of a palm tree w/ sinuous trunk and six palm fronds, w/a fox running at the circular, ringed base, topped w/a cranberry glass trumpet-shaped flower, 6 1/2" h. **$1,495**

Jewelry box, cov., Art Nouveau style, footed, decorated w/ roses, marked on bottom "92 DL," possibly a hair receiver, 2 3/4 x 2 3/4 x 3 1/2" **$165**

Match holder, model of old oaken bucket w/two branch handles on sides, sitting on raised base ribbed for striking matches, 4" l. **$325**

Napkin ring, domed stepped circular base holding cockatoo perched on stylized branch, ring resting atop tail, marked "738," 4" h. **$595**

Salt cellar, in the form of a dolphin carrying a shell on its back, rimmed base w/design depicting ocean waves, handle in the form of a ribbed leaf, 2 x 2 3/4 x 4 1/2" **$275**

Teakettle on stand, cov., footed paneled bulbous body w/a wide conforming shoulder centering a short rolled neck, hinged pointed & domed cover w/pointed finial, a fixed reeded loop overhead handle, scroll-trimmed serpentine spout, raised on open serpentine side supports on a paneled round base centered by a burner, mark of Reed & Barton, late 19th - early 20th c., overall 13" h. **$230**

Napkin ring, stepped base holding reclining lion figure, ring resting on lion's back and engraved with "HEP" and floral motifs, 1 1/4 x 2 1/4 x 2 1/2" **$475**

Smoking accessory, consisting of model of owl on branch attached to three hollow tree stumps w/ removable inserts for holding cigarettes, matches & ashes, 5 x 7 x 7 1/2" **$750**

Napkin ring, triangular shape on claw-and-ball feet, w/pierced floral rims and crossed wishbones forming a border around engraved leaf frond decoration & "Best Wishes," made by Meriden, style number 630, 1 7/8 x 2 3/8 x 3" **$175**

Tea set: cov. teapot, cov. sugar, creamer & rectangular tray; Art Deco style, each piece w/a squatty slightly flaring rectangular body & wide tapering shoulder, low domed cover w/reddish amber rectangular Bakelite finials, teapot w/angled Bakelite handle, tray w/cut corners & matching Bakelite squared end handles, England, ca. 1925, tray 15" l., the set **$196**

←

Teakettle on stand, cov., Victorian, Orientalist taste, the decagonally paneled body tapering to a short neck w/thin pierced gallery & hinged domed & stepped cover w/spherical finial, a pointed Arabesque arch fixed overhead handle, serpentine spout, the panels engraved as arches enclosing ornate quatrefoils above a chain band, raised on a platform base w/a wide top & thin gallery around a narrower pierced & paneled pedestal enclosing the burner, the wide dished & paneled base w/short columns forming the feet, by Elkington & Company, Birmingham, England, 1854, overall 10 1/2" w., overall 8 1/2" h. **$1,150**

Teapot, cov., round flat base below the wide rounded lower body w/a gadrooned medial band below the tall tapering sides w/a flaring rim, hinged domed cover w/knob finial, tall slender serpentine spout, C-scroll handle, trademark w/a lion on either side of a shield above "Silverplated - Est. 1905," early 20th c., 9 1/4" w., 9 3/4" h. **$65**

Teapot, cov., round foot below the wide squatty bulbous body tapering to a short flared neck w/a domed hinged cover, leafy scroll-trimmed spout & C-scroll handle, marked on bottom "Silver on Copper [crown] S [shield]," probably England, late 19th - early 20th c., 8" h. **$100**

Teapot, cov., squatty bulbous boat-shaped body w/widely flaring flanged rim & hinged stepped, domed cover w/wooden disk finial, ribbed serpentine spout, pointed angular handle, the sides w/an ornate engraved floral cartouche enclosing a gift inscription dated 1911, marks for an English silver plate firm, 11 1/2" l., 5 3/8" h. **$85**

Toothpick holder, figural, round stepped base holding figure of monkey holding staff & carrying on its back a basket w/basketweave decoration & rope twist rim, Meriden, 3 1/3" h. **$550**

Toothpick holder, model of a billy goat next to a large sack w/flared rim, Meriden, 2 1/4 x 2 3/4 x 3" **$375**

Do not store silver in plastic bags, as moisture can't escape. Instead, wrap them in tarnish-resistant cloth, which will not only allow the silver to breathe, but will protect it from scratches as well.

Warming platter, oval frame raised on scroll feet, the scroll-cast side fitted w/a small filling hole, ornate scrolled end handles, fitted w/a well-and-tree insert, base marked "D & S," England, early 20th c., 17 1/2 x 24", 3 1/2" h. **$575**

Tin & Tole

Box, cov., rectangular shape w/ domed lid, the lid w/ring handle & hasp, decorated w/red fruit & green & mustard leaves & feather design on copper lustre-type ground, a red swag border on the lid, 3 x 6 1/2", 3 1/2" h. **$1,035**

Box, cov., rectangular shape, the lid w/clasp & ring handle, the front panel w/colorful mustard & red fruit & flowers w/green leaves, the edge w/vine border, all on black ground, 4 3/4 x 8 3/4", 5 1/2" h. **$1,438**

Chamberstick, tin, the conical base tapering to a tall cylindrical socket fitted w/a flat drip pan issuing a flattened S-scroll strap handle attached to the center of the base, minor dents, 19th c., 5 1/2" h. **$230**

Document box, cov., rectangular w/domed lid, the lid w/ring handle, the lid & sides decorated w/ crisscross decoration in mustard yellow, the front w/brightly colored large round red flowers, green leaves & yellow sprigs, all on black japanned ground, 19th c., 5 x 9", 4" h. **$403**

Tray, tole, four-lobed shape, the rim decorated w/band of red apples & green leaves, the center w/leaf & line highlights on brownish-copper ground, 12 1/2" d., 2 1/2" h. **$300**

Tray, tole, rectangular shape w/ rounded corners & raised rim, the rim decorated w/stenciled gold leaves & black & red highlights on black ground, the interior w/painted landscape w/woman tending goats & cows in pastoral wooded setting, first half 19th c., 16 1/2 x 21 3/4" **$403**

Tray, tole, rectangular w/rounded corners, the black ground decorated w/ delicate gold leafy scrolls around the sides, the center painted w/a large colorful bouquet of flowers topped by a perched exotic bird, England, third quarter 19th c., on a later stand, 22 x 30" **$1,265**

Tray, tole, rectangular w/rounded corners, the black ground decorated w/delicate gold leafy scrolls around the sides, the center painted w/a large romantic landscape w/a lake w/bridges & a boat & building & trees on the left shore, England, late 19th c., 22 3/4 x 28 3/4" **$1,150**

MODERNISM MARKET REPORT

Noah Fleisher of Heritage Auction Galleries (www.ha.com) in Dallas, Texas, and author of *Warman's Modernism: Furniture and Accessories*, explained that Modernism is appealing for a number of reasons. Collectors can find something at every price, "from $20 pieces at flea markets to $20,000 to $30,000 pieces by top designers." And since Modernism is eclectic and not dominated by a particular design element, people can express their unique tastes. In addition, Fleisher pointed out that Modern pieces are "practical works of art that have the clean lines and sturdy construction that make them easy to clean and able to survive dogs, cats, and kids."

The lower end of the market is mass produced, which keeps prices down, yet the wide variety of styles allows individuality. The top of the market, which can reach six figures, is comprised of one-of-a-kind, handmade investment quality pieces by renowned designers. While others may imitate their materials and designs, the original pieces "are all about the hand of the master."

Fleisher predicts that the market for Modernism will stay healthy. In fact this category is not only stable, it's continuing to grow. Modernism will continue to dominate pop culture because of its simplicity and individuality.

Fleisher recommends buying and selling through auction houses and reputable dealers because they provide a service as well as a product. They are interested in their customers developing as collectors, increasing their knowledge and range of tastes. Good dealers and auction houses will work with their customers, share their expertise, and stand behind their goods. Fleisher also advises that collectors buy the best they can afford.

According to D. Scott Adams of The Gallery Kathlyn, in the Heart of Ohio Antique Mall, Springfield, Ohio (http://www.heartofohioantiques.com), Modernism is selling briskly. Adams sells smalls like glassware, pottery, lighting, art, posters, and jewelry. His low end pieces range from $40 to $80, his mid range from $100 to $300 and his high end $400 and up, with his most expensive piece ever selling for $2,500.

Adams said "buyers in their 30s and 40s who have stable jobs, are well established in their careers, and have discretionary income are looking for functional and decorative pieces from the classic sleek designs of the '50s to the funky designs of the late '50s and early '60s." He added that "discriminating buyers look for pieces associated with particular designers because they know they hold their value." Adams doesn't usually sell furniture, but noted that those who do have no difficulty selling top-notch pieces.

One of Adam's biggest challenges is acquiring Modern items. It is hard to find them in his area, and it is forcing him to travel to bigger cities. Modern pieces can be found at estate sales, but since they are most likely encountered within the setting of an overall Modern theme, collectors will likely find a feast or famine situation, with either a lot of Modern or no Modern, depending on the decorating taste of the homeowner.

The large metropolitan areas on the East coast have a much greater supply of Modern design, perhaps in large part because the movement took a deeper hold there in the '50s and '60s than in the more conservative, less fashion conscious, and less affluent Midwest.

Adams encourages buyers to purchases what they like, not just what they think others will like or what they think will appreciate in value.

MODERNISM

The scope of this section covers 1945 to 1985, give or take a decade or two on either side where necessary. It is, however, wrong to suggest there is not much great Modernism pre-1930 or post-2000. "Modernism" didn't just one day emerge, say Jan. 1, 1950, fully realized, from the mind of its remote creators. It is the stuff of the 1933 Chicago World's Fair "Century of Progress," the boundless optimism of post-World War II America, the sleek comic lines and manic music of Tex Avery's MGM 1949 "House of Tomorrow" cartoons, and the ever-present acres of the suburban ranch house that subsequently spread endlessly across the nation. That form, those colors, the unbridled enthusiasm and audacious hope represented therein ... It all hearkens back to post-War 1950s America, when the West was ready to embrace the new realities of easy living and convenience.

Modernism has never gone out of style. Its reach into the present day is as deep as its roots in the past. Just as it can be seen and felt ubiquitously in the mass media of today – on film, television, in magazines and department stores – it can be traced to the mid-1800s post-Empire non-conformity of the Biedermeier Movement, the turn of the 20th century anti-Victorianism of the Vienna Secessionists, the radical reductionism of Frank Lloyd Wright and the revolutionary post-Depression thinking of Walter Gropius and the Bauhaus school in Germany. There is no end to the ways in which the movement of Modernism, its evolution and continuing influence, can be parsed. To that end, there is more than a little irony in the fact that, in the world of collecting, Modern has a retro connotation.

Modernism is everywhere in today's pop culture. Austere Scandinavian furniture dominates the television commercials that hawk hotels and mutual funds. Post-war American design ranges across sitcom set dressings to movie sets patterned after Frank Lloyd Wright houses and Hollywood Modernist classics set high in the hills. No corporate headquarters is complete without "Modern" art on its walls, and chairs and tables straight out of the van der Rohe, Wormley, Knoll and Perriand catalogs. Similarly, apartments and dorm rooms are adorned with Modern mass-produced products of IKEA, Target, Design Within Reach, and the like.

Lisanne Dickson, Director of 1950s/Modern Design at Treadway-Toomey said, "The modern aesthetic grew out of a perfect storm of post-war optimism, innovative materials and an incredible crop of designers." Regarding the range of value for Modern pieces, she pointed out that the early original examples have the highest prices. "The closeness of an example to the original intentions of the designer is critically important. The earliest version of a design is most likely to represent the designer's true intention. Later modifications were likely made to enhance the bottom line, or ease production." The later designs are where an education can be had, collections formed and bargains found.

For more information, consult Warman's Modernism Furniture and Accessories by Noah Fleisher.

Beds, Bedroom Furniture, and Daybeds

Bruno Mathsson, queen size bed with mattress and orange slip cover (not shown), 22" x 62" x 79" **$2,000**

→

Charlotte Perriand, pine wardrobe with single sliding slatted door concealing four black tray drawers and storage compartments, on cylindrical black metal legs, 68" x 58" x 21" **$2,100**

Dresser and mirror, 1940s, Italy, cabinet 62" x 23" x 36", mirror 50" x 31", overall 67"..... **$1,200**

George Nakashima, walnut twin-size platform bed and headboard with sliding doors; bed 10" x 54" x 74 1/2", headboard 32" x 54" x 12".............. **$4,750**

George Nelson/Herman Miller, Thin Edge bed with caned headboard, 33" x 53" x 85"............... **$1,300**

Finn Juhl/Baker, full-size bed in teak and maple with slatted headboard, marked with Baker metal tag, 31.5" x 57" x 88".. **$1,700**

George Nakashima, walnut storage headboard with double bed platform, 1959, 36" x 56" x 87"...........**$3,000**

Hans Wegner/Getama, twin bed with caned headboard, and integrated single-drawer nightstand, on tapering dowel legs. Nightstand has branded mark............. **$1,700**

Hannes Wettstein, Xen platform bed, 84 1/2" x 69" x 32"..................**$2,600**

Jean Royere, daybed with tan cushion and bolster pillows on oak frame with inset cobalt glass panels, 32.5" x 65" x 32 3/4" **$4,000**

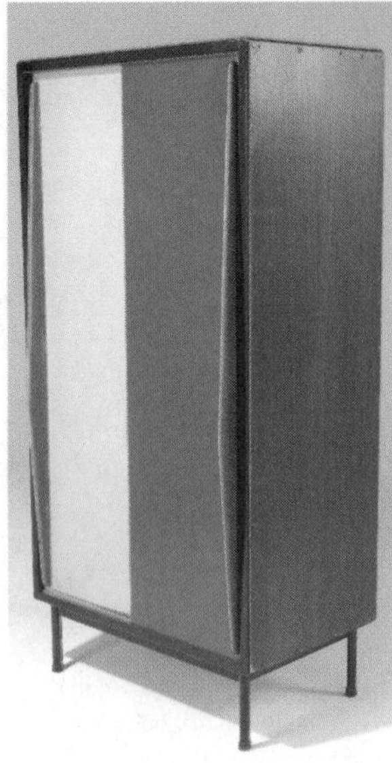

Willy Van Der Meeren, mahogany veneer wardrobe with sliding enameled metal doors concealing a clothes bar on one side, and fixed shelf on the other, 63" x 32" x 21" **$1,500**

Peter Hvidt, daybed by France and Sons, 75" x 29 1/2" x 16" **$500**

Desks and Credenzas

Birch credenza with burlwood veneer inlay on an ebonized platform base, Denmark, 47" x 65" x 16 1/4" **$1,250**

Desk, single-drawer, in wood veneer, one end faceted, the other curved, 29 1/2" x 45 1/2" x 22.5" **$1,000**

Edward Wormley, desk with inset leather top, 43 3/4" x 24" x 30 1/2" **$75**

Edward Wormley/Dunbar, desk and file cabinet in ebonized wood and mahogany, with armchair, Dunbar metal and paper tags, desk 29" x 44" x 27", cabinet 23" x 15" x 25" .... **$1,000 set**

Edward Wormley/Dunbar, rosewood veneer L-shaped desk with oak tambour doors and interior, Dunbar brass tag, 53" x 60" x 82" **$2,600**

George Nelson, L-unit desk by Herman Miller, 69" x 54" x 30" **$650**

George Nelson/Herman Miller, swag-leg desk with two shallow drawers, 34 1/2" x 39" x 28 3/4" **$3,750**

George Nelson, home office desk with tan leather covering on sliding doors and writing surface, a lift-top storage compartment, and mesh Pendaflex file, 40 1/2" x 54" **$6,500**

George Nakashima, walnut credenza, with two grass cloth-backed grilled doors enclosing two drawers, 28 1/2" x 22" x 20" **$7,500**

George Nakashima, double-pedestal desk with rare Persian walnut free-edge top, circa 1969, 30" x 110" x 36" **$35,000**

Gilbert Rohde, Paldao desk, 56" x 28" x 29"...... **$4,500**

Gio Ponti/Singer & Sons, two-drawer rosewood desk with tooled leather top and integrated magazine rack, circa 1950, 28 3/4" x 53 1/4" x 25 1/2" **$19,000**

Franco Albini, credenza in walnut veneer, parchment and chromed steel, the central compartment papered in red with glass doors and shelf, 38" x 106" x 21" **$11,000**

Florence Knoll/Knoll, eight-drawer walnut credenza on polished steel frame, 25 1/2" x 74 1/2" x 18"..... **$2,100**

Portenzac, single-pedestal desk covered in composite with six shaped drawers and steel leg, 30" x 63" x 26 3/4" **$6,500**

Hans Wegner/Ry Mobler, oak credenza with two sliding doors enclosing four sliding trays and four adjustable shelves, with contrasing oak feet, stamped RY, 31" x 78 3/4" x 19 1/4" **$2,500**

Milo Baughman, executive desk, 78" x 36" x 29 1/2" **$1,600**

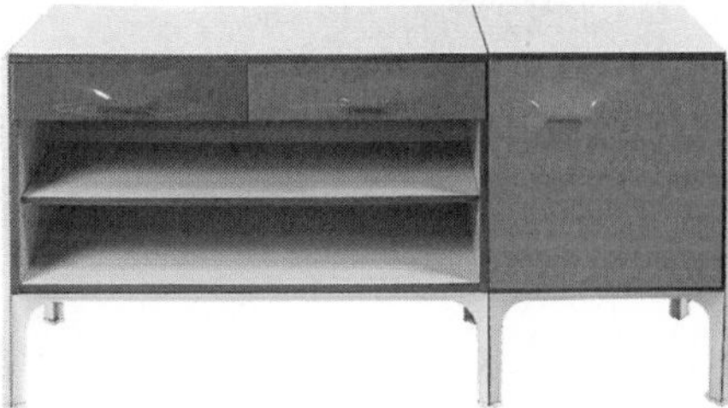

Raymond Loewy, DF2000 desk/cabinet, red molded plastic, 61" x 22 1/2" x 30 1/2" **$1,800**

Warren McArthur, desk with ebonized wood top and drawers on aluminum frame, 28 1/2" x 44" x 24" **$1,000**

Homeowners should make sure all their property is insured against fire, theft, and natural disater. Standard household policies generally do not cover antiques and collectibles. A rider or separate policy will likely be needed for these items. For those who have considerable value in their antiques and collectibles, it may be worth hiring a professional appraiser. Also, be sure to inventory and photograph property that is not appraised because insurance reimbursement will not be made for property that isn't claimed. In the aftermath of a loss, when coping with stress, it can be difficult to try to recall all the contents of a home. It is much easier to do this before a loss occurs.

Desk and Table Lamps

George Nakashima, burlwood lamp with cylindrical parchment shade over a single socket, circa 1969, 29 3/4" x 16" **$8,000**

Greta von Nessen, "Anywhere" lamp, 12" x 12" x 14" **$475**

Gio Ponti, "Bilia" table lamps, 7 1/2" x 17 1/4" (one shown) .... **$650 pair**

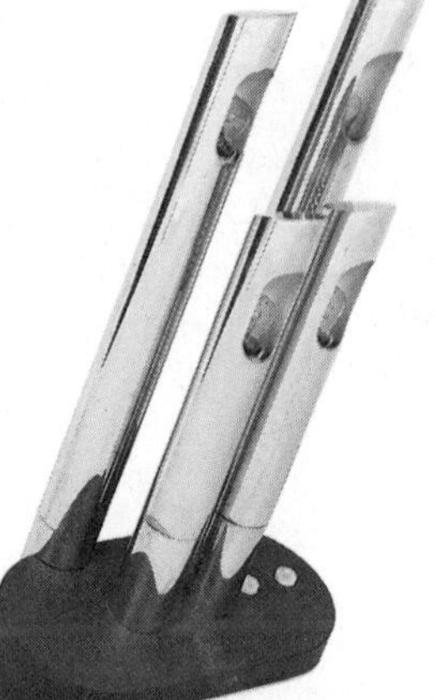

Gianfranco Frattini, table lamp, by Luci, 7 1/2" x 16 1/2".......... **$1,000**

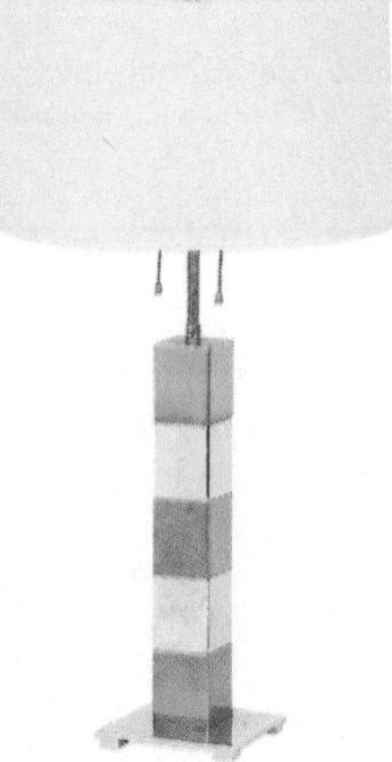

Paul Evans, table lamp, 16" x 29 1/2" **$600**

Pierre Cardin, lumico brushed steel table lamp with white glass shade, signed, 10 3/4" x 10 1/4" x 4" **$850**

Table lamp, Laurel, 12" x 10" x 35" **$100**

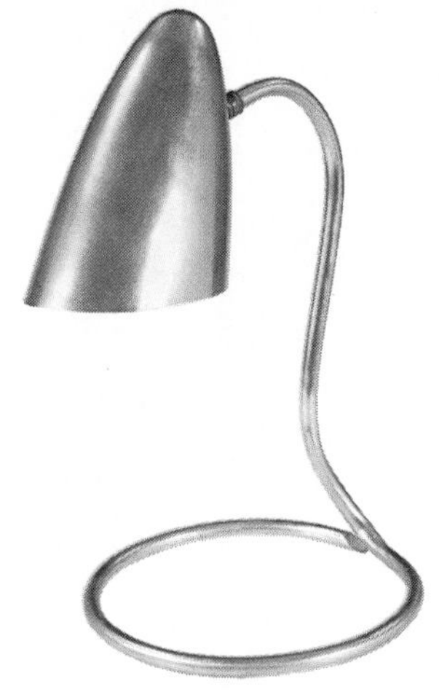

Russell Wright, aluminum desk lamp, coiled base, 12"x 16 1/2" **$150**

Table lamp, linen shade, 1950s, 6" x 6" x 14" **$275**

Table lamp, textured clear plastic panels, France, 11" x 5" x 13 1/2" **$225**

T Bönan, table lamp, 15.25" x 25.25" with shade, base is 15"......... **$400**

Sergio Asti, table lamp, 16" x 41 1/2" **$450**

Vico Magistretti, Dalu table lamps, 7 1/4" x 10 1/2" (one shown) .... **$400 pair**

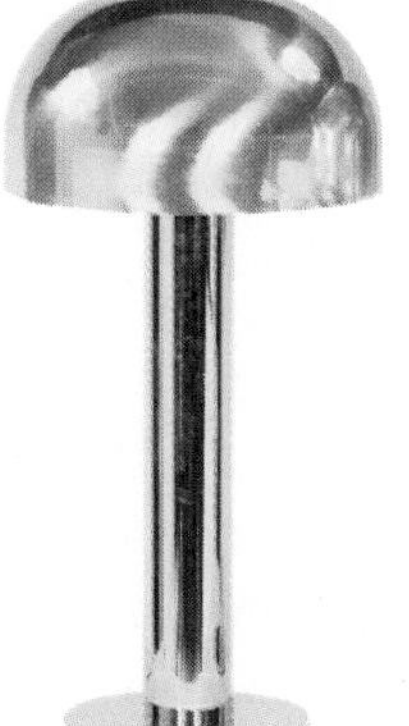

Table lamps, aluminum and chrome, 1960s 17" x 34" (one shown) .... **$700 pair**

Floor Lamps

Angelo Lelli, floor lamp, three directional light sources, 12 1/2" x 79" **$1,900**

Arredoluce, Triennale floor lamp in brass and enameled metal with three adjustable arms, 59" x 32" **$8,000**

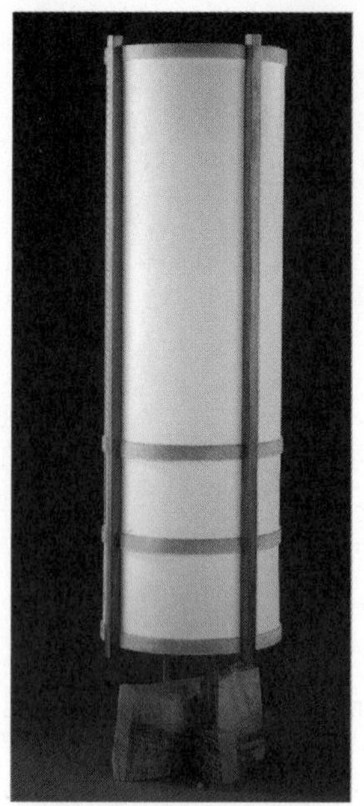

George Nakashima, Kent Hall rosewood and holly floor lamp with cylindrical paper shade and cruciform base of English and Persian walnut, 57 1/2" x 16 1/2" **$10,000**

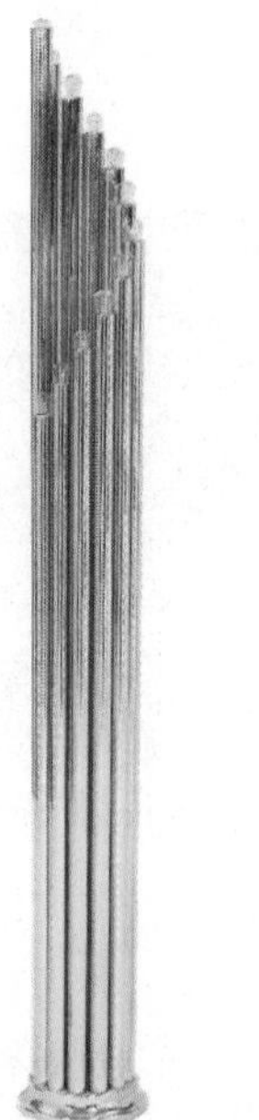

Floor lamp, 1970s, Italy, 7" x 63 1/4" **$450**

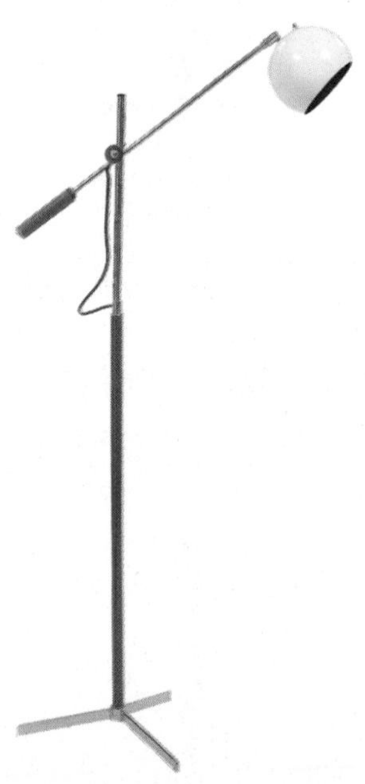

Koch and Lowy, floor lamp, 34" x 63 1/2", shade 7" **$400**

Gino Sarfatti/Arteluce, floor lamp, spiraling brass stem with nine adjustable enameled metal shades, stamped Arteluce Made in Italy, 81" x 14"................ **$8,500**

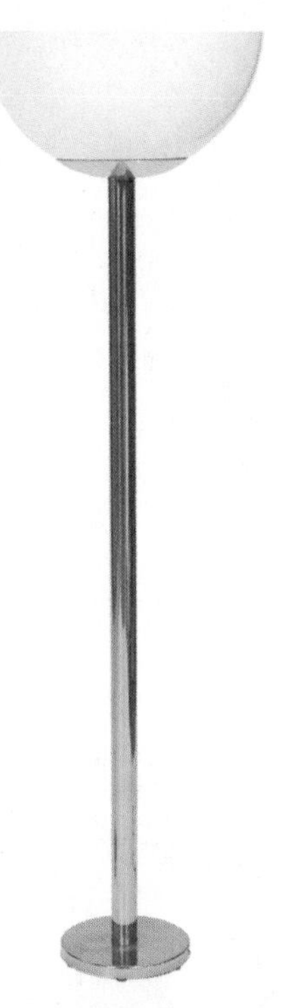

Koch & Lowy torchieres, 19 3/4" x 66" (one shown) ....**$300 pair**

Isamu Noguchi, floor lamp with spherical mulberry paper shade on bamboo shaft with weighted black metal base, 76 1/2" x 19 1/2" **$325**

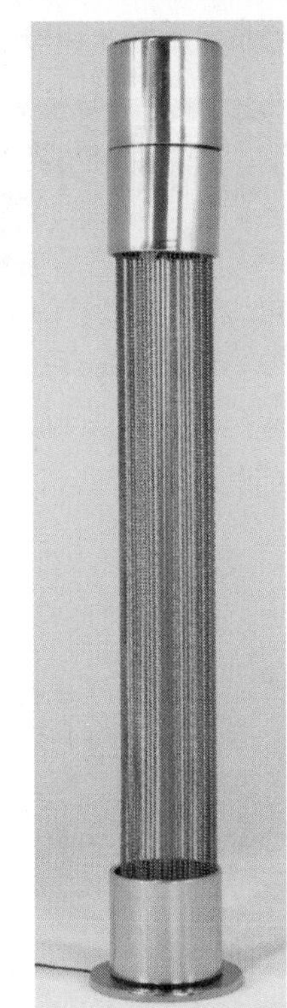

Pierre Cardin, aluminum floor lamp with beaded metal shade, signed Pierre Cardin, 64" x 11" **$2,100**

Stilus Milano, aluminum floor lamp with four pivoting sections, and five sockets, approx. 57" x 17" x 12" **$1,000**

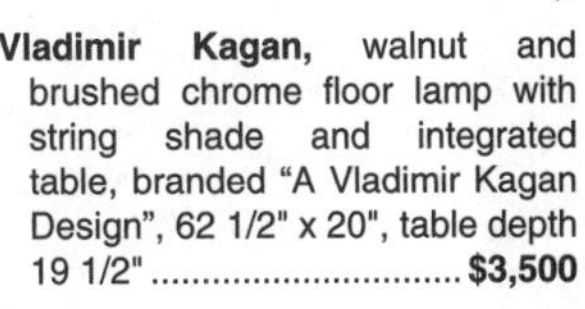

Vladimir Kagan, walnut and brushed chrome floor lamp with string shade and integrated table, branded "A Vladimir Kagan Design", 62 1/2" x 20", table depth 19 1/2" **$3,500**

Hanging Lamps and Fixtures

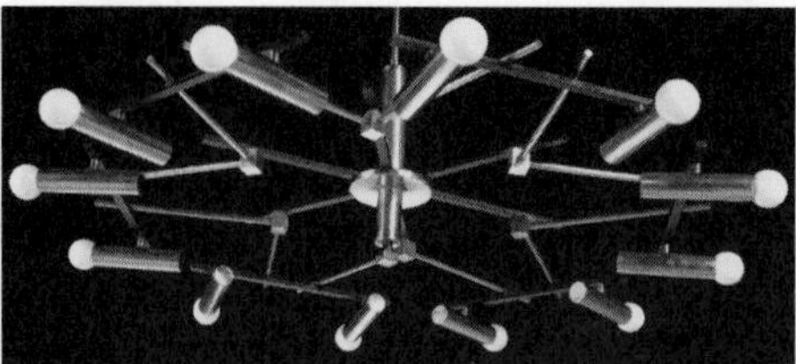

Arteluce, chandelier with 12 brass sockets radiating outward on a black enameled metal frame, approx. 28" x 34" **$4,750**

Edward Wormley, hanging fixture by Lightolier, 25" x 13" **$250**

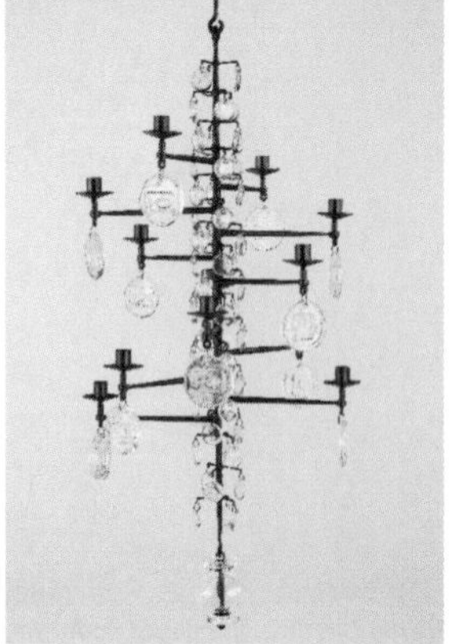

Erik Hoglun/Boda Afors, 12-arm iron chandelier with drop crystals, and clear glass discs impressed with fish and primitive faces, 39" x 19" **$19,000**

Gaetano Sciolari, hanging fixture, 27" **$1,600**

Soren Henningsen, hanging light numbered 18/20, 8" x 8" x 10 1/4" **$800**

Pierre Cardin, chromed steel and aluminum hanging fixture with beaded metal fringe, signed Pierre Cardin, 36" x 20".................. **$850**

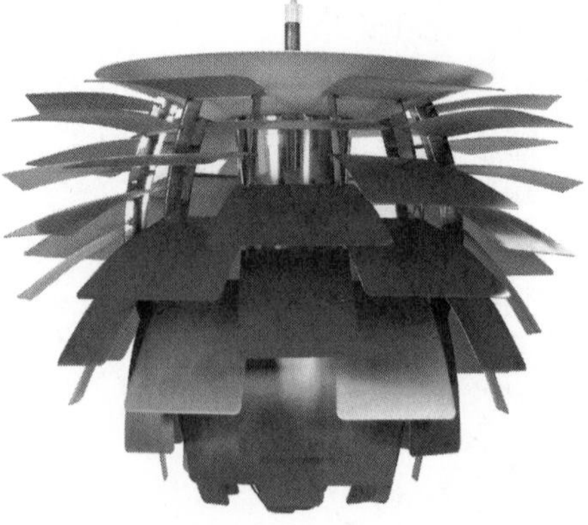

Poul Henningsen, Artichoke hanging lamp, 24" x 18" **$4,500**

Seating

Charles and Ray Eames, 670/671 lounge chair and ottoman, chair 33" x 35" x 32", ottoman 26 1/2" x 21" x 17 1/2" **$1,500**

George Nelson, steelframe chair, 29" x 27" x 27" **$375**

George Nelson/Herman Miller, coconut chair upholstered in black boucle, 34" x 40" x 29" **$1,500**

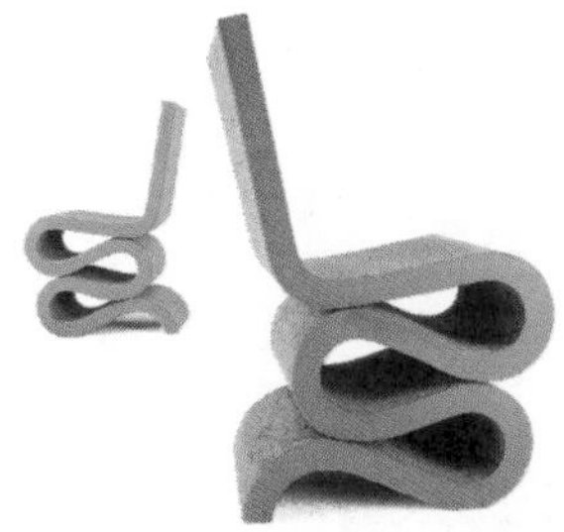

Frank O. Gehry/Easy Edges, corrugated cardboard Wiggle Chairs, 33 1/2" x 15 1/2" x 22" .... **$2,500 pair**

George Nakashima, walnut Conoid chair with hickory spindles, 36" x 20 1/2" x 21 1/2" **$5,000**

Jean Gillon, teak lounge chair with corded sling seat and burgundy leather cushions, with ottoman, chair 32 1/2" x 43" x 36".............................. **$1,000**

L. Meher, custom walnut plywood and steel rocker, signed L. Meher 78, 37 1/2" x 21 1/2" x 30" **$1,000**

Le Corbusier, LC/1 Basculant chairs brown leather, 25" x 27 1/2" x 26" .... **$550 pair**

Le Corbusier, LC/2 chairs, pair, cream-colored leather, 29 1/2" x 27 1/2" x 27" (one shown) .... **$1,900 pair**

Milo Baughman/Thayer Coggin, polished steel armchairs upholstered with woven ecru fabric, 28" x 26 1/4" x 31 1/2" .... **$1,400 pair**

Osvaldo Borsani/Tecno, steel reclining chair with rubber armrests, brass hardware marked T, 38" x 28" x 42" **$2,100**

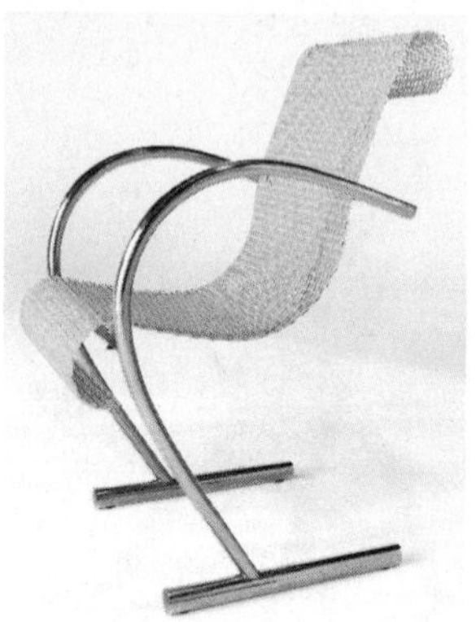

Shiro Kuramato/XO, "Sing, Sing, Sing" anodized steel armchairs, marked XO, 33 1/2" x 20 1/2" x 23 1/2" (one shown) ...**$2,700 pair**

Teak wing-back chairs upholstered in cream chenille. Danish control tags, 39" x 34" x 30" (one shown) .... **$2,300 pair**

Wendell Castle, sculpted oak sleigh chair with hard leather sling seat, 1963, signed WC 63, 34 1/2" x 29" x 51 1/2" **$170,000**

Benches, Settees, and Sofas

Charles Eames/Herman Miller, group lounge sofa with channeled black leather upholstery, 33 1/2" x 73" x 30" **$5,000**

Edward Wormley/Dunbar, ebonized wood bench with brass stretcher, 15 1/2" x 56" x 18" **$600**

Edward Wormley/Dunbar, ebonized wood bench with brass stretcher, 15 1/2" x 56" x 18" **$600**

Eero Saarinen/Knoll, womb settee upholstered in green fabric on black metal frame, 35" x 60" x 32" **$3,250**

Finn Juhl/Niels Vodder, sculpted teak settee upholstered in tan leather, branded mark, 23.5" x 55" x 25" **$6,500**

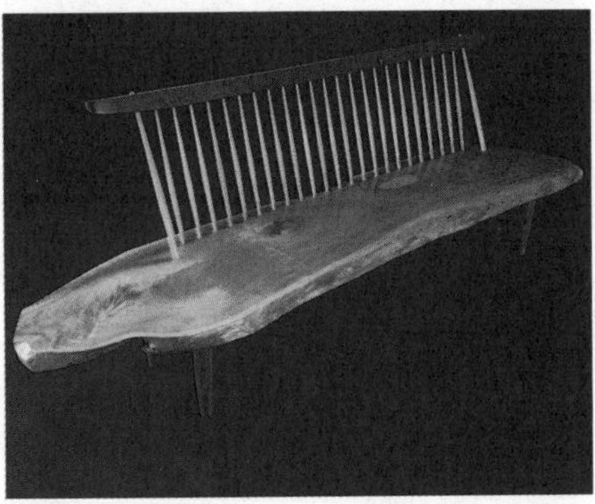

George Nakashima, Conoid bench with back in butternut, free-edge seat with single rosewood butterfly key, 31 1/2" x 90" x 23" **$32,500**

Mario Bellini, "Amanta" modular chairs, brown/oatmeal, each 33" x 34" x 28" (one shown) .... **$600 pair**

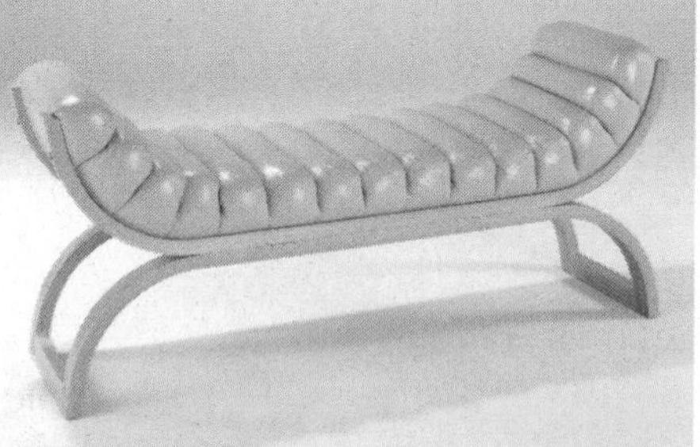

Jay Spectre, curved bench with lobed buff leather cushion on laminated oak frame, 29 1/2" x 64" x 18 1/2" **$1,250**

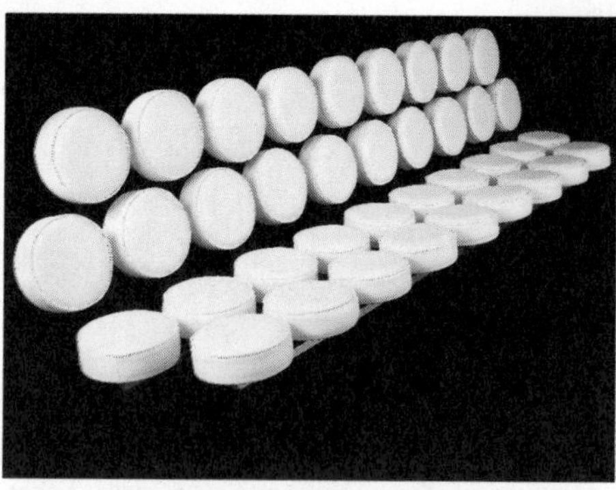

Irving Harper/George Nelson and Associates, Marshmallow sofa upholstered in white vinyl on brushed and enameled steel frame, signed Irving Harper (possibly the most famous Modernist sofa ever made), 30 1/2" x 103" x 30" **$37,500**

Nelson, Platform Bench, birch top, 48 1/4" x 18 1/4" x 14" **$750**

Vladimir Kagan, omnibus settee upholstered in striped Knoll fabric on Plexiglas base, re-upholstered in Knoll fabric, 28" x 85" x 32" **$1,500**

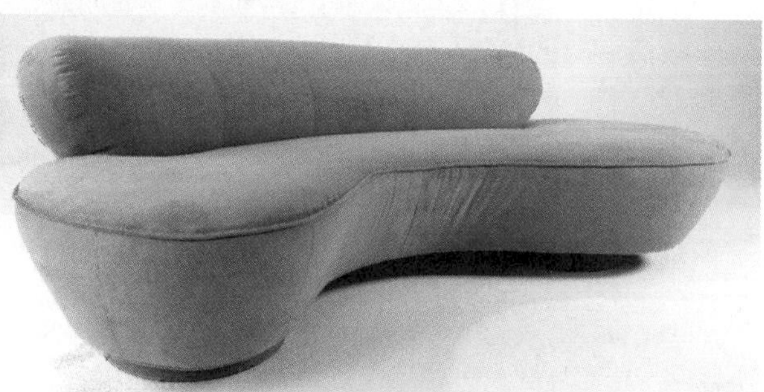

Vladimir Kagan/Directional, curvilinear sofa upholstered in grey ultras-uede, Directional label, 29" x 94" x 40 1/2" **$2,000**

Shelving and Storage

Cabinets, Donald Deskey style, exotic wood veneer, each 36" x 14 3/4" x 21" (one shown) .... **$425 pair**

Charles and Ray Eames/Herman Miller, first edition ESU 201, circa 1952, 32 3/4" x 47" x 16" **$4,250**

Edmund Spence, cabinet, one center door, 72" x 20" x 32" **$600**

Ettore Sottsass/Memphis, Carlton multicolored and patterned laminate bookcase unit, 77 1/2" x 75" x 15 3/4" **$8,000**

George Nelson, display cabinet, 34" x 12" d x 23" **$200**

George Nelson, Basic Series cabinets, 34" x 18 1/2" x 24" .... **$550 pair**

Gio Ponti/Singer & Sons, Italina walnut breakfront, the china cabinet with glass shelves and doors atop a server with three doors enclosing interior drawers and shelves, 63 1/2" x 70" x 18 3/4" **$10,000**

John Kapel, sideboard, 80" x 20" x 30" **$800**

T.H. Robsjohn-Gibbings/Widdicomb, walnut six-drawer sideboard with trapezoidal top, Widdicomb fabric label, 34 1/2" x 66" x 21" **$4,250**

Vladimir Kagan, walnut chest with eight drawers, 36" x 72" x 18" **$1,250**

Wall unit, rosewood, 1960, 87" x 16 1/2" x 73".... **$1,400**

Printed auction catalogs may seem expensive at $20 to $40 but are important tools to help the collector study the items being offered before the sale. They can be used to jot notes to refer to during the sale to verify lot numbers and prevent overbidding. Customers who order an auction catalog are usually sent a list of realized prices after the auction.

Tables

Coffee table, round top, rust, brown and yellow, 1960s, 30 1/4" x 13" **$225**

Coffee table, 1960s, 43" x 14 3/4" **$500**

Charles Eames/Herman Miller, surfboard coffee table with black laminate top on wire base, oval Eames/Herman Miller metal tag, 10" x 89 1/2" x 29 1/2" **$1,600**

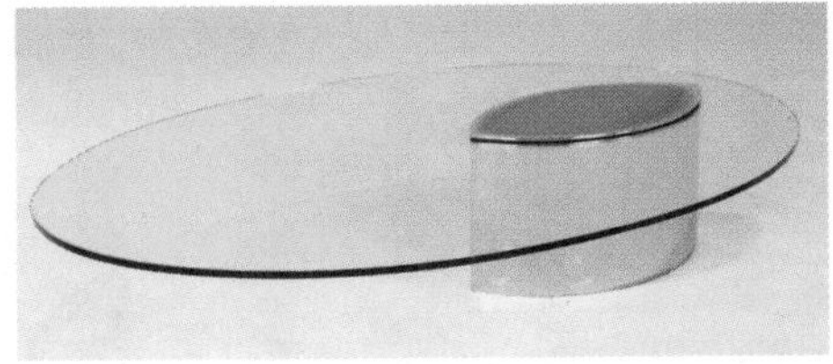

Cini Boeri, Lunaria coffee table with elliptical glass top over chromed steel base, 12 1/2" x 59" x 43 1/2" **$2,300**

George Nakashima/Widdicomb, coffee table with freeform top in Sundra finish, marked Widdicomb 12-6-200, 13" x 66" x 24 1/2" **$2,600**

Greta Grossman, side table, 18" x 31 1/2" x 20"....**$950**

George Nelson, planter table, 19" x 30" x 26"....... **$325**

Isamu Noguchi, occasional table, white laminate, birch, wire base, 23 3/4" x 20"....................................... **$950**

Isamu Noguchi/Herman Miller, coffee table with three-sided plate-glass top on ebonized base, 15" x 50" x 36 1/2" **$550**

Mira Nakashima, special redwood root burl coffee table with sled base in American black walnut, 16" x 75" x 33" **$10,000**

Paul Lazslo, occasional table, wedge shaped, 29 1/4" x 19 3/4" x 19 1/2" **$300**

Philippe Starck, steel console table with glass top, 16" x 47" x 18". **$2,000**

Roger Capron, coffee table, ceramic tiles, 40 1/2" x 36" x 11 1/2" **$800**

Silas Seandel, bronze occasional table, biomorphic top inset with two glass panels, 17" x 25" x 21" **$3,250**

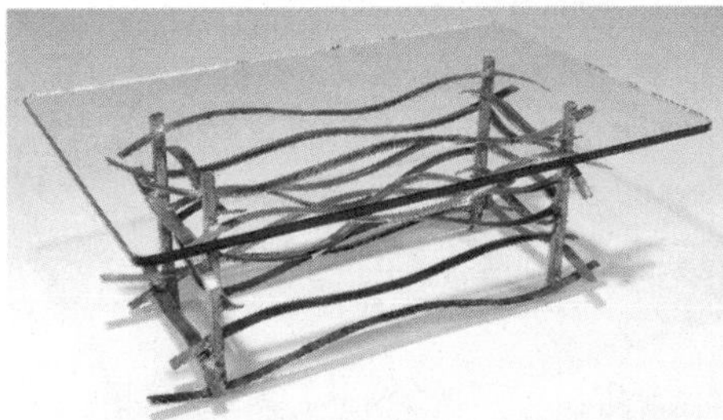

Silas Seandel, ribbon coffee table with glass top on copper, brass, bronze and steel base, 16" x 42" x 27" **$7,000**

Accessories

A.D. Copier, Serica glass footed bowl in iridescent yellow overlaid with burst-open crackle, acid-stamped triangular mark, 10 1/2" x 6 1/4" **$500**

Ceramic wall mirror, geometric cutouts, 12 1/2", 3" deep **$275**

Deruta, pitcher and set of eight cups, pitcher 12", cups 5" .... **$300 set**

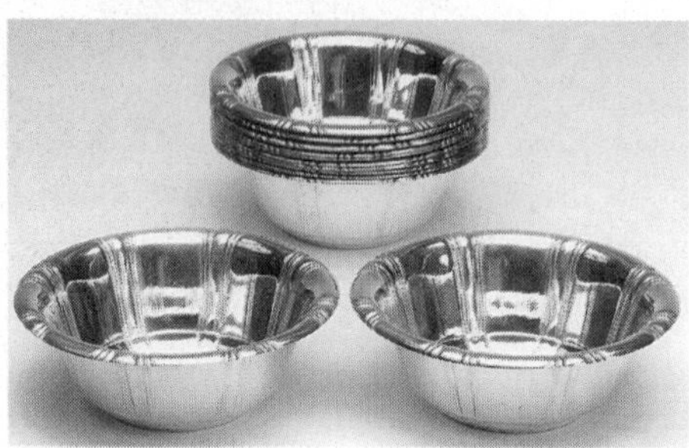

Eliel Saarinen, "Contempora" bowls, set of 12, 5 1/2" x 1 3/4" .... **$2,600 all**

Elsa Peretti, "Bone" candlesticks, pair, 14 1/4" **$350**

Franziska & James Hosken, rolling bar cart, 41" x 23" x 27" **$900**

Fulvio Bianconi, "pezzato" vase, for Venini, 7 1/2" x 8" **$9,500**

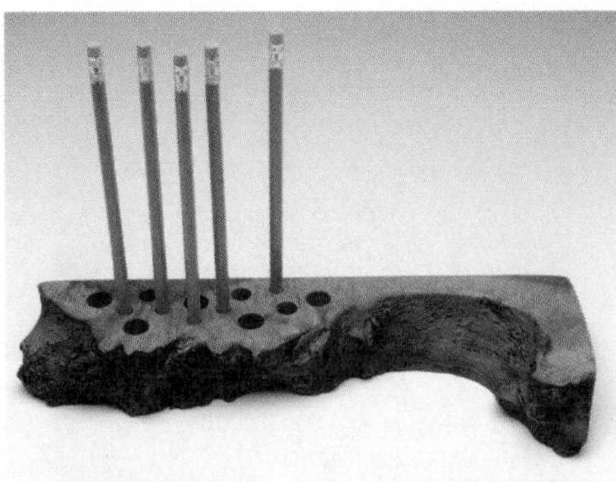

George Nakashima, burlwood pencil holder, circa 1969, 1 1/4" x 13" x 4 1/2" **$3,000**

Michael and Frances Higgins, bowl and plate, each 12 1/4" .... **$150 pair**

George Nelson, table clock, orange and white body, cone base, 5 3/4" x 6 3/4" **$1,400**

Gilbert Rohde/Herman Miller, Telechron burlwood veneer table clock with chrome-plated steel details, marked Herman Miller, 6" x 7 3/4" **$4,000**

Mathieu Mategot-style wastebasket, 10" x 15" ... **$475**

Rude Osolnik bowl, walnut, 10" x 2 1/2" **$325**

Serge Roche, wall-hanging mirror in octagonal silvered glass frame, 26" x 26".. **$5,500**

Screen, silver-leafed steel and wood frame, each panel 20" x 79 1/4" **$1,400**

Tapio Wirkkala, silver vase on teak base, signed TW with hallmarks, 10 1/2" **$650**

Art

Dorothy Morang, Conclave, 1947, oil on Masonite (framed); signed and dated, 22" x 30" **$4,500**

Hannes Beckmann, Facade, 1961, oil on Masonite; signed, dated and titled, 18" x 30" **$3,250**

Norman Carton, Blue Night, 1950s; oil on canvas; signed, 84" x 64" **$13,000**

Rex Ashlock, Dark Red on Orange with Moon, oil on canvas; dated with stamped signature and estate stamp; 1960, 80" x 70" **$3,000**

Some auction-goers intentionally discourage competition by deriding an item before it sells. After making disparaging remarks about a valuable item and scaring away potential bidders, the detractor will often be the winning bidder at a reduced price. Recognize this ploy for what it is and decide for yourself how much you want to bid.

Richard Hambleton, Untitled (Shadow Man), acrylic on canvas, 70 1/2" x 46" **$4,750**

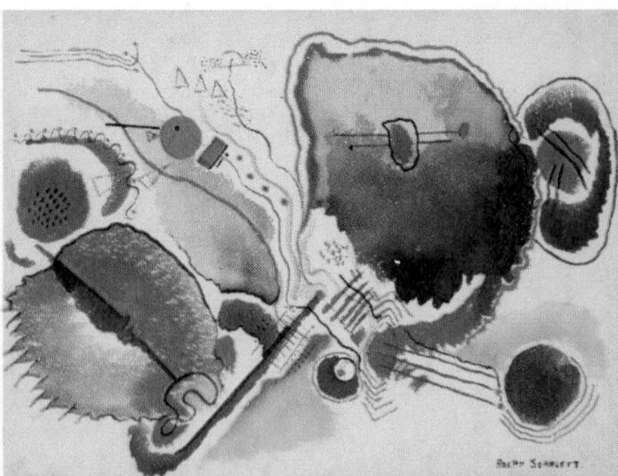

Rolph Scarlett, two works of art: Untitled; gouache and ink on paper, pictured here; signed; 9 3/4" x 13 1/2" (sheet); Untitled; gouache and ink on paper (framed); Signed **$1,600**

Stanley Twardowicz, Untitled, 1984, acrylic on paper (framed), signed and dated, 22 1/2" x 17" **$1,000**

Stephen Frykholm, Fruit Salad Annual Summer Picnic poster, 39 1/2" x 25" **$100**

Sculpture

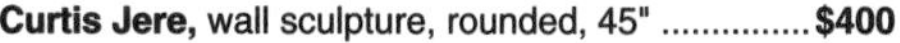

Curtis Jere, wall sculpture, rounded, 45" **$400**

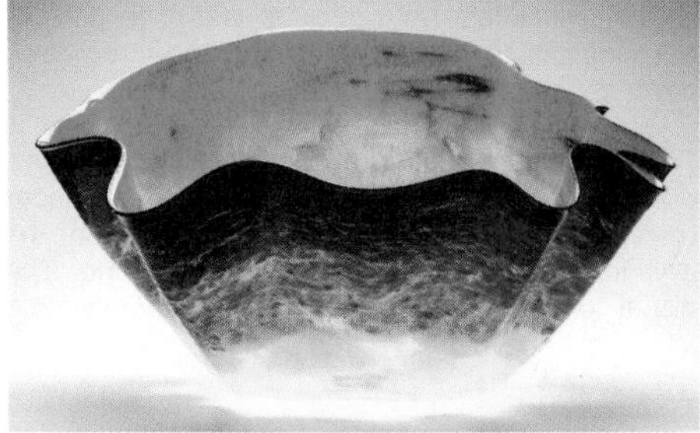

Dale Chihuly, large macchia of cobalt, vermilion and white mottled glass, acid-etched signature and date, 16" x 31" **$14,000**

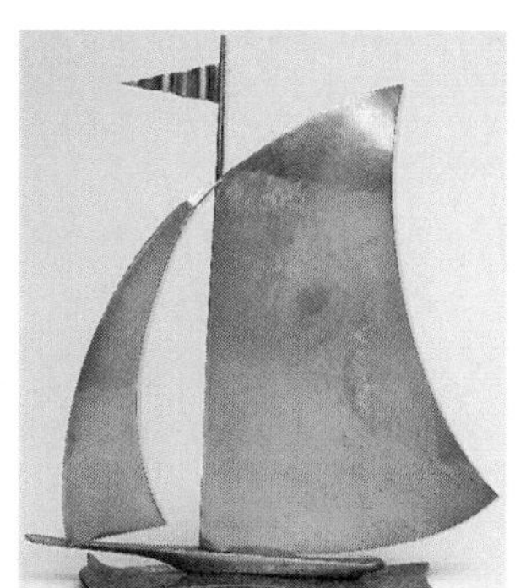

Hagenauer, boat sculpture, brass, 10 1/4" x 2" x 11 1/4" **$400**

Harry Bertoia, Willow, stainless steel, 66" h........................ **$37,500**

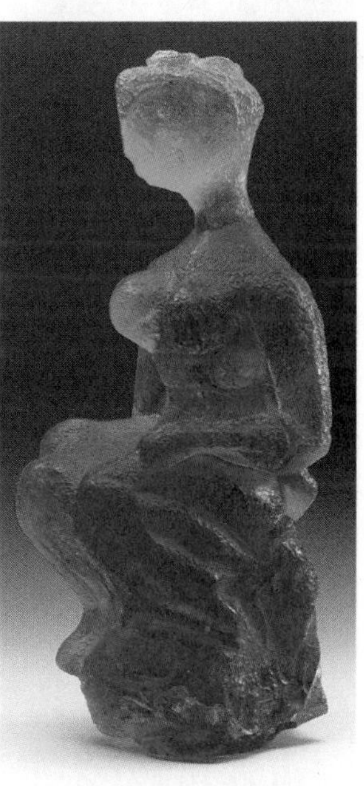

Pablo Picasso/Egidio Constantini, "Donna Seduta", blue corroso glass sculpture of a seated woman, executed for La Fucina Degli Angeli (The Forge of Angels), inscribed P. Picasso/E. Costantini/ Fucina Angeli/Venesia/P-A/1954, with copyright, 18" **$15,000**

Shady out-of-town auctioneers sometimes conduct sales on the grounds of grand homes, giving the impression the items they're selling came from the wealthy families who lived there. Furnishings sold at these auctions are hauled in and are seldom as described. This deceptive practice is called house packing. Also be wary of auctions that advertise that they are selling the assets of convicted drug dealers. These auctions are usually a ploy to sell reproductions.

MUSIC BOXES

The general term "music box" is used to describe all automatic music playing machines. The three types covered here are cylinder, disk and automaton.

Music is generated in a cylinder music box by a cylinder of metal spiked with nubs. As the cylinder rotates, one or more metal combs placed near the cylinder strike the nubs, creating the sound. The disk-type music box works in much the same way. A flat disk of metal spiked with nubs rotates and metal combs striking it again produce the sound.

Musical automatons are mechanical creations meant to imitate the motions of humans or animals playing or moving to music. The automatons can be made of wood, metal or porcelain, and generally are dressed in costumes of the era.

Mermod Freres Ideal Soprano cylinder music box, rectangular mahogany & ebonized wood case w/ band inlay & a bottom drawer w/stamped brass pulls holding three cylinders, on a matching table w/cabriole legs, ormolu mounts & a center drawer, additional wooden box w/three cylinders, music box, 19 x 42", 13 1/4" h., table 23 x 45 1/2", 31" h., the set (ILLUS. of music box) **$16,100**

Nicoles Freres Piano Forte disc music box, mahogany & rosewood long rectangular case w/ornate brass, ivory, mother-of- pearl & boulle inlaid banding & cartouche reserves on the top & front, further fine line-inlay, plays four overtures, late 19th c., minor damage, 11 1/2 x 28", 8 1/8" h. **$40,250**

Regina Corona disc music box, Model 33, floor model, mahogany upright case, the rectangular top w/a low pierced gallery of short turned spindles & fluted front corner blocks w/urn-turned finials above a deep frieze over a pair of single-pane doors w/ornate brass corner trim flanked by turned & tapering columns, the lower case w/a large rectangular glass pane acid-etched "Regina Corona" & w/ scrolled corner decoration, stepped molded flat base on casters, tag of retailer reads "From Sherman Clay & Co. San Francisco," w/29 - 27 1/2" d. discs, late 19th c., 25 x 39 1/4", 72 1/2" h. **$25,300**

Regina disc music box, Model 35, floor model, carved mahogany case, a high peaked & pierced scroll-carved crest centered by a clock dial w/Arabic numerals above a curved molded cornice above a tall curved leaded glass door decorated w/scrolls, crown & harp, ropetwist-turned columns down the sides, curved molded base molding above a conforming drawer, raised on simple cabriole legs joined by a medial shelf, w/original labels, includes 27 - 15 1/2" d. discs, 24 x 28", 71" h. **$41,400**

Automatons

Bird automaton on box, small rectangular gold-plated box w/a serpentine front, finely chased overalll w/birds & leafy scrolls, a small oval lid in the top center opens to reveal a small hand-made bird that whistles a pretty tune, plays, 19th c., 2 3/4 x 4", 1 3/4" h. **$1,668**

Birds in birdcage automaton, a gilt-metal rectangular wire birdcage w/a domed top w/knob & hanging ring, enclosing three birds w/colored plumage, two w/ moving heads & beaks, a metal perch wrapped w/a leafy vine, raised on a deep giltwood base w/ composition floral relief ornament on each side, side crank handle, the Movement Bontems, marked "Made in France 5313535," early 20th c., 19" h. **$5,975**

Cylinder Music Boxes

Baker (G.) - Troll & Co. cylinder music box, 11" cylinders w/harp harmonic piccolo, rectangular case line-inlaid w/burled walnut borders, raised on a matching table w/slender cabriole legs & a paneled & veneered apron, fine original case finish, w/three cylinders, table 22 x 42", 29" h., case 13 1/2 x 33", 8" h., the set **$8,913**

Bremond cylinder music box, 17 1/4" l. six-tune cylinder, unusual mandolin effect created by a series of sets of five teeth tuned alike, original tune card inside the lid, elaborately inlaid on the lid & fron around the keyhole & sides, very small chip on bottom front, Switzerland, 19th c., case 10 1/2 x 28", 6 1/2" h. **$3,278**

European cylinder music box, single cylinder playing six tunes, original tune card inside the lid, grain-painted wooden case w/ decal decoration, early 20th c., case 7 1/4 x 13 1/2", 5" h. ... **$777**

Swiss cylinder music box, 11" l. six-tune cylinder, fitted w/six engraved bells struck by brass birds, in a fancy burled walnut serpentine-sided case w/a black flaring stepped base, the front mounted in the center by a clock w/a beveled glass front & porcelain dial w/Roman numerals, clock strikes hour & half-hour w/a bell & playing the music, professionally refinished w/new tune card, 17 1/2 x 27", 9 1/4" h. **$17,825**

Antiques can be gently cleaned without removing patina, but the method depends on the material being cleaned. Wood, metal, jewelry, ceramics, glass, and silver each have special needs. If in doubt, don't clean at all.

Swiss cylinder music box, 17 1/4" l. twelve-tune cylinder, in a case w/an inlaid recessed top panel, front & sides w/bird's-eye maple inlay around the sides, missing tune card, separation at back left corner repaired, minor dings, late 19th c., 12 1/2 x 32", 9" h. **$1,783**

Swiss cylinder music box, rosewood-grained case, 5" l. four-tune cylinder, includes original instructions & framed tune card inside the lid, late 19th c., case 13 1/2" l. **$411**

Swiss cylinder music box, single cylinder playing ten tunes, Conchon Star works, fitted w/a double comb & nine bells, in an inlaid rosewood case, original tune card inside the lid, working, last quarter 19th c., case, 34" l., 10 1/2" h. **$4,140**

Disk Music Boxes

Mira disk music box, table model, nice tiger-sawn oak case, plays 6 3/4" d. disks, case all-original, hold-down shaft may be replaced, w/12 disks, case 8 1/2 x 10", 7" h. **$1,350**

Regina disk music box, table model, fancy carved oak case w/a medallion enclosing musical instruments centered in a lattice-carved panel w/a cherub in the upper corners, carved border bands, design repeated on all sides & the top of the lid, original paper lithograph inside the lid & two nice celluloid instruction tags inside, single-comb mechanism playing 11" d. disks, original finish on case, works restored, crank not original, w/five steel disks, late 19th c., case, 13 1/2 x 14 1/2", 9" h. **$1,725**

←

Regina disk music box, table model, oak case w/a molded base & original finish, 11" disk double-comb mechanism, original picture card inside the lid, w/eight disks, case 18 3/4 x 21", 9 1/2" h. **$2,350**

Polyphon disk music box, floor model, Model #54, tall walnut case w/a rectangular flaring top above a dentil-carved band above a narrow cornice supported on tall turned columns on blocks flanking a high arched window w/ scroll-carved upper corner panels, the stepped-out lower cabinet w/blocks & carved serpentine pilasters flanking a tall paneled storage bin, plays 24 1/2" disks, includes 12 old disks & four new disks, coin mechanism plugged, plays well, late 19th c., 22 x 33 1/2", 76" h. **$14,375**

NAUTICAL ITEMS

The romantic lure of the sea, and of ships in general, has opened up a new area of collector interest. Nautical gear, especially items made of brass or with brass trim, is sought out for its decorative appeal. Virtually all items that can be associated with older ships, along with items used or made by sailors, are now considered collectible, for technological advances have rendered them obsolete. Listed below are but a few of the numerous nautical items sold in recent months.

Boat tiller, carved wood w/a tapered form w/a turned top half ending in a carved animal head w/a wide gaping mouth holding a ball w/a five-pointed star, bronze hardware, nice old dark patina, 19th c., 59" l. **$1,840**

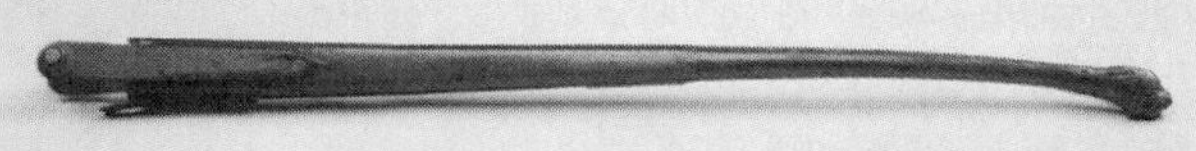

Chronometer, mahogany-cased, brass-bound double-lidded case opens to a brass movement w/engraved silver dial inscribed "Eggert & Son, New York - No. 276," w/applied ivory plaque inscribed "Eggert & Son 276 New York," early 19th c., 7 3/4" h. **$3,173**

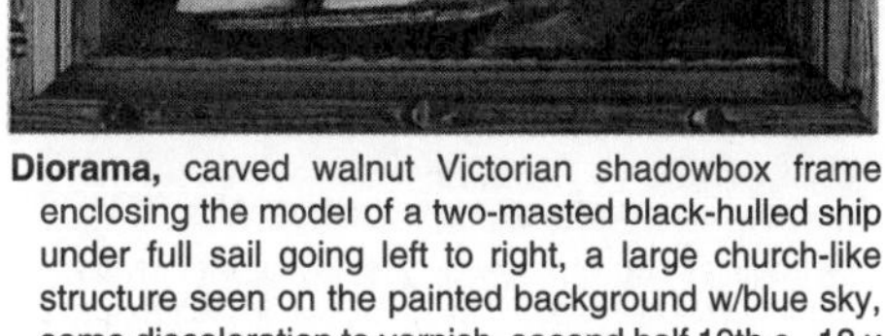

Diorama, carved walnut Victorian shadowbox frame enclosing the model of a two-masted black-hulled ship under full sail going left to right, a large church-like structure seen on the painted background w/blue sky, some discoloration to varnish, second half 19th c., 13 x 21" **$920**

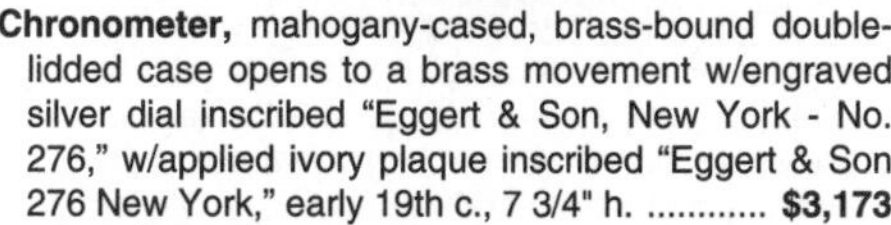

Diorama, folk art mixed media scene of the sinking of the Titanic, carved & painted wood & metal, depicting the ocean liner hitting the iceberg w/passengers, crew, lifeboats, flags & a heart w/raised inscription "S.S. Titanic Sunk in the Greatest marine Disaster in Histor (sic) April 15, 1912," in a glazed gilt gesso framed w/ metal plaque reading "Giusseppe Ruopoli 148 W. End Ave.," United States, early 20th c., 28 x 48" ... **$2,820**

Diorama, multi-ship scene in an ornate inlaid mahogany case w/a pedimented top & ball feet, the multi-ship scene features a Central American gunship sailing right to left, three masts fully rigged w/no sails, fine detailing, the other vessels encircling the warship in a celebratory manner, they include a one-masted sailboat w/American flag, a two-masted sailboart, a small one-mast dingy, a large multi-sail one-mast sailboart & a sidewheel steamship w/Navy personnel & women wearing polka dot dresses, all mounted on a painted sea w/a three-part mirrored back, the tall rectangular case w/a large window flanked by slender turned curly maple columns w/leaf block tops, the sides w/rectangular panels inlaid w/bird's-eye maple, the front base w/narrow burl mahogany inlaid panels, ca. 1810-20, 9 3/4 x 20", 20" h. **$11,500**

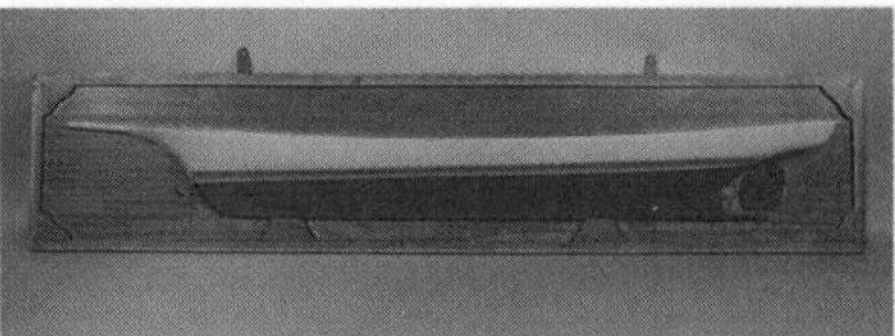

Half-ship model, huge ship builder's laminated wood model, a painted hull painted in grey, red & black, later mounted on a large mahogany board, some paint wear, late 19th - early 20th c., model 9" l. **$1,840**

Lamp, gimbaled hanging-type, large brass framework w/a long shaped harp suspending a removable brass oil lamp w/unusual burner & domed milk glass shade, weighted base, unmarked, from a ship on Lake Erie, late 19th - early 20th c., 30" h. **$230**

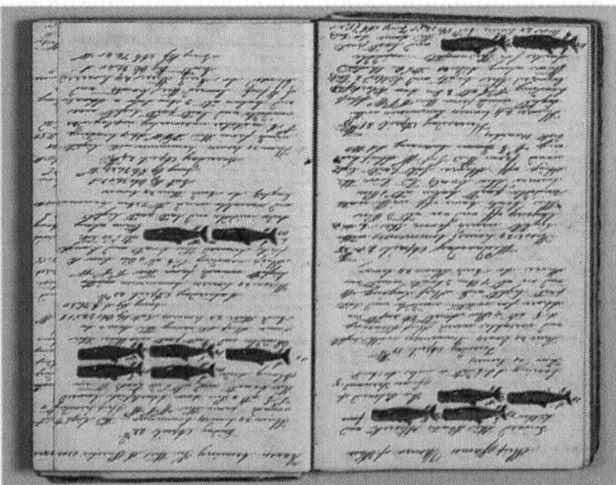

Logbook, from the whaling ship "James Monroe," hand-written w/detailed descriptions & sketches of the whales captured, Fairhaven, Massachusetts, dated 1840, together w/a group of seven carved panbone & wood stamps **$16,730**

Seaman's chest, inlaid teak, six-board construction, rectangular flat top inlaid w/three ornate compass stars, opening to an interior w/a lidded till, the front inlaid w/a light wood border band w/looping corners & across the center w/three large compass stars, each end w/a metal bail handle & another inlaid compass star, 19th c., 14 1/2 x 31", 16" h. **$1,265**

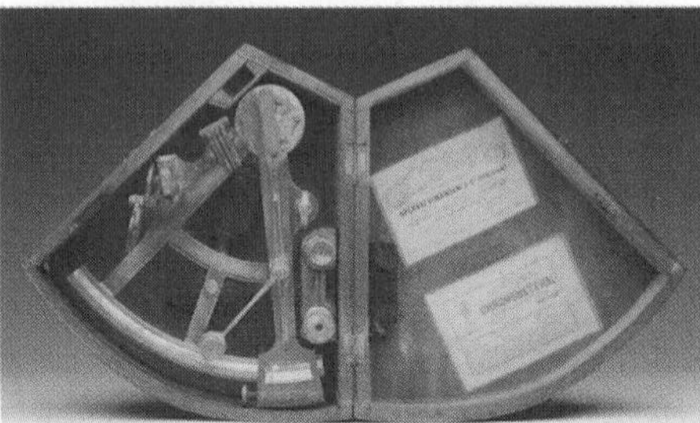

Sextant, brass instrument w/an ivory scale & turned wood handles, in a fitted hinged dovetailed mahogany case w/two labels & extra lenses, labels of Imorcy & Son Minories, London, England, includes a family history of ownership, 19th c., case 11" l. **$1,035**

Ship's wheel, brown-painted wood, paint worn & flaked, 19th c., 47" d. **$518**

An item's provenance is its pedigree or record of who owned it in the past. Sometimes an antique inadvertently acquires an embellished provenance over several generations. Because oral histories can be so unreliable, verifiable information, such as written documents, are needed to establish the authenticity of a provenance. A provenance that includes a famous historical figure, a celebrity or a major museum, can dramatically increase the value of an antique.

PETROLIANA MARKET REPORT

Petroliana is an example of "mantiques," antiques and collectibles that especially appeal to men. Mantiques are great," said Frank Fritz of the *American Pickers* television show. "That's what we deal in, that's what people view when they see us every Monday night. We've been successful with that because we're finding things that people can relate to."

"One of the cool things about petroliana is that it's something that people can still get involved in," said Fritz's partner Mike Wolfe. "We talk about getting younger people involved in collecting. There are still signs you can find at your local flea market for $50 to $75, and I think that's how a lot of people get started collecting. In a lot of genres of antiques, things have become so expensive and so rare because collectors are holding on to it, that people can't get into that category. So for younger people to get involved, it's huge."

Wolfe explained that there are two types of petroliana collectors: the older, more advanced collectors, and the younger beginning and intermediate collectors. "Advanced collectors look for pre-1920 collectibles. The younger collectors—the people who collect the more common brands like Shell and Mobil—are those who grew up in the '60s and '70s, and now they're collecting muscle cars and want to decorate their homes."

Wolfe added that a popular collecting goal is recreating a nostalgic scene. "There's two things that Frank and I come across all the time, and that's people who are trying to create a soda fountain or gas station."

While petroliana covers a broad array of collectibles, "signs are the most popular because everybody's got room in their den or garage for them," said Fritz. Gas pumps and many point-of-sale displays are big and bulky and hard to display except in a relatively large building or an outdoor area. "Most people don't want to dedicate that much room for one item," he said.

Cans and containers often feature attractive colors and graphics too, but are harder to display because they have to be placed on shelves rather than hung on walls. Signs, on the other hand, have colorful, interesting graphics and fit well into people's homes and collecting displays. Most signs are around 14 by 20 inches, which is an ideal size. Signs that are bigger than about 20 by 30 inches are harder to sell, although Wolfe pointed out that "some people have really big storage spaces to store their car or boat, so they have their collection showcased in a big area. Those guys aren't on every corner, but there are some collectors who are looking for big items."

While petroliana offers many items that are accessible to entry level collectors, it also has some rare, very valuable "holy grail" items as well. Wolfe gave the example of double clock-face pumps, while Fritz mentioned rare brands of oil cans produced by small oil companies around the turn of the century. "In the early 1900s, there were thousands and thousands of small oil companies that were bought up by the big companies," he explained. "Many of the cans produced by smaller companies were made for just a few years."

As in all antiques and collectible categories, condition plays an important role in petroliana. But the tolerance for condition varies according to several factors, including collecting level. "A lot of collectors start out with lower condition pieces. On a scale of 1 to 10, they start out with a five. Then eventually they find an 8 or 9 and sell off the 5 and upgrade," Fritz said. "But with the some of the old stuff, it's really hard to find pristine condition. If there's enough paint on it, [you should] buy it. We buy rusty signs all the time. There's all kinds of collectors. Some want to showcase their signs in their building where they have their cars and collectibles worth thousands. Other people just want to let them hang on a fence and sit outside all day, so they don't care if they have a bullet hole or some rust."

People have varying preferences concerning restoration and sometimes follow trends. Wolfe said, "[In the recent past], a lot of people were antiquing motorcycles to make them look older than they really were, where back in the '70s and '80s and even early '90s, they were over-restoring, making them look better than they did when they came off the showroom floor."

Wolfe added that sometimes people prefer to have things in their original condition. "Some people want stuff with personality. I've gone both routes of restoring signs and leaving them as is. I've completely restored pieces that go to specific collectors who wanted them for the interior of their house, and wanted them to look like a shiny new penny, but I've also left them with their patina and rust on. People can appreciate that even more because they can see the item had a life before them, there's age there, there's a story."

Both Wolfe and Fritz prefer original condition over restoration. Wolfe said, "To me, if you had ten gas pumps or signs or oil cans lined up that are restored and on the other side of the room you had ten that are beaten up and what we call 'farm fresh,' I'd much rather look at the ones that are farm fresh because they're more captivating to your eye and you have more to look at. Sometimes when you're looking at a restored item, you're taking away from the item itself and you're looking at how well done the restoration is."

Fritz agreed. "I think once someone starts painting up a sign, they've completely wrecked it. I'd just leave them alone." He added, "Sometimes we leave pieces the way they are because people like to restore them themselves and that way they feel like they found them and recreated what they want."

Rarity is another reason collectors accept less-than-ideal condition. "Sometimes things are so rare, the fact that it still exists and that you own one, even to own something that is broken, chipped, cracked, got a bullet hole in it, it's still a prized possession to most people," Wolfe commented.

Some collectors are investing their money in collectibles like petroliana rather than the stock market, Wolfe said. "A lot of people are putting their money into things that are more tangible. Things that they can put their hands on, things they can believe in, something they can enjoy, not just a dividend that they can read on the end of a page that they get monthly."

Whether collectors buy petroliana for investment or pure pleasure, they can enjoy the nostalgia and beauty of these classic collectibles. Who knows, collectors may unknowingly purchase a piece that Wolfe or Fritz discovered and picked out of a barn just a few months before.

PETROLIANA

Items in the section have primarily been selected at the high end of the market. The focus is on the top price items, not to skew the values, but to emphasze the brands and types that are the most desirable. Some less valuable items have been included to help keep values in perspecitive. For example, in many cases, even a large group of common low-end items can be worth just a fraction of a single rare piece. As with all advertising items, factors such as brand name, intricacy of design, color, age, condtion and rarity drastically affect value.

Warning: Beware of reproduction and fantasy pieces. Virtually all categories of antiques are plagued by fakes and reproductions, and petroliana is no exception. For collectors of vintage gas and oil items, the only way to avoid reproductions is experience: Mmaking mistakes and learning from them; talking with other collectors and dealers; finding reputable resources (including books and Web sites), and learning to invest wisely, buying the best examples one can afford.

Beginning collectors will soon learn that marks can be deceiving, paper labels and tags are often missing, and those that remain may be spurious. Adding to the confusion are "fantasy" pieces, globes that have no vintage counterpart, and that are often made more for visual impact than deception.

How does one know whether a given piece is authentic? Does it look old, and to what degree can age be simulated? What is the difference between high-quality vintage advertising and modern mass-produced examples? Even experts are fooled when trying to assess qualities that have subtle distinctions.

There is another important factor to consider. A contemporary maker may create a "reproduction" sign or gas globe in tribute of the original, and sell it for what it is: a legitimate copy. Many of these are dated and signed by the artist or manufacturer, and these legitimate copies are highly collectible today. Such items are not intended to be frauds.

But a contemporary piece may pass through many hands between the time it leaves the maker and winds up in a collection. When profit is the only motive of a reseller, details about origin, ownership and age can become a slippery slope of guesses, attribution and—unfortunately—fabrication.

As the collector's eye sharpens, and the approach to inspecting and assessing petroliana improves, it will become easier to buy with confidence. And a knowledgeable collecting public should be the goal of all sellers, if for no other reason than the willingness to invest in quality.

Fortunately, there are entire Web pages devoted to petroliana reproductions. A check of these resources is advised for beginning collectors.

For more information about petroliana, consult Warman's Gas Station Collectibles by Mark Moran.

Photo acknowledgments to Aumann Auctions, Rich Gannon, George Simpson, and John Hudson.

Containers

Petroliana containers are prized by many collectors. Unlike signs and globes, these were meant to be discarded after use, so they fall into the category of ephemera.

Ace High Motor Oil, quart tin can, near mint .... **$875+**

Atlantic Motor Oil, Medium one-gallon tin can, light overall wear .... **$90+**

Babolene Motor, one-gallon flat tin can, display side excellent, reverse good, worn............. **$500+**

C.A.M. (Indian Motorcycle), quart tin can, good condition .... **$200+**

Cruiser Motor Oil, quart tin can, near mint .... **$200+**

Gilmore Lion Head, "Purest Pennsylvania" tin quart, very good condition, dents and minor wear, full....................................... **$475+**

Harley-Davidson Genuine Oil, one-gallon flat tin can, very good to excellent condition, light wear .... **$2,600+**

Hudson Motor Oil, quart tin can, near mint .... **$400+**

Husky Heavy Duty Motor Oil, quart tin can, orange background, excellent condition, small dents .... **$825+**

Indian Motorcycle Oil, quart tin can, excellent condition, dent on reverse .... **$300+**

Penntroleum Motor Oil, quart tin can, excellent condition...... **$200+**

PEP Boys Pure as Gold Motor Oil, quart tin can, excellent condition, small dents .... **$150+**

Republic Motor Oil, tin quart, very good condition, small dents and some wear.......................... **$150+**

Valvoline Motor Oil, one-gallon tin can (early design), display side excellent condition, reverse fair to good .... **$150+**

Polly Penn Motor Oil, quart tin can, green stripe at top, excellent condition, light wear and dent on top .... **$875+**

Shamrock Motor Oil, tin quart, very good condition, some wear, small dents, full .... **$150+**

Vanderbilt Motor Oil, quart tin can, near mint, small dent in bottom ring .... **$400+**

Power-lube Motor Oil, five-gallon rocker can, display side excellent condition, reverse side fair .... **$2,100+**

Strata Motor Oil, quart tin can, near mint.................................. **$400+**

Wil-Flo Motor Oil, quart tin can, near mint, extra fine............ **$475+**

Displays, Holders, Racks

Although this category may be of limited interest to many collectors, those trying to assemble a well-rounded collection that approximates a working garage find them to be the perfect accessories for display. This section also includes rack tops, which many collectors use as wall-mounted decorations.

Chevron Supreme Gasoline, map rack, excellent condition, 20" x 13" .... **$300+**

Gulf, restroom tin key holder, dated 1961, excellent condition, 9" x 11" .... **$210+**

Mobil Tires, display rack with ad insert, 8 1/2" x 14" .... **$325+**

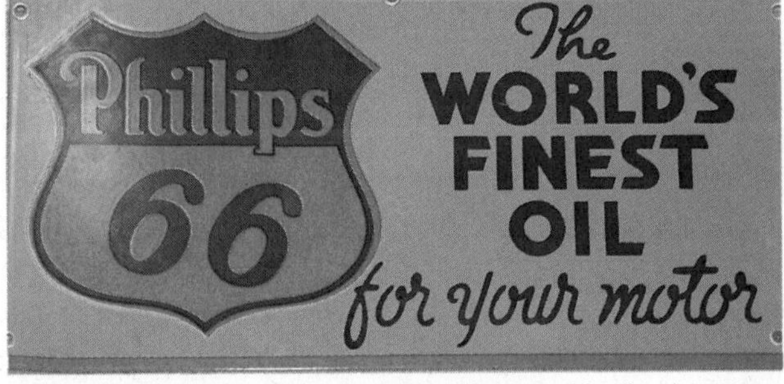

Phillips 66, The World's Finest Oil double-sided porcelain oil rack top, near mint, 12" x 20" .... **$1,300+**

Signal, metal 12-bottle oil rack with 12 generic bottle and spouts, fair to good condition .... **$575+ all**

Shell X-100 Motor Oil, display rack .... **$550+**

Socony Petroleum Products, single-sided tin die-cut display rack, good condition, chip in field, 14" x 16".. **$300+**

Globes

The globes that once decorated the tops of gasoline pumps are the holy grail for many petroliana collectors.

Early globes were a single piece of glass, often with etched or painted lettering. "Globe" is a misnomer, since none here is truly spherical, and a complete globe often has three main parts: two lenses and a body, though some came with a single lens.

The body can be made of metal, plastic or fiberglass. A high-profile body has a standing seam around the circumference. A low-profile body has a flattened seam. A gill body has a rubber or metal gasket holding the lenses in place. Later Capco bodies are molded plastic with screw fasteners at the base. A hull body accepts notched lenses, and is open where the lenses are mounted, as opposed to a glass body where the lenses rest on a low dome. Gill and hull bodies take their names from the manufacturers that created them, but as the petroliana field has grown, these names are often found with lower-case spellings.

Some collectors secure the lenses on the bodies using silicone caulk, a practice that many object to because this can contribute to paint loss and it makes the lenses difficult to examine off the bodies.

Ripple and jewel bodies are among the most desirable, and hardest to find. Ripple glass bodies have an irregular textured surface, and come clear, white, and in a range of colors. Jewel bodies have round faceted glass "jewels" set into the surface.

Globes can range in value from $50 for a common or damaged example to almost $20,000 for rarities in near-mint condition.

American Hi-Compression globe, 13 1/2" lenses in a gill-glass body, small chip on one lens..... **$1,800+**

Atlantic Gasoline, one-piece chimney-top globe, etched lettering, slight fading, chimney repainted, small chips on base .... **$5,250+**

Bay globe, 13 1/2" lenses in Capco body, good condition .... **$175+**

Buffalo Premium, single 13 1/2" lens, excellent condition ..... **$275+**

Coastal Gasoline, (with birds) globe, 13 1/2" lenses in a clear ripple body .... **$2,750+**

Conoco Gasoline, (with Minuteman) globe, 15" lenses in a high-profile metal body (repainted) .... **$5,750+**

Drake's Hi Octane Regular globe, 13 1/2" lenses in a Capco body, excellent condition........... **$3,200+**

Eagle Gasoline globe, 13 1/2" lenses on a yellow ripple gill body, excellent condition........... **$3,750+**

Fyre-Drop globe, 13 1/2" lenses, in a high-profile metal body, near mint.................................. **$2,200+**

General Gasoline globe, 15" single lens in repainted low-profile body, excellent condition.............. **$600+**

Gilmore Ethyl globe, 15" single lens in low-profile body, good condition .... **$3,500+**

Hudson Ethyl, with logo, 13" lenses in an orange ripple gill body, body cracked with paint loss around base................................. **$3,250+**

Husky Hi-Power, (with dog) globe, 13 1/2" lenses on a Capco body .... **$3,750+**

Johnson Gasolene Time Tells, (with ethyl logo) globe, 13 1/2" lenses in orange ripple gill body, metal base .... **$5,750+**

Kan-O-Tex Bondified globe, 13 1/2" lenses, in an orange ripple glass body, base chips .... **$3,000+**

Lonas Premium globe, 13 1/2" single lens in original red Capco body with some crazing, lens good condition, scratches in field .... **$100+**

Magnolia globe, with rose, 16 1/2" lenses in low-profile body, very good condition .... **$4,600+**

Mobilfuel Diesel globe, 13 1/2" lenses in Capco body, excellent condition .... **$250+**

Mohawk Gasoline, (orange background) globe, 15" lenses in low-profile metal body (repainted) .... **$8,500+**

Red Crown Gasoline globe, with crown, 15" lenses in high-profile metal body, display side excellent, reverse very good........... **$3,750+**

Shamrock oval globe, body damaged, lenses very good condition .... **$200+**

Shell globe, (West Coast), 15" single lens in high-profile body, lenses very good condition, body good original paint........... **$2,500+**

Signal globe, 15" lenses in high-profile body, lenses excellent condition, body repainted .... **$10,000+**

Sinclair Aircraft, one-piece globe, baked-on paint faded with some pinholes, chips around base .... **$6,000+**

Texaco, leaded stained-glass metal body globe, slight fading, smaller size .... **$4,500+**

White Rose globe, 13 1/2" lenses on narrow glass body, lenses caulked in place............... **$1,900+**

Pumps

Pumps are not for everybody. They are big machines that—though relatively simple—can require significant maintenance if a collector desires to keep them in working order. That's why most serve as nonfunctioning accessories. Correct components and spare parts can be expensive, and proper restoration in manufacturer's colors can take months. Pumps in untouched original condition are quite rare, and command some of the highest prices.

Some sellers, easily found on the Internet, stock reproduction parts for many gas pumps. Some also offer new-old-stock parts, used parts, and original-condition and restored pumps. Others carry globes, decals, signs, books, oil cans, road maps, and offer restoration, consultation and appraisals.

Bennett Model 748 pump, restored in Gulf colors, with reproduction globe.................................. **$950+**

M&S 80 Script Top pump, Mobilgas Special, with reproduction pump plates............................... **$1,800+**

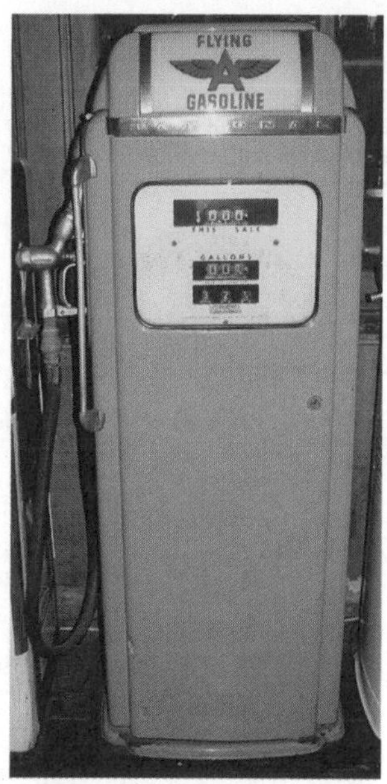

National 365 computing pump, with 64 top, Flying A ad glass, good original condition .... **$850+**

Tokheim 36-B pump, painted in Texaco colors, with reproduction globe, two original Fire Chief porcelain pump plates dated 1957 and 1962 .... **$1,700+**

Wayne 40 computing pump, fancy face bezel, original paint fair condition, Mobil shield, globe holder .... **$1,400+**

Wayne 519 10-gallon visible pump, restored in Shell colors and decal .... **$1,200+**

Wayne 60 pump, with sunburst, restored in Gilmore colors, several parts chromed, with reproduction Gilmore globe, also fitted with remote button that makes dial register .... **$3,500+**

Signs

Signs are some of the most important and desired petroliana collectibles. Their color and design are eye appealing and create wonderful wall displays. Porcelain and metal signs were intended to last for years, so they were made to endure. However, they are susceptible to scratches, chipping, rust, etc. which can dramatically lower their value. Signs in mint or near mint condition command premium prices.

Aristo Motor Oil, porcelain flange, very good condition, small chips in field, reverse has two quarter-size chips, 20" x 20" .... **$2,500+**

Calso RPM Lubrication, porcelain flange, display side excellent condition with few edge chips, reverse near mint, 19" x 22" .... **$2,500+**

Flying A Super Extra, porcelain pump plate, near mint, new old stock, 10" diameter............. **$800+**

Grizzly Gasoline, (Dubbs Cracked) Watch Your Miles double-sided tin sign, display side good condition, light wear and fading at bottom, extremely rare, 36" x 24" .... **$3,500+**

Husky Service, double-sided porcelain die-cut sign, good condition, large chips and re-drilled holes at top and small chips in field, light scratches, larger chips on reverse, 48" x 42" .... **$4,250+**

Kendall The 2000 Mile Oil, curved single-sided porcelain sign, very good condition and gloss, two quarter-size chips in field, chip at left mounting hole, 30" x 20" .... **$3,700+**

Hancock Gasoline, (early rooster) porcelain pump plate, very good condition with repaired quarter-size hole below "A" in Hancock, 12" diameter .... **$3,100+**

←

→

Magnolia Gasoline, for sale here double-sided porcelain sign, excellent condition-plus, light scratches on reverse, 30" diameter .... **$2,700+**

Red Crown Gasoline, GM Ethyl double-sided porcelain sign, professionally restored, 30" diameter .... **$1,500+**

Red Crown Gasoline Zerolene, double-sided porcelain, fair to good condition, chipping in fields and on edges, 42" diameter .... **$4,000+**

Signal Gasoline, porcelain pump plate with stoplight, excellent condition, 12" diameter.... **$2,000+**

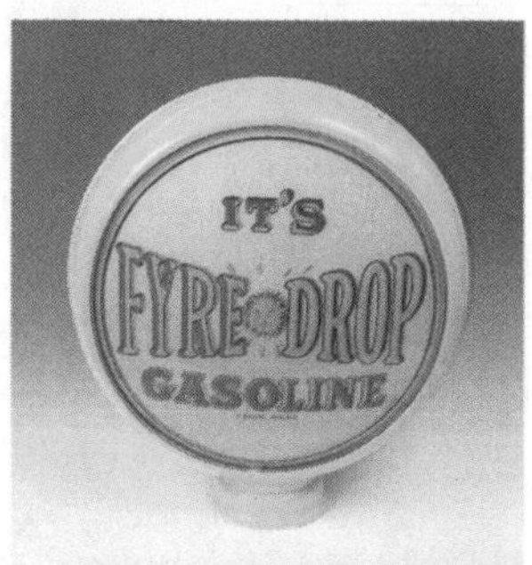

Skylark Aviation Grade Gasoline, neon sign, with plane skywriting, replaced neon and housing (or as collectors call it, the "can"), 42" x 66" .... **$8,000+**

Stanocola, Standard Oil Company of Louisiana double-sided porcelain sign, good condition, several areas professionally touched up, 30" diameter .... **$3,000+**

Texaco, (black T) Gasoline-Motor Oil double-sided porcelain sign, very good to excellent condition, two chips in field and chipping around mounting holes, 42" diameter .... **$1,250+**

Union 76 Gasoline, porcelain pump plate, very good condition, chip on one mounting hole, 11 1/2" diameter .... **$125+**

Union Oil Minute Man Service, double-sided porcelain sign, excellent condition, chips around top mounting holes .... **$7,000+**

Zerolene, The Standard Oil for Motor Cars single-sided porcelain sign, good condition, three touched-up chips around edge, 24" diameter .... **$1,900+**

←

Wil-Flo Motor Oil, double-sided tin oval sign, 17" x 23", display side restored, reverse total loss .... **$3,100+**

Related Items

"Related" collectibles—often automotive in nature—that appeal to petroliana collectors, but are not directly tied to the production of oil and gasoline, include things like tires, spark plugs, heaters, etc., and transportation in general.

Atlas Tires, clock, good condition, needs work on motor, 19" diameter .... **$325+**

Bus line guides, one Gray Line, one Pickwick Greyhound Lines .... **$35+ pair**

Champion Spark Plug, cardboard display, excellent condition, light wear, framed and matted, 32" x 22" .... **$2,100+**

Buss Auto Fuses, metal counter-top display rack, excellent condition, 7 1/2" x 8 1/2" x 3".. **$450+**

←

Firestone Tires Badge, rubber and celluloid .... **$75+**

Eveready Daylo, glass counter top show case, with mirrored back, good condition, 12" x 20" x 12" .... **$200+**

Rival Auto Lamps, Made in England cardboard display with 12 lamps, 7 1/2" x 7"...... **$225+ all**

Schrader Air Service, Kit for the Farm, excellent condition, 3" x 8" x 8"................................ **$375+**

Seiberling Steel Radial Tire, clock (clock by Sessions), working condition... **$50+**

Antique malls often have an "all sales final" policy. The policy prevents a dishonest person from buying an item of superior quality and substituting an inferior item in the return. Because antique mall personnel cannot be familiar with the condition of each piece of merchandise, they are not in the position to accept returns. The policy is also designed to prompt customers to look at potential purchases carefully.

POSTERS

Concert, "Beach Boys Show," cardboard printed in red, yellow & black on a white ground, three photos of the group, 1968 concert in Lincoln, Nebraska, near mint, 14 x 22" **$2,070**

Concert, "Pink Floyd - Atom Heart Mother Earth Tour," long narrow rectangular form printed in pink & red on white, photos of the band at the top & bottom, 1970 performance in Salt Lake City, 7 x 29" **$1,150**

Concert, colorful images of two French ladies in costume dancing, printed in red & brown "Trianon Concert - Tous Les Soirs - Tableau de la Troupe... Spectacle Variè," marked by H. Gray, style of the 1890s, ca. 1920, laid on canvas, 36 3/4 x 51 1/8" **$316**

Firearms, "Ithaca Guns," large color picture by artist Louis Agassiz Fuertes of passenger pigeons w/red wording above "Extinct Passenger Pigeon," advertising below the picture reads "Ithaca Guns - Out Shoot Them All - Authorized Agent," ca. 1910, bands at top & bottom, excellent condition, 16 1/2 x 27 3/4" **$1,540**

Liqueur, long colorful design of a horse race w/a central figure of a flying lady wearing a long flowing orange robe & holding aloft a bottle of the product, printed in French across the bottom "Premier Fils - La Vieille Marque Francaise," image by Roby, printed by L. Maboeuf, ca. 1936, framed, 51 1/4 x 79 1/2" **$1,175**

Magazine, "Le Locataire," French protest-type w/a color image of a group of poor children & their parents, title & information on a protest in black across the top, name of editor in lower left, designed by Steinler, Paris, France, ca. 1913, laid on canvas, 47 x 63" **$489**

Music festival, "Woodstock Music & Art Fair - An Aquarian Exposition in White Lake, N.Y. - 3 Days of Peace & Music," cardboard w/a red background printed in white, blue, green & black, August 1969, excellent condition, 24 x 36" **$993**

Seeds, "Ferry's Seeds," color lithograph w/artwork by Maxfield Parrish of a young girl seated beside a watering can, advertising below reads "Mary Mary quite contrary - How does your garden grow? - Plant Ferry's Seeds," framed, two horizontal creases w/ two softer vertical folds, ca. 1920, 19 1/2 x 27" **$5,520**

Stage play, "Bunco in Arizona," colorfully lithographed design of a cowboy on a bucking bronco, advertising across the top reads "J.L. Veronee Amusement Company's Original Co. in the Queen Bee of All Comedy Drama - Bunco in Arizona," wording at bottom of the scene reads "Billy Craver and His Bucking Pony 'Chub,'" American Show Print Co., Milwaukee, Wisconsin, 1902, minor edge tears, 28 x 42" **$1,485**

Stage play, "Bunco in Arizona," colorfully lithographed design w/a large oval central portrait of a pretty young woman framed by portraits of four Indian chiefs, reads "The Original Company - in The Queen Bee of All Comedy Dramas - Bunco in Arizona - Nae St. Clair Among The Red Skins," American Show Print Co., Milwaukee, 1902, 28 x 42" **$1,925**

Steamship, "Cunard Line," printed in orange & blue on a white ground w/a large image of the steamship Saxonia, reads "Cunard Line - Spend Xmas in Europe...," ca. 1885, minor wear at folds, one small internal tear, 19 x 29" **$255**

Steamship, "Red Star Line," printed in German w/black wording framing an engraving of a passenger steamship, covers trans- Atlantic passages, ca. 1875, some minor loss at folds, small ares of discoloration, 25 x 38" **$230**

Theatre, "Born Yesterday," starring Judy Holliday, Henry Miller's Threatre, colorful yellow, blue & red comic design of the star being carried by a stork, 1940s, window card-type, some minor soiling, 14 x 22" **$1,170**

Theatre, "La Yetta," long narrow color lithograph showing a full-length portrait of an exotic belly dancer in Mideastern attire, by F. Garric, Paris, France, ca. 1900, excellent condition, 22 x 61" **$690**

Theatre, "The Charity Ball," printed in color on a white ground, printed across the bottom "Daniel Frohman's Lyceum Theatre Success...," ca. 1890, minor edge loss & a small tear, gold colors, 20 x 28" **$414**

Theatre, "The Electric Spark - Atkinson's Follies," Alcazar Theatre, New York City, November 27, 1882, colorful images of the theatre interior & the crowd, the production featured illumination by Thomas Edison's new incandescent electric bulbs, mounted on board, loss to top & bottom borders, light uniform toning, w/an original four-page program for the play, 28 x 42" **$1,072**

←

Theatre, "The Squaw Man - Liebler & Co's. Production," large color image of a standing cowboy & small child w/a kneeling young woman, title across the top & image titled, Wallack's Theatre, New York City, ca. 1906, mint condition, 20 x 27" **$411**

Travel, "Red Star Line - Antwerpen - New York," lovely color scene of a mother & her young daughter looking out at an arriving ocean liner, artwork by H. Lassiers, printed in Belgium, ca. 1900, near mint, matted & framed, poster 24 x 34" **$1,150**

World War I, "Buy More Liberty Bonds," a grim color image of a young mother grasping her children, printed in the corner "Must Children Die and Mothers Plead in Vain," border tears repaired, 30 x 40" **$76**

World War I, "Boys and Girls! You can help your Uncle Sam Win the War - Save your Quarters - Buy War Savings Stamps," colorful James Montgomery Flagg image of Uncle Sam w/a young girl & boy, minor creasing, tiny corner chips, 20 x 30" **$288**

World War II, "The Four Freedoms," famous color images by Norman Rockwell, in original mailing envelope w/Office of War Information marking, set of 4 .... **$790**

←

World War I, "Remember Your First Thrill of American Liberty - Your Duty - Buy United States Government Bonds - 2nd Liberty Loan of 1917," the upper half w/a large color scene of immigrants arriving by ship w/the State of Liberty in the distance, slight border staining, 22 1/2 x 33" **$173**

RECORDS (1948-1991) MARKET REPORT

According to Martin Popoff, a record collector and editor of *Goldmine® Standard Catalog of American Records*, *Goldmine® Record Album Price Guide*, and *Goldmine® Price Guide to 45 RPM Records*, while some areas of record collecting are flat, others are seeing a lot of activity. Following is his evaluation of hot areas:

Near-mint, mint and sealed LPs. One thing that the growth of eBay has shown is that albums in truly near-mint condition, especially original editions from the 1950s through the 1970s, are extremely hard to find.

Condition has always meant a lot when it comes to records. Today, it means more than ever. Perhaps a new generation of record buyers has been spoiled by the quiet, efficient sound coming from a compact disc or a digital file and won't tolerate the pops and ticks that sometimes are audible on even the best-pressed records. Some of the prices for sealed vintage LPs border on the obscene. A couple years back, a sealed original mono copy of Pet Sounds by the Beach Boys traded for over $1,500 and a sealed stereo copy of The Beatles (The White Album) has sold for over $1,400. The only thing extraordinary about them is that they were, presumably, never opened.

"Audiophile" LPs. Albums that appeal to the audience that appreciates good sound quality are hotter than ever. This does not only apply to the records of the 1980s and 1990s that were specially licensed and marketed to appeal to this small subset of collectors. True, albums on the DCC Compact Classics label from the 1990s are almost uniformly collectible, with near-mint copies of many titles trading for three figures routinely. And many albums on the Mobile Fidelity, Nautilus and Direct Disc labels are in that range. Condition is even more important when it comes to these records, including consideration around stickers used to seal some of them, the plastic sleeves they came in, and of course, the condition of the covers.

Today, many audiophiles are paying closer attention to more mainstream albums. Indeed, the work of certain cutting engineers – the people who "translate" the sound of a master tape to the record – are becoming sought-after by this group. Often the only way these desirable pressings can be identified is by checking the trail-off wax of the albums. So far, this trend hasn't crossed over to the vast majority of record collectors, who still value a general first pressing over a specific one. But it's something we are watching closely.

Hot Genres. As one generation of record collectors passes the torch to the next, unsurprisingly, those new collectors collect what they connect with. Ergo, pre-1965 artists continue to fall off the radar, even as hot spots continue to build to their record of established high prices, in some cases continuing to march upward. Still, genres with more activity tend to begin with garage and psych, with progressive rock, punk and metal continuing to prove strong.

The Importance of Condition

Nothing is more important in determining the value of records than their condition! Yes, their relative rarity and demand is important, but a collector or dealer will pay much more for a record in Near Mint condition than one in Very Good Minus condition. Most records, especially from before the 1970s, are not in anything close to Mint or Near Mint condition. That is why a collector will pay a premium for such a disc if he or she has to have it. Records in lesser condition are worth a fraction of the Near Mint prices.

Most of the time, LPs are sold with two grades, one for the record and one for the cover. With some exceptions, albums without covers are worthless, and covers without the accompanying record are worthless. Most records are graded visually. Some defects are easy to see, such as scratches and warps. Others are subtle, such as groove wear from using a cheap or poorly aligned tone arm. Older LPs (1950s to about 1971) tend to play better than they look, and newer LPs (at least until 1989) tend to play worse than they look.

When grading your records, do so under a strong light. Some records will be worthy of a higher grade except for defects such as writing, tape or minor seam splits. Always mention these when selling a record! For some collectors, they will be irrelevant, but for others, they will be a deal-breaker. For all, they are important to know. Also note that sophisticated collectors are sometimes looking for a better sleeve to "marry" to the decent condition record they have currently housed in a trashed sleeve, and vice versa.

Also, some LPs were made for promotional purposes only. Again, always mention if a record is a promo copy when advertising it for sale! Certain promo designations tend to lower the value of a record (sawcuts, punches, cut corners and other cut-out marks), while others tend to raise the value (white labels). The gold stamp? Still debatable or often inconsequential.

Goldmine® Grading Guide

Mint (M)

These are absolutely perfect in every way. Often rumored but rarely seen, Mint should never be used as a grade unless more than one person agrees that the record or sleeve truly is in this condition. There is no set percentage of the Near Mint value these can bring; it is best negotiated between buyer and seller.

Near Mint (NM or M-)

A good description of a NM record is "it looks like it just came from a retail store and it was opened for the first time." In other words, it's nearly perfect. Many dealers won't use a grade higher than this, implying (perhaps correctly) that no record or sleeve is ever truly perfect.

NM records are shiny, with no visible defects. Writing, stickers or other markings cannot appear on the label, nor can any "spindle marks" from someone trying to blindly put the record on the turntable. Major factory defects also must not be present; a record and label obviously pressed off center is not Near Mint. If played, it will do so with no surface noise. (NM records don't have to be "never played"; a record used on an excellent turntable can remain NM after many plays if the disc is properly cared for.)

NM covers have no creases, ring wear or seam splits of any kind.

These are high standards, and they are not on a sliding scale. A record or sleeve from the 1950s must meet the same standards as one from the 1990s or 2000s to be Near Mint! It's estimated that no more than 2 to 4 percent of all records remaining from the 1950s and 1960s are truly Near Mint. This is why they fetch such high prices, even for more common items. Do not assume your records are Near Mint. They must meet these standards to qualify!

Very Good Plus (VG+) or Excellent (E)

A good description of a VG+ record is "except for a couple minor things, this would be Near Mint." Most collectors, especially those who want to play their records, will be happy with a VG+ record, especially if it toward the high end of the grade (sometimes called VG++ or E+).

VG+ records may show some slight signs of wear, including light scuffs or very light scratches that do not affect the listening experience. Slight warps that do not affect the sound are OK. Minor signs of handling are OK, too, such as telltale marks around the center hole, but repeated playing has not misshapen the hole. There may be some very light ring wear or discoloration, but it should be barely noticeable.

VG+ covers should have only minor wear. A VG+ cover might have some very minor seam wear or a split (less than one inch long) at the bottom, the most vulnerable location. Also, a VG+ cover may have some defacing, such as a cut-out marking. Covers with cut-out markings can never be considered Near Mint.

Very Good (VG)

Many of the imperfections found on a VG+ record are more obvious on a VG record. That said, VG records – which usually sell for no more than 25 percent of a NM record – are among the biggest bargains in record collecting, because most of the "big money" goes for more perfect copies. For many listeners, a VG record or sleeve will be worth the money.

VG records have more obvious flaws than their counterparts in better shape. They lack most of the original gloss found on factory-fresh records. Groove wear is evident on sight, as are light scratches deep enough to feel with a fingernail. When played, a VG record has surface noise, and some scratches may be audible, especially in soft passages and during a song's intro and ending. But the noise will not overpower the music otherwise. Minor writing, tape or a sticker can detract from the label. Many collectors who have jukeboxes will use VG records in them and not think twice. They remain a fine listening experience, just not the same as if it were in better shape.

VG covers will have many signs of human handling. Ring wear in the middle or along the edges of the cover where the edge of a record would reside, is obvious, though not overwhelming. Some more creases might be visible. Seam splitting will be more obvious; it may appear on all three sides, though it won't be obvious upon looking. Someone might have written or it or stamped a price tag on it, too.

Lower Grades

Good (G), Good Plus (G+) or **Very Good Minus (VG–)** records go for 10 to 15 percent of the Near Mint value, if you are lucky.

Good does not mean bad! The record still plays through without skipping, so it can serve as filler until something better comes along. But it has significant surface noise and groove wear, and the label is worn, with significant ring wear, heavy writing, or obvious damage caused by someone trying to remove tape or stickers and failing miserably. A Good to VG– cover has ring wear to the point of distraction, has seam splits obvious on sight and may have even heavier writing, such as, for example, huge radio station letters written across the front to deter theft.

If the item is common, it's probably better to pass it up. But if you've been seeking it for a long time, get it cheap and look to upgrade.

Poor (P) and **Fair (F)** records go for 0 to 5 percent of the Near Mint value, if they go at all. More likely, they end up going in the trash. Records are cracked, impossibly warped, or skip and/or repeat when an attempt is made to play them. Covers are so heavily damaged that you almost want to cry. Only the most outrageously rare items ever sell for more than a few cents in this condition – again, if they sell at all.

RECORDS - 45 AND LP

Music fans have been collecting records, beginning with 78 RPMs, since they were first mass produced in early 20th century. The fragile shellac 78s were eventually replaced by vinyl 33 RPM albums beginning in 1948, the 45 RPM single beginning in 1949, and the 7-inch extended play (EP) record in 1952. Later, the 8-track tape and cassette tape were introduced. They were popular because they were portable, but didn't enjoy the breadth or longevity of collecting that vinyl experienced. In the late 1980s and 1990s, digital music in the form of compact discs began to replace vinyl, and by 1991, the golden age of vinyl was over. With the rapid technological development in the music industry, CDs in turn, are being supplanted by digital downloads. Ironically, however, in recent years, music afficianados are returning to vinyl as a preferred medium because of its richer sound and its dramatic cover art. Sales of new releases in high-quality 180-gram vinyl has been growing rapidly since around 2005, although vinyl sales still comprise only a fraction of all music sales.

The following records are only a broad sampling of music produced between 1950s and the 1970s, the peak of vinyl production. To make the most of the space available, records listed here are relatively scarce and have higher than average value. Common records are often worth only a few dollars in Near Mint condition, and a fraction of that in lower condition. But some rare records in Near Mint condition sell for thousands and even tens of thousands.

Prices listed are for Near Mint (NM) condition.

Very Good+ (VG+) condition = 50 percent of Near Mint value.

Very Good (VG) condition = 25 percent of Near Mint value.

45

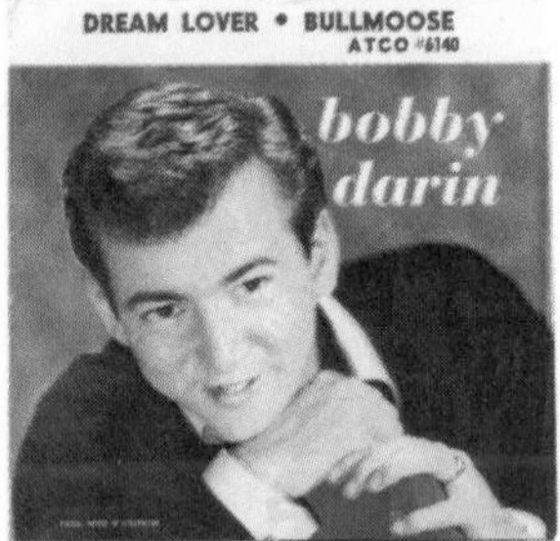

Bobby Darin, "Dream Lover," Atco 6140, 1959 .... **$50**

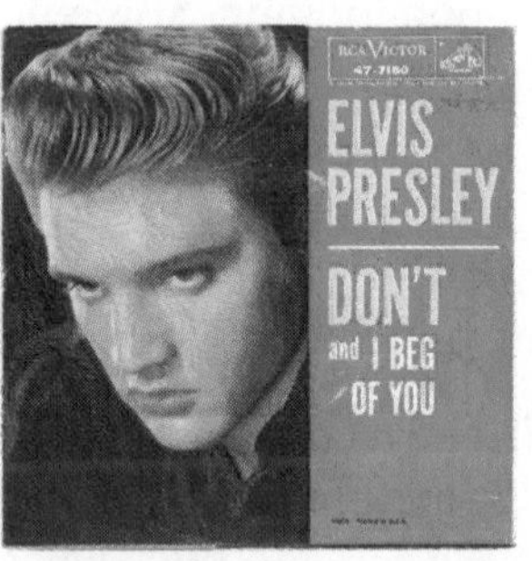

Elvis Presley, "Don't," RCA Victor 47-7150, 1958 .... **$90**

Elvis Presley, "He Touched Me," RCA Victor 74-0651, 1972 ... **$120**

Elvis Presley, "Jailhouse Rock," RCA Victor 47-7035, 1957, picture sleeve **$50-100**

Jerry Lee Lewis, "Great Balls of Fire," Sun 281, 1957.............. **$80**

John Lennon, "Mother," Apple 1827, 1970 .... **$120**

Johnny Cash, "Guess Things Happen That Way," Sun 295, 1958 .... **$40**

Ricky Nelson, "I Got a Feeling"/ "Lonesome Town," Imperial 5545, 1958 .... **$70**

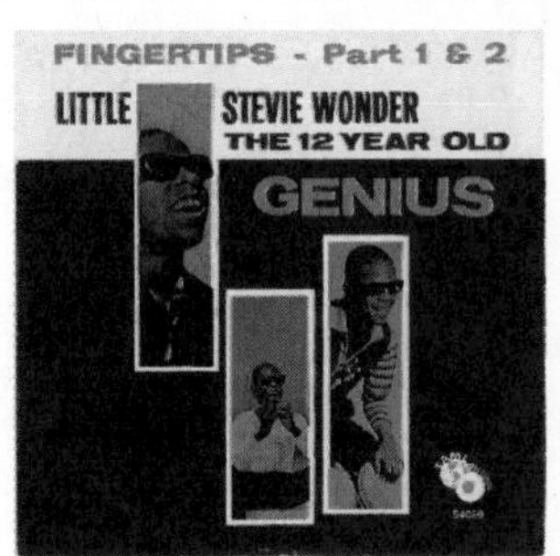

Stevie Wonder, "Fingertips Pt. 1 and 2," Tamla 54080, 1963 .... **$50**

The Beatles, "And I Love Her," Capitol 5235, 1964, picture sleeve **$60-120**

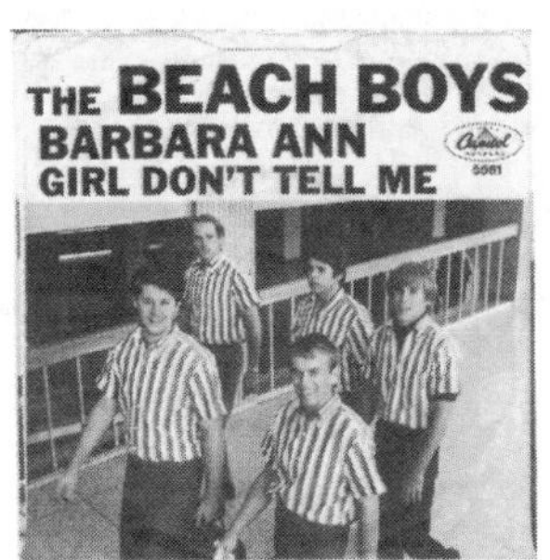

The Beach Boys, "Barbara Ann," Capitol 5561, 1965 .... **$150-200**

The Beach Boys, "It's Now or Never," RCA Victor 47-7777 1960 .... **$60**

The Beach Boys, "Ten Little Indians," Capitol 4880, 1962 .... **$200**

The Byrds, "The Times They Are a-Changin'," picture sleeve for unreleased single **$500**

The Ronettes, "Walking in the Rain," Philles 123, 1964 .... **$150**

LP

Alan Freed, Rock 'n Roll Dance Party, Coral CRL 57063, 1956 .... **$150**

Annette, Annette's Beach Party, Vista 3316, 1963 .... **$100**

Ann-Margret, The Vivacious One, RCA Victor LPM-2551, 1962 .... **$30**

Bill Haley and the Comets, Rock with, Somerset P-4600, 1958 .... **$150**

Bo Diddley/Chuck Berry, Two Great Guitars, Checker LP 2991, 1964 .... **$60**

Buddy Holly, Buddy Holly, Coral CRL 57210, 1964 .... **$100**

Buddy Holly, The Buddy Holly Story, Vol. 2, Coral CRL 57326, 1959 .... **$200**

Chuck Willis, The King Of The Stroll, Atlantic 8018, 1958 .... **$300**

Duane Eddy, The Biggest Twang of Them All, Reprise, 6218, 1966 .... **$30**

Elvis Presley, Blue Hawaii, RCA Victor LPM-2426, 1961, mono, with sticker on cover hyping "Can't Help Falling in Love" and "Rock-a-Hula Baby"....................... **$50-100**

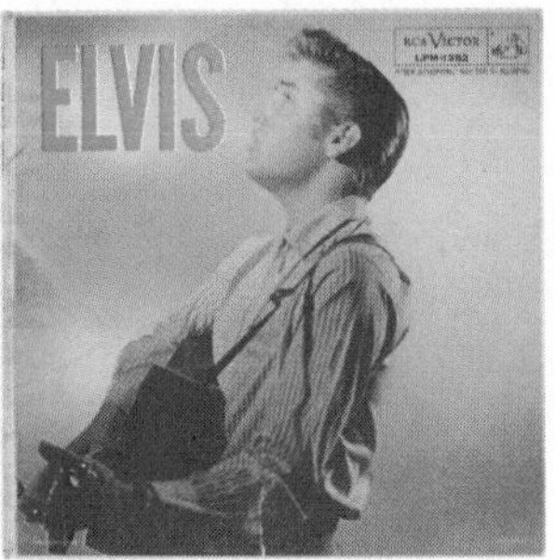

Elvis Presley, Elvis, RCA Victor LPM-1382, 1956, mono **$300-800**

Elvis Presley, Elvis' Christmas Album, RCA Victor LOC-1035, 1957, mono, with gatefold and booklet intact **$500**

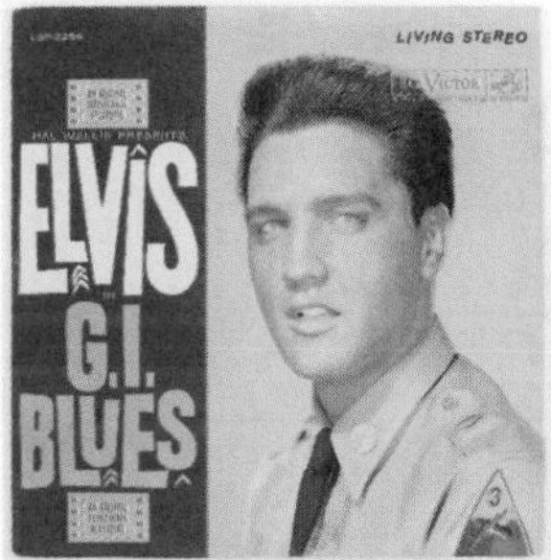

Elvis Presley, G.I. Blues, RCA Victor LSP-2256, 1960, stereo, "Living Stereo" on label, no sticker on cover........................... **$50-100**

Frank Sinatra, Swing Easy/Songs for Young Lovers, Capitol W 587, 1955, mono, gray label........... **$40**

Hank Williams, Honky-tonkin', MGM E-3412, 1957.............. **$100**

Harry Belafonte, "Mark Twain" and Other Folk Favorites, RCA Victor LPM-1022, 1954, mono.......... **$50**

James Brown, Mighty Instrumentals, King 961, 1966 .... **$100**

Jefferson Airplane, Surrealistic Pillow, RCA Victor LPM-3766, 1967, mono **$60**

LP

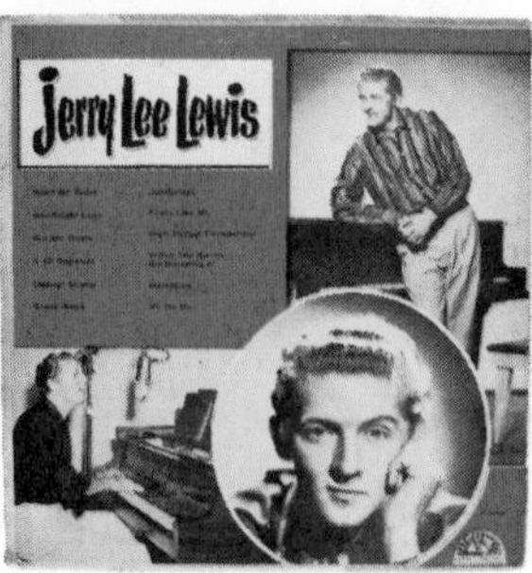

Jerry Lee Lewis, Jerry Lee Lewis, Sun SLP-1230, 1958 .... **$200**

Johnny and the Hurricanes, The Big Sound of, Big Top 12-1302, 1960 .... **$250**

Joni James, Joni James, MGM E-3346, mono, yellow label, 1956 .... **$80**

Les Paul and Mary Ford, Time to Dream, Capitol T 802, 1956 ... **$50**

Little Richard, His Biggest Hits, Specialty SP-2111, 1963........ **$50**

Little Richard, Little Richard, RCA Camden CAL-420, 1956....... **$200**

Nat King Cole, Love Is the Thing, Capitol W 824, 1957, mono, gray label....................................... **$40**

Neil Sedaka, "Little Devil" and his Other Hits, RCA Victor LSP-2421, 1961 .... **$60**

Ronnie Hawkins and the Hawks, Mr. Dynamo, Roulette, R 25102, 1960 .... **$150**

Scatman Crothers, Rock and Roll with Scatman, Tops 1511, 1956 .... **$80**

The Beach Boys, Surfin' U.S.A., Capitol ST 1890, 1963, stereo **$50**

The Beatles, Abbey Road, Apple SO 383, 1969 .... **$20-75**

The Champs, Everybody's Rockin' with the Champs, Challenge CHL-605, 1959 .... **$200**

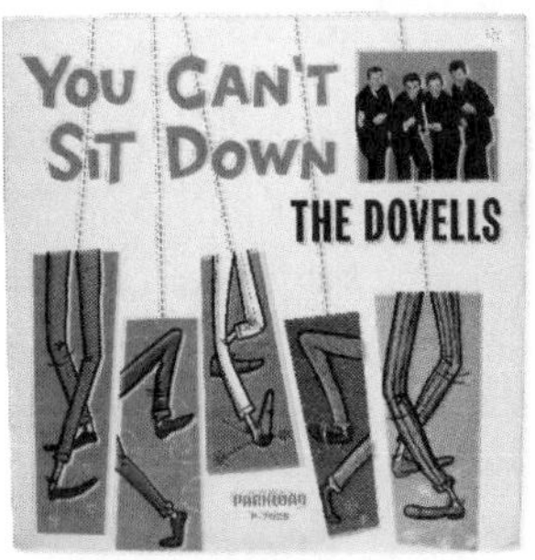

The Dovells, You Can't Sit Down, Parkway P 7025, 1963 .... **$50**

The Go-Go's, Swim with the Go-Go's, RCA Victor LPM-2930, 1964 .... **$25**

The Police, Synchronicity, A&M SP-3735, 1983, with gold, silver and bronze stripes on cover **$40**

The Shadows, Surfing With The Shadows, Atlantic SD 8089, 1963 .... **$300**

The Surfaris, Hit City '65, Decca DL 74614, 1965 .... **$40**

The Trashmen, Surfin' Bird, Garrett GA-200, 1964 .... **$220**

Soundtracks

Carousel, Decca DL 8003, 1949, original issue **$40**

House of Flowers, Columbia Masterworks OL 4969, 1954 .... **$40**

Dealers who set up at antiques shows sometimes remind their regular customers of an upcoming show by sending them a postcard provided by the show promoter. The card may specify that it be used for discount admission to the show. The dealer may add a personal note indicating he will be bringing a certain item that will be of interest to the customer.

Me and Juliet, RCA Victor LOC-1012, 1953 .... **$70**

Peter Pan, RCA Victor LOC-1019, 1954................... **$40**

SCIENTIFIC INSTRUMENTS

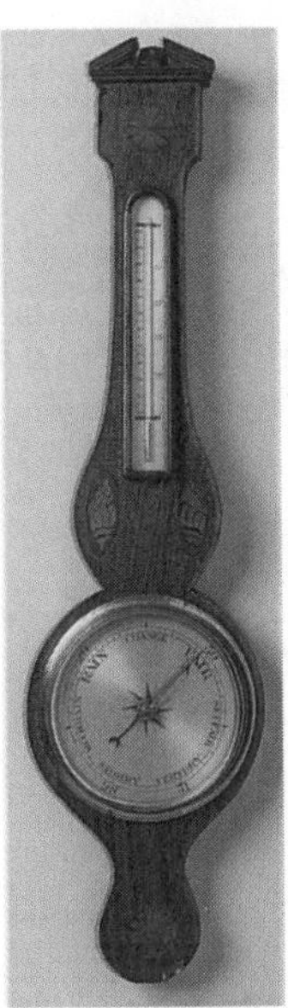

Barometer, banjo-style, inlaid mahogany, the broken-arch pediment above an inlaid rosette, the tall slender neck w/a glazed thermometer above two inlaid seashells, the lower circular silvered metal dial above another inlaid rosette, unmarked, old refinishing, minor veneer damage, probably England, 19th c., 38 1/2" h. **$316**

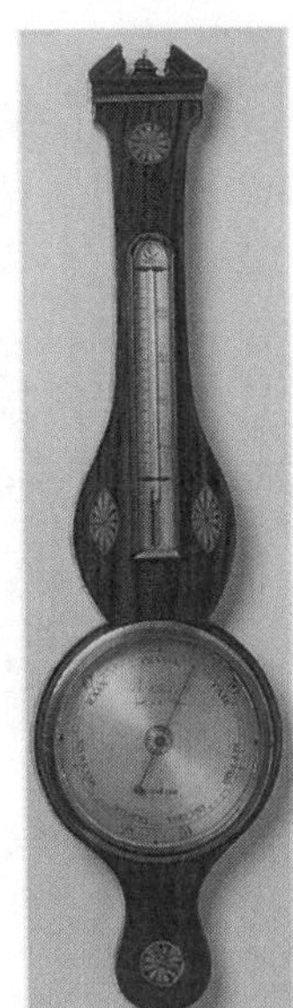

Barometer, banjo-style, inlaid mahogany, the broken-arch pediment above an inlaid rosette, the tall slender neck w/a glazed thermometer flanked by two inlaid paterae, the lower circular silvered metal dial labeled "F. Saltern & Co. London," above another inlaid rosette, thermometer damaged, some edge damage w/missing or replaced pieces of molding, England, 19th c., 38 1/2" h. **$546**

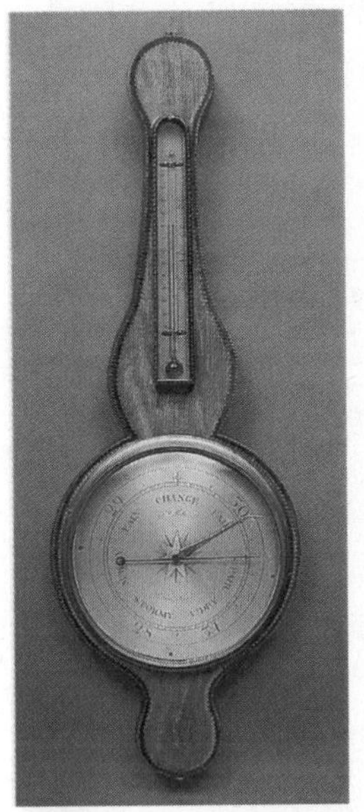

Barometer, banjo-style, inlaid satinwood, the rounded top & shaped throat mounted w/the thermometer panel above the large above the round silvered metal dial & rounded base drop,narrow mahogany banding around the whole case, dial marked by F. Molton, St. Law, Norwich, England, first half 19th c., minor loss to inlay, minor age crack, in base, 37" h. **$3,450**

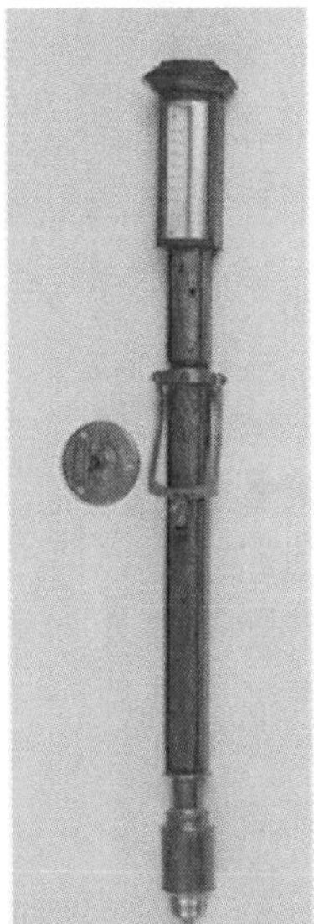

Barometer, stick-type, gimbeled marine-type, tall slender columnar mahogany case w/turned detail, ivory scale enclosed at the top, cylindrical brass cistern at the base & brass wall bracket, marked by James Bassnett, Liverpool, England, 19th c., mercury tube missing, 38" h. **$3,450**

Compass, cased model, round iron frame w/brass dial enclosed in a square mahogany case w/a hinged front window & top brass handle, a brass cylindrical oil lamp mounted on the side, ca. 1900, case 6 1/2" h. **$172**

Barometers

Stick-type

American, Simmons & Company, long narrow rectangular case w/ripple or piecrust border, Fenton, New York, 19th c. **$950**

English, Adie, rosewood case w/ stepped cornice, double vernier **$3,500**

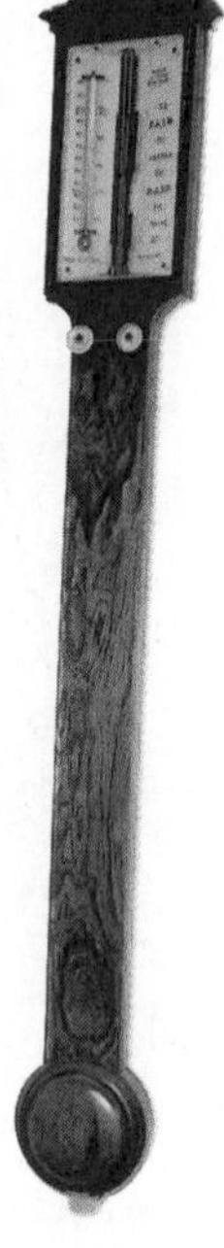

English, Admiral Fitzroy-type, marked on upper dial "Royal Polytechnic Barometer," top-of-the-line model, one of 12 types **$3,800**

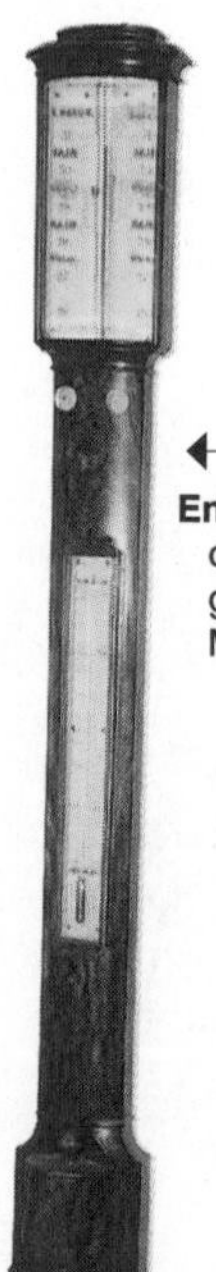

English, bow-front case w/beveled glass, double vernier, Mason of Dublin **$3,800-4,000**

English, Cremonini-Wolverhampton, dark oak case w/angled pediment centered by an urn finial above freestanding columns flanking the central thermometer over the lower case w/a large round dial **$1,800**

English, Fortin or Kew or laboratory-type, long wooden board w/milk glass inset at top **$1,000**

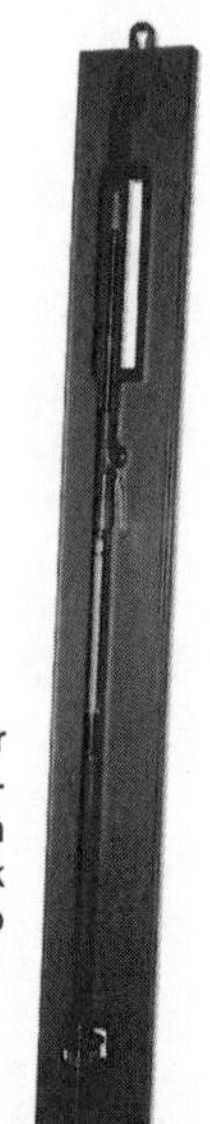

SCRIMSHAW

Scrimshaw is a folk art byproduct of the 19th century American whaling industry. Intricately carved and engraved pieces of whalebone, whale's teeth and walrus tusks were produced by whalers during their spare time at sea. In recent years numerous fine grade hard plastic reproductions have appeared on the market, so the novice collector must use caution to distinguish these from the rare originals.

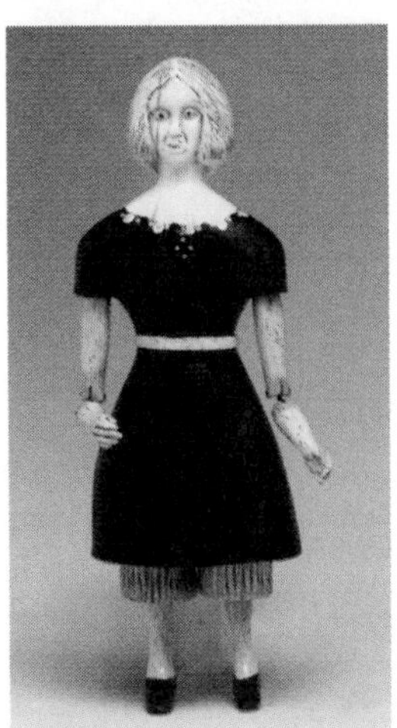

Doll, articulated figure of a lady w/ moveable lower arms, hardwood dress & shoes, inlaid collar & necklace, first half 20th c., 7 1/4" h. **$1,673**

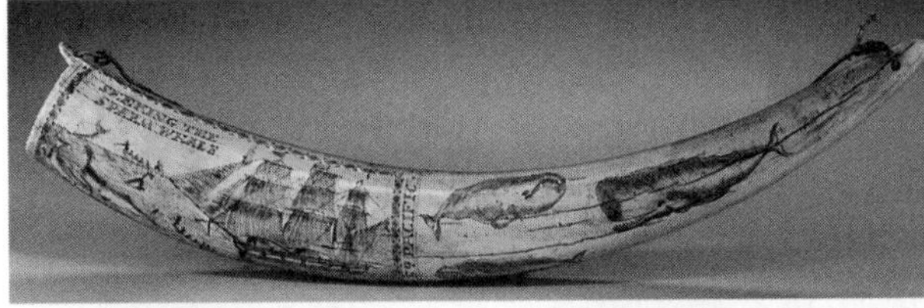

Walrus tusk, engraved on the left end w/a detailed whaling scene inscribed "Seeking The Sperm Whale" & "So. Pacific," engraved on the right end w/three large whales, probably American, 19th c., 17" l. **$4,541**

Before hiring an auctioneer, attend one of his auctions and observe him in action. The auctioneer's performance at the sale is not the only consideration, but it is one of the most important. Does the auctioneer have command over the auction and does he work in a professional manner? Is the auction well-attended? If there is any question about the auctioneer's integrity, look for someone else.

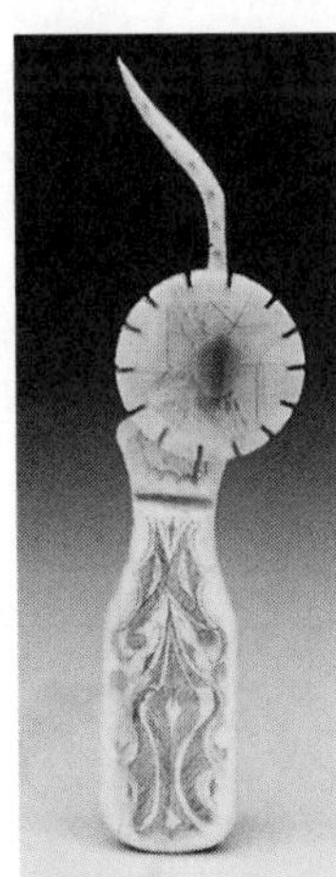

Pie crimper primitive style, a flattened oblong handle w/a long slender curved & pointed tip, mounted w/a crude notched wheel, the handle engraved w/ ornate undulating scrolls, cross-hatching on the wheel, the edge w/some dot-sized decoration & "Grace Sewell," 19th c., 5 3/4" l. **$518**

Whale's teeth, a pair, each engraved w/the figure of a Victorian lady in fancy dress, perhaps showing the same lady in daytime & evening dress, w/an inlaid row of baleen beads around the bases, polychrome highlights, late 19th c., 6 3/4" h., pr. **$15,535**

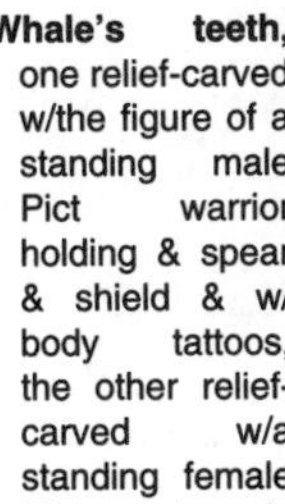

Whale's teeth, one relief-carved w/the figure of a standing male Pict warrior holding & spear & shield & w/ body tattoos, the other relief-carved w/a standing female Pict warrior w/body tattoos & holding a spear, mounted on rosewood stands, a small chip on the tip of one, American or Scottish, attributed to B. Bifer, 19th c., without the base 7" h., pr. **$27,485**

Whale's tooth, engraved w/a band of stars above a port scene inscribed "Boston," the back w/ a whaling scene, mounted on a silver base stamped "R.H. & H. Sterling," 19th c., 4 1/2" h. **$1,673**

Whale's tooth, engraved w/a band showing two horse-drawn carriages above a three-masted ship under full sail, the reverse w/the figure of a woman in fancy dress, highlighted w/polychrome, small chip at tip, base cracks, 19th c., 6 3/4" h. **$5,019**

Whale's tooth, large tooth engraved w/a scene of an amorous young couple w/tinted green & red clothing, mid-19th c, 7 1/2" l. **$1,673**

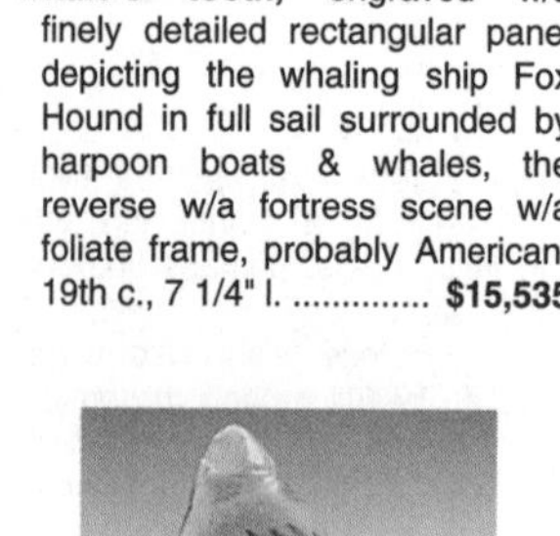

Whale's tooth, engraved w/a finely detailed rectangular panel depicting the whaling ship Fox Hound in full sail surrounded by harpoon boats & whales, the reverse w/a fortress scene w/a foliate frame, probably American, 19th c., 7 1/4" l. **$15,535**

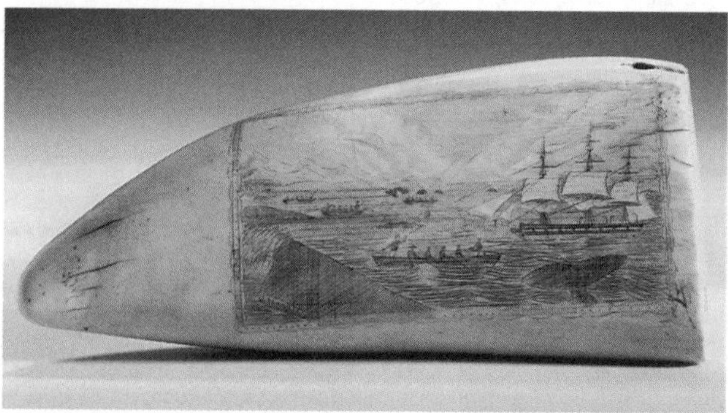

Whale's tooth, one side engraved w/a scene of an amorous couple framed by leafy branches, the reverse w/a three-masted ship in full sail flying the American flag (?) also framed by leafy branches, small old chip on tip, 19th c., 4 7/8" h. **$8,604**

Whale's tooth, engraved w/an elaborate landscape w/a large factory complex behind a row of trees & a harbor in the distance, inscribed "New England Screw Co. Providence," color-tinted, mid-19th c., 7 1/8" l. **$7,170**

TEXTILES

Needlework Pictures

Biblical scene, silk, chenille, watercolor & pencil, rectangular w/oval panel depicting the story of finding Moses in the bulrushes, a classically dressed woman standing over a basket containing the baby against a background of the river, trees, rolling landscape & blue sky, watercolor used for the woman's features, water & sky, unfinished, America, ca. 1806, 15 3/4 x 17 3/4" **$1,410**

Classical urn, silk, a scene of a large two-handled classical urn on a rectangular plinth, overflowing w/ colorful flowers, worked in shades of green, cream, brown, blue & pink silk thread on a cream silk ground, monogram on the plinth, within a rectangular reverse-painted black glass matte & giltwood shadowbox frame, 19th c., 17 5/8 x 22 7/8" (distress & foxing on ground) **$201**

Landscape with academy building, silk embroidery w/the building in gold thread w/the front door open & a horse & carriage approaching, rolling hills & fields in the foreground, painted background w/rolling hills & trees below a wide blue sky w/a single white cloud, monogrammed in lower left "EM," worked by Elizabeth Motter, Sr., St. Joseph's Academy, Emmitsburg, Maryland, retains original giltwood frame & original glass inscribed "View of Saint Joseph's Near Emmitsburg - E. Motter 1825," 17 x 23 3/4" **$50,190**

Coat of arms, rectangular, silk, gold & silver metallic thread, gold metallic cord & ink on silk, raised-work spread-winged eagle at top holding swagged floral garland in beak, over raised-work fish crest directly above the center green velvet shield showing raised-work rampant lion, the shield partly surrounded by crossed palm fronds w/encircling banner reading "REGARD - WILLIAMS - THE END" in ink above script initials "NGW," another swagged floral garland at the bottom, framed, America, ca. 1800-1810, tears, minor stains, 12 5/8 x 15 3/4" **$18,800**

Coat of arms, square, silk, gold & silver metallic thread & cord on silk, small figure of a lion at top standing over elaborate scroll, chains looping from the ends of the scroll & flanking a center shield decorated w/panels of roses, fleur-de-lis & crosses, scrolling leaves & a banner below reading "By The Name of Howard," signed "Lucy Howard" in lower right, w/related documents, America, 1806, 23 1/4" sq. **$23,500**

Landscape, a large landscape scene worked in chenille yarn of two men duck hunting from a small boat in a lake w/trees, houses & hills in the background, signed "Angelique L.C. Picot aged 9 Richmond 1 1819," framed, 19 x 19 1/2" (some water staining, tears to ground) **$7,475**

Landscape with lady, embroidered silk, a shepherdess in 18th c. costume seated overlooking a stream w/a cottage & trees in the background, watercolored silk sky & details, w/original gold-banded black liner in a modern frame, England, ca. 1810, image 16 x 18 3/4" **$633**

Old Testament story, brightly colored wool cross-stitch on a linen ground, the scene w/three angels announcing to Abraham that he & his wife, Sarah, in their old age, would soon conceive & have a son, embellished w/various animals including rabbits, a squirrel, birds & a dog, America or England, 18th c., framed, 16 7/8 x 18" ... **$3,290**

Memorial picture, silk, rectangular, depicting a willow tree overhanging two monuments, one reading "Sacred to the Memory of Mrs. Margery Clark who died Nov. 26th 1808 in the 39th year of her age," the other "Sacred to the Memory of Mr. John Clark who died March 19th 1814 in the 69th year of his age," each monument topped w/arching willow branch, spread-winged bird & the word "Hope," each base w/"MEMENTO MORI," a church, pine tree & flowers in gold, red & green at the sides, a crescent moon & stars in the sky above, "Wrought by Sarah Goodridge aged fourteen Years" at the bottom of the picture, America, early 19th c., 18 7/8 x 22" framed **$3,055**

Romantic couple, silk thread on silk ground, rectangular w/oval panel depicting woman wearing an empire-waist dress & man wearing top hat & cutaway coat in pastoral setting, the couple holding a flowering vine & wreath, a small dog at the woman's feet, painted facial features & sky, indistinct inscription in lower left corner, in molded & gilded frame, America, 1806, 16 1/2 x 19 1/2" **$5,288**

Memorial scene, depicting a woman holding a book beside a monument inscribed "Werter," mixed media w/cut-out wool felt monument, figure & background, watercolor on paper head & hands, wool & silk threads, oval format in giltwood frame, early 19th c., scene 12 3/4" d. .. **$1,175**

Shepherdess & young man, solid stitches on silk ground, rectangular, depicting a young woman dressed in white & pale yellow & holding shepherd's crook standing next to man wearing cutaway coat & playing flute, the couple flanked by two trees, five sheep in the background, painted facial features & sky, in molded & gilded frame, America, early 19th c., 13 1/4 x 14 1/2" **$5,288**

←

Patriotic, square, depicting gold & white eagle flying w/draped tasseled American flag against a sunburst, all on white silk ground, Oriental export, grain painted frame, some brown spots to background, 19 1/2" sq. **$259**

Quilts

Amish Double Nine-Patch patt., in shades of purple, red, grey & blue w/large corner blocks, Lancaster County, rayon & crepe wool, Pennsylvania, ca. 1930-40, 83 1/2" sq. **$403**

Amish Triple Irish Chain patt., in dark brown highlighted by bright blue, red & purple, cotton, Holmes County, Ohio, ca. 1981, 82" sq.................. **$259**

Appliqued Blackberry & Vine patt., sixteen white blocks each w/a vine in aqua & pendant blackberries, each block separated by an aqua grid also forming the border, white cotton backing w/intricate quilting, minor stain, 82 x 86" (ILLUS. upper right with grouping of other quilts & two coverlets) **$3,995**

Appliqued Oak Leaf patt., sixteen blocks w/a white ground decorated w/a four-leaf cross-form cluster w/square & cross at the center of each, hand-stitched, 68 x 76" **$259**

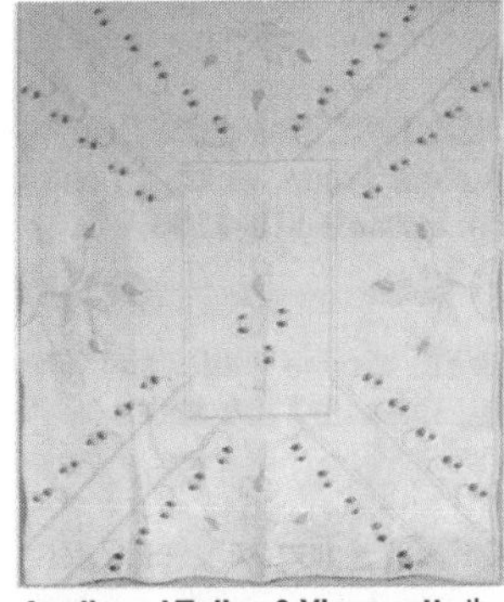

Appliqued Tulips & Vines patt., the sides w/large angled panels w/pink tulips on green leafy stems, border bands of small blue blossoms & yellow bordering, probably 20th c., faded & stained, 76 x 88" **$150**

> Many antique show managers guarantee that everything their dealers sell will be as represented. Buyers should expect to receive a brief but accurate description of the item, its approximate age and sale price. If a problem arises, you may be able to get your money back, but you must have a receipt.

Appliqued Vining Floral patt., the white ground hand-stitched w/a large arched central cluster of vining blue, yellow & red flowers & berries on leafy green vines, matching designs in each corner, scalloped border, 72 x 88" .. **$219**

Crib quilt, crazy quilt-style, rectangular, composed of a wide variety of random blocks in various materials, many finely embroidered w/roses, flowers, fans & other designs, a narrow border band of green four-leaf clusters, four corner blocks embroidered "To Edna - From Grandma - Dec. 25 - 1882," scattered losses, 35 x 52" **$2,070**

Baltimore-style quilt, appliqued in the center w/a large flower-filled basket framed w/a large leafy floral wreath within a narrow rectangular border, a boldly scalloped outer border w/green scallops each enclosing colorful floral swags, monogrammed near center, finely stitched w/eleven stitches per square inch, probably Baltimore, Maryland, ca. 1830 .... **$2,588**

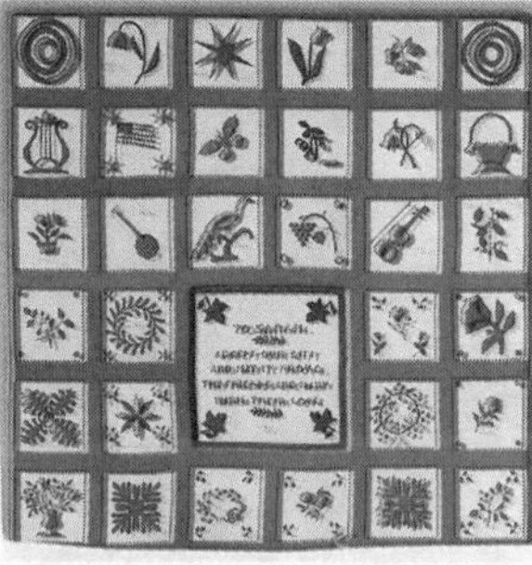

Friendship quilt top, appliquèd cotton, forty-eight blocks of red, blue & green fabrics appliquèd to white ground & separated by red cotton grid, decorated w/ naturalistic, patriotic, geometric & musical instrument designs including flowers, fruit, butterfly, peacock, flag, violin, circles & stars, the large central square w/appliquèd lettering reading "To Sarah - Accept our gift - and may it prove - thy friends are many - warm their love," & embroidered signature of "Amanda Birdsell Apr 20th, 1858," many squares w/embroidered & pen & ink signatures, mounted on wooden frame, 65 1/2 x 86" **$4,113**

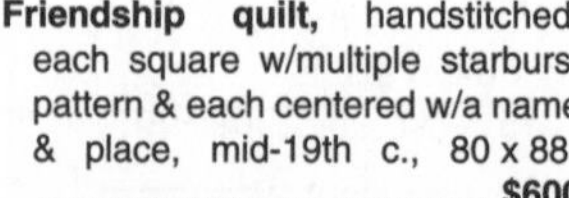

Friendship quilt, handstitched, each square w/multiple starburst pattern & each centered w/a name & place, mid-19th c., 80 x 88" **$600**

Crazy quilt, embroidered silk & velvet, multicolored design embellished w/variety of embroidery stitched & painted motifs, black satin border, stitched date of "1885," America, 64" sq. **$1,293**

Pictorial quilt, pieced cotton, center image of three-masted ship "Mary Edson" constructed of pieced rose pink calico segments on brown calico ground w/applied & embroidered silk American flag, silk magenta pennant reading "Mary Edson," blue silk flag w/thirty stars, & white silk flag embroidered "8215," the corners decorated w/hexagonal rose-pink calico rosettes, the whole bordered in same rose calico fabric, white cotton backing, made by Hope Atkins Howes, America, third quarter 19th c., 72 x 90" **$1,528**

Pieced pinwheels pattern, rows of small four-arm pinwheels arranged to form a design of blocks & half-blocks within a sawtooth inner & outer border band, worked in red print blocks on white, finely quilted ground w/trapunto border w/ baskets of flowers & meandering feather stitch, 19th c., 108 x 112" (overall wear, red slightly faded, small hanging holes in corners, stains).................................. **$770**

Pieced Tennessee Trail or Rattlesnake patt., composed of twelve large white & red lobed designs alternating w/smaller red & white crosses in squares, early 20th c., 70 x 86" **$460**

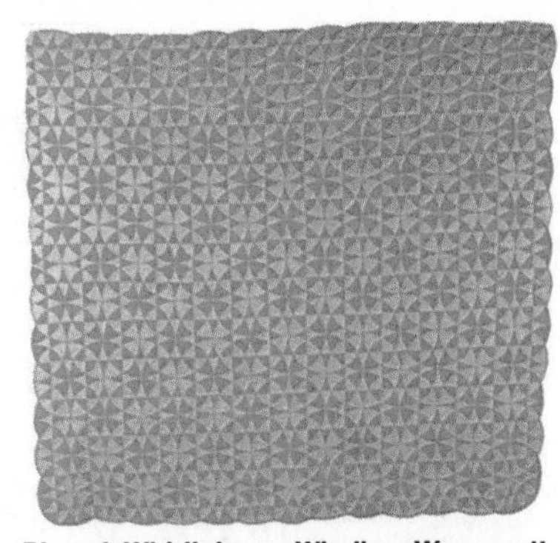

Pieced Whirligig or Winding Ways patt., overall design of small crosses alternating in red on fawn or fawn on red, scalloped border, early 20th c., 78 x 85" **$460**

"Scenes of Childhood" quilt, embroidered & appliquèd cotton, a center panel w/three figural vignettes based on illustrations from popular publications of the day w/captions & facial features inscribed in ink, panels on either side w/figures of two dogs, a cat & a cow, each corner w/a cornucopia issuing budding flowers, all worked in calico printed cotton in shades of red, green, pink & brown, green calico border, all appliquèd to a white woven cotton ground quilted w/leaf & diagonal line stitching, mounted & enclosed in Plexiglas frame, comes w/copy of book Small Endearments: Nineteenth-century Quilts For Children and Dolls, in which it appears, America, last quarter 19th c., 35 x 37" **$30,550**

Stars of Bethlehem pattern, composed of various diamond-shaped patches w/large potted flowering plants between each of the eight star points, various plain & printed cottons on a white ground, 19th c., 85 x 88" (staining, fading, scattered fiber wear)..................... **$748**

Union quilt, appliquèd & pieced cotton, central thirteen-star flag w/spread-winged eagles in each corner, all in red, white & blue cotton fabric on white field, all enclosed in red, white & blue striped border, white cotton binding & backing, overlapping circle, rosette & diagonal line quilt stitching, probably Pennsylvania, ca. 1915, 68 x 75" **$9,988**

When storing quilts, roll them rather than folding them, as the folded areas can stretch and weaken the fabric and can cause permanent creases. Store the rolled quilts in cloth bags, which will protect them from dust but also allow them to breathe. Plastic bags seal in moisture, which could cause mold or mildew.

Samplers

Alphabet & numerals above a floral bouquet, a diamond lattice border & signed at the bottom "L. Palmire 1864," color fading, staining to foundation **$345**

Alphabets & geometric designs, long narrow rectangle w/ rows of alphabets across the top, a long section w/ stylized diamond designs & flowers worked in gold, green, blue & black silk threads on a linen ground, scattered various initials & dated 1746, w/a paper label inscribed "Worked by Sarah Riddell," possibly Virginia, 1746, 10 x 19" **$10,158**

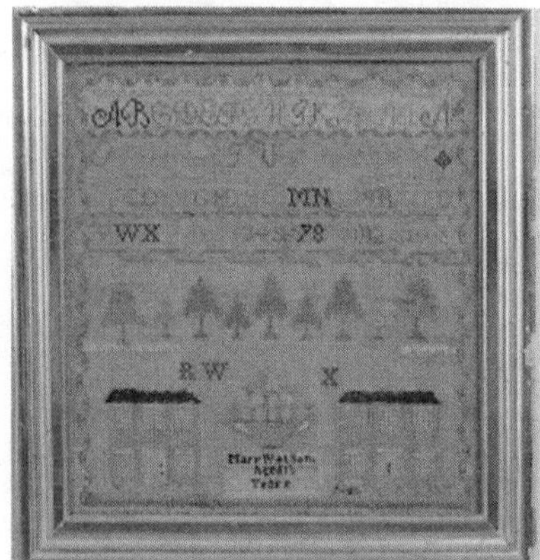

Alphabets & numerals, two alphabet rows & one numeric row, w/central row of trees of various sizes, bottom w/central basket of fruit or flowers over rectangular box w/"Mary Watson aged 16 years," flanked by colonial houses w/black roofs, double chimneys, five twelve-pane windows & front doors w/iron latches, strawberry-type vine border, presently mounted on fine linen affixed to light cardboard in lemon gold molded frame, probably Connecticut, 15 x 16" **$3,738**

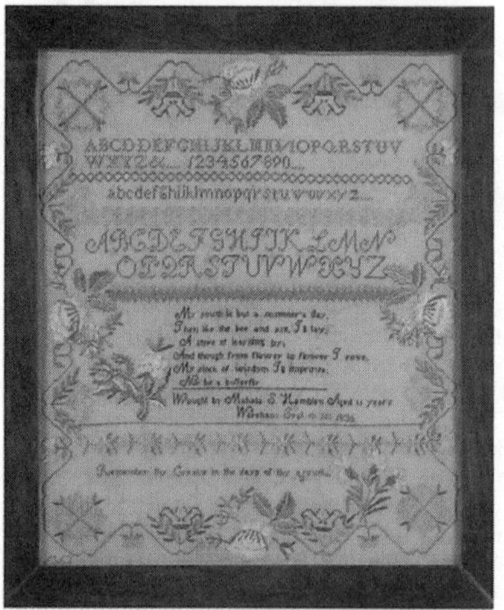

Alphabets & pious verse, silk & wool blue, white, yellow & green thread on linen, alphabet panels in upper half over verse reading "My youth is but a summer's day - Then like the bee and ant, I'll lay - A stove of learning by - And though from flower to flower I rove - My stock of wisdom I'll improve - Not be a butterfly" & "Wrought by Mahala S. Hamblen Aged 11 years Wareham Sept th 1st 1836," surrounded by floral border, framed, 17 5/8 x 21" **$8,813**

Alphabets & pious verse, silk thread on linen, alphabet panels at top under central basket of flowers & over verse reading "Remark my soul the narrow bound - Of the revolving year - How swift the weeks complete their round - How short the months appear - So fast eternity comes on - And that important day - When all the work my hands have done - Gods judgment will survey," "Wrought by Sarah Goodridge aged thirteen years" at bottom under depiction of two-story house w/double chimneys & flanked by pine trees, elaborate floral vine borders on each side, comes w/several items pertaining to Sarah Goodridge, New Hampshire, 1818, 18 7/8 x 19" framed **$3,173**

Alphabets, pious verse & landscape, finely stitched in shades of ivory, gold, green & some red silk thread on a linen ground, a large center rectangular border around the alphabets & pious verse w/the inscription "Mary B. Nath - Aged 11 Years - July 1825," all above a pair of arching willow trees, one over a memorial monument, & flanking a basket filled w/a large spray of flowers, an undulating strawberry vine border up the sides & across the top, mahogany veneer frame, attributed to coastal Maine, 18 3/4 x 19 1/2" **$6,038**

Alphabets, pious verse & landscape, silk threads on a linen ground, a central rectangular panel of alphabets above a pious verse & inscribed by Lucy Parham, born in 1811 & wrought in her 11th year, the lower border w/a landscape showing a two-story home flanked by leafy trees & small animals, each lower corner w/a large urn issuing leafy flowering vines up each side w/a flower-filled basket at the top center, by Lucy Parham, Tyngsboro, Massachusetts, 1822, toning, scattered stains, framed, 17 x 18" **$27,025**

Family tree, all stitched in silk including the gold background, a large slender tree w/leafy branches, inscribed w/various family members, Samuel & Grace Barnes, married October 22, 1774 at the bottom, the branches w/apples & the names of their eight children, the last being born in 1794, included are records of Samuel & Grace & her family line, stains, the greens w/bleeding, in mahogany flame veneer frame, 15 x 17" **$2,990**

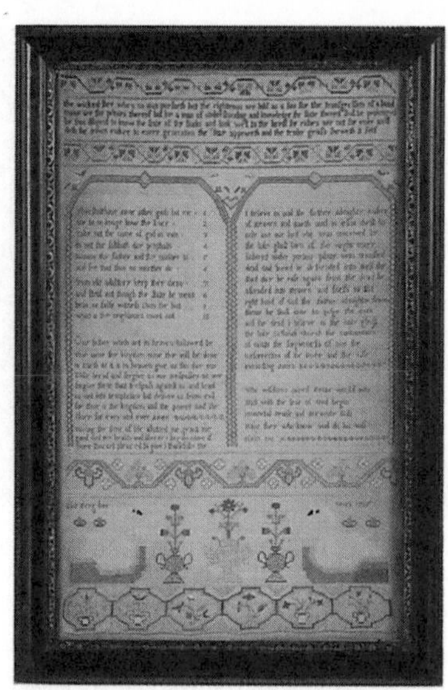

Pious verse & prayers, multicolored silk thread on linen, a pious verse over panels listing the Ten Commandments, the Lord's Prayer, the Apostle's Creed & a Psalm, floral & geometric borders accented w/ birds, hearts, swans, urns w/flowers, & crowns, signed "Eliz Berg her work 1735," 10 1/2 x 16 1/2" framed **$1,645**

Pictorial pious verse, silk thread on linen, the needlework centered by a house w/a fence & two trees & surrounded by various birds, flowers, butterflies, two verses, the signature "Susanna Stanley born October 24th __23," her parents' names, William & Rebecca Stanley, & the probable date the sampler was completed, "October 12, 1832," all enclosed in geometric floral border, probably Pennsylvania, thread losses, toning, staining, 15 3/4 x 22" **$2,233**

Pious verse & building, silk thread on linen ground, a central two-story brick house surrounded by fruit trees, birds, potted flowers, crowns & eight-pointed stars, over a pious verse & various potted flowers, trees, dogs, deer & birds, all enclosed by chain border & geometric strawberry vine, signed by "Charlotte Mussell 1839," framed, England, 15 1/2 x 12 7/8" **$1,645**

Pious verse, multicolored silk thread on linen ground, two pious verses at top & center, the bottom w/ central tree w/birds flanked by two small pine trees, deer, butterflies & two houses & surrounded by various potted flowers, baskets of fruit, birds & the figure of a man, all enclosed in geometric floral border, signed "Elizabeth Viner October The 13 1790," framed, probably England, 12 x 14 1/2" **$1,763**

TOOLS

Grandfather's old tool belt is no longer just a dust collector in the garage. From the wrenches, hammers and screwdrivers found inside to the catalog used to order them, tools and related items have become highly sought-after collectibles. Descriptions, pricing and photographs were supplied by Martin J. Donnelly Antique Tools.

Edged Tools

Axe blade, hand-wrought iron, wide blade tapering sharply to handle mount, stamped "Rotheval," early 19th c., 27 1/2" l. **$345**

Axe, copper's side-type, hand-wrought iron, stamped "Barton," mid-19th c., 16" l. **$46**

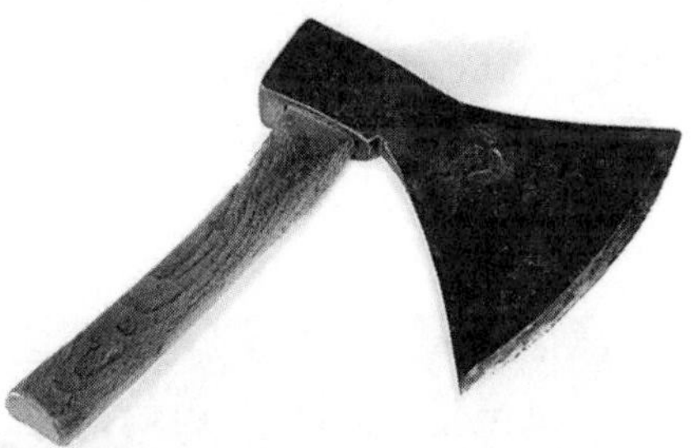

Axe, copper's side-type, hand-wrought iron, stamped "Rubin" w/wheat ears, 19th c., 14" l. **$69**

Champer knives, cooper's, hand-wrought iron w/turned wood handles, 19th c., 14" & 15 1/2" l., pr. **$46**

Planes & Scrapers

Bevel plane, brass framed w/walnut handle & nob, w/three interchangeable wood bottoms & blades w/varied radius, stamped name of owner, made by James Howarth, first half 20th c., 9 1/2" l., the set **$115**

Block plane, heavy gunmetal base w/walnut grips & wedges, brass wedge lock, blade stamped w/illegible trademark, 19th c., 7" l. **$69**

Block plane, maple base w/ivory upright front handle & blade wedge, stamped "S&S," probably early 19th c., 9" l. **$173**

Bullnose rebate plane, cast gunmetal w/ebony wedge, no blade, England, 19th c., 1 x 4 1/2" **$69**

Rabbet plane, steel shouldered rebate w/ebony wedge, mahogany slipcase w/stamped name of owner & also the maker, Spiers Ayr, early 19th c., 6" l. **$144**

Miscellaneous

Band saw, early hand-made upright style constructed of heavy oak timber w/iron hardware, twin 26" d. spoked wood wheels driven by a belted pulley, ca. 1900, 78" h. **$259**

Machinist's chest, walnut, a rectangular molded hinged top opening to a compartment w/a lock above a case w/four long, shallow drawers w/brass bail pulls, molded base, ca. 1900, 13 1/2 x 22", 14 1/2" h. **$230**

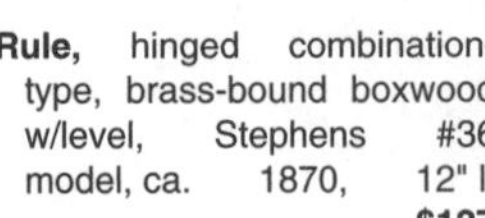

Rule, hinged combination-type, brass-bound boxwood w/level, Stephens #36 model, ca. 1870, 12" l. **$127**

TOYS

Automobile, cast metal, long stylized limousine in bright red w/white rubber tires, ca. 1930s, 5 1/2" l. **$175**

Automobile, cast spelter, four-door sedan, dark blue paint, rubber wheels, separate metal front grill w/letter "K," Tootsietoy, Model 746, original paint, ca. 1950, 6" l. **$85**

Bus, stamped metal, friction-operation, Airport Transportation Service in red on the side, dark blue & silver w/black rubber wheels, by Marx, ca. 1950s-60s, 6 1/2" l. **$145**

Delivery truck, cast iron, closed cab, orange body cast on the side "Milk - Cream," white rubber tires, ca. 1930s, 3 1/2" l. **$550**

Coal truck, pressed steel, red cab & yellow box w/red lettering, metal wheels, Wyandotte, ca. 1930s, very good condition, 11 1/4" l. **$195**

Automobile, cast spelter, early touring car, orange body & silver metal wheels, Tootsietoy, ca. 1930s, 2 3/4" l. **$125**

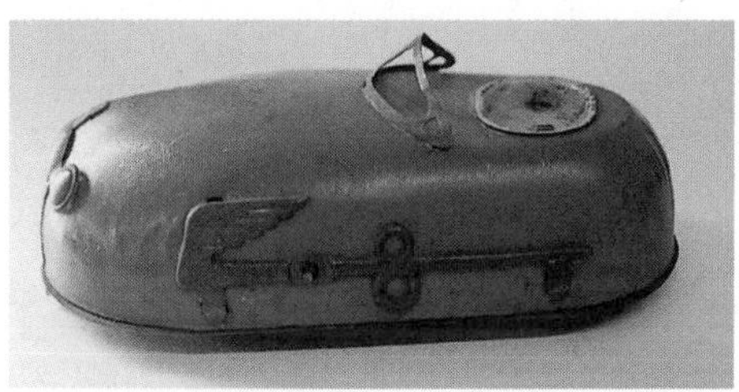

Automobile, pressed steel, friction-operated, stylized Art Deco style bubble-form body in red w/applied metal green, side exhaust pipes & windshield, original worn paint, driver missing, possibly by Wyandotte, 9" d. **$135**

Delivery truck, cast spelter, closed cab & open back, overall dark red w/decal on the side for Wrigley's Spearmint Gum, white rubber tires, Tootsietoy, Model 1010, ca. 1930s, 4 1/2" l. **$125**

Delivery truck, pressed steel, dark blue cab w/rare compartment printed in red, green, yellow, white & red, reads "Wyandotte Toys - Railway Express Agency," black rubber wheels, ca. 1930s, some overall wear, 6 1/2" l. **$65**

Delivery truck, pressed steel, friction-operated, white cab & white rear compartment w/red sides reading "Fanny Farmer Candies for Boys and Girls," black rubber tires, ca. 1950s, 8 1/4" l. **$145**

Fire ladder truck, cast metal, long red truck mounted w/removable steel ladders, black rubber tires, Hubley, marked "Made in USA," worn paint, ca. 1930s, 8 3/4" l. **$85**

Flatbed truck, die-cast spelter, yellow cab & red flatbed, black tires w/spare tire on roof turning front wheels, by Vilmer of Denmark, w/original box, ca. 1950s, 3 7/8" l. **$125**

Jeep, pressed steel, Army model w/two soldiers in seats & one in the rear aiming the large antiaircraft gun, dark green w/white trim, black tires, by Marx, ca. 1950s, 7 1/2" l. **$375**

Pickup truck, cast spelter, red cab & open rear compartment, on white rubber wheels, Tootsietoy, ca. 1930s, 5 3/4" l. **$95**

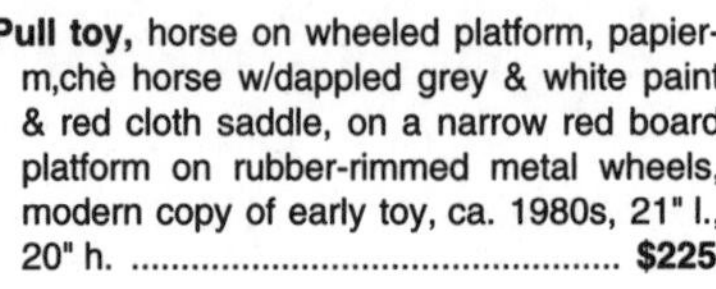

Pull toy, horse on wheeled platform, papier-m,chè horse w/dappled grey & white paint & red cloth saddle, on a narrow red board platform on rubber-rimmed metal wheels, modern copy of early toy, ca. 1980s, 21" l., 20" h. **$225**

Race car, cast aluminum, red body w/single silver side exhaust pipe, black rubber wheels, marked on the inside "Thimbledrome Special L.M. Cox Mfg. Co., Santa Ana, Calif.," worn paint, ca. 1950s, 8 3/4" l. **$120**

Race car, friction-operated, "Speed King" racer w/red & green body w/large black rubber wheels, marked "San - Made in Japan," ca. 1950s, 4 3/4" l. ... **$175**

Race car, stamped metal, long body in bright yellow & red, head of driver at top, large black & red metal wheels, ca. 1930s, slightly worn & rusted, 12 3/4" l. **$160**

Soldier on motorcycle, stamped metal, friction-powered, seated soldier w/machine gun, colorfully printed, made in Japan, ca. 1950s, 2 x 5 1/2", 3 3/4" h. **$375**

Stake truck, die-cast metal, dark green cab w/ yellow flatbed, black tires w/yellow hubcaps, spare tire on roof of cab turns front wheels, made in Denmark by Vilmer, ca. 1950s, 3 7/8" l. ... **$95**

Tanker truck, cast spelter, original dark green paint, vulcanized white rubber tires, American-made, style No. 78, ca. 1930s, 3 3/4" l. .... **$**

Toy soldier, cast lead, kneeling soldier operating field radio, wearing a separate steel helmet, worn brown paint, ca. 1930s, 2 1/4" h. **$35**

←

→

Toy soldier, cast lead, parachuting & holding rifle, brown w/silver trim, marked "M" in a circle & "Made in USA - 102," ca. 1930s, 3 1/2" h. **$60**

Toy soldier, cast lead, reclining soldier w/ machine gun, brown & silver, marked "Made in USA - 728," ca. 1930s, 4 3/8" l. **$29**

Toy soldier, cast lead, soldier pointing a searchlight, brown w/silver trim, marked "Made in USA," ca. 1930s, 2 1/2" h. **$36**

Toy soldier, cast lead, standing soldier blowing bugle, brown w/silver trim, green base, ca. 1930s, 3" h. **$22**

Toy soldier, cast lead, standing soldier leading a charge, separate steel helmet, worn brown paint, ca. 1930s, 3 1/2" h. **$23**

Toy soldiers, Britains mounted cavalry set, brown horses w/riders wearing red uniforms, in original box, first half 20th c., each figure 3" h., the set **$285**

Tractor, cast spelter, stylized red body & driver, white rubber tires, marked "Made in USA," some paint wear, ca. 1930s, 2 3/4" l. **$65**

Train accessory, coal elevator, O-gauge, grey & yellow w/red roof, operating, Lionel No. 97, 1941 .... **$275**

Train car, caboose, O-gauge, orange, maroon, yellow & black w/brass journals, Ives No. 1712, 1932 .... **$90**

Train accessory, icing station, white & red on brown base, Lionel No. 352, 1955-57 ... **$250**

Train locomotive, engine, O-gauge, GG1, 4-6-6-4, tuscan, gold "Pennsylvania" on side, Lionel No. 2340, scarce, 1955 .... **$1,350**

Train locomotive, engine, switcher & caboose, blue w/"Alaska Railroad" in yellow lettering, Lionel No. 614 (engine) & 6027 (caboose), 1959-60 .... **$425**

Train set: "The General #3" engine & tender, "W.&A.R.R." baggage car, "W.&A.R.R." passenger car, "W.&A.R.R." flat car w/horses; O-gauge, Lionel No. 8701 engine & tender, No. 9551 baggage car, No. 9552 passenger car, No. 9553 flat car w/horses, 1978-80, the set **$275**

Train set: steam engine, combination car, vista dome car, observation car; S- gauge, black engine & tender, cars all silver, American Flyer No. 322 engine, No. 660 combination car, No. 662 vista dome car, No. 663 observation car, 1950-52, the set **$420**

Truck, cast iron, stake-type w/closed cab & rails in the back, worn yellow paint, white vulcanized rubber tires, comes apart w/wire connections for chassis & frame, ca. 1930s, 3 3/8" l. **$150**

Truck, pressed steel, flatbed-type, red cab w/low-sided yellow stake back, black rubber tires, sign on cab door reading "Tri-State Lumber Co.," by Marx, made in Japan, ca. 1950s, 5" l. **$95**

Truck, pressed steel, friction-operated, flatbed rocket-carrying truck, black body w/rubber tires, mounted w/a red & white rocket marked "X-18," Cragston, Japan, w/original box, ca. 1950s, 9 1/2" l. **$250**

Truck set, cast spelter, open-cab orange truck w/three detachable back beds in various colors, in original colorfully printed box w/ label reading "Tootsietoy Truck Set," ca. 1930s, box 3 x 3 5/8", the set **$700**

Wagon, cast iron, horse-drawn stake wagon w/driver, red wagon on black metal spoked wheels, pulled by a white & black horse, early 20th c., 10 1/4" l. **$395**

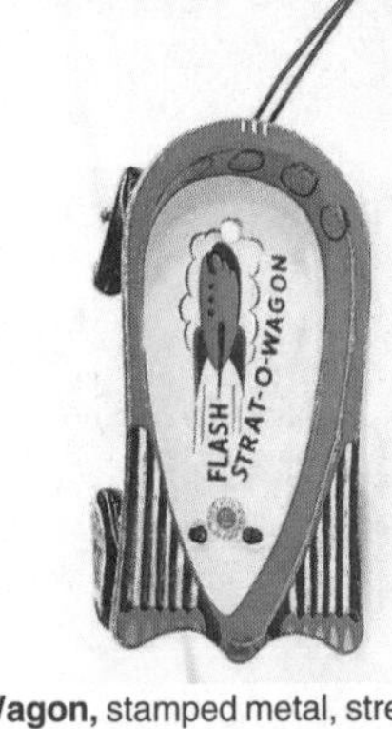

Wagon, stamped metal, streamlined bullet-shaped body printed in red, white & blue, the interior showing spaceship & reading "Flash Strat-O-Wagon," black wheels, wire bail pull handle, Wyandotte, ca. 1930s, 9 1/2" l. **$115**

Windup tin "G.I. Joe & the K-9 Pups," light green w/red & yellow trim, Unique Art Mfg. Co., ca. 1930s, 9" h. **$265**

Windup tin "Jumpin Jeep," four riders dressed in yellow in a green & yellow jeep w/oversized rear wheels & small front wheels, Marx, ca. 1940s, fine condition, 5 1/2" l. **$245**

Windup tin 1915 Ford Touring Car, dark grey exterior & red interior, black metal wheels, by Banda Baby, Japan, 1950s, mint in original box, car 7" l. **$425**

The paint on tin toys can easily be scratched by dust wiped across the surface, so be sure to wash carefully with a damp cloth. Even better, store a tin toy in a ventilated display case to prevent dust from accumulating.

Windup tin beetle pulling oak leaf, a large red stag beetle pulling a large yellow oak leaf steered by a monkey, w/two squirrels on the leaf, marked "TPS - Made in Japan," ca. 1950s, 11 1/2" l. **$275**

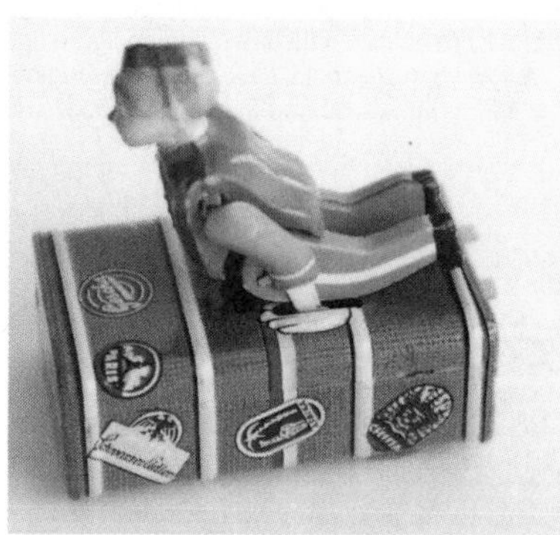

Windup tin bellhop on steamer trunk, brown trunk w/white bands, bellhop in blue outfit, bellhop first pushes then jumps on the trunk when wound, marked "Gescha. 667474 - 57-1 - Made in U.S. Zone Germany," 3" l., 2 3/4" h. **$295**

Windup tin boy on sled, large white sled w/blue top, a body dressed in a red snowsuit at the back, marked "Gescha. 57/3 - Made in U.S. Zone Germany," 1950s, 4 1/2" l. **$395**

Windup tin circus car, red vintage auto printed w/figures inside including a clown, musicians & ringmaster, black & red metal wheels, stack on roof goes up & down when wound, marked "KO Made in Japan," 1950s, near mint in original box, 5" l. **$365**

Windup tin fighting roosters, two facing birds mounted on small platforms raised on pairs of wheels & joined by a central flexible metal rod, made in Japan, ca. 1950s, 6" l. **$145**

Windup tin fire chief's car, red & white sedan w/ yellow lettering, black rubber wheels, ca. 1950, 6" l. **$95**

Windup tin fire ladder truck, red body w/open yellow back, black hard rubber tires, a Walt Reach Toy by Courtland, ca. 1950s, 8 3/4" l. **$225**

Windup tin Indian in canoe, a large white canoe w/ black rim holds a dark brown Indian figure operating yellow oars, Arnold, ca. 1930s, w/original box, 8 1/2" l. **$1,495**

Windup tin speedboat, long tapering red body w/wood-grained top, windup key at top rear, Ohio Art, ca. 1950s, 14 1/4" l. **$75**

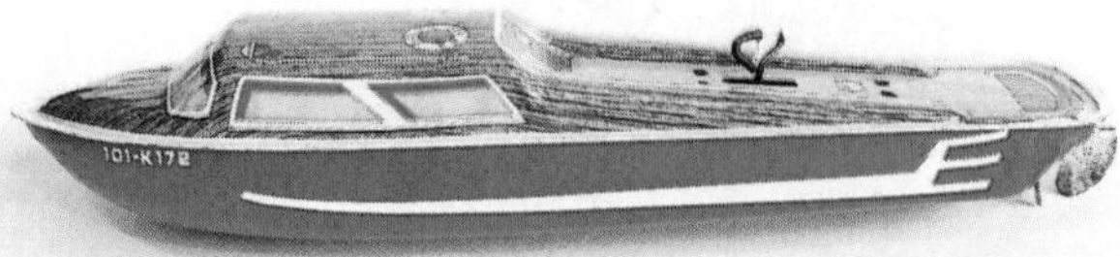

Windup tin steam engine, large model of an early steam engine in red & green, large metal wheels, probably made in Germany, early 20th c., smokestack missing, 6 1/2" l., 4 1/2" h. **$75**

Windup tin waterwheel & squirrel, long base w/lobed ends centered by a large red waterwheel, figure of a squirrel rolling around the track & through the wheel, marked "K," made in Japan, w/original box, 1950s, overall 20" l., 6 1/2" h. **$265**

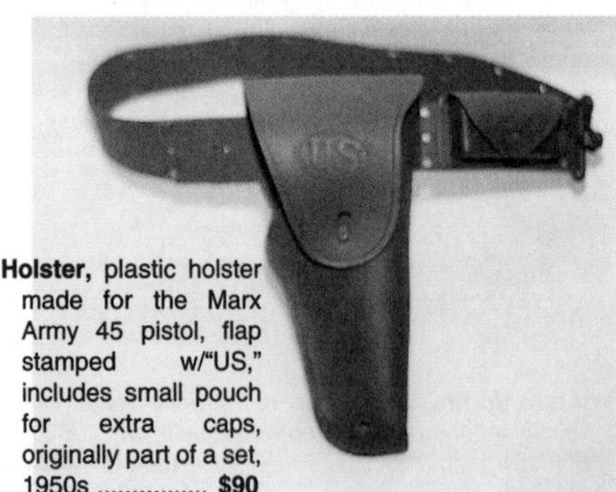

Holster, plastic holster made for the Marx Army 45 pistol, flap stamped w/"US," includes small pouch for extra caps, originally part of a set, 1950s **$90**

Pistol set, miniature Army 45 pistol, Marx, New York, New York, 1950s, 2 1/4 x 3 1/2", other models in the series include a Civil War era pistol, a Western Plains era saddle rifle & a Tommy gun, each set in original package (ILLUS. of Army 45 pistol)..................... **$125**

Pistol set, pistol & black plastic belt & holster, small size, maker unknown, 7" l. **$5**

Pistol, cast-metal w/white plastic grip, embossed w/ designs of cactus & other Western motifs, pushing down release lever opens cap compartment, unknown maker, 1950s **$40**

Pistol, detective pistol, cast-metal body w/brown plastic handle, front release on barrel opens cap compartment, Ideal, 1960s **$20**

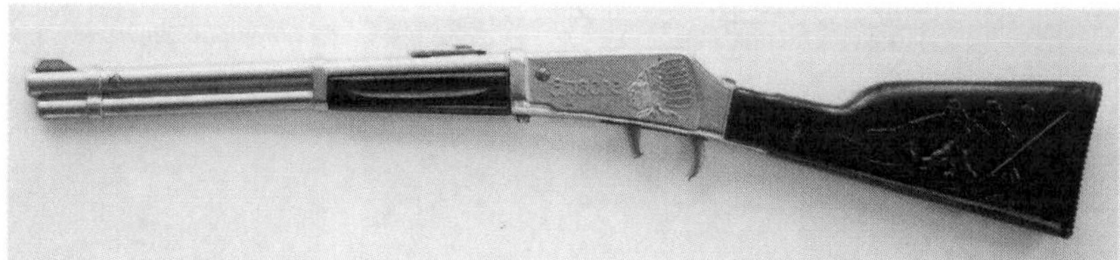

Rifle, "Apache" cap rifle, small size, metal body w/plastic handle grip, made to resemble a Winchester repeating rifle, side of body embossed w/the word "Apache" & a bust portrait of a Native American chief, the handle molded w/images of cattle & horse, 1950s, 10 1/2" l. **$7**

Rifle, BB rifle, black metal barrel & wooden stock stamped "Made in England," ca. 1940, overall 23 1/2" l. **$30**

Rifle, "Buck Jones Special - Daisy Air Rifle - No. 107," special store item sold by Daisy in Plymouth, Michigan, stock of rifle w/compass & sundial, 1936 .... **$300**

Rifle, Lone Ranger carbine-rifle, gray plastic repeating cap rifle, cap magazine dropping down for inserting roll of caps, character's name on the stock, Louis Marx, 1950s, 26" l. **$225**

Rifle, Roy Rogers carbine-rifle, gray plastic repeating cap rifle, cap magazine dropping down for inserting roll of caps, character's name on the stock, Louis Marx, 1950s, 26" l. **$225**

Germany was a major toy producer in the 19th and early 20th century. It was well known for high quality dolls, handmade marbles, tinplate and pull toys. Its numerous skilled workers could produce huge volumes at low cost for export.

Eagle Eye Man of Action, w/moving eyes, No. 7277, mint in package, 1976 .... **$180**

Land Adventurer, w/Kung Fu grip, No. 7280, in box, 1974, box damaged **$148**

Man of Action, w/lifelike hair, No. 7500, in box, 1970, no dog tags or paperwork, box damaged **$85**

Adventure Team Desert Explorer outfit, shorts & safari-style shirt, mint in package **$55**

Loose clothing w/GI Joe tags: trousers, two tops, one camouflage, pair of boots, all **$27**

Marine Demolition accessory set, w/mine detector, No. 7730, mint in package, 1966 .... **$260**

Foot locker, wood w/cardboard sleeve, hinged lid featuring name, rank & serial number in stencil-style type, strap handle on either side, 1964 .... **$202**

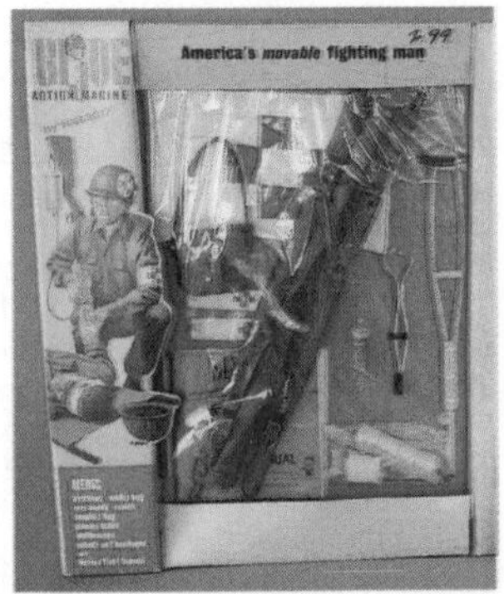

Marine Medic accessory set, No. 7719, mint in package, 1964 .... **$366**

U.S. COINS MARKET REPORT

According to David Harper, editor of *Numismatic News*, the coin market is now recovering from the recession. The drop began with middle range of the market and became the "canary in the coalmine," signaling trouble. Although the middle range dropped first, it held its value better than the top and bottom of the market. The high-end of the market dropped later. As the economy grew increasingly worse, collectors and dealers held back their valuable coins from auctions because they didn't want to risk selling at deflated prices.

The most active part of the market was in precious metals, especially gold and silver, where Harper said there was a lot of cash flow. When the stocks and currencies are weak, investors often turn to tangible commodities like precious metals. And conversely, when stocks and currencies strengthen, precious metal values begin to drop.

Through all the gut-wrenching economic woes of 2008, demand in the coin market maintained a remarkable level. "Even with tight money, major rarities are strong," said Harry Miller, market analyst for *Numismatic News*. "There is continued, broadly based demand in anything scarce."

Modern collector material—recently issued commemoratives, proof sets, mint sets, and other U.S. Mint products—have not performed as well as their more traditional scarce and rare counterparts. The U.S. Mint saw its inventories of current offerings not moving as expected and announced steps in late 2008 to reduce those stockpiles and keep them at manageable levels in the future.

Collecting Current Releases

In the last decade, coin collecting in the U.S. has received a huge boost from the popularity of several series, including the Jefferson nickels and presidential dollars, but most notably the state quarters. The state quarter series was so successful that the U.S. mint authorized the "America the Beautiful" quarter series beginning in April 2010. Each of the 56 new quarters will feature scenic views of sites such as national parks, wildlife refuges, seashores, and monuments. These recent releases, however, generally don't provide high investment potential. The circulating coins have been produced in such large quantities that even if kept in perfect condition, it's unlikely demand will increase enough to raise their values significantly. Special issue quarters that have been minted in silver will fluctuate according to their bullion value. As the value of silver rises or falls, so will the value of the quarters.

Be Cautious

It's more challenging for general antiques dealers to make a profit in coins than in decorative arts, as it's harder to find undervalued coins. Because coins are dated, have clearly defined designs, and a highly refined condition grading system, they are easier to positively identify and value. A dealer is more likely to find an overlooked rare piece of pottery than a rare coin. Also, the market is flooded with fake coins, especially from China. Some are poorly done, while others are excellent and very convincing. Be wary.

Slabbed Coins

When a dealer or collector submits a coin to an independent grading company to be slabbed, it is authenticated, condition-graded on a scale of 1 to 70, and sealed in a clear plastic case. (Nonslabbed coins are loose or enclosed in much smaller, thinner clear plastic holders with white cardboard frames that are stapled shut.) Dealers and collectors are willing to pay for extra cost of slabbing because the opinion of a neutral expert helps assure buyers that they are getting what is advertised, and helps sellers to get top prices. Because the service is relatively expensive, usually only the more valuable coins, typically $100 and up, are submitted for grading. A single coin can cost $25 or more to grade. However, when graded in bulk quantities, the charge can drop to around $6 each.

While buying and selling slabbed coins is probably the safest way for amateurs to trade high value coins, it also decreases the profit margin. Harper gave the example of a specialist coin dealer who pays $300 for an unslabbed coin or $700 for an identical slabbed coin. The specialist dealer who buys the coin will then resell it for $1,000 to one of his collector clientele. Although slabbed coins will generally sell for more, they are also harder to buy at a discount. Thus, an amateur collector or general dealer might be able to find the slabbed coin for $650 and resell it to the specialist coin dealer for $700 for only a $50 profit. There's a tradeoff between risk and reward. While the profit may be lower, it's much safer.

Commemoratives

Commemorative coins are a specialty area. Old commemoratives date from 1892 to 1954 and have the highest values. New commemoratives, released from 1982 to the present, are more common and less valuable. These coins are not encountered as often because they aren't circulating coins, so non-specialist collectors aren't likely to see them. But since they aren't as recognizable, it is possible they may be overlooked at an estate sale or local auction.

Advice

Harper recommends amateurs develop a relationship with a trusted specialist dealer who can help their customers learn the ropes. He also recommends that buyers pay close attention to condition grades and not pay uncirculated prices for circulated coins. The exception is when buying by bullion value, where buyers pay by weight, and condition is irrelevant.

U.S. COINS 1825 TO 1944

Coin collecting is one of the oldest and largest collecting categories. It can be traced back at least 500 years, and there may be as many as 100 million serious coin collectors in the world. Probably the main reason that coins are usually excluded from general antiques books is that the field is so vast that it would take a whole library to cover the topic. But since coins are found in almost all antique shops and malls, it seems appropriate to at least touch on them. While admittedly, it's difficult to give a meaningful overview of even a small segment of coins, it seems better than totally omitting them. So this year, we've decided to add a cross section of U.S. coins from the 1850s to the present to show relative values of coins in various series.

Coin prices can be as volatile as the stock market. Although some coins remain stable for years, others skyrocket during a period of popularity and then plummet when they fall out of fashion. Coins included in this section are primarily limited to older, non-circulating coins. Recent circulated coins, post-silver (after 1964) and collectors series coins such as the state quarter series, although popular for casual collecting, are excluded because the focus of this chapter is on more high-end, investment value coins.

The prices shown are guides to retail values—the approximate prices collectors can expect to pay when purchasing coins from a dealer—at the time of publication. Because the law of supply and demand ultimately rules, the final decision about a coin's value lies with the buyer and seller. Dealers are in business to make a living. This means that depending on the value and demand, a dealer will pay from 10 to 90 percent of the retail value listed here.

In most cases, the grades listed represent the conditions and corresponding values collectors will most likely encounter for a particular series in the market. In many cases, different mint marks of the same year are given to illustrate the drastic difference in value a mint mark can make.

For more detailed information, consult Krause Publications' *U.S. Coin Digest*, *North American Coins & Prices*, or *Warman's Coins and Paper Money*, available at krausebooks.com.

Coin Grading

A coin's value is determined in part by its grade, or state of preservation. Grading terms provide a concise method for describing a coin's condition, particularly when a dealer or collector advertises a coin for sale in a magazine. Several grading-guide books, which illustrate and describe U.S. coins in different series in different grades, are commonly used by dealers and collectors. Among them is The Official American Numismatic Association Grading Standards for United States Coins.

Following are commonly used grading terms and a general description of each:

Uncirculated (Unc.), or mint-state (MS), coins have no wear on them. Mint-state coins are further graded on a numerical scale from 60 to 70, with MS-70 being theoretical perfection. Although mint-state coins may show no wear from circulation, they can still vary in condition. For example, after coins are struck, they are loaded into bags and then shipped from the mint. Scuff marks occur when the coins bang into each other while being shipped in the bags. Although the coins may not show wear from circulation, these "bag marks" can detract from their condition.

Some professional grading services use all 11 increments from 60 to 70 in grading mint-state coins. Some traditionalists, however, believe it's impossible to tell a one-point difference in mint-state grades. The ANA grading guide, for example, lists and describes only MS-60, MS-63, MS-65, and MS-67.

Brilliant uncirculated (BU) refers to a mint-state coin retaining all or most of its original luster. It may have a numeric grade of MS-60 to MS-70. In the case of higher grades, many dealers prefer to use the more precise numeric grades.

MS-67 is the nearest thing to a perfect coin that is likely to appear on the market. It may have the faintest of bag marks discernible only through a magnifying glass. Copper must have luster.

MS-65 describes an exceptional coin and is most commonly the highest grade used when grading conservatively. It will have no significant bag marks, particularly in open areas such as the field or the cheek of a person portrayed on the coin. Copper may have toning. Fewer than one coin in hundreds qualifies for this grade. MS-65 coins are among the most popular sought by investors.

MS-63 coins are pleasant, collectible examples that exhibit enough bag marks to be noticed but not so many that the coins are considered marred, with particularly few on open areas, such as the fields or a cheek.

MS-60 describes coins that saw considerable scuffing at the mint before their release. They will often have nicks and discoloration. Sometimes called "commercial uncirculated," they may actually be less pleasant to behold than a higher-grade circulated coin.

About uncirculated (AU) describes coins with such slight signs of wear that a mild magnifying glass may be needed to see them. A trace of luster should be visible. One should be careful not to confuse an attractive AU coin for uncirculated.

Extremely fine (EF, XF) is the highest grade for a coin that exhibits wear significant enough to be seen easily by the unaided eye. The coin still exhibits extremely clear minute detail. In the case of U.S. coins with the word "Liberty" on a headband or shield, all letters must be sharp and clear. Many XF coins exhibit luster, but it is not necessary for the grade.

Very fine (VF) coins show obvious signs of wear. Nevertheless, most of the design detail is still clear, making for an overall pleasant coin. On American coins with "Liberty" on a headband or shield, all letters must be clear.

Fine (F) is the lowest grade most people consider collectible. About half the design details show for most types. On U.S. coins with "Liberty," all letters must be visible if not sharp.

Very good (VG) coins exhibit heavy wear. All outlines are clear, as is generally the rim. Some internal detail also shows, but most is worn off. At least three letters of "Liberty" must be legible; all letters must be present on pre-1857 copper coins and Morgan silver dollars.

Good (G) coins are generally considered uncollectible except for novelty purposes. The design usually shows no internal detail. Some of the rim may also be worn off. "Liberty" is worn off on most coins and shows just trace elements on pre-1857 copper coins and Morgan silver dollars.

About good (AG) and **fair (FR)** are grades in which only scarce coins are collected. Many collectors would rather do without the coin than to add an AG example to their collections. The rim will be worn down, and some outline of the design may be gone.

Poor (PR) is the lowest possible grade. Many coins in grade poor will not even be identifiable. When identifiable, many will still be condemned to the melting pot. Few collectors would consider owning such a coin unless it's an extreme rarity.

"Proof" denotes a special way of making coins for presentation or sale by the Mint directly to collectors. A proof coin is usually double struck with highly polished dies on polished blanks, yielding a mirrorlike finish.

In the past, matte, or sandblasted, proofs were popular. They were characterized by a non-reflective but highly detailed surface. "Cameo proofs" are struck with dies polished only in the fields. The design details, such as the portrait, have a dull finish for a cameo effect. Some cameo proofs command premium values over regular proofs.

Under the ANA grading system, proof grades use the same numbers as circulated and uncirculated grades, and the amount of wear on the coin corresponds to those grades. But the number is preceded by the word "proof"—proof-65, proof-55, proof-45, and so on. The ANA says a proof coin with many marks, scratches, or other defects should be called an "impaired proof."

Other miscellaneous factors can affect a coin's quality. The presence of all or part of the original luster usually increases a coin's value. Be careful, however, not to be fooled by a coin that has been dipped in a brightener to simulate this luster artificially.

Toning, or a natural coloration on a coin obtained over time, can be good or bad. If the toning is dull, irregular, or splotchy, it is likely to be considered unpleasant, and many collectors may choose to avoid it even if it is a high-grade coin.

On the other hand, if the toning is mild or displays a "halo effect" around a coin's edge, or is composed of pleasant iridescent shades, many collectors and dealers would pay a premium to obtain it based on its "eye appeal." Standard phrases used to denote a coin's eye appeal when grading include "premium quality" (PQ) and "prooflike" (PL).

Also, mints sometimes strike coins on blanks with minor imperfections. Poor mixing of the metals in the alloy or flaws left by trapped gas from this same process are examples. If trivial, they may be ignored on most coins, but on more expensive or high-grade pieces, concern over these flaws may increase.

Even on circulated coins, few collectors want examples with scratches or edge nicks. These will occur even more frequently on larger coins, such as silver dollars, or coins with reeded edges. Depending on extent, such coins may be discounted a little or a lot.

Of course, coins with damage are worth far less than coins without. Many coins have been mounted for use in jewelry, and even when the loop or bezel has been removed, they may still show slight signs of this unfortunate experience. A few collectors consider these situations opportunities to acquire coins with high-grade detail for a fraction of the cost. It should be remembered that the same heavy discount will apply when the collector resells the coins.

1825 Half Cent with Classic Head...... VG **$55**, VF **$110**

1828 Large Cent with Coronet............. VG **$35**, VF **$90**

1840 Large Cent with Braided Hair ......VG **$30**, VF **$35**

1858 Flying Eagle Cent........................ VG **$40**, VF **$50**

1882 Bronze Indian Head Cent, ...F **$5**, XF **$20**

1902 Bronze Indian Head Cent........... F **$2.50**, XF **$10**

1909S VDB Lincoln Cent with Wheat Ears Reverse .... VF **$1,150**, MS-60 **$1,650**

1909VDB (Not Shown).................... VF **$13**, MS-60 **$20**

The difference between the value of this penny with the "S" mintmark and without is enormous.

1922 Plain (No D) Lincoln Cent with Wheat Ears Reverse .... VF **$1,700**, MS-60 **$11,000**

1922D (Not Shown)........................ VF **$25**, MS-60 **$110**

Again, the difference between the coin with the mintmark and without is huge.

1867 Two-Cent Piece............................ F **$36**, XF **$60**

1863 Silver Three-Cent Piece with Double Border Around Star .... F **$400**, XF **$480**

1865 Nickel Three-Cent Piece................ F **$18**, XF **$35**

1896 Liberty Nickel.............................. F **$40**, XF **$100**

1907 Liberty Nickel............................ F **$4.50**, XF **$30**

1913D Buffalo Nickel....................... F **$20**, MS-60 **$65**

1937D "Three-Legged" Buffalo
.... F **$950**, MS-60 **$2,700**

This buffalo is the result of a weak die strike, which omits most of one of the legs. Because of its scarcity and value, it is frequently counterfeited.

1837 Seated Liberty Half Dime with Plain Obverse Field.. VG **$45**, VF **$135**

1855O Seated Liberty Half Dime with Stars and Arrows on Obverse.. VG **$20**, VF **$55**

1863 Seated Liberty Half Dime with Legend on Obverse.. VG **$250**, VF **$400**

1863S Seated Liberty Half Dime with Legend on Obverse (Not Shown)........................ VG **$45**, VF **$95**

1844 Seated Liberty Dime with Stars on Obverse .... VG **$350**, VF **$800**

1877 Seated Liberty Dime with Legend on Obverse .... VG **$20**, VF **$25**

1898S Barber Dime................................ F **$35**, XF **$80**

1898 Barber Dime (Not Shown) .... F **$7.50**, XF **$30**

1903S Barber Dime............................ F $340, XF **$750**

1903 Barber Dime (Not Shown) .... F **$5.50**, XF **$25**

1916D Mercury Dime.........VF **$3,850**, MS-60 **$13,200**

1916 Mercury Dime (Not Shown).....VF **$7**, MS-60 **$30**

1942/41 Mercury Dime............VF **$660**, MS-60 **$2,650**

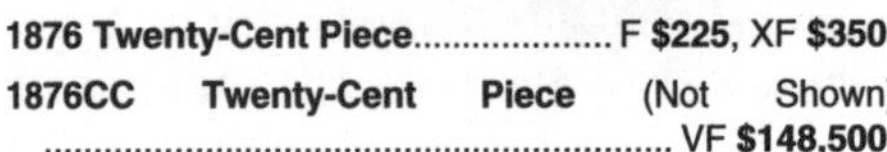

1876 Twenty-Cent Piece.................... F **$225**, XF **$350**

1876CC Twenty-Cent Piece (Not Shown) .... VF **$148,500**

The rare 1876CC was sold at an April 1977 aution.

1847 Seated Liberty Quarter with No Motto Above Eagle .... VG **$25**, VF **$50**

1853O Seated Liberty Quarter with Arrrows at Date and Rays on Reverse............................ VG **$35**, VF **$100**

1856 Seated Liberty Quarter with Arrows Removed From Date .... VG **$20**, VF **$35**

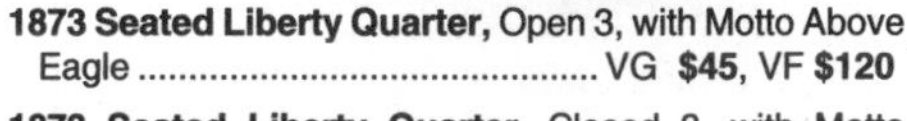

1873 Seated Liberty Quarter, Open 3, with Motto Above Eagle .... VG **$45**, VF **$120**

1873 Seated Liberty Quarter, Closed 3, with Motto Above Eagle (Not Shown) .... VG **$350,** VF **$800**

1874S Seated Liberty Quarter with Arrows at Date .... VG **$25**, VF **$70**

1879 Seated Liberty Quarter with Arrows Removed From Date .... VG **$235**, VF **$325**

1892 Barber Quarter.......................... F **$35**, XF **$100**

1903 Barber Quarter .... F **$20**, XF **$60**

1916 Standing Liberty Quarter F **$9,500**, XF **$14,500**

1917 Standing Liberty Quarter (Not Shown) .... F **$50**, XF **$95**

1927S Standing Liberty Quarter... F **$110**, XF **$1,000**

1839 Seated Liberty Half Dollar with No Motto Above Eagle and No Drapery Below Elbow .... VG **$110**, VF **$340**

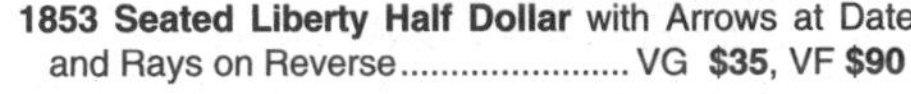

1853 Seated Liberty Half Dollar with Arrows at Date and Rays on Reverse........................ VG **$35**, VF **$90**

1854 Seated Liberty Half Dollar with Arrows at Date, No Rays on Reverse .... VG **$40**, VF **$60**

1858S Seated Liberty Half Dollar with Arrows Removed From Date .... VG **$40**, VF **$70**

1872CC Seated Liberty Half Dollar with Motto Above Eagle .... VG **$125**, VF **$400**

1872 Seated Liberty Half Dollar with Motto Above Eagle (Not Shown) .... VG **$125**, VF **$400**

1878S Seated Liberty Half Dollar with Arrows Removed From Date .... VG **$37,500**, VF **$47,500**

1878 Seated Liberty Half Dollar with Arrows Removed From Date (Not Shown) .... VG **$45**, VF **$80**

1892 Barber Half Dollar .... VG **$40**, VF **$120**

1892S Barber Half Dollar (Not Shown) .... VG **$330**, VF **$530**

1903 Barber Half Dollar .... VG **$16**, VF **$100**

1908O Barber Half Dollar .... VG **$14**, VF **$90**

1944 Walking Liberty Half Dollar............. F **$7**, XF **$9**

1845 Seated Liberty Dollar with No Motto Above Eagle .... F **$360**, XF **$540**

1871 Seated Liberty Dollar with Motto Above Eagle .... F **$330**, XF **$500**

1871CC Seated Liberty Dollar with Motto Above Eagle (Not Shown) .... F **$4,400**, XF **$14,000**

1876 Trade Dollar................................ F **$140**, XF **$175**

1881CC Morgan Dollar .... VF **$410**, MS-60 **$555**

1887O Morgan Dollar .... VF **$20**, MS-60 **$50**

1921 Peace Dollar .... VF **$140**, MS-60 **$270**

1922 Peace Dollar (Not Shown) .... VF **$15**, MS-60 **$17**

1834 Gold $2.50 with Classic Head (No Motto) .... VF **$475**, XF **$675**

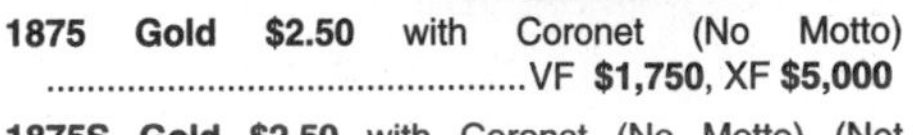

1875 Gold $2.50 with Coronet (No Motto) ....VF **$1,750**, XF **$5,000**

1875S Gold $2.50 with Coronet (No Motto) (Not Shown) ....VF **$150**, XF **$300**

1911D Gold $2.50 with Indian Head, ... VF **$2,500**, XF **$5,000**

1911 Gold $2.50 with Indian Head (Not Shown) ....VF **$175**, XF **$230**

1834 Gold $5 with Classic Head and Crosslet 4 (No Motto) ....VF **$1,650**, XF **$2,900**

1835 Gold $5 with Classic Head (Not Shown) ....VF **$390**, XF **$560**

1841 Gold $5 with Coronet (No Motto) ....VF **$400**, XF **$875**

1866 Gold $5 with Coronet and Motto ....VF **$800**, XF **$1,650**

1908 Gold $5 with Indian Head........VF **$280**, XF **$290**

1849O Gold $10 with Coronet (No Motto) ....VF **$695**, XF **$2,450**

1873CC Gold $10 with Coronet and Motto ....VF **$6,000**, XF **$13,500**

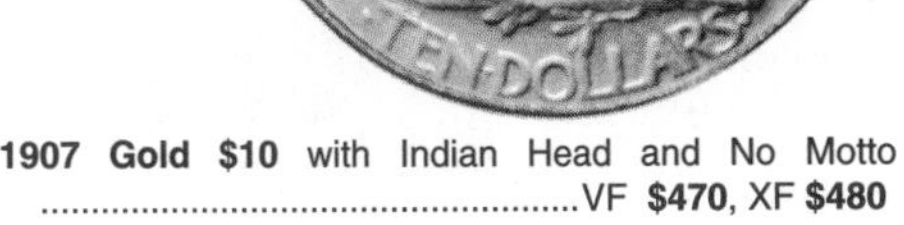

1907 Gold $10 with Indian Head and No Motto ....VF **$470**, XF **$480**

1850 Gold $20 with Liberty Head ....VF **$1,235**, XF **$1,325**

1907 High Relief Saint-Gaudens Gold $20 with No Motto ....VF **$7,500**, XF **$8,350**

1909 Saint-Gaudens Gold $20 with Motto ....VF **$1,030**, XF **$1,050**

WATCHES

Lady's hunting case watch, Elgin, delicately engraved gold-filled Dueber case, keywind mechanism, late 19th c., 1 3/4" d. **$173**

Lady's hunting case watch, pendant-style, 18k gold case polished & set w/a diamond, sapphire & ruby accent, the white enameled dial w/Arabic numerals, jeweled & adjusted damascened lever escapement movement, late 19th - early 20th c. **$264**

Lady's hunting case watch, the round case decorated in green guilloche enamel centered by a rose-cut diamond starburst & bordered by tiny diamonds, suspended from a double old European- and rose-cut diamond-mounted chain & bail joined to an enameled baton & seed pearl necklace, the silvertone dial w/ Arabic numerals, platinum & 18k gold mount, some enamel loss, Edwardian, England, early 20th c. **$3,878**

Lady's hunting case watch, Vacheron & Constantin, 18k gold case w/three bands of rose-cut diamonds ending in cabochon garnets, the white enamel dial w/Arabic numerals, a jeweled nickel movement, suspended from a scrolling openwork gold pink trimmed w/cabochon garnets & tiny diamonds, triple signed, fitted box, early 20th c. **$2,585**

Lady's pendant watch, hunting case, platinum w/the case decorated in light blue guilloché enamel w/a floral diamond central mount & frame, accompanied by a platinum & diamond chain w/ American hallmark, Starr & Frost, early 20th c., overall w/chain 21" l. **$3,290**

Lady's open face watch, pendant-type, enamel, platinum & diamond, the back of the platinum-topped 18k gold case in marine blue guillochè enamel centerd by a square set w/rose-cut diamonds & bordered by a narrow white enamel Greek key band, the goldtone dial w/Arabic numerals, suspended from a platinum, enamel baton & rose-cut diamond fancy link chain, Edwardian, England, early 20th c., overall 22" l. **$2,468**

Lady's pendant watch, Art Deco style, the round silvertone engine-turned dial w/Arabic numerals, a jeweled damascene nickel movement, platinum matte polished hunting case bow-set w/ rose-cut diamonds & sapphires w/ a cabochon sapphire in the center, w/a 14k white gold & sapphire bar pin, case interior inscribed "Paris," ca. 1920s **$2,115**

Jewels are used in watch movements to reduce friction. They resist wear and can be polished very smooth.

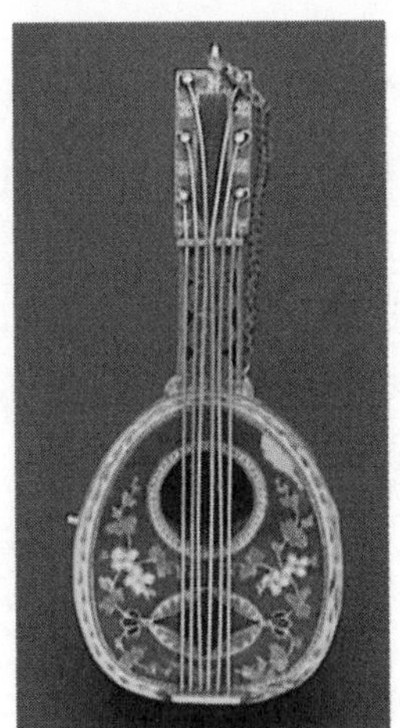

Lady's verge watch, L'Epine, Paris, France, designed in the shape of a mandolin w/multicolored enamel decoration on the 18k gold ground, opens to revealed a signed gilt movement, suspended from a trace link chain, late 19th - early 20th c. **$4,700**

Man's hunting case watch, E. Howard Watch Co., seventeen jewel movement, 14k yellow gold case w/central shield on engine-turned ground, case marked "Keystone," ca. 1903 .... **$805**

Man's hunting case watch, Elgin, lever-set movement, in a finely engraved 14k gold case applied w/an elk head, w/original Elgin mahogany case, late 19th c., w/ short watch chain **$460**

Man's hunting case watch, Illinois, lever-set movement, finely engraved 14k yellow gold case, slight case wear, minor hairlines in dial, ca. 1880 .... **$1,035**

Man's hunting case watch, Waltham, 14k tri-color gold case engraved w/foral & leaf designs among interlocking circles, the white enamel dial w/Roman numerals & subsidiary seconds dial, jeweled adjusted nickel movement, late 19th - early 20th c. **$646**

Man's open-face watch, Art Deco-style, 14k gold, goldtone metal dial w/Arabic numerals & subsidiary seconds dial, stepped bezel, enclosing a 17-jewel nickel lever escapement movement, w/ rectangular trace link fob chain, w/Dreicer & Co. box, ca. 1930s (ILLUS. of watch)................ **$323**

As their name suggests, hunting-case pocket watches were made with a lid to protect them from the elements during outdoor use. Other pocket watches, mainly used indoors, were left open faced for aesthetic reasons. Railroad pocket watches, which had to meet stringent requirements to ensure rail safety, had to be open-faced so their dials would be visible at all times.

Man's open-face watch, E. Howard Watch Co., open-faced w/marked dial w/Arabic numerals, small seconds dial, seventeen jewel movement, 14k yellow gold case marked "KW.C.C.O.," minor hairline in dial, tiny fleck at numeral 4, ca. 1900 .... **$403**

Man's open-face watch, Patek Philippe, 18k yellow gold, the silvertone dial w/Arabic numerals enclosing an 18-jewel eight adjustment damascened nickel movement, the reverse w/worn monogram, 20th c., triple-signed, boxed **$1,880**

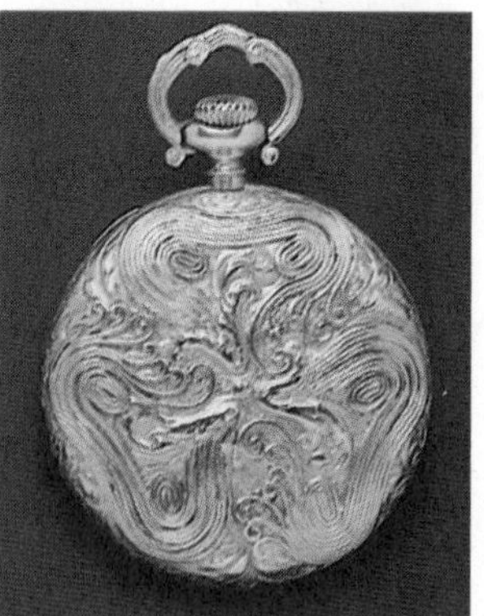

Man's open-face watch, Tiffany & Co., 18k yellow gold & platinum, Art Nouveau design, gold case w/ applied platinum wire in a looped clover-style design against a chased & rèpoussè ground w/a small bird, the gilt dial w/applied free-form Arabic numerals, curved & scrolling bi-color hands, subsidiary seconds dial, jeweled & damscened nickel lver escapment movement, ca. 1890s, triple-signed (ILLUS. of back) **$35,250**

Man's open-face watch, Vacheron, 18k gold, the white enamel dial w/Roman numerals & a subsidiary seconds dial, enclosing a jeweled lever escapement movement, early 20th c. **$646**

Cartier, lady's Art Deco style, the diamond-shaped silvered dial w/Roman numerals framed by rose-cut diamonds & onyx tablets framed by more diamonds, rose-cut diamond winding stem, completed by a later strap, the platinum-topped 18k gold case enclosing a 19-jewel movement, eight-adjustment, signed by Cartier, Paris, ca. 1920 .... **$15,275**

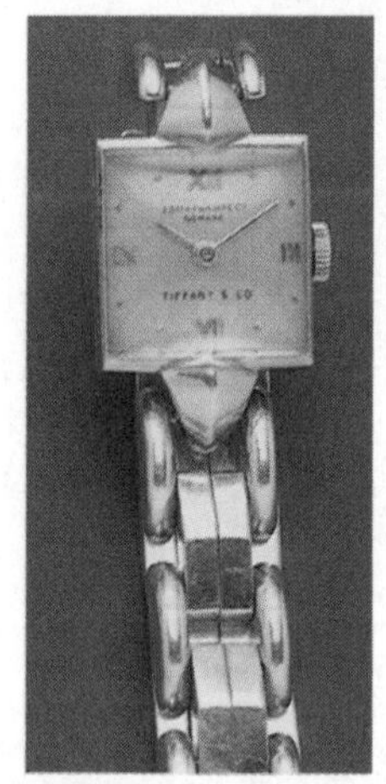

Patek Philippe, man's Retro style 14k gold, the square silvertone dial w/Roman & abstract numerals under a domed crystal, on a shaped end lugs attached to a pyramidal arched bracelet, an 18-jewel damascened movement, Tiffany & Co., mid-20th c., 6 1/2" l. **$1,880**

The earliest pocket watches were made by German locksmith Peter Henlein in the the early 1500s. Pocket watches remained in style until after World War I, when wristwatches came into vogue.

WEATHERVANES

Weathervanes were widely popular with American farmers at a time when agriculture dominated the workforce of America in the 19th and early 20th centuries. This rooftop adjunct was not only decorative but provided a reliable guide to wind direction from afar. Today farming employs less than 5% of the American workforce but the old adage, "You can take the boy out of the farm, but not the farm out of the boy" still holds true as evidenced by the continued popularity of farm-related antiques. Today valuable old weathervanes adorn walls above fireplaces, in kitchens and family rooms and even, on a few rooftops.

As in the past, vanes in the forms of animals remain the most popular with collectors. Farmers sometimes used vanes which represented the stock they raised, so cows and horses were the most common forms, with chickens and pigs also widely seen. Eagles, of course, were popular with the patriotic-minded. Sheep, ears of corn and mules can also be found quite often but more rare are beavers, fish, and wolverines.

Today when you are looking at old weathervanes you are likely to find them with bullet holes since they were popular targets for little boys and hunters of the past. The rarest examples can be found in undamaged condition with an original finish and perhaps traces of original gilding. In addition to animal-form vanes, beautiful glass-tailed arrow vanes were popular. Found in basically two shapes, rectangular and kite-tail, the framed, colored glass was often etched. Often reproduced, an original glass-tail vane should show the stains that result from the rusting of the frame around the glass, unless the arrow frame is of a later example made of aluminum.

—Phil Steiner.

American Indian, gilt molded copper & sheet copper, "Massasoit" version, standing figure of a stylized warrior w/feathers atop his head, a long arrow in one hand & a very long bow in the other, atop w/arrow pointer, Harris & Co., Boston, late 19th c., 40 1/2" w., 39 3/4" h. **$66,000**

Centaur, molded copper & cast lead, the flattened full-body figure drawing a bow & arrow w/molded sheet copper tail, the surface w/vestiges of yellow sizing, gilt, verdigris & black paint, attributed to A.L. Jewell & Co., Waltham, Massachusetts, 1852-67, repairs, 39 1/4" l., 32 1/4" h. **$51,700**

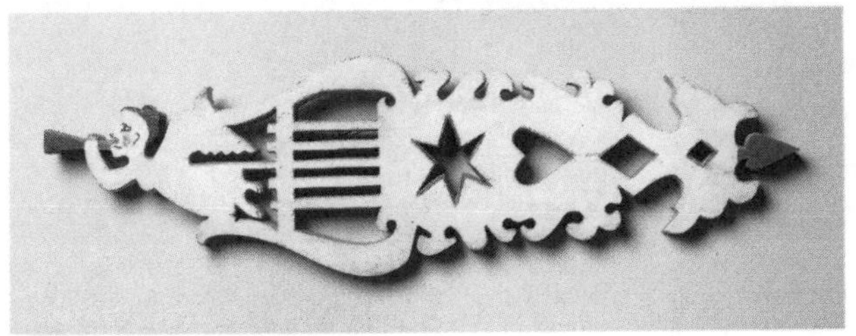

Banner, cut-out & painted wood, long form w/a cut-out figure of the angel Gabriel blowing horn issuing from a lyre at one end, the front end w/a red pointed arrow, ornately scroll-cut edges & cut-out center designs of a star, heart & diamonds, old white paint, attributed to New York, 19th c., 26 1/4" l. **$4,600**

Cow, molded copper, old yellow paint, standing animal w/applied horns & tail, on a modern base, possibly Cushing & White, Waltham, Massachusetts, late 19th c., 32" l., 18 3/4" h. **$8,365**

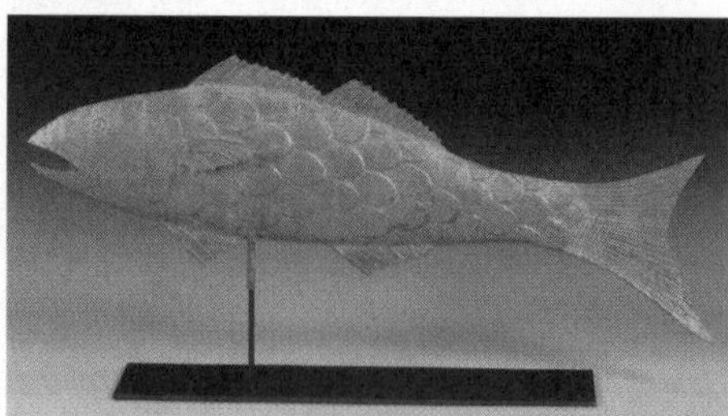

Fish, gilt molded & sheet copper, the detailed body w/large scales, fins & tail, probably Cushing & White, Waltham, Massachusetts, late 19th c., 42" l. **$24,000**

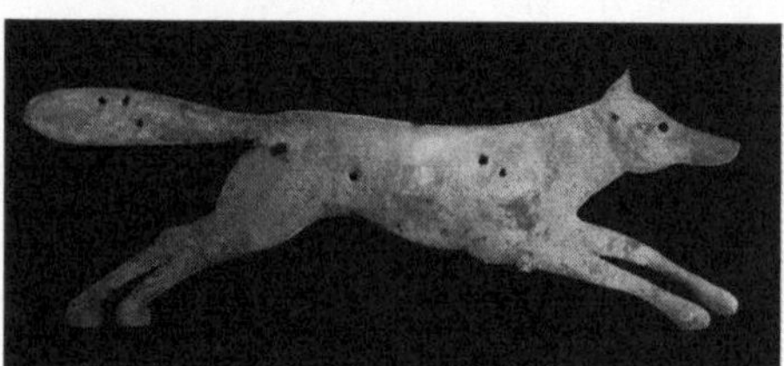

Fox, leaping, cast & molded copper, hollow-cut eyes & ear & cut tail, old holes, attributed to A. Jewel & Co., Waltham, Massachusetts, mid-19th c., 42 1/2" l., 15 1/2" h. **$20,315**

Gamecock, molded copper w/a flattened full-body w/ sheet copper tail & embossed detailings, gilt finish, mounted on an arrow w/iron point & corrugated sheet copper tail, weathered surfance, no stand, American, second half 19th c., 25 3/4" w., 21 1/2" h. **$11,750**

Goddess Liberty, gilt molded copper & painted sheet iron, the classical lady standing wearing a long flowing dress, shoulder banner & Liberty cap, one arm pointing forward, the other holding up a large American flag, together w/original iron, copper & wood post, ball directionals & a period photo of the vane in situ, William Henis, Philadelphia, mid-19th c., 29" w., 30" h. **$1,080,000**

Horse & rider, molded copper & zinc, the male riding holding the reins, rust on his head & shoulders, attributed to J.W. Fiske & Company, New York, New York, late 19th c., 37 1/2" l., 18 1/2" h. **$15,535**

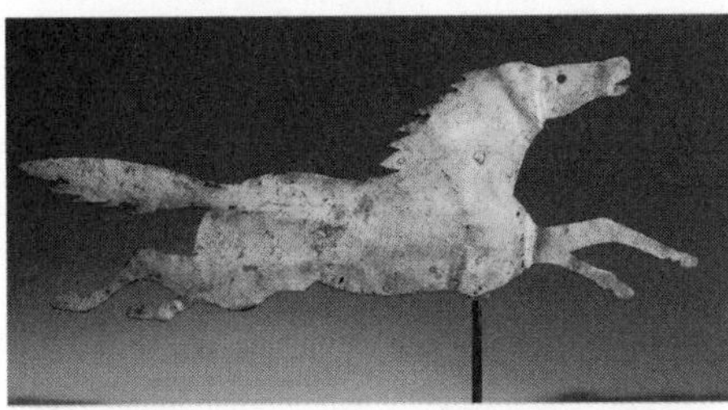

Horse, running, sheet metal, painted w/worn gold, w/a straight tail & head looking up, American, second half 19th c., 51 1/2" l. **$2,390**

Rooster, gilded sheet copper, stylized bird w/low serrated comb & crest feather, high around & deeply cut-out tail, weathered gilded surface w/verdigris, w/ weighted three-dimensional head & breast, w/a black metal stand, 19th c., 23 1/2" l., 23" h. **$7,638**

Snake, cut & painted sheet iron, the long flat serpentine & looped body painted w/alternating wide bands of green & white w/thin yellow accent bands, 19th c., 56 1/4" l., 45 1/2" h. **$14,400**

Ram, molded copper, full-bodied form w/articulated mouth, eyes, hairs & curled horns, New England, 19th c., on rod support w/modern base, 35" w., 28 1/2" h. **$13,145**

Sailboat, molded copper, fully rigged w/rippling metal sheet sails, American, late 19th - early 20th c., 37" l., 36 3/4" h. **$7,768**

Stag, leaping pose, full-bodied w/a cast zinc head & brass antlers, by Fiske, late 19th c., good deail, mounted on new wooden base, 29 1/2" l., 27 1/4" **$7,475**

WOODENWARES

The patina and mellow coloring, along with the lightness and smoothness that come only with age and wear, attract collectors to old woodenwares. The earliest forms were the simplest, and the shapes of items whittled out in the late 19th century varied little in form from those turned out in the American colonies two centuries earlier. A burl is a growth, or wart, on some trees in which the grain of the wood is twisted and turned in a manner that strengthens the fibers and causes a beautiful pattern to be formed. Treenware is simply a term for utilitarian items made from "treen," another word for wood. While maple was the primary wood used for these items, they are also abundant in pine, ash, oak, walnut and other woods. "Lignum Vitae" is a species of wood from the West Indies that can always be identified by the contrasting colors of dark heartwood and light sapwood and by its heavy weight, which causes it to sink in water.

Bowl, turned burl, wide round shallow form w/wide molded rim, traces of red on the exterior, good color & figure w/good patina on exterior & lightly scrubbed interior, age splits, 14 1/2" d., 4 1/2" h. **$4,140**

Cake board, painted, a large round board w/ small shaped & pointed handle at one side, centered by a polychrome painted basket of flowers above the painted date "1831" surrounded by a stylized green wreath of a yellow ground, age cracks, American, 19th c., 31 1/2" w. **$115**

Cutlery box, tiger stripe maple, rectangular w/low canted sides, a tall center divider w/a turned bar grip over a rectangular cut-out, 19th c., refinished, 10 1/4 x 14", 5 1/2" h. **$823**

Cutlery tray, cherry, a rectangular base with below gently canted dovetailed sides & a central divider w/a high arched & shaped central handle w/heart-shaped hand grip, each side w/a hinged flat lid, American, early 19th c., 8 3/4 x 13 1/4", 10" h. **$374**

Dough box on legs, walnut, rectangular deep box w/canted sides & a one-board top, raised on frame w/a curved apron fitted w/a single drawer & raised on simple cabriole legs, French Provincial, late 19th c., 20 x 50 1/2", 32 1/2" h. **$2,070**

Dough box on stand, mixed wood, the rectangular board top overhanging the dovetailed deep box w/canted sides & a molded base, resting on a base w/a deep canted apron on canted baluster- and knob turned legs w/peg feet, early to mid-19th c., 18 3/4 x 37 1/2", 29" h. **$633**

Drying rack, slender side posts tapering slightly w/rounded tops joined by three slender rack bars tenoned through the side posts, raised on cast-iron trestle-type feet, nice patina, first half 19th c., possibly Shaker, 28" w., 37 1/2" h. **$115**

Grain shovel w/wall peg, painted maple shovel carved from a single piece of wood w/a deep arched blade & long slender handle w/cut-out hand grip, painted red, w/narrow board w/a hanging peg, minor losses to shovel edges, 19th c., peg 13 1/2" l., shovel 36" l., 2 pcs...................................... **$529**

Flax hatchel, oak & wrought iron, the thick rectangular plank top w/rectangular top handle incised w/a band of hearts & rosettes above the row of long iron comb teeth, early 19th c., 2 3/4" thick, 23" l. **$173**

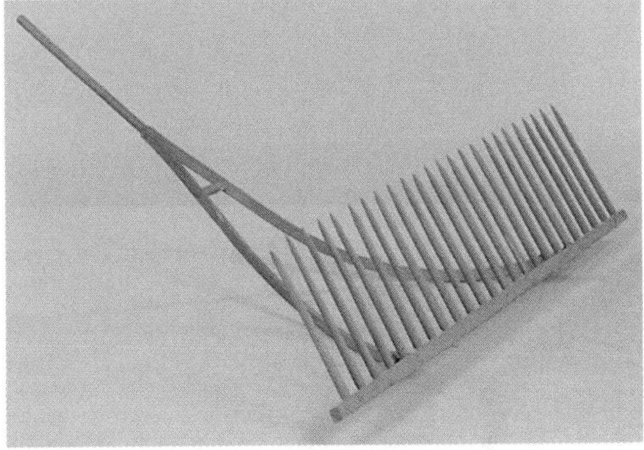

Hay rake, the curved forked handle ending in a long thin crossbar fitted w/numerous long pointed teeth, 19th c., 73" w., 67" l. **$1,195**

Jar, cov., turned, round foot & squatty bulbous body w/incised bands, low domed cover w/ pointed button finial, wire bail handle w/wooden hand grip, light varnish finish, attributed to Pease of Ohio, age split, second half 19th c., 5 1/4" h. **$173**

Peat bucket, brass-bound mahogany, slightly tapering cylindrical ring-turned design wrapped w/three wide brass bands, lion head & ring brass side handles, raised on small brass paw feet, possibly Dutch, early 19th c., 9 1/2" h. **$777**

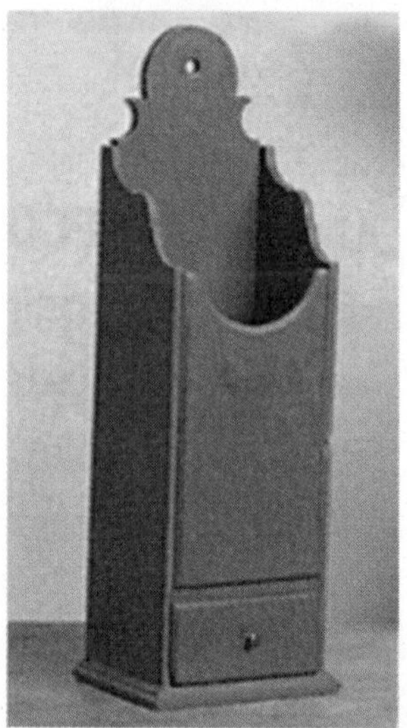

Pipe box, painted walnut, hanging-type, the tall box w/an arched backboard w/small hanging hole above scallop-stepped sides & concave-topped front board, a small drawer in the bottom w/ original small brass pull, molded base, old dry red paint, drawer bottom damaged, minor chip on one scallop, New England, late 18th - early 19th c., 5 3/8 x 6 3/4", 20" h. **$8,338**

Pipe box, hanging-type, red-stained, upright nearly square form constructed w/rose-head nails, serpentine-cut sloping top rims w/a round backboard top w/a hanging hole, a small dovetailed drawer w/ring handle at the base, early, 4 1/2 x 5 1/2", 18" h. **$4,313**

Scoop, hand-carved burl, one-piece construction, a wide curved shallow bowl w/a long turned angled handle at one end terminating in a curved hook, early 19th c., 9 3/4" l. **$1,528**

Wall box, the tall peaked backboard w/a hanging hole, the open box w/slanted sides, original dark reddish finish, 19th c., 6 x 12 3/4", 13 3/4" h. **$805**

WORLD WAR II MARKET REPORT

"As in all collecting hobbies during a recession, middle-of-the-road, mediocre pieces are not selling, and prices are down, but prices for high-end, really desirable pieces are going up quickly. There is a clamor for really high quality," said John Adams-Graf, author of *Warman's World War II Collectbles*, and editor of the *Military Trader* magazine (www.militarytrader.com).

Within the U.S. World War II collecting market, several areas are experiencing above average growth, including engraved, identified purple heart groups. While even unidentified purple hearts are desirable, the medals are even more in demand when documented identification of the owner is available, and the owner's name is engraved on it. Value increases even more for groupings, which are accompanying related items that belonged to the same individual, such as dog tags, canteens, cartridge belts, etc. Purple hearts can vary from $65 to $85 for a non-engraved medal to $185 for a medal accompanied by documentation of the circumstances of the wound, $265 to $350 for a purple heart associated with a soldier killed in action, and as much as $500 to $700 for a purple heart connected to a soldier who earned it while fighting in a famous unit like the 82nd or 101st Airborne.

According to Graf, technically, these medals fall under the 2006 Stolen Valor Act, which prohibits the unauthorized wear, manufacture, sale, or claim (either written or verbal) of U.S. decorations and medals. He explained, however, that it was intended to stop fraudulent claims of heroism, not to hinder collecting, and that those who drafted the law have said as much. So far, the law has not been enforced against collectors, since that wasn't its purpose, but because the law is on the books, there's no guarantee that it couldn't be enforced that way in the future.

Graf pointed out that although it may seems callous for relatives to sell a deceased family member's medals, the family often treasures memories more than the physical artifacts. Fortunately, serious collectors are researchers and historians who consider it an honor to maintain the record of a soldier's service. Thus, the aritfacts are often much better documented and preserved by collectors than by family members. The items are carefully researched, catalogued, and displayed, rather than stored in a forgotten trunk in an attic. Once a piece comes into the possession of a serious collector, it will most likely only pass to another serious collector, never to be mothballed again. Some families do search online for their deceased loved one's medals, which accounts for a segment of the medal sales.

Another collecting area that's growing fast is uniforms and related equipment, especially painted M1 helmets. Helmets are an area rife with fakes and forgeries, however, so it isn't for the novice, and it's not a good idea to buy them on eBay, where they can't be personally inspected first. A common painted M1 helmet can fetch $400, while helmets painted with designations of elite units garner a premium—up to $1,000 for a paratrooper helmet. Early helmets with welded chip-strap loops are also more valuable. Later helmets had swivel chin-strap loops.

Uniform groups are hot, too, with a premium being given to documented identified groups. Values rise signficantly when the unforms include the insignia—chevrons, service stripes, collar disks, pilot wings, and patches (especially bullion embroidered patches).

According to Graf, World War II re-enactors sometimes wear original uniforms, which he strongly discourages. As a former museum curator, he knows from personal experience that uniforms are fragile, as they weren't designed to last for decades. In the past, original uniforms were so common that people used them fairly casually, not thinking about their historical or collector value. With the passage of nearly seven decades since the end of the war, many have been lost or degraded and aren't so common any more. To preserve original uniforms, he encourages re-enactors to purchase and wear reproductions, which are widely available now.

Weapons and blades have always been steady sellers, and are relatively abundant since they survived at high rates. M1 rifles and carbines range from $700 to $5,000, with the value closely tied to details such as serial number (low, early numbers are more valuable than higher, later ones), variations, and manufacturer's stamps. Bayonet are another big growth area, with M1 bayonets in the lead. More desirable early 13-inch models typically cost $150, while less desirable 10-inch models from 1942 and later are valued at around $65 to $75. Other factors affecting values are the manufacturers, which are rated according to a hierarchy among specialist collectors, and the shape and style of the blade point. If you're collecting weapons, be sure to comply with federal, state, and local laws.

Of the three major wars that have a collector following—the Civil War, World War II, and Vietnam—World War II has the strongest market. In comparison to World War II collectibles, Civil War items are—not surprisingly—generally rarer and more expensive, so Civil War collecting has been harder hit by the economy. The Vietnam market is also weaker than World War II because it still carries a stigma, with the current controvery over the wars in Iraq and Afghanistan likely slowing the process of healing. Plus, being more recent, it hasn't had quite as much time as World War II to develop nostalgia.

Although Civil War collectibles have a weaker market, Civil War re-enactments are more common than World War II re-enactments, with few Civil War participants wearing original uniforms. A genuine Civil War-era forage cap could cost $2,000, so it would be an expensive and risky proposition to wear one into mock battle.

Vietnam re-enactments are relatively scarce because of the war's stigma and because it is difficult to replicate a battle, as the terrain and vegetation are very different in the United States. According to Graf, most Vietnam re-enactments that do take place re-act movies, not battles. Vietnam re-enactors number less than 10,000 nationwide, far less than the number of Civil War re-enactors, which Graf said is close to 100,000. During the 1998 Gettysburg re-enactment, from 30,000 to 41,000 re-enactors participated in the mock battle, with an equal number of spectators watching.

With the sizable number of re-enactments and participants, and the corresponding amount of both genuine and reproduction gear needed to outfit the soldiers, collectors should be very careful to distinguish between the real and repros and pay the appropriate price for each.

WORLD WAR II

During the sixty-plus years since the end of World War II, veterans, collectors and nostalgia-seekers have eagerly bought, sold and traded the "spoils of war." Actually, souvenir collecting began as soon as troops set foot on foreign soil. Whether Tommies from Great Britain, Doughboys from the United States or Fritzies from Germany, soldiers eagerly looked for trinkets and remembrances that would guarantee their place in the historic events that unfolded before them. Helmets, medals, Lugers, field gear, daggers and other pieces of war material filled parcels and duffel bags on the way back home.

As soon as hostilities ended in 1945, the population of defeated Germany and Japan quickly realized they could make money selling souvenirs to the occupation forces. The flow of war material increased. Values became well established. A Luger was worth several packs of cigarettes, a helmet, just one. A Japanese sword was worth two boxes of K-rations, while an Arisaka bayonet was valued at a Hershey's chocolate bar.

Over the years, these values have remained proportionally consistent. Today, that "two-pack" Luger might be worth $4,000 and that one-pack helmet, $1,000. The Japanese sword might fetch $1,200 and the Arisaka bayonet $85. Though values have increased dramatically, demand has not dropped off a bit. In fact, World War II collecting is the largest segment of the miltaria hobby.

Surprisingly, the values of items have been a closely guarded secret. The hobby, unfortunately, has relied on paying veterans and their families far less than a military relic is worth with the hope of selling later for a substantial profit. This attitude has given the hobby a bad reputation.

The advent of the Internet, though, has significantly leveled the playing field for sellers and buyers. No longer does a person have to blindly offer a relic for sale to a collector or dealer. Simply logging onto one of several Internet auctions will give the uninitiated an idea of value.

The value of military items is greatly affected by variation. Whether it is a difference in manufacturing technique, material or markings, the nuances of an item will determine the true value. Also, the amount of World War II material is vast. Following is just a representative sampling of various items from the four of the most commonly collected nations that participated in the war: Germany, Japan, the United Kingdom, and the United States. Readers can get an idea of the relative values of various items from these countries. For more information, consult Warman's World War II Collectibles by John Adams-Graf. Photos courtesty of www.advanceguardmilitaria.com, Rock Island Auction Company, Hermann Historica OHG, Charles D. Pautler, Minnesota Military Museum, Colin R. Bruce II, and John F. Graf.

Germany

Army medical officer's visor cap $650-900

Artillery soldier's Waffenrock $475-600

German paratrooper's camouflage jump smock $5,500-6,000

Hobnailed "jackboots" **$300-400**

German Luftwaffe Model 40 single decal helmet **$400-650**

Luftwaffe Fallschirmjäger gravity knife **$350-650**

Officer's map case **$95-150**

German proficiency badge of the SS in bronze **$6,500-7,500**

Stamped steel Heere belt plate on black leather belt **$100-175**

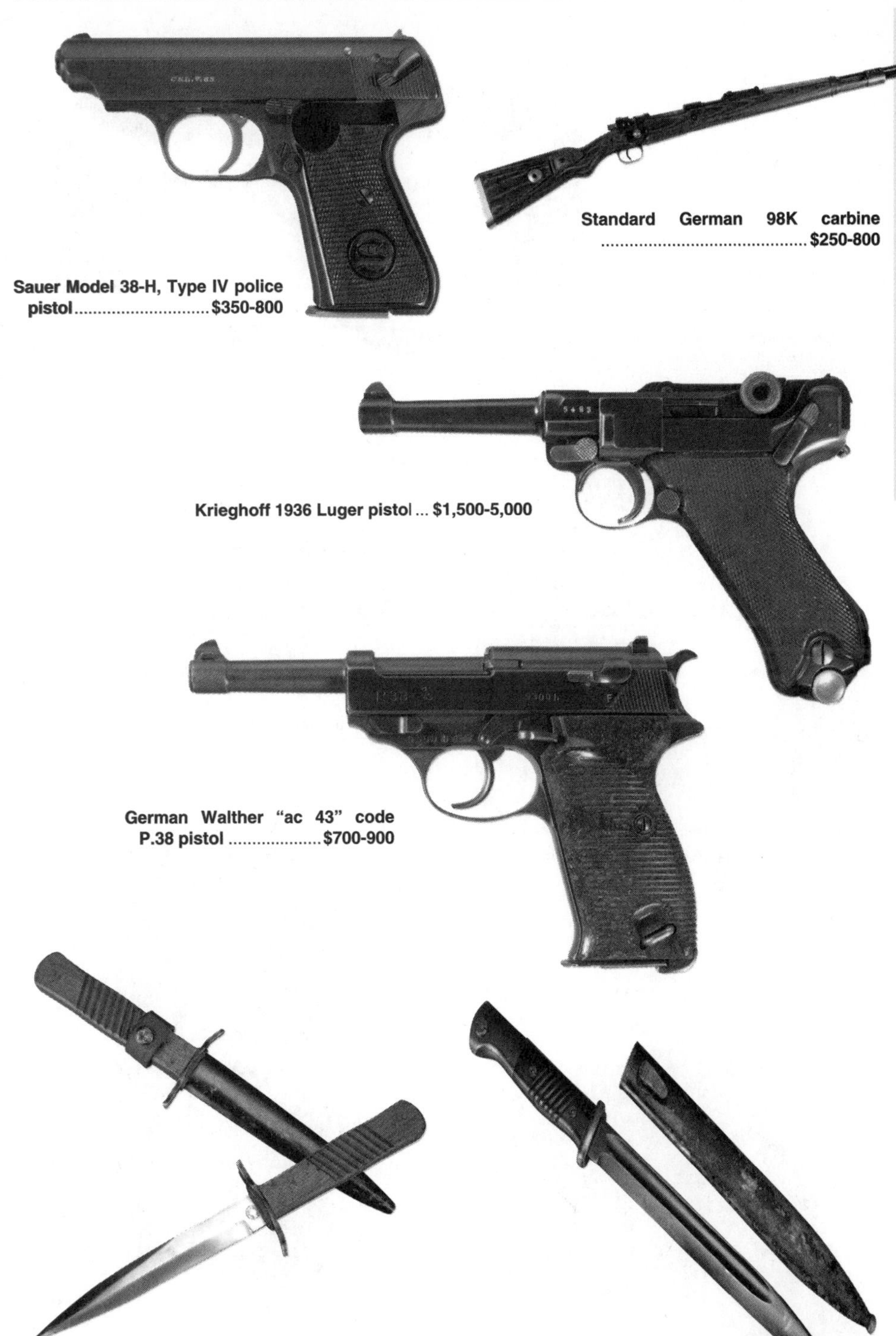

Standard German 98K carbine $250-800

Sauer Model 38-H, Type IV police pistol $350-800

Krieghoff 1936 Luger pistol ... $1,500-5,000

German Walther "ac 43" code P.38 pistol $700-900

German soldier's fighting knife.................... $150-250

84/98 Mauser rifle bayonet by "Hörster" with scabbard $65-85

Japan

Aviator goggles $300-350

Japanese Tabi toe shoes $150-200

Japanese tanker's jacket $400-475

Japanese Order of the Rising Sun, 5th Class $400-450

Model 1937 Army field cap $275-350

Japanese Kamikaze headband......................**$300-450**

Japanese "Baby Nambu" pistol..............**$3,000-5,500**

Japanese Papa Nambu pistol..................**$1,500-2,700**

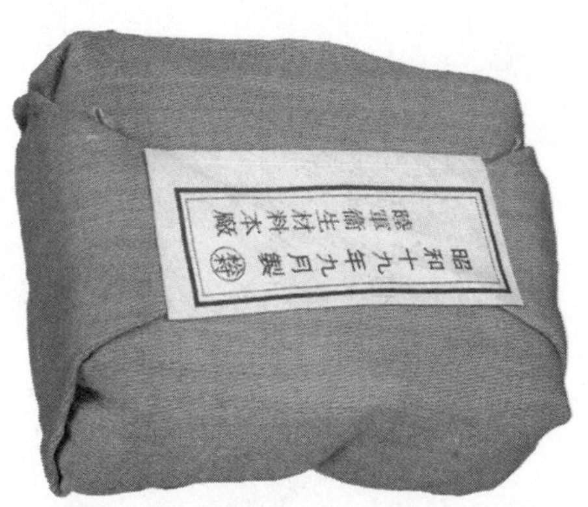

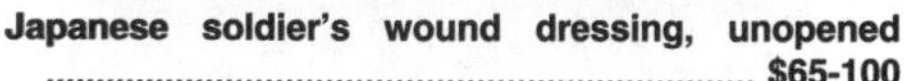

Japanese soldier's wound dressing, unopened **$65-100**

Japanese Type 30 bayonet, with a National Denki hallmark...**$85-135**

Japanese Navy pattern canteen with adjustable sling........ **$100-135**

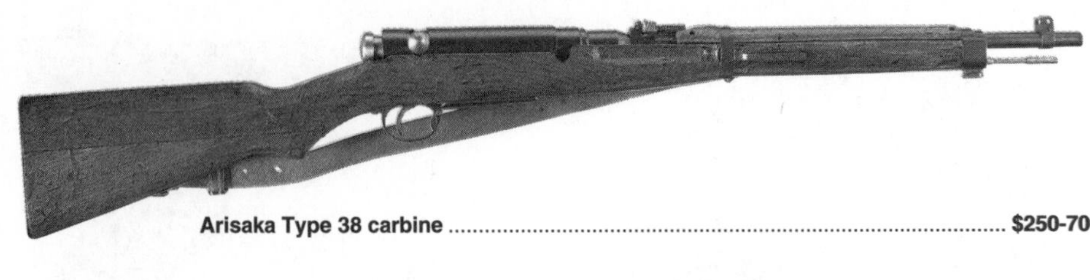

Arisaka Type 38 carbine $250-700

Japanese Type 2 paratrooper rifle $3,000-3,500

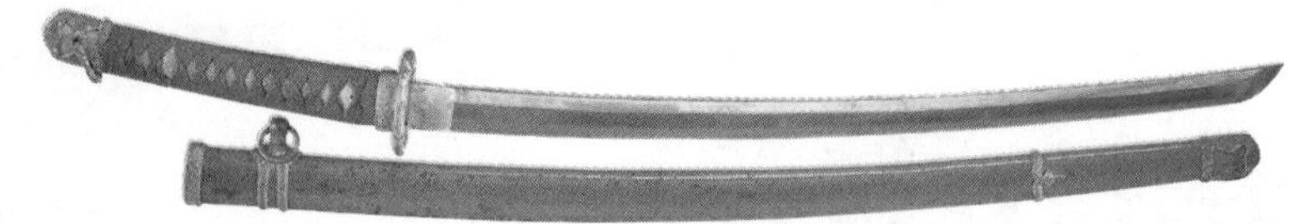

Unsigned 23-1/8" blade with unnumbered military mounts $400-600

United Kingdom

British paratrooper "Denison" smock $550-700

British Auxiliary Territorial Service bush jacket $175-250

British Women's Auxiliary ankle shoes $65-95

British enlisted man's Model 1940 battle dress tunic.........$100-150

British MK II helmet...$75-150

British ATS wool service dress cap, first pattern.... $175-225

MK IV gas mask and pouch.............. $100-125

Smith & Wesson Model 10 M&P revolver, British RAF issue **$650-1,000**

Mk V flare pistol manufactured by I.L. Berridge $250-350

Great Britain War Medal, 1939-45, cupro-nickel $20-30

Enfield No. 4 Mk I, with a later No. 32 Mk II scope and bayonet.. **$2,500-3,500**

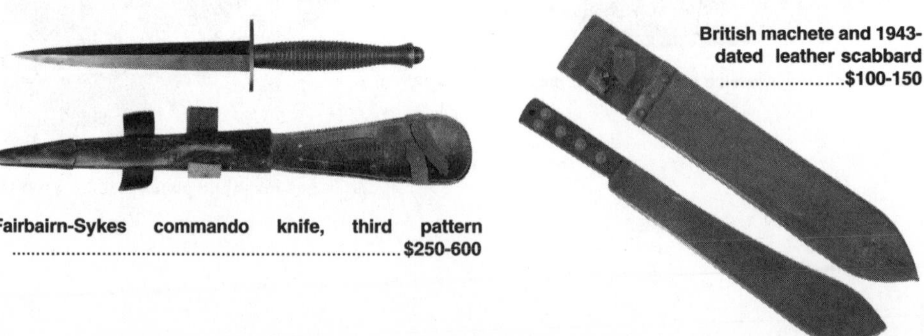

British machete and 1943-dated leather scabbard $100-150

Fairbairn-Sykes commando knife, third pattern $250-600

United States

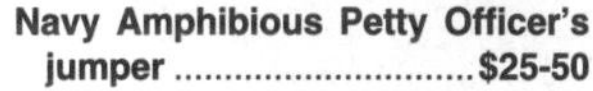

Navy Amphibious Petty Officer's jumper **$25-50**

A-2 jacket, with a painted squadron insignia **$1,500-2,500**

40th Division sergeant's Ike jacket, with bullion patch and combat artilleryman badge **$75-100**

Army Nurse Corps captain's uniform, complete with matching skirt, shirt and necktie.... **$300-350**

Model 1944 shoepacs......... **$50-75**

WAC brown leather shoes **$25-50**

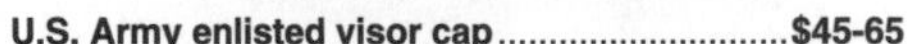

U.S. Army enlisted visor cap............................**$45-65**

U.S. Navy officer's khaki cap........................**$145-295**

Navy white fatigue hat...**$5-10**

USMC officer's visor cap with white removable cover...**$275-325**

M1 fixed bail helmet, with painted 2nd Infantry Division insignia on shell and liner.......................... **$895-1,200**

Enameled canteen, cup, and cover..............**$100-165**

Radio Receiver and Transmitter BC-611-E, ("Handie-Talkie") **$250-325**

M1943 folding shovel $25-45

Army Signal Corps compass $65-95

U.S. Army Purple Heart with Oak Leaf cluster, signifying an additional receipt of the award $75-100

U.S. Distinguished Service Cross, numbered $300-350

Colt U.S. Army Colt Commando Model revolver $500-900

Union Switch & Signal Company M1911A1 pistol $2,000-3,000

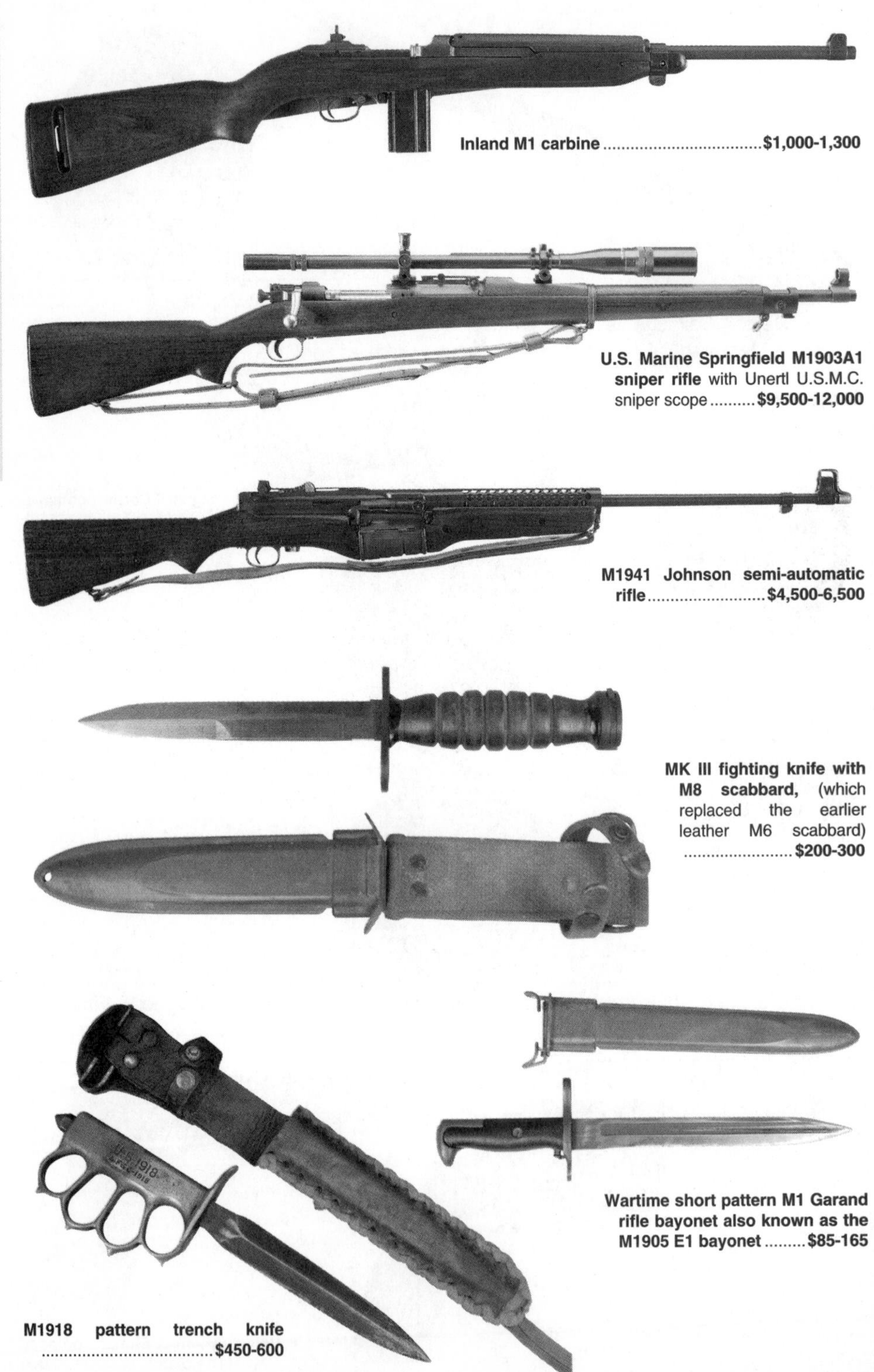

Inland M1 carbine..................................**$1,000-1,300**

U.S. Marine Springfield M1903A1 sniper rifle with Unertl U.S.M.C. sniper scope..........**$9,500-12,000**

M1941 Johnson semi-automatic rifle..........................**$4,500-6,500**

MK III fighting knife with M8 scabbard, (which replaced the earlier leather M6 scabbard) **$200-300**

Wartime short pattern M1 Garand rifle bayonet also known as the M1905 E1 bayonet.........**$85-165**

M1918 pattern trench knife **$450-600**

INDEX